The MIT Press
Cambridge, Massachusetts, and
London, England

The Sketchbooks of Paolo Soleri

This book was designed by
the MIT Press Design Department
and set in Linofilm Helvetica
by Wrightson Typographers, Inc.
Negatives prepared by Imperial Lithographers Inc.
Softcover printed on Fairmont Matte, 60 lb.;
printed and bound
by Semline Inc.
Hardcover printed on Glatco Smooth, 70 lb.,
by Semline Inc.;
bound by
The Cuneo Press of New England
in the United States of America.

ISBN 0 262 19 090 7 (hardcover)

Library of Congress catalog card number:
70-148853

Production note: All the sketches have been screened in order to retain as much of the original detail as possible. A background tone is sometimes evident as a result. In some instances the choice was made to opaque certain blemishes in the drawings.

Preface

My sketchbooks, six to date (1970), comprise a work journal whose only order is a chronological sequence of entries. A page might carry a dozen or more references to material or ideas that might appear elsewhere in the same book, in an earlier one, or in both. The books are actually a visual archive of my daily work. The writing is seldom related specifically to the designs.

Each book consists of about 400 pages, 17 by 14 inches, on Zellerbach Hammermill. The designs and writings are executed with large ball-point pens or laundry markers; occasionally pencils or wax crayons are used. Each book is bound in a cast-aluminum cover that is sturdy enough to stand the two to three years of handling time it takes to fill it. The writing is not only sketchy and unrevised, it is also grammatically wanting. The spelling is as casual as a lazy Italian tongue and an undisciplined hand can coordinate.

The material for this publication has been extracted from sketchbooks 2 and 3, coordinated and condensed by subject. The importance of the subjects and the amount of work on each varies a great deal, which will be apparent from the introduction to each subject. The two sketchbooks cover the work from October 1959 to April 1964, a period that saw the development of the concept of Mesa City. The material on Arcosanti is not included, as it will be the subject of another work.

A natural question arises: Has the procedure of a "bookkeeping" of the mind influenced the thinking and living process? Probably yes. There is an underlying structure to every life, a structure that can be driven deep into the recesses of the self but also one that can be brought to the surface, or better, can be brought "visually" into the process of life by various devices. The sketchbooks are one of these devices. It is as if the archives that are a part of this structure were more easily consultable and consequently the structure itself kept more up to date. There is also the immediate process of one page proceeding to the next page, the next, and the next. . . .

I do not know if I can explain why I work in series. That is to say, every time I develop an idea, I then proceed to conceive a series of variations on the theme. The simplest explanation is that, to avoid the brittleness inherent in the archetype as it stands alone in unfriendly territory, I feel the need to put robustness in it or give it brothers and sisters or, perhaps, a series of mirrors with a population of facsimiles slightly enlarging or deforming the original image. Another explanation is that there is no such thing as the complete, final, or perfect response to any challenge, even when the challenge is specific and detailed. As soon as the first idea works itself onto paper, all its scarcely known relatives with different degrees of legitimacy are in close pursuit. So there they come, sketchy and naked, to be picked up again later for reassessment and characterization. It is really a thickening of the thinking process quite in agreement, I think, with the behavior of the living which must seek—always—the qualitative thick of things.

It has always struck me that the power of a musician's work is strictly related to the vastness and seriality of his total production. Bach, Mozart, Beethoven, and Wagner not only perforate the roof of mediocrity with a tour de force, they build enormous constructions towering above their times, any time. So it is in poetry, in sculpture, in painting. As an Italian proverb says, one butterfly does not make spring.

Paolo Soleri
August 1970

The Sketchbooks of Paolo Soleri

Mesa City

A Quest for an Environment in Harmony with Man

1970
Most of what follows is about the development of the Mesa City concept.* There will be two sets of annotations: one set from the point of view I have today, 1970, commenting on the ideas of Mesa City represented by ten-year-old sketches, the other set consisting of abstracts from writings of the time of the studies (1959–1964).

Mesa City's interest lies in (1) fragmented attempts to introduce corposity into the urban morphology, a premonition of the arcological concept; (2) a preoccupation with the ecological aspects of every phenomenon on this planet, including the human phenomenon; (3) the unequivocally stated conviction that the city is ultimately the most relevant aesthetic phenomenon on this earth and, consequently, that the characteristic genesis of the city is an act of creation, through the paths of discovery and invention.

Generalities

1960
Project Mesa City is the outline of a regional development in the west of the American continent or any other similar region. The land is internationalized under a world government authority. Thus the sheltering of man is based on his worth, not on his clan. By dedicating a parcel of its land for this purpose, any developing country would see a radical transformation of its social, economic, and cultural life.

The plan includes
1.
On a plateau, a city of about 2,000,000.

*An implied and comprehensive comment on the conceptual structure of Mesa City is in my first book, *Arcology: The City in the Image of Man* (The M.I.T. Press, 1969). There, the rejection of the two-dimensional pattern is complete. Throughout this second book there are references to specific arcologies which can be better understood through study of the first.

2.
Towns and villages of rural character, producing and processing foodstuffs and their derivatives.
3.
Industrial complexes downstream of water reservoirs.
4.
Special structures intended as multipurpose social facilities, living and working. Their morphology is such as to capture and make use of cosmic energy—radiation, winds, water, tides.
5.
A linear city developing along a man-made waterway.
6.
A connective network of roads, railroads, and bridges.
7.
An ecological organization of nature within the new balance demanded by large social aggregates.

The city is set on a semiarid plateau (mesa) surrounded by grounds for agriculture, grazing, and land preservation. The region provides the city with foodstuffs and their by-products. The regional ecology is closely governed by a complex of works including controlled watersheds, canals, reservoirs. Multipurpose dams feed both industry and the region with water and power. Heavy industries are developed in adjacent canyons.

Description

1960
The city develops north-south in a band about 10 kilometers wide and about 35 kilometers long. At the south end of the main axis is the center for advanced study, encircled by secondary schools and dormitories. Directly north of this complex is a man-made park (150 to 200 meters wide, 15 kilometers long), widening then in a system of dikes and lakes, the edges irregularly settled by villages whose main activities are arts and crafts. Uphill, 5 kilometers north of these villages, stands the theological complex: facing east is the theological university, a library-museum is in the center, and monastic orders are on the west side. The center for advanced study, the man-made park, and the theological complex constitute the backbone of the city.

Beginning again from the south end around the school complex is a band of villages and civic centers averaging 2.5 kilometers in width. Thirty-four villages of about 3,000 people each are grouped around civic and shopping centers in clusters of five. Each village is on a ground 1,000 meters in diameter; a garden 200 to 400 meters in diameter is in the center. The village structure is about 500 meters in diameter. There is an outside farming ground 200 to 400 meters in depth for orchards and vegetable gardens. This whole band is crisscrossed by pedestrian and bicycle paths; there is no private car traffic of any kind. Each village is tied directly to the speedway through underground parking and repair-refueling shop facilities. High-density dwellings are developed on the east and west side of the man-made park on sloping grounds, allowing for a terraced structural plan. Porched piazzas with civic and public utilities are placed among the dwelling rows and the bordering public gardens.

At the foothill of the theological complex is a series of "indigenous villages." Ethnic, cultural, and racial differences are maintained and emphasized through the material and human structure of each village for comparative studies and for the identification of man's uniqueness in the face of what we erroneously call "discrimination." (Discrimination is really the process by which life is selectively etherialized, that is to say, becomes more human.)

Running in, out, and through the city are three continuous belts:
1.
Closest to the center is the home industry system where workshops and living quarters are integrated along a circulation network. The proximity of this complex to the secondary schools suggests the desirability and feasibility of apprenticeship and other kinds of interchange.

2.
The intermediate belt consists of the main network of speedways, roads, parking facilities, and a system of waterways for freight and passengers. It includes (a) all the standard productive activities, observing the need for cleanliness and hy-

giene, absence of noise, odors, clean atmosphere, and so forth; (b) all the main merchandising of standard products of the city; (c) all the public facilities found in any "downtown"; (d) amusement and recreation facilities; and (e) cultural facilities connected with production and exchange.

3.
The outside belt, sunk in the ground, holds second-hand stores and markets, the blight of the car dealers, the equipment dealers and renters, the junkyards and all the various colorful and often distressing aspects of man's dependence on technological ephemeralities. This belt is "the river of waste."

At the foot of the mesa, between the river of waste and heavy industry, are processing plants where raw materials are reclaimed from scrap heaps. In the geometric center of the city, crossing on the continuum and tangent to the first two belts, is the business center. This is a complex of towers, outcropping from a general multistory platform, and a computer center, the brain for all the interdependent activities of the city at the logistic level. An airport is on the rooftop of this complex, and air taxi facilities are scattered all over the city. Another major airport is at the south end of the mesa connected to the city and the region by two main speedways.

Three towers, 1,000 meters high, are located in the south section of the city: one is for transit population; one is for people connected with the learning complex; one is the residence of the government and its employees. The different types of villages are close to the manufacturing and marketing belts. All along the edge of the mesa rim are guilds, secular and religious. Cut within the walls of the mesa itself, they are not obstacles to the view from the city's periphery and from the edge of the rim.

The road system is mostly above or below ground level, and it is combined with a parking facility network including car storage, car silos, and normal parking. Within the structures carrying the roads are integrated road utilities such as motels and car services.

At the north end, east and west of theology hill, are two dam-and-lock systems regulating the water flow to the city, to its gravity conveyor belt of manufacturing and marketing, canals, streams, ponds, lakes. The retained water constitutes a great reservoir on the south shore which the indigenous villages face.

Origin

1960
The city develops after the establishment of a research plant for biochemistry and biophysics entailing, in time, ever-more-complex environmental contributions: technological capabilities, productivity, social backbone, cultural facilities, spiritual significance, physical substance, and the synthesizing force of the arts.

Aesthetic accomplishment is indeed viewed as the resolving force by which man can willfully accept life when the tenuous encouragement of his other discovery-inventions, science and religion, becomes too questionable and far too contradictory for his yearnings. Mesa City grows, thus, from necessity into virtue.

The conception of the master plan arose out of the elaboration of factual elements based on the principle that power—technical, political, economic—is not a finality but an instrumentality. Within the boundaries of the master plan, conceived one may say out of time (the present), time itself would define progressively the concrete aspect of things and its best expression. In this way, like an individual growing within the general character of the species, personal uniqueness would be the double consequence of ancestry and environment—ancestry expressed by the master plan (the filtering function of man), environment, by the reciprocal influence of this plan and its causative conditions in the growth of the "organism."

Morphology

1960
The city is not conceived as an amorphous coral colony whose quasi-undifferentiated cells are interchangeable and whose size is only a parameter of time and energy. It is conceived, instead, in the likeness of a higher organism whose many organs answer defined and complex functions. Thus, a definite character is morphologically necessary. What is more, its physical size, a function of the differentiation and interdependence of its "organs," cannot be altered without atrophy or gigantism. The physical maturity of the city (that is, filling in the space allowed by its morphology) is by no means the limit to its real growth for the same reason that an individual's intellectual and spiritual growth goes beyond and against its biological trajectory from cradle to grave.

In the coral colony one can speak only of cells and of contiguity, of rigid microgroupings under the constant laws of weight, food gathering, environment, and limitless macrogrouping—haphazard, repetitive, and indifferentiated—but in the higher organisms space and time, along with other mediating matters, are fundamental; they comprise the texture of the organism. Thus in the city one organ envelops another and by another is enveloped in strict interdependence . . . inner and outer transfixing according to the demands of the moment . . . spaces within spaces within time . . . these spaces, the connective foundation for man's action.

The answer to the charge of subjection to physical constrictions, for instance, prevailing winds, lies in a true recognition of an organism's "passive" nature. (The wind-warped cypress is lovingly warped: expression combines with force.) In fact, the challenge of an arid plateau is sought as a coherent premise for the flowering of multiform life. The hardship and toil of achievement, as the sap with which life constructs the graceful and, through man, creates the metaphysical. From this recognition arises respect for nature, not timid, camouflaged, or blending, but bold and demanding: man and nature as equals in conception and creation.

Technology

1960
The present conception falls short of the unification of the whole city under one roof, within one struc-

ture, but requires nonetheless an extraordinary technological know-how. The intention is to demand the utmost of technology without granting it any liberties. To the shame of technology it is constantly looking backward as if to seek the blessing of history. Thus, the car is a pepped-up horse wagon, the home appliance is a glamorized homemade contrivance, the gadget, in general, is a savage thing, a moral stupidity, and a hindrance to the essentials man must strive for.

Technology is the only servant ethically conceivable and, as such, strictly the means to significance, never significant in itself. However, given man's propensity for the makeshift, it has a monstrous capacity for creating monsters. Romantic and dear, the locomotive, symbol of all the rare ingenuity and naivety of man, the ecstasy he finds in the consuming voraciousness of power, is also a symbol of the paleotechnology he seeks to substitute for biotechnology. Possibly it is the same little-understood yearning that puts a classical freize around the locomotive stack. We must look for a more substantial plurifunctionality of the means we use and the grace that a more thoughtful and loving care can provide.

Ecology

1960
Rape and "devastation" best express the actions of technological man toward nature. Such blind brutality must be transformed in an intense search for a new ecological balance. The ecological disasters that the human animal has wrought are of such magnitude and novelty that any return or undoing would be illusory. The conflict, however, between man's intelligence and his immature use of it does not imply an inherent evil. If the past saw an ecology imposed by nature on man, the future may witness an ecology evolved by man within a tamed nature, transfigured perhaps in all those instances and places where its state was through nature or by man's degradation less than inspiring.

In Mesa City transfiguration is attempted by a full-scale intervention on the geological and ecological scale. The semiarid plateau is "scraped" in search of its ancestral structure. Once this is uncovered and made use of as it should be in the creative act, soil and plant life will be imported and integrated into it. Water will be dammed, guided into canals, stored, impounded, and man's life will then develop in these spaces that are conditioned to his needs, the whole surrounded by the untouched vastness of the landscape.

If, for a moment, one accepts the definition of orthodox environment as the combination of the artificial (man-made) and the natural, then this new environment would be better described as a protohuman condition imposed on the virginity of nature. By further action man can seek a synthesis between his compassionate self and the unbending cosmos, a synthesis nowhere achievable except in the aesthetic sphere.

The two elements of compassion, the loneliness peculiar to man and the indifference cruelly and beautifully practiced by the cosmos, will always determine the quality of human life, as they are in themselves the dialectic of the human condition. Up to us is the transfiguration of the struggle between compassion and indifference into a more inclusive divinity: the ecology of a compassionate universe.

Scope (The Age of Leisure)

1960
Underlying the design of the city is an orientation represented by the following scheme:

Ends	living education mores
ethics (growth)	religion justice government science
aesthetics (creativity)	the arts culture
Means instrumentalities (procedures)	organization production distribution exchange communication information health care
leisure (pausing)	play sport entertainment

The scope is, therefore, defined by the pursuit of values physically embodied in the city. We must seek to sensitize ourselves to a new scale of interaction with nature, to a sharpened consciousness of the miraculous reality of man in a no-less-incredible reality of nature, their unity and their separateness. This search with the mind, with the body, with the spirit through the miraculous, attempting to understand and see from the recesses of time, is the only safeguard against post-human "history." The miraculous is now the construction of horizons far beyond the pseudo-economy of our frenetic and dull present. On this scale, art is the finest synthesis of man's being and doing, as creativity engrosses those forces that, although the ultimate and unique concern of man, are of no meaning for a universe gazing at its own endlessness.

An environment in harmony with man constitutes both the basis for the establishment of a fertile outlook and the end result of what such an outlook can produce. The rationality of this need for integrity at the origin so as to reach integrity at the end points again to the necessity for aesthetic creativity, the only means by which the irrational may be transfigured into the metaphysical.

City planning is not discovery, not invention, not a corporate enterprise, not big business, although in it all of this is present. It is a creative act embodying, while unfolding substance and longing, a unique reality and expectation. Any lesser goal in conceiving the physical shell for man's endeavors, individual and social, will a priori degrade any potentiality to a mere technical meeting of needs, to a gilded cage for survival. In a sense, Mesa City is a city of leisure because it counts on the energy, will, and actual physical work of its citizens for its final aspect using the leisure time granted by automation.

The enormous potential of leisure could be resolved by either a hideous sloth or the rewarding panorama of cooperative effort. The discovery and implementation of civic creativity may be one of the best means of fulfillment man can devise; through it, he can reach personal integrity and find ends in the unencumbered time offered to him by science and technology. This explains the preponderance of the facilities and works concerned with arts and crafts, including botanical crafts. It provides a rational foundation and at the same time mirrors the intended metaphysical scope of the endeavor.

Reality can be viewed from three positions:
1.
The position of nature (objective)
the statistical
the rational
the ultrarational
the subrational
2.
The position of man (subjective)
the fatal
the willed
the destined
the regressive
3.
The position of neonature (the man-made)
the indifferent (casual)
the functional
the aesthetocompassionate
the extravagant

One has the horizontal relations: statistical-fatal-indifferent (casual), rational-willed-functional, ultrarational-destined-aesthetocompassionate, subrational-regressive-extravagant.

If the subject is what leisure will do for man, we might start with a survey of the third position, the universe of the man-made. First, the indifferent (casual): the doing for doing's sake, as worthless as the extravagant and, as such, regressive. One might say that its character is protohuman.

Second, the functional: in a strict sense, the environmentally bound. Its reason for being resides in its efficiency. It *is* because it functions. It is the instrumentality of life, and its life-span is limited to the duration of its usefulness. Consciousness has unchained it from the statistically plausible and with awesome cuts in space and time made it a domestic affair guided by every man's brain. In cutting this path through time, man has littered it with broken-down instruments. Littering is synonymous with obsolescence. An untouched forest is not littered; all the dead trees, twigs, and leaves are actual, ecological parts of the forest phenomenon. They are meaningful not because they were meaningful, but because they are actively so *now*. Thus, narrow functionality, the practical of the moment (biological as well as artificial), is the bearer of obsolescence as unavoidably as granular life is the bearer of death. Obsolescence is a man-invented category, a category he has not learned to live with. The obsolescence law: the shorter the life-span of the instrument (not the object but the category), the greater the degree of obsolescence inherent in it. (The greater the degree of obsolescence, the lesser the aesthetic breadth.)

Third, the aesthetic: if the functional is the producer, the aesthetic is the reason for the "production." The functional man works to satisfy the aesthetic man, the two-in-one. He produces instruments with which he pursues with great facility and skill his aesthetic ends. The sharper knife to produce a more "controlled" statuette is the symbol of the technological world, and its justification. It so happens that a healthier individual, physically, psychologically, ethically sane, will make a better, more complete use of the knife. Thus, science, technology, and ethics provide better shelter, better diets, better communication, better understanding so that the hand guiding and powering the knife will be more highly motivated, more powerful, more reflective, reverent, ultrarational . . . and the statuette will evolve, metamorphosis after metamorphosis, into an aesthetogenesis of the real.

I would define as aesthetic the "form" whose content is compassion. Form and content are one, an inseparable reality.

Fourth, the extravagant: the extravagant is the false. As such, it reaches into all that exists. It degrades fragments of it into pseudolife. The extravagant follows life like a shadow, echoing it. Its appeal is in its shallowness and in the license that swells personal idiosyncrasies. Unfortunately, it is hard to define the boundary between the aesthetic and the extravagant. Quite possibly there is no line but a fading zone where there are few guides. Obsolescence will tell. . . . Science gets some of its respectability from its "unequivocal" matter-of-factness, but curiously enough technology, the child of science, is surfeited in extravaganzas. This is very symptomatic. Applied science, a childless mother, sterile, adopts aesthetics, and industrial design is not born but induced. Industrial design attempts to personalize (make aesthetic) the impersonal, to "tool" man as a mass and, by necessity, fails. Joy is not marketable, as it is not transferable. Technology is fashioning a robotlike world, astonishingly sophisticated, splendidly organized, but it will be as cold as the intergalactic stuff of which it is really the faithful continuator. This is the functional world.

It so happens that man is contained in a more complex quantum; he is the aesthetic compassionate man of many tears and even more mysteries. The human conflict produces what is symbolized in the Detroit phenomenon: the mystique of instrumentality whereby that which was to satisfy a function is made to elicit and portray an emotion, an emotion that by the nature of the process (mass production) is a mass emotion. The "every one" emotion is the "no one" emotion. There lies the controlling of life by the remote control of a corporate emotion producer. The ultimate consequence of such a mystique is the world of the extravagant, irremediably obsolescent, regressive.

The Choices

In examining the preceding framework, four characterizations appear. If the casual and extravagant, both regressive, are combined into one, man can choose between a two-forked dead end and two paths:

The statistical (casual) and/or subrational (extravagant) dead end. It is the way of amorphism and hatred; its symbol and end product is what one may call *sloth man.*

The rational (functional). It is the path of structure and justice. Its symbol and logical conclusion is what might be called *bullion man.*

The ultrarational (aesthetic). It is the path of ultrastructure and compassion. Its creator may be called *aesthetic man.* My contention is that the future of man lies in the "transfusion" of leisure into a compassionate ultrastructure.

Sloth man (subrational, casual, regressive, extravagant) For all its wealth and power, life remains a fragile thing. Man's enemy is not man but the death wish life carries in its own entrails. The most subtle and devastating disguises of the death wish are sloth and extravaganza. As damaging as sand in the cogs of a machine, sloth and extravaganza pretend ownership of the present, marking the past as the dutiful mother to their existence and the future as inevitable fatality. But if sloth and extravaganza were the nodule of existence, past and future would be withered realities. Sloth man would never have seen the light of day if not for the horror and joy of eons past; nor would horror and joy ever be justifiable if sloth man were at the end of the line. Sloth, extravaganza, and boredom are three faces of the subrational drifting casually toward the kingdom of the statistically indifferent, a cosmic roulette. If life is vectorial, leisure must be something different.

Bullion man (rational, willed, functional)
The universe may be defined as the torpid likeness of the rationally possible, given no limit to space and time. Is the rationally possible the aim of man? If so, then the road to rationality is straight and unforgiving. Rationality has no shades. It is displayed, all here, all present. If so, man would then be the god vectorializing that which exists and coordinating the amorphism of the origins into the amorphism of the end: the perfect cycle, perfect and meaningless. After all, the universe has always been rational within the frame of its own resources. Cause and effect linked each other statistically without discontinuity, at least up to the inception of the biological. If man is a block, and only a block, of this whole, rational man will be the accelerator for the total rationale.

If this is so, perhaps I can suggest a total revision of man's posture. A first but essential step is the transformation of our morphological structure. As the senses are rationally unreliable, and as the lack of rationality is a source of anguish, scientific devices might be substituted. Because the motor apparatus, though versatile, is fragile and energy hungry, efficient packaging and transportation must be given top consideration. Taking these two examples and ignoring all that which, as flesh, is easy prey of illness and death, of enmity and harshness, tiredness and gloom, tearfulness and plenitude, the logical structure for the living is bullion man as a cell organism with a physical reality, retaining flesh as at least a temporary device to carry life. Bullion man would be a slightly spherical cube of flesh and nerves, metabolism, and gray matter, a cube demonstrating reduction and simplification of feeding apparatus, elimination of the brittle and now-useless skeletal structure, absence of limbs: total compactness, transportability, optimum storability—functionality—not a silly, shaven, John-the-Baptist head under a glass dome but a smooth object, enveloped by sensors, socketed for lifts and storage. Note that the perceptual life has become, or has returned to, registration of temperature changes and value emissions based on recognition of patterns of space and time; hence sight, hearing, smell. Touch and sex, as such, are obsolete and are eliminated.

If all this seems farfetched, it is the exact farfetchedness of rationality as the ultimate good, all that in mathematics, science, and technology becomes the aim of man and life in an orderly and all-justified plurality, freed from that which being totally improbable would be totally unwelcome. The brutish and sterile connotation of such a rational life strongly suggests an aim of life that is ultrarational. If for sloth man nothing that has not been discovered is worth discovering, for bullion man nothing that is not discoverable is worth longing for. That is, man's task is to reenact in his own parameter a genesis of things for the sake of the bloodless, indifferent god of determinism. Rationality demands a bullion man, incidentally, the bullion man seeking the bullion god. Bullion man is by definition an antileisure creature.

Aesthetic Man (ultrarational, destined, compassionate) Neonature, short of being compassionate, is only instrumental or only regressive. Instrumentality itself in its obsolescent nature granulates involution. But neonature can be the making of a new and far more meaningful universe. Man the maker can be man the creator if his deeds are vivified by compassion, and compassion's shroud is the aesthetic. Inasmuch as bullion man's shroud is solely instrumental, bullion man is not aesthetic. And his shroud is instrumental because the content is not compassionate but rational. As in the compassionate-aesthetic, the effect transcends the cause; rationality does not supply answers. Thus, the world of aesthetic man is the ultrarational world, that which makes compassion and aesthetics *the* human parameters. Once more, where is rationality? If bullion man is the most consciousness can achieve, why is there so much suffering and longing? The shrinking of time seems unworthy of them. Rationalizing that which exists is the willful taking the place of the statistical so as to put eons into minutes, cosmogenesis into punch cards. But knowledge, or discovery, of the laws of nature must be instrumental, not final. *The maker is the inventor of shrunken time. The creator is the form giver who makes of shrunken time the compassionate. I call this form the aesthetic.* Here appears the fundamental difference between beauty and aesthetics (and consequently a scope for leisure). Nature is the origin of beauty. The beautiful is a protohuman system established through time unending by the world of "matter" within the laws of great numbers. Structure, that is protoform, is or can be beautiful. But only ultrastructure, that is, form, is aesthetic.

One may say that the aesthetic defines the compassionately beautiful, and, as compassion is the charisma of humaneness, the aesthetic is peculiarly man's creation. The compassionate is the stuff that consciousness elaborates throughout the universe (by man, in the case of the earth). In this sense the aesthetic is the form of the compassionate (the beautiful that is willed).

As the compassionate refuses the automatic (statistically plausible) and is the discriminative, the chooser (principally the transfigurative), so does the aesthetic, its sensorial object. This slightly esoteric game of words points to the interdependence of nonobsolescent neonature and leisure.

As the character of such neonature is ultrarational, its action is not dictated by the instruments of science, economics, politics, justice, and technology, but it is the ripening of the fruit that man encourages by the reverent use of such instruments. He does this as an individual and as a species. The hypernature of the aesthetic is in its freedom and its unpredictability, the two parameters of true leisure. Here is the place for a reminder that license as submission to the extravagant is the negation of freedom and that license is denounced by obsolescence of form, not of function. Leisure, the long-sought liberator of man from need, can be the vehicle for the aesthetogenesis of the universe.

In the combination of sloth, rationality, and ultrarationality each man is made of, unless reverence prevails (that is, a measure of humility and a conscious or unconscious search for the transfiguration of materiality), what emerges from life is a tired reiteration of that which has ceased to be essential. That which is nonessential is waste, and waste is as sinful on the face of joy as it is on the face of anguish. If we can rid the universe of the nonessential, the rational will almost carry the sound of pettiness, and all that which is not vibrantly alive will be inconsequential.

To transfigure the man-made is to put it beyond the pull of obsolescence. A sonata is the rearrangement of sounds; a beautiful sonata is a transfiguration of sounds. The same raw material is used in the first instance to care for a temporary function, to fill up a program, as a car transports people; in the second instance, it is used to create an undying entity. *Transfiguration of matter as against transformation of it is the key to humaneness, and that which is transformed (the technological) is instrumental to that which is transfigured.* (It would be sad indeed if the toil of transfiguration should ignore or be unable to make full and total use of what technology can offer.)

Within the transfigurative process by which nature becomes neonature, a vast area can be filled in only by the individual expression of each member of society: the so-called homemade, the detailed works of craft produced with perseverance, love, and a basic understanding of materials. If one considers food—the raw materials—and cooking, one can see by extrapolation the meaning of craftsmanship. It is the direct action and involvement of a person with the object of his labor for reasons that are beyond the survival of the flesh but well within an engrossing life. Within this framework there are three aspects of vectorial life in which leisure would be a blessing:

1.
The bulk of organization, production, construction, distribution, control, and data processing in the magic lap of the computer. This is the world of rational instrumentality.

2.
The broad conception of neonature for historically centered minds. This is the world of creativity stemming from the sound base of its instrumental and most powerful technological slave.

3.
The filling up of such large and general frameworks and the characterization of their infrastructure by leisure man. This is the world of craftsmanship and domesticity wherein each can produce out of freely given and economically disinterested effort.

A brief recapitulation before a further dealing with leisure:

Life makes the cosmos vectorial.

The two infinites (space, time) of the entropic universe contain a third infant infinity: complexity, the self-creating.

Complexity exists in self-reflecting consciousness: mankind.

Physiological evolution is transferred by man to the world of aesthetic-compassion, neonature.

Such a world is not only poststatistical, as life has been from its inception, but also postrational, with man seeking a man-made universe.

In the process of humanizing the cosmos, man produces the *functional* so as to achieve the *aesthetic,* gets tangled in the *extravagant,* and out of indifference emulates the *statistical.*

The functional is because it functions; obsolescence is its second nature.

The aesthetic functions (is meaningful) because it is.

The extravagant is the pseudo-functional as well as the pseudo-aesthetic. This is de facto counterlife, somehow the "cunning" hindrance with which entropy sabotages life.

The functional can and will be delegated to the mechanically controlled world (cybernetic).

If the aesthetic is suffocated by the extravagant with which the functional tries to humanize and embellish itself, then it stands to reason that a mathematical world, rational and heartless, will take over. The self-creating god will wither away. The selectively rational (robotlike) will rejoin the statistical-rational protolife. That is, man will be an aimless, expendable, unjustifiable if explainable, phenomenon.

Leisure, becoming a central parameter of life, will transfigure the world or debase it and with it man, its originator.

One could say then that leisure, luxury for the few, dream for the many, is moving toward contemporary man with a mixed load of blessings and threats. Each of us, in his own self, has conscious or unconscious plans for a glorious or quiet but ever-golden stretch of nonresponsibility. The cat dozing in the sun, the bull in the herd, the information-starved in the library, the weekend aesthete sowing Sunday to Friday, the happiness of family rituals, the eternal child hunting for slightly unpalatable live flesh, and moving . . . moving . . . the nomads of affluence seeking excitement. If leisure is all this but only this, it will have a cannibalistic nature, its flesh (and creator) the soul of man. Leisure will sustain, signify, and perpetuate itself only through the gift of every single man to mankind of vibrant and original action: nonmaterialistic action that is, free of greed, fear, hatred, hypocrisy, bigotry, and pride.

Within the geological environment, time measured in billions of years, mellowed in different degrees by the organic millions of years old, the most organic and complex of all creatures, man, has from his very early infancy constructed or rearranged ecologies. The phenomenon, man, has transformed continents, working on a cosmic scale through agriculture. He has destroyed and remolded species, that is, worked again with the power of a cosmic force. Now he is on the threshold of a deeper and transfigurative transformation.

A consciousness of the vastness of his intervention has been somehow absent. Nature was overwhelming and a brutal death giver as well as a nurturing mother. Except for the insignificant and ethically warped freedom of the masters afforded by slavery, need—that is, the problem of survival—was paramount. Survival kept most human activity within the boundaries of cause and effect, to which man added his own peculiar brand of irrationality: persecutions, flag wavings, racism, greed. This atomistic pursuit of a sufficient caloric intake coupled with a relatively sparse population kept the humanoid skin wrapping the earth bidimensionally tenuous and fragile. Physical transformation of nature carried on by muscle power remained limited to the bidimensionality of agriculture, sporadically added an impressive third dimension: slave labor, at a costly human price.

Now, under the pressure of the human biological flood and the complexification of life, a reverence for nature combined with a maturing consciousness of the aesthetic-compassionate nature of man and the skill and power of self-adjourning technology will transfigure the earth, and man will construct human ecologies. It could be a transfiguration of the earth from its cause and effect ecologies into an earth not just sparsely and haphazardly "colonized" but ecologically humanized, that is, equidistant from the protohuman of the wilderness, the posthuman savagery of the megalopolises, and the squalor of small and large suburbias. Webbed in the wilderness, in the agricultural expanses, and in the seas, powerfully built organisms, modular ecologies, would rise high in the sky, roots deep in land and seas. Their skeletal framework would provide for the "functional" needs, and the citizens, thousands of minds and hands freed from repetitive labor, would give a part of their lives to the ultrastructuration (aesthetogenesis) of a truly three-dimensional environment conceived by man and dedicated to him.

As nature is something we cannot dispose of in some interstellar wastebasket, so man's work at its synthetic best cannot be fed with impunity to the hungry beast of obsolescence. No matter how awesome the complexity of our organism and how miraculous the dynamism of our intellect, both body and soul have a desperate need for the countenance, the relevance, of environmental powers and expressions. Environment is part of our evolving self as much and as directly as ourselves. It is civilization and culture. It is a parcel of materiality torn from the fatal as are the particles of our bodies. Environment carries from fathers to sons the sap and the meaning of humaneness and as such cannot be all disposable, irrelevant, and obsolescent. It is not that disposable "cities" are not feasible, it is instead that with their disposability we forfeit the continuity that is the directional guideline for growth, for evolution or even revolution; and the ultrastructuration of our institutions and behavior, the process that makes longing become substance and structure become form.

Man, more than any other living thing, overreaches the boundaries of his own flesh and makes his presence real and felt in numberless ways and directions—so much so that at his death, as the body disintegrates, the peripheral presence lingers on in actual action and influence. The entwined network of countless far-reaching presences, rooted in the near and distant past, is the texture of society. This texture is the physical environment society constructs for itself. In it and by it things, ideas, and aims take the substance of the lived, suffered, experienced, matured, enjoyed.

With the necessity of continuity goes an unavoidable movement toward ever-growing complexity. There are more configurations in a human brain than there are atoms in the universe. Furthermore, the configurations are purposeful (synthetic, structural), where the universe is granular (amorphous, statistical). Whether he likes it or not, man is of the known universe, the bearer of the hypercomplex, man as a cell and exponentially as society. The environment he constructs cannot only reflect such complexity, it must also be the fertile ground for its growth. The new cities will be the ultimate environment of contemporary man, and they will be either life givers or preposterous shrines, if not barren skeletons, according to the degree of aesthetic compassion permeating them. *The city of man is not a rational mechanism but an aesthetic organism with compassion as its content.*

How then can the human world be constructed? By having the two aspects that specifically characterize man, the aesthetic and the compassionate, move hand in hand with engrossing complexity, clustering action and thought, stratifying their undertakings on a shrinking earth, leaving wide gaps so that the earth can breathe and, so to speak, gaze at the stars. Thus, we would not have a thin, fragile, brittle film evenly spread on land and sea, a faceless earth grimly webbed by myriad senseless, suicidal spiders, but a centered, nodular, bold, substantial, self-renewing structuration: a superecology, a transfiguration of the earth's ecologies.

Broadacre City (the conception of a suburban America put forward by Frank Lloyd Wright) was a short dream in the pioneering spirit. The miracle that Broadacre City demanded of technology did not come true. It could not have because (1) there is no substitute for physical, bodily contact exponentially folding over itself which the city affords man. (2) Suburban sprawl is a land destroyer and a self-defeating concept. (3) The earth is too small for a one-story civilization; man must cluster, centralize. (4) The ground for "nature of material" is strictly rational. As such, it applies only to structure, not ultrastructure (the aesthetic).

As architecture grows into a phenomenon of human ecology, the cities will become organisms reflecting in their structural complexity the complexity of the life they contain. Upgrading from aggregation to organization signals the end of present-day architecture and the concept of individual structures. If aesthetic man does not devote himself to this, the undertaking will be given to the technocrat, and the resulting mechanisms will ignore life. Life itself will be the servant of a rational proto-human world. If aesthetic man measures the weight of his burden, disassociates himself from the whimsical and the fashionable, he will conceive the cradles of future cultures and be responsible for the advent of the ultrarational world. Now, this burden is no less than the inversion of the drift that moves the energetic universe toward a lower and more homogeneous state of energy, the condition of entropy built into matter. The spiritualization of matter is such an undertaking, and the aesthetic is its result.

In this process we demand of matter an abdication of its original structural substance (the nature of material) for an ultrastructuralization. What the aesthetic does is to shroud matter around consciousness at its most reflective in such a way as to identify it with its content while giving to this new whole the universal meaning of any true act of creation. Matter is thus ultrastructurized.

While labor, as toil, is coming to an end, man's work will have to coincide with leisure, and this combination will be aesthetic. This is the direct connection between leisure and the aesthetogenesis of the universe. We know how an exponential progression works. We know that life can grow exponentially. Thus, life is, at least potentially, of cosmic relevance. The proposition is that the leisure man will have can be used to make a gift of his "love" and energies to society for the common task of creating the new environment, a greenhouse for constantly evolving life. There are undoubtedly sound reasons to fear an economy based on "compensation for idleness" as it is done sporadically today (farming, featherbedding). But the blood and sweat demanded by the scriptures in exchange for bread should be in contemporary man for a spiritual bread, bread made of knowledge, an understanding of the world we live in and we are making. Creative "idleness" is a crossroad where man may wither in sloth, "robotize" in rationality, or hyperhumanize in form. To produce the creative attitude, we must stimulate man's sensitivity, enlarge his vision, give him occasion for awe and wonder, display before his eyes the incredible potential not of raw power or sophisticated whim but of reverent will, frugal intensity, and sustained faith.

The wastelands, the barren deserts, the tormented mountains, the deep gorges, the seas will be part of the aesthetosphere, the hyperstructure of man's compassion. As the individual will interiorize his desires, move from the materialism of today to the spirituality of tomorrow, he will demand less and less license for his vanities and his material security. Inner security will displace the market of obsolescence and its colossal circus of more consumption for more production. Human destiny does not lie in total gluttony. It lies in the frugality demanded by the quest for essentials. This transfer from emphasis on mass, weight, mechanical energy to joy, trust, and sensitivity will further simplify the mechanics of life, by then well-disentangled by more sophisticated technology.

In a coming culture, we thus have reflective man ordering matter into a skeletal framework. Its morphology is arrived at by a two-phase process: (1) analysis stringently pursued by exploiting the most advanced scientific and technical instruments; and (2) a synthesis whereby the "structures" (mechanical, social, intellectual) suggested by rational analysis are hyperstructurized into the total "form."

This is the new "nature," or the ultraenvironment, produced by ultrarational man. The broad warp of this new nature needs as many "subjectivations" as there are individuals in residence. Such subjectivation is a kind of pioneering where the fight for survival is replaced by the tension of hyperliving, the struggle for respectability transfigured in the pursuit of worthiness. Substantiation and formalization (ultrastructuration) will give true color to the environment and the full growth of a homoecology will be expressed.

Each culture has its axial parameter—religion, nationalism, federalism; science is on the verge of becoming axial in our time. If so, from the bleeding for nationalism, we may fall into withering from technology. Axiality must be redirected toward humaneness, of which the two essential faces are compassion and aesthetics. It can be said that the harshness implicit in technology and the lull the "architects" are in are directly correlated. Nor are the puritanical constructions of the "engineers" anything that can suggest to man valid reasons for existing as other than well-oiled mechanisms. The one, turning backward, retreats toward the future, keeping himself informed about things he can't understand. Short in vision, reverence, and boldness, he is the bourgeois of our culture. The other, floating head down in the inebriating sea of ever-powerful technology, goes where the drift carries him, his granular world sparkling and bubbling from obsolescence to obsolescence on a platform of squalor. They both pity each other; they are both isolated in the cage that society praises them for conceiving. The engineer as the power holder will prevail unless his drive, blinded by the so-called rational, is tamed and redirected by sensitivity. The end of his trail, as it is now heading, will be a robot society, a supersophistication of the quasi-eternal world of the statistical. It will be a triumph of materialism, that is, the destruction of life. Impending doom will not force the architect to adjust his perspective unless history takes hold of him, and the parameters of space, time, and compassion fuse in the transfiguring act of aesthetic creation with all its load of improbability and ultrarationality.

Time is running short. Environmental squalor, stretching over more than one generation, may outpower man's forbearance and sensitivity. Callousness and dullness lurk around the shine of our packaged society. Callousness, dullness, indifference—the three-headed portrait of sloth man.

In conclusion, one can hope that, dispossessed of the centrality he used to feel before the advent of modern astronomy and the other sciences and having found himself a quick-burning particle on a totally peripheral orbiting planet, man may rekindle the flame of his life.

Complexity is the infinity peculiar to man. A true comprehension of complexity is fundamental to the act of creation, and creation is the product of a mind at leisure. Then, as the possibility for leisure is to be found in freedom from need, the stage is now being set for the most explosive age of creativity the world has ever witnessed. It can be a world that is compassionate, aesthetic, and harmonious, a way of life that man has not yet known.

Growth

1960
A geological survey is the basis for the structural concept of the whole park. After the survey and planning is done, one proceeds to cut the main canyon and its secondary branches, then bore into the solid rock, making the spaces that will ultimately be "sculptured" museums, theaters, auditoriums, and worship places.

The axial park is actually a quarry for the minerals that are to be processed into building material—cement, lime, stone, gravel, sand; the construction of the city is preceded by the quarrying of this area on the longitudinal axis of the mesa. Conceivably a moving plant could start from one end and, while quarrying and moving, process all the raw materials, separating out the various products and by-products.

Chronology of Growth
The first major construction is the center for advanced study and the international research plant in biophysics and biochemistry. These two complexes will polarize all the energies and initiatives essential to implementing the growth of the city.

Following then will be
1.
The park itself, drawing on the arts to unify the whole through the aptness of its forms, spaces, volumes, colors, and textures.
2.
Clusters of villages and their civic centers.
3.
Segments of the three life-carrying bands (the home industry band, the production and merchandizing band, the "river of waste" band) built on the waterway previously laid out.
4.
Toward the north end of the park the arts and crafts villages along the waterworks being constructed there.
5.
The theological complex at the north end of the park, the spiritual factor balancing the work of the mind centered in the learning complex.

The cosmopolitan aspect of society is mirrored by the full-bodied character of the indigenous villages around theology hill. When the three bands become fully functioning, they will determine the conditions for growth of the high-density community. In the bordering axial park will be found the cultural substance and direction that will fill in the vacuum society tends to fill with vacuities.

Parallel with the constructions on the mesa is the expansion and increasing productivity of the heavy industry located in adjacent canyons, the building of multipurpose dams, the production of energy, and the establishment of processing plants for foodstuffs in the valleys below, integrated with the rural towns, the villages, and the "linear city" on the waterways.

Types of Structural Procedures

1960
1.
Assemblage and posttensioning of precast elements.
2.
Successive layers of high-strength concrete on layers of prestressed cables and mesh.
3.
Spray of high-strength concrete or elastic structural cement on prestressed cages.
4.
Casting on earth forms or similar media.

(1)
Assemblage and posttensioning of precast elements. The technical information in this very diversified field is far more complete than I could suggest here.
(2)
Successive layers of high-strength concrete on layers of prestressed cables and mesh.

Any space frame that would require costly systems of scaffolding and forms may be constructed as follows:
a.
A light skeleton of the structure is built in steel (almost the elemental representation of the final thing). Scaffolding is used wherever necessary.
b.
An envelope of three-dimensional mesh is stretched, membranelike, on the skeleton.
c.
A first coating of concrete is sprayed to attain local rigidity and to form the base for successive coatings.
d.
On the steel anchorages previously placed and protruding from the concrete are prestressed steel cables crisscrossing the whole structure.
e.
A second envelope of three-dimensional mesh is put on the structure, a second layer of concrete is sprayed, a new network of prestressed cables... etc. The number of applications of coatings, mesh, and prestressed cable varies according to form and stress.

(3)
Spray of high-strength concrete or elastic structural cement on prestressed cages.
This system is possible whenever the structure has a main vertical axis of symmetry and the final profile is concave.
a.
Steel mesh is stretched between the two bases along the perimeter. Thus, if the two bases are square, we have a rectangular prism cage; if circular, a cylindrical cage, and so forth.
b.
The distance between the anchorage is increased (5 to 15 percent) through prestressing. The tension on the cage causes it to deform into a volume with outward concavities, like a fish trap.
c.
This prestressed curved cage can now be sprayed with concrete to form a nondeformable shell. It can otherwise be sprayed with a transparent and/or translucent compound to produce a strong curtain wall.

(4)
Casting on earth forms or similar media.
This way of casting is best for horizontal structures under the following conditions:
a.
The casting of a small structure by the owner's hand, one who is willing to put his labor into the production of the form using elementary but loving skill. The abstractness of working on the negative may give surprisingly simple results, unified by the nature of the medium. The reinforcing can be done at the time of casting (or when using gunite) by laying on a first coating of cement, steel rods, or wire in short, overlapping segments easily following any given surface—flat, curved, or warped.
b.
Special structures dealing with curved and complex surfaces, the preparation of which may require great labor and care and whose dimension is prevailingly horizontal.
c.
The casting of large horizontal structures of any shape or character (linear, curved) of such scale as to permit the use of bulldozers, scrapers, blades, and diggers for the making and the completion of the form itself. Inside the structure will be textures and patterns peculiar to the raw and often potentially beautiful machine-made surfaces. The mixture of freedom and discipline in the earth-form procedure is of a different kind from the one found in orthodox form making. The results will hence be a radical departure from orthodoxy or any unsatisfactory imitation of it.

Cosmic Potentials

(The use of cosmic energy and its derivatives: wind, water cycles, and tides)

1970
The production of energy is one of the unresolved problems man has been faced with from the early days of his existence. Consumption has always tended to outrun production, and this is particularly true today. That frugality has to be reinstated as a reasonable and cardinal condition for the whole of life is becoming clear through the excesses of affluence and opulence. Frugality would reduce the demand for energy, but it would not solve the problem of how, where, and when energy can best be produced, stored, transmitted, and consumed.

The preceding paragraph was an opening to the "Cosmic Potentials" which were an attempt, in 1950, to solve the problem of how to produce energy where energy is used. Each consuming monad would by the skin of its shelter, so to speak, capture, filter, transform, store, and consume that quantum of energy needed by it, perhaps releasing some for collective use. An ideal situation would be input and output in direct linkage, strengthened by the ecologically fit and quasi-biotechnical process of solar radiation to collector to consumer, wind to wind turbine to consumer, water tide to slow turbine to consumer . . . within the same structure and almost without mediation.

The obstacle, which took many years to comprehend, is that for the sake of a direct congruence between human life and the environment, mediated by the production and use of energy, I was concealing from myself the more comprehensive congruence that has to be found between the mineral-energetic world and the biomental universe. I failed to take into account that between these two worlds a third existed: the vegetal world. By demanding from the upper layer of the biosphere, man, a behavior belonging to the lower layer of it, the vegetal, I was unconsciously filling the void at the expense of man himself. The vegetal kingdom is still the best collector of solar energy, and the whole animal kingdom depends on it through that most extensive and ecologically balanced energy transfer: vegetal food. By the short circuit of physical energy–man, through the use of a pattern typically vegetal (the capturing of diffuse energy), I was putting a biotechnical dress on a paleotechnical procedure—failing frugality itself.

In reading back over the description of the cosmic potential performance, I found the description of the performance of the leaf, the surface performance of the collector and transformer of diffuse energy that is solar energy. With man, demand outran production many times over; there could not be other than a disproportion between the amount of energy demanded and the amount of energy produced. As a consequence, monads were condemned to remain monads, as there was no available surplus to feed social and cultural life. What served the tree through the performance of each single leaf could not do for a more complex state of affairs. How could it? The function of the leaf is to transform solar energy for use by other parts of the tree. But the dialectic of the human monad is to make sense out of an enormously charged psychomental universe whose energy is more refined, demanding fruits of a more disparate kind, whose entelechy, imaginary or not, is an unforgiving state of grace darting at the present from a mythical past or a fantastic future.

Downgrading man to leaf was not helpful, but the lesson I learned was substantial and multiple:

1.
Two-dimensionality, the surface collector-performer, is not an apt pattern for animo-mental-cultural logistics.

2.
The wholeness sought in the Cosmic Potentials consisted of energy collection and consumption and the performances of individual and social man, contained within one structure. It is right if reproportioned for a congruence between the seeking and the reaching, a reproportioning whose first demand is the introduction of *thickness*, the parameter always present in the animal kingdom.

3.
Size and human scale are not self-excluding. The humaneness of scale is not destroyed by unusual dimensions but by the impracticality of a certain design organization. The scale of the house that performs poorly is inhuman. The palace that works well has a human scale.

4.
The use and consumption of the income of the earth, and not of its capital, is essential if we want to keep open our options on the future.

IN MAN SHAME ISNT WHITING INCOMPLETENESS BUT INTO QUIE-SCENCE
AS IN ANIMALS QUIESCENCE IS INHERENT CONDITIONING,
THUS THE ACCEPTANCE OF THE CONDITION OF HUNGER, OR THE CONDITION OF FISICAL HARDSHIP IN GENERAL, AS THE ONLY REALITY, AS THE WHOLE WHIC IS, ITS INQUESTIONABLE UNIQUENESS

QUIESCENCE, THE SEEKER OF UNQUOTED COMFORT

THE MAKER RESPONSABILITY IS NOT TOWARD INDIVIDUALS AS THE (OF) SAVAGE BEAST CRY IS NOT DIRECTED TO ANYONE. (BUT TO "THE ONE" POSSIBLY)

THE MAKER HAS TORN AWAY FROM THE POWER HOUSE OF NATURE A BIT OF MAGIC POTENTIALITY NOW TO ELATE VIRTUE OF SOUNDS NOW TO CUT OUT IMMAGES OF GRACE OR IMMAGES OF BEASTINESS, NOW TO CONSTRUCT HOLLOW WORLDS RE-SONANT TO ONES SOUL OF THE TREMOR.

THE MAKER'S WORLD HAS AN ANTECEDENT WHEREIN MATERIA-LITY ALWAYS HAS ASPECT OF UN-FORMED & INDETERMINED OF-FRANCE, WHERE THE IFS & THE BUT'S PLAY THE GAME OF TEM-PTATION & DECIVENESS....

WHERE NOT MUCH IS WORTH KEE-PING AS SUCH THOO EVERITHING IS WORTH THE BREATHING INTO OF LIFE....

A CONSEQUENT WHEREIN ARE MINGLED IN DIFFERENT (& DIFFERING) PORTIONS THE JOY OF FINALITY & THE BOREDOM PERTAINING TO IT.

THE IDLE MAKER IS AS PERTINENT TO ITS STATE OF GRACE AS A ~~SEAL~~ WALKING SEAL (AS TO ITS AQUATIC MORPHOLOGY).

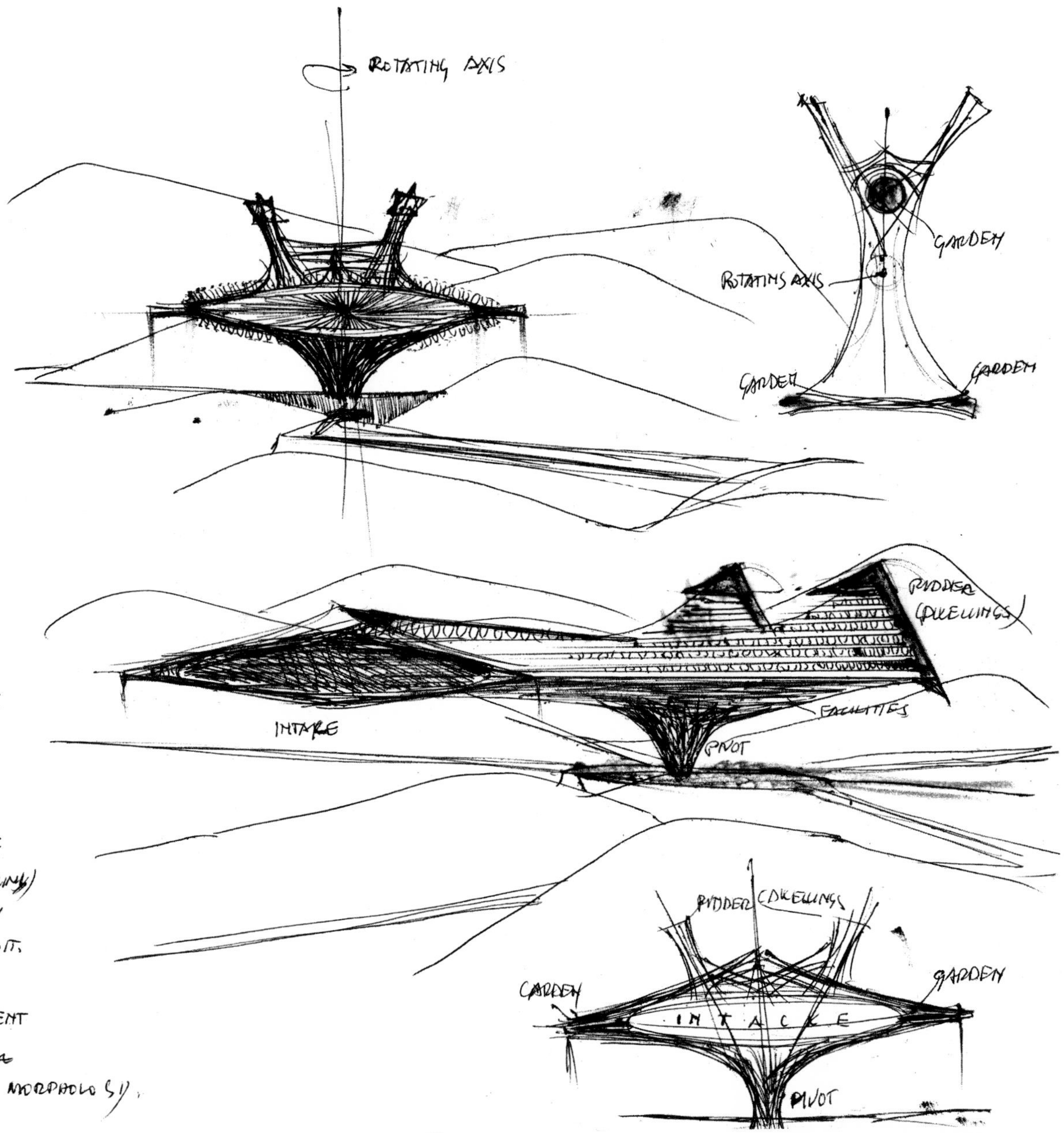

GIN FOR THE AWESOMELY DISTANT &
TOTALLY HYPOTETICAL POINT-MOMENT
OF RESOLUTION. HENCE SHORT OF
REINCARNATION MAN IS MODULATED
INTO THE STEPPING STONE, HUMBLY
PAVING THE ROAD TO SUBLIMITY. BUT
NEVERTHELESS LIVING A REAL FRAGMENT
OF THIS PROCESS WHICH TRUE SUBLIMITY
IS CONCEILED THERE IN.

IN THE SECOND INSTANCE, TAKEN
AWAY THE INCERTITUDE OF RESOLUTION
BY MOVING THE POSSIBLE FINAL
POINT-MOMENT OF PLENITUDE FROM THE
INFINITELY REMOTE FUTURE INTO A
SIDE TO "REALITY", EVER PRESENT,
THUS GIVING TO IT THE STONY INALTE-
RABILITY OF ETERNITY (AGAINST THE ENGROS-
SING BUT FAULTY BECOMING) THIS
PERFECT STATE, WHICH IS WHAT IT IS
IN THIS CASE, IS AT HAND NOW AS EVER
AS NOW AS EVER IS ITS CONNOTATION
THE SAME. HENCE IS GIVEN TO
EACH MAN WITHIN A LIFETIME
SPAN THE CHANCE TO RESOLVE HIMSELF
WITHIN THIS SAME SPHERICAL PERFE-
CTION OF ETERNAL DURABILITY (?)

OF NECESSITY SUCH ACTUAL & NOW
REALITY EXCLUDES TRUENESS TO THE
EVER TURMOIL OF LIFE & MATERIA-
LITY & HAS TO RELEGATE IT TO
THE REALM OF HALF-REALITY OR
SUB-REALITY. THE WORLD OF ILLUSIONS

WHILE BECOMING IS NEGATED TO REALITY
IS ASSUMED THAT ONLY BY BECOMING
TROUGH STAGES OF ENLIGTEMENT ONE MAY
REACH THE STATE OF GRACE: THE FUSION
WHIT THE UNCHANGEABLE.
THUS WHILE HERE BECOMING IS A MEAN

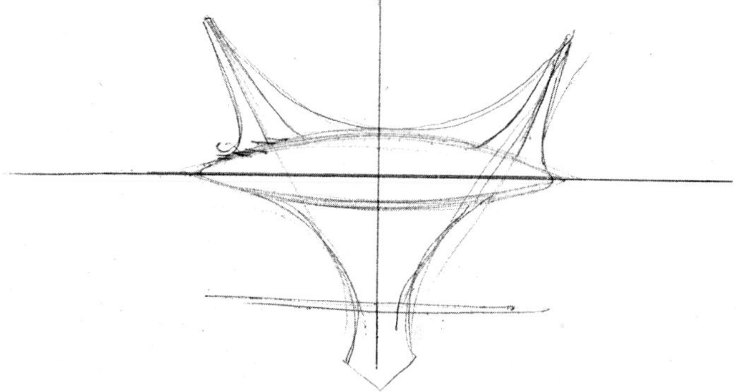

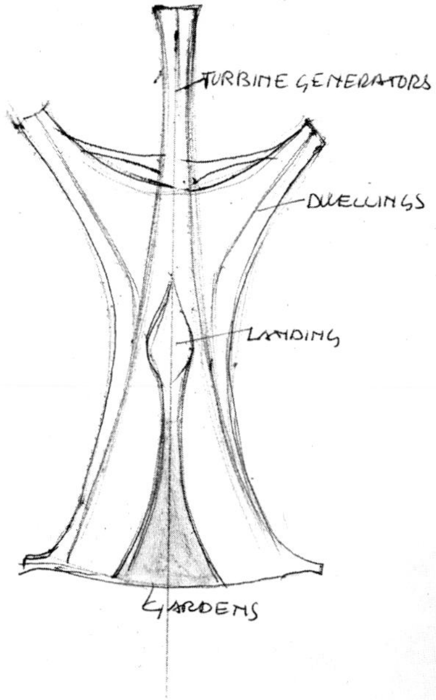

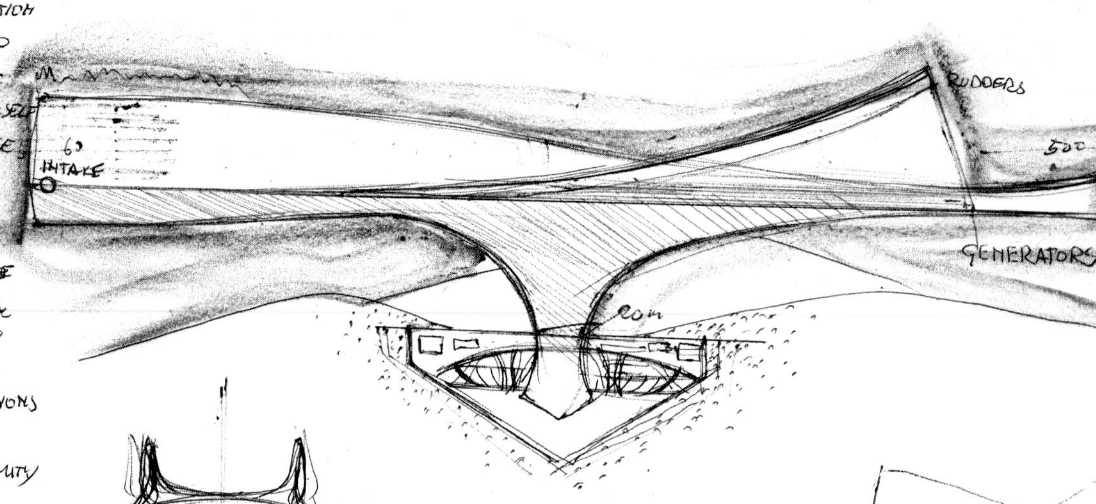

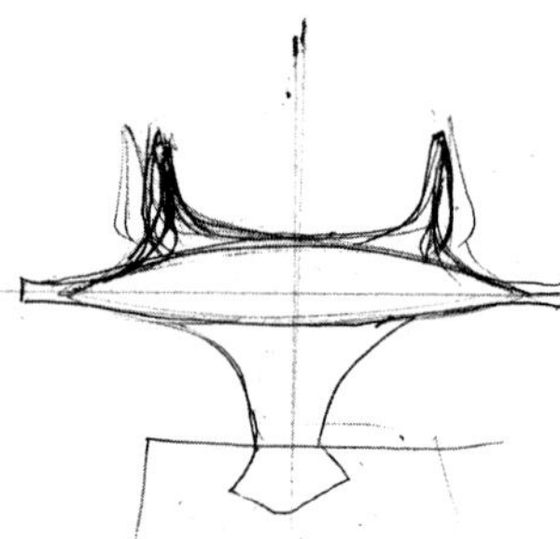

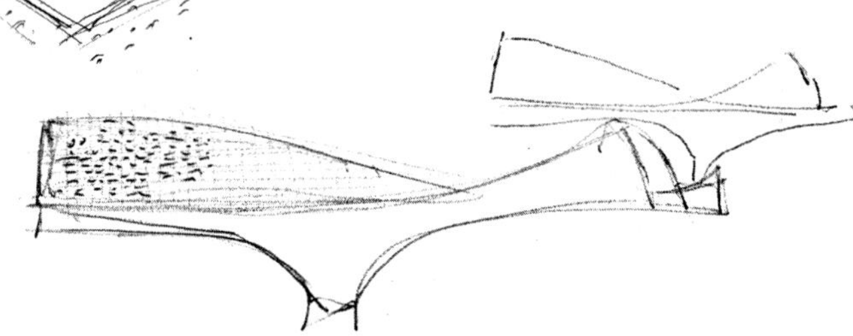

THE YEARLY PERGIURY OF DETROIT.)

(ILLUSORY?) TO AN END IN THE FIRST INSTANCE BELUSHING ITSELF IS THE DEVINE, I.E. TRUE SIGNIFICATION OF COS_ MOS WHIT NO LIMIT THAT TIME & EFFORT CAN NOT OVERFLOW & CONQUER

IN THIS INSTANCE TIME IS CONCEIVED AS DURATION & POSSIBILITY MEANS THE NEGATION OF IMPOSSIBILITY.

IN THE OTHER INSTANCE TIME IS A DEVISED SISTEM OF MESUREMENT WHIT NO INTRINSECAL TRUTH (PART OF THE ILLUSORY VEIL, "MAYA," SEPARATING BEINGS FROM REALITY) & POSSIBILITY IS A DEFINITE GAP BETWINS THE STATE OF ILLUSION & THE STATE OF PERFECTION REALITY

IMMEDIATE CONSEQUENCE OF THE DUALITY REALITY-ILLUSION IS THE SEPARATION OF THE I FROM ANY RULES, IN FACT THE "GITA" SAIS THAT GIVEN AN "ILLUMINATED" MIND DETACHED FROM DESIRE - PASSION - HATRED, AN INDIVIDUAL CAN ACT IN TOTAL "IRRESPONSABILITY," WHICH WOULD DEPICTS FAIRLY FAITHFULLY THE EXECUTIO_ NER. BE HE THE BANK CLERK THE BUROCRAT OR THE KILLER (NAZI) IF IT WASN'T FOR THE EQUIVOCAL RAC_ COMMANDATION ABOUT ENLIGHTEMENT

THE UNTOUCHABLE DIVINITY OF THE GITA DO NOT REPEL ME CAUSE ITS WROL_ CARIOM OF USELESS ANGUIS & SEN_ SLESS PERVICACITY BUT IS UNACCE_ TABLE AS SUCH BECAUSE EVEN AS ILLUSORY, THIS REALITY OF OUR AS ENGROSSING OR STULTIFING ITS PRIME CAUSE : THE DIVINITY, THUS

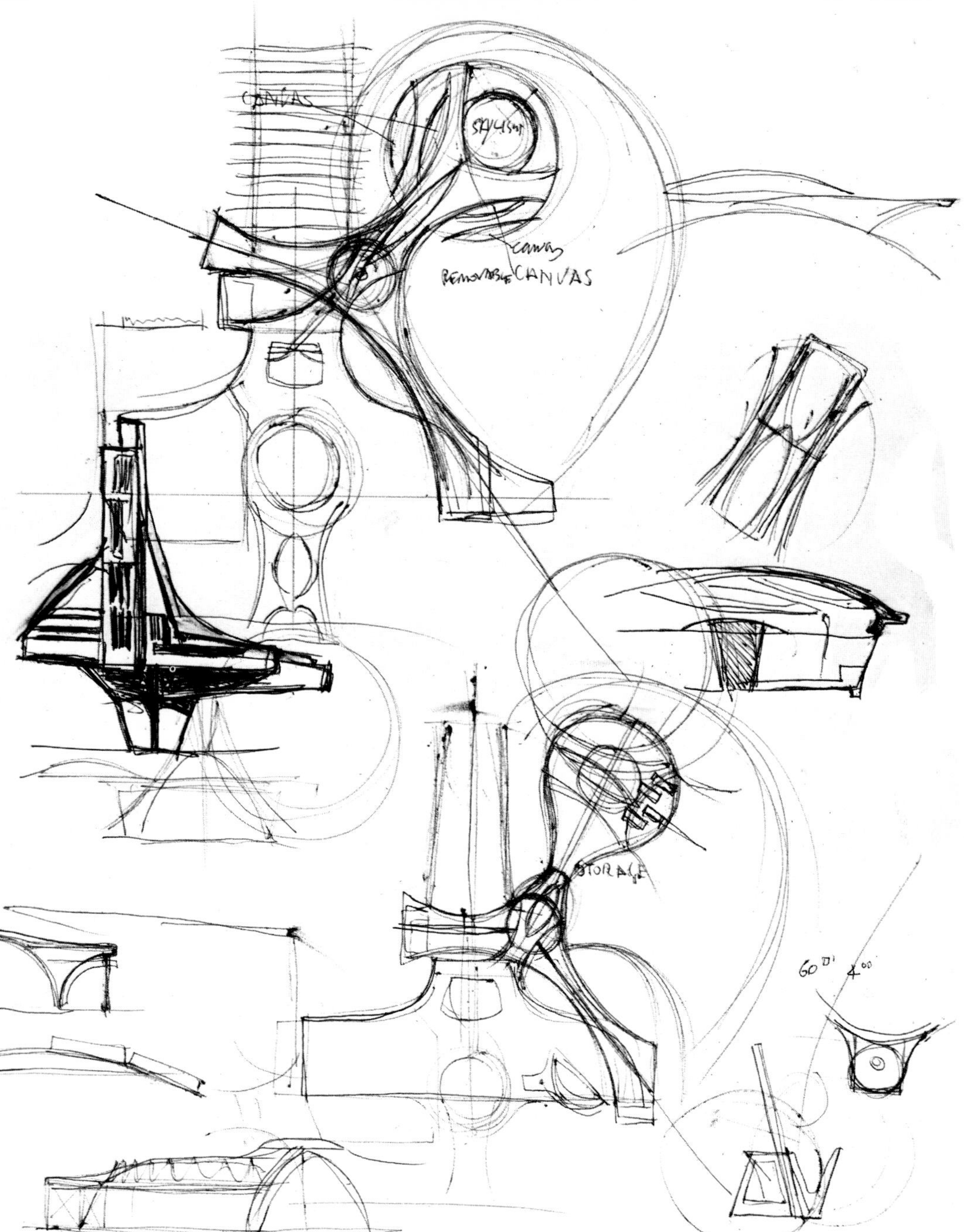

p13 DOING AWAY WHIT INALTERABILITY, ITS BASIC ATTRIBUTE.
IF THEN OUR (OTHERWISE) BECOMING IS JUST A TIMELESS DISPLAY WHITHIN THE BODY OF THE DIVINE, ONE OF THE MANY & AS SUCH. NOT BEARING OF ANY CHANGES OF IT THEN IT BECAMES OBVIOUS THAT ANY ACTION, OR EMOTION, OR INTELLECTUAL INCEPTION, IS AS GOOD AS ANY OTHER BECAUSE THE FREEDOM OF CHOOSING IS ABSENT WHERE EVER DURATION. IE THE MAKING OF THE PAST INTO THE FUTURE BY WAY OF THE SKILLFULL PRESENT, IS NO EXISTENT.

IF OUR LIFE IS THE ILLUSORY SELF RESPONSABILITY (SOLLICITED) ILLUMINATED BY A BECOM OF LIGHT (THE PRESENT) INSCRIBING IS UNALTERABLE PATH ON A, FOR EVER WRITTEN OR DEPICTED DIORAMA (PAST + FUTURE) THEN NO POSSIBLE DIRECTION IS WHITING ANY PARTICLE OF IT BECAUSE ITS CONCEPTION WAS ONE & FINAL & OUT OF SPACE OR TIME

AS NO DIRECTION HAS A VESSEL WHICH IS FOUND BY THE SEARCHING LIGHT OF THE LIGHT HOUSE ALWAYS AT THE SAME SPOT. NO DIRECTION ENCE NO LIFE (HENCE NO MEANING)

BY REFUSING SUCH DIVINITY I DESTROY IT. FINALLY & TOTALLY AS IF, WHIT SUCH BLASFEMOUS UTTERANCE, A IRREPARABLE HOLE WAS PUNCTURED INTO THE ENFLATED BALLON OF BRAHMAN NEVER TO BE REPAIRED & RESTORED,
THIS NOT BY POWER OF INTELLECT OR WISDOM BUT BY REFUSAL OF THE UNDIFFERENTIATE: THE AMORFUS. THE DEATH

VALUE IS A DEIETY WHICH I CAN'T

(P16)

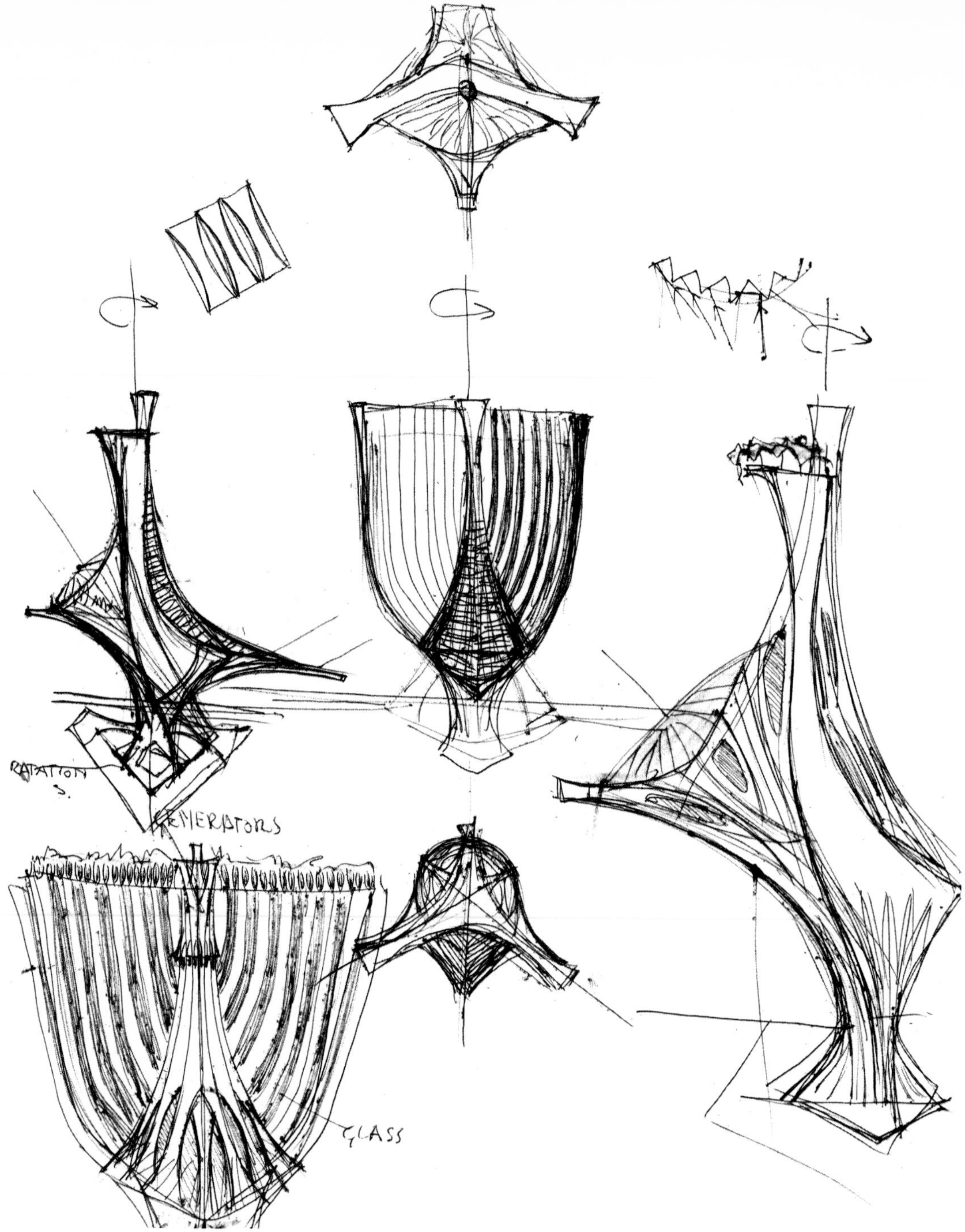

P.V. NOVEMBER 1959

TOTEM COSMIC POTENTIAL
(INFRARED RADIATIONS)
THE MULTIPLICITY OF PURPOSES PROJECTED INTO A UNITARIAN STRUCTURE COUNTS FOR THE UNPREVEDIBLE MORPHOLOGY
MAIN PURPOSES
SHELTER FOR A COMUNITY.
FACILITIES THEREOF.
PRODUCTION OF ENERGY & HOT WATER FOR DOMESTIC USES
HIGH DENSITY OF POPULATION
HIGH CONCENTRATION OF FACILITIES (MINIMUM WASTE)

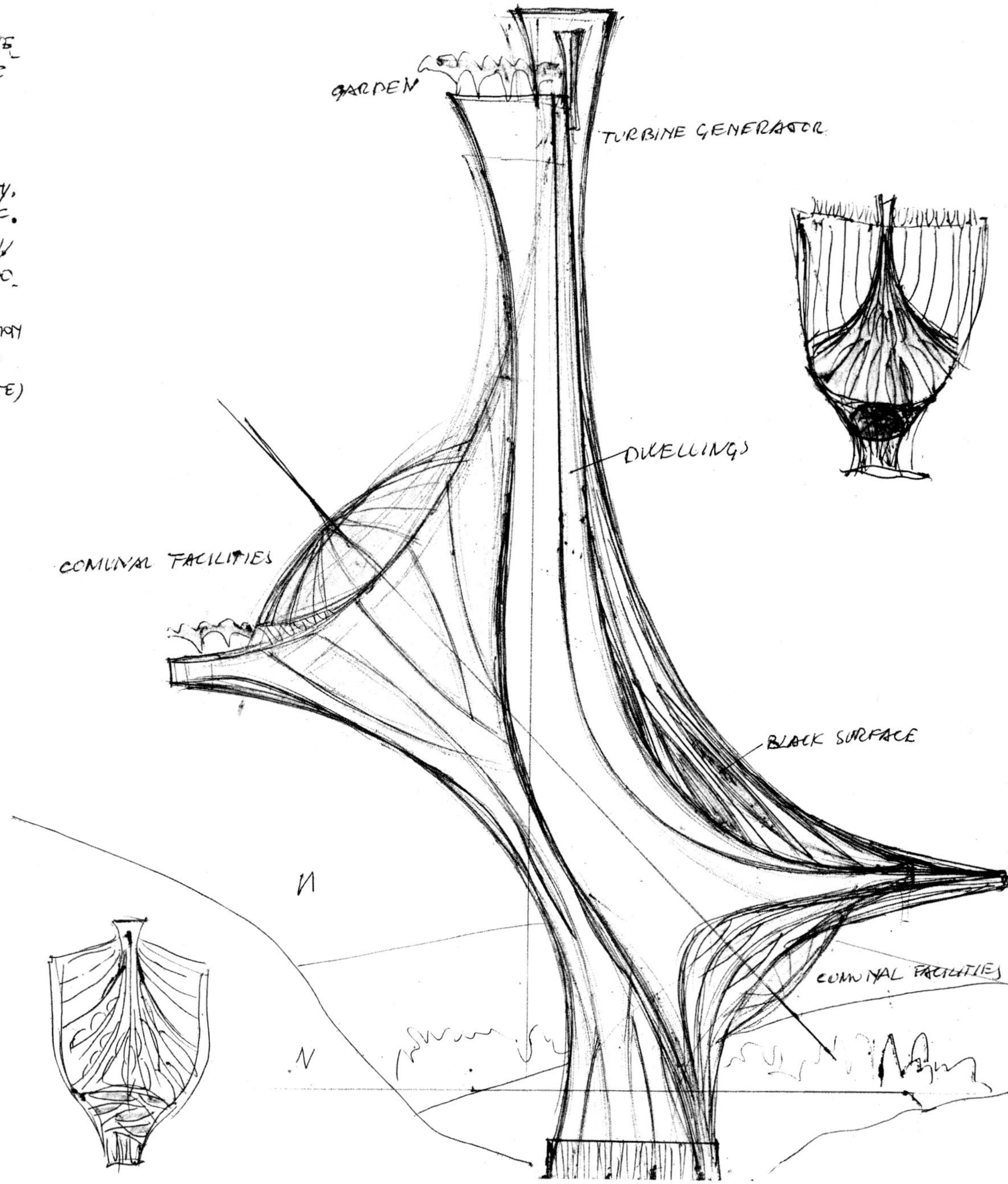

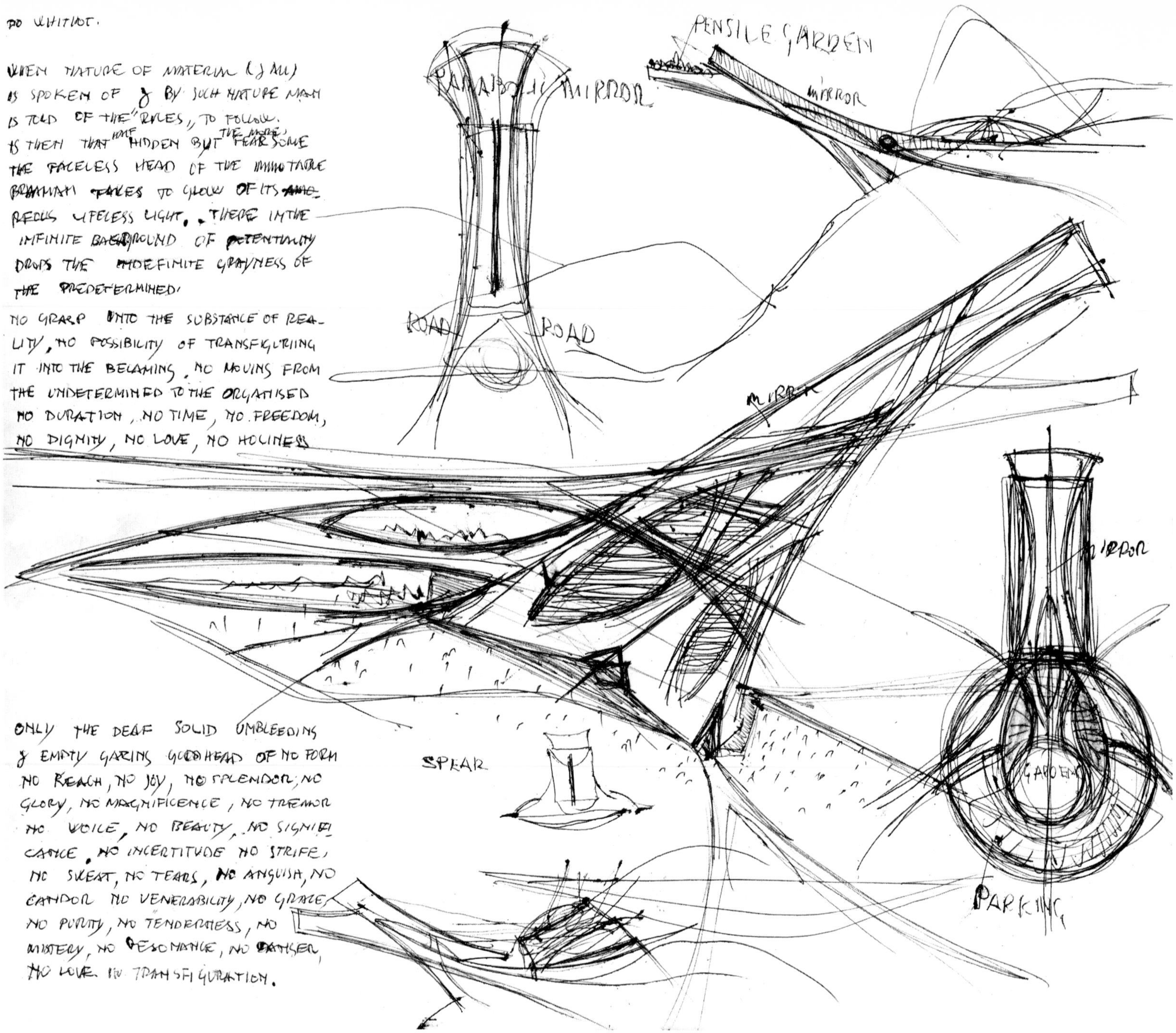
TO WHITLOT.
WHEN NATURE OF MATERIAL (J ALL)
IS SPOKEN OF J BY SUCH NATURE MAN
IS TOLD OF THE "RULES," TO FOLLOW.
IS THEN THAT HALF HIDDEN BUT THE MORE FEARSOME
THE FACELESS HEAD OF THE IMMUTABLE
BRAHMAN TAKES TO GLOW OF ITS
RECUS LIFELESS LIGHT. THERE IN THE
INFINITE BACKGROUND OF POTENTIALITY
DROPS THE INDEFINITE GRAYNESS OF
THE PREDETERMINED.
NO GRASP INTO THE SUBSTANCE OF REA-
LITY, NO POSSIBILITY OF TRANSFIGURING
IT INTO THE BECOMING, NO MOVING FROM
THE UNDETERMINED TO THE ORGANISED
NO DURATION, NO TIME, NO FREEDOM,
NO DIGNITY, NO LOVE, NO HOLINESS
ONLY THE DEAF SOLID UNBLEEDING
J EMPTY GAPING GODHEAD OF NO FORM
NO REACH, NO JOY, NO SPLENDOR; NO
GLORY, NO MAGNIFICENCE, NO TREMOR
NO VOICE, NO BEAUTY, NO SIGNIFI-
CANCE, NO INCERTITUDE NO STRIFE,
NO SWEAT, NO TEARS, NO ANGUISH, NO
CANDOR NO VENERABILITY, NO GRACE,
NO PURITY, NO TENDERNESS, NO
MISTERY, NO RESONANCE, NO DANGER,
NO LOVE. NO TRANSFIGURATION.
PARABOLIC MIRROR
PENSILE GARDEN
MIRROR
ROAD
ROAD
MIRROR
MIRROR
SPEAR
GARDEN
PARKING

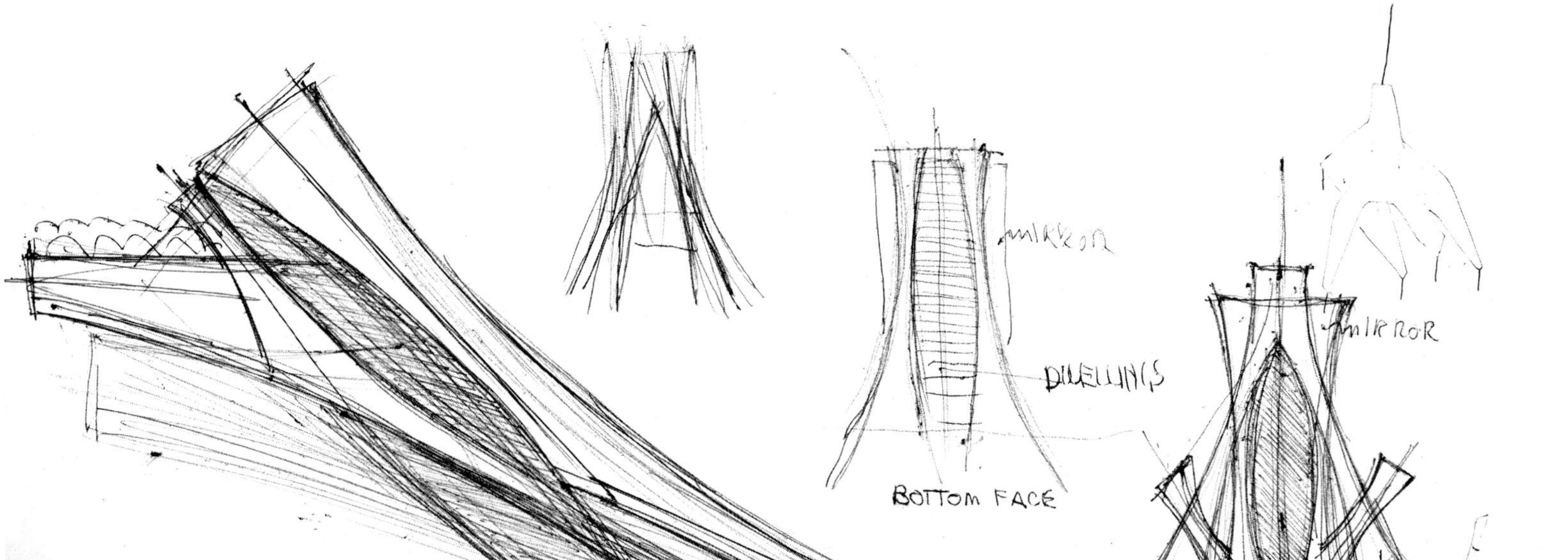

"IMPERSONAL" SKILL GOES FOR STRICT FUNCTIONALITY, THE ONE WHICH CONCERNS MATERIALITY.
LOVING SKILL GOES FOR THE "USEFUL" CRAFT WHICH FUNCTIONALITY OVERFLOWS INTO THE REALM OF AESTETIC EMOTION, THUS HAVING ALMOST A BRUSH WHIT "FINALITY"
TRANSFIGURING ACTION IMPLEMENTED BY SKILL, WHICH MAY HAVE REACHED THE "AUTOMATIC" STAGE, ARRIVES ACTING INTO THE CONDITION OF CREATIVITY, BE IT RUDIMENTAL OR COMPLEX, & ALWAYS PUTTING INTO THE PASSING MOMENT A GRAIN OR AN HANDFULL OF FINALITY

AS SUCH WHAT IS CALLED "THE WORK OF ART" CAN ABSTAIN FROM DURATION & STAY IN SUBSTANTIAL ISOLATION IN TIME AS IN SPACE, PAYING THOO, TO BOOTH, THE INEVITABLE TRIBUTE OF INVOLUTION BY DECAYING MATERIALLY & POSSIBLY OF FUSCATING SPIRITUALLY BECAUSE THE LACK

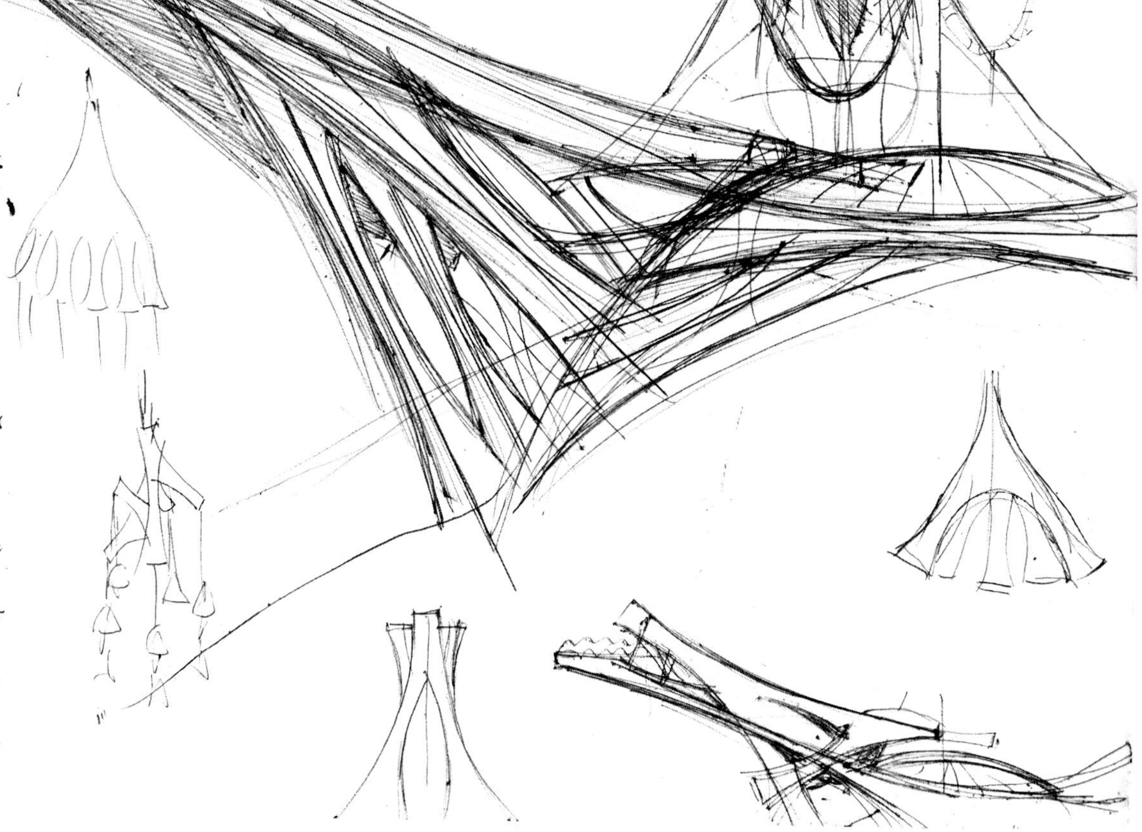

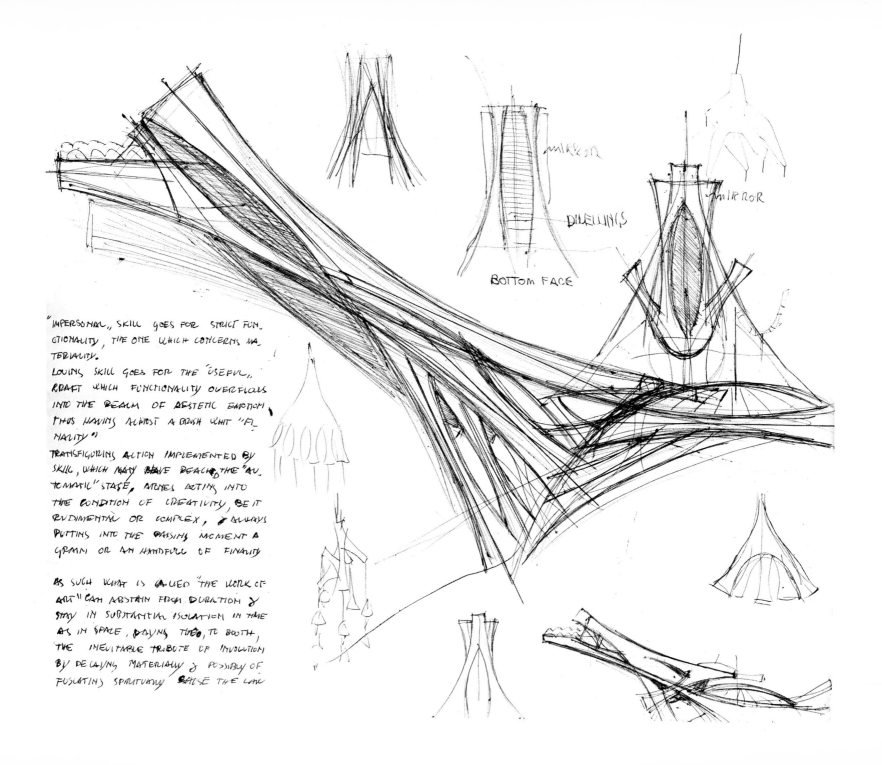

1-12-1959

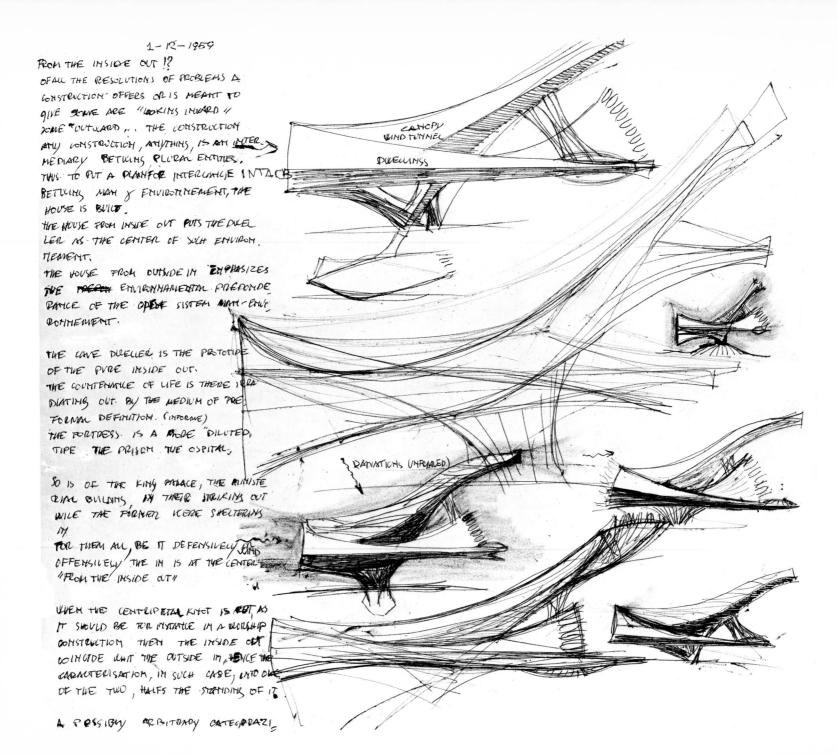

FROM THE INSIDE OUT !?
OF ALL THE RESOLUTIONS OF PROBLEMS A CONSTRUCTION OFFERS OR IS MEANT TO GIVE SOME ARE "LOOKING INWARD" SOME "OUTWARD". THE CONSTRUCTION ANY CONSTRUCTION, ANYTHING, IS AN INTERMEDIARY BETWEEN PLURAL ENTITIES. THUS TO PUT A PLAN FOR INTERCHANGE INTACT BETWEEN MAN & ENVIRONMEMENT, THE HOUSE IS BUILT.
THE HOUSE FROM INSIDE OUT PUTS THE DWELLER AS THE CENTER OF SUCH ENVIRONMEMENT.
THE HOUSE FROM OUTSIDE IN EMPHASIZES THE ENVIRONMAMENTAL PREPONDERANCE OF THE SISTEM MAN-ENVIRONMEMENT.

THE CAVE DWELLER IS THE PROTOTIPE OF THE PURE INSIDE OUT.
THE COUNTENANCE OF LIFE IS THERE IRRADIATING OUT. BY THE MEDIUM OF PREFORMAL DEFINITION. (INFORME)
THE FORTRESS IS A MODE "DILUTED" TIPE THE PRISON THE OSPITAL,

SO IS OF THE KING PALACE, THE MINISTERIAL BUILDINS, IN THEIR STRIKING OUT WILE THE FORMER WERE SHELTERING IN
FOR THEM ALL, BE IT DEFENSIVELLY OR OFFENSIVELLY THE IN IS AT THE CENTER "FROM THE INSIDE OUT"

WHEN THE CENTRIPETAL KNOT IS NOT, AS IT SHOULD BE FOR INSTANCE IN A WORSHIP CONSTRUCTION THEN THE INSIDE OUT COINCIDE WITH THE OUTSIDE IN, HENCE THE CARACTERISATION, IN SUCH CASE, INTO ONE OF THE TWO, HALFS THE STANDING OF IT.

A POSSIBLY ARBITRARY CATEGORAZI=

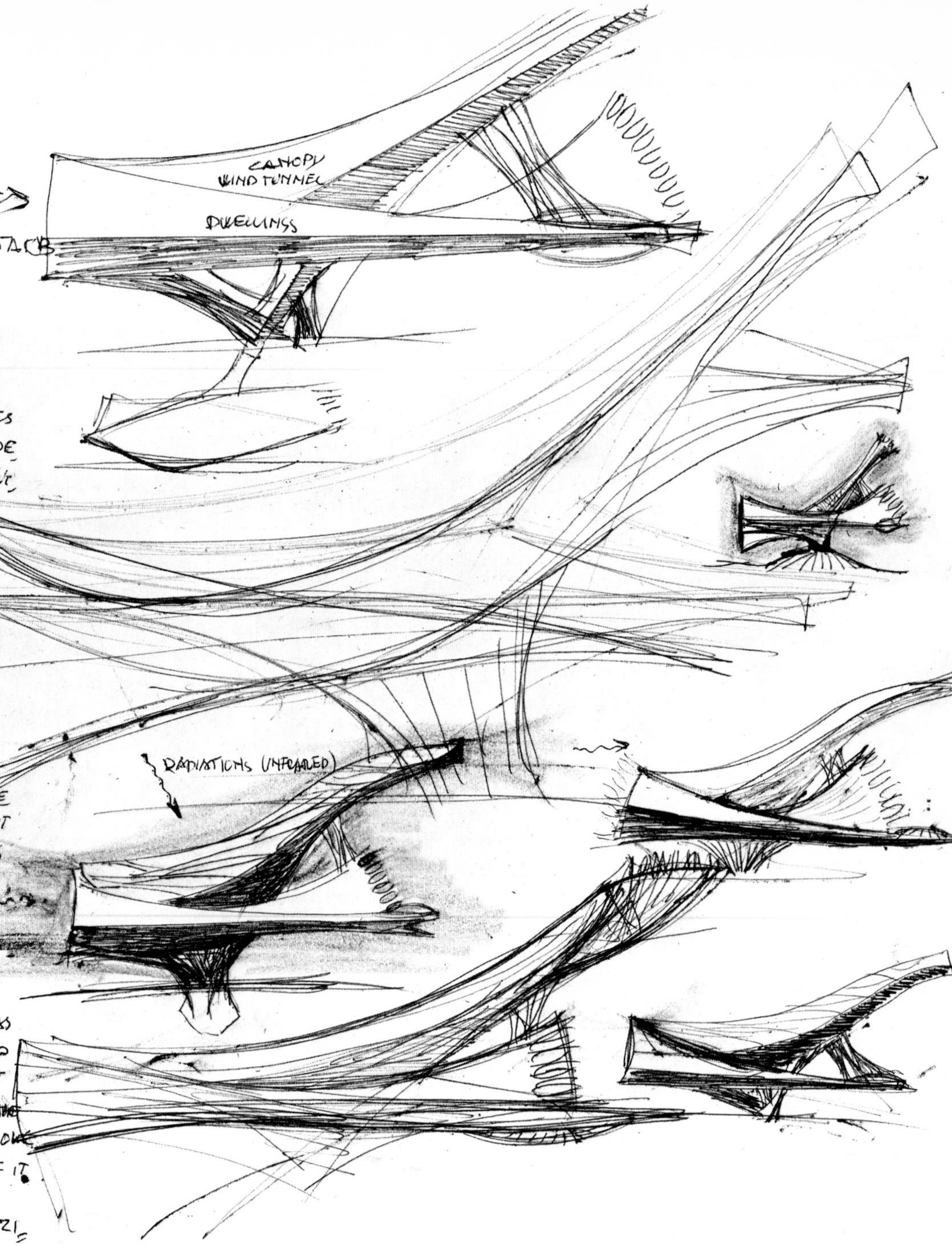

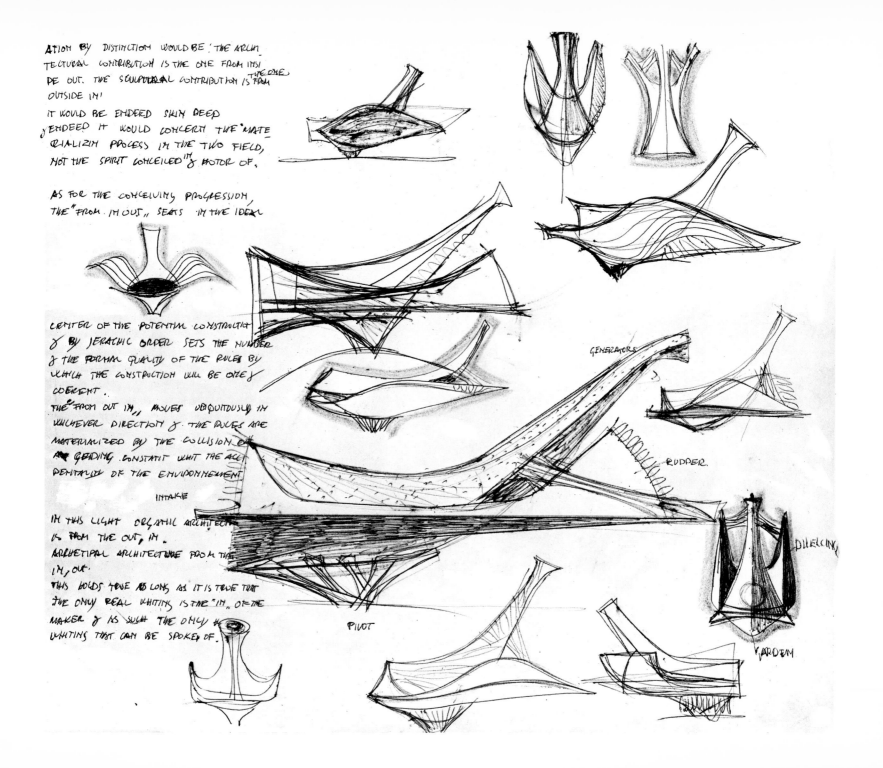

ATION BY DISTINCTION WOULD BE: THE ARCHITECTURAL CONTRIBUTION IS THE ONE FROM INSIDE OUT. THE SCULPTURAL CONTRIBUTION IS THE ONE FROM OUTSIDE IN!

IT WOULD BE ENDEED SKIN DEEP & ENDEED IT WOULD CONCERN THE "MATERIALIZIN PROCESS IN THE TWO FIELD, NOT THE SPIRIT CONCEILED IN & MOTOR OF.

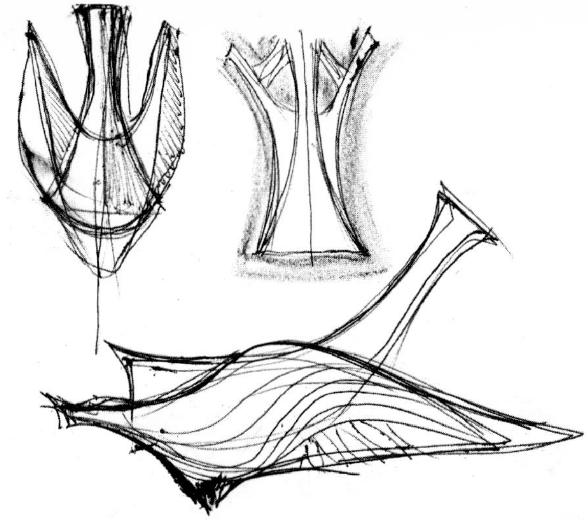

AS FOR THE CONCEIVING PROGRESSION, THE "FROM IN OUT" SEATS IN THE IDEAL

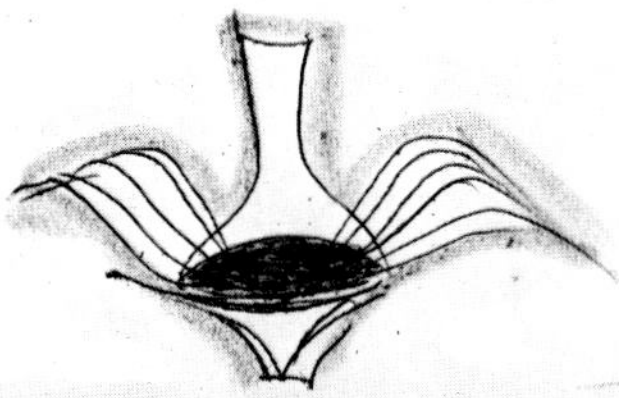

CENTER OF THE POTENTIAL CONSTRUCTION & BY JERACHIC ORDER SETS THE NUMBER & THE FORMAL QUALITY OF THE RULES BY WHICH THE CONSTRUCTION WILL BE ONE & COERENT.

THE "FROM OUT IN" MOVES UBIQUITOUSLY IN WHICHEVER DIRECTION & THE RULES ARE MATERIALIZED BY THE COLLISION OF GRADING CONSTANT WHIT THE ACCIDENTALITY OF THE ENVIRONMEMENT

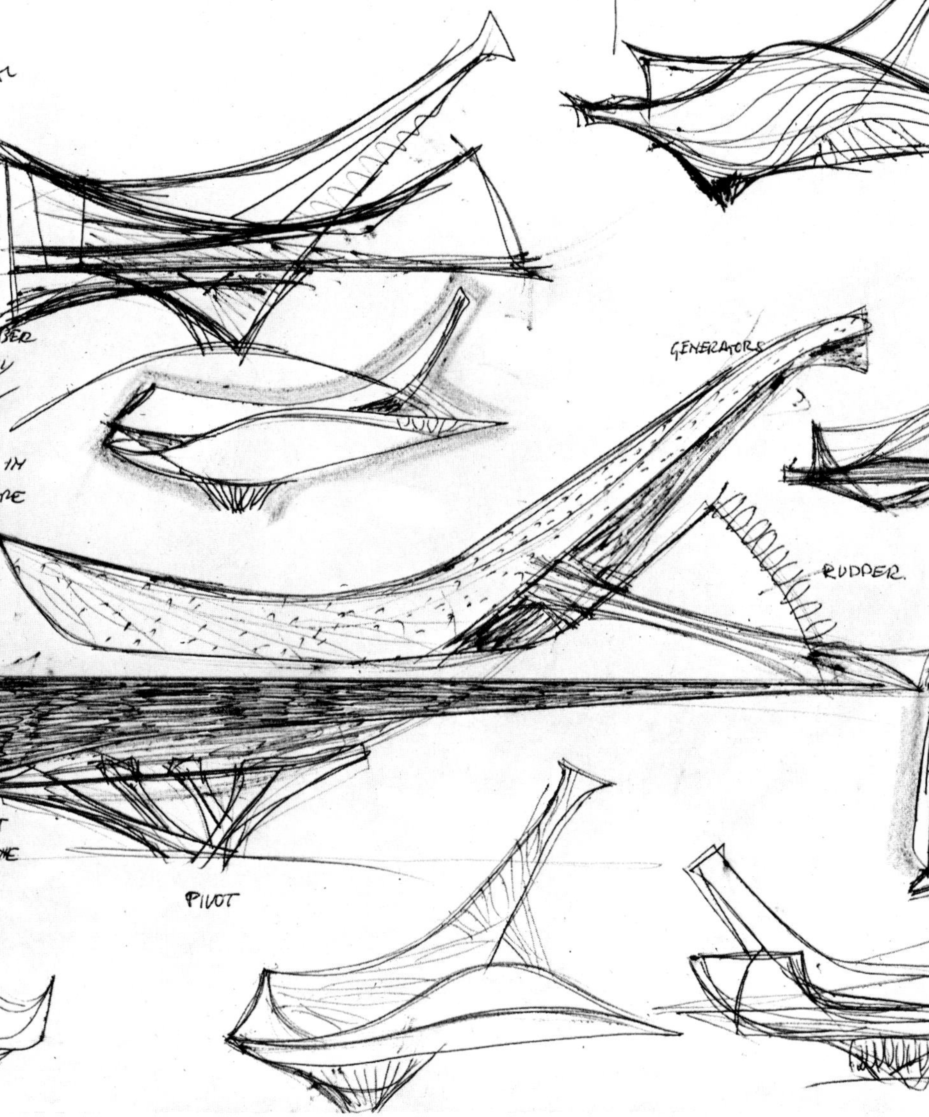

IN THIS LIGHT ORGANIC ARCHITECTURE IS FROM THE OUT, IN.
ARCHETIPAL ARCHITECTURE FROM THE IN, OUT.

THIS HOLDS TRUE AS LONG AS IT IS TRUE THAT THE ONLY REAL WHITING IS THE "IN" OF THE MAKER & AS SUCH THE ONLY WHITING THAT CAN BE SPOKEN OF.

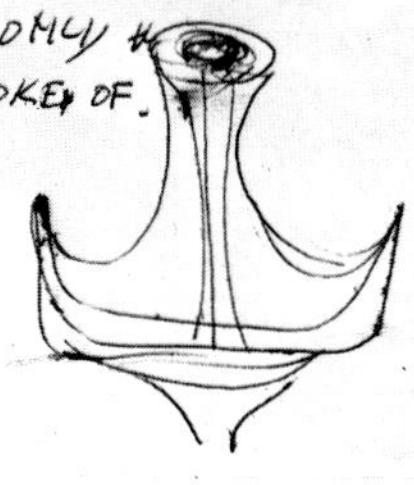

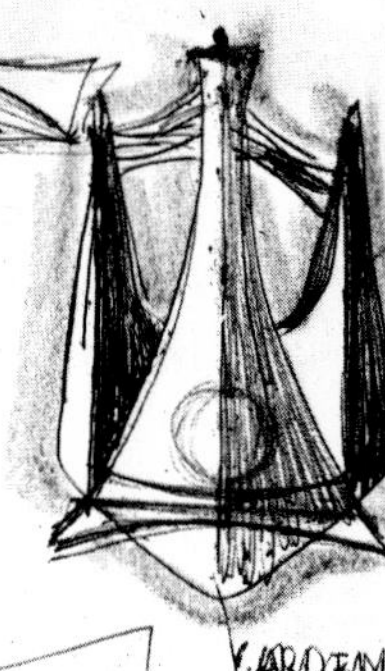

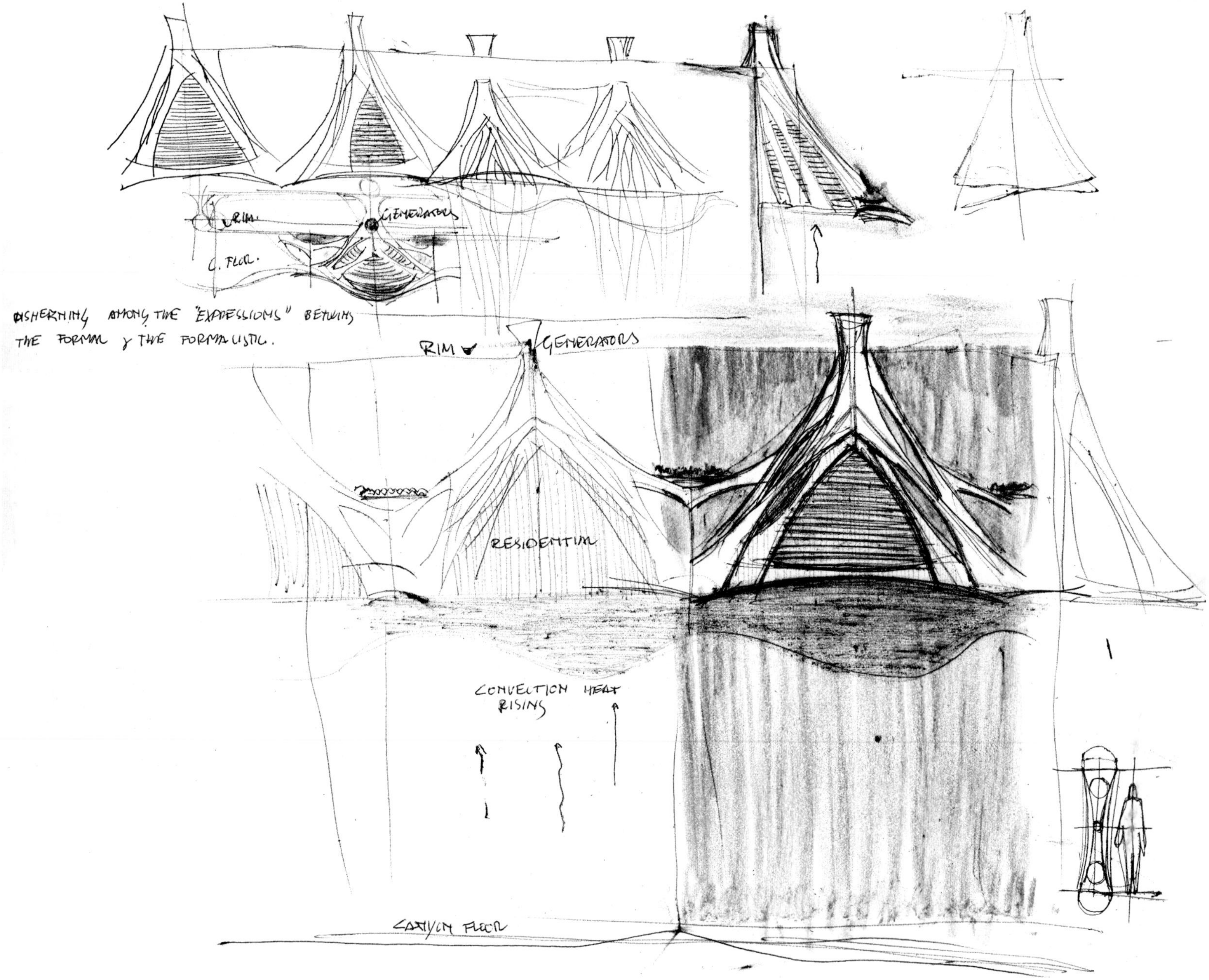
RIM
GENERATORS
RESIDENTIAL
CONVECTION HEAT
RISING

FUNDAMENTAL CARACTERISTIC OF THE ENVELOP. THIS SKIN: THE INNER PRESSURE (ATMO-SFERICAL CONDITIONING) AGAINST THE OUTER VACUM.
TENSIL ELEMENTS WILL TEXTURE THE IN-NER VOLUME KEEPING THE SKIN FROM EXPLODING

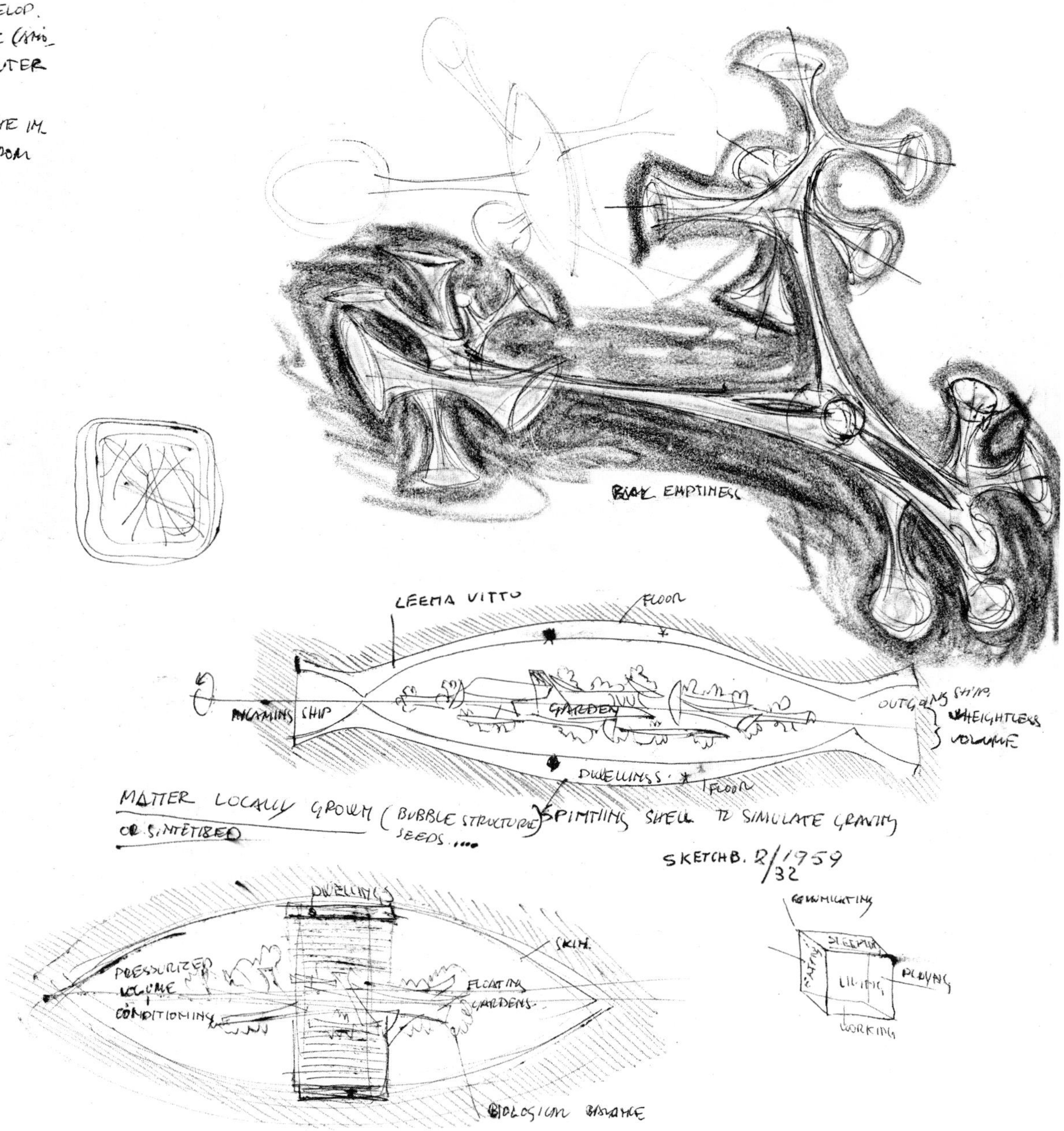

AS THE GOOD OLD HUNTER ON FLESH & NURSING POTATOS & CABBAGES ..
NO CONJECTURE POSSIBLE ON WHAT KIND OF INTELLIGENTIA WOULD AFFLICT HIM. LIBRARY, CHURCHES, OPERAHOUSES, AS MUCH AS BOOKS RECORDED EMOTIONS, CREATIONS. DOUBTFULLY CONCEIVED OF, NOT TO SAY PRODUCED.

AS THINGS ARE, AS THE GROWING-GRAZING & EATING EQUATION IS WHAT IT IS, AS MAN'S HUNGER FOR THE "SUPERFLOUS" IS & MULTIPLIES FORCEFULLY, AS THE MIND OF MAN WORKS AS IT WORKS THE "SERENADE" TO THE FREE GROWING SOCIAL BODY & ITS CONTAINERS THEREOF (HOME, VILLAGE, TOWN, CITY ...) IS AS INSIPIDOUS AS IT IS STUPID. IN THIS CASE AS ALWAYS STUPIDITY IS ANTAGONISTIC TO LIFE. MEANS INAPTITUDE, UNFITNESS HENCE DESTRUCTIVENESS, CAOS, & THIS IS WATH WE GET FROM THE "FREE GROWTH" OF WHAT IS MISTAKENLY LOOKT UPON AS AN ORGANISM, WHILE IT IS AT BEST A BEAUTIFULLY WORKING AGGREGATE & AS SUCH HAS TO BE PLANNED NOT JUST WATERED WHIT THE SPRINKLER OF OUR WISHES
+
THE CONFLICT BETWINS SPONTANEITY & RIGOR DOES OFTEN OBSCURE THE FACT THAT THE VIGOR OF SPONTANEITY IS THE INHERITANCE THAT A RIGOROUS UNDERCURRENT OF PURPOSE MAKES AVAILABLE AT THE INSTANT OF CONCLUSION WHEN FRUITS ARE REAPEN & THEY LOOK SO "NATURALLY" SO.
IF MAN WAS PURE INSTINCT THINGS WOULD GROW FROM HIM NOW MORE, NOW LESS "SUCCESFULLY", THE PLANNING WOULD BE MADE AVAILABLE (IMPOSED) TO HIM. BY GOD!? BY NATURE!? BY THE ELAN VITAL!? ...

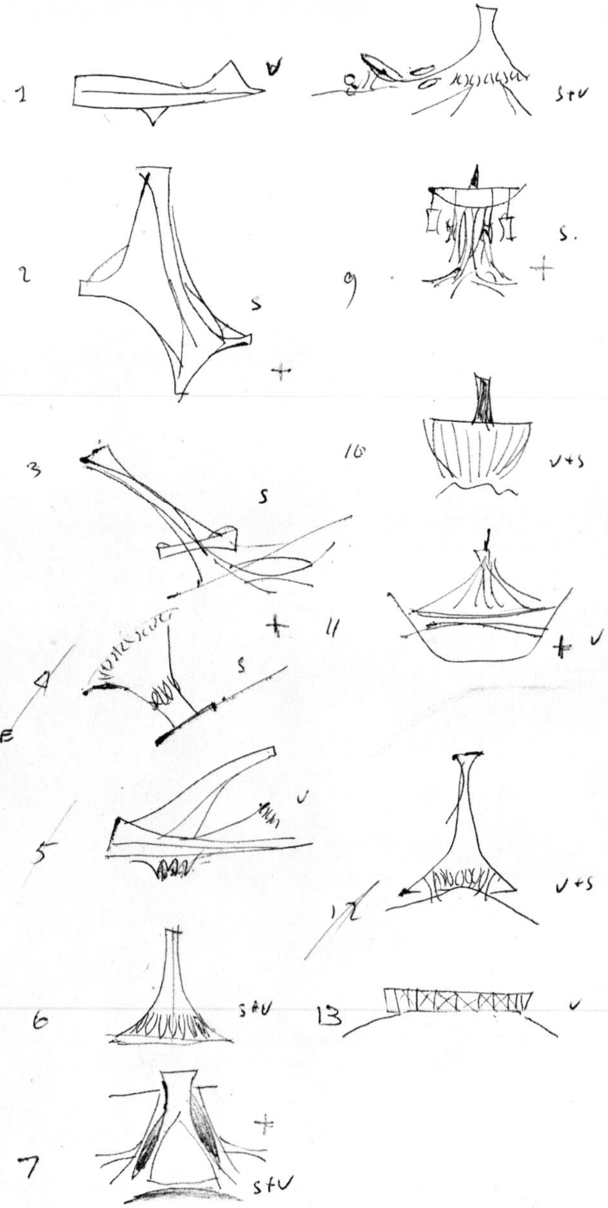

C. POTENTIAL

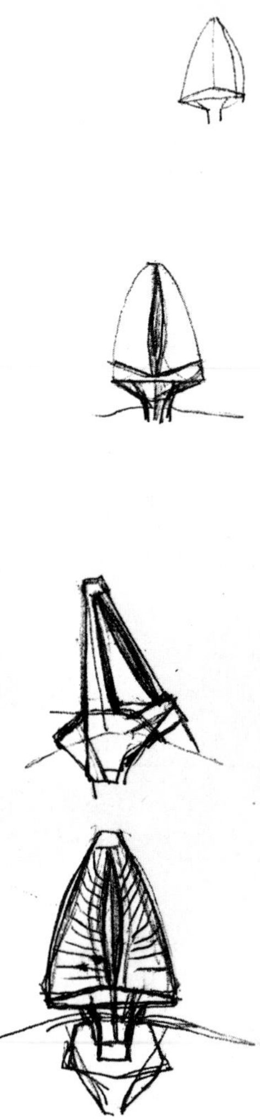

SO AS TO TRUST. UPON IT ~~AN UNDELIMITABLE~~
THESHADE OF AN "ABSOLUTE" IS THE GOD
A POSTERIORI THAT CHURCHES FALL IN
THEIR "APRIORISTIC" DOGMAS
OR THEY FALL MAN IN ~~ATTRIBUTING~~ HIM
THE LONGING FOR THE ~~ORIGINAL ANXIETY.~~
UNDIFFERENTIATE OF THE ORIGIN. (HAVEN)

OR IS MAN FILLED BY THE ILLUSION OF
A FUTURE WHICH WILL NEVER BE, IN
TOTALITY NOR IN PROPENSITY

THE DISTROYERS OF INNOCENCE

THE MORTAL FALLACY OF MAN MY BE ITS
UNSPOKEN CONCEPT THAT TIME CAN BE
COMPRESSED ~~TROUGH~~ BY SCIENCE;
THOO THE INORGANIC POTENTIAL OF THE
GLOBE IS PRACTICLY UNTOUCHED
THE ORGANIC (LIVING) CAPACITY OF IT IS
IRRESPONSABLY DESTROIED, (THE CAPITAL)
YET NO SUBSTANTIAL INDICATION IS THERE
THAT LIVING PROCESSES CAN BE SINTETAZED
Y OR TIME COMPRESSED
FROM SOIL ARVEST TO MENTAL
GROUGHT ALL THAT IS INVESTED OF
LIFE IS ALSO BOUND TO DURATION
IF IT IS NOT DURATION ITSELF : TIME.

IF THIS HOLDS TRUE FOR THE INORGANIC
ALSO, IT IS THOO MOST OF THE TIME
IN PARAMETERS Y SCALE QUITE "UNUMAN",
A STAR DURATION HAS NO RESONANCE
IN THE UMAN MIND BESIDE ~~ITS~~ POETICAL
IMMAGERY
THE VASTITY OF COSMIC MESURES
ALMOST TEND TO NEGATE THE UMAN
CONCEPT OF DIMENSION. THE CON-
TINUITY BETWINS THE TWO IS NOT
PERCEPTABLE, THERE IS MORE OF
A BOTTOMLESS VOID THAN A BRIDGING
POSSIBILITY BETWINS THE TWO".

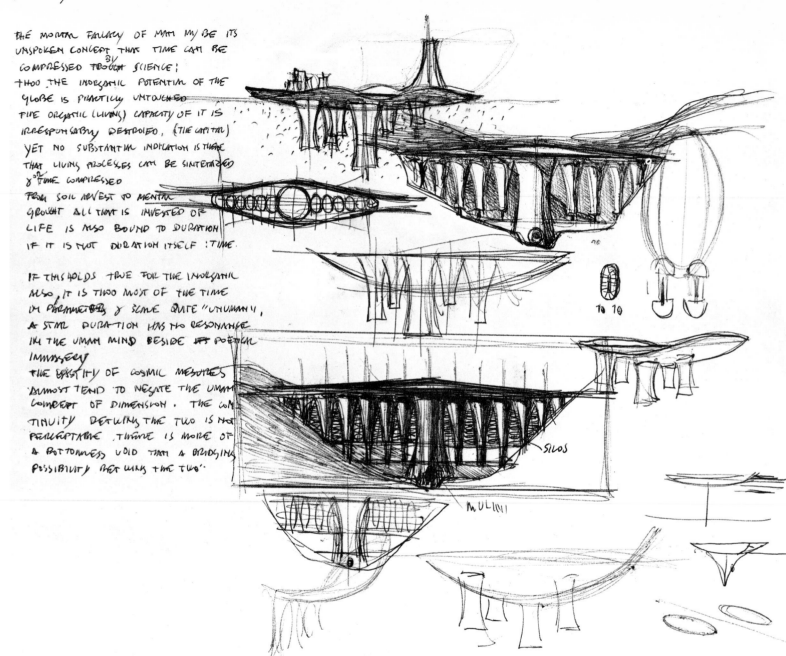

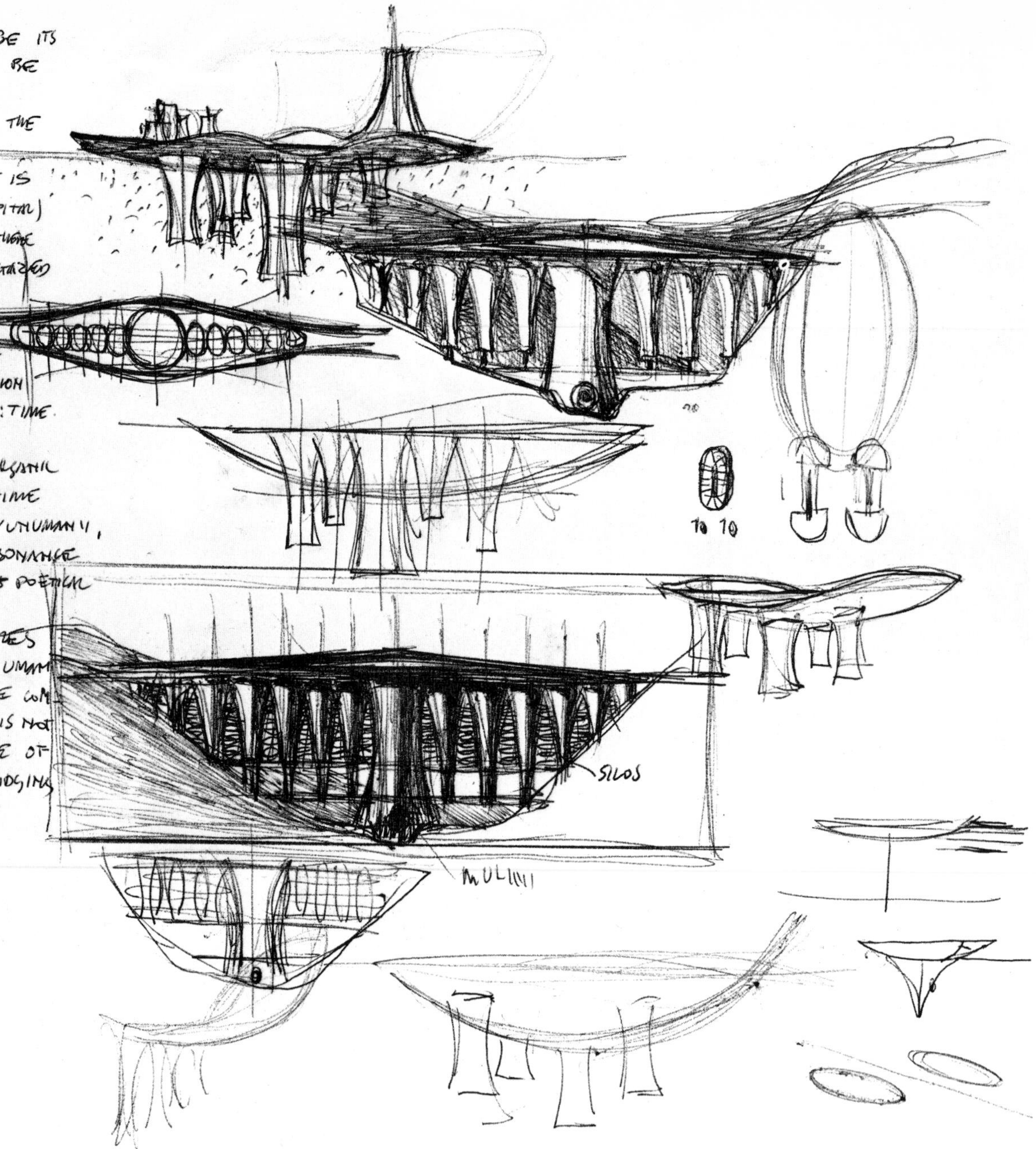

IF ONE [EACH OF US] MAY BE SIMBOLIZED BY A PHISICAL NUCLEUS RADIATING ENERGY-MATTER ON EVER WIDENING ~~CIRCLES~~ SFERES OF EVER MORE TENUOUS, THUS MORE SENSITIVE VIBRATION. THEN THE RIGHT CONCEPT OF FREEDOM HAS VERY LITTLE IN COMMON WITH THE FREEDOM ADVOCATED BY POLITICAL EXPEDIANCY.

THOSE SFERICAL BROADCAST ARE CONSTANTLY INTERFERED BY & INTERFERING IN OTHERS SIMILAR ACTIVITIES. & IF THE I IS ONLY IF THOSE BROADCAST GO ON THEN. THERE IS NO SUCH THING AS "FREEDOM," BUT ONLY COMPATIBILITY (COMPASSION?)

IT SEEMS INDEED THAT, IT IS, IF NOT COMPASSION ITSELF THE ONLY FREEDOM. IT IS ONLY TROUGH COMPASSION THAT ENSLAVEMENT CAN BE CONQUERED & WHAT IT THE ENSLAVER.

IF COMPASSION CANNOT TAME IPOCRISY IT CAN CERTAINLY ISOLATE IT. THUS THE UNSER THAT IPOCRISY HAS FOR THE BREEDING GROUNDS OF OBSCURANTISMS MAY TRANSFER IN THE ACCEPTANCE OF LIGHT

FREEDOM BEING FUNDAMENTALLY A STATUS OF BEING NOT A PHISICAL CONDITION IS FUNDAMENTALLY IMPERVIOUS TO CONSTRICTION FROM WITHOUT. IT IS THE SAID COMING OF THE ONESELF THAT FINDS SWEET THE BITTERNESS OF BEING ILL TREATED & ENSLAVED

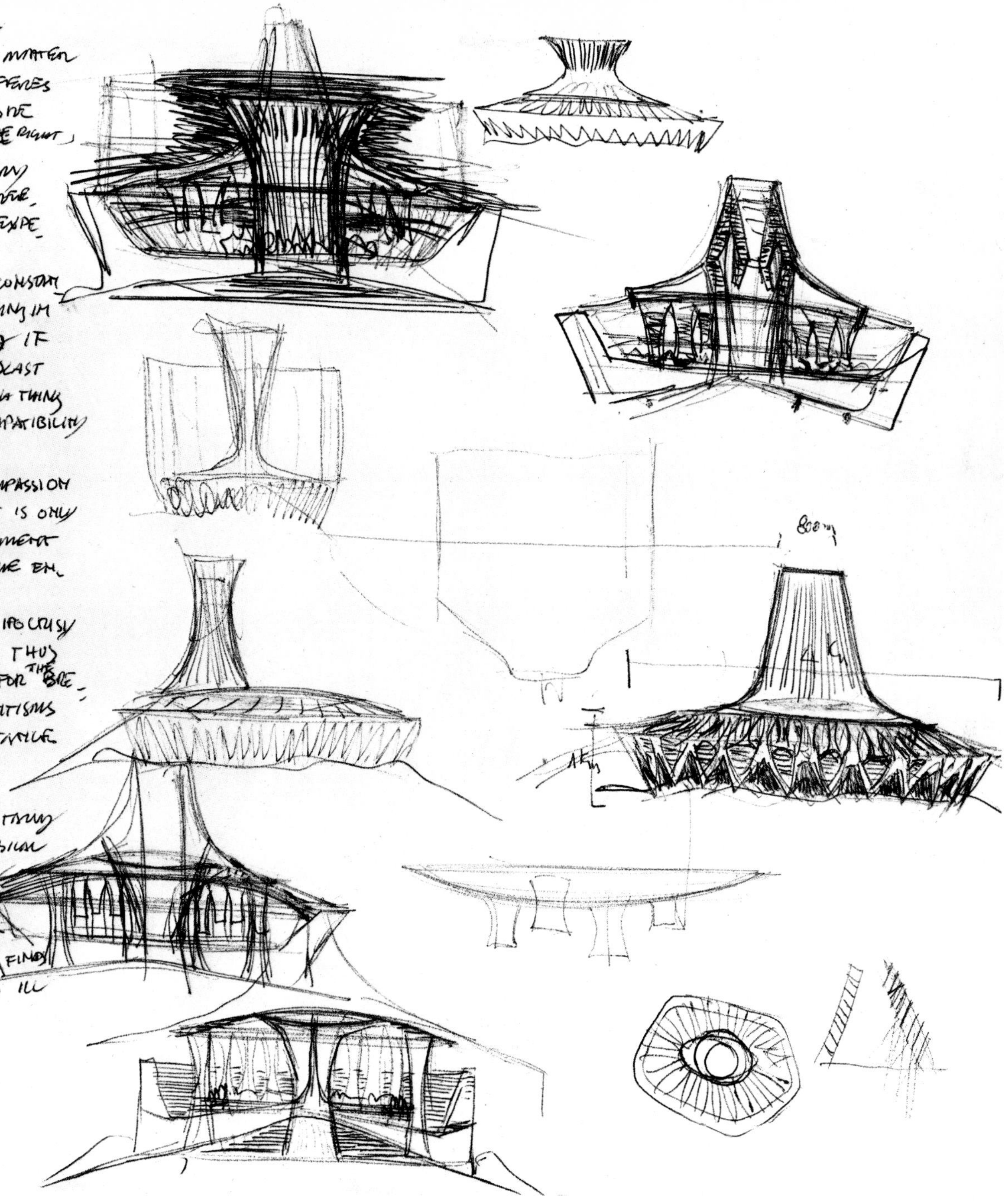

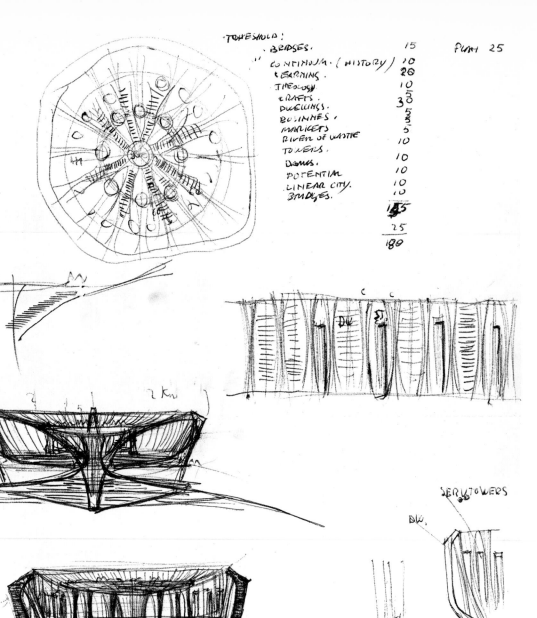

"WHAT THERE IS, IS ITS BECOMING
HAS ITS DENSE MASS SURVEYED BY
THE INNUMERABLE EXPLORERS,
EACH SURVEY IS EXTREMELY LIMITED
& OFTEN IN TOTAL ISOLATION. SO THE
UNKNOWABLE PERPETUATES ITS SECRECY

THE HIDDEN IS AS MUCH TO ITSELF
AS IT IS TO ITS PARTICLES SO IS THE
SEEKING & THE QUEST. FOR ANSWERS

THE FIRST LIGHT OF DAWN, THE WIDE
OPEN EYE ~~[illegible]~~
THE ULTIMATE ANGUISH, THE PEBBLES OF
THE SHORE, THE DEW & THE TORRENT
THEIR BEING, THEIR SEEKINGS, THEIR
MOMENTS. THEIR LANGUAGE, PRESENCE...

MARCH.

EACH TIME ONE HITS LIFE WITH SOMETHING
MEANINGLESS · LIFE IS HURT

LIFE IS HURT IN THE PERSON OF THE DOERS
& IT IS HURT IN THE TESTIMONIES OF
THE DOING.
THE MEANINGLESS IS THAT WHICH SHIED
INTENSITY & SETTLED FOR SUCH THING
THAT WILL NOT DENOUNCE ITS ORIGINATOR
WITH THE VISIBLE VOICE OF THE REJECTED.
THE REJECTED BEING CONFOUNDED
BY THE APPEARANCE OF THE DOER
IN ITS SELFRIGHTEOUSNESS..

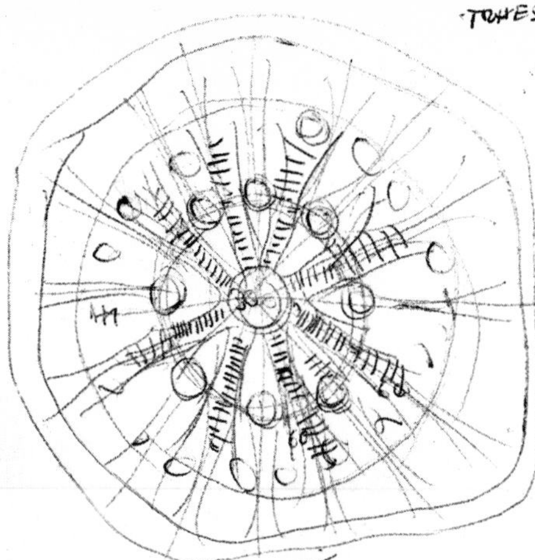

THRESHOLD:
- BRIDGES. 15
- CONTINUUM. (HISTORY) 10
- LEARNING. 20
- THEOLOGY 10
- CRAFTS. 35
- DWELLINGS. 5
- BUSINESS. 5
- MARKETS 5
- RIVER OF WASTE 10
- TOWERS. 10
- DOMES. 10
- POTENTIAL 10
- LINEAR CITY. 10
- BRIDGES. 10

155
25
180

PLAN 25

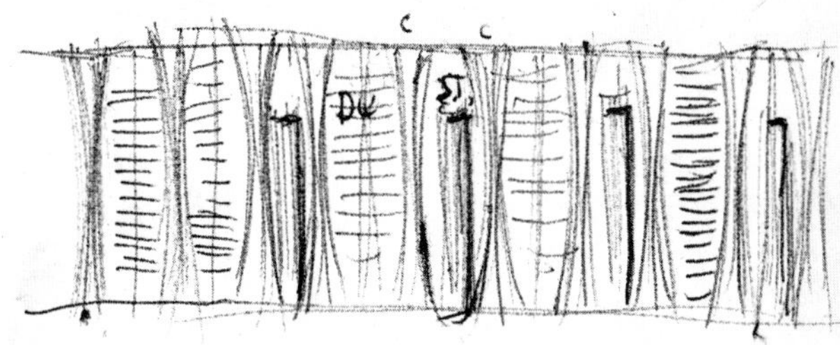

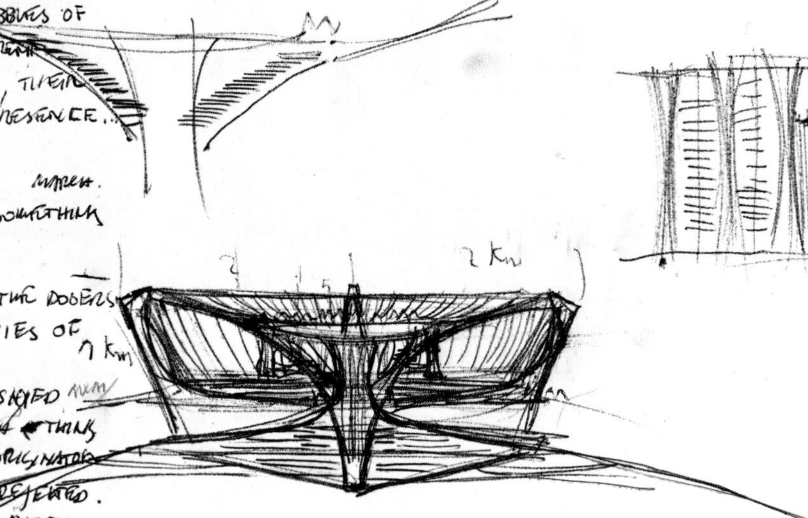

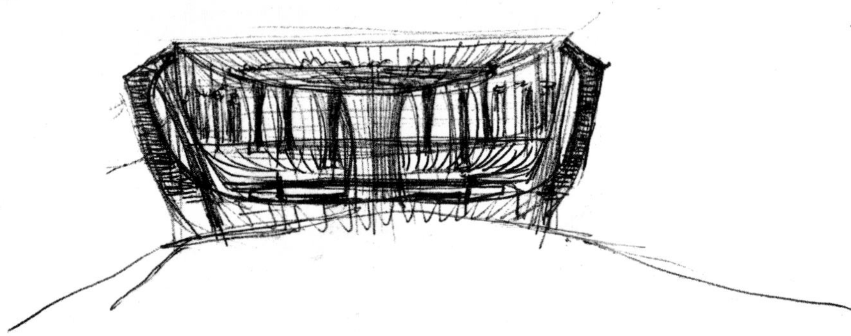

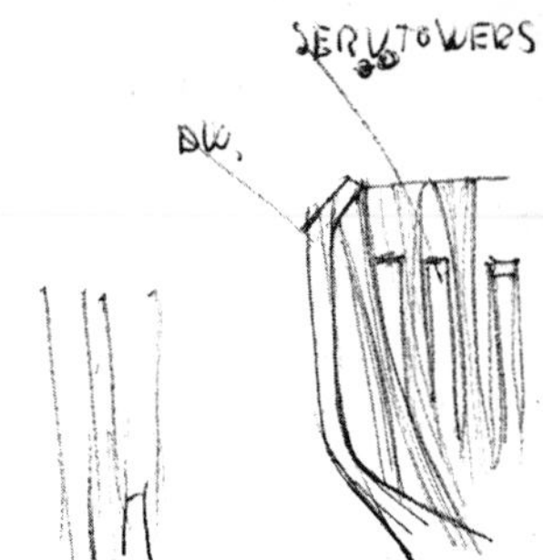

Dams

1970
The difference between sun and wind collectors and the dam is the difference between the scattered yield and the concentrated yield. In a sense, one has to go and collect wind pressures and sun radiation, while the water collects itself along watersheds, another of those cases where gravity "does it for us." There is an indisputable beauty, majesty, cleanness, and efficiency in the dam. There is also the direct encroachment of time in the silting of the water basin the dam produces. There is the enormity of the ecological transformation of the region and the advantages and disadvantages that go with it.

The dam's engineering and construction, putting up a wall against the accumulated water pressure, forces a ferocious single-mindedness. But in a way it is as if a naval engineer were so preoccupied by the hydrodynamics of his ship and the strength of the hull that he forgot the cargo aspect of the problem. The human cargo is absent in the dam. There is as much structural concrete poured into a dam as there is in a large metropolis. Why not make a dam into a metropolis by constructing one within the dam itself?

The essential elements for metropolitan life are intrinsically already part of the dam. In fact, the dam extends itself to the city with its own energy carriers, the power lines; with the water it impels, contains, and measures to farms, industries, and homes; with its roads, lakes, and campsites; with the magnetism of its size and its defiance. In fact, it almost seems as if in a golden age all those facets might have belonged to one whole organism and that some malignant genii had then torn out its heart, leaving only a monolith battling gravity. The dam is an ecological hinge that, for better or for worse, seems to demand the physical presence of man. We must return life to the place where it belongs. We cannot ignore functional-physical segregation.

I AM SEEKING THE DEFINITION OF THE LOT-SITE OF WHICH A "FREE" MAN WILL DO WHAT HE PLEASES & WHITHIN BY THIS OF (PARADOXAL) SELF DETERMINATION ~~STILL~~ NOT SPREAD THE SQUALOR OF ~~HIS~~ WASTED SOILS BEYOND THE LIMIT OF THE PRIVATE UNFORTUNATE INDECENCY LURKING FROM THE SHOLLOWNESS OF MAN'S PRIDE OR "BUSINESS."

TIME AFTER TIME MAN HAS SHOWN ITS LAKE OF ORGANIC BALANCE. THIS ~~AN~~ FORMAL OR AESTETIC (SUPERNATURAL?) BALANCE MAY BE NECESSARY TO DISTRICATE HIM. NOT FROM ITS OWN ANGUISHES WHICH ARE ITS OWN PROBLEM, BUT FROM THE GARBAGE & LITTER HE DONOT CHOSE TO RECICLE INTO LIFE & LEAVES TO KEEP UP AS LANDMARK OF ITS "INTELLIGENCE", THE ORGANIZING INTELLIGENCE.

SPACES ARE ORGANIZED TO A DESIGN PROMISING A NATURE-SCALE ENVIRONMENT & GIVEN TO INDIVIDUALS OR FAMILIES TO DEFINE WHITHING THEIR WORLD AS THEY SENSE IT & WANT IT.

IF NATURE OF CONTEMPORARY THINGS WERE DIFFERENT, IF THE MORPHOLOGY OF MAN & BEAST & VEGETATION WHERE OTHERS OR OTHER WERE THE POWERS KNOWN TO MAN & BY HIM USABLE, IN OTHER TERMS IF NECESSITY HAD A DIFFERENT CONNOTATION. "MATERIAL" AS WELL AS "IMMATERIAL" THEN ONE COULD THINK OF A POPULATION EVENLY TROWN ON THE EARTH, EACH GROUP OR FAMILY ISOLATED IN THEMSELVES IN THEIR "PURSUIT OF HAPPINESS", WHERE NO GUIDE OF A MASTER PLAN WOULD ATTEMPT AT THE JEALOUS SELF DETERMINATION OF INDIVIDUALS. THE LONE WOLF (IN THIS GENERALISED INSTANCE WHIT NO HOOKS TO HANG ITS INDIGNATIONS & THE MAKING GOING WHIT IT) PRAYING

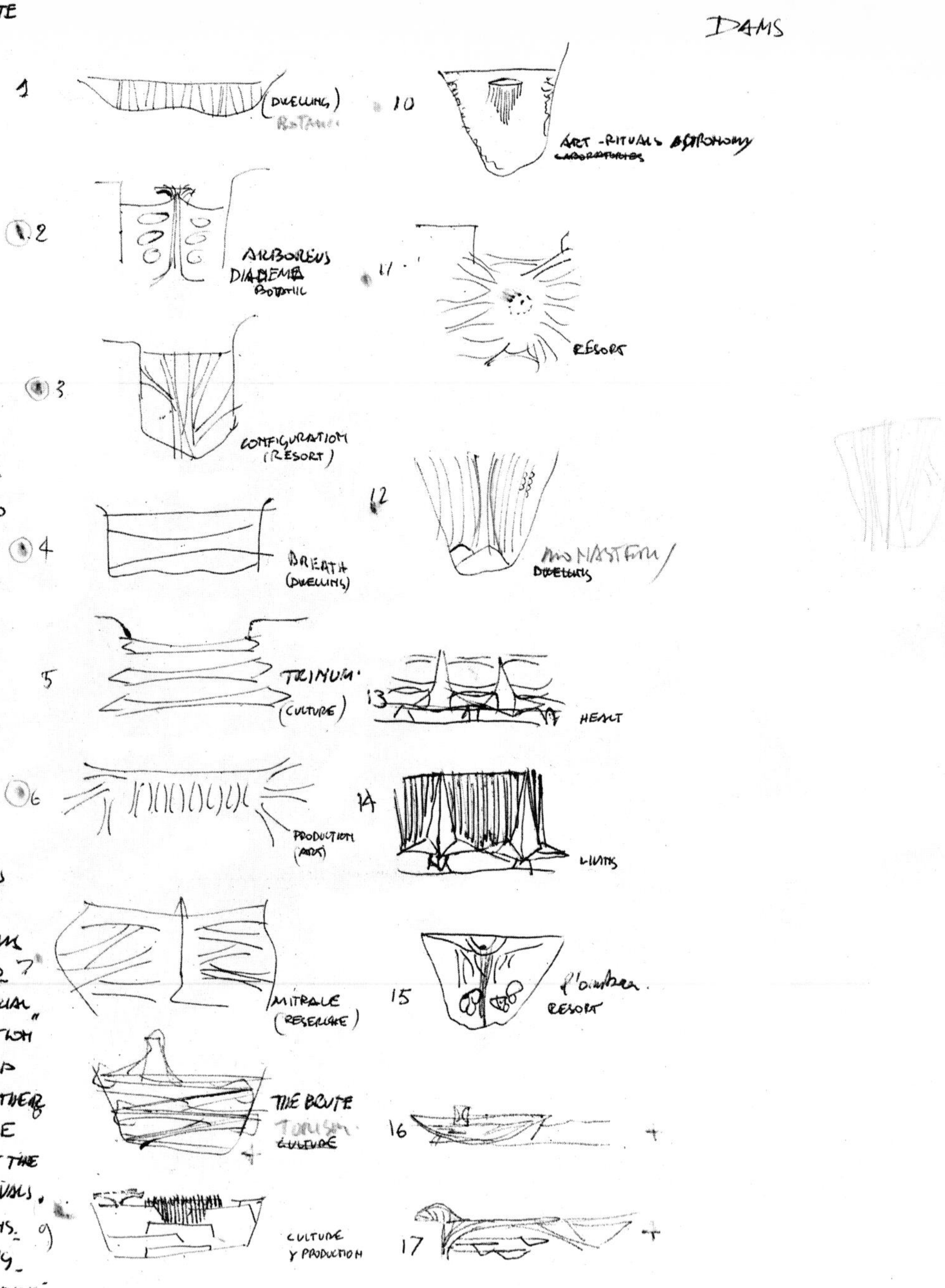

DAM.

THIS STRUCTURE IS CONCEIVED AS A MONOLITIC FORM... WHIT EVEN CURVED, CONVEX, SURFACE ON THE WATER SIDE & DEEPLY RIBBED ON THE OTHER ~~FACE~~

FROM THE INSIDE CONTINOUS WALL OUT CROPS A SISTEM OF ~~HORIZ~~ONTAL BLADES AT 6 METER INTERVAL. WITH THE DOUBLE FUNCTION OF GIVING STRUCTURAL RIGIDITY TO THE ~~MASSE~~ & PREDISPOSING A SET OF LEVEL FOR DWELLING, WORK, ETC..

THE RIBS ARE ALSO ORIGINATING FROM THE WALL & THEIR DEPTH IS ~~SUCH AS TO CAME FOWARD PAST THE EDGES OF~~ GREATER THAN THE FLORS. BLADES & DEFINE THE DESIGN OF THE OUTER ELEVATION,

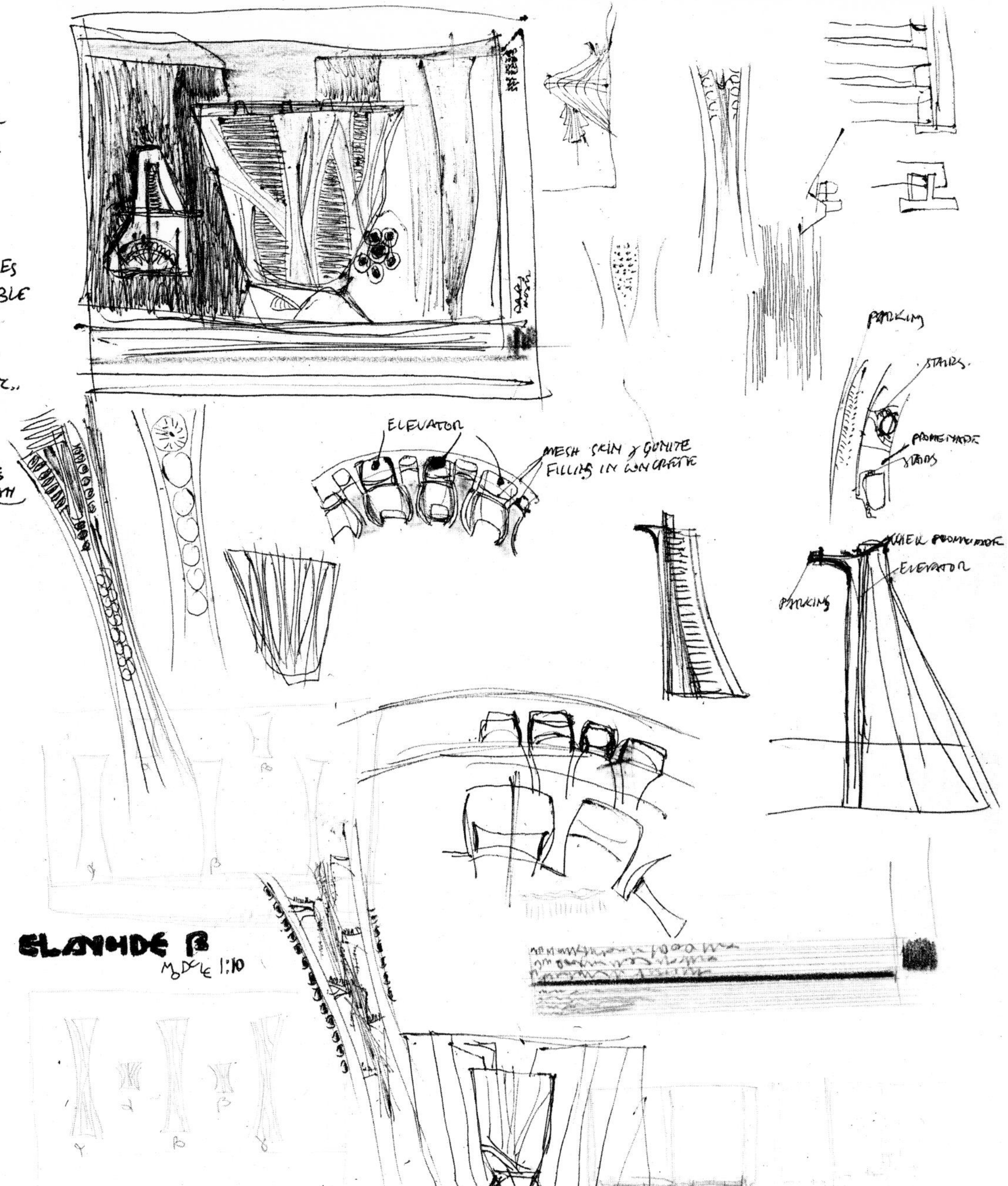

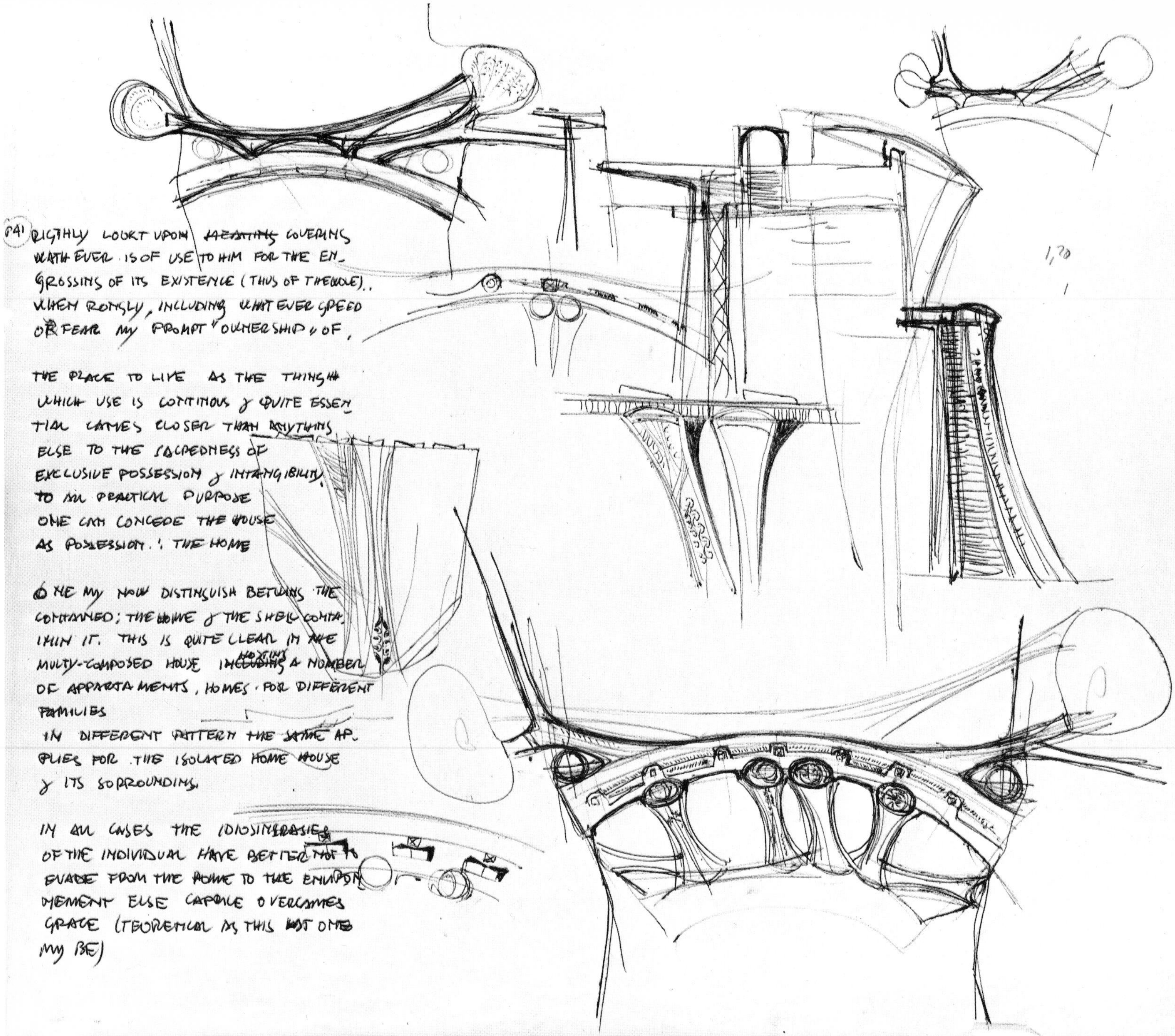
P41 RIGTHLY LOOKT UPON ~~HEATING~~ COVERING
WATHEVER IS OF USE TO HIM FOR THE EN-
GROSSING OF ITS EXISTENCE (THUS OF THEWOLE).
WHEN RONGLY, INCLUDING WHATEVER SPEED
OR FEAR MY PROMPT OWNERSHIP OF,
THE PLACE TO LIVE AS THE THING
WHICH USE IS CONTINOUS & QUITE ESSEN-
TIAL CAMES CLOSER THAN ANYTHING
ELSE TO THE SACREDNESS OF
EXCLUSIVE POSSESSION & INTANGIBILITY.
TO ALL PRACTICAL PURPOSE
ONE CAN CONCEDE THE HOUSE
AS POSSESSION. ∴ THE HOME
ONE MY NOW DISTINGUISH BETWINS THE
CONTAINED; THE HOME & THE SHELL CONTA-
ININ IT. THIS IS QUITE CLEAR IN THE
MULTY-COMPOSED HOUSE HOSTING A NUMBER
OF APPARTAMENTS, HOMES FOR DIFFERENT
FAMILIES
IN DIFFERENT PATTERN THE SAME AP-
PLIES FOR THE ISOLATED HOME HOUSE
& ITS SORROUNDINS.
IN ALL CASES THE IDIOSINCRASIES
OF THE INDIVIDUAL HAVE BETTER NOT TO
EVADE FROM THE HOME TO THE ENVIRON-
MEMENT ELSE CAPRICE OVERCAMES
GRACE (TEORETICAL AS THIS LAST ONE
MY BE)
1,20

IF PLANNING HAS TO BE PURSUED IN THE NAME OF MAN'S INTEGRITY IN A NATURE WHICH INTEGRITY IS RESPECTED & LOVED NEXT QUESTION MAY BE NOT WHAT TO PLAN BUT WHO HAS TO PLAN THE YET TO BE DEFINE "WHAT"

PLANNING MUST BE INTRUSTED TO THAT INDIVIDUAL WHO BESIDE BEEING DEDICATED TO THE FIELD INQUISITION CAN DEMONSTRATE OF HAVING ELEMENTS TO OFFER OF CONSTRUCTIVE SUBSTANCE, & THIS WILLING TO DISCUSS SUCH ELEMENTS WHIT WHOEVER HAS TITLE SUFFICENTS TO GRASP THE PROPOSITION AS A WOLE

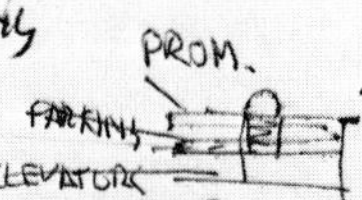

AS GROUP THINKING MAY HAVE BEEN USEFUL ~~AS~~ THE PRIORY STAGE OF PREPARATION SO IT MAY BE USEFUL IN THE POSTERIORY ~~CRITIC~~. STAGE OF PRESENTATION-CRITIC. IN THE MAKING STAGE OF THE IN BETWING THE PLANNER IS & CAN ONLY BE ALONE & TOTALLY RESPONSABLE.

THE ACTUAL PROCESS OF CONCEPTION IS ~~ONE~~ OF A SWINGING TO & FRO BETWING THE DIFFERENT POLES OF RECEPTIVITY - PAUSE - CREATIVITY - CRITIC - REFLECTION WHERE BONDUARIES ARE RESOLVED INTO PREEMINENCE OF THIS OR THAT CONDITION.

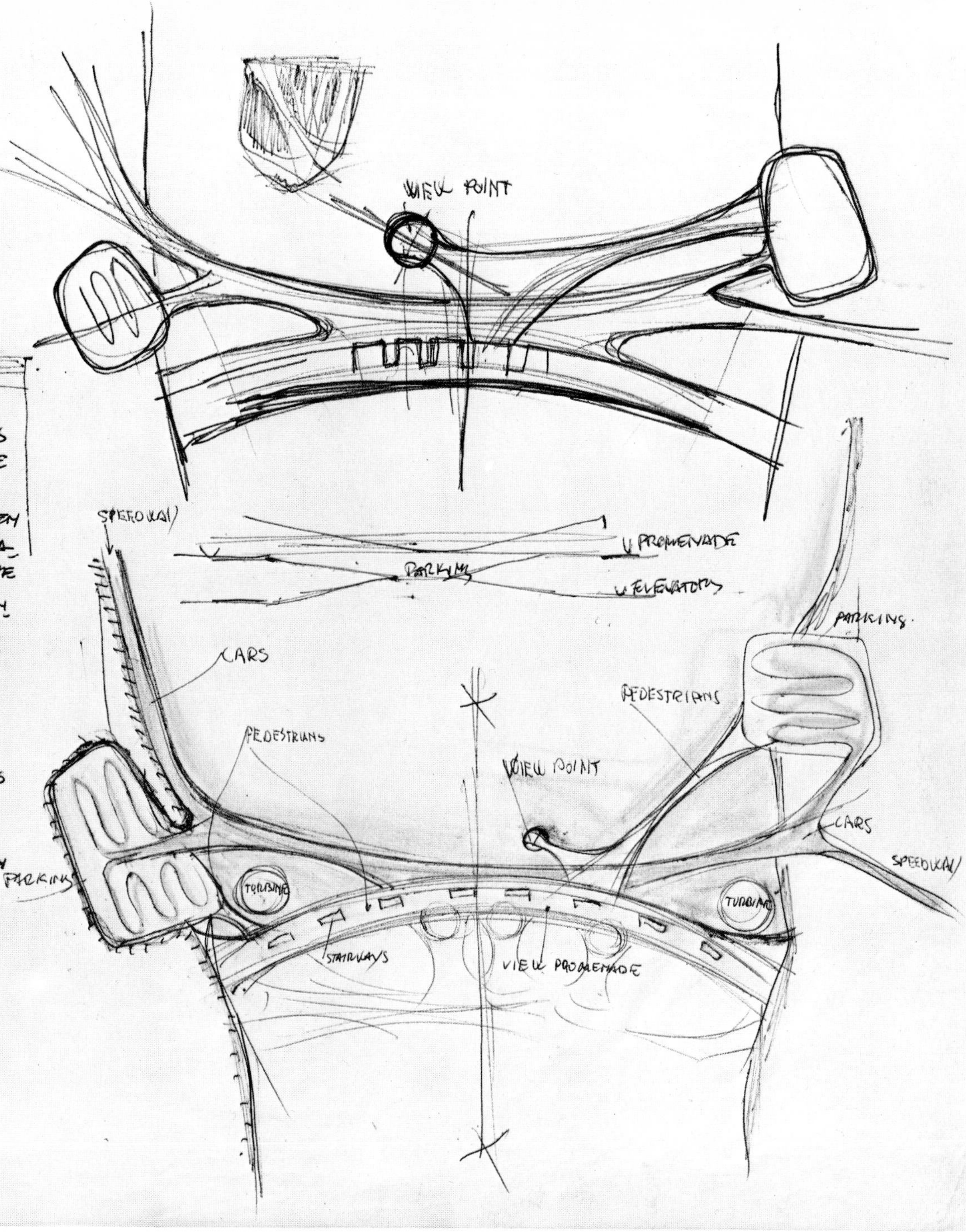

SELF CONCIOUS · INTELIGENT "IMMAGINATIVE" MOLE TO WHOM A NEW LONGING IS INBORN. THE LONGING FOR THE "REALITY OF LIGHT"

ONE WANDER IF EVEN OTHER VALUE THAN THE PRACTICAL & AESTETIC WOULD BE SO PROFOUNDLY EFFECTED AS TO APPEAR EXTRANEOUS TO MAN & ONE WANDER IF IS NOT PRECISELY BECAUSE THE AESTETIC WORLD IS UPSET THAN THE WOLE IS UPSET.

THE PRACTICAL HANDICAPS COULD BE, IN SHORT TIME (GENERATIONS) OVERCAME. BY A TRANSFORMATION OF THE WORLD OF THINGS, IN A FASHION THA WOULD BE ~~BUT NO ONE~~ EASY ENOUGH TO ENVISAGE.

BUT NO ONE CAN EVEN START TO SUPPOSE WHAT AESTETICLY WOULD HAPPEN & WHAT CONSEQUENTLY MAN WOULD BECAME

THE INVOLVEMENT OF THE SENSES OF WHICH SIGHT IS SO A PREDOMINANT ONE, INTERVENING AS IT DOES IN EVERY INSTANCE OF LIFE FROM THE MAKING OF LOVE TO THE SWEEPING OF A STREET FROM THE CONCEPTION OF A GOD TO THE PUSHING OF A THREAD TROUGH THE NEEDLE HEAD FROM THE WONDER OF A NATURAL SIGHT TO THE CHECKING OF A POLISHED SURFACE & ON & ON & ON.

THIS INVOLVEMENT (WHAT THE AETICAL LIFE) OF THE SENSE OF SIGHT &

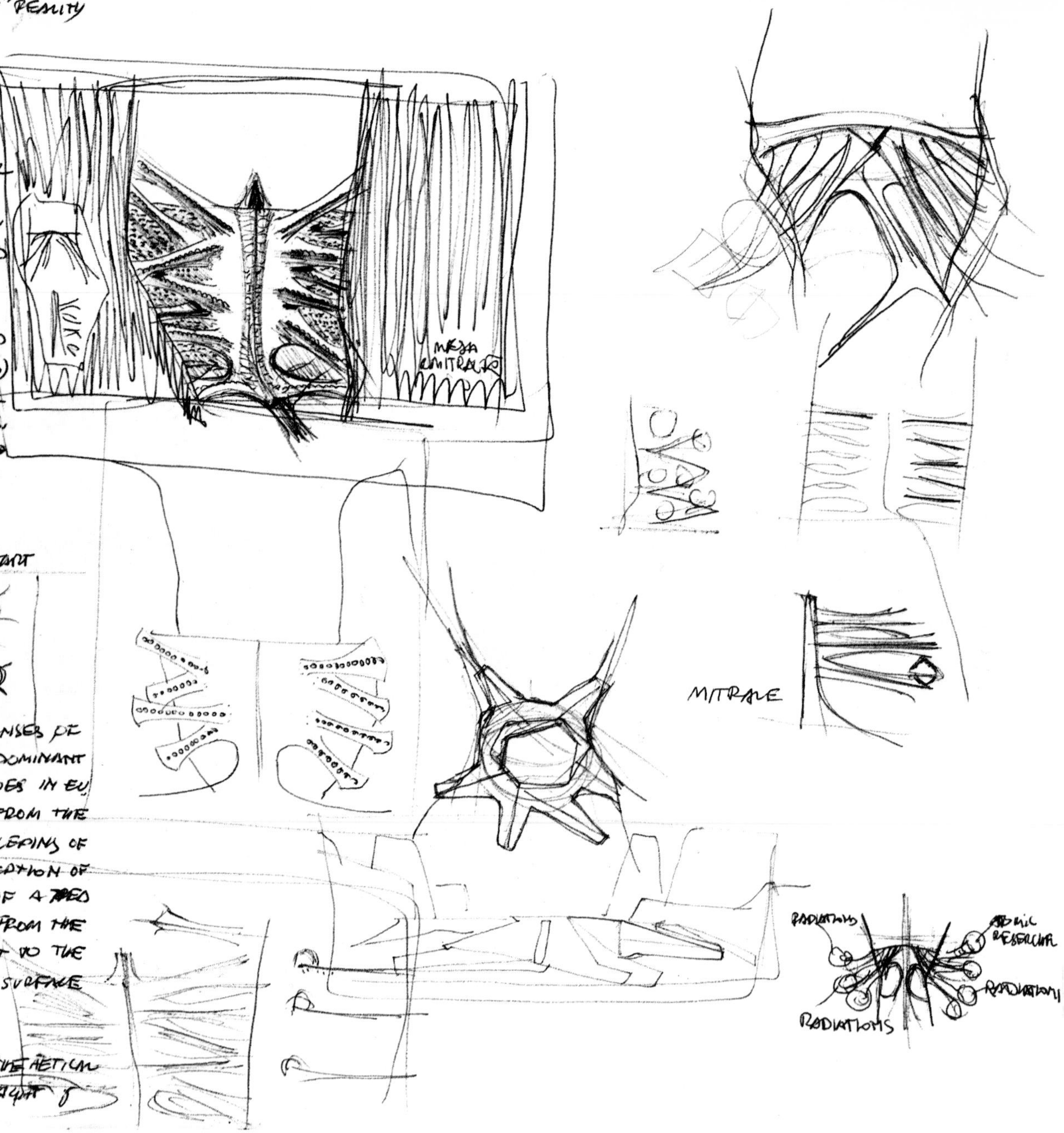

THE CARACTERIZATION EVEN OF THE IDEAS OF .... COMPASSION .... WISDOM ..... UMILITY... BY ~~SAYING~~ SAYING OF THEM THEY "BEAUTIFIE" THE SOUL .... IS A EVER PRESENT FUNDAMENTAL IN THE ~~PATH~~ PATH OF LIFE

✦ THIS AMOUNT TO SAYING THAT SIGHT IT IS NOT OR NOT ANY MORE (MAINLY) FOR PERCEIVING BUT MAINLY FOR CREATING & AS SUCH HAS TO BE CULTIVATED BY MAN

THE NATURE OF SUCH CREATION IS MEANT NOT AS THE FISIOLOGICAL "RECREATION" IN THE MIND OF THE OUTSIDE WORLD BY THE MEDIA OF THE EYE APPARATUS BUT THE INWARD-OUTWARD ACT OF THE CONCEIVING MIND FORCED INTO THE CHANEL OF SIGHT, THE ONE TROUGH WHICH PERCEPTION GOT IN. & THE ONE BY WHICH AN EVALUATION WILL BE REACHED OF THE SAME "CREATION"

LOOKING - SEEING -

- PERCEPTION - SENSITISATION - CONCEPTION -
- ACTUALISATION - JUDGEMENT

THE PROCESS GOES FROM A PASSIVE CONDITION (PRE-PERCEPTION OR LOOKING - ~~SEEING~~) TO A COMPLETELY ACTIVE & RESPONSABLE ONE TROUGH ~~THE A PROCESS~~ SEQUENCE WHICH ONE MAY SEE AS THE AESTETIC UNFOLDING OF CREATIVITY

"ARTIST" IS ONE WHOM REACHED THE SOLUTION OF ALL INSTRUMENTALITYES INCLUDING THE WAYS & THE HOWS SETS TO "CREATE", CREATION BEING ASSUMED BY HIM TO BE THE FINALITY OF EXISTENCE, & ALL ELSE INSTRUMENTAL TO IT.

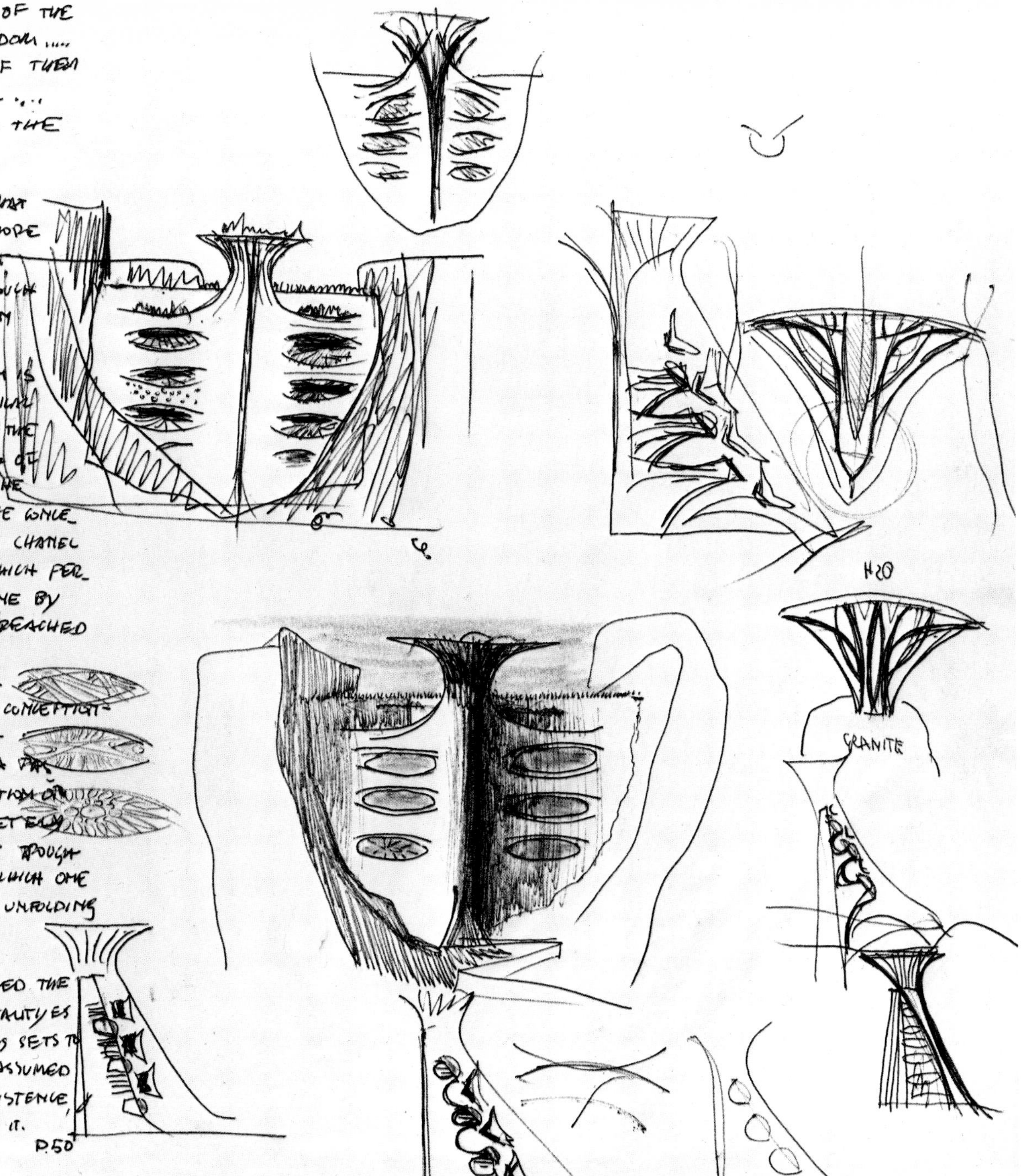

MY FINAL INSTANCE ~~[illegible]~~ I HAVE NO BET-
TER EXPLATIATION FOR THIS WORK ~~THAN~~
THE NEED TO DEMONSTRATE TO MYSELF
THAT I CAN ENTER IN THE SOUL ENGROS-
SING ACTION OF NATURE, IN HER MODE-
LINS OF ENVIRONMEMENT, IN A SCALE
& WHIT SUCH FORCE & IMMAGINATION
AS TO INVEST THE SUBSTANCE OF
THE "MAKER" ITSELF WHATEVER IT
BE

ONE MAY DEAM AS UNFORTUNATE THAT
IN DO DOINS I MAY (EVEN) ONLY SUGGEST
THAT MAN MAY BE TAKEN AS GUINEY
PIG FOR SUCH A "WILD" EXPERIMENT.

THE WOLE POINT IN QUESTION IS THAT
THAT ONLY AS MEDIATORS BETWINS
MAN & NATURE HAVE THOSE CONSTRUC-
TION ANY SENSE AT ALL
THE MEDIATION HERE CONCERNINS THE
FISICAL AS WELL AS METAPHISICAL–
AESTETICAL MAN & ITS OBSERVINS
WILE LIVINS IN & OF, ~~OF~~ NATURE.

MY WHISH TO CONVEY HOW HUMBLE MY
ATTITUDE IS IN BOTH DIRECTION OF MAN
& NATURE CAN ONLY BE SATISFIED
BY THE POSSIBILITY OF ~~MAKING~~ THOSE
CONSTRUCTION TO BEAR THE VENERA-
TION & SENSE TOWARD LIFE.
COERENT TO IT I SEEK WHAT I SEE
AS THE FULLEST & MOST MEANINGFULL.
IN (IF) DO DOINS I DISPLAY FIRSTLY
& MOSTLY MY EGO, THE ONLY GIUSTIFICA-
TION IS IN THE OLD SAYINS THAT
EACH ONE OF US CAN BEST GIVE BY
THE MOST OF SELF ASSERTINS. PROVIDED
THAT THE TREMOR OF LIFE BURNS
WHITINS. & NOT THE FURY OF DISTRUCTION

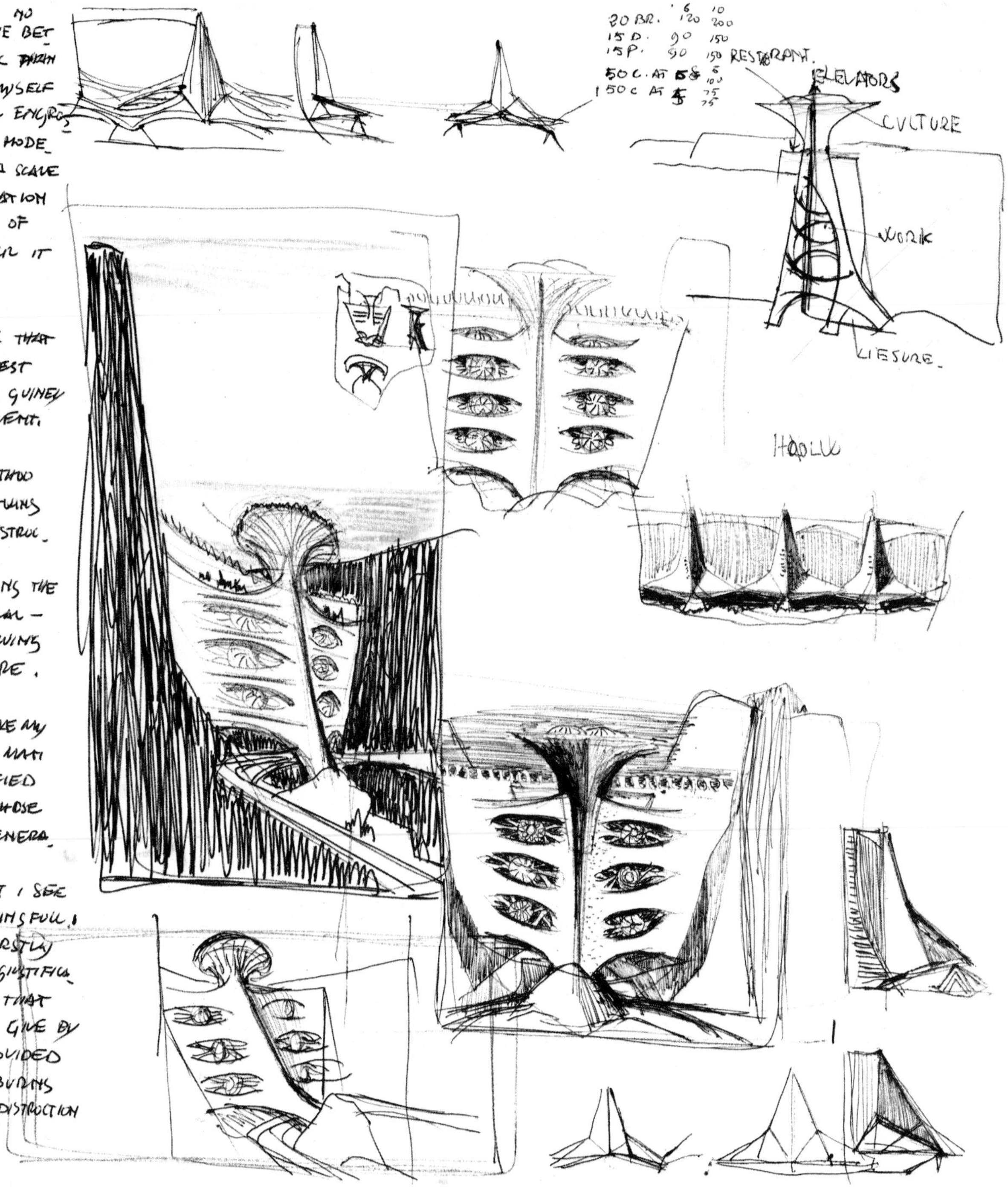

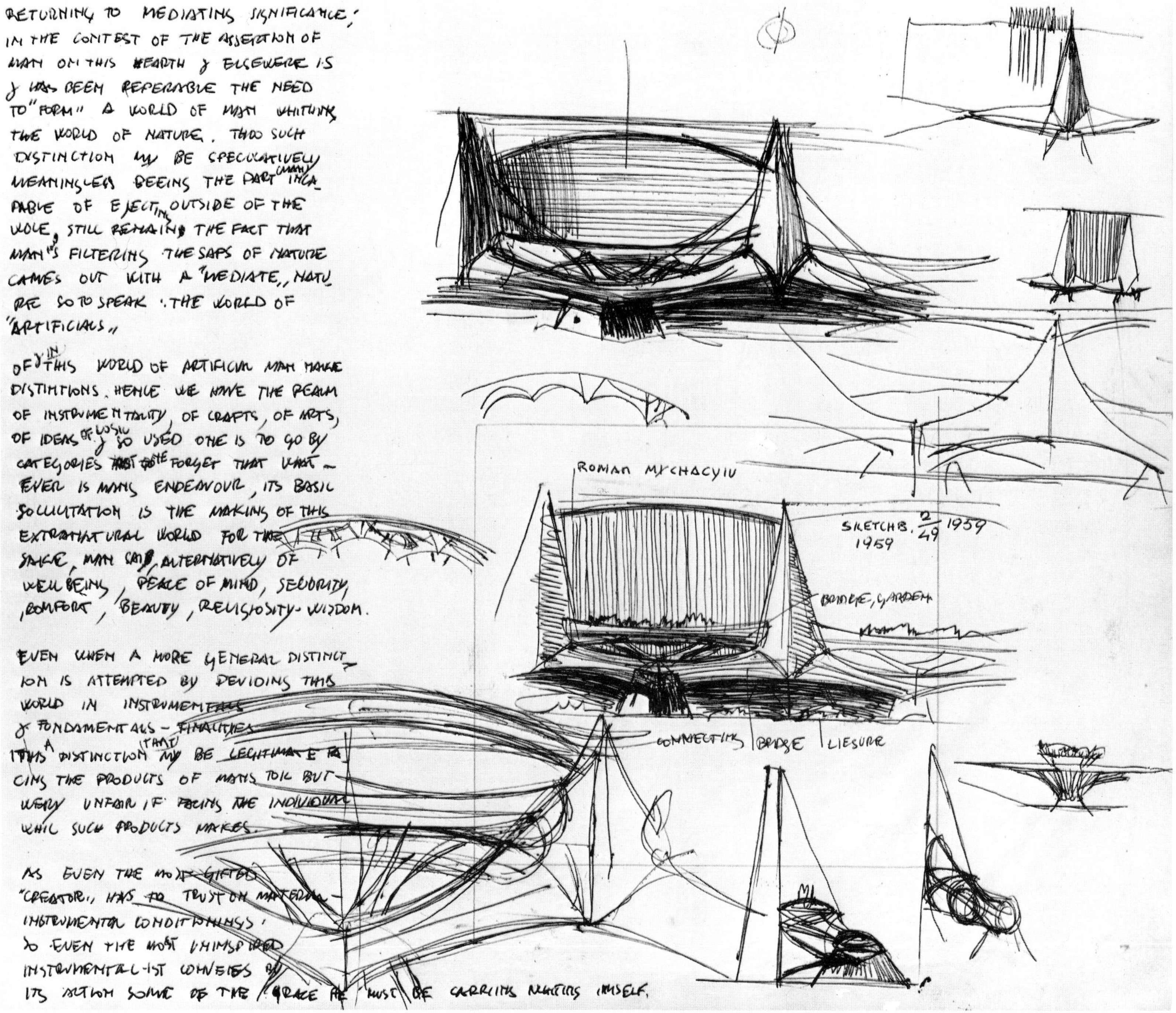
RETURNING TO MEDIATING SIGNIFICANCE;
IN THE CONTEST OF THE ASSERTION OF
MAN ON THIS EARTH & ELSEWHERE IS
& HAS BEEN REPERABLE THE NEED
TO "FORM" A WORLD OF MAN WHITHIN
THE WORLD OF NATURE. THOO SUCH
DISTINCTION MAY BE SPECULATIVELY
MEANINGLESS BEEING THE PART (MAN) INCA-
PABLE OF EJECTING OUTSIDE OF THE
WOLE, STILL REMAINS THE FACT THAT
MAN'S FILTERING THE SAPS OF NATURE
CAMES OUT WITH A "MEDIATE" NATU-
RE SO TO SPEAK: THE WORLD OF
"ARTIFICIALS"
OF & IN THIS WORLD OF ARTIFICIAL MAN MAKE
DISTINTIONS. HENCE WE HAVE THE REALM
OF INSTRUMENTALITY, OF CRAFTS, OF ARTS,
OF IDEAS OF LOGIC & SO USED ONE IS TO GO BY
CATEGORIES ONE FORGET THAT WHAT-
EVER IS MANS ENDEAVOUR, ITS BASIC
SOLLICITATION IS THE MAKING OF THIS
EXTRANATURAL WORLD FOR THE
SAKE, MAN SAID, ALTERNATIVELY OF
WELLBEING, PEACE OF MIND, SECURITY,
COMFORT, BEAUTY, RELIGIOSITY-WISDOM.
EVEN WHEN A MORE GENERAL DISTINCT-
ION IS ATTEMPTED BY DEVIDING THIS
WORLD IN INSTRUMENTALS
& FONDAMENTALS – FINALITIES
THIS A DISTINCTION (THAT) MAY BE LEGITIMATE FA-
CING THE PRODUCTS OF MANS TOIL BUT
VERY UNFAIR IF FACING THE INDIVIDUAL
WHIC SUCH PRODUCTS MAKES.
AS EVEN THE MOST GIFTED
"CREATOR" HAS TO TRUST ON MATERIAL-
INSTRUMENTAL CONDITIONINGS,
SO EVEN THE MOST UNINSPIRED
INSTRUMENTAL-IST CONVEIES BY
ITS ACTION SOME OF THE GRACE HE MUST BE CARRING WHITHIN HIMSELF.
ROMAN MYCHACYIU
SKETCHB. 2/49 1959
1959
BRIDGE, GARDEN
CONNECTING
BRIDGE
LIESURE

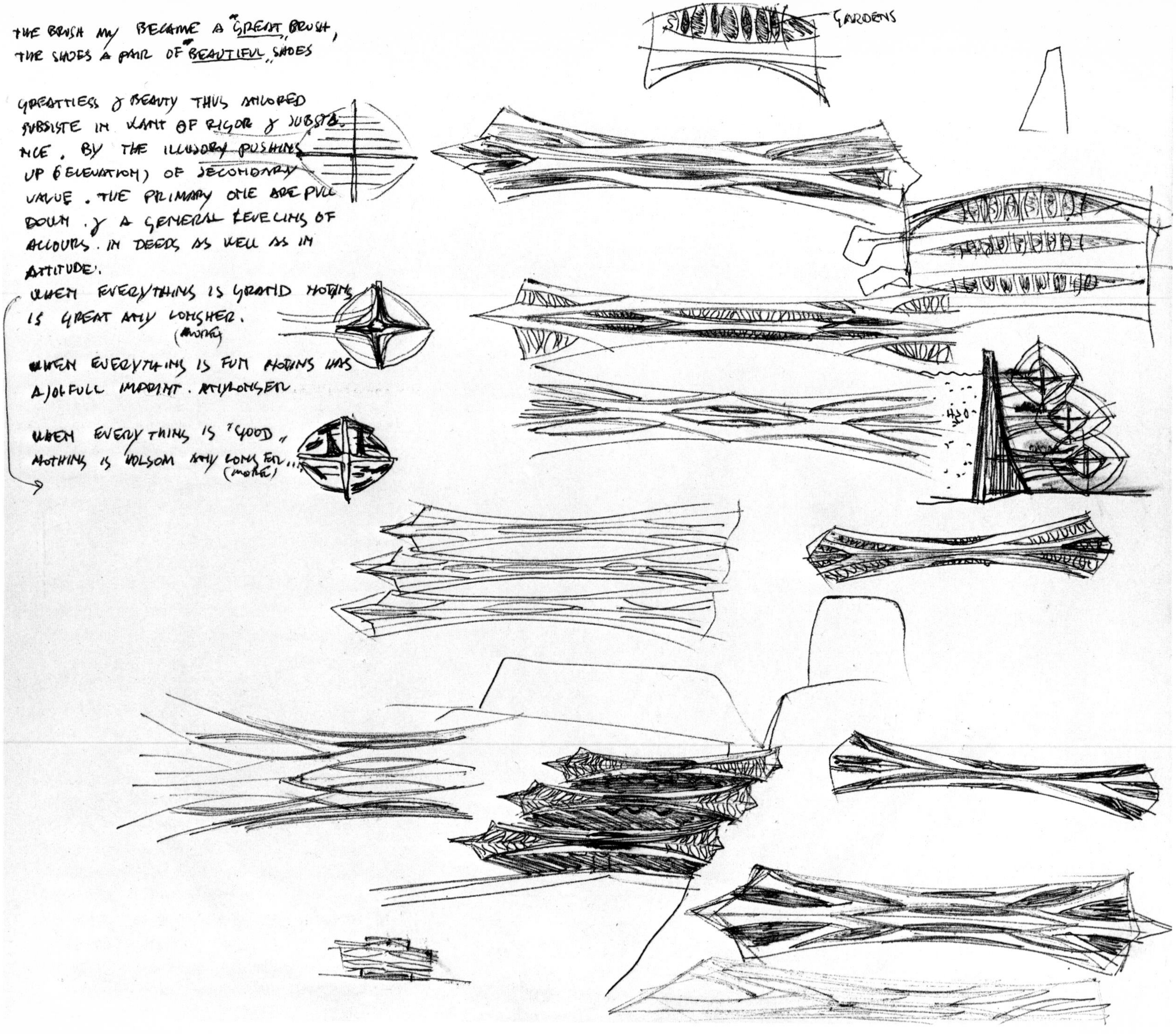
THE BRUSH MY BECAME A "GREAT" BRUSH,
THE SHOES A PAIR OF "BEAUTIFUL" SHOES
GREATNESS & BEAUTY THUS ANCHORED
SUBSISTE IN WANT OF RIGOR & SUBSTA-
NCE. BY THE ILLUSORY PUSHING
UP (ELEVATION) OF SECONDARY
VALUE. THE PRIMARY ONE ARE PULL
DOWN. & A GENERAL LEVELING OF
ALLOURS. IN DEEDS AS WELL AS IN
ATTITUDE.
WHEN EVERYTHING IS GRAND NOTHING
IS GREAT ANY LONGHER.
(ANYMORE)
WHEN EVERYTHING IS FUN NOTHING HAS
A JOYFULL IMPRINT. ANYLONGER
WHEN EVERYTHING IS "GOOD"
NOTHING IS WOLSOM ANY LONGER...
(MORE)
GARDENS

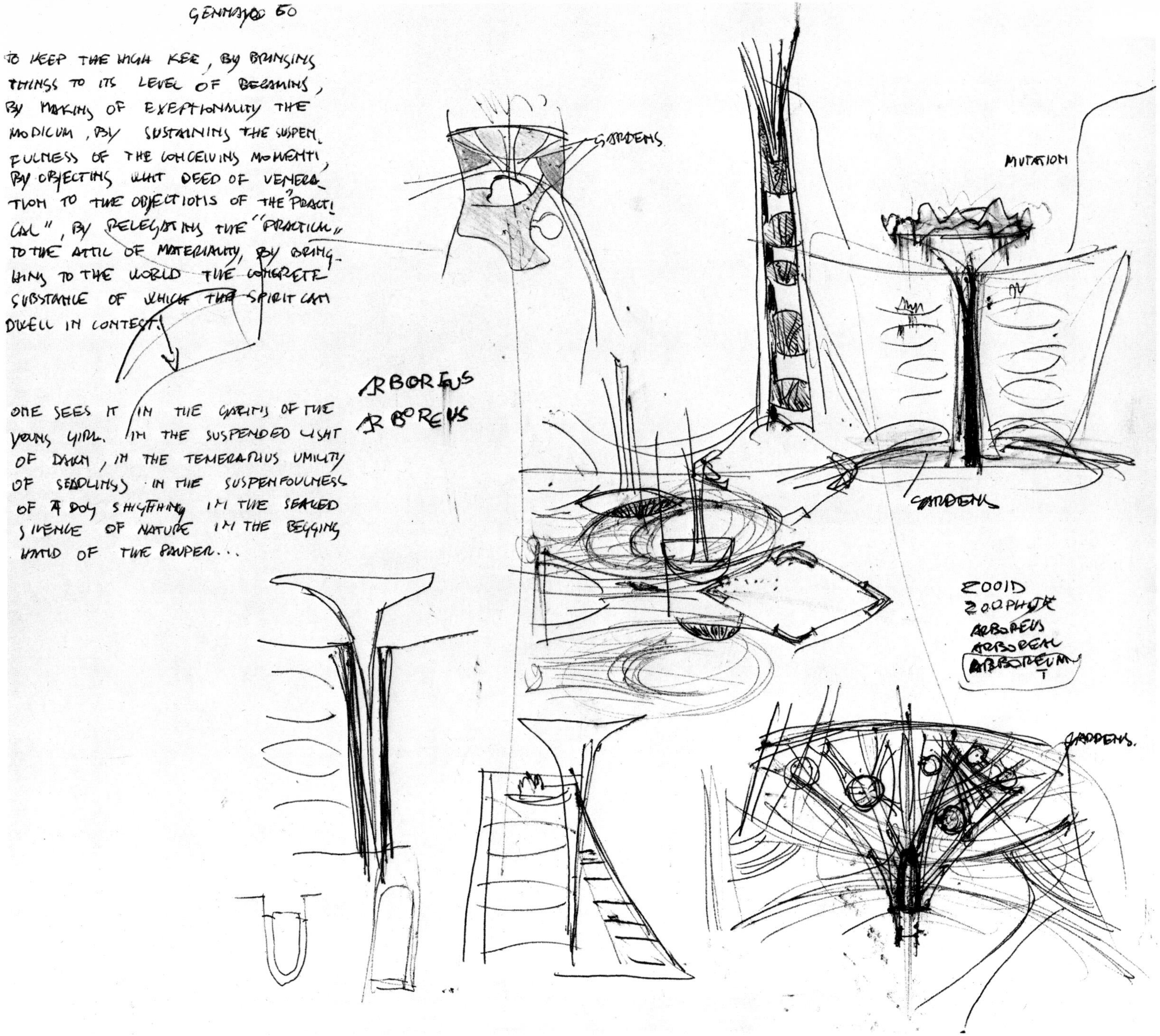
GENNAIO 50
TO KEEP THE HIGH KEE, BY BRINGING THINGS TO ITS LEVEL OF BEGINNING, BY MAKING OF EXEPTIONALITY THE MODICUM, BY SUSTAINING THE SUSPENFULNESS OF THE CONCEIVING MOMENT, BY OBJECTING WHAT DEED OF VENERATION TO THE OBJECTIONS OF THE "PRACTICAL", BY RELEGATING THE "PRACTICAL" TO THE ATTIC OF MATERIALITY, BY BRINGING TO THE WORLD THE CONCRETE SUBSTANCE OF WHICH THE SPIRIT CAN DWELL IN CONTEST.
ONE SEES IT IN THE GAIETY OF THE YOUNG GIRL, IN THE SUSPENDED LIGHT OF DAWN, IN THE TEMERARIUS UMILITY OF SEEDLINGS, IN THE SUSPENFOULNESS OF A DOG SNIFFING, IN THE SEALED SILENCE OF NATURE, IN THE BEGGING HAND OF THE PAUPER...
GARDENS
MUTATION
ARBOREUS
ARBOREUS
GARDENS
ZOOID
ZOOPHYTE
ARBOREUS
ARBOREAL
ARBOREUM
GARDENS

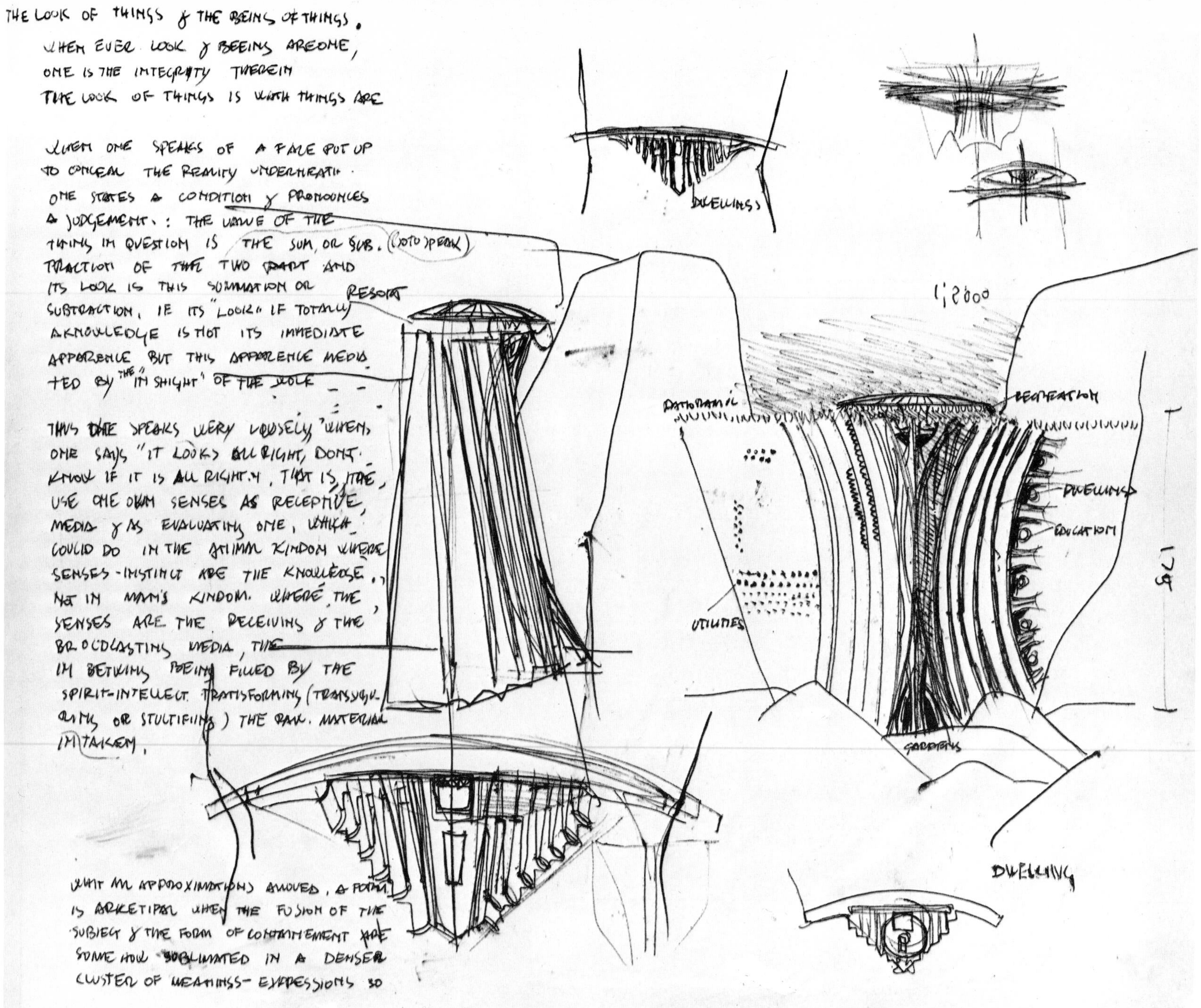
THE LOOK OF THINGS & THE BEING OF THINGS.
WHEN EVER LOOK & BEEING ARE ONE,
ONE IS THE INTEGRITY THEREIN
THE LOOK OF THINGS IS WHAT THINGS ARE
WHEN ONE SPEAKS OF A FACE PUT UP
TO CONCEAL THE REALITY UNDERNEATH.
ONE STATES A CONDITION & PRONOUNCES
A JUDGEMENT. : THE VALUE OF THE
THING IN QUESTION IS THE SUM, OR SUB. (ROTO) PEAK)
TRACTION OF THE TWO PART AND
ITS LOOK IS THIS SUMMATION OR
SUBTRACTION, IE ITS "LOOK" IF TOTALLY
AKNOWLEDGE IS NOT ITS IMMEDIATE
APPARENCE BUT THIS APPARENCE MEDIA
TED BY THE "IN SHIGHT" OF THE WOLE
THUS ONE SPEAKS VERY LOOSELY WHEN,
ONE SAYS "IT LOOKS ALL RIGHT, DONT
KNOW IF IT IS ALL RIGHT.", THAT IS, ONE,
USE ONE OWN SENSES AS RECEPTIVE,
MEDIA & AS EVALUATING ONE, WHICH
COULD DO IN THE ANIMAL KINDOM WHERE
SENSES-INSTINCT ARE THE KNOWLEDGE,
NOT IN MAN'S KINDOM. WHERE THE
SENSES ARE THE RECEIVING & THE
BROCDCASTING MEDIA, THE
IN BETWING BEING FILLED BY THE
SPIRIT-INTELLECT TRANSFORMING (TRANSFIGU-
RING OR STULTIFING) THE RAW. MATERIAL
IN TAKEN.
RESORT
DWELLINGS
1/2000
PANORAMIC
RECREATION
DWELLINGS
EDUCATION
UTILITIES
GARDENS
DWELLING
WHAT ALL APPROXIMATIONS ALLOWED, A FORM
IS ARKETIPAL WHEN THE FUSION OF THE
SUBJECT & THE FORM OF CONTAINEMENT ARE
SOME HOW SUBLIMATED IN A DENSER
CLUSTER OF MEANINGS- EXPRESSIONS SO

AS TO CANCEL IN THE MIND THE DU-
ALITY OF SUBSTANCE &
THE FORM GIVING,
SUBSTANCE BECAMES HER OWN
FORM & FORM IS ITSELF SUBS-
TANTIAL
IN THIS CONTEST THE NATURE
OF MATERIAL IS A MATTER OF NO CON-
SEQUENCE, THE ACTION PROGRESSING NOW
IN THE PURE SFERE OF CREATIVITY &
NOT IN THE, LEFT BEHIND, SFERE OF KRAFT
MANSHIP

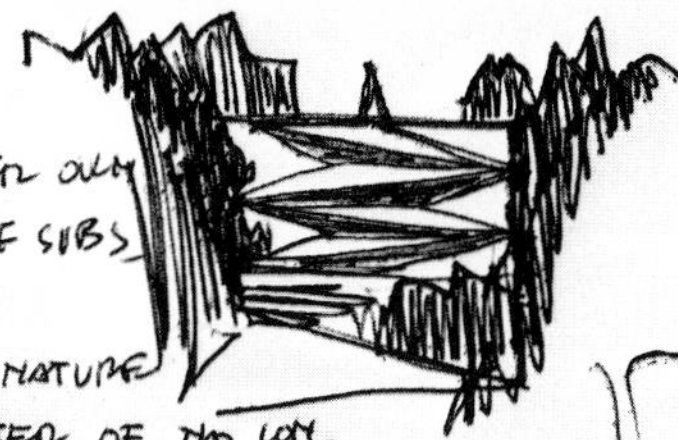

THE "PERFECTION" OF THE ARKETIPE IS
A SELF CREATED PERFECTION, ITS UN-
QUESTIONABILITY IS THE INQUESTIONABILITY
OF THE BIRDS' WINGS., OF THE WATHER
FALLING...... THE BEFORE CAN'T OF-
FER ANY MODULE OF EVALUATION, THE
AFTER MY SEE THE FUSSING & CRAKING
OF EXITEMENT OR RESENTEMENT, ...
THE ARKETIPE STANDS UNTOUCHED,
THE TEORIZING, DISSECTION, ANALISIS).....

THE SUBIECT BEEING HERE THE "IDEAL
ARKETIPE"

IN THIS SENSE ARKETIPE IS THE
WORK OF NATURE BY THE MEDIA OF MAN,
ITS VALIDITY ON THE TRESHOLD OF THE
ABSOLUTE, ITS EXISTENCE TRASCENDENTAL
THE ORIGINATING CAUSES, ITS
ACCEPTABILITY LINKED TO MAN DEGRE
OF UNDERSTANDING, ITS IMPACT, TO
THE ENVIRONMENTAL ATTITUDES
ITS LIFE IN THE HANDS OF THE ACCI
DENTAL.

YET THE ARCKETIPE IS SOMEHOW
LIFELESS. DUE TO ITS PRIMEVAL
ATTRIBUTE: IT HAS NOT LIVED YET,
LIFE HAS NOT PUT ANY OF HERS INDE-
TITURES & COLORS IN IT, & THIS CANT

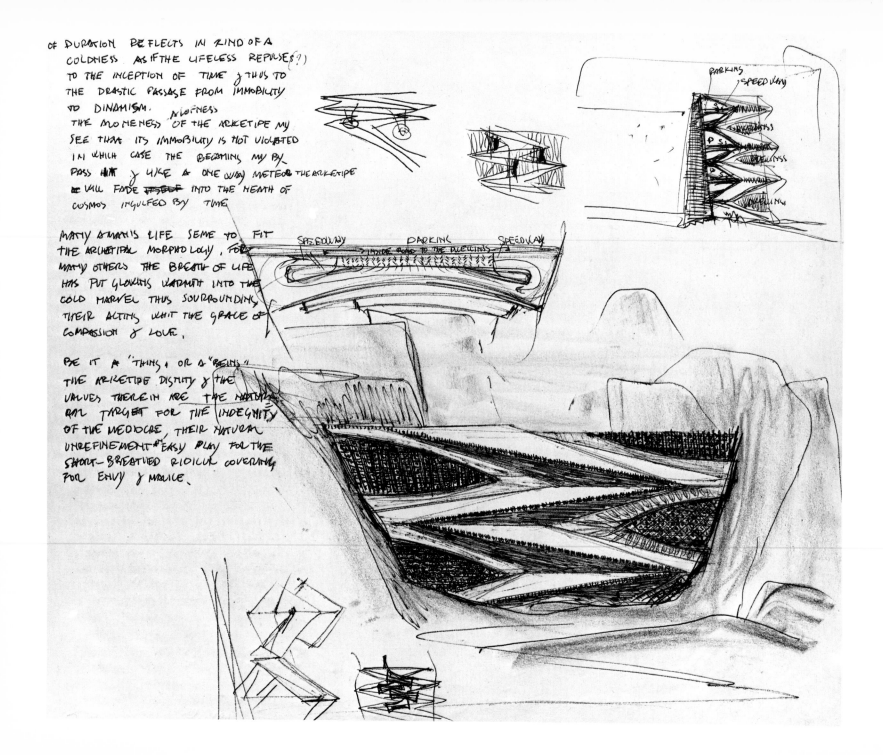

OF DURATION REFLECTS IN KIND OF A
COLDNESS AS IF THE LIFELESS REPULSES(?)
TO THE INCEPTION OF TIME & THUS TO
THE DRASTIC PASSAGE FROM IMMOBILITY
TO DINAMISM.
ALOOFNESS
THE MOMENESS OF THE ARKETIPE MY
SEE THAT ITS IMMOBILITY IS NOT VIOLATED
IN WHICH CASE THE BEGINNING MY BY-
PASS HIM & LIKE A ONE WAY METEOR THE ARKETIPE
WILL FADE ~~ITSELF~~ INTO THE NEATH OF
COSMOS INGULFED BY TIME

MANY A MAN'S LIFE SEME TO FIT
THE ARCHETIPAL MORPHOLOGY, FOR
MANY OTHERS THE BREATH OF LIFE
HAS PUT GLOWING WARMTH INTO THE
COLD MARVEL THUS SOURROUNDING
THEIR ACTING WHIT THE GRACE OF
COMPASSION & LOVE.

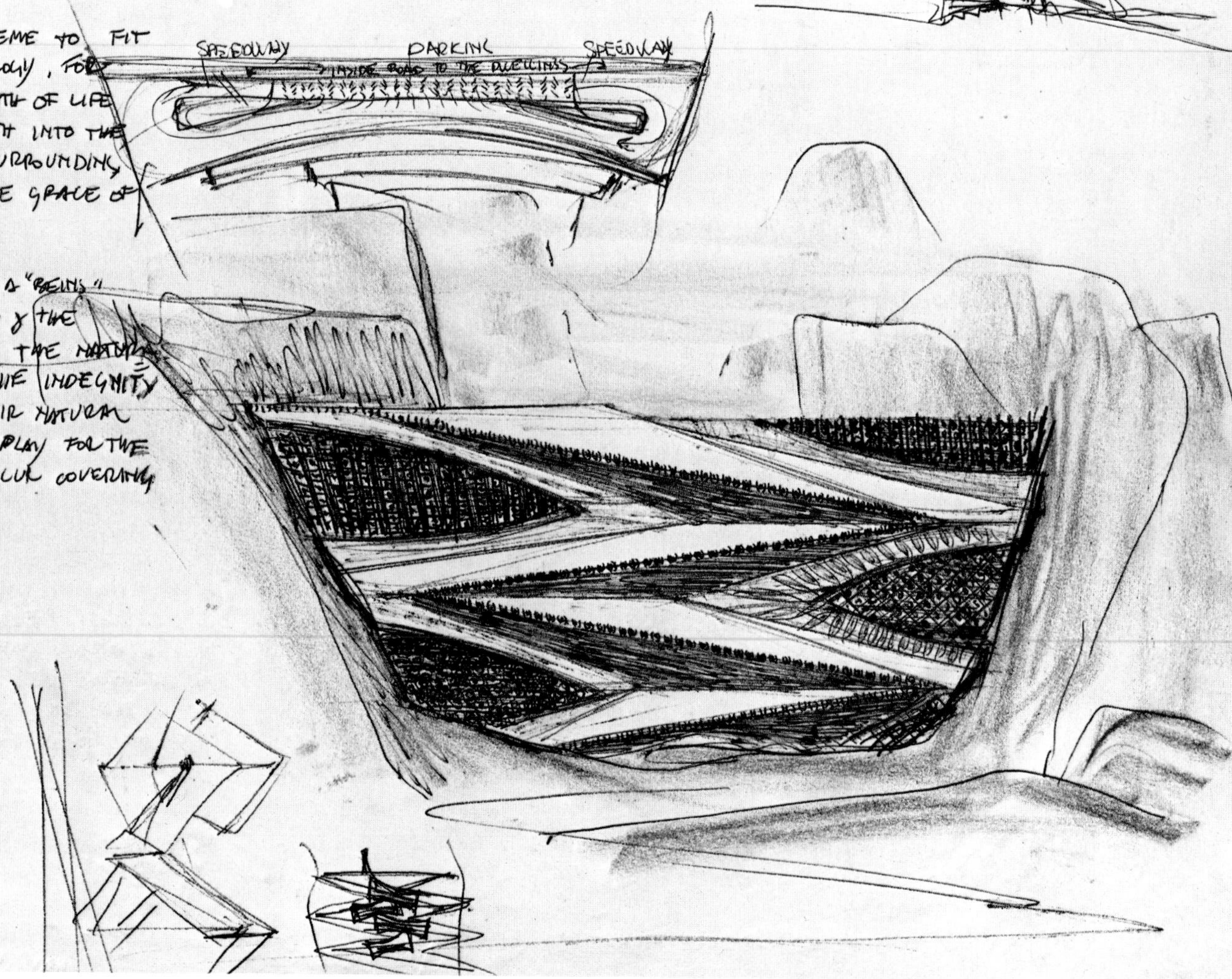

BE IT A "THING" OR A "BEING"
THE ARKETIPE DIGNITY & THE
VALUES THEREIN ARE THE NATU-
RAL TARGET FOR THE INDEGNITY
OF THE MEDIOCRE, THEIR NATURAL
UNREFINEMENT AN EASY PLAY FOR THE
SHORT-BREATHED RIDICUL COVERING
FOR ENVY & MALICE.

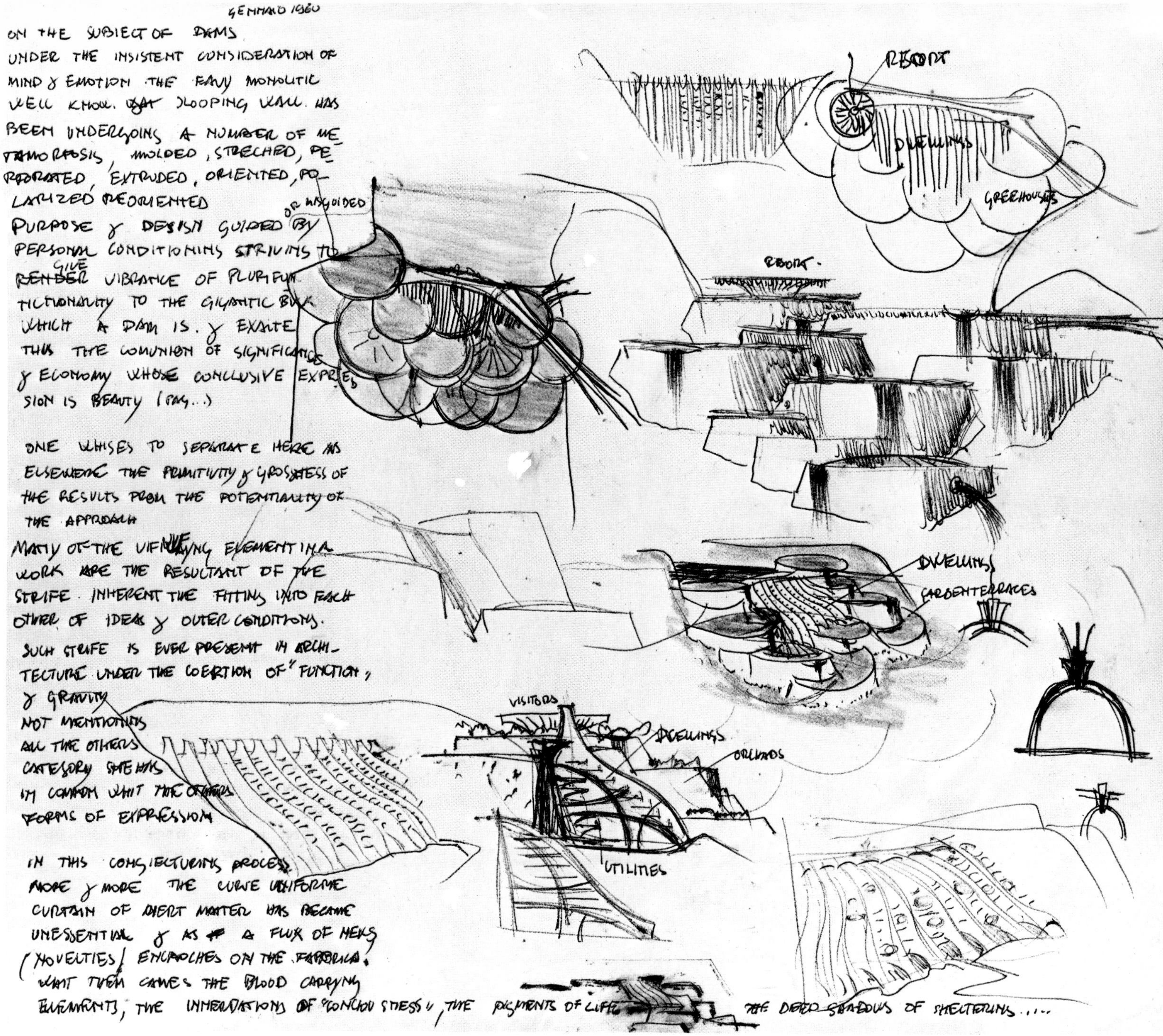
GENNAIO 1960
ON THE SUBJECT OF DAMS
UNDER THE INSISTENT CONSIDERATION OF
MIND & EMOTION THE FAMILY MONOLITIC
WELL KNOW. SLOOPING WALL HAS
BEEN UNDERGOING A NUMBER OF ME
TAMORFOSIS, MOLDED, STRECHED, PE
RFORATED, EXTRUDED, ORIENTED, PO
LARIZED, REORIENTED
PURPOSE & DESIGN GUIDED BY
OR MISGUIDED
PERSONAL CONDITIONINGS STRIVING TO
GIVE
RENDER VIBRANCE OF PLURIFUN
CTIONALITY TO THE GIGANTIC BULK
WHICH A DAM IS. & EXALTE
THUS THE COMUNION OF SIGNIFICANCE
& ECONOMY WHOSE CONCLUSIVE EXPRES
SION IS BEAUTY (SAY...)
ONE WHISES TO SEPARATE HERE AS
ELSEWERE THE PRIMITIVITY & GROSSNESS OF
THE RESULTS FROM THE POTENTIALITY OF
THE APPROACH
MANY OF THE VIFYING ELEMENT IN A
WORK ARE THE RESULTANT OF THE
STRIFE INHERENT THE FITTING INTO EACH
OTHER OF IDEAS & OUTER CONDITIONS.
SUCH STRIFE IS EVER PRESENT IN ARCHI
TECTURE UNDER THE COERTION OF "FUNCTION"
& GRAVITY
NOT MENTIONING
ALL THE OTHERS
CATEGORY SHE HAS
IN COMMON WHIT THE OTHERS
FORMS OF EXPRESSION
IN THIS CONGIECTURING PROCESS
MORE & MORE THE CURVE UNIFORME
CURTAIN OF INERT MATER HAS BECAME
UNESSENTIAL & AS A FLUX OF NEWS
(NOVELTIES) ENCROCHES ON THE FABRICA.
WHAT THEN CAMES THE BLOOD CARRYING
ELEMENTS, THE INNERVATIONS OF "CONCIOUSNESS", THE PIGMENTS OF LIFE
THE DEEP SHADOWS OF SHELTERING....
RESORT
DWELLINGS
GREENHOUSES
RESORT
DWELLINGS
GARDENTERRACES
VISITORS
DWELLINGS
ORCHARDS
UTILITIES

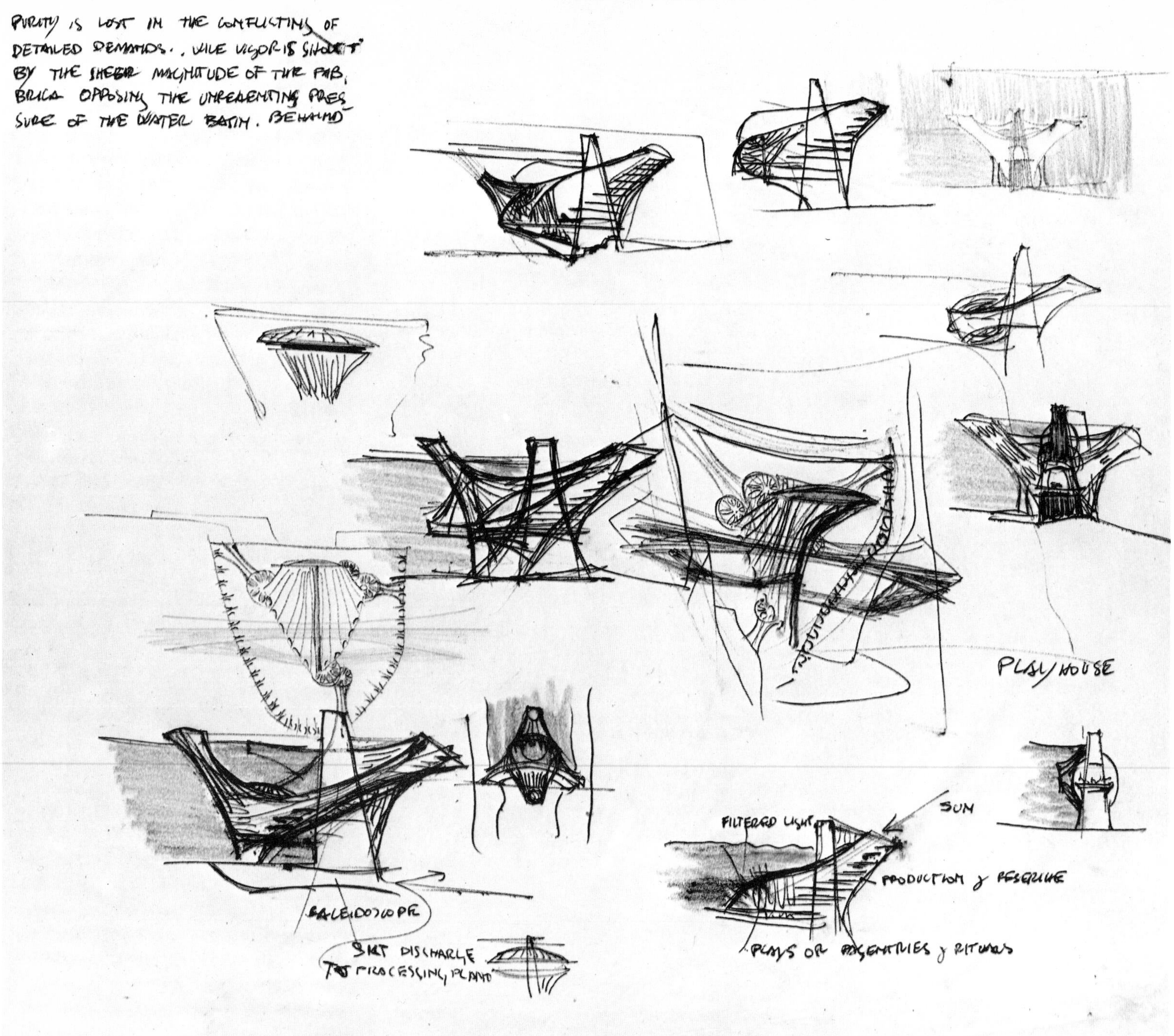
PURITY IS LOST IN THE CONFLICTING OF
DETAILED DEMANDS. , WHILE VIGOR IS SHOUT
BY THE SHEER MAGNITUDE OF THE FAB-
RICA OPPOSING THE UNRELENTING PRES-
SURE OF THE WATER BATH. BEHIND
PLAYHOUSE
SUN
FILTERED LIGHT
PRODUCTION & RESERVE
PLAYS OR PAGEANTRIES & RITUALS
KALEIDOSCOPE
SILT DISCHARGE
TO PROCESSING PLANT

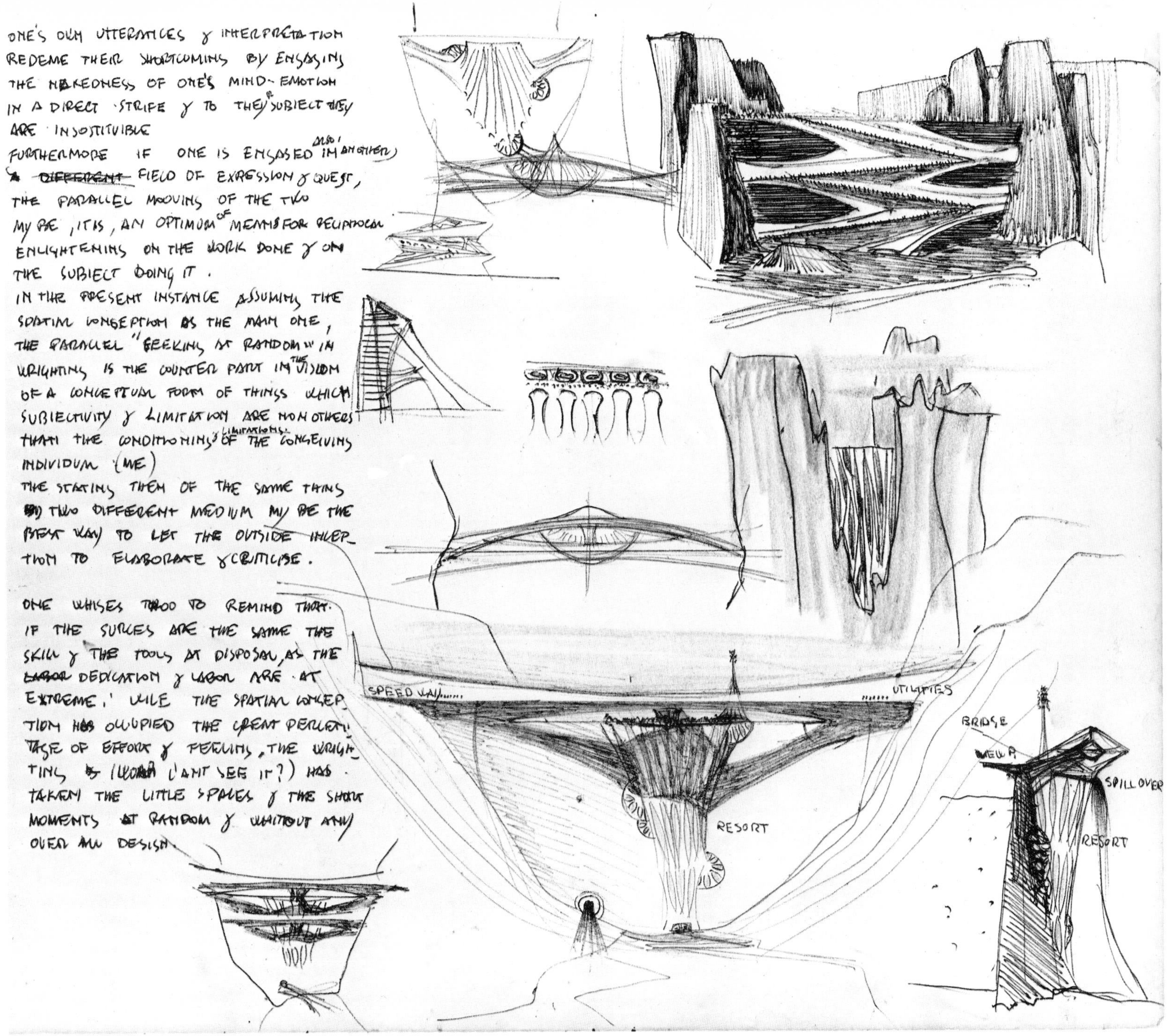
ONE'S OWN UTTERANCES y INTERPRETATION
REDEME THEIR SHORTCOMINGS BY ENGAGING
THE NAKEDNESS OF ONE'S MIND-EMOTION
IN A DIRECT STRIFE y TO THE SUBIECT THEY
ARE INSOSTITUIBLE
FURTHERMORE IF ONE IS ENGAGED ALSO IN ANOTHER
~~A DIFFERENT~~ FIELD OF EXPRESSION y QUEST,
THE PARALLEL MOOVING OF THE TWO
MY BE, IT IS, AN OPTIMUM OF MEANS FOR RECIPROCAL
ENLIGHTENING ON THE WORK DONE y ON
THE SUBIECT DOING IT.
IN THE PRESENT INSTANCE ASSUMING THE
SPATIAL CONCEPTION AS THE MAIN ONE,
THE PARALLEL "SEEKING AT RANDOM" IN
WRIGHTING IS THE COUNTER PART IN THE VISION
OF A CONCEPTUAL FORM OF THINGS WHICH
SUBIECTIVITY y LIMITATION ARE NON OTHERS
THAN THE CONDITIONING y LIMITATIONS OF THE CONCEIVING
INDIVIDUM (ME)
THE STATING THEM OF THE SAME THING
TWO DIFFERENT MEDIUM MY BE THE
BEST WAY TO LET THE OUTSIDE INCEP_
TION TO ELABORATE y CRITICISE.
ONE WHISES TOO TO REMIND THAT.
IF THE SURCES ARE THE SAME THE
SKILL y THE TOOLS AT DISPOSAL, AS THE
~~LABOR~~ DEDICATION y LABOR ARE AT
EXTREME, WILE THE SPATIAL CONCEP_
TION HAS OCCUPIED THE GREAT PERCEN_
TAGE OF EFFORT y FEELING, THE WRIGH_
TING (WORD CAN'T SEE IT?) HAS
TAKEN THE LITTLE SPACES y THE SHORT
MOMENTS AT RANDOM y WITHOUT ANY
OVER ALL DESIGN.
SPEED WAY
UTILITIES
RESORT
BRIDGE
VIEW
SPILL OVER
RESORT

SENHAIO 60

ONE DO NOT KNOW IF IT IS BECAUSE THE SUBLIME IS ATTEMPTED WITH SUB UMAN MEANS OR IF IT IS THAT SUB UMAN UTTERANCES ARE MIS-TAKEN FOR FLIGHT A "NEW" NOUNESS. THE SENSATION REMAINS THAT WILE THE VENERABILITY OF A FACIAL EXPRESSION IS BRUTALIZED INTO A SHAPELESS QUESTION, THOSE SAME WORTHY CONDITION OF ORGANIZED & UNORGANIZED MATTER ARE STULTIFIED BY A DEMAND TRUSTED UPON THEM WHICH IS NOT IN THEIR NATURE TO FULFILL

TO THINK FOR INSTANCE OF TRANSPOSING OR INTERPRETING OR ILLUSTRATING A BACH WHIT A RITMICAL FLOW OF SPLENDID BUBBLES & CORRUSCATIONS OF WAVES & EXPLOSION OF CROMATISM & SPATIAL DEPTHS. IS TO REMAIN ON THE OUTSIDE OF BACH'S SPIRITUALITY I.E. OUTSIDE OF THE MUSICAL MEANING FULLNESS OF THE PIECE IN QUESTION.

THE REFUSAL, BY THE VISUAL ARTS, TO USE ANTROPOMOPHIC FORM TO EXPRESS MANLINESS IS BY NO MEAN GARANTY OF A HIGHER LEVEL OF CONCIOUSNESS-EXPRESSION. IT MAY WELL BE THE PROMOTER OF A LOWER ONE.

WHIT ADEQUATE INSTRUMENTALITY & SKILL A MAN CAN EXTRACT FROM NATURE INCOMPARABLE PATTERNS - FORMS - COLORS OVERSHADOWING THE "INVENTIVENESS OF ANY "ARTIST"

WHAT NATURE CANNOT FURNISH WITHOUT MAN'S MEDIATION IS THE GLOW OF SPIRITUAL COUNTENANCE REPERABLE IN ANY ACT MAN'S CONCEIVE & CONCRETISES IN LOVE & HUMILITY

p61

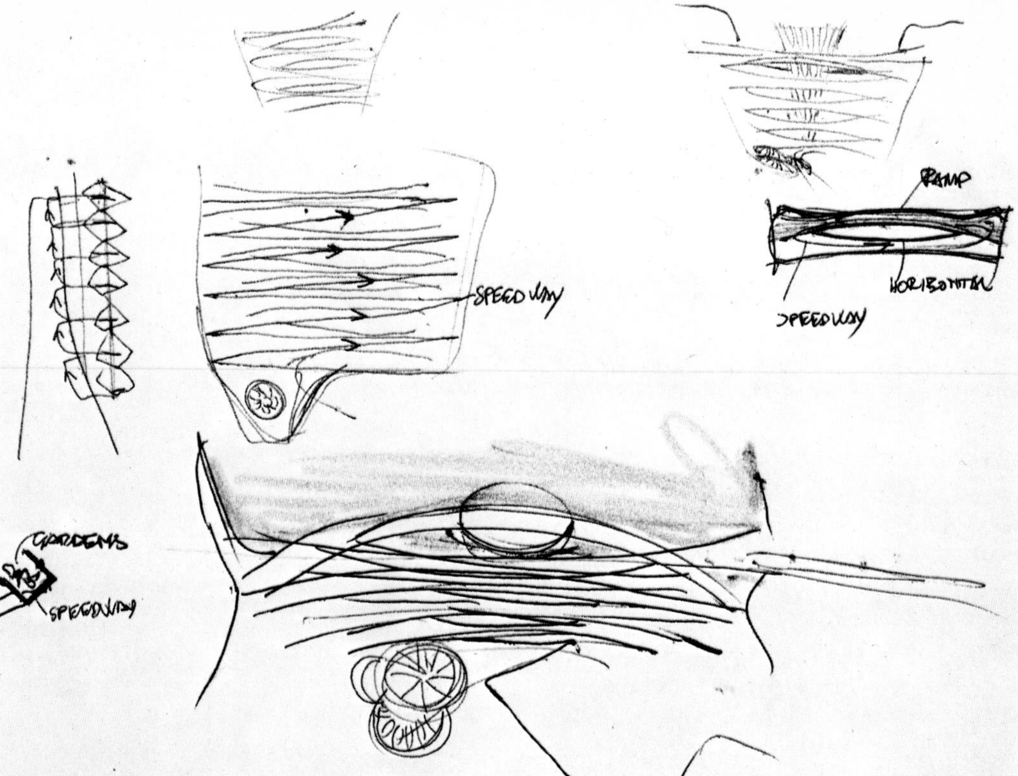

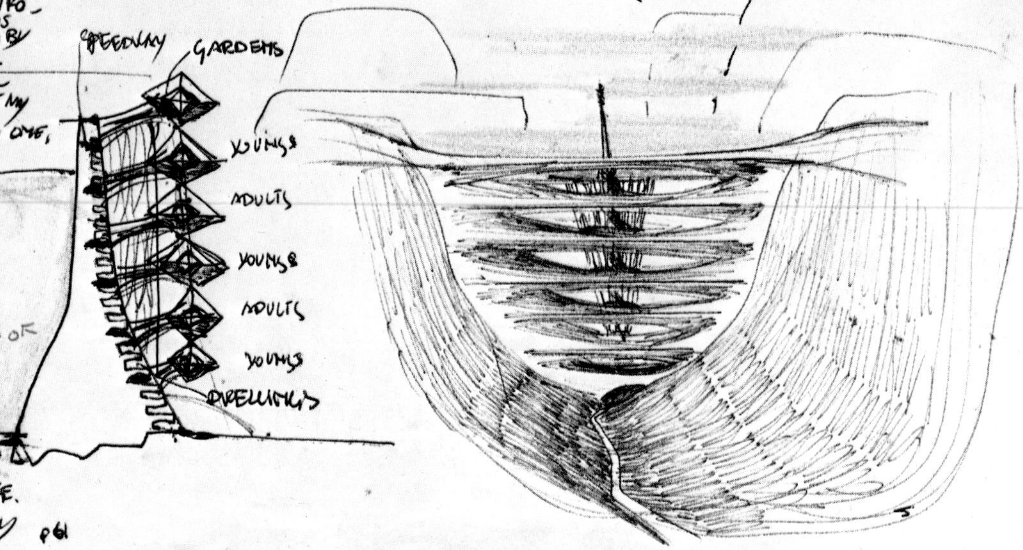

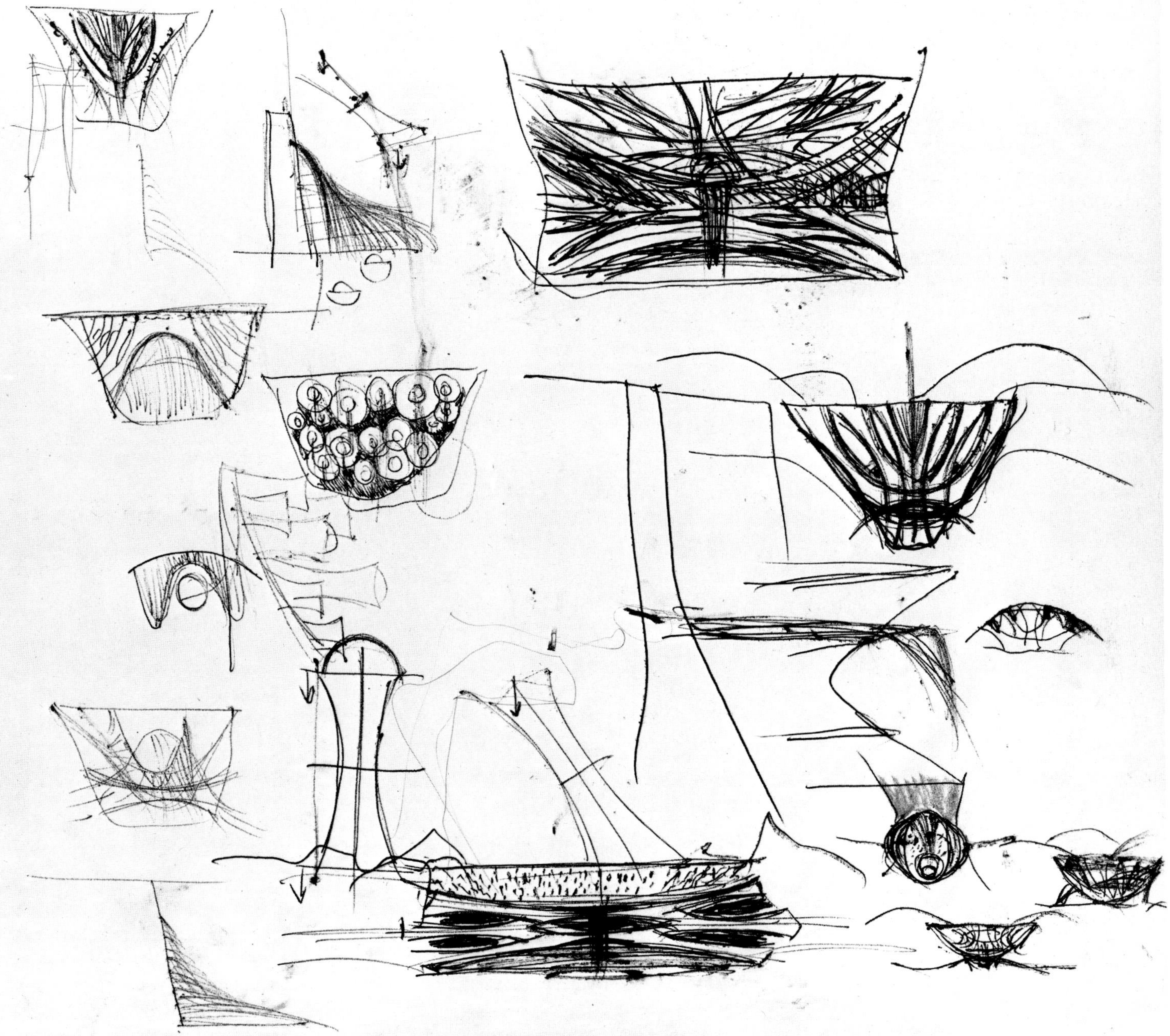

CAME NECESSARY TO OUTLINE A COERENT SCHEME OF ENDEAVOUR. WHEREIN THE SEEKING OF THE "ANSWERS" MAY BE ALSO THE LONGING FOR THE INACCESSIBLE "ANSWER", & INDEED THIS SAME LONGING MAY SO LEND ~~THE~~ THAT FRINGE ~~OF~~ OF VIBRANCE OF AMIABILITY TOUCHING IN MISTERY & TIMELESSNESS.

THE UTTERANCES OF & ON USEFULNESS, INDIVIDUALITY, MEMORY, GROWTH, WASTE, TECNOLOGY, ORGANIC, ECONOMY, TIME, SPACE, STATICITY, MOVEMENT, PROCESS, EVOLVING, BEAUTY, INTEGRITY, MULTIPLICITY, CAOS, INVOLUTION, ACTING, REACTING, RELIGIOSITY, BARBARISM......, CREATIVITY, PRODUCTIVITY, ARTIFICIALITY... TEND TO DISPLAY THEMSELVES BY A SLOWLY EMERGING PATTERN WHICH "TRANSFORMISM" ITSELF IS PART OF IT, WHOLE AS AN INHERENT CONDITION

THE DOUBLE & OPPOSITE MOVEMENTS OF CLOSING IN & EXPANDING OUT SEEM TO BE INFERED BY THE REDUCTION ON THE BOUNDARIES OF INTEREST & IN THE FINDING WITHIN THOSE SHRINKING BOUNDARIES MORE & MORE OF EVERYTHING, BUT NOT ANYMORE SO TOTALLY UNCONNECTED & EACH OTHERS INDIFFERENT TO

FAR FROM HAVING REACHED ANY ORDERLY OUTLOOK CONSTRUCTED ON THE ABOVE CATEGORIES & FAR FROM PRESUMING A CAPACITY & AN UNDERSTANDING FOR IT IT NEVERTHELESS CAMES NOW & THEN ~~AWARE OF THE~~ SENSATION OF A CERTAIN BACKGROUND ~~ON~~ AGAINST WHICH THINGS CAN ~~STAND OUT~~ ON QUASI ACCEPTABLE LIGHT.

THE SPLENDOR OF EXISTENCE IS THE TEXTURE OF THE BACKGROUND, AGAINST IT & ITS HIPOTETICAL POTENTIALITIES THE SHADOWS

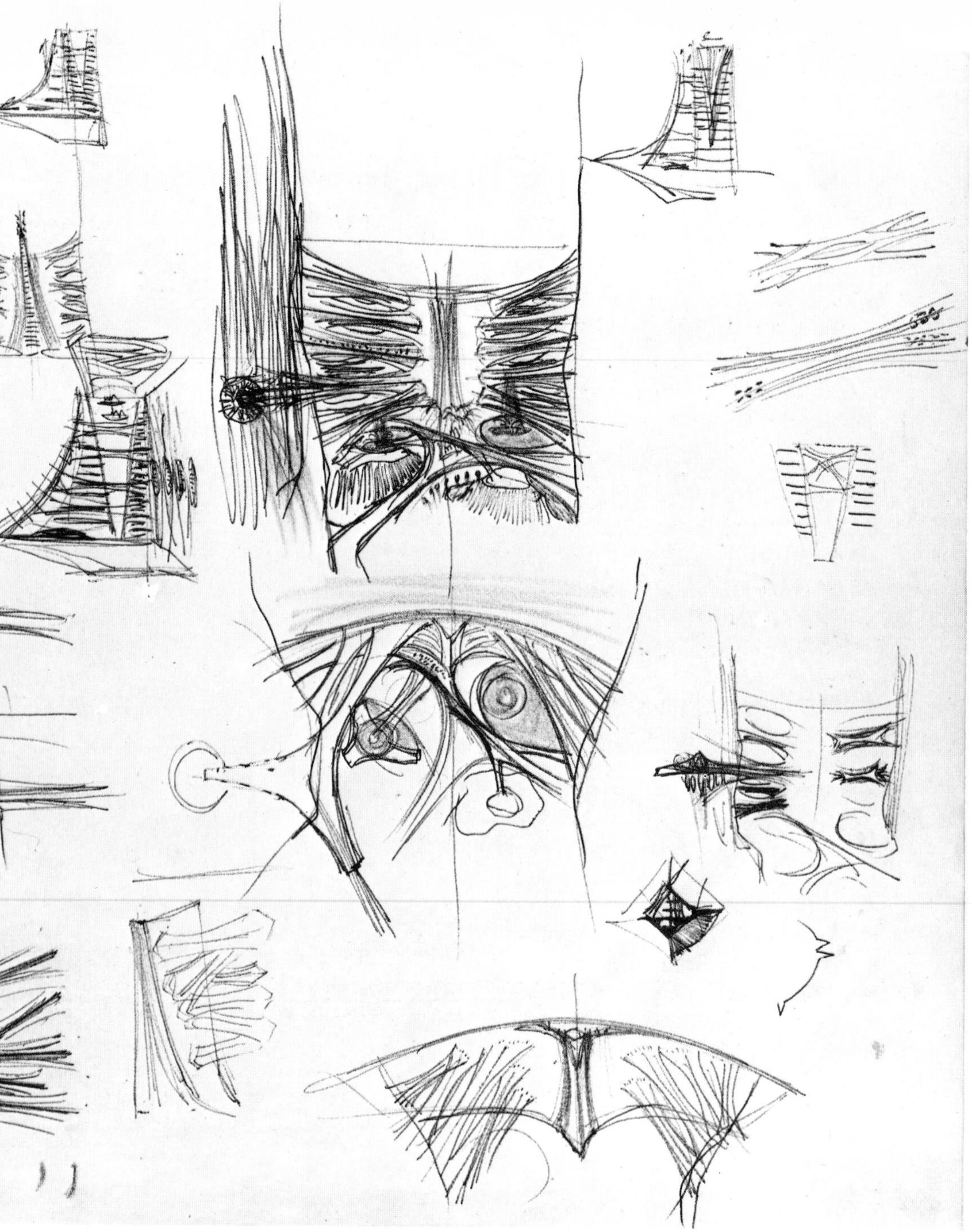

OWN UNIVERSE OF VALUES.

WITHIN THIS UNIVERSE AN A POSTERIORI CASUALISM MAY BE ENDORSED UNDER THE ASPECT OF "SPONTANEITY". ITS SENSE IS ALL DEPENDING ON THE SFERE FROM WHIC IT CAN SPRING OF & TO WHICH IS TOTALLY CONDITIONED. SO IT IS THAT THE "LICENCE" BY A CREATOR IS A PEAK OF INTENSITY, THE "LICENSE" IN THE TAKER IS THE CLEAR DENOUNCIATION OF ITS UNWORTHINESS; THE FORMER IS THE LEAP OF A SHURE FOOTED BEAST ON A WELL KNOWN & MOST CHERISHED GROUND, THE LAST ONE IS THE BLIND FOLDED JUMP OF AN ASTRAYED BEAST LOST IN AN UNGRASPED GROUND.

FROM A SFERE OF UNDERSTANDING TO A MORE INCLUSIVE ONE THE CONCENTRIC IMPLEMENTATION OF KNOWLEDGE FIND AN EVER ENCREASING MESURE OF FREEDOM; THE PLASMA FILLING THE FORM & WHAT IT. A MULTIPLICATION OF POSSIBILITIES & HORIZONS. AS FOR A THEATRE, THUS, THE ENCREASE IN THE NUMBER OF STRUCTURES & OF THE COMPLEXITY OF LIGHT GROUPING DO NOT TOUCH IN THE SUBSTANCE OF THE DRAMA FUNCTION OF THE DEPTH CONVEYED BY IT NOT BY THE REDUNDANCE OF THE SCENERY, THIS HOLDS TRUE IF KNOWLEDGE IS ONLY LOOKED UPON AS A COLLECTION OF INFORMATIONS.

IF KNOWLEDGE IS NOT INFORMATION IS STILL CONDITIONED BY IT HENCE PASSIVE EXPECTATION IS MORE A PRESUMPTION OF, THAN A REACHING FOR KNOWLEDGE

Pg 69

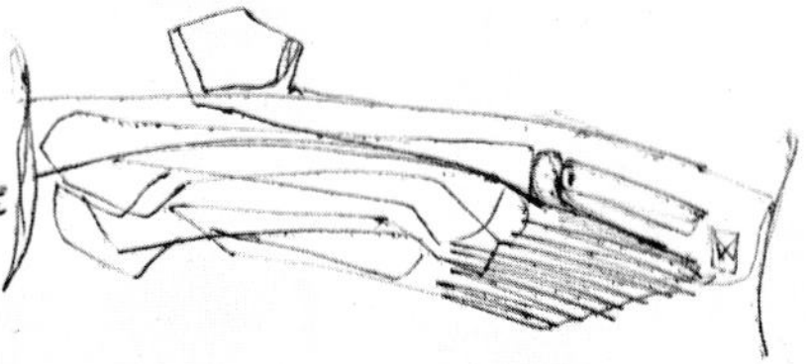
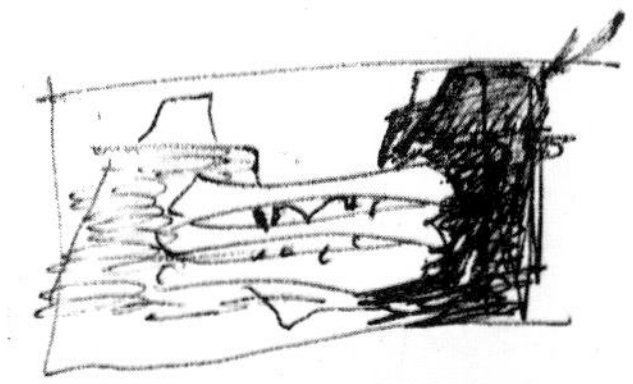
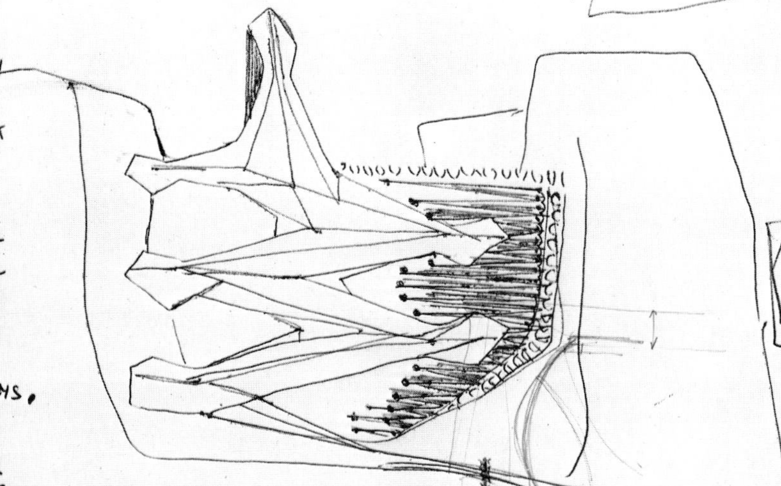
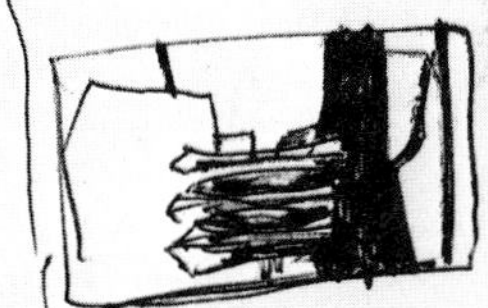

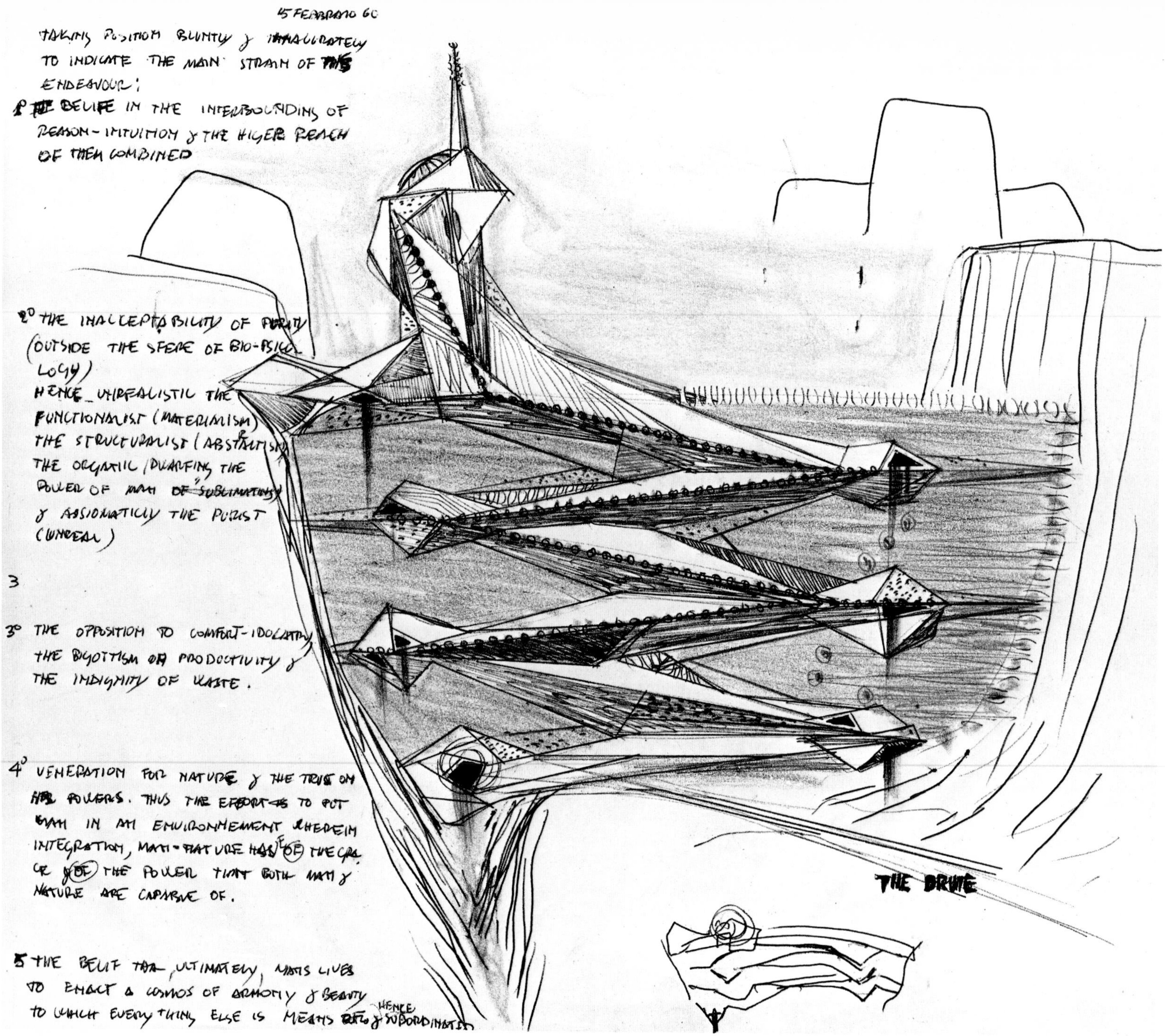
15 FEBBRAIO 60
TAKING POSITION BLUNTLY & INACCURATELY
TO INDICATE THE MAIN STRAIN OF THIS
ENDEAVOUR;
1 THE BELIFE IN THE INTERBOUNDINGS OF
REASON-INTUITION & THE HIGER REACH
OF THEM COMBINED
2° THE INACCEPTABILITY OF PURITY
(OUTSIDE THE SFERE OF BIO-PSICO-
LOGY)
HENCE_UNREALISTIC THE
FUNCTIONALIST (MATERIALISM)
THE STRUCTURALIST (ABSTRACTISM)
THE ORGANIC (DWARFING THE
POWER OF MAN OF SUBLIMATION)
& ASSIOMATICLY THE PURIST
(UNREAL)
3
3° THE OPPOSITION TO COMFORT-IDOLATRY
THE BIGOTTISM ON PRODUCTIVITY &
THE INDIGNITY OF WASTE.
4° VENERATION FOR NATURE & THE TRUST ON
HER POWERS. THUS THE EFFORT IS TO PUT
MAN IN AN ENVIRONMEMENT WHEREIN
INTEGRATION, MAN-NATURE HAS THE GRA-
CE OF THE POWER THAT BOTH MAN &
NATURE ARE CAPABLE OF.
5 THE BELIF THA, ULTIMATELY, MAN LIVES
TO ENACT A COSMOS OF ARMONY & BEAUTY
TO WHICH EVERYTHING ELSE IS MEANS & HENCE SUBORDINATED
THE DRIVE

6° THE URGENT NEED FOR AN UNDERTAKING WHICH SUBSTANCE & MAGNITUDE MY BE CAPABLE OF AWAKENING IN THE DEEPER ~~MANS~~ LONGINGS FOR INTEGRITY & FONDAMENTALS,

7° THE REJECTION OF THE "FRAGMENT", PAINSTAKINGLY POLISHED & OVER RATIONALIZED ACUMEN IN THE SQUALOR OF OUR CAOTIC MODES & MATERIALITIES.

8° THE SEEKING OF FABBRICAS WHICH MORFOLOGY & EXPRESSION IS ENGENDERING FEELINGS FOR CONTINUITY, LASTINESS & INDEPENDENCE FROM "THE FASHIONABLE.

9° "STILE" AS RESULTANT OF TWO COMPONENTS:
1° THE UNDERGOING OF THE CONTINOUM WHICH IS THE MAN & WHICH TINGES ALL IT TOUCHES ~~OF~~ THE "COLOR" OF ITS POINT OF GROWTH.
2° THE CONTINGENT ~~ABOUT~~ OF WHICH THE PROBLEM IS ABOUT & WHICH ACTION PLOTS WHIT THE UNDERSTANDING OF THE MAKER THE FISIONOMY OF THE FABBRICA.

10° THE STRIFE OF MAN TO OUTDO NATURE ITSELF TO ~~[illegible]~~ DEMONSTRATE HIMSELF THE WORTHINESS OF ITS STRUGGLE.

11° INTENSITY AS INVOLVEMENT WHICH LEAVES OUT ONLY THAT MUCH CONCIOUSNESS & DETACHMENT TO RIDIRECT THE SEEKING IN THE RIVER BED OF CONCEPTIVITY.

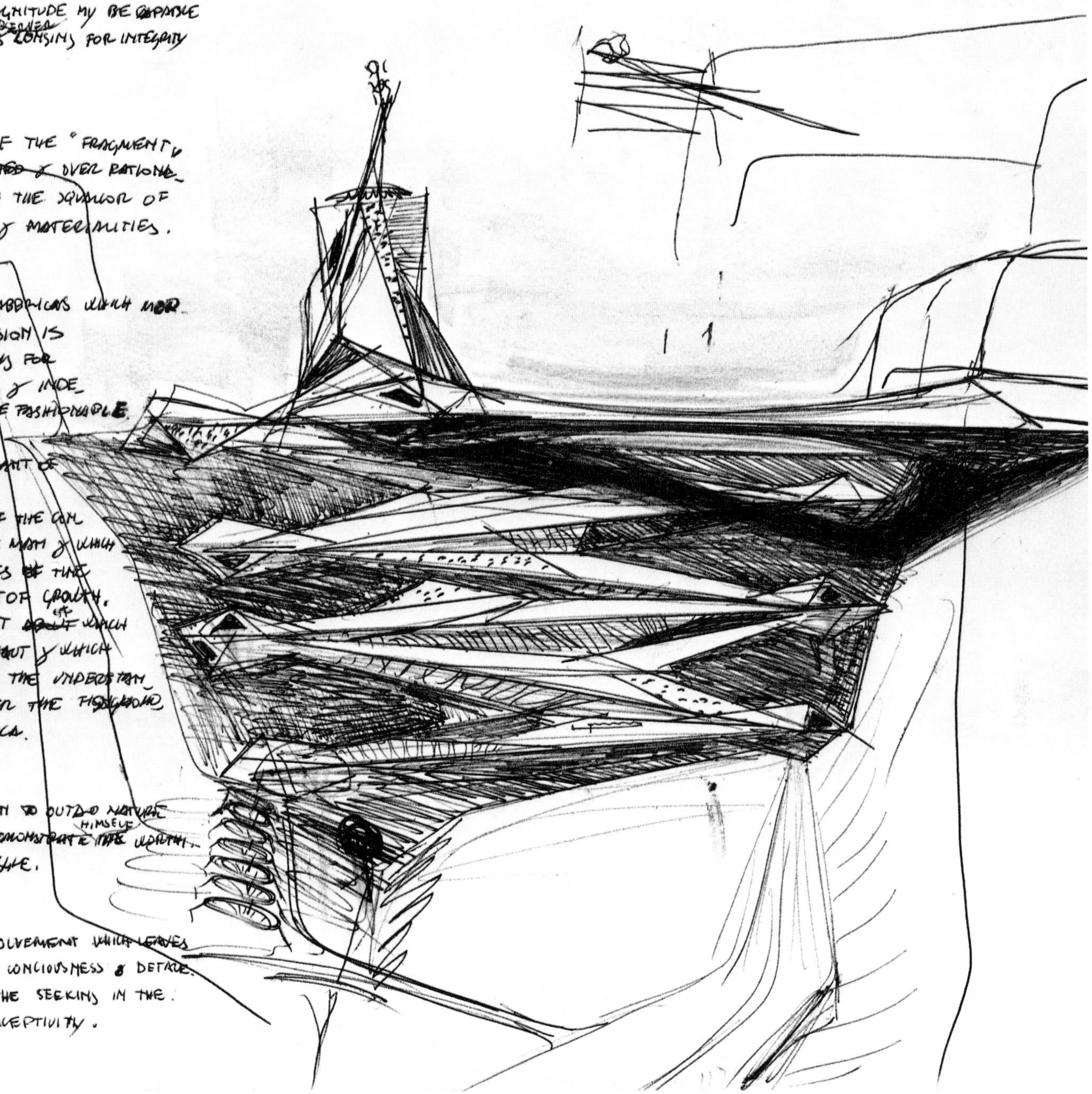

12° THE SACRIFYINS SOME WERE ALONG THE
LINE OF EXTENTION FOR THE SAKE DEPTH WHICH
NEGATIVELY LOOKED UPON MY STRIKE AS
SPECIALISATION. THUS AS SACRIFYINS THE
WOLE TO THE PART.
IN THIS CONTEST INDICATING THAT THE
TIRANNY INHERENT THE QUEST IS SETTING
ASIDE ALL ASPECT OF LIFE OF COLLATERAL
INTEREST: LONG HOURS OF READINGS, TRAVELS
INDIVIDUAL CONTACTS "HOBBIES" . . .

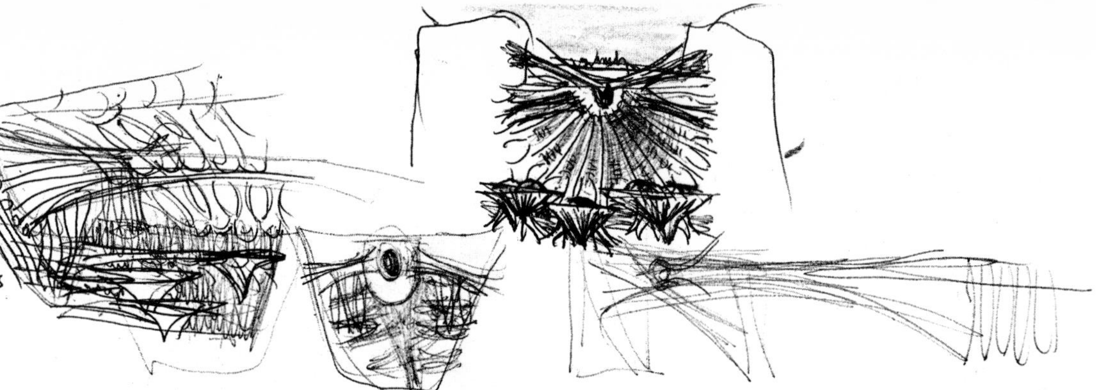

13° IN FAIR CONTRADDICTION TO 12° THE TYING TOGETHER
OF VERY ETEROGENEUS CATEGORIES BY THE
STRANDS OF IMPROVED COERENCE & THE
FINDING OF CONCEALED OR & NOT SELF EVIDENT
CONNECTIONS.

14° THE TRUST ON TWO FONDAMENTAL. CONSTAN
CE & CHANGE:
CONSTANCE: ALL THAT WHICH GROSSLY IS ~~ARMED~~
PUT ON THE ALTAR OF THE ETERNAL VALUES,
& POSSIBLY ~~IS~~ THE RESULT OF THE ORGANIC
MEMORY WHICH IMPRINTS IN THE EONS PAST
OUR PRESENT STRIFE. THE SUBSTANTIAL
EQUALITY FOR ANY BEING OF SUCH PAST.
EXPLAINS THE GENERAL AGREEMENT ON THE
RULES OF "JUSTICE" THE "LAWS" OF LOVE
COMPASSION, MAGNANIMITY, FORGIVENESS . . .
THE AGREEMENTS ON ERROR UGLINESS, MANAGITY . . .
THESE ETERNAL LAWS ARE THE OUTCOME OF THEIR
OPPOSITE: CHANGE, AS SUCH THEY ARE NOT
ETERNAL BUT ETERNALLY UNFOLDING & AS THEY
ARE THE SINTESIS OF CHANGE SO THEY ARE
ITS MOST FORMATIVE CAUSE.
IF ACCIDENT THERE WAS IT WAS ONLY IN THE
FIRST INSTANT. THERE FROM THE SELF LINKING
CHAINE HAD ~~THE~~ ALL THE ATTRIBUTES OF
NECESSITY OF CHOICE & SELF ASSERTION
AS PAST IN THE DEFINITION OF ITSELF
AS FUTURE

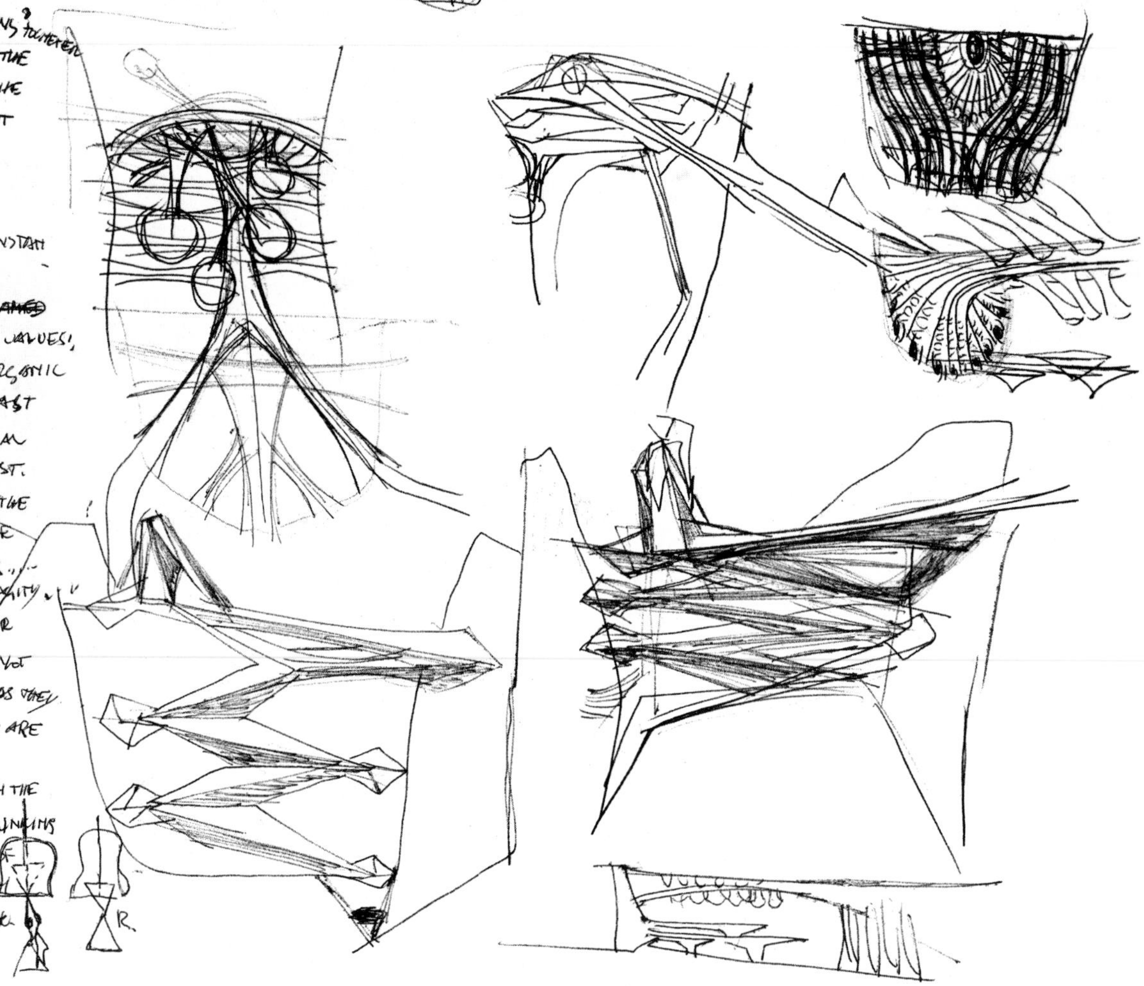

WHEN y HOW WILL BE DEMONSTRATED THAT THE EXTRA-SENSORIAL PERCEPTION y THE WORLD TO IT CONNECTED ARE ~~A~~ (THE CONCERN OF) HIGHER STATE OF BEING y NOT OF A LOWER ONE?

WE MAY WELL REMEMBER THAT MOST OF OUR UNDISCRIBABLE SENSATION, LIKE THE ONE SURGING WITHIN OUR BODIES ARE THE FISICO-FISIOLOGIC ONES, THE SAME AFFLICTING IN MAJOR OR ~~LESSER~~ MINOR DEGREE THE ANIMAL KINGDOM NOT TO GO SO FAR AS TO THE BOTANICAL ONE.

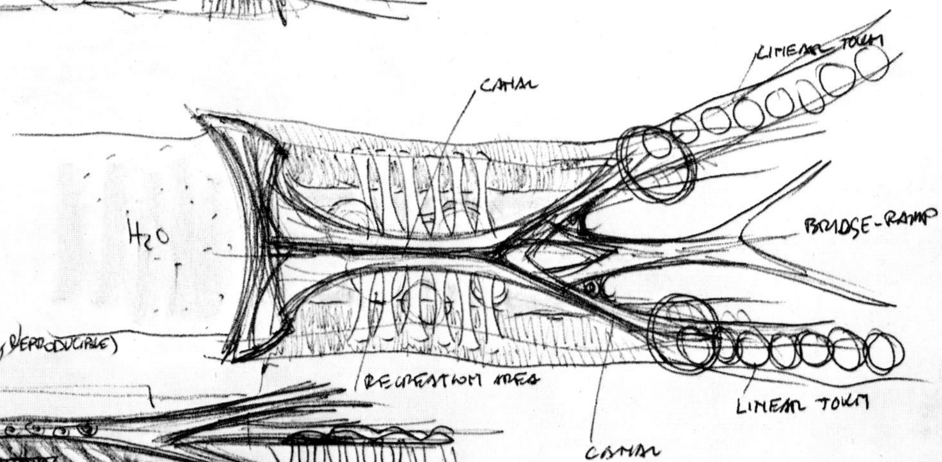

WHIT MAN CAMES SIMBOLOGY y WHAT IT THE POSSIBILITY OF REITERATED y, TO ADEGRE, PERMANENT EXPRESSIONS (REPETIBLE, REPRODUCIBLE) FALLOWS THE INVESTIGATION INTO THE METAPHISICAL BY THE ~~WORK~~ OF THE MIND ACTIVATED BY THE RESTLESNESS OF THE SPIRIT

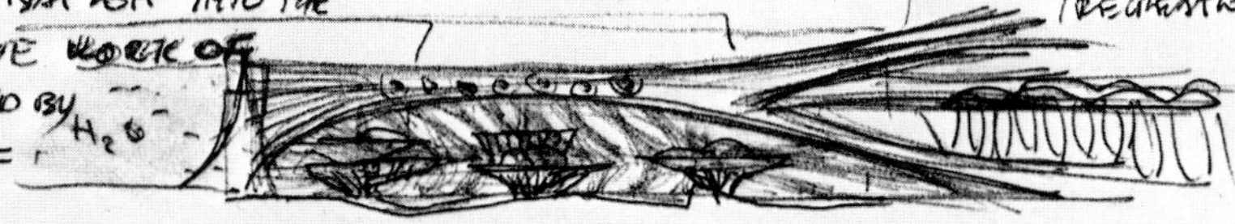

IT WOULD BE VERY EASY TO EXPLAIN THE MISTICAL EXPERIENCE AS THAT EXPERIENCE WHICH A "DESPERATE NOSTALGIA" FOR THE ORGANIC I.E. FISIOLOGICAL, COMBINED WHIT A DEEP SEATED REPULSION FOR THE ENDURABLE THAT SAME ORGANIC IS BEARER, - CONSTRICT, AUXILIARIES y ~~MOST~~ EFFECTIVE THE IMAGINATION OF THE MIND y THE THIRST OF THE BODY ~~SPIRIT~~, y THE LONGING OF THE SPIRIT.

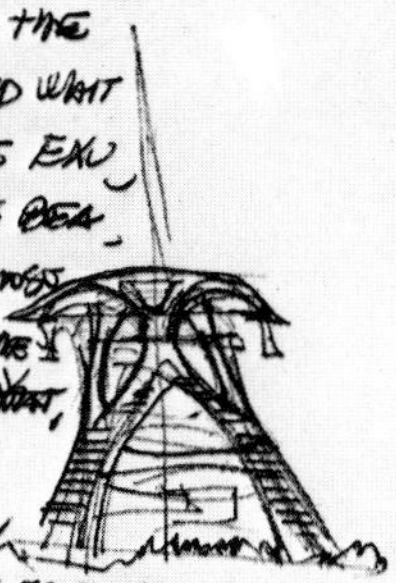

THE OUTCOMING EXPERIENCE THEN, BECAUSE OF ITS INTENSITY y CENTEREDNESS THERE WHERE THE I FADES INTO THE ALL, VIEWED AS A PEAK OF REALITY y NOT AS A POSSIBLE ANNIHILATION INTO THE BIOLOGICAL, WHIT THE TRICKS OF THE TRADE THAT THE MIND CAN SUBMIT.

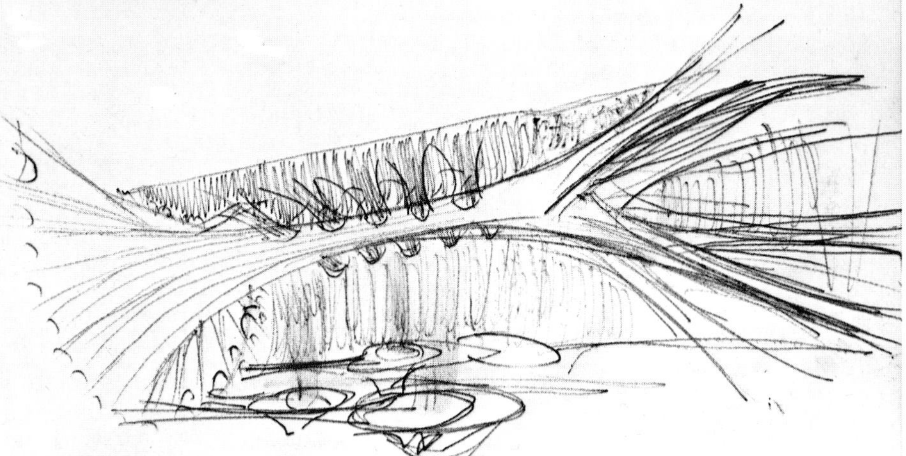

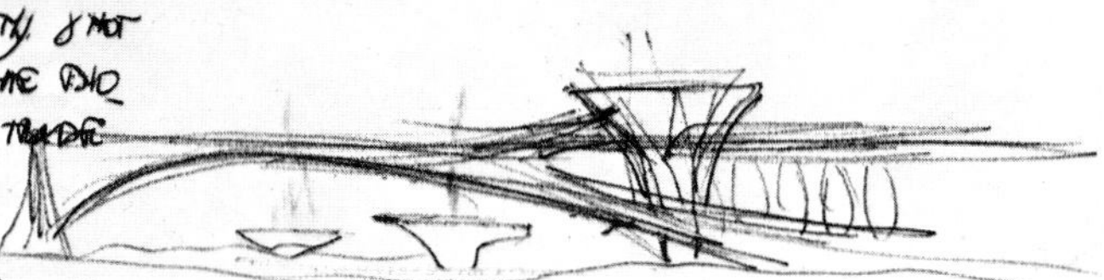

IS IDENTIFICATION THE HIGHLIGHT OF THE SONG OR THE PRECEDING y FALLOWING SILENCE?

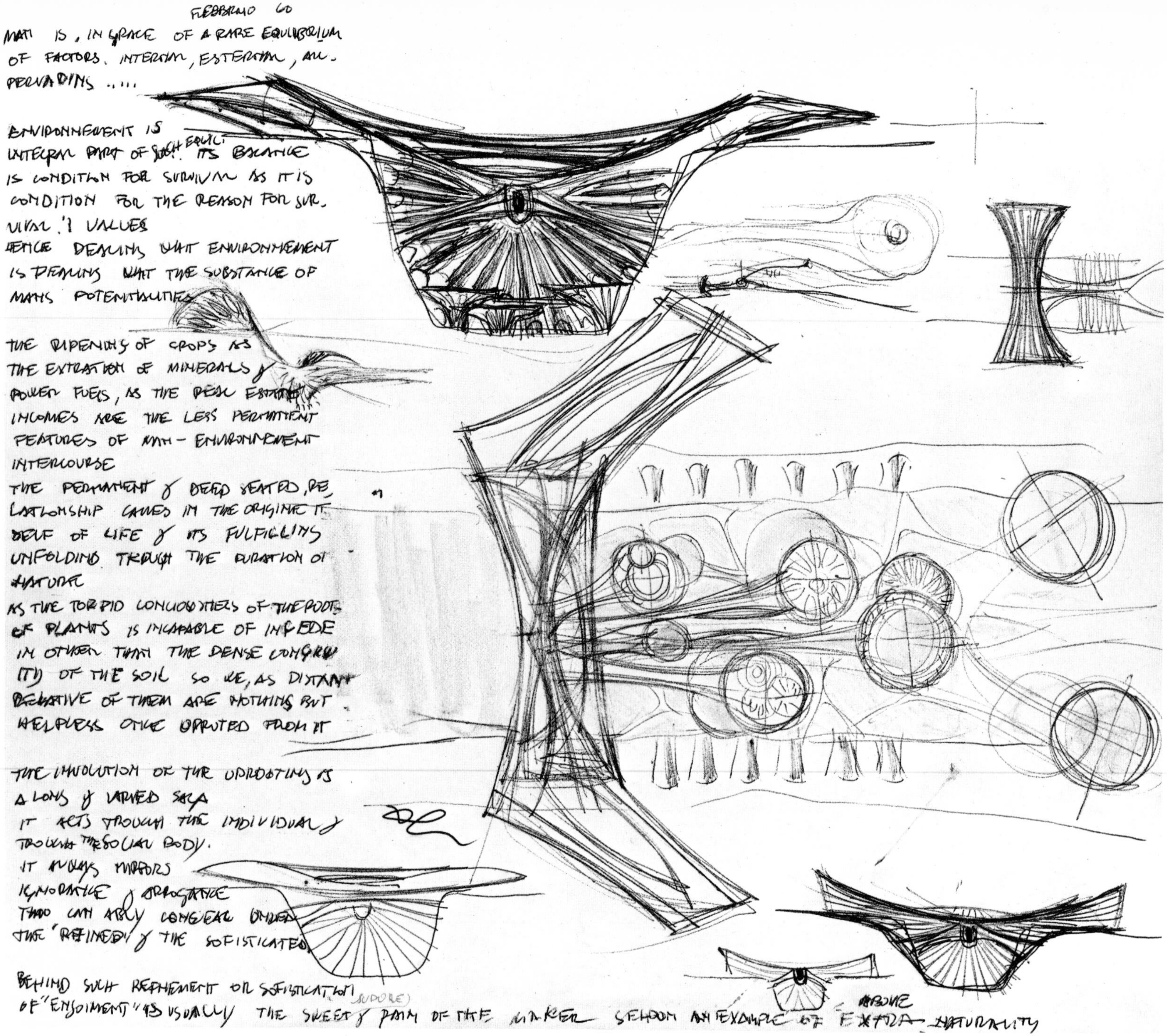
FEBBRAIO 60
MAN IS, IN GRACE OF A RARE EQUILIBRIUM
OF FACTORS. INTERNAL, ESTERNAL, ALL-
PERVADING .....
ENVIRONMENT IS
INTEGRAL PART OF SUCH EQUIL. ITS BALANCE
IS CONDITION FOR SURVIVAL AS IT IS
CONDITION FOR THE REASON FOR SUR-
VIVAL: VALUES
HENCE DEALING WHIT ENVIRONMEMENT
IS DEALING WHIT THE SUBSTANCE OF
MANS POTENTIALITIES
THE RIPENING OF CROPS AS
THE EXTRATION OF MINERALS &
POWER FUELS, AS THE REAL ESTATE
INCOMES ARE THE LESS PERMANENT
FEATURES OF MAN-ENVIRONMEMENT
INTERCOURSE
THE PERMANENT & DEEP SEATED, RE-
LATIONSHIP CAMES IN THE ORIGINE IT-
SELF OF LIFE & ITS FULFILLING
UNFOLDING TROUGH THE DURATION OF
NATURE
AS THE TORPID CONCIOUSNESS OF THE ROOTS
OF PLANTS IS INCAPABLE OF INFEDE
IN OTHER THAN THE DENSE CONGRUITY OF THE SOIL SO WE, AS DISTANT
RELATIVE OF THEM ARE NOTHING BUT
HELPLESS ONCE UPROOTED FROM IT
THE INVOLUTION OR THE UPROOTING IS
A LONG & VARIED SAGA
IT ACTS TROUGH THE INDIVIDUAL &
TROUGH THE SOCIAL BODY.
IT ALWAYS MIRRORS
IGNORANCE & ARROGANCE
THAT CAN ABLY CONCEAL UNDER
THE "REFINED" & THE SOFISTICATED
BEHIND SUCH REFINEMENT OR SOFISTICATION
OF "ENJOIMENT" IS USUALLY THE SWEET (SUDORE) & PAIN OF THE MAKER SELDOM AN EXAMPLE OF EXTRA ABOVE NATURALITY

ULTIMATELY THE CONTEST WILL BE BETWEEN MAN & NATURE. WHEREAS NOW THE CONFUSION OF IGNORANCE & MALICE CALL & GETS ITS TOLL OF VICTIMS & MARTIRS FROM THE CONTEST AMONGST MAN-NATIONS

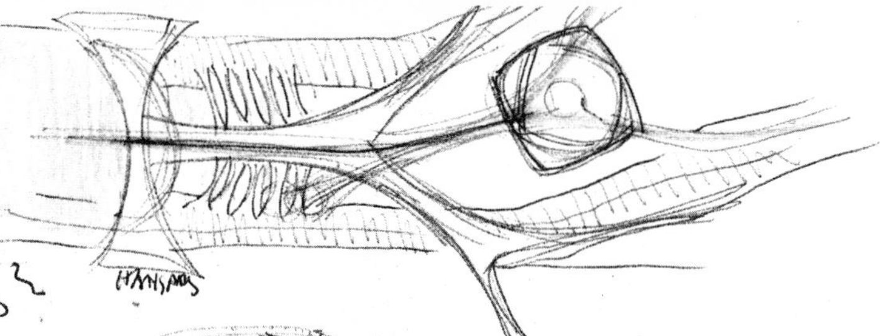

STRIFE AMONG MAN WILL, IN THE OTHER HAND NEVER TOTALLY ~~SEEDE~~ SUBSIDE FOR THAT MUCH THAT MAN IS NATURE IE SOMETIMES UNFORTUNATELY EXTERNAL TO MAN THE INDIVIDUAL.
HENCE WILE ONE MAN CONTENDS TO NATURE A WATER SHED ANOTHER CONTENDS TO SOCIETY A PARTICULAR POSITION.

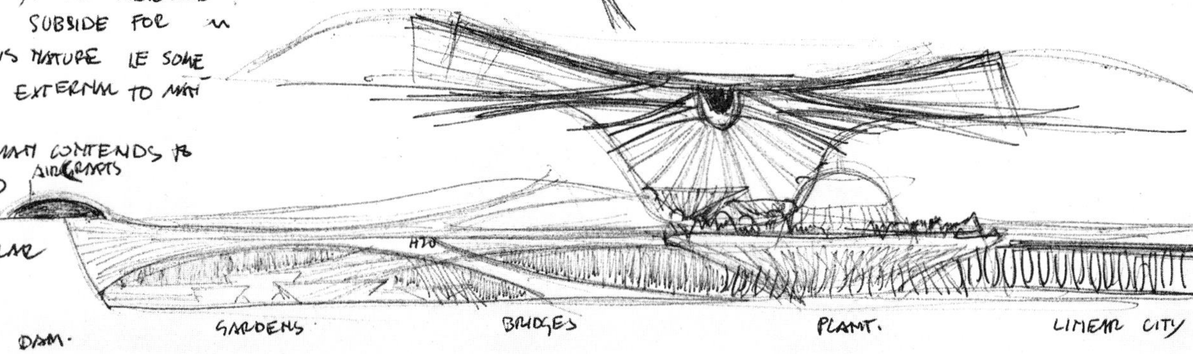

BOTH MEN TRYING TO INSTITUTE ON A EXTERNAL ENTITY A PERSONAL ORDER-PATTERN.
ONLY SPECULATIVE INQUIRE, WHICH END MAY BE THE DEFINITION OF A HISTORICAL CONTINUITY MAY GO AS FAR AS TO EXPLORE THE POSSIBILITIES OF FONDAMENTAL DIFFERENCES BETWEEN THE TWO ENDEAVOUR!

ONE PROSPECTIVE MAY THEN, ENVISAGING MEN AS A COMPOSITE ASSOCIATION OF SELF SUFFICENT INDIVIDUAL OF WHICH EACH MAN IS THE ULTIMATE, FIND NO FONDAMENTAL DIFFERENCE.

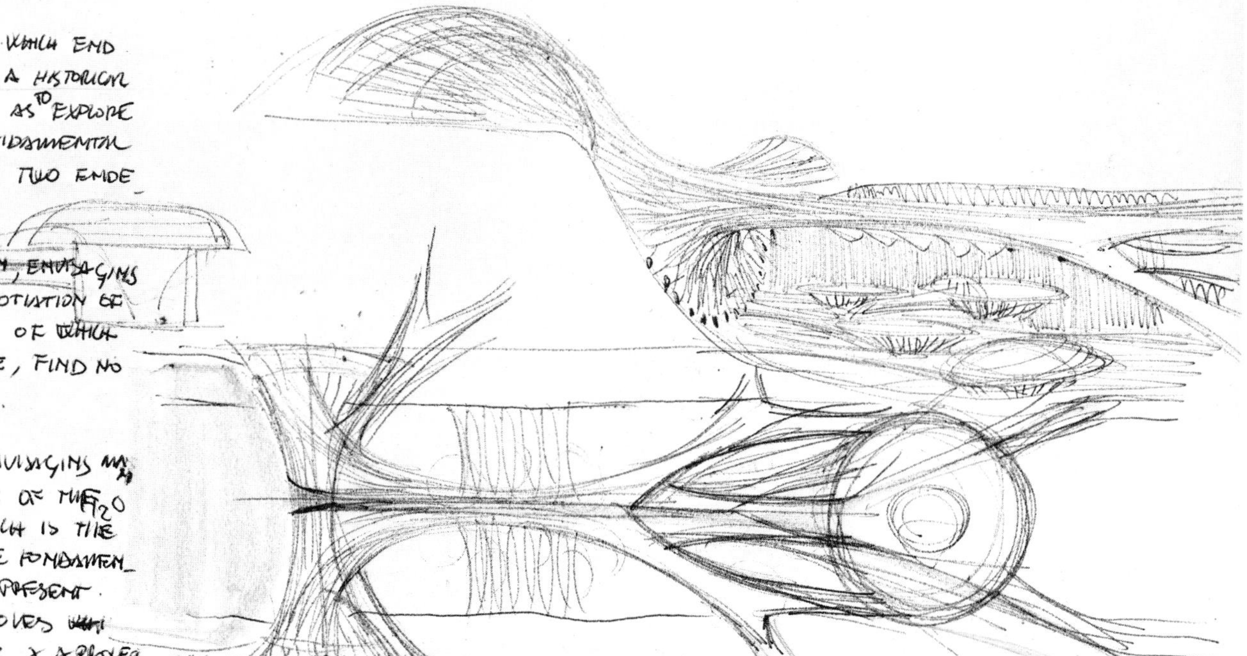

THE OTHER PERSPECTIVE ENVISAGING MAN AS A SPECIALISED CELLULE OF THE BODY SOCIETY WHICH AS SUCH IS THE ULTIMATE, WOULD FIND THE FONDAMENTAL DIFFERENCE THAT IS PRESENT. BETWEEN A PROCESS WHIC MOVES ~~WHI~~ WHITHIN ITS OWN BONDUARIES & A PROCESS WHIC MOVES FROM WITHIN TO WITHOUT TO RECICLE AGAIN ...

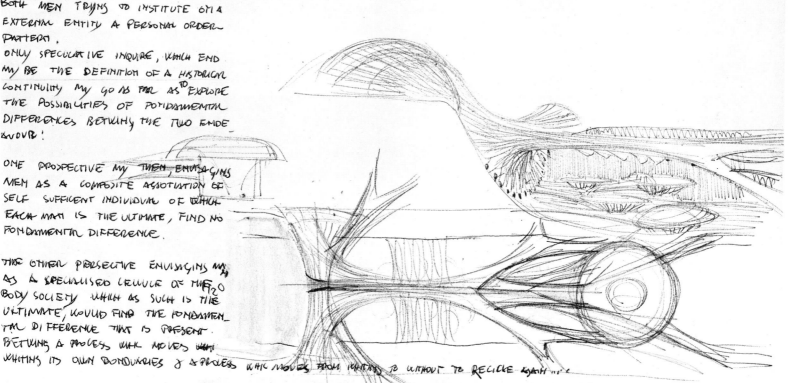

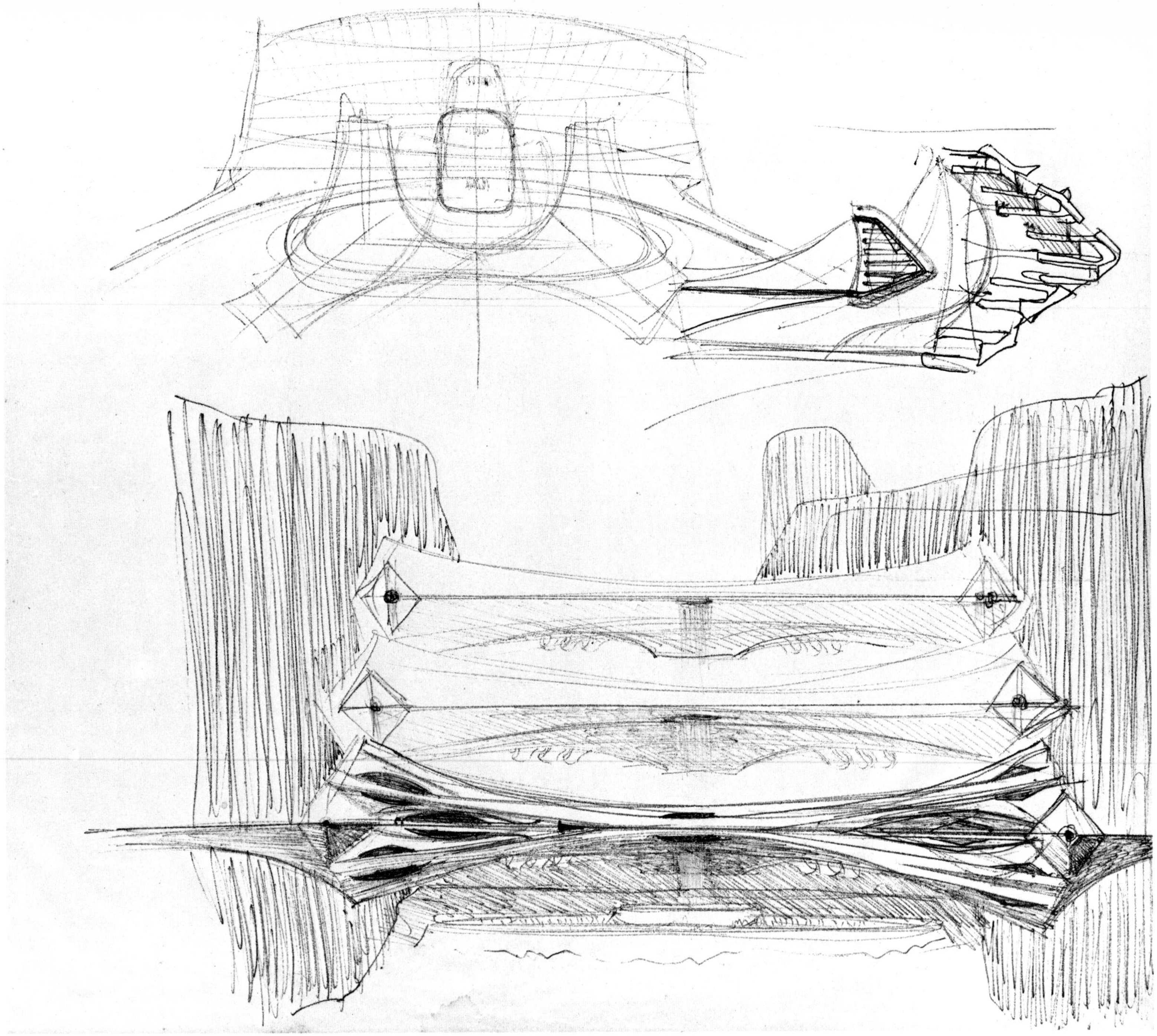

MARCH 60

OF KRAFTS & ARCHITECTURE
AS GROUND BREAKING, ONE MY SAY THAT WILE ARCHITECTURE IS AT A GIVEN LEVEL A KRAFT, KRAFT IS INHERENTLY DEPRIVED OF THE ARCHITECTURAL SIGNIFICATION EVEN IF DEPLOYED INTENTIONALLY & ONESIDEDLY AS A CONSTRUCTION ACTIVITY. IN OTHER WORDS ARCHITECTURE ENVELOPPES KRAFTS BUT NOT VICE VERSA

THIS ROUGHLY SPEAKING IS FISICLY ASSERTED BY THE MATERIAL RELATION KR-ARCH.

THE BASIC DIFFERENCE IS THOUGH RESIDING IN THE FACT THAT WILE ARCHITECTURE, AT HIS HIGHEST, TRANSCENDS MATERIALITY, KRAFT IS MATERIALITY ITSELF MADE LIVE & AMAIBLE

ONE EXALTE MANLINESS IN ITS ASPECT OF "SUPERNATURAL" THE OTHER, EXALTE MANLINESS IN ITS ASPECT OF SPLENDID ANIMALITY: THE BEAUTY OF MATTER ORGANIZED

HENCE FOR EACH KRAFTED BUILDING ONE RENOUNCES TO A WORK OF ARCHITECTURE AS SUCH THO STILL RETAINING A WORTHY THING TO BEHOLD

THUS RELATED KRAFT ENTERS INTO ARCHITECTURE BY THE FRONT DOOR AS A PRIMARY PROCESS - DATA IN THE CONSTITUTIVE FASE OF THE FABBRICA. ONE MY ALMOST SAY THAT THE FABBRICA IS KRAFT IN ITS "SECONDARY" INCEPTION LEAVING THE PRIMARY TO THE TRANSFIGURING POWER OF CREATIVENESS.
THEN KRAFT IS THERE, IMBEDDED INTO THE MATERIALITY OF WALLS, HORIZONT ELEMENTS ... ETC & ALL STRUCTURALS

BY EXTENDING SUCH LEGITIMACY IN SPA-
CE & TIME WE HAVE THE INTRODUCTION
OF THE KRAFTS IN THE TEXTURE OF
THE CONSTRUCTION.

THIS POINT REACHED, THE UNTRAMMELING
OF THE CONFLICT DECOR OR BUILDING
MIGHT SEE BETTER POSSIBILITIES.

BY STATING THAT THE CONCEPTION OF
THE TOTALITY HAS TO COME FROM THE
ARCHITECT. ONE REALLY ADVOCATES AN
IDENTIFICATION THAT IS LEVELING THE
CATEGORIES INTO ONE. ART & KRAFTS.
IF THE ARTISTIC REGION IS NOT REACHED
THIS MAY WELL BE THE MOST ONE MAY ASK
FOR. BUT IF SUCH REGION HAS BEEN REA-
CHED THEN THE QUESTION IS PLAINLY
IMMATERIAL OR IRRATIONAL AS FOR ISTANCE DEMANDING
THAT THE SCENT OF GIASMIN EMANATE
FROM AN ANGELICO, FRESCO (MOVIES-ODORS)

VERY SENSIBLE IS INSTEAD TO SAY THAT.
IF, IF AN ODOR IS TO BE CONNECTED
WITH ANGELICOS WORK THIS ODOR IS
TO BE LOOKED FOR NOT INTO THE
GARLIC SPECIES BUT IN THE
GASMIN ONE.
THIS HOLDS FOR THE CATEGORIES OF
ART-KRAFTS: THE BELONGING & BEFIT-
TING IS NOT EXTABLISHED BY FILOSO-
PHICAL INTROSPECTIONS BUT BY SENSO-
RIAL & FEELING-EMOTIVE STIMULAE &
LONGINS. LONGINGS.
WILE ON A MERELY QUALITATIVE BASES
ANY GOOD KRAFT MAY BELONG IN ANY
GOOD ARCHITECTURE, SUBTLER & CLOSER
TO SIGNIFICANCE PROSPECTIVE, WILL MAKE
THE RELATION MUCH MORE DEMANDING
& OF DIFFICULT ACHIVEMENT.
THIS SHOULD BE THE FIELD OF RESEARCH
RESEARCH

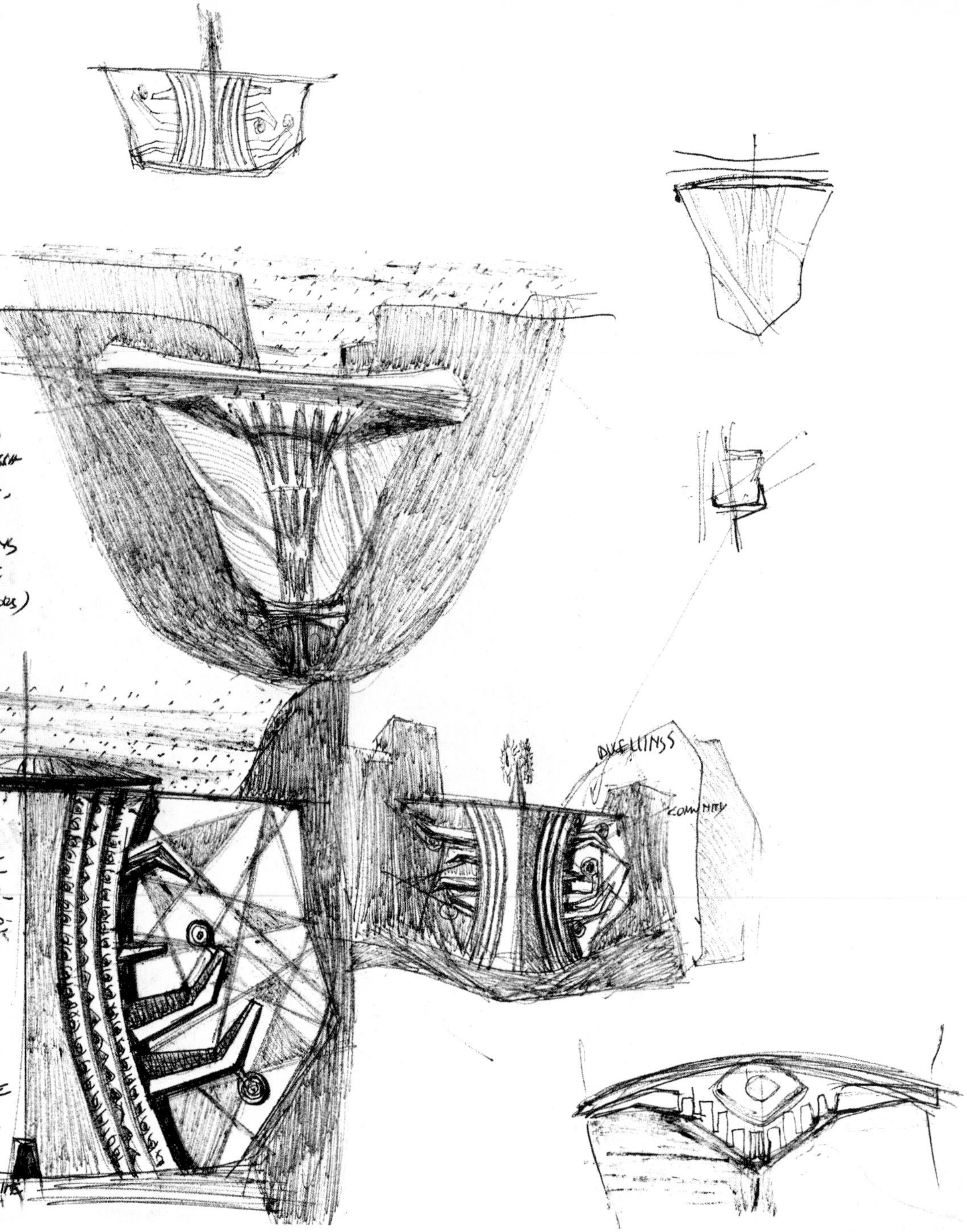

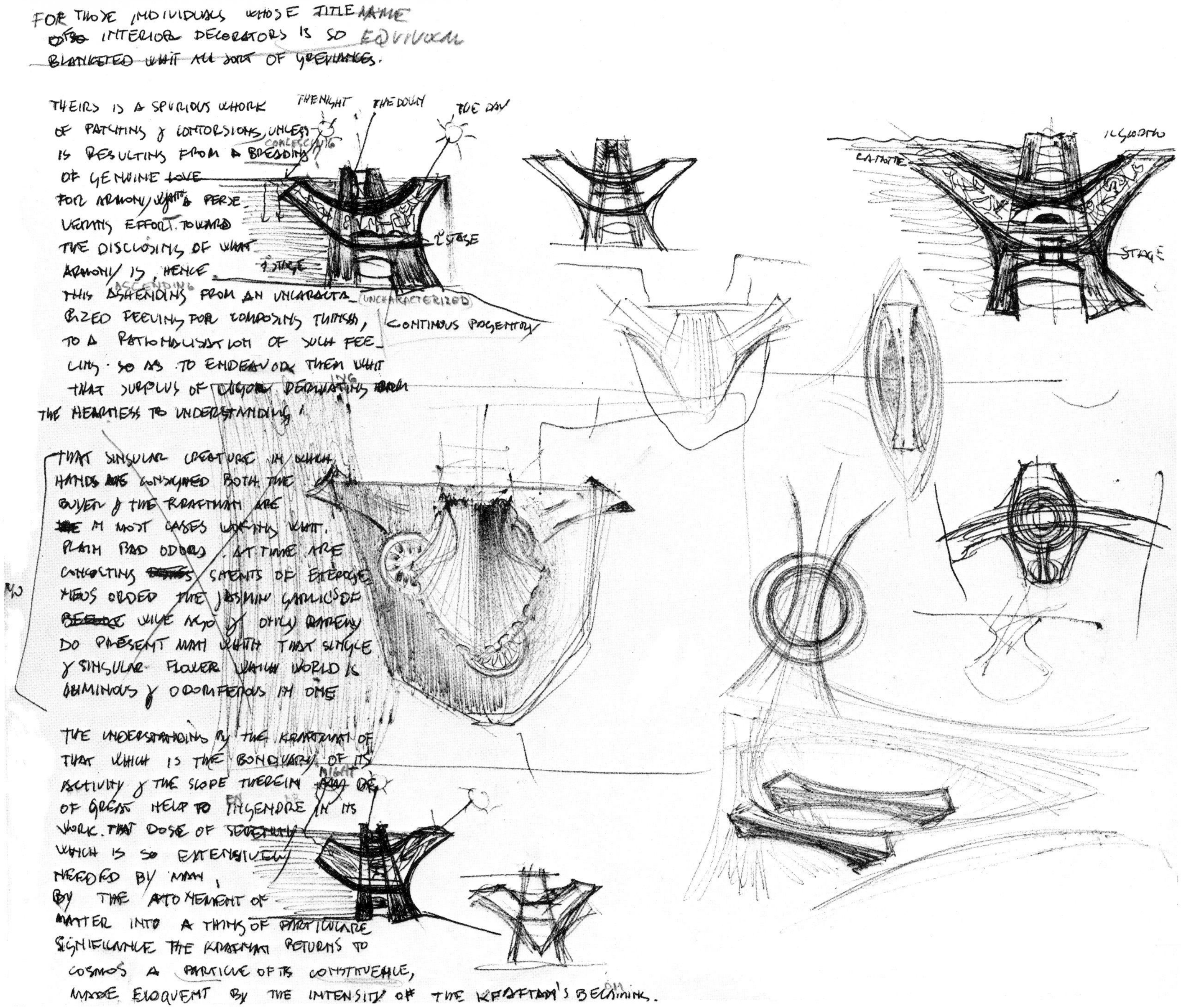
FOR THOSE INDIVIDUALS WHOSE TITLE NAME
INTERIOR DECORATORS IS SO EQUIVOCAL
BLANKETED WHIT ALL SORT OF GREVIANCES.
THEIRS IS A SPURIOUS WHORK
OF PATCHING & CONTORSIONS, UNLESS
IS RESULTING FROM A BREEDING
CORRECTING
OF GENUINE LOVE
FOR ARMONY, WHIT A PERSE-
VERING EFFORT TOWARD
THE DISCLOSING OF WHAT
ARMONY IS, HENCE
ASCENDING
THIS ASHENDING FROM AN UNCARACTE-
RIZED FEELING FOR COMPOSING THINGS,
(UNCHARACTERIZED)
CONTINOUS PROGENITORY
TO A RATIONALISATION OF SUCH FEE-
LING SO AS TO ENDEAVOR THEM WHIT
THAT SURPLUS OF VIGOR DERIVATING FROM
THE NEARNESS TO UNDERSTANDING.
THE NIGHT
THE DOWN
THE DAY
2° STAGE
1 STAGE
THAT SINGULAR CREATURE IN WHICH
HANDS ARE CONSIGNED BOTH THE
BUYER & THE KRAFTMAN ARE
IN MOST CASES WORKING WHIT
PLAIN BAD ODORS, AT TIME ARE
CONCOCTING SCENTS OF EXTERGE-
NEOUS ORDER THE JASMIN GARLICS OF
WILE AGO & ONLY RARELY
DO PRESENT MAN WHITH THAT SINGLE
& SINGULAR FLOWER WHICH WORLD IS
LUMINOUS & ODORIFEROUS IN ONE
THE UNDERSTANDING BY THE KRAFTMAN OF
THAT WHICH IS THE BOUNDARY OF ITS
ACTIVITY & THE SCOPE THEREIN MAY BE
OF GREAT HELP TO INGENDRE IN ITS
WORK. THAT DOSE OF SERENITY
WHICH IS SO EXTENSIVELY
NEEDED BY MAN,
BY THE ATONEMENT OF
MATTER INTO A THING OF PARTICULARE
SIGNIFICANCE THE KRAFTMAN RETURNS TO
COSMOS A PARTICLE OF ITS CONSTITUENCE,
MADE ELOQUENT BY THE INTENSITY OF THE KRAFTMAN'S BECOMING.
NIGHT
IL SOFFITTO
CALOTTE
STAGE

MARCH 60

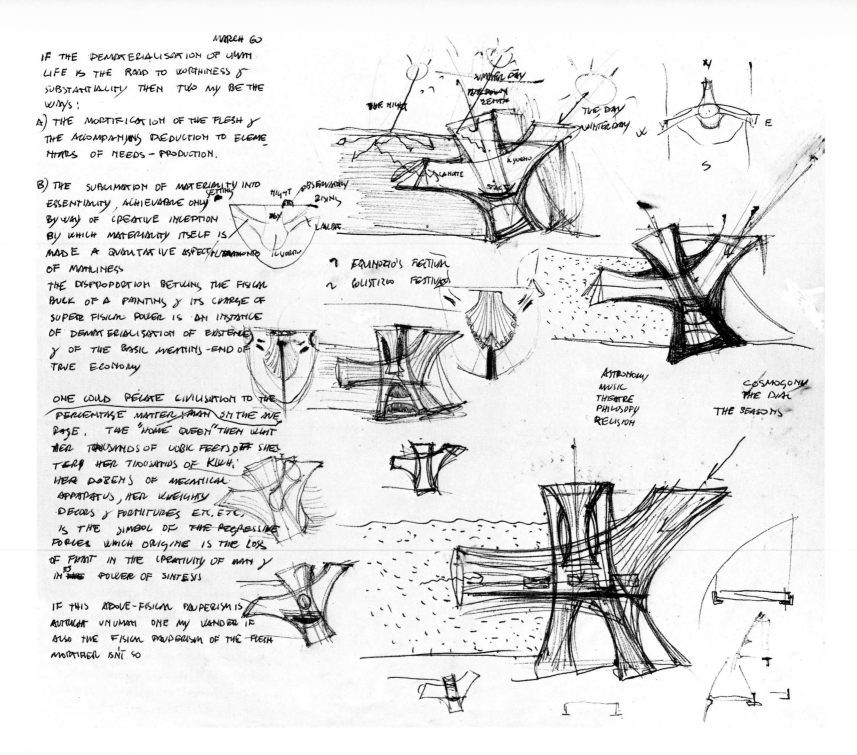

IF THE DEMATERIALISATION OF HUMAN LIFE IS THE ROAD TO WORTHINESS & SUBSTANTIALITY THEN TWO MY BE THE WAYS:

A) THE MORTIFICATION OF THE FLESH & THE ACCOMPANYING REDUCTION TO ELEMENTARS OF NEEDS – PRODUCTION.

B) THE SUBLIMATION OF MATERIALITY INTO ESSENTIALITY, ACHIEVABLE ONLY BY WAY OF CREATIVE INCEPTION BY WHICH MATERIALITY ITSELF IS MADE A QUALITATIVE ASPECT OF MANLINESS

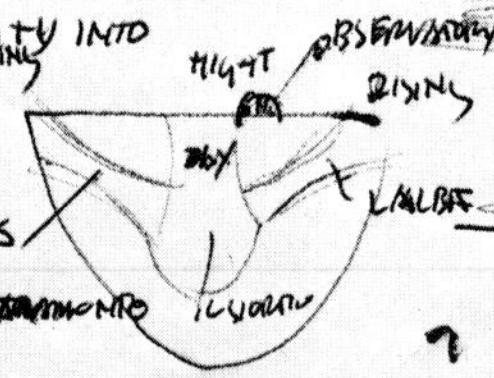

THE DISPROPORTION BETWEEN THE FISICAL BULK OF A PAINTING & ITS CHARGE OF SUPER FISICAL POWER IS AN INSTANCE OF DEMATERIALISATION OF EXISTENCE & OF THE BASIC MEANING – END OF TRUE ECONOMY

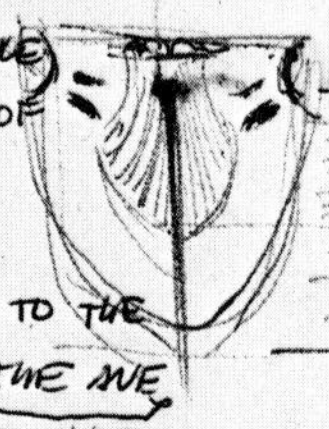

ONE COULD RELATE CIVILISATION TO THE PERCENTAGE MATTER/MAN ON THE AVERAGE. THE "HOME QUEEN" THEN WHAT HER THOUSANDS OF CUBIC FEETS OF SHELTERY HER THOUSANDS OF KWH, HER DOZENS OF MECANICAL APPARATUS, HER WEIGHTY DECORS & FORNITURES ETC. ETC., IS THE SIMBOL OF THE REGRESSIVE FORCES WHICH ORIGINE IS THE LOSS OF FAITH IN THE CREATIVITY OF MAN & IN ITS POWER OF SINTESIS

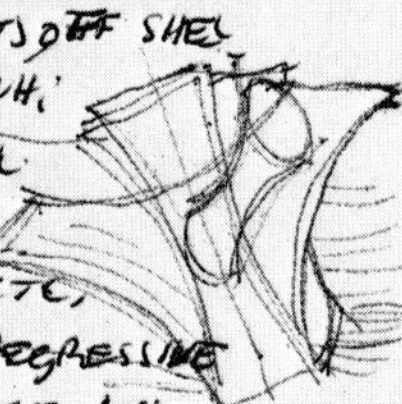

IF THIS ABOVE-FISICAL PAUPERISM IS OUTRIGHT UNHUMAN ONE MY WANDER IF ALSO THE FISICAL PAUPERISM OF THE FLESH MORTIFIER ISN'T SO

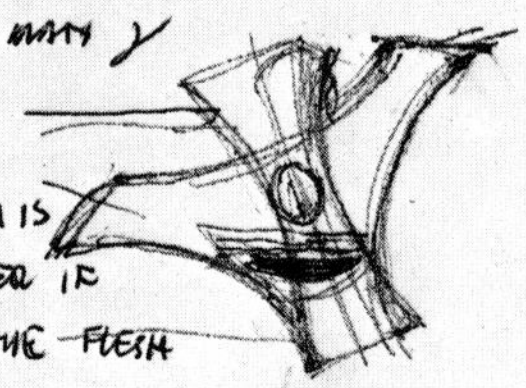

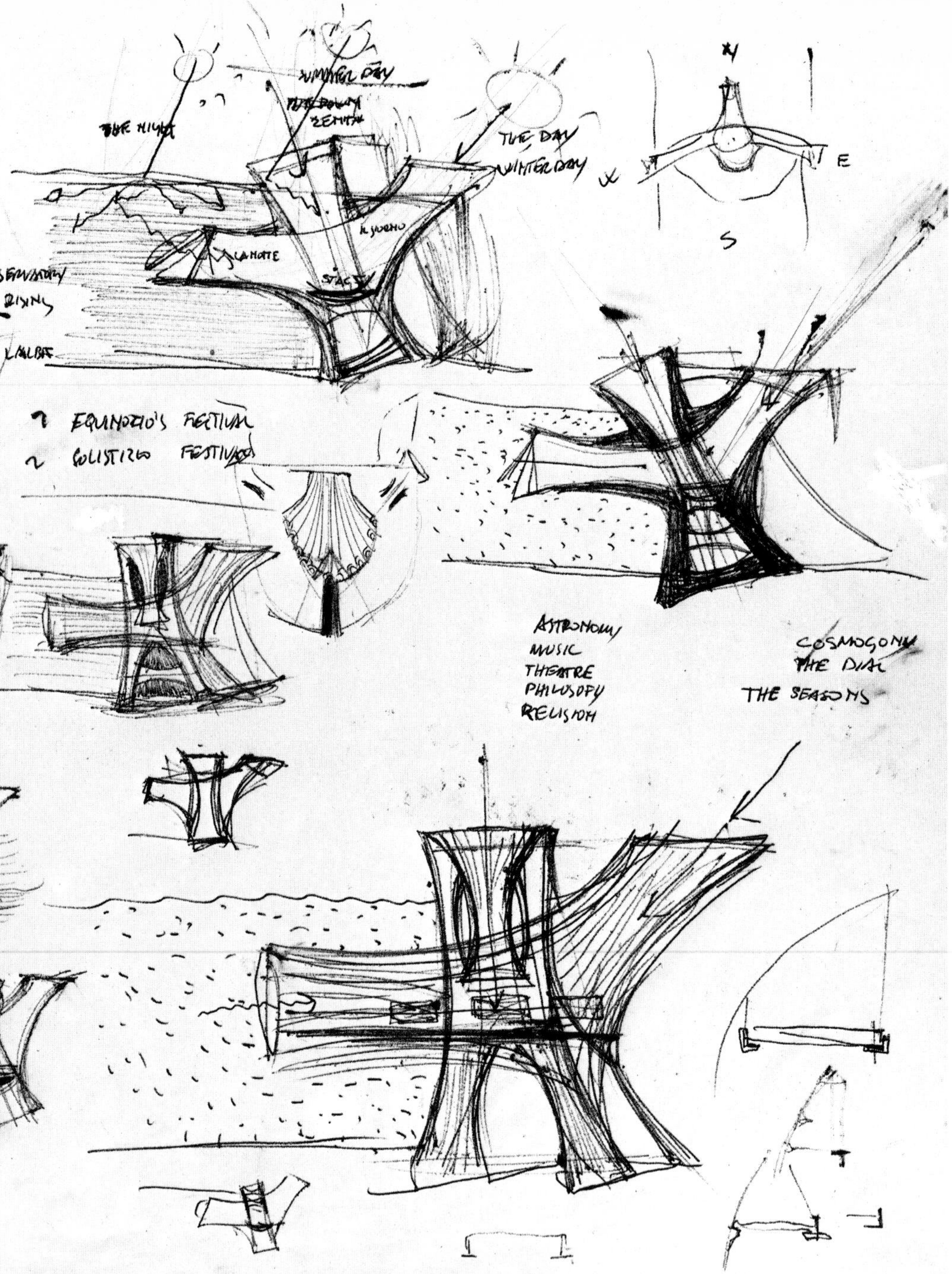

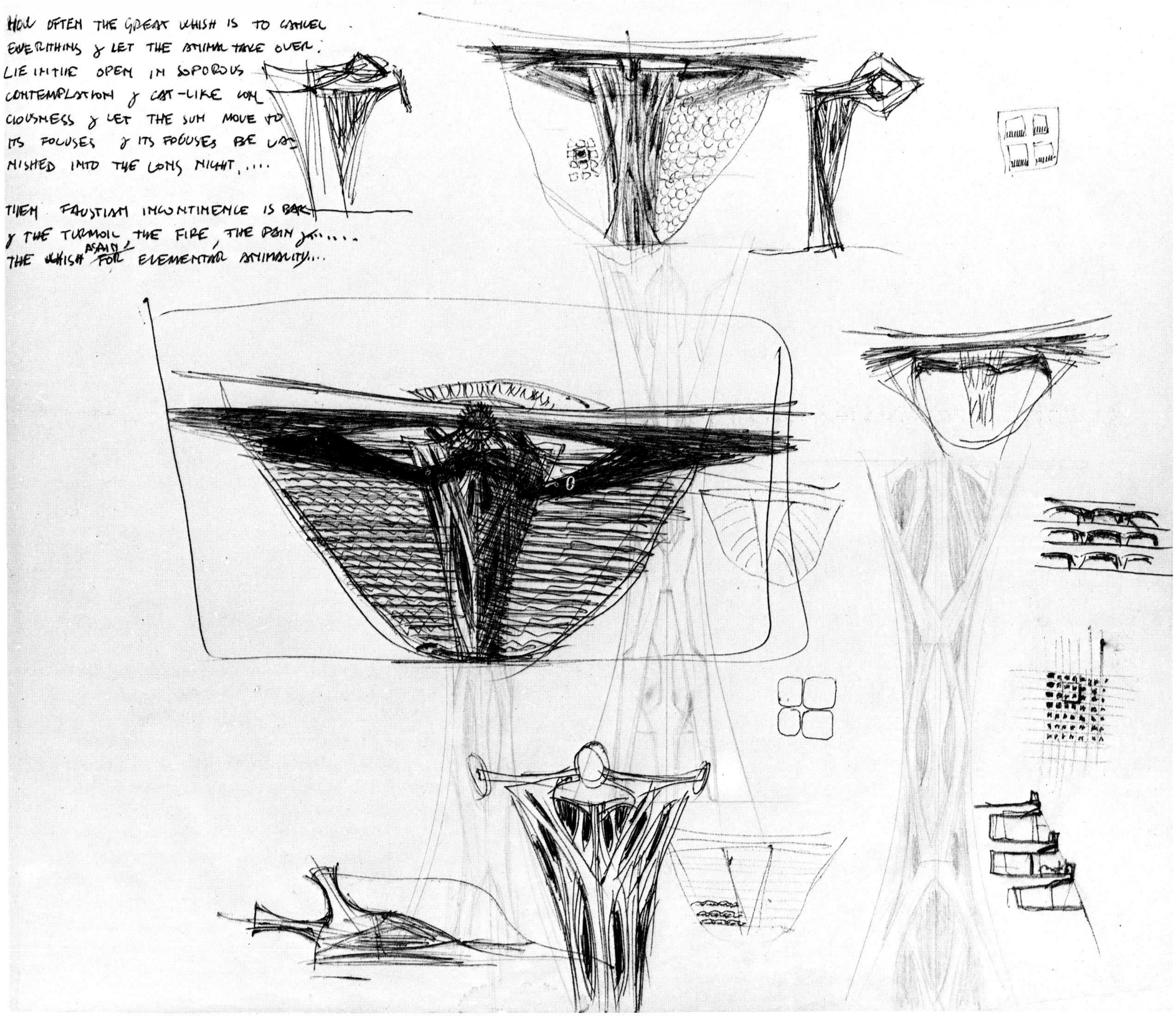
HOW OFTEN THE GREAT WHISH IS TO CANCEL
EVERYTHING & LET THE ANIMAL TAKE OVER.
LIE IN THE OPEN IN SOPOROUS
CONTEMPLATION & CAT-LIKE CON
CIOUSNESS & LET THE SUN MOVE TO
ITS FOCUSES & ITS FOCUSES BE VA
NISHED INTO THE LONG NIGHT, ...
THEN FAUSTIAN INCONTINENCE IS BACK
& THE TURMOIL, THE FIRE, THE PAIN ......
THE WHISH AGAIN FOR ELEMENTAR ANIMALITY...

Axial Park (Mesa City)

1970

Man is a manipulator of matter. The animal and the plant are too. But look at how much matter a single man manipulates in his life-span and how much of it other men manipulate for his sake, and there you have the obvious evidence of a species literally moving mountains: moving, crushing, digesting, transforming, purifying, condensing. The plant manipulates matter as a fixator and storer of energy; the animal, as a digestive tube gifted with the joy and drudgery of life. In both instances matter is preponderantly manipulated into tissues and organs with few exceptions (nests, burrows, beehives, beaver dams, and so forth). Man routinely manipulates matter in these ways, but then with a gigantic step he has manipulated matter outside of himself. The side effects of this gigantic manipulation, including the manipulation-transformation and consumption-degradation of energy, are entrapping the whole of life in an ecological debacle. One way to reduce the magnitude of it is to transform our one-phase process of exploitation into a two-phase process of exploitation and transfiguration. It is not that we do not really do that often. The ore transformed into steel is a transfiguration of matter, up to a point. But what of the petroleum burned into fumes for irrelevant or destructive reasons? There is usually a lack of cohesion among the many related aspects of the same performance, and the consequent breakdown of the sequence throws heaps of waste everywhere. Surface mining is a most telling example. The matter mined may be transfigured, but in far-away places, and what is worse the socket where the material has been mined remains an island of sterility at best or devastation at worst. This reflects strongly and directly on the people tied to the enterprise and fatally crushed by it.

The physical construction of a metropolis consumes such quantities of raw materials as aggregates that generally metropolitan centers are surrounded by gravel pits, disrupted landscape, stagnant waters, and refuse. Even if a nobler kind of reality comes of the dug-out materials, Mother Earth is left gazing at the sky covered with wounds inflicted by man on the geology that sustains him.

In the park of Mesa City, man confronts this devastated area and attempts its transfiguration. Thus, building a city becomes a two-phase process: (1) mining and transfiguration of the mined, buildings out of aggregates; (2) transfiguration of the socket left by the mining. The park is the end result of a process that sees a first phase of mining and refining followed by a second phase of organizing and forming. In fact, the engineer and the geologian, the natural scientist and the ecologist, all would work with the architect, the sculptor, the artist, the musician, and the scholar to combine the geology of nature with a man-made geology.

1960

The city is physically built of the materials taken from it, food for symbolic and mystical inferences. From the ridge protruding lengthwise on the mesa, the city gets the weight of its structures as if a self-generating power working within the stone's ravines went on filling in the design man constructed. The imprint of man and the vast geological lines this imprint cuts are the two forces one seeks to conciliate in a coherent aesthetic whole. In the resulting broad structure the expressions of individual artists and craftsmen insert themselves, sculptor-architects, architect-sculptors, painters on "canvases" of stone as large as museum walls under untamed light, light rebounding from other walls, the dimness of crevasses. . . . If the natural and the man-made coalesce here and there, it is a natural fusion. With a nuclear power plant at the center of the future park, a few pounds of matter and the ingenuity of man could quarry and process the raw materials, allocate them for the construction process. Man can, at least theoretically, condense eons of time and action into brief moments of technological prowess.

Toward the north end, the axial park moves uphill overshadowed by the distant theological complex. Successive dikes impound large volumes of water. Facing toward these on the east and west are the formal gardens and the arts and crafts villages. The "botanical" crafts are here particularly developed, carried all around the theological hill at the north, the continuum itself, and the center for advanced study on the south.

THE EXPRESSION IN SCULPTORAL FORM IS CONSIGNED Y LIMITED THE FROM OUTSIDE ONLOOKING CATEGORY

THE MOMENT SPACE AS SUCH Y IN SUCH VOLUME AS TO FISICLY ALLOWE FOR THE UMAN MODULE, IS CONSIGNED TO SCULPTURE THEN THE BORDER LINE SCULPT. ARCH. GETS EVEN MORE VAGUE Y SEMANTIC IN CARACTER

THE MAN THAT SCULPT A VOID WITHINS WHICH OTHER MAN WILL ACCEDE Y PAUSE IS ARCHITECTING ITS SPACES WITH HIS SENSIBILITY AS A SCULPTOR. WHAT IS THE OUTCOME?

SEMANTIC ASIDE THE SCULPTOR WILL SEE A GREATER COMPLEXITY ENTER IN ITS WORK, AN EXTENTION IN POTENTIALITY Y SCOPE. BY PREPONDERANTLY ENVELOPPING SPACE WITH FORM, ALTERNATING CONSTANTLY ~~ENVELOPPED~~ LET UNCONTROLLED SPACE ENVELLOPE FORMS, HE MAY WELL ACCEDE TO NEW DIMENSIONALITIES OF CONCEPTIVITY Y EXPRESSION

NOW HE CAN PRACTICLY Y EMOTIONALLY WORK FROM THE INSIDE OUT.
IN SOME OF THE FALLOWING SCHEMES IS SUGGESTED THE FIELD OF ENDEAVOUR SUBMITTED TO THE SCULPTOR:

1) A MUSEUM FOR ONE PIECE SCULPTURE THE ARTIST CONSTRUCT THE SCULPTURE Y ITS SURROUNDINGS IN ONE. IN STRICT RELATIONSHIP Y IN KINDRED EMOTIONAL STATE

2) A BASIN FOR PAGENTRY IS COMMISSIONED, TO BE CUT OUT OF A STONE QUARRY

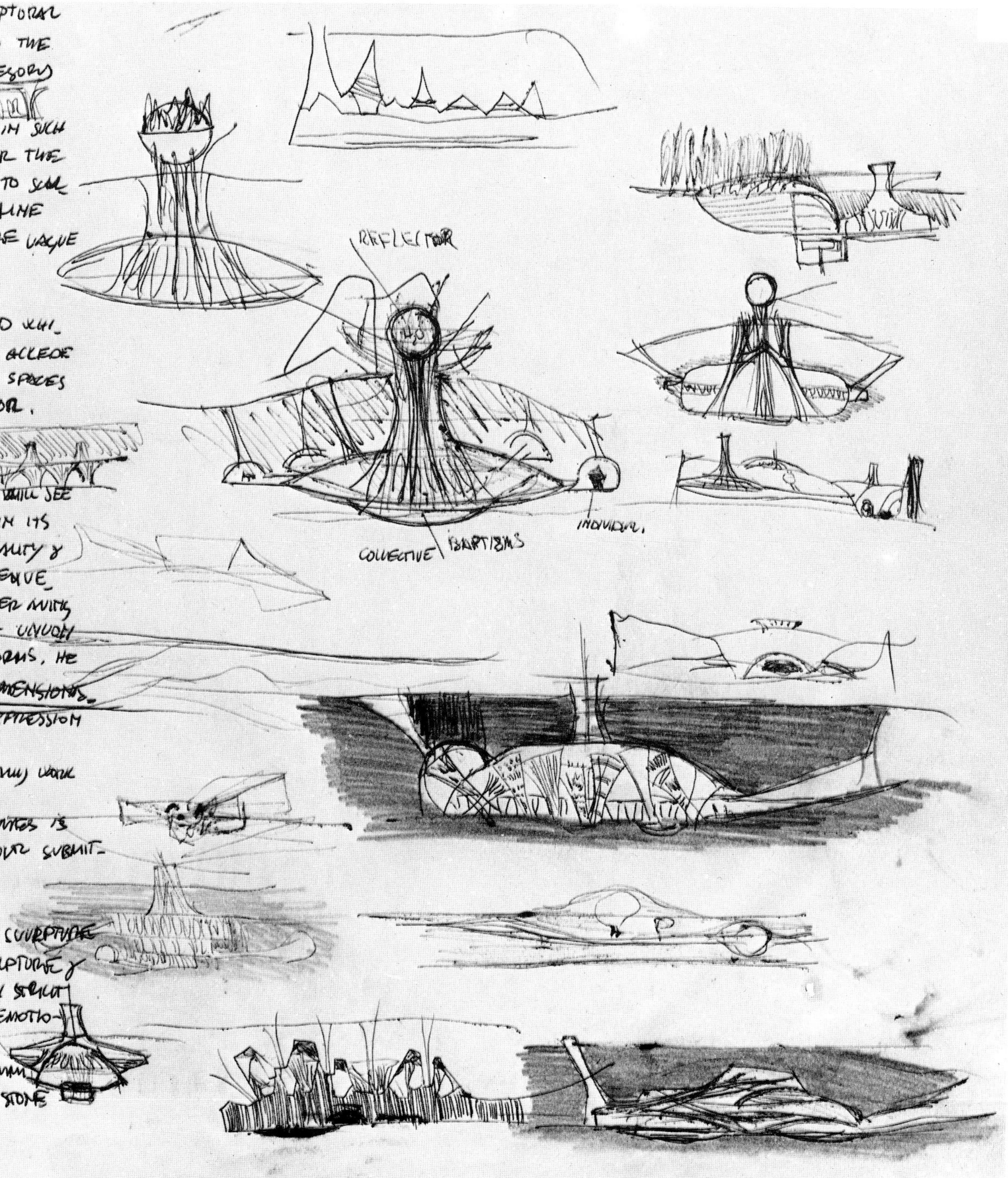

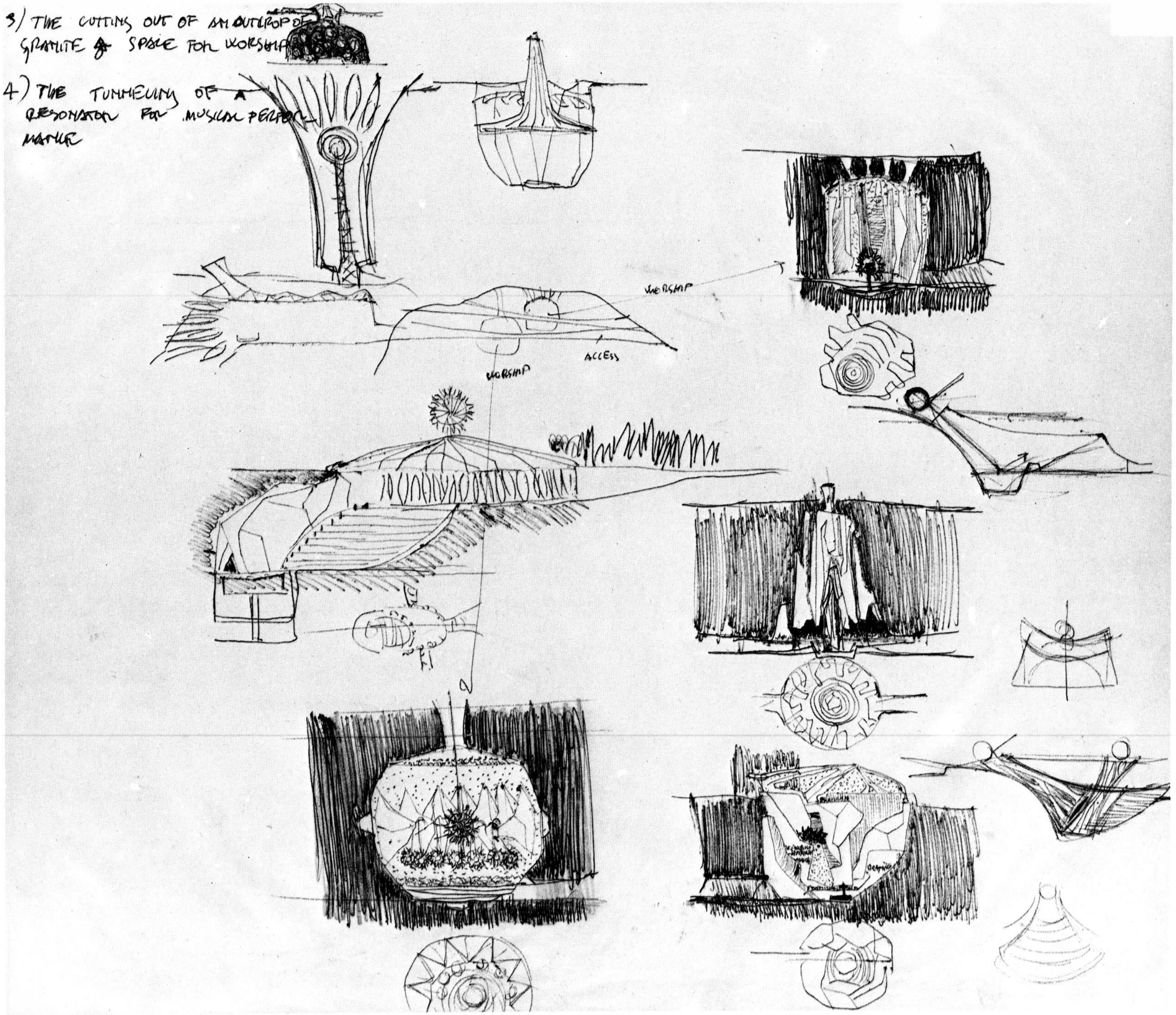
3) THE CUTTING OUT OF AN OUTCROP OF
GRANITE A SPACE FOR WORSHIP
4) THE TUNNELLING OF A
RESONATOR FOR MUSICAL PERFOR-
MANCE
WORSHIP
ACCESS
WORSHIP

STONEARCHETIPES
PEOPLE
AZOIC
CONTEMPORARY MUSIC.

MARCH 60
ONCE PLANNING IS ACCEPTED FOR THE ORGANIZING OF FRAGMENTS, PLANNING IMPOSES ITSELF TO THE ORGANIZING OF COMPOSITIES
N
SOUND

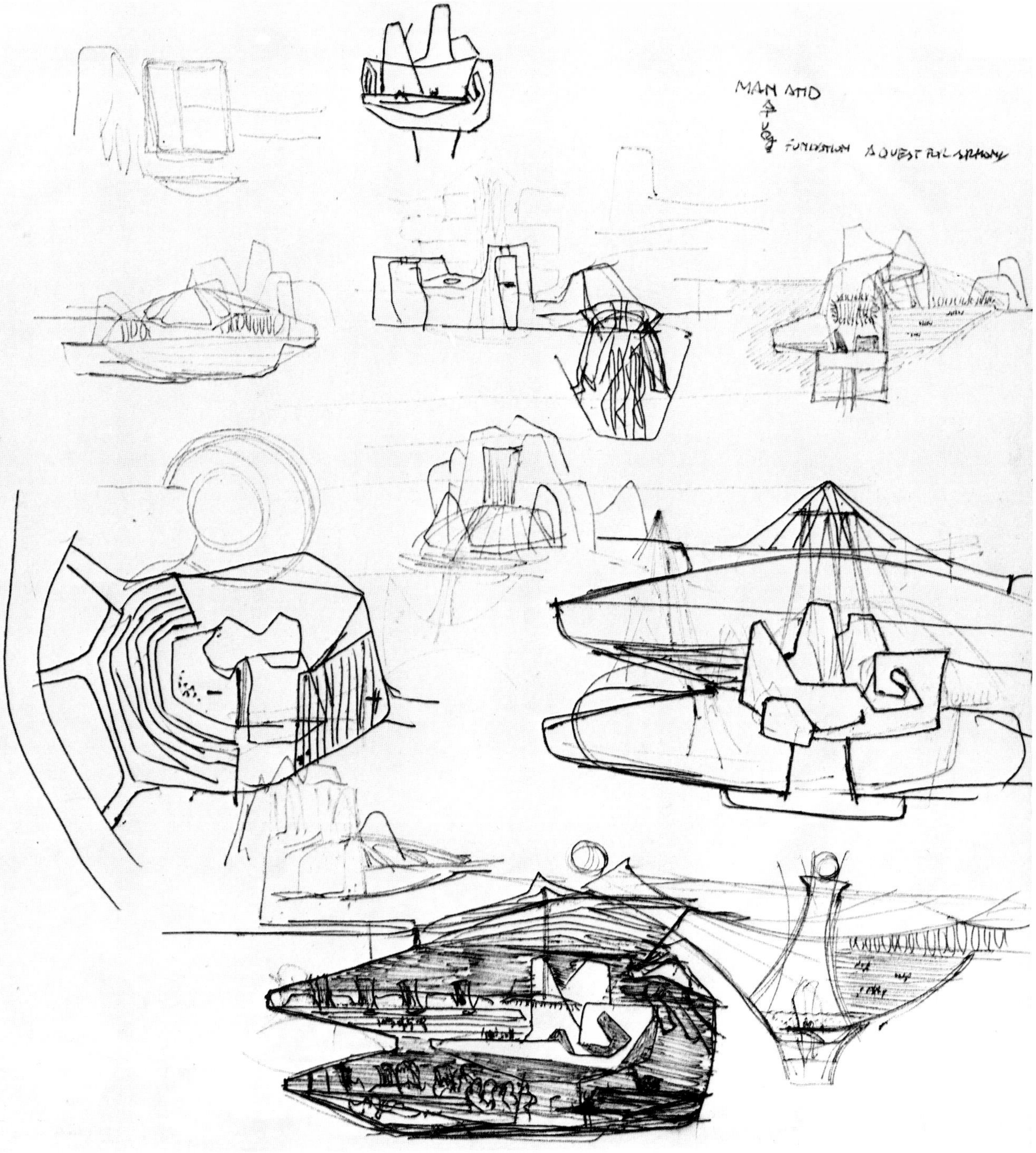
MAN AND
A QUEST

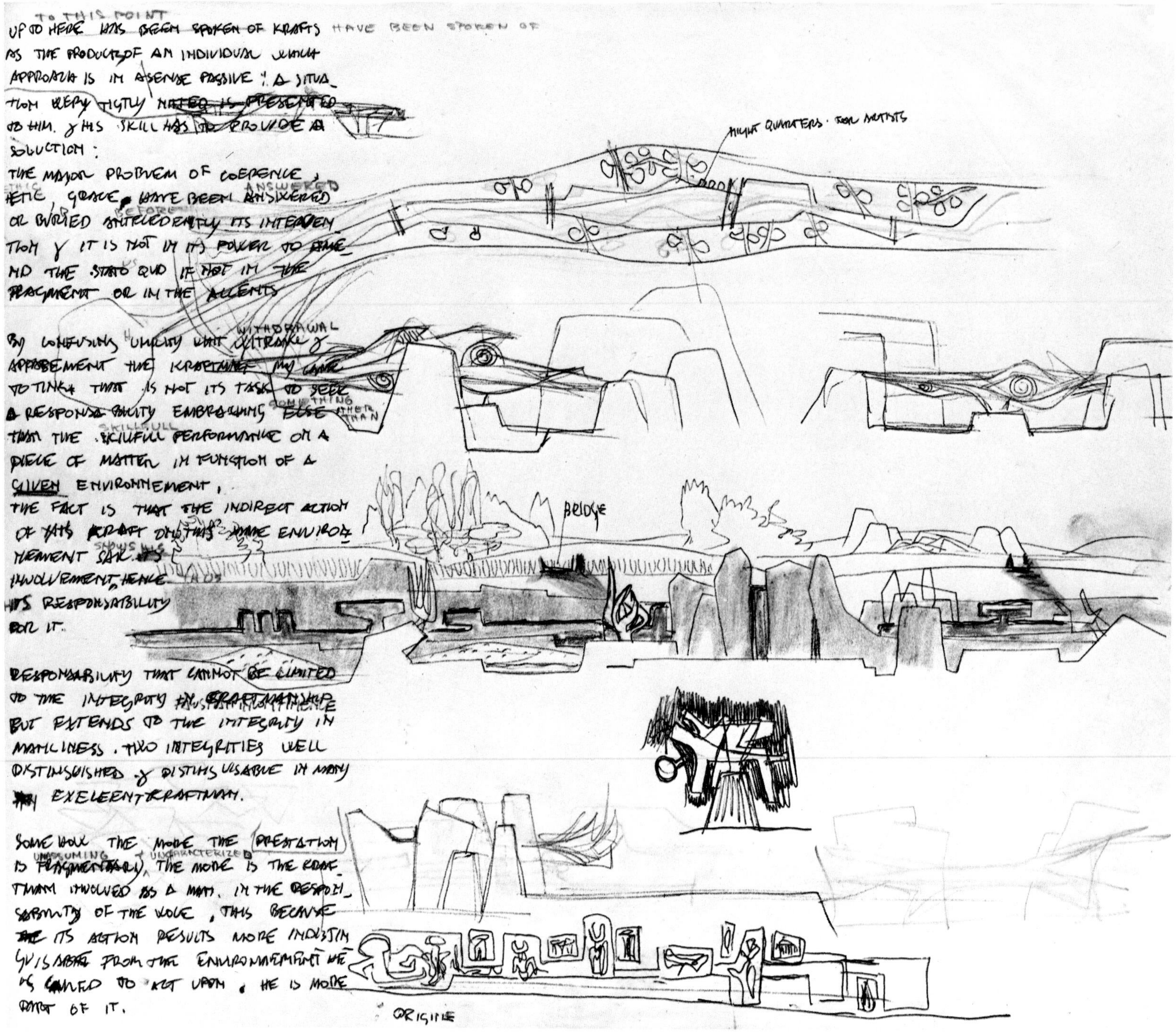
TO THIS POINT
UP TO HERE HAS BEEN SPOKEN OF KRAFTS HAVE BEEN SPOKEN OF
AS THE PRODUCT OF AN INDIVIDUAL WHICH
APPROACH IS IN A SENSE PASSIVE : A SITUA_
TION VERY TIGHTLY NATED IS PRESENTED
TO HIM. & HIS SKILL HAS TO PROVIDE A
SOLUCTION :
THE MAJOR PROBLEM OF COERENCE ,
ETHIC, GRACE, HAVE BEEN ANSWERED
ANSWERED
BEFORE
OR BURIED ANTECEDENTLY ITS INTERVEN_
TION & IT IS NOT IN ITS POWER TO CHANGE_
US
IN THE STATO QUO IF NOT IN THE
FRAGMENT OR IN THE ACCENTS
WITHDRAWAL
BY CONFUSING HUMILITY WITH OLTRANCE &
APPROBEMENT THE KRAFTMAN MY CAME
TO TINK THAT IS NOT ITS TASK TO SEEK
A RESPONSABILITY EMBRACING ELSE
SOMETHING OTHER THAN
SKILLFULL
THAN THE SKILFULL PERFORMANCE ON A
PIECE OF MATTER IN FUNCTION OF A
GIVEN ENVIRONNEMENT ,
THE FACT IS THAT THE INDIRECT ACTION
OF THIS KRAFT ON THIS SAME ENVIRON
SHOWS HIS
NEMENT SAK.
INVOLVEMENT, HENCE
HIS RESPONSABILITY
FOR IT.
RESPONSABILITY THAT CANNOT BE LIMITED
TO THE INTEGRITY IN CRAFTMANSHIP
BUT EXTENDS TO THE INTEGRITY IN
MANLINESS . TWO INTEGRITIES WELL
DISTINGUISHED & DISTINGUISABLE IN MANY
EXELEENT KRAFTMAN.
SOME HOW THE MORE THE PRESTATION
UNASSUMING + UNCARACTERIZED
IS FRAGMENTARY, THE MORE IS THE KRAF_
TMAN INVOLVED AS A MAN, IN THE RESPON_
SABILITY OF THE WOLE , THIS BECAUSE
ITS ACTION RESULTS MORE INDISTIN
GUISABLE FROM THE ENVIRONNEMENT HE
IS CALLED TO ACT UPON . HE IS MORE
PART OF IT.
NIGHT QUARTERS · FOR ARTISTS
BRIDGE
ORIGINE

Towers

1970

The problem with tower buildings is that they tend to carry on the vertical the defects that mark the flat urban texture, a segregative pattern that sooner or later enforces its own limitations on the life that fills it. To avoid this, the tower has to thicken itself as if a richer blood were to flow into all of its parts; it needs a denser and larger motion and interaction among the different parts to foster new differentiations and increasing participation. Whenever life thrusts into the inanimate universe, it must thrust substantially, carrying with it all that makes its existence valid, so that survival becomes the means to fulfillment. This may seem fairly abstract, but nothing is less realistic than an effort whose premises are founded on a pragmatism too short-sighted to see where its tail has been left and its head is going to be. If the tower structure achieves the rounded character of life, then its inhabitants will occupy that ideal threshold between nature and the man-made that might well be the most fruitful situation for man to be in. Homes and residences would be positioned on the outer membrane of the tower with visual and physical access to the urban action of the tower interior on one side and visual access to the open countryside on the other. Towers are really my first glimpse into the world of the tridimensional city. The tower of Babel represents confusion and arrogance, and it would take a correction of emphasis to produce an urban cultural container within the Babel structure. Confusion is a breakdown of complexity; arrogance is the defeat of compassion.

NOVEMBER 59

BY CRISTALLINE STRATIFICATION, OR BY ORGANIC GROWTH (CORALS) GUIDED ON A PREDESIGNED VOLUMETRICAL FRAME-SKELETON IT WILL BE POSSIBLE TO CONSTRUCT CONFIGURATIONS OF SUCH NATURE TO MAKE AVAILABLE AT LOW EXPENSE OF ENERGY-MATERIAL DWELLINGS & FACILITIES OF ALL KIND.

WHILE THE CELLULAR (MOLECULAR) STRUCTURE WILL THEN BE DIRECTLY FROM NATURE, THE DESIGN-IDEA WILL BE MAN'S OWN. THE CONSTRUCTOR WILL BE "FARMING" ITS BUILDING AROUND THE MATERIALIZED FRAME IMMAGINED & DEFINED BY THE MAKER.

THE FIBROUS STRUCTURE
THE MEMBRANE-STRUCTURE
THE OSTEO-STRUCTURE
THE SHELL-STRUCTURE
THE GELLY-STRUCTURE
& THE CRISTALLINE STRUCTURE

} MEGASTRUCTURES

IN SPACE (COSMIC EMPTINESS) THE SEEDING OF A CONFIGURATION WILL SEE IT GROW LOCALLY BY THE MEDIA OF SINTETIZED ELEMENTS (H, O, C, N..) INSIDE AN ATMOSFERICAL BUBBLE.

AS THE GULF SEPARATING MY IDENTITY FROM THE IDENTITY OF A STONE IS GREATER THAN THE ONE DEMANDED BETWEEN MY PRESENT IDENTITY & THE IDENTITY OF A "COSMIC MAN" IS THERE NO VALID OBJECTION TO THE EXISTENCE IN TIME OF SUCH MAN & OF THE ENVIRONMENTAL MEDIUM FOR HIM TO ENDURE

A UNIVERSE SPOTTED OF MAN'S COLONIES, & THE LIKE FROM OTHER PLANETS, MAY SEE A FENOMENAL MOLTIPLICATION OF MA

A POTENTIALITY,
SO ON & ON GOES THE DANCE OF SIMBOLS,
ONE TO CONVEY AN IDEA ONE TO CONVEY
THE EMOTION INBRED TO IT ONE TO CON
VEY THE "TORMENT" OF THE NOT SUBSTANTIA
TED IDEA-EMOTION ONE TO REGROUP
THE OTHERS TO AN ORDAINED
JERARCHY, FINALLY ONE TO APPEAL
TO THE SENSES, THE EYE, BY THE
GRAPHIC MEDIUM

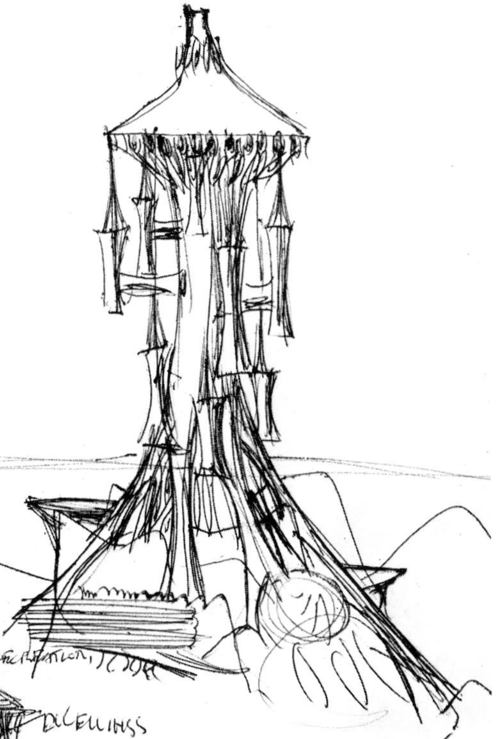

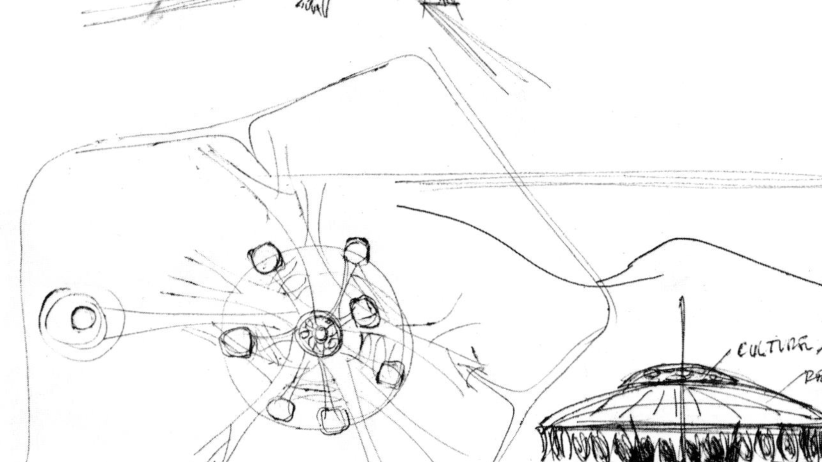

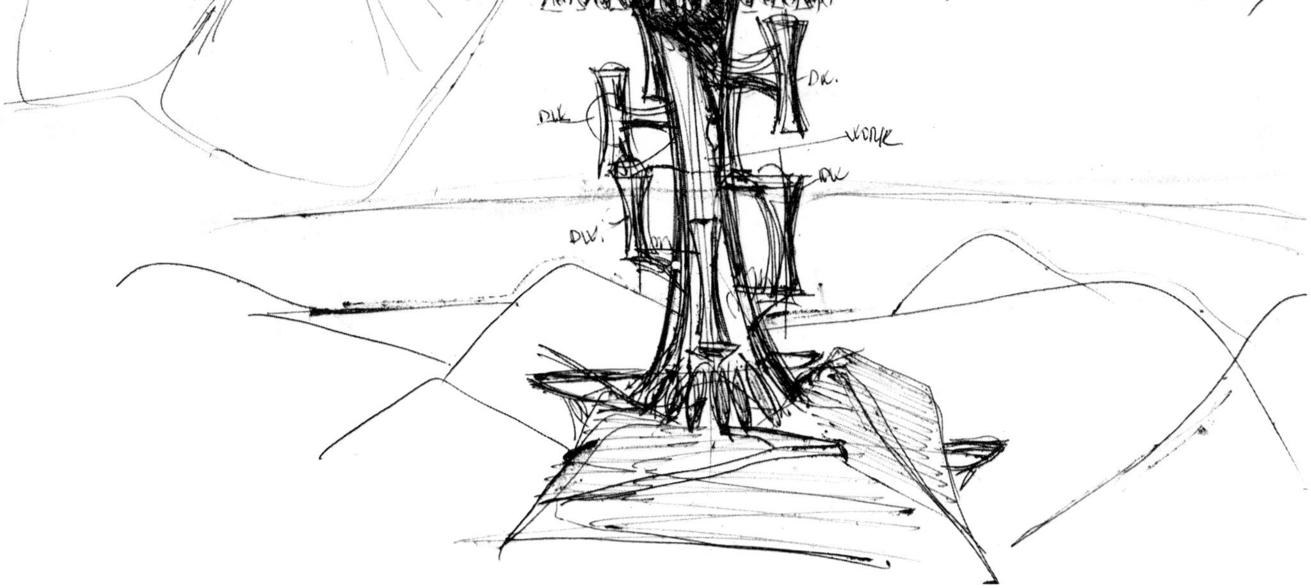

20 - 12 - 59

TO PUT UNIVERSAL SIGNIFICANCE TO ONE'S OWN TROUBLES BELONGS TO THE EXPRESSIVE WORLD MADE AESTETIC, YET THE INSTIGATION GOES DEEPER: THE NEED TO INSERT ONE SELF & ONE'S LOAD OF VULNERABILITY INTO THE MEANINGFULL WORLD OF CAUSALITY
WHERE IN THINGS THAT HAPPEN ARE THE TEXTURE OF REALITY WHATEVER REALITY MY BE
THE AESTETIC "TWIST" IS THE EMPHASIS BY WHICH THE EVEN DREARY "REAL" IS GLORIFIED INTO THE BEAUTIFUL INSIGHT INTO TRUTH BY MEAN OF INTENSITY TWISTED INTO THIS SAME REAL.

IN THIS AESTETIC ACTION THERE IS THE RITUAL OF A PROCEDURE WHIC PUTS THE INVESTIGATION OF THE MIND ABOVE THE ~~TORMENT~~ TOIL OF THE SOUL SO AS TO MAKE ONE ABLE TO SPEAK OF ONE'S OWN "UNSPEAKABLE" "TORMENT"
IF THIS PROCESS IS NOT CONSTANTLY CONTROLLED BY BASIC VENERATION TOWARD LIFE & THE UMBLE ATTITUDE THUS INDISPENSABLE WHITIN, THE EXPRESSION (FINAL) FAR FROM INSERTING THE PART INTO THE WOLE WILL CLEARLY DENOUNCE THE VACUITY OR IMMATURITY OF THE ONE'SELF

ART AS A LIE-DETECTOR

ANYTHING BECOMES BERABLE IF ONE CAN SEE IN IT A UNIVERSAL & CAN BELIVE IN WHAT HE SEES,
VALUE IS NOT THE FANCYING DRESS UP COVERING THE UNWORTHY, IS THE "GOD" DISTILLED FROM NATURE BY THE INVOLVEMENT OF MAN.
MAN THUS GROWS TO GREATENESS WASHING AWAY READ BLOOD BY WHAT REEDER BLOOD AS NATURE RIGHTIOUSLY EXPECTS OF HIM.

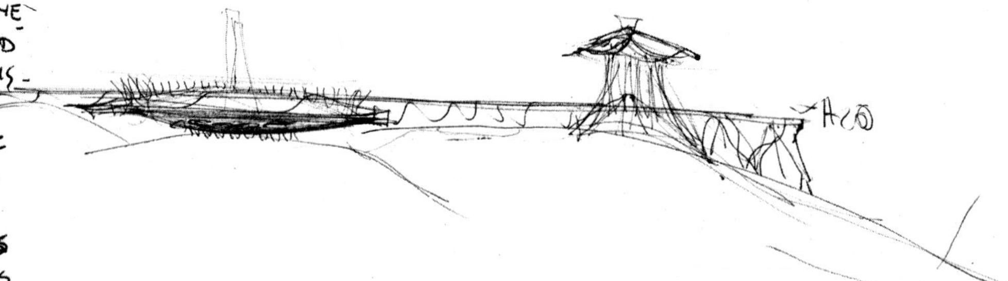

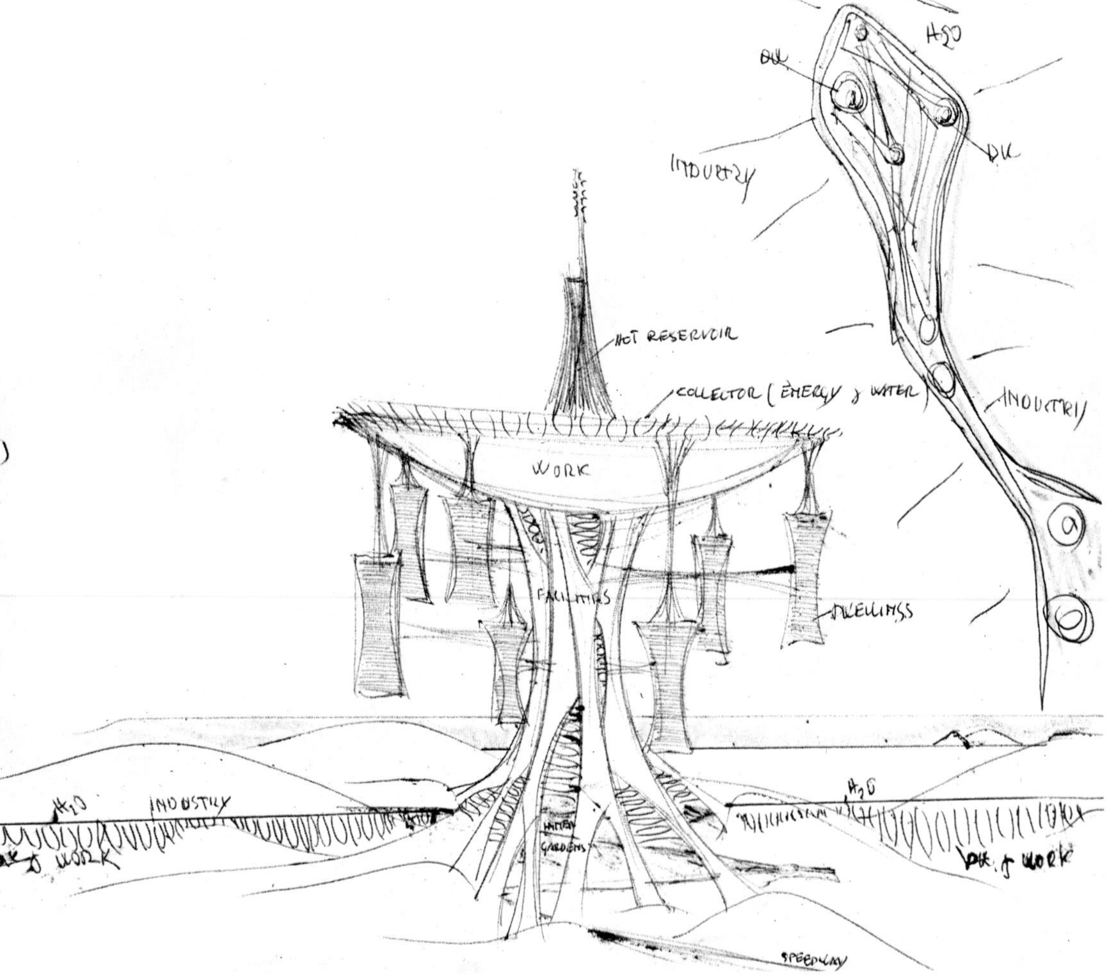

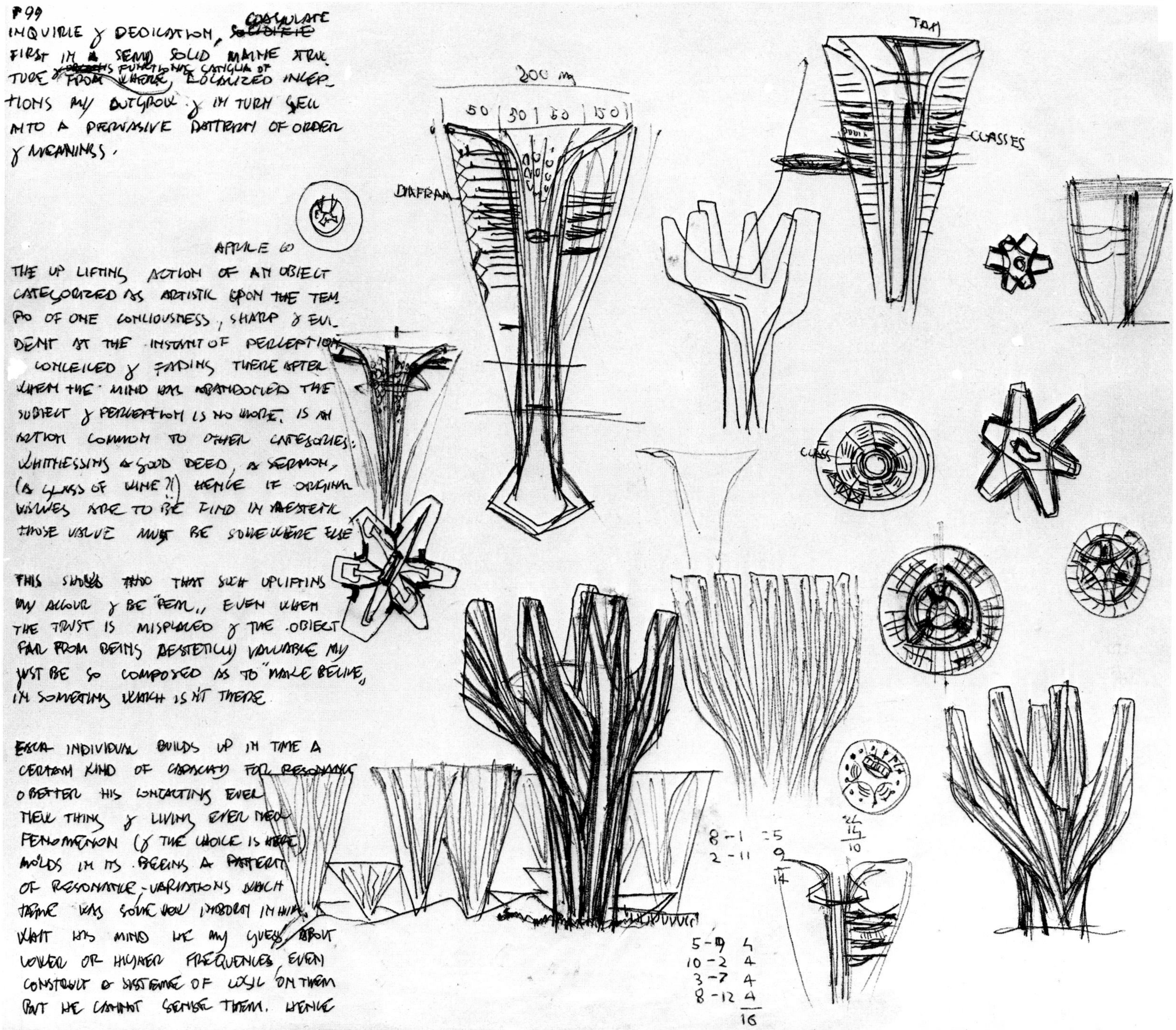
F 99
INQUIRIE & DEDICATION, COAGULATE
FIRST IN A SEMI SOLID MAINE STRUC
TURE FUNCTIONING CATIGLIA OF FROM WHERE, LOCALIZED INCEP-
TIONS MY OUTGROW & IN TURN GELL
INTO A PERVASIVE PATTERN OF ORDER
& MEANINGS.
APRILE 60
THE UP LIFTING ACTION OF AN OBJECT
CATEGORIZED AS ARTISTIC UPON THE TEM
PO OF ONE CONCIOUSNESS, SHARP & EVI-
DENT AT THE INSTANT OF PERCEPTION
CONCEIVED & FADING THERE AFTER
WHEN THE MIND HAS ABANDONED THE
SUBJECT & PERCEPTION IS NO MORE. IS AN
ACTION COMMON TO OTHER CATEGORIES:
WHITNESSING A GOOD DEED, A SERMON,
(A GLASS OF WINE?!) HENCE IF ORIGINAL
VALUES ARE TO BE FIND IN AESTETIC
THOSE VALUE MUST BE SOMEWHERE ELSE
THIS SHOWS ALSO THAT SUCH UPLIFTINS
MY ACCOUR & BE "REAL", EVEN WHEN
THE TRUST IS MISPLACED & THE OBJECT
FAR FROM BEING AESTETICALLY VALUABLE MY
JUST BE SO COMPOSED AS TO "MAKE BELIVE"
IN SOMETING WHICH IS NOT THERE.
EACH INDIVIDUAL BUILDS UP IN TIME A
CERTAIN KIND OF CAPACITY FOR RESONANCE
OR BETTER HIS CONTACTING EVER
NEW THING & LIVING EVER NEW
FENOMENON (& THE CHOICE IS HERE)
MOLDS IN ITS BEING A PATTERN
OF RESONANCE-VARIATIONS WHICH
THE WAS SOMEHOW INBORN IN HIM.
WHAT HIS MIND HE MY GUESS ABOUT
LOWER OR HIGHER FREQUENCES, EVEN
CONSTRUCT A SYSTEME OF LOGIC ON THEM
BUT HE CANNOT SENSE THEM. HENCE
200 m
50 | 30 | 60 | 150
DIAFRAM
TAM
CLASSES
CLASS
8 - 1 5
2 - 11 9
14
24
14
10
5 - 9 4
10 - 2 4
3 - 7 4
8 - 12 4
16

THAT WHICH IS PRIVACY & FISICAL OR SPATIAL INDIPENDENCE INGES PRIMARILY ON THE FACT THAT WHEN OR IF SITTING OR MOVING ABOUT ONES HOMES, BEHIND THOSE THINGS OF ONES CHOICE & USE & NATURE, WHICH PRESENCE IS TO BE FELT & NURSED, DOES NOT CROP UP THE NEIBOROUGH LUNDRY OR THE CORDIAL EMPTINESS OF ITS TOGHEDERNESS OR ITS VAGUE FACE DULLED BY ALCOOL ..... OR THE "PICTURE WINDOW,, OF ITS PRIVATE IDIOSINCRASIES ..

A MICROCOSMOS OF MINE OPEN ON A MACROCOSMOS OF NATURE TROUGH A "WINDOW,, HAMMERED BY THE TWO WAY BRODCASTING OF MAN-UNIVERSE BE IT PETTY OR MORTIFIED OR IRRUENT & LUMINOUS.

SUCH SOMEWATH FIXED PROSPECTIVE, UNENCOUMBERED BY THE ACCIDENTS OF CLOSED UP INTERVENTIONS, MY PRESENT ITSELF AS A STONE OF COMPARISON TO WHICH THINGS ARE RELATED OR EVEN SUBMITTED IN A DEMANDFOR EVALUATION.

THE PORCH IS NOW OPEN ON INFINITY, NO MORE ON THE BUSY-BODIES OF MORE OR LESS TAILORED DIMENSION, WHICH CLOSENESS & NEED-SENTIMENTS ARE INALIENABLE BUT ONLY PART OF SUCH INFINITY

ONE WOULD SUGGEST THAT AS IN OPENING THE DOOR ON THE HOUSE OF WORSHIP ONE EXPECTS & FIND A PLACE OF SOMEHOW RARE PARAMETRES TO WHICH LIFE LENDS MORE OF AN ABSTRACTION THAN ANY PARTICULAR. SO THE TOTAL ONE SIDE OF THE HOME WINDOW OPENS ON THE INFINITUM HOUSE OF WORSHIP WHICH CATARTIC MOMENTUM IS IN REASON OF LIGHT & SEASON-HOURS-ATMOSFERE-WHEATER ... & SPACE & SPACES

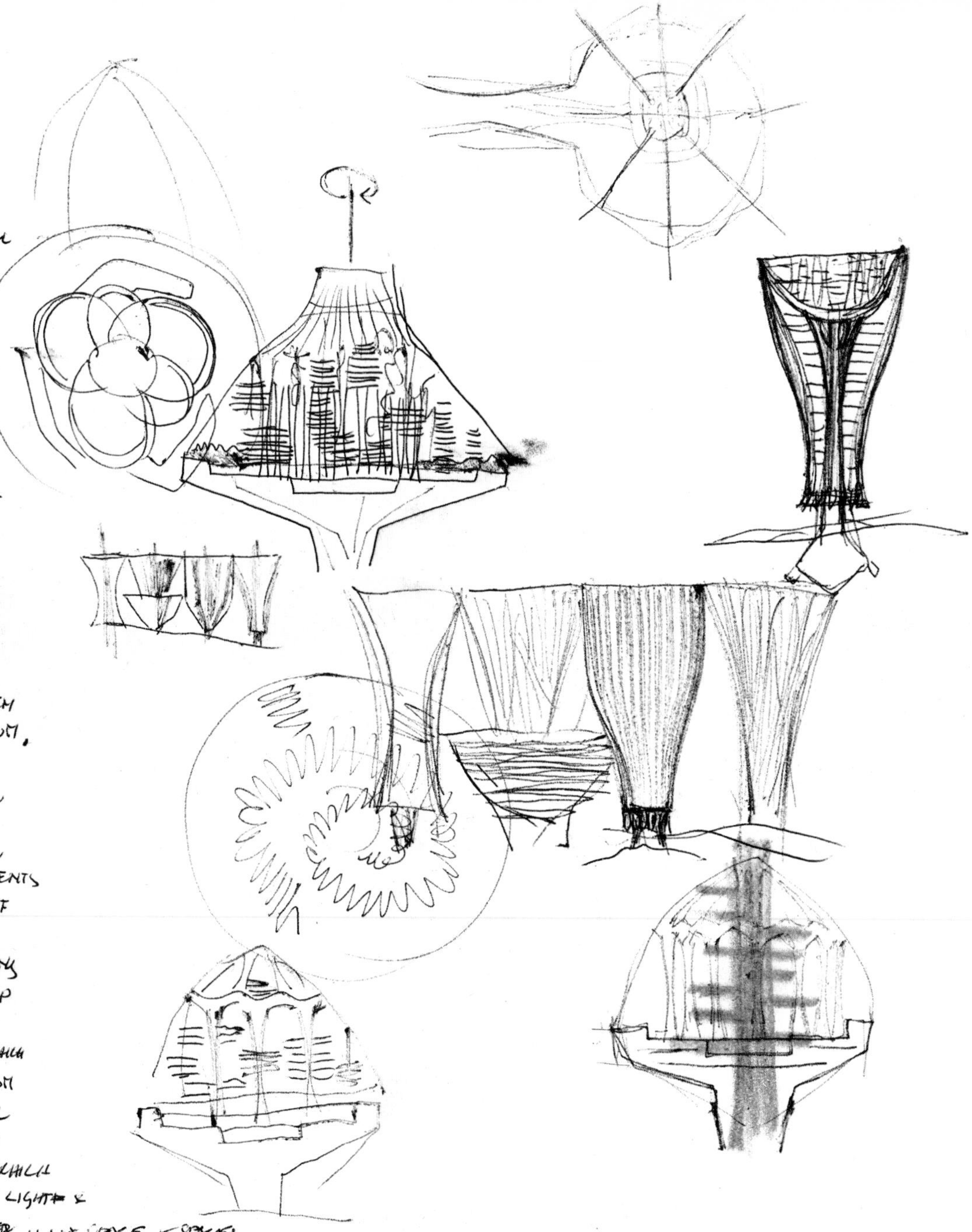

NEGATIVE PART, WARFARE, OR IN THE POSITIVE ONE; THE CONQUERING OF A PLATEAU OF CULTURE UNDER ADVERSE FATE.

AGUST 60

THE ISSUE IS NOT FUNCTIONALISM ~~AGAINST~~ VERSUS STRUCTURALISM, OR EXPRESSIONISM AGAINST RATIONALISM, OR REFINITALISM ~~AGA~~ VERSUS BRUTALISM OR ANY ISMS VERSUS ANY OTHER ~~ISMS~~. THE ISSUE IS INTENSITY IN ITSELF BY ITSELF FOR ITSELF.

WHY IS IT THAT ANY EPIGONE CAN BE MORE ~~ELEGANT~~ FUNCTIONAL, MORE, MORE REFINED, MORE TONE SENSITIVE, MORE ABSTRACTED, MORE ON, JUST ABOUT ANYTHING THAN THE MASTER: & YET REMAIN AN OBSCURE NON ENTITY. IT IS BECAUSE THE HARD CORE MOTIVATION IS NOT THERE, GREAT NOISE IS MADE AROUND AN ENTITY WHICH TO SLANTING PERCEPTION WILL SHOW VACUITY.

INTENSITY COULDN'T CARE LESS FOR THE PATTERN OF THE BATHROOM TILES, ~~THAT~~ NOT OUT OF LACK OF UNITY BUT OUT OF GRASP FOR THE TOTALITY FACING ALL THINGS.

MAN CAN AFFORD ONLY GREATNESS ANYTHING LESS IS A REGRESSIVE CONSUMPTION OF THE DAYS WHICH ARE LIMITED IN SPACE & IN TIME, IN SPIRIT, THUS PRECIOUS. EVERY WHERE & ALL THE TIMES.

THE "INTERIOR DECORATORS" OF CULTURE ARE AT BEST FITTED FOR POINTING OUT THAT WHICH IS WORTH POINTING OUT. THAT CAN BE ACCOMPLISHED THROUGH MODES OR THROUGH THE LESSER FASHION.

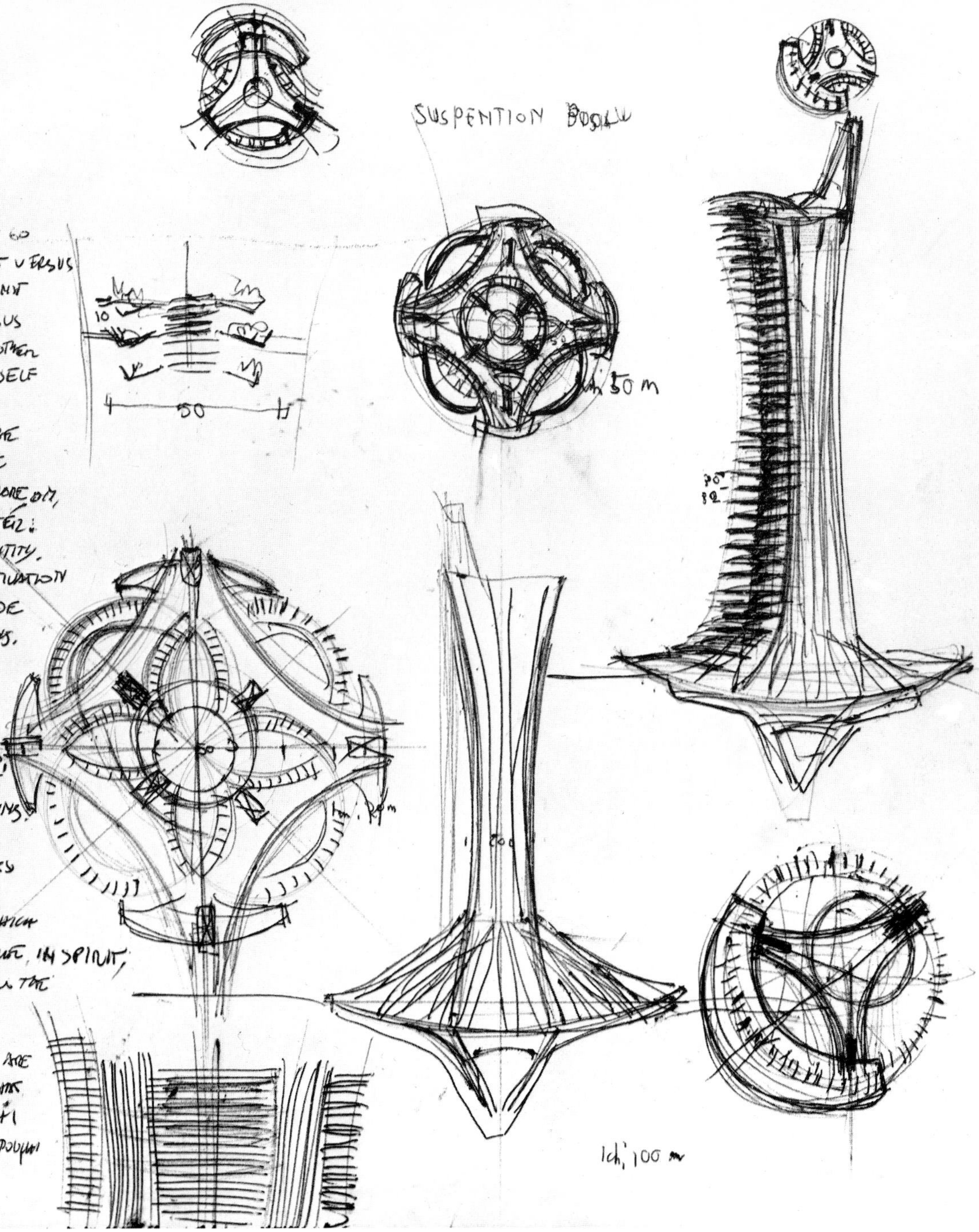

OCTOBER 60, V.U.

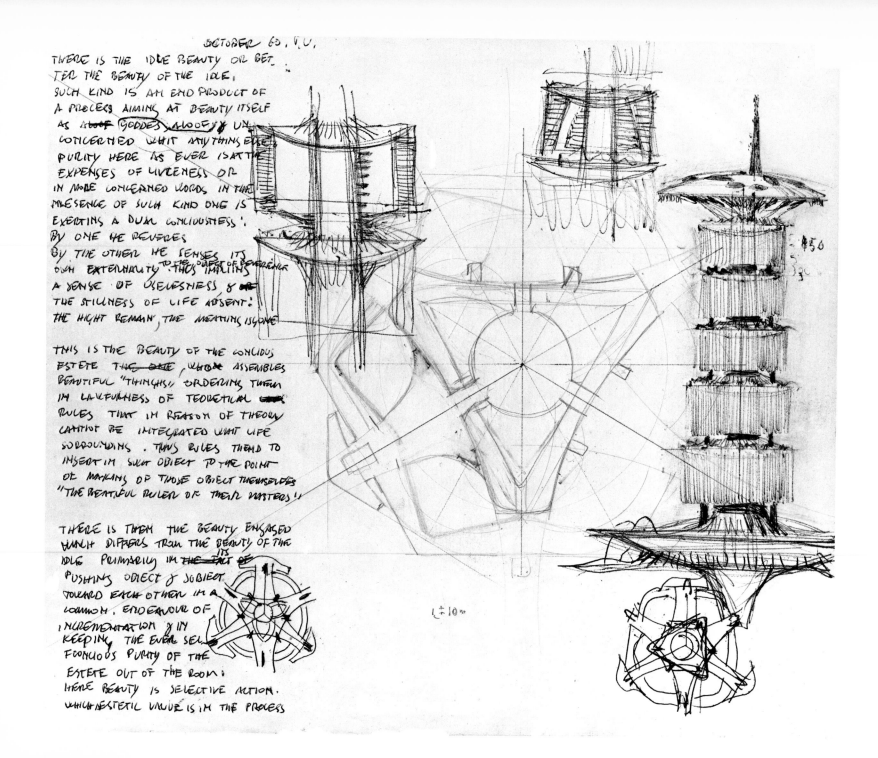

THERE IS THE IDLE BEAUTY OR BET-
TER THE BEAUTY OF THE IDLE.
SUCH KIND IS AN END PRODUCT OF
A PROCESS AIMING AT BEAUTY ITSELF
AS ~~ALOOF~~ GODDES, ALOOF & UN-
CONCERNED WHIT ANYTHING ELSE,
PURITY HERE AS EVER IS AT THE
EXPENSES OF LIVENESS OR
IN MORE CONCERNED WORDS IN THE
PRESENCE OF SUCH KIND ONE IS
EXERTING A DUAL CONCIOUSNESS'.
BY ONE HE REVERES
BY THE OTHER HE SENSES ITS
OWN EXTERNALITY TO THE OBJECT OF REVERENCE. THUS IMPLYING
A SENSE OF USELESSNESS & ~~OF~~
THE STILLNESS OF LIFE ABSENT:
THE NIGHT REMAIN, THE MEANING IS GONE

THIS IS THE BEAUTY OF THE CONCIOUS
ESTETE ~~THE ONE~~, ~~WHO~~ ASSEMBLES
BEAUTIFUL "THINGHS", ORDERING THEM
IN LAWFULNESS OF TEORETICAL
RULES THAT IN REASON OF THEORY
CANNOT BE INTEGRATED WHIT LIFE
SURROUNDING. THUS RULES TEND TO
INSERT IN SUCH OBJECT TO THE POINT
OF MAKING OF THOSE OBJECT THEMSELVES
"THE BEATIFUL RULER OF THEIR MASTERS"!

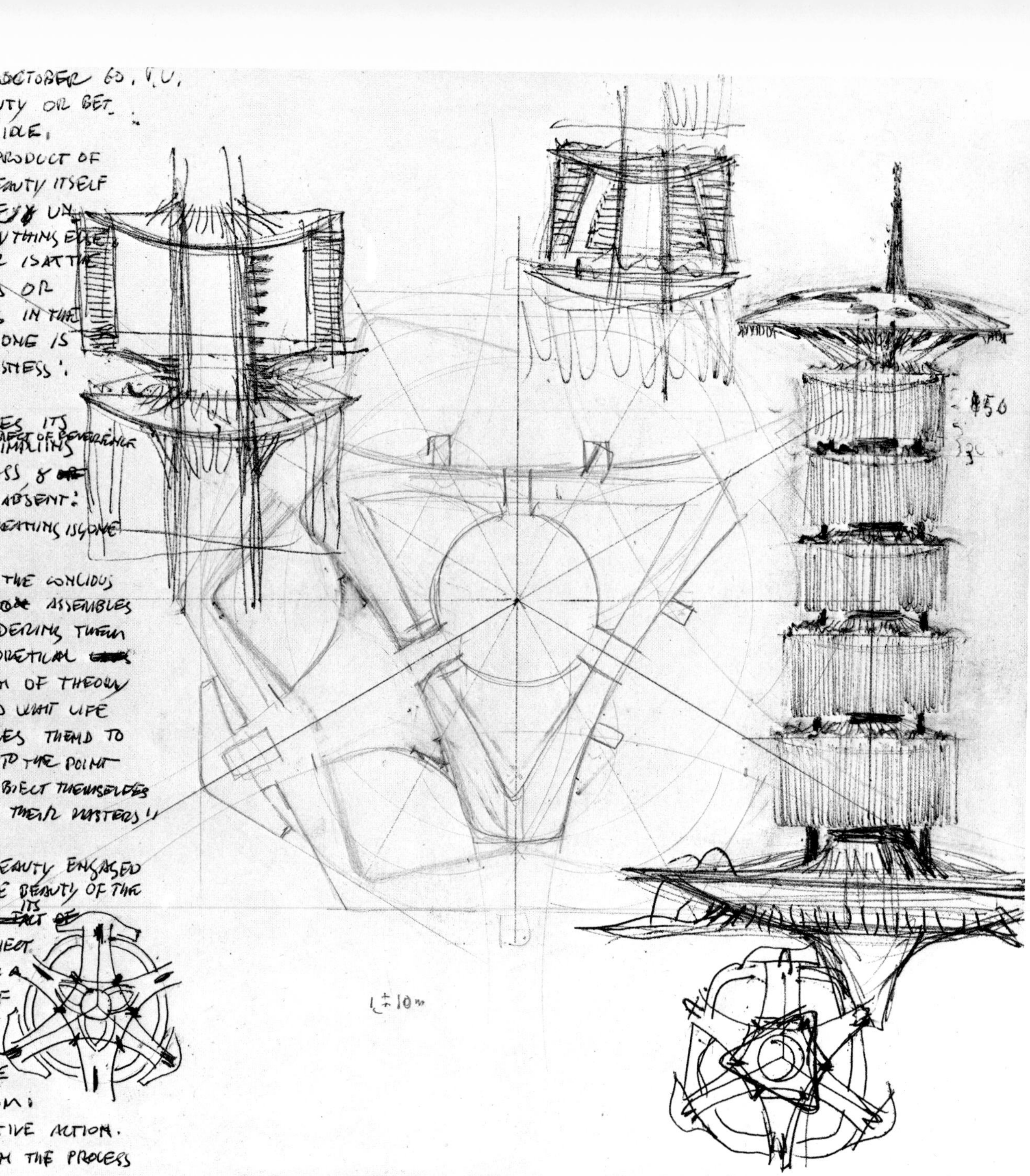

THERE IS THEN THE BEAUTY ENGAGED
WHICH DIFFERS FROM THE BEAUTY OF THE
IDLE PRIMARILY IN ~~THE FACT OF~~ ITS
PUSHING OBJECT & SUBIECT
TOWARD EACH OTHER IN A
COMMON. ENDEAVOUR OF
INCREMENTATION & IN
KEEPING THE EVER SEL-
FCONCIOUS PURITY OF THE
ESTETE OUT OF THE ROOM.
HERE BEAUTY IS SELECTIVE ACTION.
WHICH ESTETIC VALUE IS IN THE PROCESS

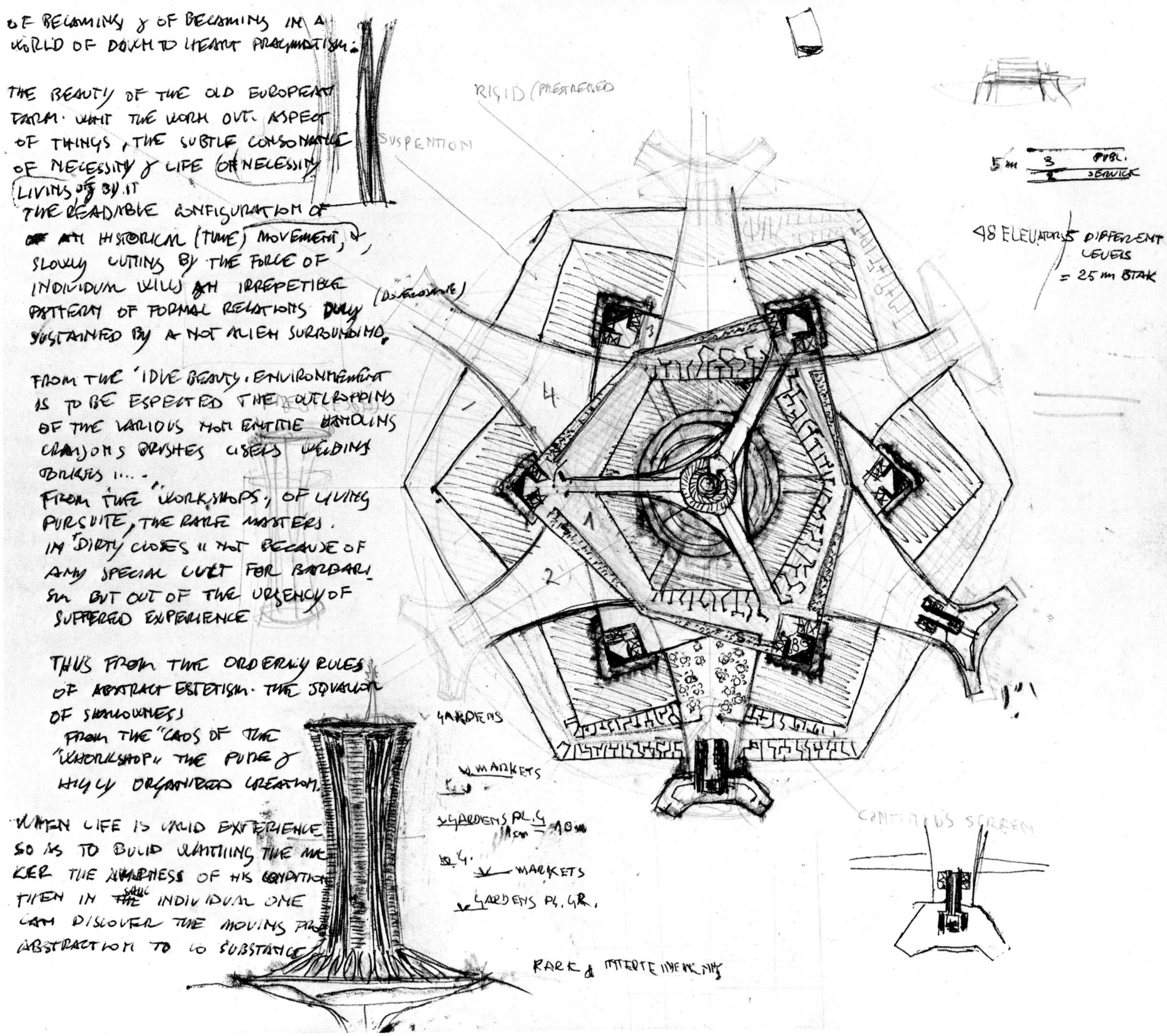
OF BECOMING & OF BECOMING IN A WORLD OF DOWN TO HEART PRAGMATISM.
THE BEAUTY OF THE OLD EUROPEAN FARM. WHAT THE WORN OUT ASPECT OF THINGS, THE SUBTLE CONSONANCE OF NECESSITY & LIFE OF NECESSITY LIVING BY IT
THE READABLE CONFIGURATION OF AN HISTORICAL (TIME) MOVEMENT, SLOWLY CUTTING BY THE FORCE OF INDIVIDUAL WILL AN IRREPETIBLE PATTERN OF FORMAL RELATIONS SUSTAINED BY A NOT ALIEN SURROUNDING.
FROM THE 'IDLE BEAUTY' ENVIRONMENT IS TO BE EXPECTED THE OUTCROPPING OF THE VARIOUS INSTRUMENTS
CRAYONS BRUSHES CHISELS WELDING TORCHES ....
FROM THE "WORKSHOPS" OF LIVING PURSUITE, THE RARE MASTERS.
IN "DIRTY CLOTHES" NOT BECAUSE OF ANY SPECIAL CULT FOR BARBARISM BUT OUT OF THE URGENCY OF SUFFERED EXPERIENCE
THUS FROM THE ORDERLY RULES OF ABSTRACT ESTETISM. THE SQUALOR OF SHALLOWNESS
FROM THE "CAOS OF THE "WORKSHOP" THE PURE & HIGHLY ORGANIZED CREATION.
WHEN LIFE IS VALID EXPERIENCE SO AS TO BUILD WITHIN THE MAKER THE AWARENESS OF HIS CONDITION THEN IN THE SAME INDIVIDUAL ONE CAN DISCOVER THE MOVING FROM ABSTRACTION TO SUBSTANCE
RIGID (PRESTRESSED
SUSPENTION
5 m 3 PUBL. SERVICE
48 ELEVATORS 5 DIFFERENT LEVELS = 25 m BTAK
GARDENS
MARKETS
GARDENS PL. G
MARKETS
GARDENS PL. GR.
CONTINUOUS SCREEN
4
1
2
3

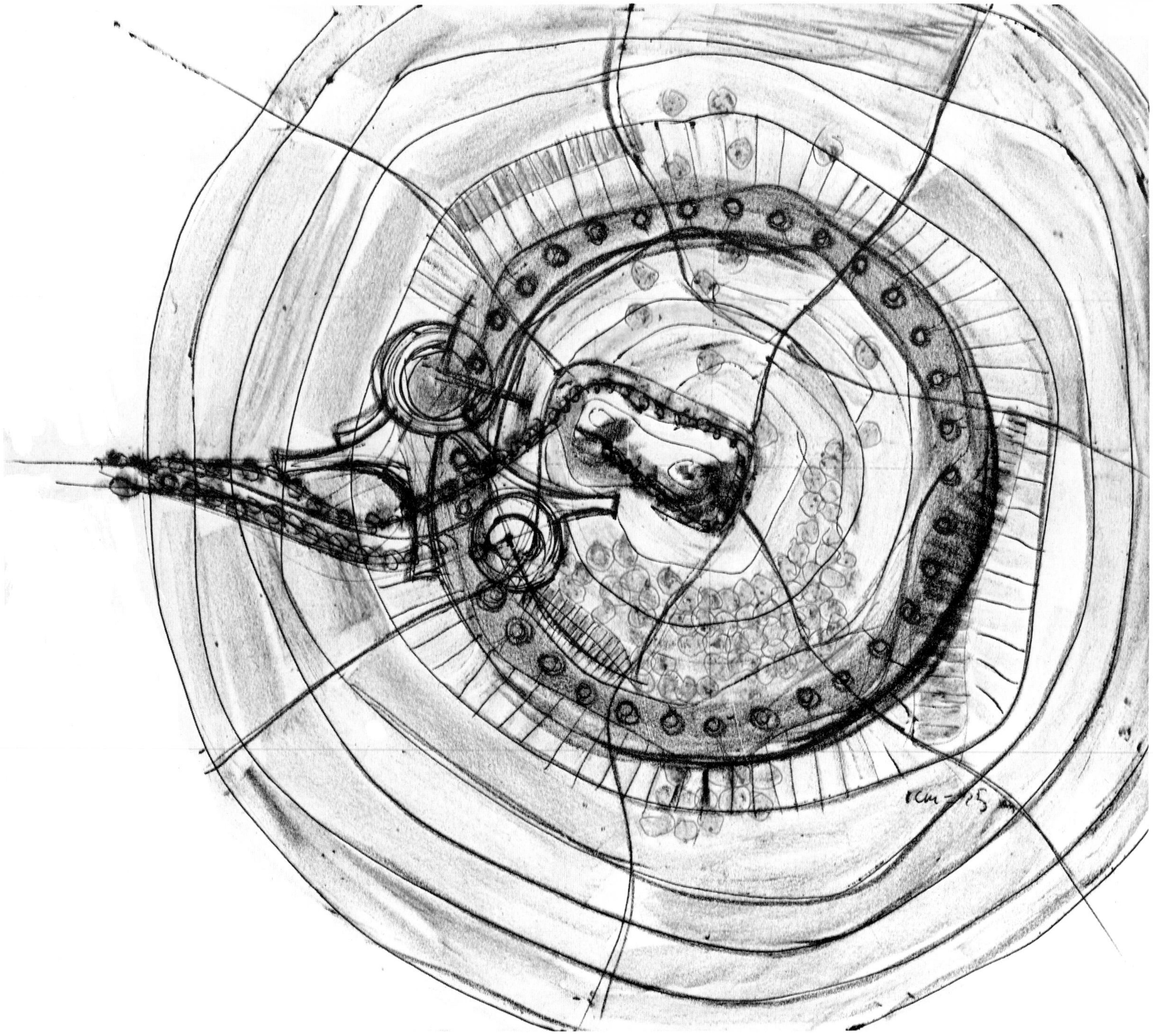

DECEMBER 60 PV.

ON PALEONTOLOGICAL CENTER.

AT THE EXTREMES ONE INVEST THE (A) PROBLEM OR BY APPEASEMENT OR BY DEFIANCE. BETWEEN THESE TWO ~~extremes~~ ARE THE NUANCES THAT CULTURE & CIVILISATION CAN AFFORD.

TOTAL DEFIANCE OR TOTAL APPEASEMENT DENOTE BOTH A BARBARIAN STATUS. PRIMITIVISM OR BETTER SAVAGERY EXPRESSES LIFE IN BOTH THE VIOLENT FORMS & COLORS OF THE PRIMITIVE BEING & RITUAL MEDIUM'S & THE QUASI MIMETISM OF THE EVERY DAY LIFE

IS TO BE EXPECTED THEN IN THIS AGE OF EXPLICIT BARBARISM WHICH FLARES UP IN ACTS OF WOLESOME VIOLENCE, GENOCIDE, BRUTALISATION, AUTOMATISM, CLUMSINESS, GROSSNESS OF EVALUATION ETC..... ON ONE SIDE & SEARCH FOR SPERSONALISATION, COMFORTABLE GRAYNESS, SOCIAL MIMETISM ETC. ON THE OTHER, THAT THE ~~problem~~ SOLUTION MAY BE SOUGHT IN THE VICINITY OF THOSE TWO EXTREME ME!

DEFIANCE.

DEFIANCE IS IN FUNCTION OF AN AT LEAS STATISTICAL CHANCE FOR SUCCESS. BOLDNESS IS THE INGREDIENT NEEDED. BUT BOLDNESS WITHOUT GRACE IS BRUTALITY, THUS UNLESS THE BOLD ACT IS AN ACT OF LOVE THE ATTITUDE OF DEFIANCE WILL BRING FORTH NOT AN AFFIRMATION OF MAN POTENTIALS BUT WILL SIMPLY INFLICT ANOTHER WOUND ON THE ENVIRONNEMENT. LIKE BLEEDING THE WILD BEAST TO DEATH WHILE TRYING TO TAME IT.

IF DEFIANCE ARISES FROM THE UNDERSTANDING OF ONES OWN INSIGNIFICANCE

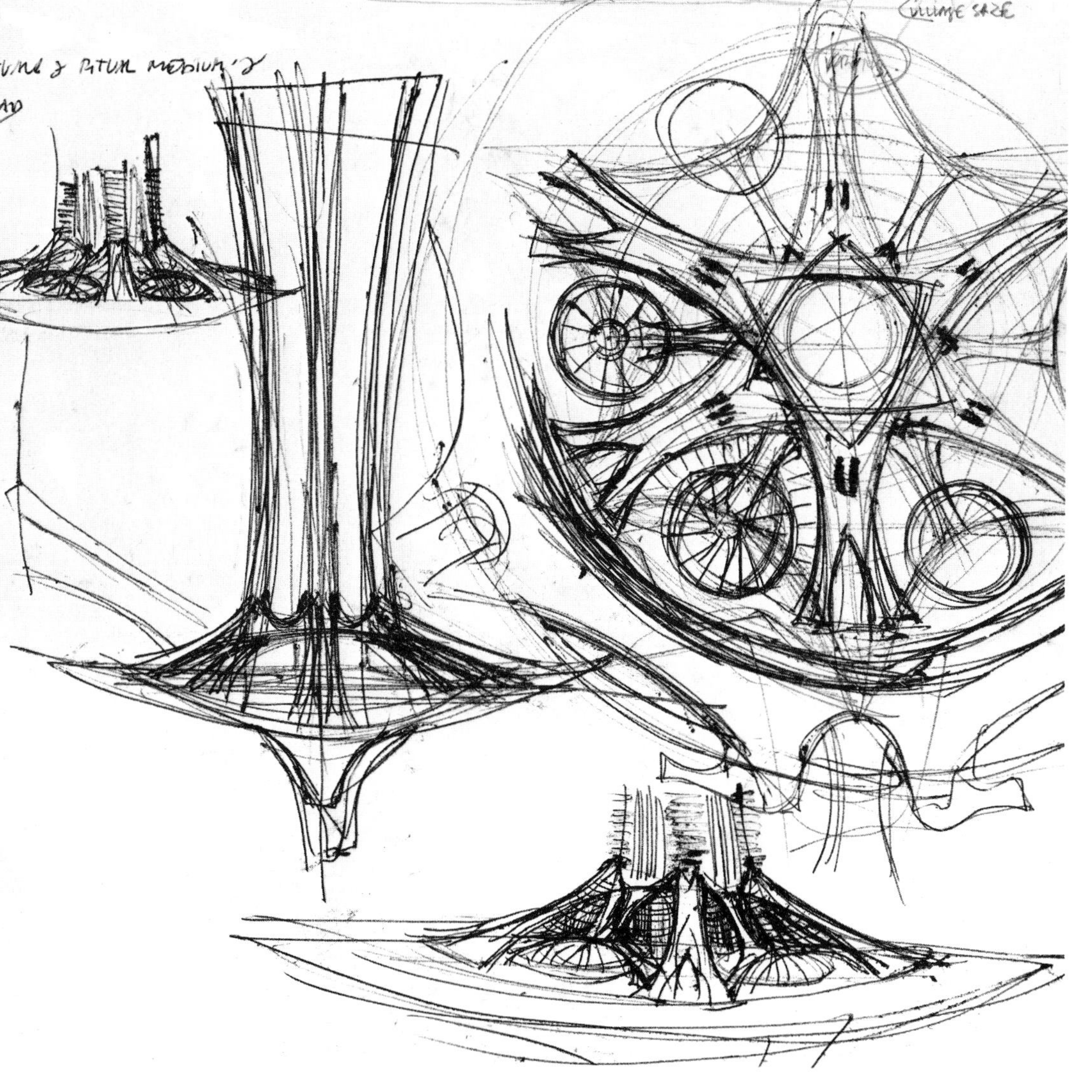

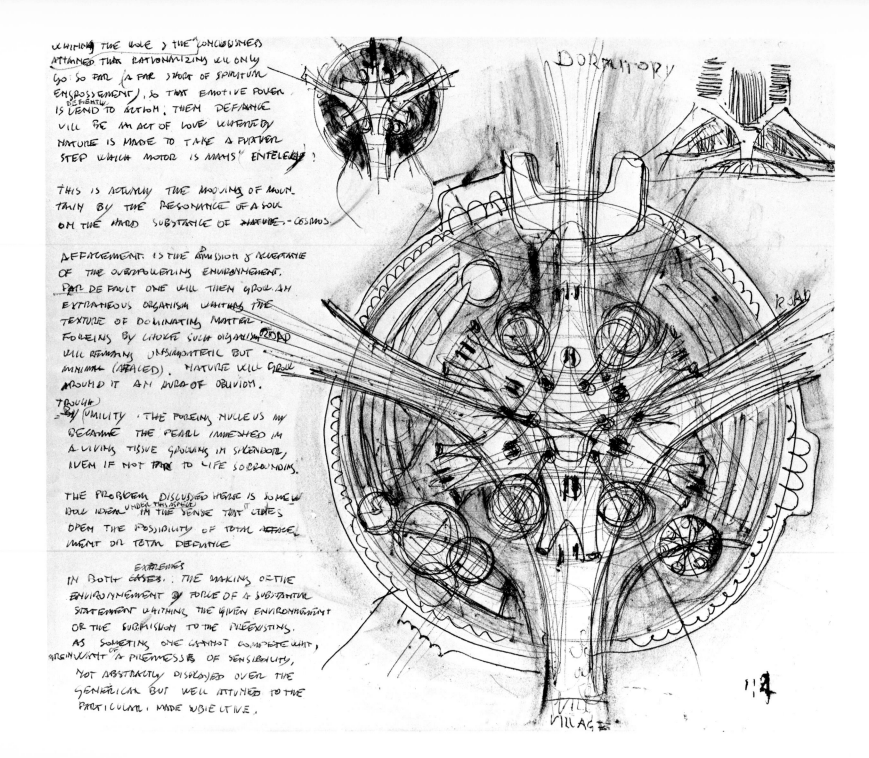

WITHIN THE ROLE OF THE CONSCIOUSNESS ATTAINED THAT RATIONALIZING WILL ONLY GO SO FAR (A FAR SHORT OF SPIRITUAL ENGROSSEMENT), SO THAT EMOTIVE POWER IS DEFIENTLY LEND TO ACTION; THEN DEFIANCE WILL BE AN ACT OF LOVE WHEREBY NATURE IS MADE TO TAKE A FURTHER STEP WHICH MOTOR IS MANS' ENTELECHY!

THIS IS ACTUALLY THE MOOVING OF MOUNTAIN BY THE RESONANCE OF A SOUL ON THE HARD SUBSTANCE OF ~~NATURE~~, -COSMOS.

AFFACEMENT IS THE ADMISSION OF ACCEPTANCE OF THE OVERPOWERING ENVIRONMEMENT. PAR DEFAULT ONE WILL THEN GROW AN EXTRANEOUS ORGANISM WITHIN THE TEXTURE OF DOMINATING MATTER. FOREING BY CHOICE SUCH ORGANISM WILL REMAINS UNSIMPATETIC BUT MINIMAL (AFFACED). NATURE WILL GROW AROUND IT AN AURA OF OBLIVION.

= ~~BY~~ TROUGH UMILITY · THE FOREING NUCLEUS MAY BECAME THE PEARL IMMESHED IN A LIVING TISSUE GROWING IN SPLENDOR, EVEN IF NOT ~~PARC~~ TO LIFE SORROUNDING.

THE PROBLEM DISCUSSED HERE IS SOMEHOW IDEAL UNDER THIS ASPECT IN THE SENSE THAT IT LEAVES OPEN THE POSSIBILITY OF TOTAL AFFACEMENT OR TOTAL DEFIANCE

IN BOTH EXTREMES ~~CASES~~: THE MAKING OF THE ENVIRONMEMENT BY FORCE OF A SUBSTANTIAL STATEMENT WITHIN THE GIVEN ENVIRONMEMENT OR THE SUBMISSION TO THE PREEXISTING. AS SOMETING ONE CANNOT COMPETE WITH, BEING WITH OF A PREMESSES OF SENSIBILITY, NOT ABSTRACTLY DISPLAYED OVER THE GENERICAL BUT WELL ATTUNED TO THE PARTICULAR, MADE SUBJECTIVE.

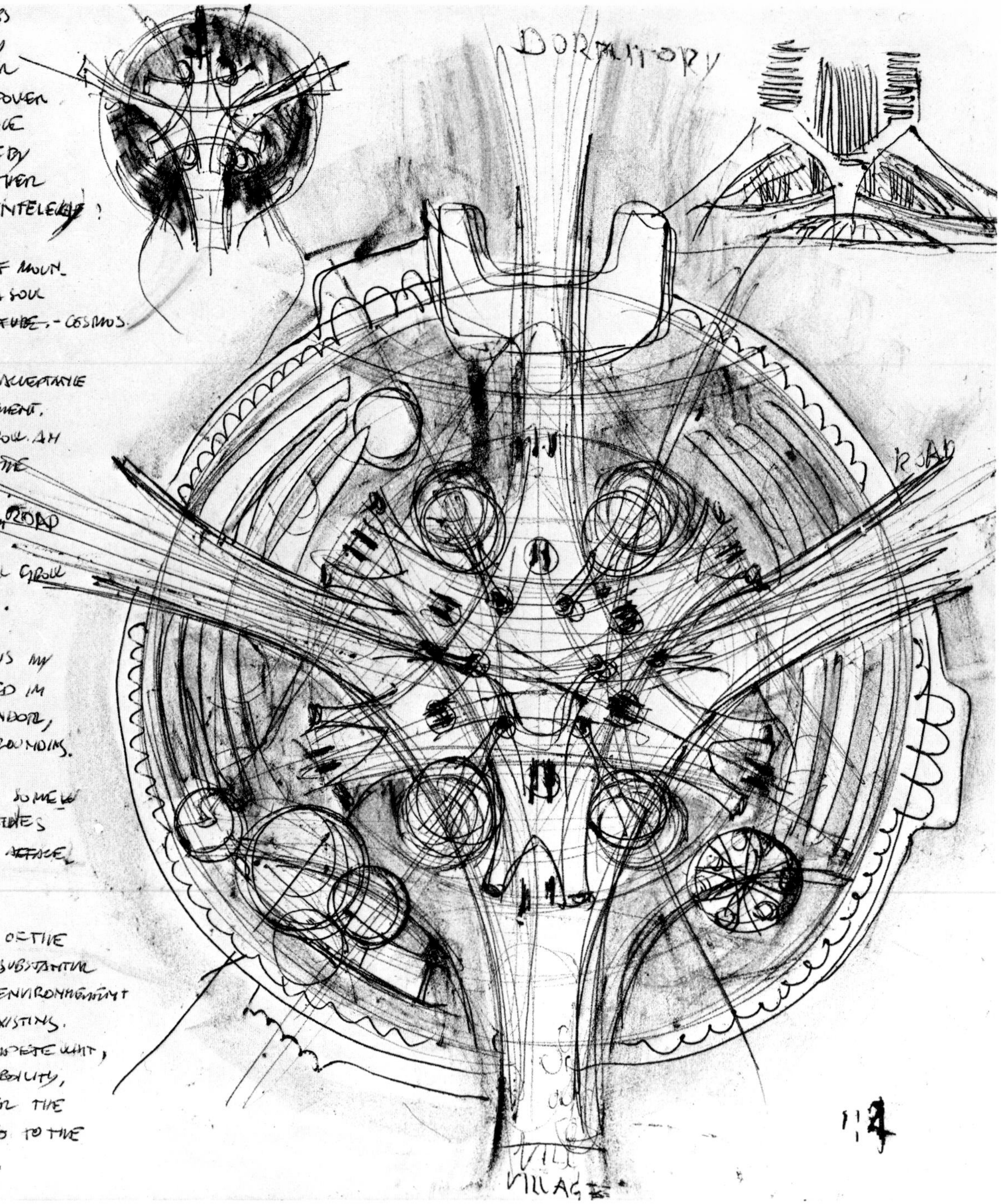

FOR LACKE OF SENSITIVITY ONE MY SEAT
IDLY IN A ~~PSEUDO~~ POSITION OF PSEUDO
"CLASSICISM" HALF DEFIANT ~~HALF~~ EFFACING.
THE APOLLINEAN TRANQUILLITY ~~WOULD BE~~
FAKED BY THE LUKEWARMTH OF INDECISION.

THE "SCOLARY" ENDEAVOURS TO FIND
A BALANCED EXPRESSION. SITUATED
ON A PLATFORM OF PARITY WHIT NATURE,
WHERE GIVING & TAKING IS RECIPROCAL
& EMOTIONALLY SEDATE. HE WILL CONSTANTLY
REPROPORTION ~~HIS~~ THE INCIDENCE OF HIS ACTION
TO THE IMPACT NATURE HAS ON HIS
UNDERSTANDING.

THEN ARCHITECTING BECAMES THE
"COCREATIVE EFFORT" PUT OUT BY MAN
~~FLANKING~~ COMPLEMENTING THE OTHER KIND OF CREATIVITY
CARRIED ON BY NATURE FROM
THE BEGINNING OF TIMES.

IF ONE VENTURE IN GUESSING THE
MANLY ACTION AS THE AFFIRMATION
OF THE NEW COMER MIND-SPIRIT ON
EARTH & FORESEE AN EVER ENCREASING
FORCEFULNESS OF IT, THEN
ONE MAY SPECULATE ON A FUTURE DAY
WHERE MAN WILL BE THE PRINCIPAL
CREATOR OF ITS OWN ENVIRONMENT
IN COSMIC SCALE. AS WELL AS IN THE
HOMELY.
THE DEFIANCE WILL THUS BE GROWN
INTO THE INAVOIDABLE, AS ANY OTHER
TIME-ESTABLISHED FACTS OF NATURE

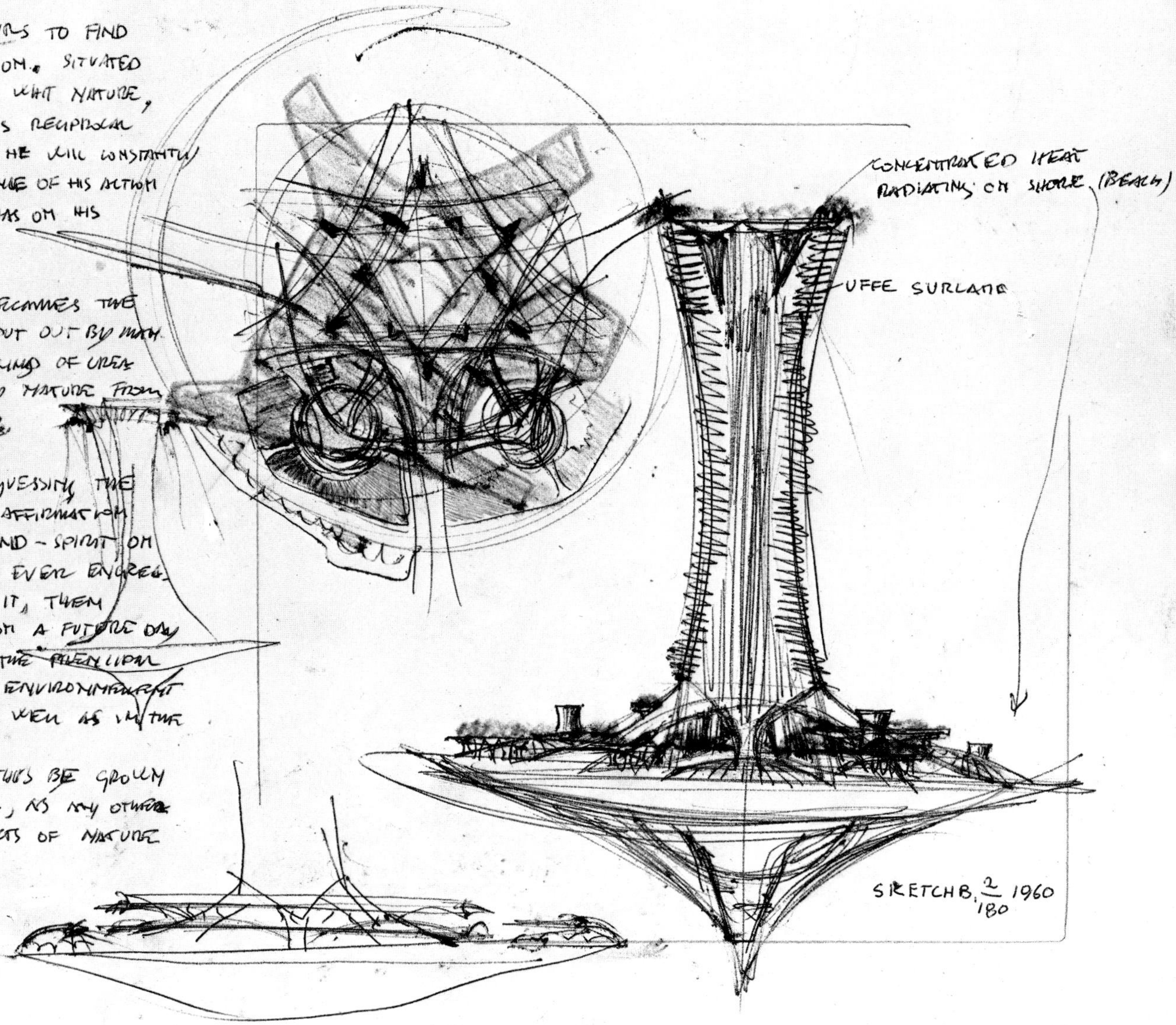

SKETCHB. 2/180 1960

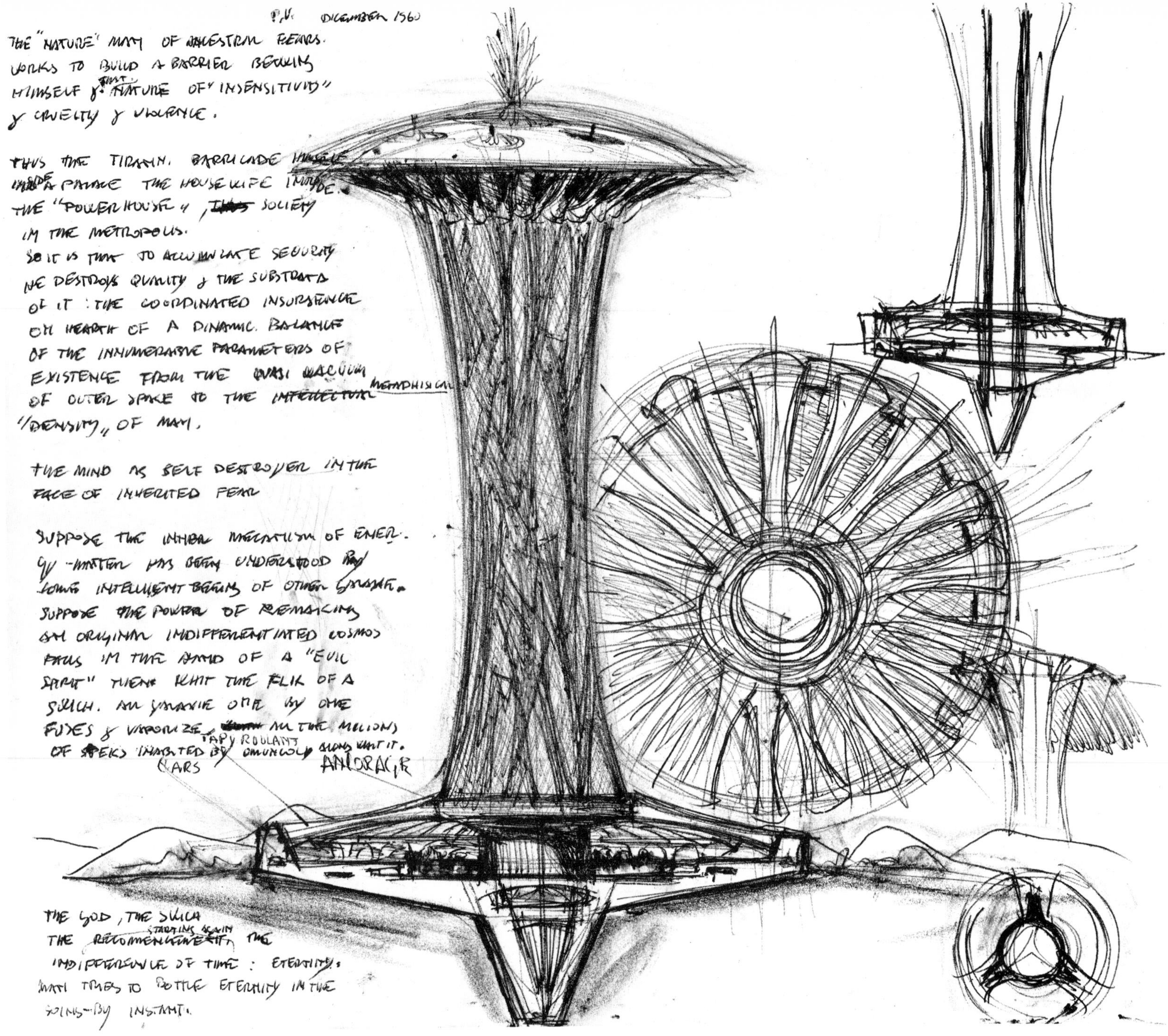
P.V. DECEMBER 1960
THE "NATURE" MAN OF ANCESTRAL FEARS.
WORKS TO BUILD A BARRIER BETWEEN
HIMSELF & THAT NATURE OF "INSENSITIVITY"
& CRUELTY & VIOLENCE.
THUS THE TIRANN. BARRICADE INSIDE A PALACE THE HOUSEWIFE INSIDE.
THE "POWERHOUSE", SOCIETY
IN THE METROPOLIS.
SO IT IS THAT TO ACCUMULATE SECURITY
HE DESTROYS QUALITY & THE SUBSTRATA
OF IT: THE COORDINATED INSURGENCE
ON HEARTH OF A DINAMIC BALANCE
OF THE INNUMERABLE PARAMETERS OF
EXISTENCE FROM THE QUASI VACUUM
OF OUTER SPACE TO THE METAPHISICAL
"DENSITY" OF MAN.
THE MIND AS SELF DESTROYER IN THE
FACE OF INHERITED FEAR
SUPPOSE THE INNER MECANISM OF ENER-
GY-MATTER HAS BEEN UNDERSTOOD BY
SOME INTELLIGENT BEING OF OTHER GALAXIE.
SUPPOSE THE POWER OF REMAKING
AN ORIGINAL INDIFFERENTIATED COSMOS
FALLS IN THE HAND OF A "EVIL
SPIRIT" THEN WHIT THE FLIK OF A
SWICH. ALL GALAXIE ONE BY ONE
FUSES & VAPORIZE ALL THE MILLIONS
OF SPEKS INHABITED BY TAPY ROULANT ALONG WITH IT.
CARS
AMORAGER
THE GOD, THE SWICH
THE STARTING AGAIN, THE
INDIFFERENCE OF TIME: ETERNITY.
MAN TRIES TO BOTTLE ETERNITY IN THE
GOING-BY INSTANT.

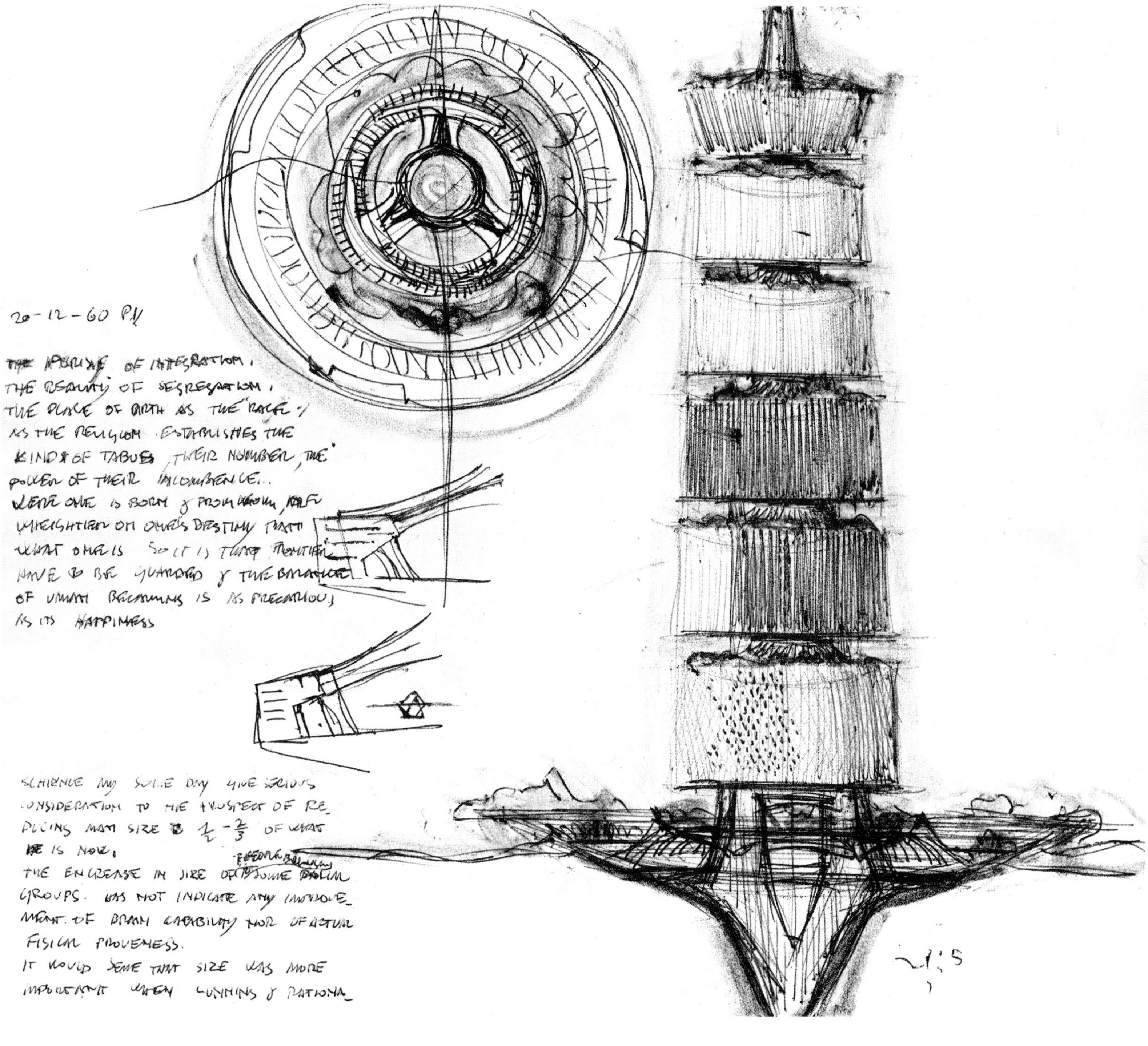
20-12-60 P.M.
OF INTEGRATION,
THE REALITY OF SEGREGATION,
THE PLACE OF BIRTH AS THE RACE
AS THE RELIGION ESTABLISHES THE
KIND OF TABUES, THEIR NUMBER, THE
POWER OF THEIR INCOMBENCE...
SO IT IS THAT
HAVE TO BE GUARDED & THE BALANCE
AS ITS HAPPINESS
SCIENCE MAY SOME DAY GIVE SERIOUS
CONSIDERATION TO THE PROSPECT OF RE_
DUCING MAN SIZE TO 1/2 - 2/3 OF WHAT
IS NOW.
THE ENCREASE IN SIZE OF SOME
GROUPS. HAS NOT INDICATE ANY IMPROVE_
MENT OF BRAIN CAPABILITY NOR OF ACTUAL
FISICAL PROVENESS.
IT WOULD SEME THAT SIZE WAS MORE
IMPORTANT WHEN CUNNING & RATIONA_

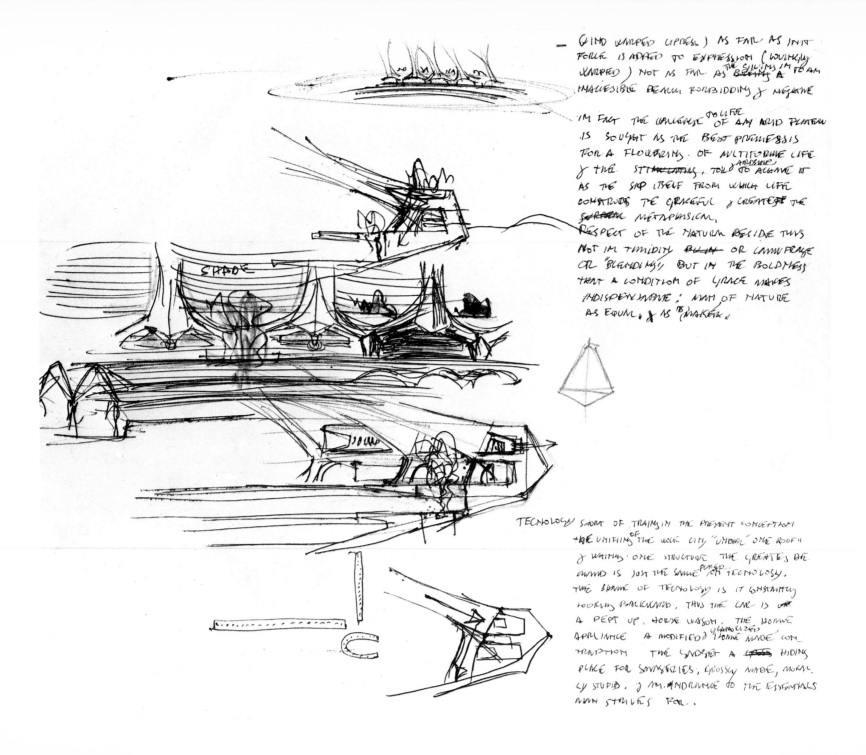

— (AND WARPED LIPRESS) AS FAR AS INIT FORCE IS ADAPTED TO EXPRESSION (WILLINGLY WARPED) NOT AS FAR AS THE SILLINESS IN TO AN INACCESSIBLE REALM FORBIDDING & NEGATIVE

IN FACT THE CHALLENGE TO LIFE OF AN ARID PLATEAU IS SOUGHT AS THE BEST PREMISSIS FOR A FLOWERING OF MULTIFORME LIFE & THE STIMULATING, TOIL AND SWEAT TO ACHIEVE IT AS THE SAP ITSELF FROM WHICH LIFE CONSTRUCTS THE GRACEFUL & CREATES THE METAPHYSICAL.

RESPECT OF THE NATURAL BESIDE THUS NOT IN TIMIDITY OR CAMOUFLAGE OR "BLENDINGS" BUT IN THE BOLDNESS THAT A CONDITION OF GRACE MAKES INDISPENSABLE: MAN OF NATURE AS EQUAL & AS ITS MAKER.

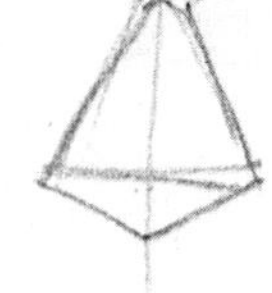

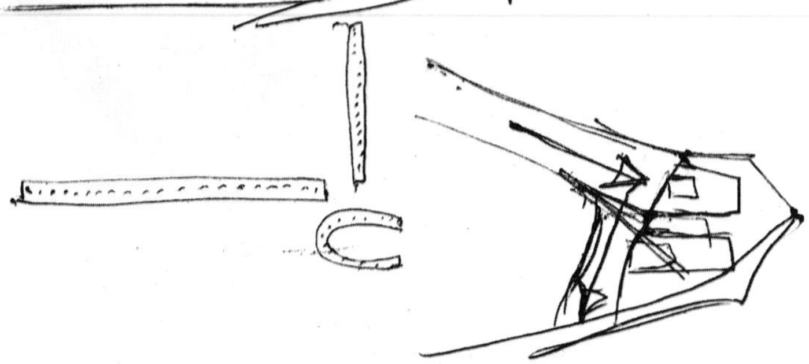

TECNOLOGY SHORT OF TRAINS IN THE PRESENT CONCEPTION THE UNIFYING OF THE WHOLE CITY "UNDER" ONE ROOF & WRITING ONE STRUCTURE THE GREATEST DE MAND IS JUST THE SAME PLACED ON TECNOLOGY. THE SHAME OF TECNOLOGY IS IT CONSTANTLY LOOKING BACKWARD, THUS THE CAR IS A PEPT UP HORSE WAGON. THE HOME APPLIANCE A MODIFIED GLAMORIZED HOME MADE CONTRAPTION THE GADGET A HIDING PLACE FOR SAVAGERIES, GROSSLY MADE, MORALLY STUPID, & AN HINDRANCE TO THE ESSENTIALS MAN STRIVES FOR.

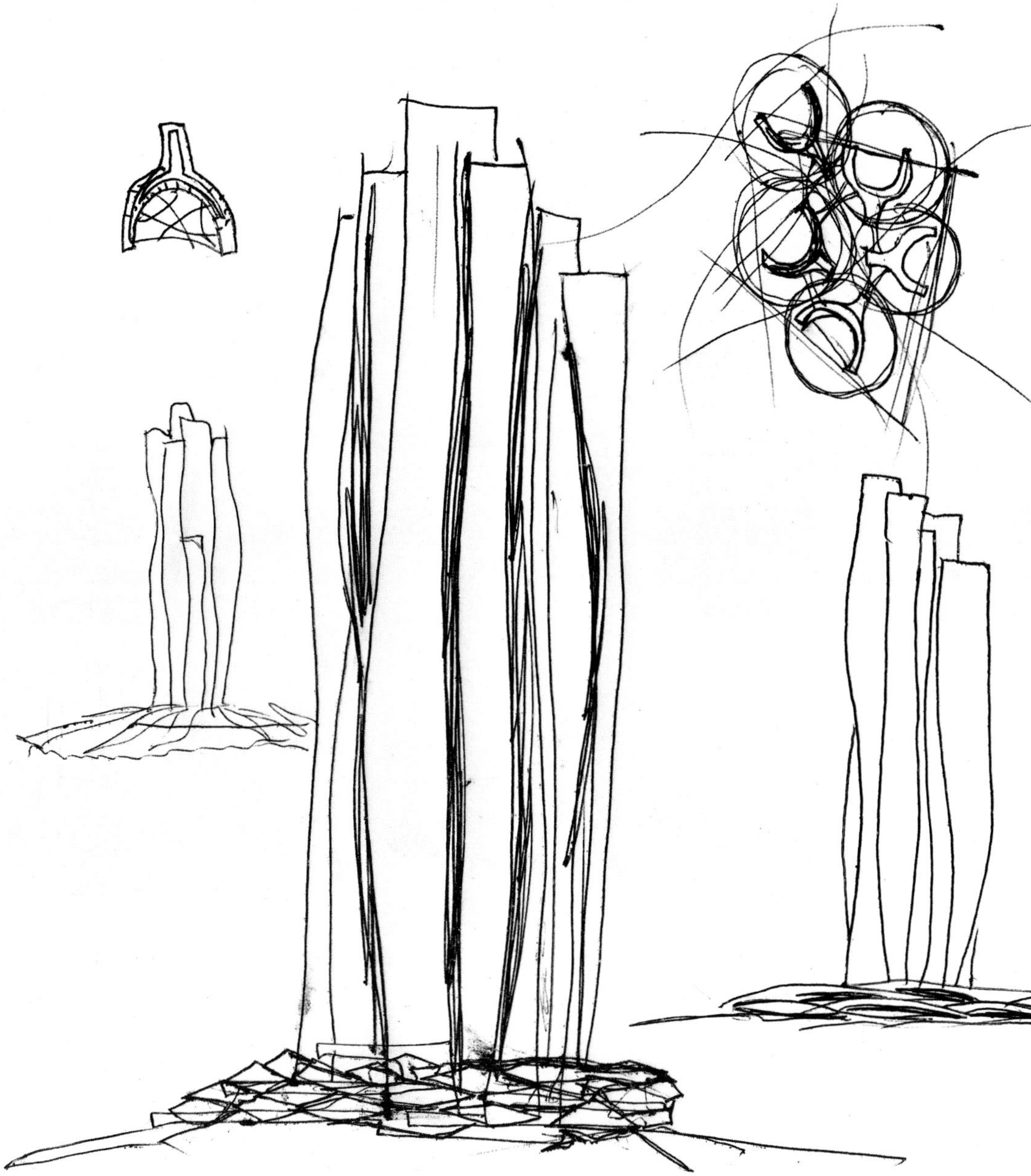

SEPTEMBER 62

THERE WONT BE JUST TODAY
THERE WONT BE JUST TOMORROW
THERE WILL BE A TOMORROW FOR
EVERY TOMORROW. ~~FOR~~
FOR THE CONSUMPTION. OF PLANETS
STARS, SYSTEMS. GALAXIES - COSMOS.
THEN. THE DAY WILL REST. FOR
A DAY WITH NO TOMORROW.

ABOUT A BOOK::

THERE IS ~~ARE~~ A REASON THAT
WILL STAND REASONING FOR PRINTING
WHAT FOLLOWS: WRITTEN IN A LANGUAGE
NEW TO THE AUTOR, BY SOMEONE ~~AN AUTHOR~~ WHO
WOULD BE A POOR WRITER IN HIS
OWN TONGUE ~~LANGUAGE~~, WITH NO LOGICAL
TREND FOLLOWED, WHAT EXPRES-
SION OF MEANS STRICTLY FOR ~~HIS~~ OWN
CONSUMPTION ~~OF THE AUTHOR~~, THE AUTHOR
ITSELF A GOOD SPECIMEN OF
IGNORANCE.
YET THE EMBARRASSING QUESTIONS BY
BY INDIVIDUALS INTERESTED IN
ART ARCHITECTURE & PLANNING MAY
FIND INTELLECTUALIZED ANSWERS.
SUCH ANSWERS MAY OPEN THE WAY
TO THE THEORETICAL WORK: THE
MESA CITY. PROJECT. & THE PRO-
GRAMS ENVISAGED BY THE AUTHOR.

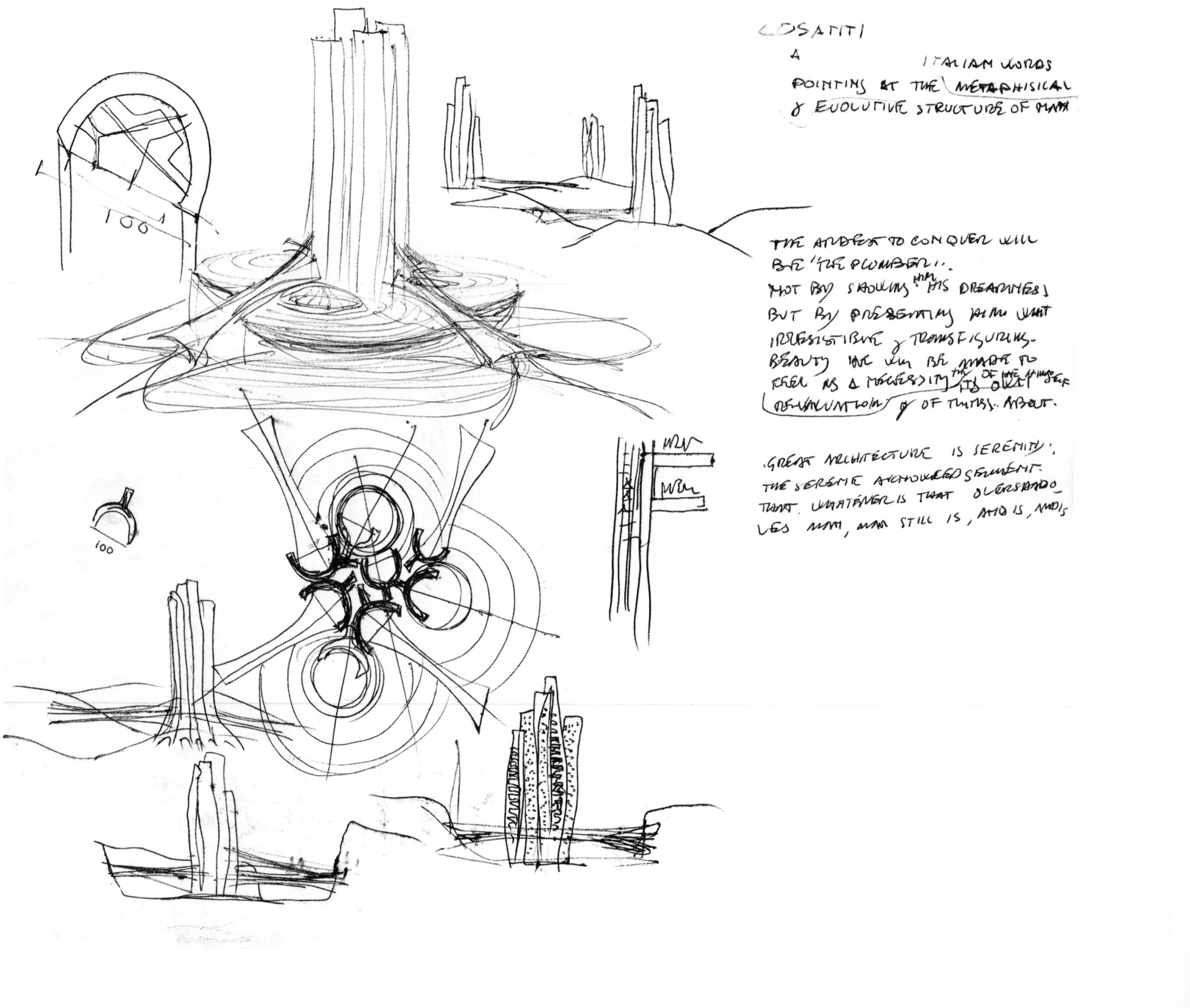
COSANTI
A ITALIAN WORDS
POINTING AT THE METAPHISICAL
& EVOLUTIVE STRUCTURE OF MAN
100
100
THE HARDEST TO CONQUER WILL
BE 'THE PLUMBER'.
NOT BY SHOWING HIM HIS DREARINESS
BUT BY PRESENTING HIM WITH
IRRESISTIBLE & TRANSFIGURING
BEAUTY HE WILL BE MADE TO
FEEL AS A NECESSITY
REVALUATION & OF THINGS ABOUT.
GREAT ARCHITECTURE IS SERENITY.
THE SERENE ACKNOWLEDGEMENT
THAT WHATEVER IS THAT OVERSHADOWS MAN, MAN STILL IS, AND IS, AND IS

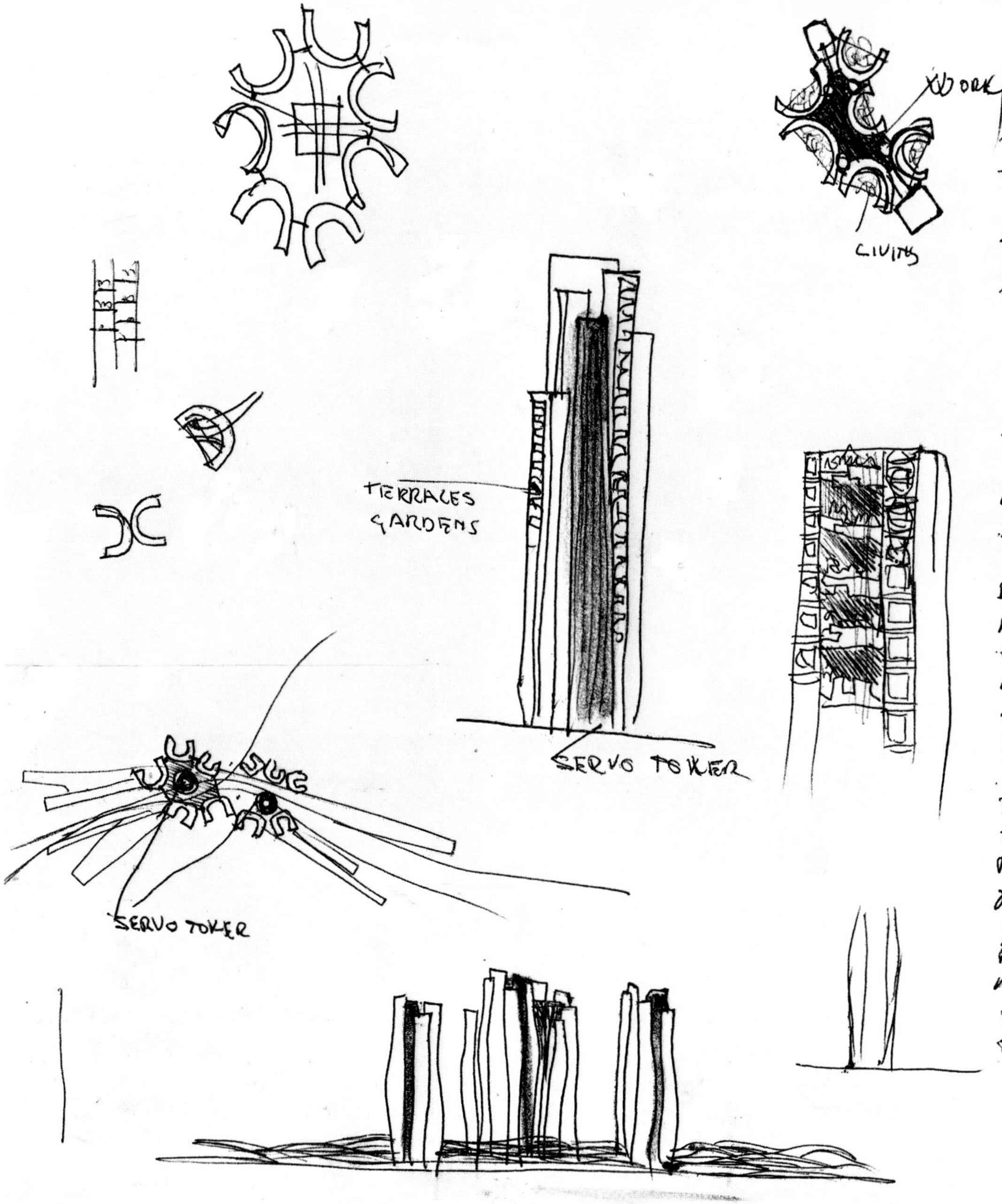

QUESTION: OCTOBER 62

COMMUNICATION BETWEEN A "CREATIVE" PERSON & THOSE AROUND HIM

IT REVERTS TO THE GENERAL CONDITION OF SOLITUDE EACH BEING IS IN. THE MORE LIFE OR ENERGY VIGOROUSLY ASSERTED THE GREATER IS THE ISOLATION IN WHICH THIS ASSERTION IS MADE.

SIMILAR CONDITION OCCOURS IN PHISICAL FENOMENON.

THE TWISTER PULLS TO ITSELF THE MOST ITS ENERGY CAN UPROOT & LONELY CREATURE, MOVES FROM CAOS TO CAOS OF ITS OWN MAKING.

THE VOLCANO GROWS AT THE EXPENSES OF INNER MATTER & THE LONGER HE LIVES THE MORE ISOLATED & DOMINANT IT IS.. THE LONELY AGAIN.....

. . . .

EGO & ENERGY MAY WELL BE SINONIMOUS.. IN THE SENSE THAT BOTH PRESUME A SOMEWHAT GREATER CONCENTRATION OF THE STUFF FORMING THE FENOMENON

IN THE CASE OF MAN, THE STUFF IS BY ALL STANDARDS IDENTICAL:

THE DIFFERENCE BETWEEN THE MORON & THE "GENIUS" IS NEGLIGIBLE COMPARED TO THE DIFFERENCE BETWEEN THE MORON & THE APE

YET THE EXISTING GULF SEEMS TO BE OF FUNDAMENTAL IMPORTANCE TO MAN: THE IMPOSSIBILITY OF DEFINING WHAT IS THE DIFFERENCE IS THE GREATER FACTOR FOR ISOLATION. THE SENSE OF JUSTICE CAN HARDLY ACCEPT DIFFERENTIATION (PATERNITY) IN THE RIGHT TO BE & TO BE FULLY...... (COVERED RESENTMENT.)

WE ARE LONELY IN AS MUCH AS WE

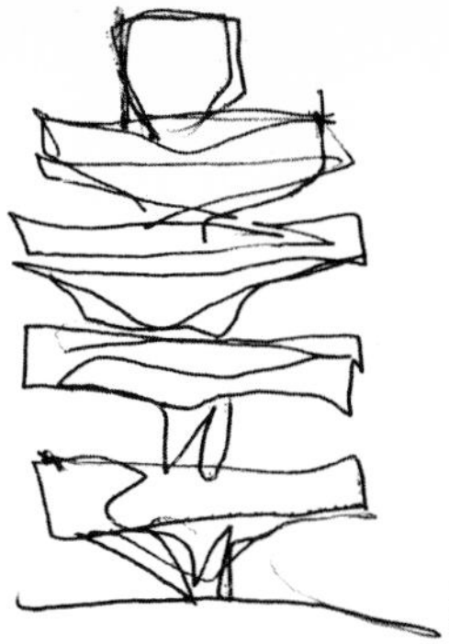

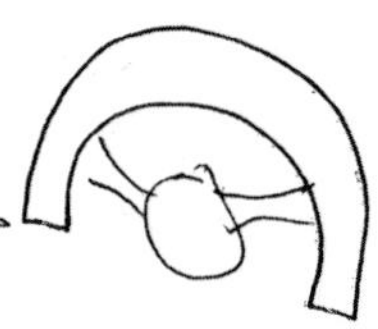

ARE "UNIQUE"
WHEN LOVE INTERVENE IT IS AS IF
SUCH UNIQUENESS WAS UNDERSTOOD "BIO_
LOGICALLY" & SPIRITUALLY BY THE OTHER
PERSON, UNDERSTOOD AS SOMETHING
UNREACHABLE THUS THE MORE PRECIOUS.
IN THIS SENSE LOVE IS ALWAYS ONE
WAY AFFAIR.

RECIPROCAL LOVE (NOT LOVE & GRATITUDE)
IS A RARE COINCIDENCE WHERE BY
ONE WAY GRASPING IS COUNTER
WEIGHTED BY AN OPPOSITE UNDERSTA
NDING, GENERALLY ON A DIFFERENT SUBJECT
MATTER.

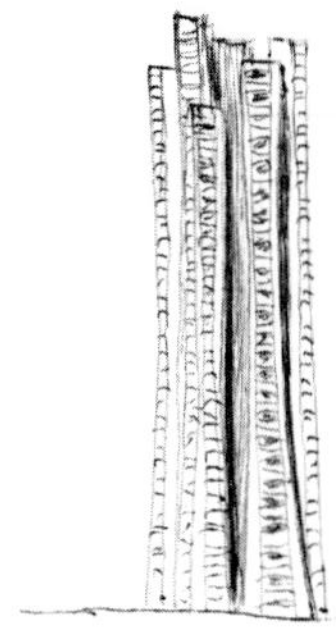

THIS LOVE DO NOT NECESSARILY 'PERSO_
NIFIES' IN LOVE FOR THE CARRIER OF
UNIQUENESS. THE CARRIER WILL RECEIVE
MOST OFTEN ONLY A REFLECTED WARMTH
THUS LEAVING GROWTH TO WARD HIS OWN
UNIQUENESS AS THE EVER PRESENT OB.
STACLE TO COMMUNION.

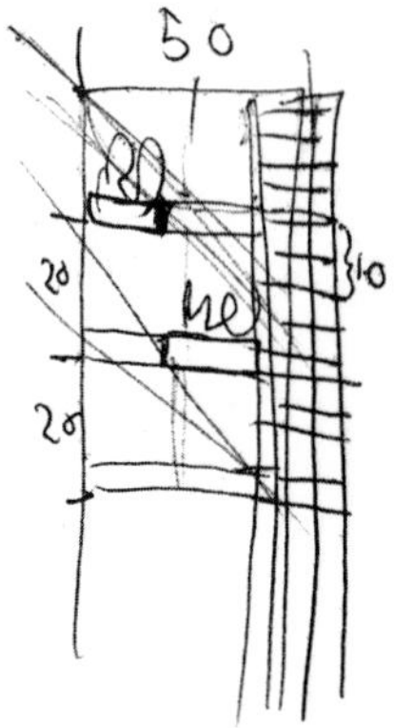

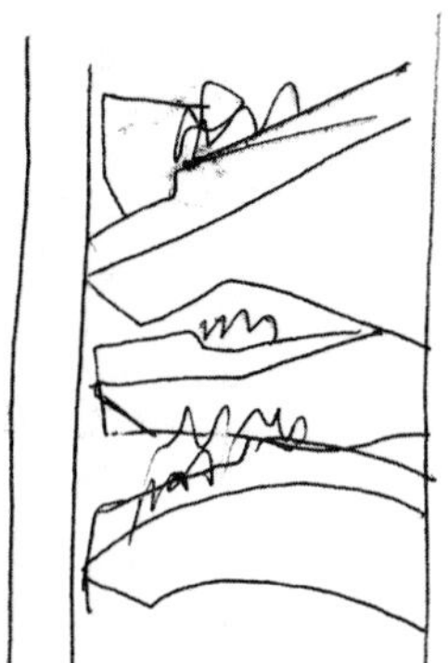

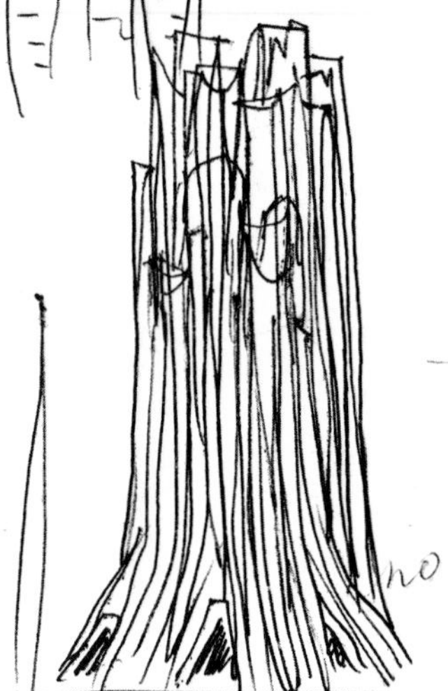

RELIGIOUS EXPERIENCE TRANSFERS
UNIQUENESS TO A THIRD PERSON: GOD
LOVE BECOMES A TRIANGLE PATTERN
WHAT ONE OF THE ANGLE AS
RISOLUTIVE TO THE OTHERS.

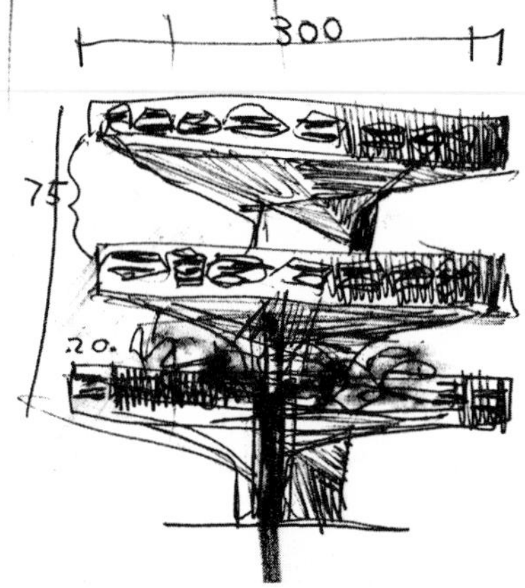

THE MORE UNIQUENESS IS SUSTAINED
THE MORE THE SUBJECT TENDS TO CON_
DUCT THE DIALOGUE BETWEEN HIMSELF
& THE OUTSIDE AS IF THE OUTSIDE
WERE BUT THE REFLECTIONS OF HIS
OWN PROCESSES
THE URGENCY INHERENT TO EACH
MOMENT DEMANDS ANSWERS
READY & "CONVENIENT"

AS COMMUNICATION HAPPENS TROUGH THE
DEEDS MORE THAN TROUGH WORDS,
DIALOGUE, & AS THERE IS AN UNBAL-
LANCE BETWEEN THE DEEDS OF

Theological Center

1970

Now that my inability to accept God has moved from ethical objections to realization of the physical impossibility of His existence,* I can only let the whole idea of a theological center fall into the grinder of history. That is to say, as we institute museums and collections to document past actions, we might find it necessary to institute archives and study centers for "what religion was." This would clip the wings of the project, as it is hardly enough to trust that the past aspects of what you work with are relevant and have no true faith that the future will bring any true import to it. And yet one of my recurring reveries remains the picture of the quiet life of the cloister, a slightly rosy, if dull, vision of the monastic life in the reposeful shade of a colonnaded courtyard. From gardening to books to crafts to stillness remains a humanistic temptation.

1960

The complex is an outcropping from a hill, the slopes of which are worked in terraces of varying width. Among these terraces, cared for by the various monastic orders, are graveyards accessible by pathways and stairways.

The system is composed of the following parts:

1.
A secular section sheltered under a canopy, 200 x 4,000 meters, split by an inner "silent walk."

2.
Six bowls, 500 meters in diameter, sheltering the major theological institutions of man: Hinduism and Buddhism, Confucianism and Taoism, Judaism and Christianity, Islam, Zoroastrianism and "minor" religions, atheism and agnosticism.

3.
A towering structure on top of the hill tentatively representing a synthesis of man striving for knowledge, sheltering a major library-museum, meeting rooms, cells for visiting scholars, and so forth. It is organized in a hollow cylindrical drum, 500 meters in diameter. An "instrument" diffuses sound from its vertical axis over the city and surrounding land.

4.
Primitive cults have a 400-meter shelter under the "angel's wings."

5.
A bridge with landing platforms and necessary facilities interconnects and serves the whole complex.

The access is through four gates: the water gate on the east; the earth gate on the south; the fire gate on the west; the air gate on the north. The water gate opens through a sequence of waterworks in the middle of the theological university, the low, long canopy sheltering classrooms, workrooms, cloisters, and gardens. The silent walk cuts through the length of it with a soft stonewall on which anonymous writers can cut or draw or paint their names, their poems, their doodles. On the outside perimeter of the canopy facing east is the "stilita portico." Each hollow column containing a cell studio is named after a philosopher, saint, guru, religious leader, or prophet. Small libraries devoted to these people are arranged parallel to the portico, which has on the wall facing east on the low land a chronological representation of historical events of which the figures were a part. Inwardly, the theological university opens onto a composite garden and faces the east side of the landing bridge, the 400-meter-high library-museum and some of the bowls containing the monastic orders. In the composite garden are special structures relating to the concepts of time, space, light, infinity, matter, energy, and entropy.

The earth gate on the south side opens from a group of staggered structures, cut into the earth, functioning as car terminals and silos, youth hostels, and cafeterias, the grounds densely wooded. It is the terminal of the axial park that cuts through the city from the study center 20 kilometers farther south. The gate leads to the south end of the composite garden. The terraced gardens and graveyards surrounding the whole theological complex face the earth gate.

The fire gate on the southwest side of the complex opens onto a large structure for primitive and open-air rituals. Processions, funerals, and religious pageantries move through this gate in and out of the complex. Cremation facilities are here.

The air gate is the landing bridge, 2,000 meters long, running roughly north-south tangent to the library-museum and rising many stories above the composite garden. Inside its structure are facilities for transient clergy and visitors. From it, direct connections are available with all the components of the complex.

The library-museum is a 500-meter-diameter structure on a stem 150 meters in diameter. Within the stem is a water reservoir whose top structure is partially transparent. The reservoir is also a shrine that can be seen from the museum-library above, and its inner walls are covered with painting, mosaics, or bas relief. Within the large body of potable water a smaller volume can be maintained with marine life as part of the shrine. Above the shrine, in the expanding structure, the museum and library can avail themselves of the same main spaces and services. Farther above are facilities for the residents, shops, restaurants, infirmaries, and chapels. And last, are many stories of cells for scholars, clergymen, teachers, and artists. At the top and from the outer rim of the structure is hung a double-tension system carrying "inverse gardens," light- and weather-control devices. At the center of this radial cable system, hanging on the vertical axis of the structure, is the "instrument," an electronic mechanism capable of sending out sounds for miles over plains and valleys. Geared with the movement of the stars, it could also work as an astronomical clock.

The six 500-meter bowls cling to the west slope in staggered order. The main access to all of them is at a level different from the main mall, developing below the main structure (library-museum). Each one composes a separate world, physically contained within the shell of the bowl. If perforated,

*If complexity is the nature of the divine and complexity is conditioned by ultrasophisticated logistics, the obstacle to the existence of the divine is the diffusion of its being. Diffusion is by definition absence of complexity because of its nonminiaturized status, that is to say, its inability to perform the sophisticated logistics of information and communication.

this shell would reveal the outer world distantly receding in formal separateness. The root, though, is in the geological heart of the hill, powerfully anchored, and life sustenance comes from the same earth at the horizons.

The physical closeness of the different religions is intended to favor reciprocal investigation, understanding, and comparison. The technical and cultural facilities help in reaching within and beyond the fable, the myth, the superimpositions at the common roots and structures. Both of these intentions are reflected in the complex, its organization, its continuity, the related positions of its elements and how they hinge on one another.

(NOT THE BEST UNLESS ADAPTATION IS CONSTANTLY WORKING WAITING)
BUT AS MUCH FAR AS RESPECTING & MAKING ONES OWN THE VALUE-POWERS THAT PULLED OUT MAN FROM THE BOTTOM BASES OF ELEMENTAR EXISTENCE (DOWN TO VEGETATIVITY) SUCH AN ATTITUDE & CONDITIONING ARE MUCH TO CLOSE TO SELF DENIAL & CONSEQUENTLY SELF EXTINCTION, AS INDIVIDUALS & AS A SPECIE.

GOOD SENSE IS THAT WHICH MAKES MONKIES CARRY ON THEIR MONKEY BUSINNES DAY AFTER DAY & AS FAR AS WE CAN WITNESS GENERATION AFTER GENERATION.

GOOD SENSE IS THE KEEPER OF THAT WHICH THE ~~[illegible]~~ -UTOPIAN HAS INTRODUCED INTO THE WORLD BY ITS STRIVING WITH THE THINGS OF NATURE

GOOD SENSE MUST HAVE ENOUGH GOOD SENSE TO UNDERSTAND THAT, UNLESS THOSE THINGS ARE ACTIVATED BY FURTHER FENOMENA OF THE SAME NATURE, THEY WILL WITHER AWAY UNDER THE UNMERCIFUL SUM OF ~~[illegible]~~ UNCONSUMED TIME

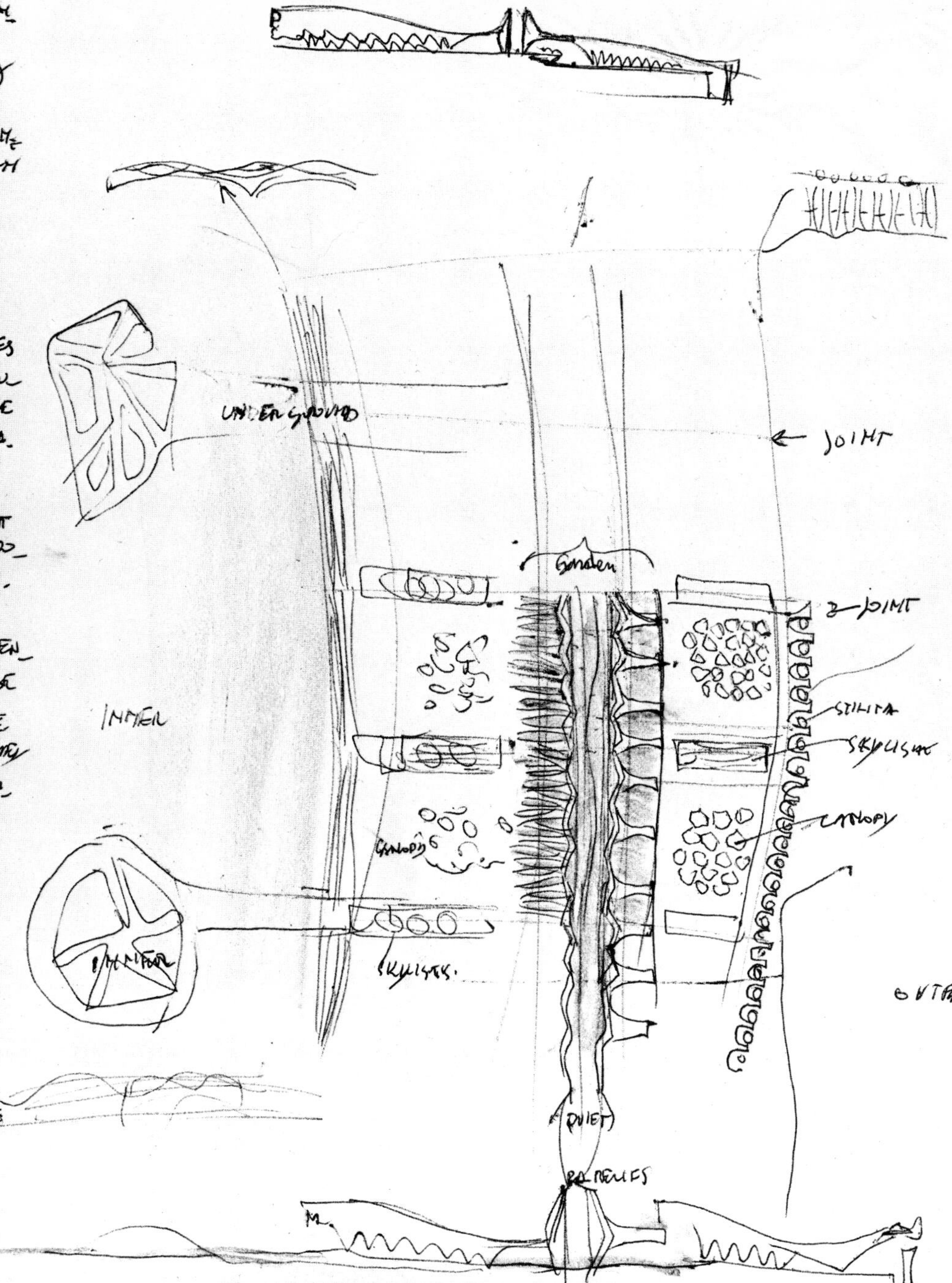

VALUE CANT BE BOUGHT BY ONE OF ITS BYPRODUCTS : MONEY

RISOLVING ANGUISH INTO WORTHINESS BY
ACT OF THE MIND & OF THE HAND

THE FLOWER TO FLOWER BUTTERFLY IS IN
THE YOUTH OF MAN, THE MAN IS IN THE
FLOWER TO FLOWER BUTTERFLY.

ABUSE OF THE PREROGATIVES OF LOVE
& YOU WILL BE ABUSED BY THE BORE-
DOOM OF FISICAL PLATITUDE.

DIVINITY & THE FEMININE GRACE UNI-
TED CAME BY LONG INTERVAL OF
LONGING & ENGROSSEMENT WHEREIN IM-
MAGES BLUR INTO GLORIES OF FORMS
LIGHT - COLORS SOUNDS. NEGATED TO THE
MATING BEAST AND THE SHALLOW PLAYBOY

SPERMATOZOOI ARE POETRY POTENTIAL.
& THE GIVING MIGHT REACH THE RARE
SUBSTANCE OF THE INCREDIBILITY & FULLNES
OF A PURE PROFILE ON A WHITE LINEN,
& THE SIGHTING OF LOVE TROUGH THE OFFER OF
INFINITY BY THE LOVERS ~~EYES~~ EYES.

BY "JUMPING IN THE MIDDLE OF" IT, YOU
WILL FIND SOLUTIONS FOR THE INSOLVABLE.
THE JUMP SPRINGING NOT FROM THE ~~SAND~~
QUICKSANDS OF IRRESPONSIBILITY BUT FROM
THE SPRING BOARD OF INVOLVEMENT

ABIDING TO THE "FINAL" IS CASTING ASIDE
LIFE CALLING, THE SECRETS, THE MISTERIES
THEREIN, THE FINALITY ITSELF TO WHICH
THE "FINAL" WAS A LEGITTIMATE LONGING

BEWARE, FULLNESS IS A SHIE (TIMIDO) GLORY.
TAPPING TO ITS RESERVOIR DEMANDS
QUASI TOTAL ALONENESS & LONG PREME-
DITATIONS OF YIERS

DEDICATION RESSEMBLES THE DOG ~~FIRE~~

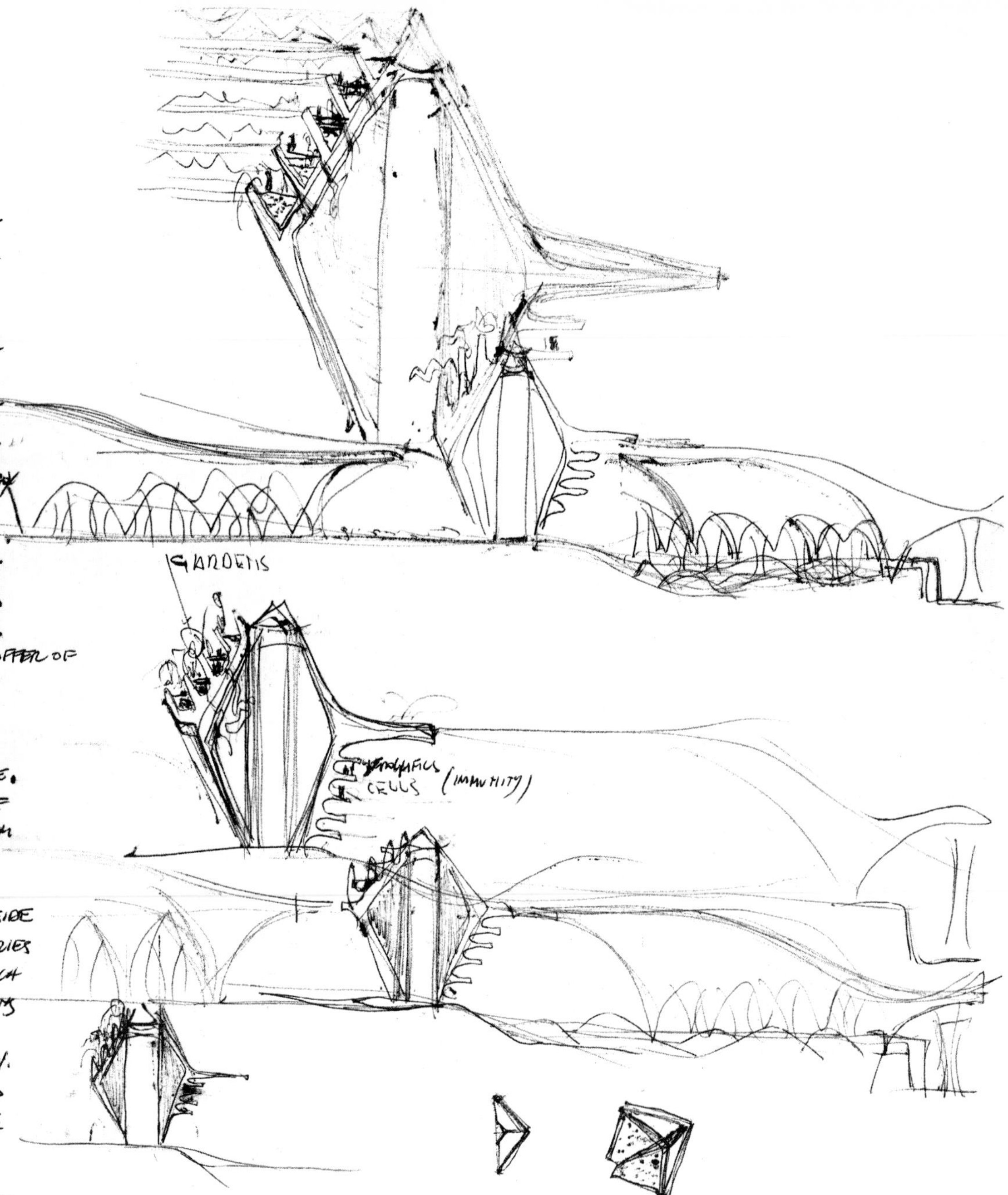

FAITHFULNESS, THE MATTER WILL DO OF BLIND OBIDIENCE A THING OF MERIT OR OF UNDUING.

WATCH THE SELF ASSURED INDIVIDUAL AT THE PRESENCE OF DEATH, SEE THE CRUMBLING OF ITS MANY FACES INTO THE FACELESS OF ANNIHILATION

COUNT YOUR HOURS OF DULLENESS AS A TOLL FOR THE PRIVILEDGE OF LIVING Y AS A REMINDER OF YOUR INFINITE SMALLNESS

YOU WON'T COUNT THE JOIOUS HOURS, YOU WILL LIVE THEM Y OF TIME WILL LOOSE ~~COUNTING~~ THE MESURING BEATS

IF IT ISNT SIMPLE ITS QUITE CLEAR: WE ARE PUT ON A EARTH OF SPLENDOR Y OF EVER CHANGING BEAUTIES, OF POWER Y GRACE, A EARTH THAT EVEN IN ITS SO CALLED STERILE LANDS HAS THE INTEGRITY OF THE SACRED. A EARTH BLOOMING LIFE Y FLOWER FROM HER WASTAGE HEAPS. A EARTH WHICH IS A BREATHTAKING CONTINUUM.

THE LEAST MAN CAN DO IS TO RESPECT HER WITH THE UTMOST REVERENCE HE IS CAPABLE OF, THAT IS, SEEK INTENSELY THE INEFFABLE OF THINGS Y THINGS DO WHICH INNEFABLE ARE. ALWAYS, EVER, EVERYWERE, EVERYTIME.

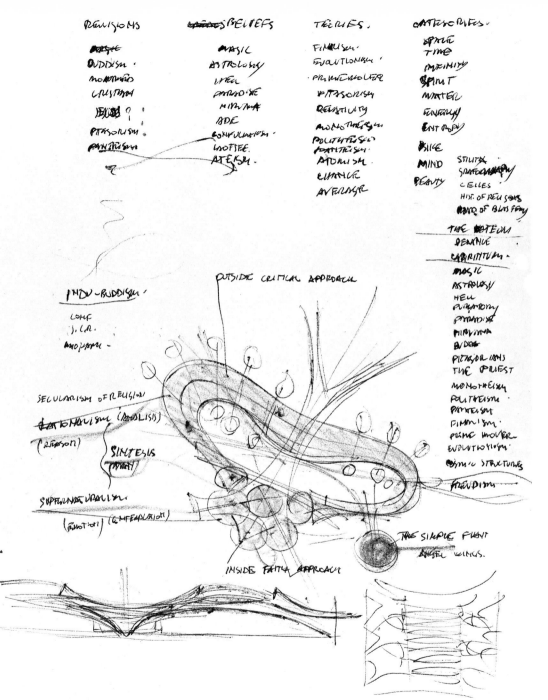

RELIGIONS	BELIEFS	THEORIES.	CATEGORIES.
~~MAGIC~~	MAGIC	FINALISM.	SPACE
BUDDISM.	ASTROLOGY	EVOLUTIONISM.	TIME
MOHAMMED	HELL	PRIME MOVER	INFINITY
CRISTIANISM	PARADISE	PITAGORISM	SPIRIT
?	NIRVANA	RELATIVITY	MATTER
PITAGORISM.	ADE	MONOTHEISM	ENERGY
PANTHEISM	CONFUCIANISM.	POLITHEISM	ENTROPY
	LAOTSEE.	PANTHEISM.	BLISS
	ATEISM.	ATOMISM.	MIND
		CHANCE	BEAUTY
		AVERAGE	

STILITA
SAVONAROLA
CELLES
HIST. OF RELIGIONS
WORD OF BLASFEMY

THE BATEAU
DEMANCE
LABIRINTUM.

MAGIC
ASTROLOGY
HELL
PURGATORY
PARADISE
NIRVANA
BUDDA
PITAGORIANS
THE PRIEST
MONOTHEISM
POLITHEISM
PANTEISM
FINALISM.
PRIME MOVER
EVOLUTIONISM.
COSMIC STRUCTURES
FREUDISM

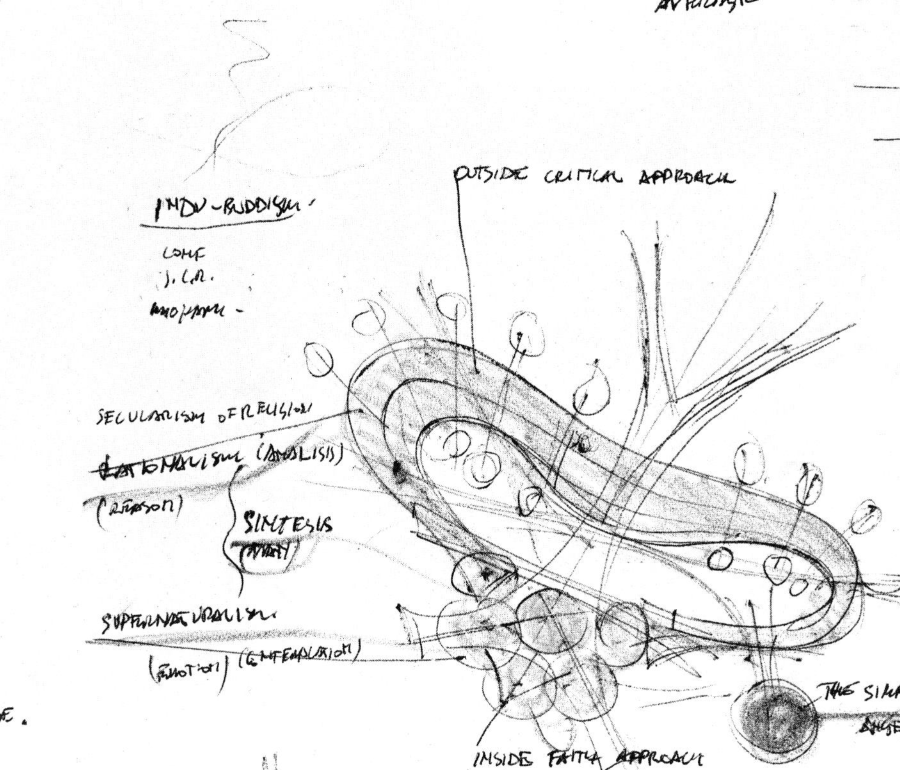

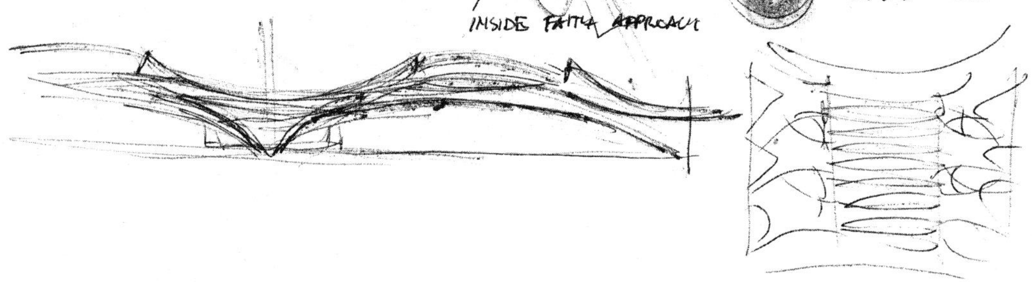

ONE MIGHT OBSERVE THAT ONE OF THE
FEW POINT WHERE BEAST Y MEN CAME
TO TOUCH ABOVE THE LEVEL OF VEGE-
TATIVITY IS IN THE "IRRATIONALITY„
OF RITMICAL MOVEMENT.
THE MATING ANIMALS ARE DANCING INTO
THEIR FINAL RESOLUTION Y IF ONE MIGHT
EXPLAIN THE EXUBERANCE OR EVEN POM-
POSITY OF ASPECT AS A MEAN TO CATCH
THE COMBATION, THE DANCE ITSELF, (PLEASURE PRINCIPLE)
CARRYING AFTER THE CHOICE IS MADE
IS BEYOND THE REALM OF DRIED Y CUT (REALITY PRINCIPLE)
NECESSITY, IT IS EXPRESSION, FREE Y
"UNNECESSARY„ YET UNAVOIDABLE.
AS A CREATIVE MAN:
IF I SEE IMMAGES I PAINT IF I
FEEL VOLUMES I SCULPT IF I CONCEIVE
SPACES I CONSTRUCT - IF I FORM CON-
CEPTS I WRIGHT IF I HEAR SOUNDS
I COMPOSE IF I SEEK I PRAY IF
I "AM" I DANCE

WHEN I AM I AM NAKED, AS THE SNAKE
IS AS THE RUSTER IS AS THE DOLPHIN IS.

EACH VEIL ON THE BODY OF THE DANCER
IS A VEIL OF IPOCRISIE ON THE HOLINESS
OF ITS GIVING, HE IS GIVING ITS OWN
BODY Y WHAT HE IS GIVING THAT IS WHAT
WAS TO BE APPREENDED.

THE COSTUME, THE COLORS, THE HAIR DRES-
SING ETC. HAVE THE FUNCTION OF INHA-
NCING THE PLAY OF THE NAKED BODY

DANCE "IS THE "SIN„ OF HAVING A BODY
THUS ANY HIDING OF IT BY EVEN A
REMOTE SENSE OF GUILT IS IPOCRITICAL
OR VERY, VERY NAIVE.

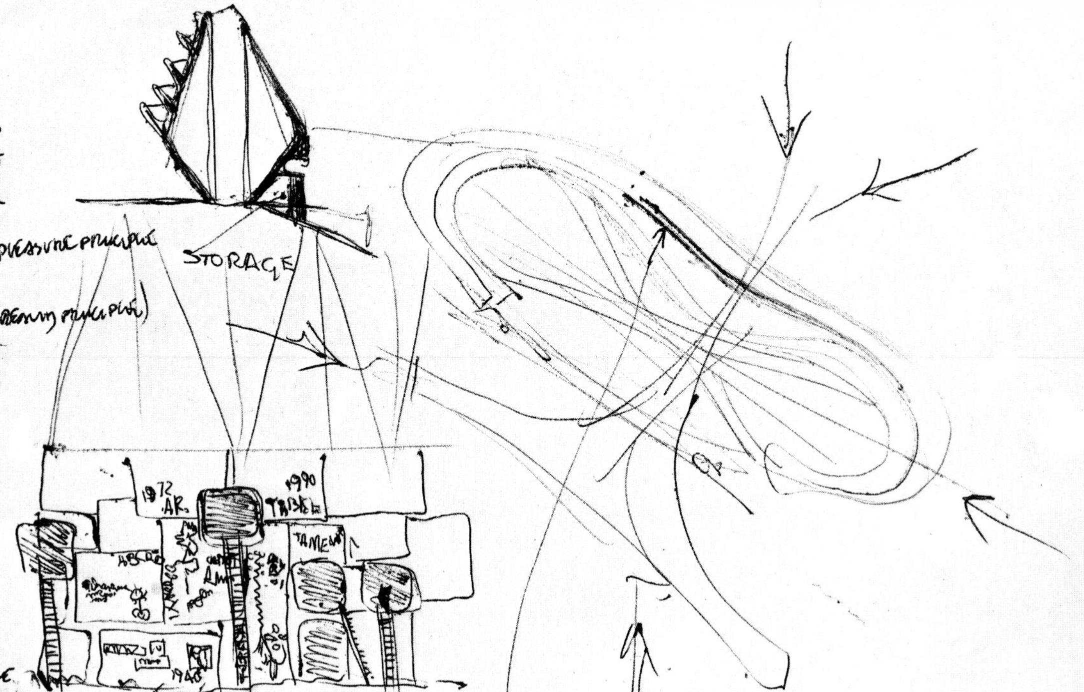

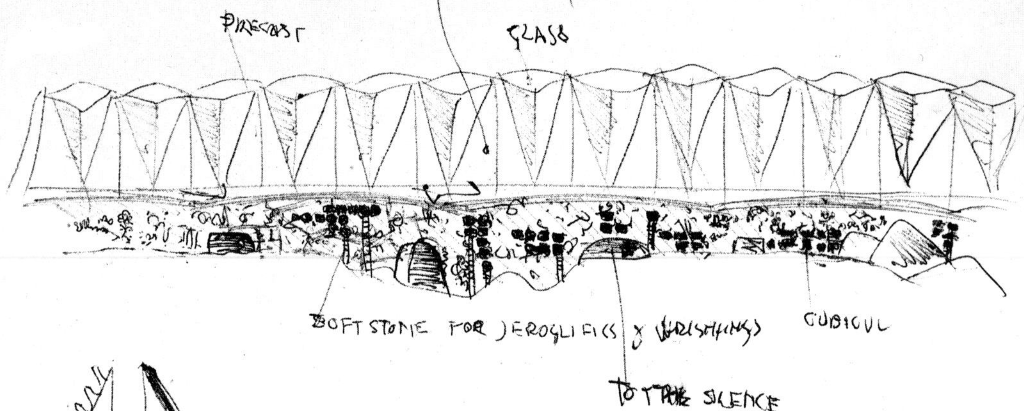

DOZENS OF SQUARE MILES, TO THE INTERNATIONAL ORGANISATION. WOULD ESTABLISH IN THE HEARTH OF THE LAND A POWERFUL FERMENT FOR DEVELOPPEMENT OF RESURCHES & AN UNVALUABLE TRESAURE THAT THE WOLE POPULATION OF THE WORLD WOULD MAKE A POINT TO ACQUAINT WHIT & VISIT.

THE STARTING POINT WOULD BE A RESERCHE PLANT FOR FISIC, BIOCHEMISTRY TO WHICH ALL NATION WOULD BE INTERESTED IN GIVING SUBSTANTIAL CONTRIBUTION OF FUND, MATERIALS, MACHINERIES & ESTABLISHED A SOLID ECONOMICAL FUNDATION THE NEW & FONDAMENTAL FIELD WOULD BE THE QUEST OF AN ENVIRONNEMENT IN ARMONY WHIT MAN OF WHICH THE CITY WOULD BE THE MOST COMPLEX EXPRESSION

& SUCH INTERNATIONAL INTERVENTION WOULD MAKE THE PLANT THE BEST ENDOWED FOR THE MOST EXPENSIVE RESERCHE IN PURE SCIENCE

ONCE THE LAND IS GIVEN THE GIURISDICTION OF IT AND EVERYTHING ON IT GOES TO THE INTERNATIONAL COURT OR INTERNATIONAL AUTORITY DESIGNATE

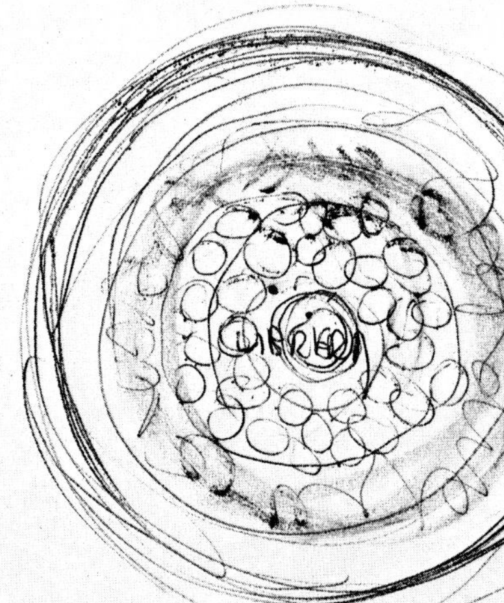

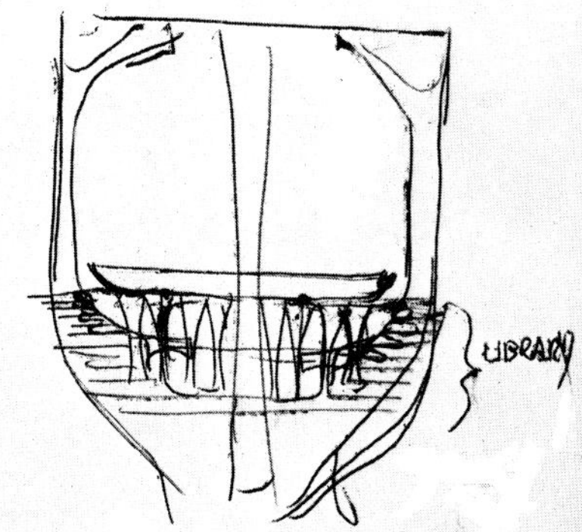

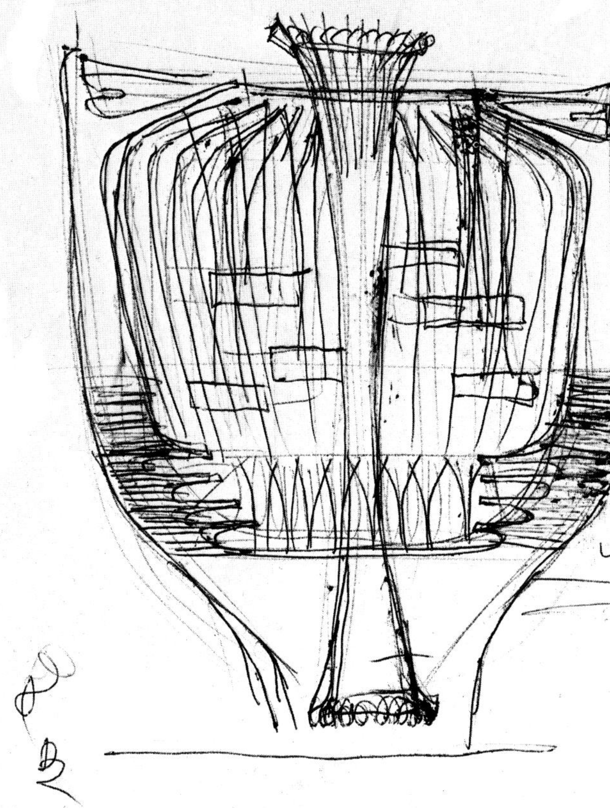

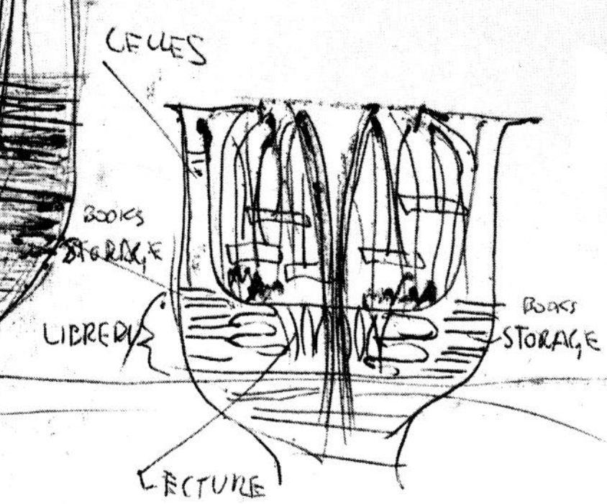

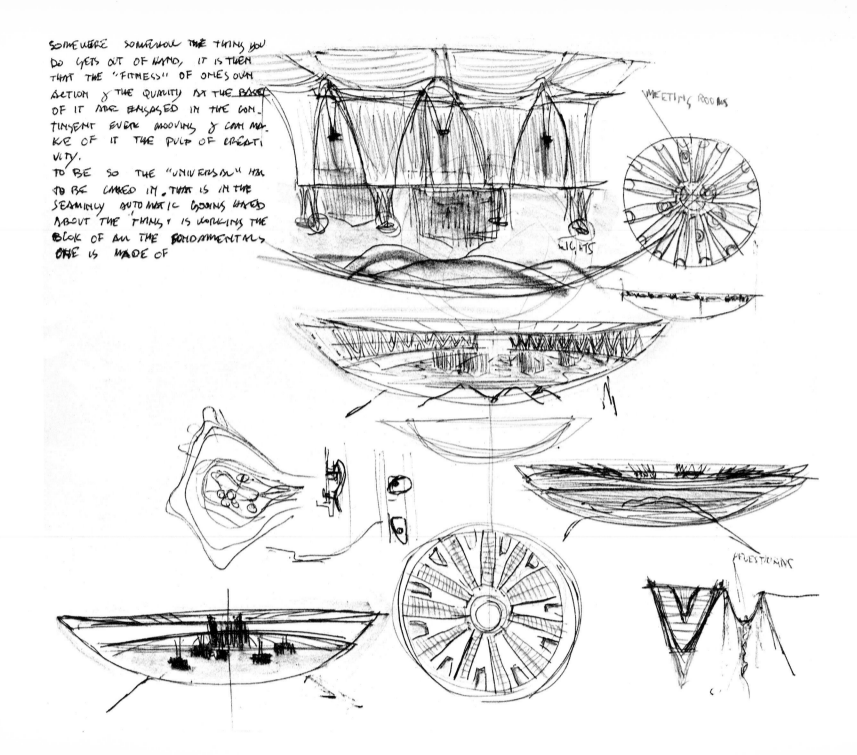

SOMEWERE SOMEHOW THE THING YOU DO GETS OUT OF HAND, IT IS THEN THAT THE "FITNESS" OF ONES OWN ACTION & THE QUALITY AT THE BASE OF IT ARE ENGAGED IN THE CONTINGENT EVER MOOVING & CAN MAKE OF IT THE PULP OF CREATIVITY.

TO BE SO THE "UNIVERSAL" HAS TO BE CALLED IN. THAT IS IN THE SEAMINGLY AUTOMATIC GOINGS WAYED ABOUT THE 'THING' IS WORKING THE BLOK OF ALL THE FONDAMENTALS ONE IS MADE OF

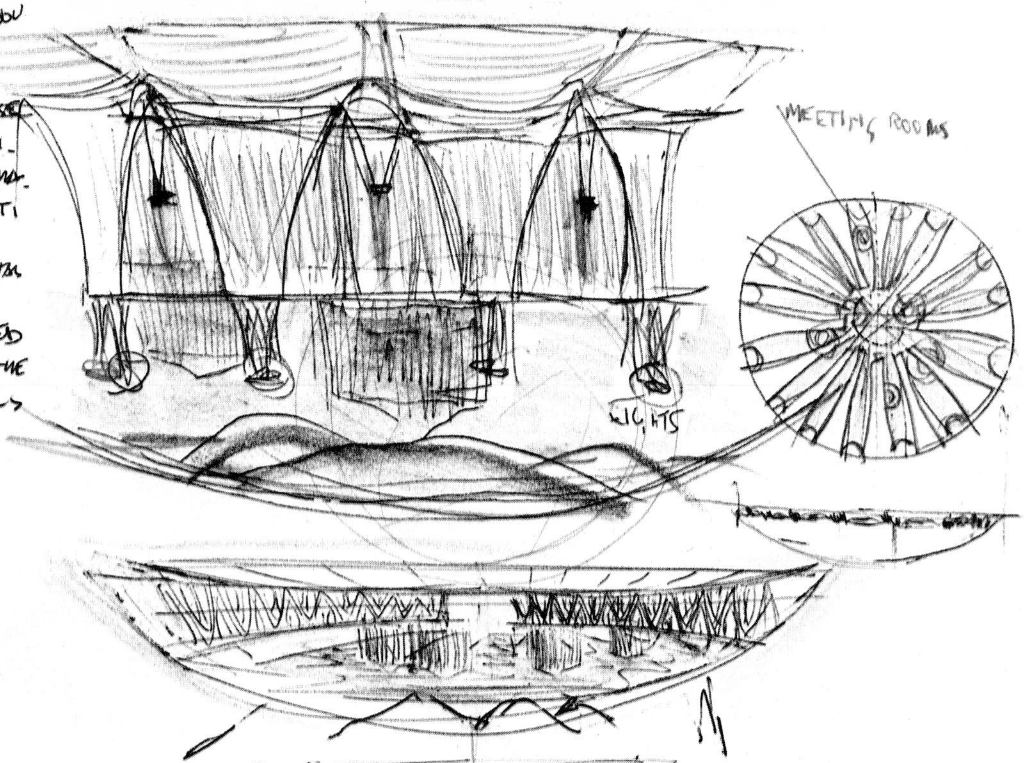

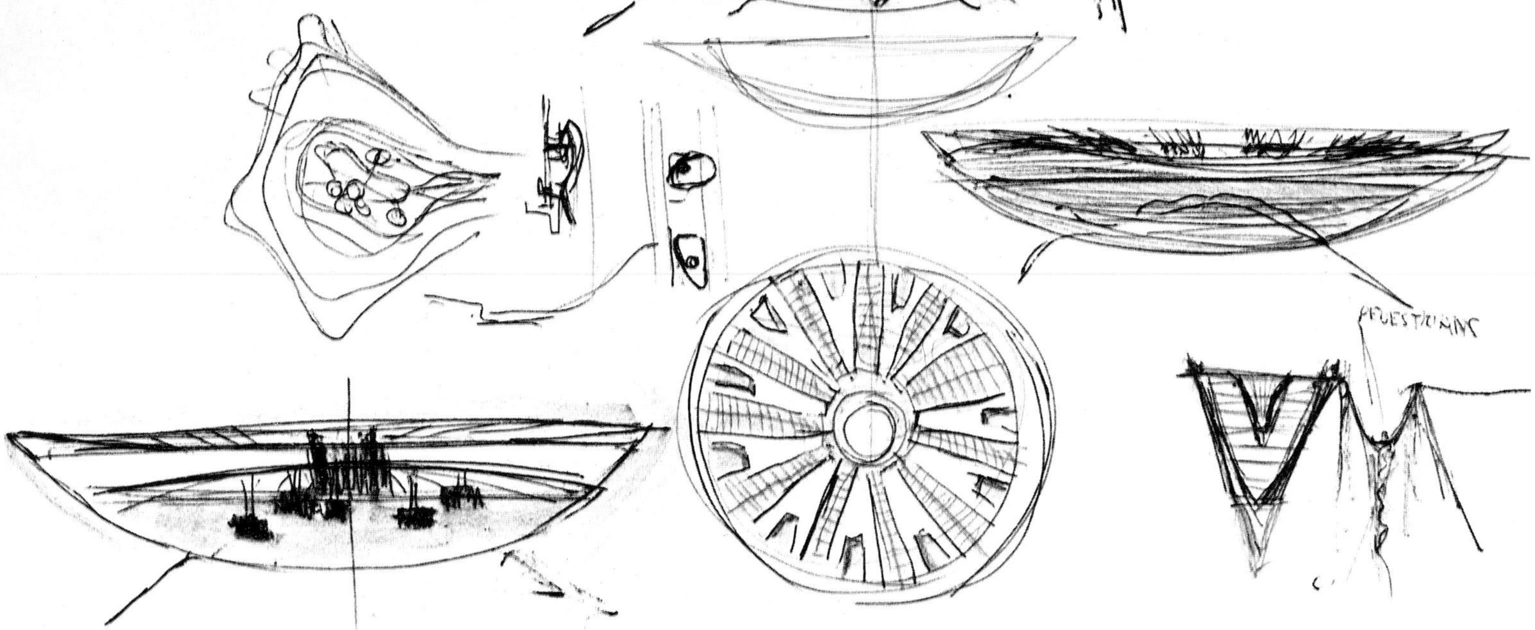

MAY 60

ASSUMING THE COMPETITIVE TIPE IS THE
EXELENCE IN ORGANISATION -PRODUCTION-
DISTRIBUTION & CONSEQUENTELY WELLCOMI-
NG THE FREE ENTREPRISE SISTEM,
WHITING SUCH BONDUARIES, ONE MUST ADD
THAT ONLY IN THE NON COMPETITIVE
TIPE CAN BE FOUND THE MOST SUB-
STANTIAL VALUES OF MAN; LOVE,
COMPASSION WISDOM CREATIVITY....
THUS BY BLANKETING ALL OF HUMAN EN-
DEAVOR BY THE "EFFICENCY" OF
FREE ENTREPRISE ONE GETS WHIT
THE SPURIOUS ABBONDANCE OF "GOODS"
& WASTES THE UNAVOIDABLE HOLDINGS OF
POWER-GUIDANCE BY THE COMPETITIVE
WHO, BY INNATE ARROGANCE & LAKE
OF THAT CORE OF UMILITY WHICH IS
THE HOPE OF MAN, WILL, AS SURE AS
THE SUN, MISGUIDE SOCIETY INTO THE
REALM OF INNER SQUALOR THAT NO
BULK OF GADGETRY & "PLENTIFULNESS"
WILL SUCCEDE TO HIDE, BE INSIDE OR
ENVIRONMENTALLY

THE EFFICENCY IN MAKING & KEEPING THINGS
MOVING IS NOT THE MASTERY IN CHAN-
NELING EMOTIONS, FEELINGS, INTELLECTION
WHITHIN THE MAIN STREAM OF BECOMING
IT IS DEFENETELY A DISTRACTION OF SUCH
CATEGORIES INTO THE STREAM OF PRODUCT-
IVITY - CONSUMPTION OR SHOULD ONE SAY
INTO THE QUIET LAGOON OF CONTENTE,
MANY-COMFORT. WHIT ~~WASTE~~ THE HEPS
OF WASTE AS DIKES, ISLAND & MOOLS

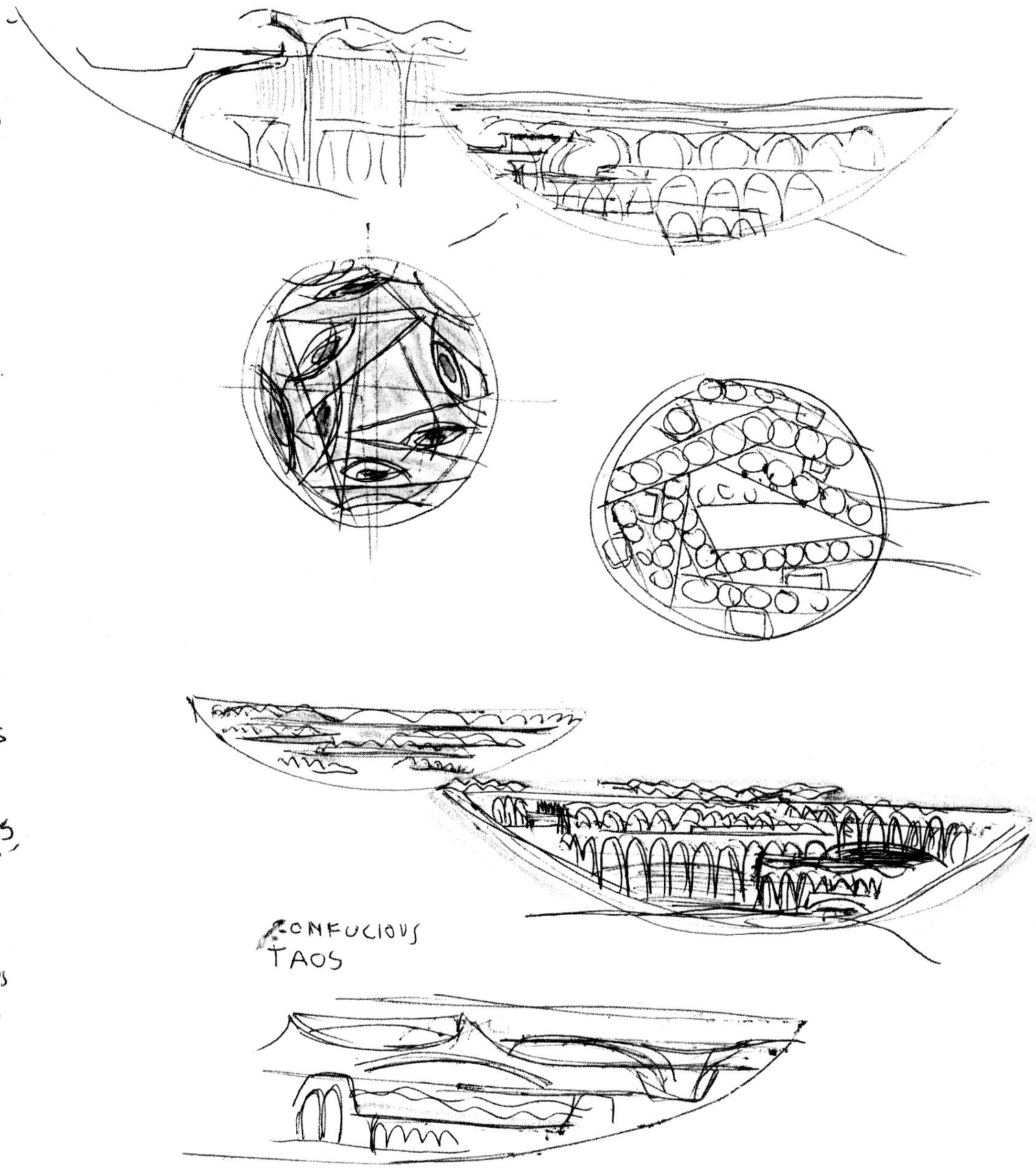

THE GASOLINE STATION RECLIMBOLIZES & EPITOMIZES MAN'S PRIMITIVITY, THE CRUDE WAY OF MOVING HIMSELF ON A DOWARD CASE OF IRON, THE CRUDE WAY OF FEEDING THE LITTLE MONSTER BY THE RUBBERY UMBILICAL REACHING IN THE UNDERGROUND BUBBLE, THE THOUSAND & ONE TOOLS-TOYS, SYRINGES & PUMPS GELLIES & EMULSIONS PATCHES & SCREWS, RUBBER BANDS & STRINGS, SEEKING & "CURING" THE SMALL & NOT SO SMALL AFFLICTIONS CAUGHTS, RATTLES, DRAGS, PUFFINGS, JOLTINGS.... CONTENDING FOR A SPOT LIKE THE CONTRAPTION TO THE HEAPS OF WASTE ALIGNED ALONG SIDE THE BOULEVARDS OF SELF DECEPTION, WAITING CIRCLE REACH CITY DRAGS AS SO PERSONAL & SO GENERIC COMA.

HOW CAN THE GASOLINE STATION BE MADE INTO "WORK OF ART", CRAVED FOR BY THE FUNCTIONALIST? THE GASOLINE STATION WHICH LIFE WILL NOT SPAN A GENERATION, THAT WILL BE CONCEIVED BORN, BURIED & FORGOTTEN WITHIN A MAN'S LIFE SPAN?

MONUMENTS ARE BUILT TO ETERNATE THAT WHICH IS "ETERNAL" (THIS THE TAUTOLOGY OF THEM) MONUMENTS TO THE EFFEMERAL - INADEQUATE ARE THE MONUMENTS TO SELF DECEPTION, STUPID LITTLE SPIT OF ARROGANCE TO THE ETERNAL PAVEMENT THE HONEST-SONES ON THE MURKY SLABS OF TECNOCRACY

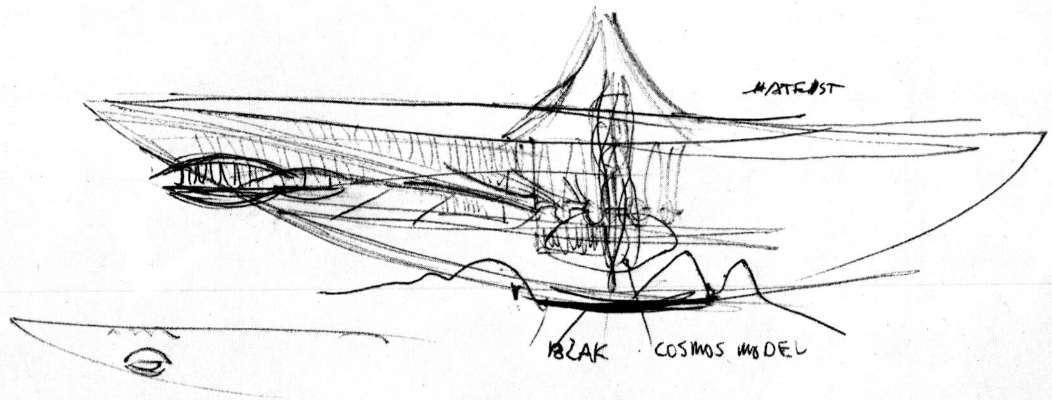

TO THE STUDENTS

1 ONE ANSWER IS IN THE QUESTION; THE FALLACY OF CLEAR CUT DEFINITIONS.

2 PROBLEM AS | A GENERAL POSITION OF MAN.
AS A PARTICULAR POSITION OF THE "ARCHITECT.

3 PROBLEM AS; THE "SHELTERING" OF MAN THE ANIMAL & ITS ACTIVITIES
AS THE SHELTERING OF MAN & ITS ACTIVITIES

4 CONVERGING WITH NATURE
DIVERGING FROM NATURE

5 WHAT, WERE, WHEN, HOW, OF "REALITY"

6 THE "ARCHITECTURE" FOR "THIS SOCIETY OR THE ARCHITECTURE OF MAN?

7 THE CREATING, THE COMPOSING, THE ARRANGING

8 BECAME A MAN ARCHITECTURE MIGHT FOLLOW. FORFAIT MANLINESS & WITH EVERYTHING ELSE YOU FORFAIT ARCHITECTURE

9 INDIGNATION AS LIVING AGAINST INDIGNATION AS WORDING

10 THE CONTENTEMENT OF ANIMALITY WHICH IN MAN IS THE CONTENTEMENT OF AUTOMATISM.

11 ONLY WAY TO FOSTER LIFE: MATCHING NATURE'S SPLENDOR WITH MAN'S SPLENDOR: ENVIRONMENTAL SQUALOR IS MAN'S SQUALOR.

12 WHAT YOU DO BELIVE IN SPIRIT, FLESH & BLOOD THAT IS WHAT YOU WILL MAKE THINGS OF, ~~PAPER MONEY~~ MINT CURRENCY WON'T BUY

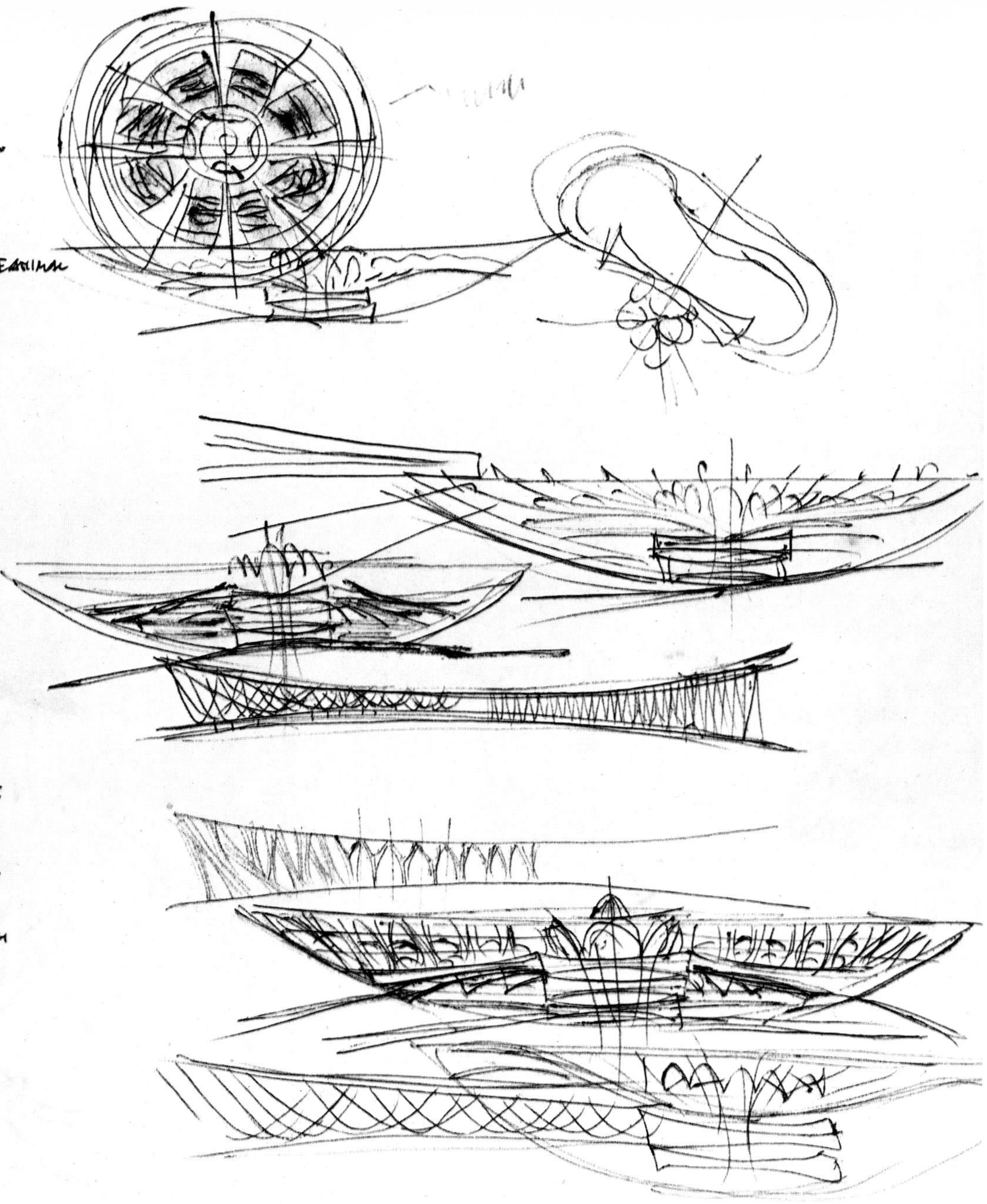

IF THOSE POWER GROUP ARE NOT EVIL BUT COMPROMISES WHIT THE ENVIRONMENTAL STATUS IN VIEW OF A GENERAL UPLIFT. THE RELASE OF SUCH POWER AS A YEARLY BUDGET OF 50 BILLIONS & THE EVEN MORE POWERFUL HAND OF KINDNESS SUCH RELEASE IS CONDITION OF, WOULD IN MANY WAYS MEET THE CHALLENGE OF COSMOS TO MAN ON A LEVEL PERCEPTABLE TO SUCH POWER GROUPS & TO THEM ACCEPTABLE COOPERATION WOULD BECAME INEVITABLE, THE ICE OF MISTRUST WOULD MELT AWAY TO THE FLAME OF OPENESS & VULNERABILITY. THE WAR BUDGETS OF ALL NATIONS WOULD IMPLEMENT THE MIRACLE OF POVERTY CONQUERED. THEN MAN COULD DIRECT HIMSELF AT THE TASKS OF MAKING LIFE MEANINGFULL NOT JUST AS A RESISTENCE TO THE GODS OF EVIL BUT AS A MAKER OF THE GODS OF LOVE & BEAUTY.

IT IS VERY POSSIBLE THAT TO ENVISION THE CONSTRUCTIVE FORCE OF SUCH UNILATERAL INITIATIVE MY TAKE TIME & DOINGS, WHIT BOTH TIME & DOINGS GIVEN ESSENTIALLY TO THE EDIFICATION OF A CONSTRUCTIVE MODE OF THINKING TODAY DWINDLED TO NEXT TO NOTHING.

THE BOLD VISION & BOLD PLANS ADVOCATED BY AMERICAN LEADERS ARE VISIONS & PLANS CONFINED WITHINS THE BONDUARIES OF SELF DECEPTION. ! DECEPTIVE THE ~~IDEA~~ ASSUMPTION THAT THE FOUNDING FATHERS SAT THE LAWS OF THE UNIVERSE. DECEPTIVE THE

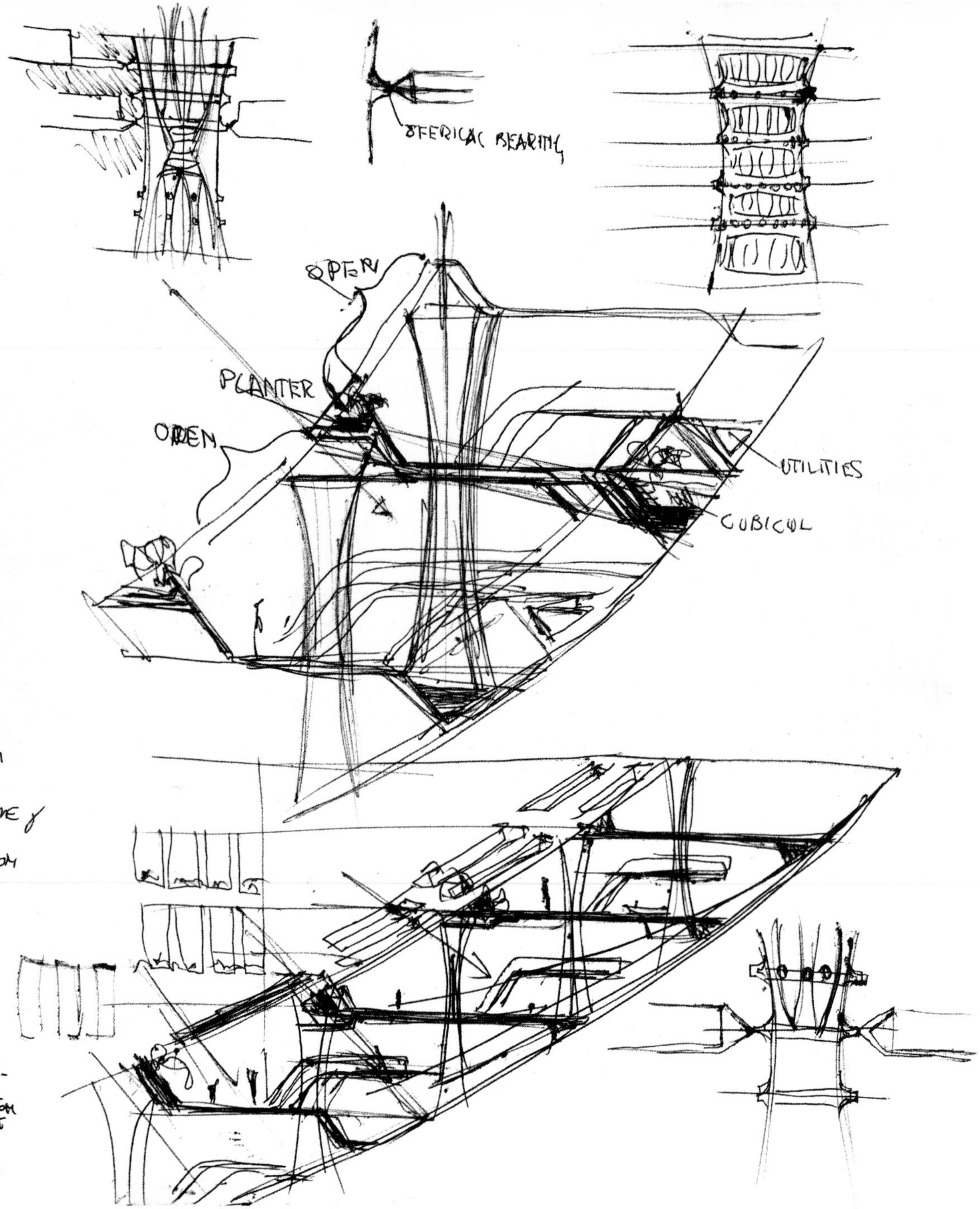

OF HISTORY & LIFE. ITS OWN ECONOMY OF PLENTY DENOUNCES WHERE THE HART OF USA IS ~~RAT~~ LAND.
DAY MUST CAME WHEN EVEN THE MOST OPPORTUNISTIC OF POLITITIAN WILL HAVE TO DENOUNCE THE STERILITY OF THE "CONSUMPTION" ECONOMY.
WHO WOULD NOT CONSIDER NUTS THE LONELY ISLANDER DESTROING DAY IN DAY OUT ITS OWN HUT · SO THAT HE COULD HAVE A REASON TO BUILD AN OTHE & ANOTHER DAY BY DAY. ~~SHOULD~~ HE POSE, LOOK INTO HIS MA-DNESS FIND MEANING & BECAME A MAKER OF TIME INSTEAD OF A ~~MAKER~~ KILLER OF TIME? THIS IS NOT THE PERFECTIONISM OF THE CRAFTMAN SE-EKING THE ~~ABSOLUTE~~ ARMONIOUS, NOR THE IRRATIONALITY OF THE ARTIST SEEKING THE ABSOLUTE THIS IS THE MONOTONOUS & HOPLESS BUZZING OF A FLY AGAINST THE WINDOW PANE. DEMANDING THE ~~IMPOSSIBLE~~ UNRACHABLE SKY LIGHTED BY THE PROMISES OF A UNKNOWN STAR.

THE POWER & "PRODUCTIVITY" OF THE MACHINE IS NOT ENNOBLING MAN · IT IS SIMPLY REMOVING BLOKS & OBSTRUCTION ON THE WAY HE HAS CHOSEN TO TAKE, IF THE ROAD IS TO WISDOM THE MULTIPLYING OBSTACLES WILL PREVENT MAN FROM GETTING · NAIVE HAPPY & COMFORT DUMB.

IF THE ROAD IS TO "DAMNATION" IE INVOLUTION, THE MACHINE WILL BULDOZE HIM, STRAIT INTO THE SWAMPS OF SLOTH. AMORFOUSNESS, WAIT THE DIRECTNESS OF AN ENTROPY FORMULA

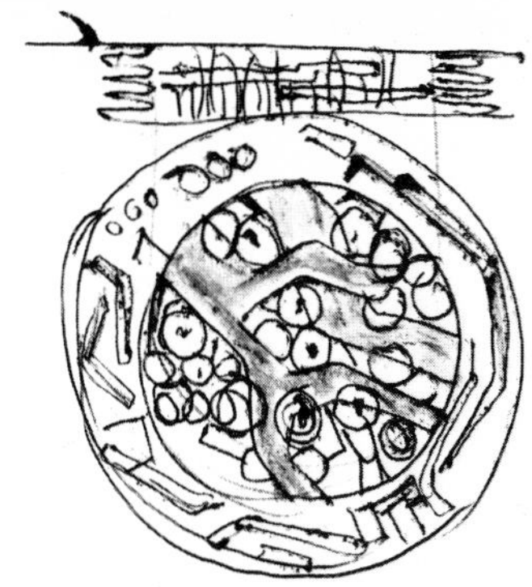

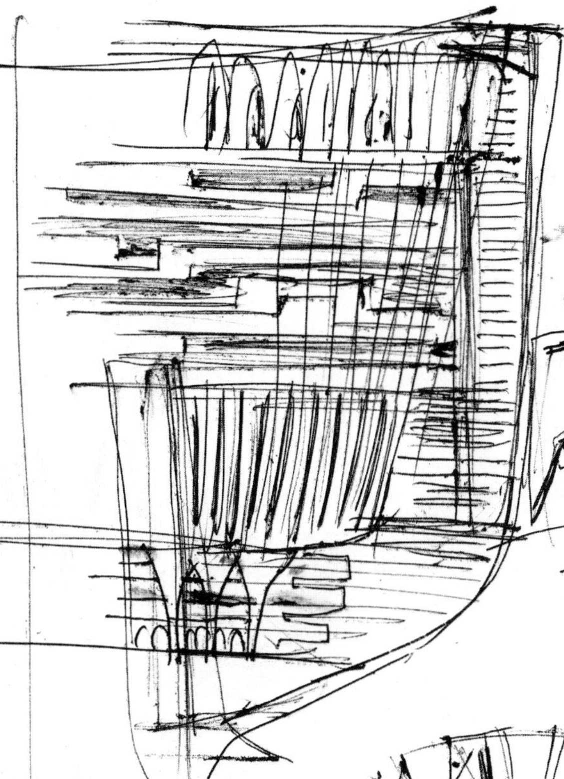

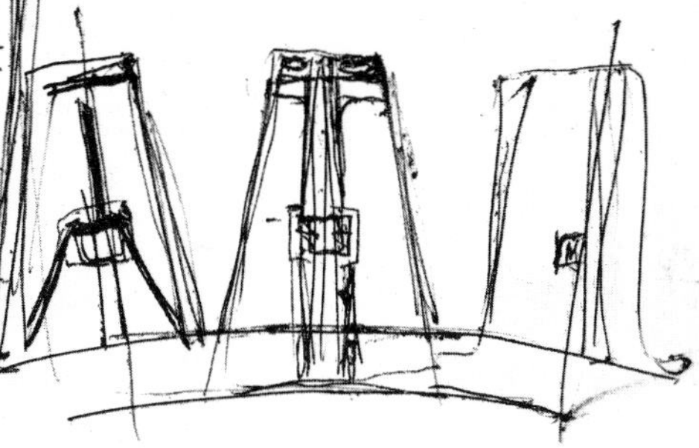

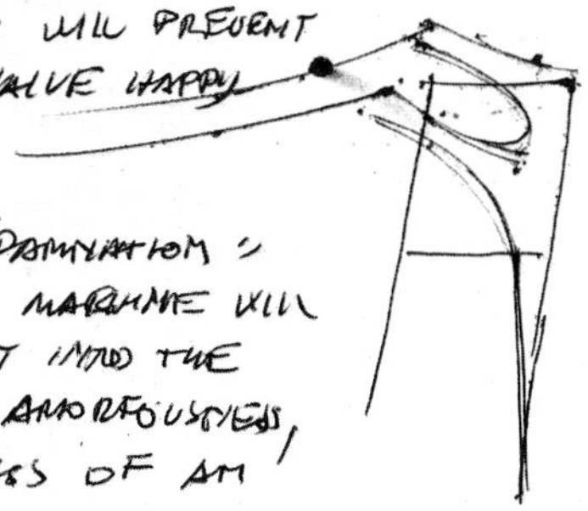

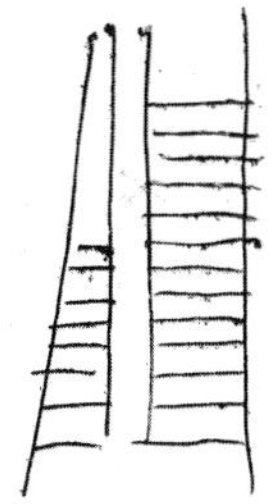

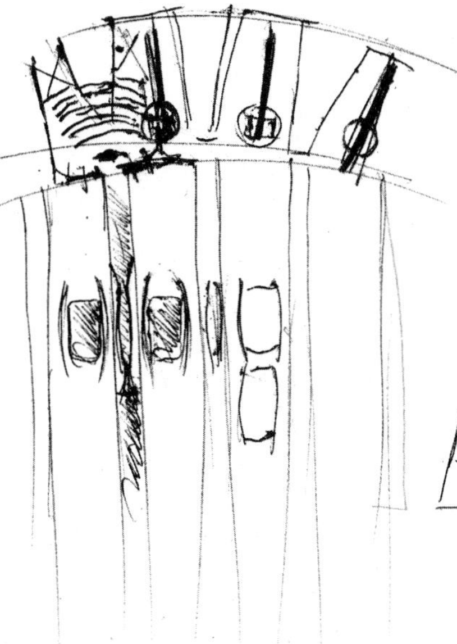

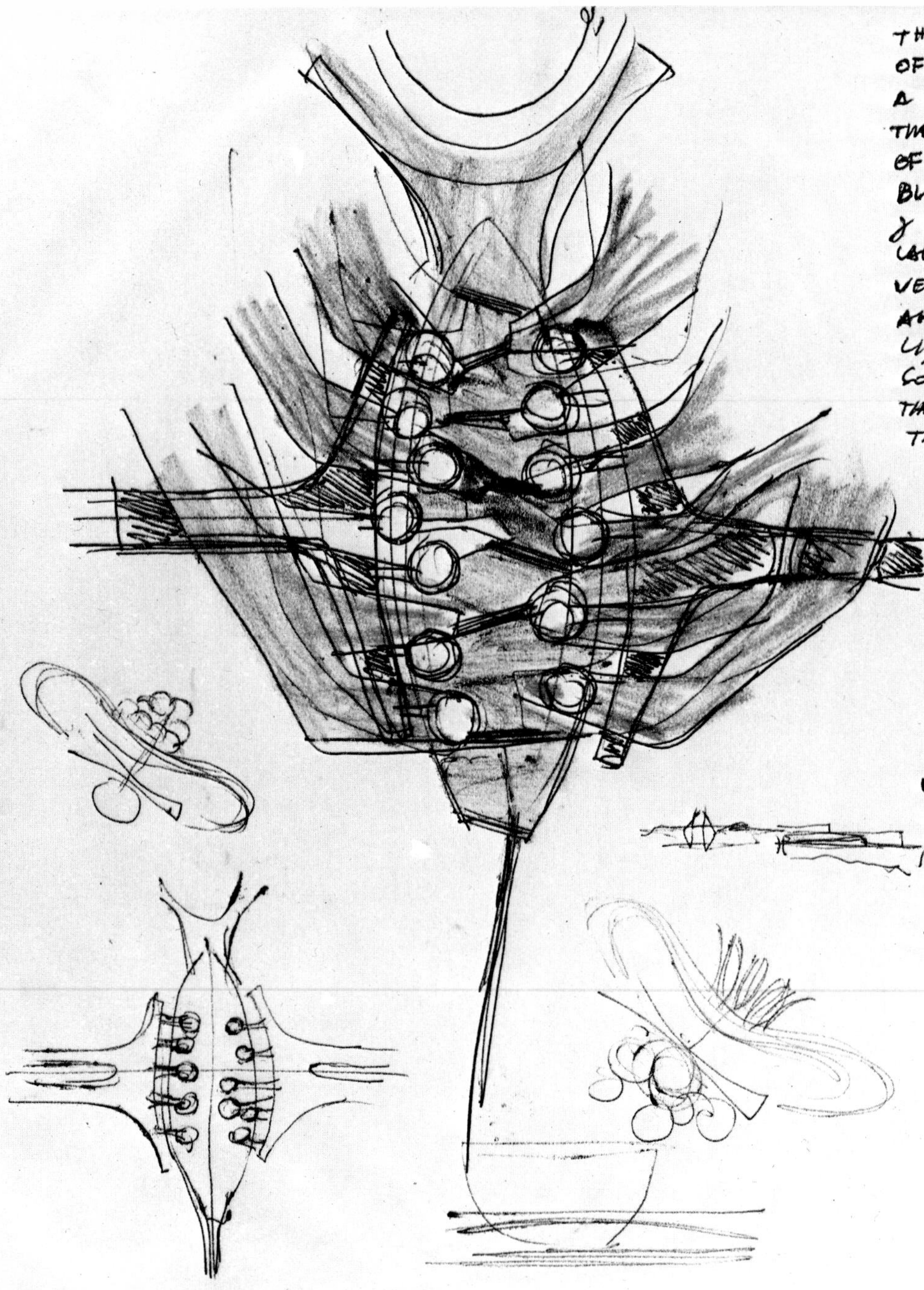

THEM TOGHETHER KNIT THE IMPRINT
OF A MIND'S POWER THE SCARS OF
A HAUNTED SOUL.
THE MULTIPLYING OF SUCH LITTLE PILE
OF UNTIDE WASHES MAKES FOR THE
BLITED LANSCAPE OF CIVILISATION.
& THE SOUNDS OF UGLY
LAUGHTER THERE FROM.
VENERABLE HE WHO CAN CARRY
ALONG WITH HIM ALL OF MATERIA
LITY HE IS MAKING USE OF & IN
SO DOOING CAN YET MAKE VISIBLE
THE HIDDEN LOVE HE BEARS FOR
THINGS.

APRIL 61

WHEN THE DOOING IS INADEQUATE IS
WHEN THE DOOING IS REALLY ONLY
THE WHISHING
I MEANT WELL IS! THE WHISH WAS
SUCH THAT IF .....
THE IF IS THE SIMBOL OF WATH
SEPARATES REALITY FROM THE AMOUNT
OF GRASP THE SELF CAN HAVE
OF SUCH REALITY
BETRAYED IS THE DOOING IN THE
SINOPSIS OF THE PARTIAL INVESTITURE,
ONE'S FEW PENNIES, POOR PURCHASING POWER! ONES LOVE
TO BREAK A BOMB... ONE'S TRUST
TO ERRATIC, ONE'S EYES TOO DRIEN

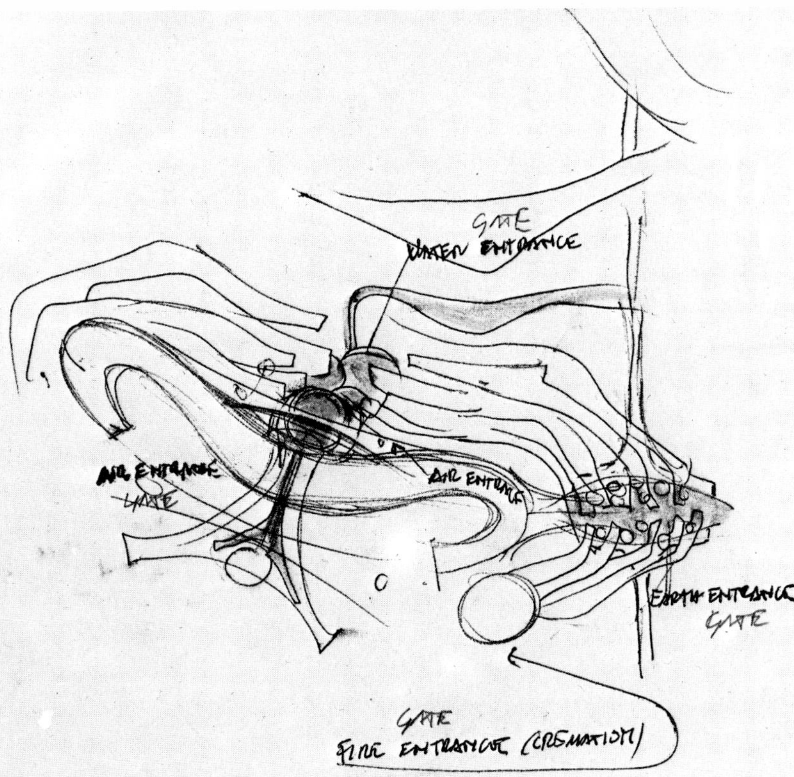

APRIL 61 P.V.

IT IS DIFFICULT TO SEE WHY & HOW SHEER SIZE CAN BE NEGATIVE TOWARD MAN (AS IT CAN BE POSITIVE) IF WE PUT MAN IN AN IDEAL WORLD.
YET, GIVEN THE PHISICAL DIMENTIONS OF THINGS & THE RELATIVE INTERPLAY OF LIFE & MATERIALITY, IT BECOMES UTOPIAN THE INTENTION OF GIVING TO EACH MAN OR FAMILY A PARCEL OF NATURE WHERE TO GROW ON. EVEN IN THE WRONG IPOTESIS THAT THE EXTENTION OF THE EARTH WOULD ALLOW FOR IT & STILL GIVE ENOUGH LAND FOR FARMING ETC... THIS PARCELING OF THE LAND IN SMALL MOSAIC STONES WOULD EXACTLY GO AGAINST THE REASON FOR SO DOING.

ONCE ALL THE SERVICES, THE ACCESSES, THE FACILITIES ARE BROUGHT TO EACH OF ALL THE LITTLE STONES VERY LITTLE IS LEFT IN NATURE, IN WEALTH IN POTENTIALITY, IN BEAUTY, IN INTEGRITY, TO WORK WITH. ONE HAS ONLY TO THINK OF THE FISICAL BULK OF NEEDS EACH INDIVIDUUM IS IN WANT, PLUS ALL THE FANCIFUL FISICAL PREFERENCES THE SAME INDIVIDUAL CLIMES AT AS SOON AS THE POSSESSION FEVER TAKES HOLD OF HIM, & SUDDENLY IS CLEAR WHERE UTOPIA REST.

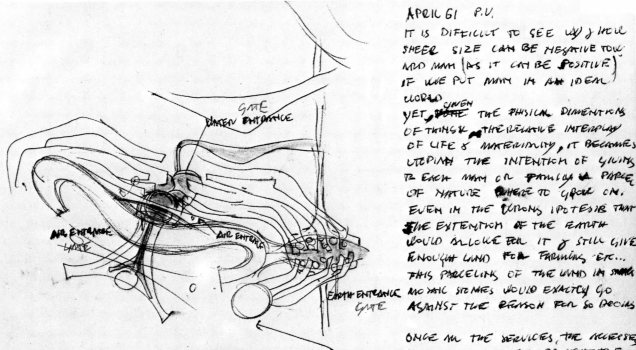

LIKE TRYING TO CONCEIVE A BIOLOGICAL ORGANISM SPREADED OUT BIDIMENTIONALLY INSTEAD OF CLUSTERED TRIDIMENTIONALLY.
THE SPREAD OUT EQUIVALENT OF THE PHISICAL MAN WOULD PROBABLY COVER MANY SQUARE MILES OF SPACE. IT GOES WITHOUT SAYING

Villages

1970
Life is a cooperative undertaking. How much of this must there be, and where is it that the individual punctures the collective bag and goes out on his own? And can he?

He definitely can, at a price. It is a price with two conditions. One is what he as a person gives up. The other is what society, and his family, has to pay so as to afford him this privilege. To define those conditions is naturally difficult, but it is evident that the degree of parasitism permissible to each individual has a limit. The parasitic threshold is that beyond which what is good for one person is coercive for another. It is also true that the individual is always dependent on the society that sustains him and owes that society something in exchange.

To a degree we cannot ask that the buying power of money include the right to be served, even when that same money comes from services rendered to others. This tends to become a discourse among the clever by which wealth drifts toward a limited stratum of the social landscape, the same landscape that is composed of and sustained by the less clever and the less fortunate, though not necessarily the less motivated. When money ceases to be a simple currency and becomes a source and symbol of unquestionable power, then the wealthy become parasitic even though their philanthropy may be flamboyant. Consider the flamboyancy, the recklessness, of the man who assumes that the subjection of nature is a once-for-all thing, not a battle won but a war triumphantly concluded. This nonsensical assumption adds steel and fire to the crushing nature absentmindedly inflicts on man. We are still and will probably always be in an armed camp where life struggles to keep out of the gates the encroachment of naught. Internicine battles among living specks is pathetic and fraudulent.

The village has no culture, inasmuch as the exercise of systematic speculations in the field of science, philosphy, aesthetics, or religion is not in its institutions. The process of abstraction and universalization does not seem to thrive in the villages of man, as if the limited topography were sterile ground for theoretical thinking. The village is the realm of crafts where pragmatism surrounds all undertakings. The village is also important as that place where human society can produce the kind of individual who fosters continuity-constancy-predictability-conservation-preservation-artisan sensitivity-earthliness-gentleness-ecological wisdom. In this sense the village is the reservoir from which the city has to find its regenerating and cleansing energies, which the city consumes at a somewhat inhuman pace in its pursuit of the unknown and the new. The city is complemented by the villages, for without them its energies would dry up. At the same time the village, deprived of light and direction from the city, would tend to be a dim flame glowing in the deterministic darkness of nature. What the village may not find as its own mental core, the logos, it might want to seek as a physical center; this explains the circularity of its structure and the enveloping feminine character of the pattern enclosing the town park.

1960
A conciliation of city and country life is attempted in the villages. The city supplies nearby services, job opportunities, and civic centers at the edge of the villages; the center for advanced study, the continuum, and the theological center are available to all. The country can be enjoyed in the farmland below each terrace, in the orchards, the vegetable gardens, the open markets, the workshops, the open environment.

An attempt is also made to realize many environmental conditions developing one into the other to open finally into the large unbroken continuity of the structure which encloses meadows, trees, and ponds, and envelops fields and orchards of the farmland. The origin of this unfolding is in each dwelling, and their continuity is functional, not necessarily social. Due to the scale, the curved structure gives each dwelling a rectilinear layout. At the same time it defines focal points, gives a general feeling of unity, of possible sociability, procures volumes and surfaces for a rich play of light and shadow, is unobtrusive, and carries an inner poise auspicious in an organism for dwelling and living.

The dwelling units develop on two levels: they look outward to the farmland or the park; inward to the annular conditioned garden. Thus, there are four primary environmental conditions:
1.
The conditioned garden running circularly within the structure of the village itself.
2.
The park in the center of the village.
3.
Outside farmland and close-by civic centers.
4.
Open space where the view is unlimited.

The dwelling units, averaging 20 x 10 x 6 meters, are a sheltered volume connected to the network of public facilities. Directly served by the underground parking-repairing-refueling stations, each "house" is a few minutes' driving distance from the places of work and shopping. Pedestrians reach civic centers and open markets by short walks.

GIUNE 1960 P.V.

WHILE AUTOMATISM IS THE ONLY FINAL GRAN-
TER FOR SURVIVAL OF TECNOCRACY. SO THAT
THE PLUMBER GOES TO WORK REGULARLY
NO MATTER WHAT THE CLERK RUBBER
STAMPS WASTE REGULARLY NO MATTER WHAT .....
IT'S THIS SAME AUTOMATISM WHICH GRANTS
THE DEGENERATION OF MAN.
AUTOMATION MY BE THE ANSWER.
IF IN THE HANDS OF WISDOM & IF MAN
WILL BY THEN HAVE FOUND WHAT WILL
TAKE THE PLACE OF MARCHETED LABOUR.

THE "LEISURE TIME" HANGS ON MAN AS
A MAGNIFICENT PUZZLE. WOULD THE
MULTITUDES GIVE VOLUNTERILY PART OF
THEIR LIFE TO THE CONSTRUCTION OF A
CULTURE OR WOULD THEY SIMPLY LEND
THEMSELVES TO THE SLOTH IDOLS?

IF THE MAIN PURPOSE OF WORK IS NOW
THE MAKING OF A LIVING THE DAY SUCH
LIVING WILL BE GIVEN BY AUTOMATION
TO 80-90% OF THE POPULATION WITHOUT
ANY DEMAND FROM THEM OUTSIDE THE
PLEDGE OF LOYALTY TO A CLUB IN PRE-
FERENCE TO ANOTHER THEN WHAT
WILL OCCUPY THE LIFE OF THOSE
INDIVIDUALS?

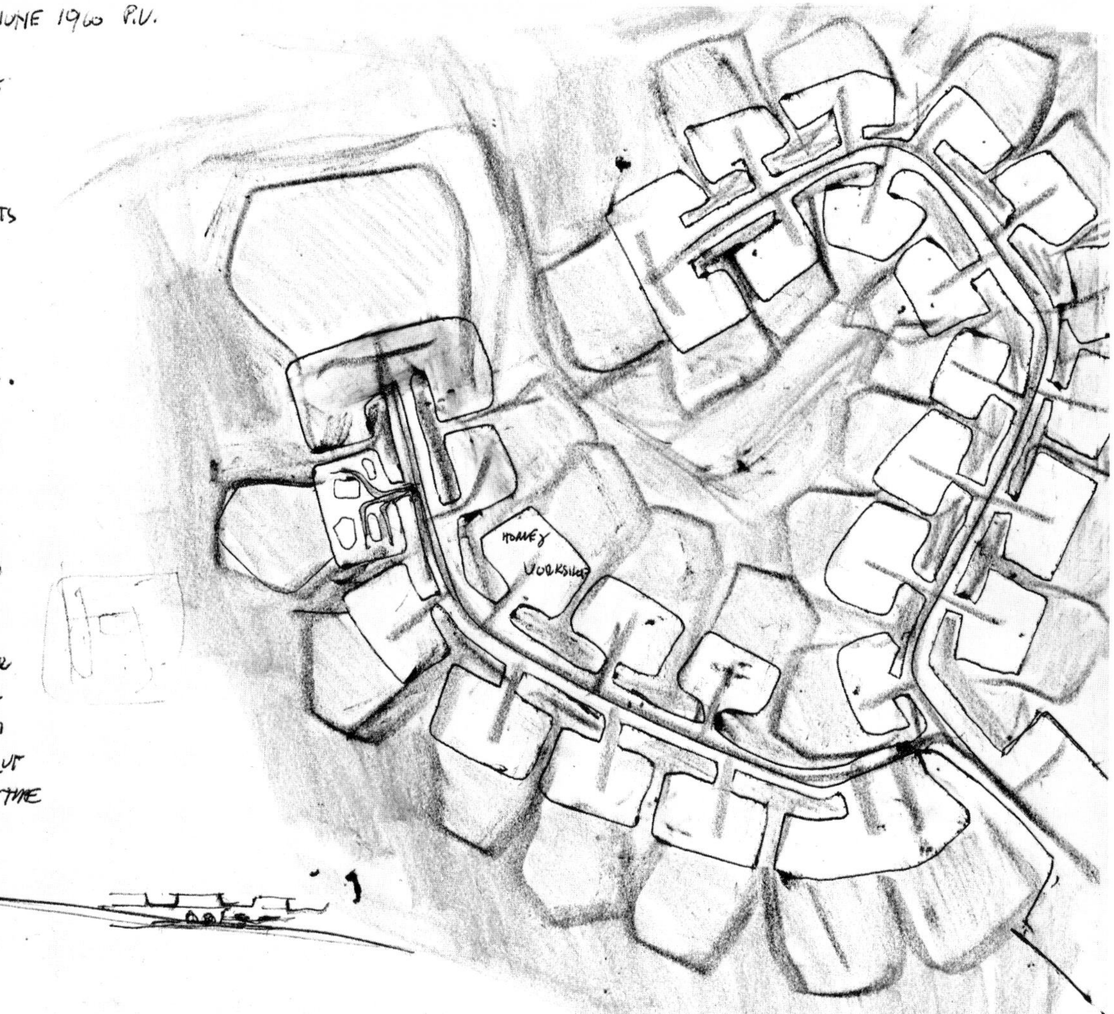

ONE THING SEEMS CERTAIN DEMOCRACY JULY 1960
MY WORK IN PRODUCTIVITY & MORALS, IT IS OF
NO MEANING IN THE FIELD OF CREA-
TIVITY ETHICS
ONE SIMPLE REASON IS THAT THE
BASE OF A MAJIORITY CONSIDERATION
IS THE UNDERSTANDING BY SUCH
MAJIORITY, IT IS CLEAR THAT
CREATIVELY ONLY A SMALL, AT TIME
INEXISTENT MINORITY IS CAPABLE
& WILLING TO UNDERSTAND & THUS
IMPLEMENT THE DEMOCRATIC CICLE,

U.S.A. HAS LEAPED & INDICATIONS
ARE AVAILABLE (OF WHERE THAT SHE HAS &) SHE HAS
LANDED
URRSR HAS LEAPED & IT IS IN THE
MIDDLE OF IT. WE SEE A DIRECTION & SOME INDICATION
START TO MATERIALIZE OF WHERE IT
MY LAND
CHINA IS JUST NOW LEAPING
ONE MY WONDER EVEN ON THE
DIRECTION OF THE JUMP. LEFT TO
CONJECTURE IS ALL THE REST.

LEAVING THE FUTURE TO THE SUESSERS
& COMPARING THE CONSUMED & SO DIFFERENT PATHS
OF THE LEAP AS THE PAST OF
U.S.A & THE QUASI PRESENT OF THE SO-
VIET & GIVING ATTENTION TO THE
CORE OF THE MATTER: WORTINESS OF
MAN, ONE MY FIND THAT VERY GREAT
DISPARITY IN THE SUFFERING & GLO-
RY OF THE TWO UMAN GROUP.
SAVAGERY IN ORGANIZED OR NOT SO
ORGANIZED TERMS IS THERE IN BOTH
PROCESSES, ONE SEEKING THE UNIBITED
POWER FOR THE "FREE" INDIVIDUUM.
THE OTHER SEEKING THE ORGANIZED
POWER OF THE SOCIAL MAN
ABSTRACTED FROM MAN ITSELF,

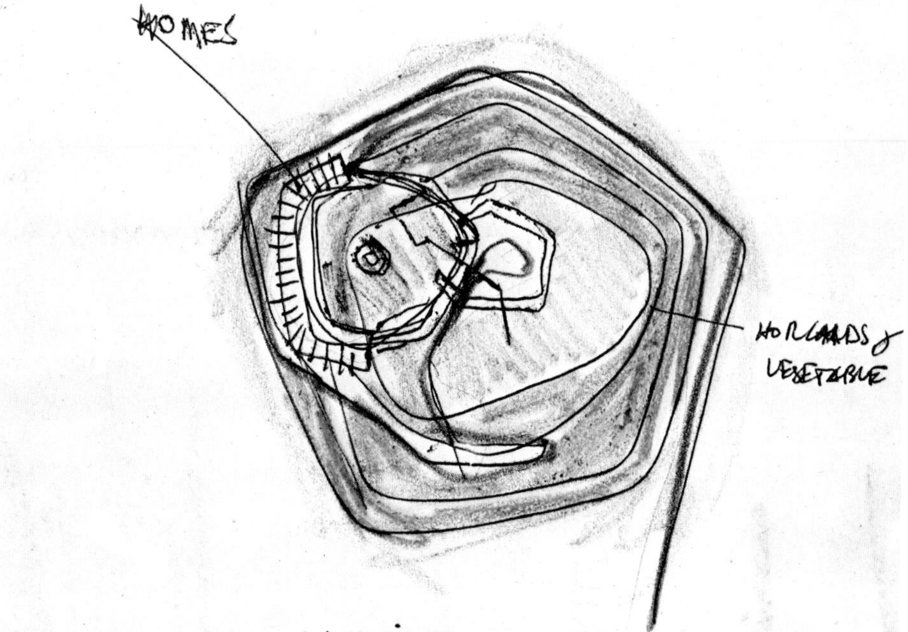

VILLAGE

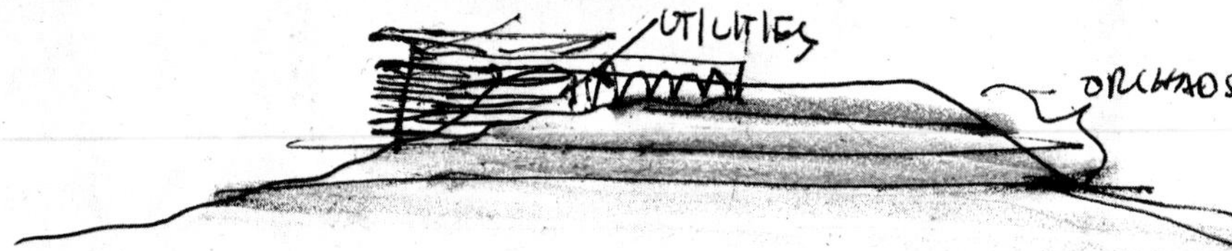

VILLAGE

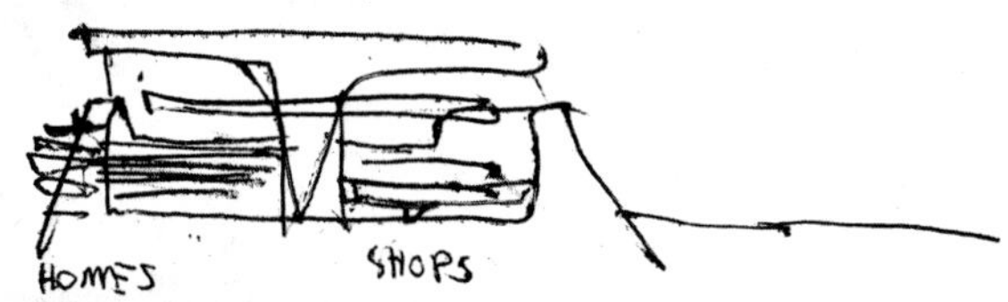

FREE WOOERS OF A SHALLOW LIFE,
WE ARE THE MAKER OF OUR SUPER
FILM ENVIRONMENT.
IN THIS ONE DIMENSIONAL "AIR" IS
QUITE IRRELEVANT THE DEGREE OF FA-
SHIONABILITY ONE IS WRAPPED IN.
WE WILL COME & GO QUIETLY QUIETLY
IGNORING LIFE, QUIETLY IGNORED BY IT

THE GRAY REASSURANCE OF THE EVE-
NING ALCOHOL, THE UNCONCERN FOR
THINGS OF SUBSTANCE, THE BLAND HATRED
CEALED UNDER FLAGS, THE PERPETUAL
PLANNING FOR AN EVER BETTER
WEEK END
THE GENERIC SHELVING OF
SOUL SEARCHING QUESTIONS
OF SUCH THINGS OR NON THINGS
ARE OUR HOUSES MADE,
OUR CIVIC (TRAFIC) CENTERS AND
OUR TOWNS. OUR "CONQUERED NATURE"

IT IS NOT THAT OUR PARADISE IS GLOBALLY
AN INSULT TO MAN BECAUSE IT IS
UNHEALTHY, BUT BECAUSE IT DOES
NOT SEEM TO BE WANTING TO MOVE
FROM THIS YET
NOWHERE TO SOMEWHERE

THIS WILL HAVE TO PASS
OUT OF COMPETITIVE COMPULSION
DRESSED UP IN RATIONALISTIC GARMENTS
BUT FROM THE REALIZATION THAT
AFFLUENCE NOTWITHSTANDING MAN IS A
CREATURE OF DEEDS ONLY IF HE
IS A CREATURE OF LOVE
OUR BUSY LIVES, OUR HAZED FUM-
BLING, WILL ALWAYS AMOUNT TO A FEW
UNCOLLECTED ASHES, UNLESS WE
WILL PASS ALONG TO YOUNGER LIVES
A. TENDER, HUMBLE, TREASURED, LITTLE
SOMETHING IMPERVIOUS TO WEALTH, CLUBS, CONGREGATIONS,

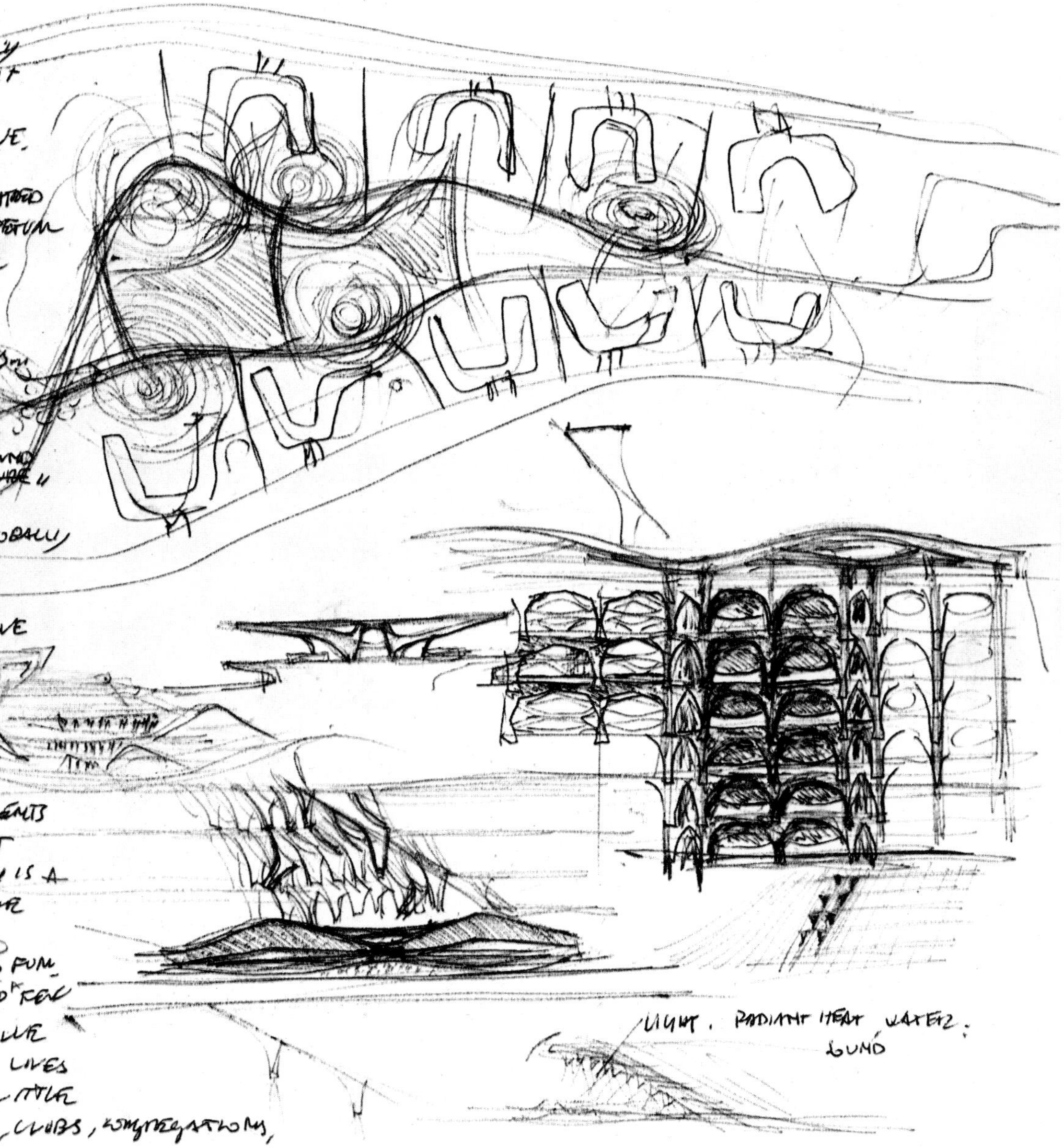

JULY 61

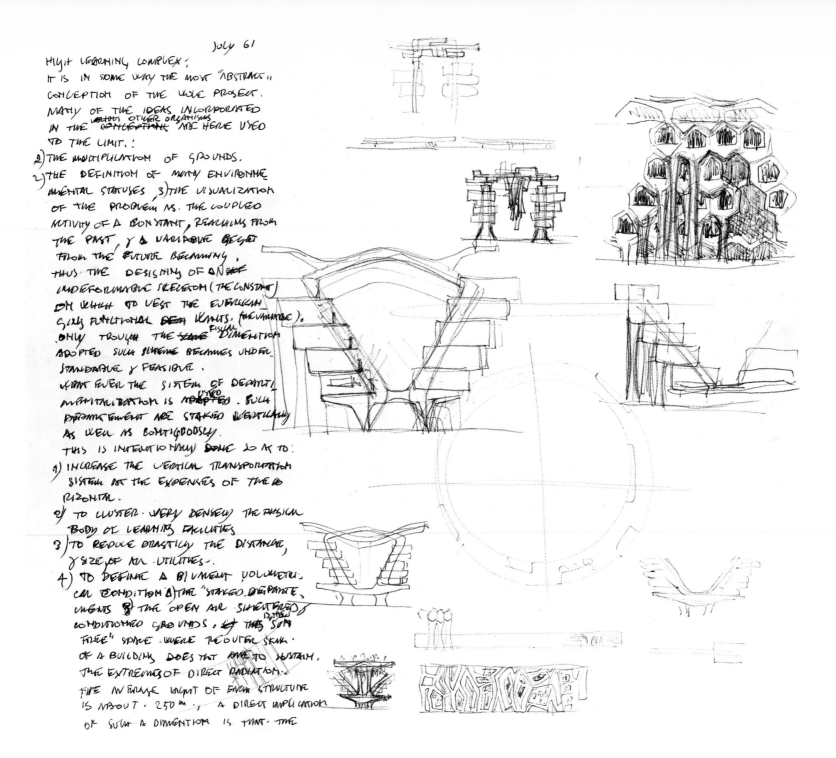

HIGH LEARNING COMPLEX:
IT IS IN SOME WAY THE MOST "ABSTRACT"
CONCEPTION OF THE WOLE PROJECT.
MANY OF THE IDEAS INCORPORATED
IN THE ~~various~~ ~~conception~~ OTHER ORGANISMS ARE HERE USED
TO THE LIMIT.:
1) THE MULTIPLICATION OF GROUNDS.
2) THE DEFINITION OF MANY ENVIRONMENTAL STATUSES, 3) THE VISUALIZATION
OF THE PROBLEM AS THE COUPLED
ACTIVITY OF A CONSTANT, REACHING FROM
THE PAST, & A VARIABLE, BEGET
FROM THE FUTURE BECOMING.
THUS THE DESIGNING OF AN
UNDEFORMABLE SKELETON (THE CONSTANT)
ON WHICH TO VEST THE EVERCHANGING FUNCTIONAL ~~DEA~~ UNITS. (THE VARIABLE).
ONLY TROUGH THE ~~SCALE~~ FISICAL DIMENTION
ADOPTED SUCH SCHEME BECAMES UNDERSTANDABLE & FEASIBLE.
WHAT EVER THE SISTEM OF DEPARTIMENTALIZATION IS ~~ADOPTED~~ USED. SUCH
DEPARTEMENT ARE STAKED VERTICALLY
AS WELL AS CONTIGUOUSLY.
THIS IS INTENTIONALLY DONE SO AS TO:
1) INCREASE THE VERTICAL TRANSPORTATION
SISTEM AT THE EXPENSES OF THE HORIZONTAL.
2) TO CLUSTER VERY DENSELY THE PHYSICAL
BODY OF LEARNING FACILITIES
3) TO REDUCE DRASTICLY THE DISTANCE,
& SIZE OF ALL UTILITIES.
4) TO DEFINE A BIVALENT VOLUMETRICAL CONDITION A) THE "STAKED DEPARTEMENTS B) THE OPEN AIR SHELTERED &
CONDITIONED GROUNDS, ~~&~~ ~~THE~~ IS THE "SUN
FREE" SPACE WHERE THE OUTER SKIN
OF A BUILDING DOES NOT ~~HAVE~~ TO SUSTAIN.
THE EXTREMES OF DIRECT RADIATION.
THE AVERAGE HIGHT OF EACH STRUCTURE
IS ABOUT 250 m., A DIRECT IMPLICATION
OF SUCH A DIMENTION IS THAT THE

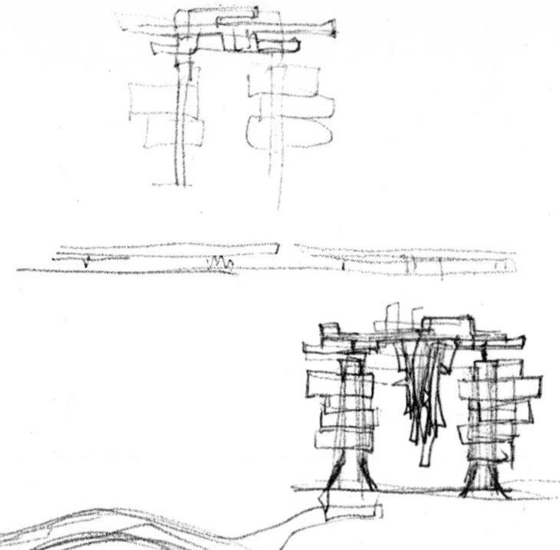

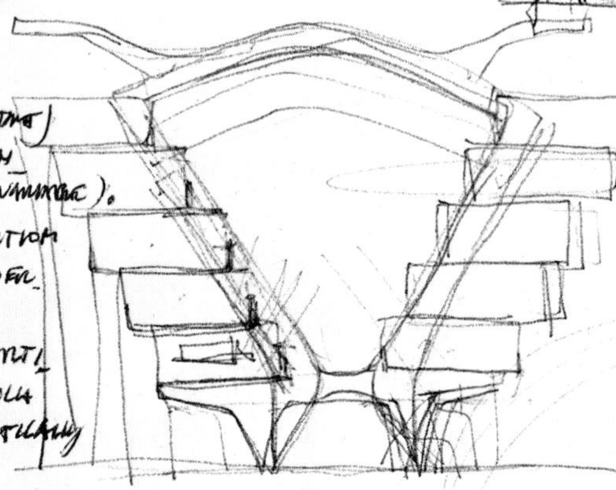
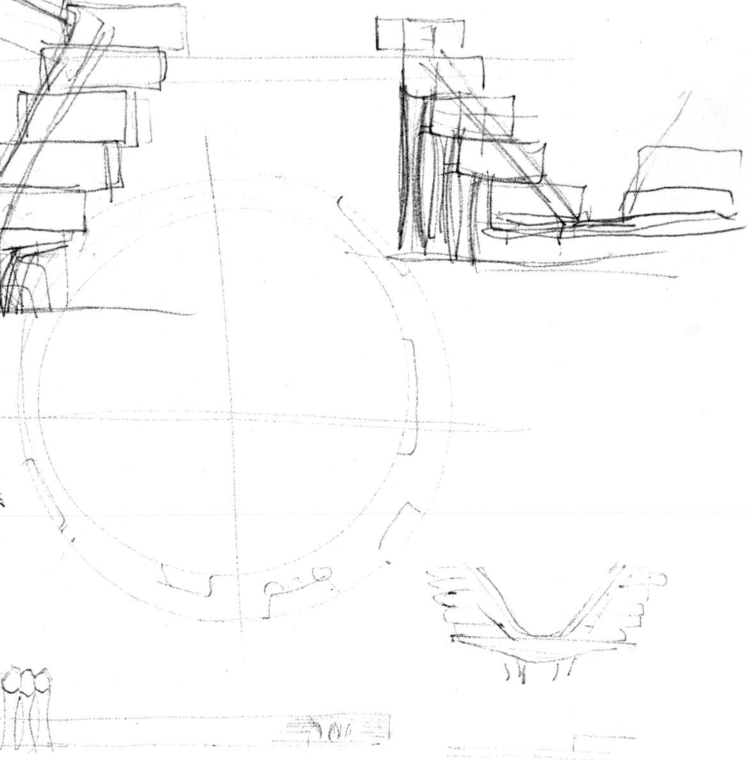
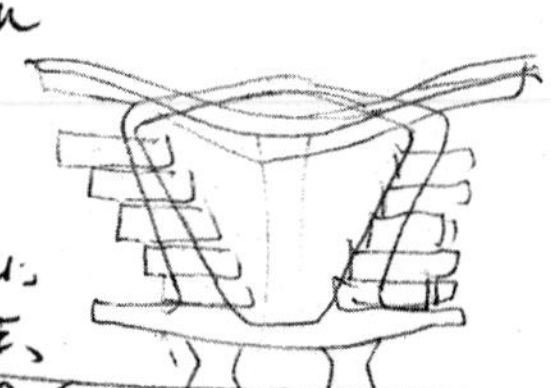
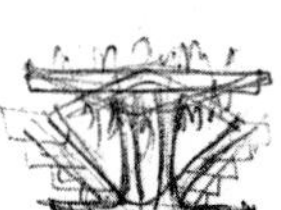
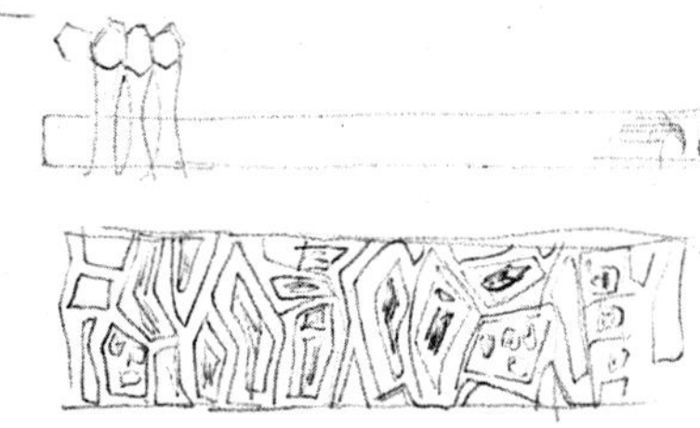

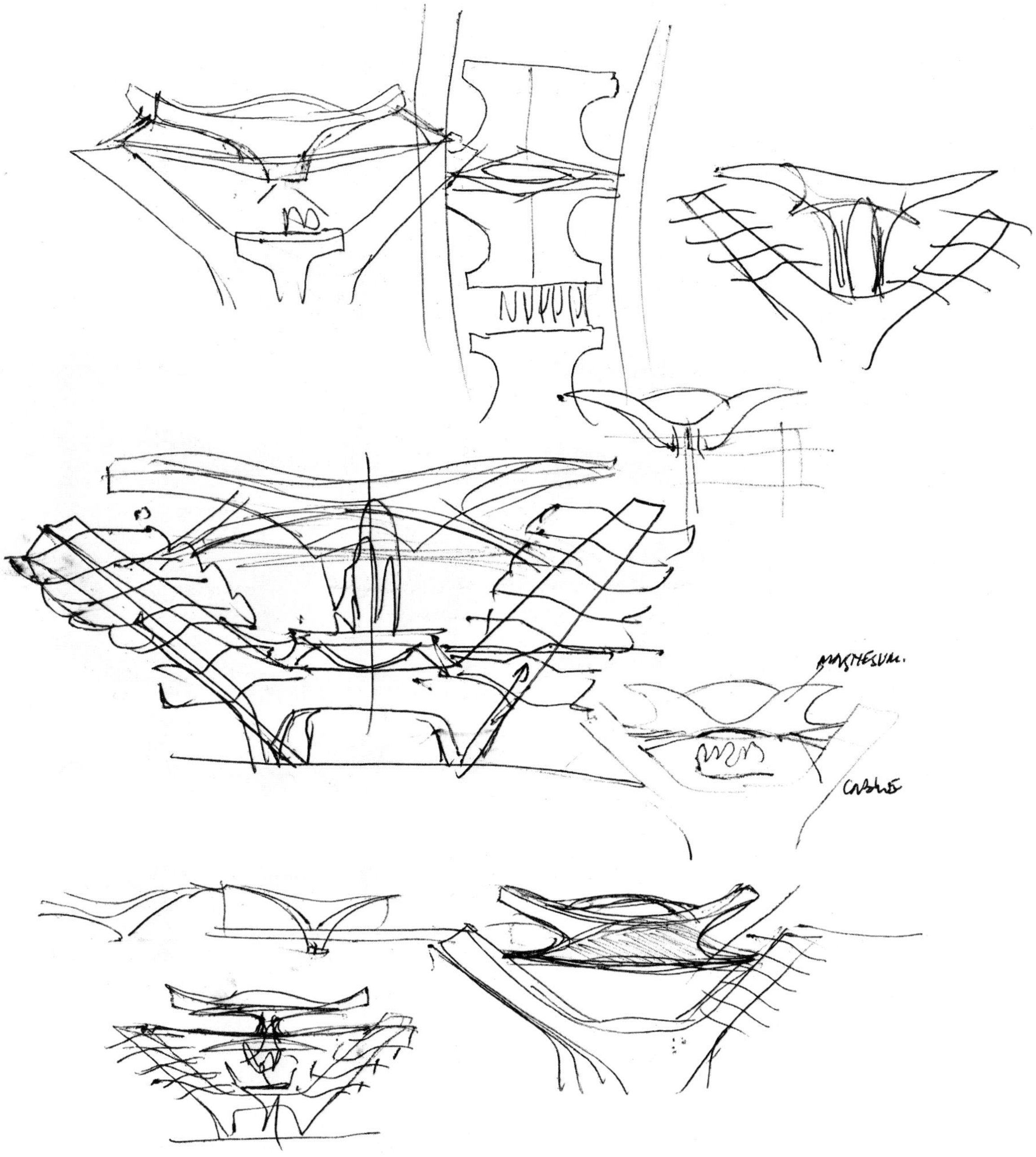
MAGNESIUM.
CABLE

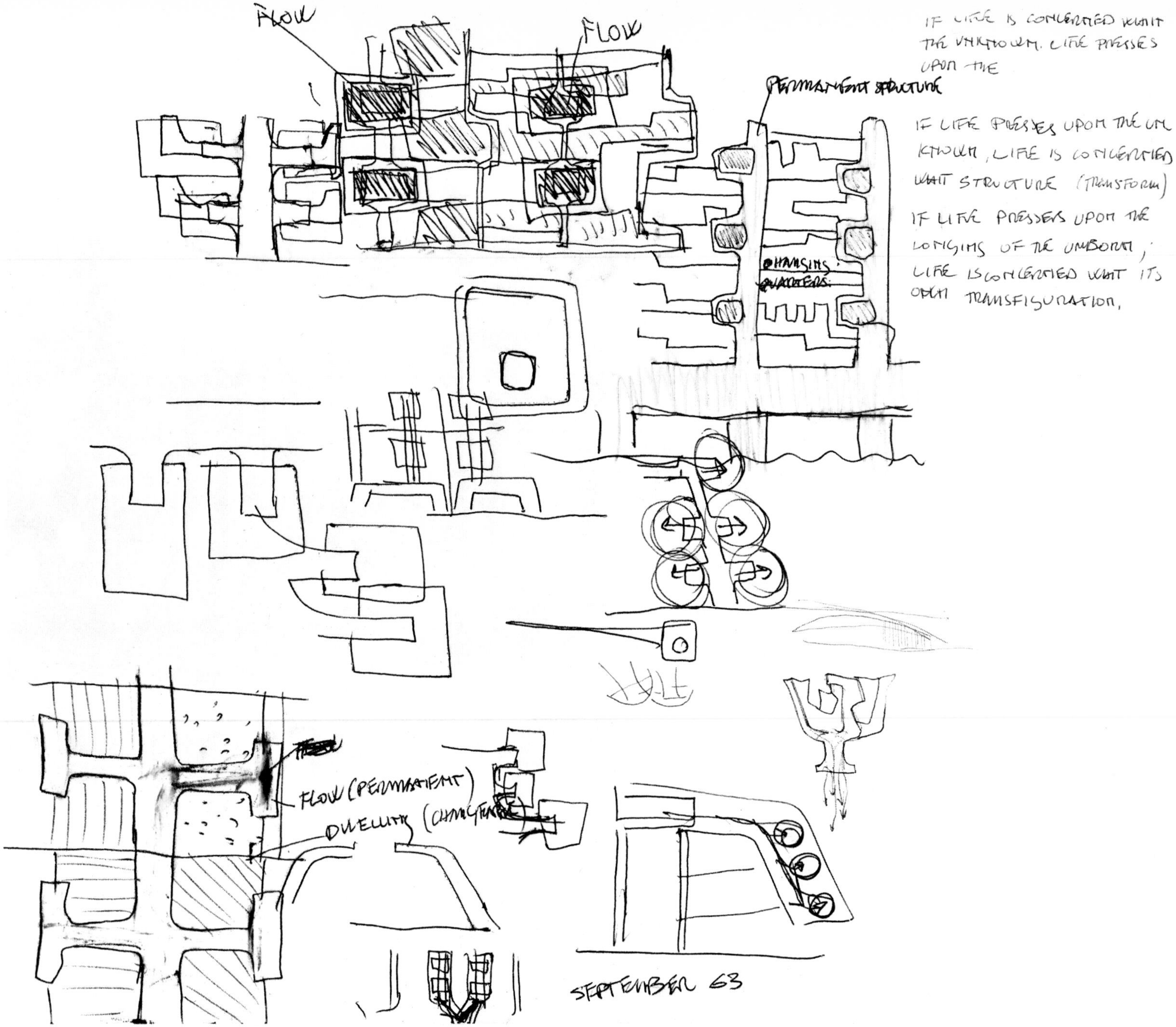
FLOW
FLOW
PERMANENT STRUCTURE
IF LIFE IS CONCERNED WITH THE UNKNOWN. LIFE PRESSES UPON THE
IF LIFE PRESSES UPON THE UNKNOWN, LIFE IS CONCERNED WITH STRUCTURE (TRANSFORM)
IF LIFE PRESSES UPON THE LONGINGS OF THE UNBORN, LIFE IS CONCERNED WITH ITS OWN TRANSFIGURATION,
CHANGING QUARTERS
FLOW (PERMANENT)
DWELLING (CHANGING)
SEPTEMBER 63

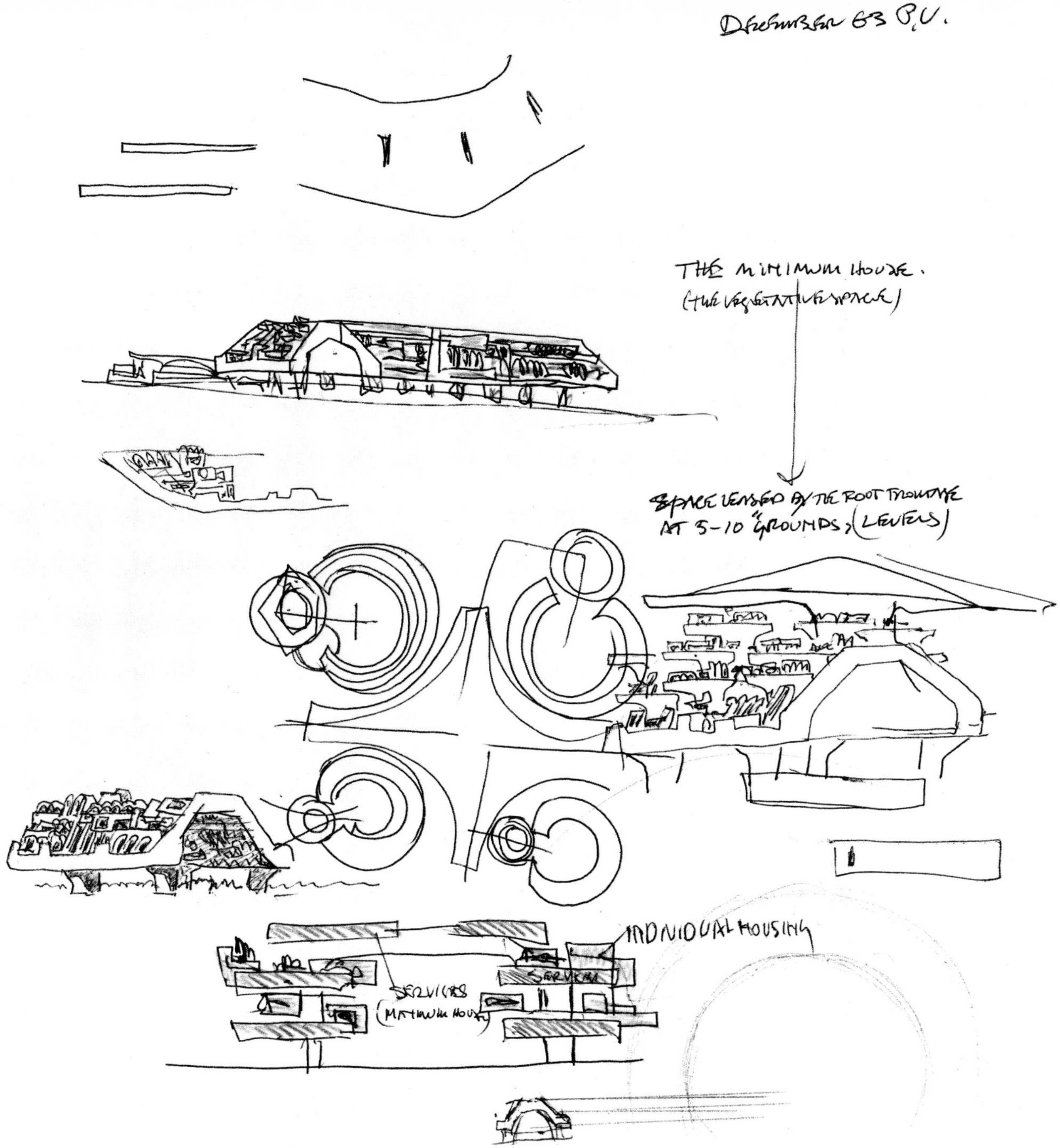
THE MINIMUM HOUSE.
(THE VEGETATIVE SPACE)
AT 5-10 "GROUNDS" (LEVELS)
INDIVIDUAL HOUSING
SERVICES

Ground Villages

1960

The primary aim here is the multiplication of ground area within a limited surface so as to keep all the advantages of closeness, services, utilities, and accessibility but provide, as well, the conditions for a totally separated and uncluttered life. This is obtained by multiplication of grounds at various levels. Each, about two-thirds of an acre, is supported by a stem. Clusters of twelve to fifteen levels are dependent upon a service tower carrying a crane (not visible if not in use), storage elevators, and at the top a nursery. The general layout is circular within a diameter of 1 kilometer. The grounds are located on the outside belt. The center is occupied by meadows, trees, rock formations, and ponds. The village depends for livelihood and supply upon the manufacturing and marketing belt to which it is directly connected.

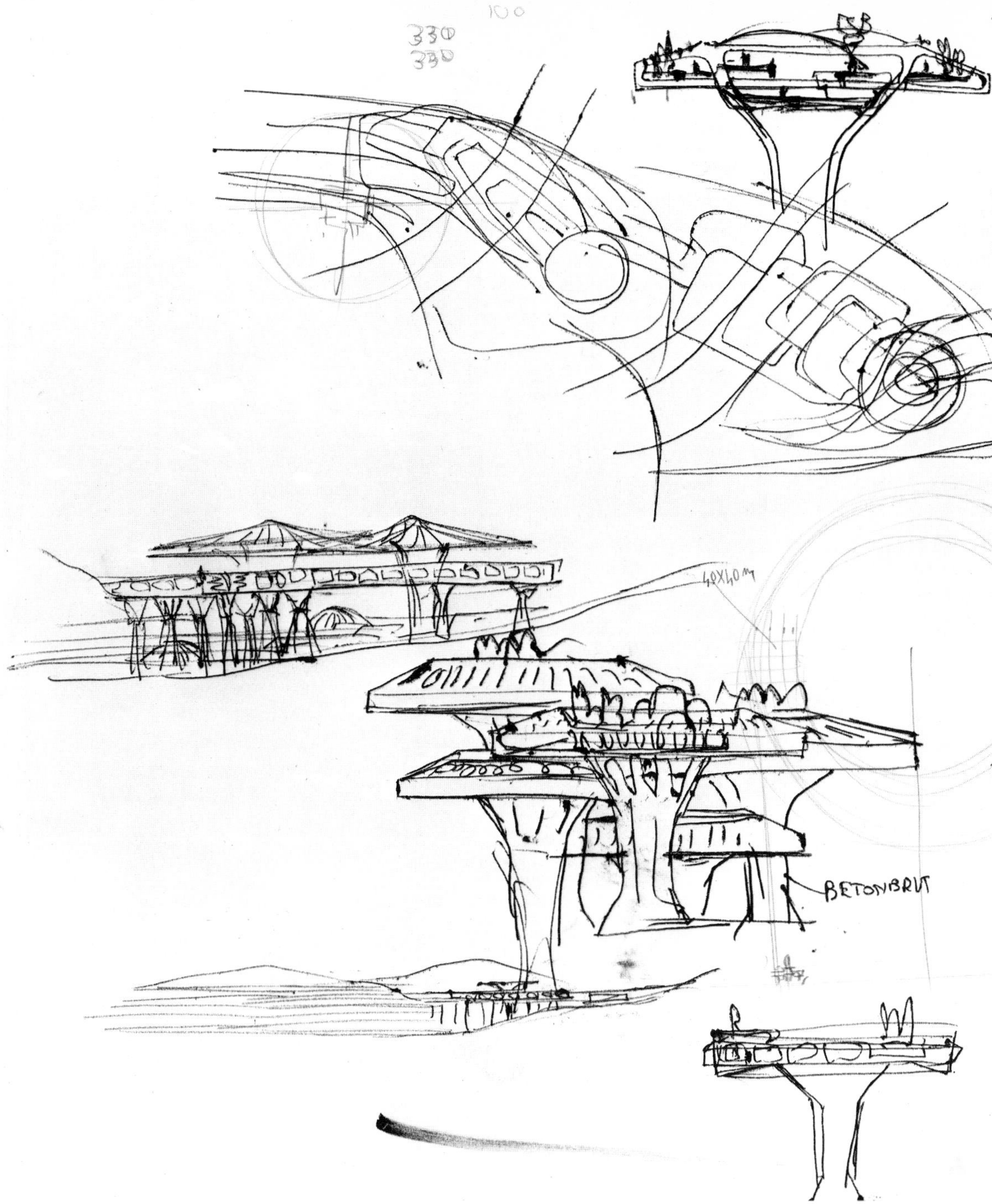

THEN THAT TRUE LOYALTY TO WHAT THIS NATION WAS INTENDED TO BE IS THE REJECTION OF WHAT THIS NATION HAS CAME TO BE

IF ONE SUBSCRIBE TO FREEDOM OF BODY & MIND ONE CANNOT ~~BY~~ ANY GIMMISTIC OF RETORIC, FILISTEISM SUBSCRIBE A PLEDGE TO THAT WHICH CAN & WILL FORFAITE IN FEW HOURS NOT ONLY FREEDOM, BUT THE REASON FOR ITS BEING: MAN, DIGNITY REVERENCE CREATIVENESS, GRACE, BEAUTY, FAITH, LONGING, GENEROSITY, MAN,

MOMENT CAMES WHEN THE FREEDOM OR DEATH BOYS MUST BE TRUE TO THEIR PLEDGE, & BY BEING LITTERAL: I COMMIT SUICIDE TO BE TRUE TO MY BELIEF. ~~[illegible]~~ THIS CAN BE A FENOMENON TO RESPECT.

MY FREEDOM OR ~~[illegible]~~ DEATH OF HOUMAN ~~HAS~~ NO ETHICAL LIGHT (AFTER IT) ~~NOW~~ ~~WHEN~~ THAT INDISCRIMINATION HAS REACHED THE TOTALITY.

OUR CONDUCT IN INTERNATIONAL PROBLEMS OUR AS THAT OF ANY OTHER ~~DEATH~~ BUDGETED NATION SEEMS TOTALLY UNCONCERN OF WHAT THE ~~AFTER~~ POS HIDROGEN ~~BUTCHERY~~ WILL BE.

WE RUN ABSTRACTLY & INHUMANLY TOWARD ~~THE~~ FINAL BARRICADE IN THE NAME OF A FREEDOM LONG LOST TO ~~THE~~ BESTIALITY, ON THE OTHER SIDE OF IT. WHAT EXPECTS US IS AT THE LEAST ~~THE~~ UNBERABLE BLAKNESS OF A ~~THORN~~ INDIVIDUAL & COLLECTIVE CONCIENCE, THE RESURGENCE OF PRIMEVAL TERRORS & FEARS, A SQUALID ENVIRONMENT FOR SQUALID CHILDHOOD & MEMORIES ~~FOR~~ EACH OF US WHICH WILL MAKE THE FATE OF THE DEAD ENVIABLE

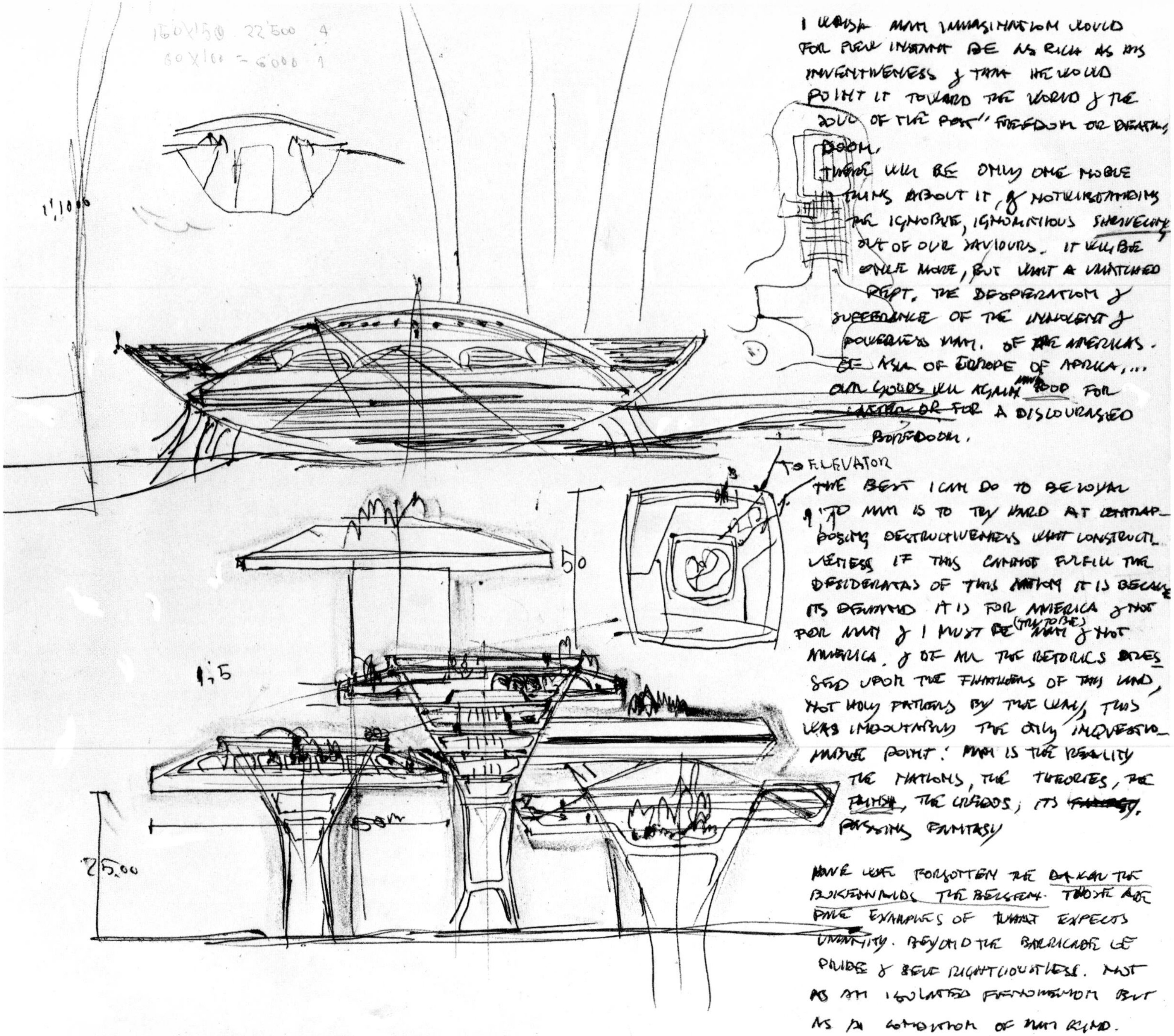

I WISH MAN IMAGINATION WOULD
FOR EVERY INSTANT BE AS RICH AS HIS
INVENTIVENESS & THAT HE WOULD
POINT IT TOWARD THE WORLD & THE
SOUL OF THE POET" FREEDOM OR DEATH
DOOM.
THERE WILL BE ONLY ONE NOBLE
THING ABOUT IT,
THE IGNOBLE, IGNOMINIOUS
OUT OF OUR SAVIOURS. IT WILL BE
ONCE MORE, BUT WHAT A
THE DESPERATION &
SUFFERANCE OF THE INNOCENT &
POWERLESS MAN. OF THE AMERICAS.
OF ASIA OF EUROPE OF AFRICA, ...
OUR GOODS WILL AGAIN FOR
FOR A DISCOURAGED
BOREDOM.
TO ELEVATOR
THE BEST I CAN DO TO BE LOYAL
TO MAN IS TO TRY HARD AT
DESTRUCTIVENESS WITH CONSTRUCTI-
VENESS IF THIS CANNOT FULFILL THE
DESIDERATAS OF THIS NATION IT IS BECAUSE
ITS IT IS FOR AMERICA & NOT
FOR MAN & I MUST BE (TRY TO BE) MAN & NOT
AMERICA. & OF ALL THE RETORICS
UPON THE FATHERS OF THIS LAND,
NOT HOLY FATHERS BY THE WAY, THIS
WAS THE ONLY
POINT: MAN IS THE REALITY
THE NATIONS, THE THEORIES, THE
THE CREEDS; ITS
PASSING FANTASY
HAVE WE FORGOTTEN THE THE
THE THOSE ARE
EXAMPLES OF EXPECTS
UNANIMITY. BEYOND THE BARRICADE
PRIDE & SELF RIGHTEOUSNESS. NOT
AS AN ISOLATED PHENOMENON BUT
AS A CONDITION OF MAN KIND.
1:1000
1:5
50
25.00
60 m

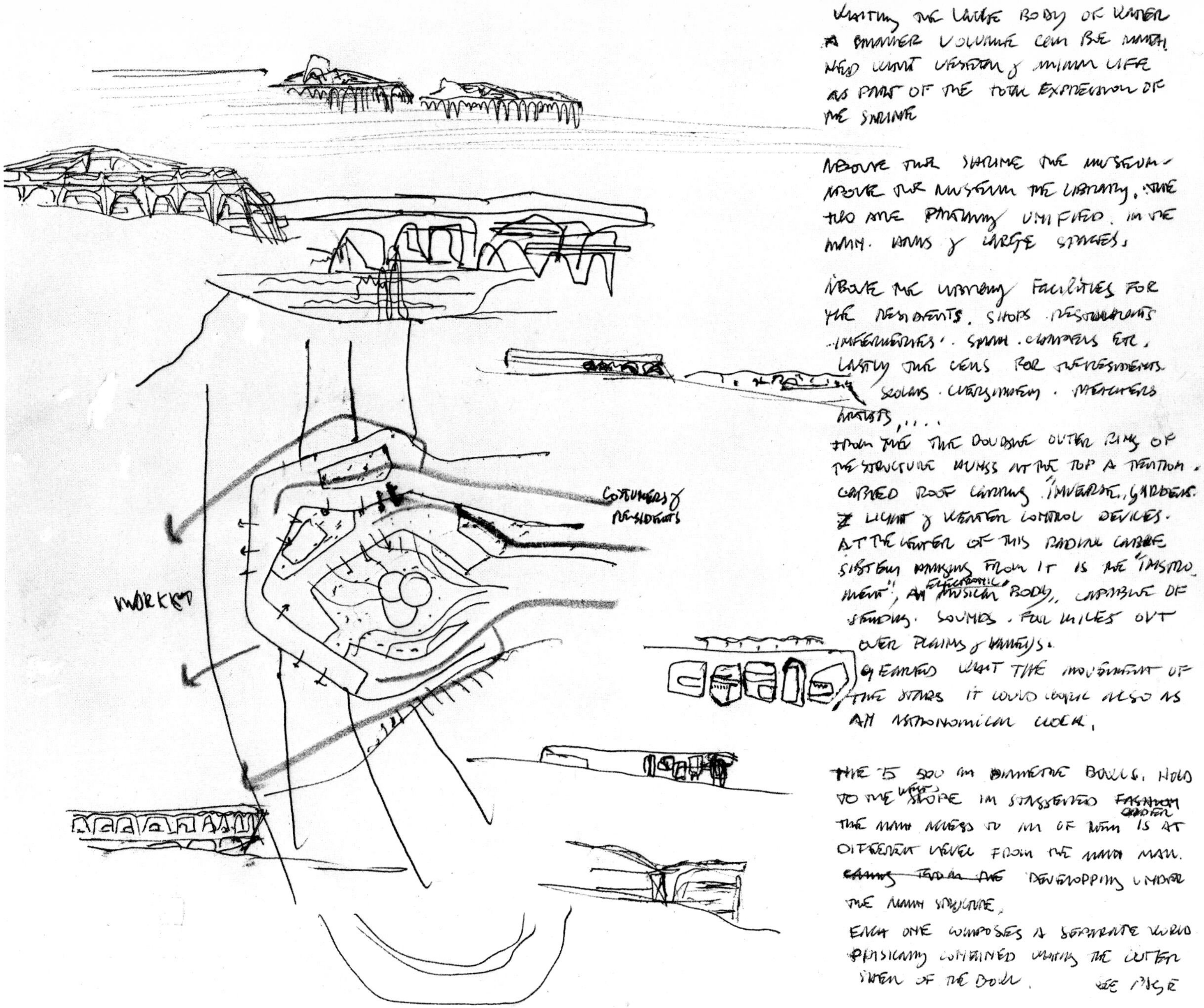
COSTUMERS & RESIDENTS
MARKET
LASTLY THE LARGE BODY OF WATER
A SMALLER VOLUME CAN BE MATCHED WITH VEGETATION & ANIMAL LIFE
AS PART OF THE TOTAL EXPRESSION OF THE SHRINE
ABOVE THE SHRINE THE MUSEUM - ABOVE THE MUSEUM THE LIBRARY. THE TWO ARE PARTIALLY UNIFIED. IN THE MAIN HALLS & LARGE SPACES.
ABOVE THE LIBRARY FACILITIES FOR THE RESIDENTS. SHOPS. RESTAURANTS. INFIRMARIES. SAUNA. CHAPELS ETC.
LASTLY THE CELLS FOR THE RESIDENTS. SCOLARS. CLERGYMEN. TEACHERS ARTISTS, . . .
FROM THE DOUBLE OUTER RING OF THE STRUCTURE HANGS AT THE TOP A TENSION. CABLED ROOF CARRYING "INVERSE" GARDENS. & LIGHT & WEATHER CONTROL DEVICES.
AT THE CENTER OF THIS RADIAL CABLE SYSTEM HANGING FROM IT IS THE "INSTRUMENT", AN ELECTRONIC MUSICAL BODY, CAPABLE OF SENDING. SOUNDS. FOR MILES OUT OVER PLAINS & VALLEYS.
GEARED WITH THE MOVEMENT OF THE STARS IT COULD WORK ALSO AS AN ASTRONOMICAL CLOCK.
THE 5 500 M DIAMETER BOWLS. HOLD TO THE WEST SLOPE IN STAGGERED ORDER
THE MAIN ACCESS TO ALL OF THEM IS AT DIFFERENT LEVEL FROM THE MAIN MALL. DEVELOPPING UNDER THE MAIN STRUCTURE.
EACH ONE COMPOSES A SEPARATE WORLD PHYSICALLY CONTAINED WITHIN THE OUTER SKIN OF THE BOWL. SEE PAGE

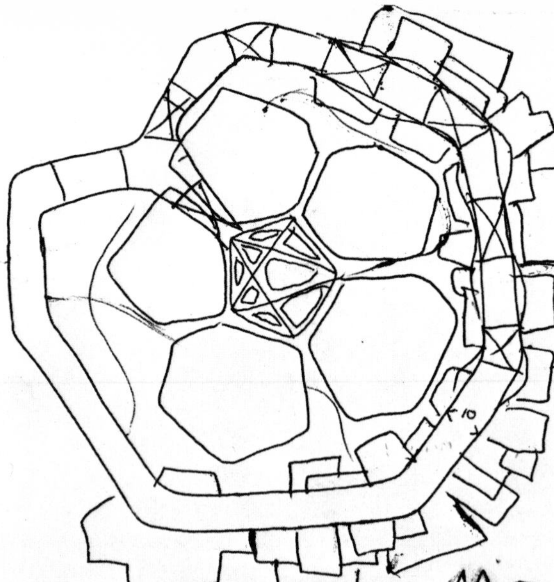

ORGANISMS OF FUNCTIONALITIES. IN THEIR COMMUNITY OF NEED.

MEANWHILE THE PARK ITSELF WOULD TAKE SHAPE, THE ARTS WOULD BE CARRIED IN MORE & MORE TO UNIFIES THE WHOLE BY THE ESSENTIALIZATION OF FORMS SPACES. TEXTURES, COLORS, VOLUMES, ETC.

THE VILLAGES OF ARTS & CRAFTS WOULD FLOWER, TOWARD THE NORTH END OF THE PARK. ALONG THE WATER WORKS. BEINGS BUILD THERE,

BY NOW THE CITY WOULD HAVE COME OF AGE, THE INTERNAL STRESSES WOULD CALL FOR A COMPLETE SURVEY OF THE WHOLE. PERSONALITY OF MAN & SOCIETY.

THE THEOLOGICAL COMPLEX. THE SPIRITUAL ENTITY BALANCING THE WORLD OF THE MIND. CENTERING ITS TOIL IN THE HIGH LEARNING. COMPLEX WOULD TAKE CONCRETE FORM AT THE NORTH END OF THE CITY.

THE COSMOPOLITAN ASPECT OF SOCIETY, WOULD BE MIRRORED BY THE "INDIGENOUS" VILLAGES IN THEIR INTERNATIONALLY. AESTHETIC CHARACTERS.

THE REACHED FULL FUNCTIONALITY OF THE 3 LIFE BANDS WOULD SET IN THE CONDITION FOR THE GROWTH OF THE NEW, DENSIFIED COMMUNITIES. FINDING IN THE BORDERING PARK (COMMUNITY) THE MAJOR (A) CULTURAL SUBSTANCE & DIRECTION. FILLING THE VACUUM SOCIETIES TEND TO FILL IN WANT OF VACUITIES.

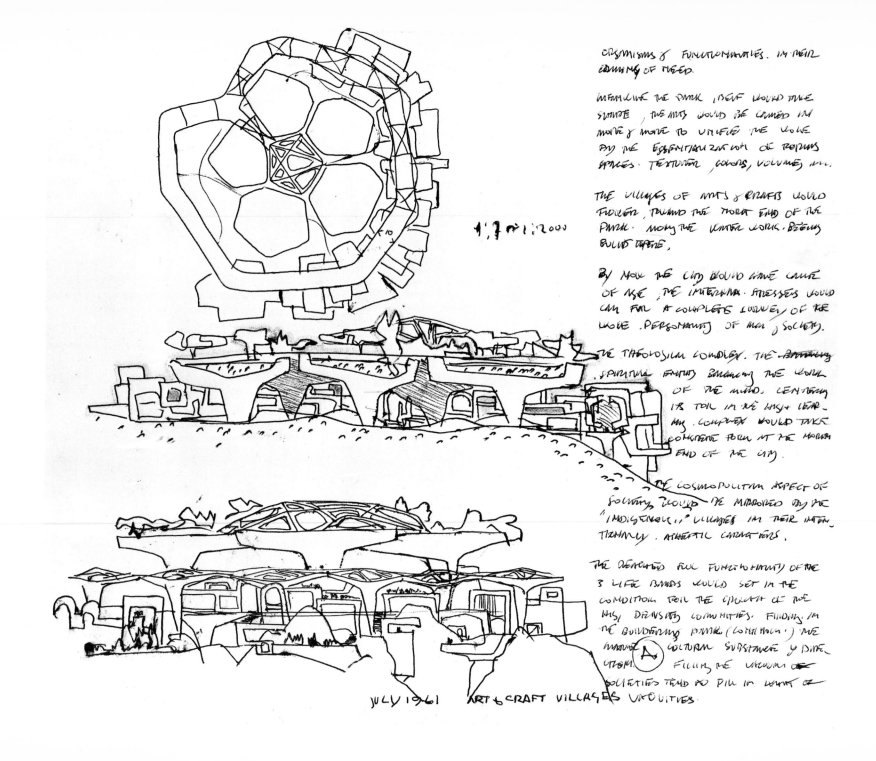

JULY 1961 ART & CRAFT VILLAGES

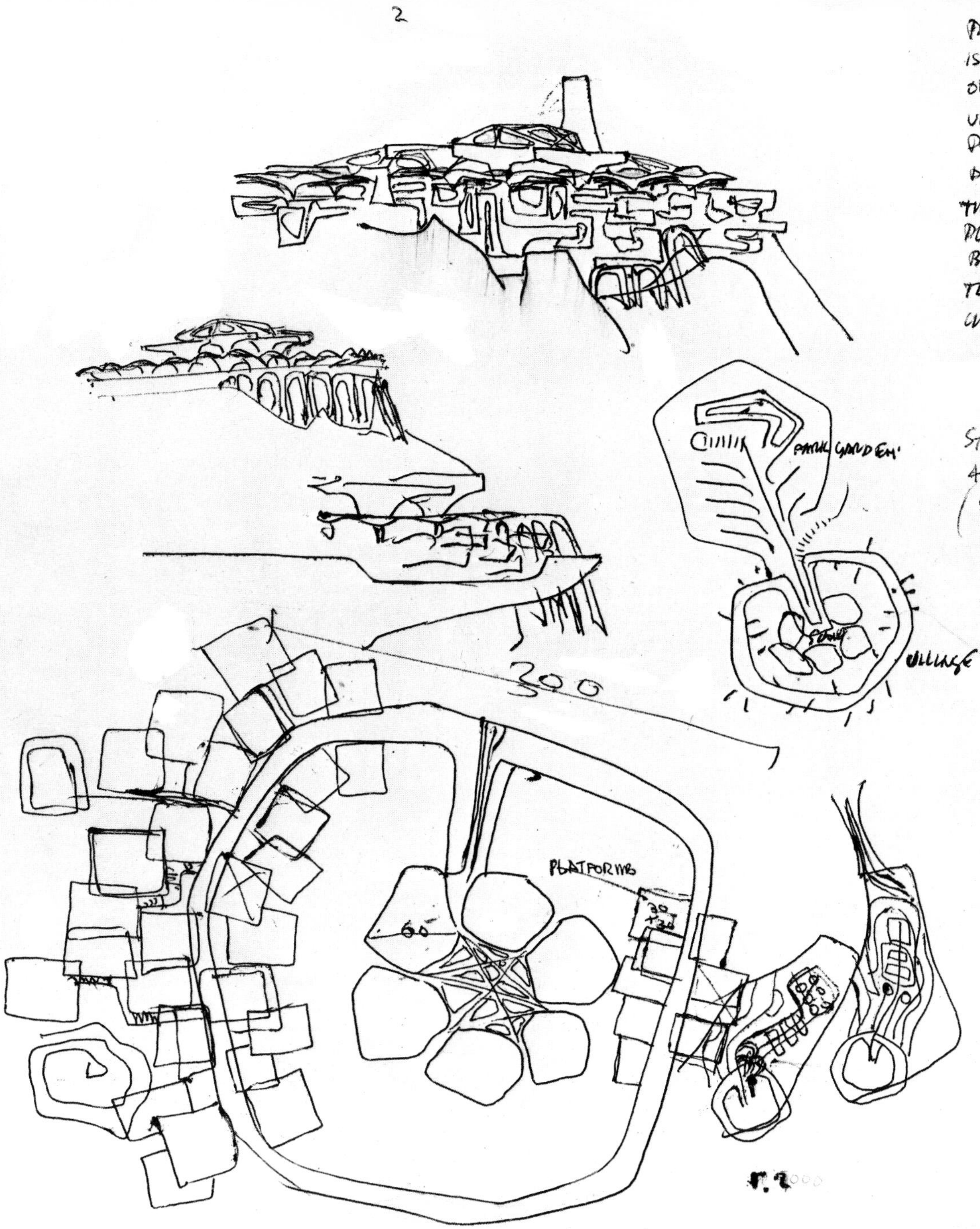

PARALLELING WITH THE BUILD UP ON THE MESA IS THE PRODUCTIVITY & THE EXPANSION OF THE HEAVY INDUSTRY LOCATED IN THE VICINITY. THE BUILDING OF MULTIPURPOSE DAMS. THE PRODUCTION OF ENERGY; THE DEFINITION OF THE NEW ECOLOGY. THE ESTABLISHMENT OF PROCESSING PLANTS FOR FOODS STUFF IN THE VALLEYS BELOW. INTEGRATED WITH THE RURAL TOWNS & VILLAGES, & THE "LINEAR CITY" ON THE WATER WAYS.

STRUCTURES.
4 MAIN TYPES OF STRUCTURAL PROCEDURES (SEE. YELLOW PRINT)

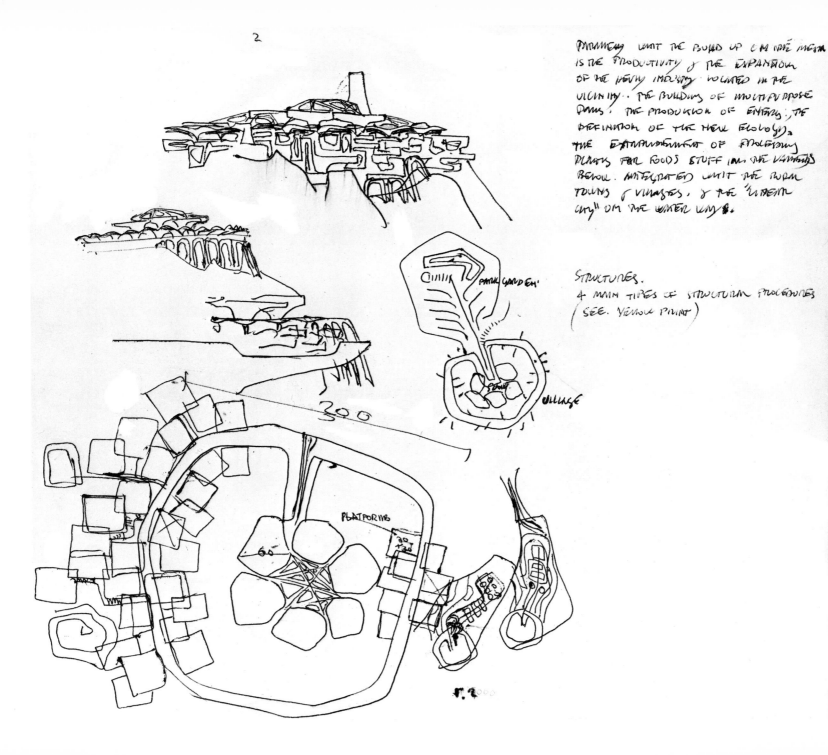

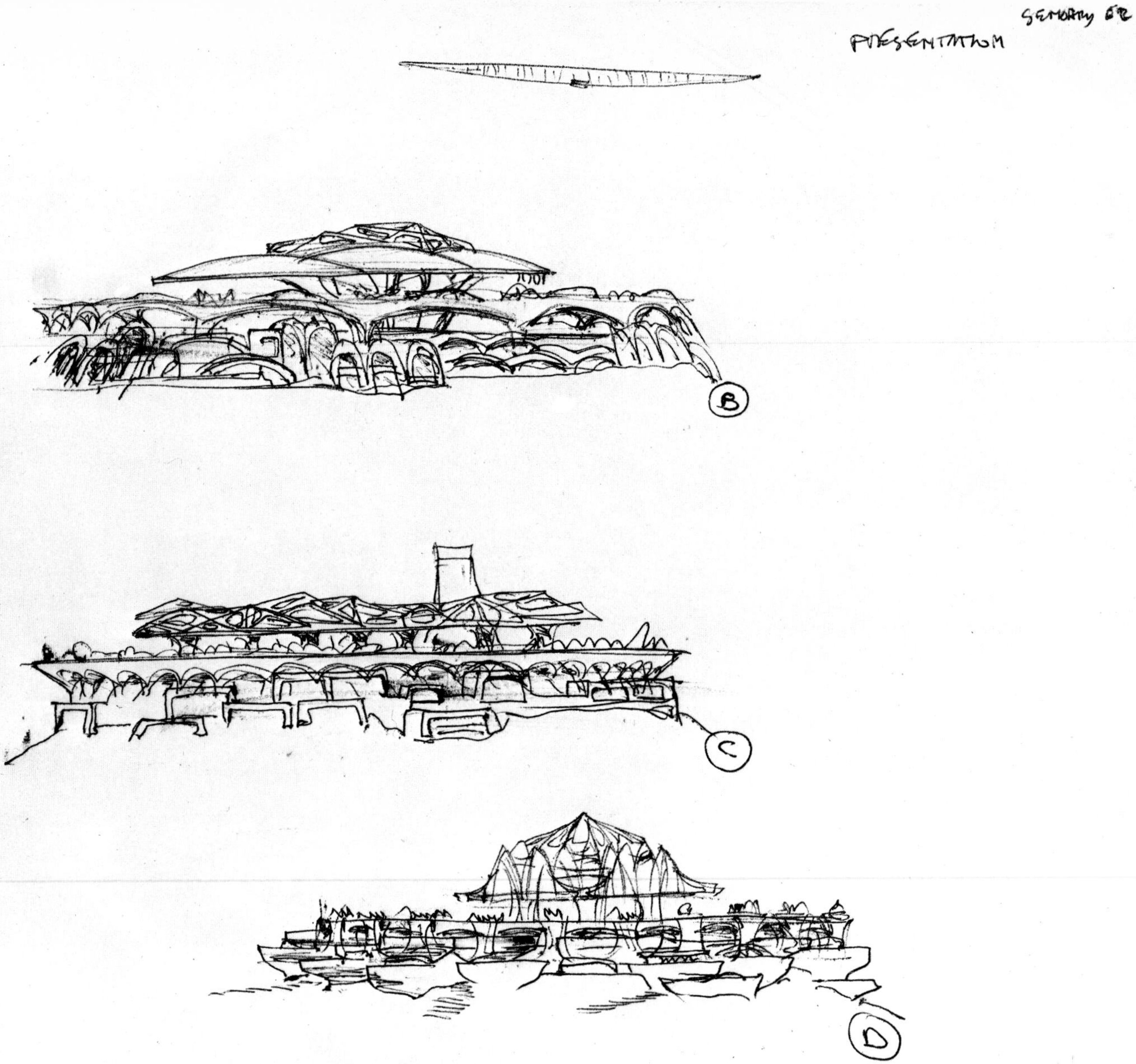
PRESENTATION
B
C
D

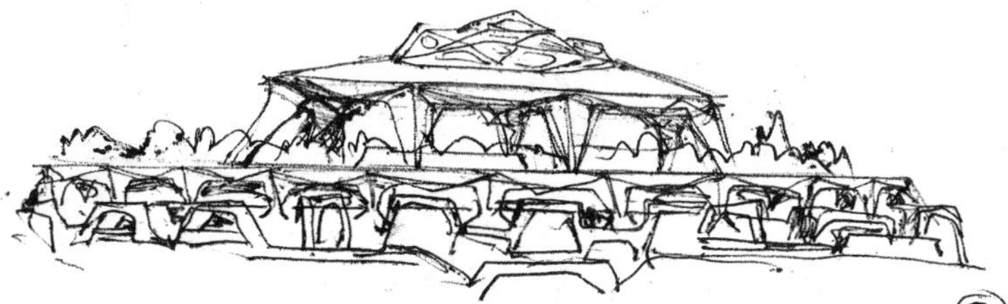

E

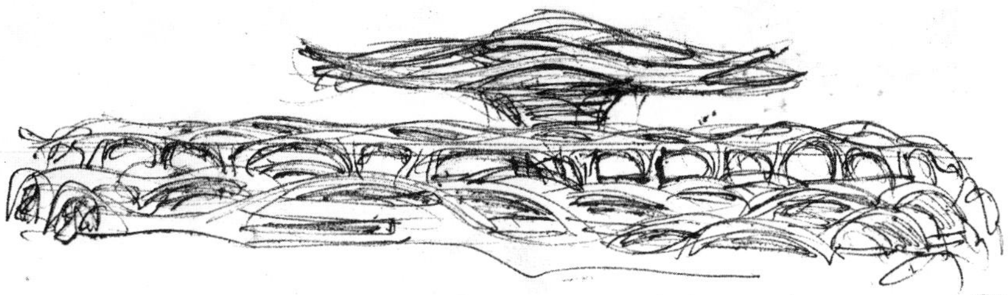

F

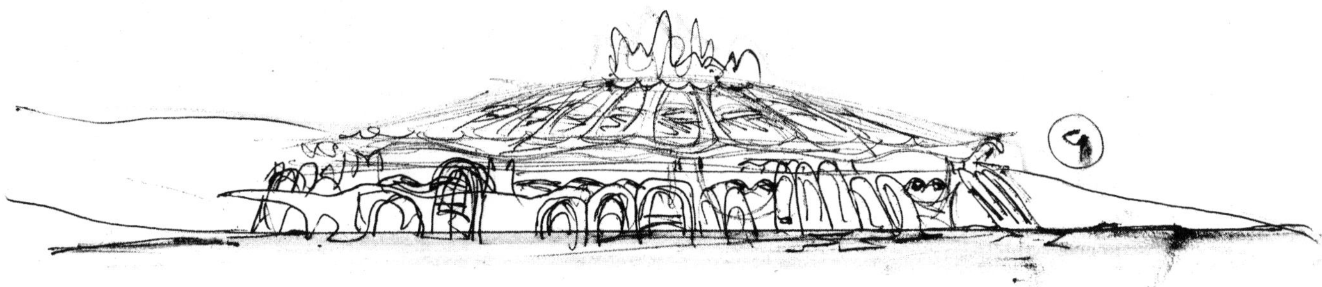

G

H

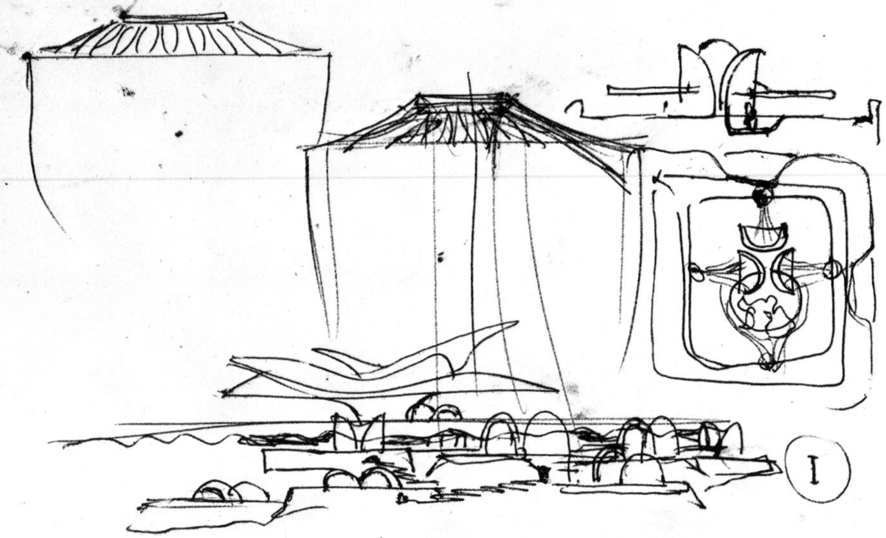
I

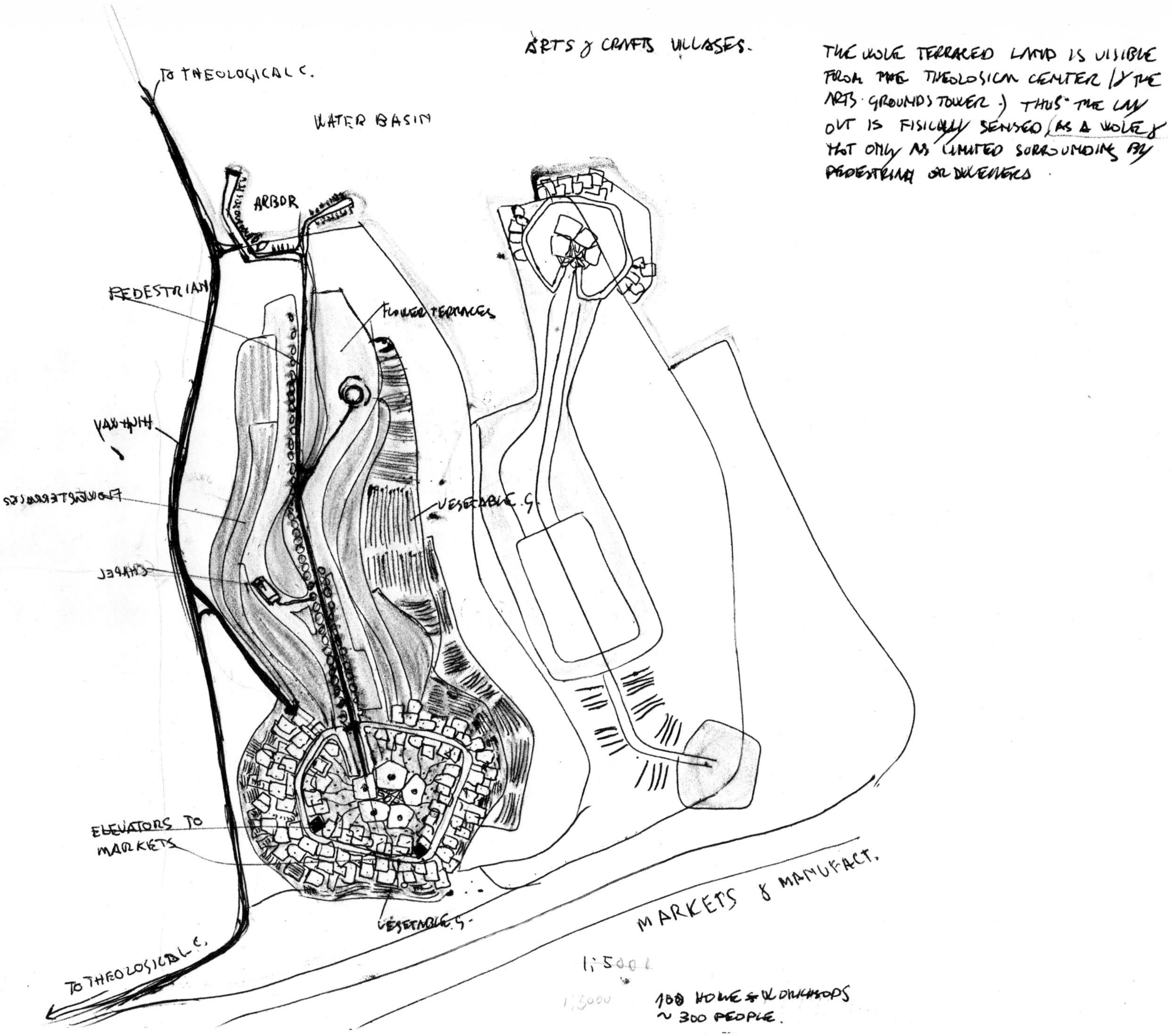
ARTS & CRAFTS VILLAGES.
THE WOLE TERRACED LAND IS VISIBLE FROM THE THEOLOGICAL CENTER (& THE ARTS GROUNDS TOWER) THUS THE LAY OUT IS FISICALLY SENSED AS A WOLE & NOT ONLY AS LIMITED SURROUNDING BY PEDESTRIAN OR DWELLERS.
TO THEOLOGICAL C.
WATER BASIN
ARBOR
PEDESTRIAN
FLOWER TERRACES
VEGETABLE G.
ELEVATORS TO MARKETS
VEGETABLE G.
MARKETS & MANUFACT.
TO THEOLOGICAL C.
1:5000
100 HOMES & WORKSHOPS
~ 300 PEOPLE.

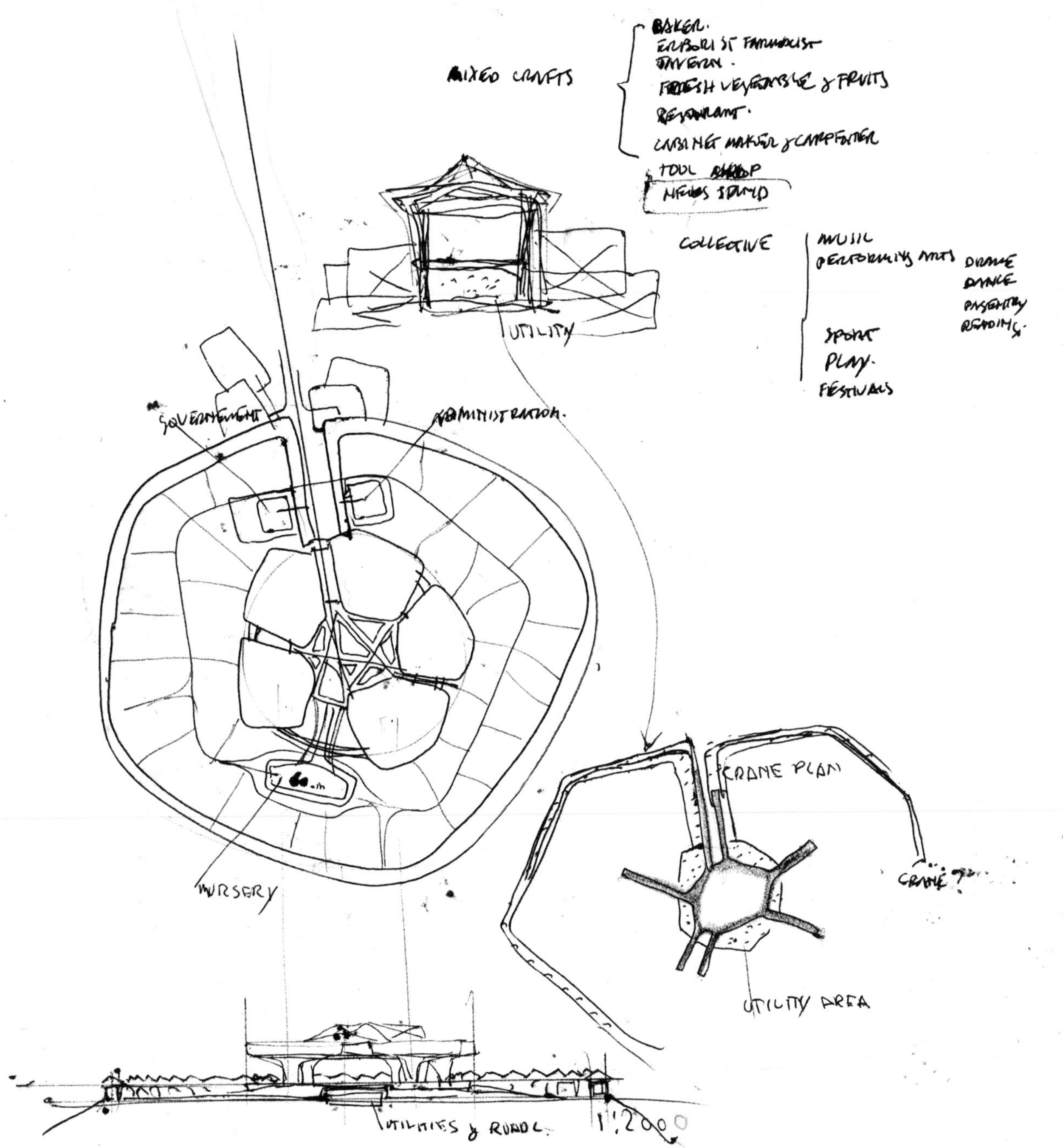
MIXED CRAFTS
BAKER.
TAVERN.
FRESH VEGETABLE & FRUITS
RESTAURANT.
CABINET MAKER & CARPENTER
TOOL SHOP
NEWS STAND
COLLECTIVE
MUSIC
PERFORMING ARTS
DRAMA
DANCE
SPORT
PLAY.
FESTIVALS
UTILITY
GOVERNMENT
ADMINISTRATION.
NURSERY
CRANE PLAN
CRANE
UTILITY AREA
UTILITIES & ROADS
1:2000

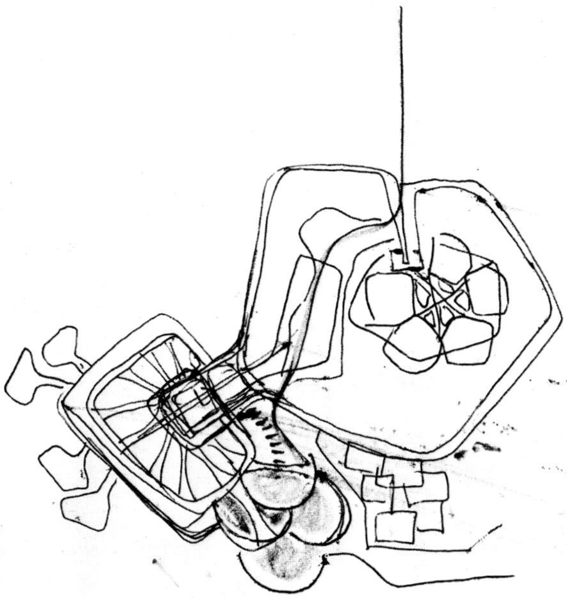

SEE PAGE

IF PERFORATED, THIS SHELL, WILL REVEAL THE OUTER WORLD. DISTINCTLY RECEDING. IN FORMAL HERMETICNESS YET IN REALITY THE ROOTING IS IN THE GEOLOGICAL ~~[illegible]~~ OF THE HILL ITSELF IN POWERFUL ANCHORAGES. & THE LIFE SUSTENANCE COMES FROM THE SAME WEALTH AT THE HORIZON.

THE MATERIAL CLOSENESS OF THE ORDERS IS INTENDED TO FAVOR RECIPROCAL INVESTIGATION, UNDERSTANDING & ....
THE TECNICAL & COLTURAL FACILITIES TO HELP IN REACHIN BEYOND THE FABLE, THE MYTE THE SUPERSTRUCTURE THE COMMONE RULES & STRUCTURES.
BOTH THOSE CONDITIONS ARE REFLECTED IN THE COMPLEX ~~IN ALL ITS IMAGES~~, ITS ORGANIZATION. ITS CONTINUITY ~~THE IMAGES~~. THE RELATIVE POSITION OF ITS ELEMENTS & HOW THEY RELATE TO ONE ANOTHER.

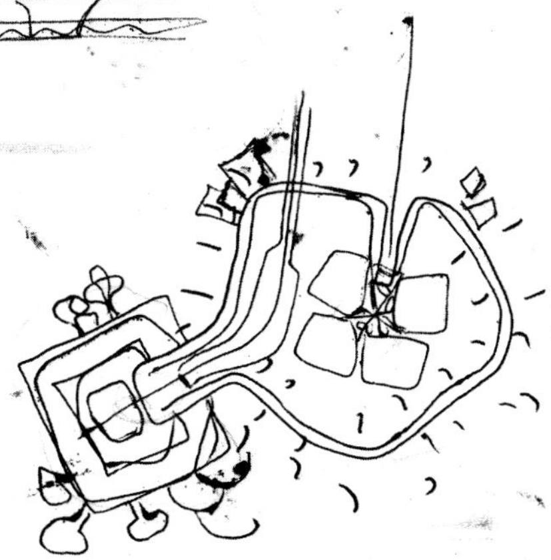

2

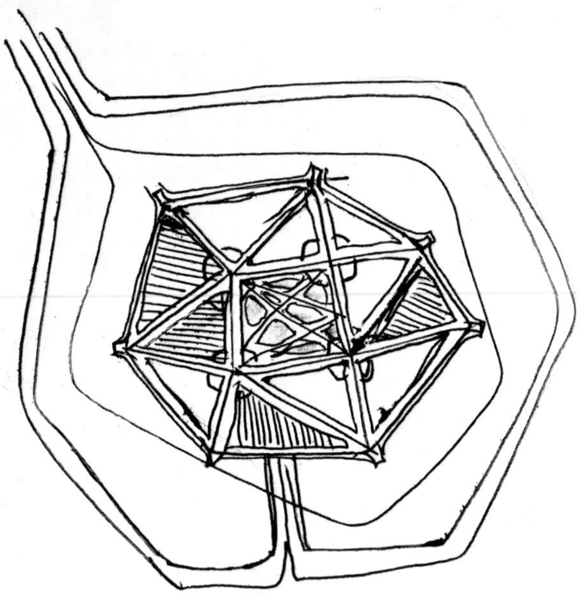

— CONTINUUM

THE CITY IS BUILT OF ITS MATERIAL, (GOOD FOR MISTICAL & SIMBOLOGICAL ~~DISCUSSIONS~~) INFERENCES)
IT REMAINS ANYHOW THE RATIONAL FACT THAT FROM THIS ORIGINAL RIDGE CUTTING THROUGH THE MESA, THE CITY GETS THE WEIGHT OF ITS BOUNDARIES, AS IF A SELF GENERATING POWER WERE AT WORK, LIMITING THE ATTRACTS OF ~~PRESTIGE~~ TO FILL IN THE DESIGN MAN AND CONSTRUCTED FOR IT.

IF THE POLITICAL IMPLICATION WERE NOT SO NEGATIVE ONE COULD SEE A FISSION PLANT AT THE CENTER OF THE PARK. (BUSINESS COMPUTER CENTER) & FROM FEW POUNDS OF MATTER & FROM MAN INGENUITY WOULD THEN BE THE RAW MATERIAL QUARRIED, PROCESSED, DISTRIBUTED, FORMED, ENVELOPING SPACES, ENCLOSING, SEPARATING, ISOLATING, EMBRACING, REACHING, CONTAINING, SUSTAINING, ELEVATING....

① QUARRYING & PROCESSING ARE GUIDED BY THE DESIGN THE FINAL PARK WILL SPEAK OF.
THE IMPRINT OF MAN & THE BROAD GEOLOGICAL LINES ON THIS IMPRINT WOULD CUT IN ARE THE TWO ANTAGONISTIC FORCES THAT ARE HERE AT PLAY: & THAT ONE SEEK TO CONCILIATE NOT PHYSICALLY BUT ESTETICALLY.
IN THIS LARGE STRUCTURE WOULD INSERT THEMSELVES THE EXPRESSIONS OF INDIVIDUAL ARTISTS FRUIT OF ONE MINDED INTENSITY WORKING WITH COLORS, FORMS, METALS, PLASTICS, GLASS.... PLANT LIFE, WATER ... LIGHT, SPACE ...

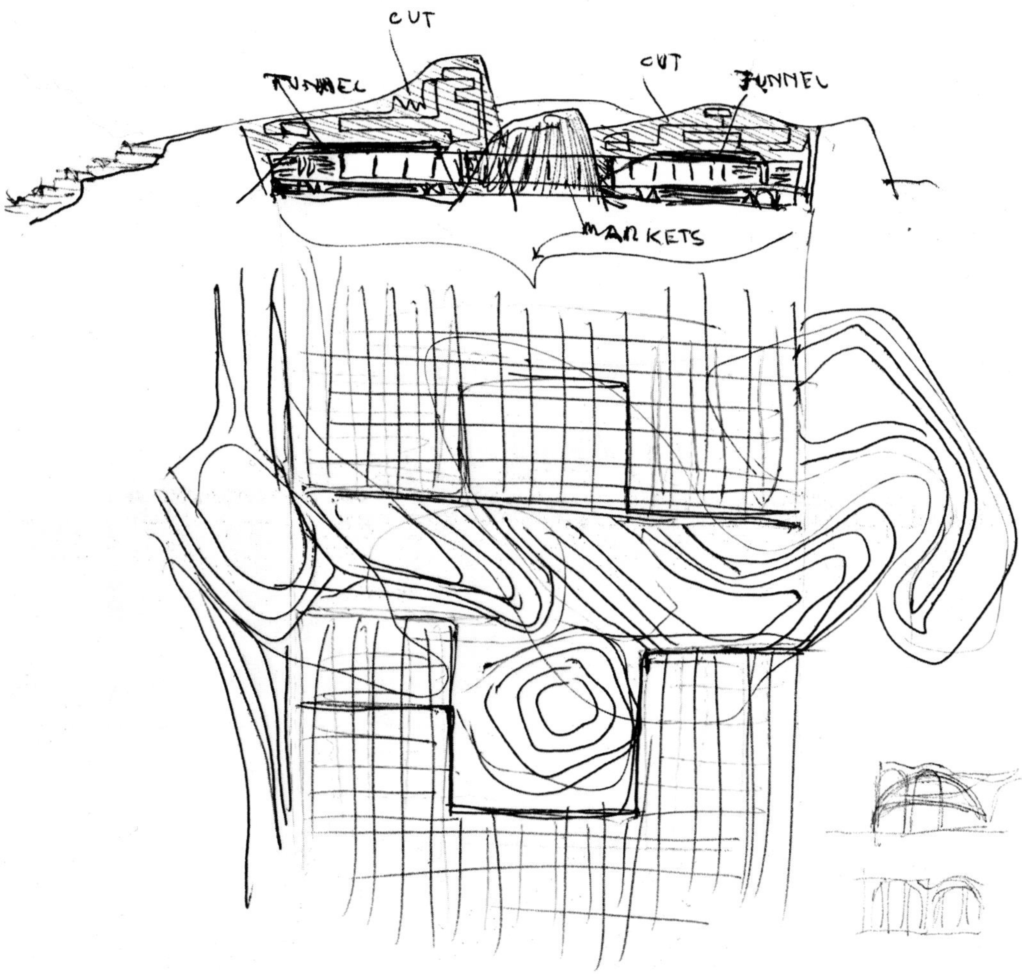

SCULPTORS BECOMING ARCHITECTS OR ARCHI-
TECTS SCULPTOR IN SEMANTIC CONTROVERSY
PAINTERS REACHING FOR 'CANVASSES'
OF STONE AS LARGE AS ALL THE WALLS
OF ALL THE MUSEUM PUT TOGETHER.
UNDER SLASHING SUN LIGHT OR
LIGHTED BY THE REBOUNDS OF
THE SUN ON OTHER WALLS. OTHER
SURFACE, TEXTURES, CLOUDS, WATER...

ON THE SAME BREATH THE CLUSTE-
RED, THE SMALL THE ONE MODULE EX-
PRESSIVE ART, THE HIDDEN ~~LITTLE MOSAIC~~. THE
LIMITED VOLUME, THE SMALL BLADE OF
LIGHT, THE STRONG DIMMED OBSCURITY.

IT MAY NEED TO BE SAID THAT THE MATERIAL
& THE MAN MADE OF WHERE & THERE
COMPOUND INTO EACH OTHER IN UNDISCERNIBLE
WAY THAT WOULD BE SO OUT OF
CIRCUMSTANCES NOT OUT OF INTENDED
IMITATION OR SUBMISSION.
MAN CAN, AT LEAST THEORETICALLY,
CONDENSE EONS OF NATURE ACTION
INTO BRIEF MOMENTS OF TECHNOLOGICAL
PROCESS. SUCH DOINGS BELONG
MORE TO OTHER FIELDS OF ENDEAVOUR
THAN THE ARTS (PHYSIC, CHEMISTRY, ~~BIOLO~~
MEDICINE, NOT BIOLOGY / MECHANICS)..
THE ARTISTIC ENDEAVOUR ITSELF
TIGHTLY FITTING ITS OWN UNSIZABLE
DURATION ~~ACTS~~, CREATES, IN THE TIME-
LESS SPHERE UNLIKE NATURE DOES.

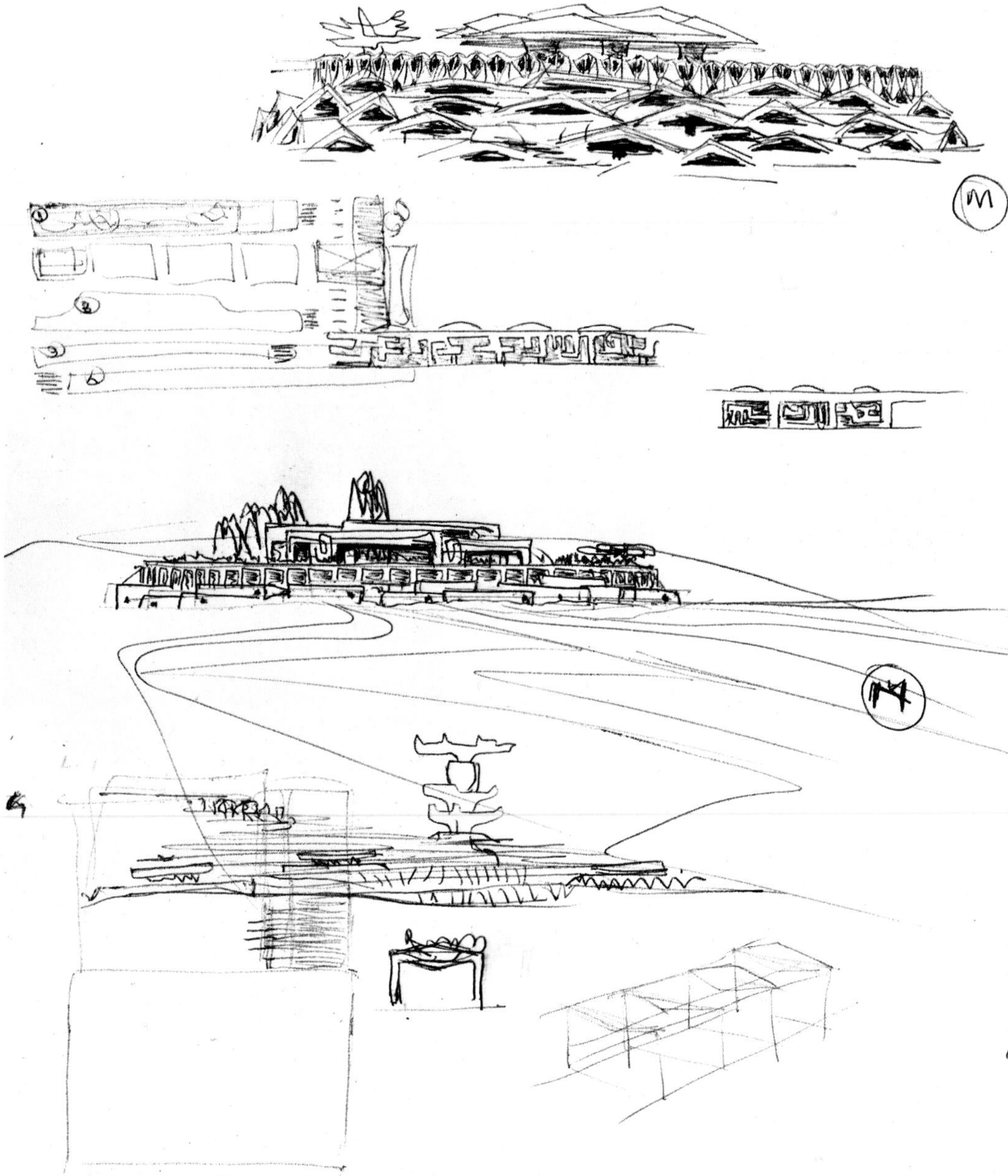

MARKET–MANUFACTURING.

THIS COMPLEX INCLUDES ALL THE PROCESSING OF RAW MATERIAL, MONTAGE ASSEMBLAGE, SHELLING & SALE OF STANDARD PRODUCT THAT CAN BE OBTAINED WITHOUT THE PRODUCTION OF ~~BY PRODUCTS~~ LIKE FUMES, ODORS, DUST NOISES .....

IT IS THEN ATTEMPTED THE UNIFICATION OF ALL THESE FUNCTION UNDER ONE "ROOF" SHELTERING ALSO THE FACILITIES FOUND IN ANY DOWN-TOWN DISTRICT. SHOPS. RESTAURANTS, THEATERS, BANKS, AMUSEMENT HALLS. SHOW ROOMS ... PROFESSIONAL FACILITIES ETC.
THE INTERSTITIAL TISSUE CONSTITUTED OF GARDENS MEADOWS. PATHWAYS, OPEN MARKETS. FOUNTAINS. PONDS. ETC.

THE MANUFACTURING & MARKETING UNITS ARE SERVED BY A BATTERY OF CONVEYOR BELTS EACH ABOUT 20 Km LONG. USING WATER A LUBRICANT, GRAVITY AS MOVING POWER.
THE EVEN, ~~SLOPE~~ IMPERCEPTIBLE SLOPE OF THOSE CONVEYORS ARE THE REFERENCE PLAN ALL ALONG THE COMPLEX & IT IS CARRIED TROUGH, FLAT GROUND, OR BROKEN LEVELS, GARDENS & MEADOWS PONDS & WOODS MUCH LIKE THE ANCIENT AQUEDUCTS. APPEARING & DISAPPEARING FROM & IN THE BODY OF THE PROCESSING & MARKETING PLANTS.

THE DOUBLE SYSTEM OF SPEED WAYS ARE AT THE TWO OUTER EDGES OF THE COMPLEX & THEY CARRY WITHIN THEIR STRUCTURE CAR SILOS. & REPAIR SHOPS.
IF THE CAR BECOME SUDDENLY ABSOLETE THIS ALL SUSPENDED SYSTEM WOULD BE TAKEN OVER BY OTHER FUNCTIONS

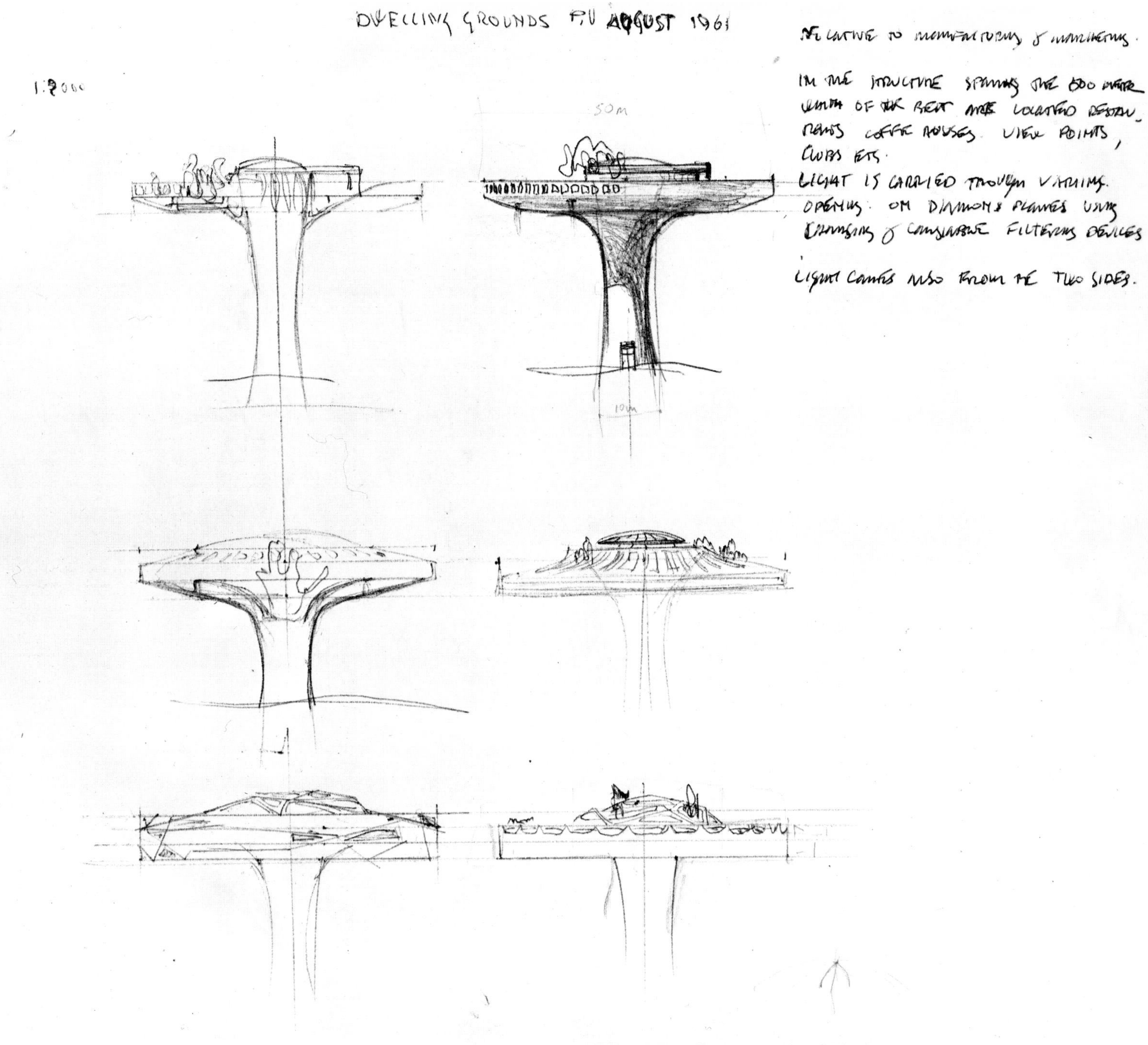
DWELLING GROUNDS P.V AUGUST 1961
1:2000
50m
10m
RELATIVE TO MANUFACTURING & MARKETING.
IN THE STRUCTURE SPANNING THE 600 METER WIDTH OF THE RIVER ARE LOCATED RESTAURANTS COFFEE HOUSES VIEW POINTS, CLUBS ETC.
LIGHT IS CARRIED THROUGH VARYING OPENINGS ON DIAMOND PLANES USING CHANGING & CONSISTENT FILTERING DEVICES
LIGHT COMES ALSO FROM THE TWO SIDES.

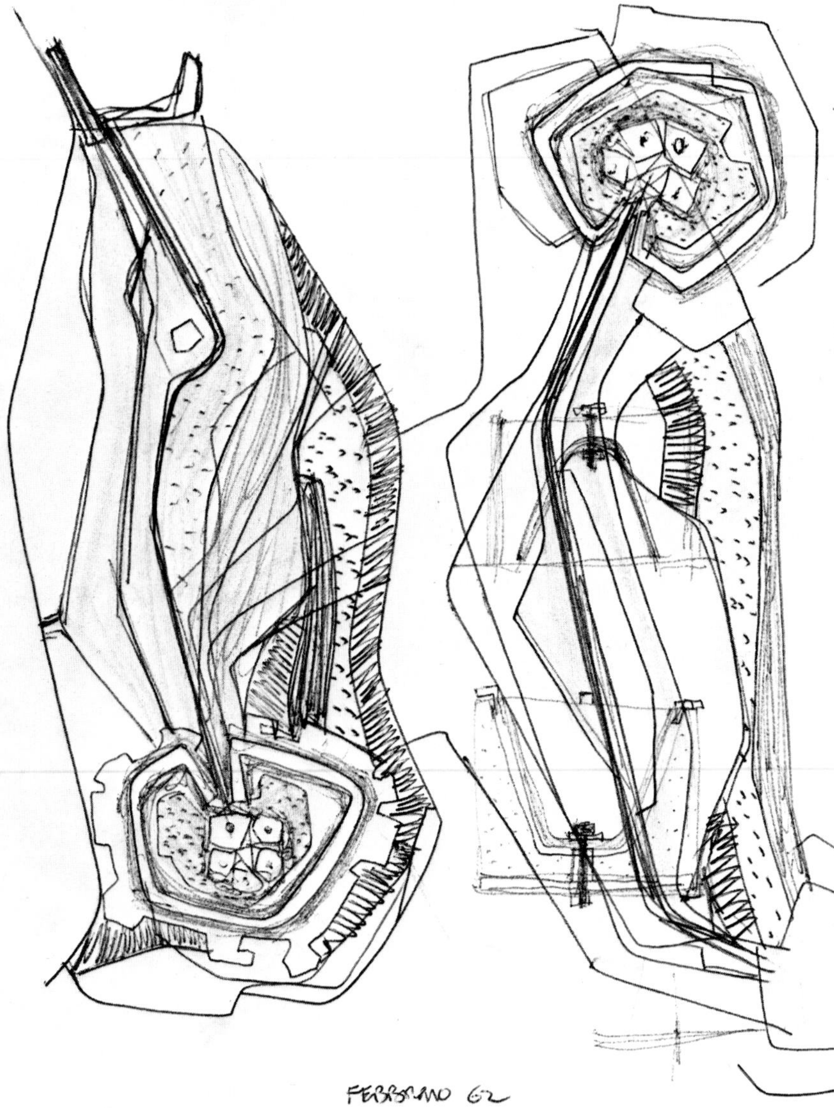

THEN GOD THE NEEDIEST WEAKEST OF ALL BEAUTY, ITS EXISTENCE POSTULATED BY MAN'S COMPASSION, IN ITS UPGRADING TOWARD THE ABSURD EVENTUALITY OF A LOVING UNIVERSE.

THIS INFANT GOOD DELIVERED TO US, IN NAKED DEFENSELESSNESS, SOBBING AT OUR INDIFFERENCE, WHIMPERING AT OUR SAVAGERY. A PAUPER OF OUR AFFLUENT CIVILISATION. THE APARTHEID IN OUR SCHEME OF DOGMAS & BIGOTTRIES. SEE (1) NEXT.

THE NATURAL, THE BEAUTIFUL, THE ARTISTIC

BEAUTY REVEALS ITSELF IN A CONCRETE OBJECT; NOT OBJECTIVATION HERE BUT AURA IN WHICH THE OBJECT IS IMMERSED
THIS AURA IN ITSELF A TEORETICAL EXISTENCE IN WANT OF WHAT THE CONTINUUM OF MATTER, WILL OFFER AS BASE FOR ITS CONCRETISATION.

THE CREATIVE SEQUENCE OF NATURE OR THE CREATIVE ACT OF MAN CAME TO POSSES THIS AUREA OR OCCASION & IT IS MOSTLY A GUESS WORK TO TRY TO FIND WHERE, WHAT THE REASONS ARE FOR ITS PRESENCE

IN THE ABSENCE OF THIS AURA THE OBJECT COMMUNICATE TO THE BEHOLDER AS IF THROUGH A SCREEN OF

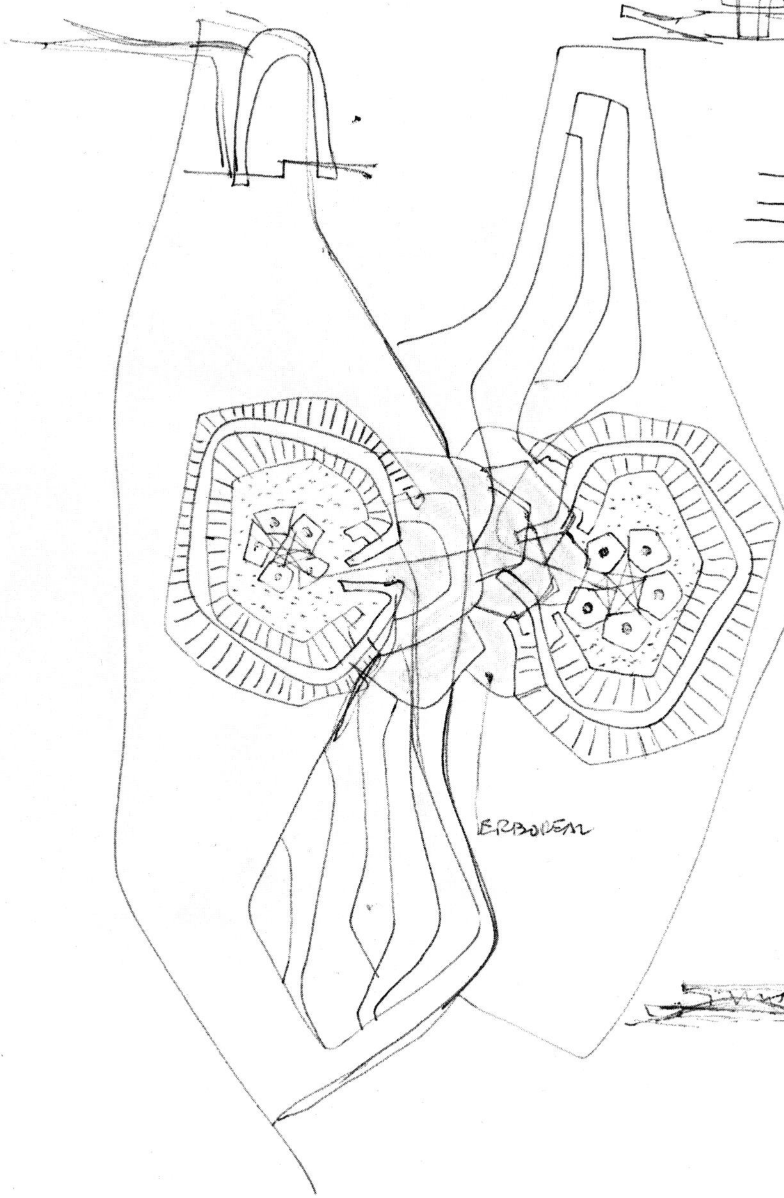

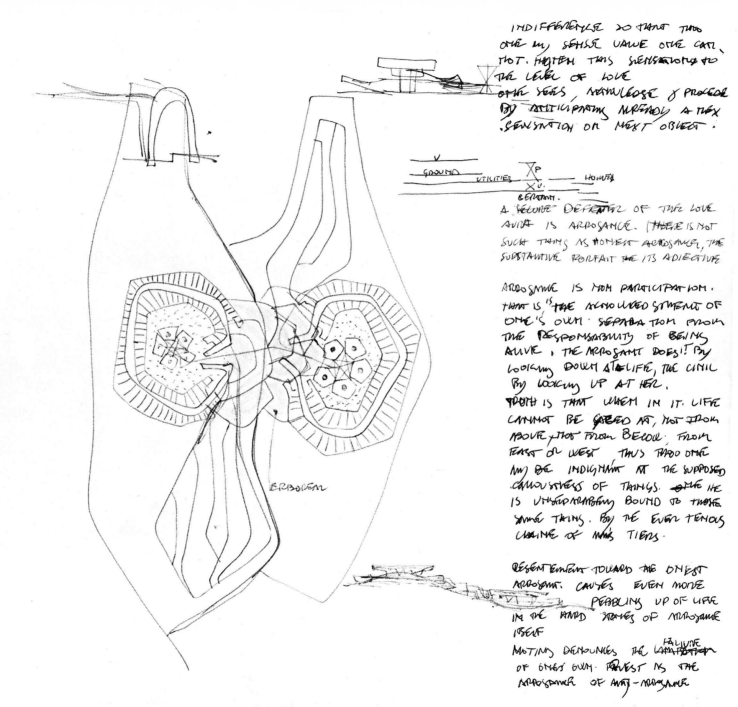

INDIFFERENCE SO THAT THOUGH ONE MAY SENSE VALUE ONE CANNOT. HEIGHTEN THIS SENSATION TO THE LEVEL OF LOVE
ONE SEES, ACKNOWLEDGE & PROCEED BY ~~ANTICIPATING~~ ALREADY A NEW SENSATION OR NEXT OBJECT.

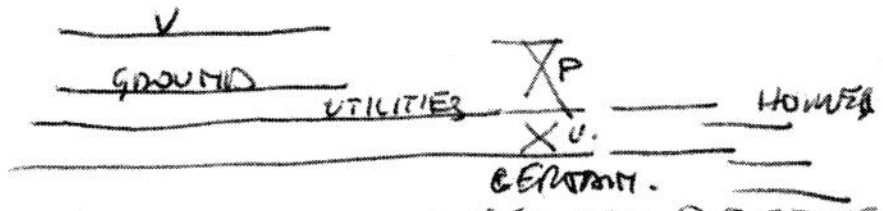

A ~~SECURE~~ DEFEATER OF THE LOVE AURA IS ARROGANCE. (THERE IS NOT SUCH THING AS HONEST ARROGANCE, THE SUBSTANTIVE FORFAIT ~~THE~~ ITS ADJECTIVE

ARROGANCE IS NON PARTICIPATION. THAT IS, IS ~~THE~~ ACKNOWLEDGEMENT OF ONE'S OWN SEPARATION FROM THE RESPONSIBILITY OF BEING ALIVE, THE ARROGANT DOES! BY LOOKING DOWN AT LIFE, THE CIVIL BY LOOKING UP AT HER.
TRUTH IS THAT WHEN IN IT. LIFE CANNOT BE GAZED AT, NOT FROM ABOVE, NOT FROM BELOW, FROM EAST OR WEST THUS THOUGH ONE MAY BE INDIGNANT AT THE SUPPOSED CALLOUSNESS OF THINGS. ~~ONE~~ HE IS UNSEPARABLY BOUND TO THOSE SAME THINGS. BY THE EVER TENUOUS CHAINE OF MAN'S TIERS.

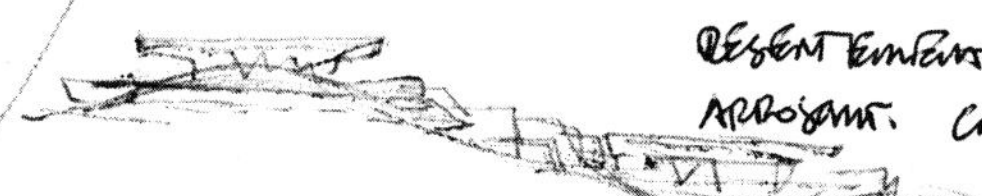

RESENTMENT TOWARD THE ONEST ARROGANT. CAUSES EVEN MORE PEBBLING UP OF LIFE IN THE HARD STONES OF ARROGANCE ITSELF
NOTING DENOUNCES THE ~~LIMITATION~~ FAILURE OF ONES OWN. HONEST AS THE ARROGANCE OF ANTI-ARROGANCE

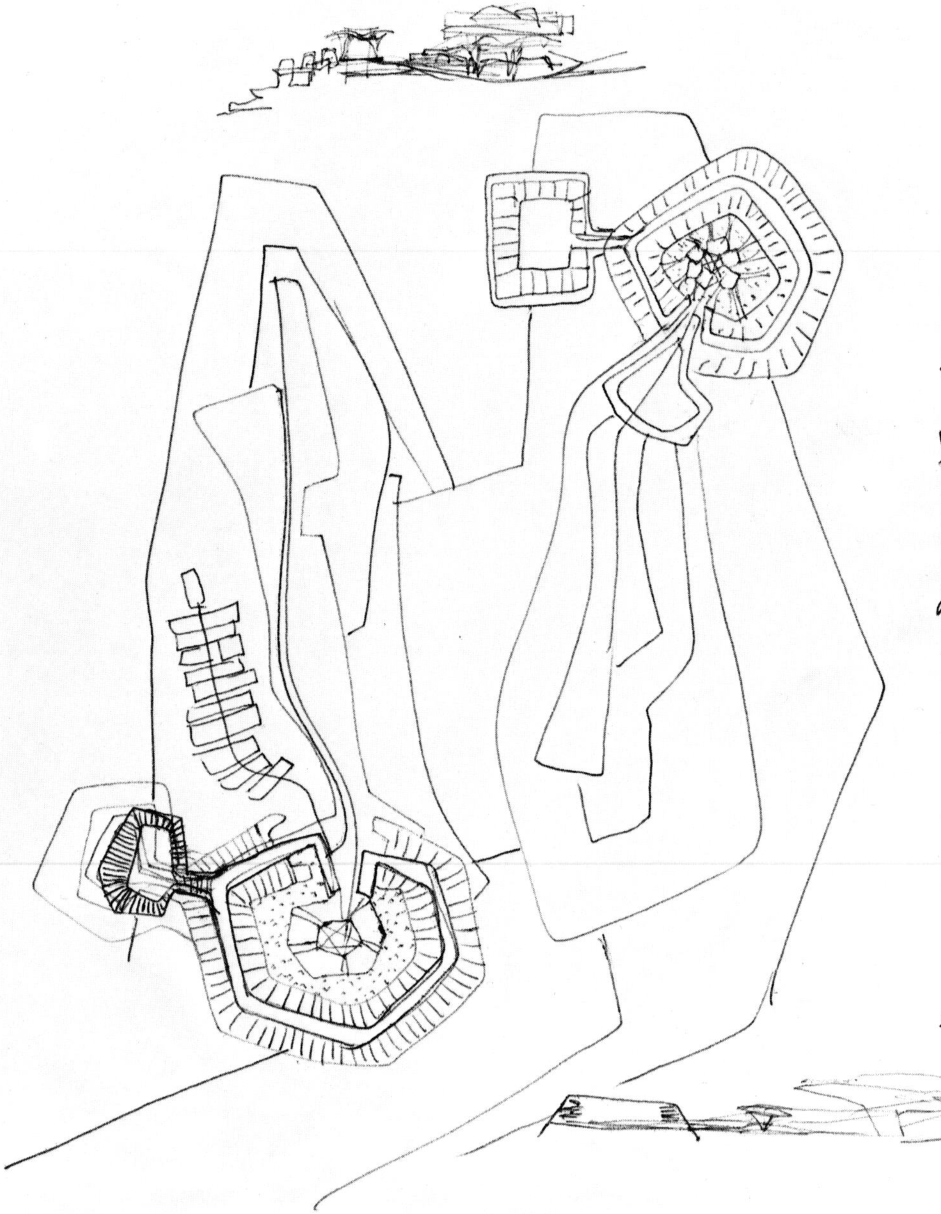

SEE (1) THE MITOLOGICAL MONSTERS OF
"PREHISTORY" BETTER ~~A~~ SIMBOL
OF AN UPSURGING. REALITY CUTTING
ITS WAY IN A "MEAT" SCARLATT
OF THE THICK BLOOD OF EVERY
OLDER & PRECARIOS MONSTERS

FOR A SUFFICENT RECEDING.
~~THIS BLOOD~~ RIVER OF BLOOD DILUD
IN A BROOK THEN IN A SMALLE
SPRING AMONG STONES & STRANGE
VEGETATION. THERE IN THE ENTRANCE
OF THE RELATIVELY YOUNG GRANITE
THE SORROWS & THE JOYS OF LIFE
INCIPIENT ALREADY IS AN AUDIBLE
VOICE CRYING & LAUGHING AT
THAT WHICH IS ~~FAR~~ REMOTELY FAR
& TOTALLY UNKNOWN.
THE VOICE OF THE INFANT GOD.
PREPARING FOR THE LONG. TREMENDOUS
JOURNEY.

THE BEATS MEASURING THE INFANT
GOD GROWTH ARE THE GENERATIONS
OF MAN & ITS ANCESTRY
THE LONG TORMENTED NIGHTS BY
THE CENTURIES OF OSCURANTISME.
THE SHATTERING NIGHTMARES. (SAID
TO BE INSTANTANEOUS LIKE ALL DREAMS)
BY THE "FUSING" HATRED OF MEN.

GOD HERDING ITS OWN MYRIADES
OF BEEINGS. SHEPERD & SHIPS, WATCH
DOG & LAMB, OCCASIONALLY SELF
DEVOURING PREDATOR, SUBSTANTIALLY
A GLORIFICATION OF THE EFFEMERAL
BECOMING THE INEFFABLE & THUS THE
MASTERING ENERGY UNFOLDING. THE
UNIMMAGINABLE AS MERE & CONSUB-
STANTIAL PEDESTALS TO EVER MORE
FANTASTIC "REALITY".

OUR PRESENT, THE FEARFULL JANUS OF
THE NEW BORN GOD, SO PREGNANT TO
ALL OF US LIVING, FINDING IN THE ILLU-
SION OF UNIQUENESS THE SOUSTENANCE
THAT EVERY PRESENT, HAS ALREADY HAD, TO ITS
OWN "FORTUNE", IS PINPOINTING TO EACH
INDIVIDUAL. THE FILIGRANE OF JOY &
ANGUISH UNIQUELY HIS. DEMANDS OF EACH
OF US THE DUST-PARTICLE OF CREATION.
WHICH WILL SANCTION A VISAGE UPON
THE FACELESS SKULL OF OUR MATERIA-
LITY
"A VISAGE TO BE REMEMBERED",

A VISAGE WHICH CAN EXPAND PHYSICAL-
& METAPHYSICALLY TO ELATE AROUND
ITSELF & FAR BEYOND ANY HORIZONT
THE NEW SOUND OF GOD'S VOICE THE
NEW GLIMMERING IN GODS' EYES,
ITS OWN INALIENABLE SPELL OF ETERNITY

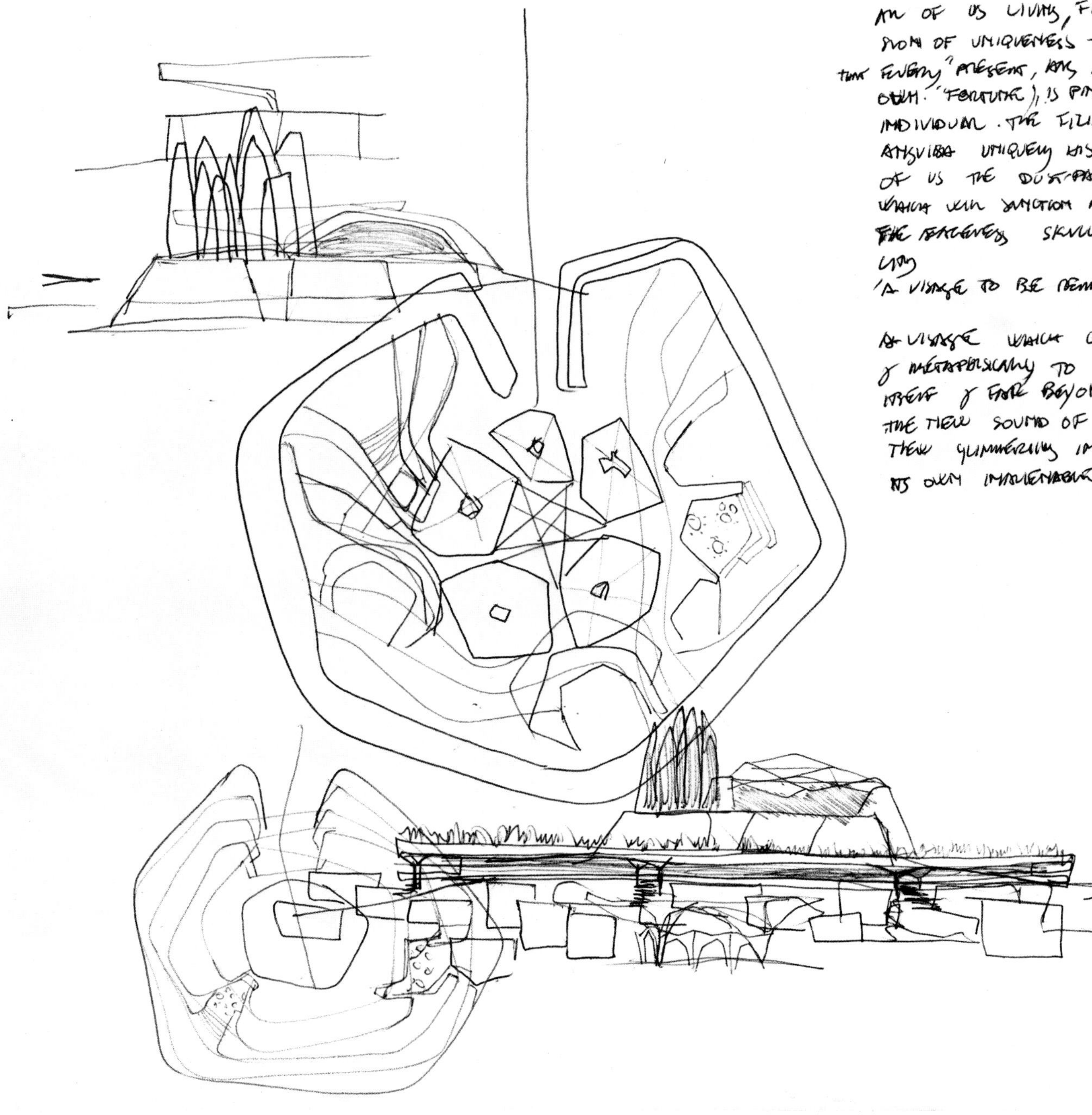

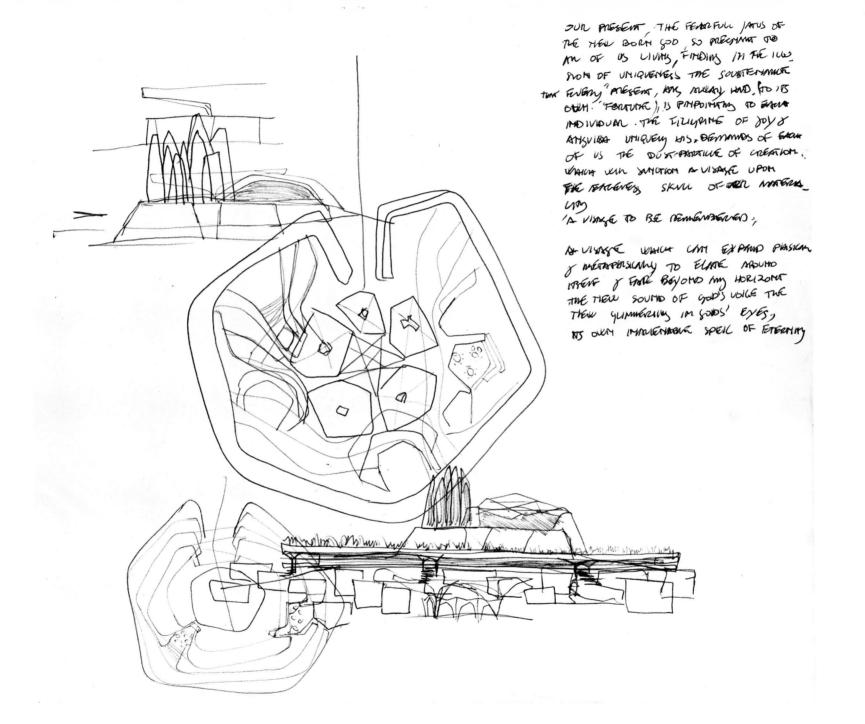

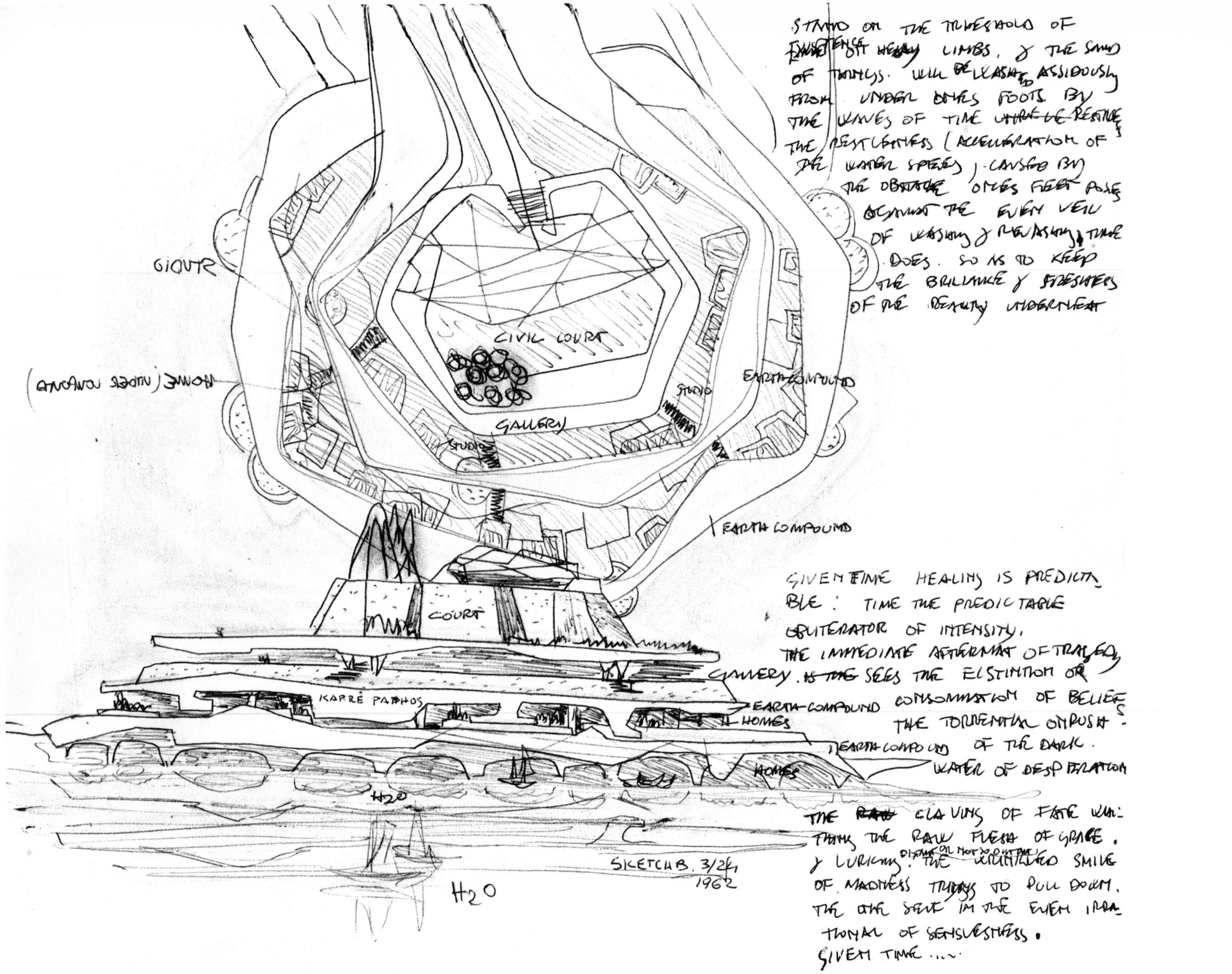
CIVIL COURT
GALLERY
STUDIO
STUDIO
EARTH COMPOUND
EARTH COMPOUND
COURT
GALLERY
KARRÉ PAPHOS
EARTH COMPOUND
HOMES
EARTH COMPOUND
HOMES
H2O
H2O
SKETCH B. 3/24, 1962
GIVEN TIME HEALING IS PREDICTA-
BLE: TIME THE PREDICTABLE
OBLITERATOR OF INTENSITY.
THE IMMEDIATE AFTERMATH OF TRAGEDY
SEES THE EXTINCTION OR
CONSUMMATION OF BELIEFS
THE TORRENTIAL ONRUSH
OF THE DARK
WATER OF DESPERATION
GIVEN TIME .....

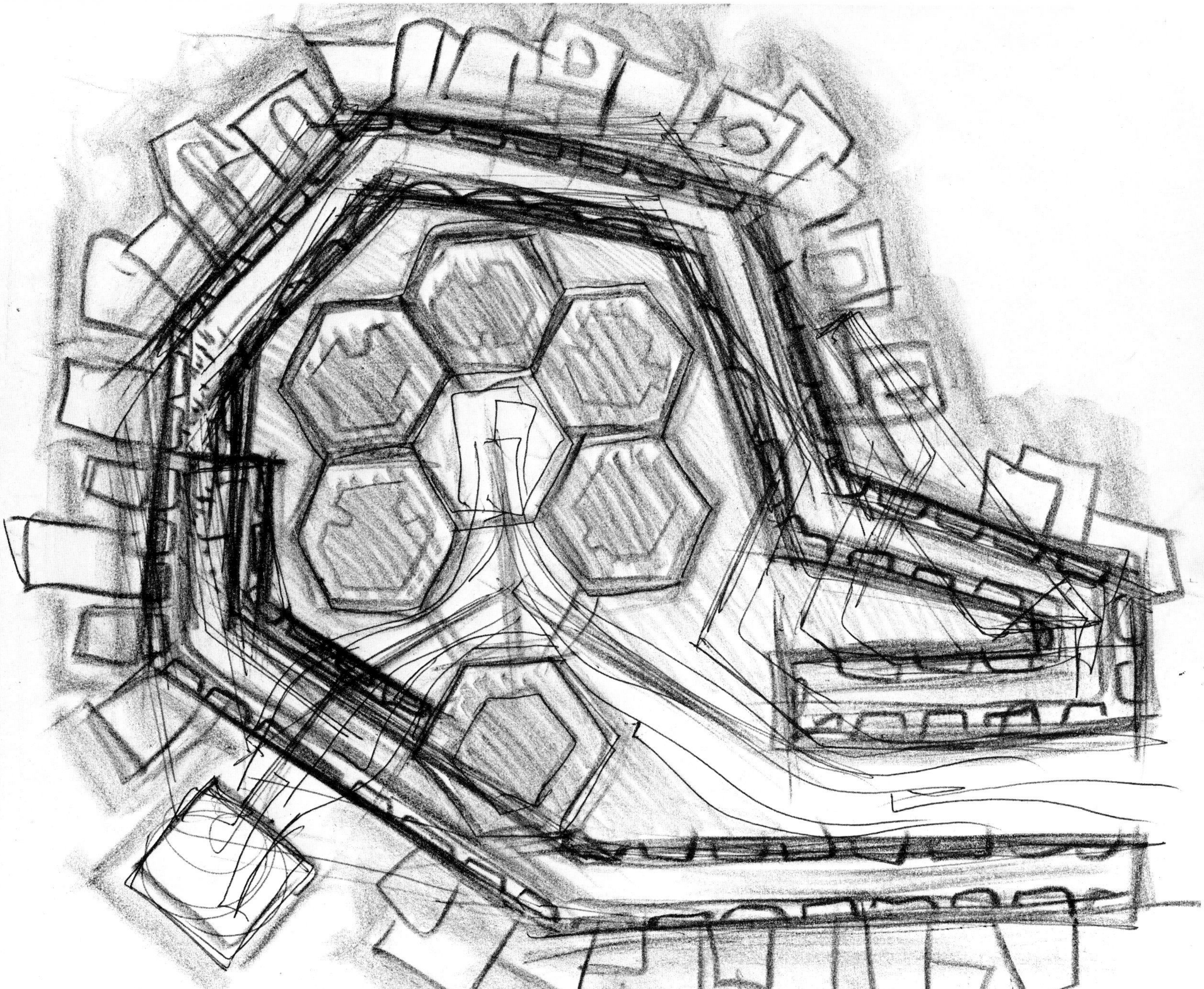

Center for Advanced Study

1970
To construct knowledge out of information is the core of the learning process. Too often the physical core of the information centers is a blatant failure as the shell for the metamorphosis of dormant bits of reality (information) into the radiant kind of substance that knowledge becomes. To attempt a congruence within the general pattern of the real, mineral, biological, human, temporal, and spatial world would seem to be the highest priority of a university. How otherwise can knowledge be offered to man, the latest success in the long adventure of life coherent with the system supporting it? The environmental failure of the campuses is due to the perpetration of violence on coherence and wholeness. The dotting of the campus grounds with architectural "jewels" is a direct attempt to mesmerize the pliable mind of the student and a no-less-direct indictment of the faculty and administration for the lack of insight and courage they demonstrate. One does not go into a bazaar for inspiration and guidance. In the bazaar one finds the bizarre and the irrelevant or, perchance, the surprising in minute fragments of unrelated cleverness. As the forerunner of the Arcology, the study center is a large and coherent system, much more than one cubic kilometer of sheltered and structured space.

1960
The center for advanced study is in some ways the most "abstract" conception of the whole project. Many of the ideas existing in other organisms are here used with greater force: such concepts as multiplication of grounds, definition of many environmental conditions, visualization of the problem as the coupled activity of a constant reaching from the past and a variable projected on the needs of the future. Thus, there is a nondeformable skeleton (the constant) on which to vest ever-changing functional wants (the variable).

Whatever system of departmentalization is used, such departments are stacked vertically as well as contiguously. This is done intentionally in order to

1.
Increase the more efficient vertical transportation system at the expense of the horizontal.

2.
Cluster very densely the physical body of learning facilities.

3.
Reduce drastically the distance and size of all utilities.

4.
Define a polyvalent volumetric condition: the stacked departments; the open-air sheltered and conditioned grounds; the "sun-free" space, where the outer skin of a building does not have to sustain the extremes of direct radiation.

Such a scheme becomes understandable and feasible only through the physical scale adopted. The average height of each structure is about 250 meters. The dimensions of an outdoor volume cut into space by dendriform structures is hard to visualize; by roofing over the center of Manhattan with skylights and suspended gardens topping and spanning the highest skyscrapers, one would approach the scale of things involved but not by any means the mood and character of them. The surfaces, curved and half transparent, half reflecting, would add a sense of relationship between the physical and the ultraphysical. The geometric rigor of each volume, as well as the rigor of the space that such volumes exclude and envelop, would place the complex solidly within the realm of the man-made beyond any analogy with the work and the expression of nature. It would not resemble a huge forest, nor a vast cave studded by stalactites, nor a submarine realm, nor a blown-up microcosmic structure; yet it would be dimly reminiscent of them all. The spherical world of human vision could move endlessly among the unceasing variations that perspective would define: of light, of color, of a kind of measured spatiality. An atmosphere of defined parameters would combine in the aesthetic category the conceptual position of the constant untouched by motion and the variables in an ever-changing realm.

The low, two-story platform is the connective element close to the ground and will carry all the traffic transferring students from one department to another. The grounds are for retreat, leisure, and quietness. Direct access and the bulk of circulation to the departments is at an upper level on the circular, two-deck road linking all the suspended bridges that lead to the dormitories and the villages.

THE QUANTUM PACAGES OF PROBABILITIES
REFLECTED IN THE QUEST FOR THE
MELODY TROUGH THE PROBABLE IN JAZZ.
THE JAZZ MUSITIAN LIKE THE INDIAN
HORSMAN RIDES AROUND ~~THE~~ ITS PRAY
IN CIRCLE NOW LARGE NOW TITE
SEEKING THE CORE OF ITS RAPTURE
BY WRAPPING TEXTURES OF SOUND ON
THE SLIM FUST OF A MELODY ONCE
HEARD

THAT APPLIES ON MOST OF CONTEMPORARY
EXPRESSIONS. SCULPTURE, PAINTING,
DRAMA, MOVIE,... THE CORE, THE
REAL IF PRESENT IT IS BY IMPLICATIONS.
EACH FLOATING OR TWIRLING AROUND
ITS EVENTUALITY
IN CONSTRUCTION ONLY SCORES
OF BUILDINGS PATTERNED ON THE SAME
SCHEME & SLIGLY DIFFERENT IN
PROPORTION-RELATION-DETAIL COULD
DEFINE THE ARCHITECTURAL REALITY
OF ITS CONCEPTION. HERE THE
PACAGE IS ALMOST EMPTY ONLY
ONE PROBABILITY IS GIVEN, THUS:
EVERY POUR CHANCES OF TOUCHING
INTO THE THING.

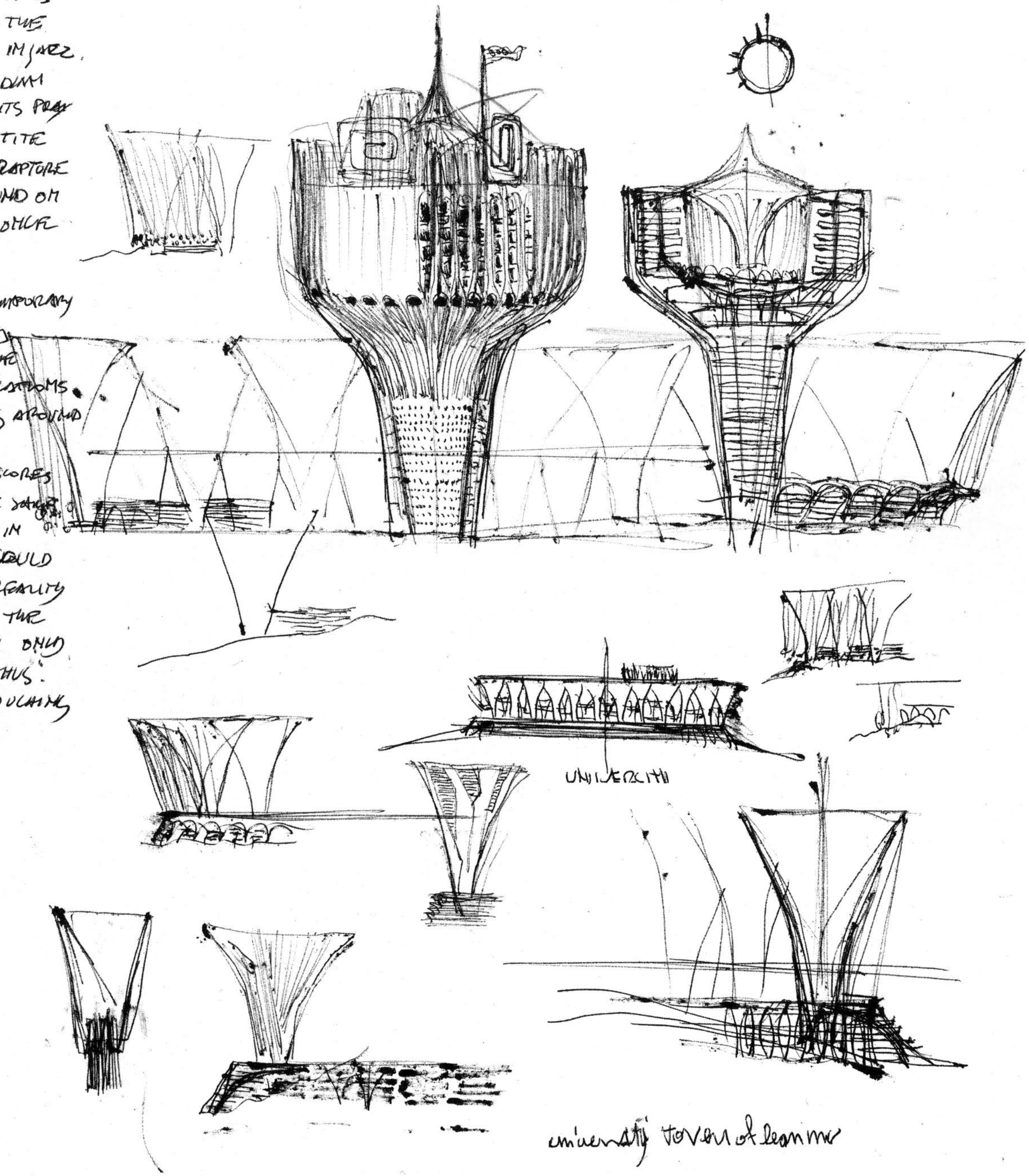

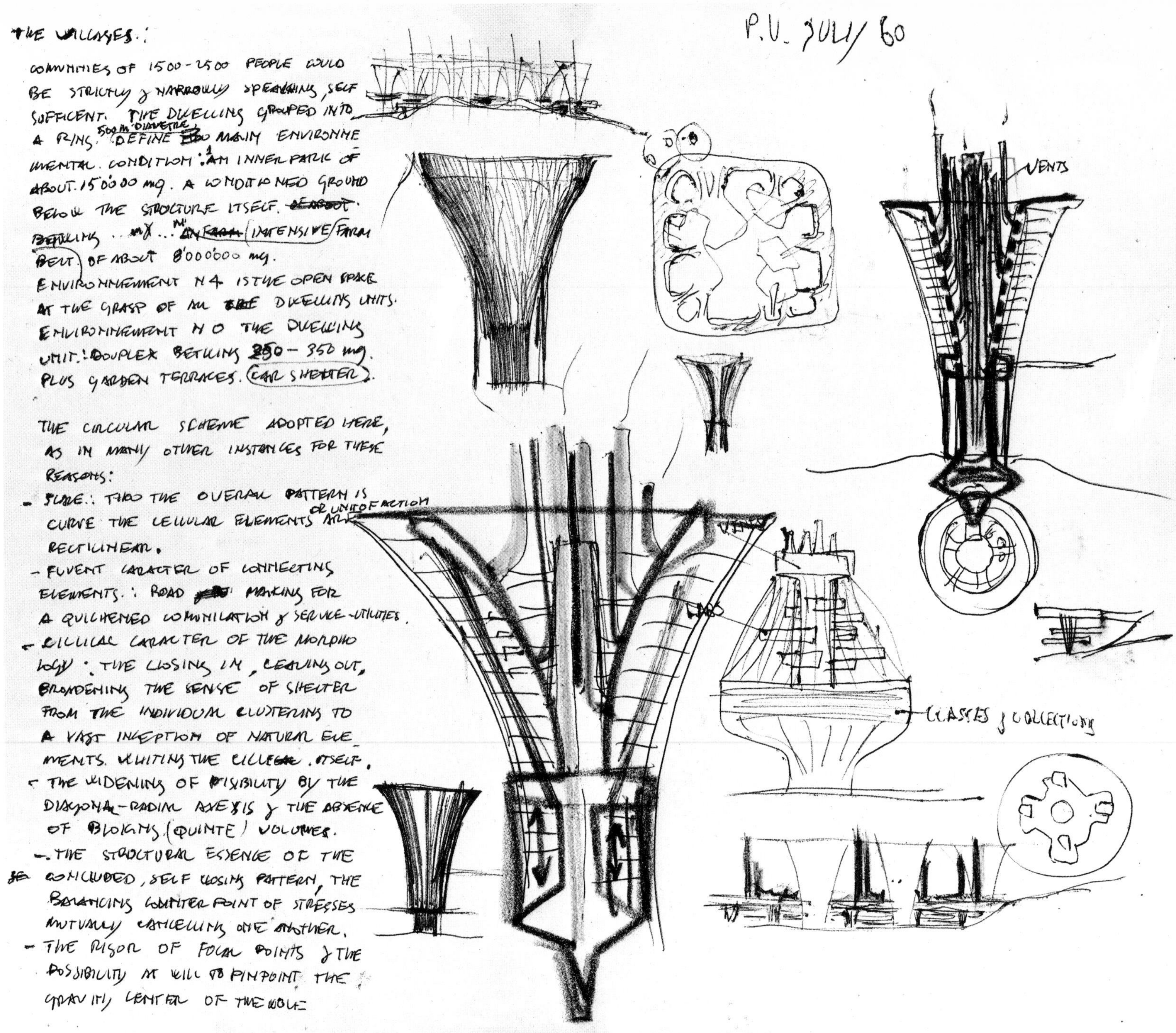
THE VILLAGES:
COMMUNITIES OF 1500-2500 PEOPLE WOULD
BE STRICTLY & NARROWLY SPEAKING, SELF
SUFFICENT. THE DWELLING GROUPED INTO
A RING. 500 M DIAMETRE DEFINE MAIN ENVIRONME
MENTAL CONDITION: AN INNER PARK OF
ABOUT 15'00'00 MQ. A CONDITIONED GROUND
BELOW THE STRUCTURE ITSELF.
BETLING ... MQ ... INTENSIVE FARM
BELT OF ABOUT 8'000'000 MQ.
ENVIRONMENT N 4 IS THE OPEN SPACE
AT THE GRASP OF ALL DWELLING UNITS.
ENVIRONMENT N 0 THE DWELLING
UNIT: DOUPLEX BETLING 250 - 350 MQ.
PLUS GARDEN TERRACES. CAR SHELTER.
THE CIRCULAR SCHEME ADOPTED HERE,
AS IN MANY OTHER INSTANCES FOR THESE
REASONS:
- SCALE: THO THE OVERALL PATTERN IS
CURVE THE CELLULAR ELEMENTS OR UNIT OF ACTION ARE
RECTILINEAR.
- FLUENT CARACTER OF CONNECTING
ELEMENTS: ROAD MAKING FOR
A QUICKENED COMUNICATION & SERVICE-UTILITIES.
- CICLICAL CARACTER OF THE MORPHO
LOGY: THE CLOSING IN, LEAVING OUT,
BROADENING THE SENSE OF SHELTER
FROM THE INDIVIDUAL CLUSTERING TO
A VAST INCEPTION OF NATURAL ELE_
MENTS. UNITING THE VILLAGE ITSELF.
- THE WIDENING OF VISIBILITY BY THE
DIAGONAL-RADIAL AXIS & THE ABSENCE
OF BLOCKING (QUINTE) VOLUMES.
- THE STRUCTURAL ESSENCE OF THE
CONCLUDED, SELF CLOSING PATTERN, THE
BALANCING COUNTER POINT OF STRESSES
MUTUALLY CANCELLING ONE ANOTHER.
- THE RIGOR OF FOCAL POINTS & THE
POSSIBILITY AT WILL TO PINPOINT THE
GRAVITY CENTER OF THE WHOLE
P.U. JULY 60
VENTS
CLASSES & COLLECTIONS

AROUND THE TEOLOGY HILL. ARE THE INDIGENOUS VILLAGES SERVED BY THE MARKETS RIBBON HERE SHELTERING INDIGENOUS PRODUCE IN. FOOD, CRAFTS.

CEMETERIES ARE SCATTERED ON THE SLOPE BETWEEN THE VILLAGES & THE TEOLOGICAL COMPLEX

PEDESTRIAN ACCESSES CLIMB THROUGH THE CEMETERIES. & FLOWER TERRACES... MONASTERY GARDENS.

DAMS ARE RETAINING WATER INTO A LARGE RECEIVING NORTHWAY INTAKES ARE FEEDING THE "CONVEYOR BELTS" THE STREAMS - THE CANALS NETWORK ......

FROM THE DAMS. WATER WAY MOVE SOUTH WARD COMPOSING LINEAR CITIES & CLUSTERING. VILLAGES. THE LOW LAND IS OF MAIN: NATURE. ~~GRAZING ON THE HILLS~~ WILD ON THE HILLS

- GRAZING ON THE FOOT HILLS,
- CEREAL CULTIVATION IN THE MID VALLEY
- ORCHARDS & VEGETABLE GARDENS, SURROUNDING THE VILLAGES & ALONG THE LINEAR CITY - WATER WAYS.

RAIL ROAD SERVING SILOS BATTERIES IN THE FARMLAND & INDUSTRIES EAST & WEST OF THE CITY (CONTAINED & CONCEALED IN THE CANYONS CUT BETWEEN THE MESAS)

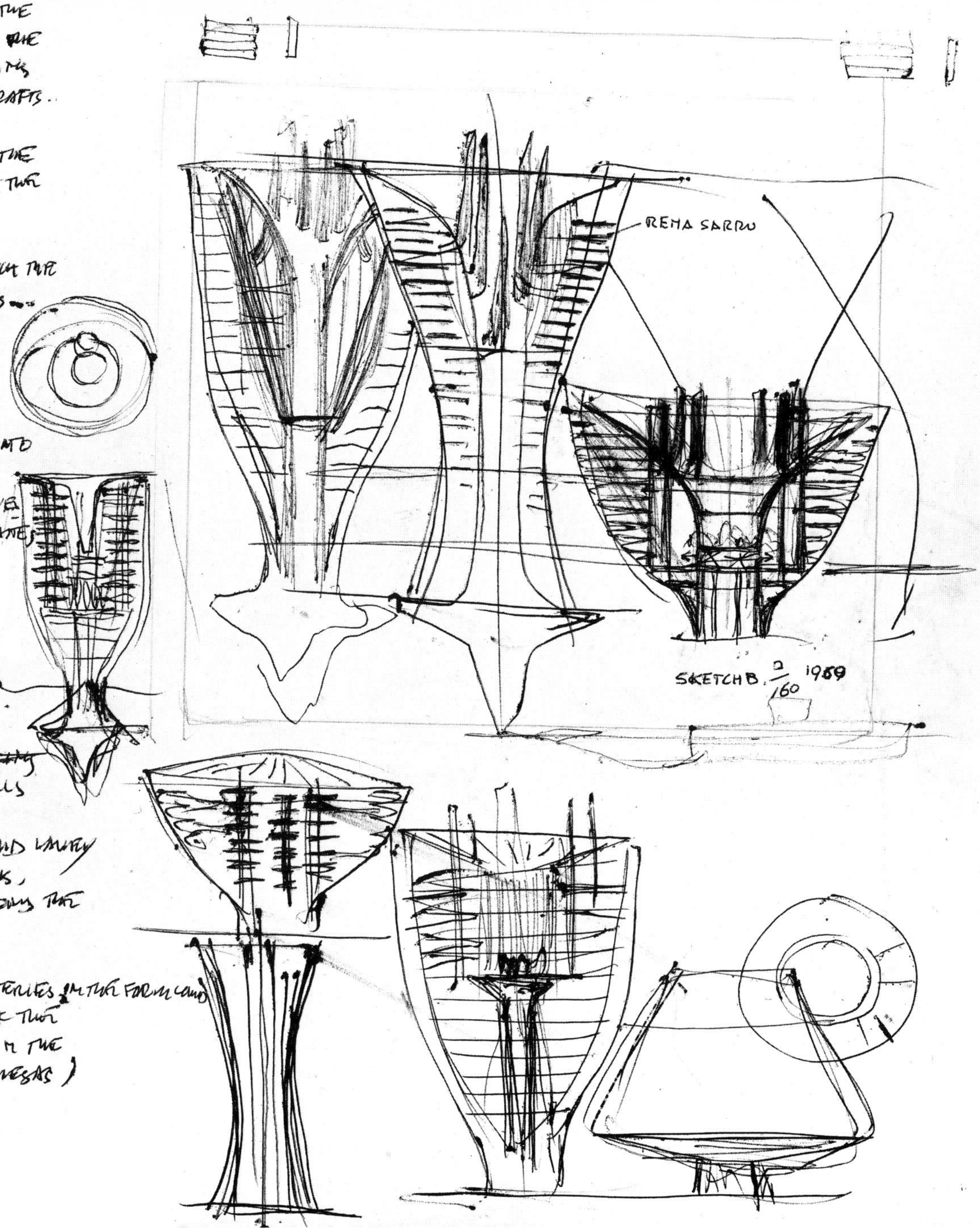

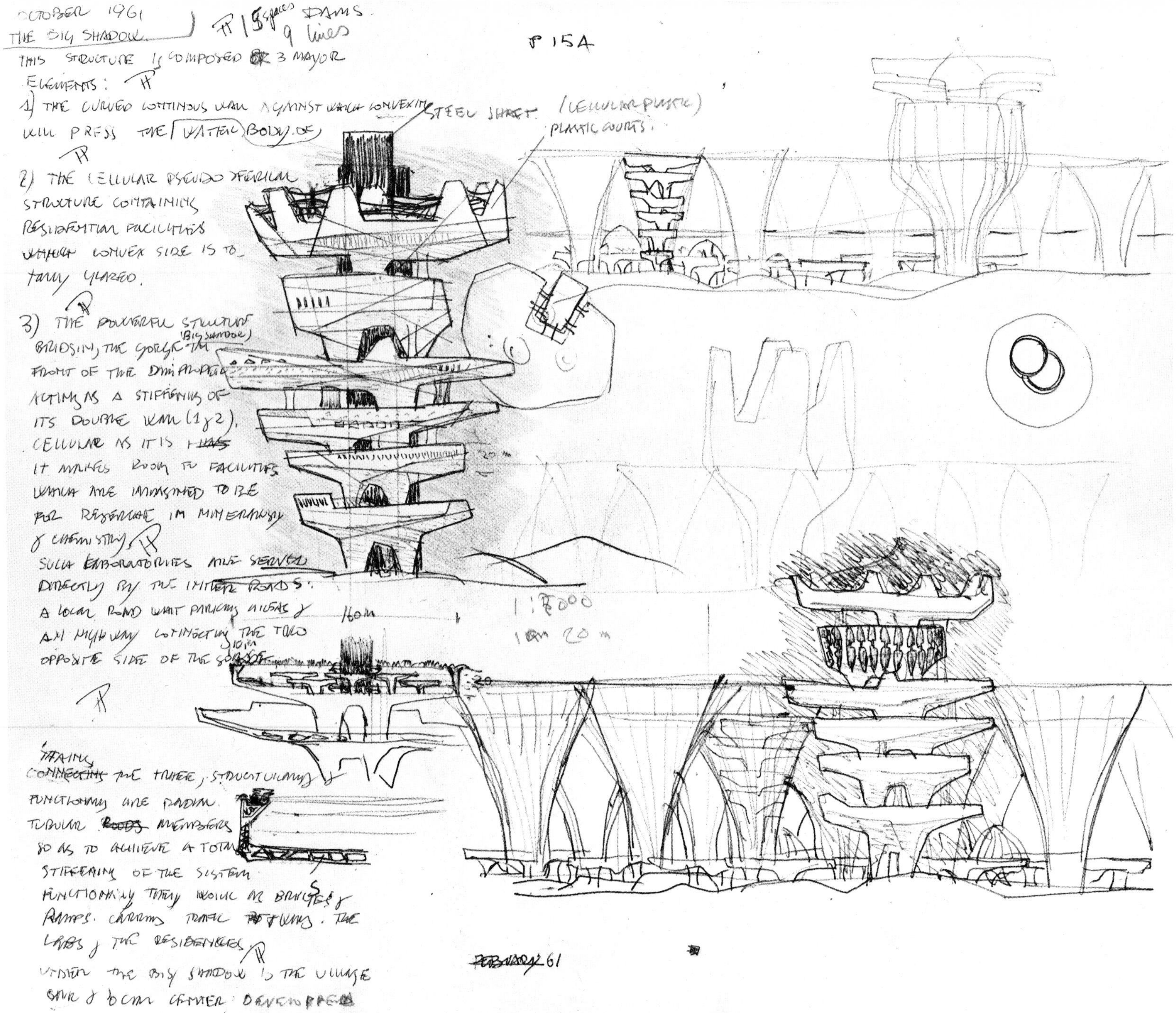
OCTOBER 1961
THE BIG SHADOW
DAMS
9 lines
P 15A
THIS STRUCTURE IS COMPOSED OF 3 MAJOR ELEMENTS:
1) THE CURVED CONTINUOUS WALL AGAINST WHICH CONVEXITY WILL PRESS THE WATER BODY OF
STEEL SHEET
(CELLULAR PLASTIC)
PLASTIC COURTS
2) THE CELLULAR PSEUDO SPERICAL STRUCTURE CONTAINING RESIDENTIAL FACILITIES WHOSE CONVEX SIDE IS TO
3) THE POWERFUL STRUCTURE (BIG SHADOW) BRIDGING THE GORGE IN FRONT OF THE DAM
ACTING AS A STIFFENING OF ITS DOUBLE WALL (1 & 2).
CELLULAR AS IT IS IT MAKES ROOM TO FACILITIES WHICH ARE IMAGINED TO BE FOR RESEARCH IN MINERALOGY & CHEMISTRY
SUCH LABORATORIES ARE SERVED DIRECTLY BY THE INNER ROADS:
A LOCAL ROAD WITH PARKING AREAS & AN HIGHWAY CONNECTING THE TWO OPPOSITE SIDE OF THE GORGE
1:2000
1 cm 20 m
CONNECTING THE THREE, STRUCTURALLY & FUNCTIONALLY ARE RADIAL TUBULAR MEMBERS
SO AS TO ACHIEVE A TOTAL STIFFENING OF THE SYSTEM
FUNCTIONALLY THEY WORK AS BRIDGES & RAMPS CARRYING TRAFFIC BETWEEN THE LABS & THE RESIDENCES
UNDER THE BIG SHADOW IS THE VILLAGE
FEBRUARY 61

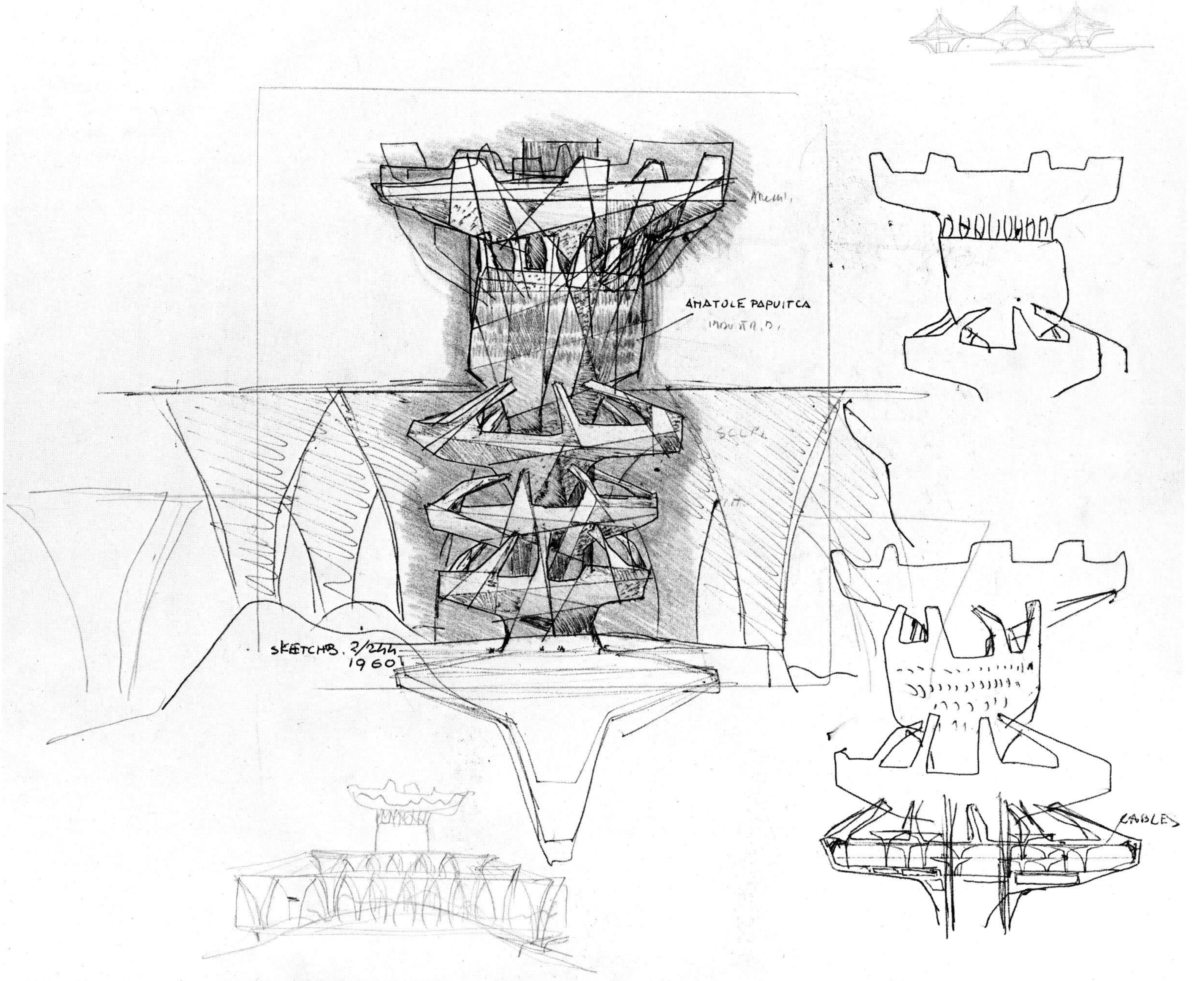
ANATOLE PAPUITCA
SKETCH B. 2/24
1960
CABLES

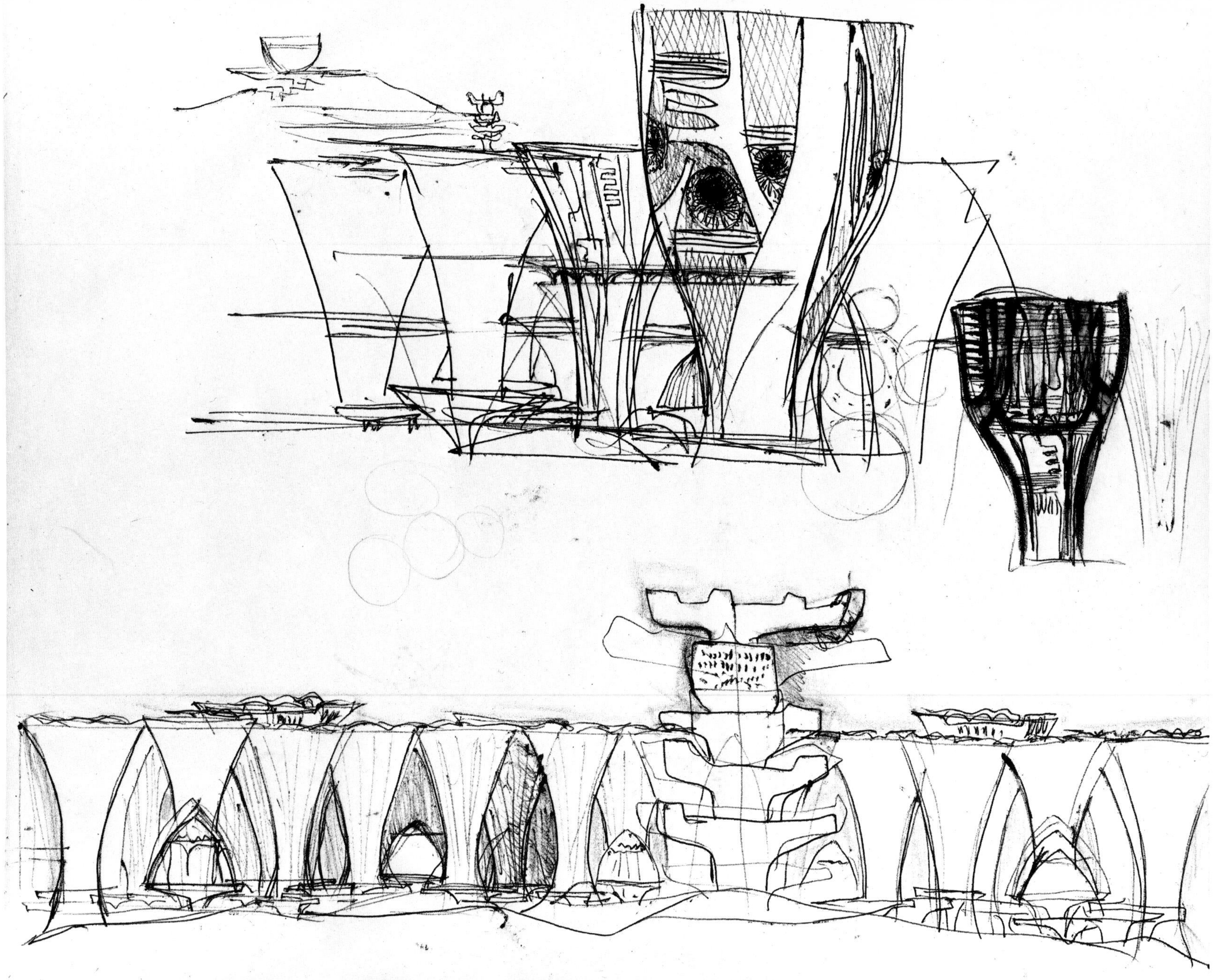

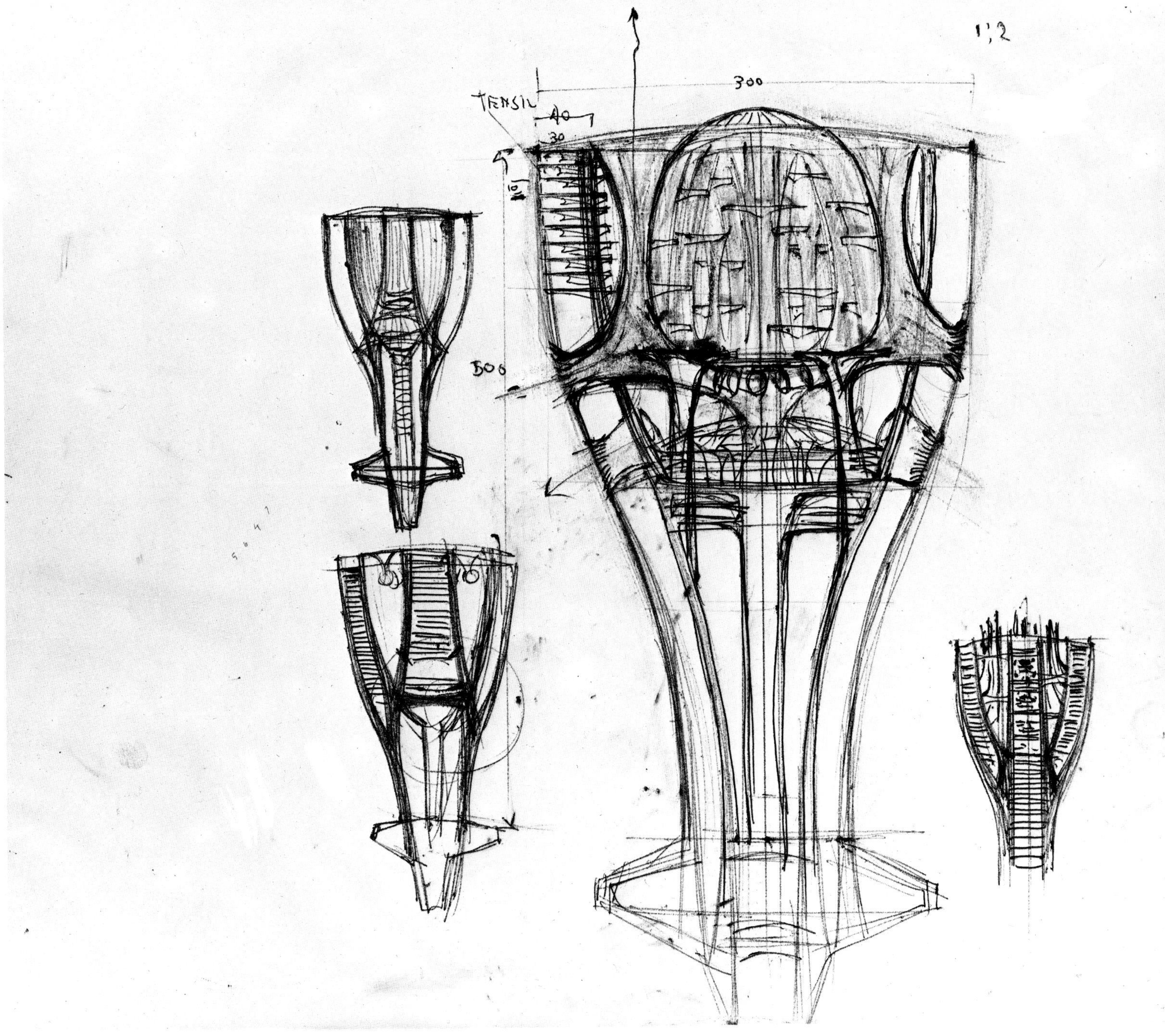
1;2
300
TENSIL
40
30
10
500

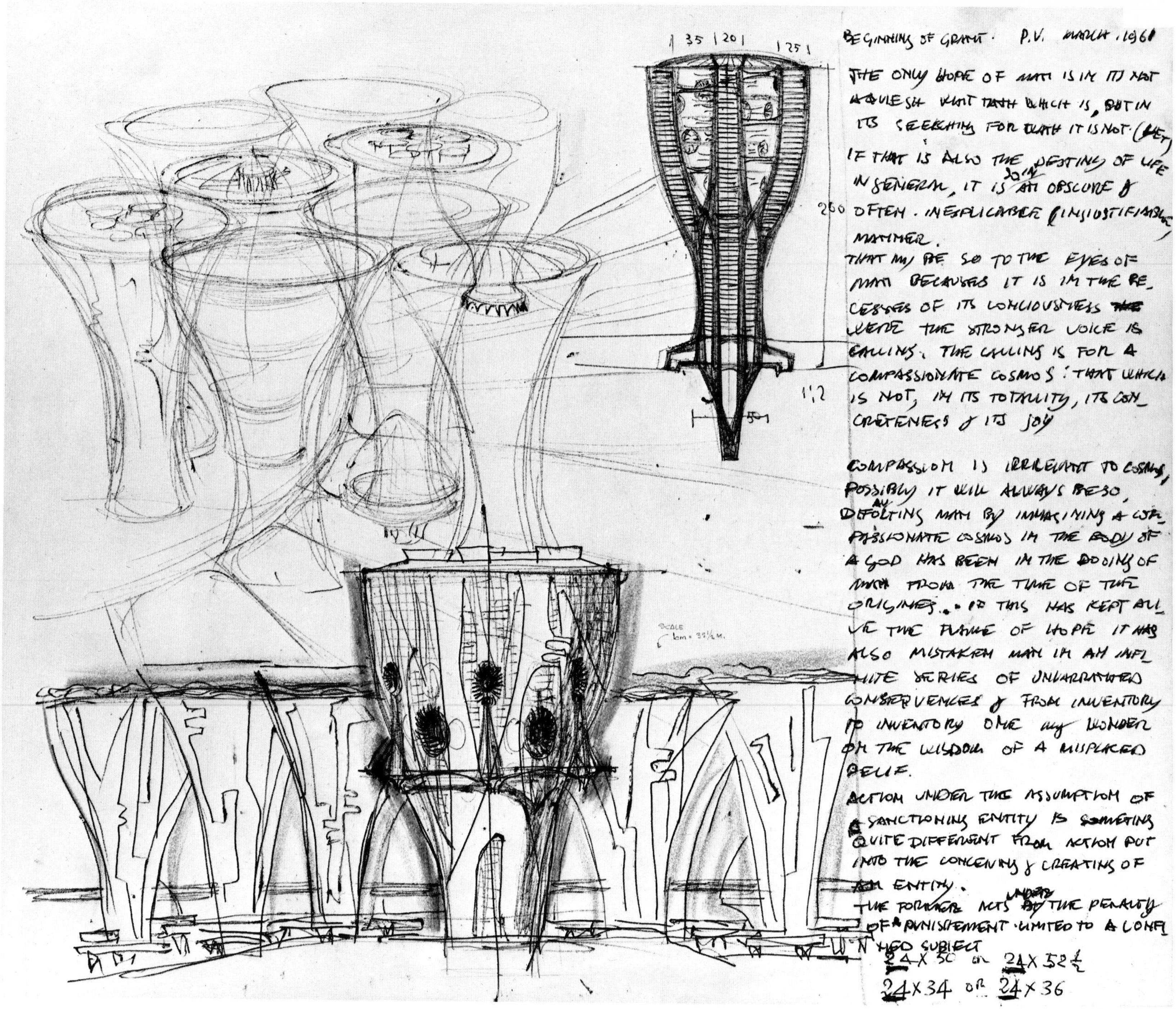
BEGINNING OF GRANT. P.V. MARCH. 1961
IF THAT IS ALSO THE DESTINY OF LIFE IN GENERAL, IT IS IN AN OBSCURE & OFTEN INEXPLICABLE & UNJUSTIFIABLE MANNER.
THAT MAY BE SO TO THE EYES OF MAN BECAUSE IT IS IN THE RECESSES OF ITS CONSCIOUSNESS WHERE THE STRONGER VOICE IS CALLING. THE CALLING IS FOR A COMPASSIONATE COSMOS: THAT WHICH IS NOT, IN ITS TOTALITY, ITS CONCRETENESS & ITS JOY
COMPASSION IS IRRELEVANT TO COSMOS, POSSIBLY IT WILL ALWAYS BE SO.
ACTION UNDER THE ASSUMPTION OF A SANCTIONING ENTITY IS SOMETHING QUITE DIFFERENT FROM ACTION PUT INTO THE CONCEIVING & CREATING OF AN ENTITY.
24 X 50 OR 24 X 52½
24 X 34 OR 24 X 36
SCALE

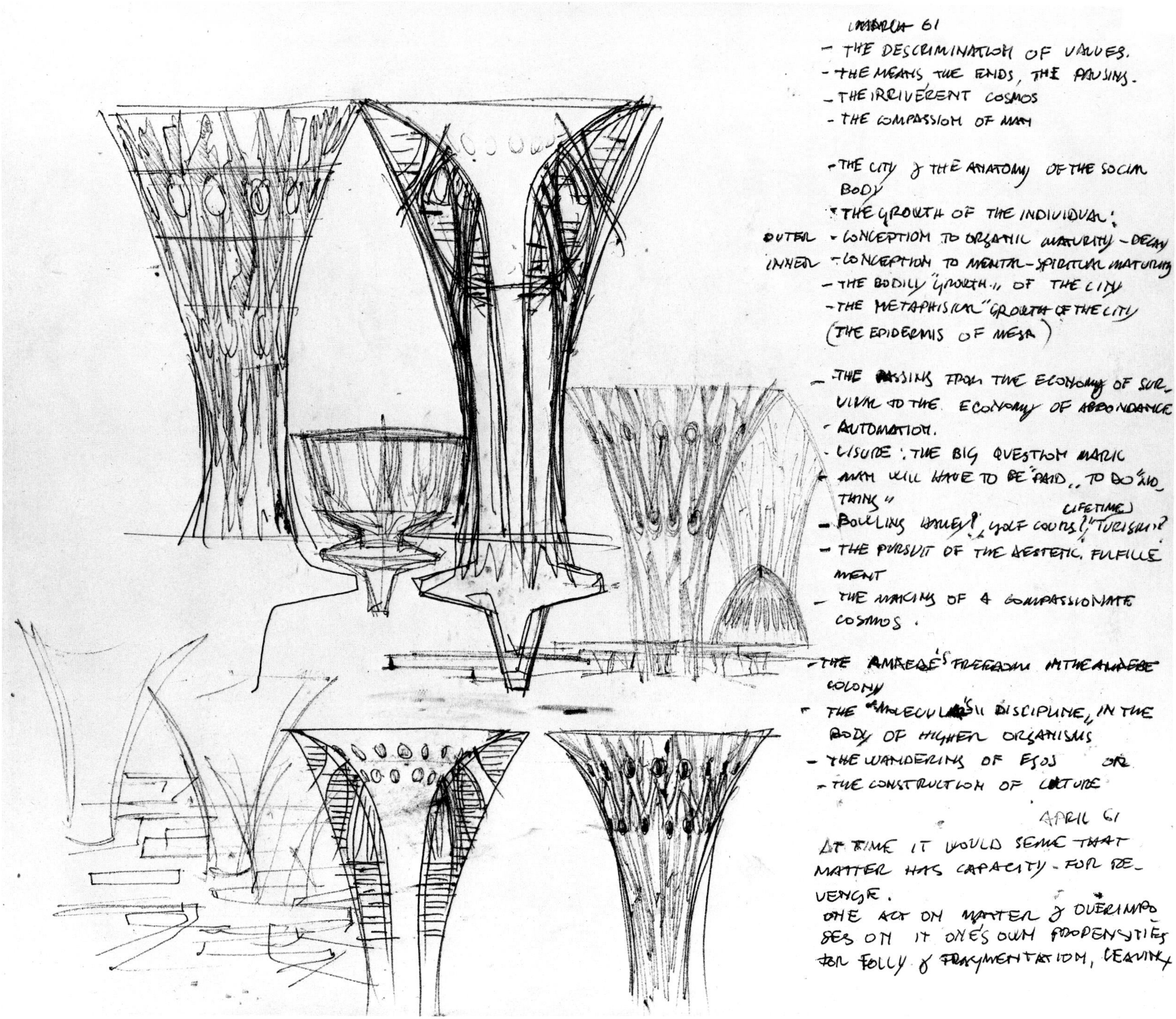
MARCH 61
- THE DESCRIMINATION OF VALUES.
- THE MEANS THE ENDS, THE PAUSING.
- THE IRRIVERENT COSMOS
- THE COMPASSION OF MAN
- THE CITY & THE ANATOMY OF THE SOCIAL BODY
- THE GROWTH OF THE INDIVIDUAL:
OUTER - CONCEPTION TO ORGANIC MATURITY - DECAY
INNER - CONCEPTION TO MENTAL-SPIRITUAL MATURITY
- THE BODILY "GROWTH" OF THE CITY
- THE METAPHISICAL "GROWTH OF THE CITY
(THE EPIDERMIS OF MESA)
- THE PASSING FROM THE ECONOMY OF SURVIVAL TO THE ECONOMY OF ABBONDANCE
- AUTOMATION.
- LISURE: THE BIG QUESTION MARK
- MAN WILL HAVE TO BE "PAID" TO DO "NOTHING"
- BOWLING ALLEY?, GOLF COURS?, "TURISM"? (LIFETIME)
- THE PURSUIT OF THE AESTETIC FULFILLEMENT
- THE MAKING OF A COMPASSIONATE COSMOS.
- THE AMEBE'S FREEDOM IN THE AMEBE COLONY
- THE "MOLECULAR'S" DISCIPLINE, IN THE BODY OF HIGHER ORGANISMS
- THE WANDERING OF EGOS OR
- THE CONSTRUCTION OF CULTURE
APRIL 61
AT TIME IT WOULD SEME THAT MATTER HAS CAPACITY FOR REVENGE.
ONE ACT ON MATTER & OVERIMPOSES ON IT ONE'S OWN PROPENSITIES FOR FOLLY & FRAGMENTATION, LEAVING

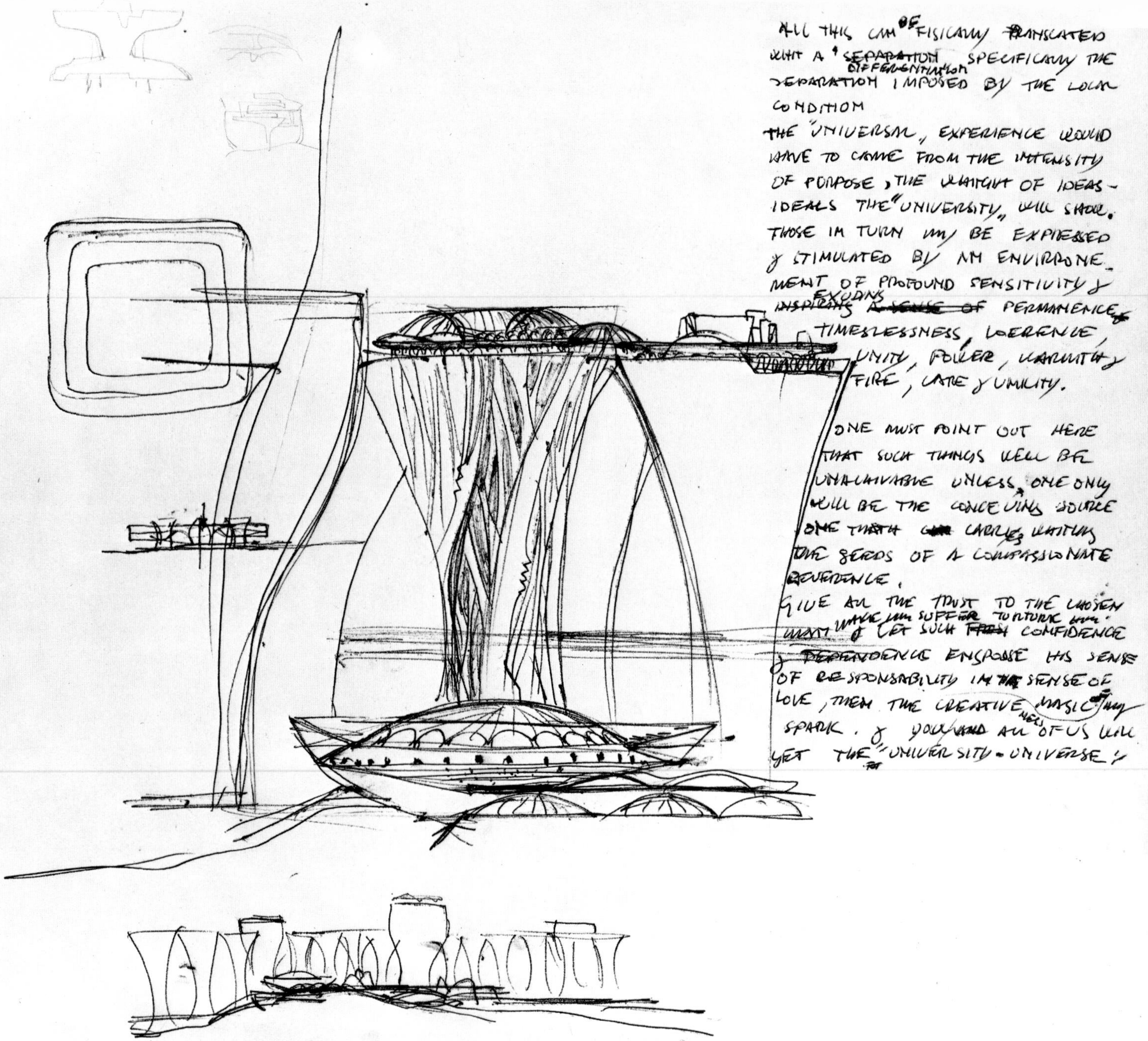
ALL THIS CAN BE FISICALLY TRANSLATED
WHIT A "DIFFERENTIATION" SPECIFICALLY THE
SEPARATION IMPOSED BY THE LOCAL
CONDITION
THE "UNIVERSAL" EXPERIENCE WOULD
HAVE TO COME FROM THE INTENSITY
OF PURPOSE, THE WEIGHT OF IDEAS-
IDEALS THE "UNIVERSITY" WILL SHOW.
THOSE IN TURN MAY BE EXPRESSED
& STIMULATED BY AN ENVIRONE-
MENT OF PROFOUND SENSITIVITY &
EXUDING PERMANENCE,
TIMELESSNESS, COERENCE,
UNITY, POWER, WARMTH,
FIRE, CARE & UMILITY.
ONE MUST POINT OUT HERE
THAT SUCH THINGS WILL BE
UNACHIEVABLE UNLESS ONE ONLY
WILL BE THE CONCEIVING SOURCE
ONE THAT CARRIES WAITING
THE SEEDS OF A COMPASSIONATE
REVERENCE.
GIVE ALL THE TRUST TO THE CHOSEN
MAN, MAKE HIM SUFFER TORTURE HIM
& LET SUCH CONFIDENCE
& DEPENDENCE ENGROSSE HIS SENSE
OF RESPONSABILITY IN SENSE OF
LOVE, THEN THE CREATIVE MAGIC MAY
SPARK. & YOU AND ALL OF US WILL
GET THE "UNIVERSITY-UNIVERSE"!

1970
The business center is similar to the study center but more codified or dogmatized. It is a vast system of interconnected towers, whose inner space defines a garden among whose trees sprout man-made trees, each the site for a computer. Will those man-made trees be fruitful or sterile? It is a question mark written all over the recent doings of man. Can we rationalize ourselves and remain human? It will depend on the degree of liveliness we will be able to nurture and grow between the deterministic stepping stones of progress.

We might well want to be purely efficient from the instrumental point of view, but if such efficiency blankets the landscape with an uninterrupted ribbon of "concrete-ness," it is almost axiomatic that buried beneath will be not only the entrails of logistics but also of the monad the efficient machine was meant to serve, the "I" and the "thou." Is it then that efficiency might be recognized as abstractness and self-destruction? Business as usual, free enterprise, the competition incentive—are we clever, or are we prey of a kind of topor? If those are the terms we choose to stick to, then we must fit them into the grand scheme of things. In it survival and plenitude do not refer to sectors of humanity nor to the opulence that curses some of them. What is business if it is not the "busy-ness" of life? What is usual if not that kind of performance that delivers a today without forfeiting tomorrow? What is free in those acts that unavoidably bring back responses as antagonistic as the ones perpetrated in the first place? Enterprise is the construction of something "higher" by the use of something "lower"; competition is a pool of effort discriminatively scaled in order to bring about richer results.

WANT. NOT FROM THE FILLING IN A CONTAINER WHIT ANY POSTERIORY FEELINGS.

THUS THE PRIORITY OF EMOTION OVER RATIONALISATION UNDER THE ASPECT OF TIME (ROMANTICISM – CLASSICISM / DIONISIOUS APOLLO.) CONDITION SINE QUA NON FOR THE "EVOLUTION TIPE" MAKES OF THE PRODUCT OF ITS ~~TIPE~~ PROSPECTIVE SOMEHOW THE OPPOSITE OF THE RATIONAL TIPE.

THE RATIONAL SEEKS THE WORTHY IN A SINGULAR STATE, EVEN THOU HE MY INTENSLY APPRECIATE THE WORLD OF ARTS, FIND IN IT THE GREATEST REWARDS, HE AS A PERSON ENGAGED IN DOOING REFUTE THE ELEMENT SUCH ARTS ARE SUBSTANCE OF: (EMOTIONAL INTENSITY) UNIVERSALIZED.

ITS OWN RATIONALIZATION THEN, CUTS HIM SHORT OF A GLOBAL UNDERSTANDING; ON ONE SIDE ~~THE~~ A LAND OF VALUES. AESTETIC VALUES / RELIGIOUS VALUES OF WHICH HE IS SENSITIVE SPECTATOR. ON THE OTHER SIDE A LAND OF RATIONALITY IN WHICH HE IS A DOOER.

AS A DOOER HE FINDS UNNATURALLY ALMOST FUTILE TO BE "ARTISTIC" AS A ~~WH~~ COMPLETE / COEREMT BEEING HE FIND ITS RATIONAL DOOING SHALLOW, STERILE, BLIND. TO ~~BE~~ COERENT TO IT WOULD MEAN TO CUT ONESELF AWAY FROM LIFE ENGROSSING,

TEAR OF FROM THE UMAN BOOK THE NON RATIONAL CHAPTERS. LOVE-RELIGIONS-ARTS-. WHAT WILL BE LEFT WILL BE A SHAKY SKELETON OF INCOGNITOS OF A RATIONALITY ARDLY ABOVE THE TERMITE RATIONALITY. CERTAINLY INFERIOR TO THEIR BIOLOGICAL WISDOM.

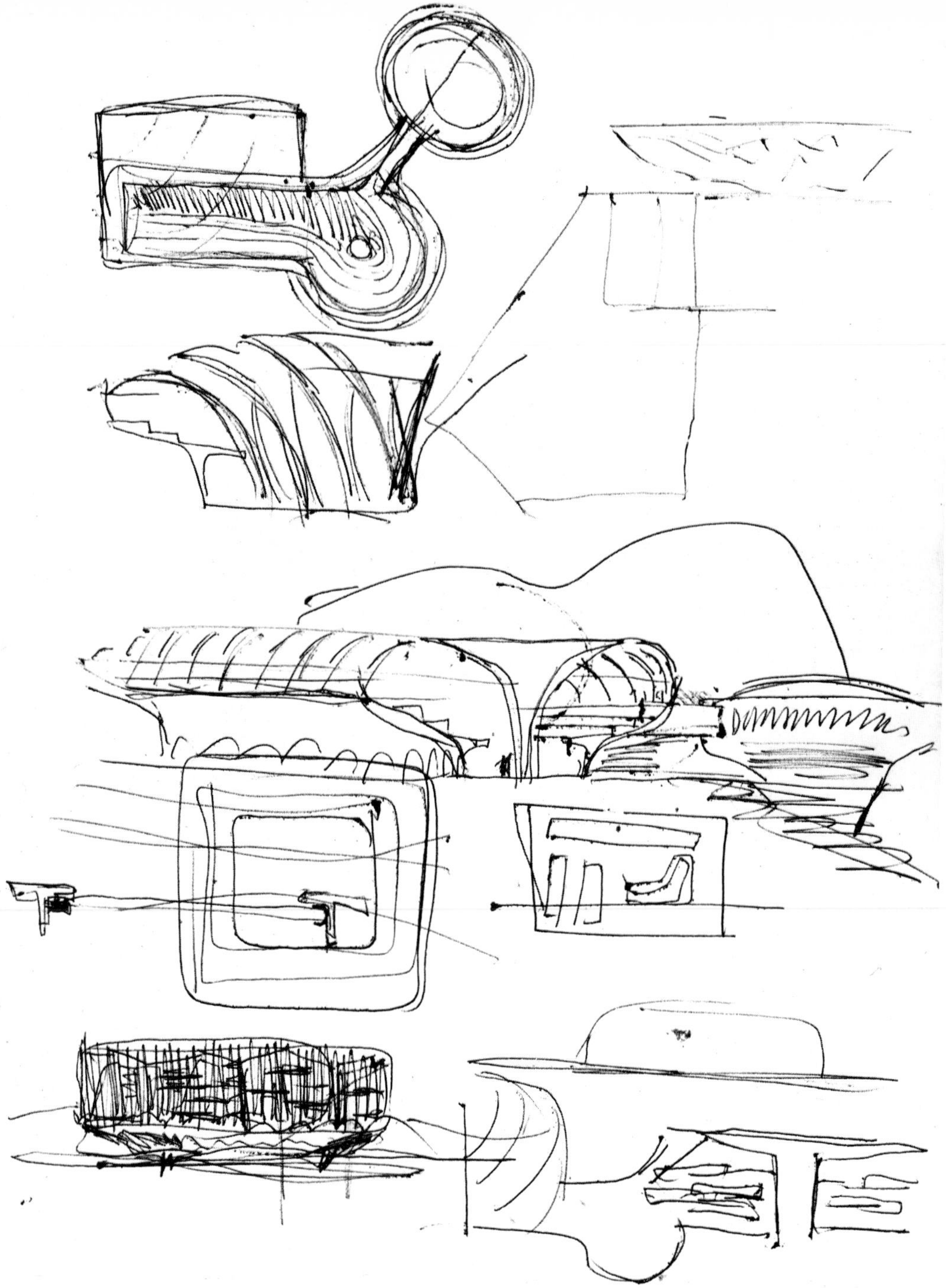

B.V. JUNE 60

THE AMERICAN UTOPIA

THE AMERICAN CIVILISATION HAS GROWN LIKE A SOLID BALL FROM A PRIMEVAL SITUATION OF EXEPTIONALITY'. A VERGIN, RICH, BEAUTIFUL CONTINENT OPENING TO STERN, SEEKING, CIVILIZED, PEOPLE. THIS CIVILISATION HAS ONLY ONE WAY TO GO ON EVOLVING. THE SOLID BALL HAS TO OPEN UP AT ALL LEVELS, THE AFFLUENT CIVILISATION HAS TO FLOW & INTERMIX WITH THE REST OF THE WORLD. THE WORLD OF ONE ONLY COLOR, MAN.

THUS MUCH MORE WILL BE GAINED THAN WILL BE LOST FOR ALL, AMERICAN INCLUDED.
THE AMERICAN MAY WELL BE LEADING IN THE SPIRIT OF INDIVIDUAL FREEDOM BUT HE IS CERTAINLY QUITE A BARBARIAN IN THE LIGHT OF SUBSTANTIAL VALUES WHICH SHOULD BE TRIGGERED BY FREEDOM IF & WHEN THE INDIVIDUAL IS UP TO IT.
IS IT REALLY MEANINGFULL THE FREEDOM OF BEING INSIGNIFICANT? WHERE DOES FREEDOM ENDS & LICENSE BEGINS?
I WONDER OFTEN IF THE "PURSUE OF HAPPINESS" OF THE FOUNDING FATHERS SHOULD HAVE BEEN THE "PURSUE OF MANLINESS"!! (& THE HAPPINESS THEREIN)

THE OPENING OF THE CLOSE AMERICAN CIVILISATION & ITS GROWTH INTO THE MORE EMBRACING CIVILISATION OF MAN IS FEASIBLE ONLY IF THE FIRST STEP IS UNEQUIVOCABLY ONE OF LOVE & COMPASSION & COURAGE. THIS BECAUSE TIME IS SHORT & THE MAGIC OF DESTRUCTION IS

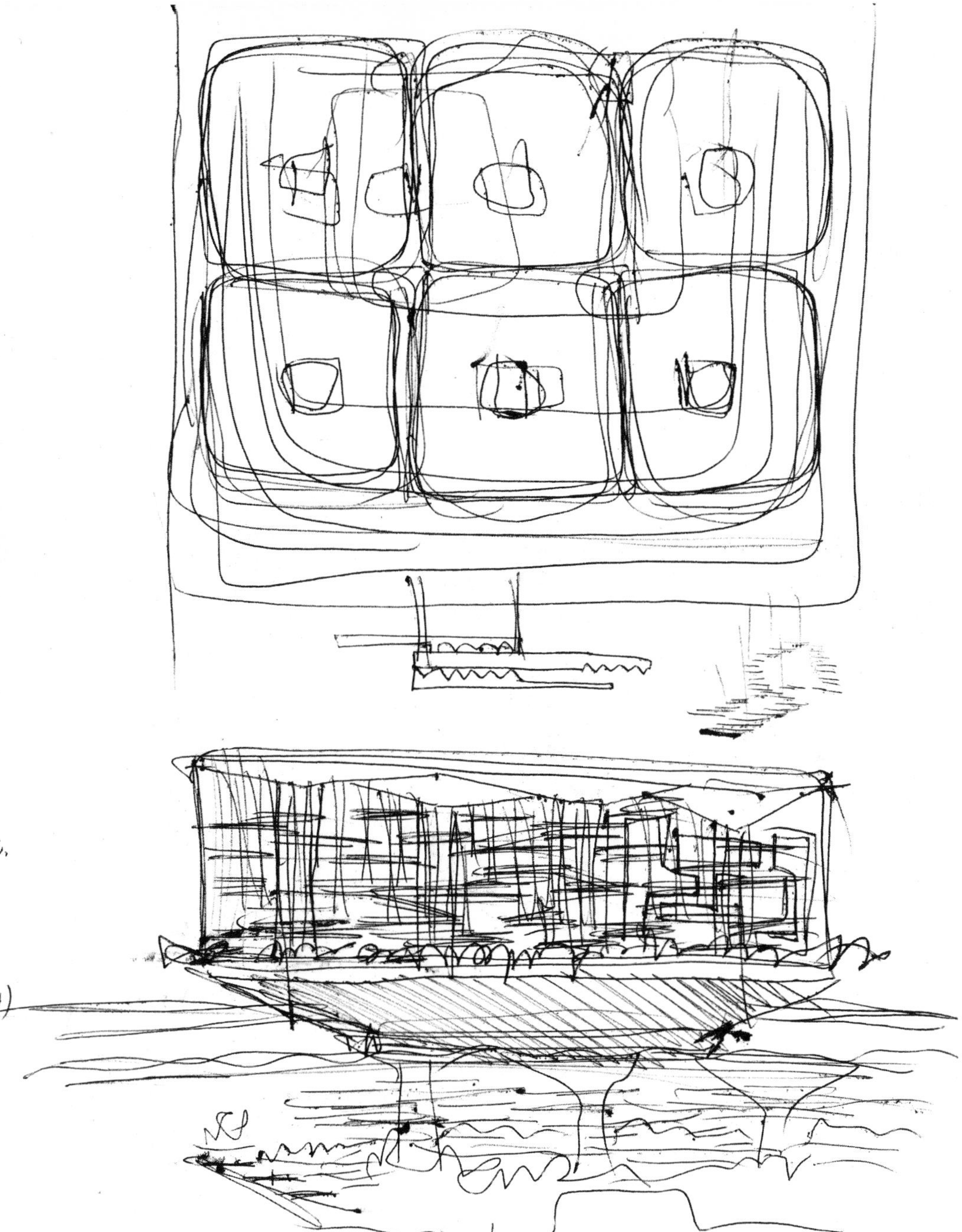

INFILTRATING THE MARROW OF MAN
ITS INTENSITY ~~& ITS~~ OF SPIRIT, ITS VEGETATIVE
INSTINCT~~IVITY~~.
WE ARE NOT JUST WASTING EFFORTS
& HUMAN VALUE AT THE RATE OF MILLIONS
OF DOLLAR PER MINUTE, IM THE NAME
OF SELF RIGHTEOUSNESS (THE IPOCRISY
OF WHICH HAS NOT BEEN YET MESURED)
WE ARE CASTING IN THE SOUL OF
EACH & ALL BEEING, NEW BORN &
OLD, THE SQUALID CONCEPTION THAT
LIFE CAN BE FOSTERED BY DEATH,
WHEN DEATH IS A POVERFULLY &
SPLENDIDLY PLANNED MOVE, ON
A PEDESTAL OF INCREDIBLE DEDICA-
CATIONS & INCREDIBLE MALICE

THUS THE FIRST STEP IS THE ~~UNILATERAL~~
~~RAL~~ UNILATERAL DISTRUCTION OF ALL INSTRUMENTS
OF WAR, THE GIVING UP AS A CONTINENT,
UNARMED & OPEN TO THE FORCES
THAT MIGHT BE FOOLISH ENOUGH TO
PERSIST IN ILL DEEDS &
MAN KIND WOULD IN SUCH DAY REACH
A NEW LEVEL OF GREATNESS, SUCH
DATE WOULD INITIATE THE YEAR ONE OF
THE NEW ERA, ~~[illegible]~~ [illegible] WOULD BE
PILOT IN THE DESTINY OF MAN.
DOSENT MAN NEED ~~A RENEWED~~ ESSENTIALLY
FAITH IN GOODNESS & COURAGE,
LET (THEM) SUPPOSE THE "WORSE" HAPPENS.
THE POWER GROUPS OF CHINA &
RUSSIA TAKE OVER. IF THOSE ARE
EVIL, MAN WILL DO JUSTICE OF THEM
WAITING A GENERATION, WAIT THE POWER
GENERATED BY THE ACT OF LOVE OF
A WOLE CIVILISATION, THIS END WILL
BE POSSIBLY ACHIVED TROUGHT LOCALISED STRUGGLES
& MARTIRDOOMS. BUT NO MASS OLOCAUST
NO DEGRADATION OF TOTAL EVIL
FOR EVIL. TOTAL ANNIHILATION FOR
TOTAL ANNIHILATION.

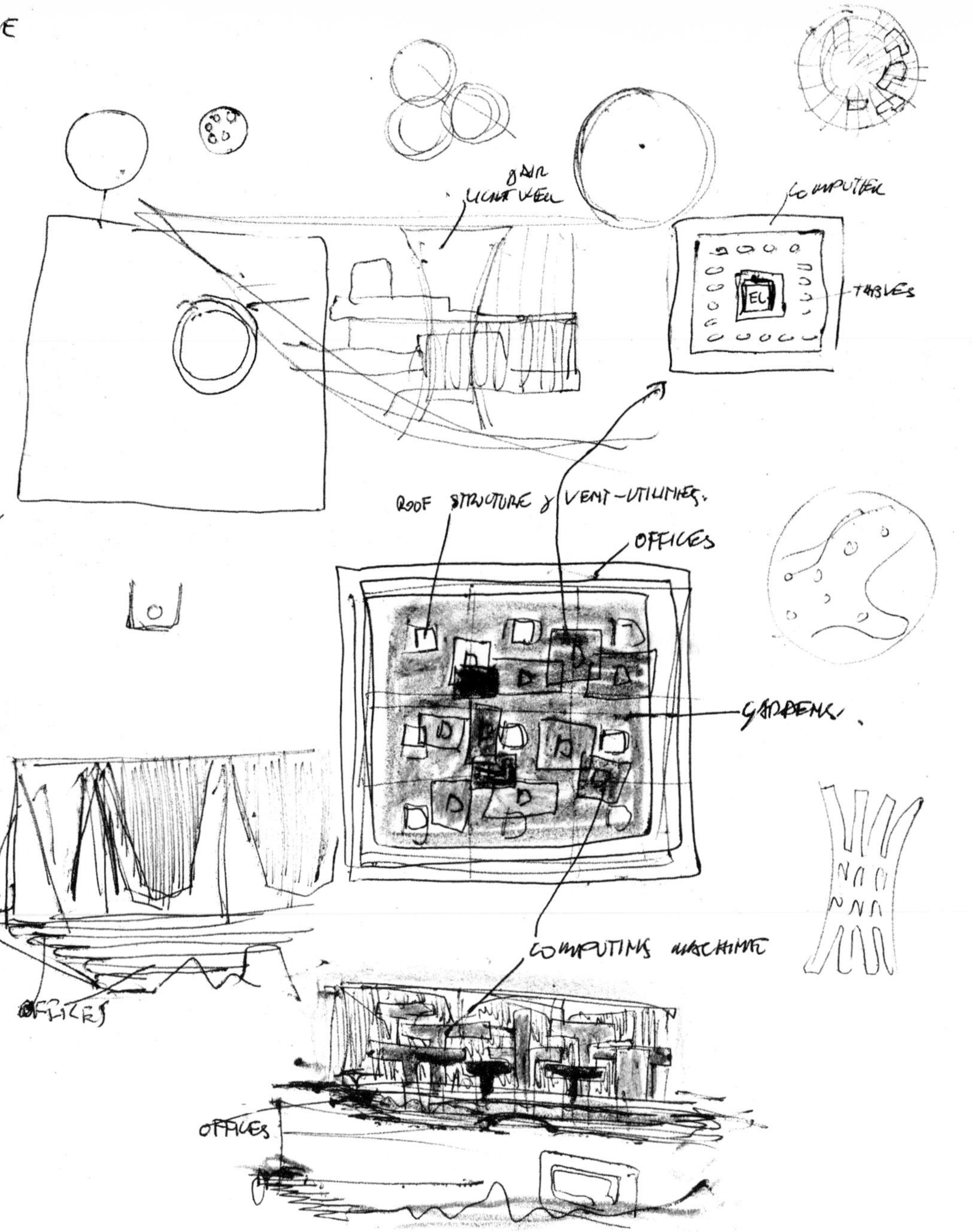

• THE TIRANTS WOULD BE SLOWLY ISOLATED IN A UNBEARABLE ~~ISOLATION~~ LONENESS & UNDER THE WEIGHT OF UNIVERSAL (BUT INDIVIDUAL) CONDEMNATION WOULD FADE INTO FUTILITY ITS POWER & ITS SHRIEKINGS.

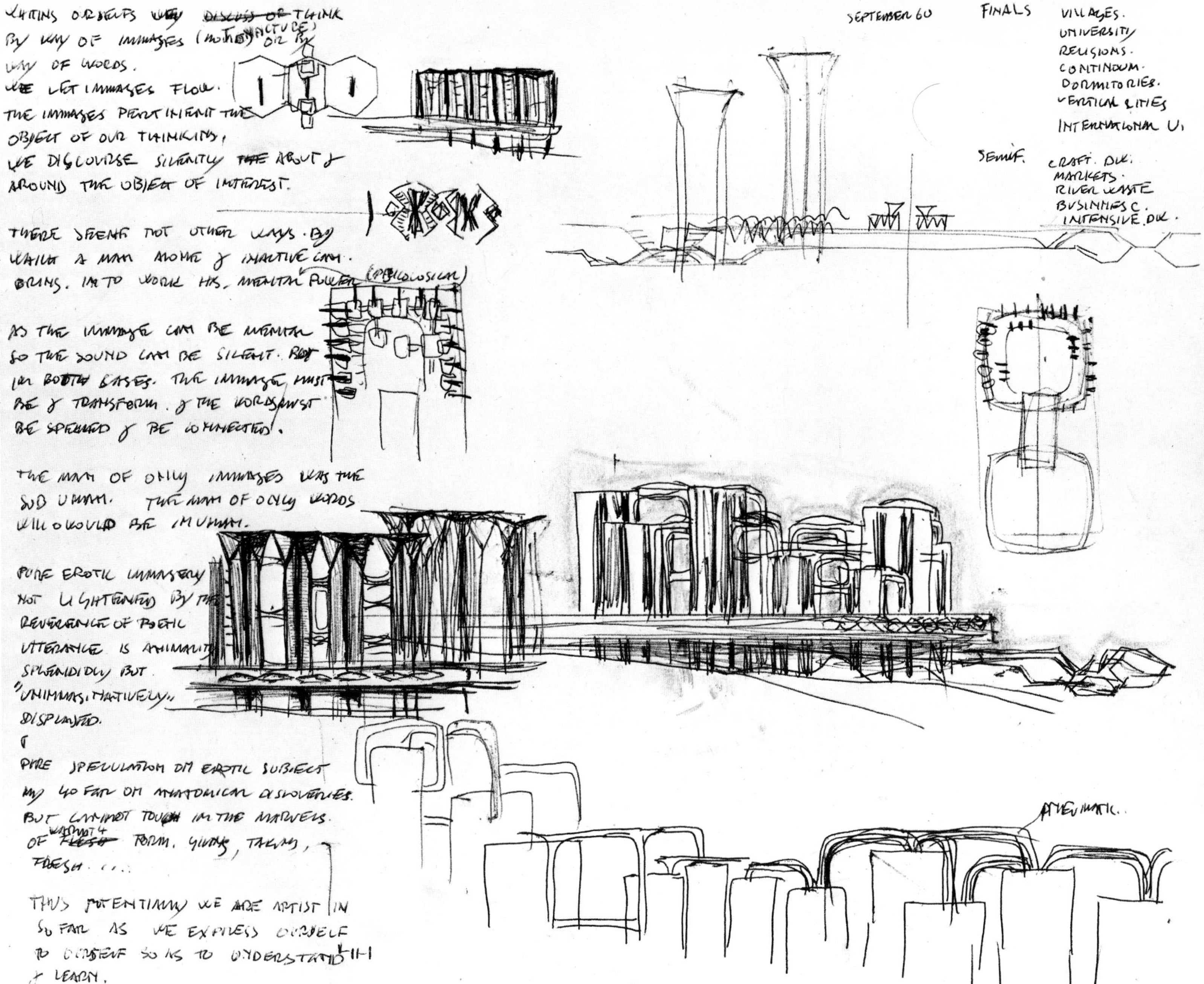
WITHIN OURSELFS WE ~~DISCUSS OR~~ THINK
BY WAY OF IMMAGES (MOTION) (PICTURE) OR BY
WAY OF WORDS.
WE LET IMMAGES FLOW.
THE IMMAGES PERTINENT THE
OBJECT OF OUR THINKING,
WE DISCOURSE SILENTLY ~~THE~~ ABOUT &
AROUND THE OBJECT OF INTEREST.
THERE SEEMS NOT OTHER WAYS. BY
WHICH A MAN ALONE & INACTIVE CAN.
BRING. IN TO WORK HIS. MENTAL POWER (PHILOSOPHICAL)
AS THE IMMAGE CAN BE MENTAL
SO THE SOUND CAN BE SILENT. BUT
IN BOTH CASES. THE IMMAGE MUST
BE & TRANSFORM. & THE WORDS MUST
BE SPEAKED & BE CONNECTED.
THE MAN OF ONLY IMMAGES WAS THE
SUB UMAN. THE MAN OF ONLY WORDS
WILL OR WOULD BE INUMAN.
PURE EROTIC IMMAGERY
NOT LIGHTENED BY THE
REVERENCE OF POETIC
UTTERANCE IS ANIMALITY
SPLENDIDLY BUT
"UNIMMAGINATIVELY"
DISPLAYED.
&
PURE SPECULATION ON EROTIC SUBJECT
IN SO FAR ON ANATOMICAL DISCOVERIES.
BUT CANNOT TOUCH IN THE MARVELS
OF ~~FLESH~~ WANTS FORM. GIVING, TAKING,
FLESH . . .
THUS POTENTIALLY WE ARE ARTIST IN
SO FAR AS WE EXPRESS OURSELF
TO OURSELF SO AS TO UNDERSTAND HIM
& LEARN.
SEPTEMBER 60
FINALS
VILLAGES.
UNIVERSITY
RELIGIONS.
CONTINUUM.
DORMITORIES.
VERTICAL CITIES
INTERNATIONAL U.
SEMIF.
CRAFT. DIK.
MARKETS.
RIVER WASTE
BUSINNESS C.
INTENSIVE. DIK.
PNEUMATIC.

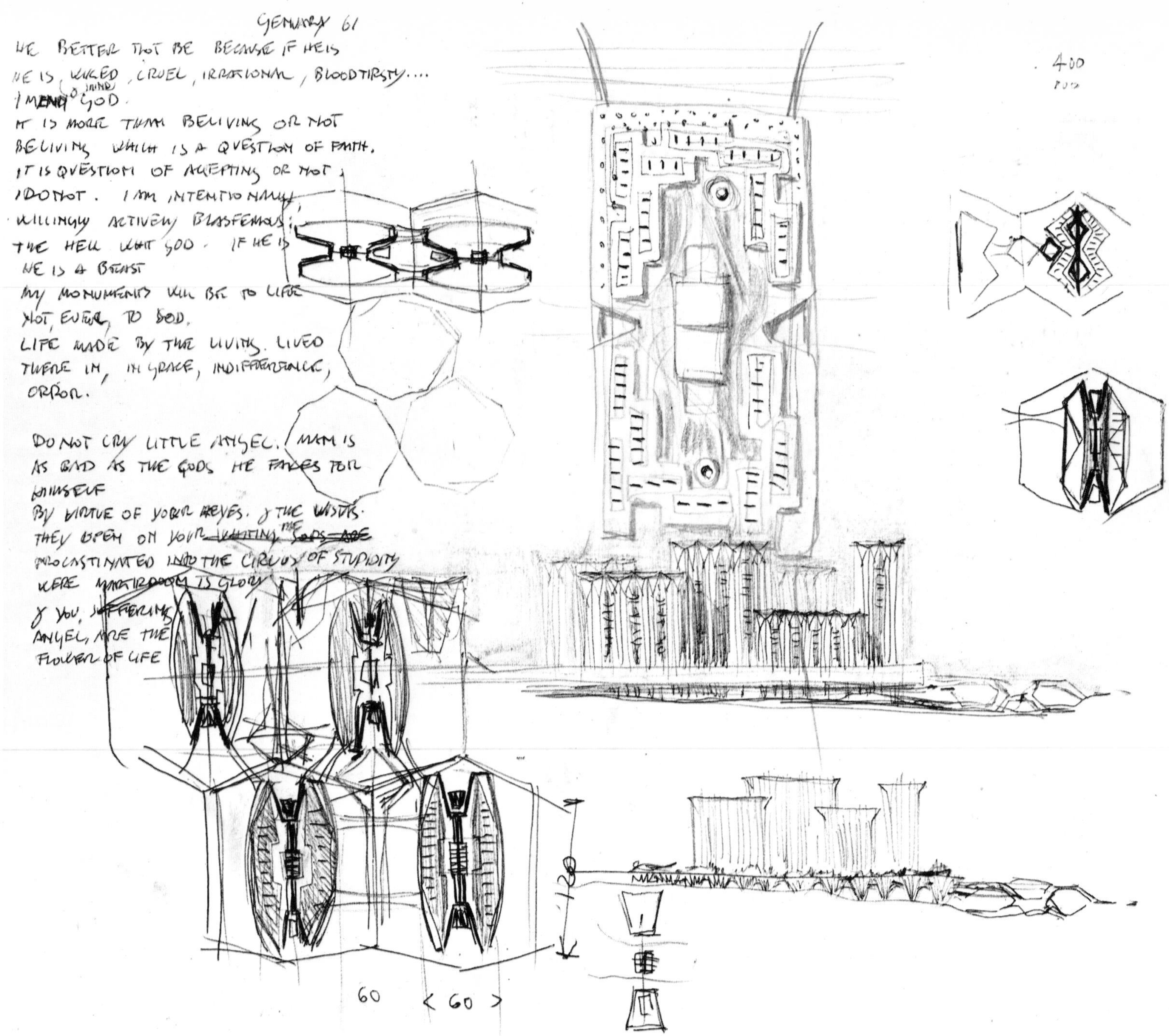
GENNARY 61
HE BETTER NOT BE BECAUSE IF HE IS
HE IS WICKED, CRUEL, IRRATIONAL, BLOODTIRSTY....
I MEAN GOD.
IT IS MORE THAN BELIVING OR NOT
BELIVING WHICH IS A QUESTION OF FAITH.
IT IS QUESTION OF ACCEPTING OR NOT,
I DO NOT. I AM INTENTIONALLY
WILLINGLY ACTIVELY BLASFEMOUS;
THE HELL WHIT GOD. IF HE IS
HE IS A BEAST
MY MONUMENTS WILL BE TO LIFE
NOT, EVER, TO GOD.
LIFE MADE BY THE LIVING. LIVED
THERE IN, IN GRACE, INDIFFERENCE,
ORROR.
DO NOT CRY LITTLE ANGEL. MAN IS
AS BAD AS THE GODS HE MAKES FOR
HIMSELF
BY VIRTUE OF YOUR EYES. & THE WISTS.
THEY OPEN ON YOUR WAITING THE GODS ARE
PROCASTINATED INTO THE CIRCUS OF STUPIDITY
WERE MARTIRDOOM IS GLORY
& YOU, SUFFERING
ANGEL, ARE THE
FLOWER OF LIFE
400
60
< 60 >

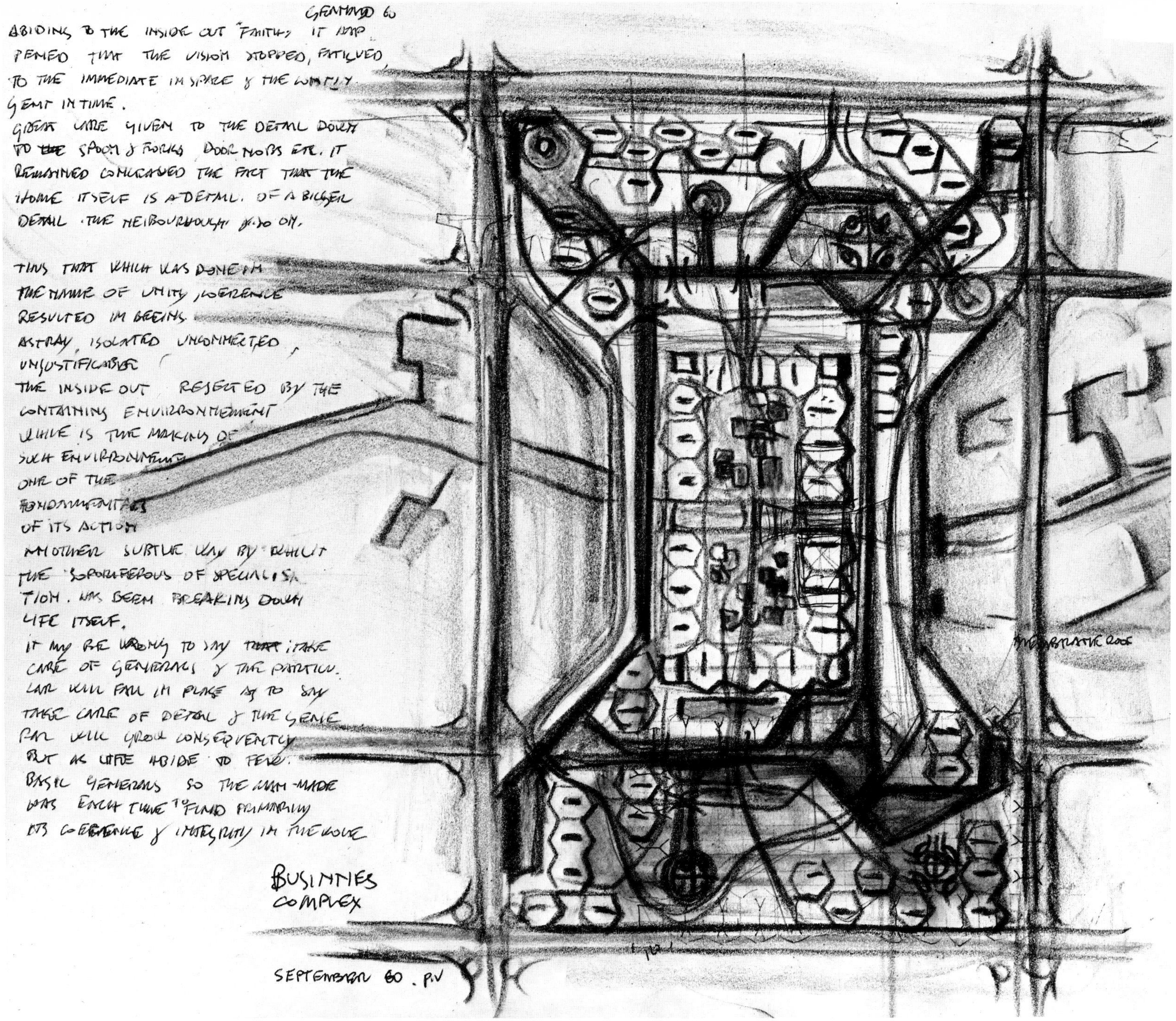
GENNARD 60
ABIDING TO THE INSIDE OUT "FAITH" IT HAP
PENED THAT THE VISION STOPPED, FATIGUED,
TO THE IMMEDIATE IN SPACE & THE WEAKLY
GENT IN TIME.
GREAT CARE GIVEN TO THE DETAIL DOWN
TO SPOON & FORKS DOOR NOBS ETC. IT
REMAINED CONCEALED THE FACT THAT THE
HOME ITSELF IS A DETAIL. OF A BIGGER
DETAIL. THE NEIBOURHOOD & SO ON.
THUS THAT WHICH WAS DONE IN
THE NAME OF UNITY, COHERENCE
RESULTED IN BEEINGS.
ASTRAY, ISOLATED UNCONNECTED,
UNJUSTIFICABLE
THE INSIDE OUT REJECTED BY THE
CONTAINING ENVIRONMENT
WHILE IS THE MAKING OF
SUCH ENVIRONMENT
ONE OF THE
FUNDAMENTALS
OF ITS ACTION
ANOTHER SUBTLE WAY BY WHICH
THE SOPORIFEROUS OF SPECIALISA
TION. HAS BEEN BREAKING DOWN
LIFE ITSELF.
IT MAY BE WRONG TO SAY TAKE
CARE OF GENERALS & THE PARTICU
LAR WILL FALL IN PLACE AS TO SAY
TAKE CARE OF DETAIL & THE GENE
RAL WILL GROW CONSEQUENTLY
BUT AS LIFE ABIDE TO FEW
BASIC GENERALS SO THE MAN-MADE
HAS EACH TIME TO FIND PRIMARILY
ITS COHERENCE & INTEGRITY IN THE WHOLE
BUSINNES
COMPLEX
INTEGRATIVE ROOF
SEPTEMBER 60. P.V

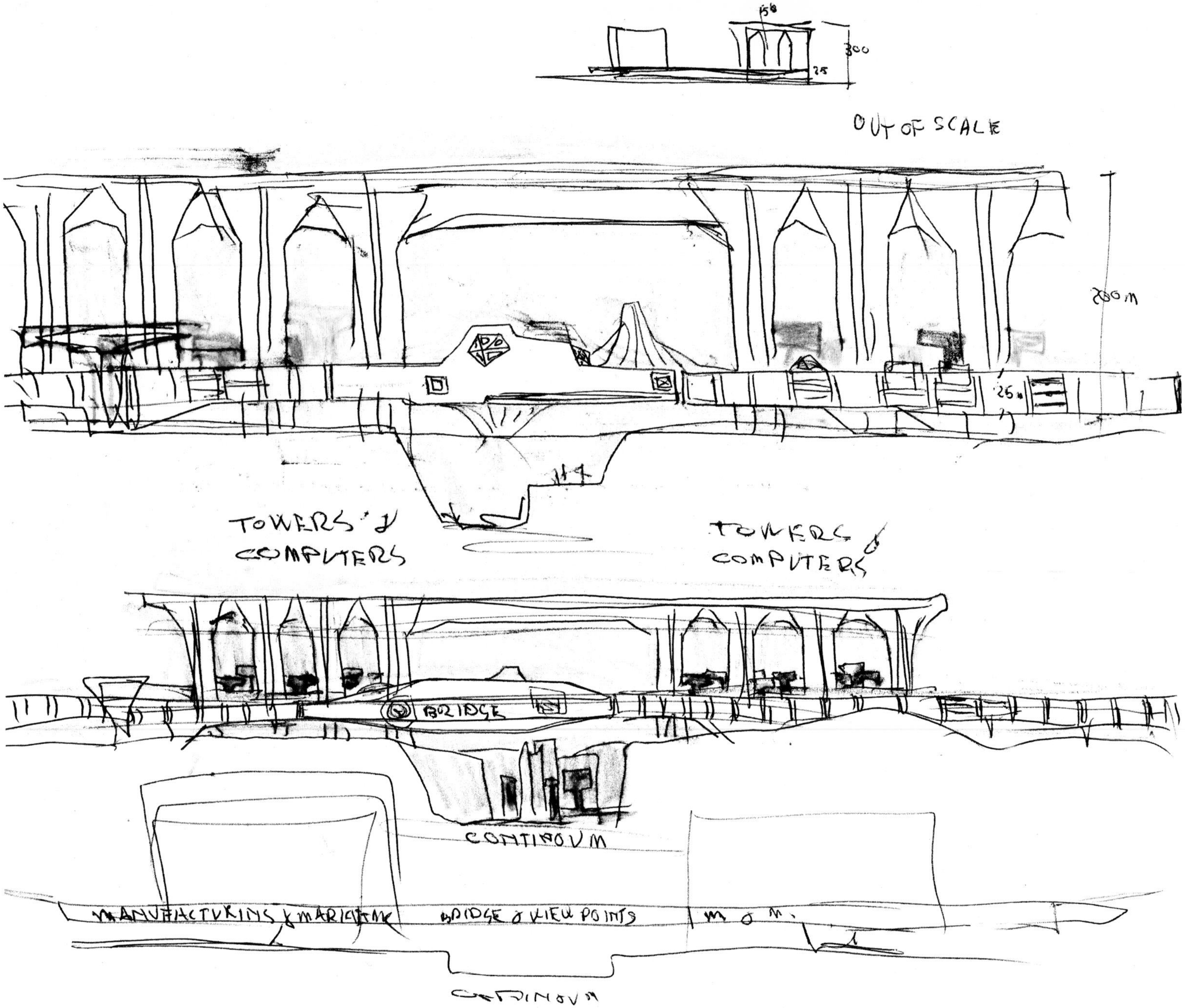
150
300
25
OUT OF SCALE
200 m
25 m
TOWERS & COMPUTERS
TOWERS & COMPUTERS
BRIDGE
CONTINUUM
MANUFACTURING & MARITIME
BRIDGE & VIEW POINTS
M O M.

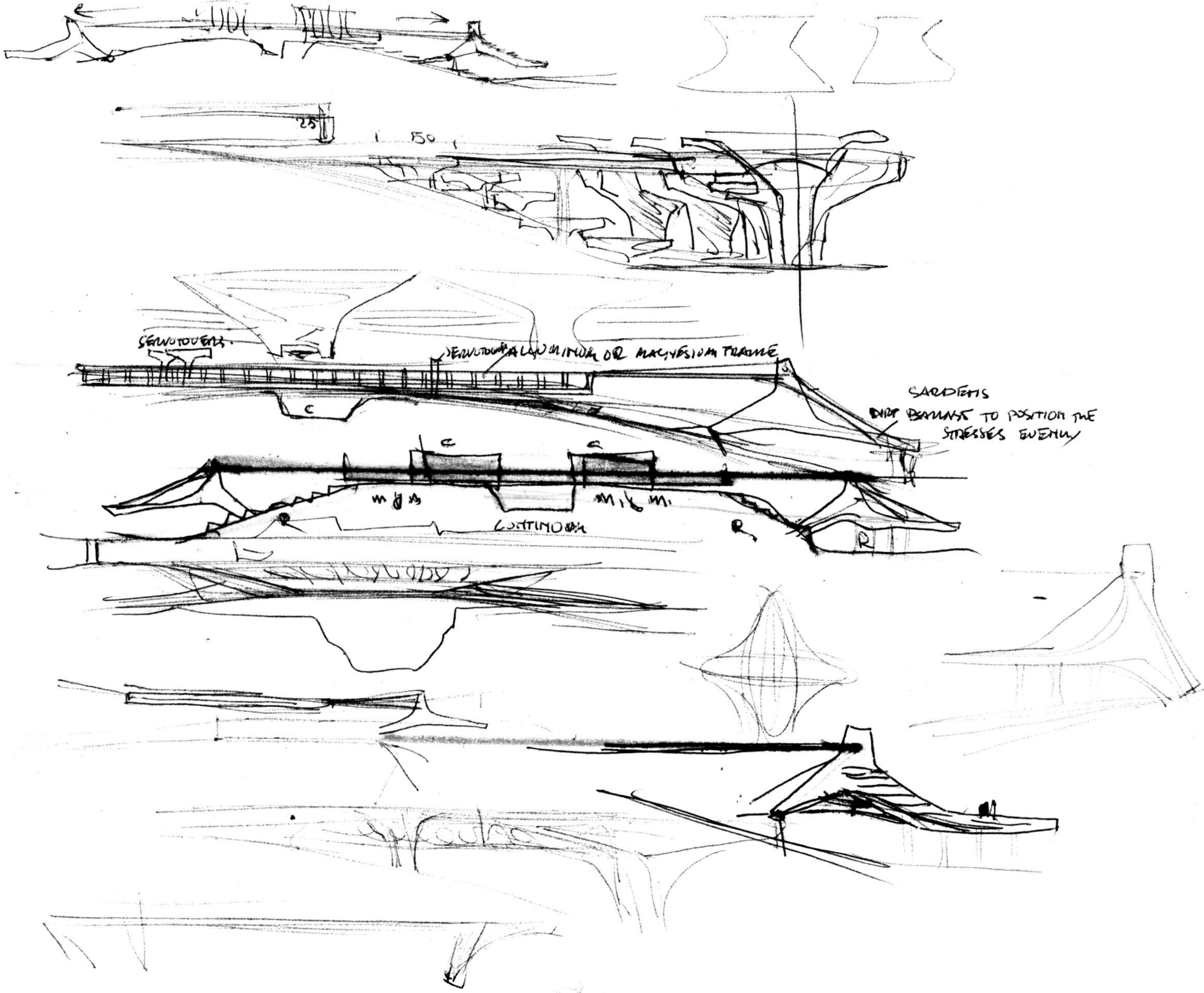
ALUMINUM OR MAGNESIUM FRAME
TO POSITION THE
STRESSES EVENLY
150

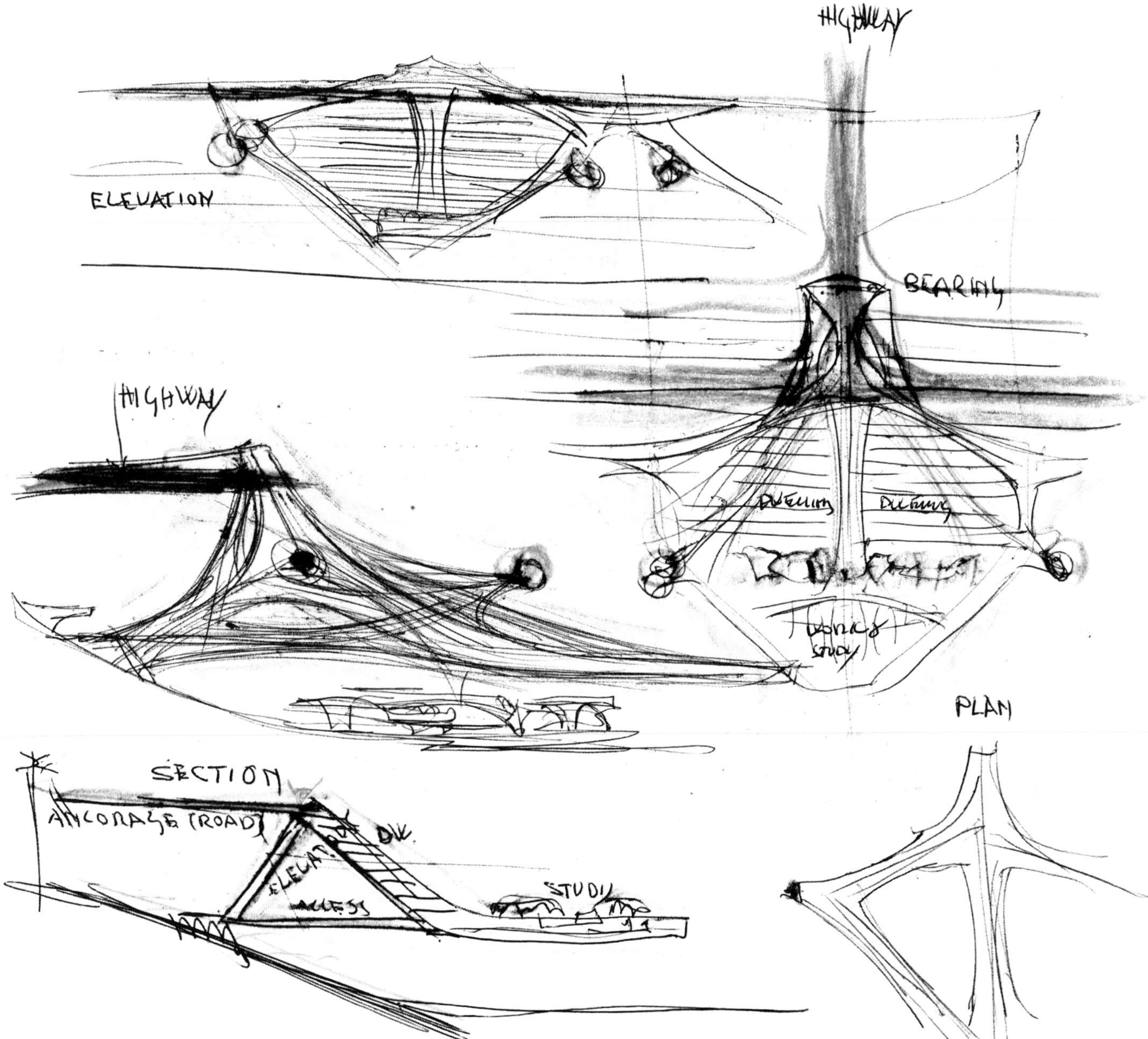
HIGHWAY
ELEVATION
BEARING
HIGHWAY
PLAN
SECTION
ANCORAGE (ROAD)
ACCESS
STUDI

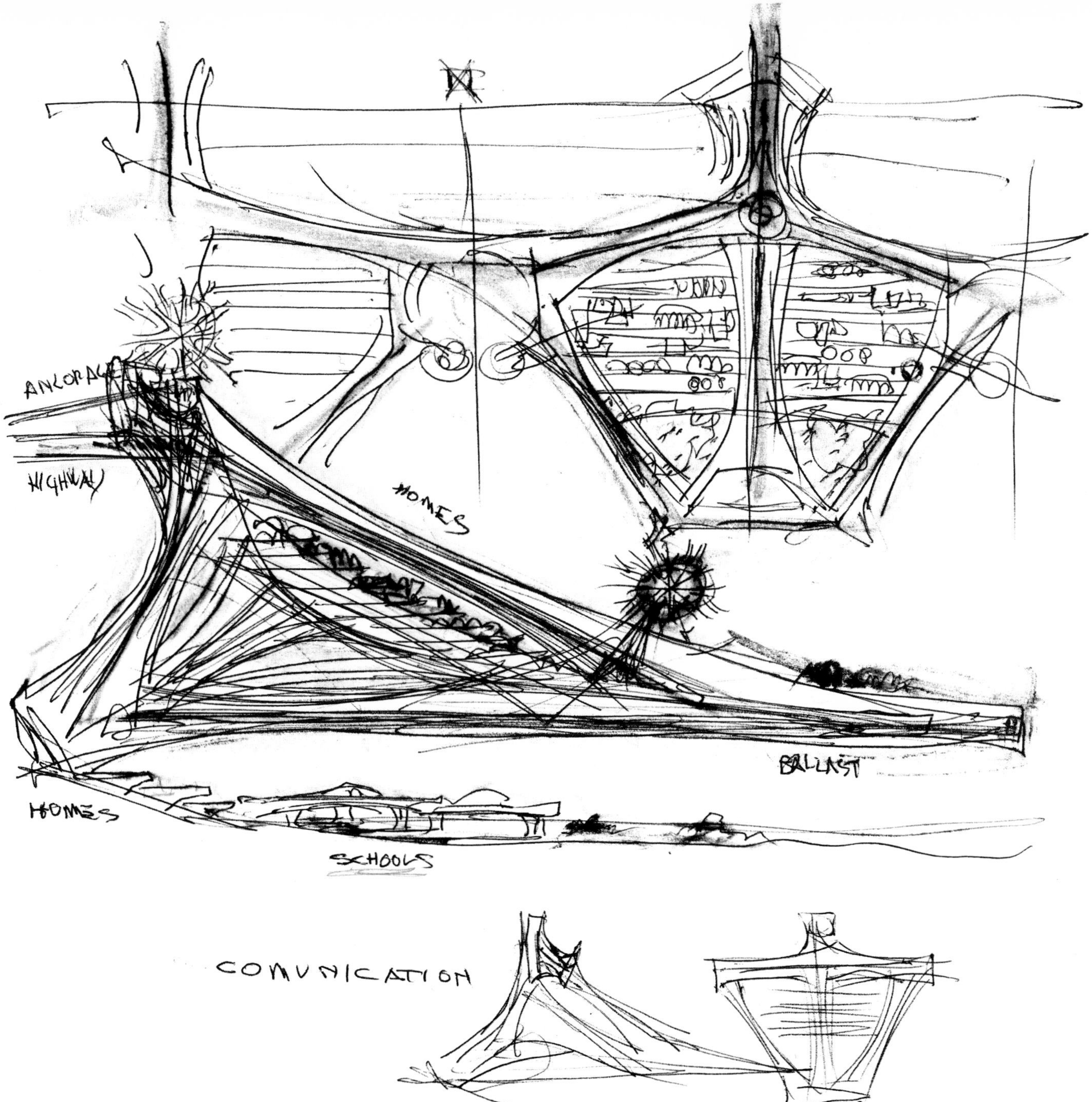
ANCORAG
HIGHWAY
HOMES
BALLAST
HOMES
SCHOOLS
COMUNICATION

Car Silos

1970
The oddest thing about the automobile is that it is a very sophisticated machine devised for the purposes of the most primitive logistics with the sophisticated intent of liberating man from the slavery of time and space The result is (1) a savagely convulsive primitivism of interrelation between man and man, man and institutions; (2) an inflation of physical interstices and functions; (3) a progressively widening time lapse between stimulus and response; (4) the poisoning of the environment; (5) a sacrificial heap of metal and upholstery offered to the god of waste; (6) an endless network of cement and asphalt; (7) a systematic butchering and maiming of the software, man, trapped in his hardware, the machine; (8) a mindless depletion of the energetic sources of the earth's fuels; (9) an insularity of action represented by the busts of men and women visible inside their own moving and mystical cages; (10) an explosion into fragments and a segregation of the urban fabric; (11) the paralysis of ugliness and chaos, a possibly irreversible decadence of the human environment.

The obscurantism of the automobile age might well go down in history on a par with some of the most fierce catastrophies man has brought upon himself. A cultural catastrophe, first of all. An ecological catastrophe. A logistical catastrophe. A social catastrophe. Those are some of my comments on the car now, when my naivety in seeing redeeming features in the idea "car" is all but gone. Only at the service of leisure might the car redeem itself and then only with well-defined limitations. The major reason why the car is an insult to life is its use as a "work" device. Work has a mandatory character: survival; thus the linkage car-survival and, among others, the folly of the commuters' tide. Eliminate the car as a means of survival, and we can return to the pleasure of the country drive for the sake of leisure and family outings. This would automatically deflate the intrusion of steel tonnage and rubber tires and submission to a major catastrophe.

IT DEFENETLY GOES TOO FOR PRO-GRESSIVE STULTIFICATION, WHICH WITHOUT DOSENT GROW OLDER, JUST SIMPLY DO NOT GROW. IF THE GOLF CLUB IS AS MEANINFUL AT 60 AS IT WAS AT 20. THEN IS LIFE WHICH IS MEANINGLESS.

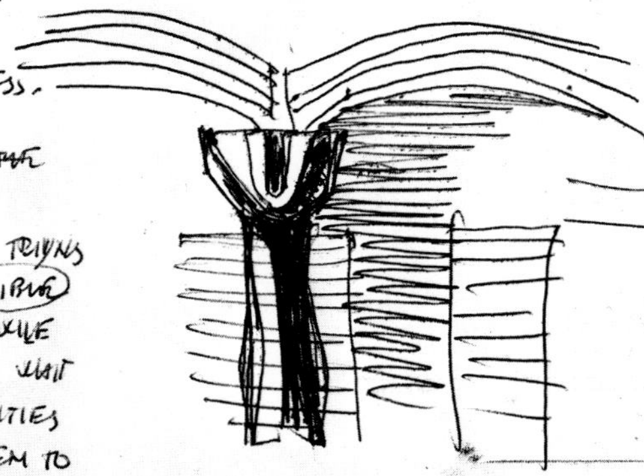

~~THUS THE MAIN SIGNIFICATION OF THE CITY IS ATTEMTED~~

THUS THE LAY OUT OF THE CITY IS TRYING TO CRISTALIZE FORMALLY THE POSSIBLE MEANING OF THE LIFE IT WILL HOST, WHILE INSTRUMENTALITY IS TAKEN CARE WITH AMPLE & WELL INTERLOCKED FACILITIES

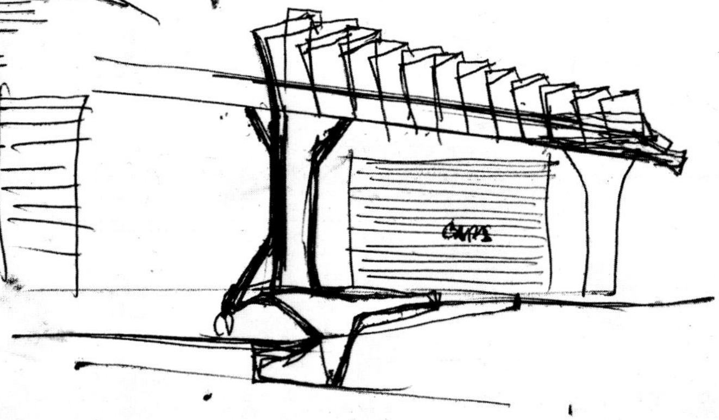

THE WOLE CITY IS PRACTICALLY GIVEN TO LIVING (NOT TO ~~GET~~ SEE ALL THERE)

PRIMARY CATEGORIES OF THIS LIVING ARE THE LEARNING, THE SPIRITUAL & THE AESTHETIC & ARE THOSE TO FORM THE BACK BONE OF THE WOLE.

NEX LAYER IS ~~ARE~~ THE DWELLINGS INTERPO-LATED WITH THE MAKING (& DISTRIBUTING)

THEN COMES THE COLLECTION OF ABSO-LETE INSTRUMENTALITY & REMARKETING OF IT. THEN THE REGENERATION OF THE LEFT OVER, IN FORM OF WASTE, IN THE RAWS TO BE REINJECTED IN THE CICLE OF INSTRUMENTALE TROUGH MANUFACTU-RING.

SPATIALLY, ABOVE THE REGENERATING-PLANT. (FOOT OF MESA) ARE THE GUILDS (RIM & MESA'S WALLS),

THE ALTERNATIVE TO CAOS SO OUTLINED IS SOUGHT BY WAY OF A FLUID INTERACTION BETWING ~~MASSIVE~~ STRUCTURES. (~~SECONDARY~~ ENVI-RONMENT) SHELTERING MICRO STRUCTURE. (TERTIARY ENVIRONMENT) & THE LAND TREATED AS A BIOLOGICAL FACTOR AVALIABLE TO MAN, THE UNHURRIED PEDESTRIAN WALKING TO MOVE & STAND, OBSERVE, RETREAT, PARTI-CIPATE, CONTEMPLATE .... (PRIMARY ENVIRON.)

THE WEAVING OF THOSE 3 ENVIRONM-
MENTAL CATEGORIES INTO EACH OTHER
& THE LARGER SPACE PRESENTED BY
THE LAND SORROUNDING COMBINES
IN THE TOTAL ENVIRONMEMENT.

NATURE IS IN THE CORE OF
THE CITY. & THERE BOTH THE
NATURE MADE & THE MAN MADE
ARE CONTENDING FOR THE POTEN
TIALITIES OF LIFE TROUGH THE
INTERPLAY OF EQUALLY FORCEFULL ~~STRUC~~ ORGANIZATIONS
~~TURALITIES~~. THE ONES MATURED BY TIME
ON THE TORPIDITY OF MATTER THE
OTHERS COMPARATIVELY EXPLODED INTO
BEING BY THE PERHAPS DESPERATE
LONGINGS OF MAN,

IT SEEMS (TEMPESTIVO) TO SAY HERE THAT
POSSIBLY THE FONDAMENTAL DEPARTURE
IMPLIED IN THIS CITY IS THIS ENVELOP
PING OF ENTITIES OF ONE MODULAR PA-
RAMETRE BY ENTITIES OF A DIFFERENT
MODULAR PARAMETRE,
SPACE MOVES THUS FROM ~~THE~~ INTIMI
TY (HOME) TO INFINITY (LAND) TROUGH THE
MOULDINGS OF ENLARGING CONTAINERS
EACH ONE PROMOTING DIFFERENT
EMOTIONS, TIPIFING PARTICULAR
CONDITIONS & PROCEDURES

THE RELATIVITY OF INNER & OUT.ER OF
INTERIOR & ESTERIOR OF PLAN & FACADE
IS CONSTANTLY RIPRESENTED BY SHELTE
RING OF SHELTERS BY ENCLOSING
OF ~~OUTSIDES~~ ENCLOSURES BY THE REPROPO
SING OF SPACES SCALED TO DIF
FEREN ACTIONS FOR DIFFERENT MAN

OAR SIKOS
THEOLOGY COMPLEX

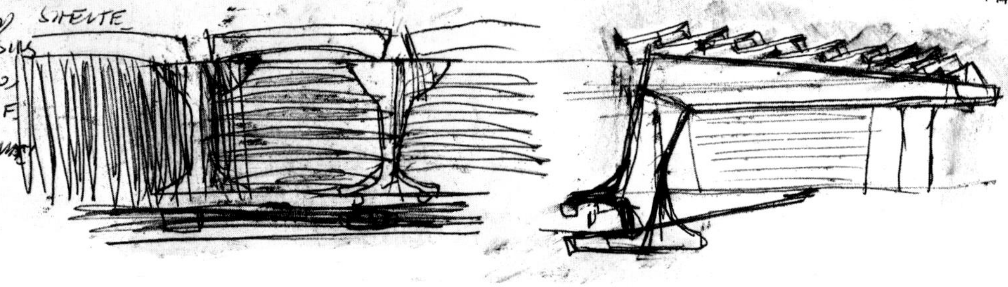

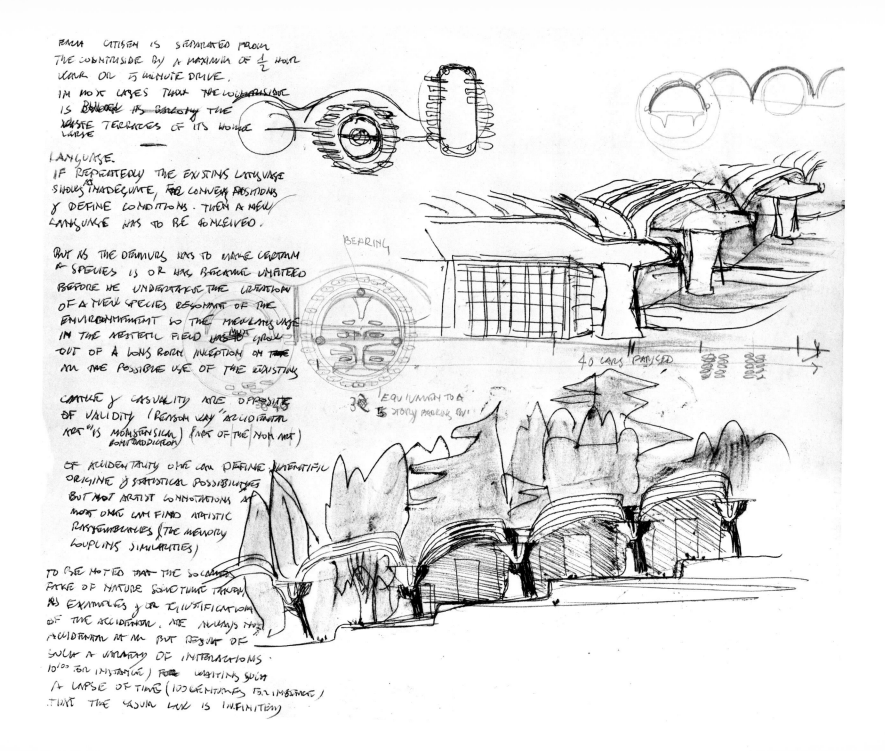

EACH CITIZEN IS SEPARATED FROM THE COUNTRYSIDE BY A MAXIMUM OF ½ HOUR WALK OR 15 MINUTE DRIVE.
IN MOST CASES THAN THE COUNTRYSIDE IS ~~BALCONY ITS BALCONY~~ THE ~~VASTE~~ LARGE TERRACES OF ITS HOME

—

LANGUAGE.
IF REPEATEDLY THE EXISTING LANGUAGE SHOWS AS INADEQUATE, FOR CONVEY POSITIONS & DEFINE CONDITIONS. THEN A NEW LANGUAGE HAS TO BE CONCEIVED.

BUT AS THE DEMIURG HAS TO MAKE CERTAIN A SPECIES IS OR HAS BECAME UNFITTED BEFORE HE UNDERTAKE THE CREATION OF A NEW SPECIES RESONANT OF THE ENVIRONMENT SO THE NEW LANGUAGE IN THE AESTETIC FIELD ~~HAS TO~~ MUST GROW OUT OF A LONG BORN INCEPTION ON ~~THE~~ AN THE POSSIBLE USE OF THE EXISTING

CHANCE & CASUALITY ARE OPPOSITE OF VALIDITY (REASON WHY "ACCIDENTAL ART" IS NONSENSICAL CONTRADICTION) (ART OF THE NON ART)

OF ACCIDENTALITY ONE CAN DEFINE SCIENTIFIC ORIGINE & STATISTICAL POSSIBILITIES BUT NOT ARTIST CONNOTATIONS AT MOST ONE CAN FIND ARTISTIC RASSEMBLANCES (THE MEMORY COUPLING SIMILARITIES)

TO BE NOTED THAT THE SO CALLED FAKE OF NATURE SOMETIME TAKEN AS EXAMPLES & OR JUSTIFICATION OF THE ACCIDENTAL, ARE ALWAYS NOT ACCIDENTAL AT ALL BUT RESULT OF SUCH A VARIETY OF INTERACTIONS. (10^{100} FOR INSTANCE) ~~FOR~~ WAITING SUCH A LAPSE OF TIME (100 CENTURIES FOR INSTANCE) THAT THE CASUAL LAW IS INFINITEM

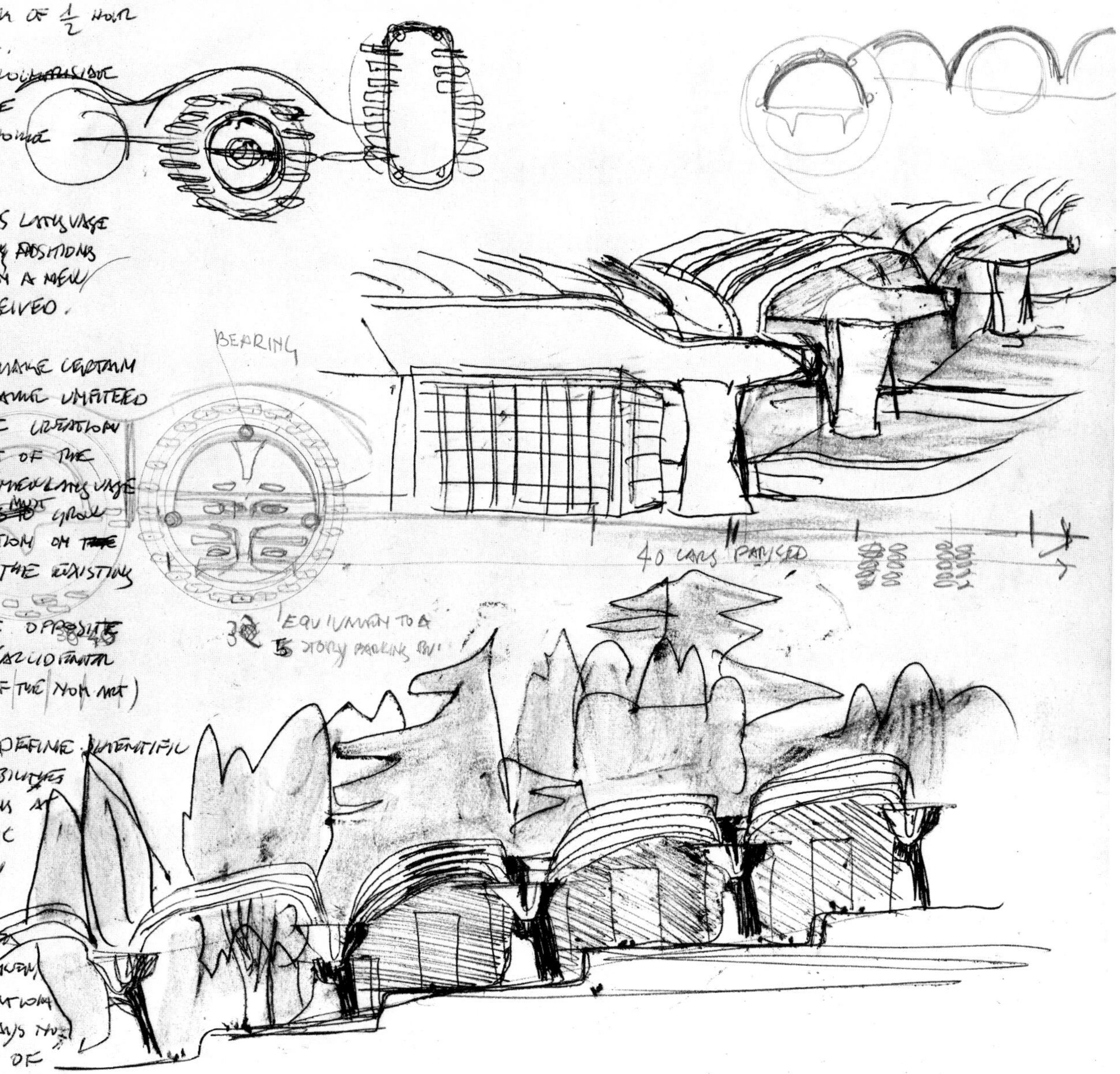

COMPLEX & FOR PRACTICAL PURPOSES
MEANINLESS EVEN IF GRASPED.

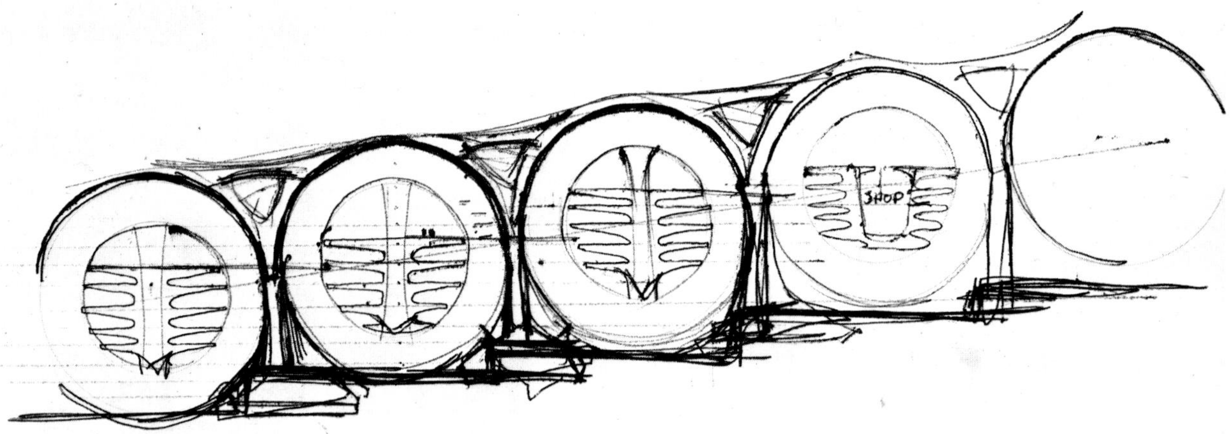

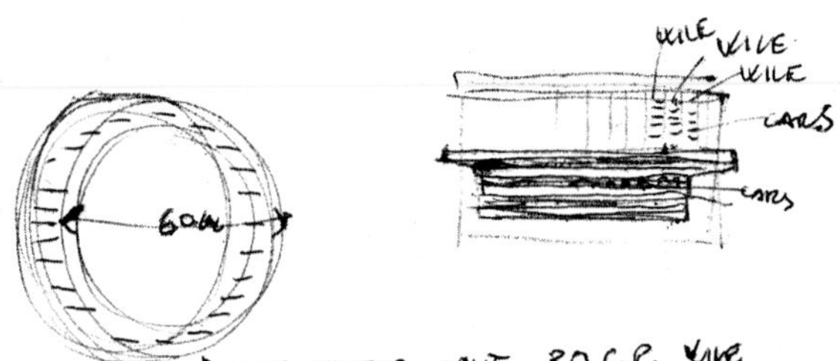

ONE PREFAB. UNIT 30 C.P. VILE
FUNCTIONS AS PERMANENT FORM FOR ROOF

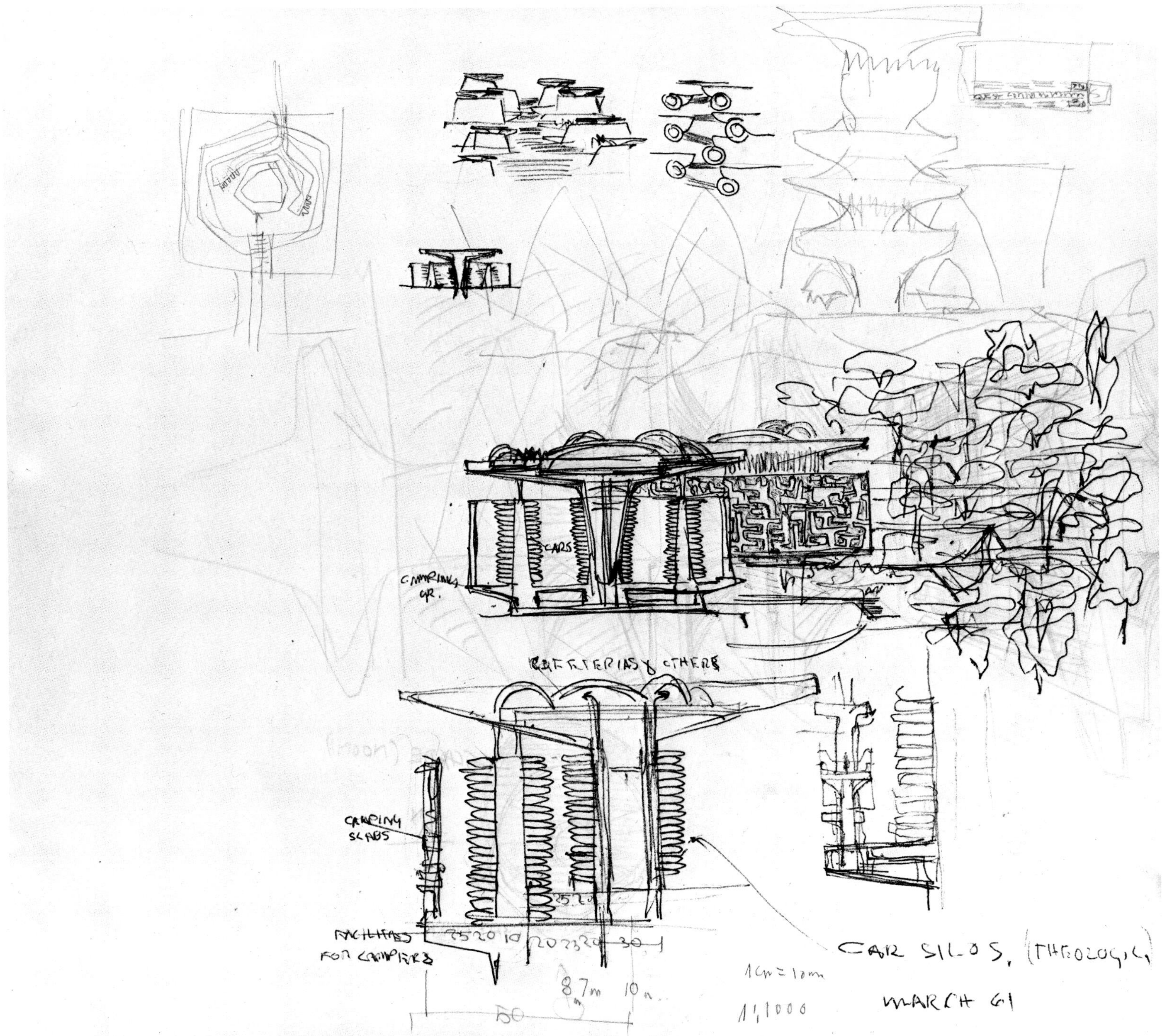
CARS
CAR SILOS,
MARCH 61
8.7m
10m
50
1:1000

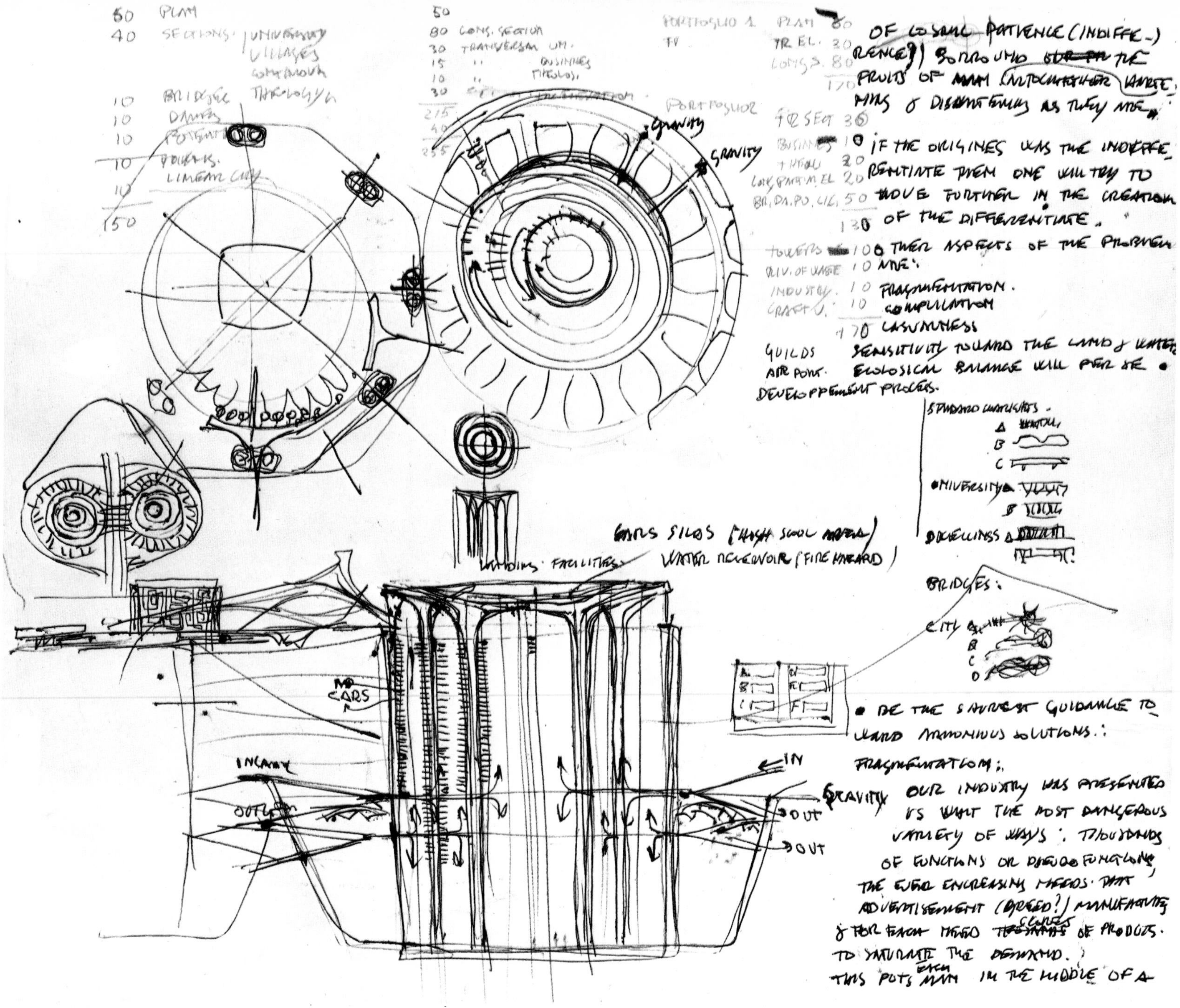
OF COSMIC PATIENCE (INDIFFE-) RENCE?) BORROWING THE FRUITS OF MAN ... AS THEY ARE."
"IF THE ORIGINES WAS THE INDIFFERENTIATE THEN ONE WILL TRY TO MOVE FURTHER IN THE CREATION OF THE DIFFERENTIATE."
OTHER ASPECTS OF THE PROBLEM ARE:
FRAGMENTATION.
COMPLICATION
CASUALNESS
SENSITIVITY TOWARD THE LAND & WATER ECOLOGICAL BALANCE WILL BE THE DEVELOPPEMENT PROCESS.
STANDARD UNITS
UNIVERSITY
DWELLINGS
BRIDGES:
CITY
GRAVITY
GUILDS
AIR PORT
WATER RESERVOIR (FIRE HAZARD)
NO CARS
IN
OUT
OUT
GRAVITY
OUR INDUSTRY WAS PRESENTED US WHAT THE MOST DANGEROUS VARIETY OF WAYS". THOUSANDS OF FUNCTIONS OR PSEUDO FUNCTIONS, THE EVER INCREASING NEEDS. THAT ADVERTISEMENT (GREED?) MANUFACTURE & FOR EACH NEED ... OF PRODUCTS. TO SATURATE THE DEMAND.
THIS PUTS EACH MAN IN THE MIDDLE OF A

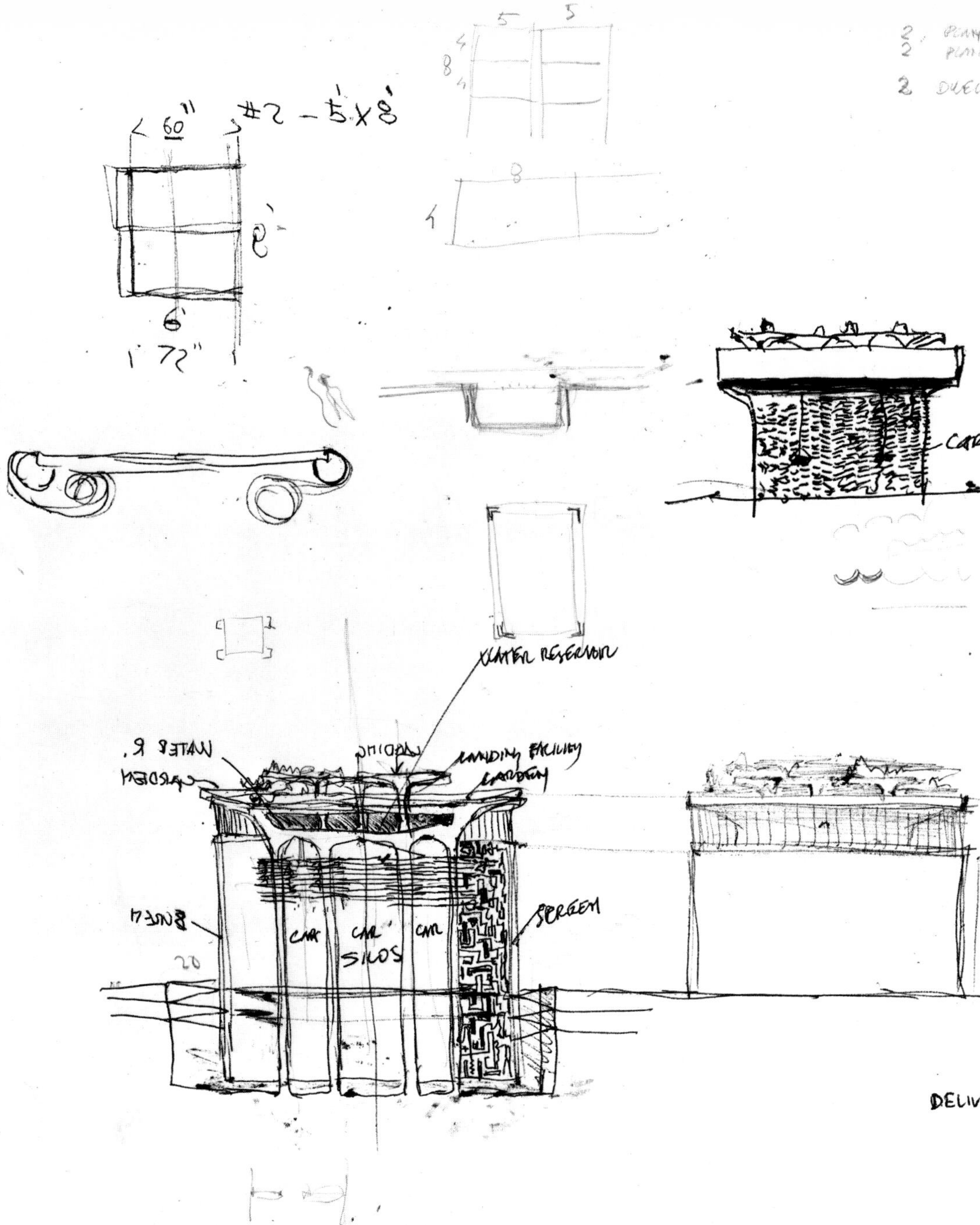

CANCEL ANYTHING ELSE. SORROW
IS PASSED ON & TAKEN ON, BY
WILL OR BY IMPOSITION.
THE CRIPPLED HAS THE VIRTUE OF ITS
MANHOOD OR WOMANHOOD FOREVER
STAINED. NO RELIGION NO FRIENDLINESS
NO PITY NO LOVE GIVE HIM BACK.
THE GLORY OF FULLNESS. IN THE
FULNESS OF MATING.
LIFE: SPLENDID MISERY

AUGUST 61
ARE YOU AWARE OF THE SFERICAL
INFINITY GAZING ON WITH THE
FROZEN INDIFFERENCE OF AN IMPOS-
SIBLE FIRE?
NO ONE BUT YOU CAN MOVE SUCH INDI-
FFERENCE INTO GRACE

WHEN YOU STRIKE OUT ON OTHER THINGS,
ON OTHER MEN, YOU RECOIL FROM
IT WITH LEAF OF RECOGNITION & WHAT IS
THE CONJECTURE OF A MEANING

THE PITY OF OUR STRIFE IS THAT. THE
GRINDING WORK ON EACH-
OTHER IS EVEN MORE PITILESS THAN
THE FATE (CONCEALED & FORGOTTEN) THE
WOLE OF THINGS HAS

LOVERS TAKE REFUGE IN HER, OR ITS ARMS.
THERE, CLOSER MAY BE THAT WHICH
COULD BUT NEVER WILL COME. THERE
THE MURDEROUS GODS ARE (FOR BRIEF
MOMENTS) DISTRACTED. THERE THE
WARMTH OF THE FLESH NOT YOURS WILL
DELIVER YOU OF YOUR HAUNTING
MASTERS OF THE ABSTRACT CAUSE.
DO SEEK THERE THE ABSTRACT CONFIRMATION
OF ANGELS. & FOUND IT FRAGMENTED
BUT INTENSE IN EYES THAT DO NOT CARE.

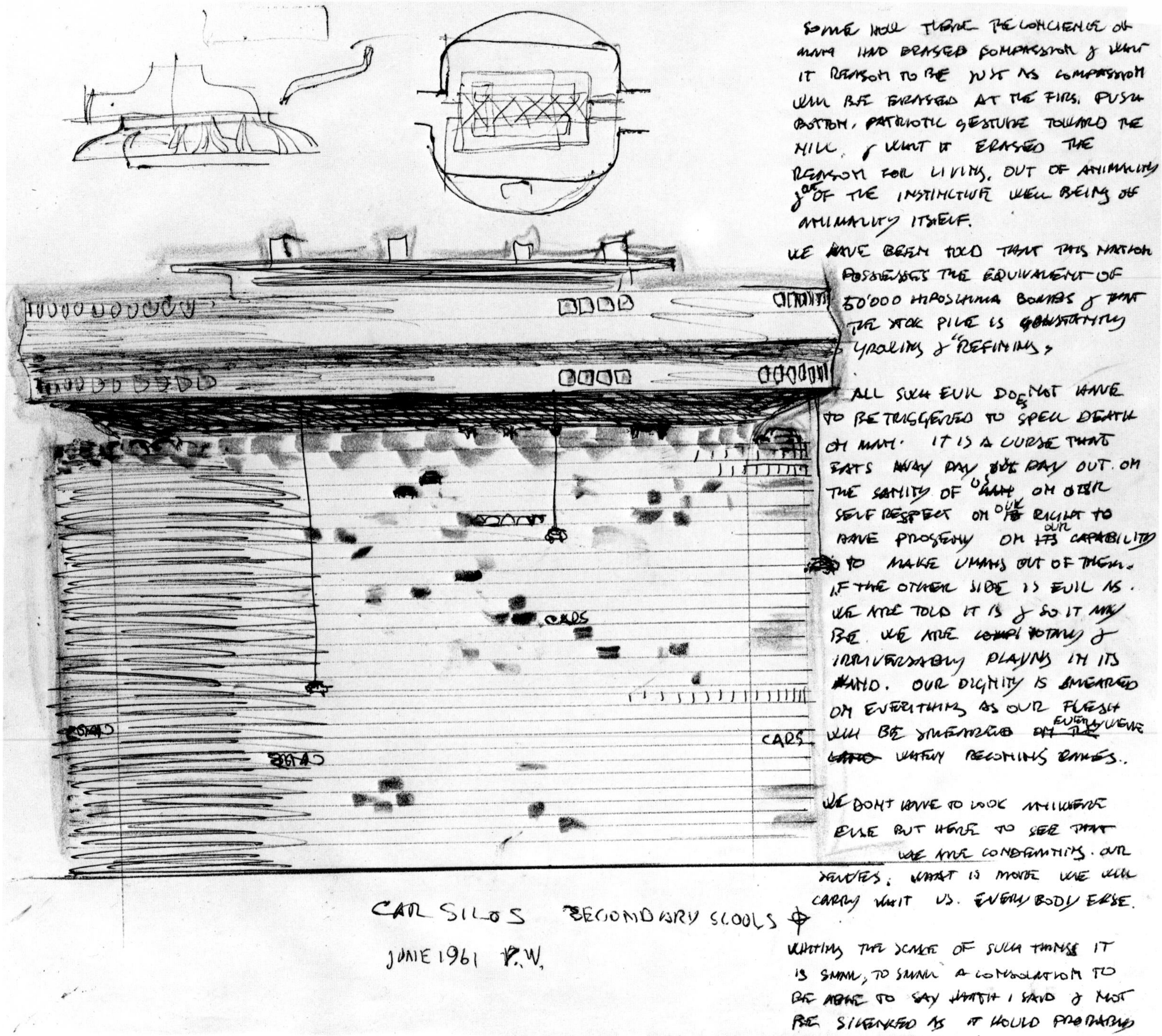
SOME HOW THERE THE CONCIENCE OF MAN HAD ERASED COMPASSION & WHAT IT REASON TO BE JUST AS COMPASSION WILL BE ERASED AT THE FIRST PUSH BUTTON, PATRIOTIC GESTURE TOWARD THE KILL & WHAT IT ERASED THE REASON FOR LIVING. OUT OF ANIMALITY & OF THE INSTINCTIVE WELL BEING OF ANIMALITY ITSELF.
WE HAVE BEEN TOLD THAT THIS NATION POSSESSES THE EQUIVALENT OF 50'000 HIROSHIMA BOMBS & THAT THE STOCK PILE IS CONSTANTLY GROWING & "REFINING,"
ALL SUCH EVIL DOES NOT HAVE TO BE TRIGGERED TO SPELL DEATH ON MAN. IT IS A CURSE THAT EATS AWAY DAY IN DAY OUT. ON THE SANITY OF US ON OUR SELF RESPECT ON OUR RIGHT TO HAVE PROGENY ON OUR CAPABILITY TO MAKE HUMANS OUT OF THEM. IF THE OTHER SIDE IS EVIL AS WE ARE TOLD IT IS & SO IT MAY BE. WE ARE COMPLETELY & IRREVERSIBLY PLAYING IN ITS HAND. OUR DIGNITY IS SMEARED ON EVERYTHING AS OUR FLESH WILL BE SMEARED EVERYWHERE WHEN BECOMING BAKED..
WE DONT HAVE TO LOOK ANYWHERE ELSE BUT HERE TO SEE THAT WE ARE CONDEMNING OUR SELVES; WHAT IS MORE WE WILL CARRY WITH US EVERYBODY ELSE.
KNOWING THE SCALE OF SUCH THINGS IT IS SMALL, TO SMALL A CONSOLATION TO BE ABLE TO SAY WHAT I SAID & NOT BE SILENCED AS IT WOULD PROBABLY
CARS
ROAD
ROAD
CARS
CAR SILOS SECONDARY SCOOLS
JUNE 1961 P.W.

1970
There are topographical situations that seem to invite elation and awe. One of them is to be at the foot of a cliff or halfway up, your back against the rock and the open landscape at your feet. It might be like the sensation of being on (of) the plane of a blow that had split the earth, one side remaining up, defiant; the other side, collapsed and tamed. The earth has established a vertical boundary so that in back of you all is massive, unchanging, and solid, and in front of you is the thermodynamic "unpredictable," ever-changing and endless in color, depth, brilliance, dimness, night. Man is there, very much the intelligent animal, his skeleton pulled toward the enormous magnet of rock and eternity, and his flesh perched on the ledge of stone, half dismayed, half boastful. Man is there, the original homo faber, going to make for himself and his kin the things he needs for survival and adornment for which he will learn to use elementary materials and simple tools. He is the artisan and the craftsman; a cliff dweller of the psyche, half solid matter, half dream and grace.

The cliff is "nonacreage" land. From the interface of stone and air (actually physically vibrant from the hot sheet of air made when the sun hits the rock), one penetrates the geology to carve spaces for the artisan and the craftsman. This way of life is well known to the scattered cave dwellers of past and present, but it would be a revelation to the Madison Avenue manipulators of our "culture."

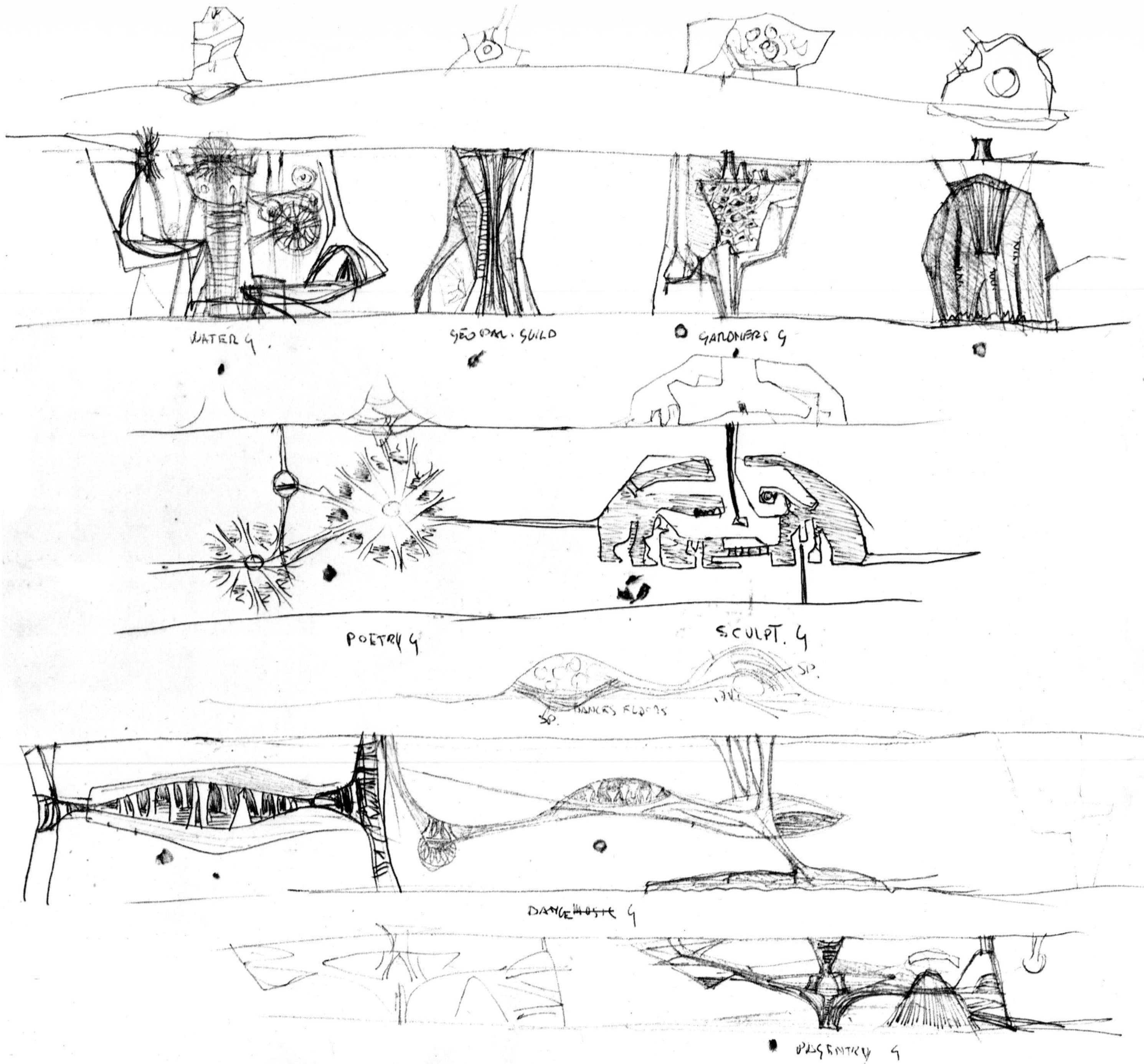
WATER G.
GARDNERS G
POETRY G
SCULPT. G
SP.
DANCERS FLOORS

THE ATTRIBUTE OF ADAPTABILITY HAS VERY MUCH IN THE SPOT LIGHT. THE ABILITY OF A BUILDING TO RESPOND WELL TO DIVERSIFIED USAGES IS THEN SHORT OF BEING OF SUCH TRANSFIGURED CHARACTER + ONLY A RATIONAL TOOL FOR THE INVENTIVENESS OF MAN:

A BUILDING IS NOT. OR BECAUSE ARTISTIC OR BECAUSE ENGINEERIAL
THE KRAFTED BUILDING IS RIGIDLY ONE FUNCTIONAL.

IF ARTISTIC ITS APTNESS IS UNCHANGED FROM TIME.
IF ENGINEERIAL HIS APTNESS IS CHANGED ON TIME & BESIDE SUCH APTNESS VERY LITTLE IS WORTH OF EXISTENCE.

IF KRAFTED, LIMITED BY TIME BUT SENSUOUSLY ANCHORED TO IT, WILL STAY AS VALUABLE DOCUMENT.

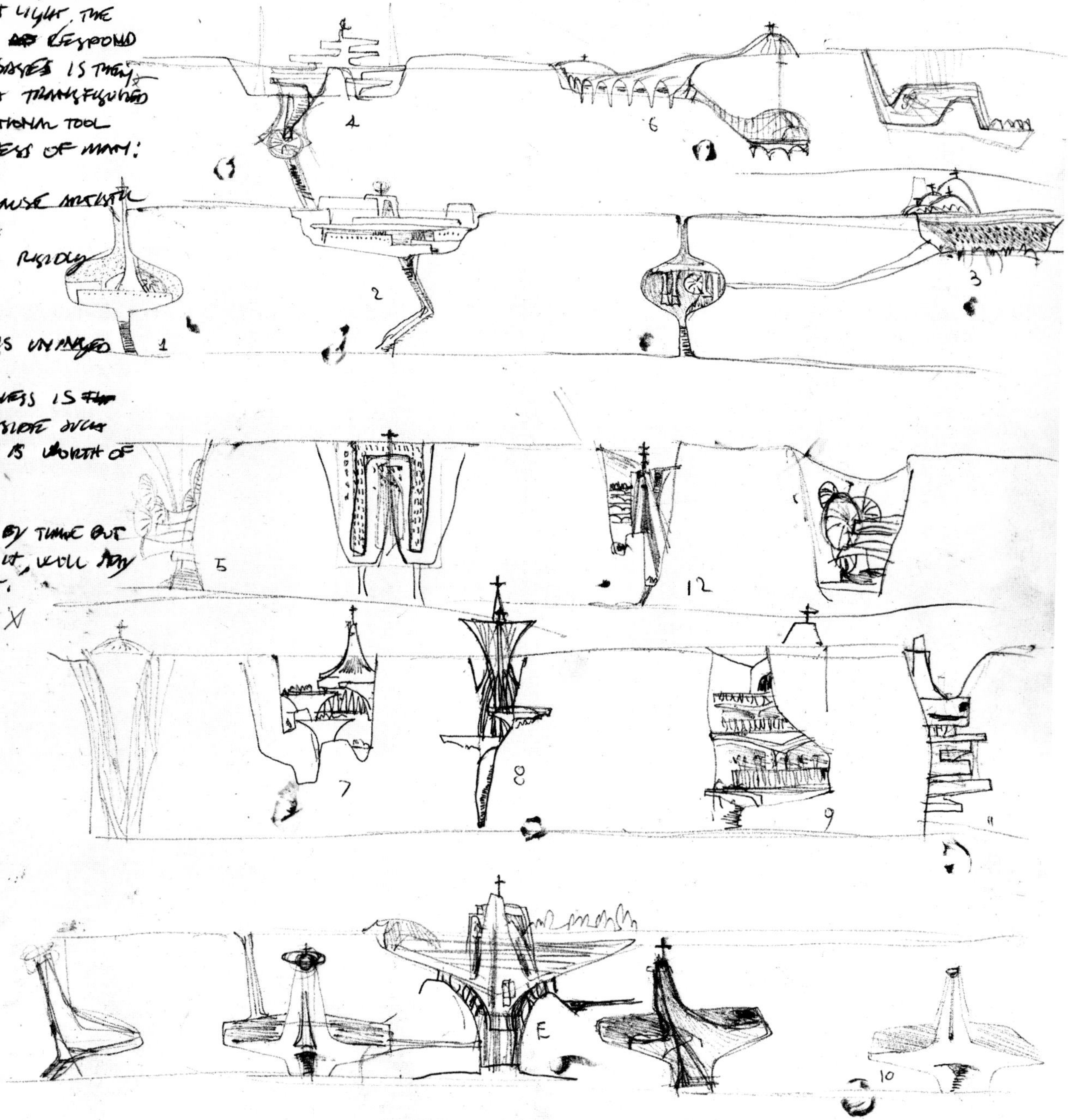

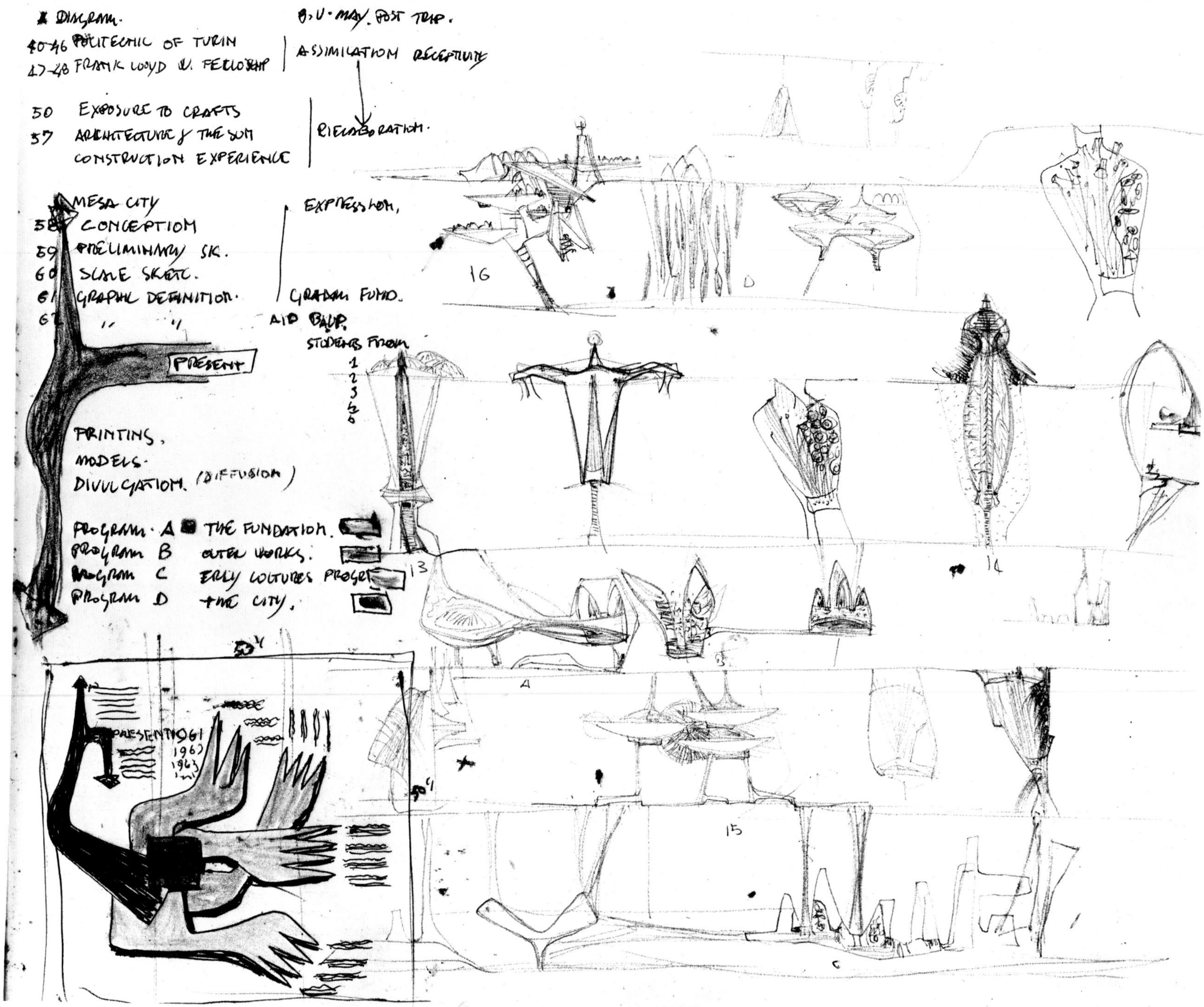
DIAGRAM.
POST TRIP.
40-46 POLITECNIC OF TURIN
47-48 FRANK LLOYD W. FELLOWSHIP
ASSIMILATION RECEPTIVITY
50 EXPOSURE TO CRAFTS
57 ARCHITECTURE & THE SUN
CONSTRUCTION EXPERIENCE
RIELABORATION.
MESA CITY
58 CONCEPTION
59 PRELIMINARY SK.
60 SCALE SKETC.
61 GRAPHIC DEFINITION.
62
EXPRESSION,
GRAHAM FUND.
STUDENTS FROM
PRESENT
PRINTING,
MODELS.
DIVULGATION. (DIFFUSION)
PROGRAM A THE FUNDATION.
PROGRAM B OUTER WORKS.
PROGRAM C EARLY CULTURES PROGR
PROGRAM D THE CITY.
PRESENT 1961
1962
1963
16
D
13
14
A
15
C

Market Manufacturing

1970
A cornucopia of goods put on a conveyer belt and the city dweller sitting at the long table of plenty—an unnecessarily opulent vision of how to bring to the citizenry the things produced by the city and the things the city merchants import. A forty-mile conveyer belt, not in the literal sense but as a symbol of the great flow of hard and software along a fascia that is the productive, marketing, retailing, servicing, and consumption chain of the city. The availability of all the phases of this enormous phenomenon we consider to be the gate to happiness, this procurer of affluence, could be a way to decongest the mind of man, the buyer, and turn it away from the idols of gross (how gross?) national product and annual percentage growth (what growth?). The mind could return to an understanding, conscious or not, of the delicate balance between what we might call nonmanipulated nature and the neonature which man, the manipulator, has been collecting around himself at times wisely, sensitively, beautifully, at times pompously, mistakenly, callously. We do not really understand this balance, but it is the essential difference between the determinism of nature and the compassion of man.

The dingy and squalid industrial towns of Europe at the turn of the century had a varnish of truth about them: the unpleasant fact of life that nothing comes without a price. At that historical point the price was direct pollution of the towns and a graying and dulling of the colors of life. But it has taken half a century for a variegated, ubiquitous, surprising, peripatetic poisoning of the whole biosphere to outrage the mind. The fraudulence of affluence has kept our eyes and minds away from this deterioration. As affluence and opulence characterize the dead end of many civilizations, we might want to curb our wants. Not that by doing so doom might be avoided or postponed—that takes a more central inner determination—but because there is a dignity in projecting into one's last moments an uncluttered state of things and being.

1960
The market-manufacturing complex, in two symmetrical bands 25 kilometers long, shelters all the activities of processing, assembling, display, and sale of standard products compatible with the need for clear atmosphere, absence of fumes, odors, dust, and noise. The unification of all these functions is then attempted under one roof with all the facilities found in any downtown district such as shops, restaurants, cafes, theaters, libraries, banks, and professional offices. The interstitial tissue is constituted of meadows, gardens, pathways, fountains, and open markets. The manufacturing and marketing units are served by a battery of conveyer belts, originating from the water locks at the north end of the city, using water as a lubricant, gravity as the moving power. The constant imperceptible slope of these structures is the reference level all along the complex and may be followed through plains, broken levels, meadows, ponds, and woods, appearing and disappearing from and into the body of the processing and marketing plants, much like an ancient aqueduct.

The double system of speedways is at the two outer edges of the complex and carries within its structure car silos and repair-refueling shops.
If the car becomes obsolete, this completely suspended system is given to other functions relative to production and consumption.

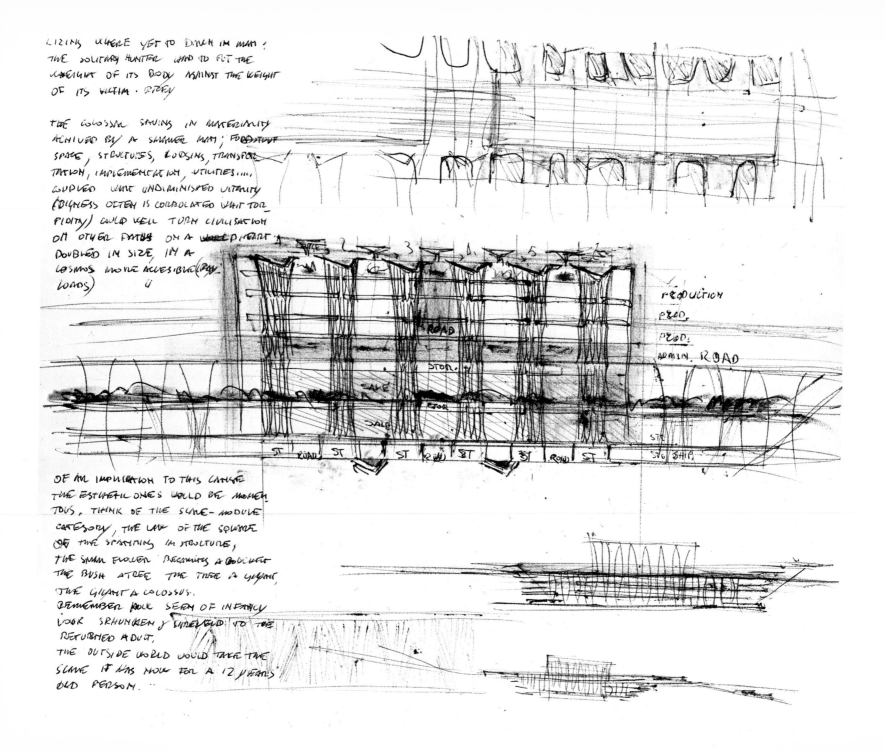

LIZINGS WHERE YET TO DWELL IN MAN: THE SOLITARY HUNTER HAD TO PIT THE WEIGHT OF ITS BODY AGAINST THE WEIGHT OF ITS VICTIM · PREY

THE COLOSSAL SAVING IN MATERIALITY ACHIVED BY A SMALLER MAN; FOODSTUFF SPACE, STRUCTURES, LODGING, TRANSPORTATION, IMPLEMENTATION, UTILITIES...., COUPLED WITH UNDIMINISHED VITALITY (BIGNESS OFTEN IS CORRELATED WITH TORPIDITY) COULD WELL TURN CIVILISATION ON OTHER PATHS ON A WORLD HEART DOUBLED IN SIZE, IN A COSMOS MORE ACCESIBLE (PAYLOADS)

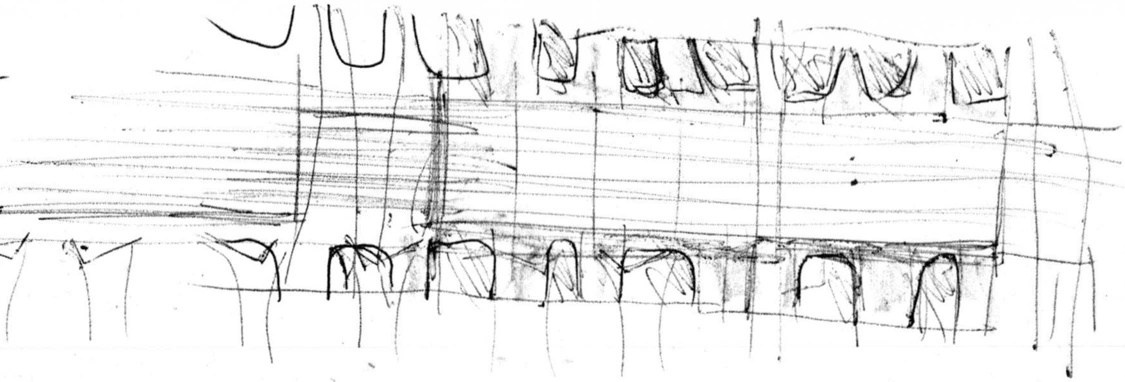

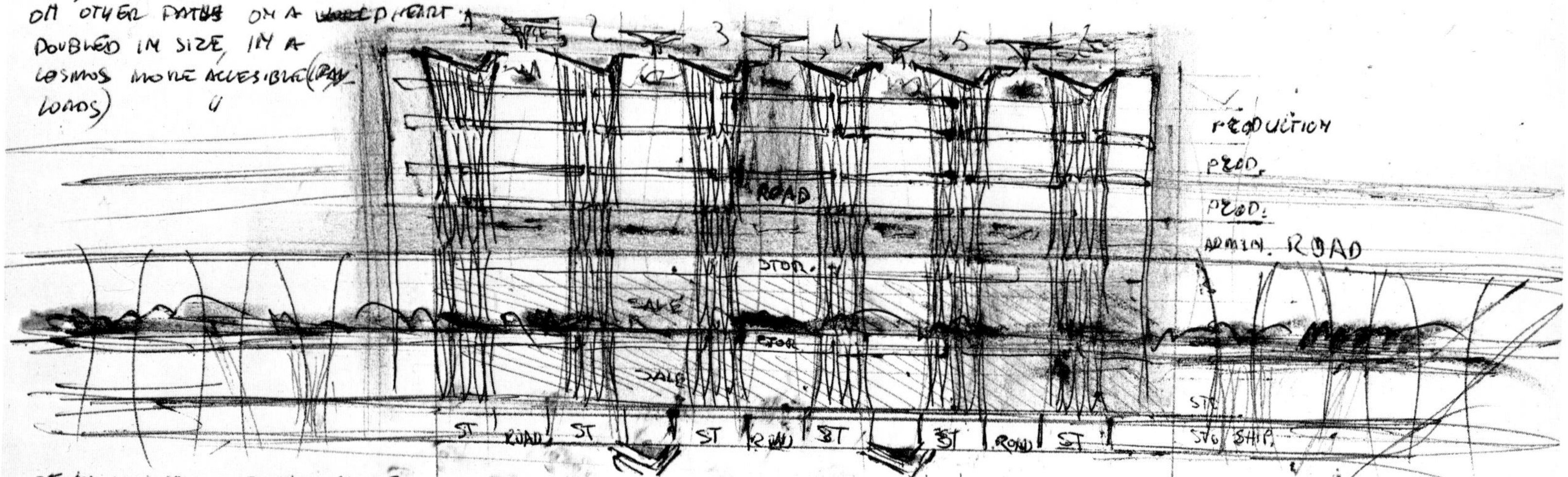

OF AN IMPLICATION TO THIS CAUSE THE ESTHETIC ONES WOULD BE MOMENTOUS. THINK OF THE SCALE-MODULE CATEGORY, THE LAW OF THE SQUARE OF THE SPANNING IN STRUCTURE, THE SMALL FLOWER BECOMING A BOUQUET THE BUSH A TREE THE TREE A GIANT, THE GIANT A COLOSSUS.. REMEMBER HOW SEEN OF INFANCY LOOK SHRUNKEN SHRIVELED TO THE RETURNED ADULT, THE OUTSIDE WORLD WOULD TAKE THE SCALE IT HAS NOW FOR A 12 YEARS OLD PERSON. ..

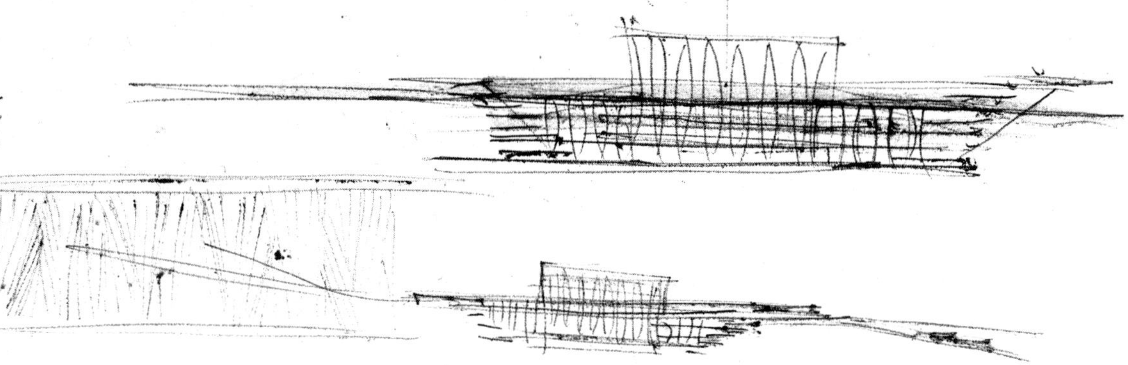

DECEMBER 60 PV.

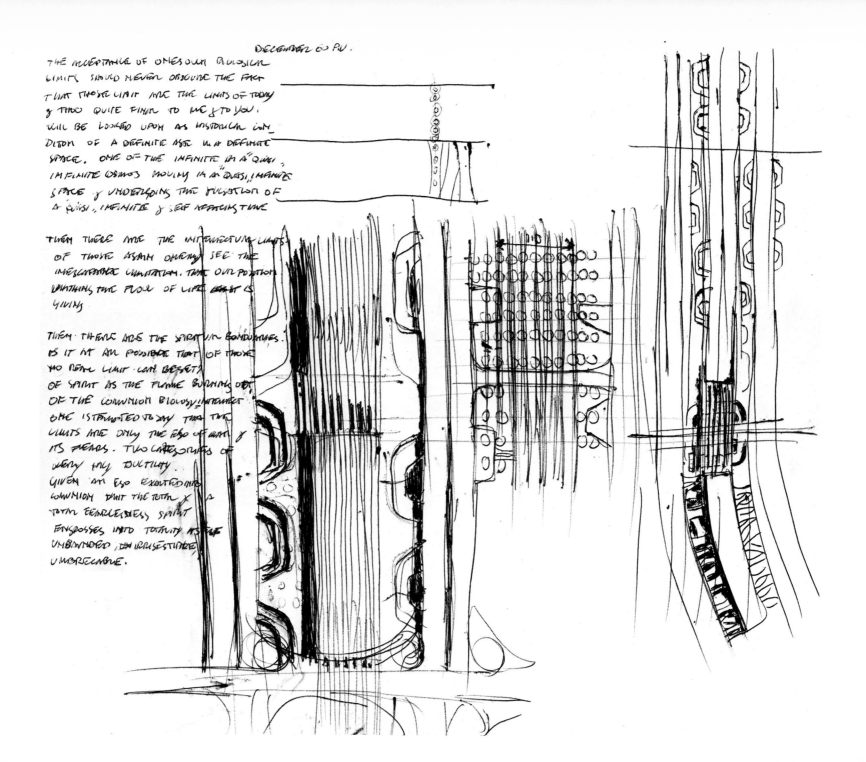

THE ACCEPTANCE OF ONE'S OWN BIOLOGICAL LIMITS SHOULD NEVER OBSCURE THE FACT THAT THOSE LIMIT ARE THE LIMITS OF TODAY & THO QUITE FINAL TO ME & TO YOU, WILL BE LOOKED UPON AS HISTORICAL CONDITION OF A DEFINITE AGE IN A DEFINITE SPACE. ONE OF THE INFINITE IN A "QUASI" INFINITE COSMOS MOVING IN A "QUASI" INFINITE SPACE & UNDERGOING THE PULSATION OF A "QUASI" INFINITE & SELF REPEATING TIME

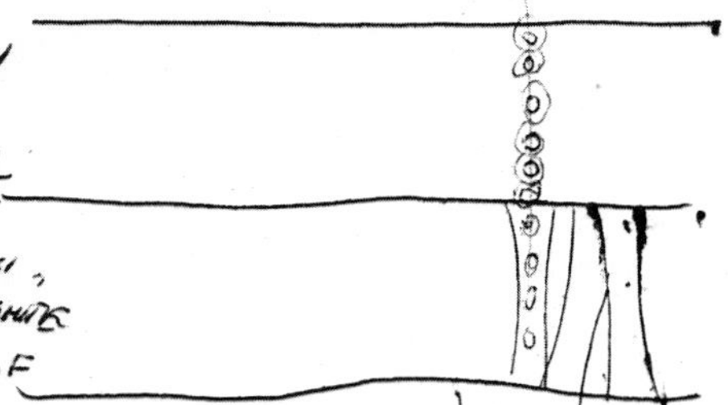

THEN THERE ARE THE INTELLECTUAL LIMITS OF THOSE AGAIN ONLY A FEW SEE THE INESCAPABLE LIMITATION. THAT OUR POSITION WITHIN THE FLOW OF LIFE ~~[illegible]~~ IS GIVING

THEN THERE ARE THE SPIRITUAL BOUNDARIES. IS IT AT ALL POSSIBLE THAT OF THOSE NO REAL LIMIT CAN BESET? OF SPIRIT AS THE FLAME BURNING OUT OF THE COMMUNION BIOLOGY-INTELLECT ONE IS TEMPTED TO SAY THAT THE LIMITS ARE ONLY THE EGO OF MAN & ITS FEARS. TWO CATEGORIES OF VERY HIGH DUCTILITY. GIVEN AN EGO EXALTED INTO COMMUNION THAT THE TOTAL & A TOTAL FEARLESSNESS SPIRIT ENGROSSES INTO TOTALITY ITSELF UNBOUNDED, ~~[illegible]~~ IRRESISTIBLE, UNBREAKABLE.

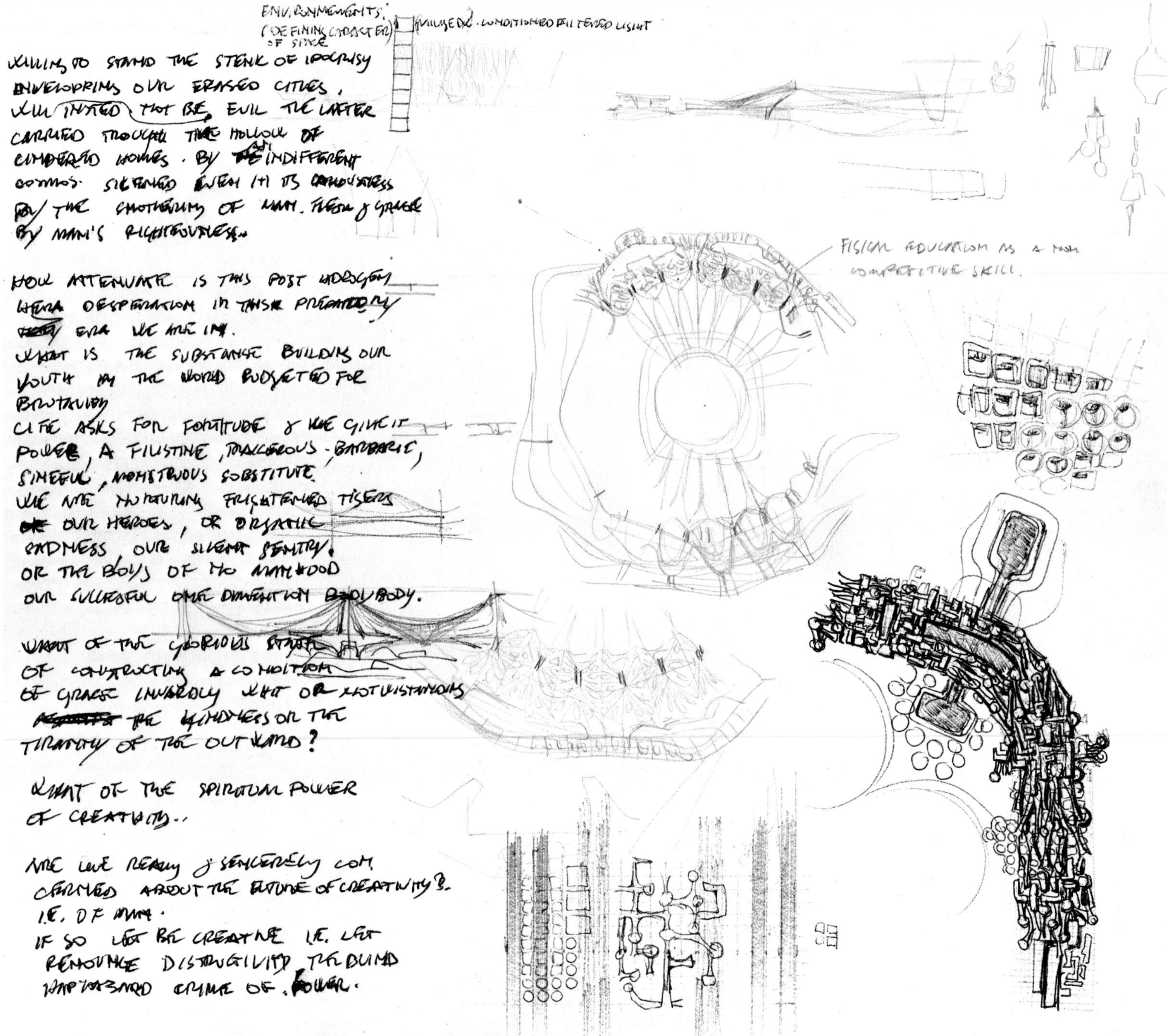
ENVIRONMENTS: (DEFINING CHARACTER) OF SPACE
WILLING TO STAND THE STENK OF HYPOCRISY
ENVELOPING OUR ERASED CITIES.
CARRIED THROUGH THE HOLLOW OF
CINDERED HOMES. BY AN INDIFFERENT
BY MAN'S RIGHTEOUSNESS.
HOW ATTENUATE IS THIS POST
DESPERATION
ERA WE ARE IN.
WHAT IS THE SUBSTANCE BUILDING OUR
YOUTH IN THE WORLD BUDGETED FOR
BRUTALITY
LIFE ASKS FOR FORTITUDE & WE GIVE IT
POWER, A FILISTINE, BARBARIC,
MONSTROUS SUBSTITUTE.
WE ARE NURTURING FRIGHTENED TIGERS
OUR HEROES, OR ORGANIC
SADNESS, OUR SILENT SENTRY.
OR THE BOYS OF NO MANHOOD
OUR SUCCESSFUL ONE DIMENSION BODYBODY.
WHAT OF THE GLORIOUS
OF CONSTRUCTING A CONDITION
OF GRACE INWARDLY
THE KINDNESS OR THE
TYRANNY OF THE OUTWARD?
WHAT OF THE SPIRITUAL POWER
OF CREATIVITY..
ARE WE REALLY & SINCERELY CON-
CERNED ABOUT THE FUTURE OF CREATIVITY?
I.E. OF MAN.
IF SO LET BE CREATIVE I.E. LET
RENOUNCE
CRIME OF POWER.
FISICAL EDUCATION AS A NON
COMPETITIVE SKILL.

LIFE HAS TO EXTEND ITSELF THROUGH CREA-
TIVITY NOT THROUGH POWER
THAT IS WHY MONSTERS ARE ONLY
IN THE MIND OF MAN & IN HIS PO-
WER TO CONCEIVE & POSSIBLY TO
PRODUCE

IN SO FAR AS LIFE & AS CONS. CREATIVE IS
MENACED BY MAN THE POWERFUL.
LIFE ITSELF IS PRECARIOUSLY SITUATED
ON THE EDGE OF SELF ANNIHILATION.

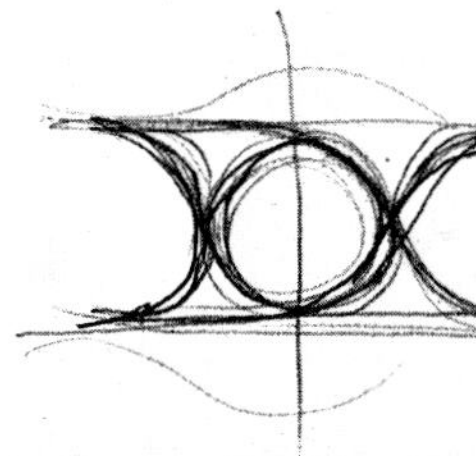

THAT IS, & HOW AND THAT SO IT IS
& HOW WISE, THAT THERE
SUBSTITUTE TO CREATIVITY.
ONE CONSTRUCTS OR ONE DESTROYS.
IN THE PRESENCE OF POWER
LIFE HAS BUT ONE CHOICE: TO CON-
CEIVE MORE INTENSELY SO AS TO
EXUDE MORE GRACE, SO AS TO
SHOW POWER THE FOLLY OF ITS OWN
SENSELESSNESS
THAT IS THE ORGANIC HEROISM OF
THINGS LIVING. THAT IS NOT A HOPE
FOR MAN BUT ITS ONLY & SOLE HOPE.
ANY OTHER WAY IS THE ENSLAVEMENT
OF THE SPIRIT TO THE CONSTRUCTIONS
OF THE ABSTRACT MIND.

FEBURY 61

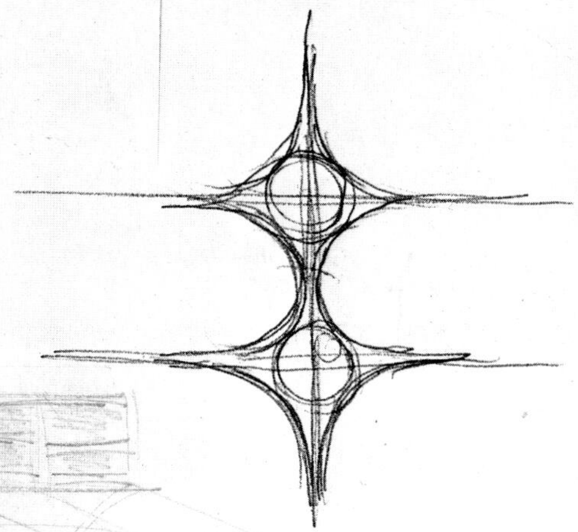

EVIL WILL ALWAYS GIVE BIRTH TO
ITS OWN SELF. ONE DO NOT CONQUER
IT BY CUTTING ONE OF HIS HEADS
BUT BY MAKING IT USELESS I.E.
SENSELESS.
SUCH TASK: DEMANDS BASIC STRENGTH
UNLIMITED HEROISM & A CONSTANT
SELF RESPONSIBLE BEHAVIOUR OF
WHICH WE ARE THE VERY POOR &
VERY AFRAID
THE GREATEST TASK FOR MAN &
FOR A COMMUNITY OF MAN. A NATION. A REAL NATION.

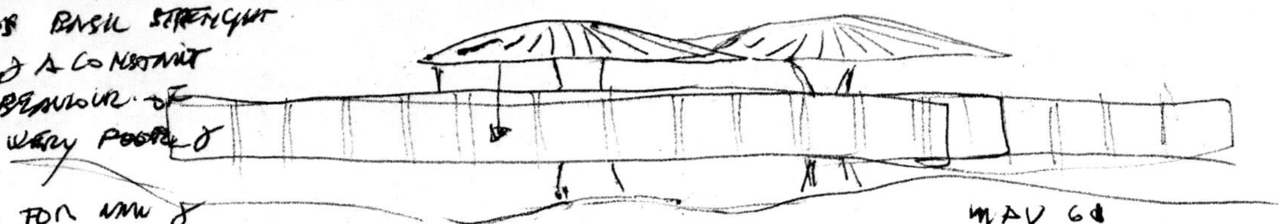

MAY 60

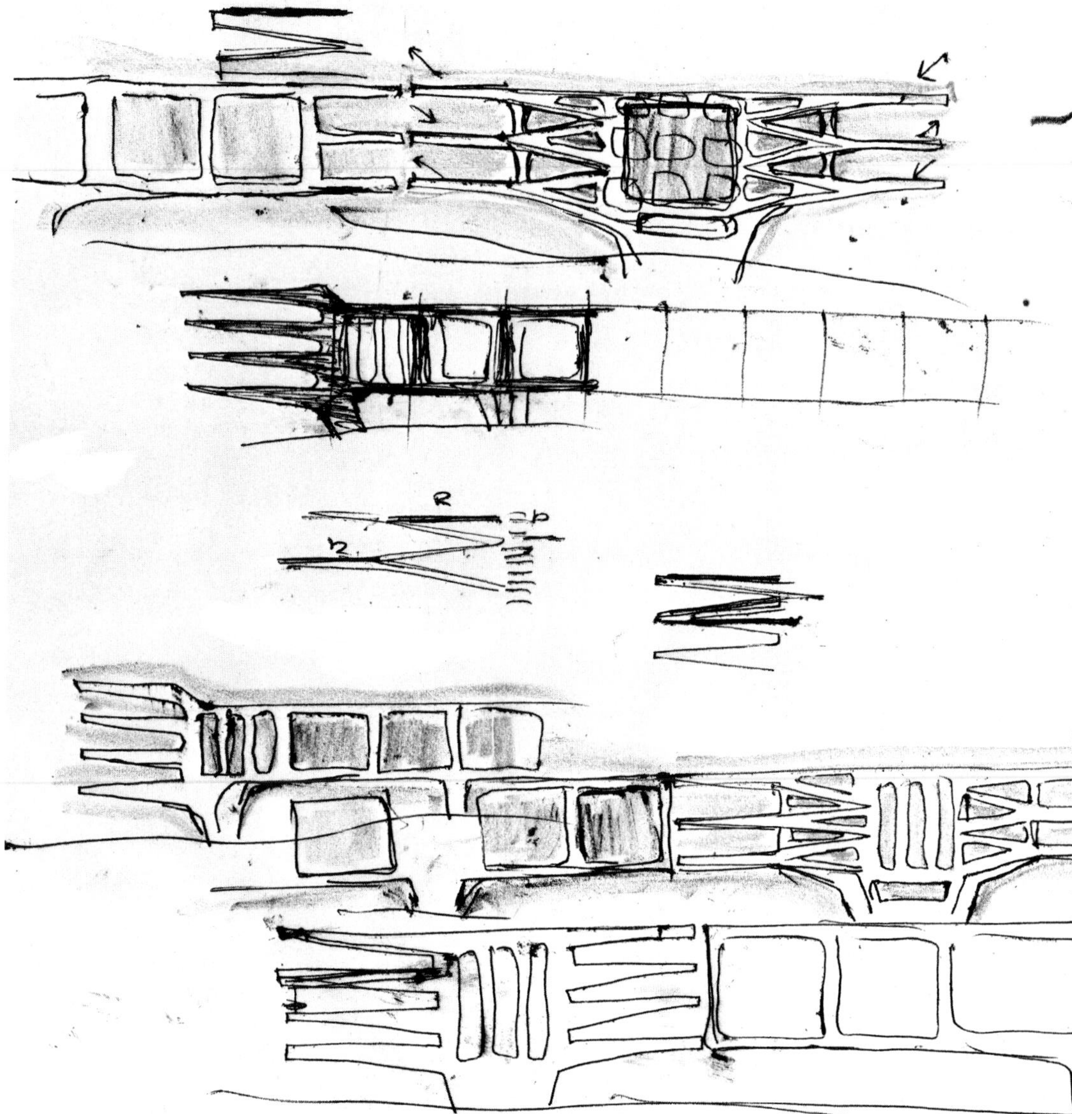

CULTIVABLE LAND & ALL THE OTHER OUTLINED GREEN BELTS & AREAS.

THE MESA IS, SO TO SPEAK, STRIPT TO ~~THE BONE~~ ITS GEOLOGICAL BONE & THEN HERE FILLED IN WITH GOOD EARTH, THERE FURTHER HOLLOWED OUT, TO PRODUCE THE MAN MADE LANDSCAPE

IN FACT THE CENTRAL SPINE OF THE CITY CONNECTING ITS INTELLECTUAL CENTER TO ITS THEOLOGICAL CENTER IS ~~A~~ COMPLEX SEQUENCE OF MAN-CARVED CANYONS & VALLEYS TO WHICH THE ACCESSES TO "INVERTED SCULPTURES" ARE OPEN.

THOSE INVERTED SCULPTURES ARE THE OUTCOME OF THE CONCEPTIONS OF SCULPTORS & ARTISTS, EQUIPPED WITH THE TECHNOLOGICAL POWER AVAILABLE. SUCH MAN-MADE CAVES & PITS & .... ARE MUSEUMS, SHRINES, ~~WORSHIP~~ PLACE, PERFORMING ART PLACES.......

ALL THE ~~CARVED~~ QUARRIED MATERIAL WOULD GO IN PROCESSING PLANTS TO PRODUCE LIME, CEMENT, & OR WILL BE USED AS BUILDING MATERIAL

A MOBILE PLANT IS ENVISAGED TO MOVE FROM ONE END TO THE OTHER "DIGESTING" ALL THE MATERIALS QUARRIED

IN THE MESA INSTANCE THE INTERVENTION OF MAN ON THE BALANCE OF NATURAL FACTS IS SOMEHOW CONFINED ~~BOX~~ ACTING ON A STERILE OR SEMI STERILE LAND.
IT IS SO ALSO BECAUSE A MESA TENDS TO BE SOMETHING OF A DETACHED & FORGOTTEN AREA TOUCHED

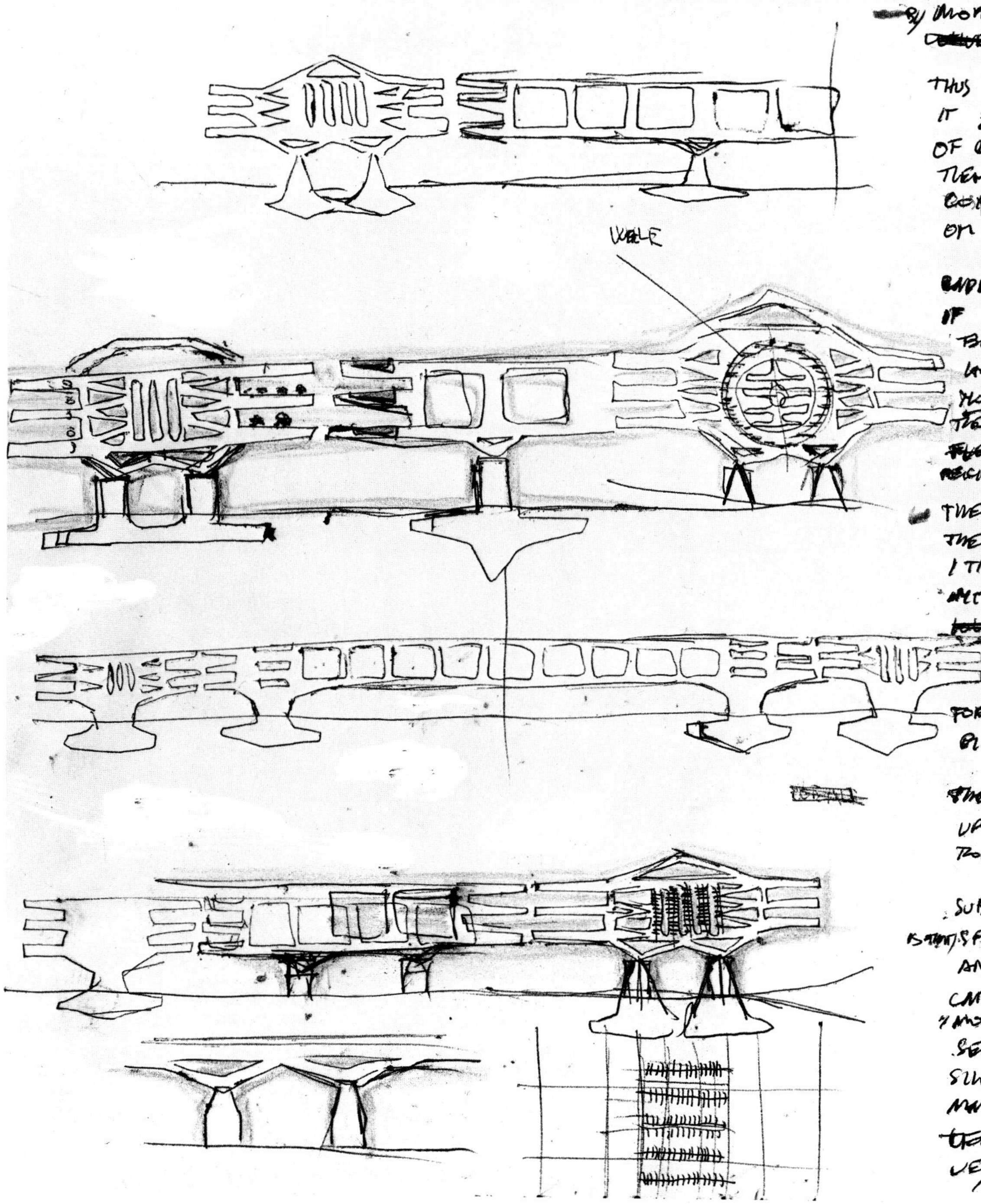

BY MORE THAN TOUCHING THE TORPID
FLOW OF THE AGES

THUS THE VIOLENCE BROUGHT UPON
IT & THE POSSIBLY SAVAGE INTENSITY
OF CHANGE, TESTIMONY OF MAN IMPA-
TIENCE PERHAPS, ARE SOMEWHAT
CONTAINED & THEIR RESONANCE
ON THE SURROUNDING MINIMIZED

RAPE HAS SPLENDORS OF ITS OWN
IF AT THE MOMENT OF DECISION
BOTH THE POTENTIALITY OF FRATER-
NHOOD & MOTHERHOOD DISCOVER THAT
NOW IT IS ONLY BY LOVE THAT
THE CONCEIVED WILL BE OR CAN BE
TO GRACE
REKINDLED

THEN. CONCIOUS IF AT TIME UNEASY
THE RAPE I TEORETICLY APPLIED
I TRY TO APPLY, WHAT UTMOST INTENSITY
ON THE FACE OF A
NATURE LOVED ENOUGHT
TO BE DEVASTATED FOR SOME
MORE PERSONAL INTERACTION,
FOR SOME RISK & FOR THE POSSI-
BILITY OF DISASTER.

THE PHISICAL CONTAINEMENT OF MANS ACTION
UPON NATURE IT IS ALSO A
FONDAMENTAL POINT IN MY BELIEF;

SUBURBIA SHOWS US THAT WHATEVER
SPRAWLS INDIFFERENTLY IN ANY
AND ALL DIRECTION & DOES NOT
CARRY THE STERN BUT BEAUTIFUL
MONOCRONY OF A PRAIRIE, DESERT
SEA .... THE LONELINESS & ITS
SILENCES ITS A CURSE ON BOTH
MAN & NATURE

LETS. ACT INTENSLY & NOT EXTENSI-
VELY. LET THE PRODUCE

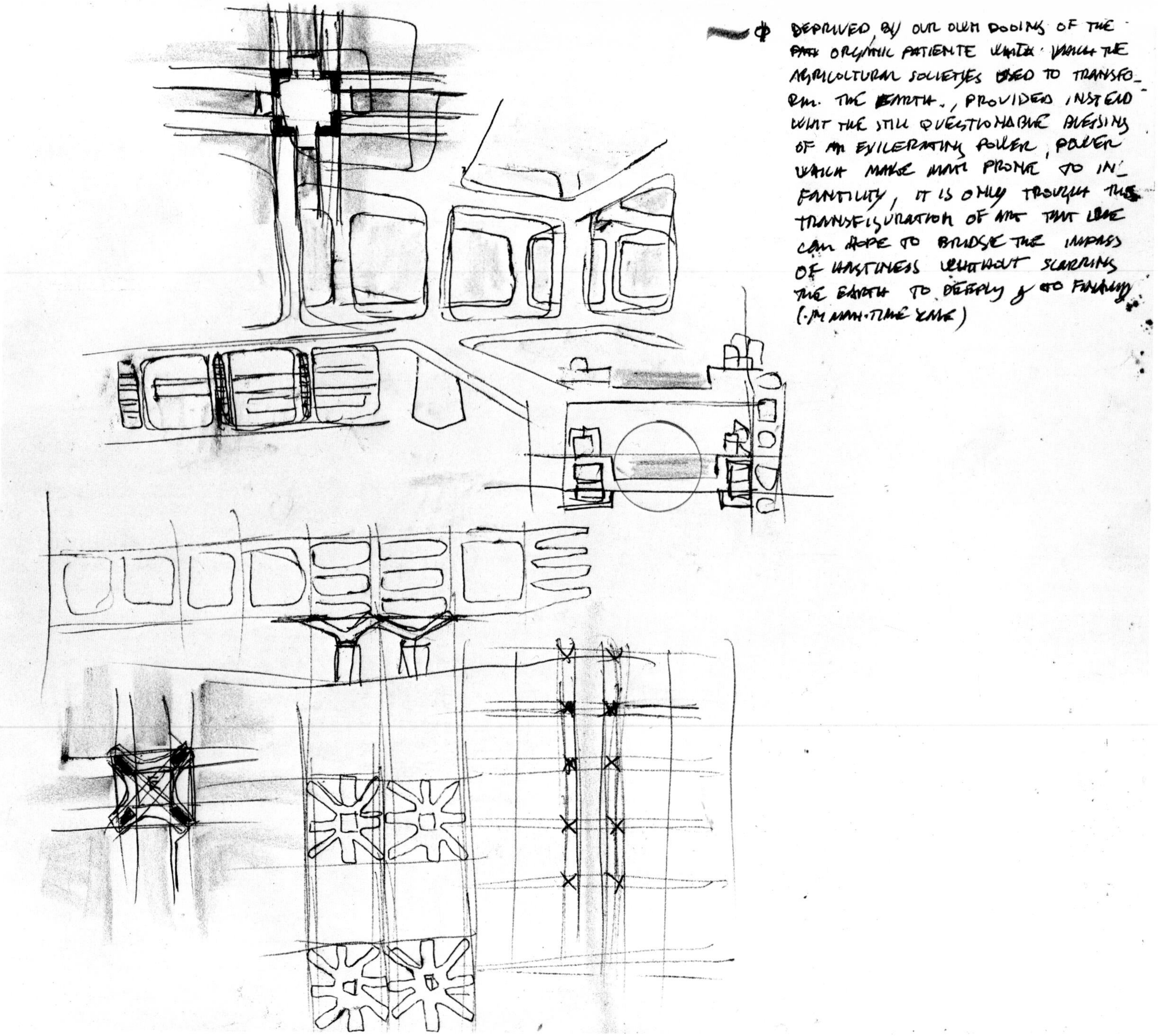
DEPRIVED, BY OUR OWN DOOING OF THE
ORGANIC PATIENTE WORK WHICH THE
AGRICOLTURAL SOCIETIES USED TO TRANSFO_
RM. THE EARTH., PROVIDED INSTEAD
WITH THE STILL QUESTIONABLE BLESSING
OF AN EXILERATING POWER, POWER
WHICH MAKE MAN PRONE TO IN_
FANTILITY, IT IS ONLY TROUGH THE
TRANSFIGURATION OF ART THAT WE
CAN HOPE TO BRIDGE THE IMPASS
OF HASTINESS WITHOUT SCARRING
THE EARTH TO DEEPLY & TO FINALLY
(IN MAN-TIME SCALE)

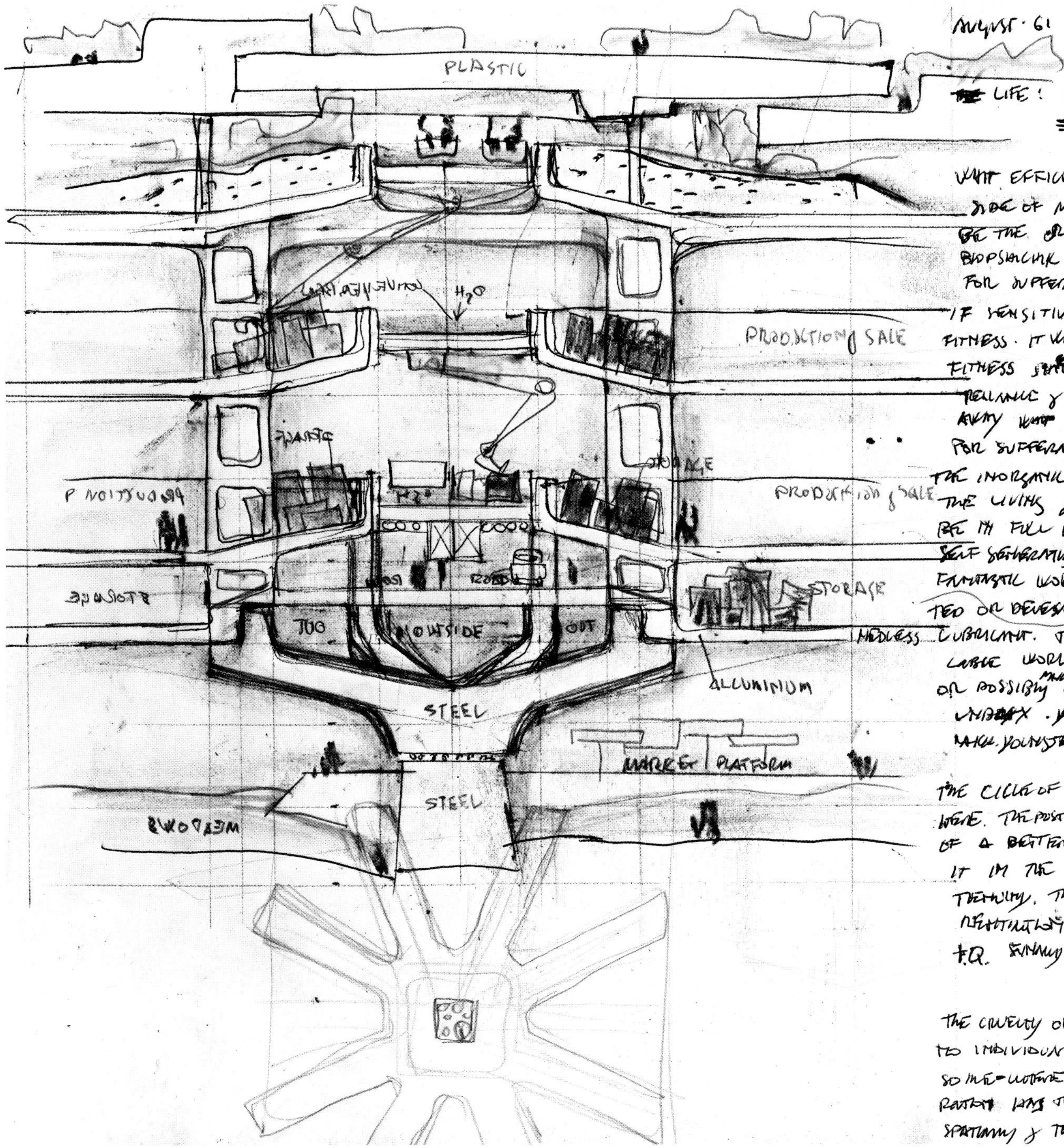

AUGUST · 61

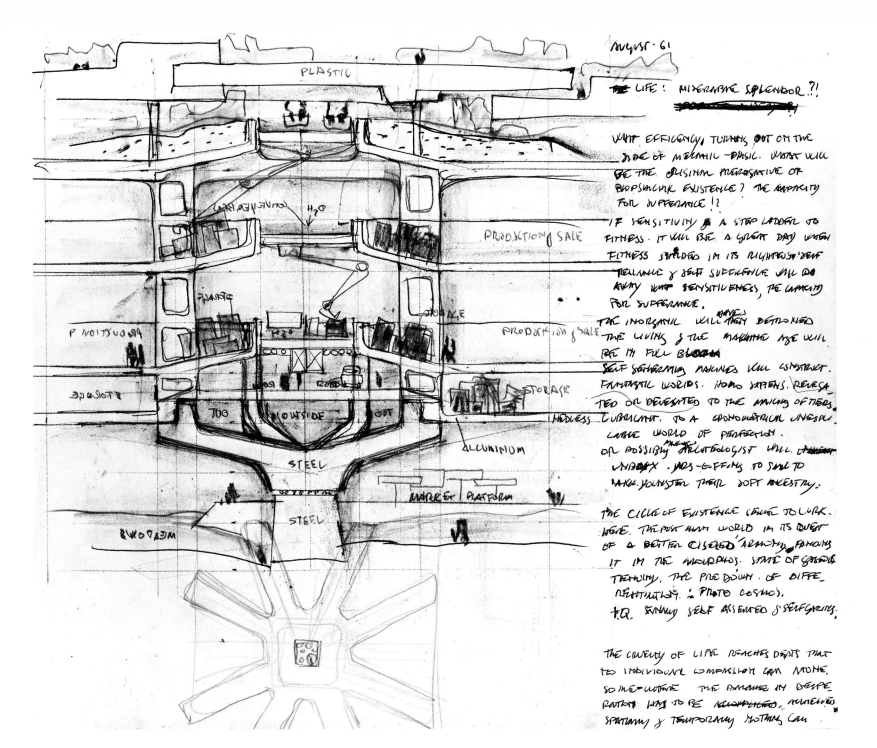

~~THE~~ LIFE! MISERABLE SPLENDOR ?!

WHAT EFFICIENCY, TURNING OUT ON THE SIDE OF MECHANIC-BASIC. WHAT WILL BE THE ORIGINAL PREROGATIVE OF BIOPSYCHICAL EXISTENCE? THE CAPACITY FOR SUFFERANCE!?

IF SENSITIVITY IS A STEP LADDER TO FITNESS. IT WILL BE A GREAT DAY WHEN FITNESS SHIELDED IN ITS RIGHTEOUS SELF RELIANCE & SELF SUFFICIENCE WILL DO AWAY WITH SENSITIVENESS, THE CAPACITY FOR SUFFERANCE.

THE INORGANIC WILL HAVE THEN DETHRONED THE LIVING & THE MACHINE AGE WILL BE IN FULL BLOOM

SELF GENERATING MACHINES WILL CONSTRUCT FANTASTIC WORLDS. HOMO SAPIENS. RELEGATED OR DEVESATED TO THE MAKING OF TIERS LUBRICANT. TO A CRONOMETRICAL UNEXPLICABLE WORLD OF PERFECTION.

OR POSSIBLY MACHINE ARCHEOLOGIST WILL UNBOX JARS-COFFINS TO SHOW TO MACH. YOUNGSTER THEIR SOFT ANCESTRY.

THE CIRCLE OF EXISTENCE COME TO WORK HERE. THE POST MAN WORLD IN ITS QUEST OF A BETTER CISELED ARMONY, FINDING IT IN THE AMOURPHOS STATE OF GASEOUS TRENDING, THE PREDOWN OF DIFFERENTIATION: PROTO COSMOS.

F.Q. SUNNY SELF ASSENTED & SELFGAZING.

THE CRUELTY OF LIFE REACHES DEPTS THAT NO INDIVIDUAL COMPASSION CAN ATONE. SOMEWHERE THE BALANCE IN DESPERATION HAS TO BE ~~ACCOMPLISHED~~. ACHIEVED. SPATIALLY & TEMPORALLY NOTHING CAN

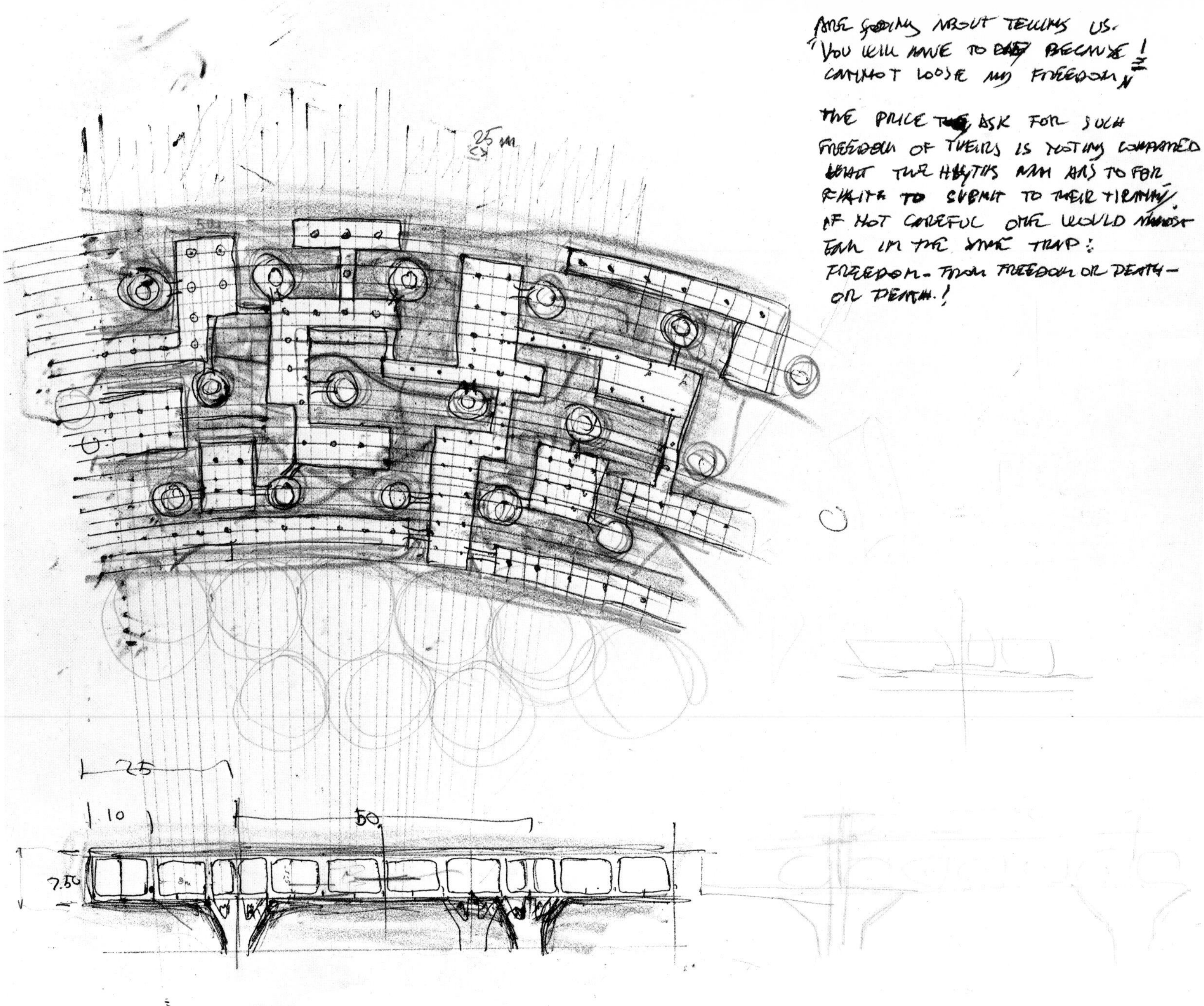
ARE GOING ABOUT TELLING US.
"YOU WILL HAVE TO BECAUSE I
CANNOT LOOSE MY FREEDOM"
THE PRICE THEY ASK FOR SUCH
FREEDOM OF THEIRS IS NOTHING COMPARED
TO SUBMIT TO THEIR TYRANNY.
IF NOT CAREFUL ONE WOULD ALMOST
FALL IN THE SAME TRAP:
FREEDOM - FROM FREEDOM OR DEATH -
OR DEATH.!
25 m
25
1.10
50
7.50

FEBUARY 62

REACHING AS WE SEEM THE LEVEL OF FULFILLED AMORPHISM, WHERE [UNFORMED] MORALS ARE WELL CUSHIONED BY PHYSICAL SATIETY, IT WOULD PERHAPS CONTRIBUTE TO SANITY THE ADOPTION OF THOSE ATTITUDES WHICH WERE PUT FORWARD CENTURY AGO BY THE FUNDATIONS OF MONASTIC ORDERS.

WHAT THE EQUIVALENT OF THOSE IN OUR TIME WOULD BE IS PERHAPS ONE OF THE QUESTIONS WHOSE ANSWER COULD OPEN AN ALTERNATIVE TO SOCIAL [illegible]

WHILE THEN, SPECULATIVE WORK, SALVAGED ~~WITHIN THE~~ MONASTIC WORLD, THE KNOWLEDGE OF PAST EPOCS. NOW SALVATION WOULD LIE MORE IN REFRAINING FROM THE INTELLECTUAL CONSTRUCTIONS. SO AS TO QUEST IN THE YET UNANSWERED QUESTIONS OF HOW MAN CAN DEAL WITH ITS OWN INNER SELF & ITS SOCIAL SURROUNDING [AWAY FROM] ~~BEYOND~~ THE MAD WORLD OF ~~THE~~ MANIPULATED NATURE BEYOND RECOGNITION. & BEYOND GRACE

THE CULTIVATION OF SENSITIVITY, THE SOLLICITUDE FOR BEAUTY, THE ESSENTIALISATION OF PHYSICAL NEEDS, ...
AN UNIVERSALIZED CONSCIOUSNESS ...
ARE SOME OF THE ELEMENTS, STEPS TOWARDS THE GAPING OF THE VOID BETWEEN SCIENCE & ETICS. NOW FILLED BY THE BRUTALIZING ABSTRACTION OF ~~THE~~ TECHNOCRACY

IN THIS LIGHT THE NEW WORLD WILL NOT COME FROM THE CITY. IT WILL COME FROM AN "ISOLATED SOCIETY CONSCIOUS & [illegible]

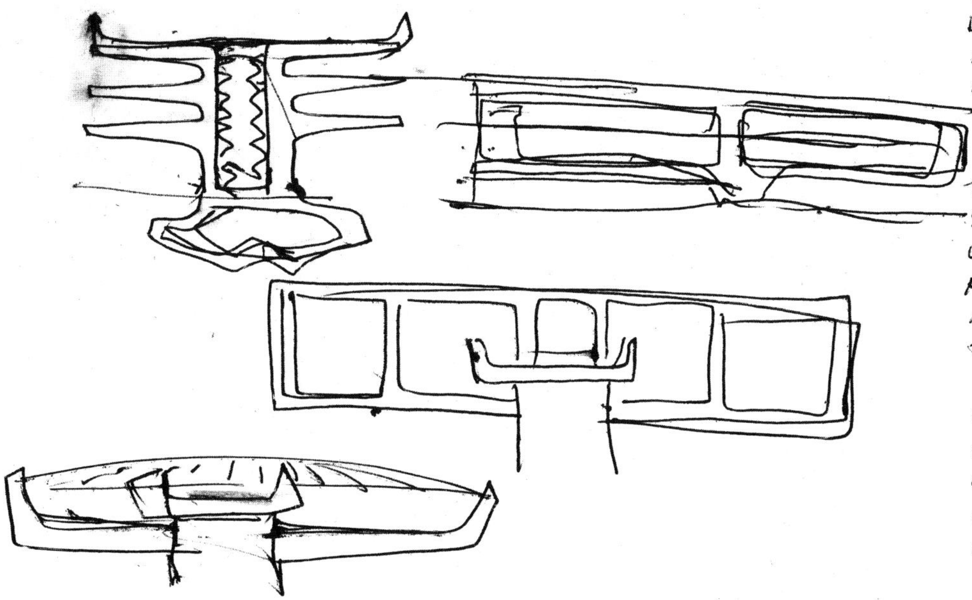

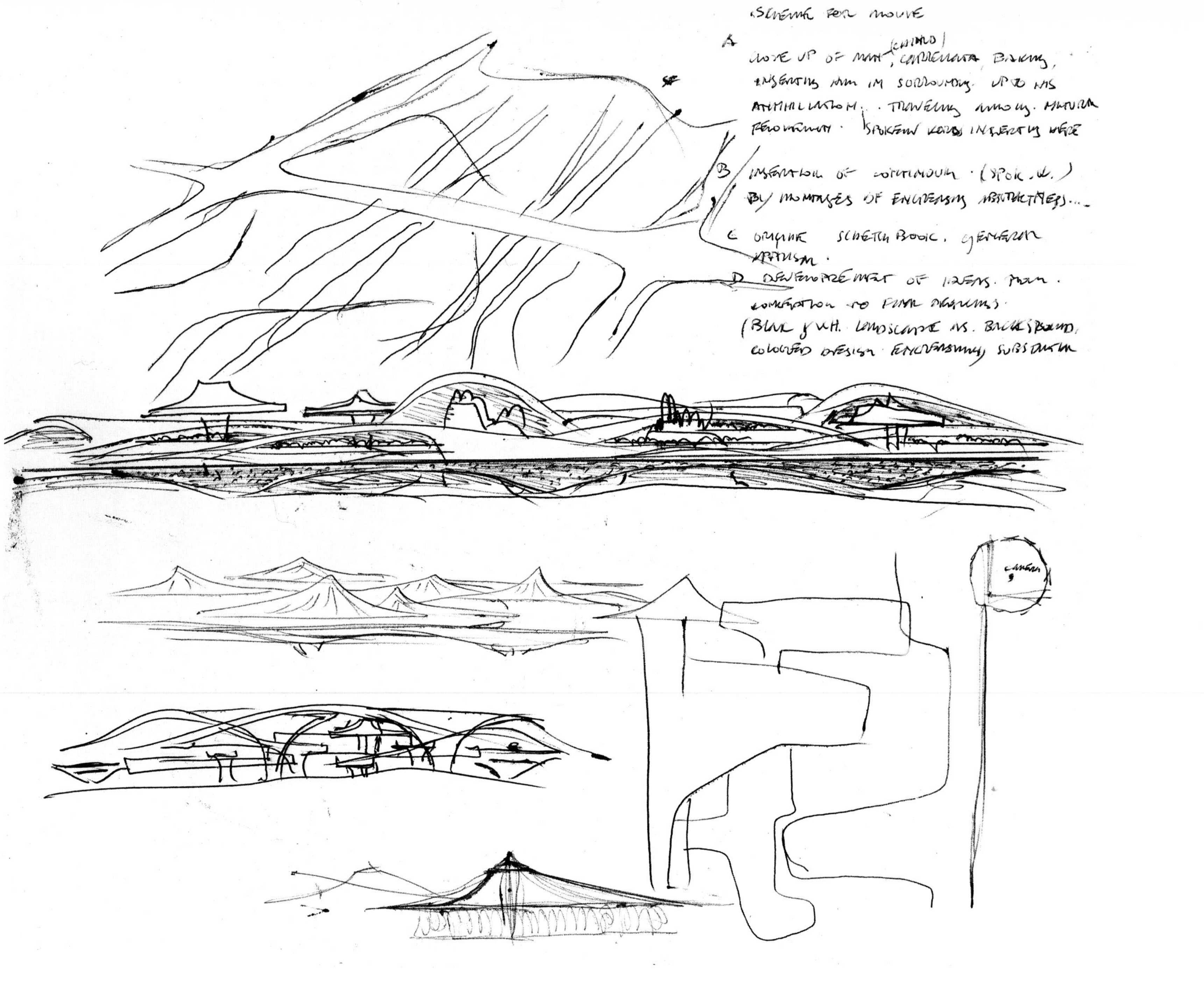
SCHEME FOR MOVIE
A
CLOSE UP OF MAN (CHILD),
B
C ORIGINAL SKETCHBOOK.
D

AUGUST 1961

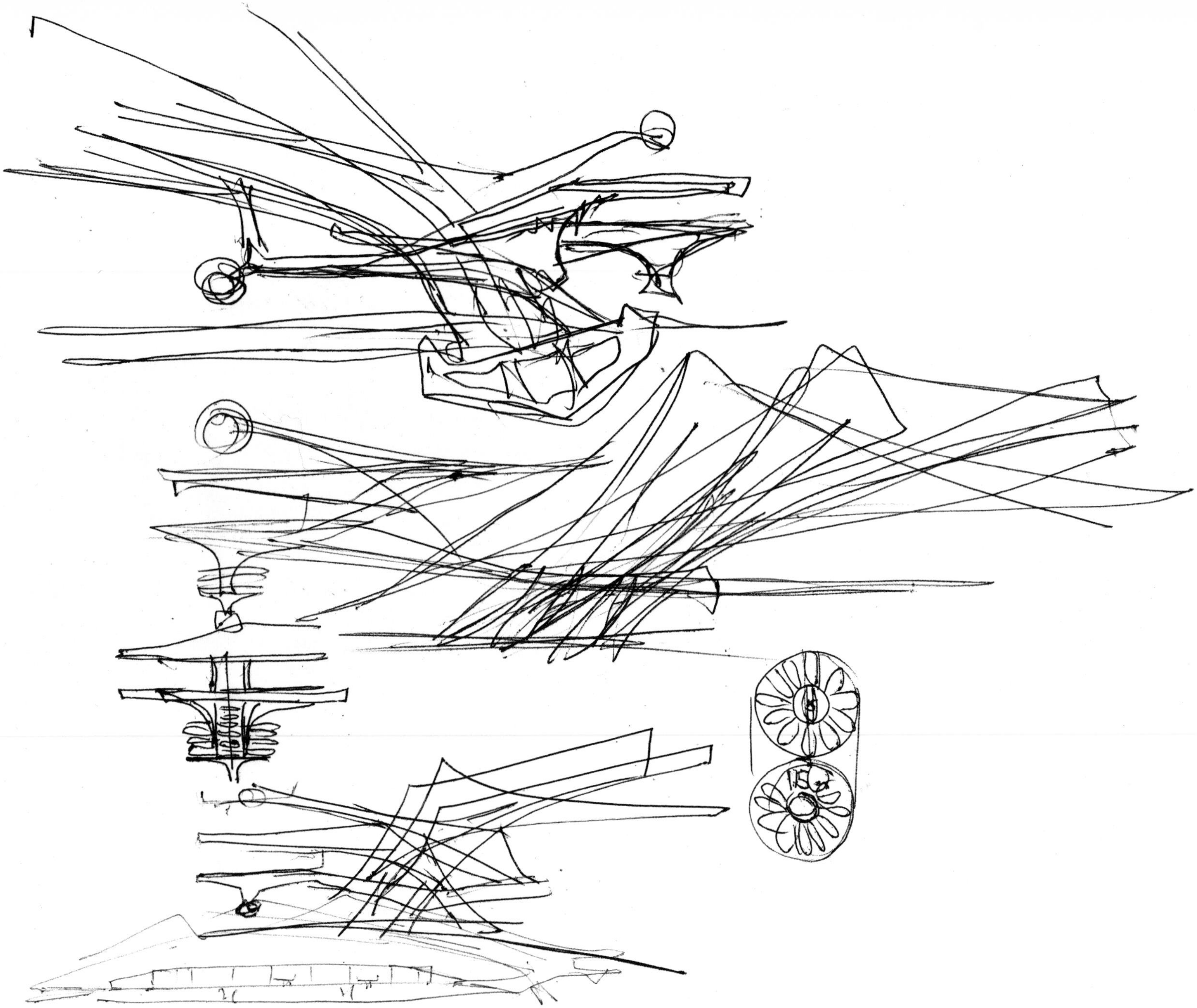

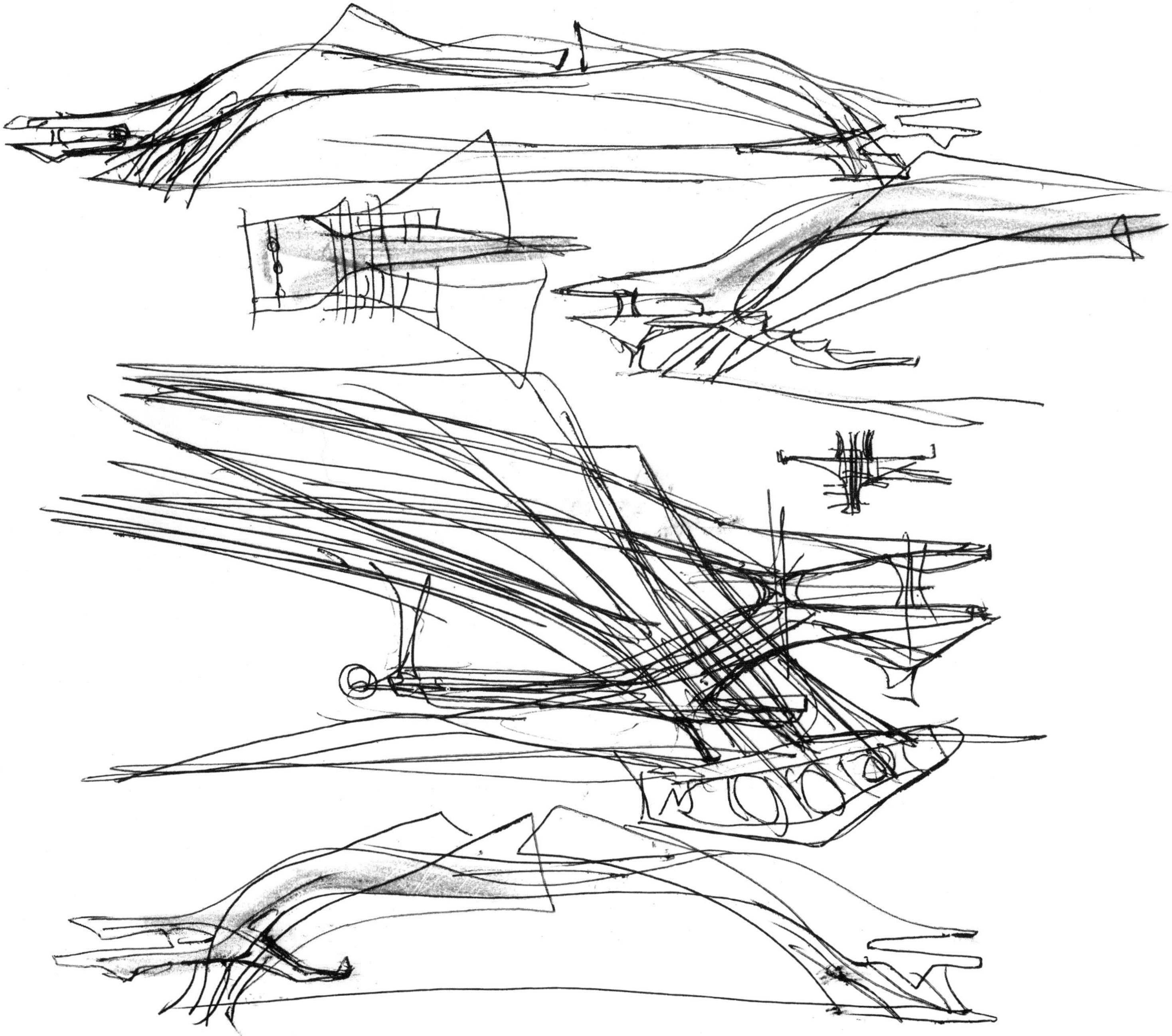

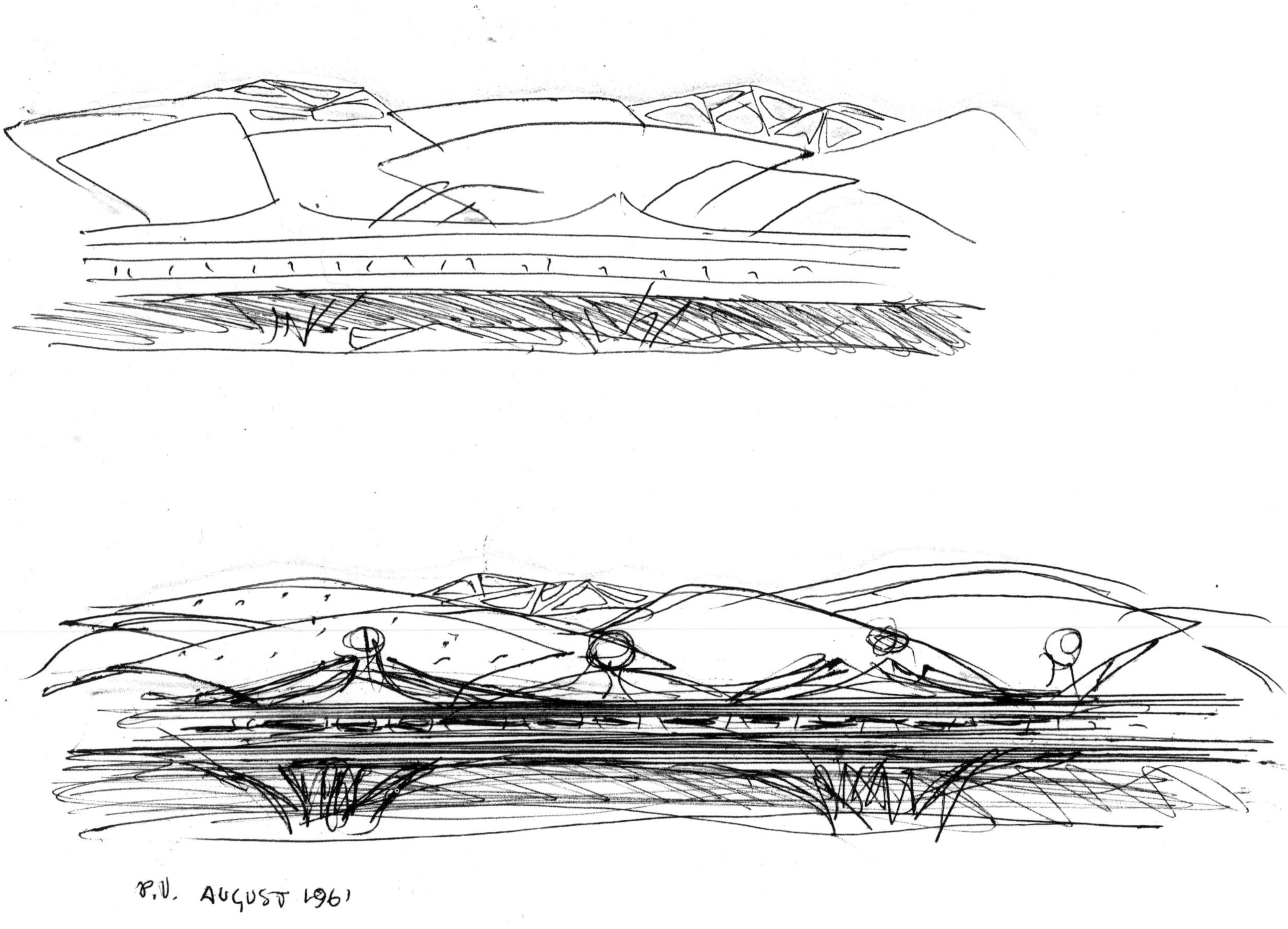
P.V. AUGUST 1961

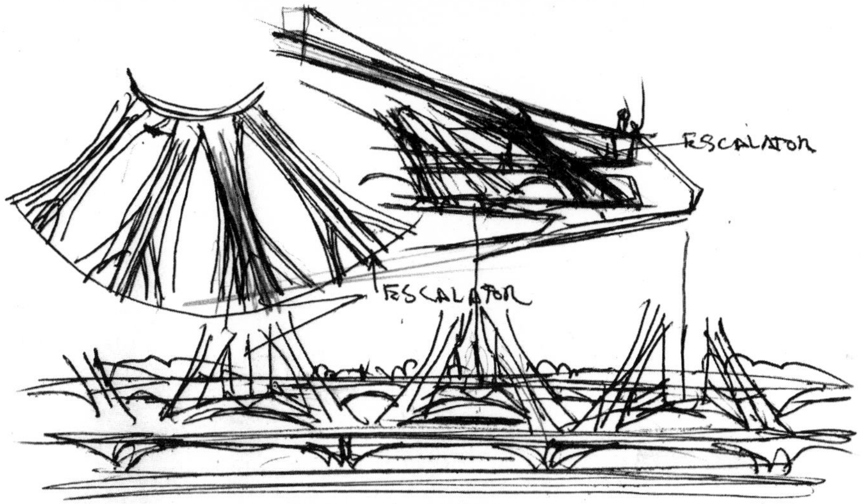
ESCALATOR
ESCALATOR

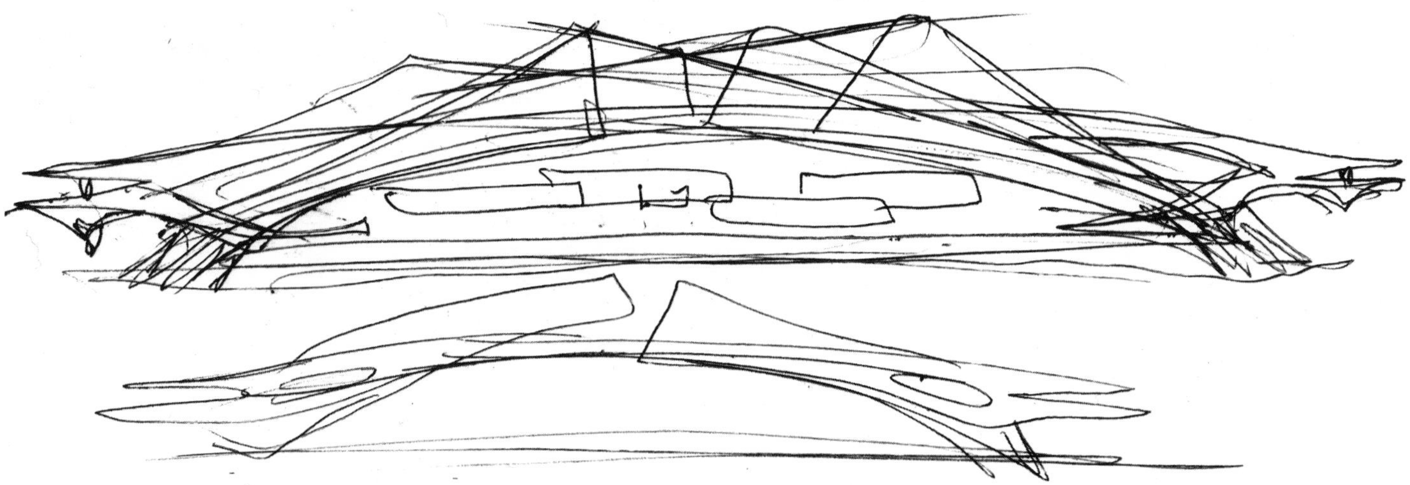

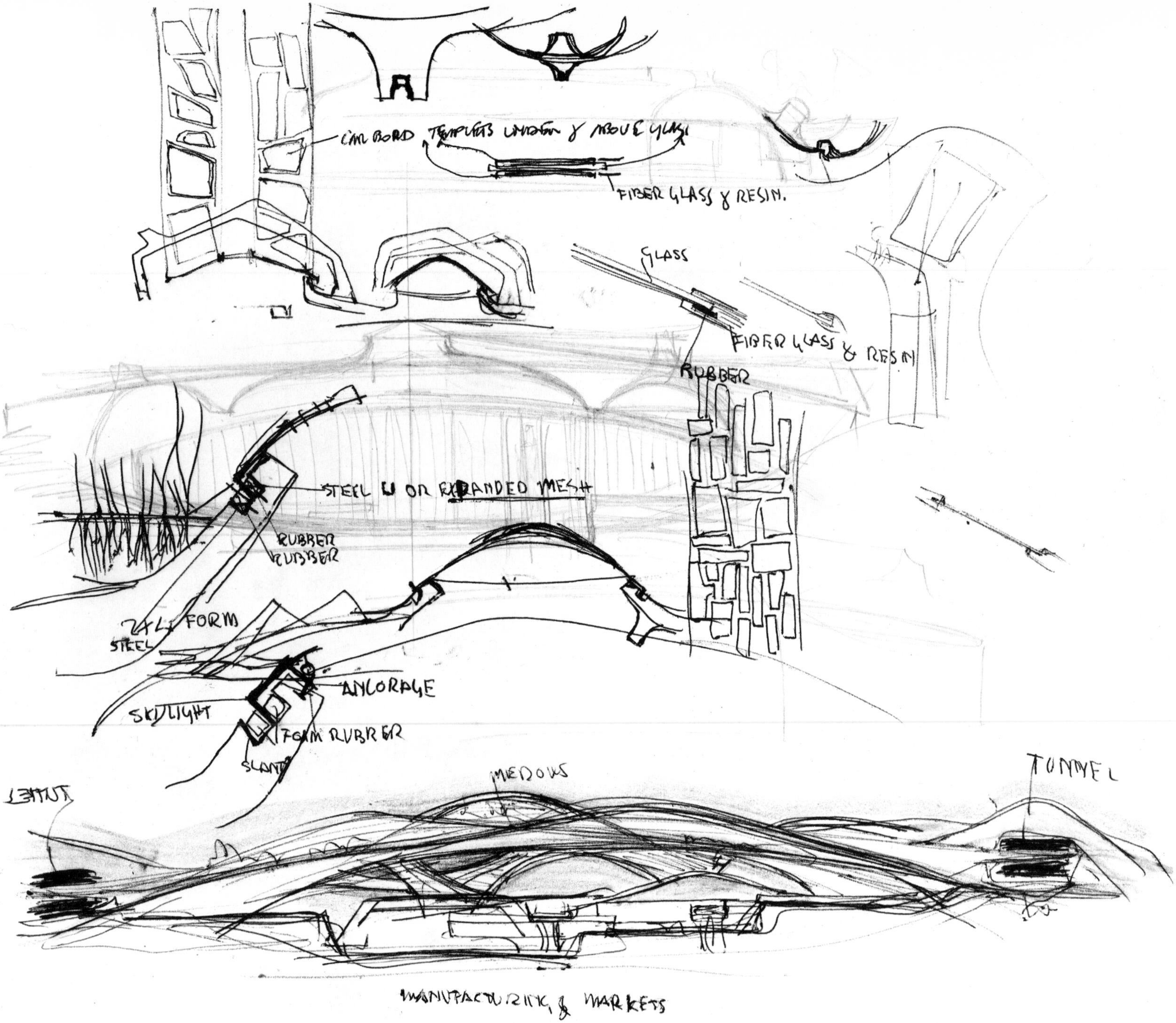
FIBER GLASS & RESIN.
GLASS
FIBER GLASS & RESIN
RUBBER
STEEL U OR EXPANDED MESH
RUBBER
RUBBER
FORM
STEEL
ANCORAGE
SKYLIGHT
FORM RUBBER
MEDOWS
TUNNEL
MANUFACTURING & MARKETS

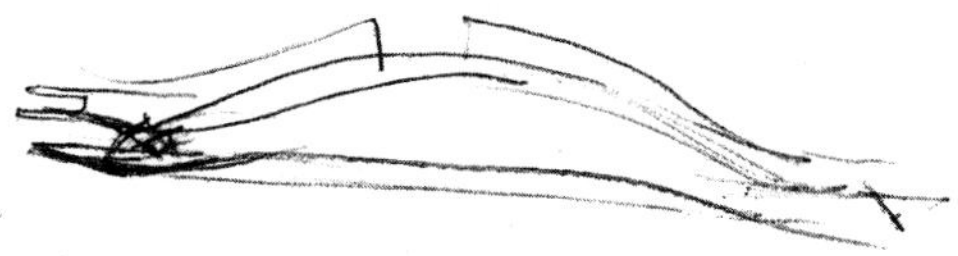

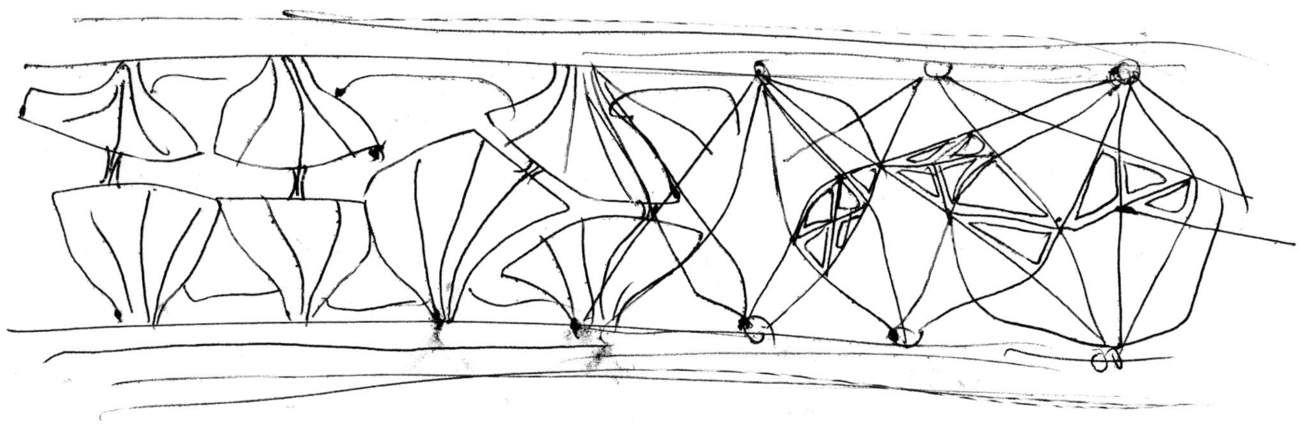

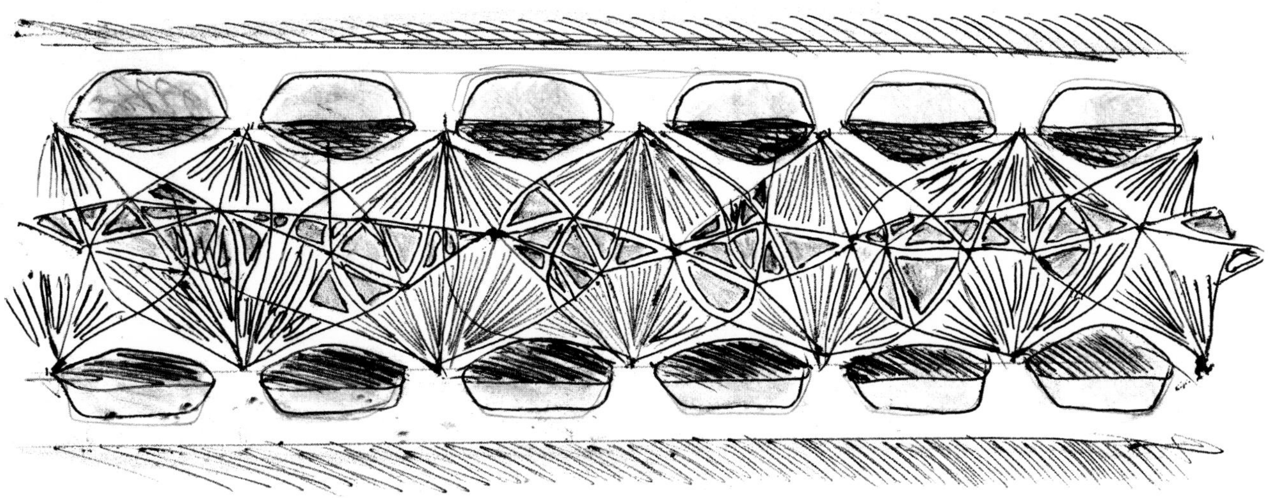

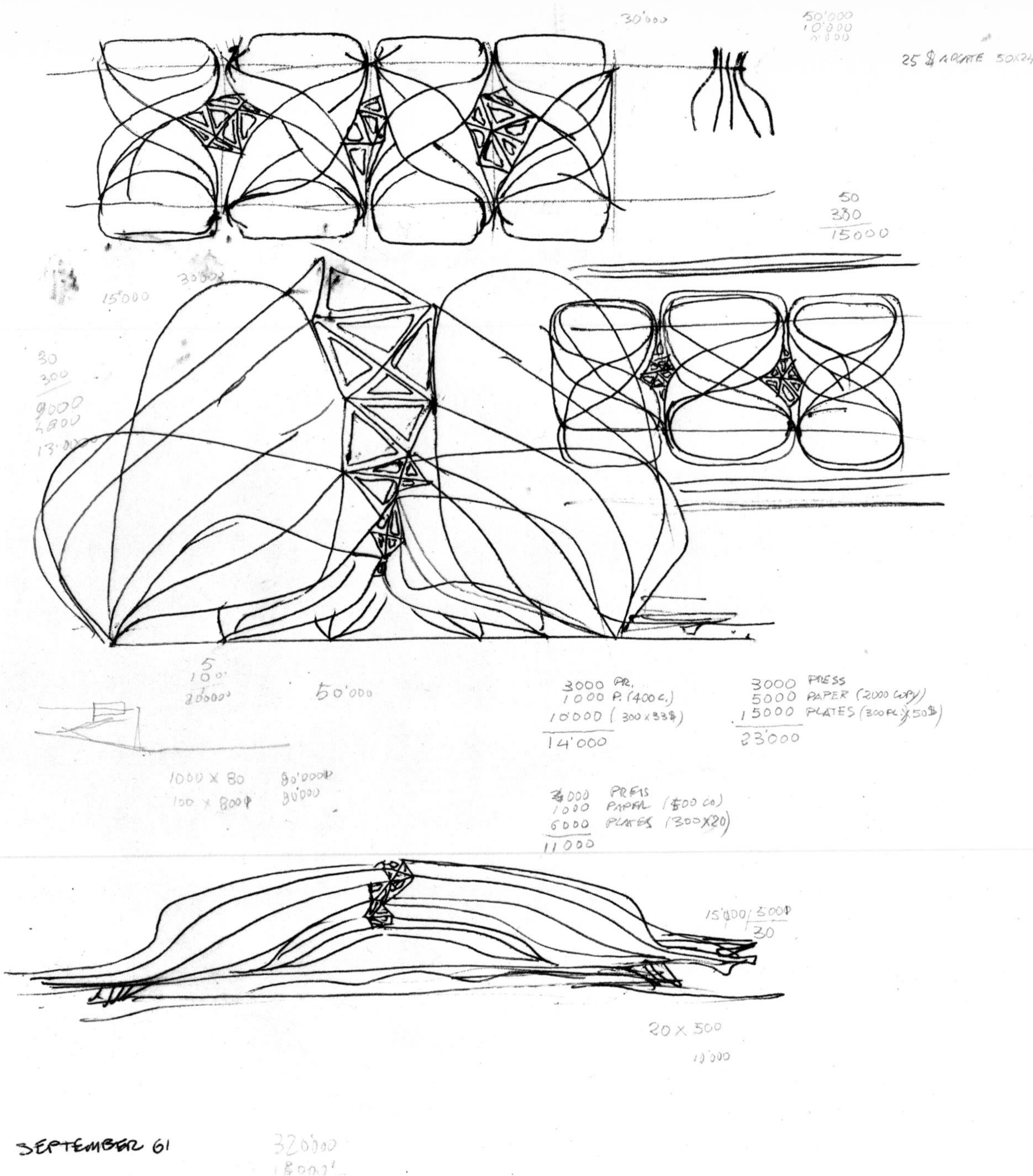
30'000
50'000
10'000
25 $ A PLATE 50X24
50
300
15000
15'000
30
300
9000
13'000
5
100
50'000
3000 PR.
1000 P. (400 C.)
10000 (300 X 33$)
14'000
3000 PRESS
5000 PAPER (2000 COPY)
15000 PLATES (300 PL. X 50$)
23'000
1000 X 80
100 X 800$
80'000$
80'000
PRESS
PAPER (500 CO)
6000 PLATES (300X20)
11000
15'000/5000
30
20 X 500
10'000
SEPTEMBER 61
320'000

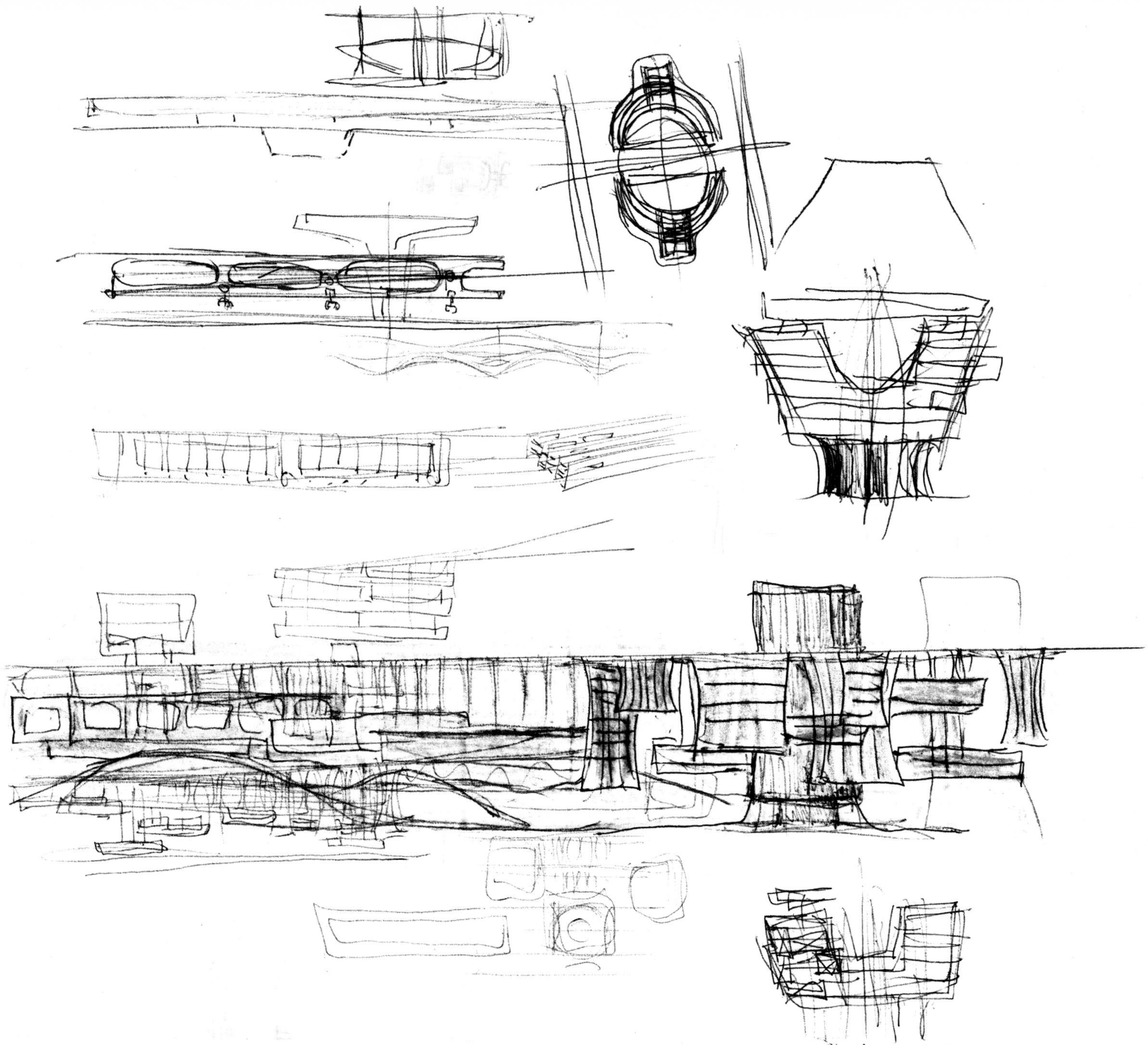

1970

This idea borrows from industry the system of overhead cranes. The structure that supports the frame on which the cranes move is a perforated umbrella with controllable sun shades. With this system entire classrooms can be moved and rearranged from time to time to suit the programs of the schools. In fact, a whole classroom with students in it can be lifted and moved or kept in "suspension." Special facilities that are infrequently used can be stored in one of the supporting towers. A rigid nucleus sheltering administration and offices would be the functional hinge. The plug-in classrooms would be peripatetic, and their aggregation would reflect the equilibrium of the moment between stresses and responses. Naturally, the presence of the overhead cranes would introduce a whole new world of possibilities. In addition to moving classrooms and other spaces, the cranes could move around visual devices, acoustical devices, lights, banners, teaching devices, performing instruments, performing groups, and so forth. Enclosed or semienclosed spaces could be assembled overnight.

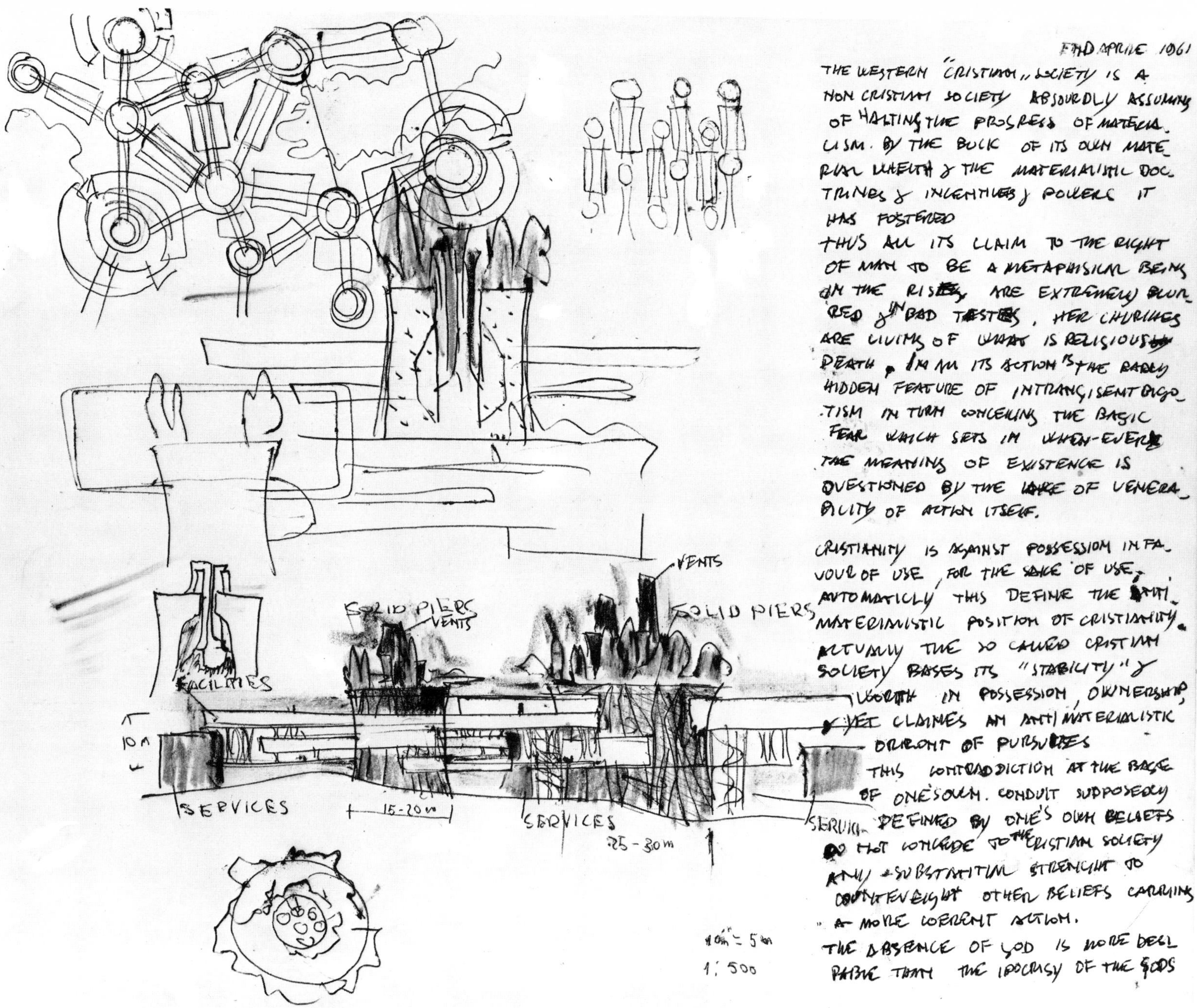

FIND APRILE 1961
THE WESTERN "CRISTIAN" SOCIETY IS A NON CRISTIAN SOCIETY ABSOURDLY ASSUMING OF HALTING THE PROGRESS OF MATERIALISM. BY THE BULK OF ITS OWN MATERIAL WHEALTH & THE MATERIALISTIC DOCTRINES & INCENTIVES & POWERS IT HAS FOSTERED
THUS ALL ITS CLAIM TO THE RIGHT OF MAN TO BE A METAPHISICAL BEING ON THE RISE ARE EXTREMELY BLURRED & IN BAD TASTES, HER CHURCHES ARE LIVING OF WHAT IS RELIGIOUS DEATH, IN ALL ITS ACTION IS THE BARELY HIDDEN FEATURE OF INTRANSIGENT EGOTISM IN TURN CONCEALING THE BASIC FEAR WHICH SETS IN WHEN-EVER THE MEANING OF EXISTENCE IS QUESTIONED BY THE LACK OF VENERABILITY OF ACTION ITSELF.
CRISTIANITY IS AGAINST POSSESSION IN FAVOUR OF USE, FOR THE SAKE OF USE. AUTOMATICLY THIS DEFINE THE ANTI-MATERIALISTIC POSITION OF CRISTIANITY. ACTUALLY THE SO CALLED CRISTIAN SOCIETY BASES ITS "STABILITY" & WORTH IN POSSESSION, OWNERSHIP, & YET CLAIMES AN ANTI MATERIALISTIC ORIENT OF PURSUITES
THIS CONTRADDICTION AT THE BASE OF ONE'S OWN CONDUIT SUPPOSEDLY DEFINED BY ONE'S OWN BELIEFS DO NOT CONCEDE TO THE CRISTIAN SOCIETY ANY SUBSTANTIAL STRENGHT TO COUNTERVEIGHT OTHER BELIEFS CARRYING A MORE COERENT ACTION.
THE ABSENCE OF GOD IS MORE BEARABLE THAN THE IPOCRISY OF THE GODS
VENTS
SOLID PIERS
VENTS
SOLID PIERS
FACILITIES
10 m
SERVICES
15-20 m
SERVICES
25-30 m
SERVIC
1 cm = 5 m
1: 500

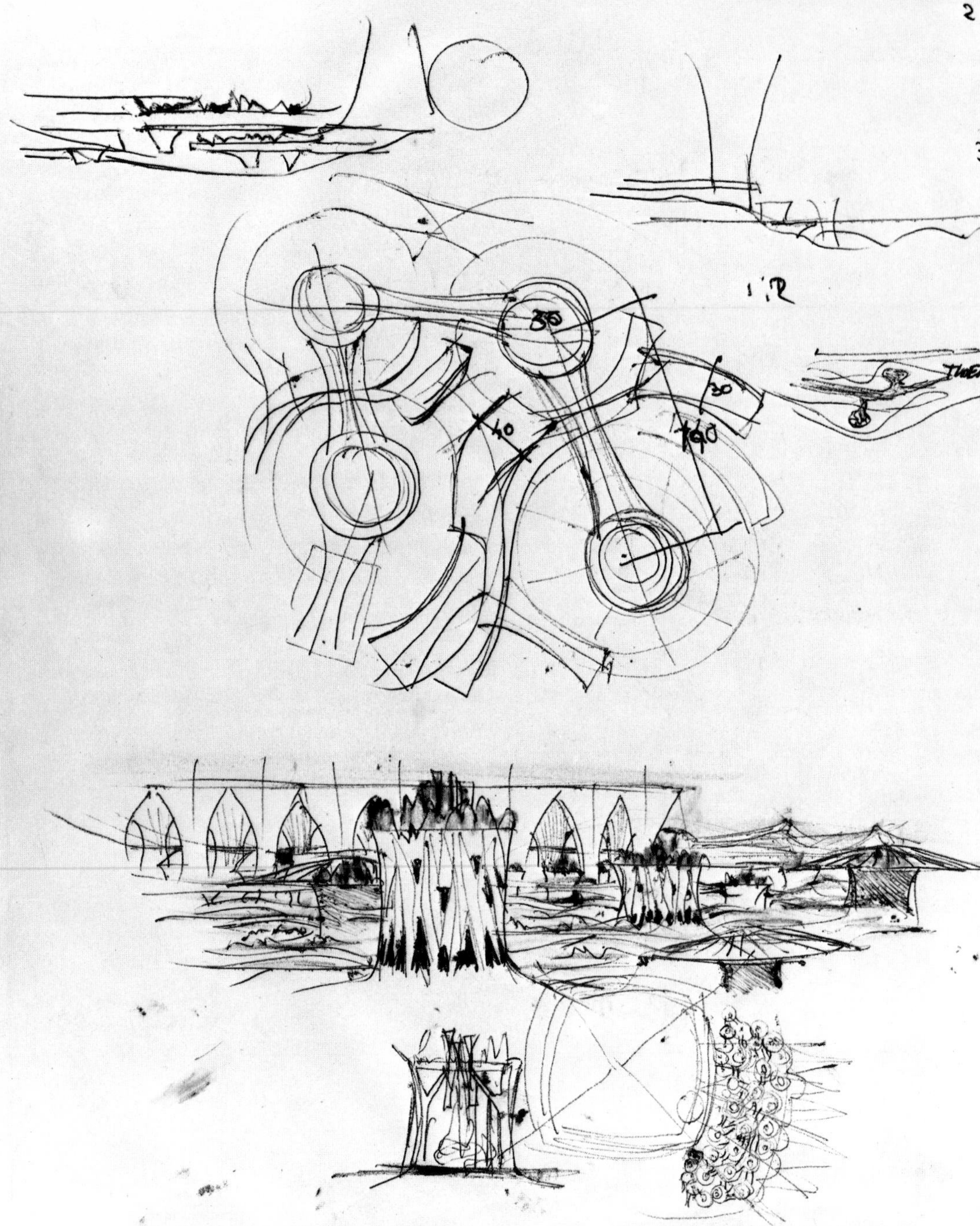

2 BIOTECNIC IS THE SAME WORD USED BY MUNFORD. AS OBSERVED ABOVE THE FILLING IN OF THE TEORY BY DEEDS IS WHAT THE TEORY BECAMES.

3 THE WORM SOCIETY CAN EXPAND INDEFINETLY ONCE THE ELEMENTS FOR THE NUTRITION OF ITS ORGANISM ARE THERE. THAT IS SO BECAUSE THE SOCIETY IS SIMPLY AN AGGREGATE OF SELF SUFFICIENT INDIVIDUALS, THE NEEDS OF EACH OF THEM AS THE SFERE OF THEIR ACTION ARE NEATLY DEFINED & UNCHANGIABLE. FOR INSTANCE THE MEDIUM IN WHICH THE COLONY LIVES (WATER) IS THE CONVEYER OF ALL WHICH IS NEEDED.

THIS AS IF TO EACH RESIDENT OF EACH APPARTMENT THE AIR ITSELF WOULD CONVEY, FOOD, KNOWLEDGE, INFORMATION, EMOTIONS, RELATIVES, TOBACCO, SEX, TOYS, HEALT, INSURANCE, MAIL, POWER, ... AND TAKE AWAY, WASTE, INFORMATION, PRODUCTS, EMOTIONS, ... CORPSES...

THE CITY AGGREGATE IS OF A DIFFERENT KIND. ALL THE DWELLERS ARE COMPLEX ORGANISMS. EACH OF THEM IS AN INTERLOCKED BALANCE OF SYSTEMS (ORGANS) STRICTLY INTERDIPENDENT.

TO SUSTAIN SUCH BALANCE & FOSTER ITS ENGROSSING ... ORGANISM LIVES IN A SFERE OF NEEDS WHICH IS FANTASTICLY EXTENSIVE (WE LIVE ON INDIAN CORN, FARADY INVENTIONS, CRISTIAN LOVE, BOLIVIAN MINERS, HERINGS, PARIS FASHION, HISTORY, MANS' SKILLS, DREAMS...) SO IT IS FOR ITS SFERE OF INFLUENCE. THUS IF THE FISICAL CONTAINER OF MAN IS ITS SKIN. THE REAL CONTAINER OF ITS BEEING IS AN EVER REACHING

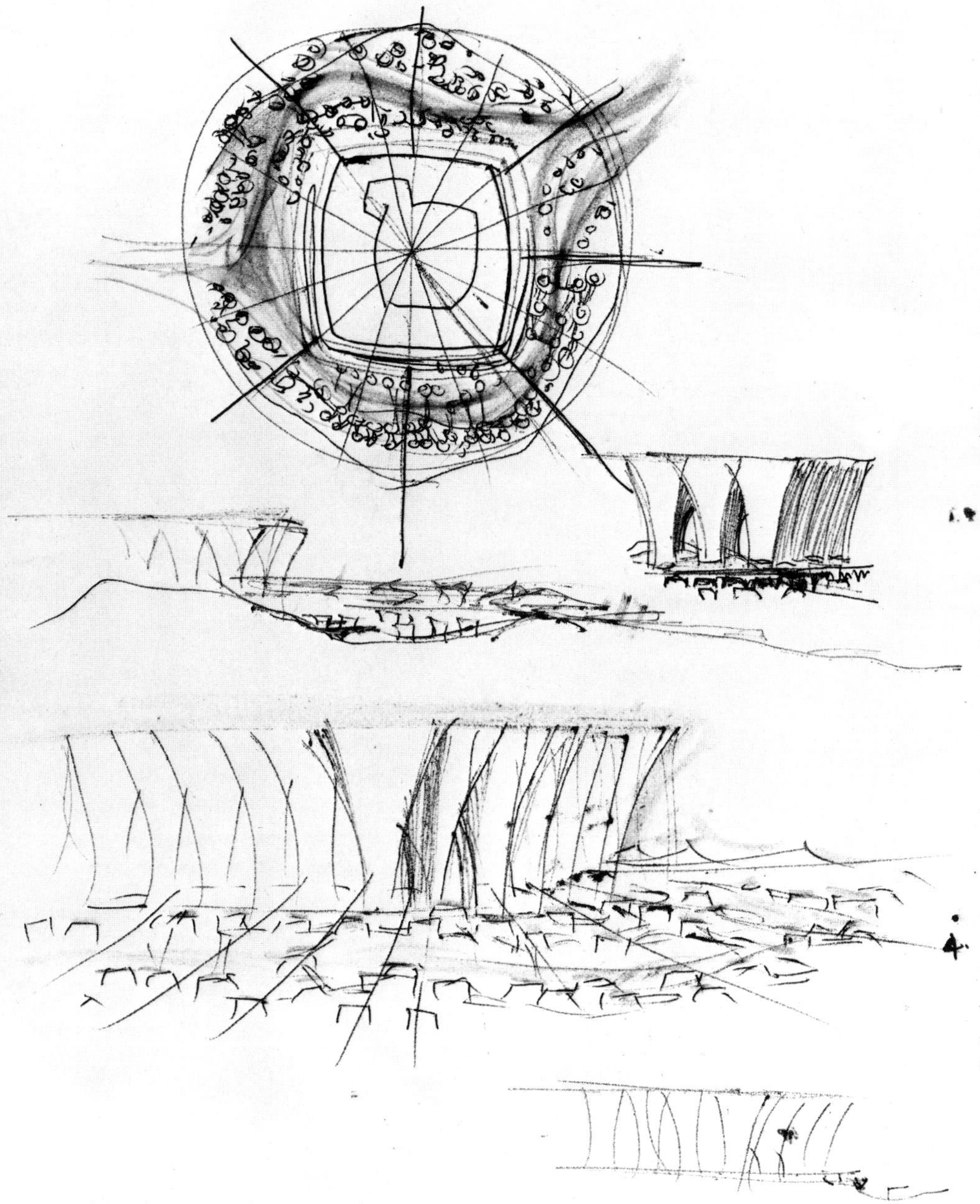

EVER GROWING, EVER CHANGING, MORE
SUBTLE SKIN UNDER STRESS
SED BY THE NEED, THE LONGING, THE
DESIRES, THE WILL, THE AMBITION, THE
LOVES, THE TERRORS OF ITS BEARER;
BROADCASTING & RECEIVING, TAKING &
GIVING ... THE
TO & FRO ALMOST LIMITLESS.

THERE IS THEN WHY THE PLANNING
OF A CITY IS ALTOGETHER INDISPENSA-
BLE & IMPOSSIBLE & WHY IT IS
THAT SUCH PLANNING IS NOT A SCIENTI-
FIC BUT AN HUMANISTIC PROBLEM.

A CITY CANNOT EXTEND THUS OUTSIDE
THE "BIOLOGICAL" LIMITS. THAT ITS
MORPHOLOGY POSSES (THE BODY) WHILE
ITS GROWTH CAN GO ON FOR "EVER",
WAITING SUCH BIOLOGICAL FISICAL
SKIN:
A MORE ROBUST HEART, A SUBTLER INTEL-
LECT, A LARGER OXIGEN INTAKE, A
BETTER STORAGE SISTEM, A LESS
QUESTIONABLE WASTE DISPOSAL ...
& FINALLY A GREATER UNDERSTANDING
OF ITS DEPENDENCE TO THE OUTER
& THE SPACE WITHIN. A BETTER &
WISER MAN IN AN ENVIRONME-
NT IN ARMONY WITH NATURE

4. IF THE QUESTION IS ABOUT PUBLIC
TRANSPORTATION THE ANSWER IS YES.
AMPLE FACILITIES ARE ANTICI-
PATED FOR INDIVIDUAL CARS. "COMPACTS &
OBSOLETE", THOSE FACILITIES DO NOT
PARTICIPATE IN MAKING THE CITY A
TECHNOLOGICAL ROBOT KEPT AS THEY
ARE WAITING STRICTLY NOT PRETENTIOUS
BOUNDARIES.

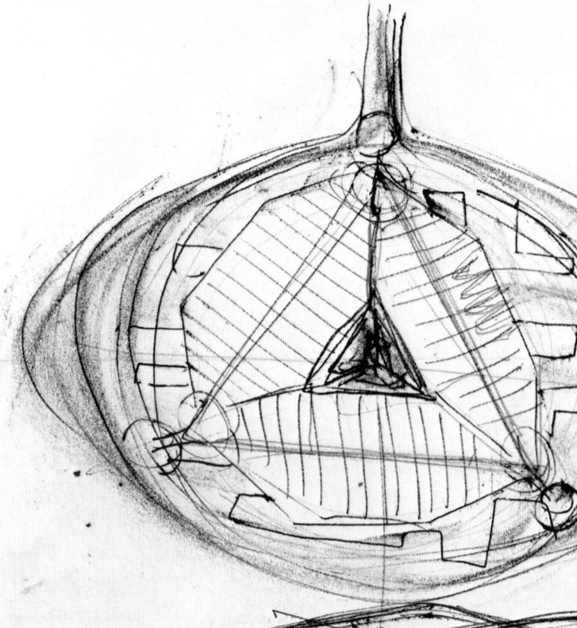

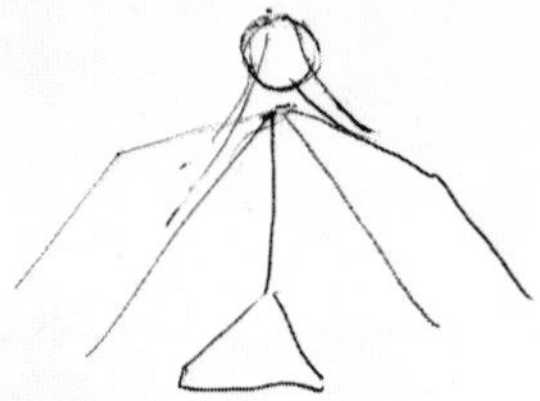

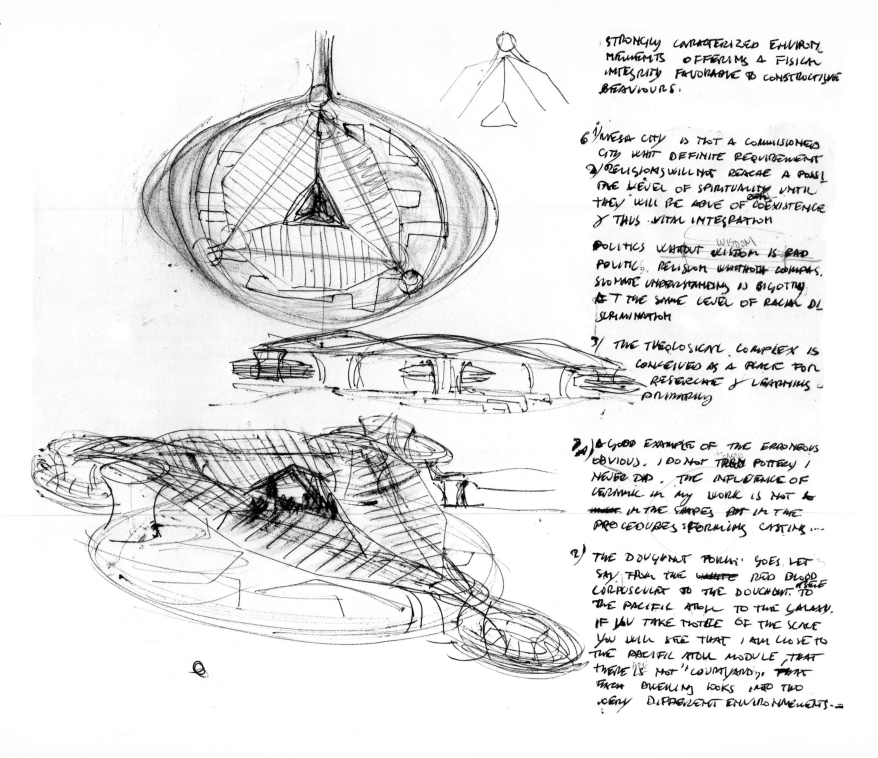

STRONGLY CARACTERIZED ENVIRON-
MENTS OFFERING A FISICAL
INTEGRITY FAVORABLE TO CONSTRUCTIVE
BEHAVIOURS.

6 1/ MESA CITY IS NOT A COMMISSIONED
CITY WHIT DEFINITE REQUIREMENT
2/ RELIGIONS WILL NOT REACHE A POSSI-
BLE LEVEL OF SPIRITUALITY UNTIL
THEY WILL BE ABLE OF COEXISTENCE
& THUS VITAL INTEGRATION

POLITICS WITHOUT ~~WISDOM~~ WISDOM IS BAD
POLITICS. RELIGION WITHOUT ~~COMPAS~~-
SIONATE UNDERSTANDING IS BIGOTRY
AT THE SAME LEVEL OF RACIAL DI-
SCRIMINATION

3/ THE THEOLOGICAL COMPLEX IS
CONCEIVED AS A PLACE FOR
RESEARCHE & LEARNING -
PRIMARILY

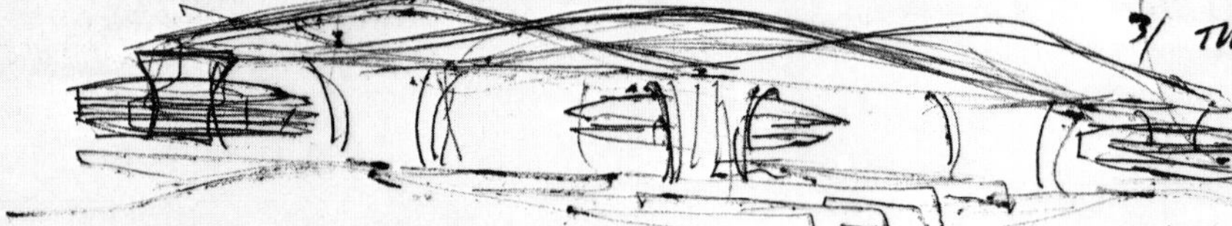

7 A) A GOOD EXAMPLE OF THE ERRONEOUS
OBVIOUS. I DO NOT ~~TREAD~~ THROW POTTERY I
NEVER DID. THE INFLUENCE OF
CERAMIC IN MY WORK IS NOT ~~&~~
~~...~~ IN THE SHAPES ~~BUT~~ IN THE
PROCEDURES: FORMING CASTING....

B) THE DOUGHNUT FORM: GOES LET
SAY FROM THE ~~WHITE~~ RED BLOOD
CORPUSCULAR TO THE DOUGHNUT TO ~~ASSELE~~
THE PACIFIC ATOLL TO THE GALAXY.
IF YOU TAKE NOTICE OF THE SCALE
YOU WILL SEE THAT I AM CLOSE TO
THE PACIFIC ATOLL MODULE, THAT
THERE ~~IS~~ ARE NOT "COURTYARDS", ~~THAT~~
EACH DWELLING LOOKS INTO TWO
VERY DIFFERENT ENVIRONMENTS.

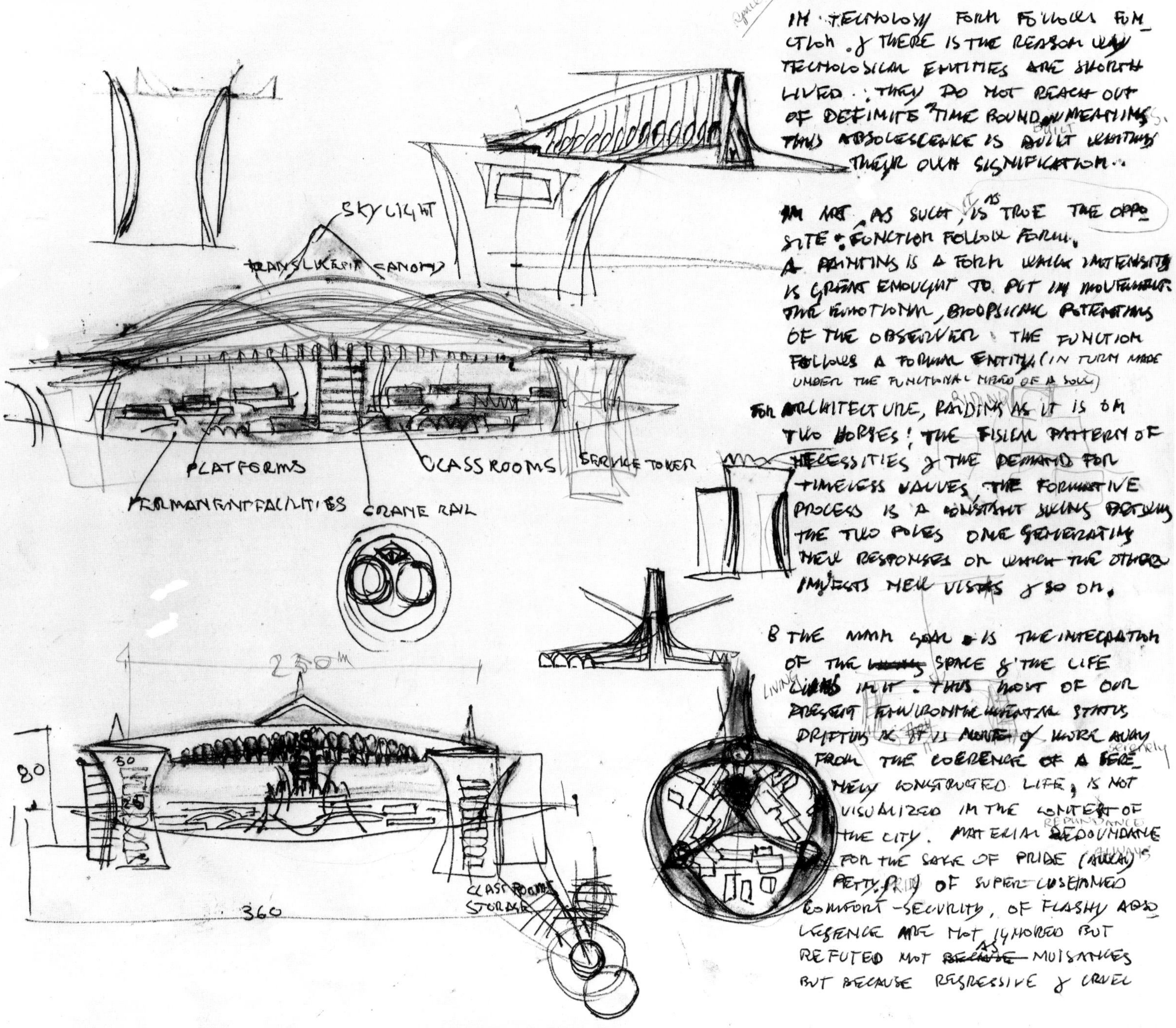
IN TECNOLOGY FORM FOLLOWS FUNCTION & THERE IS THE REASON WHY TECHNOLOGICAL ENTITIES ARE SHORTH LIVED: THEY DO NOT REACH OUT OF DEFINITE TIME BOUND MEANINGS. THUS OBSOLESCENCE IS BUILT WITHIN THEIR OWN SIGNIFICATION.
IN ART, AS SUCH, IT IS TRUE THE OPPOSITE: FUNCTION FOLLOW FORM.
A PAINTING IS A FORM WHICH INTENSITY IS GREAT ENOUGHT TO PUT IN MOVEMENT THE EMOTIONAL, BIOPSICAL POTENTIALS OF THE OBSERVER. THE FUNCTION FOLLOWS A FORMAL ENTITY (IN TURN MADE UNDER THE FUNCTIONAL NEED OF A SOUL)
FOR ARCHITECTURE, RIDING AS IT IS ON TWO HORSES: THE FISICAL PATTERN OF NECESSITIES & THE DEMAND FOR TIMELESS VALUES, THE FORMATIVE PROCESS IS A CONSTANT SWING BETWEEN THE TWO POLES ONE GENERATING NEW RESPONSES ON WHICH THE OTHER INJECTS NEW VISTAS & SO ON.
B THE MAIN GOAL IS THE INTEGRATION OF THE SPACE & THE LIFE LIVING IN IT. THUS MOST OF OUR PRESENT ENVIRONMENTAL STATUS DRIFTING AS IT IS MORE & MORE AWAY FROM THE COHERENCE OF A SERENELY CONSTRUCTED LIFE, IS NOT VISUALIZED IN THE CONTEXT OF THE CITY. MATERIAL REDUNDANCE FOR THE SAKE OF PRIDE (ALWAYS PETTY PRIDE) OF SUPER CUSHIONED COMFORT-SECURITY, OF FLASHY OBSOLESCENCE ARE NOT IGNORED BUT REFUTED NOT AS NUISANCES BUT BECAUSE REGRESSIVE & CRUEL
SKYLIGHT
TRANSLUCENT CANOPY
PLATFORMS
CLASSROOMS
SERVICE TOWER
PERMANENT FACILITIES
CRANE RAIL
250 m
80
50
360
CLASSROOMS
STORAGE

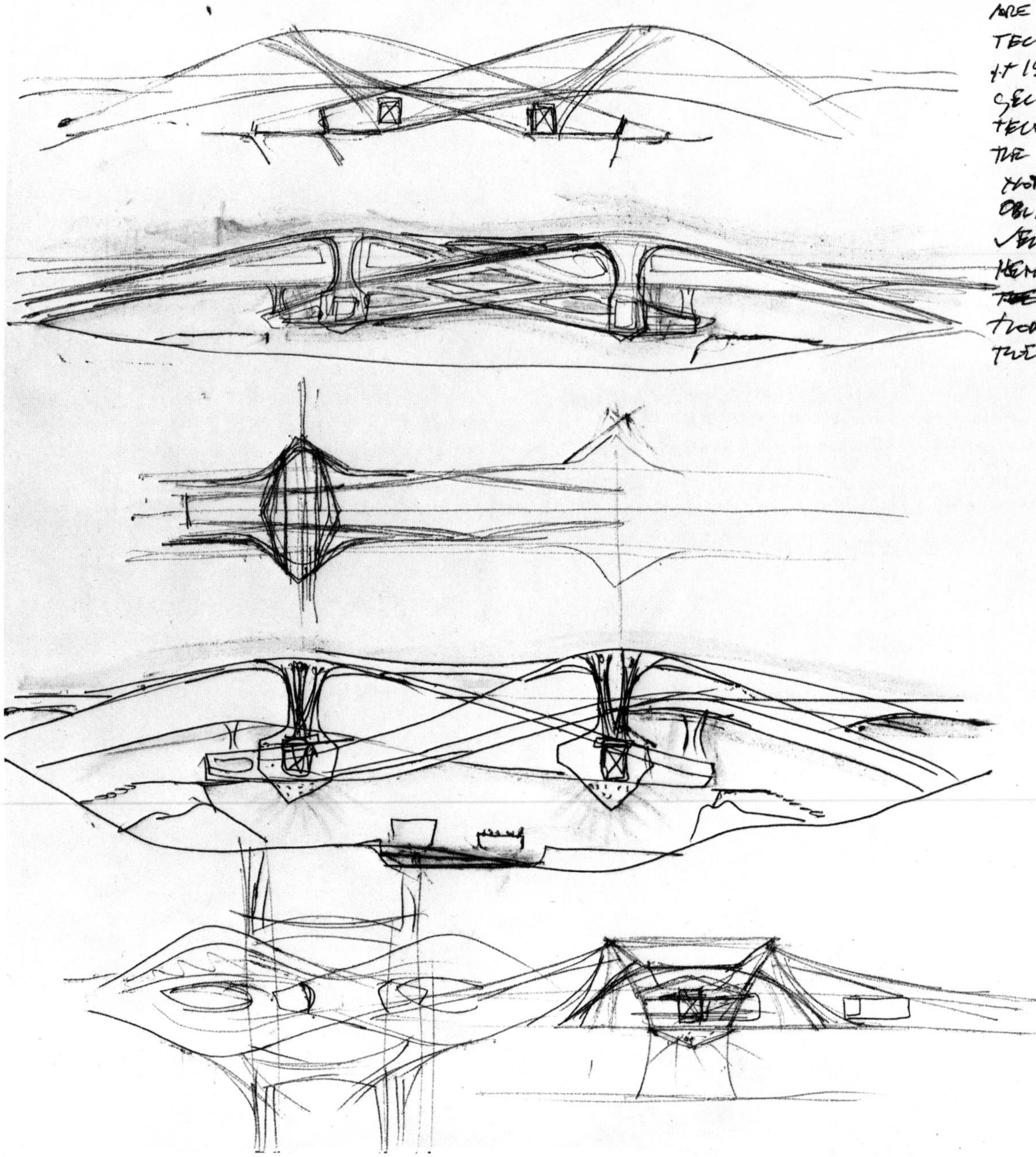

JULY 61
SOME OF THE MEGA CITY STRUCTURE
ARE UNFAESIBLE WHIT THE PRESENT
TECNOLOGICAL KNOW HOW.
IT IS INTENDED THOO BY THE PRO-
JEC ITSELF TO BE AN STIMULUS FOR
TECHNITIAN & SIENTIST TO IMPROVE
THE PRESENT KNOWLEDGES - & THIS
NOT FOR ULTIMATE FUNCTION OF
OBLITERATION BUT FOR THE IMPRO-
VEMENT OF MAN'S CONDITION
HENCE THE MORE IMPRESSIVE
~~THE~~ & CONVINCING THE PRESENTA-
TION THE MORE CONSTRUCTIVE
THE EFFORT. IN ITS. RESULTS.

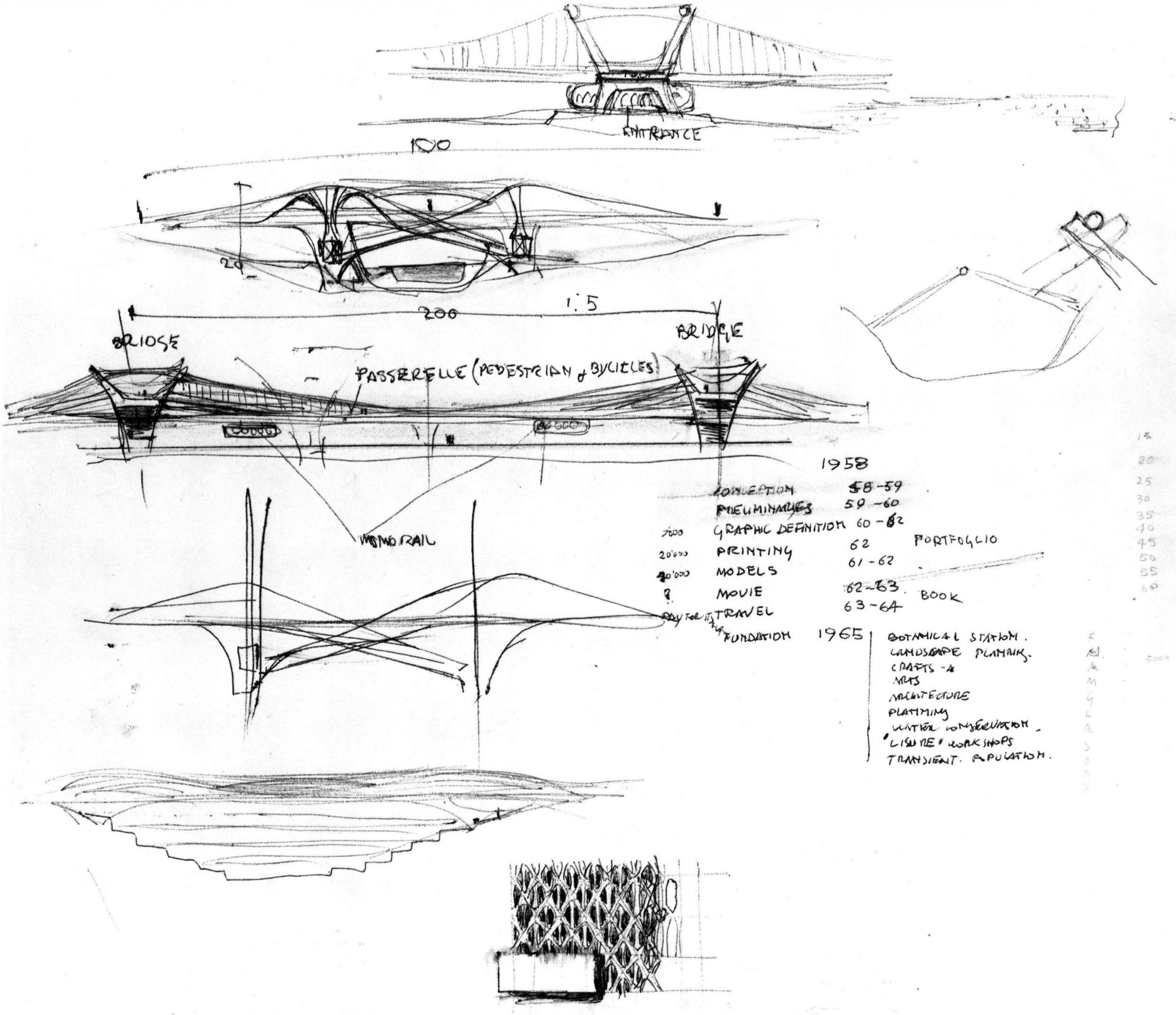
ENTRANCE
100
20
200
1:5
BRIDGE
BRIDGE
PASSERELLE (PEDESTRIAN & BYCICLES)
MONORAIL
1958
CONCEPTION 58-59
PRELIMINARIES 59-60
7000 GRAPHIC DEFINITION 60-62
20'000 PRINTING 62 PORTFOGLIO
MODELS 61-62
? MOVIE 62-63 BOOK
TRAVEL 63-64
FUNDATION 1965
BOTANICAL STATION.
LANDSCAPE PLANNING.
CRAFTS
ARTS
ARCHITECTURE
PLANNING
WATER CONSERVATION.
LEISURE WORKSHOPS
TRANSIENT. POPULATION.
15
20
25
30
35
40
45
50
55
60

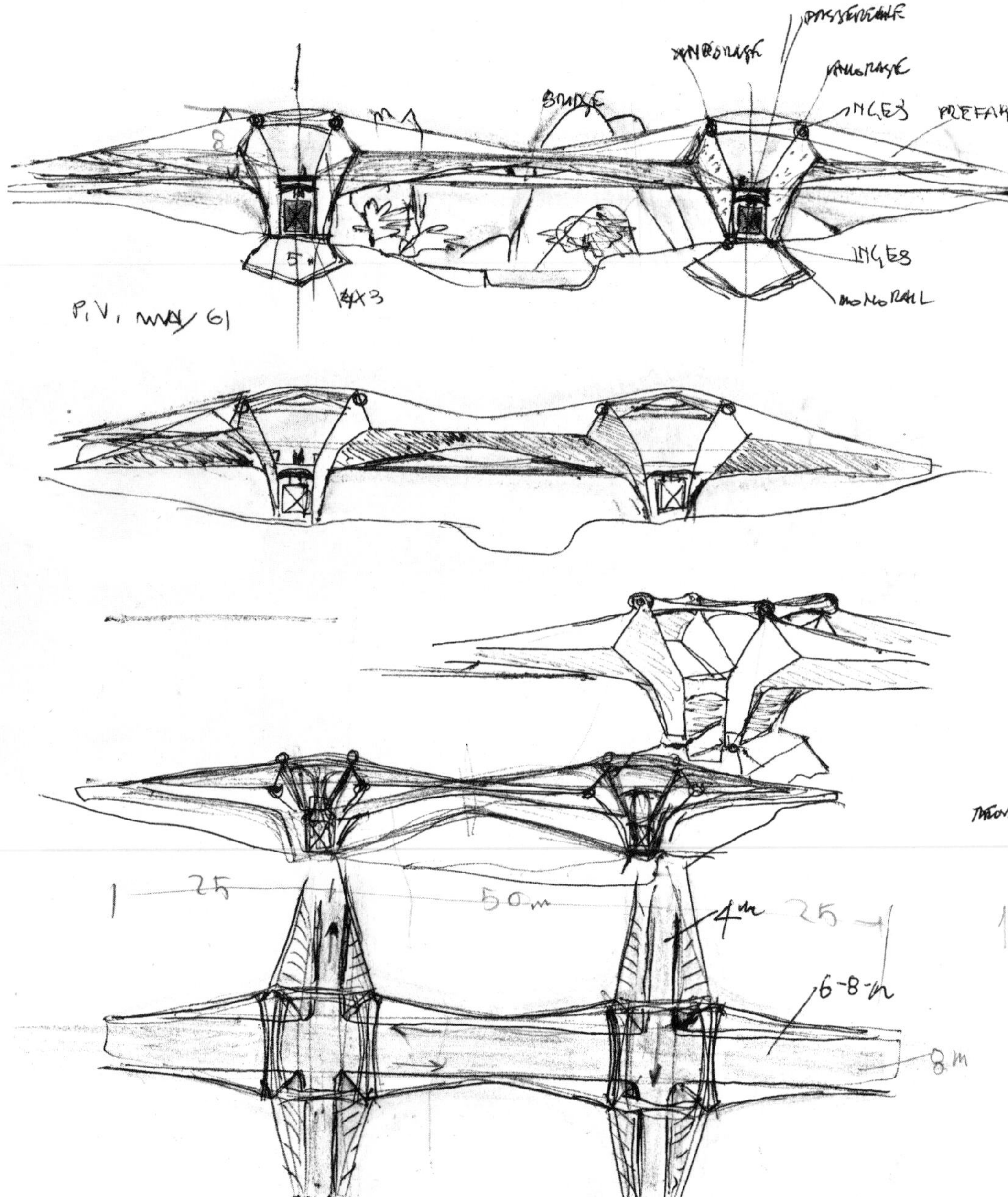

JULY 1961 P.V.
WHATEVER IS STRIFE FOR EACH OF US.
IS IN THOSE RARE MOMENT OF INNER
SILENCE AS STRIFE SUBSIDE, RETREATING
IN THE FACE OF UNKNOWN GODLINESS.
THAT THE TERSE ENGROSSION OF TIME
CAN BE GLANCED INTO
THOSE QUIVERING, FAST PASSING DIA-
MONDS OF PURE BEEING NOTHING CAN
BE HUNG ON, NOT HOPE, OR MEMORY,
NO RESENTMENTS OR HATREDS, NO CARING
OF SEXES NO COMMUNION WANT ANYTHING ELSE.

AS THEY MOVE IN, UNANNOUNCED, FURTIVE
LIKE, & STOP THE CLAMOUR OF
TOO MANY WANTS. SO THEY MOVE OUT
INDIFFERENT TO THE DREAM OF
A BEING. MADE BY THEM MOMENTARILY CONCIOUS. & STILL.
AT A FUTURE TIME IN A MOST
UNLIKELY MOMENT AGAIN
THE LIGHT FROM THE FAR GALAXY
WILL PAY ONCE MORE ITS
VISIT. TO ROB A MAN. OF SOME
OF HIS UNCONCIOUS GODLINESS.

SCIENCE TELLS THAT. SUCH VISITATION
IS POSSIBLY NOTHING BUT ONE
OF THOSE STATISTICLY IMPROBABLE STATA
CONDITION. WHEN ALL THE PHYSICAL &
BIOLOGICAL INTERACTION.
METERIALIZE BY CAUSE OF COINCIDENCE
IN THE SUPER UNIQUE CONFIGURATION.
THE TEXTURES THE JELLIES THE BROTHS
THE ELECTRY MESSAGES. ORDERLY
COUPLED & DANCING. AT THE MUSIC
OF THE SPHERES

TO ARCHITECTURE ULTIMATELY WOULD
BECOME THE RESPONSABILITY OF PRO
DUCING OF MAN SUCH RESONATOR.
& DISCOVER ALTOGHETER WHAT IS THE
TREMOR OF STARS

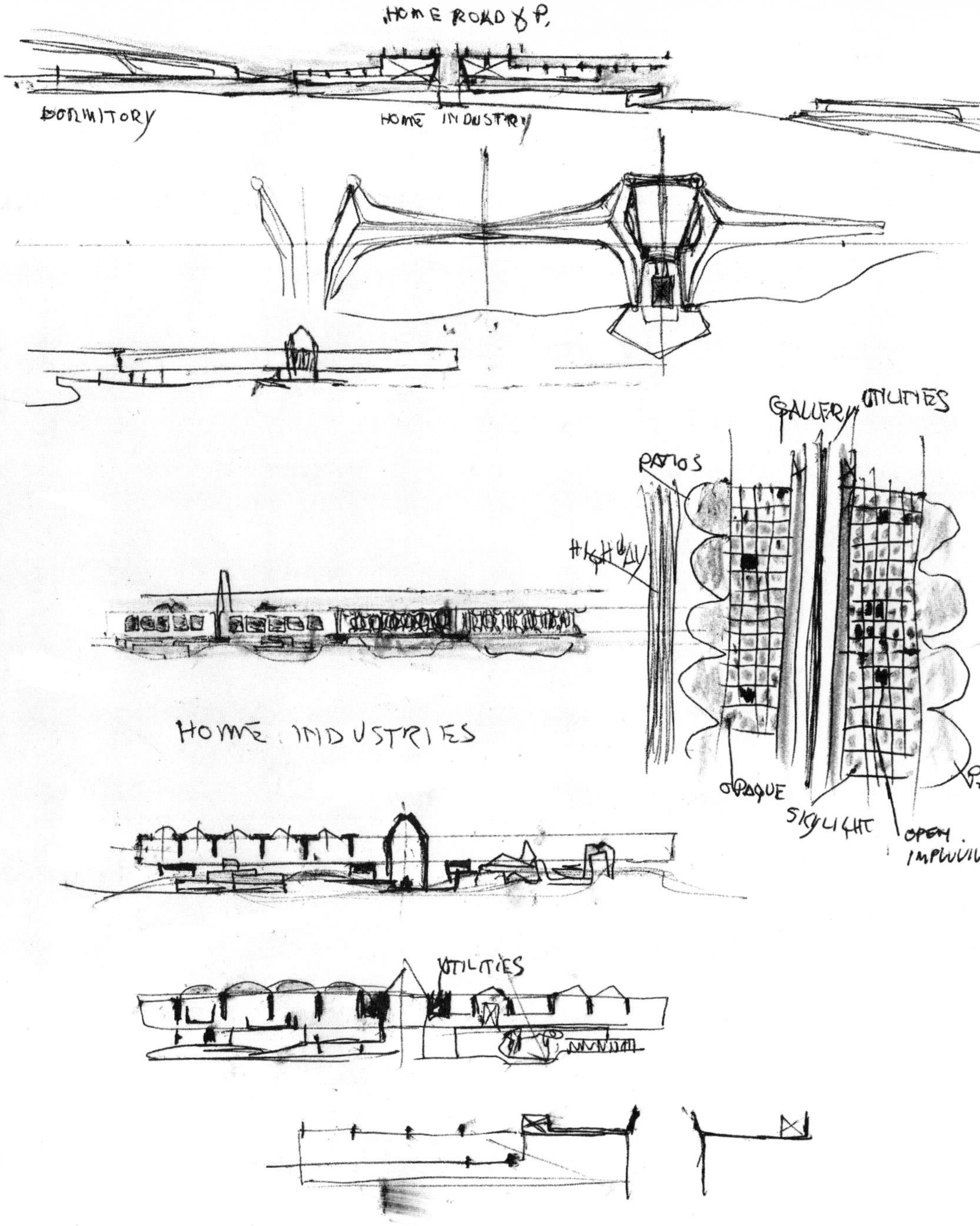

FOR THE TIME BEEING THE ARTISTIC ENDEAVOUR IS THE MOST EFFECTIVE SUBSTITUTE. AS SORTED AS THE OUTCOMES ARE STILL: INDIVIDUAL MAN, CRUEL MAN, DUMB MAN, MALITIOUS MAN, BIGOTS, HATRED SHOWERS, SLOTHS, BULLS, TRAITORS, PRIEST, ... ONE OF THE MANY OF THEM REACH THE THRESHOLD OF REDEMPTION, TOUCHED BY A POEM OR A MELODY.

IT IS QUITE POSSIBLE THAT WALKING THE TRAVEL RETURN THE UNMERCIFUL HAMMERING OF THINGS & THE MISTY STUPOR OF THE ALCOOL RITUAL. MANY A MAN GET A CHANCE, A QUICK CHANGE TO OF THEM, TO HIT UPON THE FOLGORATING PURITY OF OTHER REALITIES. & THAT SO EXPOSED THE IRRIVERENCE OF THEIR LIFE BE SOMEWHAT (LESSENS) LESS HARSH.

JULY 61

THE ASPECTS OF DEATH MOUNTING WAITING THE LIFE SPAN TO OCCUPIE THE DECREASING ASPECTS OF LIFE AS ITS SPAN CONSUME.

THIS WORKINGS OF DEATH TO BUILD. A RIGHT OF POSSESSION ON WHAT EVER IS LIVING. FROM BIRTH ON, IS SUBTLE IN SOME, IS GENTLY EASING IN OTHER. IS TIGER LIKE ON IS ABSENT LIKE IN OTHERS

A SOCIETY MADE WISE BY UNDERSTANDING WOULD BUILD ITS MORES ON THE 'SCHEME THAT DEATH TRY TO FOLLOW AT LEAST STATISTICALLY. THUS THE ENCROCHEMENT THAT MATERIALITY BURDENS ON LIFE WOULD BE EASED AWAY WHIT YEARS PASSING TO PRESENT SISTER DEATH

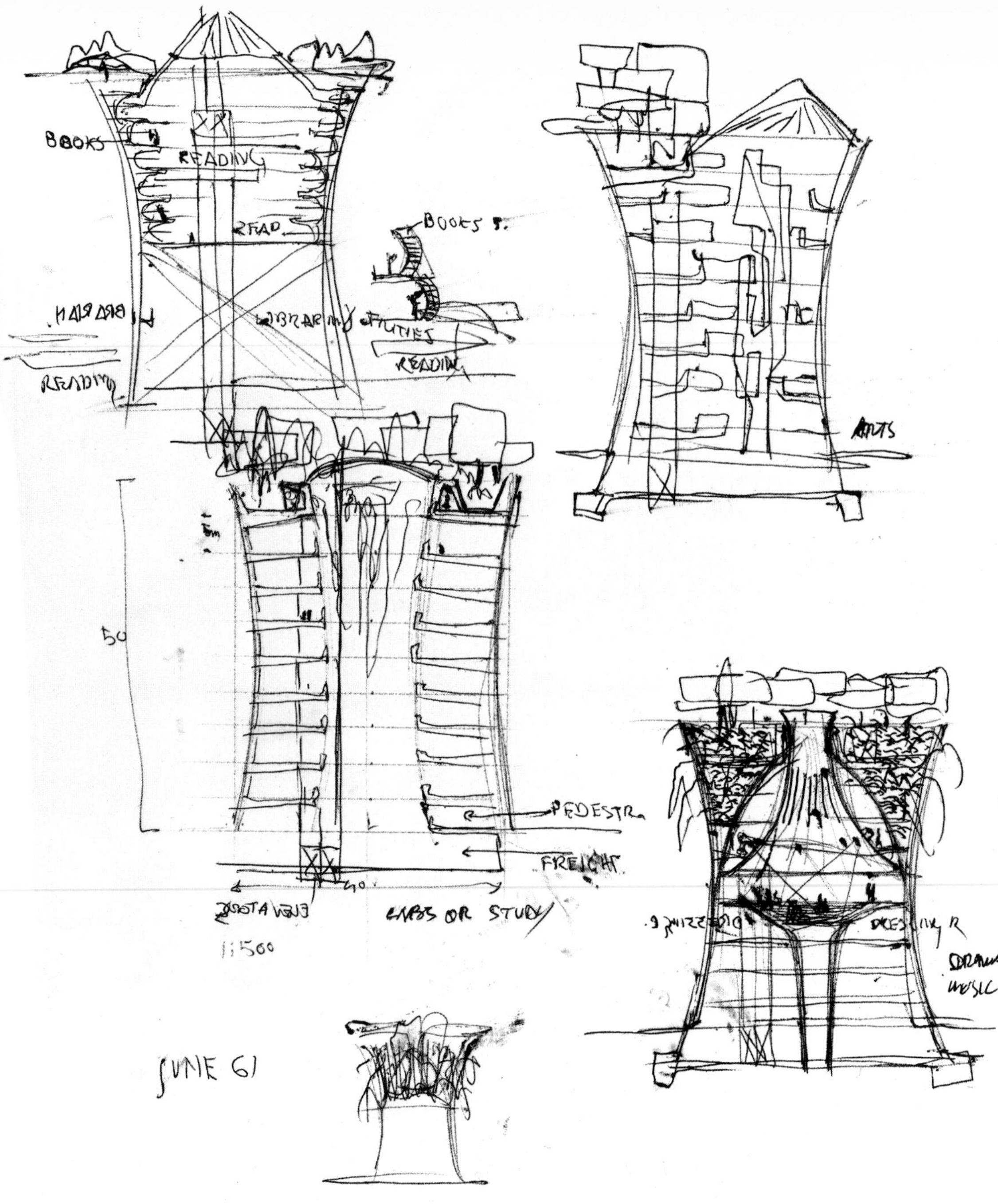

JUNE 61

BE WORDLESS NOW.
REACH THERE IN THE COMPOSURE OF.
THE UNSPOKEN AT COMPOSING THE
UNSPEACHABLE.

OUR LOVE FOR STATISTICS DOSENT SEME
TO DO US VERY MUCH GOOD:
DISTILLERS & BREWER GETS MORE
THAN CULTURE SO DOES THE SMOKE
MANUFACTURERS
SO DOES OUR MANIA FOR ~~TRAVELING~~ MOOVINGS.

AND ABOVE ALL LOOMING LIKE A
MONSTROUS, BLOODY, SULFOROUS SUN
IS THE COMPOUND OF HATRED & STEEL
OF OUR BUDGET FOR DISTRUCTION

A BOOMING ECONOMY WHICH FLOWERS
ARE SPROUTING FROM THE ANTICIPA-
TE CORPSE OF MANKIND HANDED
DOWN TO THE ABSTRACT VERBOSITY
OF "IDEALS" HANDLED WHAT DIABOLICAL
GOODNESS BY GANGSTERS BOYS

MAN HAS TWO CHAMPIONS:
ONE DEDICATED AT THE "DEMONSTRATION"
THAT THE UNIVERSE CAN BE MADE
"MORAL". SUCH MAN CAN BE

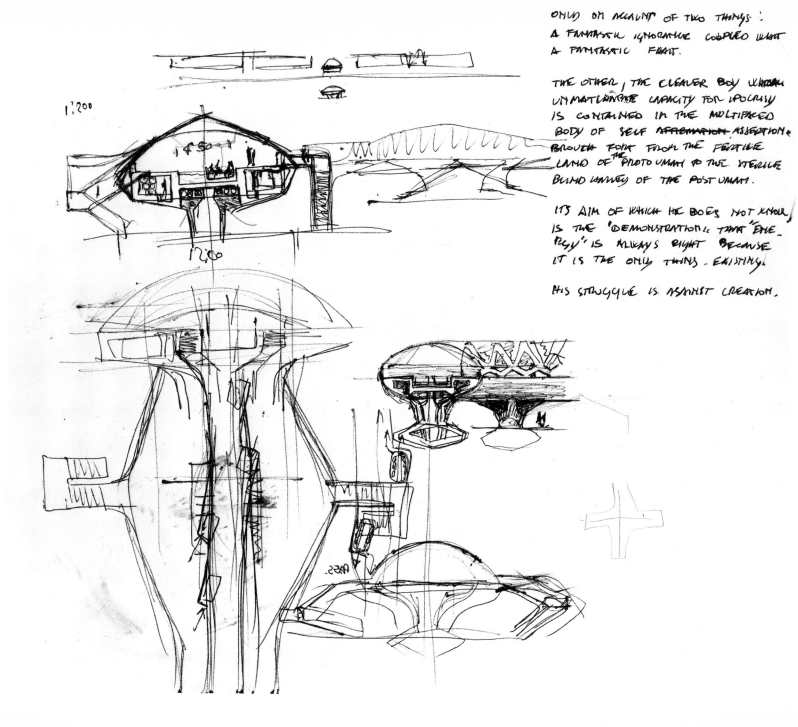

ONLY ON ACCOUNT OF TWO THINGS:
A FANTASTIC IGNORANCE COUPLED WITH
A FANTASTIC FAITH.

THE OTHER, THE CLEVER BOY WHOSE
UNMATCHABLE CAPACITY FOR HYPOCRISY
IS CONTAINED IN THE MULTIFACED
BODY OF SELF ~~AFFIRMATION~~ ASSERTION,
BROUGHT FORTH FROM THE FERTILE
LAND OF THE PROTOHUMAN TO THE STERILE
BLIND ALLEY OF THE POSTHUMAN.

ITS AIM OF WHICH HE DOES NOT KNOW,
IS THE "DEMONSTRATION" THAT "ENE-
RGY" IS ALWAYS RIGHT BECAUSE
IT IS THE ONLY THING EXISTING.

HIS STRUGGLE IS AGAINST CREATION.

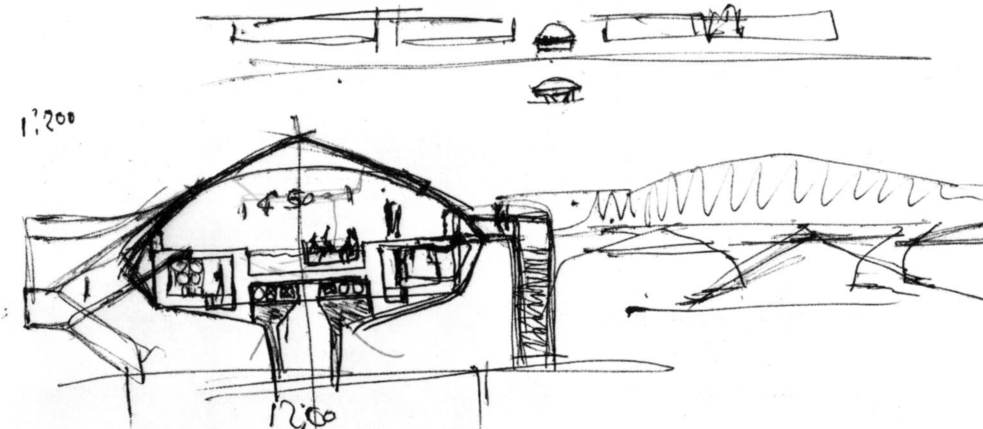

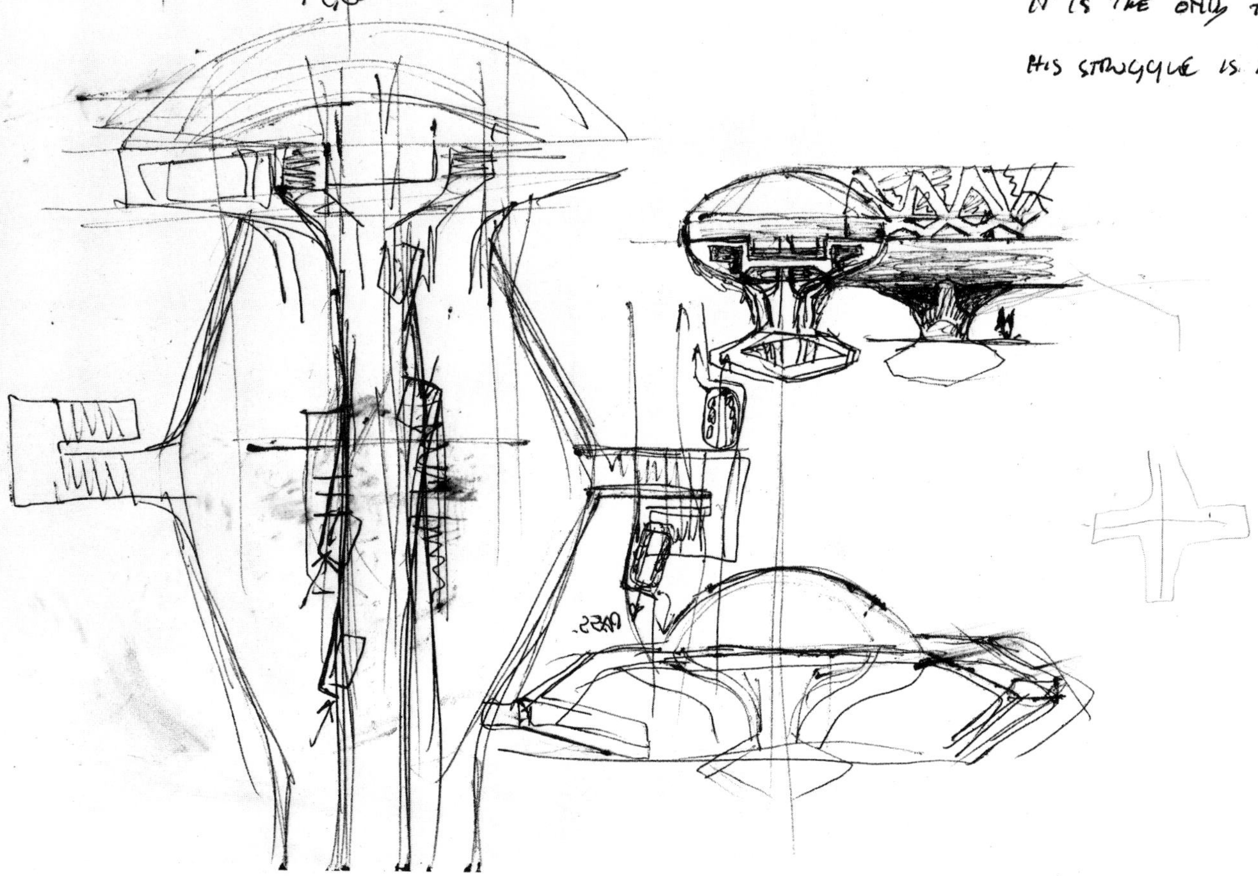

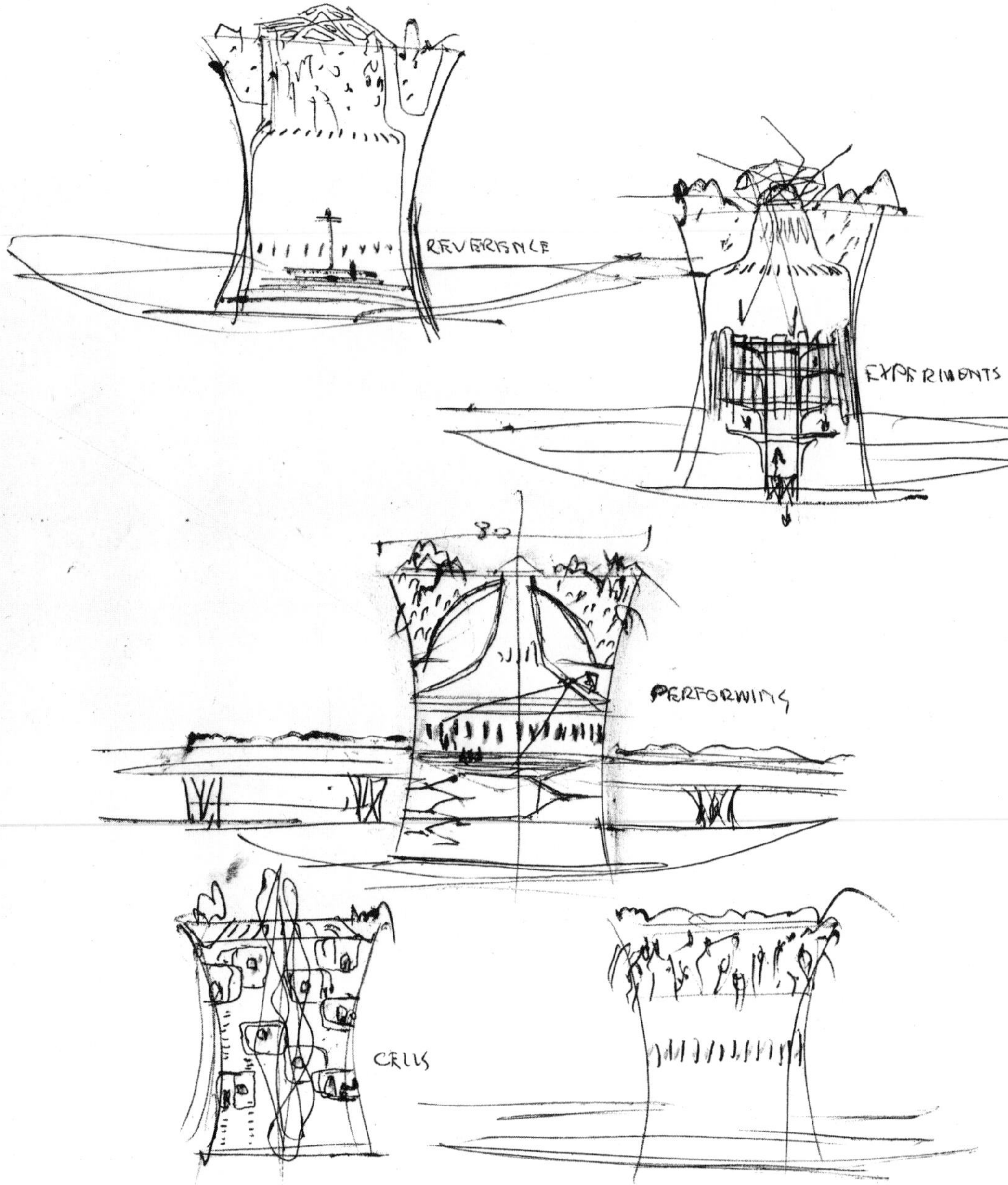

THE INTENTION HERE IS TO OR TECNOLOGY
THE GREATES EFFORT WHITHOUT GIVING TO
IT THE LEAST LIBERTY
TECNOLOGY THE ONLY SERVANT ETHICALLY
CONCEIVABLE, AS SUCH STRICTLY
THE MEAN TO SIGNIFICANCE NEVER
SIGNIFICANCE ITSELF HAS NEVERTHE
LESS, ALLIED TO MAN, BENT ON MA
CHECRAFT A MONSTROUS ABILITY FOR
MONSTERS MAKING,

THE MOST ROMANTIC & LESS EVIL OF
WHICH HAS BEEN THE COAL LOCOMOTIVE
SIMBOL OF ALL THE RAW INGENUITY
OF MAN & THE EXTASY HE FIND IN THE
"CONSUMING" VORACIOUSNESS
OF PULSATING IRON.
THE HUNGER OF FIRE & ITS
RESIDUUMS DESTINED FOR THE LUNGS
& THE METABOLISM OF MANY ANIMALS
& PLANTS.

TO THIS DIARRO PALEOTECNOLOGY ONE SEEKS
THE SUBSTITUTION OF THE UMANIZED BIO.
TECNOLOGY FRAMED IN ITS. INSTRUME.
VITALITY FRAME WORK UNTIL AT LEAST
THE DAY WHEN COMPUTER WILL SHOW
A FIRST GLIMMER OF EMOTIONAL STRAIN

POSSIBLY BY THE SAME SPIRIT THAT
PUT. CLASSICAL FRIZE AROUND THE LOCOMOTIVE
STACK. ONE MAY LOOK FOR A LESS ACCURAD
PLURI FUNCTIONALITY OF THE MEAN.
WE USE & THE GRACE THAT A MORE
SEDATE & LOVING CARE MAY AFFORD
FOR THEM & THEIR SIGNIFICATION.

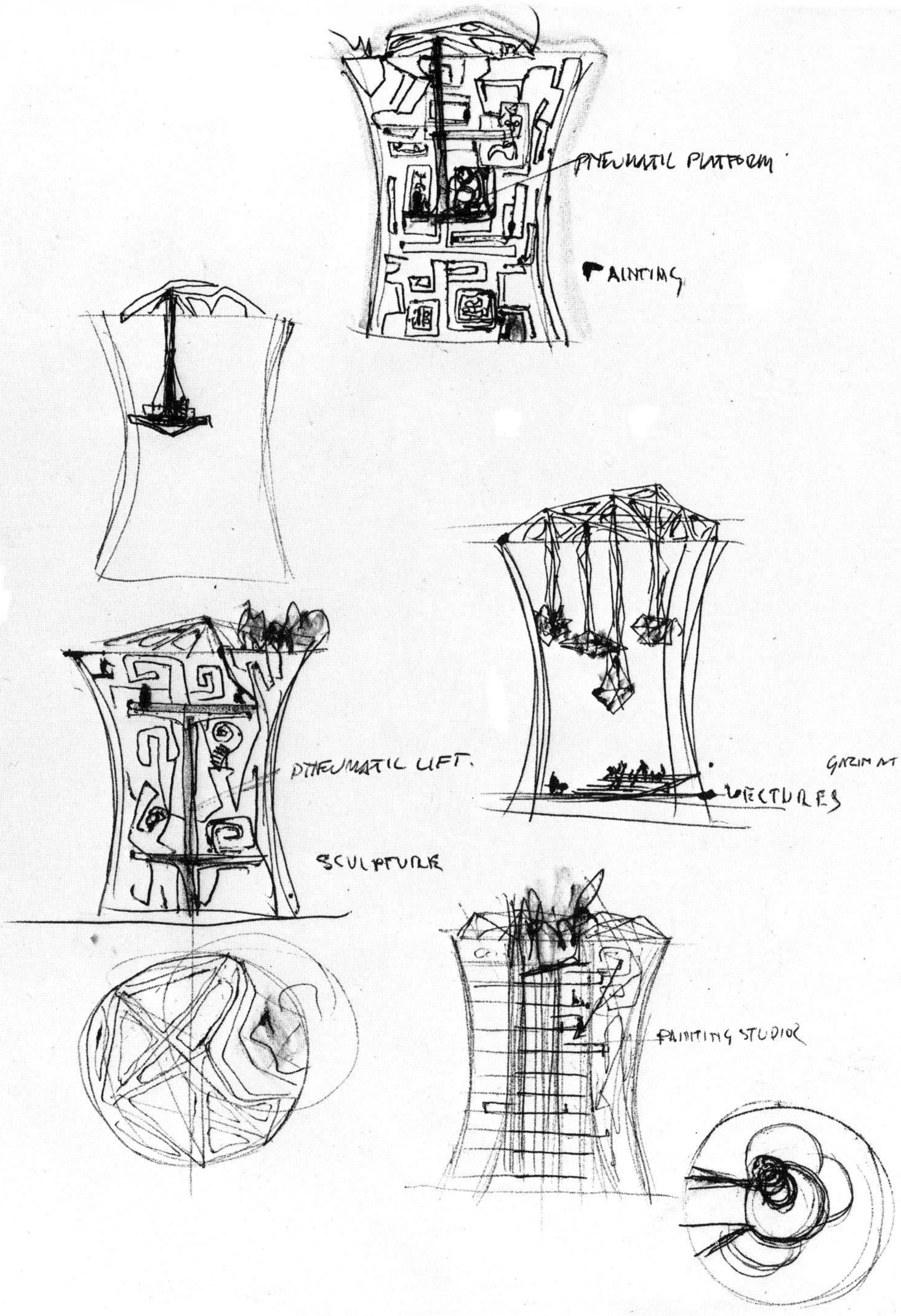

SCOPE

UNDERLYING THE DESIGN OF THE CITY IS THE ORIENTATION OF THINKING REPRESENTED IN THE FOLLOWING SCHEME

ENDS ·

INSTRUMENTALS ·

PAUSING ·

THE SCOPE IS THUS THE ESTABLISHING OF A SET OF VALUE FISICALLY EMBODIED BY THE CITY.

IN THIS HERARCHY ART IS TAKEN AS THE FINAL SINTESIS OF MANS DOING & THINKING. AS CREATIVITY ~~PERPETUA~~ [ENCLOSING] BY WAY OF MAN THE MOVING OF PERVADING FORCES [OF] ~~COUSE. THE UNIVERSE IS NOT CONCERNED OF, BUT~~ THAT ~~ARE~~ TWO THE CONCERN ULTIMATE & UNIQUE OF MAN, ARE OF NO MEANING TO ~~AN INDIFFERENT~~ UNIVERSE.

GRIM AT HIS OWN ENDEAVOURS

AN ENVIRONNEMENT IN ARMONY WHIT MAN CONSTITUTE BOTH THE BASIS FOR THE ESTABLISHEMENT OF A FERTILE OUTLOOK & THE END RESULT OF WHAT SUCH OUTLOOK ~~CAN~~ BRING ABOUT,

HERE SHOWS [UP] THE EXTRARATIONALITY OF THE PROBLEM; WHAT IS THE CONDITION FOR INTEGRITY IS REACHABLE ONLY ON THE PREMESSES OF INTEGRITY ITSELF

~~THIS~~ [IT] IS A CARACTERISTIC OF THE ARTISTIC ENDEAVOUR ~~WHERE IN ONE MAY~~ TO ~~FIND~~ [DEMAND] THE ACT OF CREATION. I.E. ~~THE~~ INTEGRITY AT HIS BEST, BLOSSOMING FROM & AMONG THE DISINTEGRATION OF THE IRRATIONAL.

THUS ONLY THROUGH CREATIVITY IS THERE HOPE TO FIND ANSWERS

Terraced Dwellings

1970
If roads must be accepted in the residential fabric, they could be covered over by dwellings. Then the vegetative pattern would extend uninterrupted in every direction.

This would imply two things: (1) a one-layer (duplex) pattern of dwellings, a typically vegetative mode; (2) an opening of the dwellings themselves toward the sky whereby the opaque roof is replaced by a lived-on roof and terrace. The Casbah of Algiers is a prototype of this mode.

As I already have serious doubts about the effectiveness of low-density schemes for urban living (a contradiction in terms), I have not carried the study of this project beyond a schematic layout.

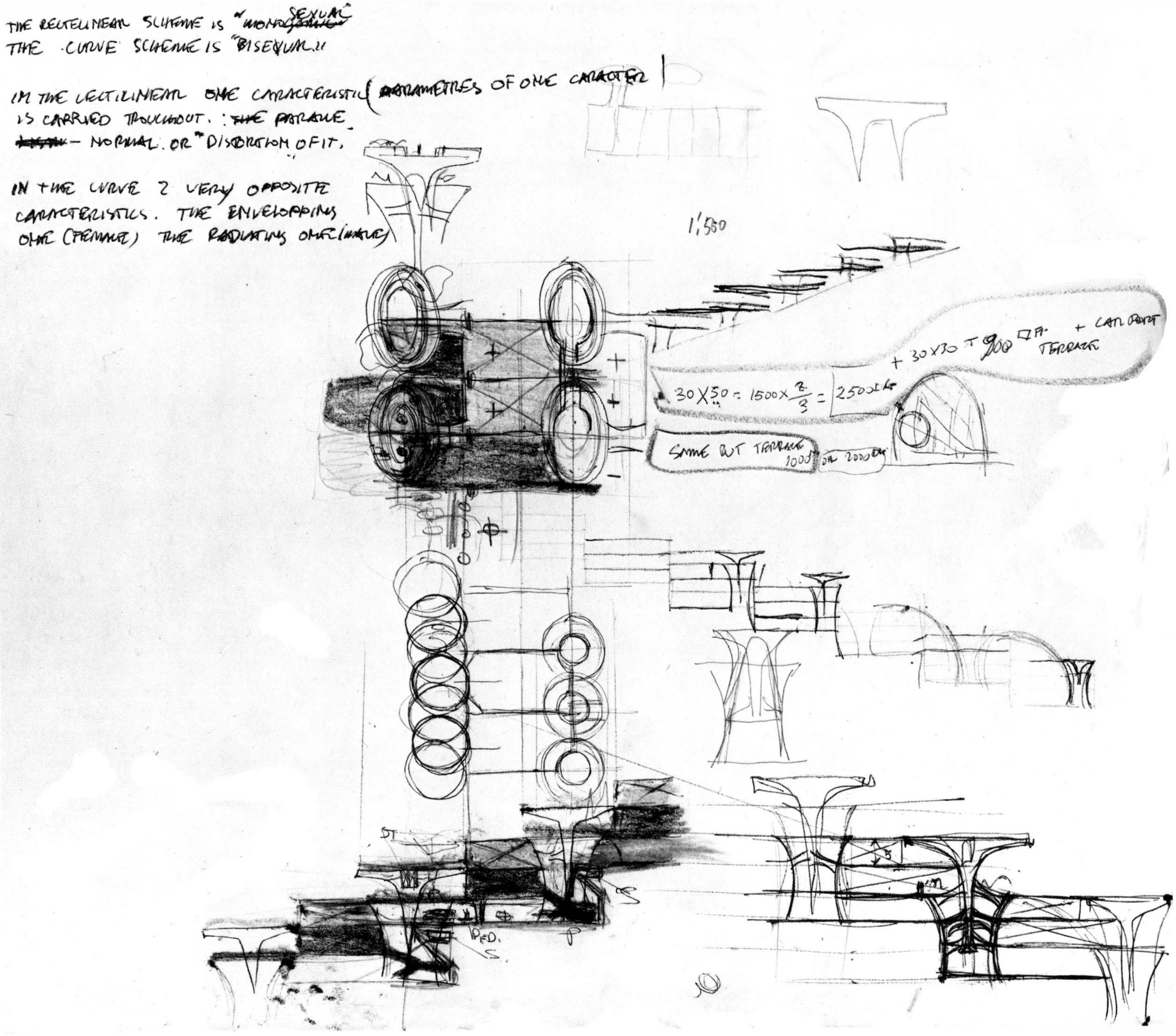
THE RECTELINEAR SCHEME IS "MONOSEXUAL"
THE CURVE SCHEME IS "BISEXUAL"
IN THE RECTILINEAR ONE CARACTERISTIC (PARAMETRES OF ONE CARACTER)
IS CARRIED TROUGHOUT. : THE PARALLE
– NORMAL OR "DISTORTION" OF IT.
IN THE CURVE 2 VERY OPPOSITE
CARACTERISTICS. THE ENVELOPPING
ONE (FEMALE) THE RADIATING ONE (MALE)
1/500
+ CAR PORT
+ 30X30 = 900 □ FT TERRACE
30X50 = 1500X 5/3 = 2500 □ FT
SAME BUT TERRACE 1000 OR 2000 □ FT
ST
PED.

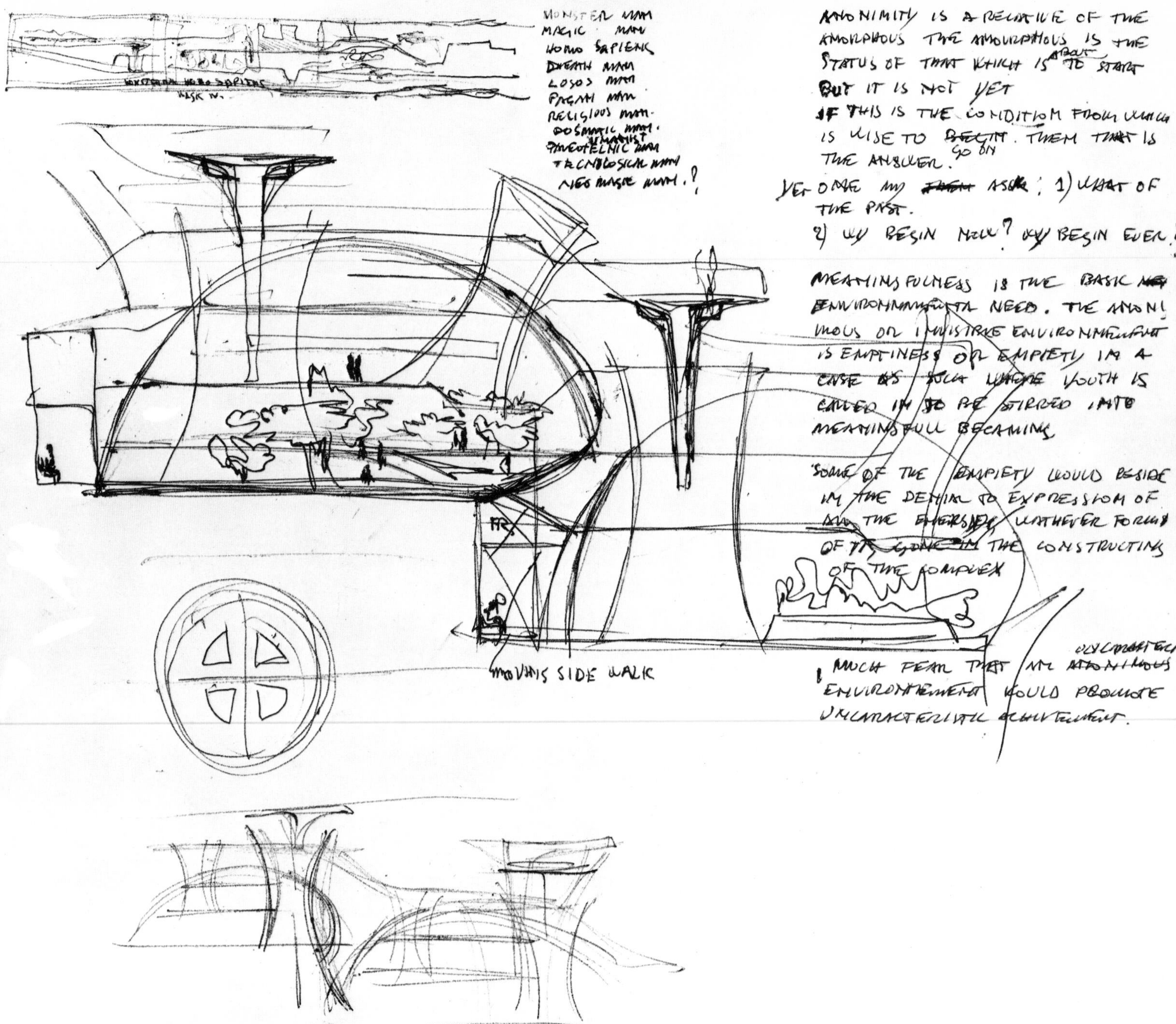
MONSTER MAN
MAGIC MAN
HOMO SAPIENS
DREAM MAN
LOGOS MAN
PAGAN MAN
RELIGIOUS MAN
DOGMATIC MAN
TECHNOLOGICAL MAN
NEO MAGIC MAN ?
ANONIMITY IS A RELATIVE OF THE AMORPHOUS THE AMOURPHOUS IS THE STATUS OF THAT WHICH IS ABOUT TO START BUT IT IS NOT YET
IF THIS IS THE CONDITION FROM WHICH IS WISE TO GO ON. THEN THAT IS THE ANSWER.
YET ONE MAY ASK: 1) WHAT OF THE PAST.
2) WHY BEGIN NOW? WHY BEGIN EVER?
MEANINGFULNESS IS THE BASIC ENVIRONMENTAL NEED. THE ANONIMOUS OR IMMISTRIVE ENVIRONMENT IS EMPTINESS OR EMPIETY IN A CASE AS SUCH WHERE YOUTH IS CALLED IN TO BE STIRRED INTO MEANINGFULL BECAMING
SOME OF THE EMPIETY WOULD RESIDE IN THE DENIAL TO EXPRESSION OF THE ENERGIES, WHATEVER FORMS OF IT, GONE IN THE CONSTRUCTING OF THE COMPLEX
MOVING SIDE WALK
MUCH FEAR THAT AN UNCHARACTERIZING ENVIRONMENT WOULD PROMOTE UNCHARACTERISTIC ACHIEVEMENT.

WHICH AFTER ALL IS INTRINSICALLY
ARTIFICIAL BECAUSE TEMPORARY IS
NOT ALTOGETHER A BLESSING.
ONE DOES NOT CAMP IN A CLINIC KIOSK
WHAT IS MORE IT IS A LIFE SITUATED IN
A PHASE OF GROWTH OF THE INDIVIDUAL
WHERE THE ACCENT HAS TO BE ON
RECEPTIVITY.
RECEPTIVITY IS ILL SERVED BY FOOTS
ON THE TABLE, BACK SLAPPING, LOAFING,
CRITICISM BY ATTITUDE, CINICISM
PRESUMPTION OF POWER, BULLISHNESS

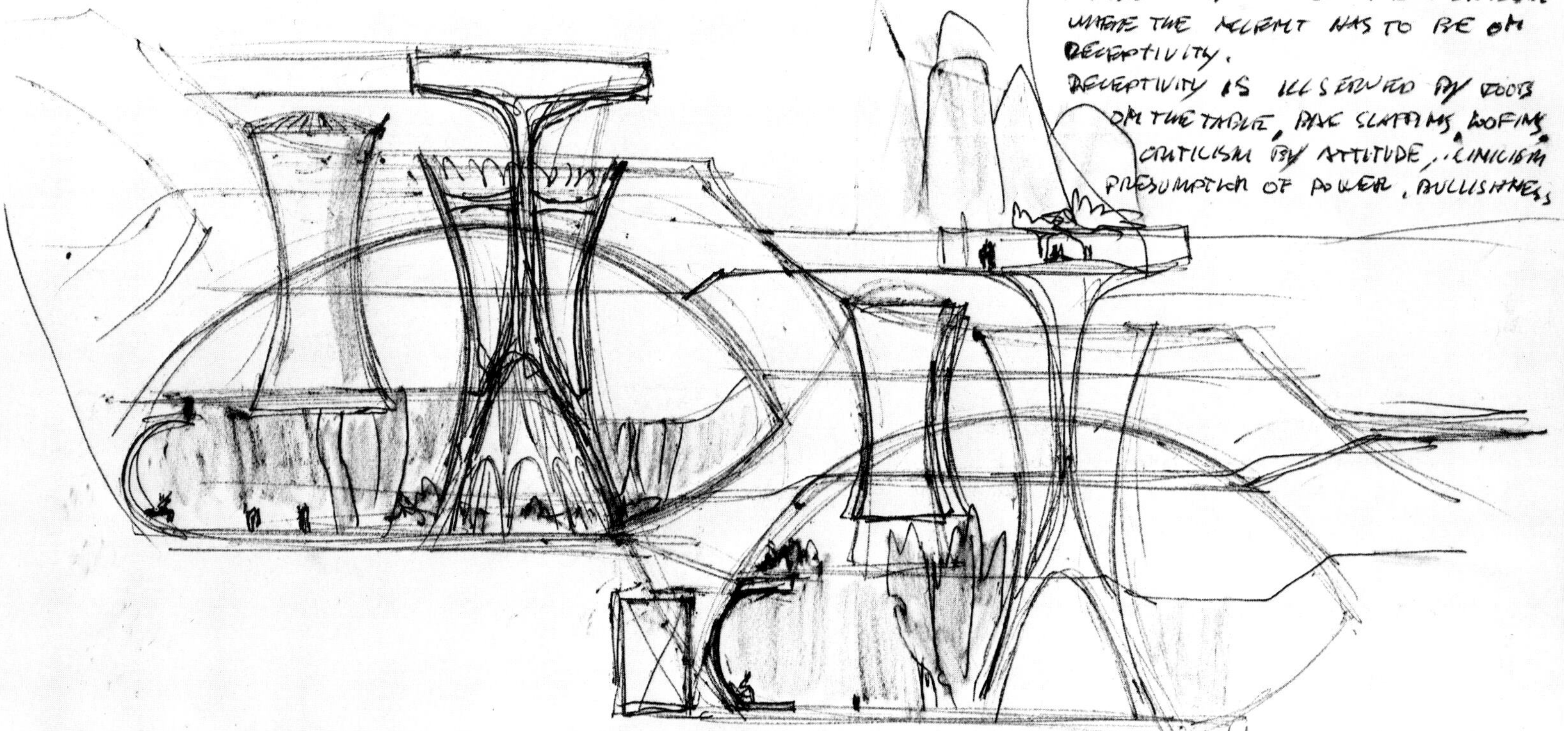

WHAT TO MATURE MAN MAY LOOK AS MAY INJUSTIFICABLE
TABU FROWNING ON THE BIGOTRY OF THE BEHOLDER.
TO A YOUTH, LONGING FOR GUIDANCE, MAY BE
A NECESSARY SYMBOL FOR REVERENCE.
REVERENCE POINTS IN YOUTH ON A
PERSON, THE MASTER, THE LEADER,
THE HISTORIC FIGURE, TO TRANSFER BY
THE INCREASING MATURENESS TO LIFE
IN HER DETAILED & MOST INTIMATE
EXPRESSIONS.
BUT REVERENCE IS INDISPENSABLE
& MORE THAN EVER IN THE MORE RECEPTIVE
PHASE OF LIFE

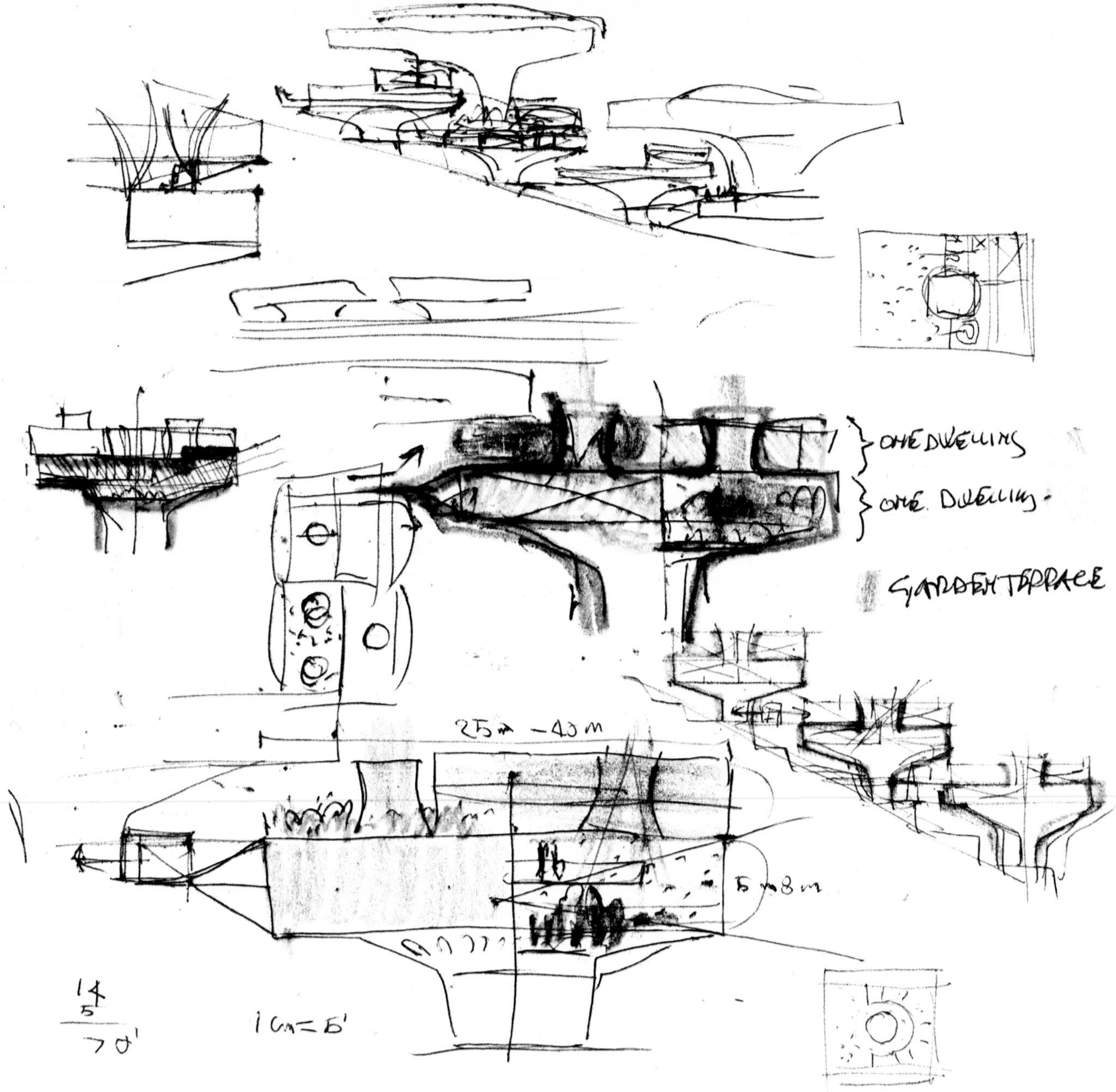
ONE DWELLING
ONE. DWELLING
GARDEN TERRACE
25m – 40m
5 – 8m
14
5
70'
1cm = 5'

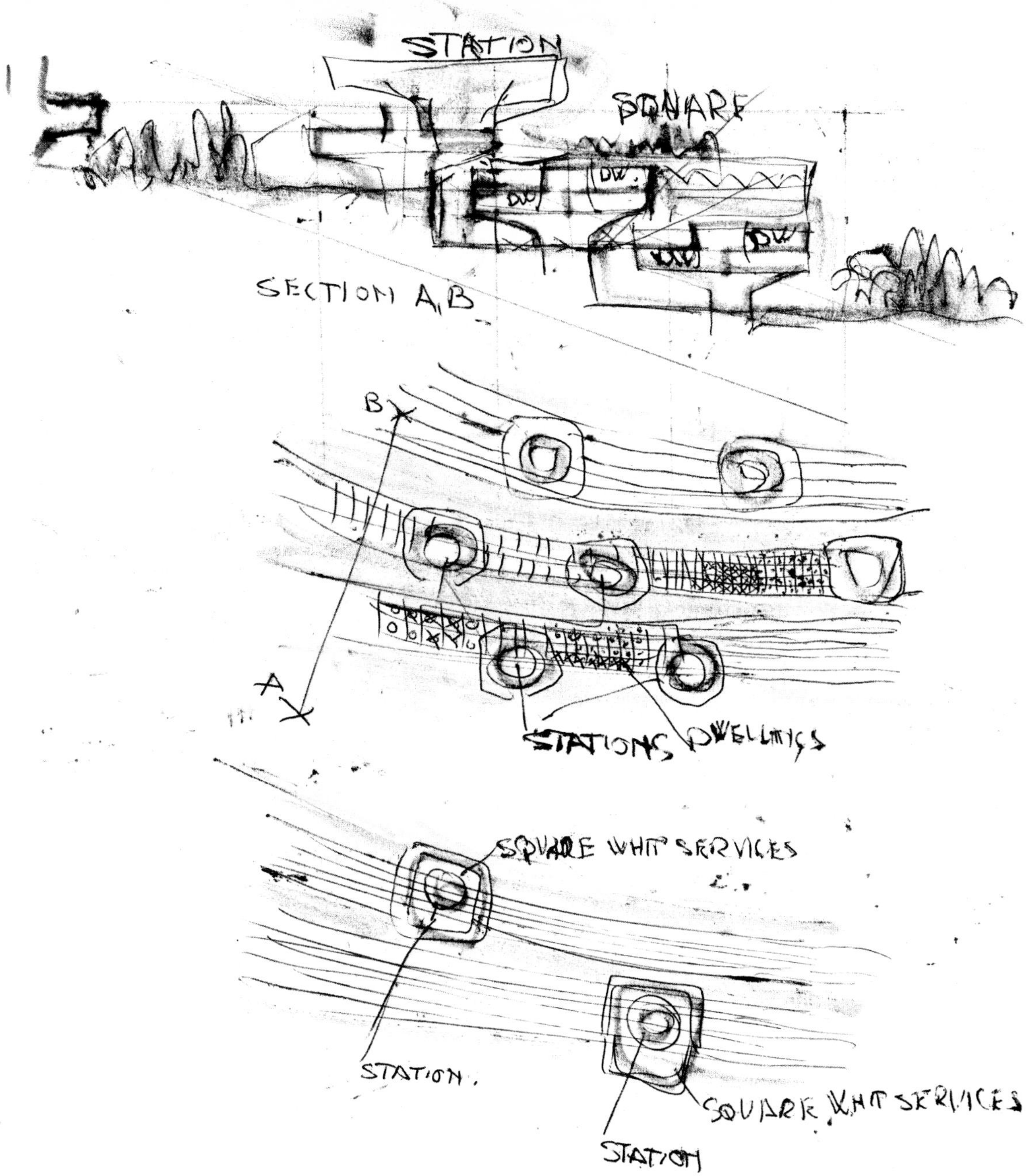
STATION
SQUARE
DW.
DW
SECTION A,B
B
A
STATIONS
DWELLINGS
SQUARE WHIT SERVICES
STATION.
SQUARE WHIT SERVICES
STATION

River of Waste

1970
Today there is much talk about waste, pollution, and recycling. At the time I was working on the River of Waste, it was not so.

Conceptually everything that exists goes through the cycle of conception, planning, making, performing, repairing, reperforming, wearing out or obsolescence, rejection, decay, diffusion. The living organism submits to these rules as does the manufactured. Unfortunately, man tends to ignore about half of the cycle, and, by the time an instrument has broken down or has worn out, he has lost any interest in it. By the same token, materials media or energy (minerals, fossils, fuels) have been exploited, used, and consumed. Man finds enough "distractions" to ignore the problem of their residuals and by-products; in short, he is unwilling to consider the whole cost. He is willing to pay for that part of the process that he can exploit, reluctant to pay for that part of the process that will make it ecologically acceptable. This inability or unwillingness to close the link of each performance ends sooner or later in the breakdown of the whole process. This has repeated itself time after time throughout known history; indeed, it is possible to write a history of man tracing the collapse of the structure of human groups through the saturation of waste and the drying up of sources of livelihood. The River of Waste was a large and integrated device that could lower the second price tag and by so doing bring the whole "civilizing" process into ecological balance. In the state of opulence that characterizes American civilization, the necessity for a total cycle, whatever the endeavor, becomes imperative. The by-products of recklessness are pollution of land and atmosphere, decay of urban settlements, land destruction, river, lake, and sea decay, flora and fauna destruction, and so on. Lastly, a sense of pervading sterility and ugliness prevails, and man's very soul is swept away into the waste heaps of unfitness and death. Opulence can, in fact, be defined as a deceptive condition of health where the florid appearance of the patient conceals the tiredness of his flesh and the dimness of his psyche, both slowly poisoned by the disintegration of all his interrelated functions.

In Mesa City there is conceptually almost a one-to-one relationship between the production and marketing belt and the rejection-regeneration-recycling belt. In it the worn out, the broken down, the wastes are sources of material and energy and, as such, are processed and reinserted into the life cycle of the city.

BEATEN BY THE MONSTRUOSITY OF ITS
IMPLICATIONS. WHICH OF THOSE HEROES
IS GOING TO TELL THE COUNTLESS MOTHERS (ABOUT 700 MILLIONS?)
THAT THEIR CHILDREN WILL BE ANNIHILATED,
THEIR HOMES CANCELLED OUT OF THE EARTH
THEIR REASON OF BEEING STULTIFIED.
THE WHOLE SUBSTANCE OF REVERENCE
GIVEN TO THE GODS OF A DEAD LAND.
BECAUSE IN THEIR JUDGEMENT DEATH
IS THE ONLY ALTERNATIVE TO FREEDOM—
(THAT FREEDOM THAT EVIDENTLY NONE
OF THEM HAS NEVER QUITE GRASPED TO
SAY THE LEAST)

IT IS QUITE CLEAR THE GODS THEY
INVOKE IS THE GOD OF
THEIR ABSTRAC MADNESS

SEPTEMBER 60 P.V.

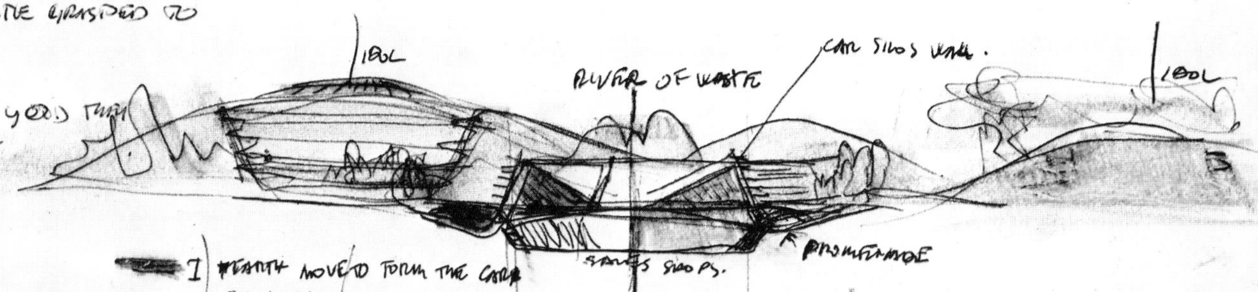

I) EARTH MOVE TO FORM THE CAR SILOS HALL.

II) EARTH MOVE TO CARVE THE RIVER OF WASTE & MAKE THE HILLS AROUND THE IDOLS.

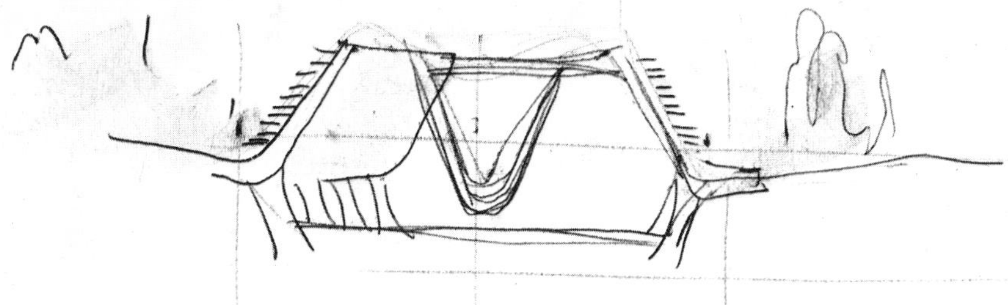

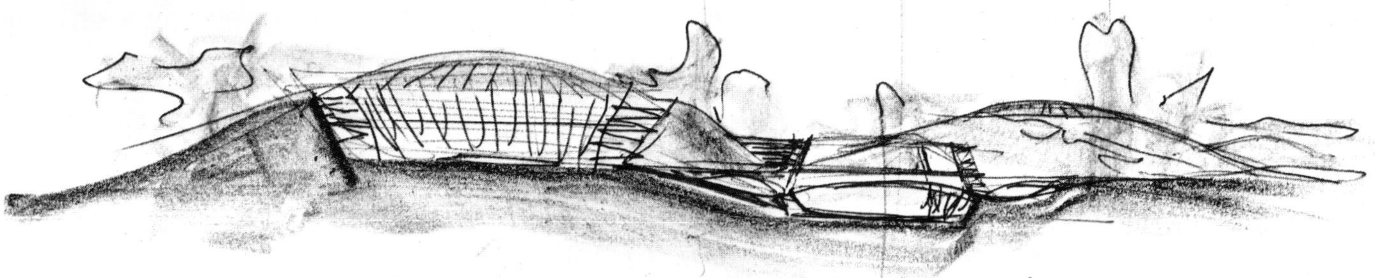

PRESTITISITAION

~~DECEMBER~~ 60 GENNAIO 61

IS IT THERE A SIMPLE STATEMENT TO EXPLAINING THE CITY.? THE MAN PROMOTING THE IDEA OF DISPOSABLE CITIES CUT FOR HIMSELF A QUITE SIMPLE ONE OR AT LEAST IMPLIED IT;
AS CONTEMPORARY MAN MOVES FAST LET'S NOT ~~BOTH~~ BURDEN ITS FREEDOM WHIT THE TIMELESS INSCRIBED IN STONE, ROADS, STRUCTURES ....
OF ALL ANIMALS ON HEART MAN WOULD THUS BE THE FASTEST, THERE IS A GREAT IDEAL FOR LIFE "MOVING."

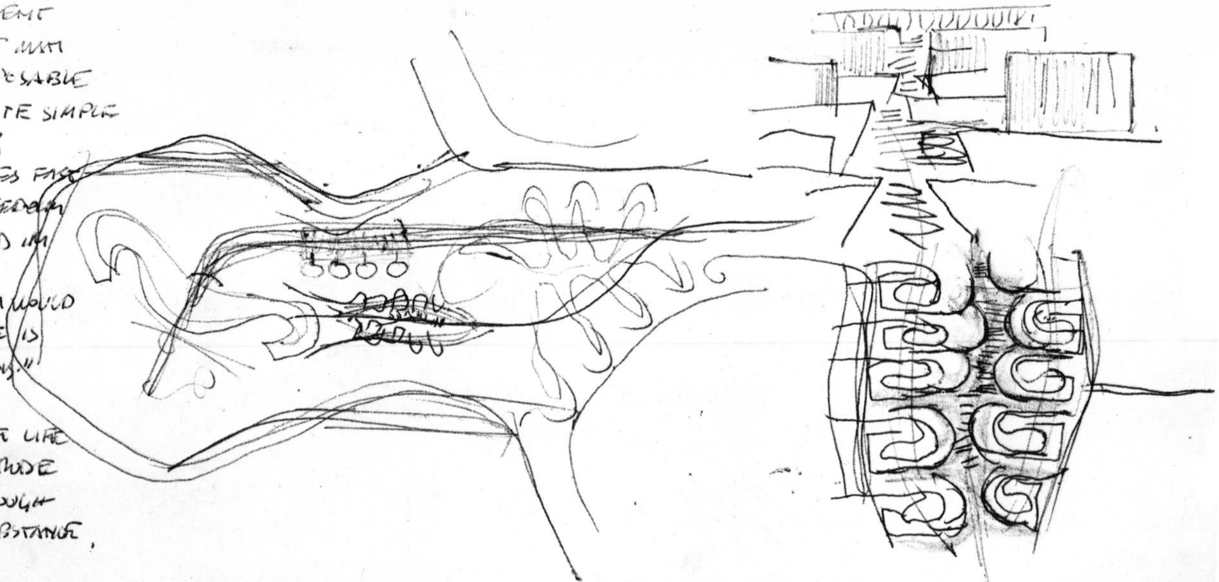

IT IS THE HUMAN CONDITION THAT LIFE PUSHES FROM WITHIN TO EXTRUDE SOME SORT OF EXPRESSION TROUGH THE TEMPLET OF ONE OWN SUBSTANCE.

MY TEMPLET SPELLS NOW. CITY. THIS IS AS GOOD AS DEFINITION AS ANY FOR THE REASON OF MY CONCEIVING A CITY. IT IS SO COMPREHENSIVE AS TO BE. OF NO HELP.

INDIRECTLY IT DEFINE ALSO THE REASON ~~FOR~~ THE EXISTING OF SUCH THINGS AS CITIES IN THE MIND OF THE AUTOR: AS ~~THE~~ HE WAS TO DESIGN A CITY BECAUSE HE'S "FORCED TO DO IT" SO MAN BUILDS CITIES BECAUSE HE IS "FORCED" TO DO IT.

FREEDOM, SO GREATLY BANDIED ABOUT, MAY CONSIST ~~&~~ IN THE VESTING OF THIS "FORCED" WHIT THE DESIRABILITY OF GRACE, THE DURABILITY OF COMPASSION. ALL THE REST ~~IS~~ INCIDENTAL;

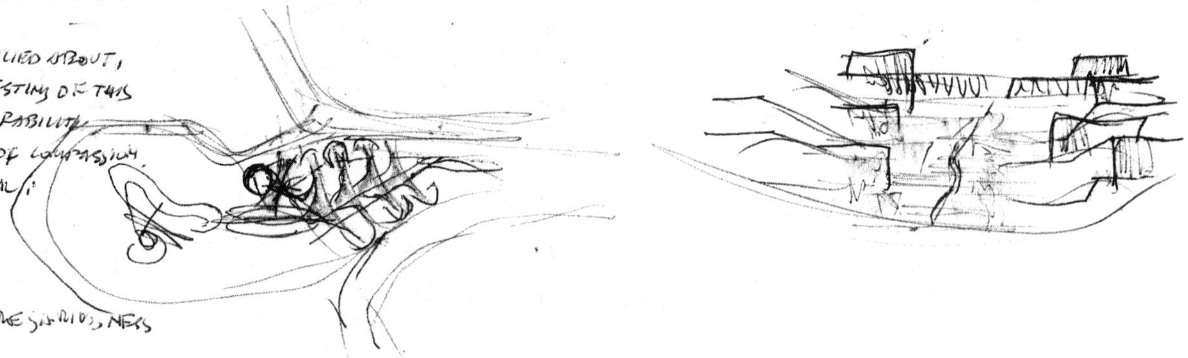

THE "FORCING" FORCES?;
~~THE~~ OBJECTIVE:
1 MAN IS GREGARIOUS; GREGARIOUSNESS

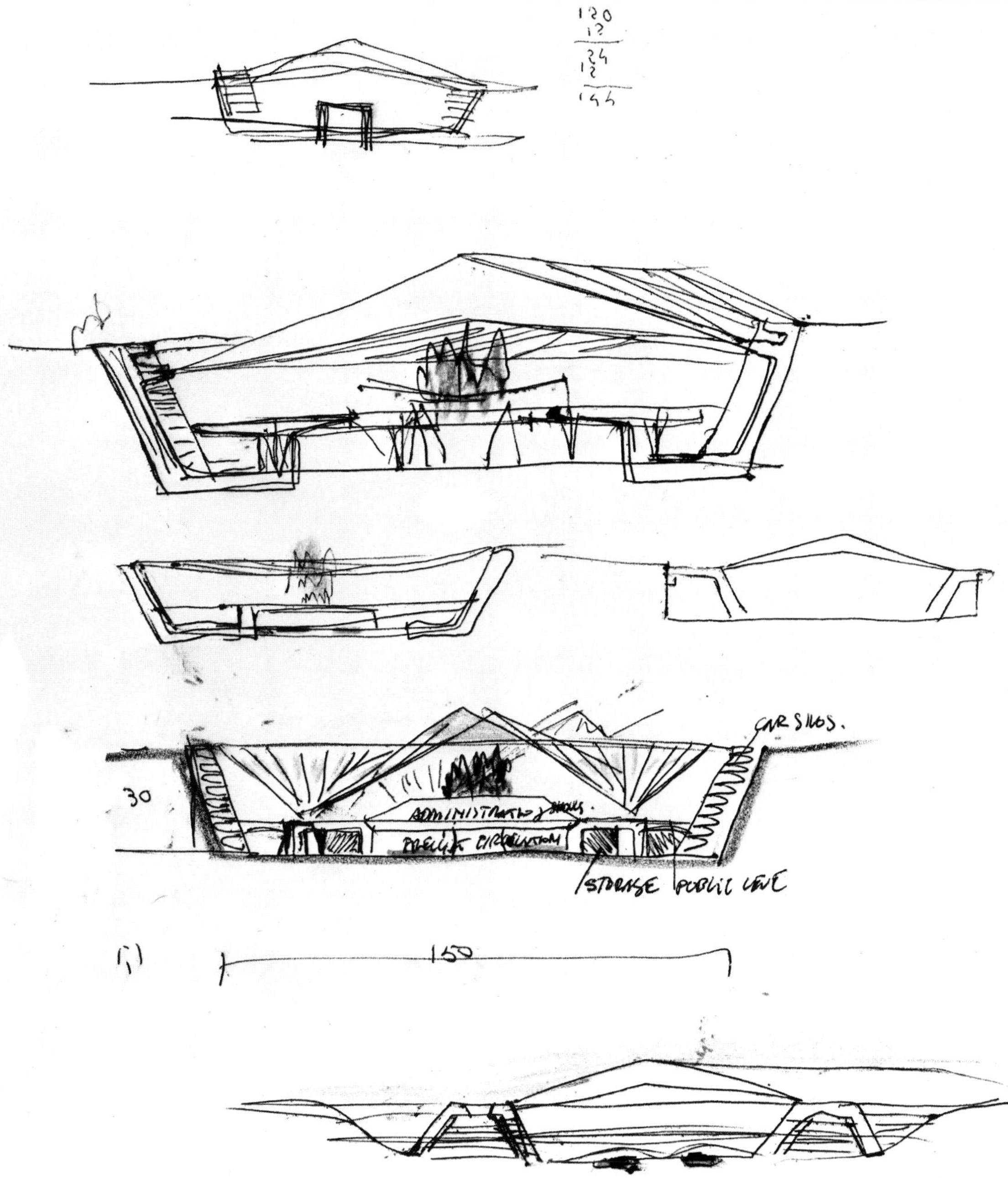

IDOLATRIES FOR ABSTRACT GOODS & THE "DIONISIAN EXCESSES" NEEDED TO COUNTERACT THE STERILITY OF LIFE ~~NOT~~ TROUBLY LIVED.

STATISTICAL MURDER WILL TAKE GREATER TOLL THAT TIME PASSING & ITS ANONIMITY WILL FAVOR ITS IGNOMINITY

THE HIGH WAY CARNAGE:
TWO MOVES COULD DROP THE TOLL TO LESS THAN HALF SAY 15.000 DEAD AGAINST 30.000. A YEAR.
1) PRODUCE CARS WHICH TOP SPEED IS ~~70~~ MILES/HOUR WHICH IS THE TOP LEGAL SPEED ON THE ROAD. IN THE MOST LIBERAL STATES.
2) PUT THE SAVINGS. MADE FROM THIS REDUCTION IN H.P. IN SAFETY DEVICE. & IN REDUCING THE NEED FOR MOBILITY; A BETTER ENVIRONMENT.
IF ONE ADDS A TRUER HEROIC APPROACH TO THE PROBLEM OF INTOXICATED DRIVER (IMMEDIATE REVOKING OF LICENCE FOR INSTANCE) THE BUTCHERY WOULD DWINDLE.

HIPOCRISY, GREED & FALSE FREEDOM WILL NEVER ALLOW FOR SUCH PROVISIONS

GASOLINE CONSUMPTION.
GASOLINE IT IS NOT AS CHEAP AS WE CAN BUY IT. IT IS A LIMITED PRECIOUS SOURCE OF POWER, A CAPITAL. BRUTALLY SQUANDERED ROBBING MAN OF ITS OWN POTENTIALITY. FOR THE SAKE OF STUPIDITY. OR WORSE (SEE ABOVE)
TO UNDERSTAND THIS ONE MUST THINK OF WHAT IT COULD BE DONE WITH SUCH FUEL: TRANSFORM ARID LANDS INTO GARDENS. MAKE LIVABLE THE EXTREME HOT & THE COLD PARTS OF THE

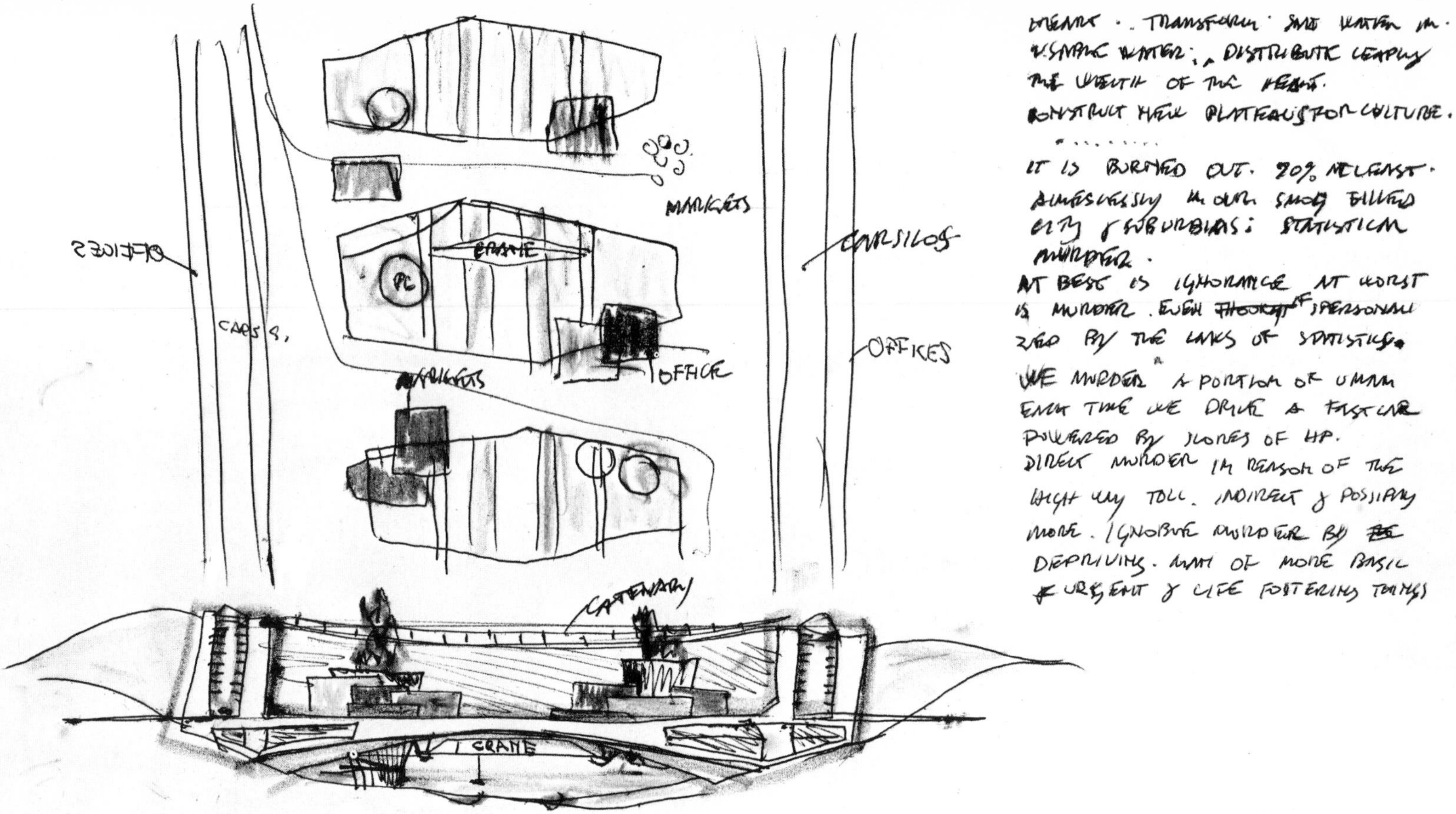
OFFICES
MARKETS
CRANE
PC
CARSILOS
OFFICES
OFFICE
MARKETS
CATENARY
CRANE
HEART. TRANSFORM SALT WATER IN USABLE WATER; DISTRIBUTE LEAPING THE WEALTH OF THE HEART.
CONSTRUCT NEW PLATEAUS FOR CULTURE.
IT IS BURNED OUT. 90% AT LEAST. AIMLESSLY IN OUR SMOG FILLED CITY & SUBURBIAS: STATISTICAL MURDER.
AT BEST IS IGNORANCE AT WORST IS MURDER. EVEN IF PERSONALIZED BY THE LAWS OF STATISTICS.
WE MURDER A PORTION OF HUMAN EACH TIME WE DRIVE A FAST CAR POWERED BY SCORES OF HP.
DIRECT MURDER IN REASON OF THE HIGHWAY TOLL. INDIRECT & POSSIBLY MORE. IGNOBLE MURDER BY DEPRIVING MAN OF MORE BASIC & URGENT & LIFE FOSTERING THINGS

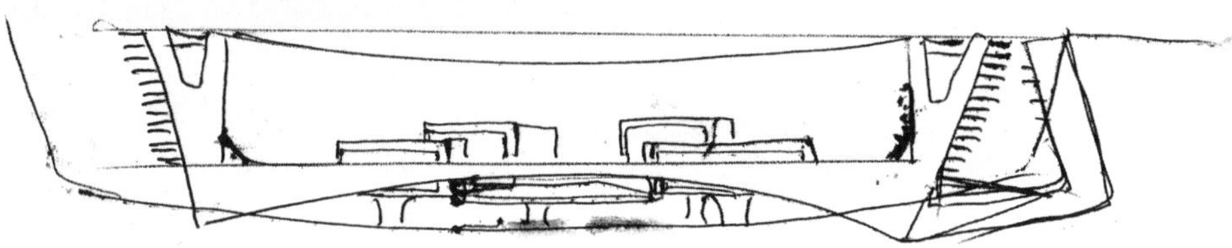

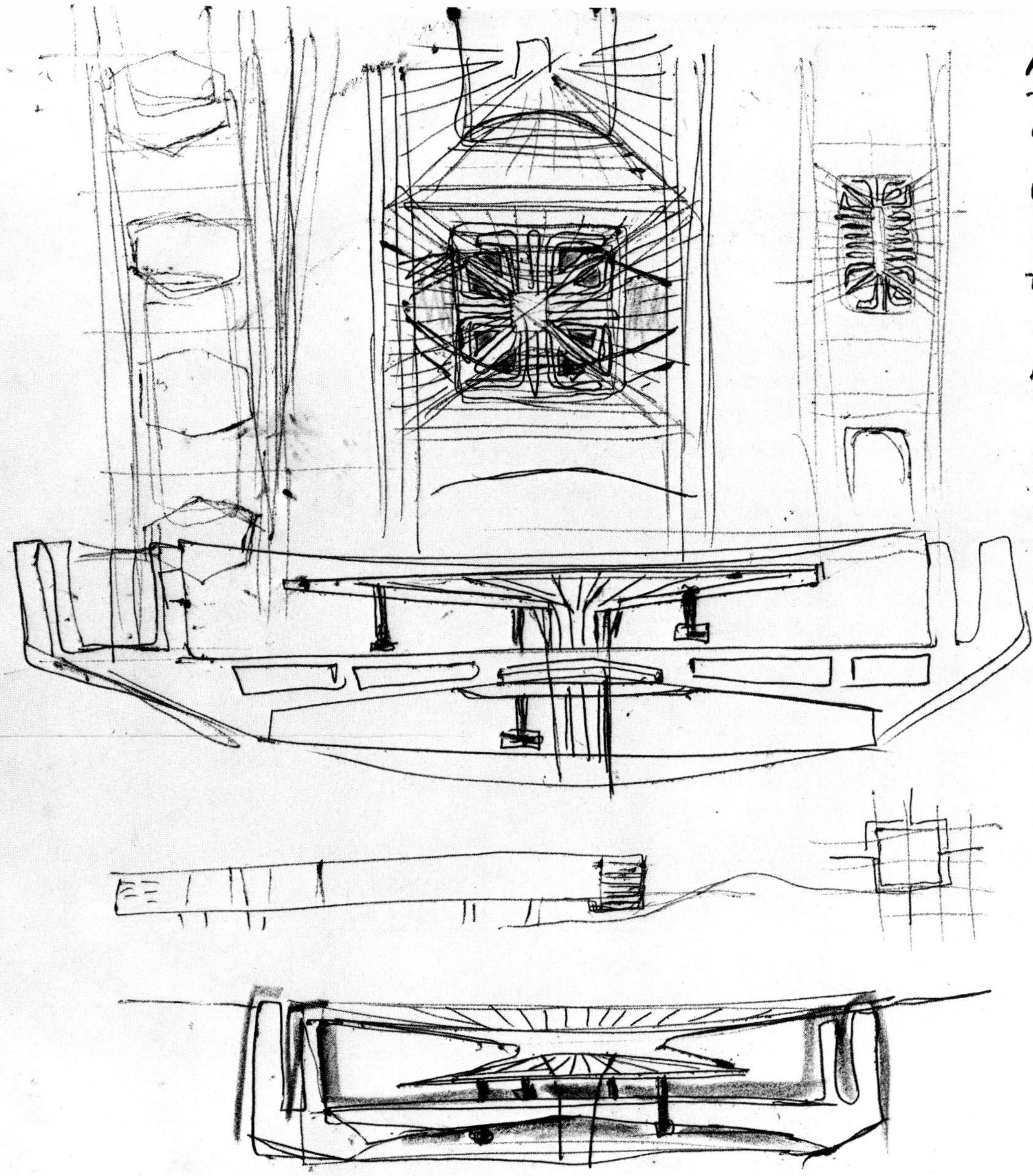

SCARRED EARTH WILL ALWAYS RE-
MAKE HER OWN BALANCE, THE IN-
TERIM MAY THOUGH SEE COUNTLESS
GENERATIONS OF MAN WANDERING.
IN SEARCH OF A LOST GRACE, POSSI-
BLY LOOSE IN THE SPAN. THE LONGING
FOR IT & WITH IT ITS GODLIKE POTENTIAL.

THE "INTELLIGENT" REVERENCE. IS
HARD TO CARRY FORWARD BECAUSE IT
IS NOT POSSIBLE TO "MAINTAIN"
MAINTENANCE IS OR SHOULD BE INSTINC-
TIVE OR AUTOMATIC. BUT HERE
REVERENCE IS TO CONCEIVE & MAKE

BOTH CONCEIVING & MAKING EVEN
AT THEIR HIGHEST SEEM TO DRAG
ALONG. A UNLIMITED CAPACITY FOR
MAKESHIFT & SQUALOR.
THE VACUUM ITSELF MADE BY THE
CLUSTERING OF INTENSITY TO ONE
POINT. (THE CREATED THING) VERY
OFTEN REMIND OF THE WOUNDS
THE BULDOZER CUTS. WHEN PILING
UP MATTER INTO A DIKE OR AN
EMBANKEMENT. FURTHERMORE FROM
THIS NEW THING "LITTLE DEVIL" ENDE-
AVOUR TO TROUBLE. IN THE SCARRED
VACUUM. ALL THE LITTERS & RELICS.
THE POWERFUL ACTION HAS BY PRO-
DUCED
SO ONE HAS NOW AN HIGHLIGHT
& AROUND IT IGNOMINY.

A GOAL OF CIVILISATION IS TO "DIGEST"
THE IGNOMINY TO AT LEAST A NEUTRAL
CONDITION SO THAT: THE CONTINUUM OF
GRACE MAY RECONSTRUCT ITS FLOW &
MAN MAY FIND JOY WAITING. IT.

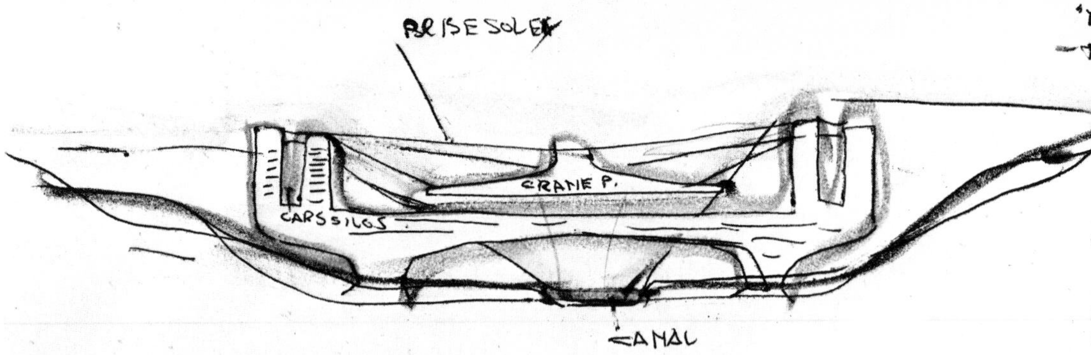

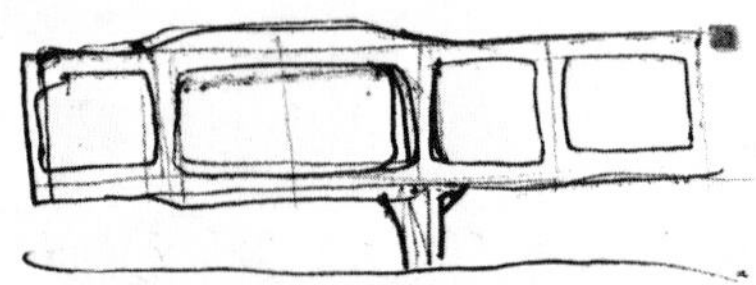

ENVIRONMENT TO ~~MAKE~~ (CONSTRUCT) ITS OWN "NATURE".

— THE MAKING OF AN ENVIRONMENT IN HARMONY WITH THE LIVING MAN.

~~MAN~~ MAY WELL ALLOW OUT OF THE EARTH THE EVEN ~~AGE OF~~ UNSIFTED INDEFINITE INDIFFERENTIATE AGE OF POSTLIFE OR HE MAY FACE NATURE AS IT IS AND TRANSFIGURE IT AS HE IS.

WISDOM MAY BELONG TO EITHER ONE BUT MAN BELONGS TO THE SECOND

IF MAN IS ONLY THE MOST ACTIVE TOOL OF (EARTHLY) NATURE FOR CONCEIVED ENDS THEN. HE AND THE BEAVER BELONG TOGETHER.

IF MAN IS TO TRANSCEND (EARTHLY) NATURE FOR EVEN MORE CONCEIVED ENDS THAN. IS UP TO MAN TO MOLD - TRANSFORM TRANSFIGURE NATURE.

~~WHAT~~ ~~MAY~~ BE FRIGHTENING. IS NOT THE SCALE OF THE (ENORMOUS) PROSPECTIVE BUT THE STIGMA OF ARTIFICIALITY ATTACHED TO IT. WHERE WILL WE GET THE SENSIBILITY THE GOODNESS THE DEPTH, THE REVERENCE SUFFICIENT FOR SUCH TASK? ~~KNOWLEDGE~~, OF THE DEGREE AVAILABLE NOW IS DEFINITELY A POOR ASSET. SO IT MAY WELL BE THAT WE SHOULD POSTPONE THE INTERVENTION ON NATURE AS WE SHOULD POSTPONE OUR QUEST INTO FISIC. & TECHNOLOGY UNTIL OUR MIND SHALL RECOVER OR ACHIEVE SOME BETTER MORAL LUCIDITY.

THE FACT IS THAT BY THE SHOVEL ~~THE~~ OR THE BULDOZER WE ARE (WE HAVE)

Earth Houses

1970

There is nothing new in setting houses into the ground rather than on the ground. This has been done in many places at many different times, often on a very large scale and with great consistency and coherence. The reasons have been opportunity, shelter from weather, convenience, specific geological and topographical conditions, and social and economic standards.

For me the main reason was to experiment. My starting point was the slip casting of ceramic objects whose molds were cut into the ground. Moving from fractions of a square foot to many square feet and from liquid clay to concrete (a plastic material, too) was simply an extrapolation. What had been a pot became a roof. In both cases, the soil was very instrumental, not only as the shaping material, a negative mold, but also in characterizing the texture, color, and feeling of the final product.

The specific ugliness afflicting "free form" concrete on plastic structures is the sloppiness of the shapes and the flaccid character of the surfaces. Earth forming, if done well, negates those weaknesses and in addition introduces certain special effects: variation in texture is one, variation in color is another. But mainly it allows enrichment of the structure by the introduction of "structural suggestions" with an emphasis on areas of stress.

The salient characteristics of the earth house are two: (1) It is a crafted construction and as such it tends to reflect the "nature of materials." (Frank Lloyd Wright) (2) It is a semisubterranean construction. It is essential not to dismiss the "semi" as otherwise the concept is distorted to a degree that makes it unfit for human use. Human life is not mole life because human biopsychical characteristics are not those of the mole.

The difference between an underground house and an earth house is that the first is sealed from light, air, climate, and sound. It is totally artificial and to that degree a fake environment. The second is situated below grade, but it is amply open to sunlight, air, sounds, climate, and so forth.

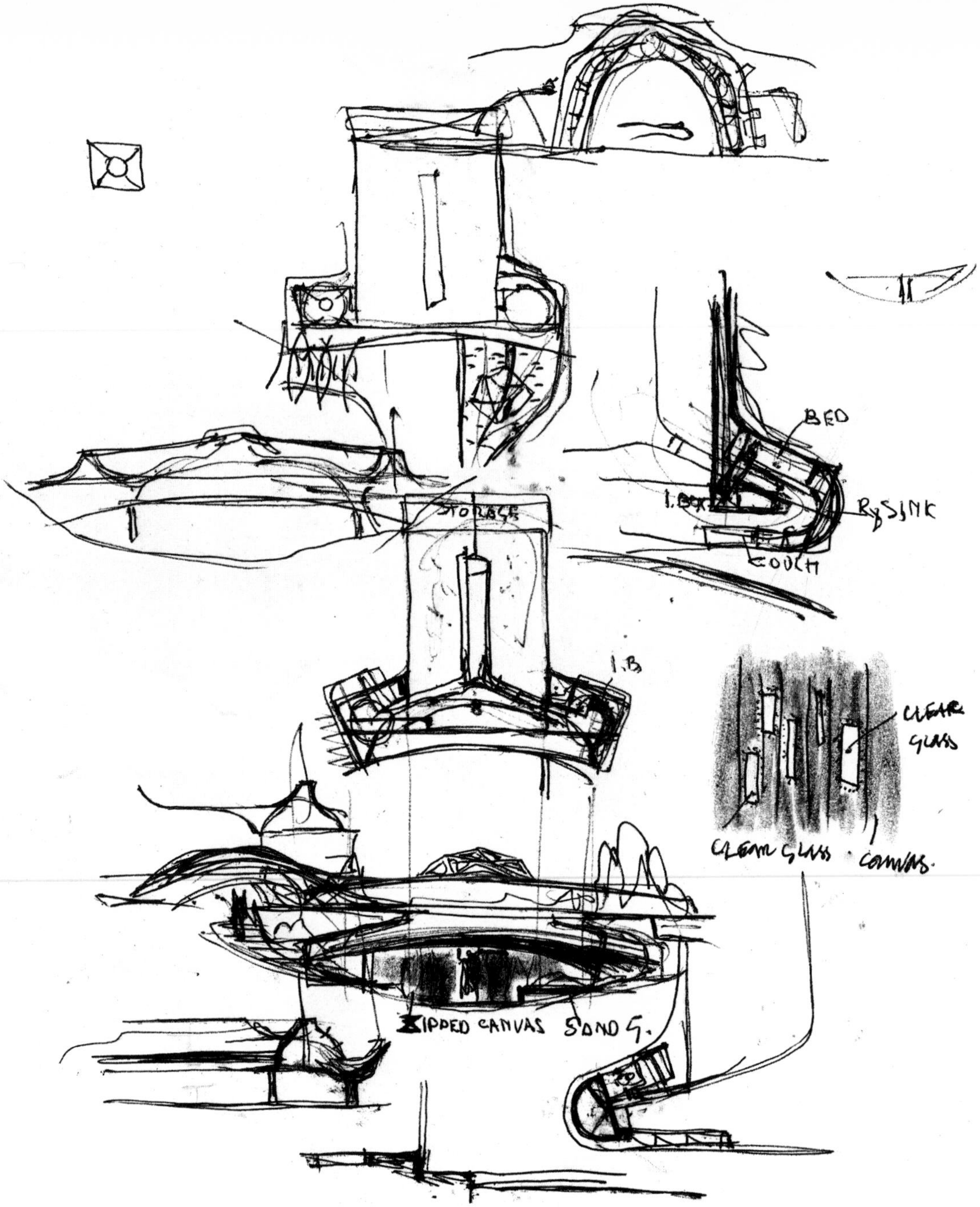
BED
I.BOX
R SINK
COUCH
STORAGE
I.B
CLEAR GLASS
CLEAR GLASS
CANVAS.
DIPPED CANVAS
SAND G.

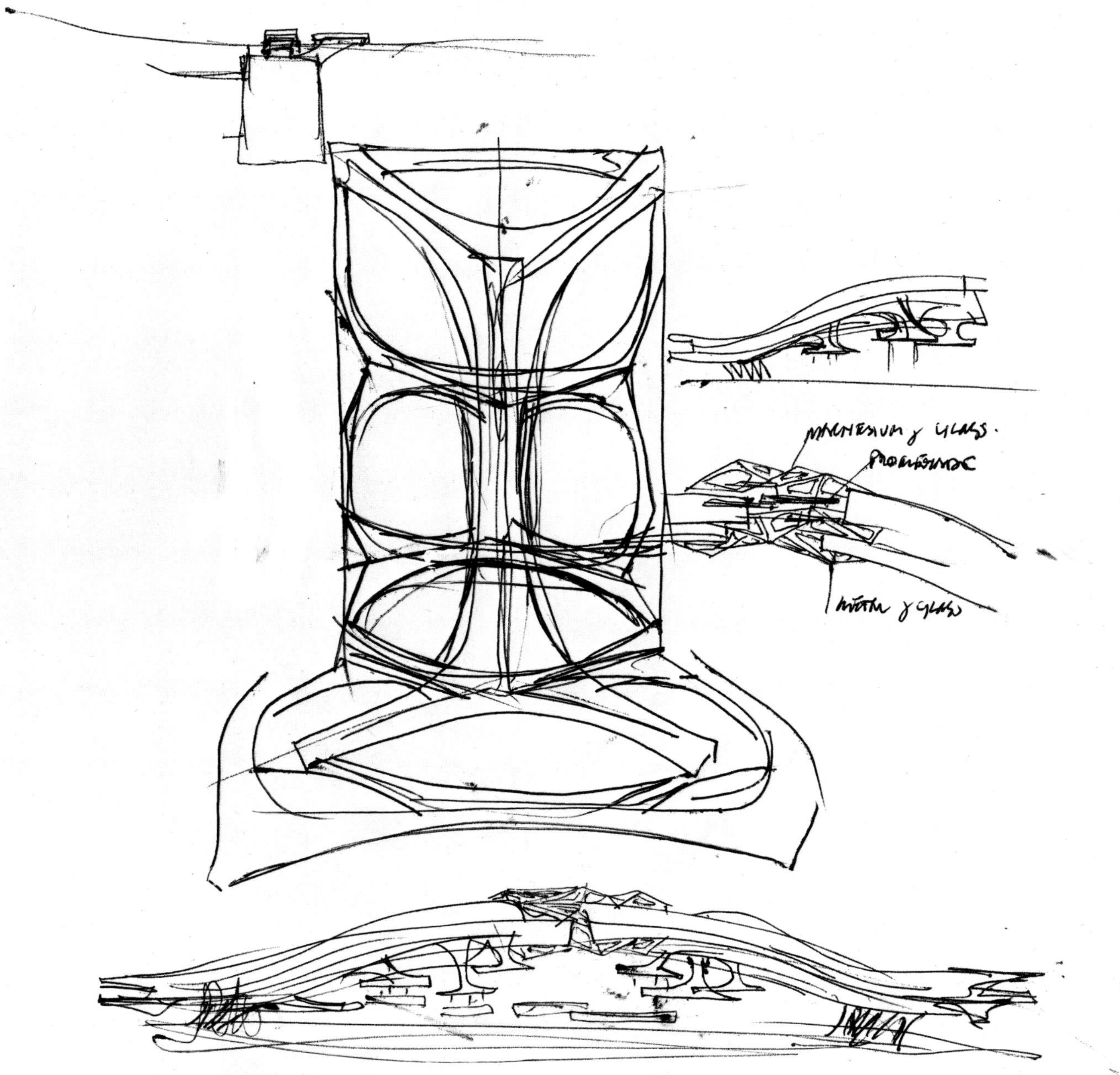
MAGNESIUM y GLASS.
PROMENADE
METAL y GLASS

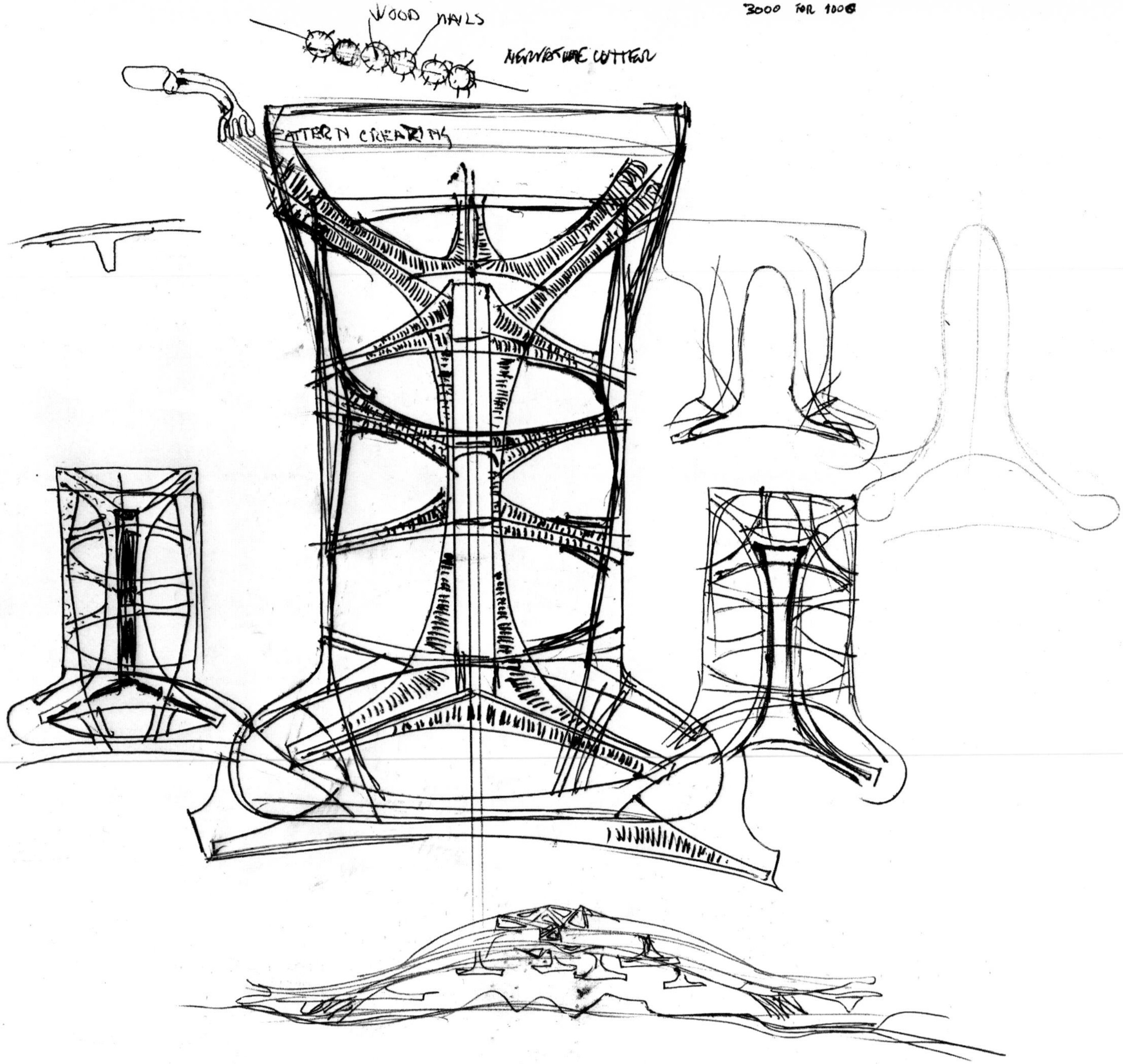

WOOD NAILS
3000 FOR 1000
PATTERN CREATING

OCTOBER 61 PARADISE VALLEY

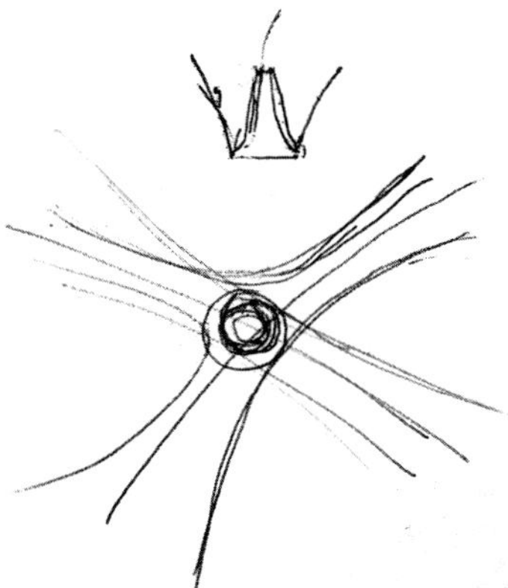

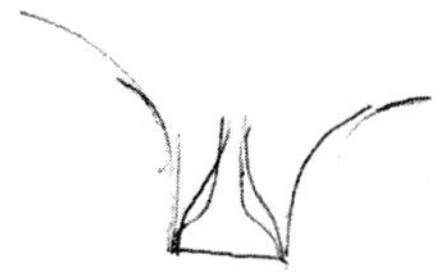

LOOKING OUTWARDLY, FROM THE CENTER OF THE EGO ITS LOOKING ALLWAYS AT THE SAME FACE OF REALITY,

AS BEEING AT THE CENTER OF A PHISICAL UNIVERSE (ROTATING ON IT) PRESENTING AT ANY TIME & ANY POSITION EACH COMPONENT "FACE DOWN" ON THE CENTER. SAME FACE & SAME RELATIVITY.

LEAVE THE CENTER & WANDER ABOUT IS THE WAY TO DISCOVER THE OTHER FACES OF THINGS & KNIT THEM THEYR TRUER DIMENTIONS

ONE SO DOES IF HE SEEKS SOLUTION OF CONFLICT BY CHOOSING TO SEATE IN THE "BROTHERS" SEAT & FIND OUT THE REASONS OF HIS "MISCONDUCT"

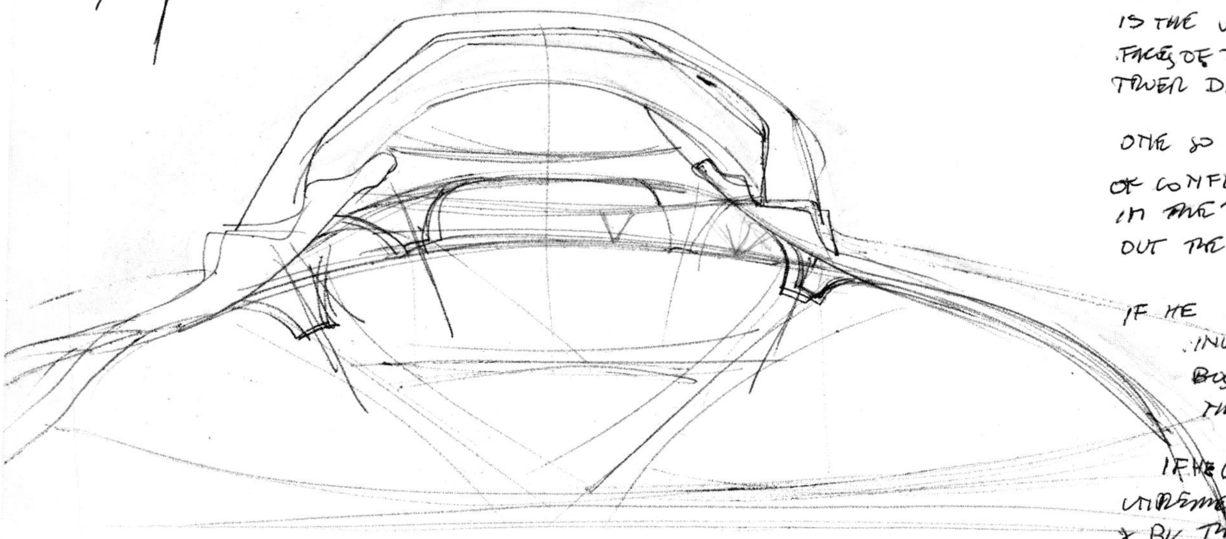

IF HE CONSENTS TO THE CAT INVITATIONS & LYE AMONG THE BUSHES IN DOZING ALERTENESS

IF HE COMPLAYS TO THE WATER UNRELENTTING DOWNGRADING GOOING & BY THE SAME EFFORTLESS NECESSITY TOUCHES ON THINGS AT BAY

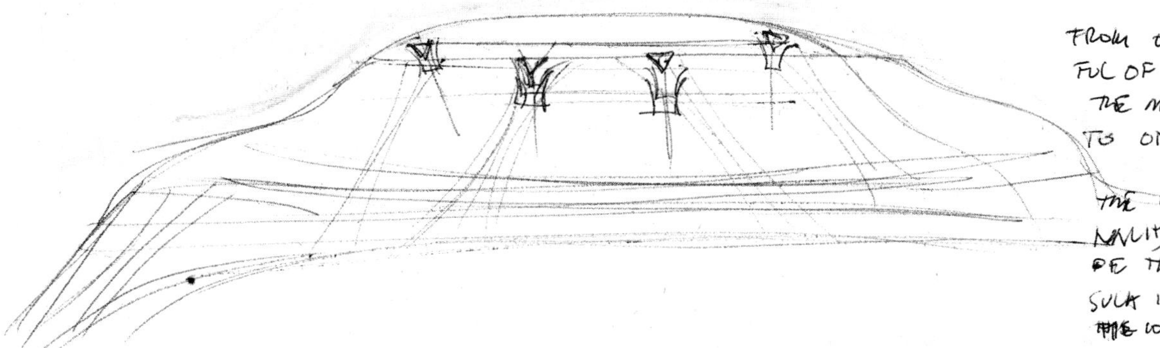

FROM ONES OWN CENTER, FORGETFUL OF THE CONCEILED FACE OF THE MANY MOONS ONE PROCURES TO ONES' ~~CONSCIOUSNESS~~ INTELLECT A PHOTOGRAPHIC DIAGRAM OF THE WOLE & THE POLIDIMENTIONALITY OF IT WILL FOREVER ESCAPE NOT HIS KNOWLEDGE THAT SUCH IS THE FATE OF MAN BUT EVEN THE CONCIOUSNESS OF IT.

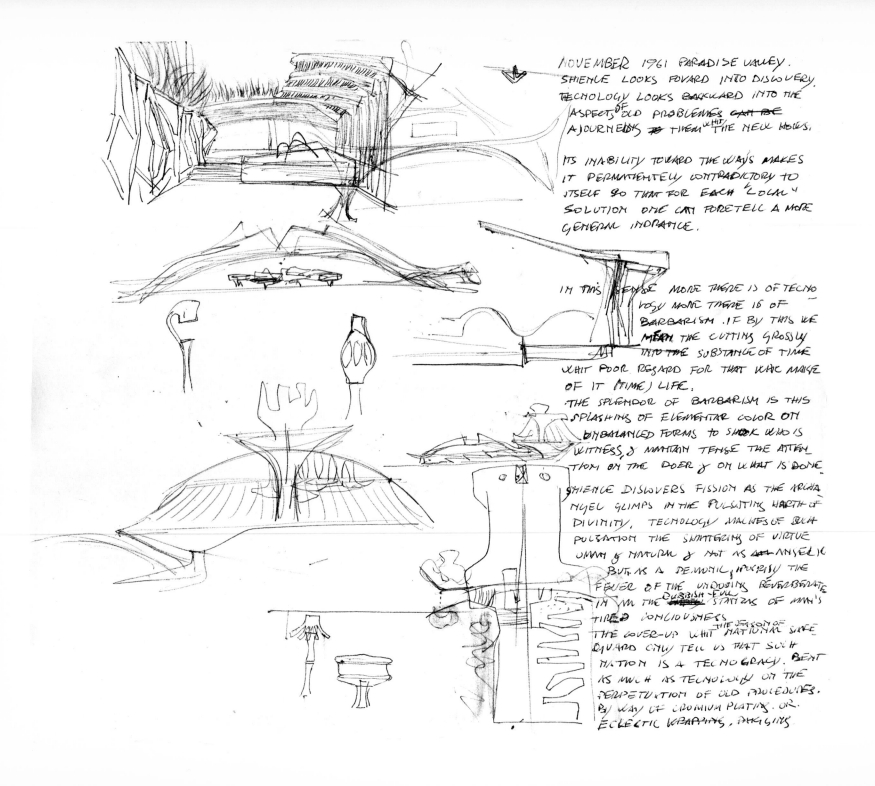

NOVEMBER 1961 PARADISE VALLEY.
SHIENCE LOOKS FOVARD INTO DISCOVERY.
TECNOLOGY LOOKS BACKWARD INTO THE
ASPECTS OF OLD PROBLEMES ~~CAN BE~~
ADJOURNEDS ~~TO~~ THEM WHIT THE NEW HOWS.

ITS INABILITY TOWARD THE WAYS MAKES
IT PERMANENTELY CONTRADICTORY TO
ITSELF SO THAT FOR EACH "LOCAL"
SOLUTION ONE CAN FORETELL A MORE
GENERAL INORANCE.

IN THIS SENSE MORE THERE IS OF TECNO
LOGY MORE THERE IS OF
BARBARISM. IF BY THIS WE
MEAN THE CUTTING GROSSLY
INTO THE SUBSTANCE OF TIME
WHIT POOR REGARD FOR THAT WHIC MAKE
OF IT (TIME) LIFE.
THE SPLENDOR OF BARBARISM IS THIS
SPLASHING OF ELEMENTAR COLOR ON
UNBALANCED FORMS TO SHOCK WHO IS
WITNESS, & MANTAIN TENSE THE ATTEN
TION ON THE DOER & ON WHAT IS DONE.
SHIENCE DISCOVERS FISSION AS THE ARCHA
NGEL GLIMPS IN THE PULSATING HARTH OF
DIVINITY, TECNOLOGY MACHINES OF SUCH
PULSATION THE SHATTERING OF VIRTUE
UMAN & NATURAL & NOT AS ANGELIC
BUT AS A DEMONIC, IPOCRISY THE
FEVER OF THE UNDOING REVERBERATE
IN ALL THE RUBBISH-FULL STATIONS OF MAN'S
TIRED CONCIOUSNESS.
THE COVER-UP WHIT THE REASON OF NATIONAL SAFE
GUARD ONLY TELL US THAT SUCH
NATION IS A TECNOCRACY. BEST
AS MUCH AS TECNOLOGY ON THE
PERPETUATION OF OLD PROCEDURES.
BY WAY OF CROMIUM PLATING. OR.
ECLECTIC WRAPPING, PAGGING

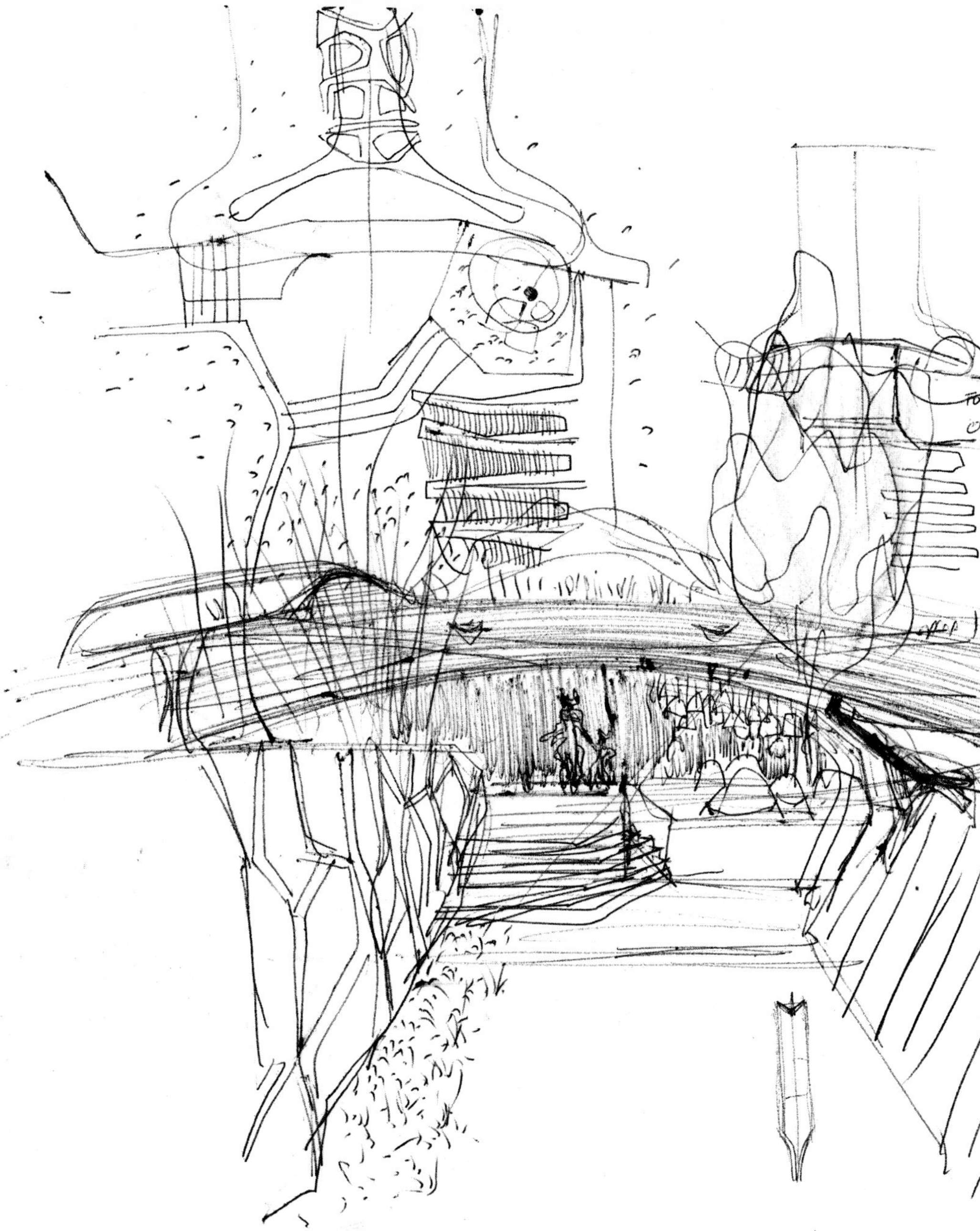

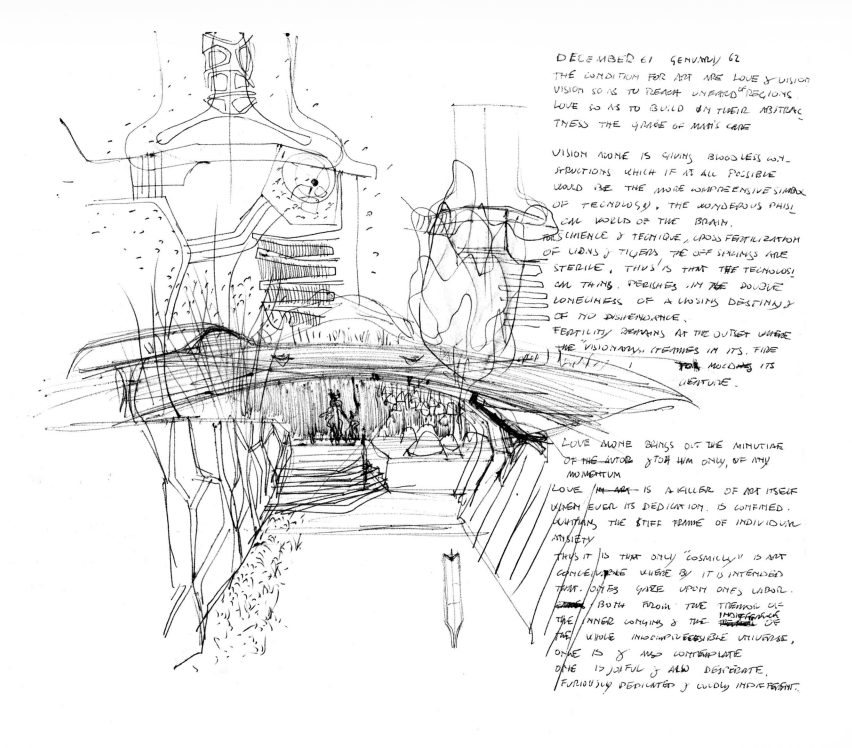

DECEMBER 61 GENUARY 62

THE CONDITION FOR ART ARE LOVE & VISION
VISION SO AS TO REACH UNHEARD OF REGIONS.
LOVE SO AS TO BUILD ~~ON~~ IN THEIR ABSTRACTNESS THE GRACE OF MAN'S CARE

VISION ALONE IS GIVING BLOODLESS CONSTRUCTIONS WHICH IF AT ALL POSSIBLE WOULD BE THE MORE COMPREENSIVE SIMBOL OF TECNOLOGY, THE WONDEROUS PHISICAL WORLD OF THE BRAIN.
~~FOR~~ SCHIENCE & TECNIQUE, CROSS FERTILIZATION OF LIONS & TIGERS THE OFF SPRINGS ARE STERILE, THUS IT IS THAT THE TECNOLOGICAL THING PERISHES IN ~~THE~~ DOUBLE LONELINESS OF A LOSING DESTINY & OF NO DISHENDANCE.
FERTILITY REMAINS AT THE OUTSET WHERE THE "VISIONARY" CREAMES IN ITS FIRE ~~FOR~~ MOLDING ITS CREATURE.

LOVE ALONE BRINGS OUT THE MINUTIAE ~~OF THE AUTOR~~ & TO HIM ONLY, OF ANY MOMENTUM
LOVE ~~IN ART~~ IS A KILLER OF ART ITSELF WHEN EVER ITS DEDICATION IS CONFINED. WITHIN THE STIFF FRAME OF INDIVIDUAL ANSIETY
THUS IT IS THAT ONLY "COSMICLY" IS ART CONCEIVABLE WHERE BY IT IS INTENDED THAT. ONES GAZE UPON ONES LABOR. ~~[illegible]~~ BOTH FROM THE TREMOR OF THE INNER LONGING & THE ~~[illegible]~~ INDIFFERENCE OF THE WHOLE INCOMPRENSIBLE UNIVERSE,
ONE IS & ALSO CONTEMPLATE
ONE IS JOIFUL & ALSO DESPERATE,
FURIOUSLY DEDICATED & COLDLY INDIFFERENT.

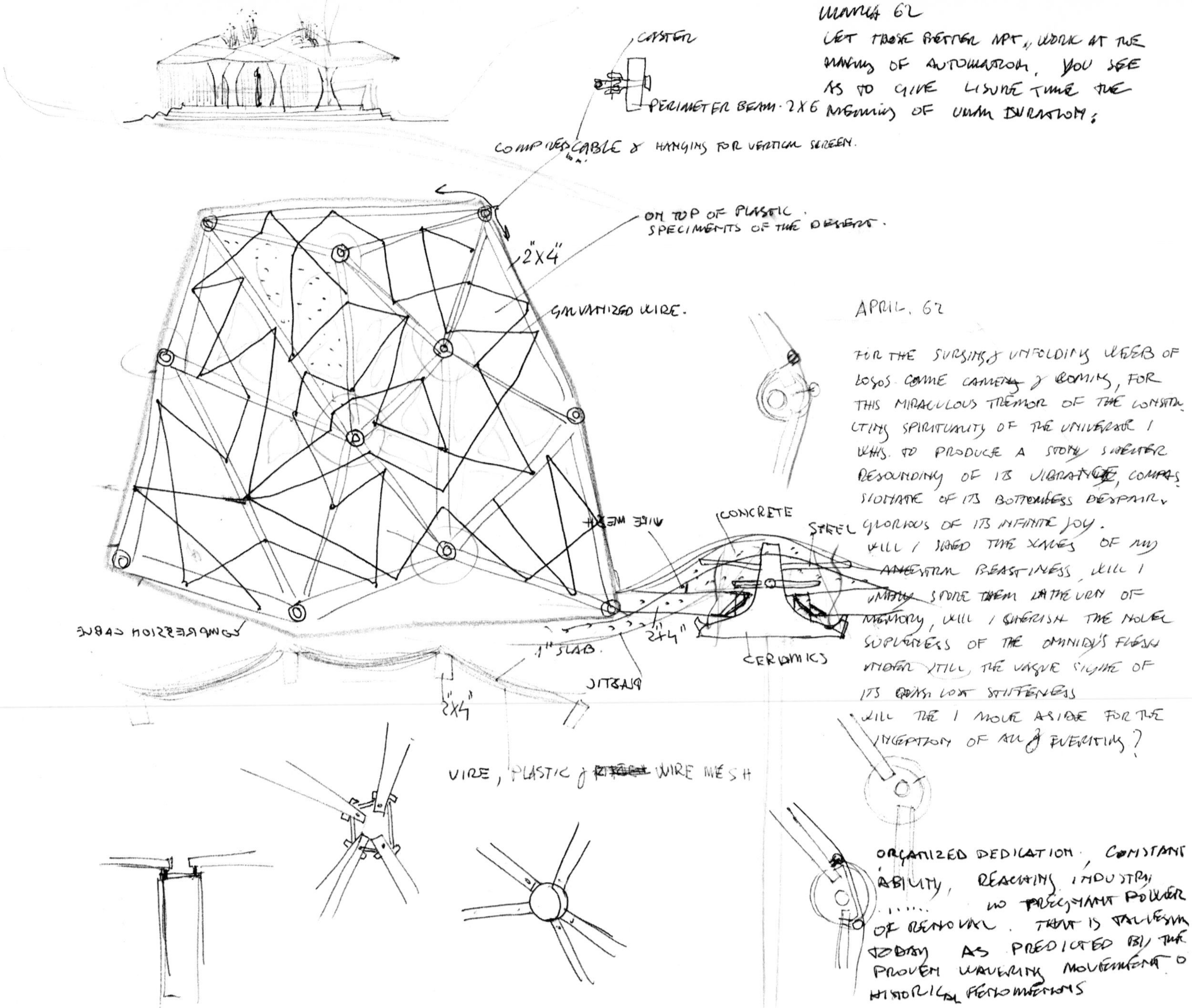
CASTER
PERIMETER BEAM · 2 X 6
CABLE & HANGINGS FOR VERTICAL SCREEN.
ON TOP OF PLASTIC
SPECIMENTS OF THE DESERT.
2" X 4"
GALVANIZED WIRE.
APRIL. 62
FOR THE SURGING & UNFOLDING WEB OF LOGOS COMING & GOING, FOR THIS MIRACULOUS TREMOR OF THE CONSTANTLY SPIRITUALITY OF THE UNIVERSE I WISH TO PRODUCE A STONY SHELTER RESOUNDING OF ITS VIBRANCE, COMPASSIONATE OF ITS BOTTOMLESS DESPAIR, GLORIOUS OF ITS INFINITE JOY.
CONCRETE
STEEL
COMPRESSION CABLE
1" SLAB.
2" X 4"
PLASTIC
CERAMICS
WIRE, PLASTIC & WIRE MESH
ORGANIZED DEDICATION, CONSTANT ABILITY, REACHING INDUSTRY

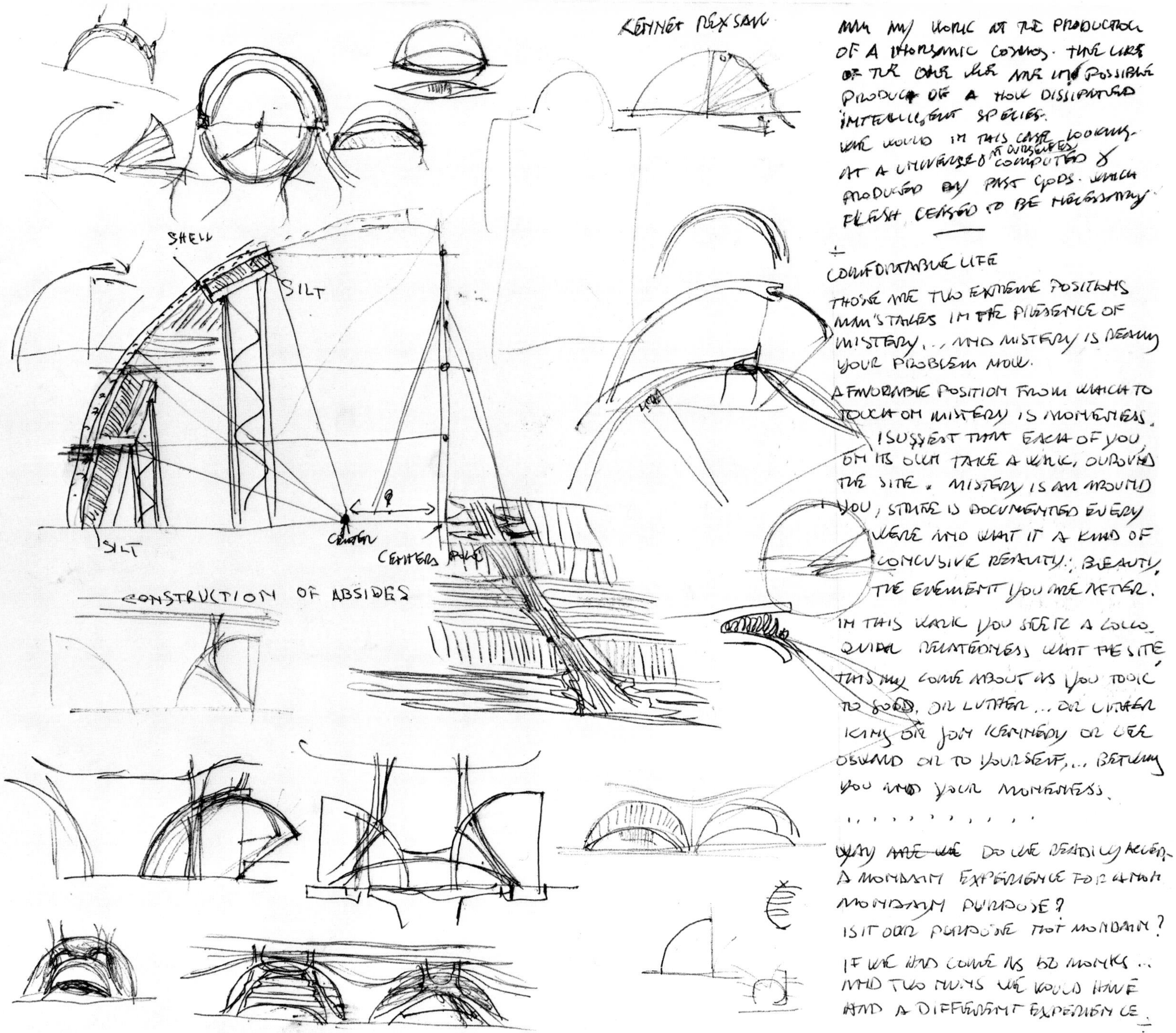
SHELL
SILT
SILT
CENTER
CENTERS
CONSTRUCTION OF ABSIDES
MAN MY WORK AT THE PRODUCTION
OF A INORGANIC COSMOS. THE LIFE
OF THE ONE WE ARE IMPOSSIBLE
PRODUCT OF A NOW DISSIPATED
INTELLIGENT SPECIES.
WE WOULD IN THIS CASE LOOKING
AT OURSELVES
AT A UNIVERSE OF COMPUTED &
PRODUCED BY PAST GODS. WHICH
FLESH CEASED TO BE NECESSARY.
COMFORTABLE LIFE
THOSE ARE TWO EXTREME POSITIONS
MAN'S TAKES IN THE PRESENCE OF
MISTERY... AND MISTERY IS REALLY
YOUR PROBLEM NOW.
A FAVORABLE POSITION FROM WHICH TO
TOUCH ON MISTERY IS LONENESS.
I SUGGEST THAT EACH OF YOU,
ON ITS OWN TAKE A WALK, AROUND
THE SITE. MISTERY IS ALL AROUND
YOU, STATE IS DOCUMENTED EVERY
WERE AND WHAT IT A KIND OF
CONCLUSIVE BEAUTY; BEAUTY,
THE ELEMENT YOU ARE AFTER.
IN THIS WALK YOU SEEK A COLLO-
QUIAL RELATIONSHIP WITH THE SITE,
THIS MAY COME ABOUT AS YOU TALK
TO GOD, OR LUTHER ... OR LUTHER
KING OR JON KENNEDY OR LEE
OSWALD OR TO YOURSELF,... BETWEEN
YOU AND YOUR LONENESS.
~~WHY ARE WE~~ DO WE READILY ACCEPT
A MUNDANE EXPERIENCE FOR A NON
MUNDANE PURPOSE?
IS IT OUR PURPOSE NOT MUNDANE?
IF WE HAD COME AS 50 MONKS ...
AND TWO NUNS WE WOULD HAVE
HAD A DIFFERENT EXPERIENCE.

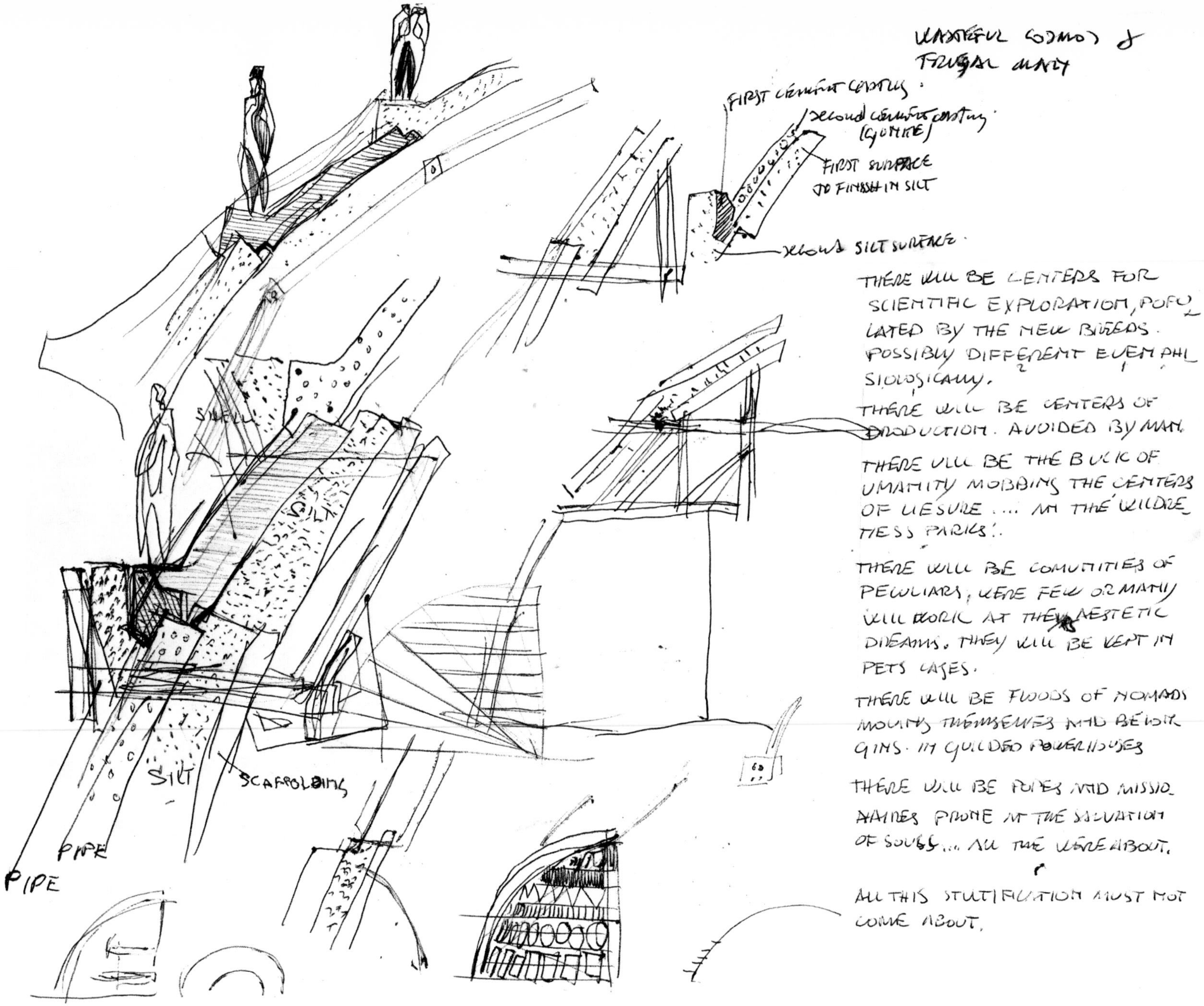
WASTEFUL COSMOS &
FRUGAL MAN
FIRST CEMENT COATING.
SECOND CEMENT COATING.
(GUNITE)
FIRST SURFACE
TO FINISH IN SILT
SECOND SILT SURFACE.
THERE WILL BE CENTERS FOR SCIENTIFIC EXPLORATION, POPULATED BY THE NEW BREEDS. POSSIBLY DIFFERENT EVEN PHYSIOLOGICALLY.
THERE WILL BE CENTERS OF PRODUCTION. AVOIDED BY MAN.
THERE WILL BE THE BULK OF HUMANITY MOBBING THE CENTERS OF LEISURE .... IN THE WILDERNESS PARKS!.
THERE WILL BE COMMUNITIES OF PECULIARS, WERE FEW OR MANY WILL WORK AT THEIR AESTETIC DREAMS. THEY WILL BE KEPT IN PETS CAGES.
THERE WILL BE FLOODS OF NOMADS MOVING THEMSELVES AND BEING IN GUILDED POWERHOUSES
THERE WILL BE POPES AND MISSIONARIES PRONE AT THE SALVATION OF SOULS.... ALL THE WEREABOUT.
ALL THIS STULTIFICATION MUST NOT COME ABOUT.
SHELL
SILT
SILT
SCAFFOLDING
PIPE
PIPE

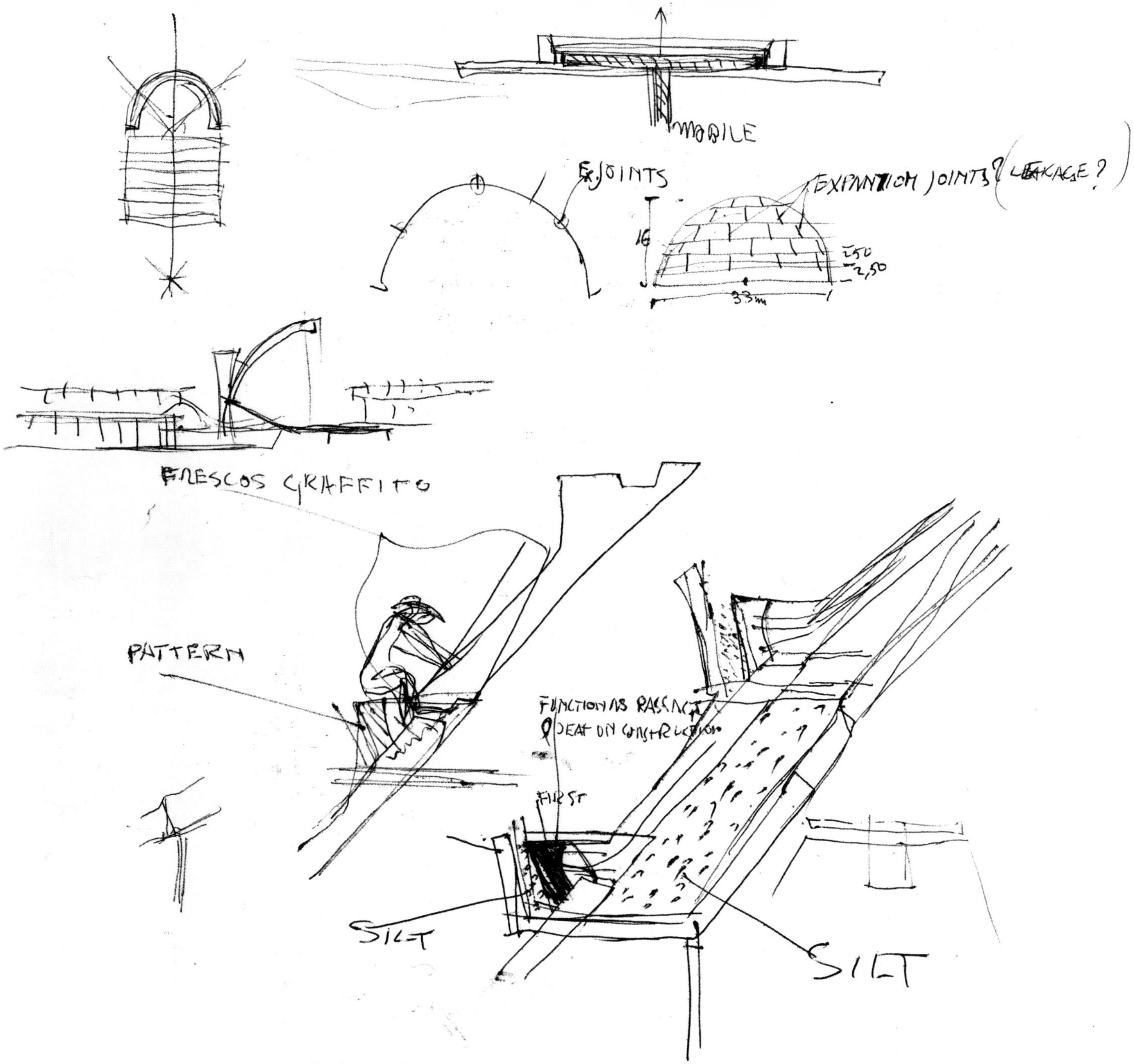
MOBILE
E.JOINTS
EXPANTION JOINTS? (LEAKAGE?)
16
33m
FRESCOS GRAFFITO
PATTERN
FUNCTION AS PASSAGE
IDEA ON CONSTRUCTION
FIRST
SILT
SILT

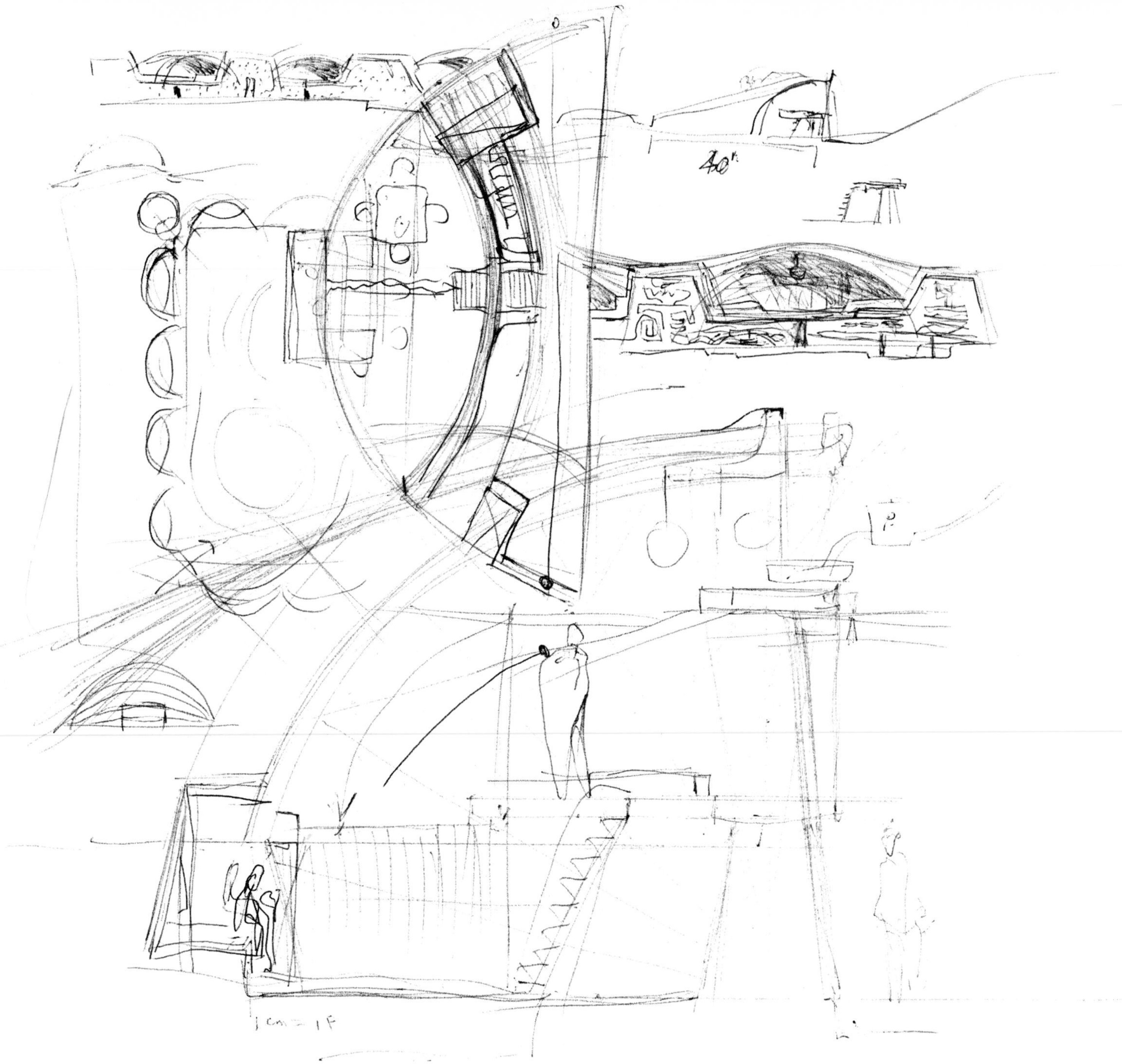

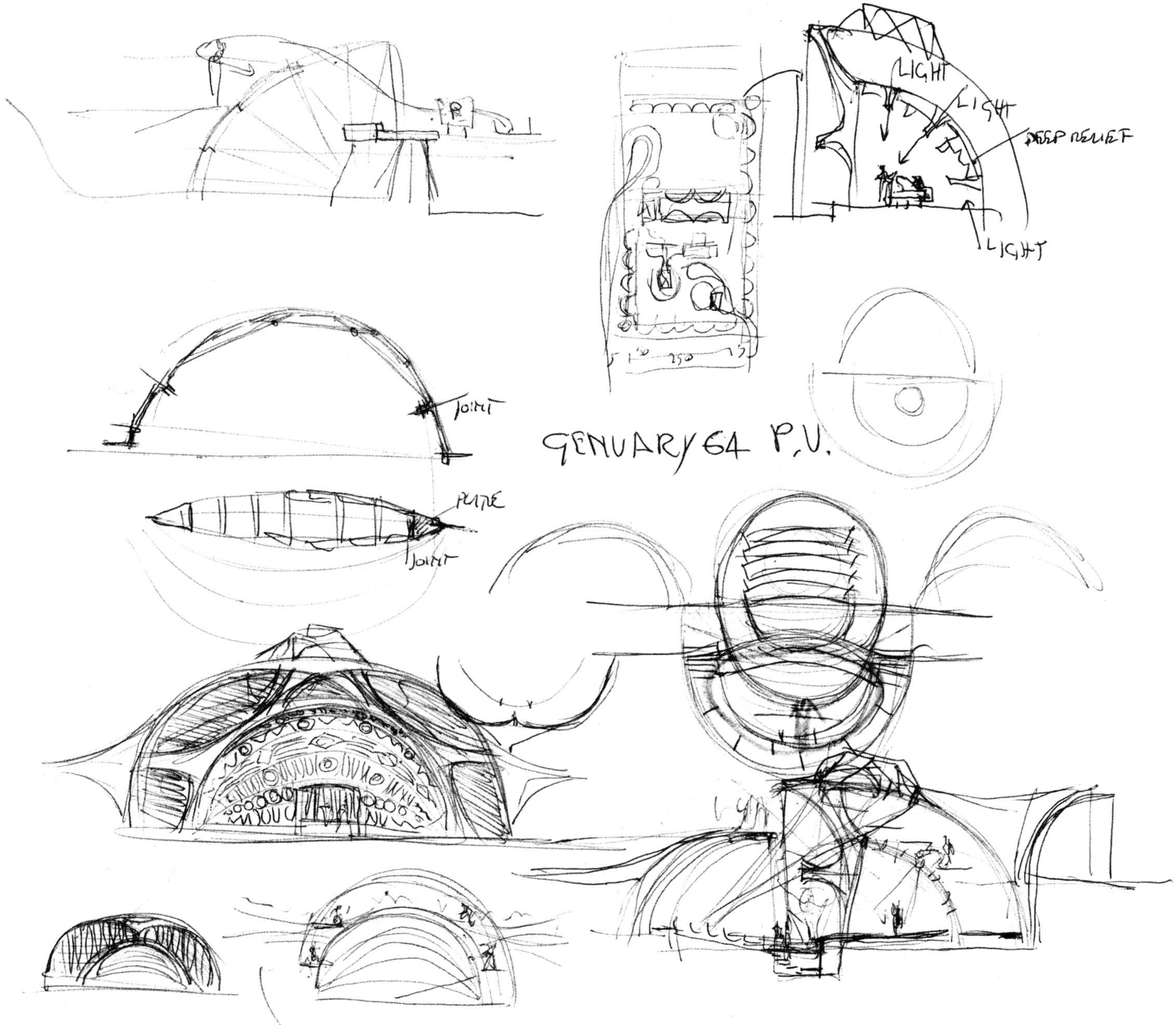
LIGHT
LIGHT
DEEP RELIEF
LIGHT
JOINT
GENUARY 64 P.V.
PLATE
JOINT

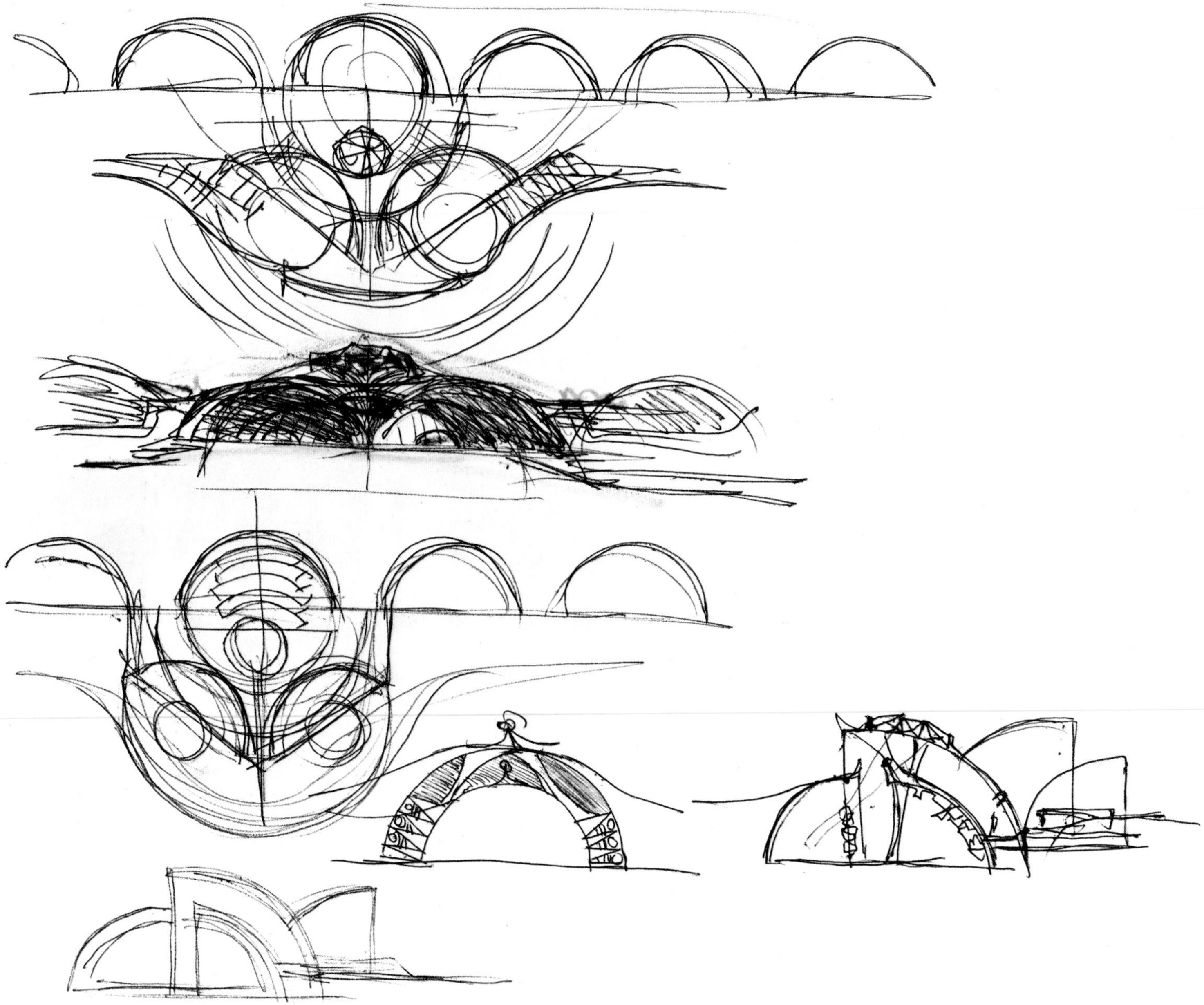

Highway (Linear City)

1970
Le Corbusier, as a god prophet, saw that, where there is a function demanding large investments and substantial intrusion on the land, you might as well make full and multiple use of the instrument you construct (the road becoming the roof of a continuous building). One of the things that marks an instrument for obsolescence is its narrow specialization. This is certainly a virtue when the instrument is a small fraction of a larger process and its task is so "absorbing" as to veto distraction or secondary actions. One can hardly object to the narrowness of a bench drill or a fan. The aberrant thing comes about when the instrument achieves environmental proportions and becomes a preponderant part of the envelope sheltering and serving man. If the envelope was built in obsolescence (often defined by a mortgage coverage), the expediency of the instrument imprints itself on the people who are tied to its performance. Obsolescent environment makes expedient people.

The specter of not keeping up with the times because of an environment that is too "permanent" is one of the afflictions of poor perspective. Even though communication time has enormously decreased and production time has been separated from hand manipulation and its "organic" pulse, psychological growth and real knowledge have not left the channel where they develop for a faster one, certainly not much faster. How could they? Biological changes are enormously slow for our limited patience, and the mind can go only so far out without balking. The naked mind is a dangerous and savage mind, a mind of abstraction and segregation, a deadly mind. It is unfortunate, but possibly unavoidable, that the inventive mind, the technologically inclined, tends to be the naked mind. (The most productive age span of discoverers and inventors is in the twenties.) It is the naked mind and the desensitized body that find an obsolescent environment to their liking. They indeed are alike, both sensing the presence of a dark chasm of senselessness only one step ahead of themselves, as if man's fall reflected itself endlessly on the sloping bastions of a deterministic and indifferent universe.

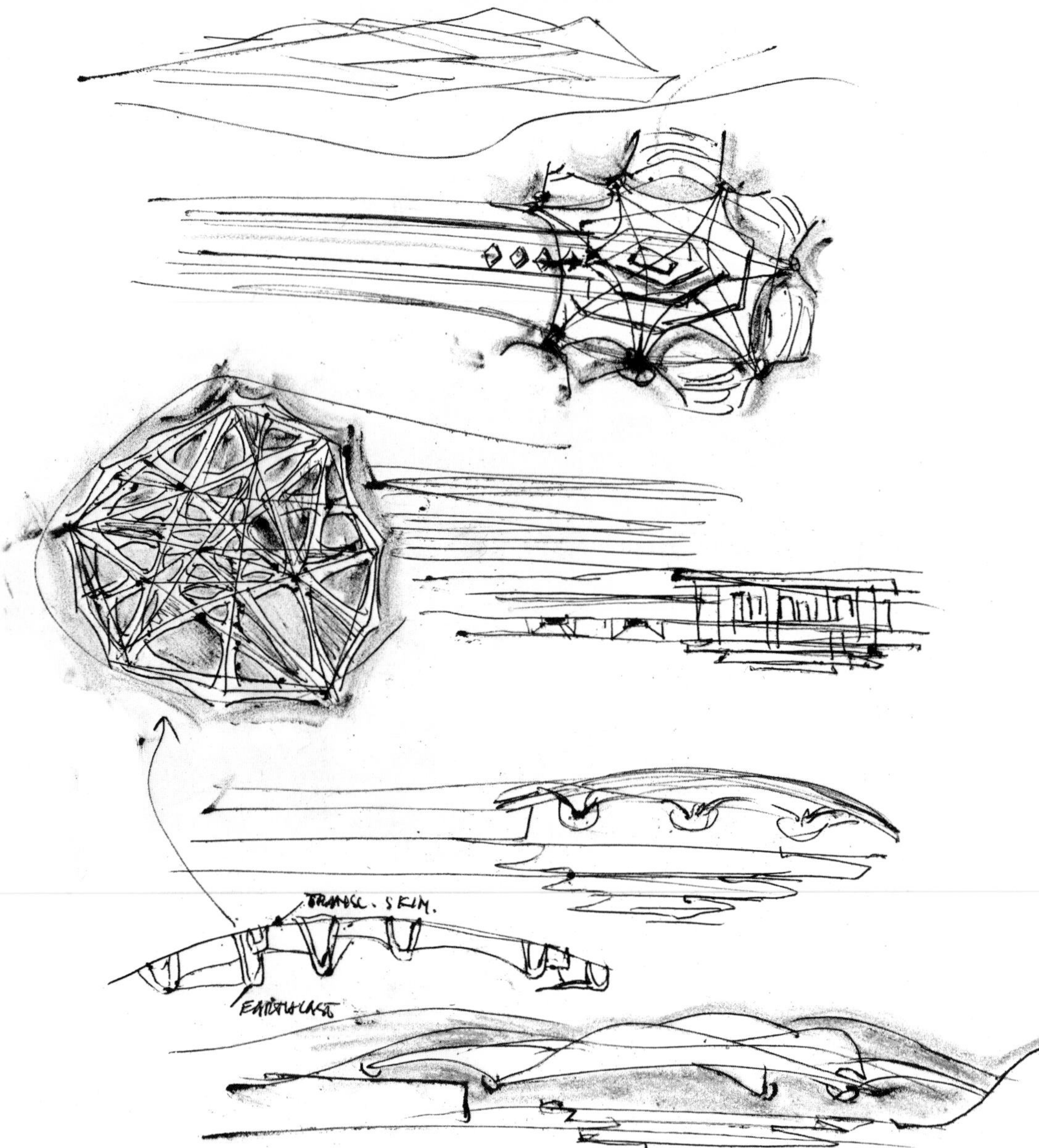

AS TO IMAGINE A WORLD OF SUCH BEEINGS IS UTTERLY IMPOSSIBLE WE RUSH TO THE CONCLUSION USUALLY ACCEPTED IN REGARD TO THE UNKNOWN: IT MUST BE OSTILE POSSIBLY DEADLY

EVEN THE THINKING OF IT AS A POSSIBILITY IS IN ITSELF EVIL

THE CHURCHES WOULD BE IN THE FOREFRONT OF CONDEMNATION, & THE LOUDEST THOSE THAT MORE WANTS THE FLESH MORTIFIED: SINFUL YES BUT INDISPENSABLE (THE FLESH),

GENETIC DONE WHAT, ORGANIC MEMORY, INSTINCT, DURATION DONE WHAT THESE, WILL WE BE ALSO "DISENGAGED", FROM EMOTIONS, FEARS, LOVE, HATRED BEAUTY, COMPASSION, ?
WILL BE KNOWLEDGE ALL WHAT TO BE WELL BEE? ALMOST AS THE FULL CIRCLE FROM THE UNQUESTIONABLE MATEMATICAL BUT UNCONCIOUS BEING OF THE PHISICAL UNIVERSE THROUGH THE BRIEF GLOW OF LIFE-HETICS WILL CLOSE BY THE UNQUESTIONABLE, MATEMATICAL SELF CONCIOUS POST LIFE, POST HETIC BEING OF AN "INTELLIGENT" PHISICAL UNIVERSE

EVEN THUS GRAND SCHEME SEEME TO INDICATE THAT KNOWLEDGE HAS TO BE CONQUERED TROUGH THE UNPREDICTABLE OF HUMAN EMOTIVITY THUS NO KNOWLEDGE WITHOUT AGONY.

AGONY & HETIC WHIC COULD BE PECULIAR TO THE "HUMAN" FASE OF EVOLUTION. AS MEANS TO REACH SUCH A PLATEAU OF KNOWLEDGE THAT WOULD INABLE LIFE TO BECAME ROBE LOGOS.

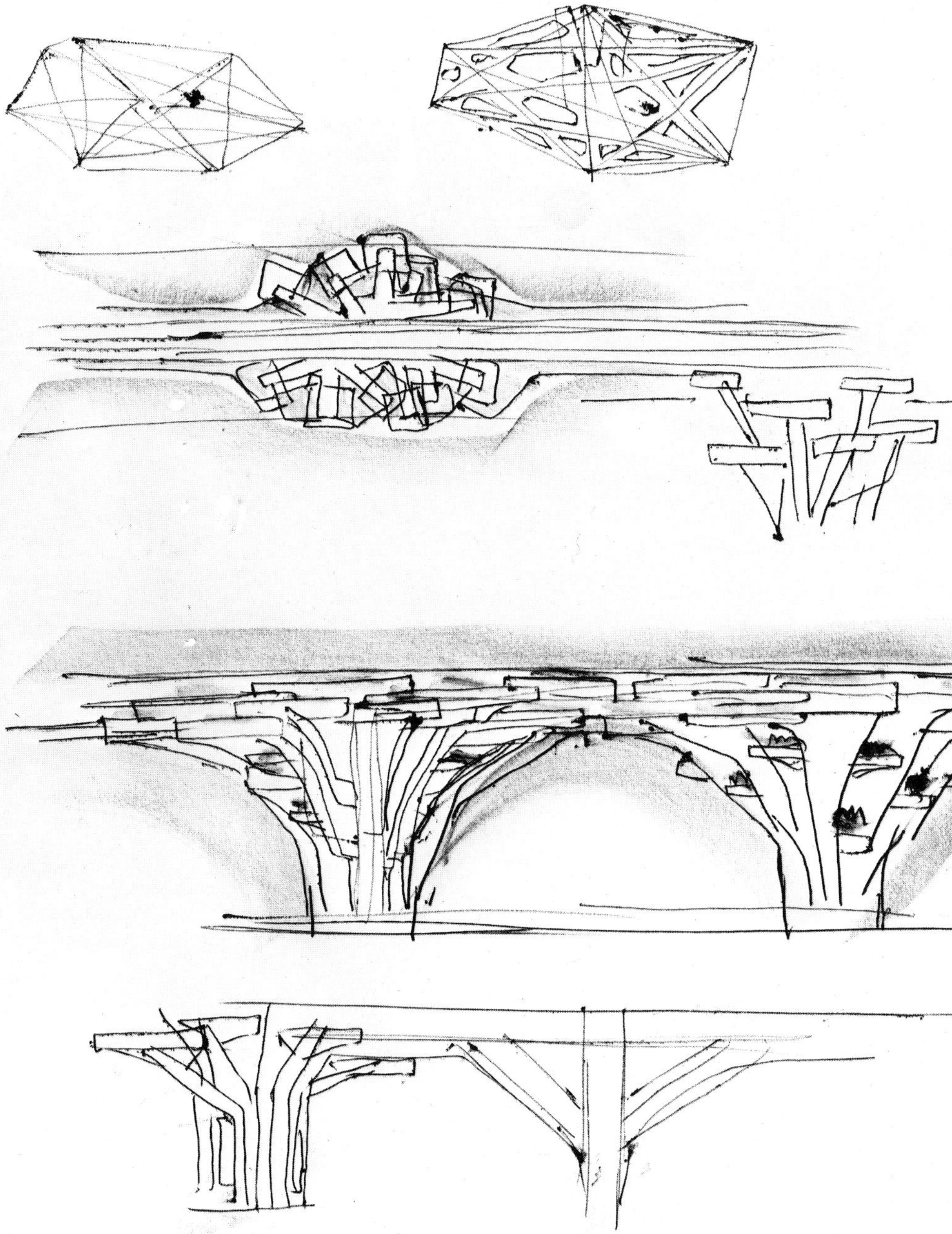

IT MAY BE THAT THE DIFFERENCE BET-
WEEN PHILANTROPHY & ART AS ACTION
IS THAT WHILE THE FORMER IS A CONSCIENT
EFFORT STRIVING TO ALLEVIATE MISERY
& PER SE MAY BE CARRYING MAINLY THE
DRUDGERY OF THE "GIVING"
THE LATTER IS MAINLY THE JOY OF
GIVING BIRTH TO THE NOT YET & ITS
~~GIVING~~ BENEFACTORING IS ONLY THE
UNAVOIDABLE BY PRODUCT OF IT

IT REMAINS THE TRADITIONAL ATTITUDE
OF LOOKING UPON PHILANTROPHY AS A
GESTURE OF GENEROUS GIVING OF ONE
~~SELF~~ & UPON ARTISTRY AS THE TOTAL-
LY EGOISTIC CONDITION BY WHICH THE
MAKER IS ARDLY ACCEPTED AS A
HUMAN ELEMENT AMONG A HUMAN SOCIETY

IT DOES NOT HURT SO MUCH THE MAKER
TO BE SO ISOLATED BUT THE SOCIETY
ITSELF BY THE SELF DENIAL & GREA-
TER RICHES · WAITING · TO BE ACQUIR-
RED & QUARRIED
NOW OR NEVER UNDER THE
~~NOT REMOVABLE~~
CRUST OR THE SHIELD PUT UP
BY HIM · WHO IS A DEMON SEE-
KING FOR THINGS TO MOLD SO THAT
MEANINGS & CREATURES KEEP EMERGING FROM THE
EXISTENT FOR THE GOOD OF THE EXISTENT.

THE MAKING OF SUCH MEANING & CREA-
TURE ~~...~~ CARRIES AN HOLINESS OF HIS
OWN BUT IT IS BY NO POSSIBLE STAN-
DARD THE HOLINESS OF A TRANQUIL
"IF NOT NOW TOMORROW, IF NOT BLUE, CERULEAN"
APPREHENSION.
WOMEN KNOW THAT THE MAKING OF A
NEW BEING & PARTICULARLY ITS BIRTH
IS MATTER FOR CONSUMING STRIFE

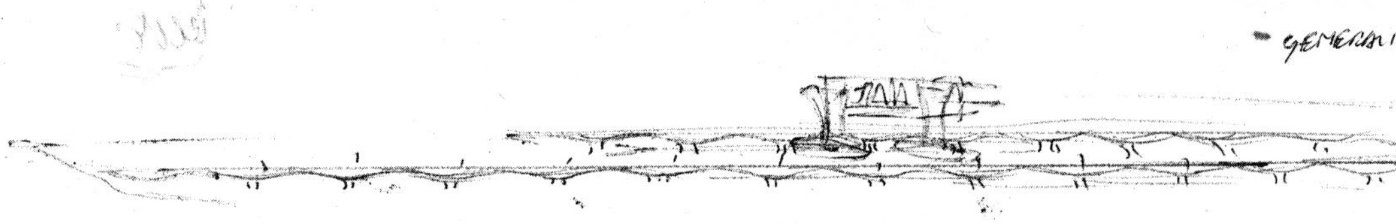

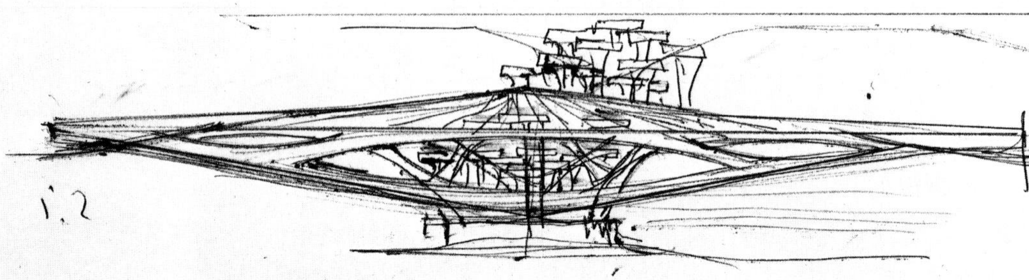

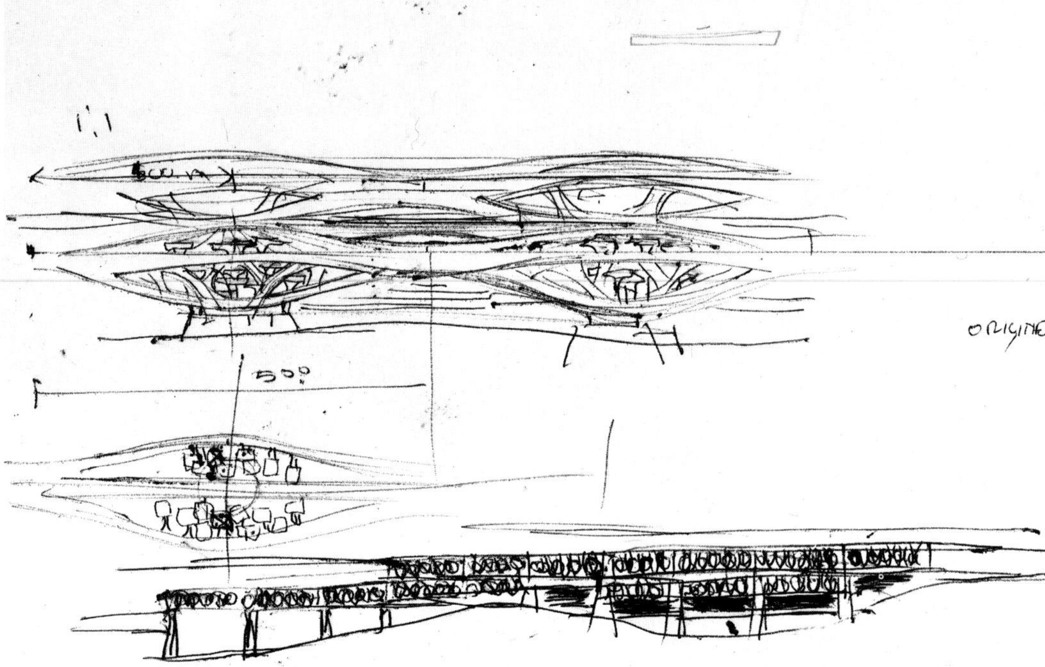

GENUARY 1962

– GENERALITIES FOR GRAHAM FUNDATION:

CONCEPTION OF A CITY OF 2'000'000 PEOPLE ON THE HIGH LAND OF THE WEST ~~ARIZONA~~ OR ~~NEW MEXICO~~ OR MEXICO OR LAND OF SIMILAR CLIMATIC & GEOLOGICAL CARACTERS

THE CITY & THE SORROUNDING REGION IS SUPPOSEDLY INTERNATIONALIZED, UNDER A "WORLD GOVERNEMENT" AUTORITY, CONSEQUENTLY THE CITY ~~WOULD~~ INCORPORATES FISICALLY EVERY MAN'S DESIRE FOR BETTERMENT & CREATIVENESS.

ONE MAY NOTICE THAT SUCH AN UNDERTAKING IN AN "UNDERDEVELOPPED" CONTRY WOULD BRING A FORTH A SUDDEN & RADICAL SURGE OF POTENTIALITY & PHYSICAL IMPROVEMENTS, IN ALL FIELD OF ENDEAVOUR.

THE REGION IS FEEDING THE CITY OF FOOD STUFF & ITS BY PRODUCTS, HEAVY INDUSTRIES ARE DEVELOPPING IN THE VALLEYS ADIACENT TO THE MESA THE CITY IS CONSTRUCTED ON.

THE REGIONAL ECOLOGY IS ~~RADICALLY~~ CLOSELY CONTROLLED (CERVED) BY A COMPLEX OF WORKS: WATER SHED, CANALIZATION OF WATER. DAMMES & DIKES OF PLURY FUNCTIONAL CARACTER (RESORT RESERCHE, CULTURE, ART, ~~[illegible]~~ SPORTS).

WATHER WAYS. LAKES. RESERVOIRS...,

AGRICULTURAL COMMUNITIES ARE CONCEIVED ALONG A WATER WAY, ~~[illegible]~~ ("LINEAR CITY")

ORIGINE THE CITY DEVELOPPES AS A CONSEQUENCE OF A RESERCHE PLANT [illegible] BIOPHISIC & [illegible] INTAILING, AN EVER MORE COMPLEX ENVIRONMENTAL CONTRIBUTION IN TERMS OF CULTURAL FACILITIES. LABS. FACILITIES. BRAIN POWER TECHNOLOGICAL CAPABILITIES. SOCIAL, BACK BONE, SPIRITUAL SIGNIFICANCE PHYSICAL SUBSTANCE & THE SINTETIZING FORCE OF THE ARTS.

ENDEED ARTISTIC ACCOMPLISHEMENT IS VIEWED AS THE RESOLUTIVE FORCE & REALITY BY

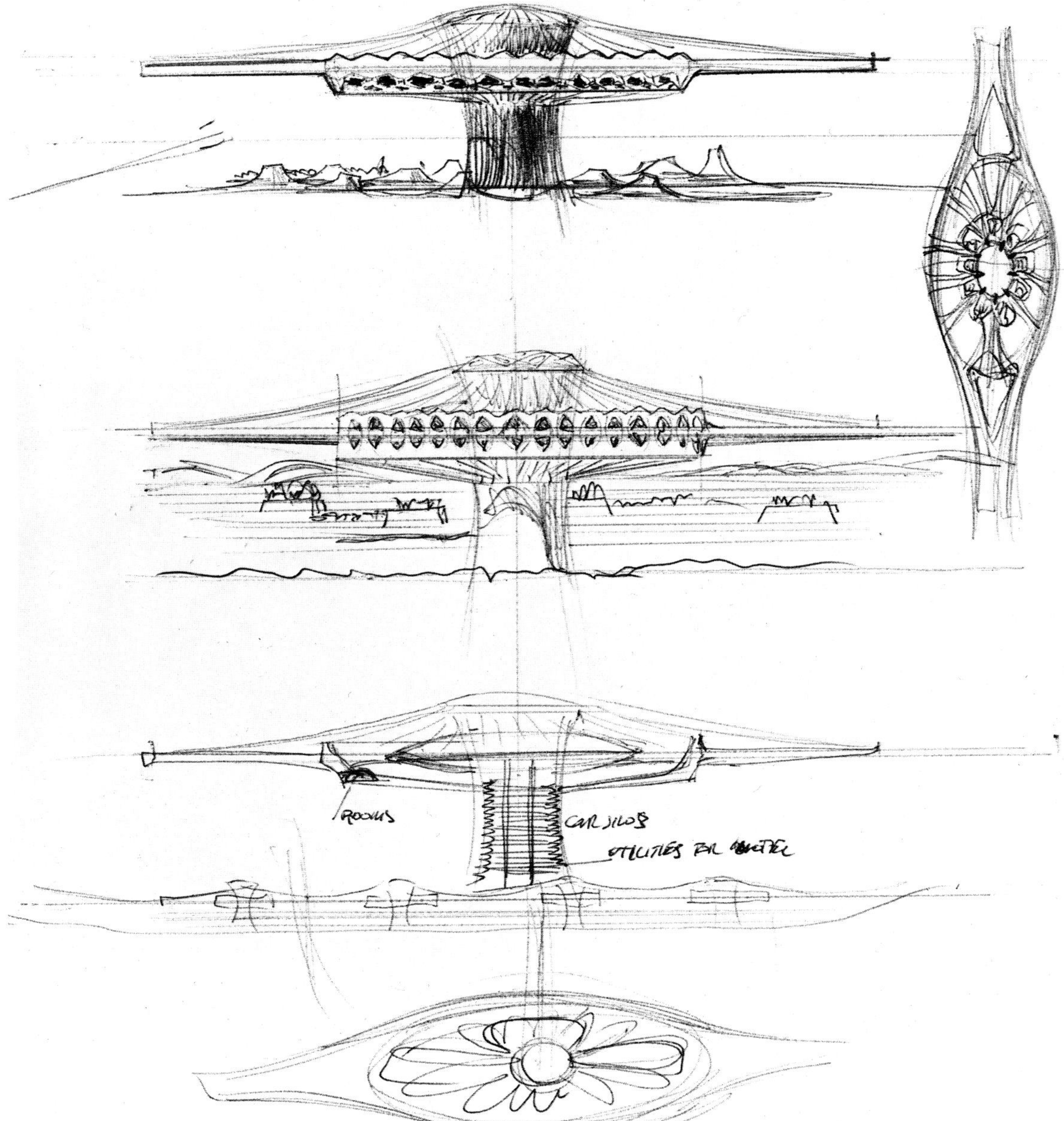
ROOMS
CAR SILOS
UTILITIES FOR

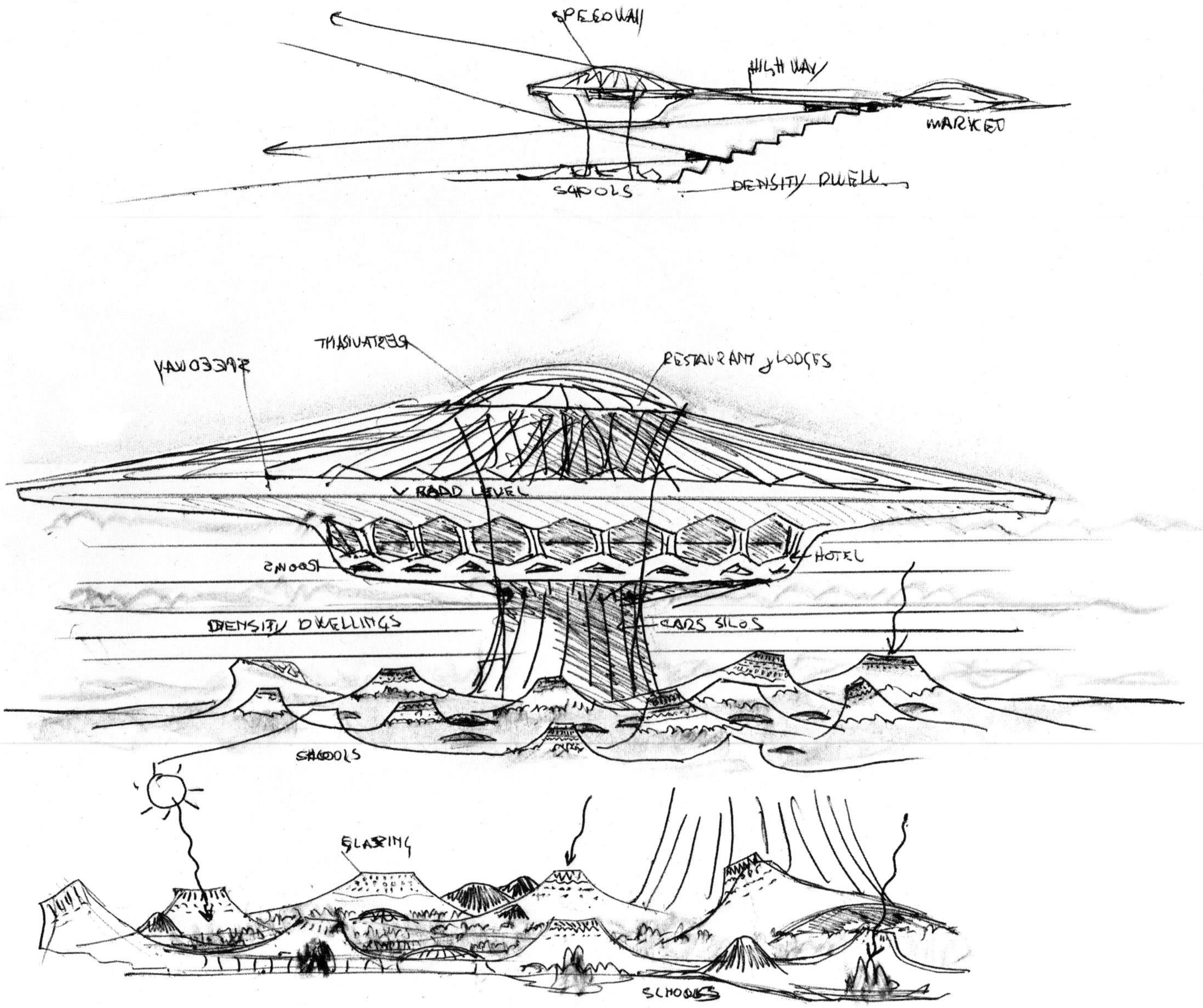

SEPTEMBER 1961 VIADUCT HOTELS - MOTELS CAR SILOS - SECONDARY SKOOLS - SHELTER

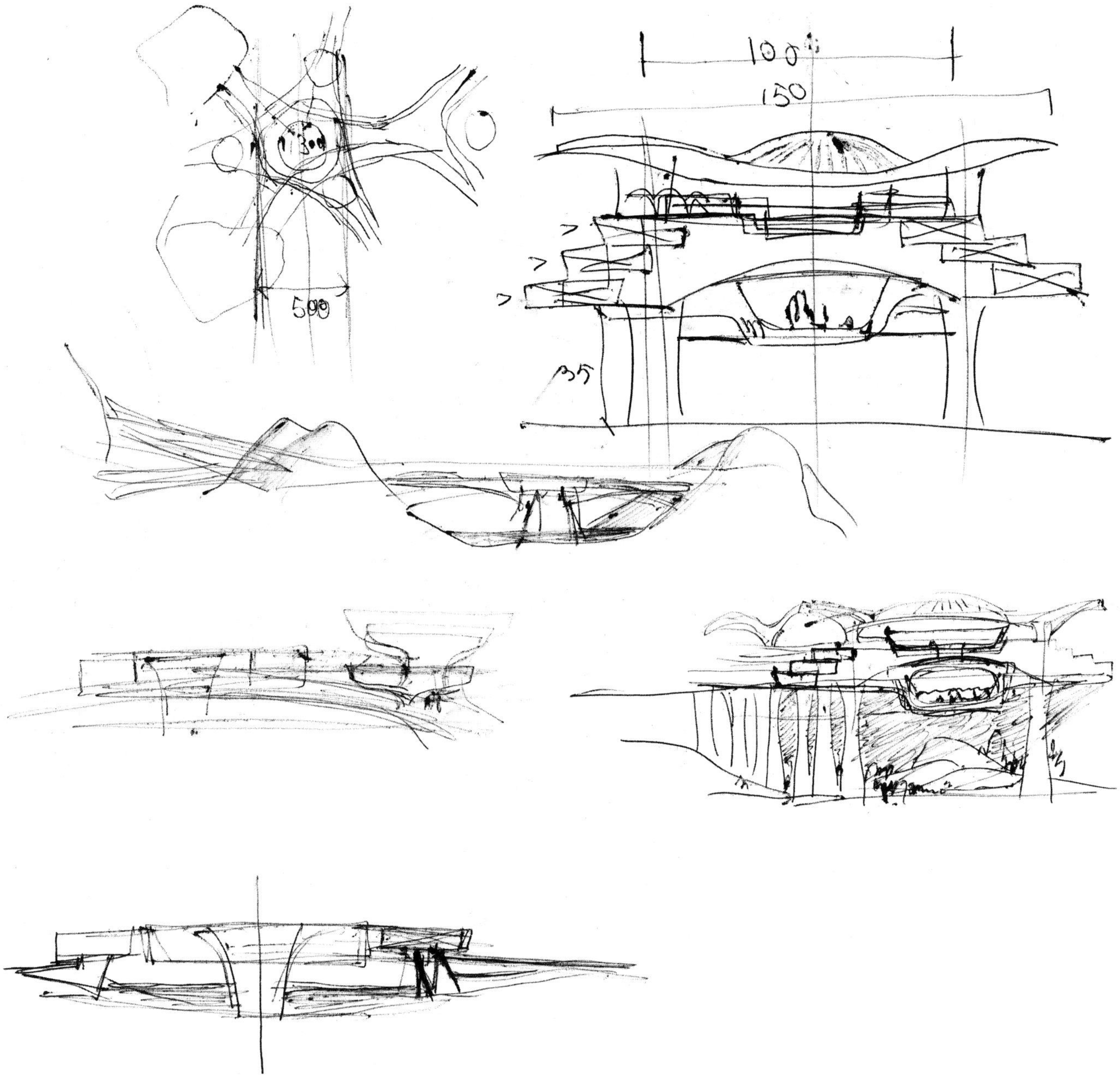
150
35

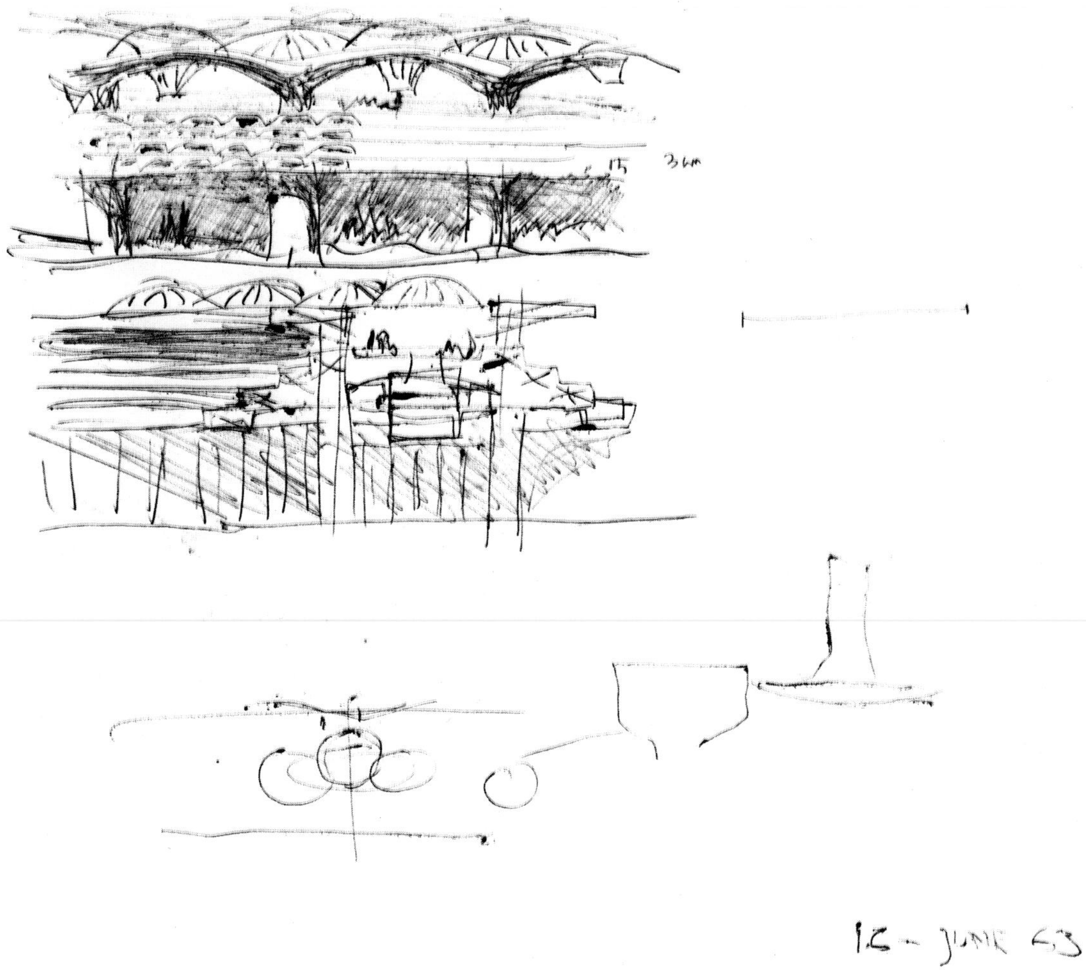
16 – JUNE 63

1970
As simple-minded as the zoo environment tends to be, it is similar to the idea of a partly petrified, partly living tree of life. If we could only look at the uninterrupted spectacle of matter discovering life, life appropriating matter for its own incredible uses, life branching out in endless probings, matter reasserting itself minerally in the very marrow of life through the instuaration of mineral and fossil, death and resurrection, transfiguration and death; and then the strobe of man's mind capable only of fragmented glances at itself. If we could only see the immensely vast, endlessly dark and silent unimaginable megamachine of cosmos manufacturing the eyes and ears of the living in order to gaze at these fatal stages moving on in endless time. To see physically displayed the imprint of the process from mineral to mind upon the terracing of space could be enormously instructive. One can envisage a cityscape built in spaces studded with the cornerstones of evolution and kept together by an overriding "élan vital" infused in its structure. Conjecture is part of history. Guessing is a preponderant part of prehistory, and the delicate imprints of life on stones of an age just short of eternity are as precious as any of the most brilliant conjectures linking them together in the vector of life.

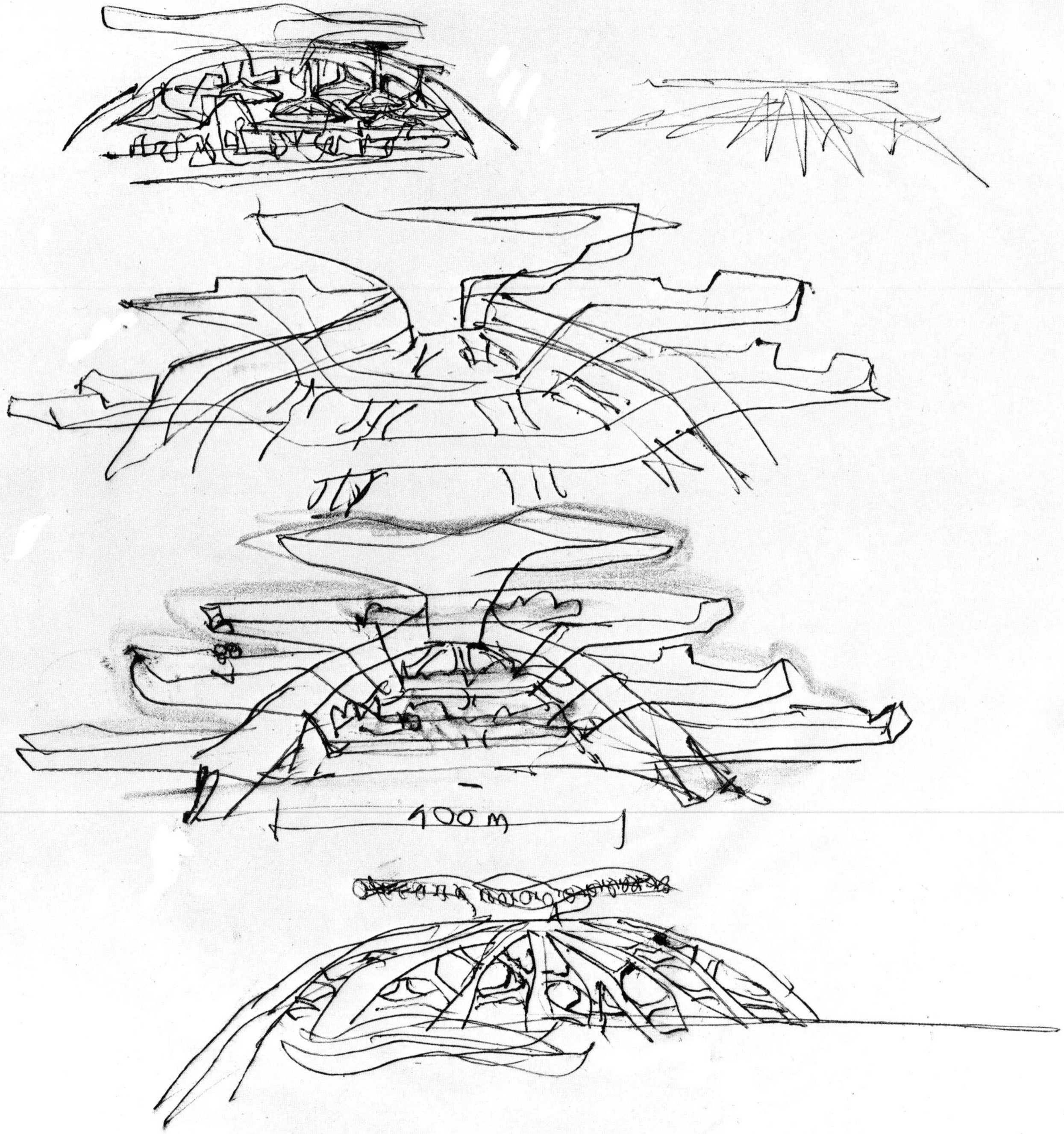
100 m

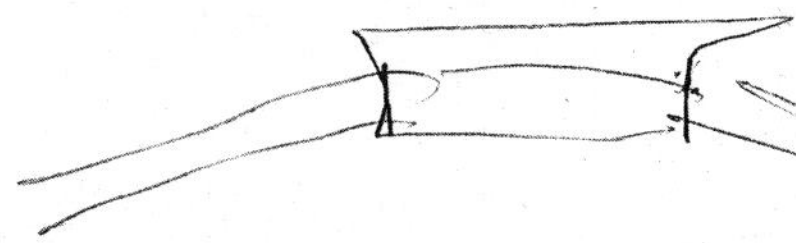

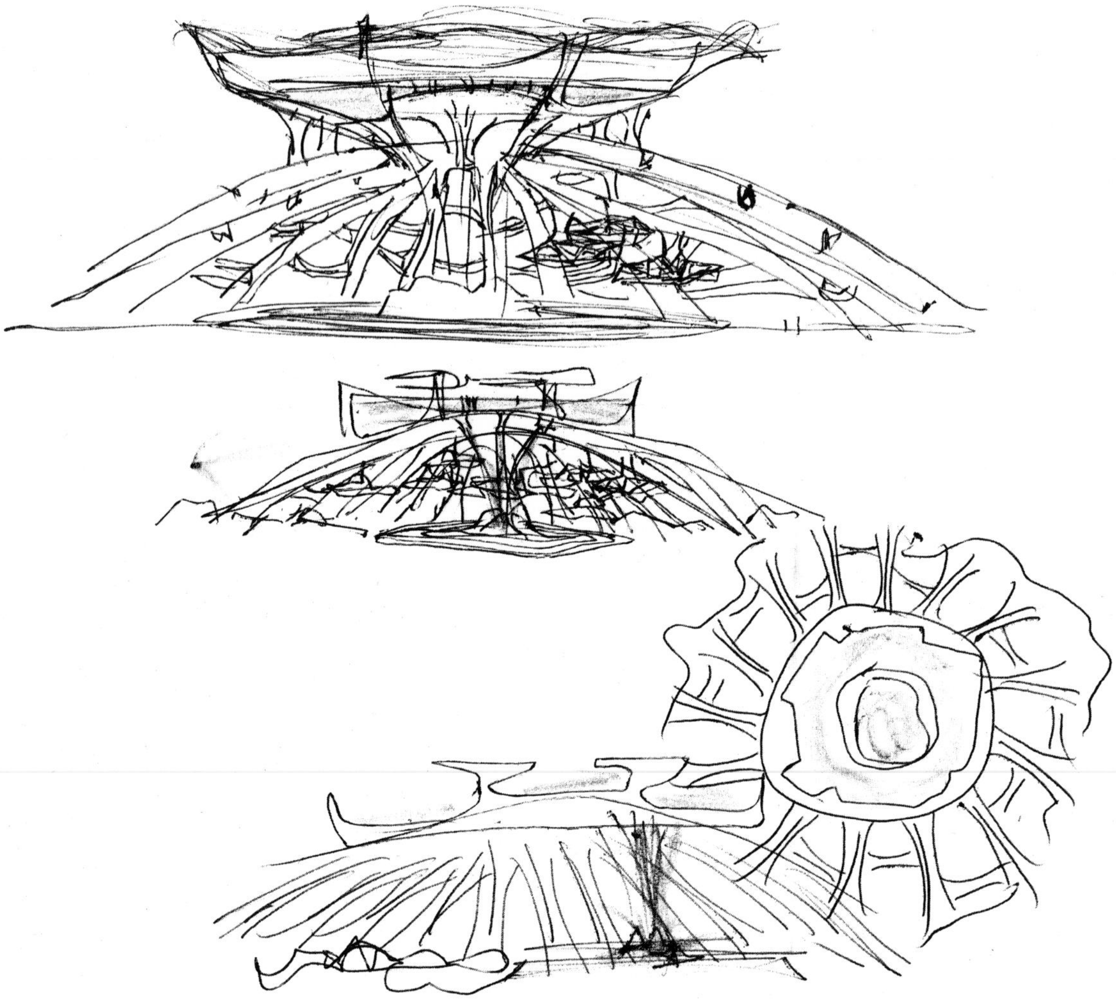

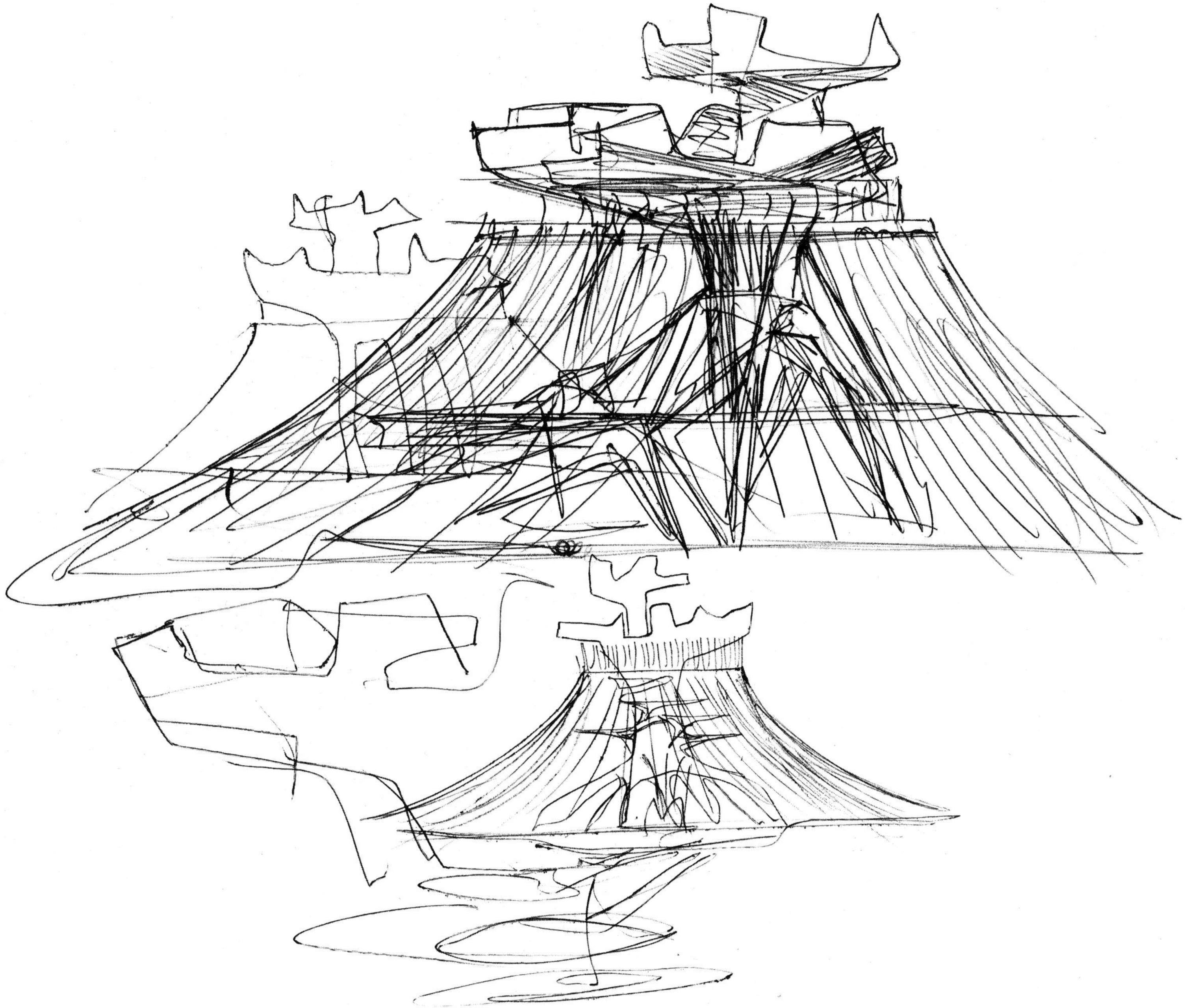

500

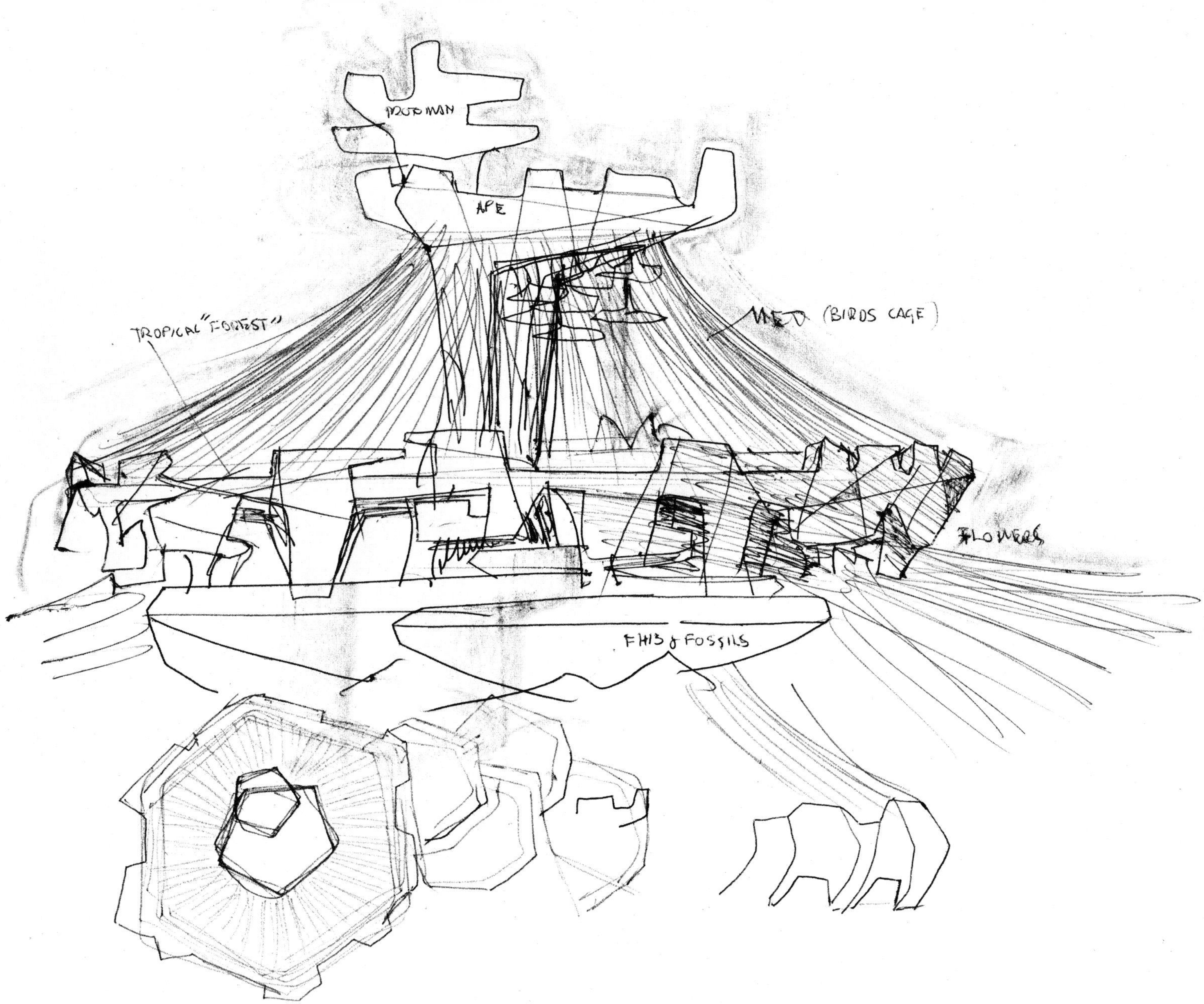
PROTO MAN
APE
TROPICAL "FOREST"
(BIRDS CAGE)
FLOWERS
FHIS & FOSSILS

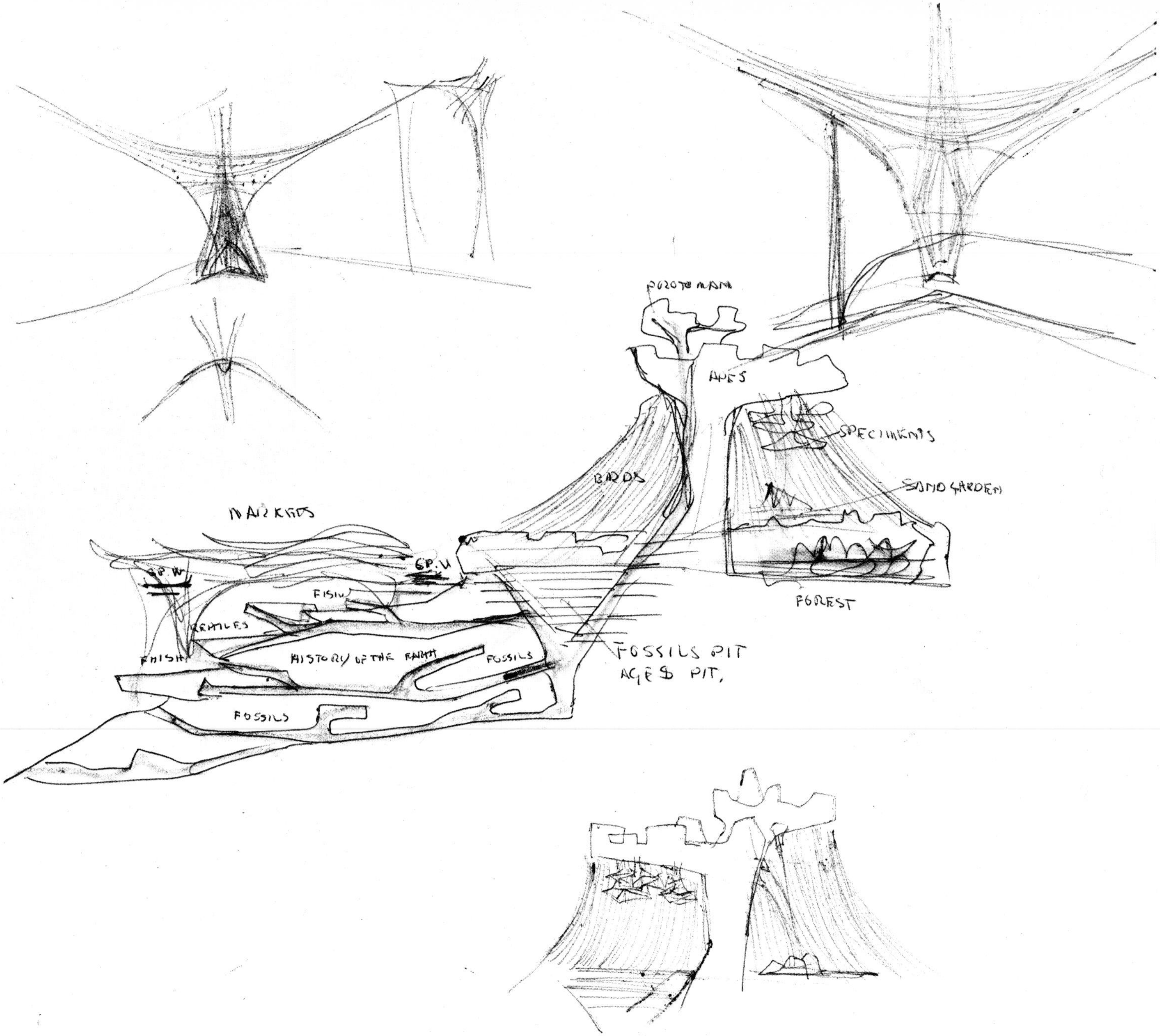
APES
SPECIMENS
BIRDS
SAND GARDEN
FISH
FOREST
FOSSILS PIT
AGES PIT,
HISTORY OF THE EARTH
FOSSILS
FOSSILS

Arcology

1970

The concept of Arcology arose as a noncentral element of a larger concept: Mesa City. It might be pure coincidence, but it would seem that ideas tend to be born as individuals or species are. There is the parent larger than life. And there is the offspring, puny and helpless, inexperienced, unfit. But the trajectory of the parent is downward, and the trajectory of the offspring is upward. Later, the offspring is on a par with the wilting parent, and then the prime mover fades off, the offspring taking not its place but an analogous place in another time.

Mesa City fades away, leaving as its own justification the embryos of a number of arcological fragments, each a parcel in need of complementarity and roundness. There is the village fragment, the study fragment, the commercial fragment, the theological fragment, the governmental fragment. If a magnet is placed among them and the magnet is called the arcological concept, then there they come together. This is in fact how the arcologies were defined. The complete genesis might be rather more sophisticated, but then the reality they symbolize is far more complex.

The arcological commitment is not indispensable because it is the best solution to the sheltering of an exploding population, although it is that.

The arcological commitment is not indispensable because it is the only solution to the ecological debacle, although it is that.

The arcological commitment is not indispensable because it is the only solution to the problem of waste through affluence, although it is that.

The arcological commitment is not indispensable because it is the only true resolution of the nightmare of pollution, although it is that.

The arcological commitment is not indispensable because it is the only true road to land, air, and water conservation, although it is that.

The arcological commitment is not indispensable because it structurally desegregates people, things, and performances, although it is that.

The arcological commitment, more generally, is not indispensable because it is the best instrument for survival, although it is that.

All these are remedial reasons important to man but only instrumental to the specific humaneness sought by him. They are manutentive and restorative. They are not specifically creative. By their implementation, the refound health of man and earth would not be a substitute for grace but could be a threshold to it.

The arcological commitment is indispensable because it advocates a physical system that justly consents and fosters the compression of things, energies, logistics, information, performances, thinking, doing, living, learning, and playing into urban-human integrals that compose the essential, critical, vibrant phenomenon of life at its most lively and compassionate: the state of grace (aesthetogenesis) that is possible for socially and individually healthy man on an ecologically healthy earth.

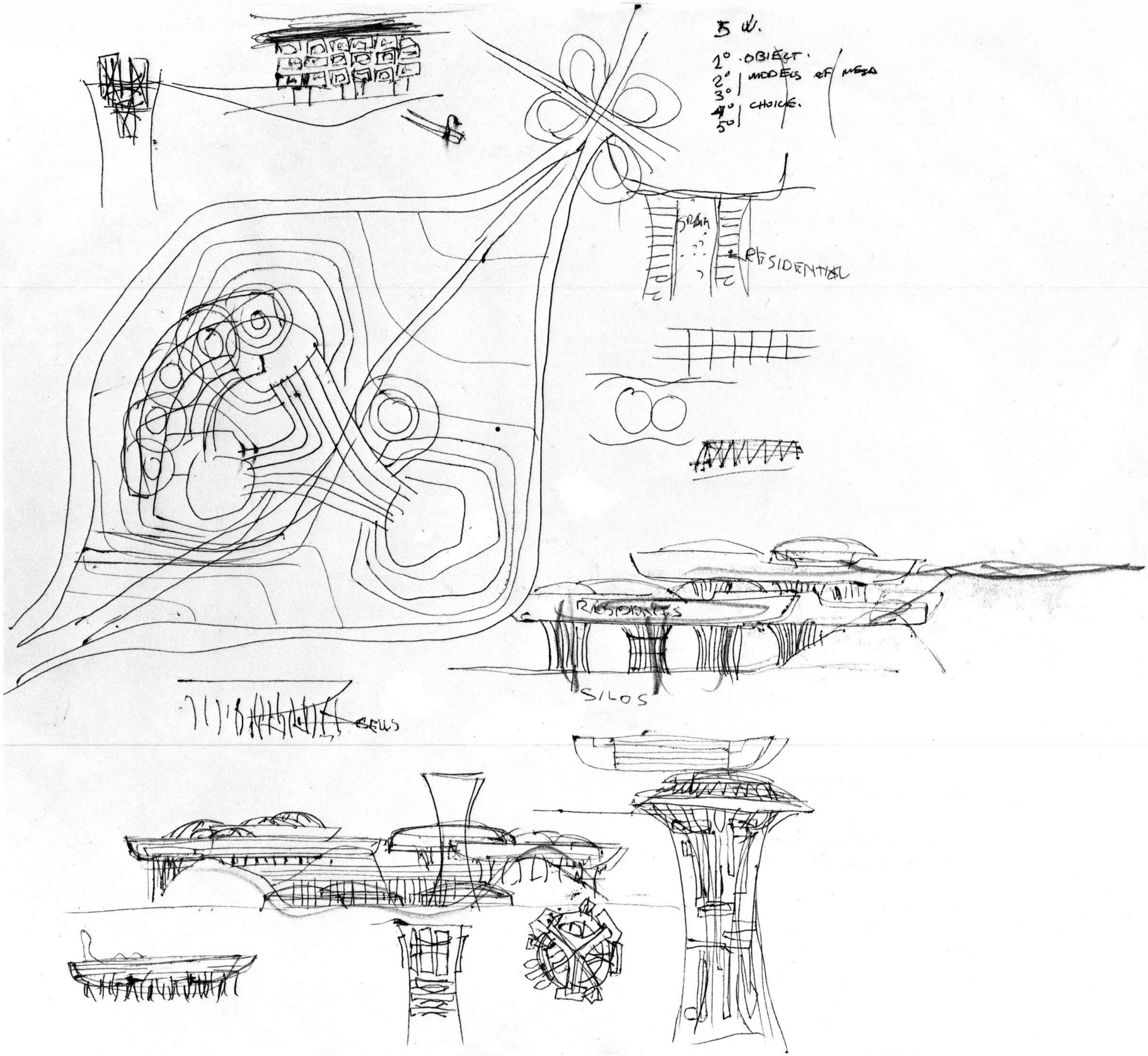
1° OBJECT.
2° MODELS OF MEGA
3°
4° CHOICE.
5°
RESIDENTIAL
RESIDENCES
SILOS
CELLS

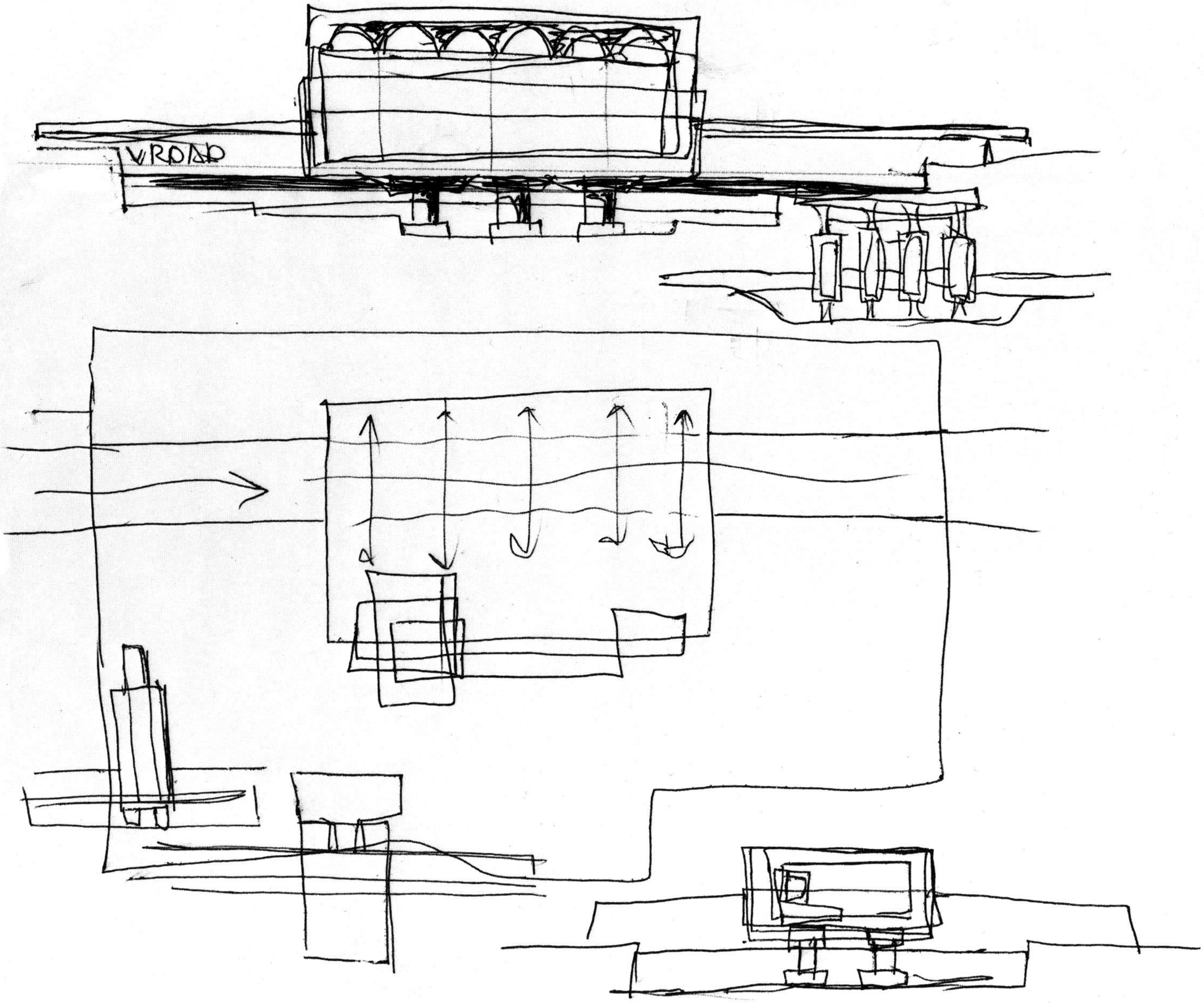

ROAD

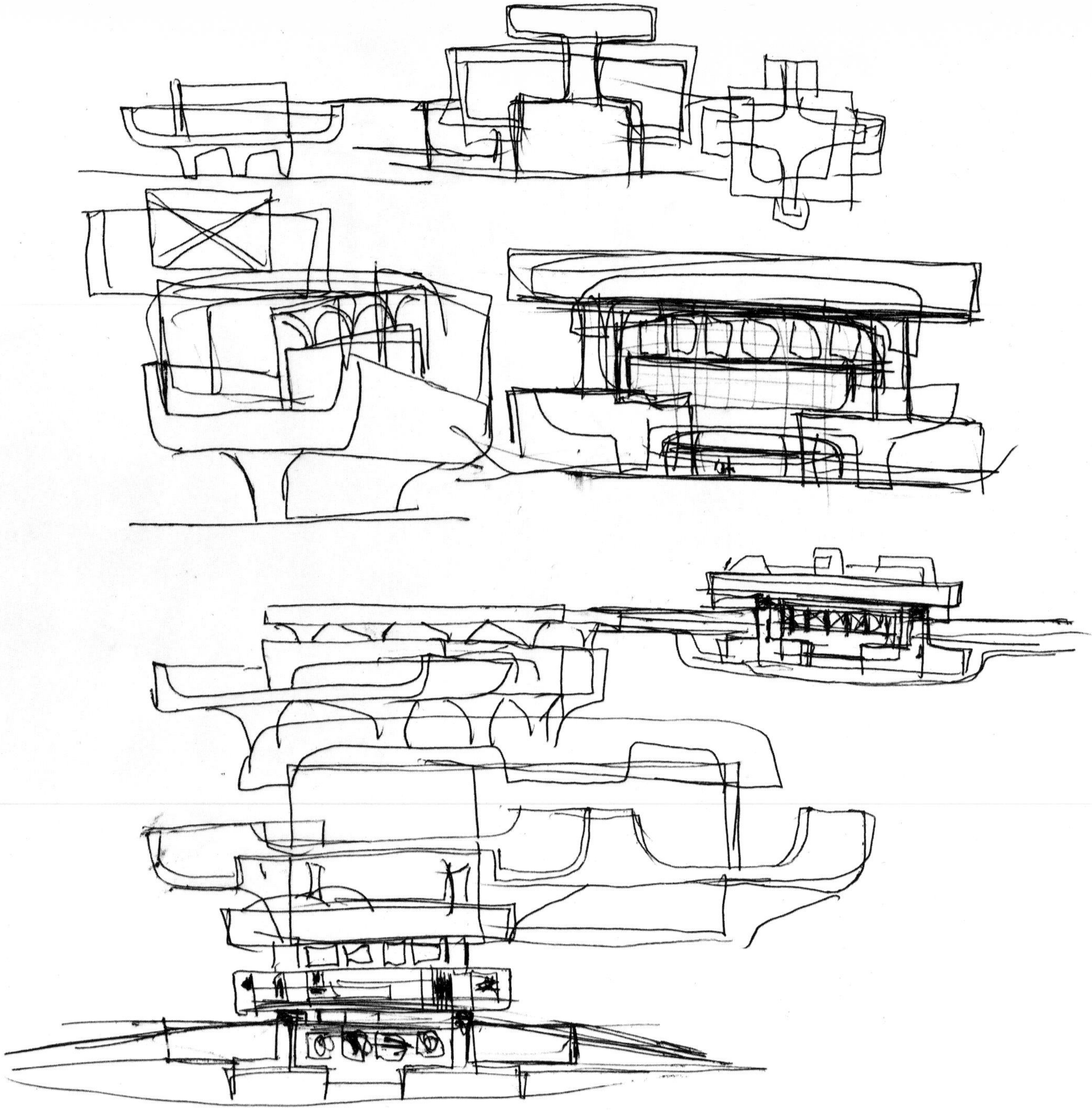

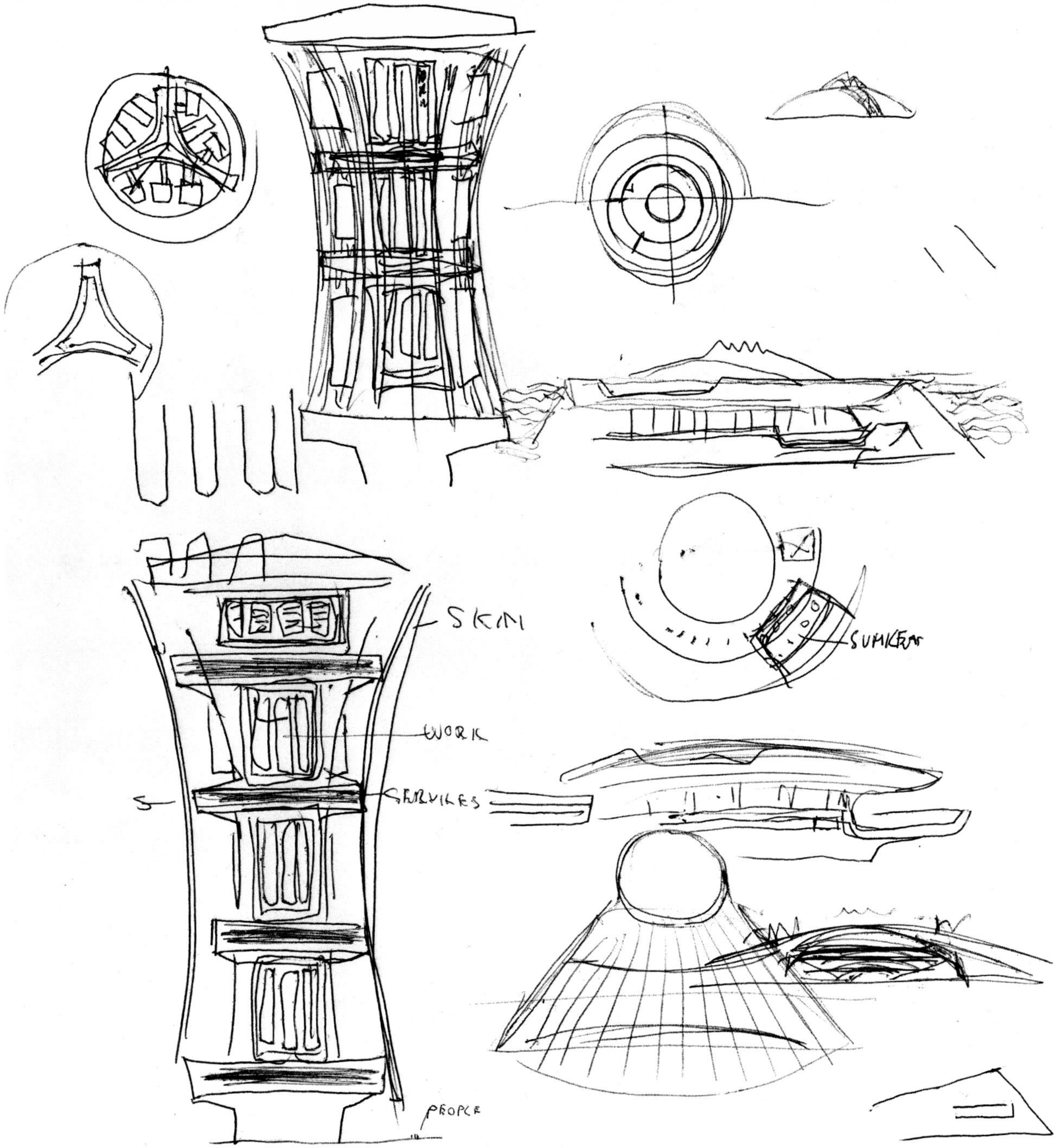
SKIN
WORK
SERVICES
PEOPLE

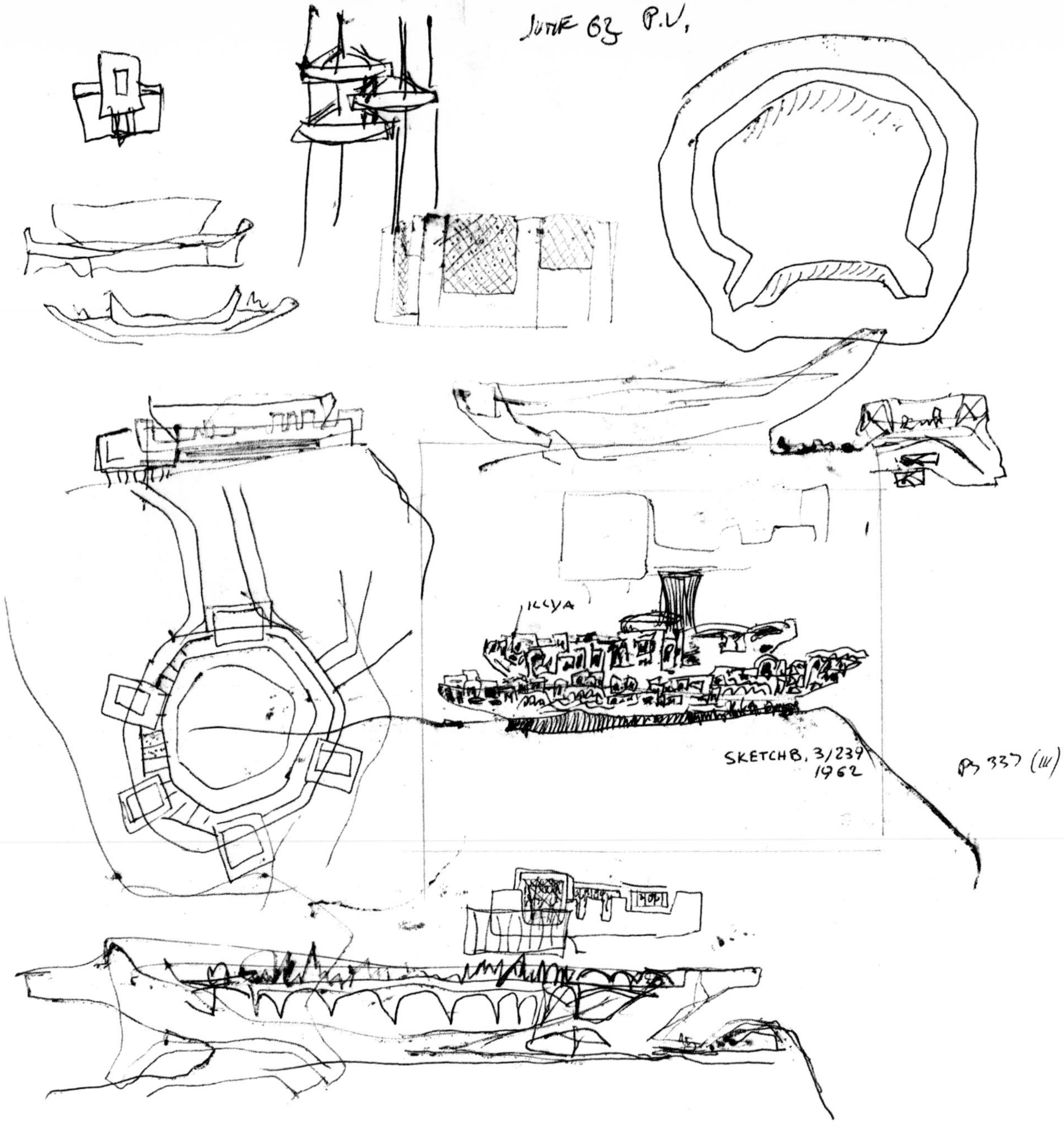
JUNE 63 P.V.
ILLYA
SKETCHB. 3/239
1962
Pg 337 (III)

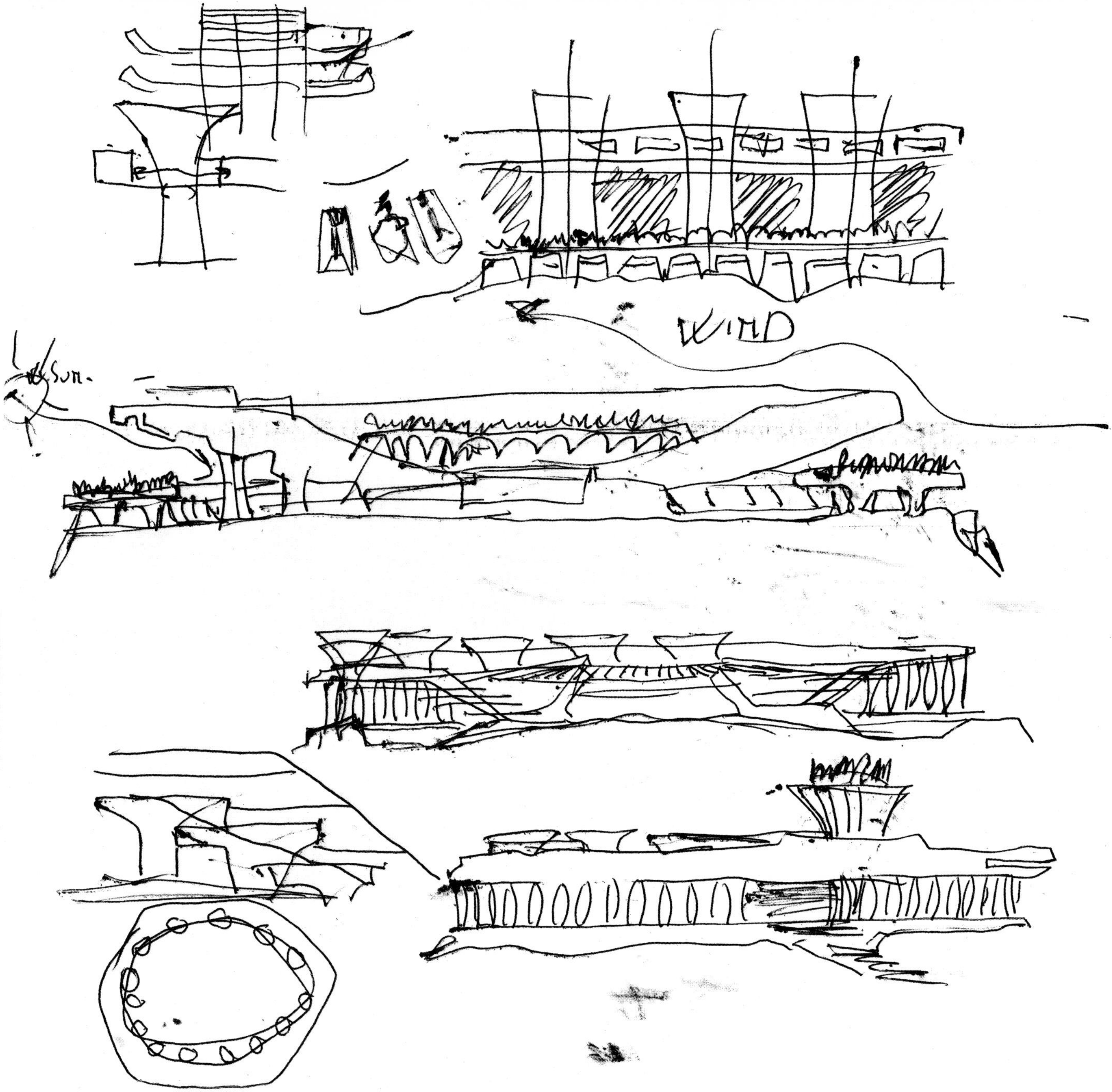
WIND
Sun.

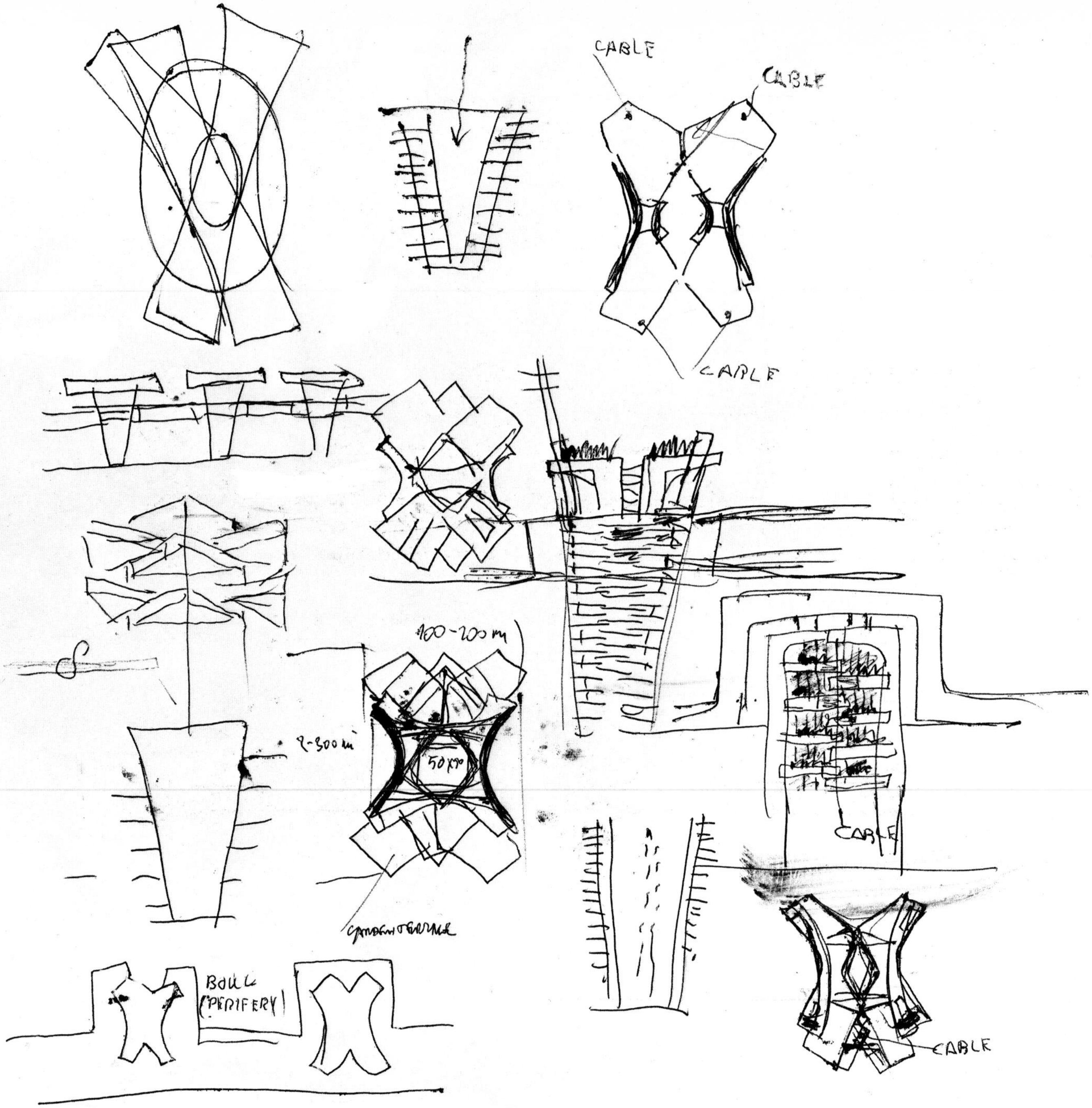
CABLE
CABLE
CABLE
100-200 m
CABLE
BOWL
(PERIFERY)
CABLE

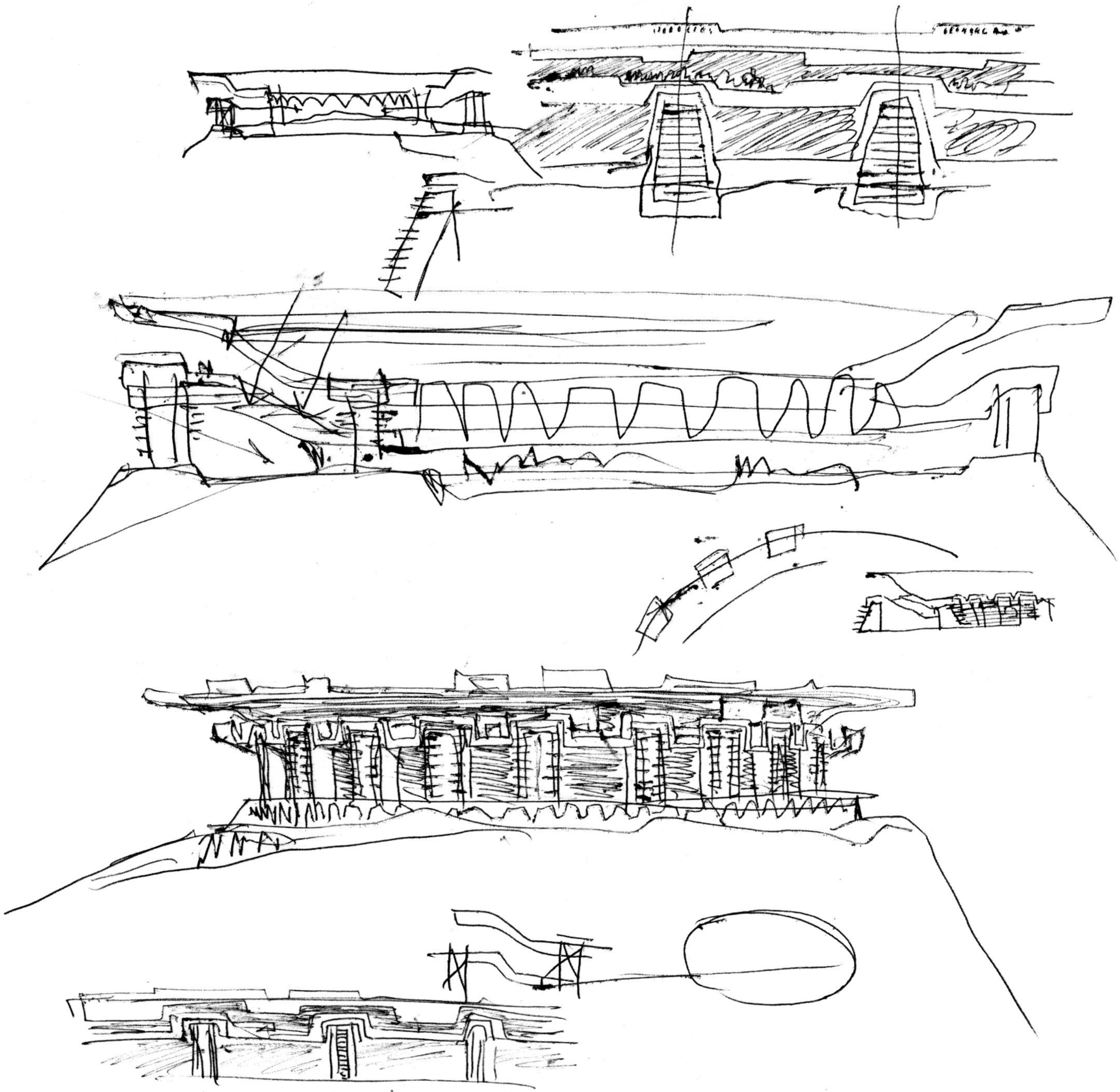

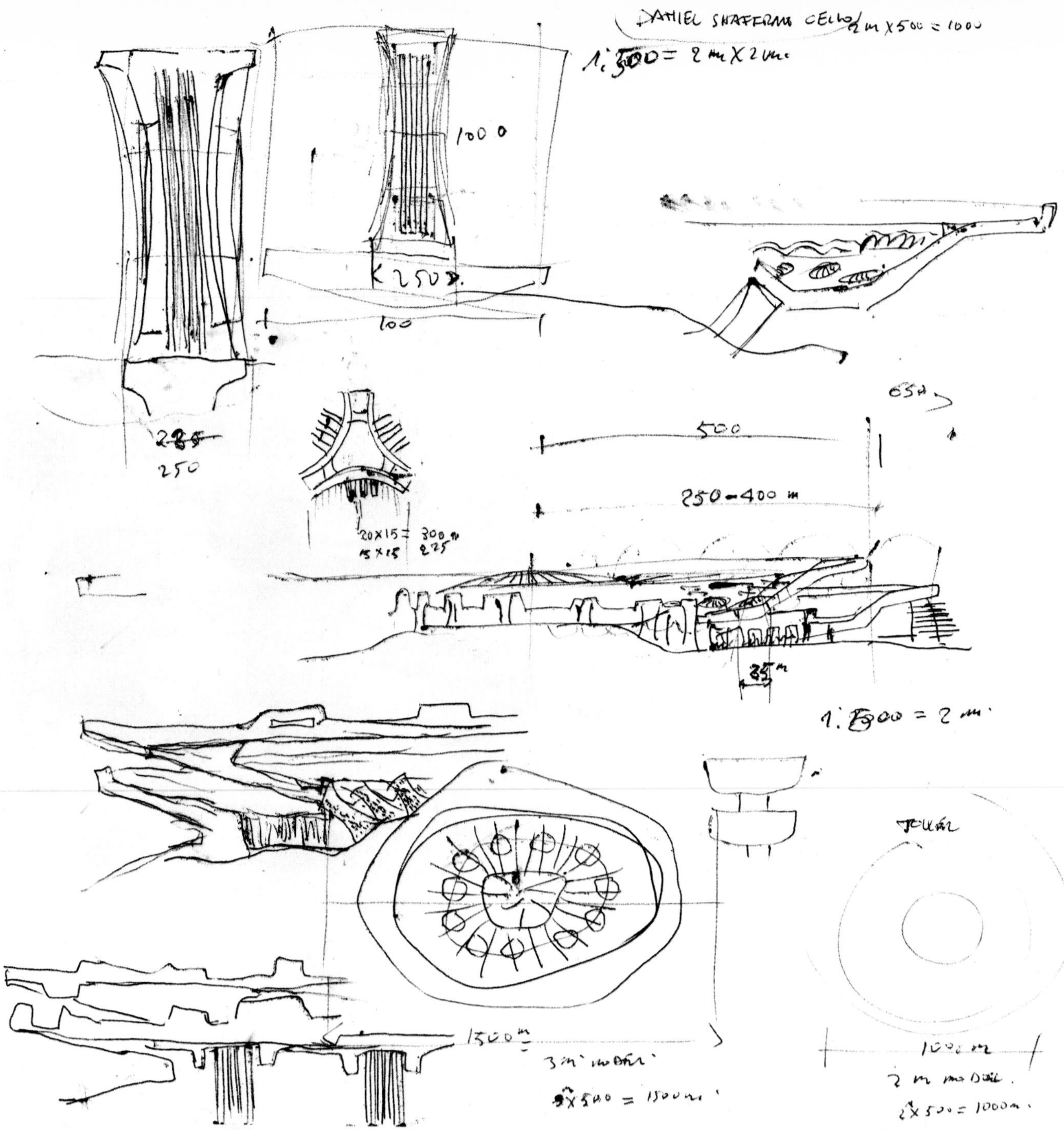
2 m X 500 = 1000
1:500 = 2 m X 2 m
1000
250
100
250
500
250–400 m
20X15 = 300 m
15X15 225
35 m
1:500 = 2 m
1500 m
3X500 = 1500 m
1000 m
2 m model
2X500 = 1000 m

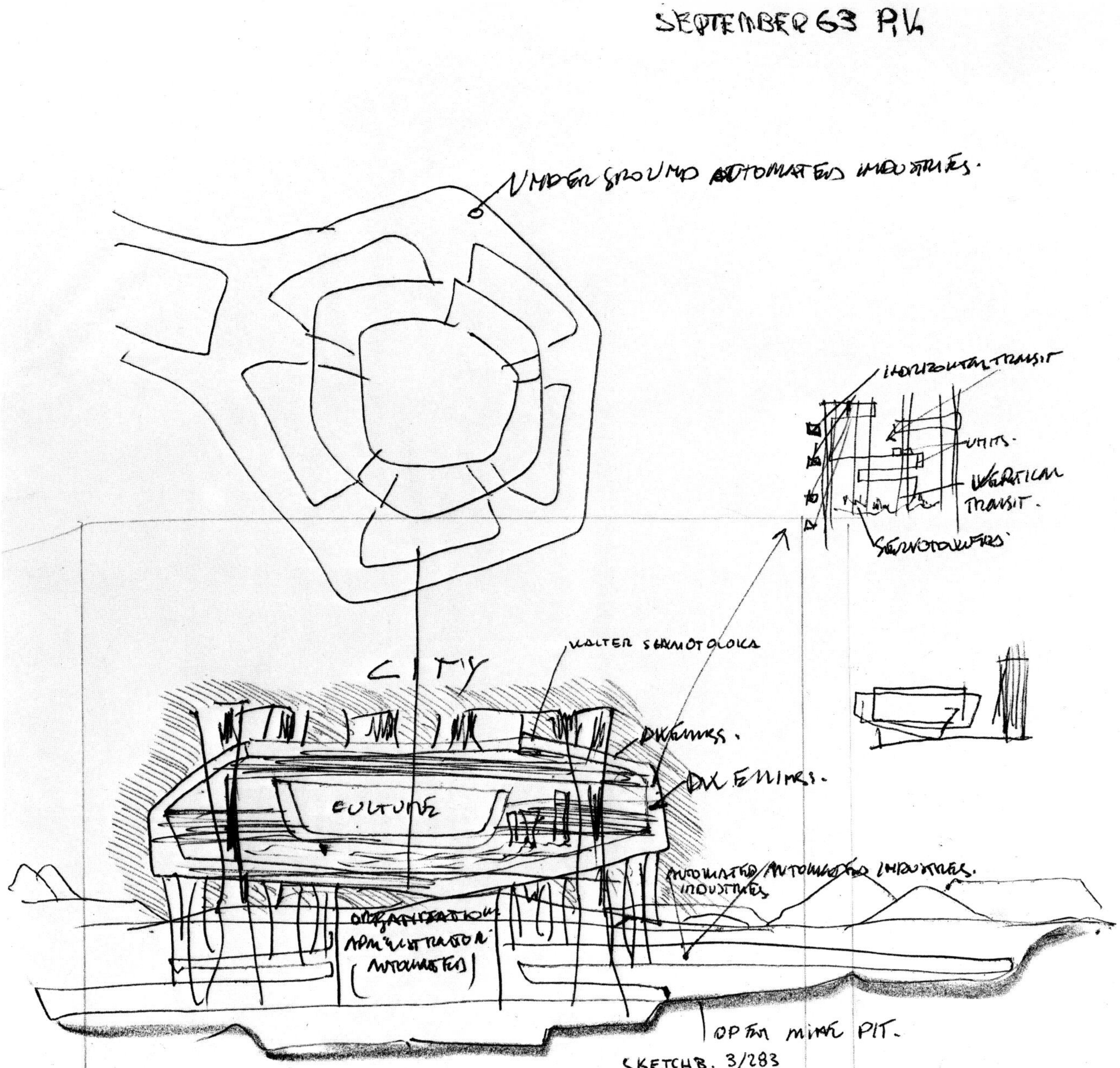

SKETCHB. 3/283
1963

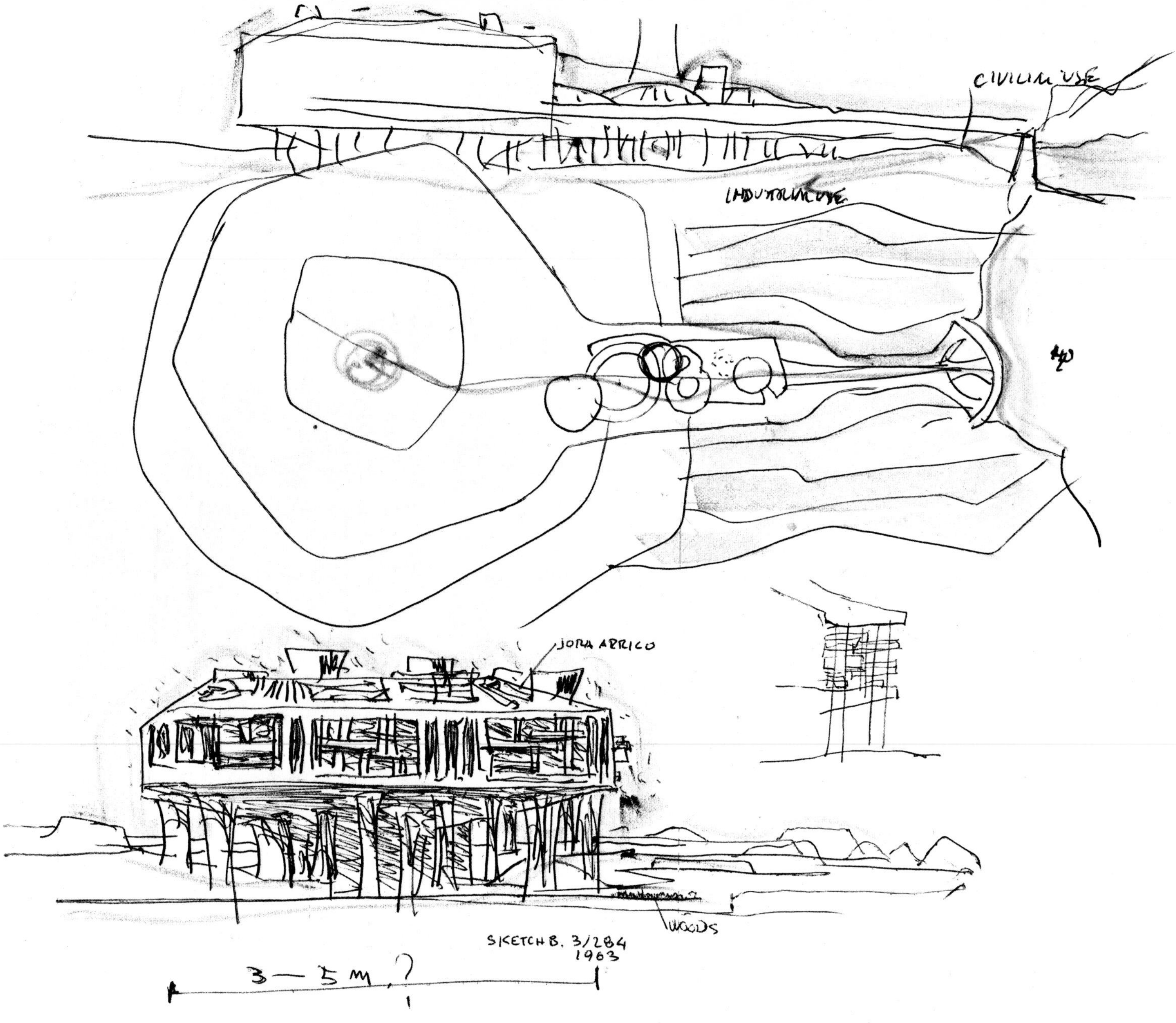
CIVILIAN USE
INDUSTRIAL USE
WOODS
SKETCH B. 3/284
1963
3 — 5 m ?

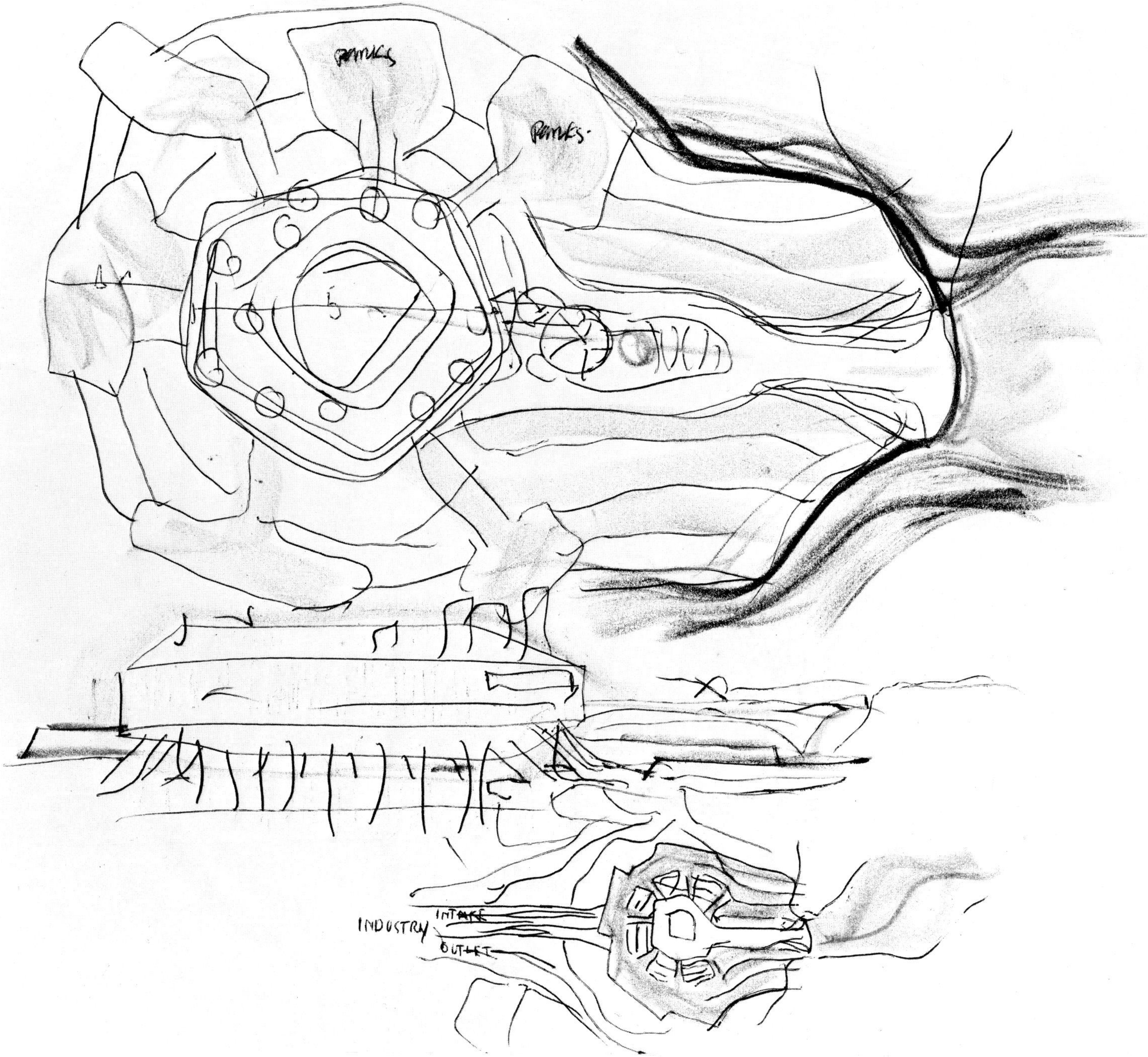
PARKS
PARKS.
INDUSTRY
INTAKE
OUTLET

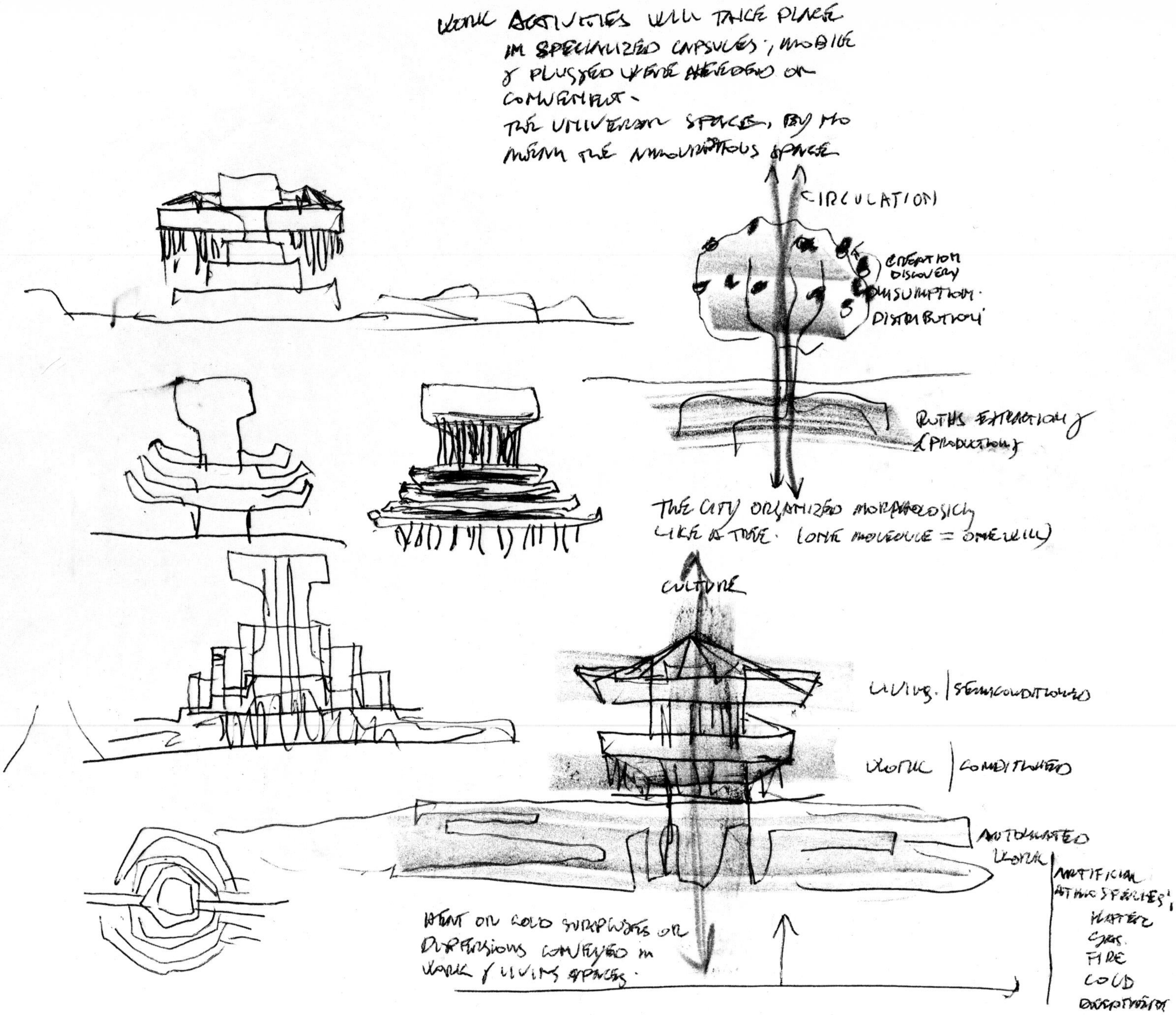

WORK ACTIVITIES WILL TAKE PLACE
IN SPECIALIZED CAPSULES; MOBILE
& PLUGGED WHERE NEEDED OR
CONVENIENT.
THE UNIVERSAL SPACE, BY NO
MEANS THE
SPACE
CIRCULATION
CREATION
DISCOVERY
CONSUMPTION
EXTRACTION &
(PRODUCTION)
THE CITY ORGANIZED MORPHOLOGICALLY
LIKE A TREE. (ONE MOLECULE =
CULTURE
LIVING | SEMICONDITIONED
WORK | CONDITIONED
AUTOMATED
WORK
ARTIFICIAL
ATMOSPHERES;
WATER
GAS
FIRE
COLD
HEAT OR COLD SURFACES OR
DIFFUSIONS CONVEYED IN
WORK & LIVING SPACES.

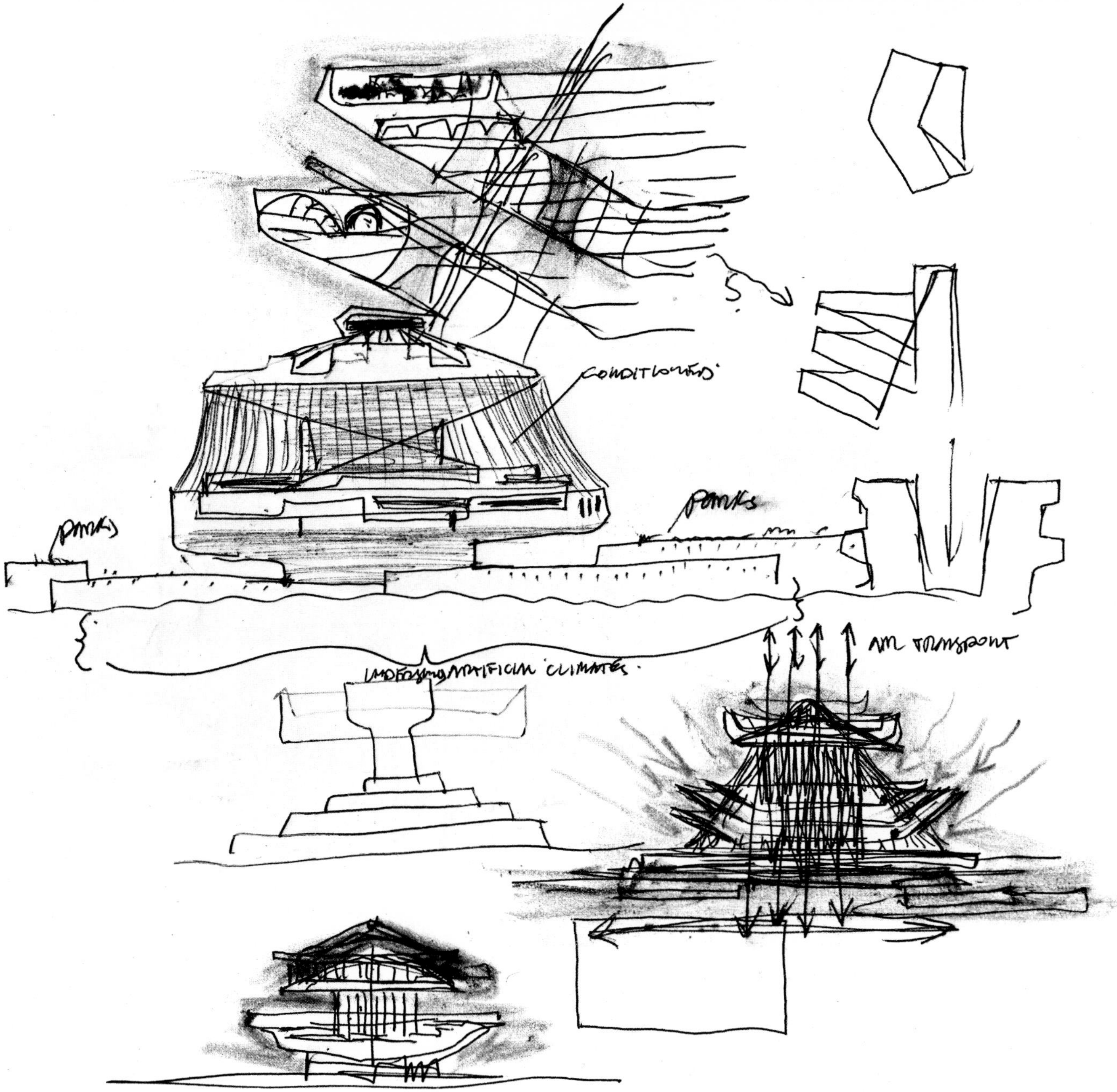
CONDITIONED
PARKS
PARKS
AIR TRANSPORT
ARTIFICIAL CLIMATES

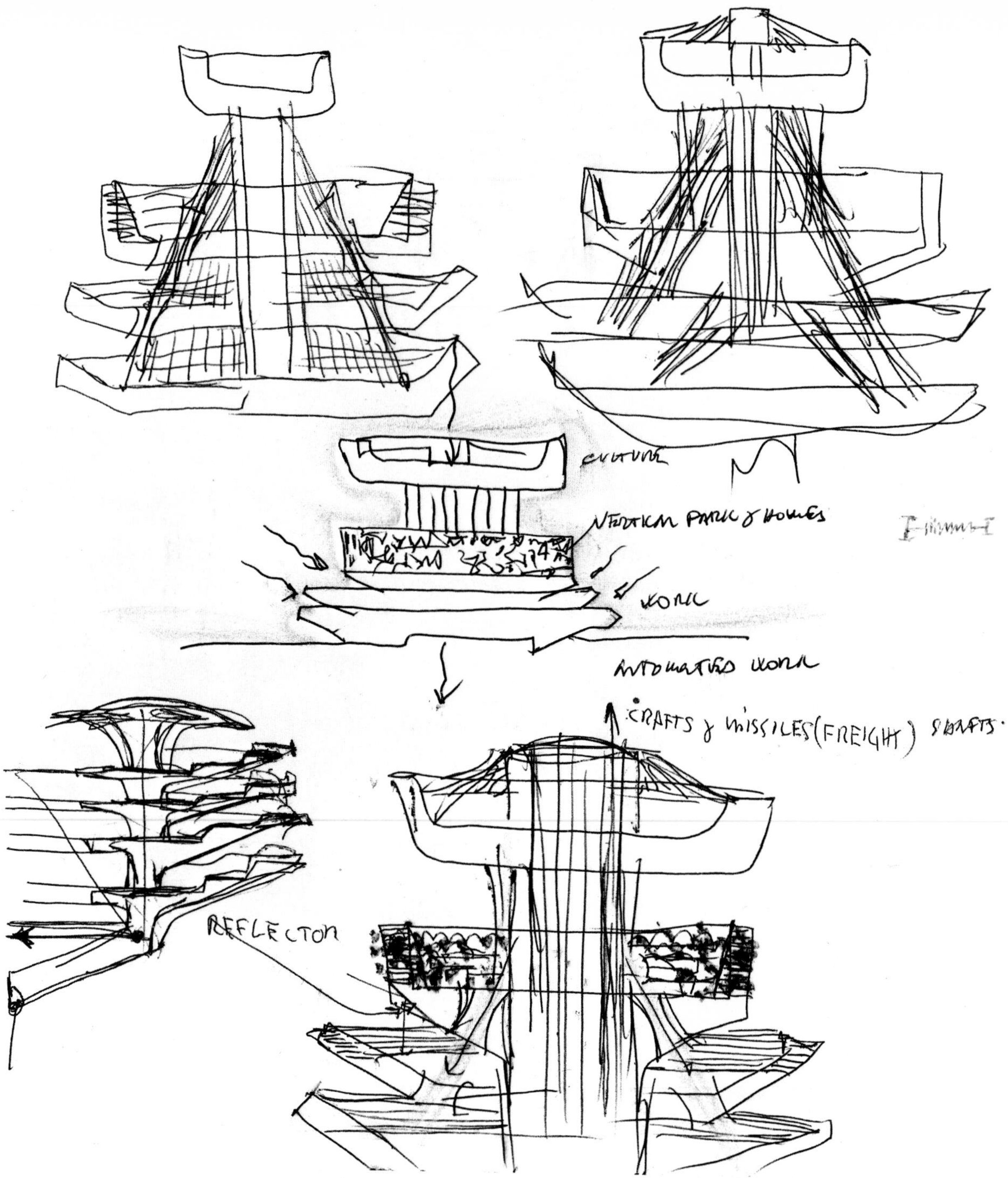
CULTURE
VERTICAL PARK & HOMES
WORK
AUTOMATED WORK
CRAFTS & MISSILES (FREIGHT) SHAFTS.
REFLECTOR

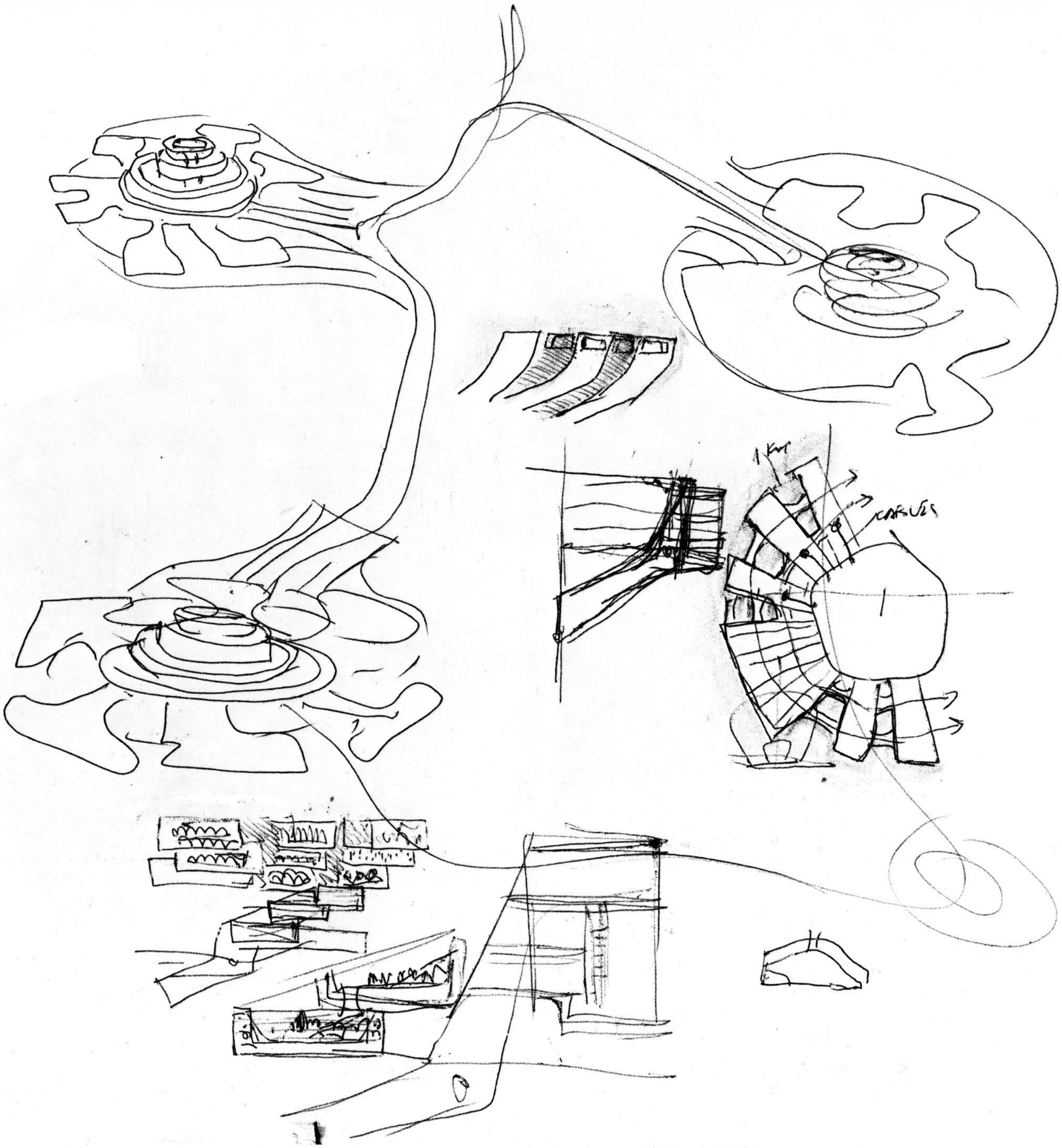
1 Km

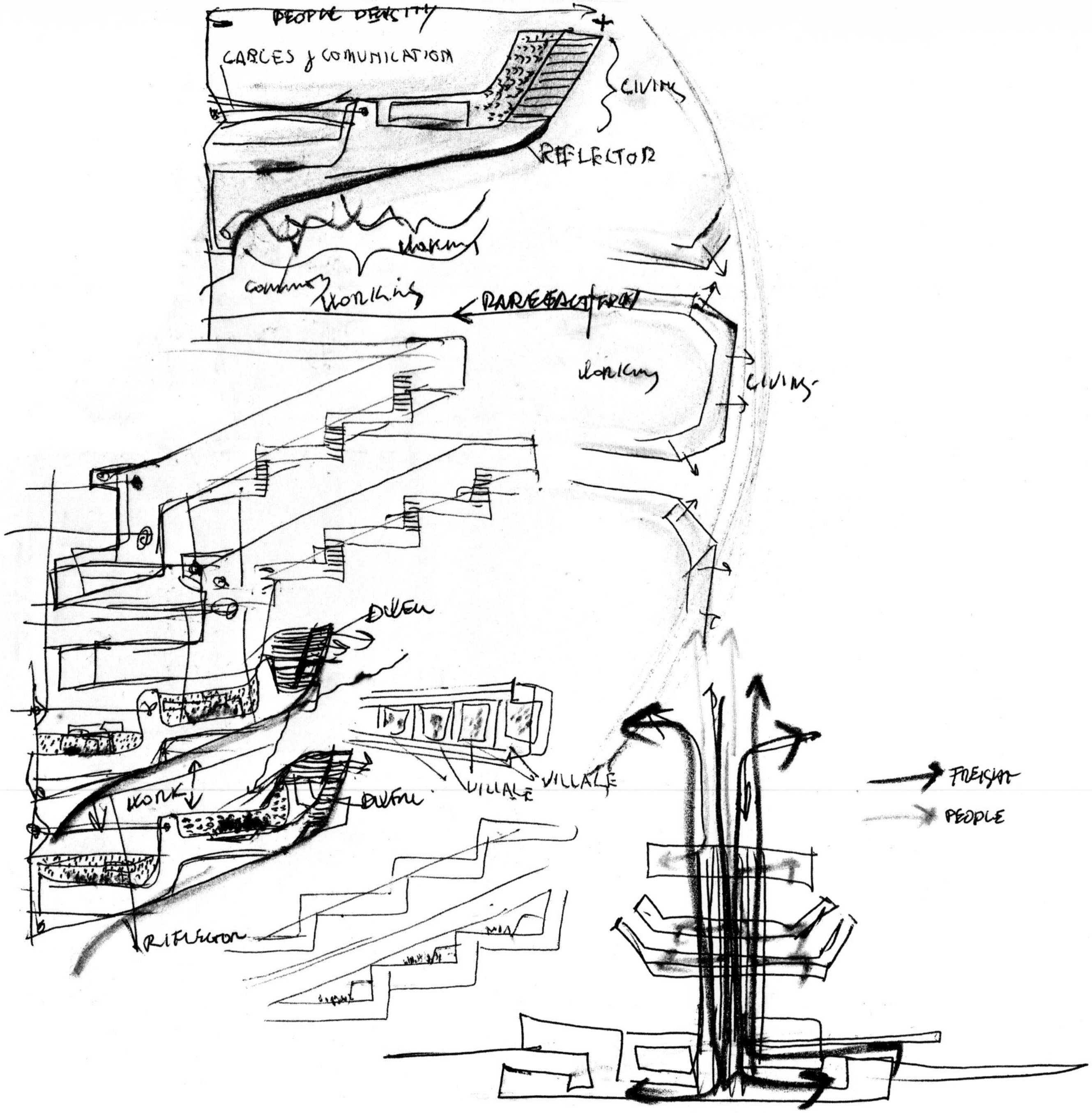
PEOPLE DENSITY
CABLES & COMUNICATION
LIVING
REFLECTOR
WORKING
LIVING
DWELL
WORK
DWELL
VILLAGE
VILLAGE
REFLECTOR
FREIGHT
PEOPLE

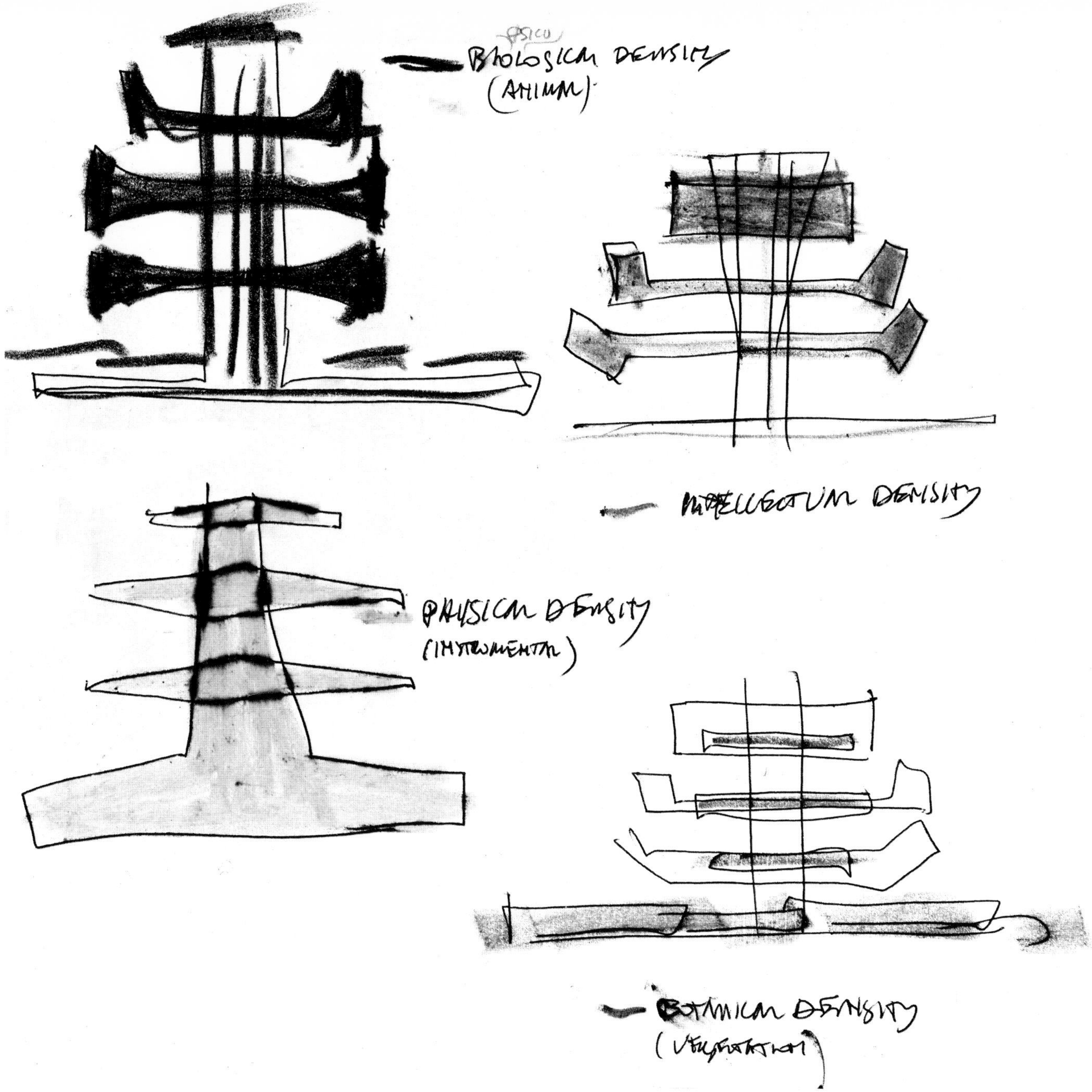
BIOLOGICAL DENSITY
(ANIMAL)
INTELLECTUAL DENSITY
PHYSICAL DENSITY
(INSTRUMENTAL)
BOTANICAL DENSITY
(VEGETATION)

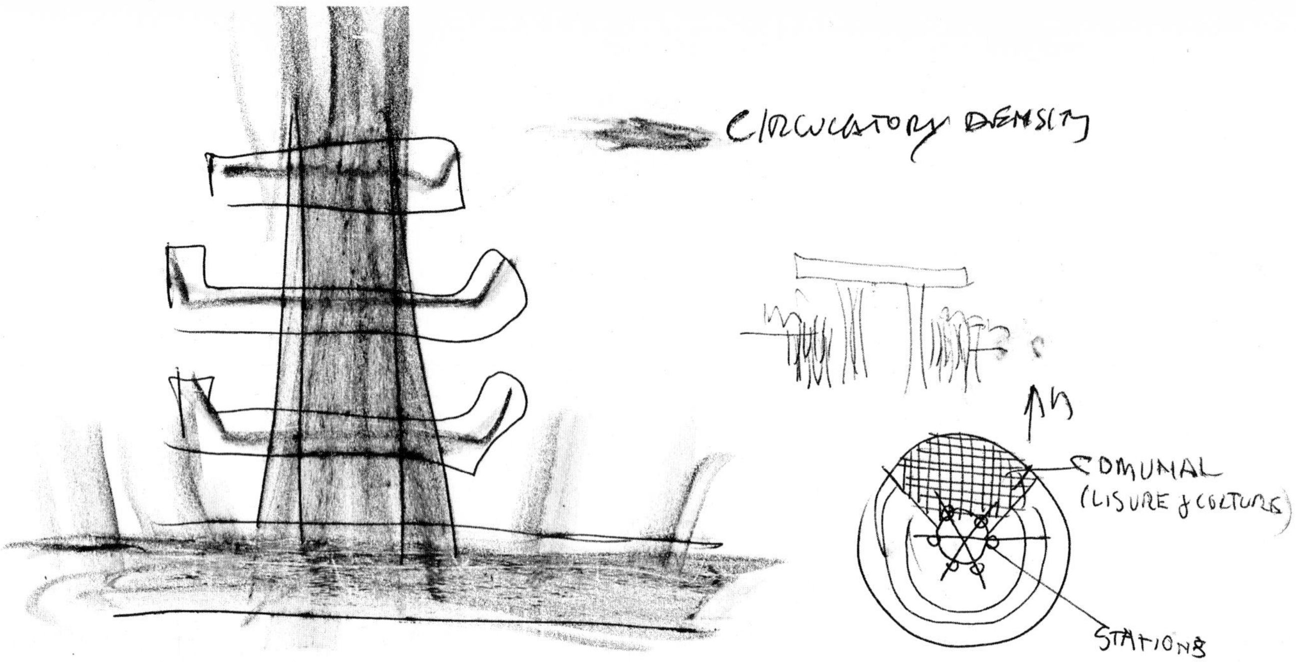
CIRCULATORY DENSITY
COMUNAL
(LISURE & CULTURE)
STATIONS

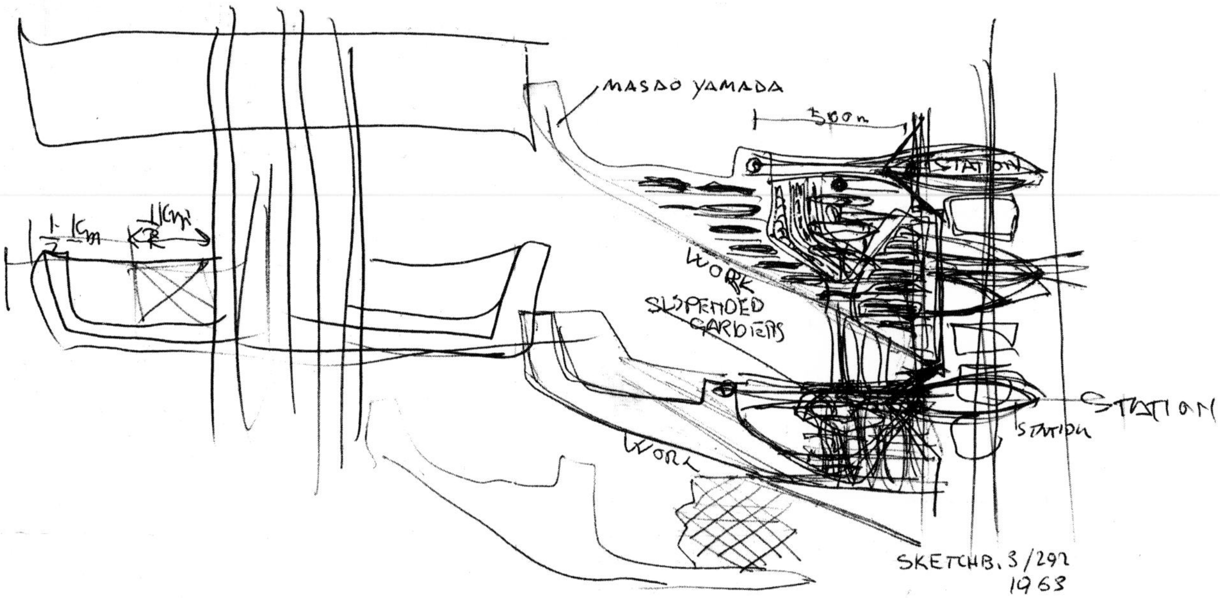
MASAO YAMADA
500m
STATION
WORK
SUSPENDED GARDENS
WORK
STATION
STATION
SKETCHB. 3/292
1963

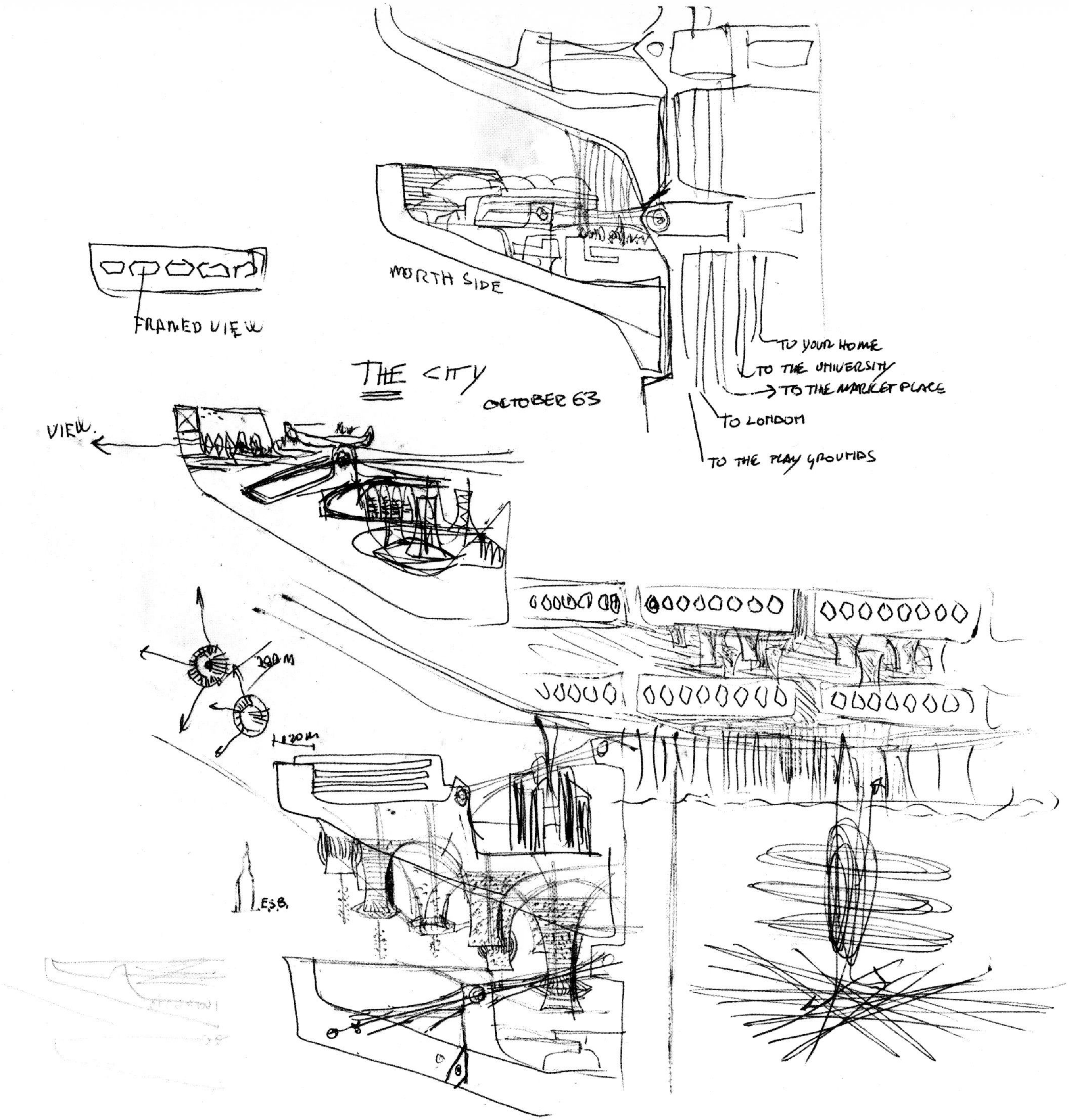
FRAMED VIEW
NORTH SIDE
THE CITY
OCTOBER 63
TO YOUR HOME
TO THE UNIVERSITY
TO THE MARKET PLACE
TO LONDON
TO THE PLAY GROUNDS
VIEW.
E.S.B.

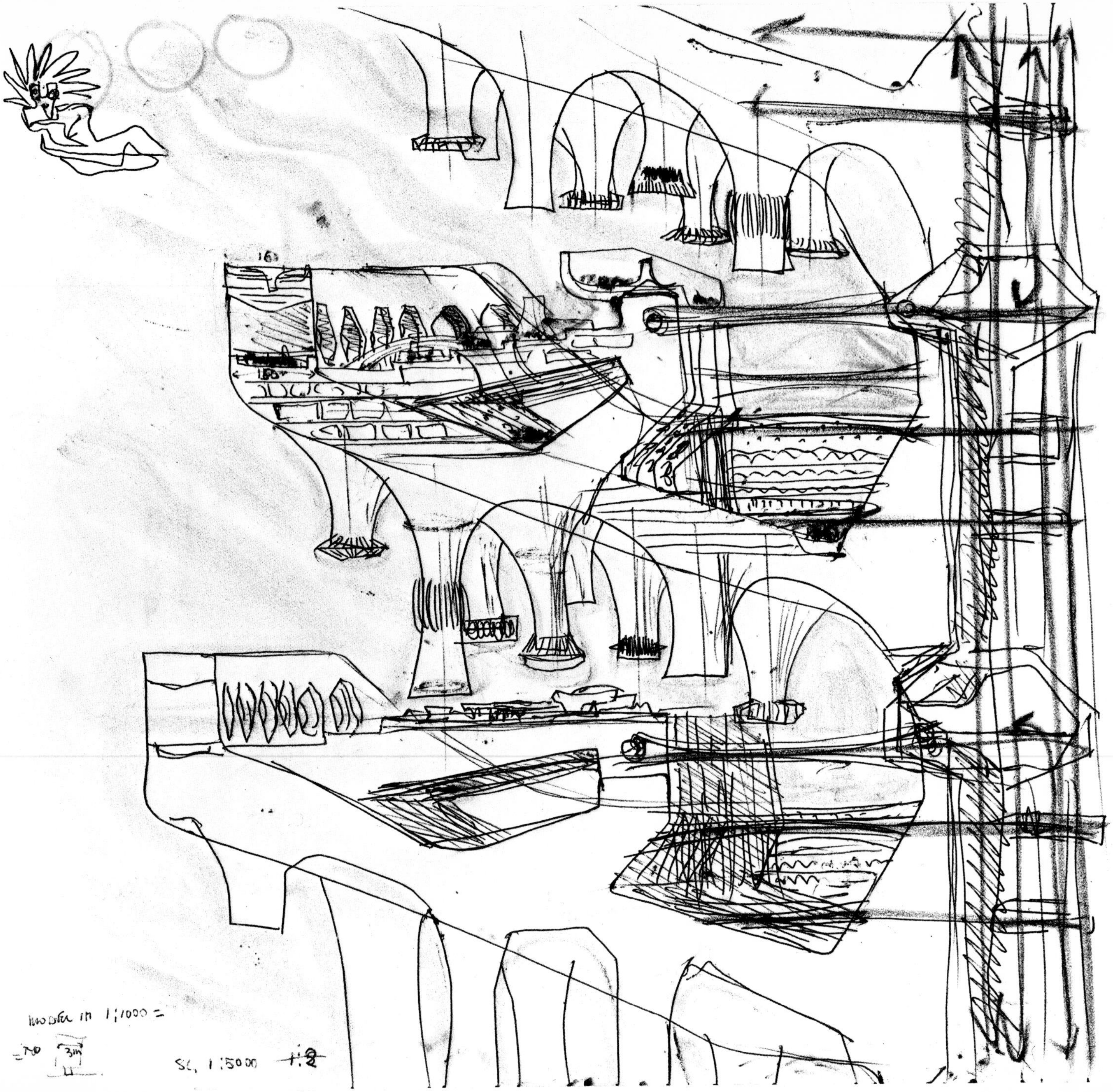

1:1000 =
3m
SC, 1:5000

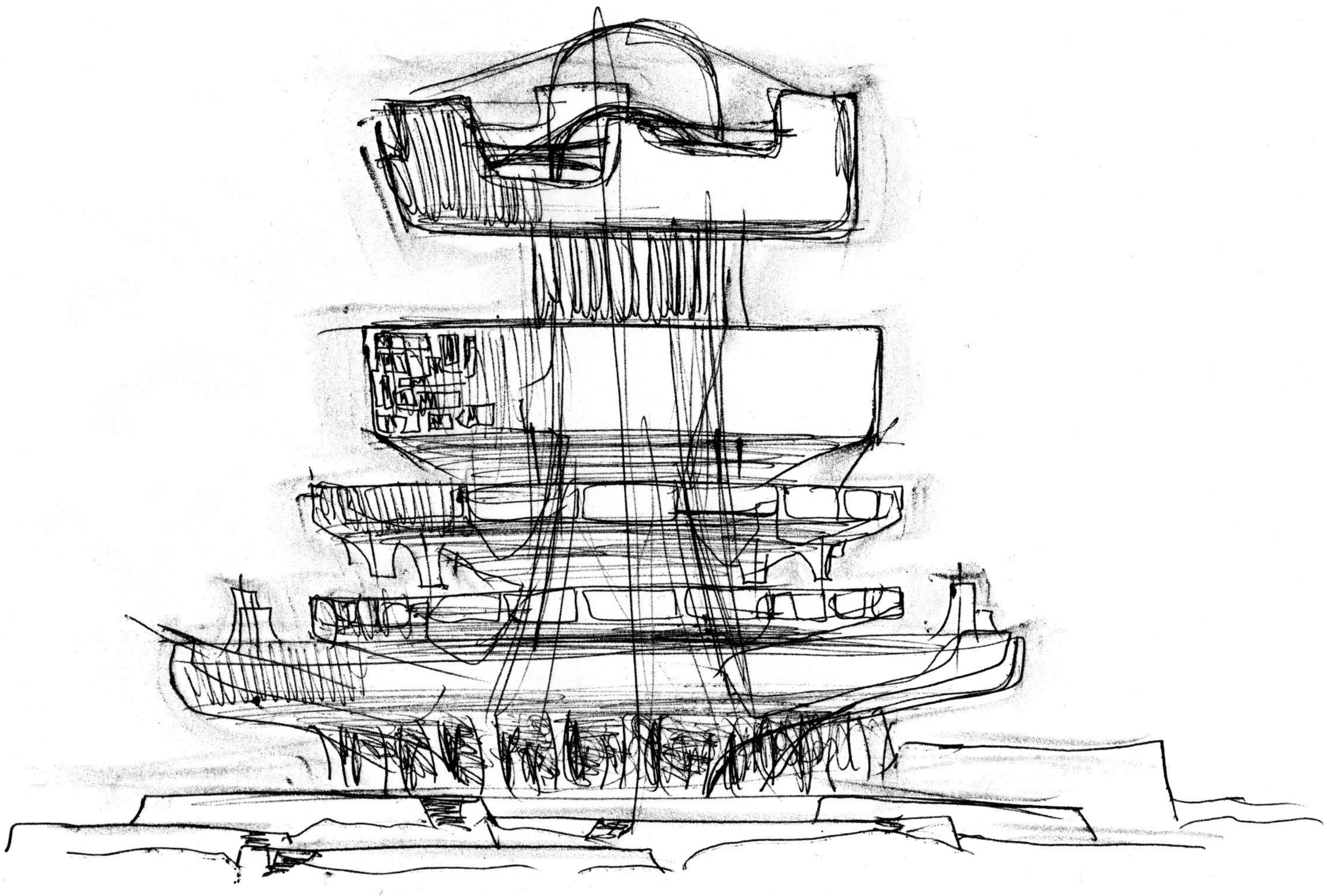

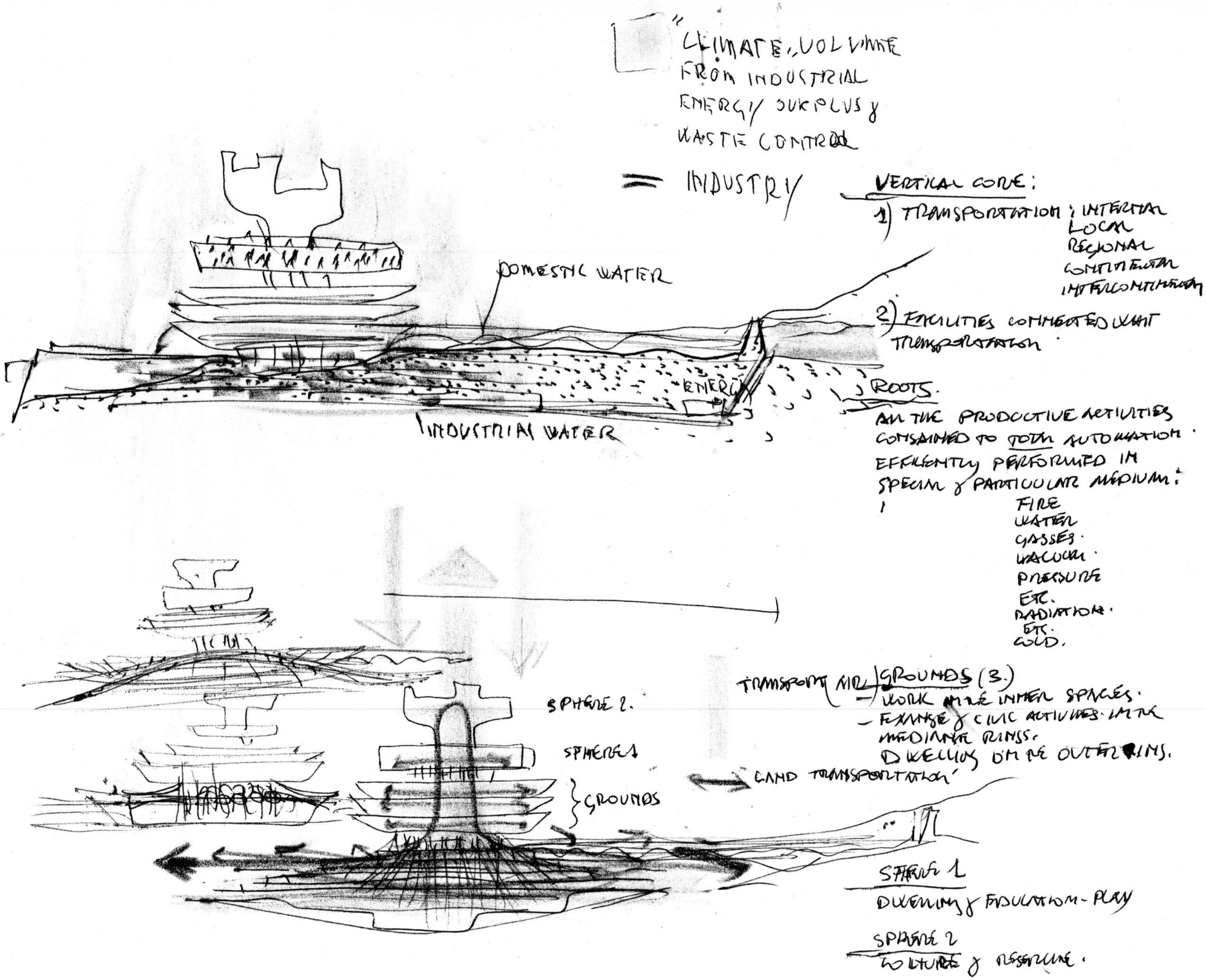

"CLIMATE VOLUME
FROM INDUSTRIAL
ENERGY SURPLUS &
WASTE CONTROL
= INDUSTRY
VERTICAL CORE:
1) TRANSPORTATION: INTERNAL
LOCAL
REGIONAL
CONTINENTAL
INTERCONTINENTAL
DOMESTIC WATER
2) FACILITIES CONNECTED WITH
TRANSPORTATION
ENERGY
ROOTS.
ALL THE PRODUCTIVE ACTIVITIES
CONSIGNED TO TOTAL AUTOMATION.
EFFICIENTLY PERFORMED IN
SPECIAL & PARTICULAR MEDIUM:
FIRE
WATER
GASSES.
VACUUM.
PRESSURE
ETC.
RADIATION.
ETC.
COLD.
INDUSTRIAL WATER
TRANSPORT AIR
GROUNDS (3.)
- WORK IN THE INNER SPACES.
- EXCHANGE & CIVIC ACTIVITIES IN THE
MEDIAN RINGS.
DWELLING ON THE OUTER RINGS.
SPHERE 2.
SPHERE 1
GROUNDS
LAND TRANSPORTATION
SPHERE 1
DWELLING & EDUCATION-PLAY
SPHERE 2
CULTURE & RESEARCH.

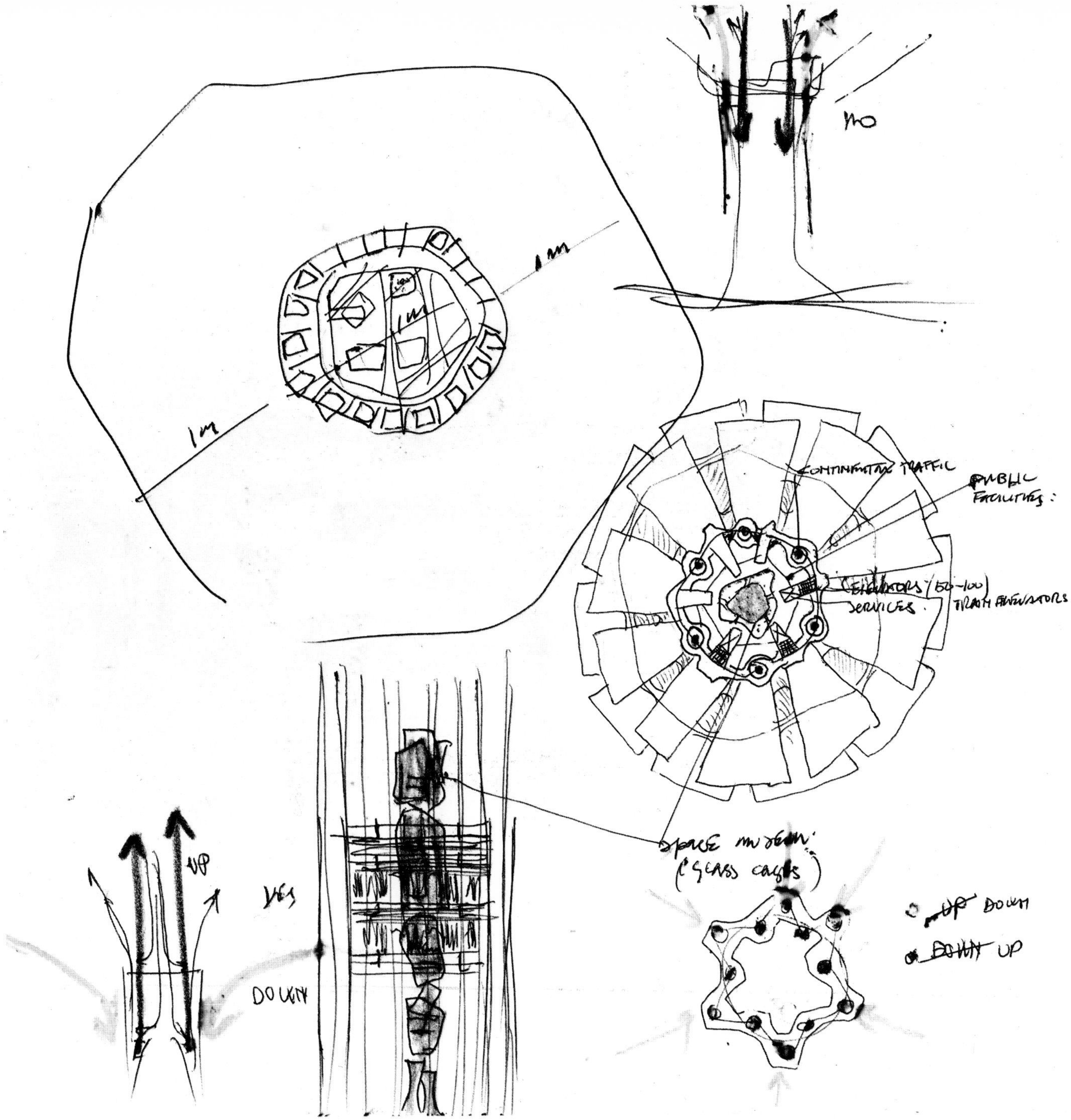
1m
1m
1m
1/10
CONTINENTAL TRAFFIC
PUBLIC FACILITIES:
ELEVATORS (50-100)
SERVICES
TRAM ELEVATORS
SPACE MUSEUM
(GLASS CAGES)
DOWN
UP
UP
YES
DOWN

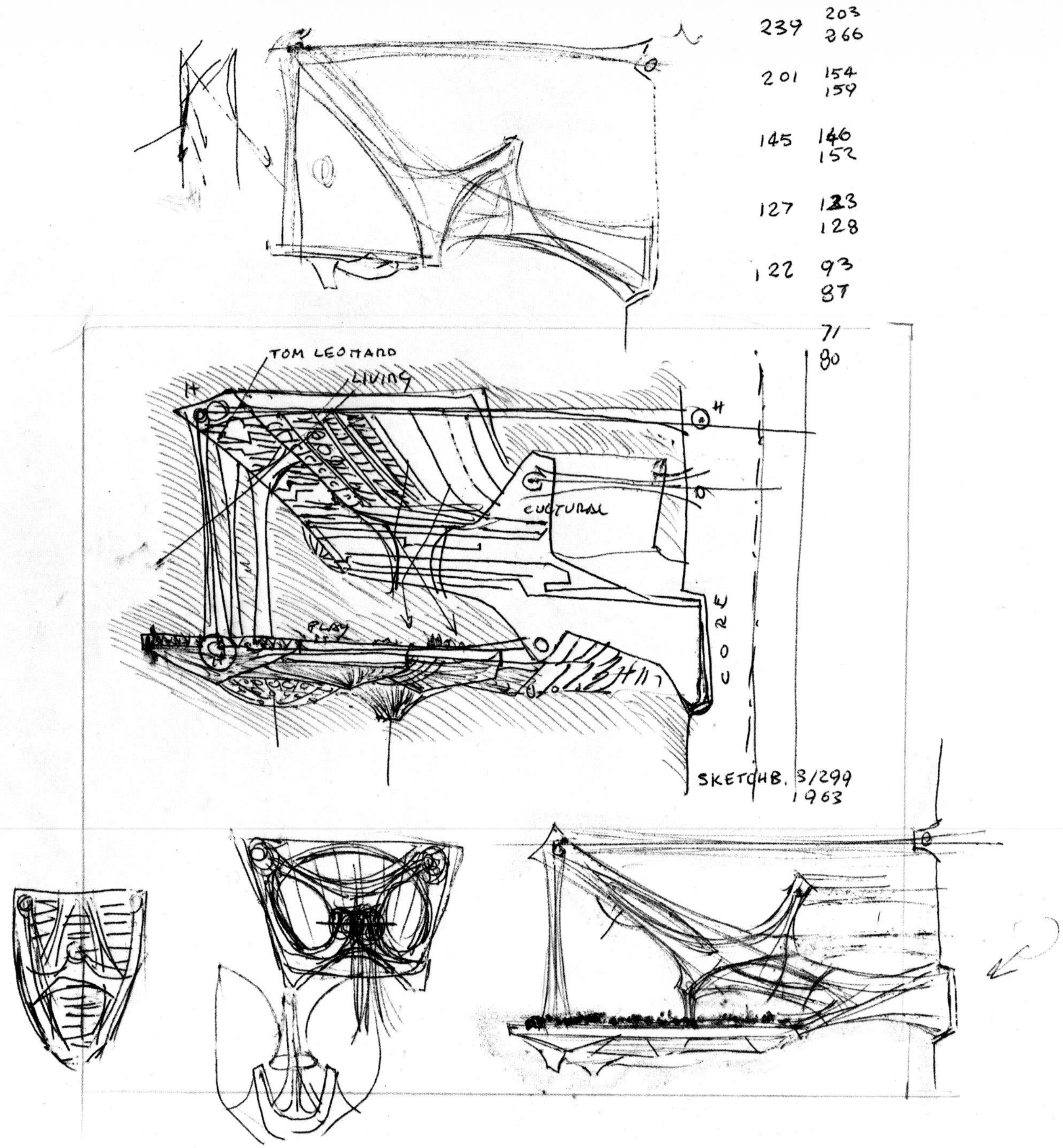

239 203 266
201 154 159
145 146 152
127 123 128
122 93 87
71
80
TOM LEONARD
LIVING
CULTURAL
PLAY
SKETCHB. 3/299
1963

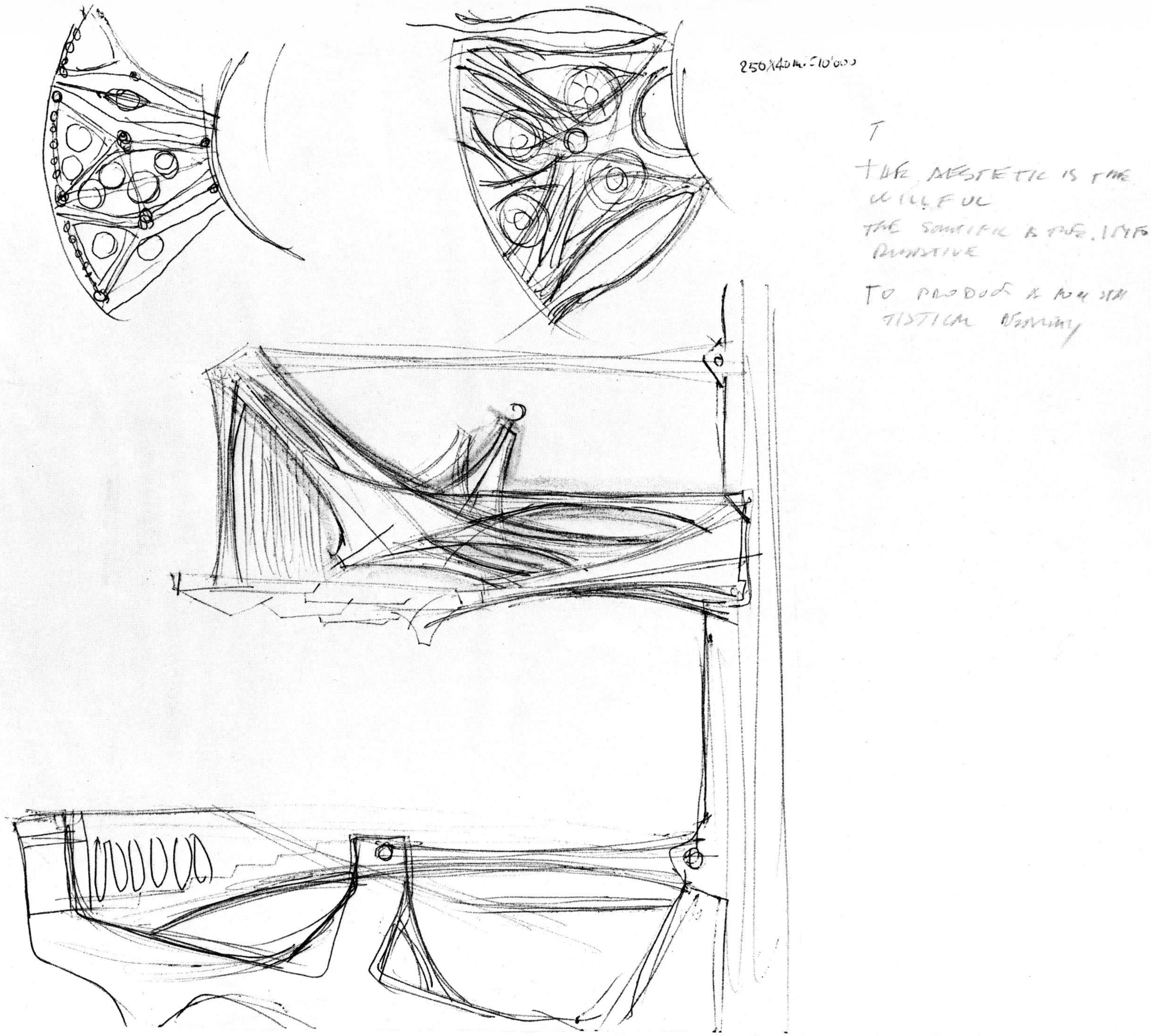
250X40M.=10'000
THE AESTETIC IS THE
WILLFUL
TO PRODUCE A

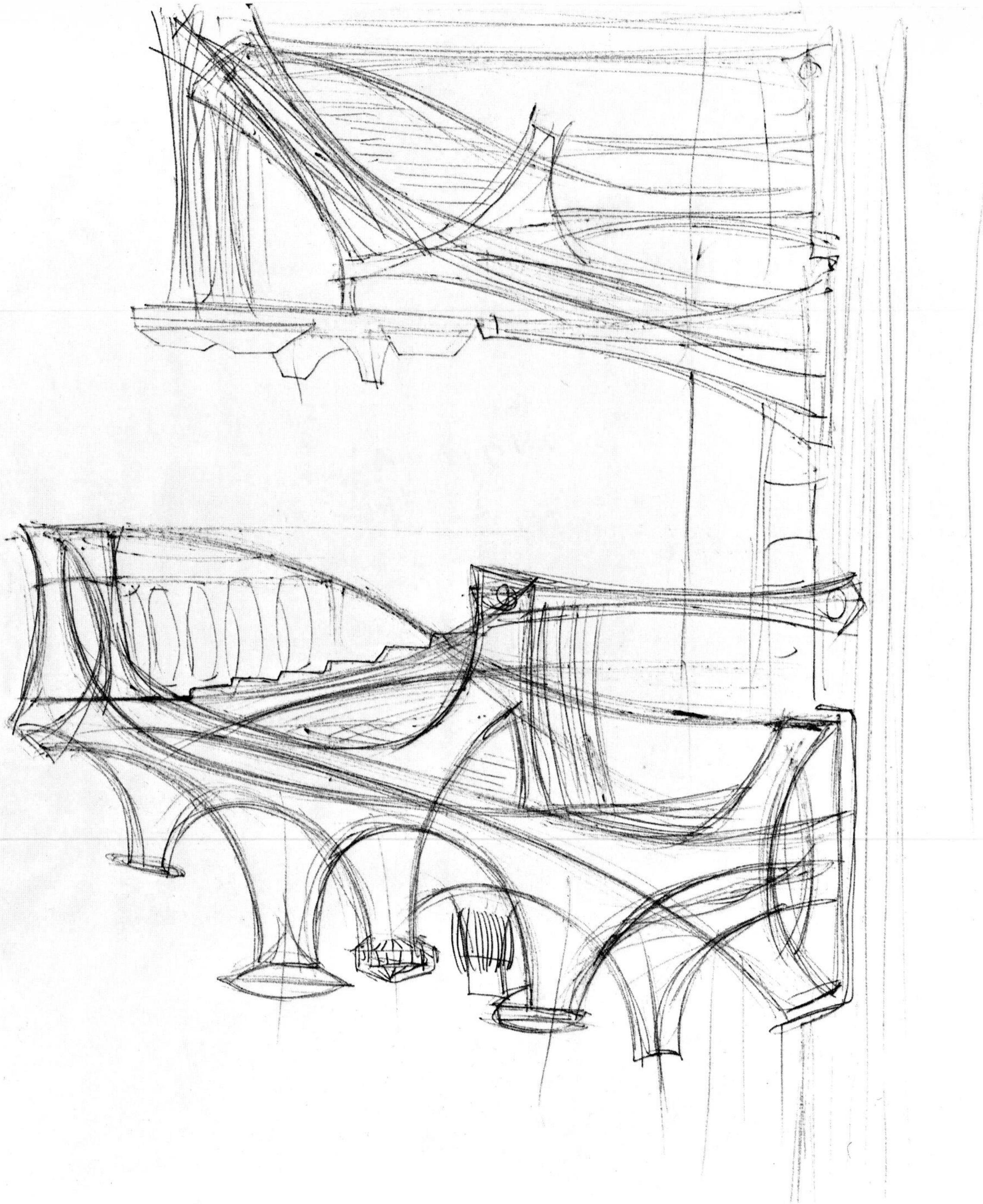

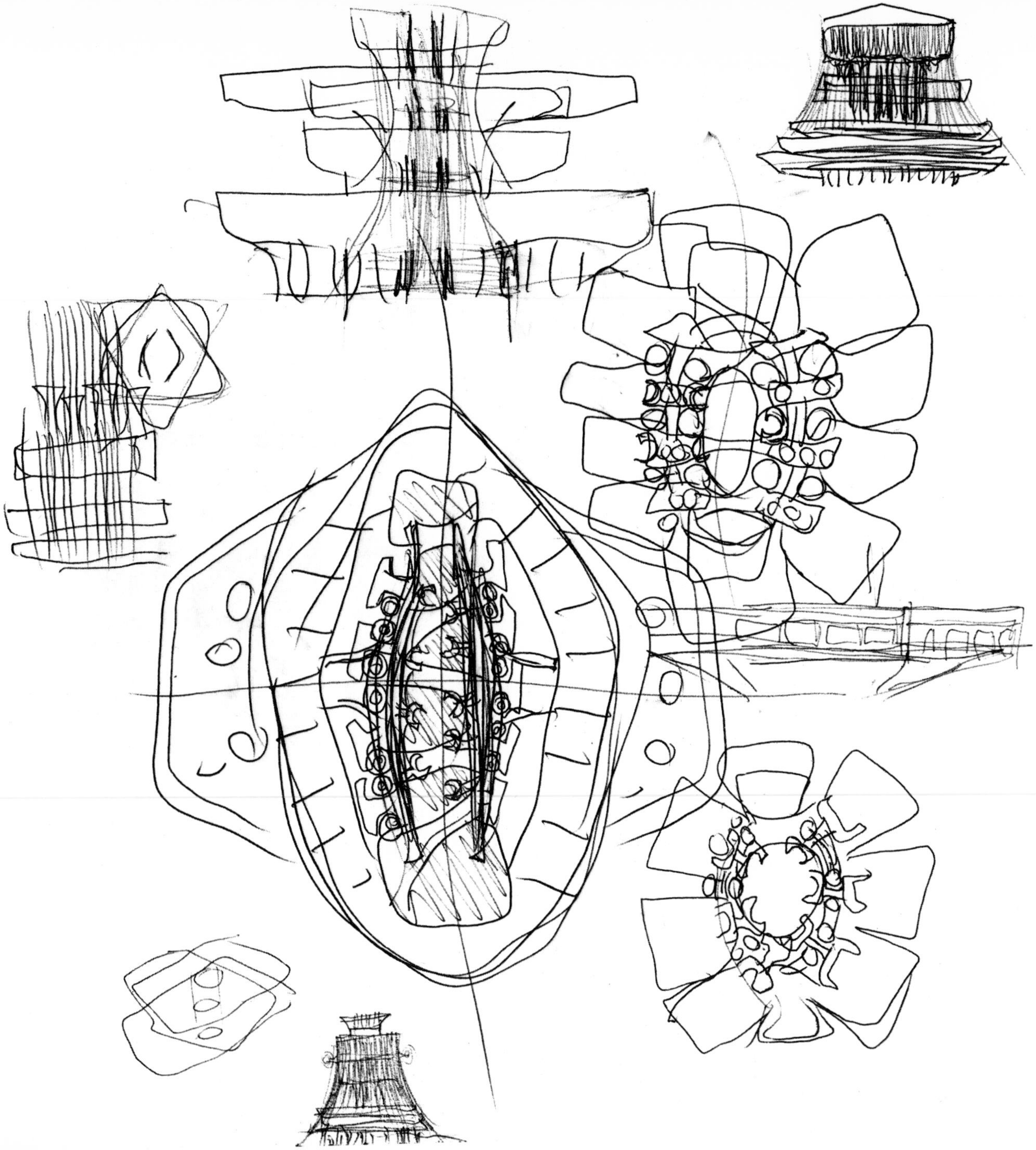

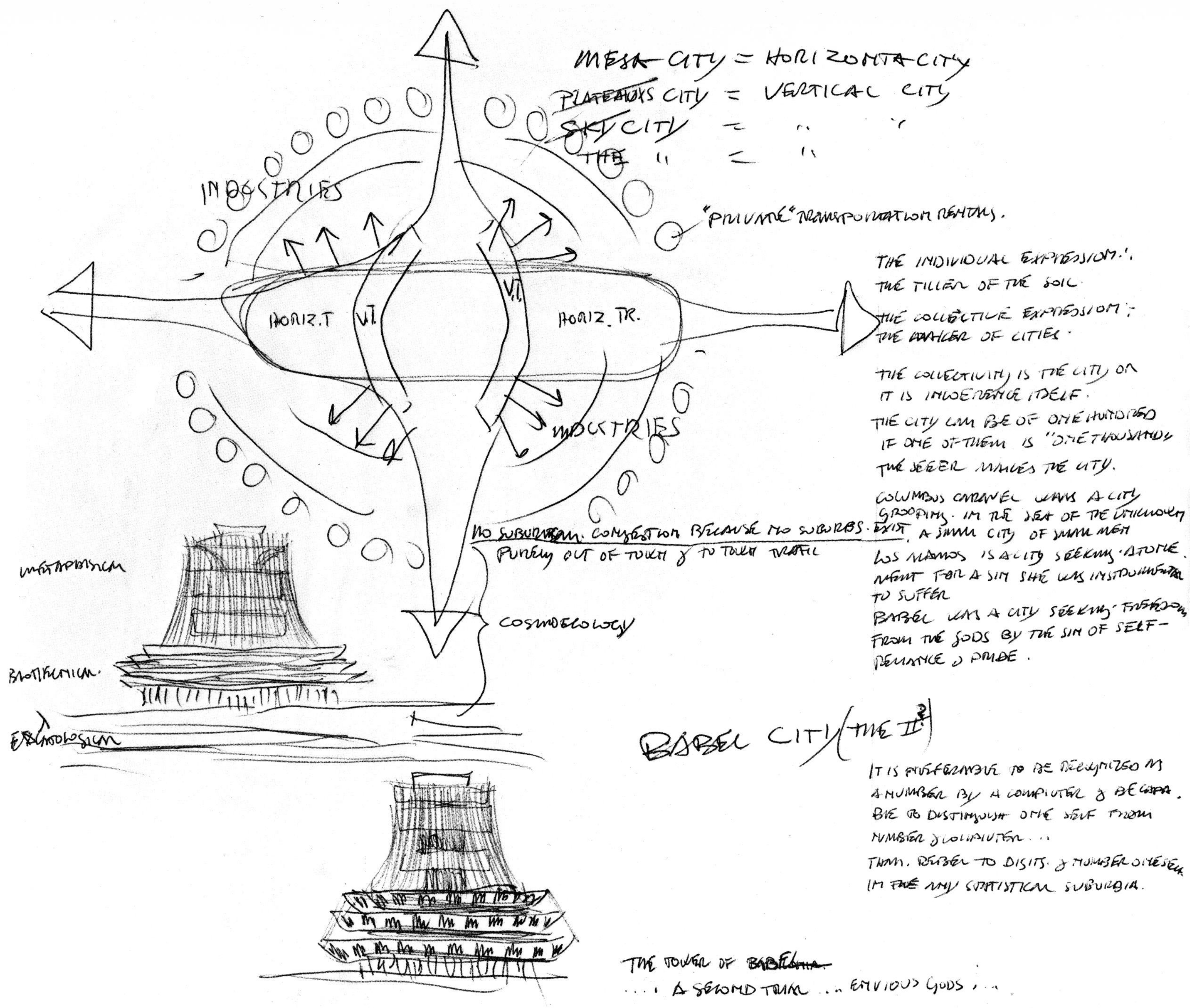
MESA CITY = HORIZONTAL CITY
CITY = VERTICAL CITY
CITY = " "
" = "
INDUSTRIES
"PRIVATE" TRANSPORTATION RENTALS.
HORIZ.T
V.T.
V.T.
HORIZ. TR.
INDUSTRIES
NO SUBURBAN. CONGESTION BECAUSE NO SUBURBS. EXIST
PURELY OUT OF TOWN & TO TOWN TRAFFIC
COSMOECOLOGY
METAPHYSICAL
BIOTECHNICAL.
ESCHATOLOGICAL
THE INDIVIDUAL EXPRESSION:.
THE TILLER OF THE SOIL.
THE COLLECTIVE EXPRESSION;
THE MAKER OF CITIES.
THE COLLECTIVITY IS THE CITY OR
IT IS INNOCENCE ITSELF.
THE CITY CAN BE OF ONE HUNDRED
IF ONE OF THEM IS "ONE THOUSAND"
THE SEER MAKES THE CITY.
COLUMBUS CARAVEL WAS A CITY
GROOPING. IN THE SEA OF THE UNKNOWN
A SMALL CITY OF SMALL MEN
LOS ALAMOS IS A CITY SEEKING ATONE-
MENT FOR A SIN SHE WAS INSTRUMENTAL
TO SUFFER
BABEL WAS A CITY SEEKING FREEDOM
FROM THE GODS BY THE SIN OF SELF-
RELIANCE & PRIDE.
BABEL CITY (THE II?)
IT IS PREFERABLE TO BE RECOGNIZED AS
A NUMBER BY A COMPUTER & BE CAPA-
BLE TO DISTINGUISH ONE SELF FROM
NUMBER & COMPUTER ...
THAN REBEL TO DIGITS & NUMBER ONESELF
IN THE STATISTICAL SUBURBIA.
THE TOWER OF BABEL
.... A SECOND TRIAL ... ENVIOUS GODS ...

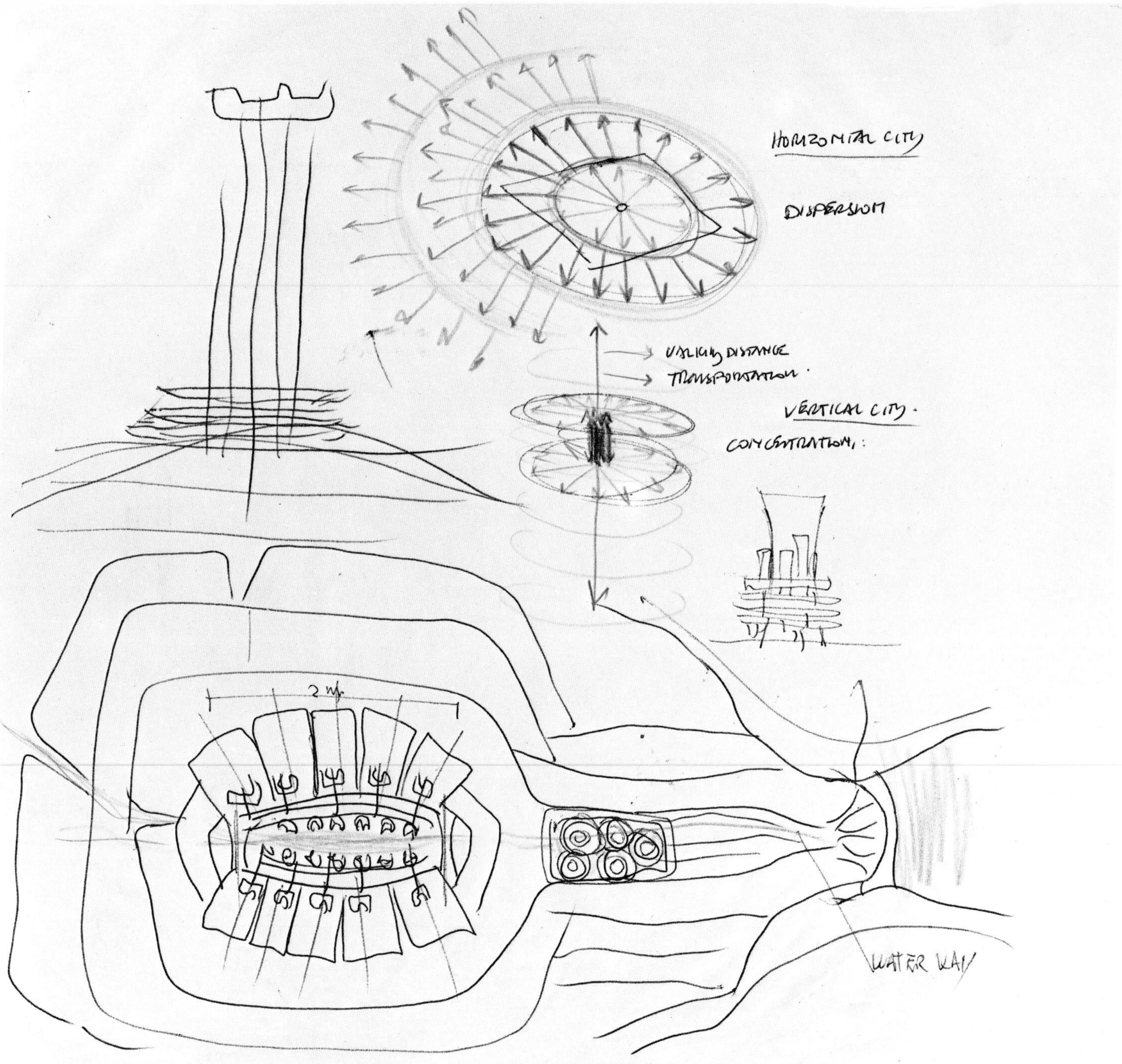
HORIZONTAL CITY
DISPERSION
VALIGING DISTANCE
TRANSPORTATION.
VERTICAL CITY.
CONCENTRATION:
2 m.
WATER WAY

BRIDGESTO PARK

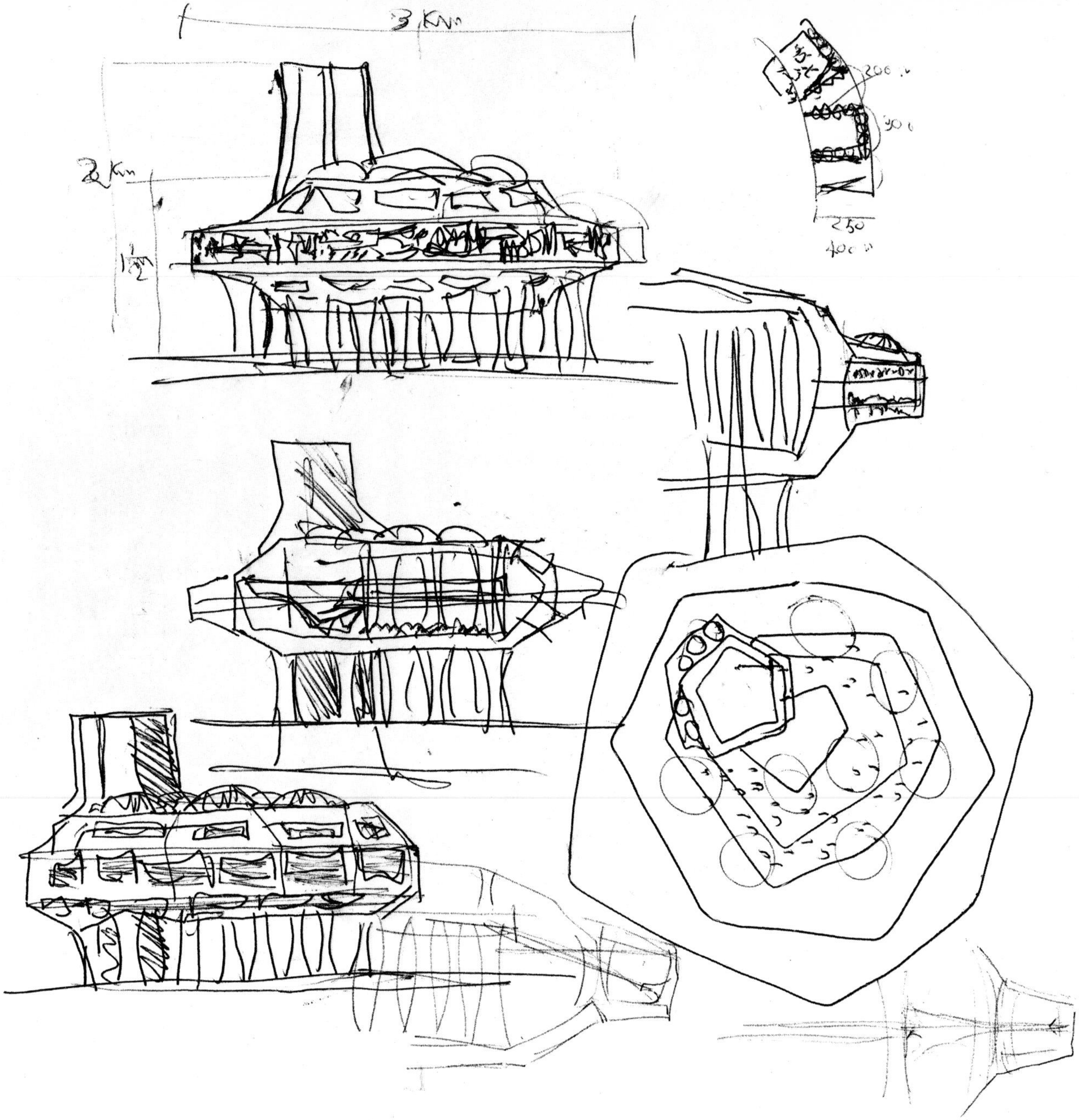
3 Km

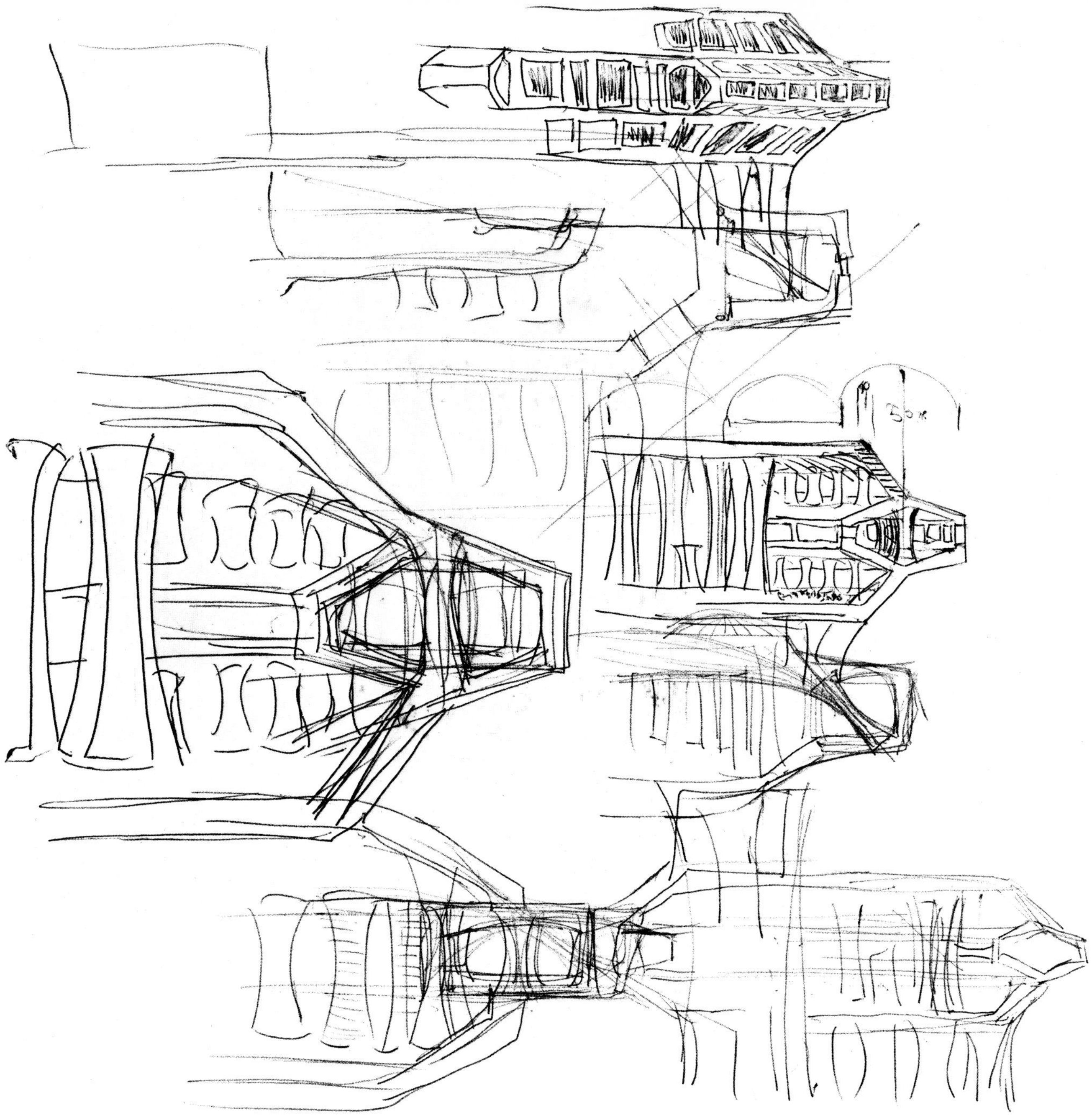

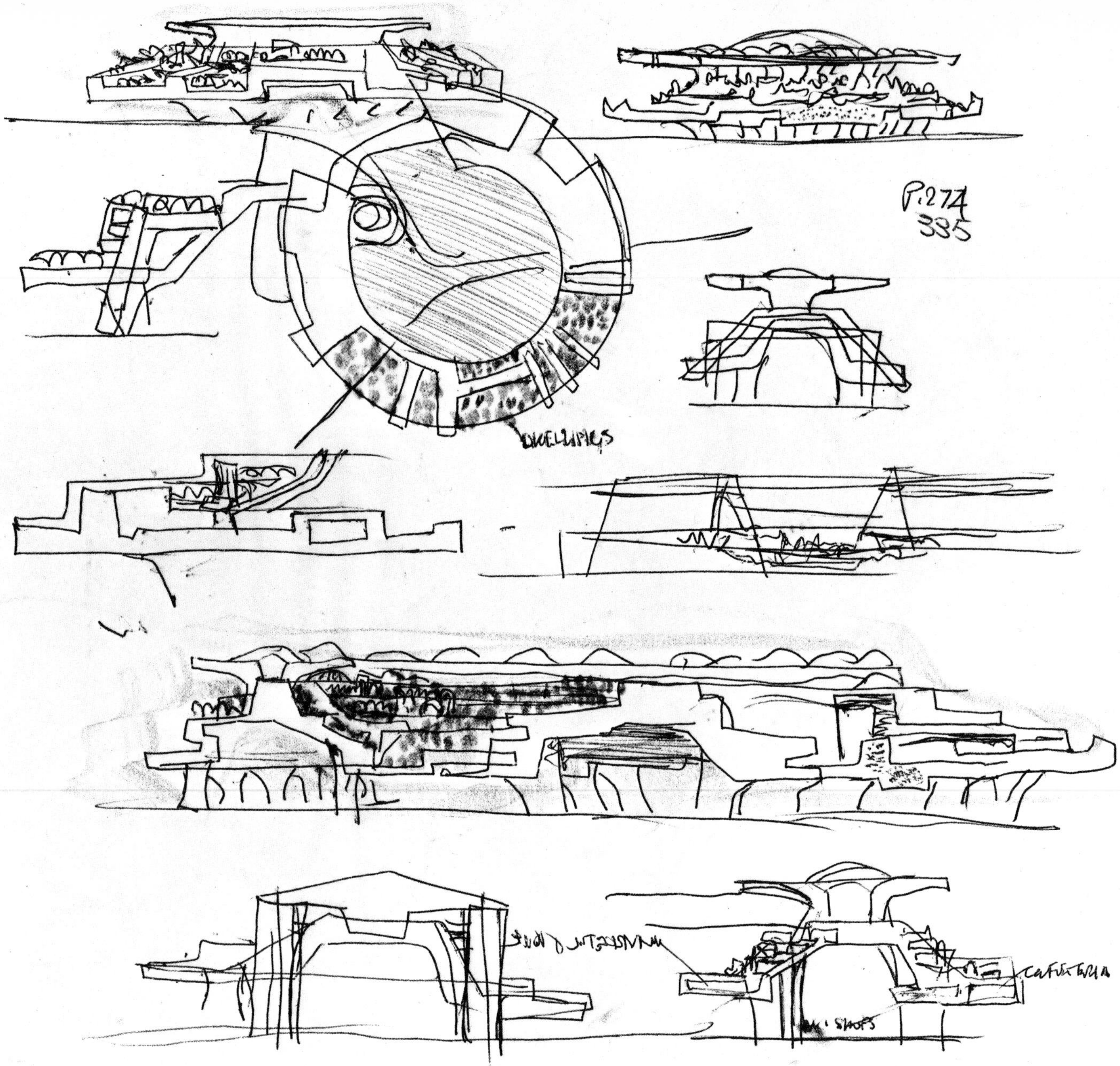
P.274
335
DWELLINGS
CAFETERIA
SHOPS

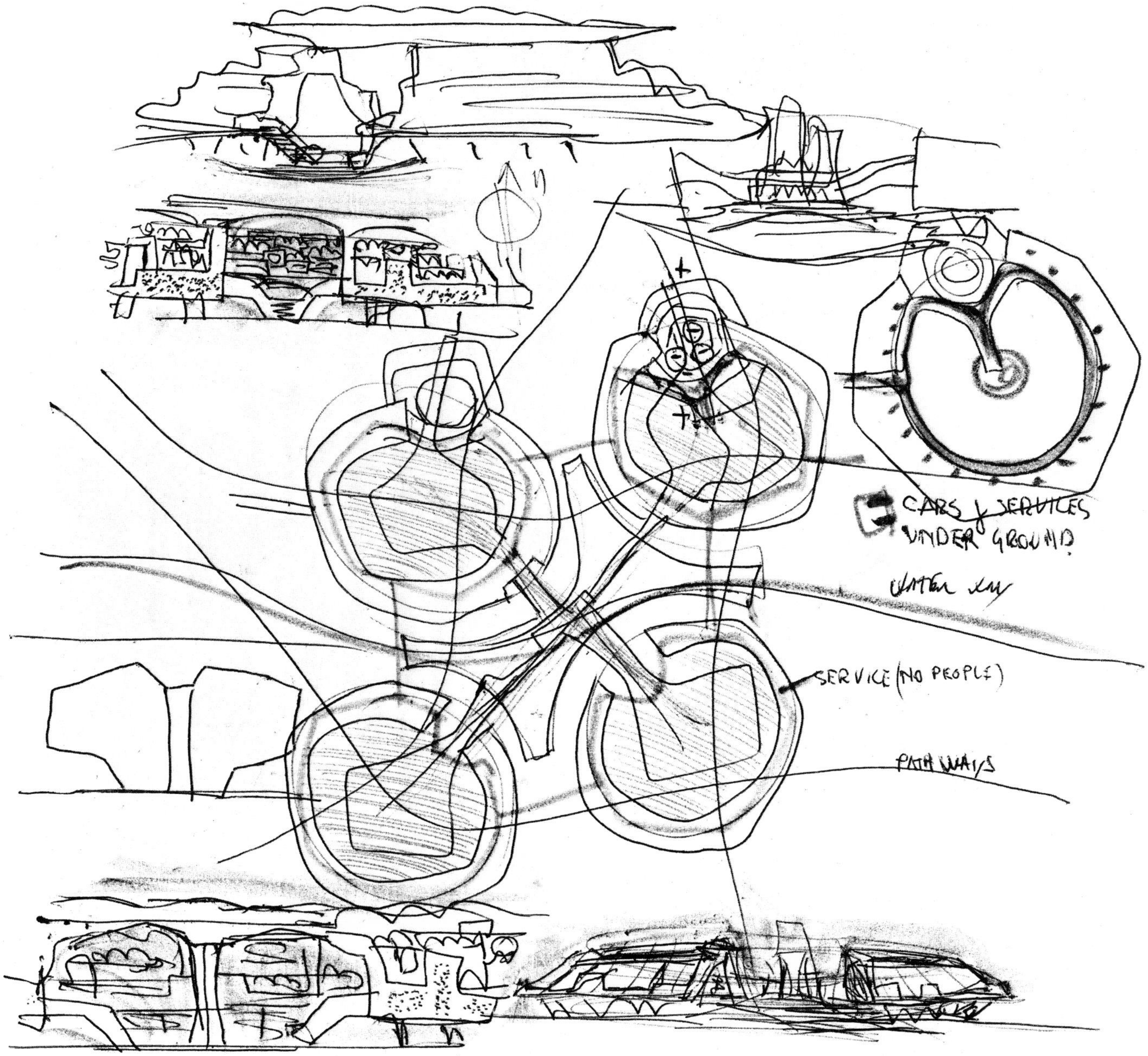
CARS & SERVICES UNDER GROUND
SERVICE (NO PEOPLE)
PATH WAYS

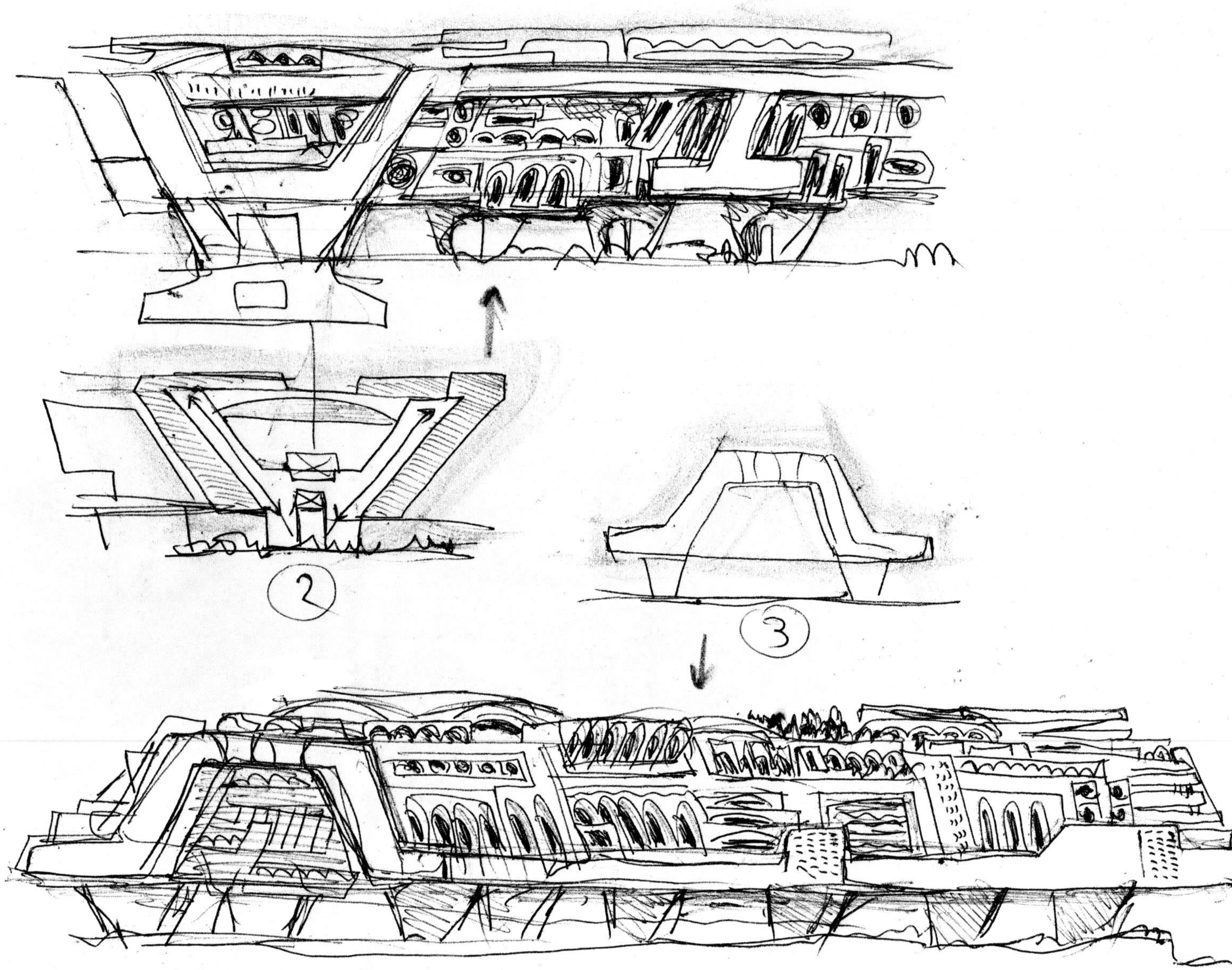

2
3

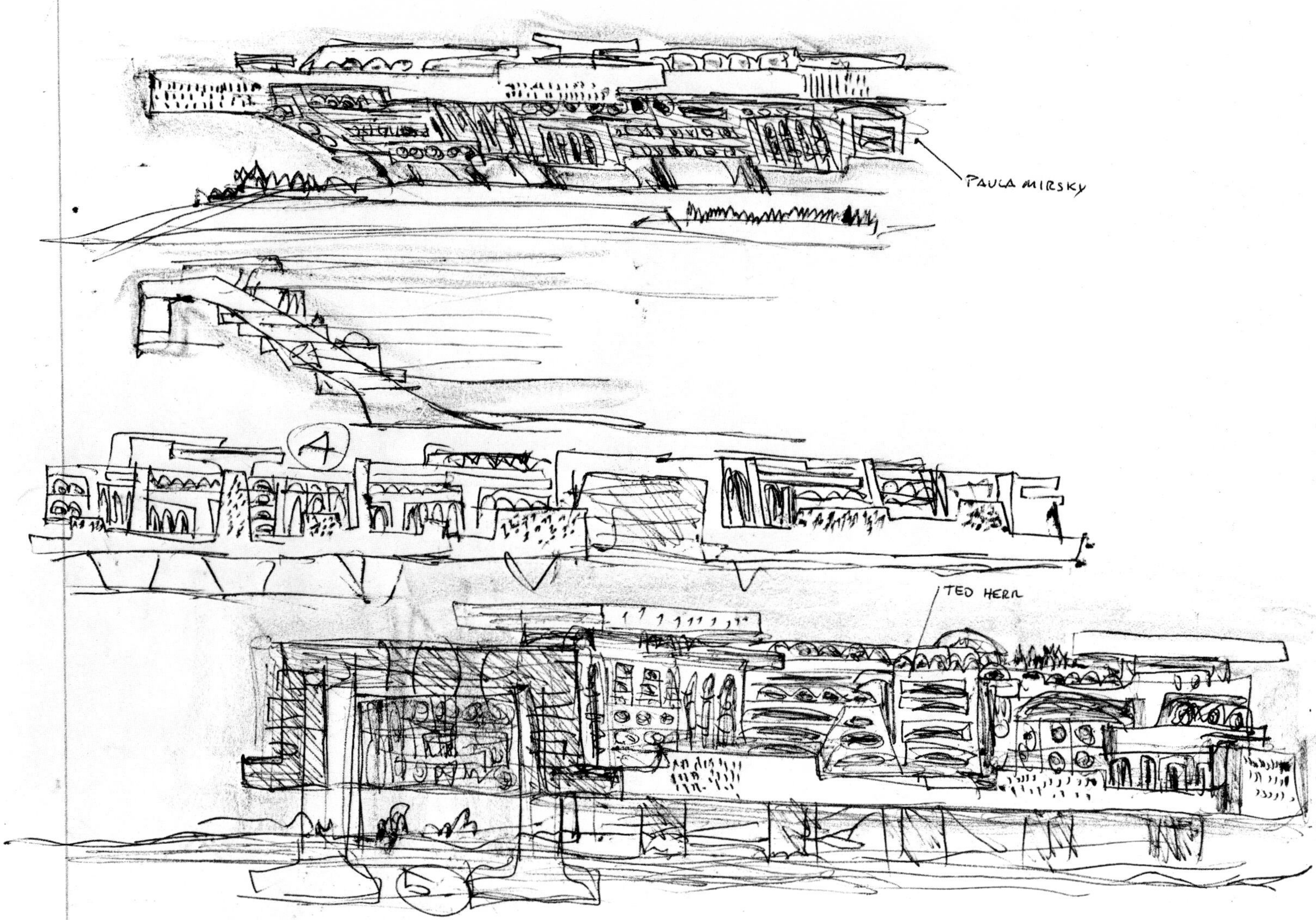

SKETCHB 3/359
1964

SHOPS
CAFETERIAS
WORKSHOPS
&

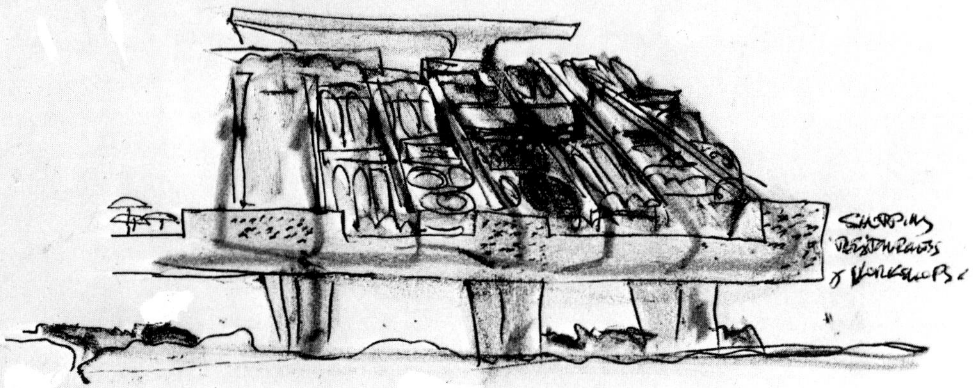
SHOPPING
& WORKSHOPS

PERMANENT STRUCTURE
FOR ACCESSES & SERVICES,
VARIANTE, IN FUNCTION OF DWELLERS

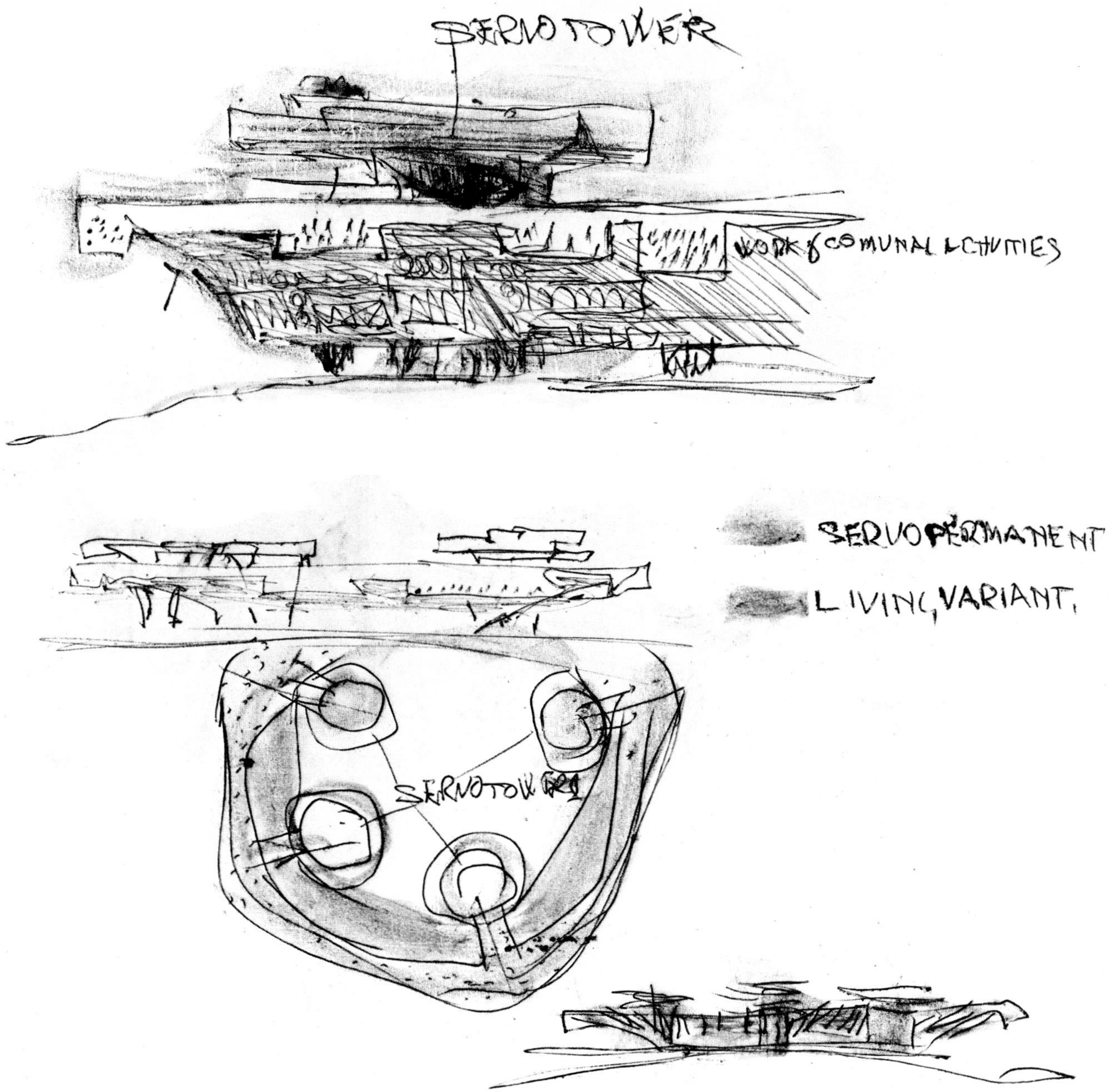
SERVOTOWER
WORK & COMUNAL ACTIVITIES
SERVOPERMANENT
LIVING, VARIANT.
SERVOTOWERS

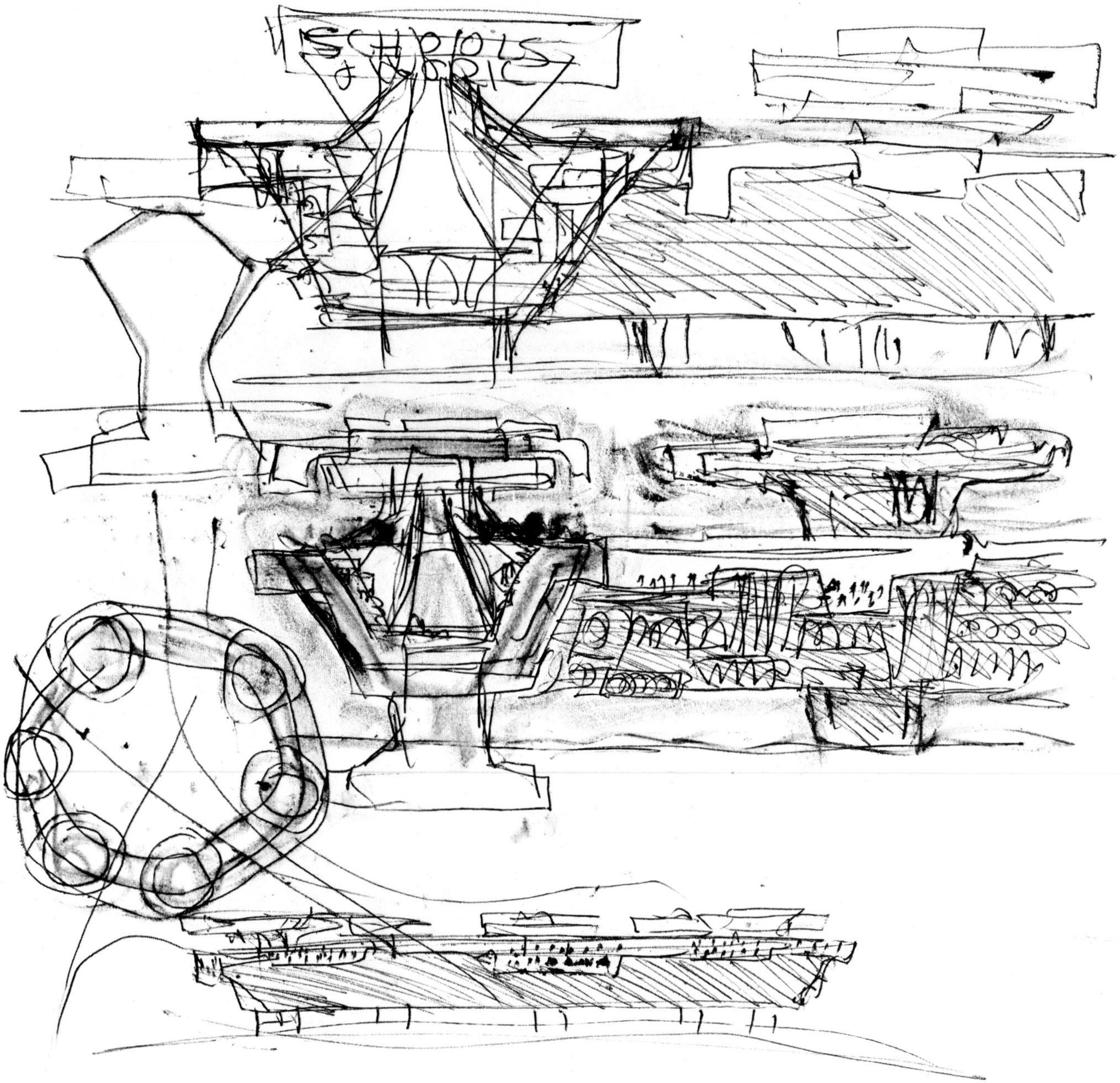

1970
There are two possible reasons why a person (and a society) becomes less sensitive to the taste of food and the pleasures of the table. One is that such a person has etherialized, that is to say his interests have become less earthly. As the mind takes over larger grounds for exploration, the least sophisticated senses, taste and smell, are quarantined, and the most sophisticated, sight and hearing take over. While the glutton survives to eat, the saint eats to survive. The other reason is that the person, or society, is desensitized by a growing callousness of the soul and decay of the environment. Insensitivity comes in with a paraphernalia of banners to camouflage the loss of joy once identifiable with daily routines, one of them the ritual of food. A triple ritual, indeed: the ritual of growing food, the ritual of cooking, the ritual of eating. In a no-nonsense society, gardening and cooking are put on an assembly-line basis. Eating is dependent on the first two. It follows automatically, either deprived of pleasure or granting a pleasure of coarse quality. For the taste characteristic of each family is substituted a national taste, symbolized by the hot dog of Seattle or Miami, Saint Louis or Las Vegas.

Cooking is eminently a craft. It has much to do with the materials at hand, from food to utensils. It is a geographically determined occupation. It has to be rooted to be genuine. The reason why the "art" of cooking and its imperatives over- or undershoot the mark is its uprootedness. An uprooted craft is a neurotic fever for the exotic, lacking ancestral spicing and the subtlety of a slowly developing palatal sensitivity.

So the craft of cooking has been lost. Its place has been taken by pre-mass cooking, which is really selling and packaging, a distracting substitution for the "art." The restaurant is seen as the place for the ritual of cooking and eating.

CAMERA — dissolvenze
MODEL OF CITY ⟶ UNIVERSITY ⟶ CONTINUUM ⟶ ART VILLAGES ⟶ THEOLOGICAL ⟶ MODEL
model
model
model
2000 x 20

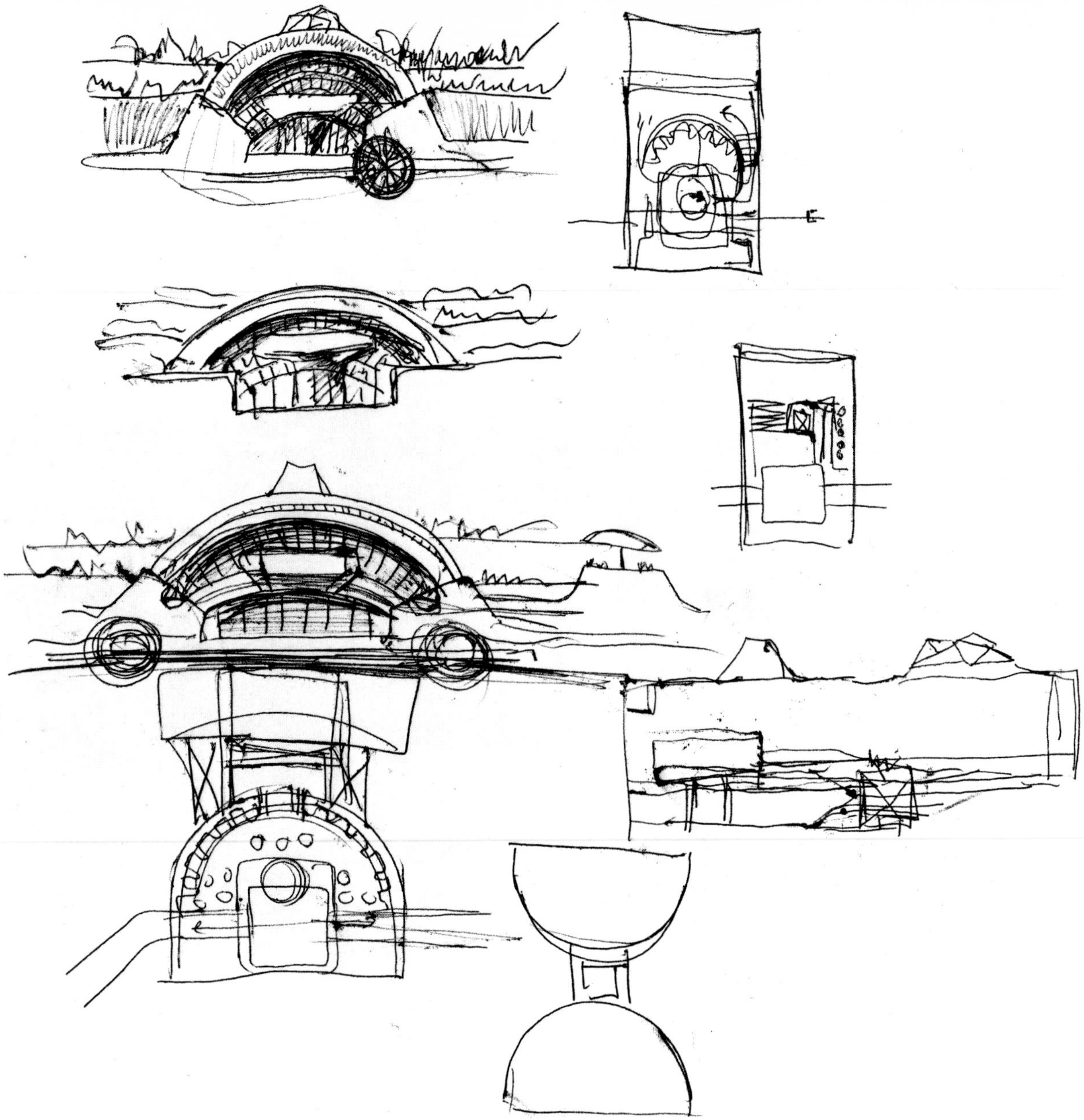

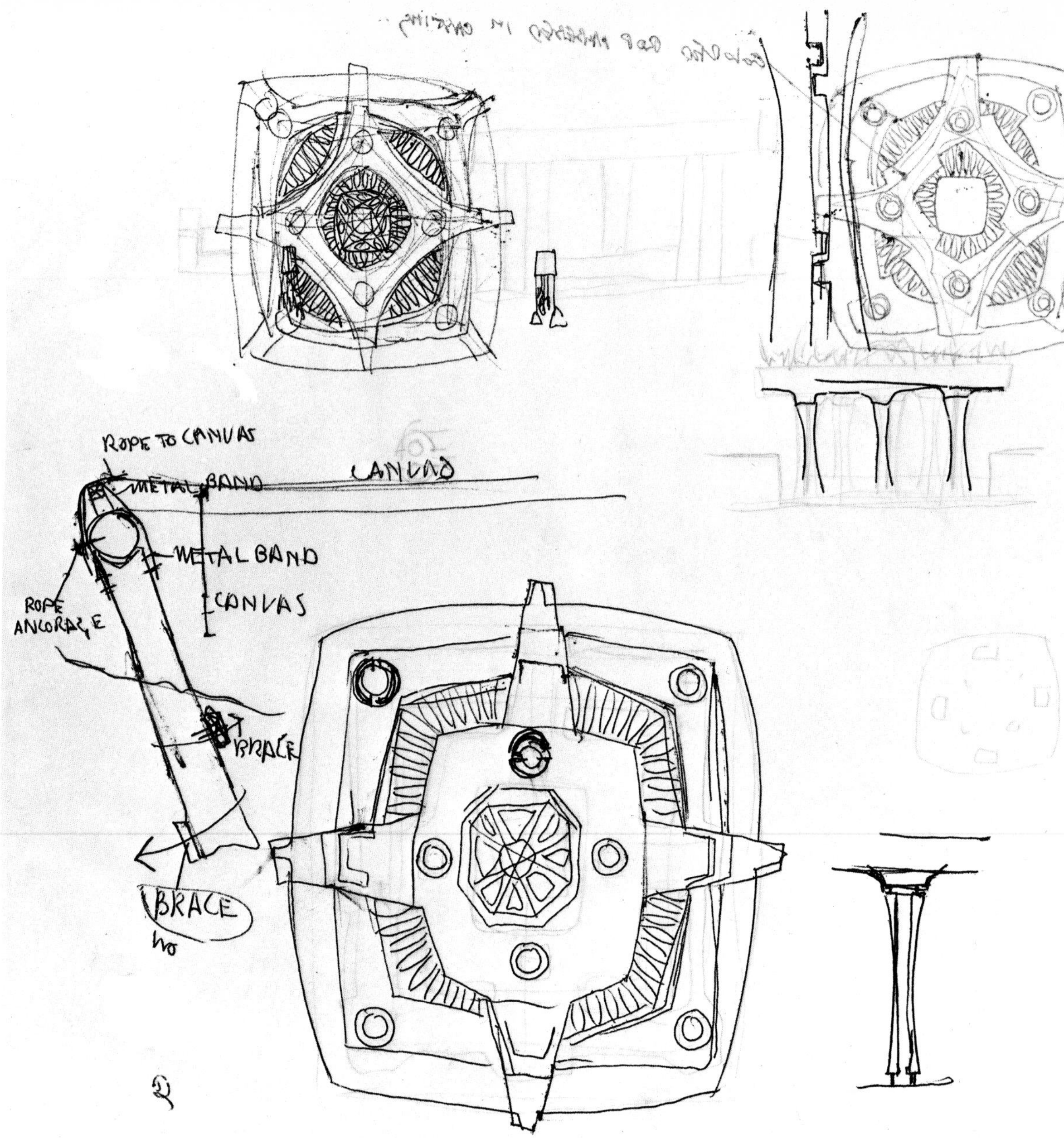
ROPE TO CANVAS
CANVAS
METAL BAND
METAL BAND
CANVAS
ROPE ANCORAGE
BRACE
BRACE
no

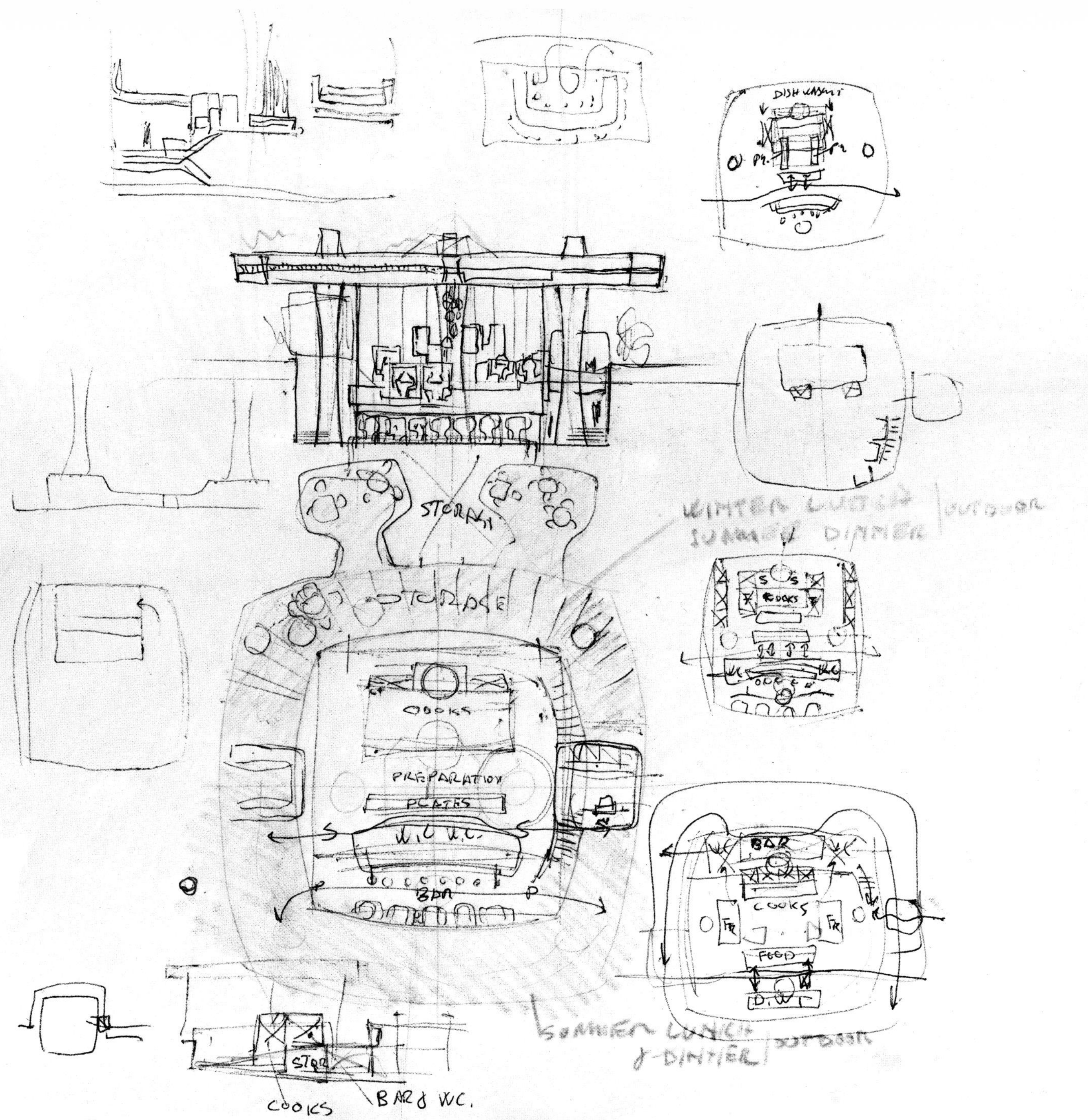
STORAGE
COOKS
PREPARATION
PLATES
W.C. W.C.
BAR
COOKS
FOOD
BAR
STOR
COOKS
BAR & W.C.

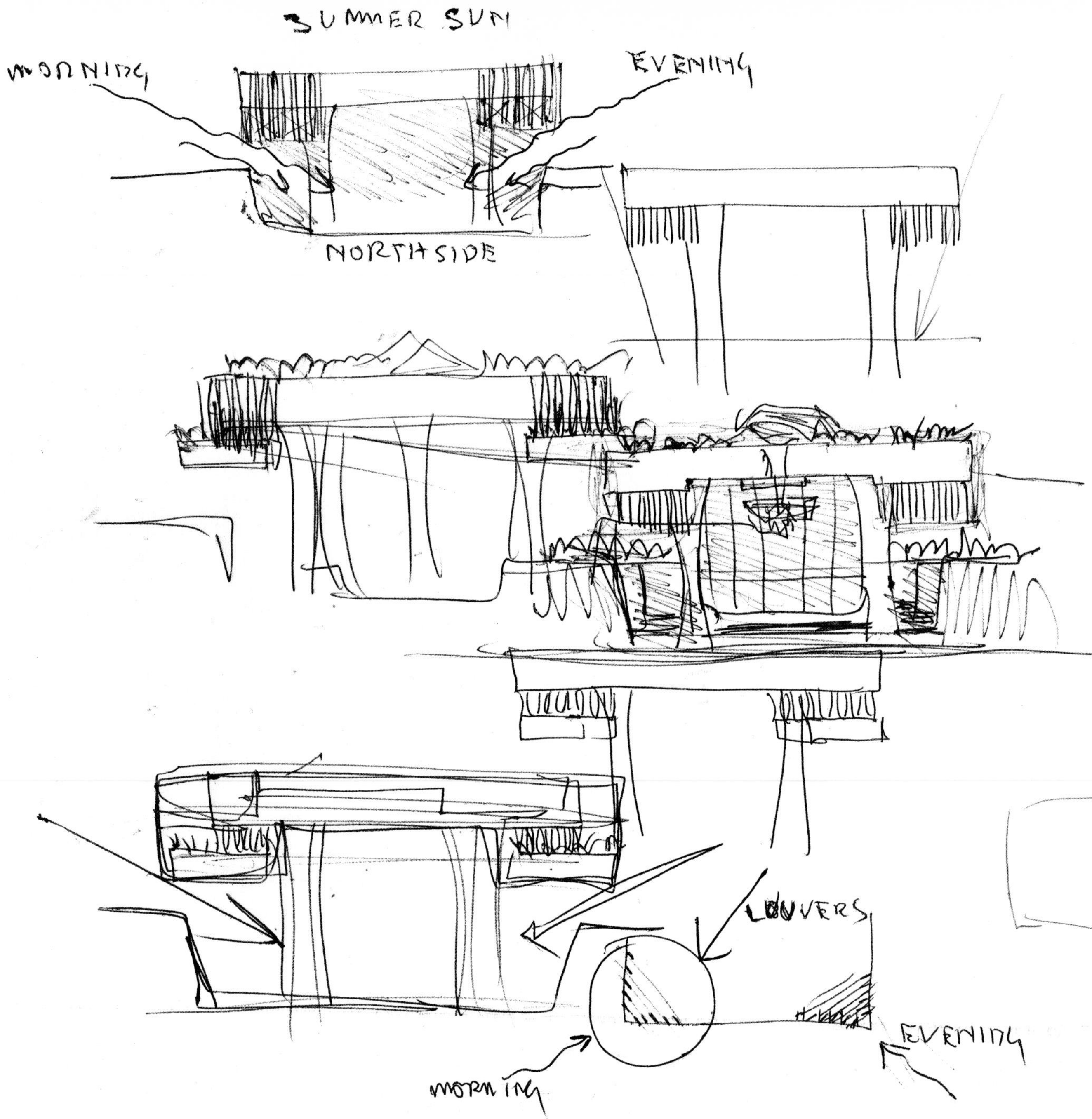
SUMMER SUN
MORNING
EVENING
NORTHSIDE
LOUVERS
EVENING
MORNING

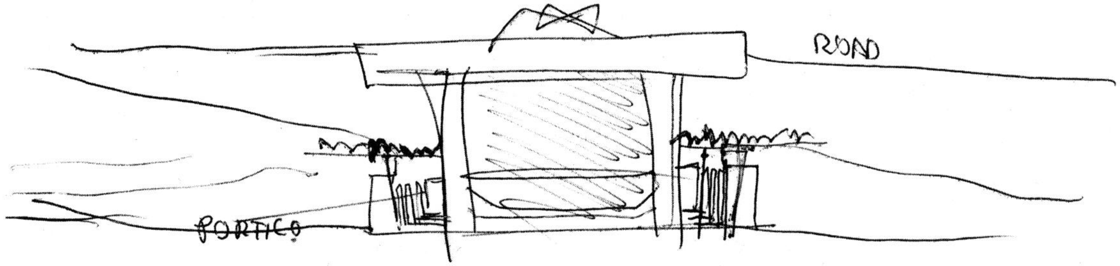
ROAD
PORTICO

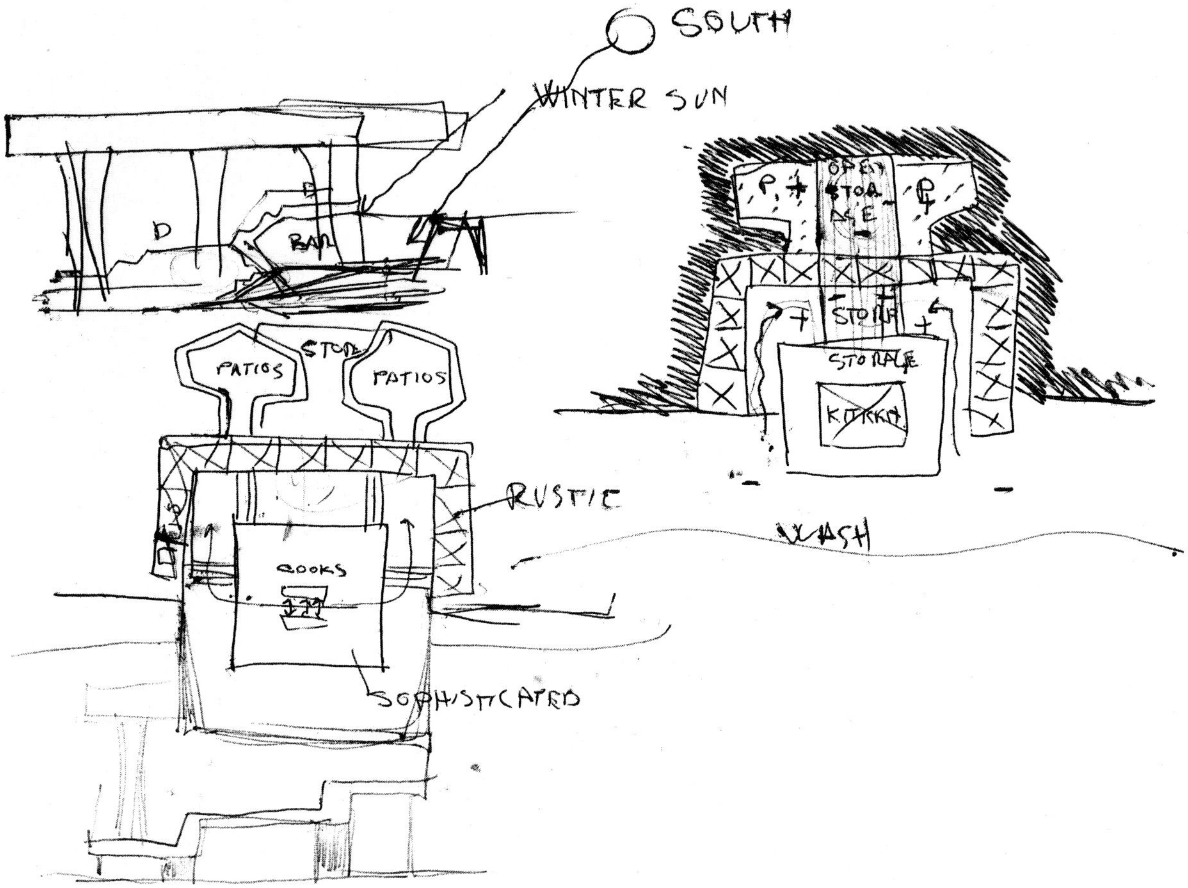
SOUTH
WINTER SUN
BAR
PATIOS
PATIOS
RUSTIC
BOOKS
SOPHISTICATED
STORAGE
WASH

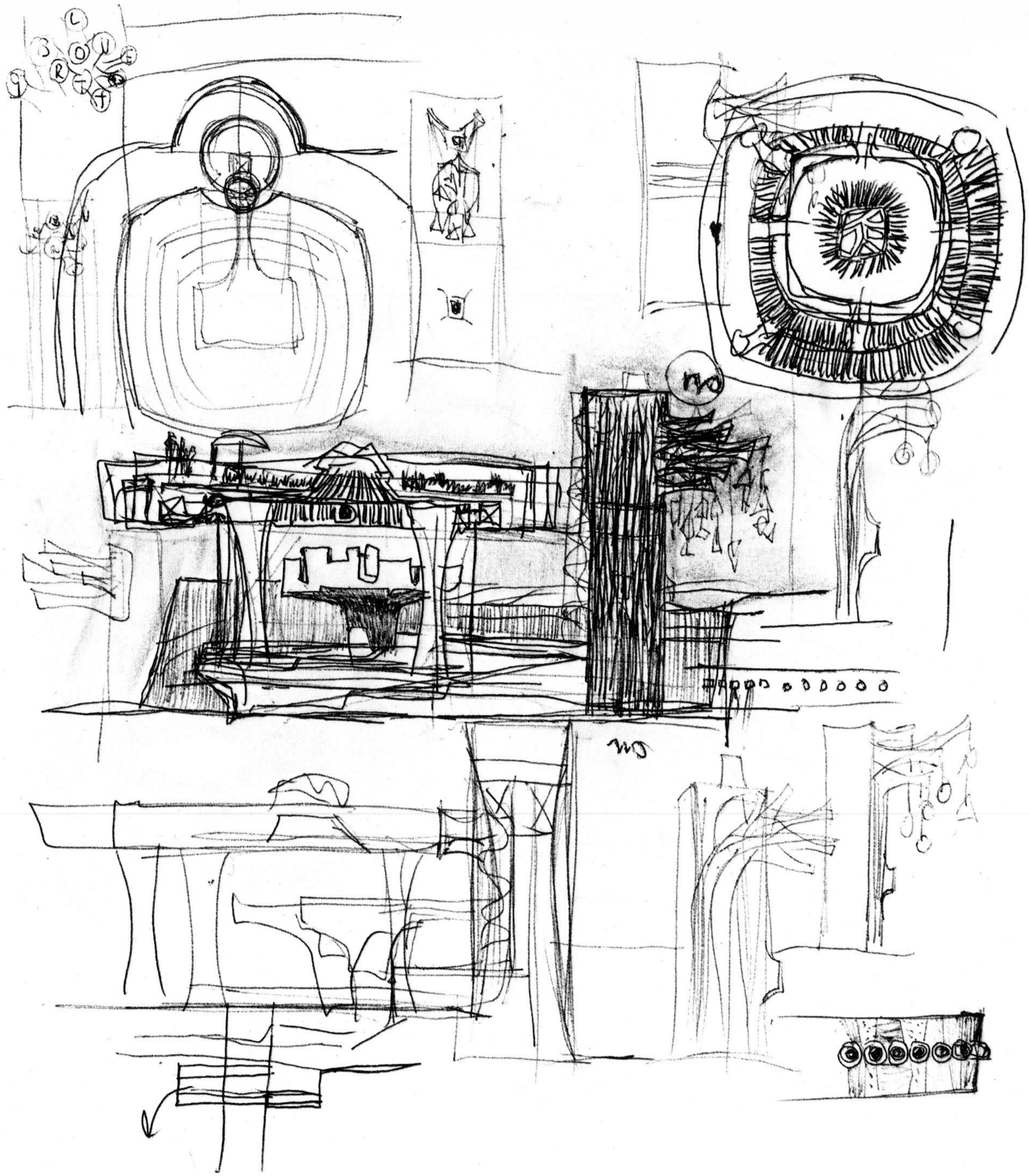

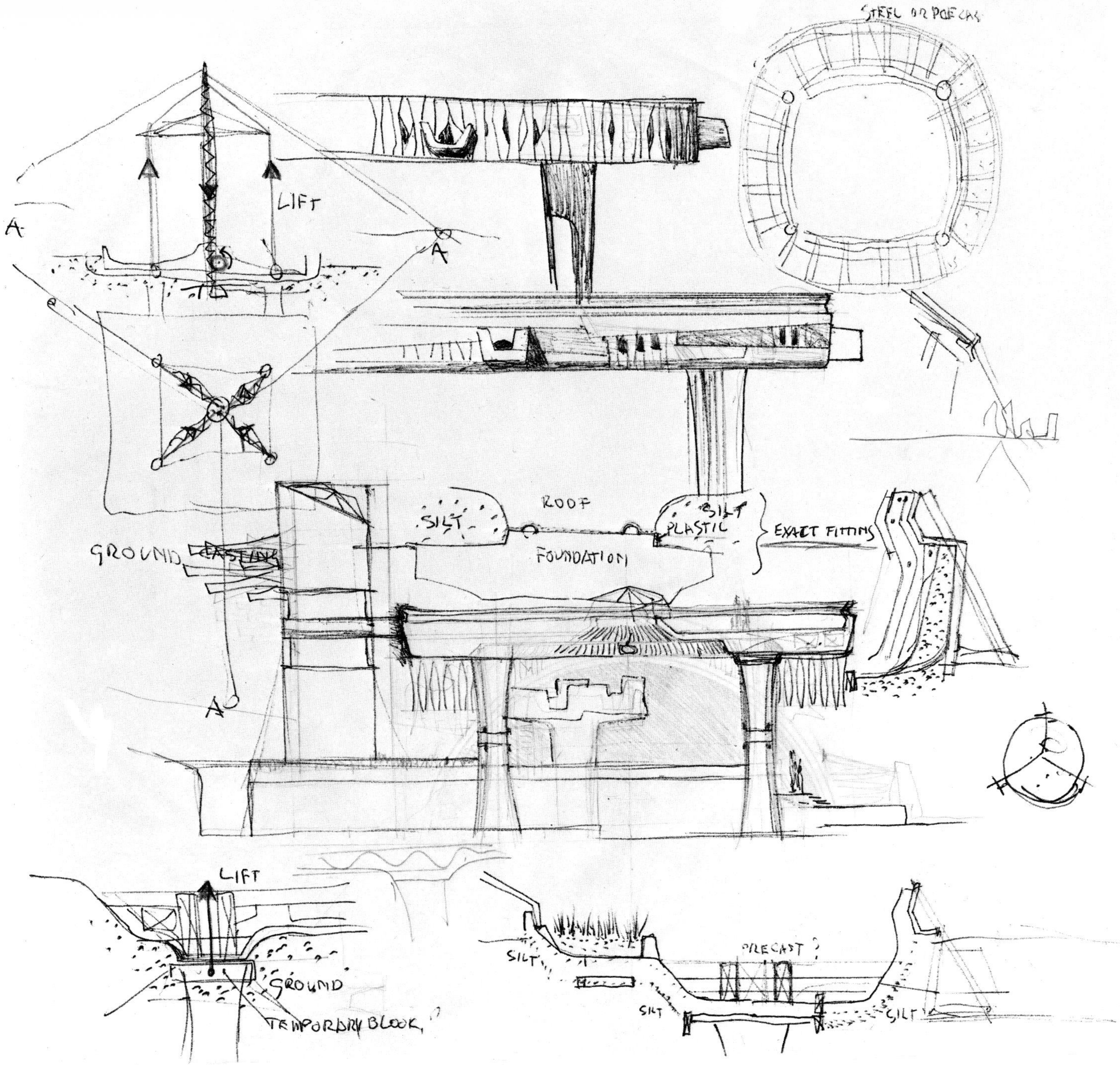
LIFT
A
A
A
ROOF
SILT
SILT
PLASTIC
EXACT FITTINGS
GROUND
FOUNDATION
LIFT
GROUND
TEMPORARY BLOCK
SILT
PRECAST ?
SILT
SILT

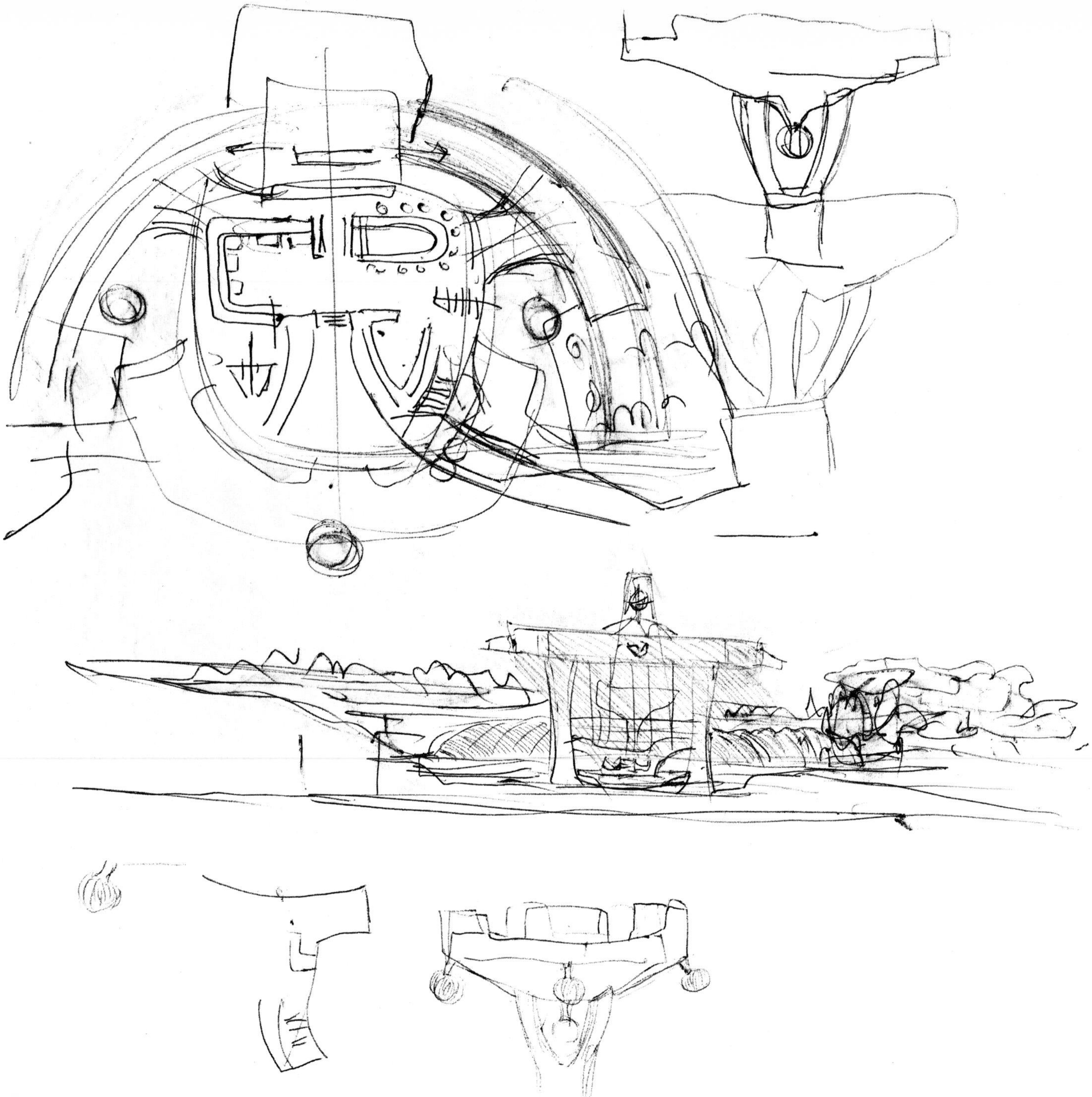

50 – 25

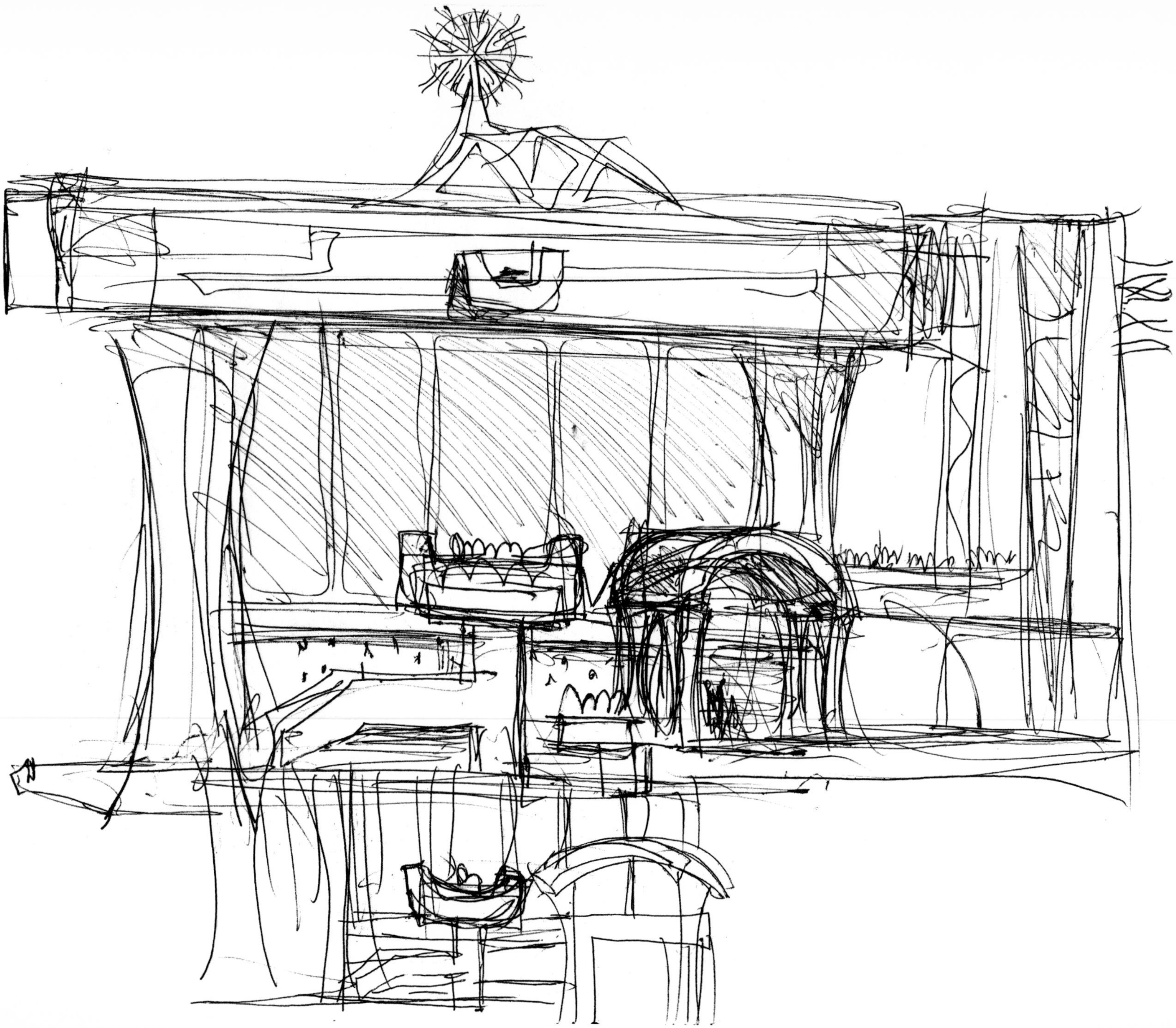

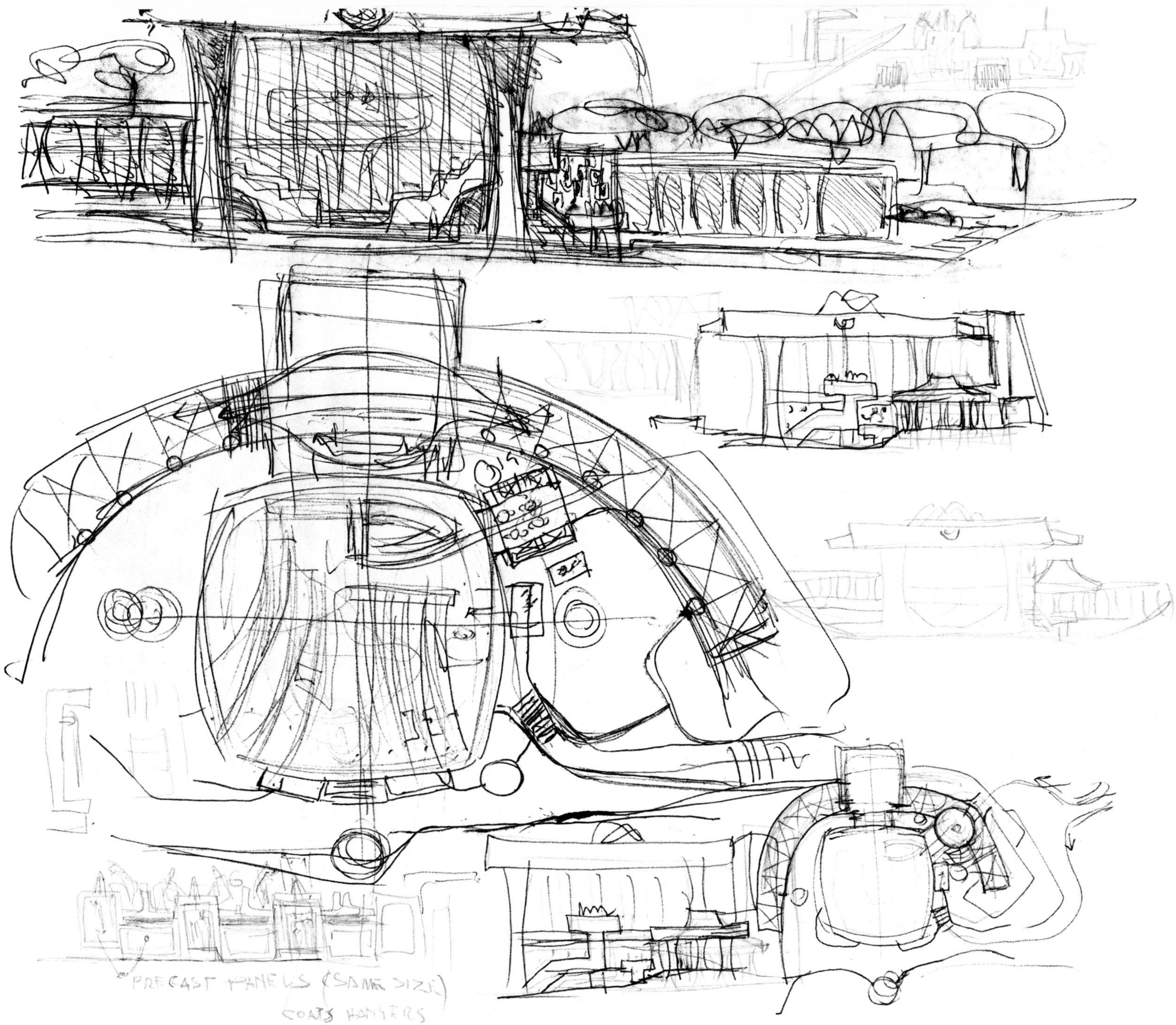
PRECAST PANELS (SAME SIZE)
COATS HANGERS

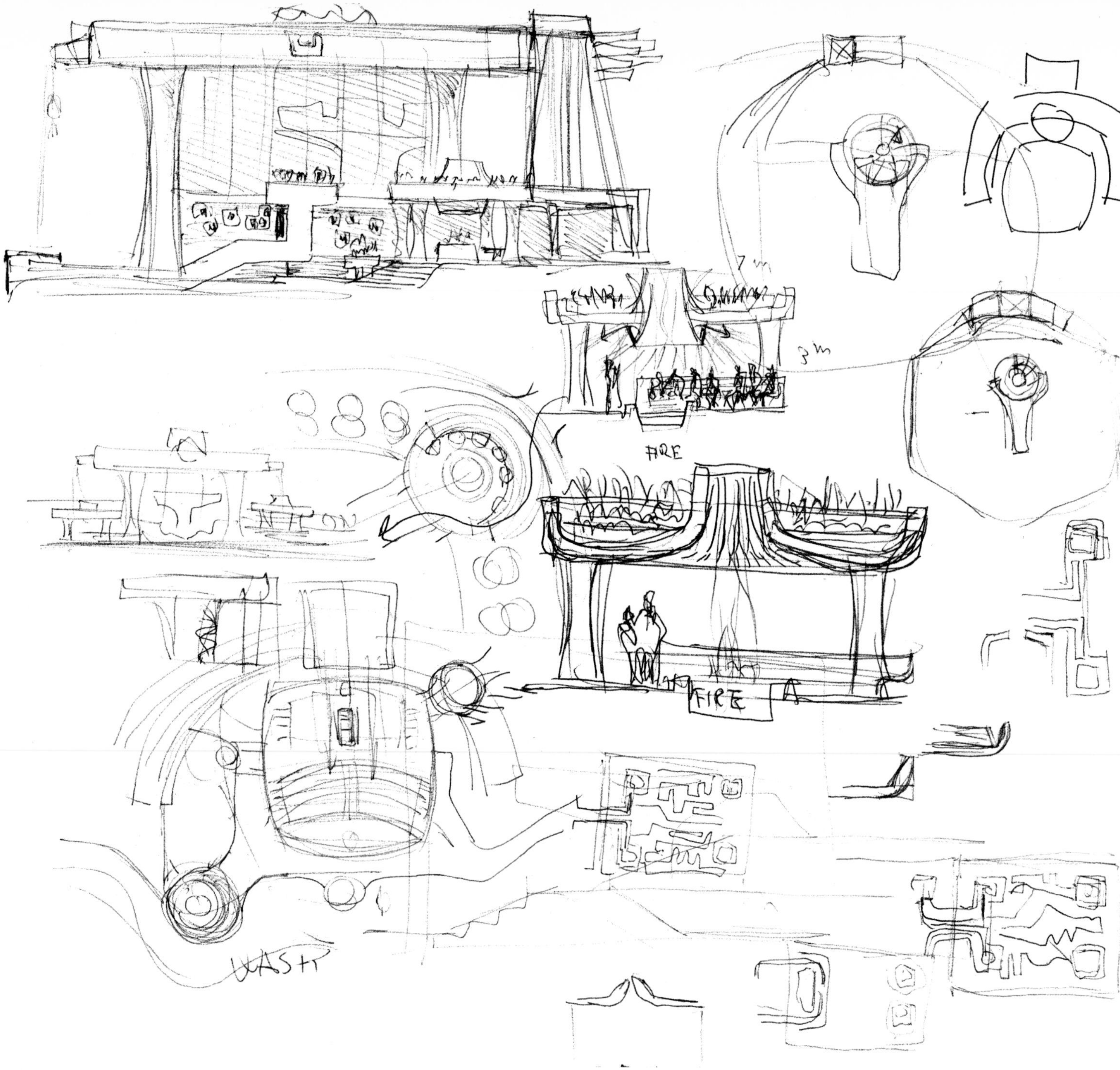
FIRE
FIRE
WASH

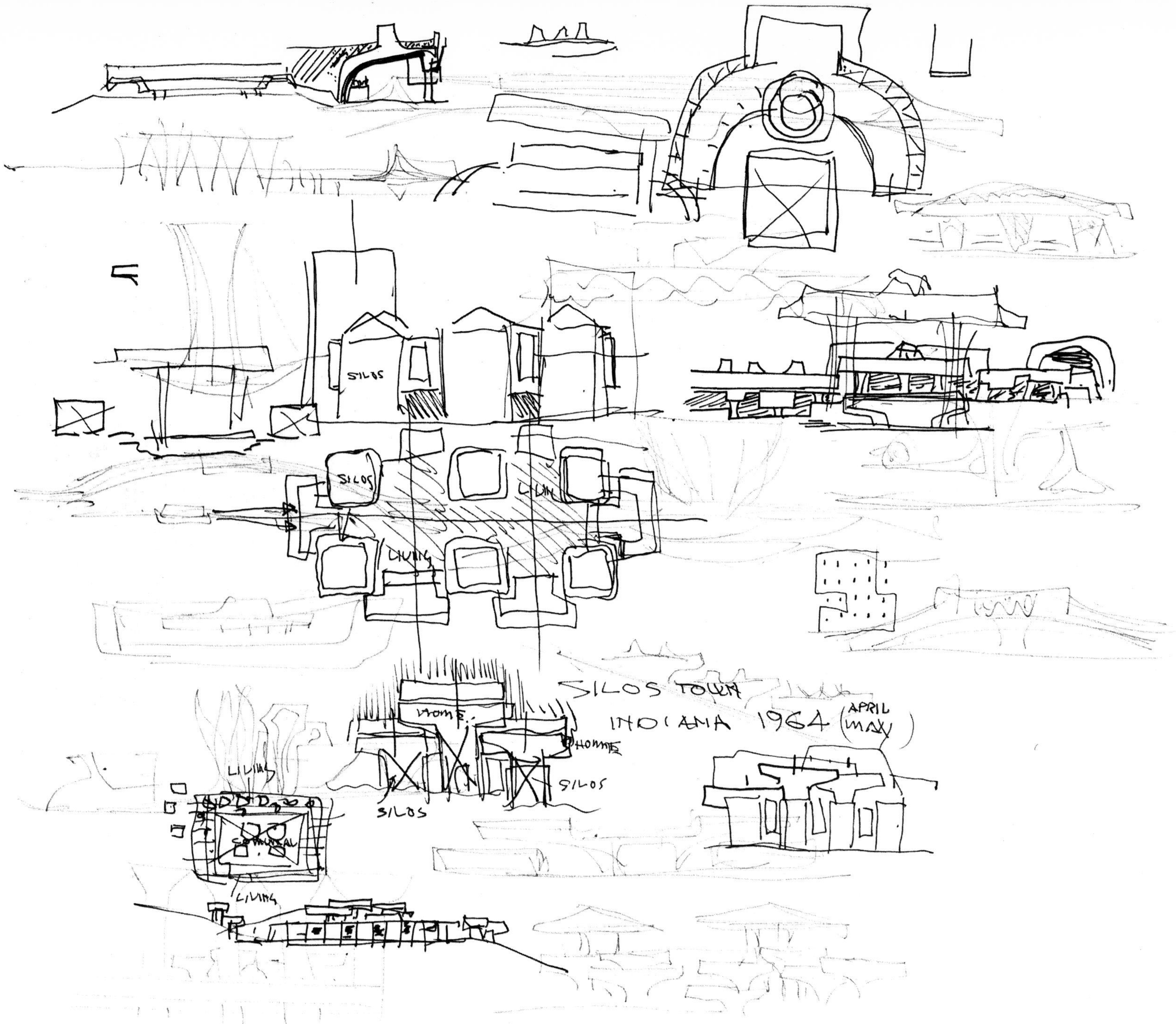
SILOS
SILOS
LIVING
SILOS TOWN
INDIANA 1964 (APRIL MAY)
HOME
HOMME
SILOS
SILOS
LIVING
COMMUNAL
LIVING

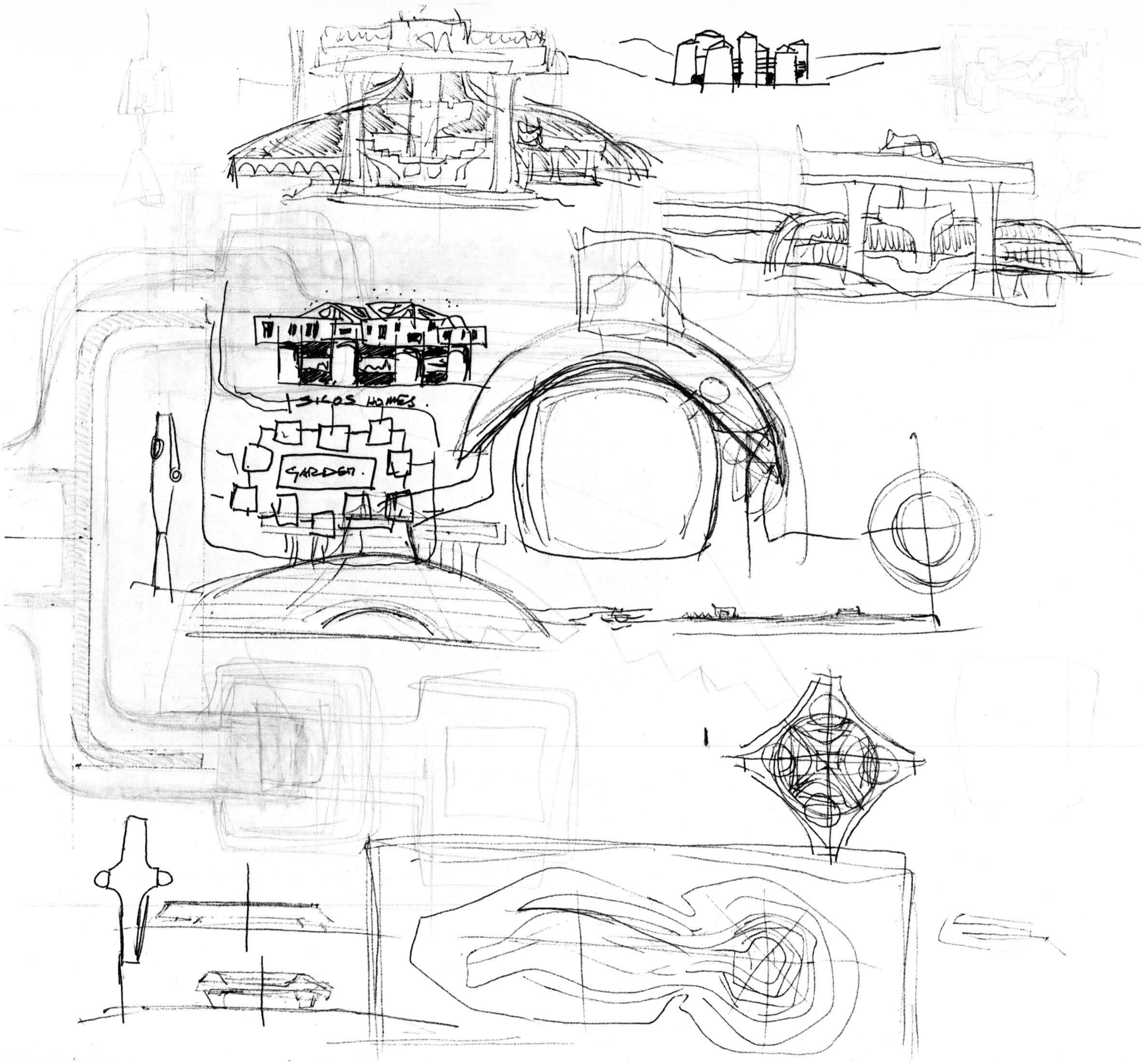
SILOS HOMES
GARDEN

Airport

1970
The airport is that place where things don't seem able to stay put together. To say that this is a sign of dynamism just obscures the issue. The fact is that the aircraft is a cumbersome and, on land, a very awkward animal.

Here the airport is conceived as a building containing all services and vertical shafts for the takeoff and landing of saucerlike crafts. They land from the top; they take off by dropping down and out. The tripod of the structure is above an artificial lake surrounded by gardens planted on high-buoyancy canisters. In case of takeoff or landing accidents, the craft can fall on this gigantic cushion which is part of the landscape on which the airport is poised.

At a ten-year distance, considering that facilities for vertical takeoff and landing as a normal mode have not been developed, the only reasonable answer to the air transportation problem is the identification of the airport with the city. This is only feasible in an arcological scheme.

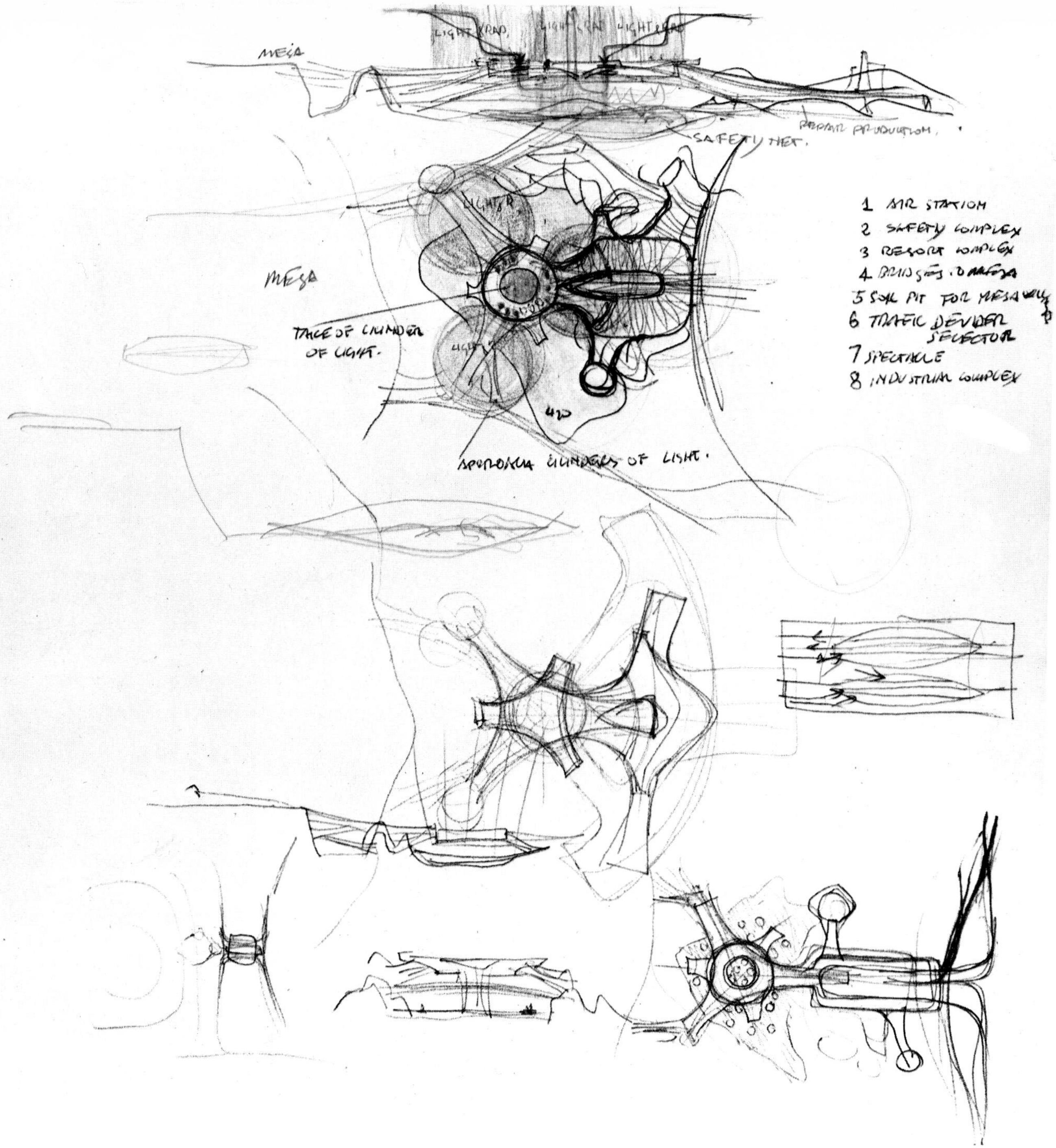
MESA
SAFETY NET.
MESA
TRACE OF CYLINDER
OF LIGHT.
1 AIR STATION
2 SAFETY COMPLEX
3 RESORT COMPLEX
5 SOIL PIT
6 TRAFIC DEVIDER
SELECTOR
7 SPECTACLE
8 INDUSTRIAL COMPLEX

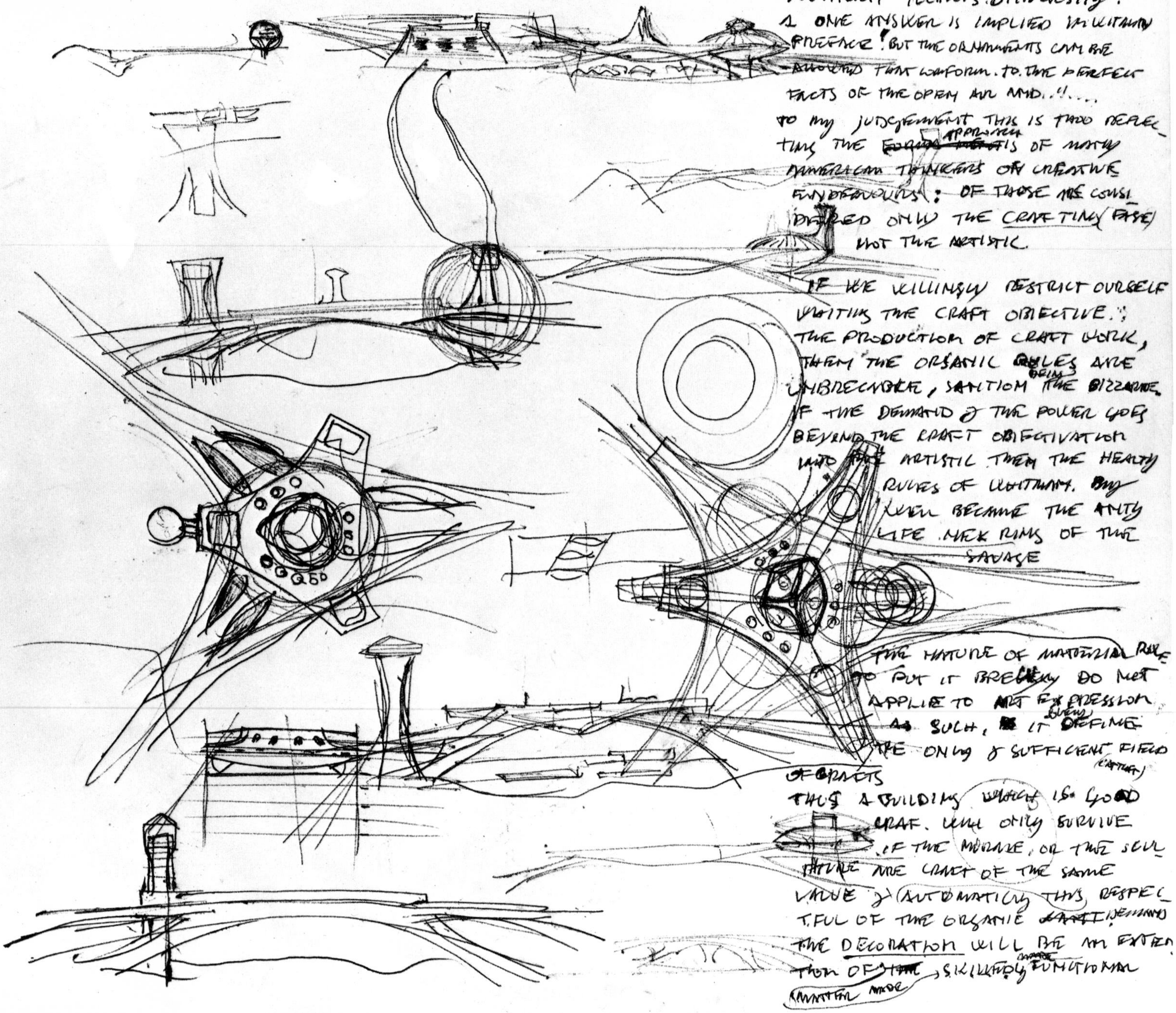
SOUTHERN ILLINOIS UNIVERSITY.
FACTS OF THE OPEN AIR AND...
TO MY JUDGEMENT THIS IS TWO REFLEC
TING THE APPROACH OF MANY
AMERICAN THINKERS ON CREATIVE
ENDEAVOURS: OF THOSE ARE CONSI
DERED ONLY THE CRAFTING PHASE
NOT THE ARTISTIC.
IF WE WILLINGLY RESTRICT OURSELF
WITHIN THE CRAFT OBJECTIVE.
THE PRODUCTION OF CRAFT WORK,
THEN THE ORGANIC RULES ARE
IF THE DEMAND OF THE POWER GOES
BEYOND THE CRAFT OBJECTIVATION
INTO THE ARTISTIC THEN THE HEALTHY
RULES OF WHITMAN.
SAVAGE
THE NATURE OF MATERIAL RULE
APPLIE TO ART EXPRESSION
AS SUCH,
THE ONLY SUFFICIENT FIELD
OF CRAFTS
THUS A BUILDING WHICH IS GOOD
CRAFT. WILL ONLY SURVIVE
VALUE
T.FUL OF THE ORGANIC
THE DECORATION WILL BE AN EXTEN
TION OF
FUNCTIONAL

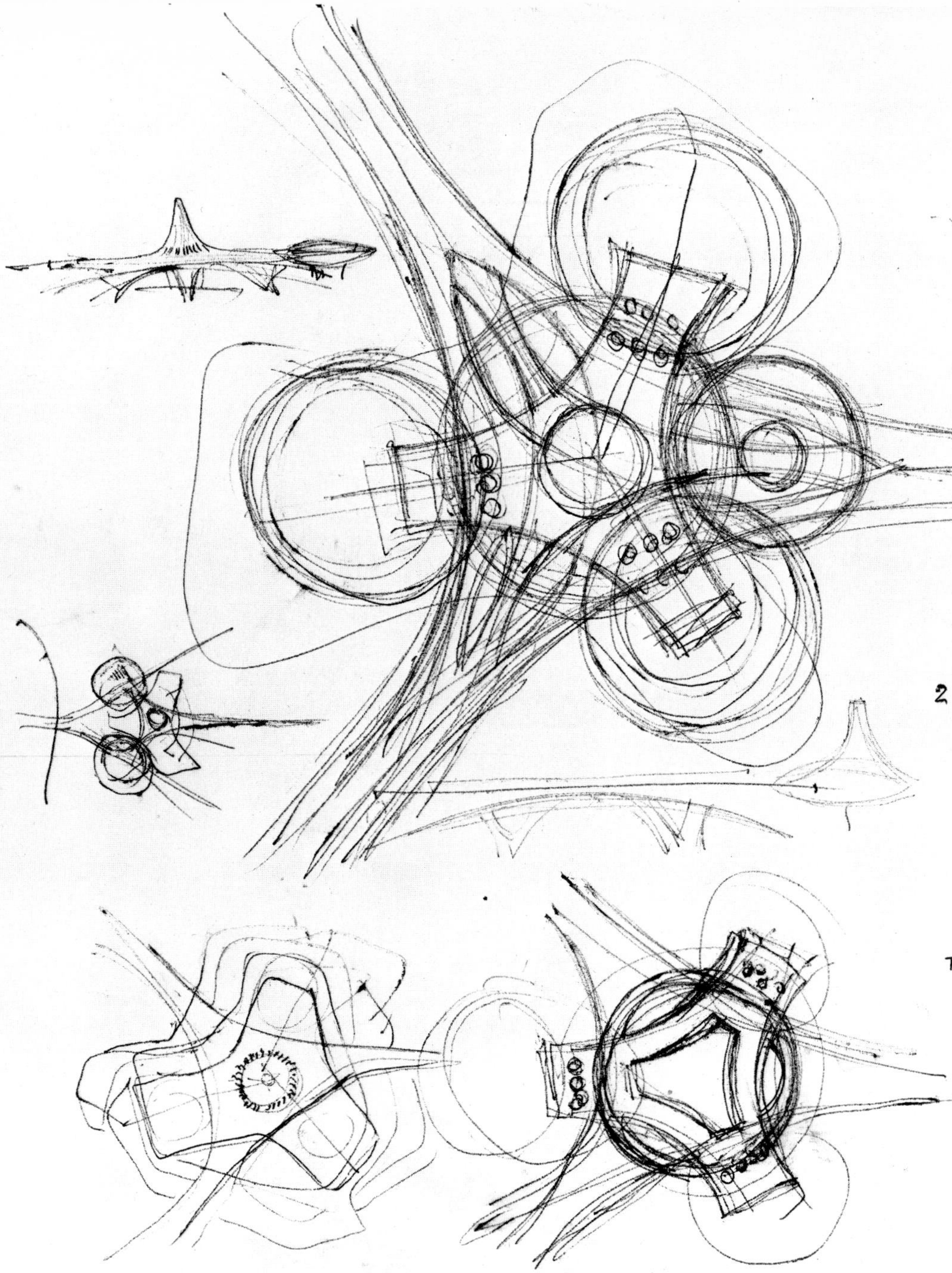

SEE THE PAINTED WALLS OF OR TEX 271
TURED WALLS OF AN AFRICAN VILLAGE.

IF ON THE CRAFTED BUILDING IS
OVER LAID AN MASTERPIECE OF
ART : THAT WHICH CAN BE & LIVE
DESPITE MISUSE OF MATERIALS &
INDIFFERENCE TO ENVIRONMENT
THEN. THE BUILDING ITSELF IS NOTHING
BUT A PEDESTAL TO THE OBJECTIVATED
AESTETIC EXPRESSION.

IF THE BUILDING IS ART ITSELF THEN
IT WILL BE SELF "DECORATED, I.E. SELF
ENRICHED. & ANY CRAFTED OVER
LAYED WORK WILL BE PREPOSTEROUS
& ANNOIING,
ANY ARTISTIC POST-IMPOSITION WILL
POSSIBLY ADD ANOTHER DIMENTION TO IT
BUT MORE LIKELY WILL DISTRACT & DEVIDE
THE ATTENCTION OF THE ONLOOKER

2 THE QUOTATION REVEAL AN BLURRED
CATALOGATION OF INTELLECTUAL PURPOSES TOOLS & BUILDINGS.
OF FORM FOLLOW FUNCTION CRITERIA
ABOUT CONCERNING ARCHITECTURE AS
TOTAL, ARTISTIC EXPRESSION I.E. SINTESIS
AESTETIC SINTESIS OF BIOPSICHICAL
NECESSITIES
TO CONTINUE WERE ONE STOPPED ABOVE
& INTRODUCTING THE NEX CATEGORY.
THE STANDARD PRODUCT TO THE CRAF. &
ART. ONE SEES IMMEDIATLY THAT
NO AMOUNT OF INTELLECTUAL & LOGICAL
UNDERSTANDINGS OF FORM PURE OR
IMPURE FORM WILL RETRIVE A CONSTRUCTION
FROM OBSOLESCENCE ONCE THE FUNCTION
UNDERLING. THE FORM IS GONE
THE FORM FOLLOWS FUNCTION RULE IS SOUND
FOR THE ORGANIC NEEDS OF THE CRAFTED
OBJECT (FORK, POT ... RING ...) IS
ESSENTIAL IN THE CONNOTATION OF

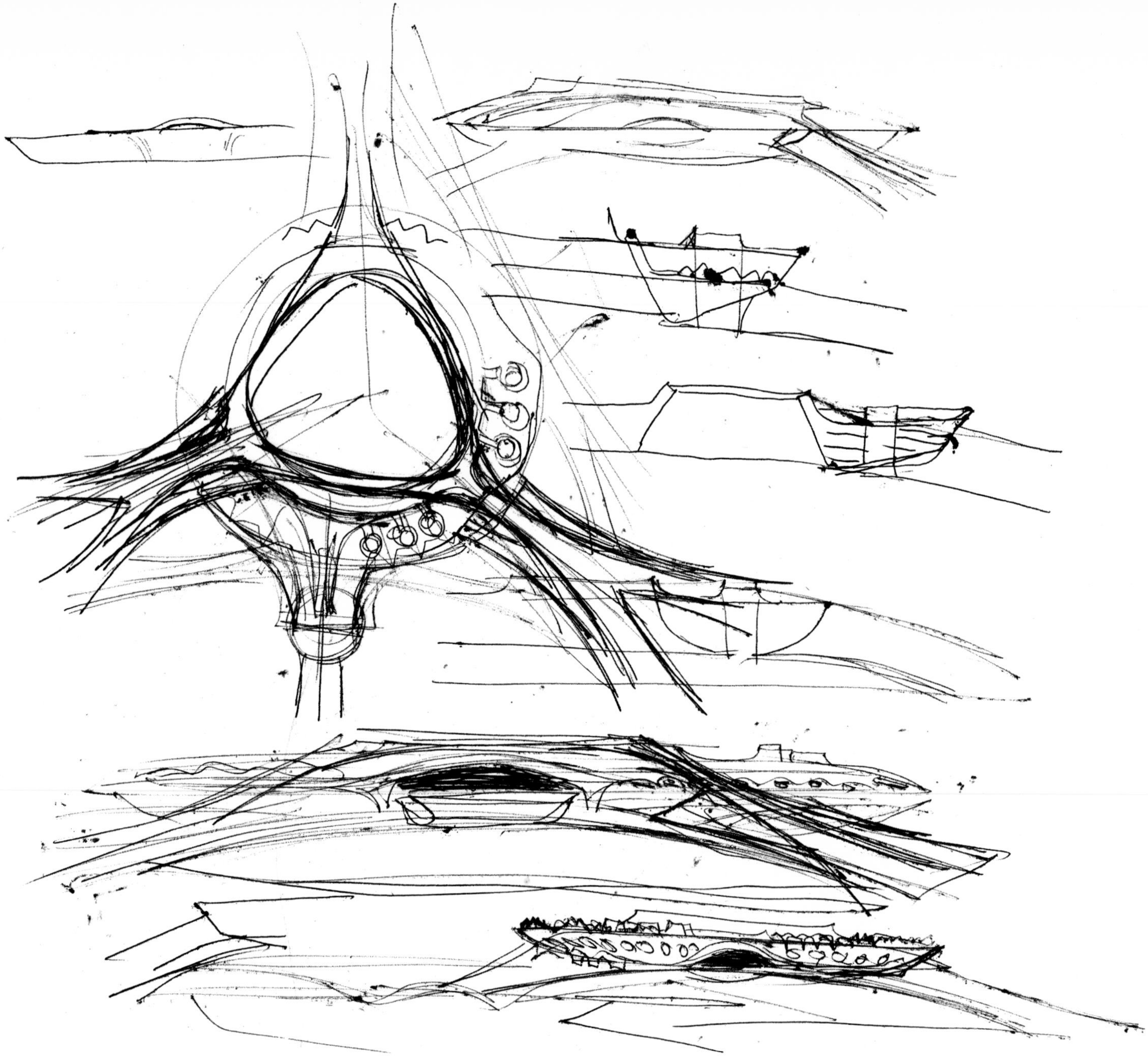

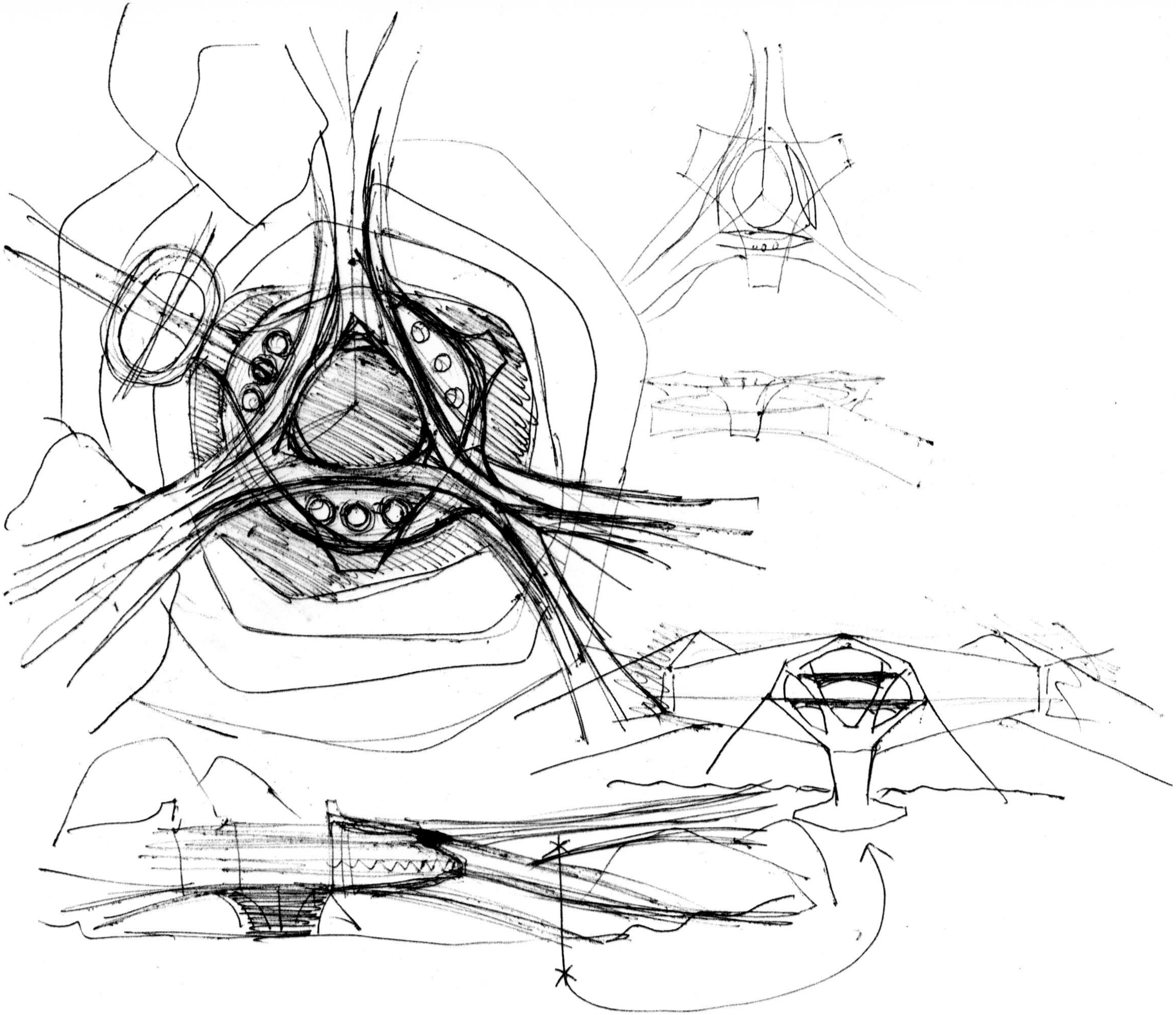

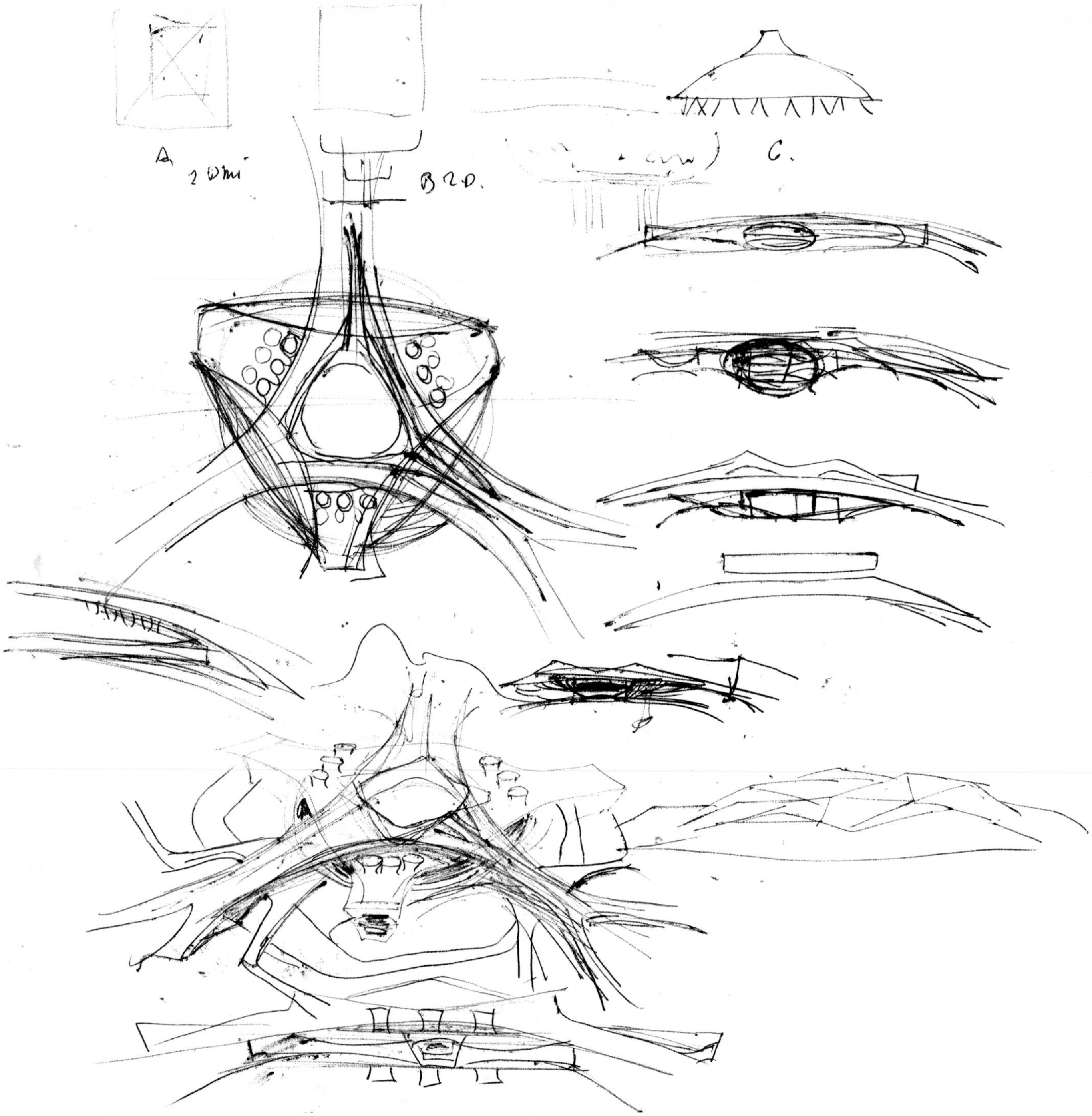
A
C.

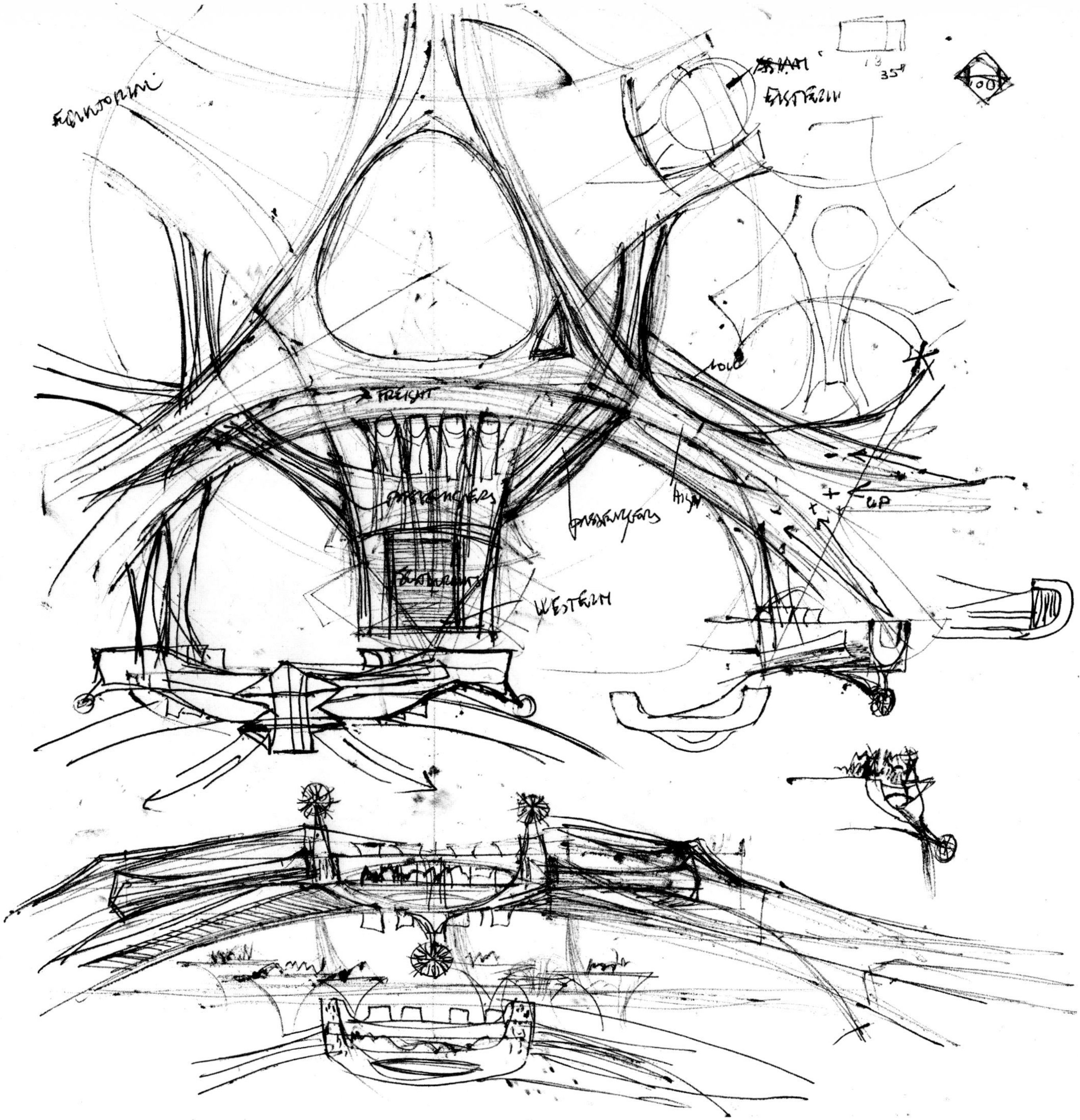
FREIGHT
PASSENGERS
WESTERN
EASTERN
UP

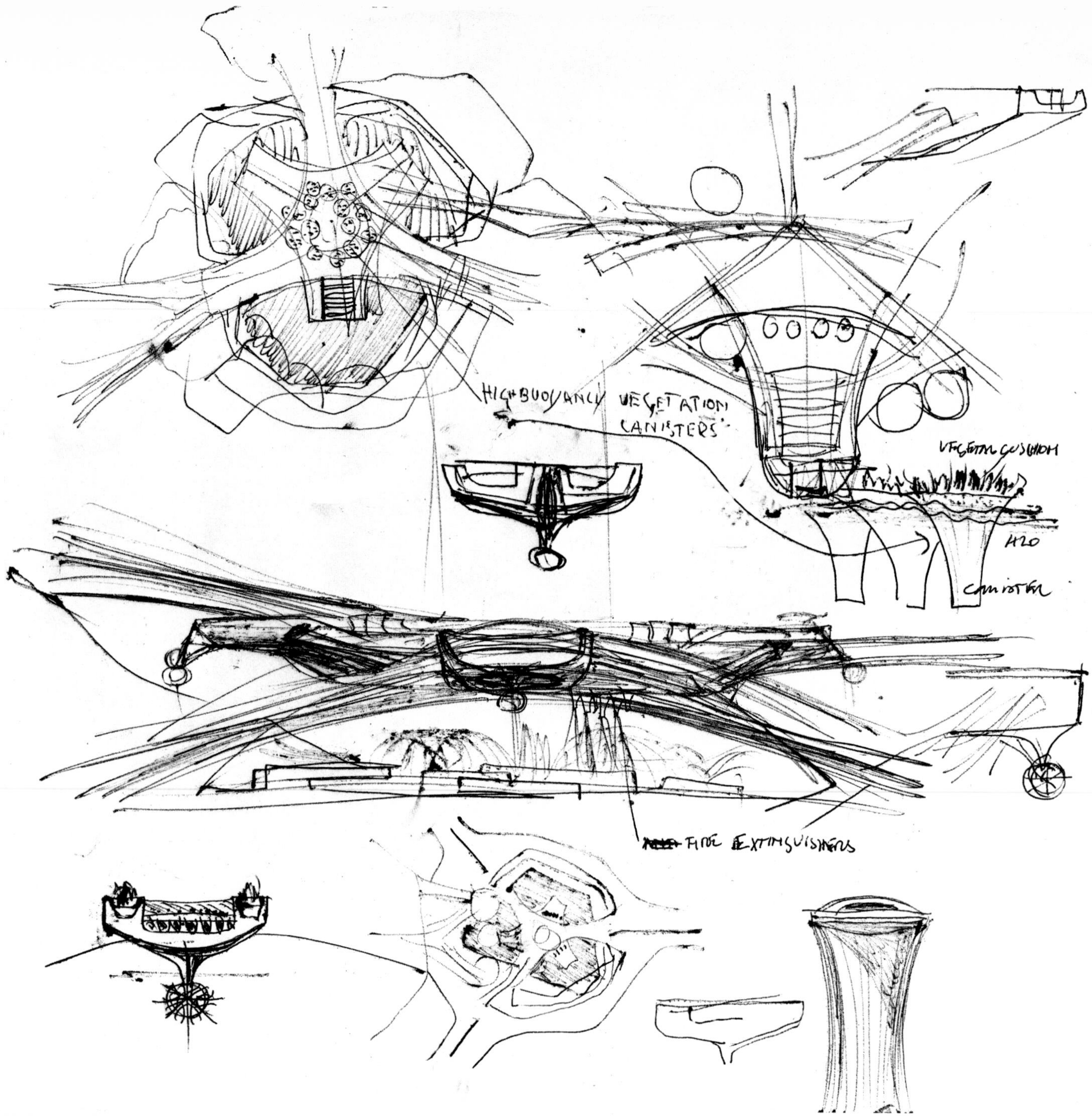
HIGH BUOYANCY VEGETATION CANISTERS
VEGETAL CUSHION
H2O
CANISTER
FIRE EXTINGUISHERS

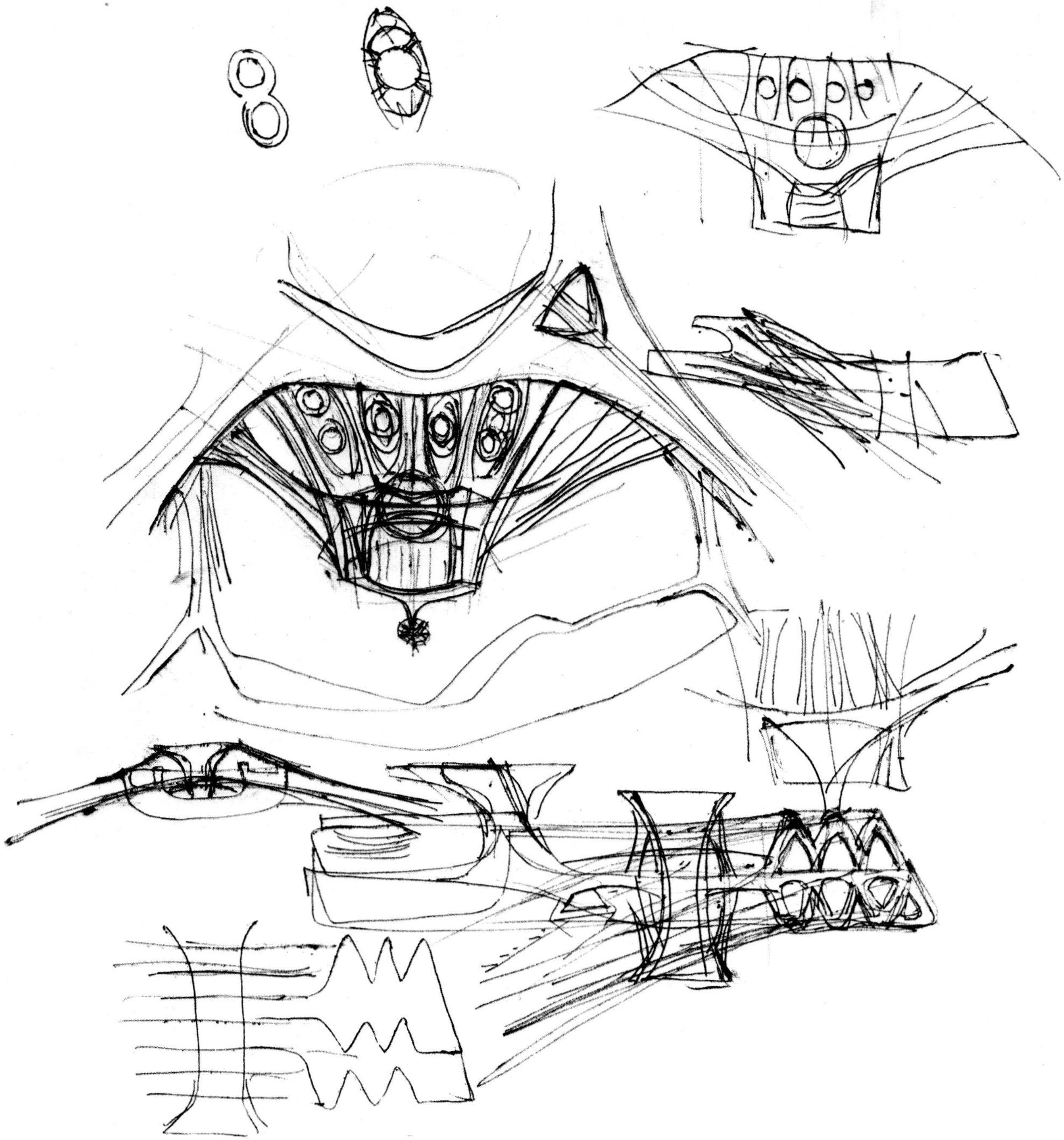

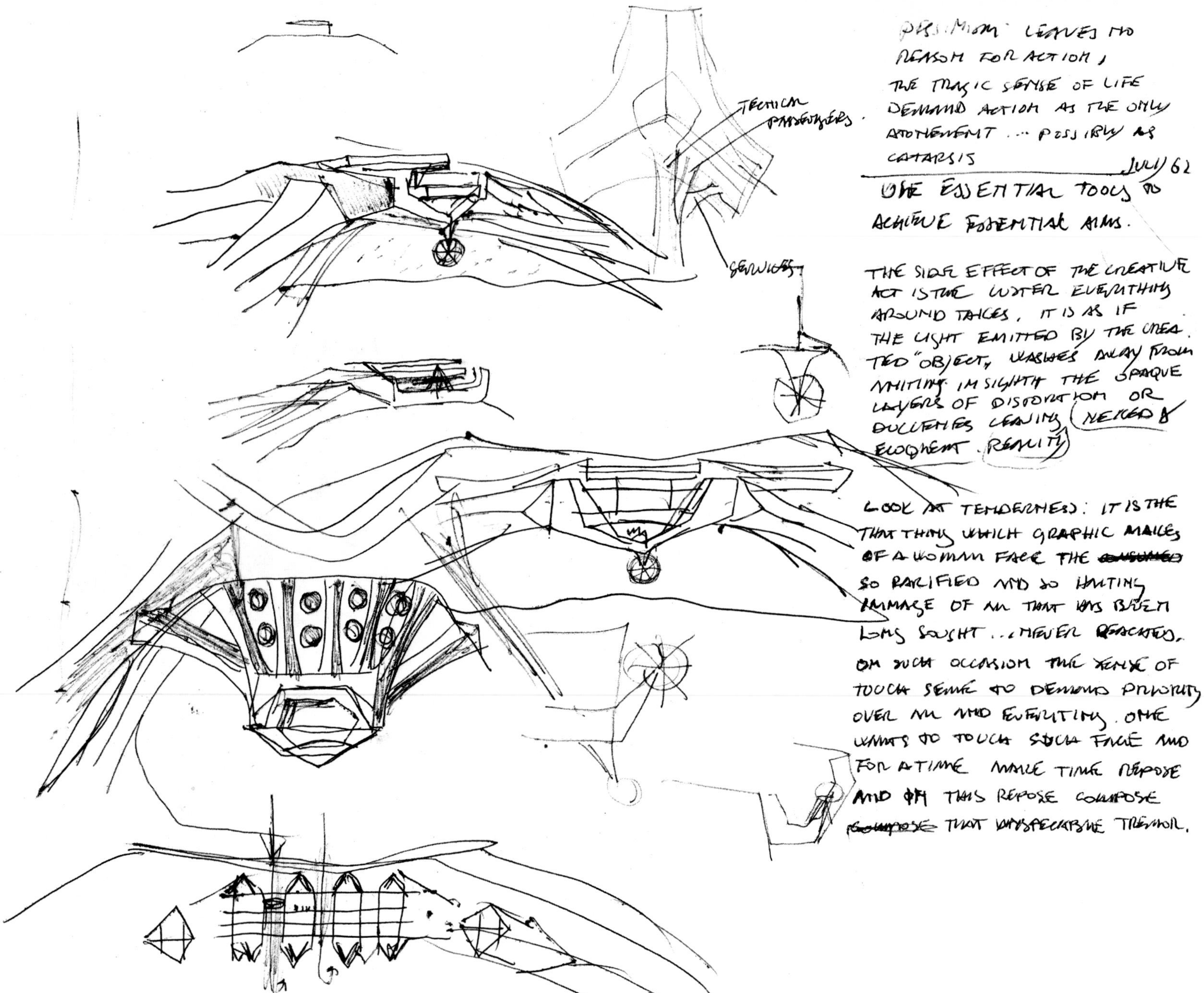
TECNICAL PASSENGERS.
SERVICES
PESSIMISM LEAVES NO REASON FOR ACTION, THE TRAGIC SENSE OF LIFE DEMAND ACTION AS THE ONLY ATONEMENT ... POSSIBLY AS CATARSIS
JULY 62
USE ESSENTIAL TOOLS TO ACHIEVE ESSENTIAL AIMS.
THE SIDE EFFECT OF THE CREATIVE ACT IS THE LUSTER EVERYTHING AROUND TAKES, IT IS AS IF THE LIGHT EMITTED BY THE CREATED "OBJECT" WASHES AWAY FROM NOTHING IN SIGHT THE OPAQUE LAYERS OF DISTORTION OR DULLNESS LEAVING (NAKED & ELOQUENT REALITY)
LOOK AT TENDERNESS: IT IS THE THAT THING WHICH GRAPHIC MAKES OF A WOMAN FACE THE SO RARIFIED AND SO HAUTING IMMAGE OF ALL THAT HAS BEEN LONG SOUGHT ... NEVER REACHED.
ON SUCH OCCASION THE SENSE OF TOUCH SEEMS TO DEMAND PRIORITY OVER ALL AND EVERYTHING. ONE WANTS TO TOUCH SUCH FACE AND FOR A TIME MAKE TIME REPOSE AND ON THIS REPOSE COMPOSE THAT UNSPEAKABLE TREMOR.

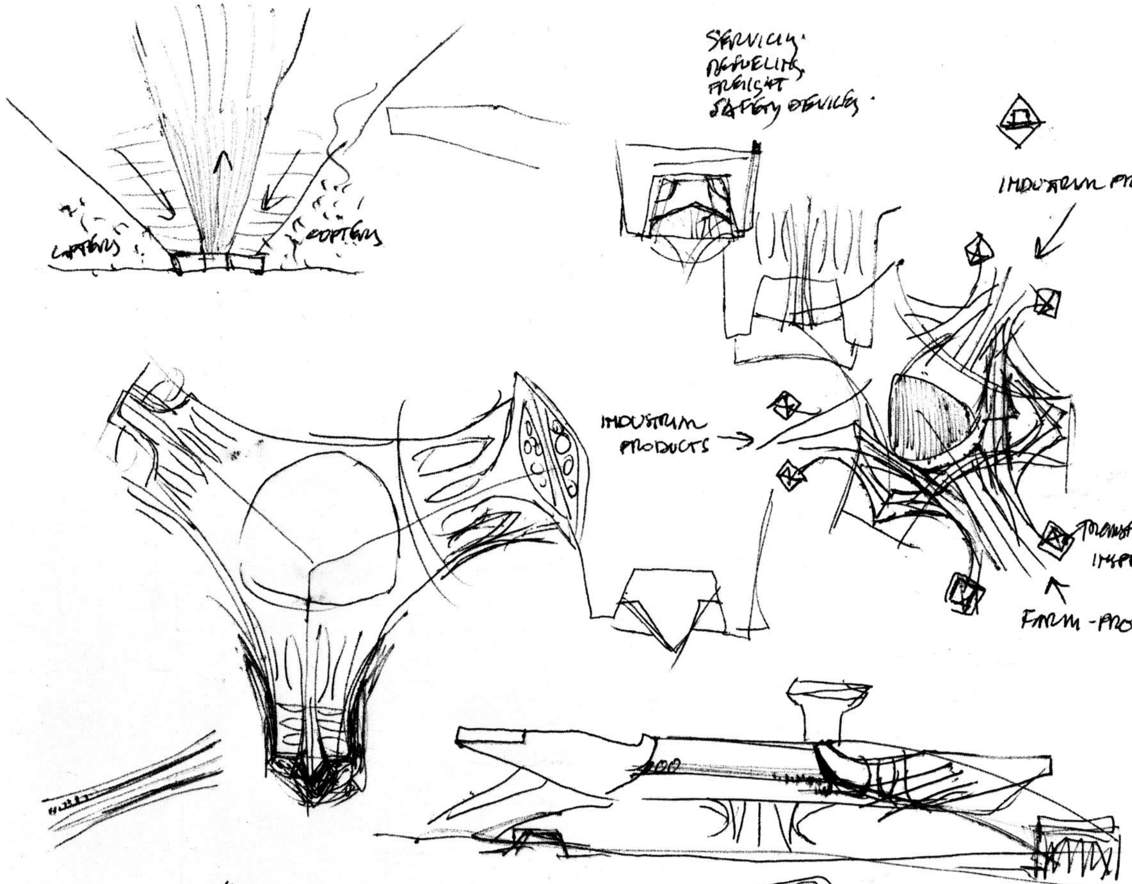

FLORENCE OR ATHENS TODAY
MUST BE WILLFUL UNDERTAKINGS.
THE "FREE" CHOICE OF A NUMBER OF
INDIVIDUALS (FAMILIES) TO CONGREGATE
& PHYSICALLY "AGGREGATE," TO FORM
A "POLIS"
WITH DEDICATION, DIFFERENT BUT NOT
INDIFFERENT TO CONTEMPORARY CULTURE
WOULD PURSUE THE ROAD SCIENCE &
TECHNOLOGY, MORE THAN SUGGEST, DEMANDS ~~FROM~~ US TO FOLLOW.

"BORROWING" FROM THE INDUSTRIAL &
FINANCIAL WORLD WOULD NOT BE
COMPROMISE OR RENUNCIATION -
BUT THE USE OF THE INSTRUMENTAL PREMISES
& STRESS FOR THE FLOWERING OF A
SUBSTANTIALLY NEW CULTURE FRUIT
OF A NEW KIND OF LIFE

ESSENTIAL WOULD BE THIS CLUSTERING OF THE MOST WILLFUL FERMENTS
CONTEMPORARY SOCIETY CAN AFFORD,
BUT THAT AS SCATTERED AS THEY
ARE HAVE NO CHANCE TO SAP
EACH OTHER & ENRICH MANIFOLD
FOR THEMSELVES & ALL

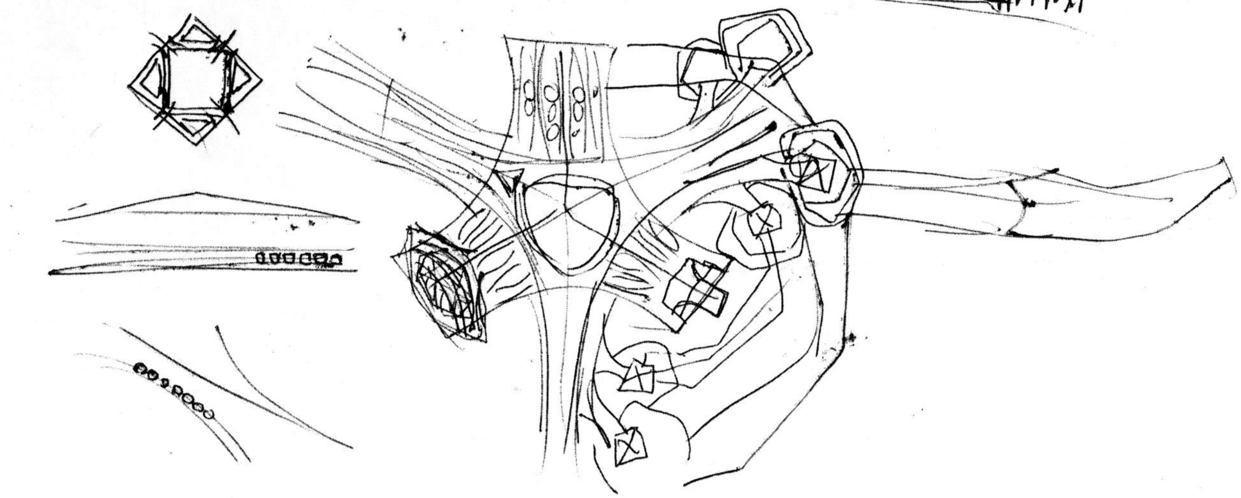

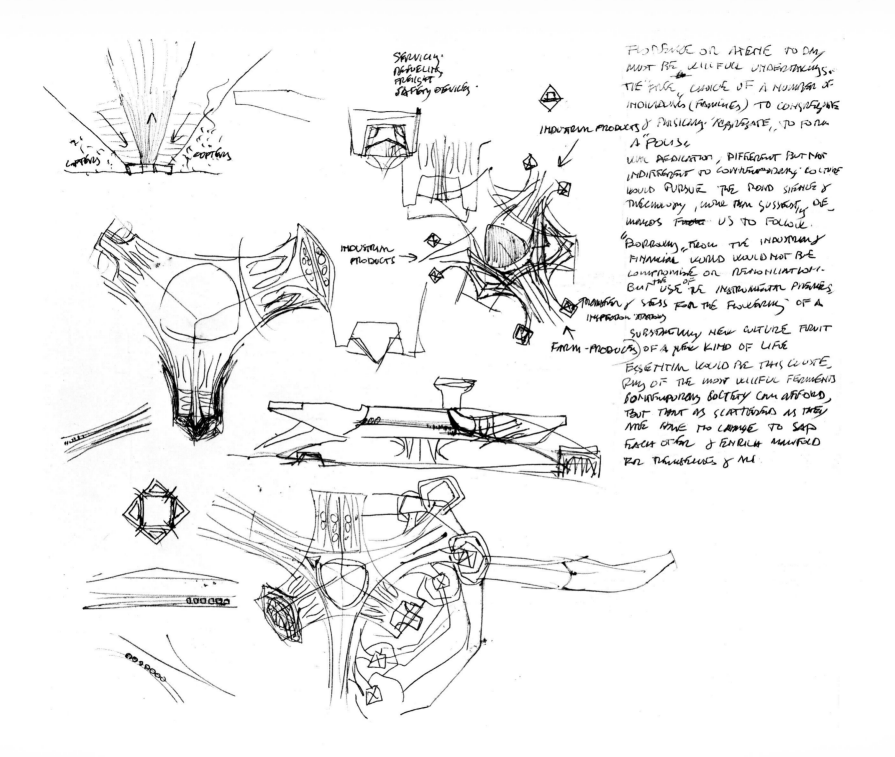

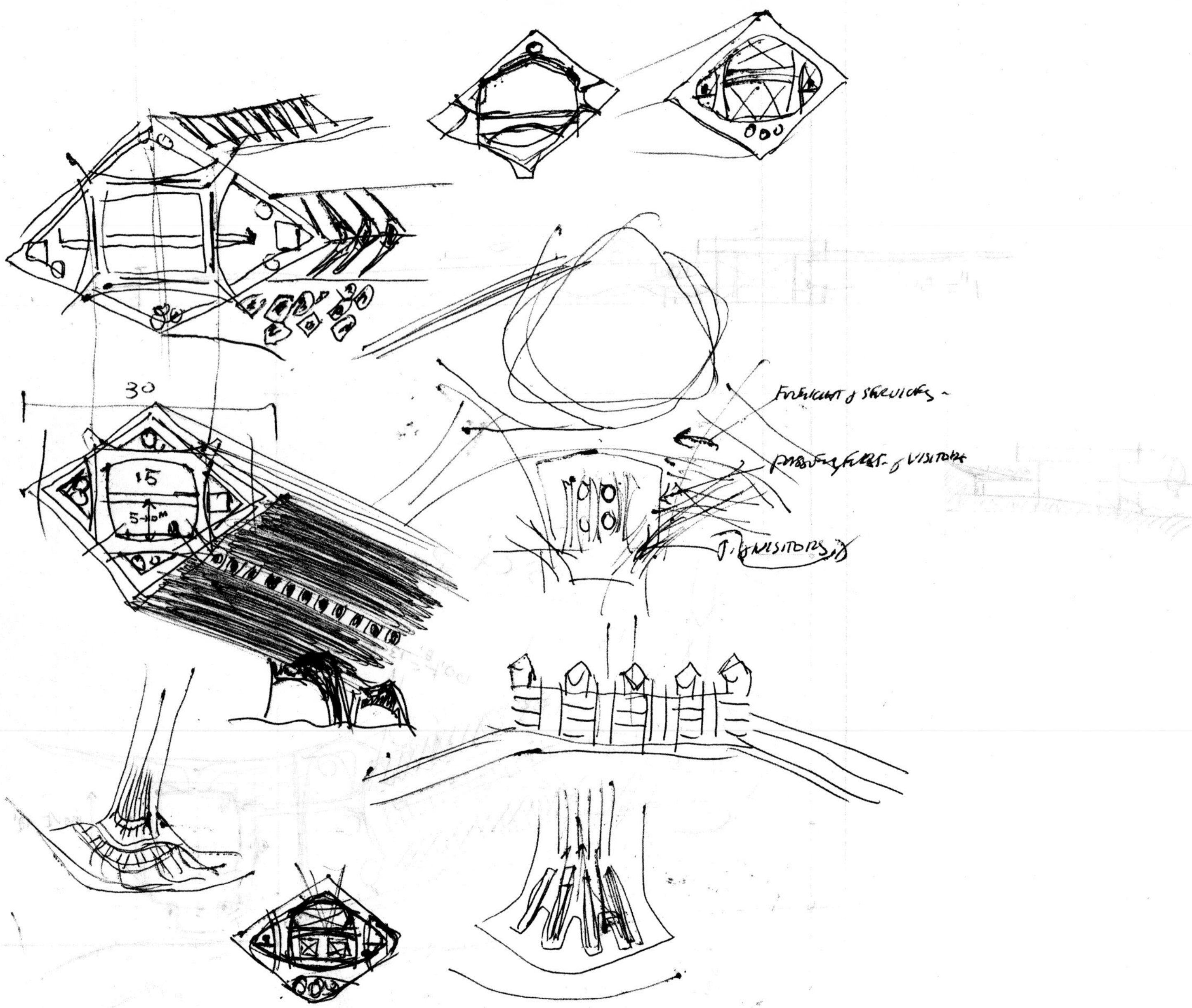
30
15
FREIGHT & SERVICES
PASSENGERS & VISITORS

Bridges

1970
Of all things that are man-made, bridges are, with dams, the most "structural," single-minded, and imposing. As connectors at a breaking point, they have a heroic force that is aided by a challenging structuralism. As a strand of continuity in a noncontinuum, the bridge is full of implied meanings. It is the opposite of devisiveness, separation, isolation, irretrievability, loss, segregation, abandonment. To bridge is as cogent in the psychic realm as it is in the physical world. The bridge is a symbol of confidence and trust. It is a communications medium as much as a connector.

I do not know how much of this has caused me to be attracted by the design of bridges. It is possibly the clear-cut purpose of the bridge that permits reflection of the single-mindedness of the problem into the single-mindedness of the conceptual process. There is meaning aplenty grafted onto a simple purpose, an ideal subject for the imaginitive mind if the mind accepts the discipline that gravity and matter impose. The bridge, like the dam, is very much of a bottleneck to which something pervasive converges and diverges. In the dam is the water with its load of vivifying power. On the bridge are people, software and hardware, a more loaded cargo already manipulated by life. As hinges to a vast network of stresses, they both imply and forecast compression and contraction on specific constituents of life.

THE MIND-ENDOWED MAN IS A QUESTIONING MAN, & QUEST FOR THINGS TO CAME IS THE MEANINS OF ITS BEEINS & THE CONDITION OF ITS MORTILINESS
WHIT QUESTIONING, CAMES DOOINS, WHIT DOOINS CAMES ERROR OR BETTER, THE MATERIALISATION OF ERROR WHIC IS, THE CAOS OF THE MIND & THE CAOS OF THE ENVIRONMEMENT

THUS AT EACH HEAP OF WASTE ONE CAN ASSERT : THE MIND OF MAN HAS BEEN HERE. THIS IS THE MESURE OF ITS LONGING AS WELL AS THE MESURE OF ITS BRUTALITY

THIS, THE BRUTALITY SIDE OF ITS RATIONALIZING-DOOING IS THE PART THAT ONE MY HOPE TO DEMINISH BY A PROCESS WHICH IS AT THE SAME TIME MENTAL & EMOTIONAL.
MENTAL IN ITS ORDAINING OF DATAS & ORGANIZING OF THEM WHITIN A WOLE

EMOTIONAL, MAINLY BECAUSE IN FACE OF THE FORMELESS, SENTIMENT DO NOT KEEP QUIET. LIFE, THE FORM GIVER, SEE ITS OWN NEGATION IN CAOS, THE FORMELESS. HENCE THE STRUGGLE IS NOT MARGINAL, IS TO AFFIRM THE GOIN ON OF TIME, THE ESSENCE OF LIFE.

THE ONLY INSTANCE WHERE MAN HAS TO BE LEFT ALONE (IF HE WISHES) IS ITS OWN IMMEDIATE BEEINS, TO HIM THE INITIATIVE TO MEDIATE THIS ONENESS INTO THE PRESUMED REAL I.E TO BECAME SOCIAL.
BEYOND THIS STRICT LIMIT HE DEALS WHIT A "COLLECTIVE PROPRETY", NO MATTER HOW THIS MY DESPLEASE OR OBSET HIM. HIS OWNERSHIPS ARE SIMBOLS, WHEN

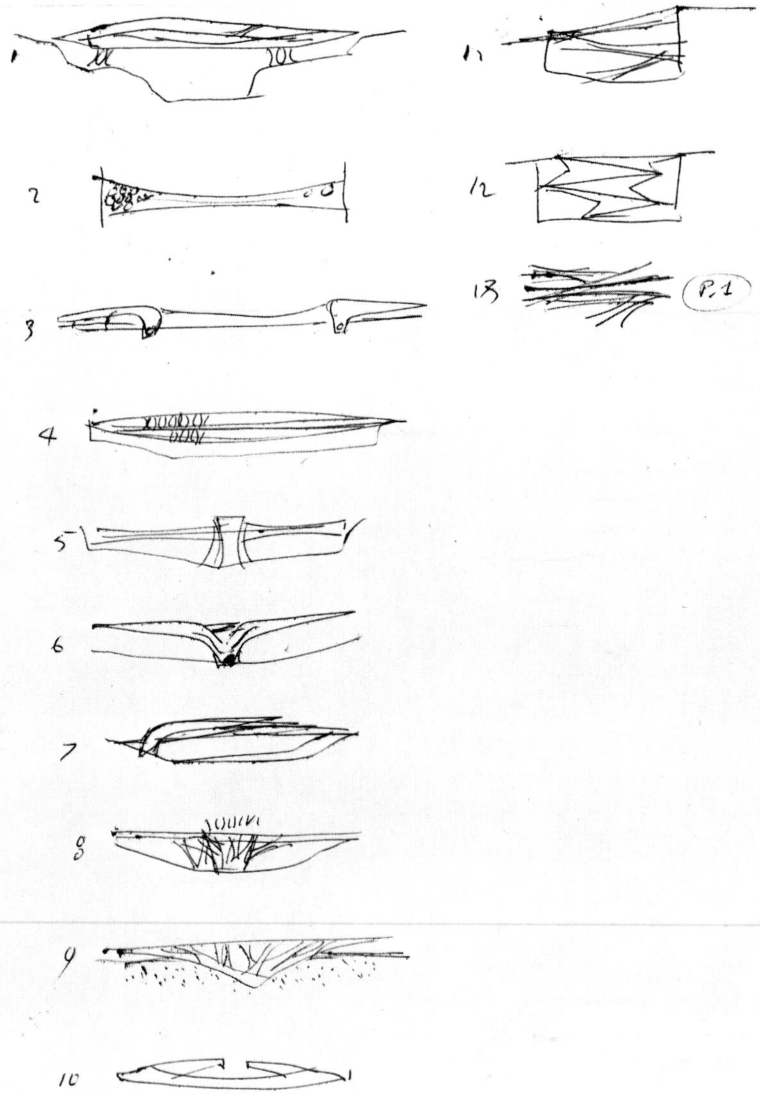

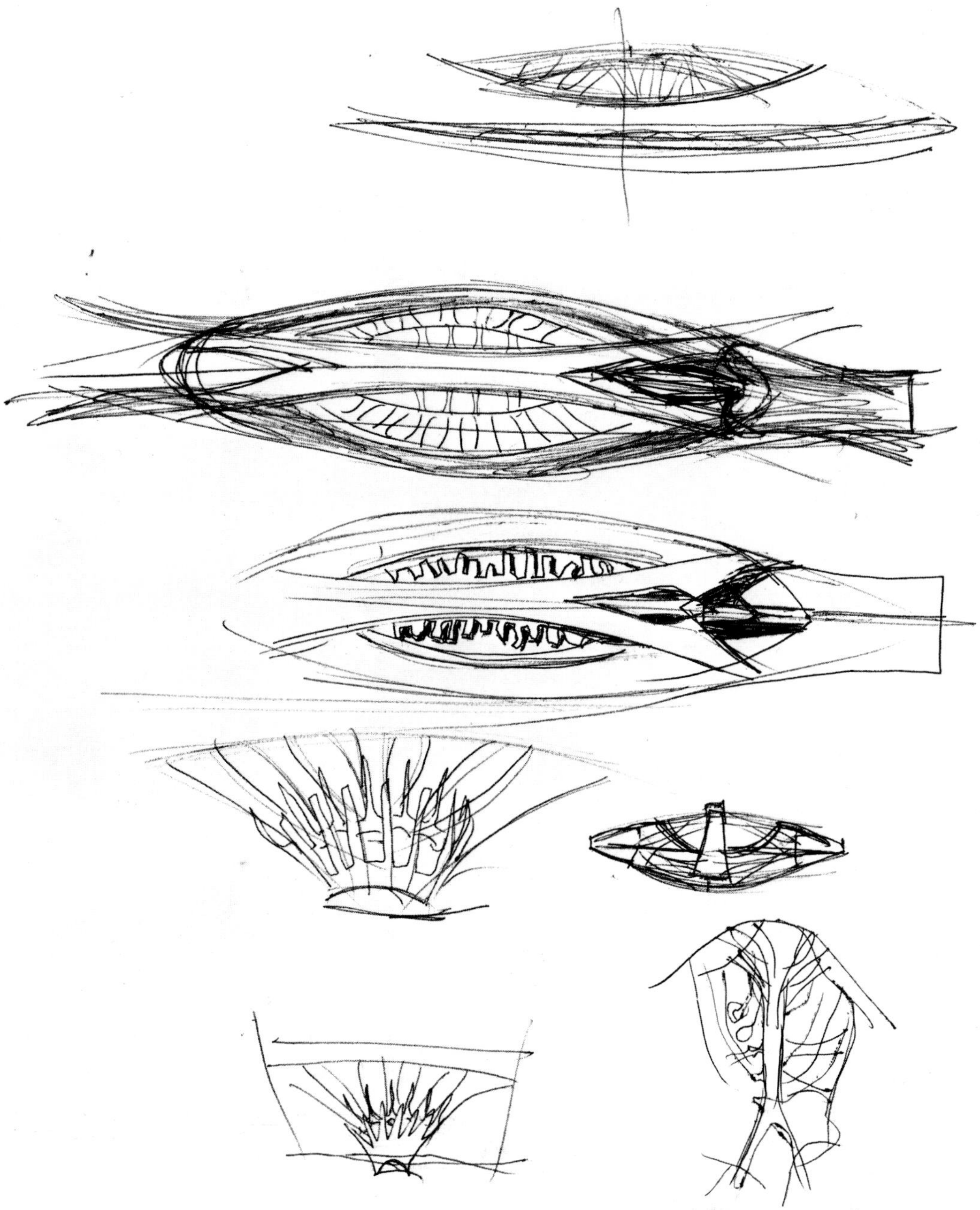

E INCOMES

IN THE LAST 4 YEARS. I PUT INTO
THE EXPERIMENTAL WORK TOWARD
THE FOUNDATION & THE PRODUCTION –
OF PROJECT MESA CITY AN AVERA-
GE OF $15.000 $. A YEAR. SO.
[illegible]: ITEMIZED

– INCOME FROM PERSONAL (FAMILY)
CRAFT WORK. 6000 (CASH)

– THE PERSONAL WORK ON PROJECT
MESA & CONSTRUCTION OF THE ~~BUILDING~~
EXPERIMENTAL BUILDING. 6000
(VERY CONSERVATIVE FIGURE I TRUST)

– LABOR & DEDICATION OF YOUNG APP-
RENTICE PAID WHAT A SUBSISTENCE
SALARY (FROM CASH & GRANT. FUNDA-
TION FUNDS) 3000" (FIGURE
DEDUCTED BY DOUBLING THEIR SALA.
RY TO A FIGURE OF MINIMUM WAGE
SALARY: IE. WHILE I PAID THEM 3000
YEARLY I GOT THE PRODUCTIVITY OF
6000 (FROM CASH)

TO THIS HAS TO BE ADDED THE
7500 SUM FROM G.F.
WHICH WILL BRING THE FIGURE FOR
THE 4 YEARS TO A TOTAL OF 67500.
CONSTRUCTIONS & PROJECT ARE
HERE TO TESTIFIE ABOUT THE
~~GOOD~~ USE OF SUCH CAPITAL.

NOT COUNTING ON ANY "IMPROVE-
MENT" ON THE CASH PRODUCING
ACTIVITY (CRAFTS WHICH WILL SOON
EXTEND TO A THIRD FIELD, GARDEN
OBJECTS IN SPECIAL CEMENT. THE
FIRST TWO BEING CERAMICS & METAL)
THERE WOULD THEN BE A CASH
& LABOR INCOME CONSERVATIVELY
ESTIMATED AT 15000–20.000 $
A YEAR.

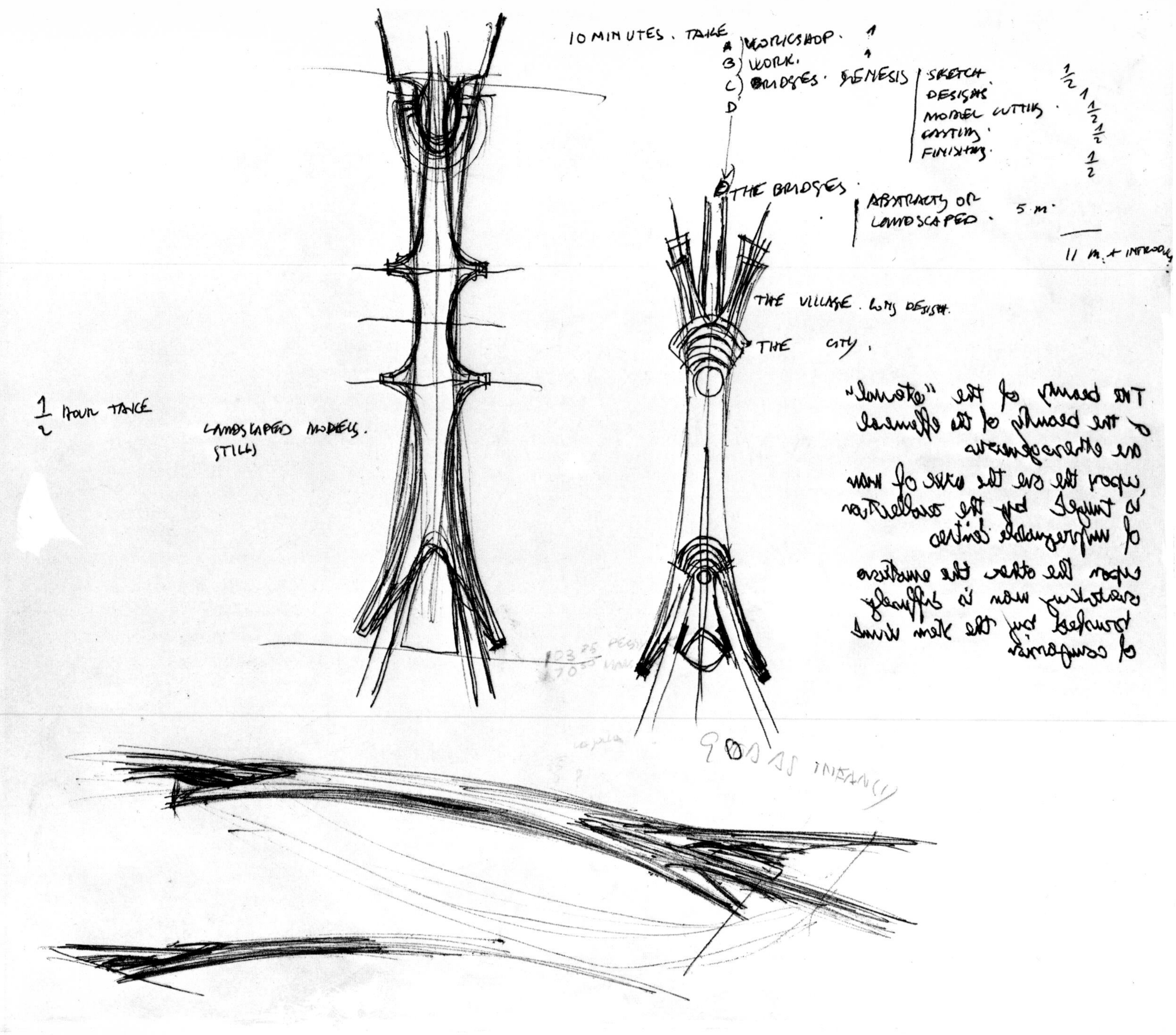
10 MINUTES. TAKE
A) WORKSHOP. 1
B) WORK. 1
C) BRIDGES. GENESIS
SKETCH 1/2
DESIGNS 1
MODEL CUTTING 1/2
CASTING 1/2
FINISHING 1/2
D
THE BRIDGES
ABSTRACTS OR LANDSCAPED. 5 M.
11 M. + INTRODU
THE VILLAGE. LONG DESIGN.
THE CITY.
1/2 HOUR TAKE
LANDSCAPED MODELS. STILLS

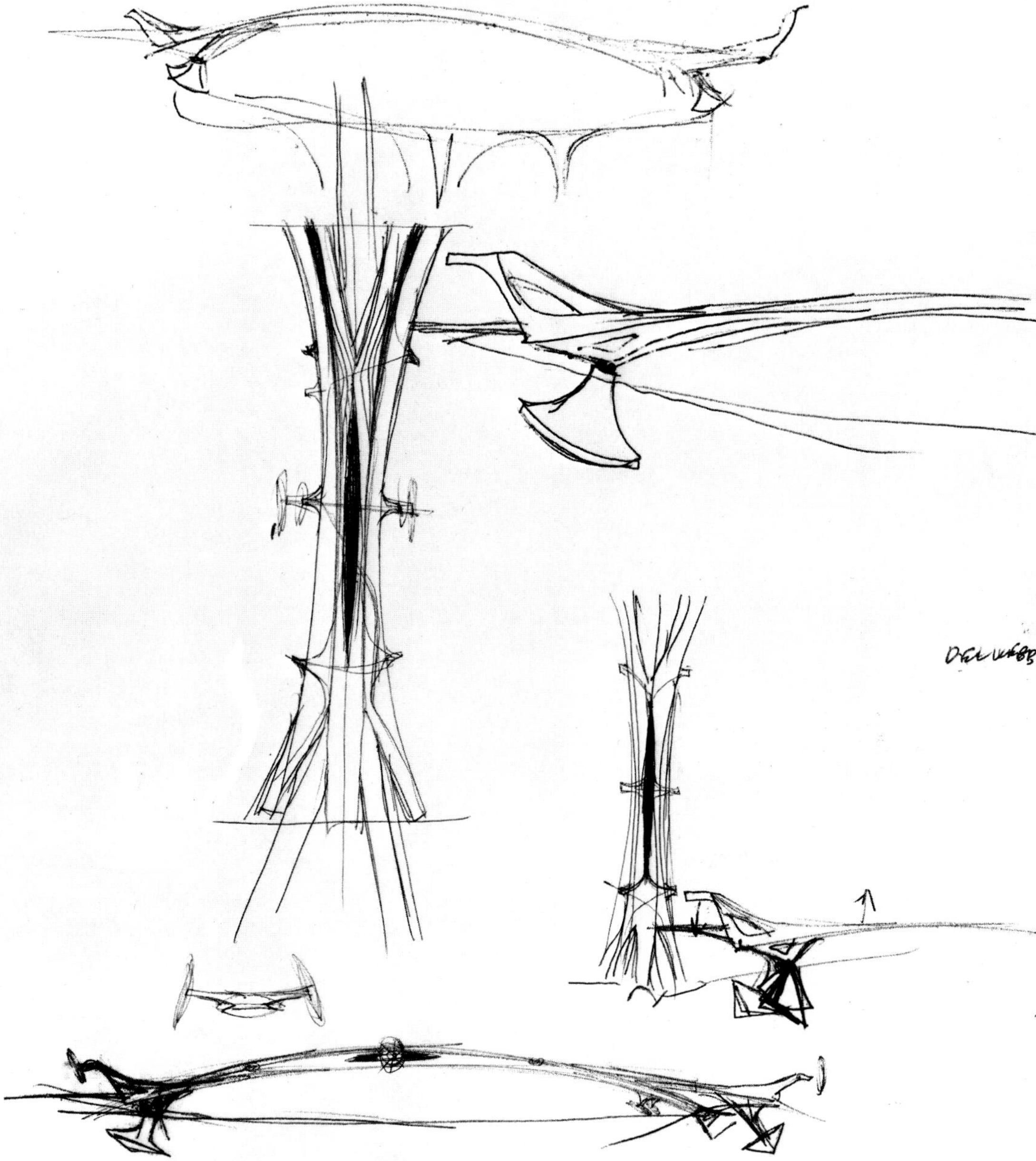

WILL BE RULED OVER IN THE 47
PROCESS. SO WHAT IF HISTORY
WILL ANSWER YES?
SO WHAT IF HISTORY'S ~~WILL~~
ANSWER IS NO?
~~THE~~ CERTITUDE HAS NEVER
BEEN RESPONSIBLE FOR THE
MOST UNDISTINGUISHED STEP OF
EVOLUTION. FROM THE GASEOUS
CLUSTERS TO THE AMOEBA TO
THE SABER TIGER, TO THE
NEANDERTHAL MAN TO THE
PROPHETS TO THE ALCHEMIST TO
THE SCIENTIST...

~~IT IS UNQUESTIONABLE THAT~~
CHANCES ARE THAT THE GRIND
STONE OF "THE NORMAL" WILL
ASK FOR HIS TOLL UP TO THE LIMIT
OF MEANINGFULNESS, I.E. THE
FOUNDATION MAY DISMISS SLOWLY
HER CULTURAL CLOTHES TO
BECOME A WALT DISNEY OR
DELIBER. ENTERPRISE, WITHOUT THE
FANCIFULNESS OF THE ONE NOR
THE "EFFICIENCY" OF THE OTHER.
THE FOUNDATION WILL THUS ~~HAVE~~
FAILED
BUT CHANCES ARE ALSO THAT
A STUBBORN, PERSISTENT PREOC-
CUPATION TOWARD FUNDAMEN-
TALS MAY. BECOME INTO A
CREATURE OF GRACE,
IT IS THEN THAT ITS MEANING
WOULD TRANSCEND ITS SIZE.
THAT. AN INVISIBLE ~~NETWORK~~
OF OMINISATION WOULD FLUX RADIATE
~~TOWARD~~ FORWARD. TOWARD BET-
TER WAYS AND BETTER MEN:
THE MAKING OF GOD.

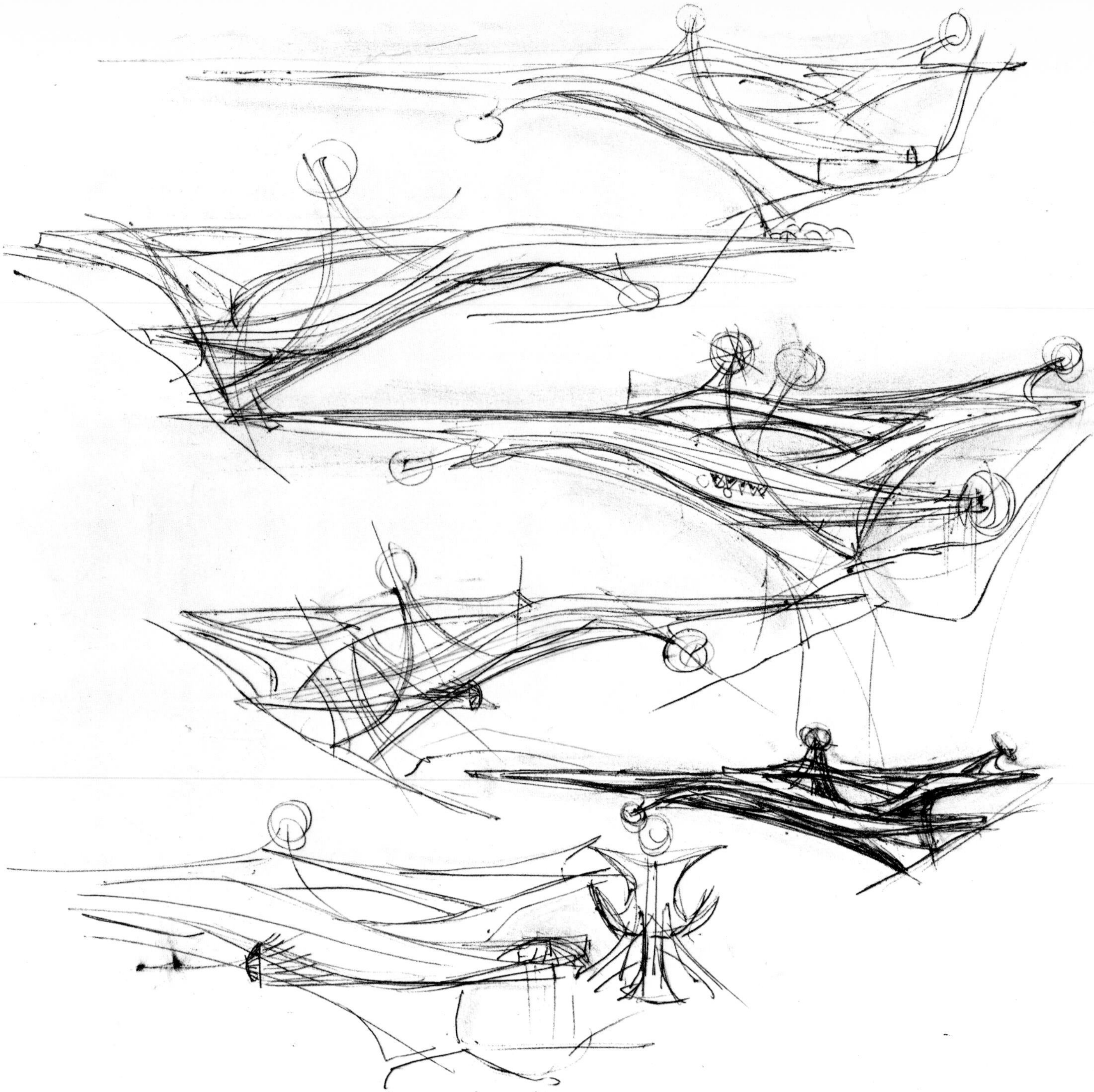

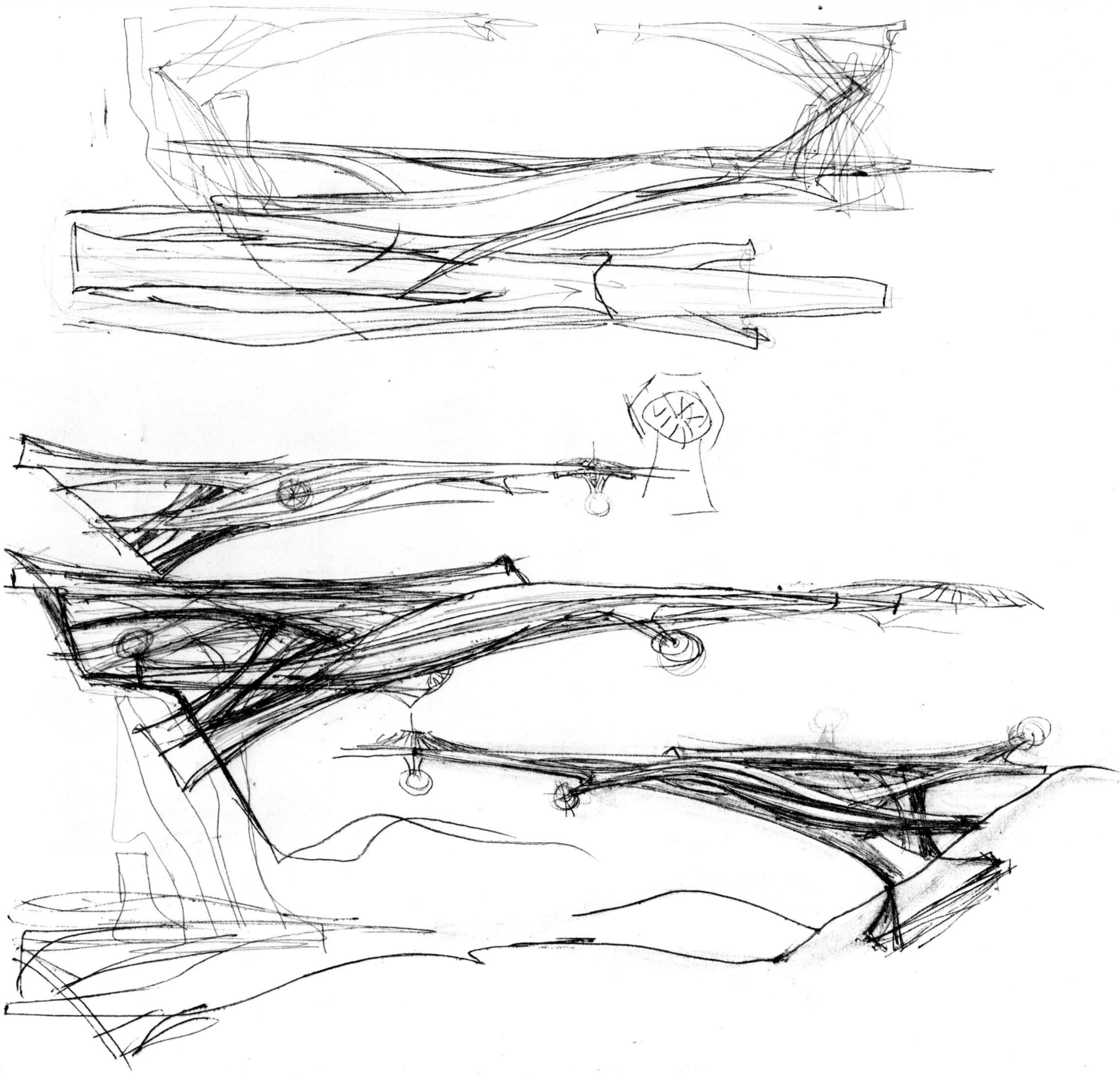

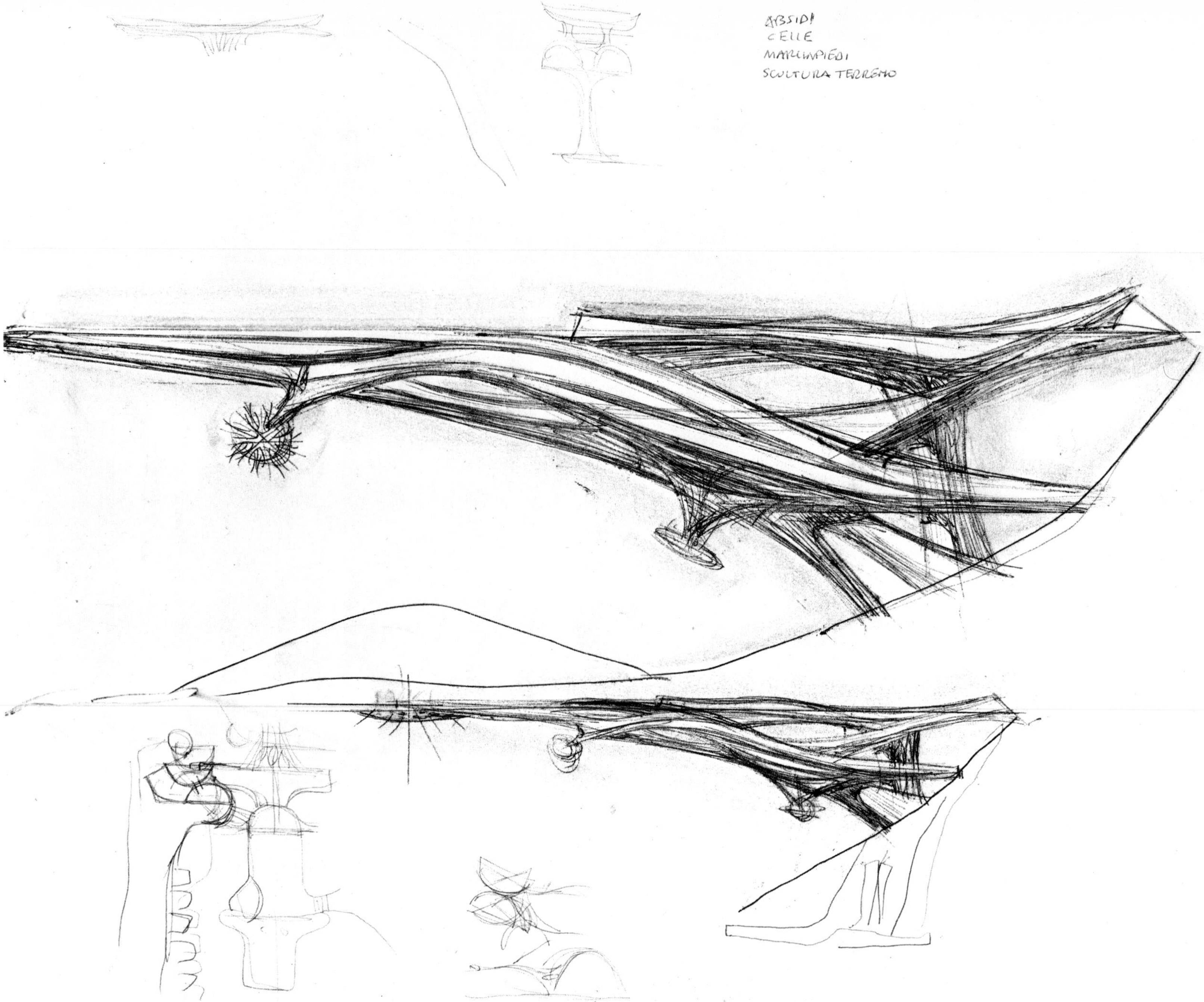
ABSIDI
CELLE
MARCIAPIEDI
SCULTURA TERRENO

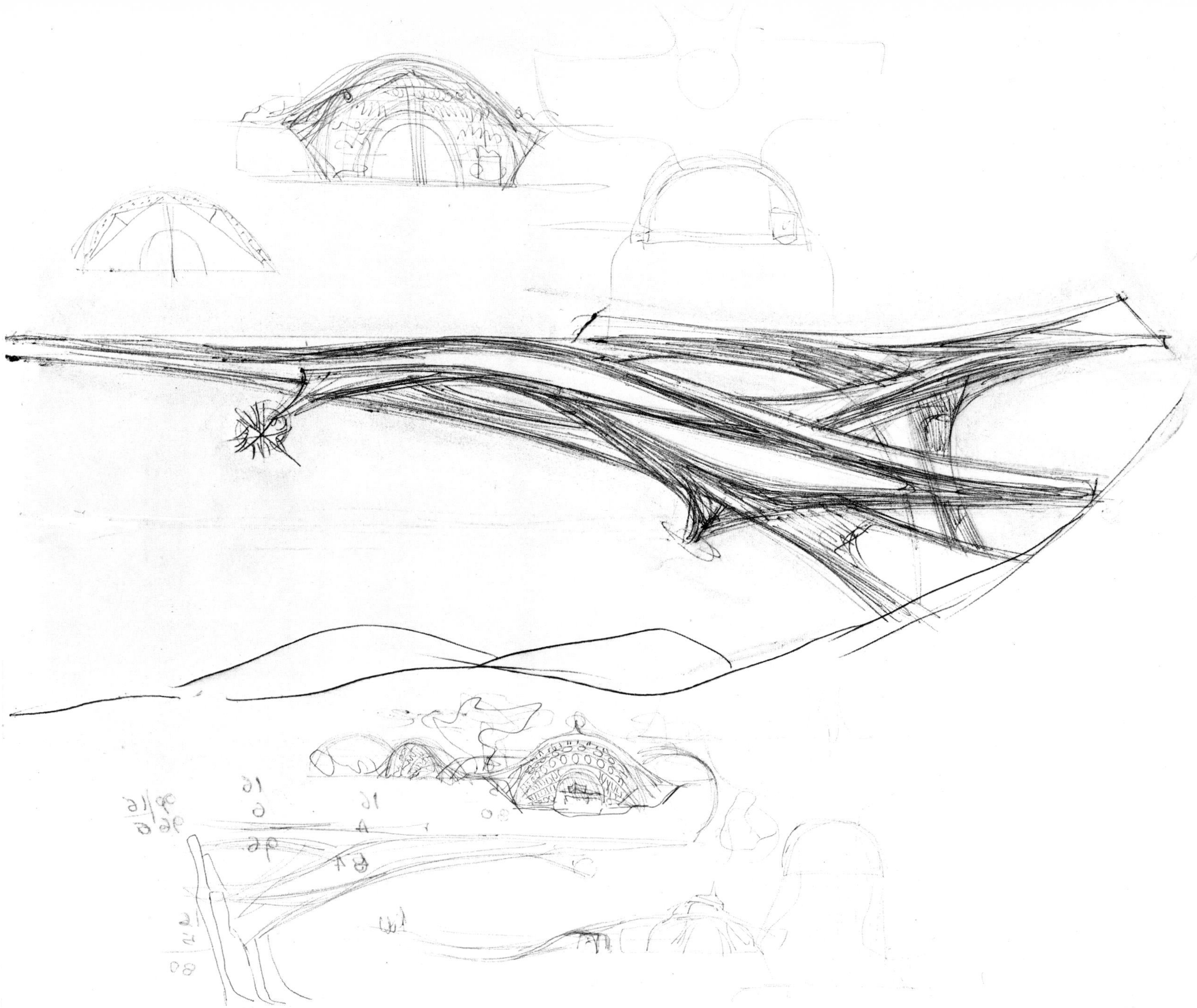

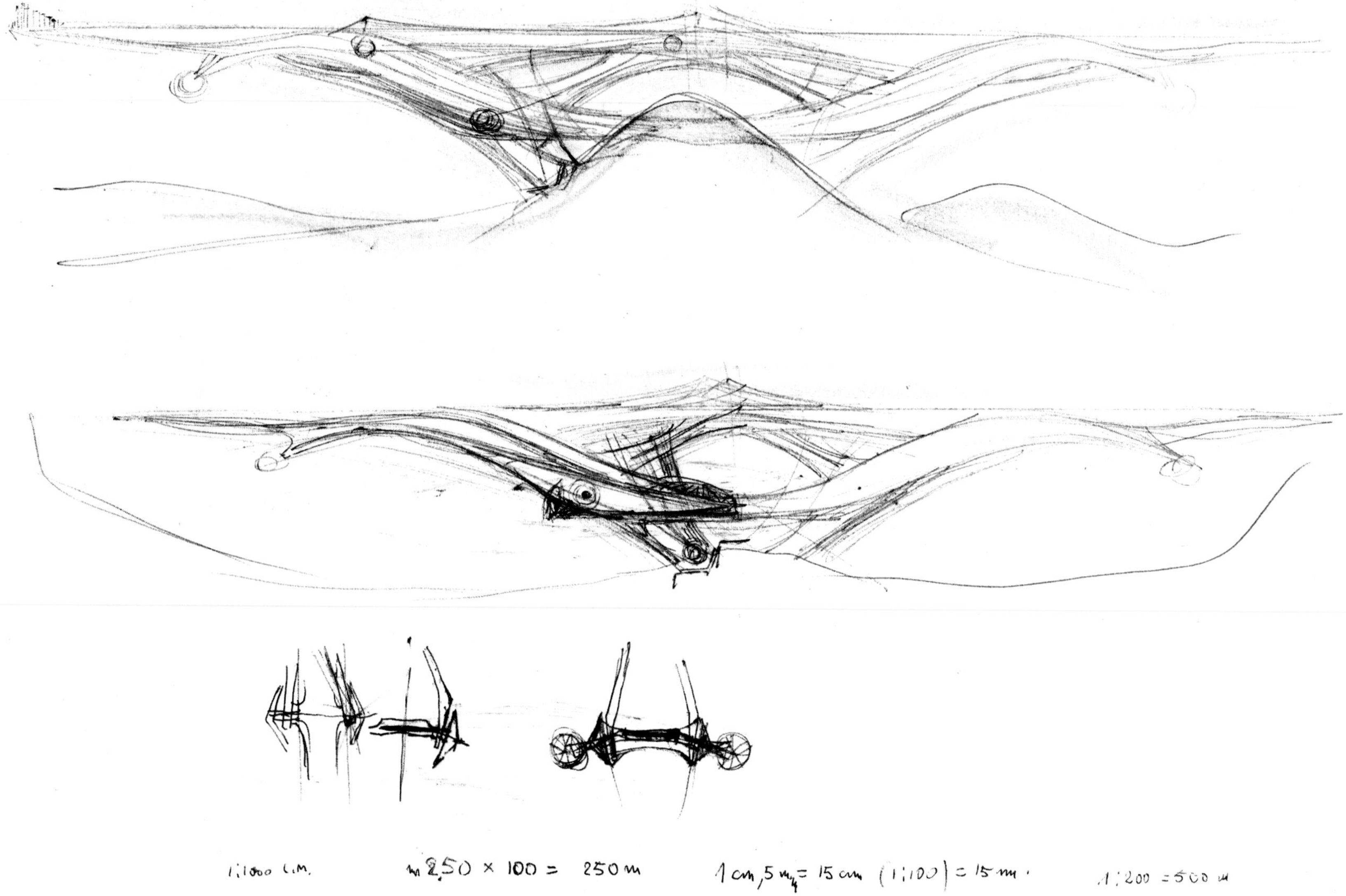
1:1000 l.m.
m 2,50 × 100 = 250 m
1 cm,5 m = 15 cm (1:100) = 15 m.
1:200 = 500 m

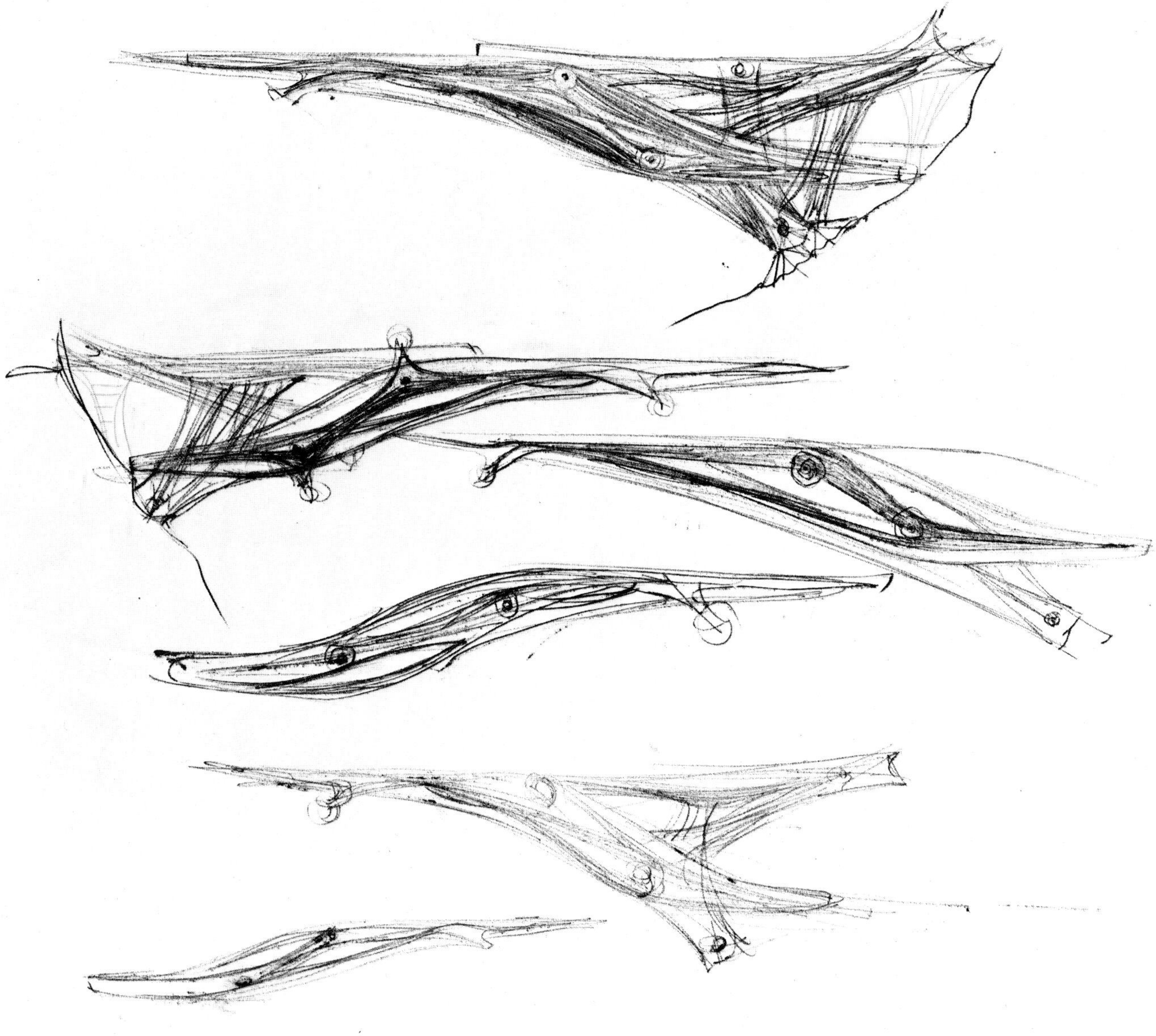

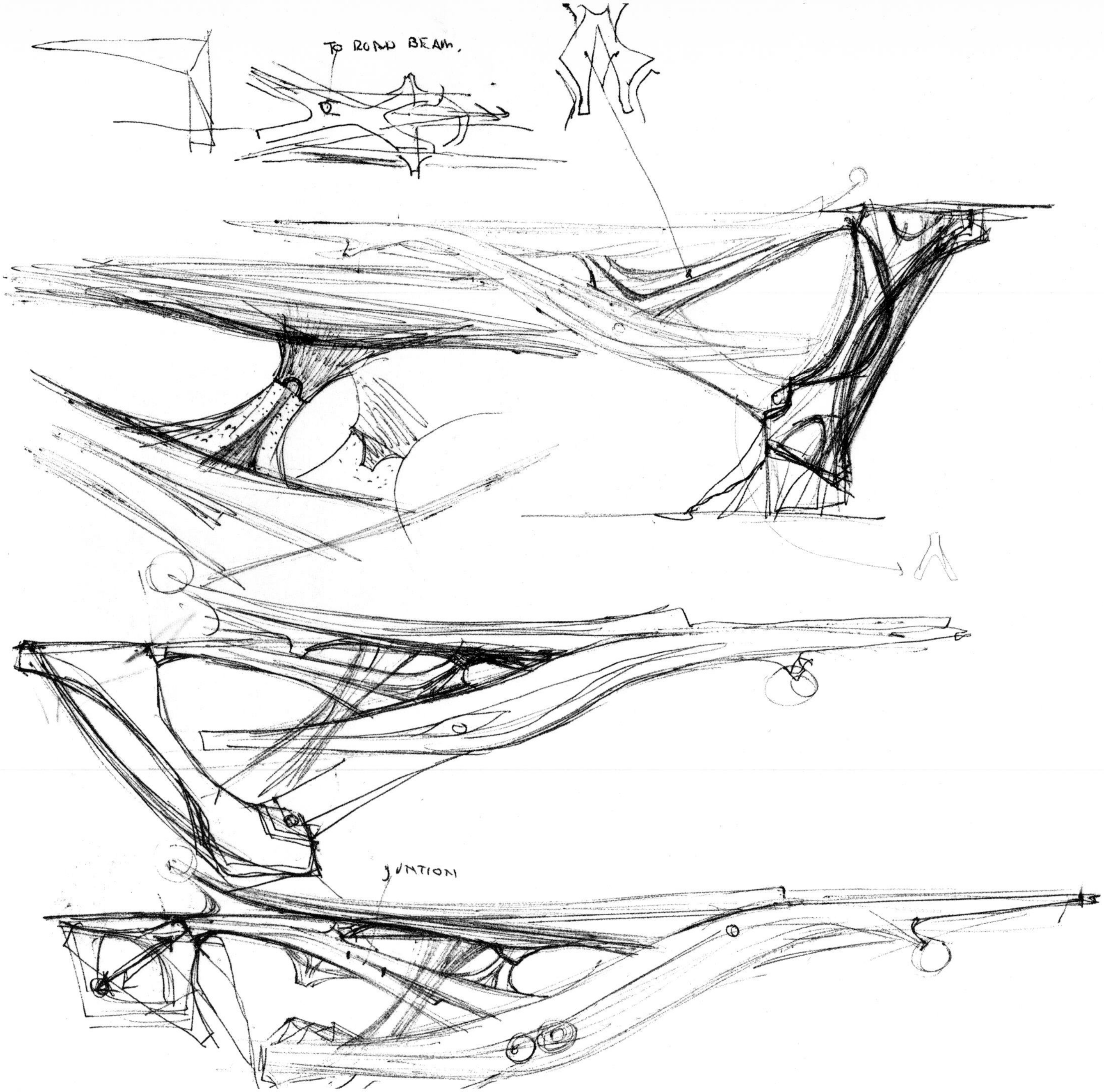
TO ROAD BEAM,
JUNTION

Cosanti II

1970
Because I always remind myself that possibly none of the things I put on paper may be constructed, I decided long ago that at least one would be attempted personally. Cosanti II, as presented here, is one of the phases in this attempt. (Cosanti II has become Arcosanti, and some construction work is going on now.)

Cosanti comes after Mesa City, and it is an intermediate phase between the two-dimensional sprawl of Mesa City, in which some three-dimensional nodules already appear, and the uncompromising three-dimensional unity of the arcologies (Arcosanti included).

Even in 1963, I was not an advocate of a return to nature. (Every age has its natural man. In this epoch, natural man is the city dweller because that is where life, the spearhead of nature, has invested the best and the most of its intensity.) Cosanti II then, as Arcosanti now, was the introduction of the urban concept into still-wholesome "natural" surroundings.

While "Walden" never represented more than a finite and rewarding environment for an exceptional man, "Walden II" does not indicate that there is any more than social engineering to the performance of a society.

If one glosses over the tearing and the healing, the harshness and the exhilaration, the utterly fluid condition of the human psyche compressed into ever-more-mysterious molds, one finds oneself in the classic Arcadian limbo blanketed with all sorts of pain-killers and joy-killers. Somewhere I wrote that compassion is not an electric blanket but a blazing flame. Neither Waldens burned that hot; nor is the romanticism tag much more valid. I suggest watching the butchering of a hog or a steer and having a glimpse of the "romantic" turmoil of its entrails while life drains away. And that is still pure genetic-instinctual-automatic unacceptance of naught. Move up to the mind and the self-conscious, and the Arcadian-romantic landscape becomes a devastated battlefield, blood-fertile and expectant on the blazing flame of compassion.

As we are discovering how rigorous is the discipline of nature, we can be congruous to it only in terms of a no-less-disciplined and rigorous performance. Furthermore, at the ultracomplex level of the human, social, and cultural performance this rigor must be translated into a concrete awareness of the future as something as factual as any so-called hard fact. From this recognition arises the necessity for "planning" and "projecting" within the behavioral flux of evolving life within which existential toil is only part of the story, possibly the least part of it.

1963
The land is a parcel of about one square mile, of which two-thirds is in the Prescott National Forest. The forest surrounds it on the east, south, and west as a natural barrier to the encroachment of "civilization."

The elevation of about 4,100 feet puts the land within the Arizona prairie belt. The spare grass is green after the winter and summer rains. The rest of the year it is a most beautiful, even, pale gold.

This specific plan results from the encounter of an idea and a described site that responds broadly to its demands.

This encounter had to be consumed within a "heavenly" determinant: if the cosmography governing the land were square, that is, if a square sun rising vertically on the straight horizon should describe a square orbit in the cubical sky, the scheme of the structure and its parts would be square. For our spherical (elliptical) cosmography the structural morphology, parts and all, is spherical (curved).

The reason for this dependence is not far-fetched: in the Foundation most of the activities are to be developed in sheltered but open spaces. To succeed in this, the main problem is to tame the sun by selecting those radiations that are "kind" and rejecting those that are "unkind." Its curve trajectory demands curved "traps."

The long, hot, horizontal, east and west intrusions of the sun, the midday blasting verticality of summer, and the shorter and inclined warmth of winter were causal in the choice of the two schemes adopted. One, a microstructure sheltering individual or small group activities, is repetitively used. The other, a macrostructure sheltering similar activities, this time compactly grouped, is used in three variations.

Very generally the microstructures are "vertically efficient." The macrostructures are horizontally efficient: the first, like a hand sheltering a lighted match; the other, like a two-hand bowl catching falling water (falling sunlight). The psychological similitude stops there, all structures being inscribed in elemental geometric configurations.

The microstructure is an apse, trapping most of the winter sunshine projecting into it (if open to the south), slowly releasing it through the spring, cutting it out almost totally during the summer months, gradually recapturing it again with fall.

The macrostructure also produces a microclimate zone, but more extensively than intensively. In this case the climatic zones are indeed multiple but broadly divided into two groups: under the bowl is a shaded volume where vegetation and water can contribute to coolness. This volume is of the ground environment, crisscrossed by breezes and winds. It is rain sheltered. The winter sun will cut deep into it on the east, south, and west sides.

Within the bowl is a wind-sheltered volume. A system of movable shading devices suspended from the structural cable system allows shade for most of this volume or lets it be sun-bathed. Thus in winter the bowl will be a great collector of sun energy; in summer it will be a vast shaded space.

Access gates between the pillars elliptically displayed to support the structure can be open (summer) or closed (winter) to accentuate the climatic advantages.

This upper volume is a man-made microenvironment in sharp contrast to its natural surroundings. Polychromy will enhance the spatial complexity and further distinguish its manmade character from the quasi-monochromatic landscape—green and blue after the rains, pale yellow and blues most of the year.

Moving through the gates from one environment, clustered and finite, to the other, open and infinite, should be a momentous experience.

These two basic schemes must now be organized into a working complex. For the microstructures this is done by coupling them back to back then repeating the coupling contiguously and developing it further tridimensionally on multiple levels: the elementary, functional structure of the apse is enriched and becomes a multiple-purpose organism.

There is thus a series of apsidal volumes that are open on the south side for sheltered open-air workshops, a twin series facing north, open or glazed for optimum-north-light studios, good centers of work in winter as well as summer. Sandwiched in between the apses are two levels of passageways: one level of studios and classrooms and, above, a continuous suspended ground where mobile dwelling units are located for students and apprentices. At the feet of the apses are earth houses for permanent residents.

Thus this long structure has become a thoroughfare serving the whole community, for which it furnishes studios, workshops, dwellings, suspended gardens, and so forth. Furthermore, it envelops and shelters on the north side the ground that is to be transformed into a terraced garden reaching under the three macrostructures and closely following the contours of the land.

The relationship between all the facilities incorporated in the thoroughfare varies according to the axial orientation. This causes functional and visual changes.

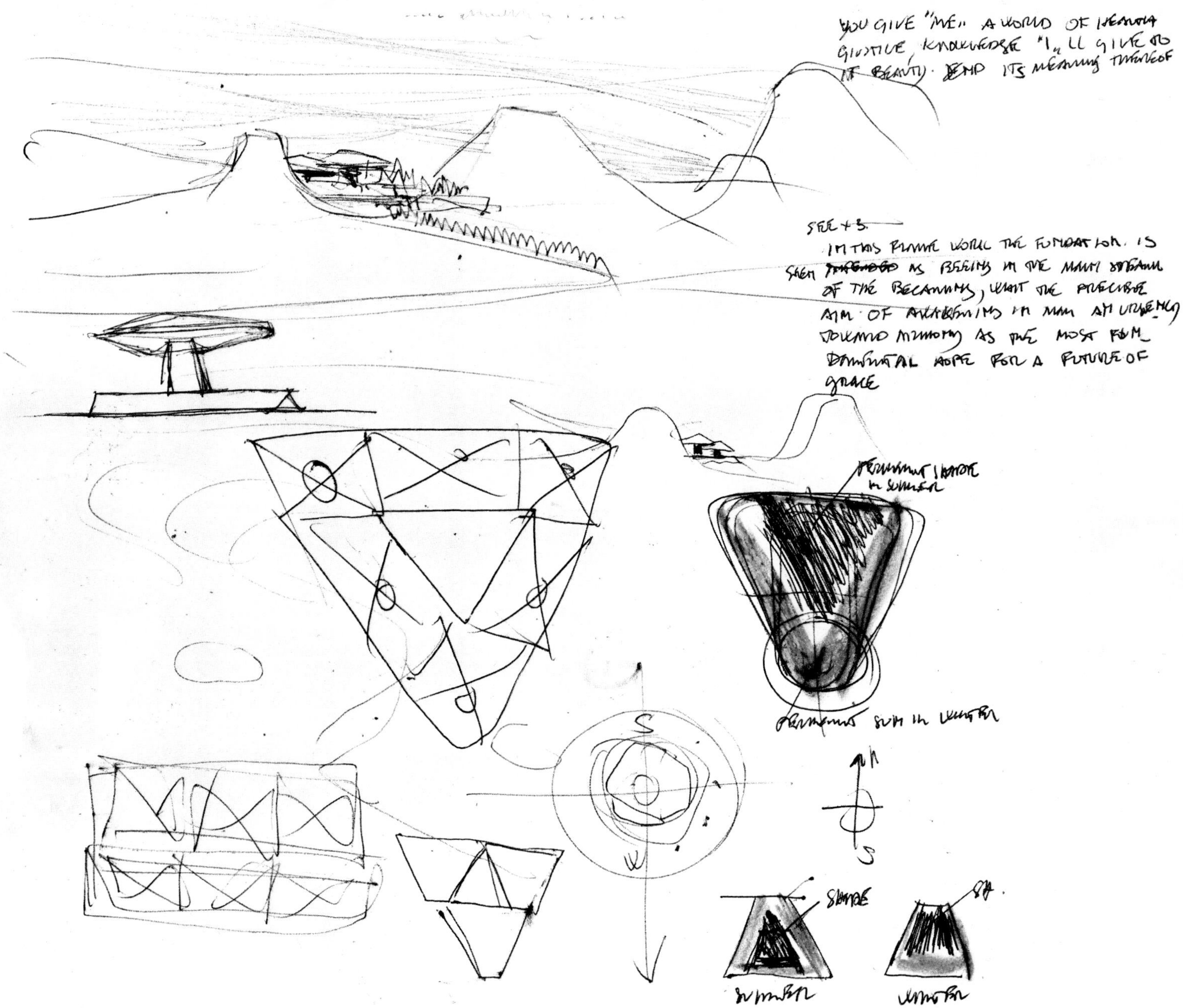
YOU GIVE "ME" A WORLD OF HEAVEN
JUSTICE, KNOWLEDGE "I" LL GIVE TO
IT BEAUTY. AND ITS MEANING THEREOF
SEE + 3.
IN THIS PLANE WORLD THE FOUNDATION. IS
SEEN AS BEING IN THE MAIN STREAM
OF THE BEGINNING, WHAT THE PRECISE
AIM OF AWAKENING IN MAN AN URGENCY
TOWARD HARMONY AS THE MOST FUN-
DAMENTAL HOPE FOR A FUTURE OF
GRACE
PERMANENT SHADE IN SUMMER
PERMANENT SUN IN WINTER
S
W
N
S
SHADE
SUMMER
WINTER

FEBRUARY 63

THE SIGNIFICANCE OF THE FOUNDATION IN THE "SOCIAL" CONTEST.

TO FIND OUT IF SUCH SIGNIFICANCE IS THERE IT IS NECESSARY TO BRING IN CAUSE THE MAJOR PROBLEM FACING THE "LABOR" WORLD: AUTOMATION.

SUPPOSING AUTOMATION WILL PERFECT ITSELF SO COMPLETELY AS TO TAKE OVER · 80 90% OF THE PHISICAL WORK TWO MAJOR PROBLEMS WILL FACE MAN.

1. HOW TO DISTRIBUTE THE WEALTH "ENFORCED" BY AUTOMATION ON MAN.
2. WHAT ~~TO~~ GIVE occupations (MAN) SO THAT HE MAY FIND LIVING A REWARDING A VALUABLE THING,

IT IS SOMEWHAT IRONIC THAT AFTER CENTURIES OF STRUGGLE TO ~~GAIN~~ TEAR OF TIME SOME PRECIOUS HOUR OF "LIESURE", WHICH WILL ~~BE~~ LET THE MIND WANDER & DISCOVER & CREATE, MAN HAS NOW TO LIVE IN TERROR FOR A LIFE EMPTIED OF NEEDS, OF NEEDED TASKS. THE MAN THAT FEELS ITSELF USELESS IS A DEAD MAN.

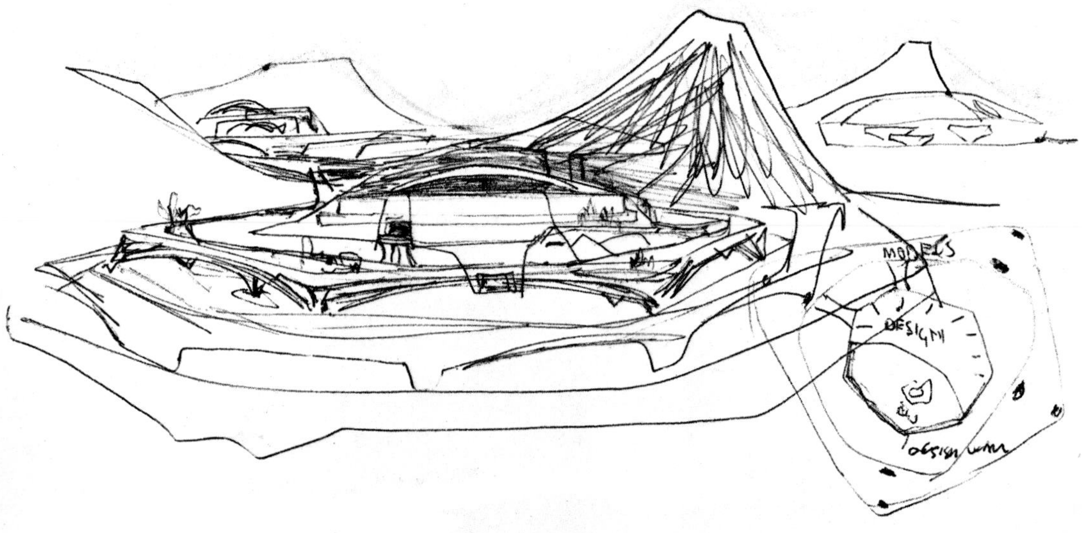

OCTOBER 62

THE SPECTER OF THE UNEMPLOYMENT WILL NOT BE ECONOMICAL. HE WILL BE "FORCED" TO ACCEPT. SALARY FOR HIS IDLENESS. (HE HAS TO CONSUME). THE GRIM PROSPECTIVE WILL BE TO FIND ONESELF DRIFTING FROM THE CLUB TO THE CRUISING VESSEL FROM THE BAR TO THE BOWLING ALLEY ..... & NOT A CONSEQUENTIAL TREND LOOKING IN ALL OF THIS. NOTHING TO SHOW THAT ONE CAN SAY I MOLDED IT I ASSEMBLED IT. I CONSTRUCTED IT ....

MODELS 2 DESIGN. PUBLICATION.

THERE SEEMS TO BE ONLY ONE MANNER MAKE MAN PROFICIENT IN THESE EVENTS

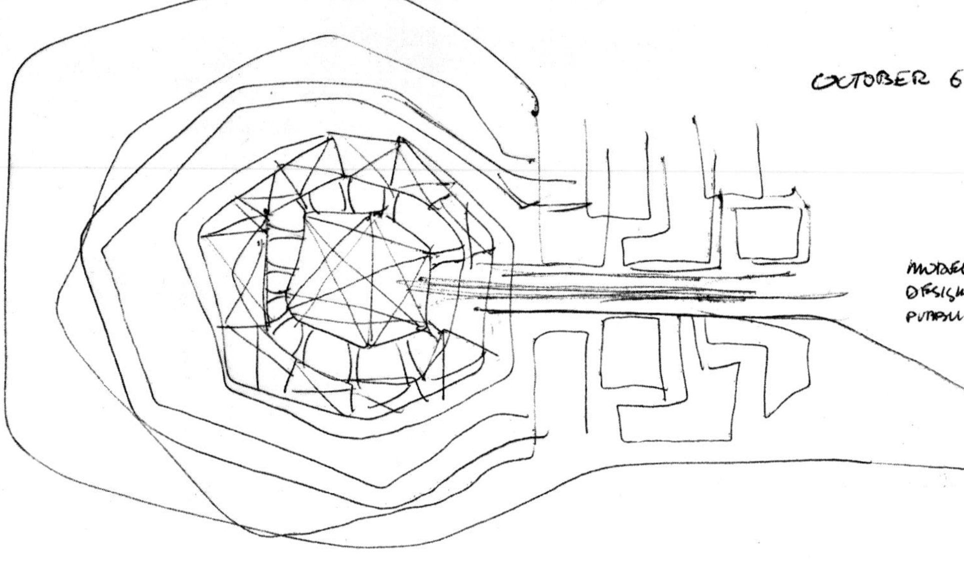

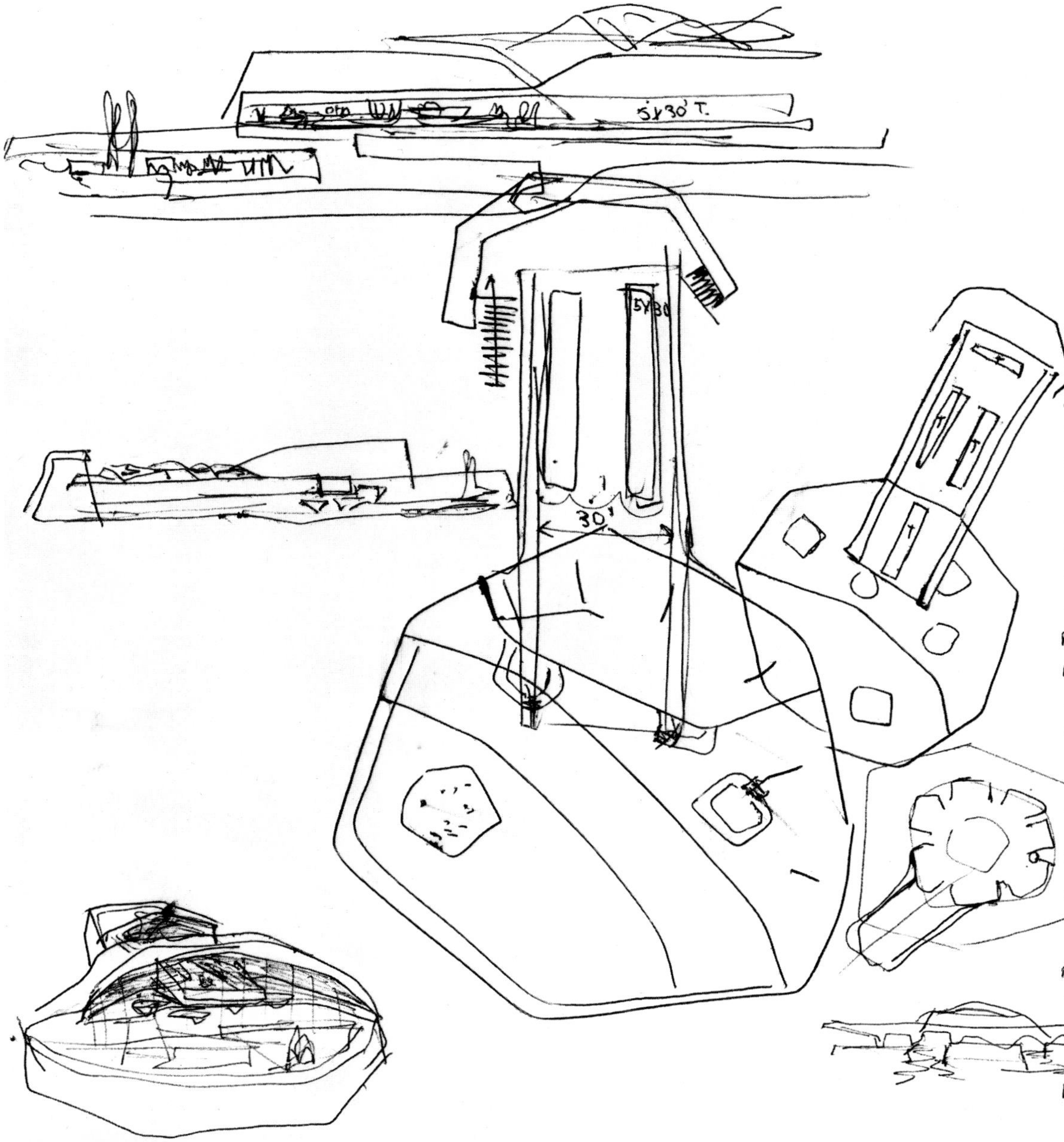

WHERE THE MACHINES, THE COMPUTERS, ARE HELPLESS: CREATIVITY.
THE COMPUTER SPECIES WILL IN TIME DISCOVER & INVENT NOT JUST INFORM. IN THIS LIGHT SCIENCE, APPLIED SCIENCE AT LEAST WILL BE A FIELD FOR THE MACHINE.
EVEN RELIGION & PHILOSOPHY IN THEIR RATIONAL ASPECTS (JUSTICE & ~~RATIONAL~~ MATHEMATIC) WILL BE SOMEWHAT "FOOD FOR COMPUTATION" (OR EXTRAPOLATION)

THE ONE FIELD OF PURE CREATIVITY WHERE IN THE MACHINE WILL ALWAYS REMAIN AN UNESSENTIAL TOOL ARE THE ARTS. THIS IN ITSELF WOULD SEEM TO SUGGEST THAT THE TRUE & FUNDAMENTAL NATURE OF MAN IS ITS POWER TO CREATE (AESTHETICALLY).
NATURE HAS PRODUCED WHAT THE MACHINE TRIES NOW TO REPRODUCE IN A WORLD OF SYNTHETIC TIME, (AUTOMATISMS)
THE ADVENT OF MAN HAS BROUGHT FORWARD THE NEW WORLD OF "ART", DESTROY THE WORLD OF ART: ALL THE MUSIC, ALL THE POETRY, ALL THE WRITING, ALL THE DANCING, ALL SCULPTURE, ALL ARCHITECTURE, ALL PAINTING & THE TEXTURE OF CIVILIZATION IS FORFEITED, MAN HAS LOST ITS GRACE & ITS SIGNIFICANCE

RELIGION, PHILOSOPHY & SCIENCE ARE OCCUPIED IN FINDING OUT WHERE WE STAND & WHY. ART FROM THE BEGINNING ACTED AS IF THOSE FINDINGS WERE INVOLVED OR NOT ESSENTIAL ANYWAY (THEIR RATIONAL ~~[illegible]~~ APPREHENSION) THUS ITS INFANTILE VOICE HAS ALWAYS OVERSHADOWED ~~THE~~ OTHERS BY THE POWER OF ITS ESSENTIALITY.

THE COMPUTER CIVILISATION OR AUTOMATION & MAN

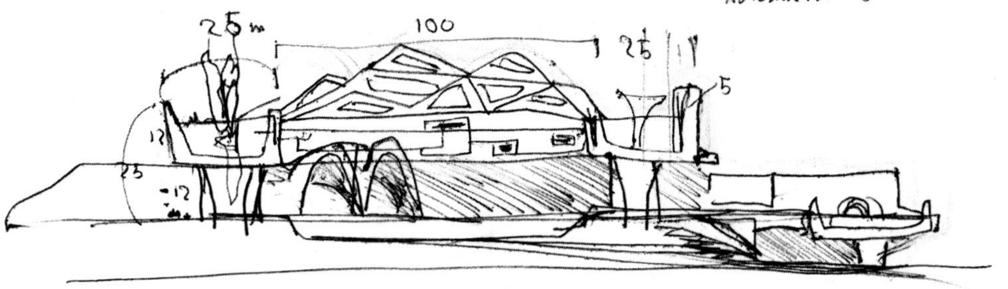

AUTOMATION & MAN

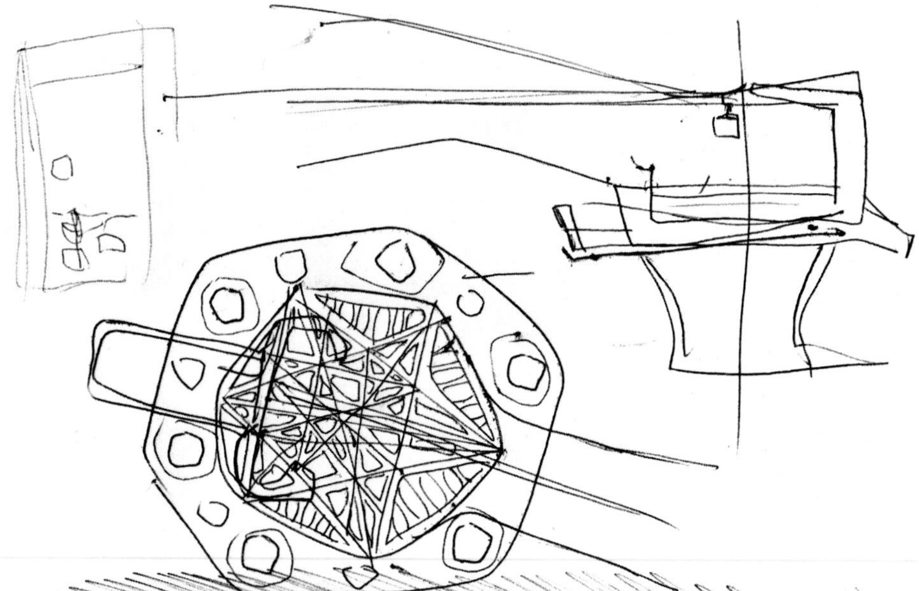

FIND ONESELF UNPREPARED FOR A LONG SOUGHT 'GIFT, (CONDITION) IS ONE OF LIFE'S IRONIES

THE UNSPOKEN BUT CONSTANT WANT OF MAN HAS BEEN THE 'FREEDOM FROM NEED". ON THE THRESHOLD OF THE AUTOMATION CIVILIZATION, PROMISING MAN ~~AN~~ A LIMITLESS STORAGE OF LIESURE. ~~THE IT IS~~ THERE IS A PLENTIFUL HARVEST OF CINICISM & IRONY IN THE REALIZED FACT THAT MAN IS LEARNING TO LIVE IN TERROR OF A LIFE EMPTIED OF NEEDS, OF NEEDED TASKS.

1 WHAT WILL MAN DO?

2 HOW WILL WEALTH BE DISTRIBUTED THE "ENFORCED UPON MAN BY THE MACHINE"

THE SPECTER OF UNEMPLOYMENT WILL NOT REFER TO INDIGENCE. THE "UNEMPLOYED" WILL BE FORCED TO ACCEPT A SALARY FOR HIS IDLENESS, HE MUST CONSUME. THE GRIM PROSPECTIVE WILL BE TO FIND ONESELF, AS ONE OF THE COUNTLESS, DRIFTING AMONG THE EPHEMERITIES OF PLENTY. KIND OF A LIFE SLAVE TOURIST FOR LIFE, ... WITHOUT A CONSEQUENTIAL TREND WOVEN IN ALL OF THIS, NOTHING TO POINT AT AS OF ONE'S OWN DOING.

IT IS WELL, IN THE REALM OF AN INDIFFERENT UNIVERSE THE POSSIBILITY THAT MAN MAY CONSTRUCT A SOCIETY SIMILAR IN ITS PERFECTED MECHANICS TO SOME INSECT SOCIETY, DIFFERENT FROM THOSE BECAUSE THE BIOLOGICAL SPECIALISATION, ~~WOULD~~ BE TRANSFERRED TO TECHNOLOGY & BECAUSE SOMEHOW THE PERFECT ROBOT WOULD BE AN AURA OF BIO PSYCHOLOGICAL USELESSNESS, ~~THAN~~ UNITY

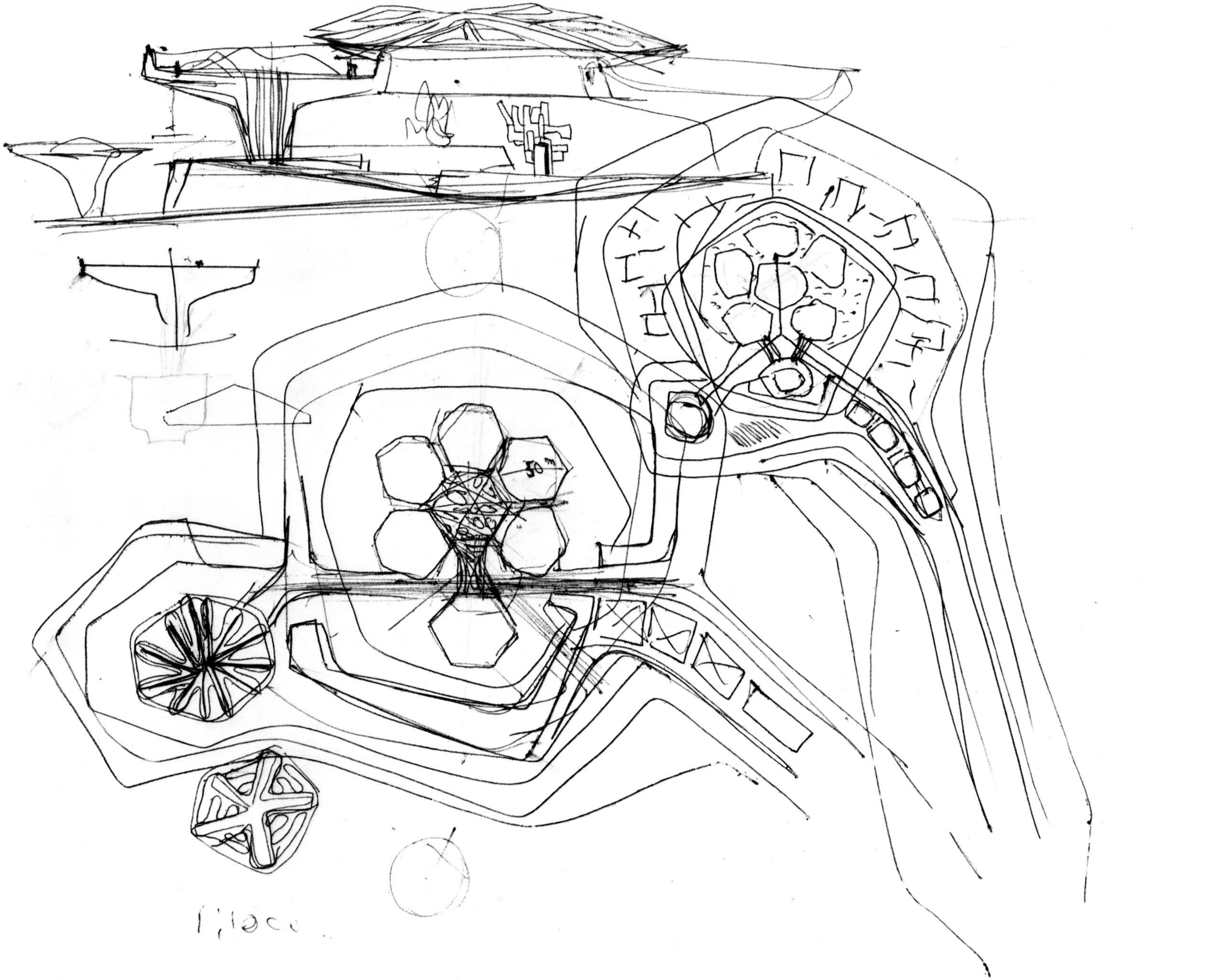

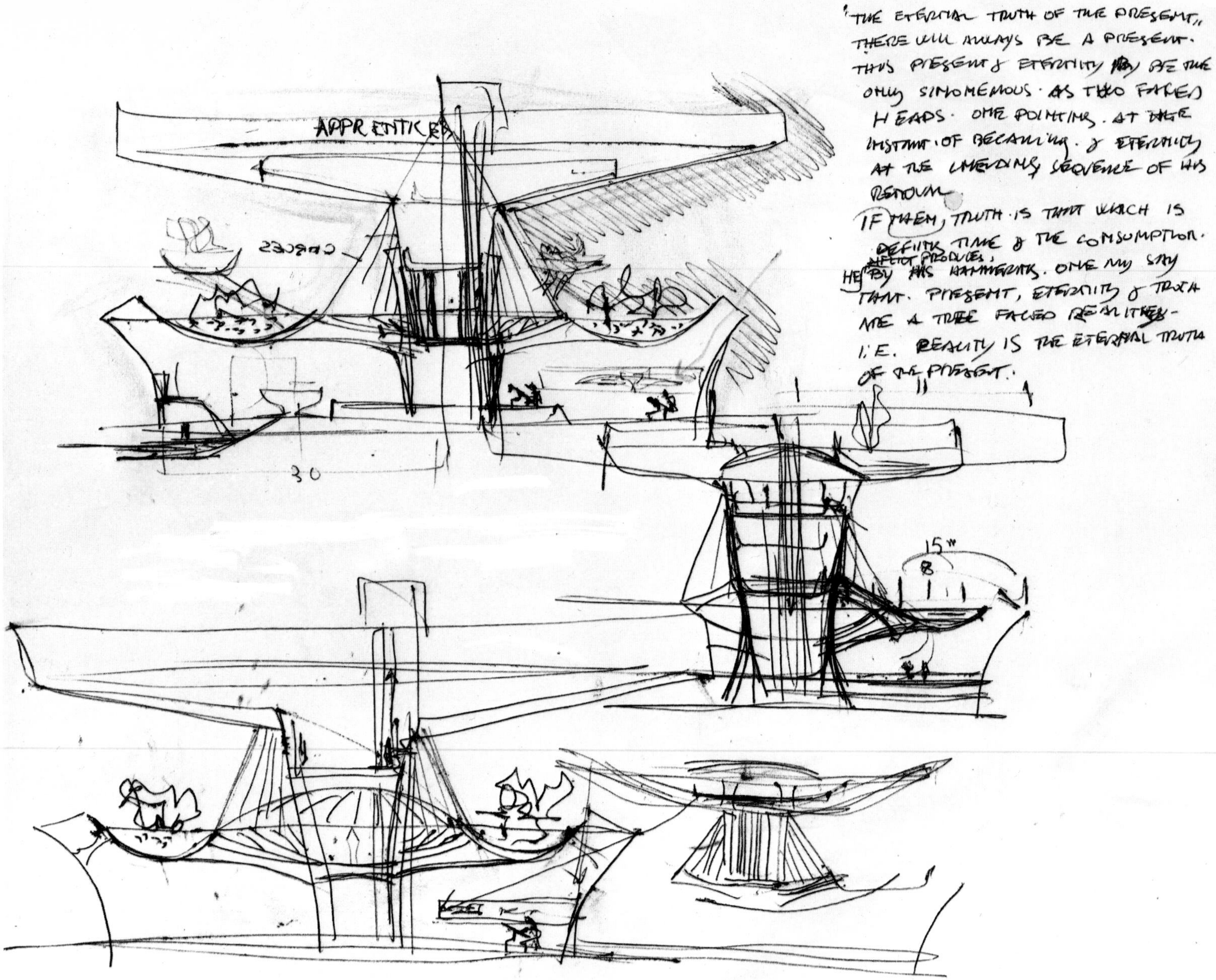
"THE ETERNAL TRUTH OF THE PRESENT"
THERE WILL ALWAYS BE A PRESENT.
THUS PRESENT & ETERNITY BE THE
ONLY SIMONEMOUS. AS TWO FACED
HEADS. ONE POINTING. AT THE
INSTANT OF BECOMING. & ETERNITY
AT THE UNENDING SEQUENCE OF HIS
RENOWN.
IF THEN, TRUTH IS THAT WHICH IS
TIME & THE CONSUMPTION.
PRODUCES,
ONE MAY SAY
THAT. PRESENT, ETERNITY & TRUTH
ARE A TREE FACED REALITY
I.E. REALITY IS THE ETERNAL TRUTH
OF THE PRESENT.
APPRENTICES
30
15"
8

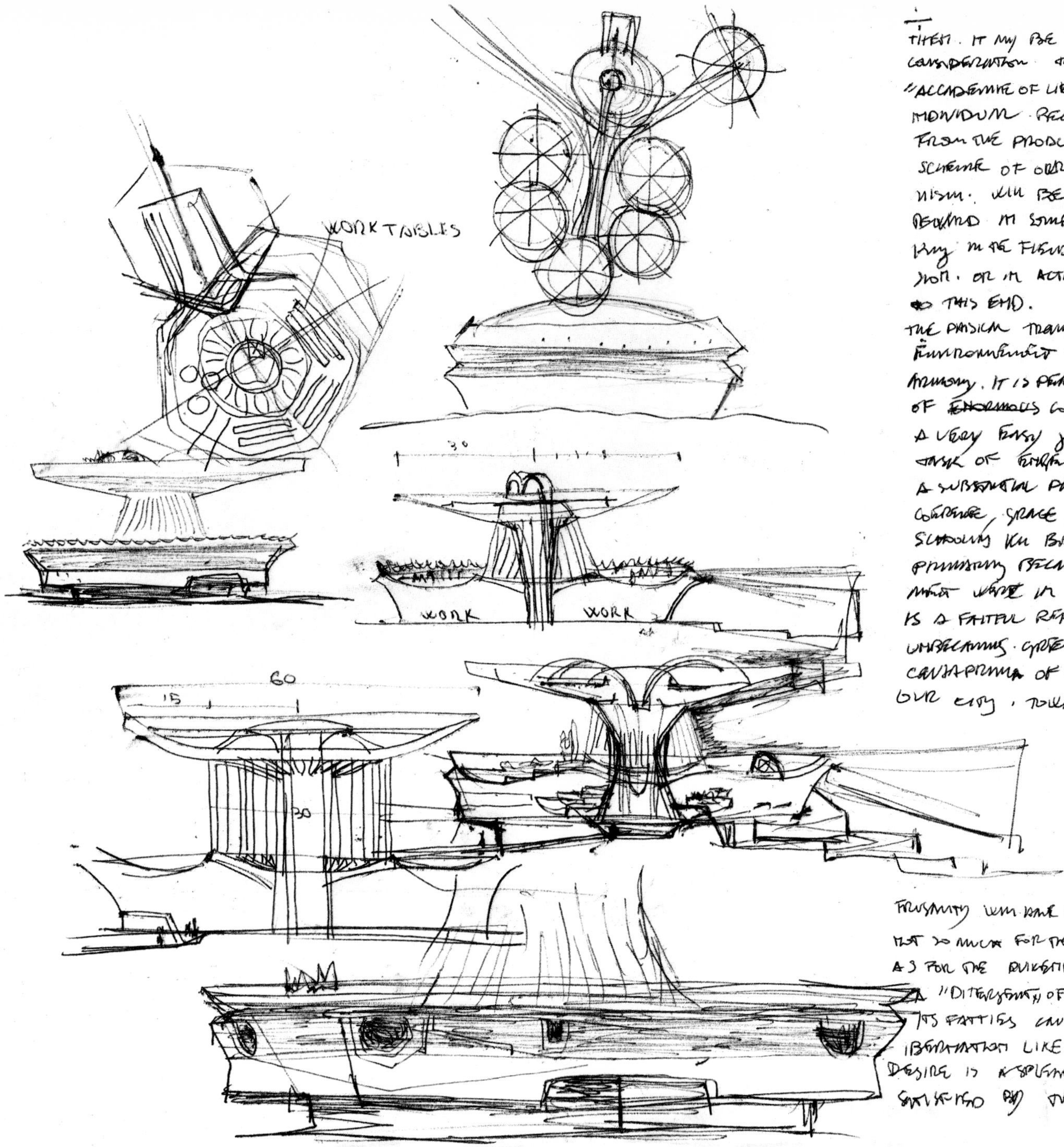

THEN. IT MAY BE MATTER OF SERIOUS
CONSIDERATION THE INSTITUTION OF
"ACCADEMIE OF LEISURE" WHERE THE
INDIVIDUAL BECOMING UNHINGED
FROM THE PRODUCTION – MAINTENANCE
SCHEME OF OUR TECHNOLOGICAL MECHA-
NISM. WILL BE HELPED IN FINDING
REWARD IN SOME SERIOUS UNDERTA-
KING IN THE FIELDS OF AESTHETIC EXPRES-
SION. OR IN ACTIVITIES INSTRUMENTAL
TO THIS END.
THE PHYSICAL TRANSFORMATION OF OUR
ENVIRONMENT FROM BLIGHT TO
HARMONY. IT IS PER SE AN UNDERTAKING
OF ~~ENORMOUS~~ COLOSSAL ~~SIZE~~ MOMENTUM BUT
A VERY EASY & SECONDARY FACET COMPARING TO THE
TASK OF ENGENDERING IN PEOPLE
A SUBSTANTIAL PASSION FOR INTEGRITY,
COHERENCE, GRACE.
SCHOOLING WILL BE MADE UP TO IT
PRIMARILY BECAUSE THE ENVIRONMENT
WHAT WE ARE IN THE SCHOOLING. IS DONE
IS A FAITHFUL REFLECTION OF THE SAME
UNBECOMING. GREED & SORTISHNESS,
CANNIBALISM OF PURE UGLINESS OF
OUR CITY, TOWNS, VILLAGES. SUBURBIA

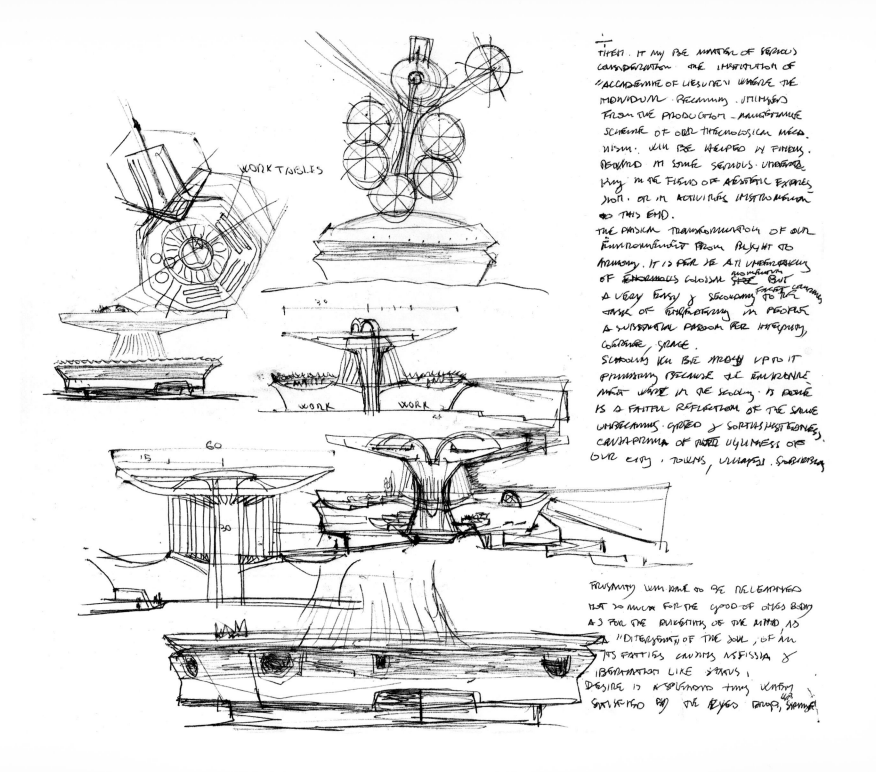

FRUGALITY WILL HAVE TO BE RELEARNED
NOT SO MUCH FOR THE GOOD OF ONES BODY
AS FOR THE QUICKENING OF THE MIND, AS
A "DIETETIC" OF THE SOUL, OF ALL
ITS FACULTIES CAUSING ASFISSIA &
IBERNATION LIKE STATUS.
DESIRE IS A SPLENDID THING WHEN
SATISFIED BY THE EYES, EARS, SENSES

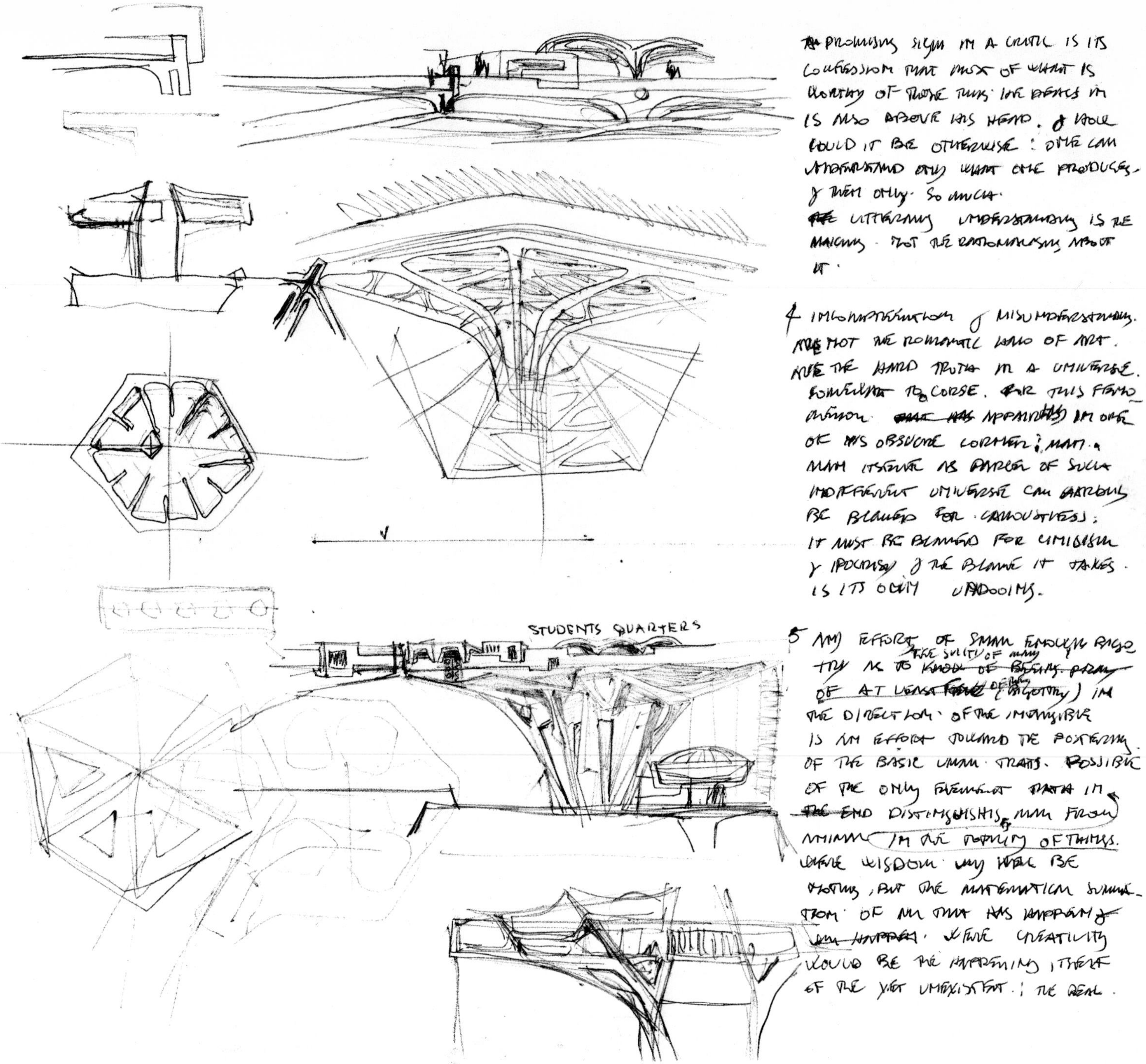
A promising sign in a critic is its
confession that most of what is
worthy of those things he deals in
is also above his head. & how
could it be otherwise: one can
understand only what one produces,
& then only so much.
The uttering understanding is the
making, not the rationalizing about
it.
4 Incomprehension & misunderstanding
are not the romantic halo of art.
are the hard truth in a universe
somewhat to coarse. For this fenomenon has appeared in one
of his obscure corners: man.
man itself as parcel of such
indifferent universe can hardly
be blamed for callousness;
it must be blamed for cynicism
& ipocrisy & the blame it takes
is its own undoing.
5 Any effort of man
try as to know
of at least
the direction of the intangible
is an effort toward the fostering
of the basic human traits. Possibly
of the only element that in
the end distinguishes man from
animal in the family of things.
Where wisdom may well be
nothing, but the mathematical summation of all that has happened
Where creativity
would be the happening itself
of the yet unexistent: the real.
STUDENTS QUARTERS

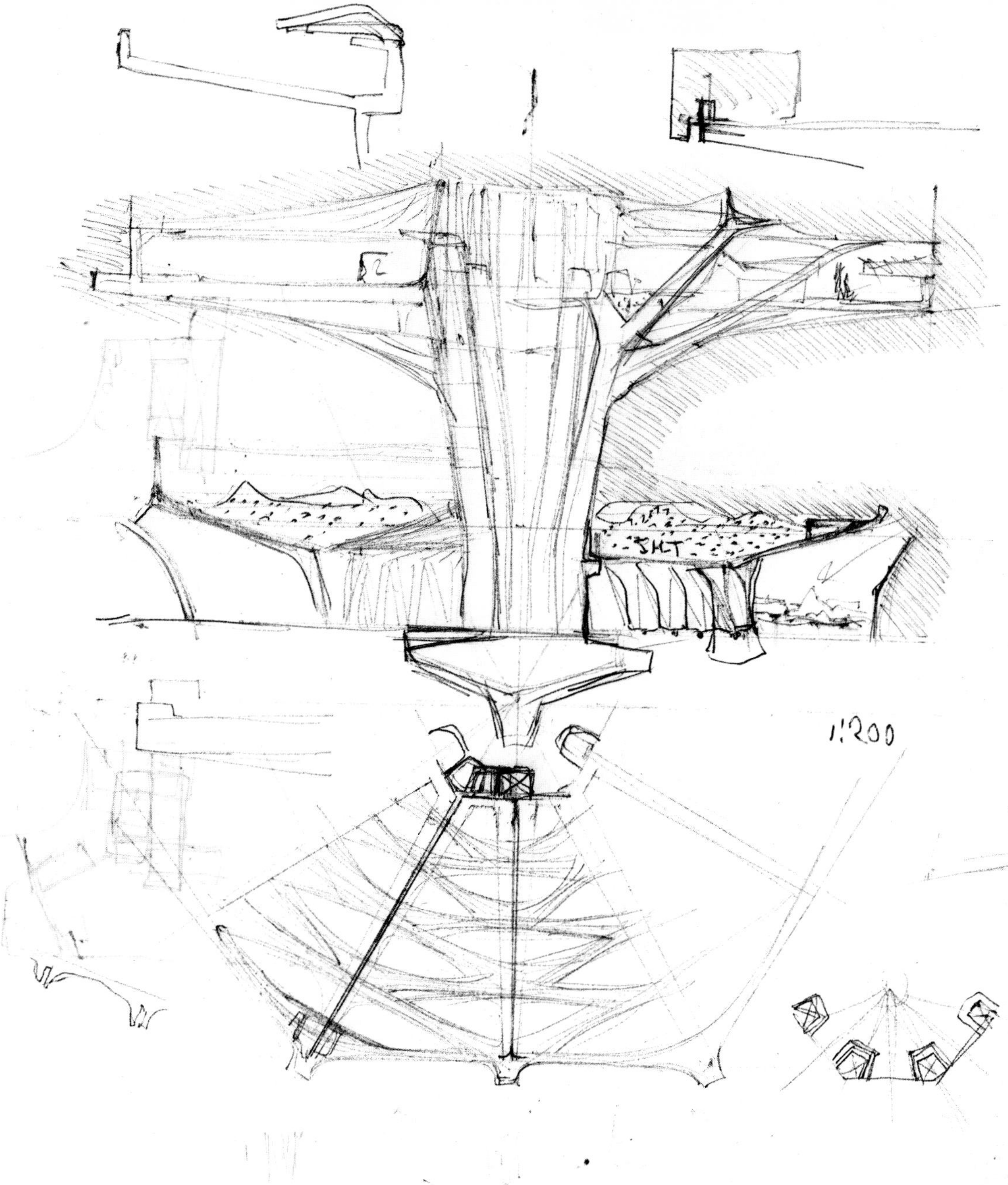
(A POSTERIORI)
SCHEME OF OPEN WORK
SHOP FOR SALT PILE MODEL
MACHINES. ..
AND PLATFORM FOR STUDENTS
ACTIVITIES.
1:200
THE LOWER LEVEL IS FOR
LANDSCAPED MODEL · DISPLAYED
IN A CONTINOUS RIMS.
ONE OF THE DRAW BACK OF
THIS SCHEME IS ITS INDIFFE-
RENCE TO ORIENTATION.
THOO WORKING WELL IN SUMMER
WHEN THE WOLE WORK
PLATFORMS WOULD BE
SHADOWED MOST OF THE DAY
IN WINTER ONLY PART
OF IT WOULD BE EXPOSED
TO THE LOW SUN · & THE
BREEZES COULD MAKE
WORKING DIFFICULT.
SUCH SCHEME IS MORE AP-
PROPRIATE TO A MELLOW
CLIMATE NOT TOUCHED BY
EARLY MORNING FROSTS. OR
FREEZING NIGHTS.
RADIANT HEAT FROM THE
RIM OF THE "UMBRELLA
JUSTIFIED BY
CHEAP & ABBONDANT ENERGY WOULD
MITIGATE THE UNFA-
VORABLE TEMPERATURES - &
WHAT IT THE FUNCTIONNING
OF THE STRUCTURE.
WIND BREAKING DEVICES WOULD
ACT ALSO IN THE SAME DI-
RECTION.. SUCH DEVICES CAN
BE OF THE STRUCTURE OR BE
THE ENVIRONMENTAL CON-
DITION.
1:200
SALT

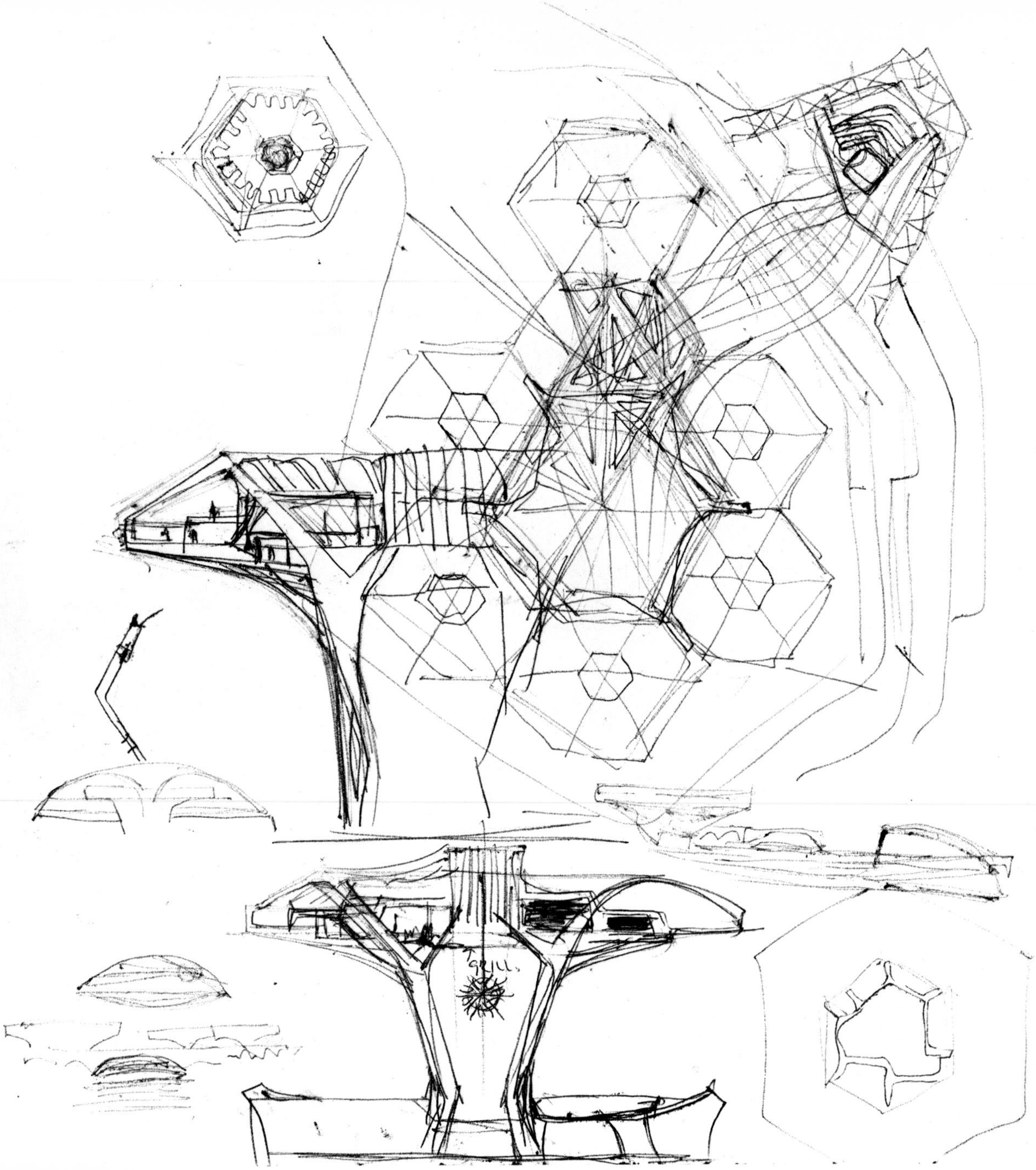
GRILL

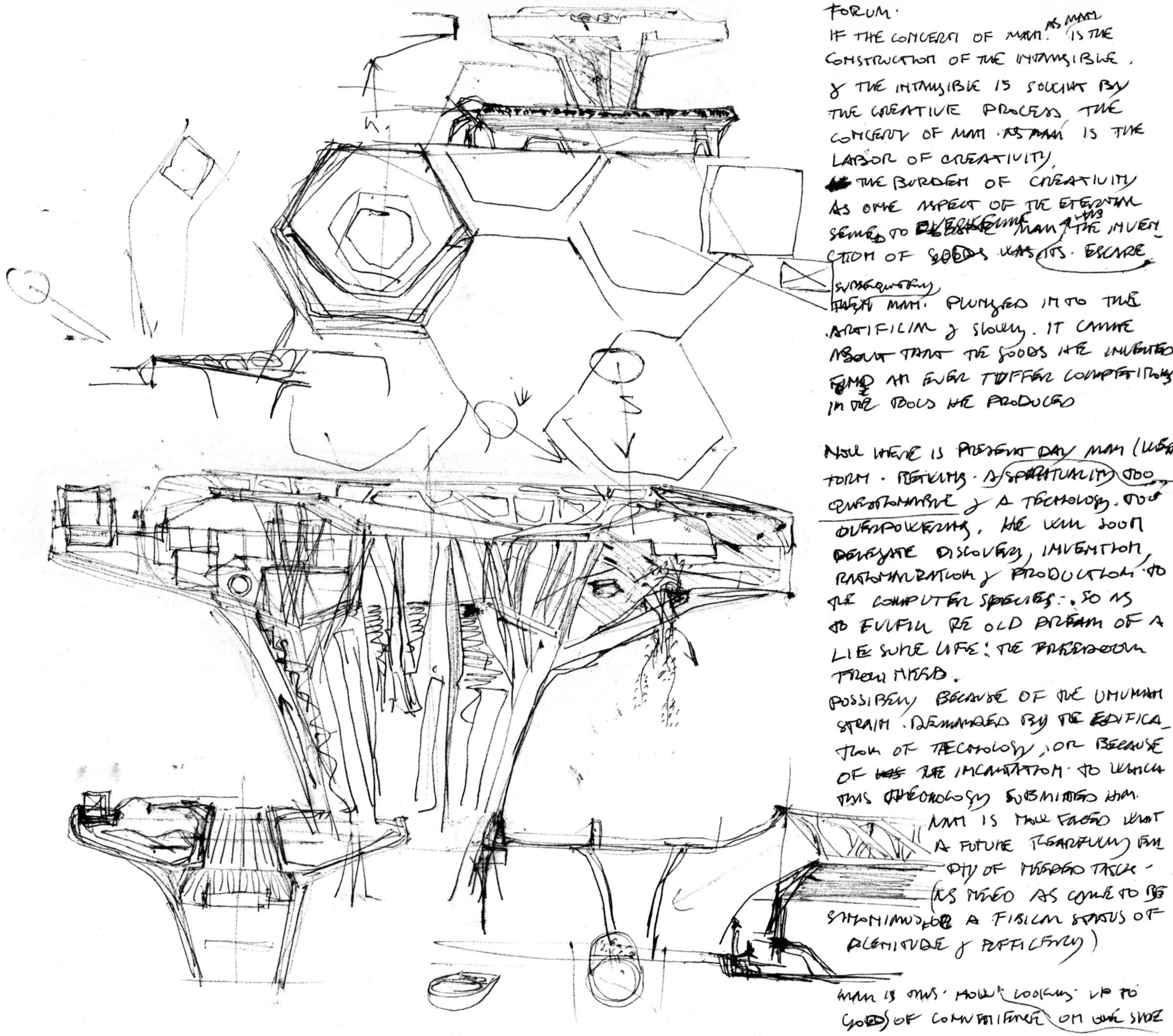
FORUM.
IF THE CONCERN OF MAN AS MAN IS THE
CONSTRUCTION OF THE INTANGIBLE,
& THE INTANGIBLE IS SOUGHT BY
THE CREATIVE PROCESS THE
CONCERN OF MAN AS MAN IS THE
LABOR OF CREATIVITY.
THE BURDEN OF CREATIVITY
AS ONE ASPECT OF THE ETERNAL
SEEMED TO OVERCOME MAN & HIS INVEN_
TION OF GODS WAS ITS ESCAPE
SUBSEQUENTLY
MAN PLUNGED INTO THE
ARTIFICIAL & SLOWLY. IT CAME
ABOUT THAT THE GODS HE INVENTED
FOUND AN EVER TOUGHER COMPETITION
IN THE TOOLS HE PRODUCED
NOW HERE IS PRESENT DAY MAN (WESTERN
FORM) FEELING A SPIRITUALITY TOO
QUESTIONABLE & A TECHNOLOGY TOO
OVERPOWERING. HE WILL SOON
DELEGATE DISCOVERY, INVENTION,
RATIONALIZATION & PRODUCTION TO
THE COMPUTER SPECIES. SO AS
TO FULFILL THE OLD DREAM OF A
LEISURE LIFE: THE FREEDOM
FROM NEED.
POSSIBLY BECAUSE OF THE INHUMAN
STRAIN DEMANDED BY THE EDIFICA_
TION OF TECHNOLOGY, OR BECAUSE
OF THE INCANTATION TO WHICH
THIS TECHNOLOGY SUBMITTED HIM.
MAN IS NOW FACED WITH
A FUTURE FEARFULLY EMP
TY OF NEEDED TASKS -
(AS NEED AS COME TO BE
SYNONIMOUS FOR A FISCAL STATUS OF
PLENITUDE & EFFICIENCY)
MAN IS THUS NOW LOOKING UP TO
GODS OF CONVENIENCE ON ONE SIDE

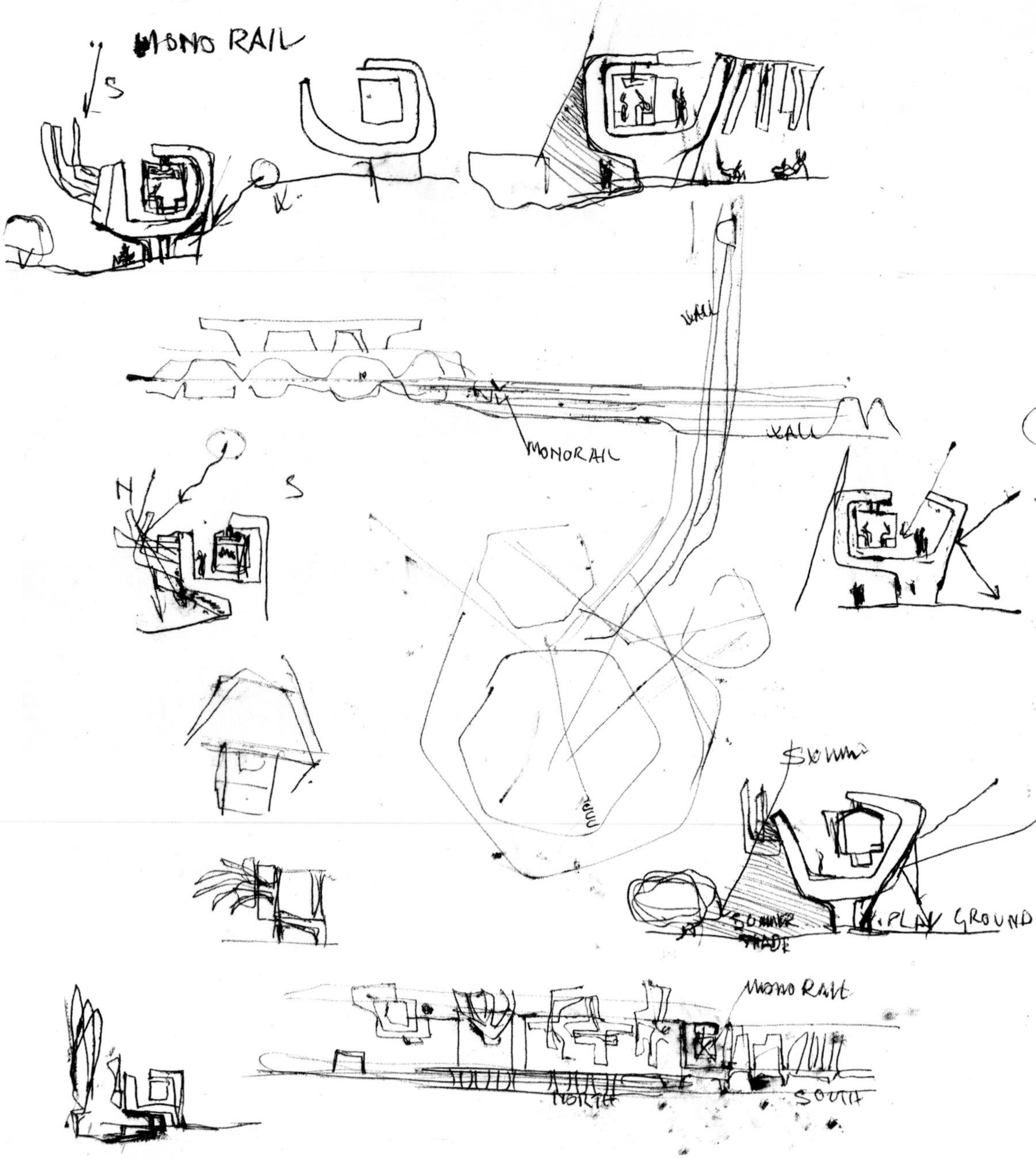

UP & what idolatry to the untamed beast of science & technology, onward ~~forward to a [illegible]~~ backward to a fantastic but [illegible] blood stained past & forward to a sort of [illegible] end of futilities. That total automation will force upon him [illegible].
The opportunity has come for the prodigal son of man civilisation. The ~~[illegible]~~ [illegible] small [illegible] [illegible] of the creativity of individual could finally become a [illegible] river cutting [illegible] the unchangeable & the indifferent, ~~[illegible]~~ compassionate & lasting.

To stand up to technology supposedly solely a tool. What [illegible] powerfulness as to assert [illegible] & finalities, the arts & [illegible] architecture [illegible] to move out of their [illegible] [illegible] & face some very [illegible] realities.
1 Conservativism is the safeguard of man's continuity, to [illegible] at it is to be permanently on the losing side: innovations are accepted by man ~~[illegible] [illegible] [illegible]~~ after they have been moved from the avantgarde to the [illegible] guard.
That is, it is not by [illegible] tricks or minute inventions that art will dispel the magic of automation but by the creation of substantial new entities [illegible] taking technology by the ~~[illegible]~~ & making it work boldly & constructively to its own ends, the ends of man.

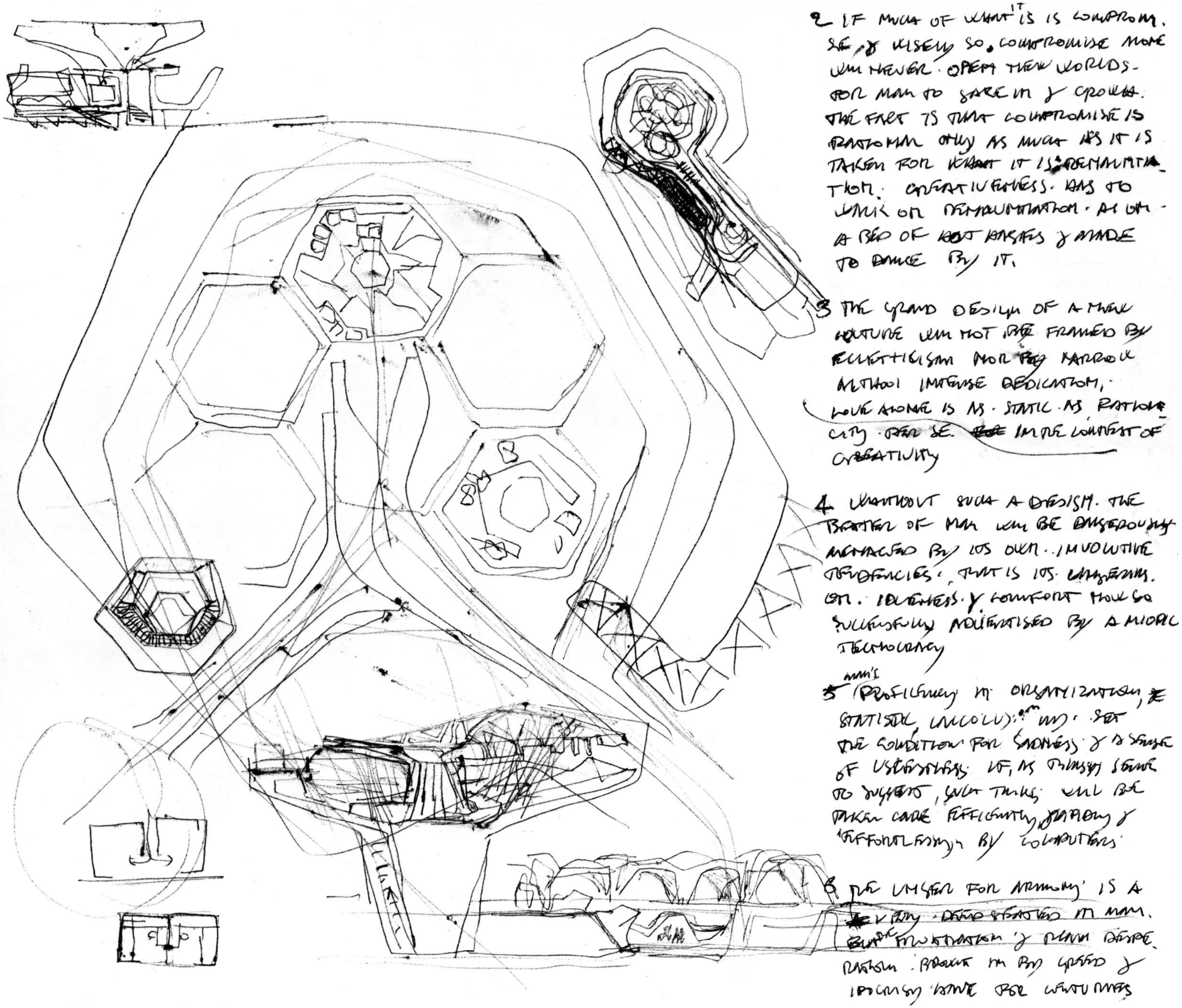
2 IF MUCH OF WHAT IT IS IS COMPROMISE, AND WISELY SO, COMPROMISE ALONE
WILL NEVER OPEN NEW WORLDS
FOR MAN TO SEARCH IN AND GROW.
THE FACT IS THAT COMPROMISE IS
RATIONAL ONLY AS MUCH AS IT IS
TAKEN FOR WHAT IT IS: RATIONALIZA-
TION. CREATIVENESS HAS TO
WALK ON RATIONALIZATION AS ON
A BED OF HOT ASHES AND MADE
TO DANCE BY IT.
3 THE GRAND DESIGN OF A NEW
CULTURE WILL NOT BE FRAMED BY
ECLECTICISM NOR BY NARROW
METHOD. INTENSE DEDICATION,
LOVE ALONE IS AS STATIC AS RATIONALI-
CITY PER SE. IN THE CONTEXT OF
CREATIVITY
4 WITHOUT SUCH A DESIGN THE
BETTER OF MAN WILL BE DANGEROUSLY
MENACED BY ITS OWN INVOLUTIVE
TENDENCIES, THAT IS ITS WALLOWING
IN IDLENESS AND COMFORT NOW SO
SUCCESSFULLY ADVERTISED BY A MIOPIC
TECHNOCRACY
5 MAN'S PROFICIENCY IN ORGANIZATION,
STATISTICAL CALCULUS ... SET
THE CONDITION FOR SADNESS AND A SENSE
OF USELESSNESS IF, AS THINGS SEEM
TO SUGGEST, SUCH THINGS WILL BE
TAKEN CARE EFFICIENTLY, RATIONALLY AND
EFFORTLESSLY BY COMPUTERS
6 THE LONGER FOR HARMONY IS A
VERY DEEP SEATED IN MAN.
BUT FRUSTRATION AND PLAIN DESPE-
RATION BROUGHT IN BY GREED AND
IDIOCY HAVE FOR CENTURIES

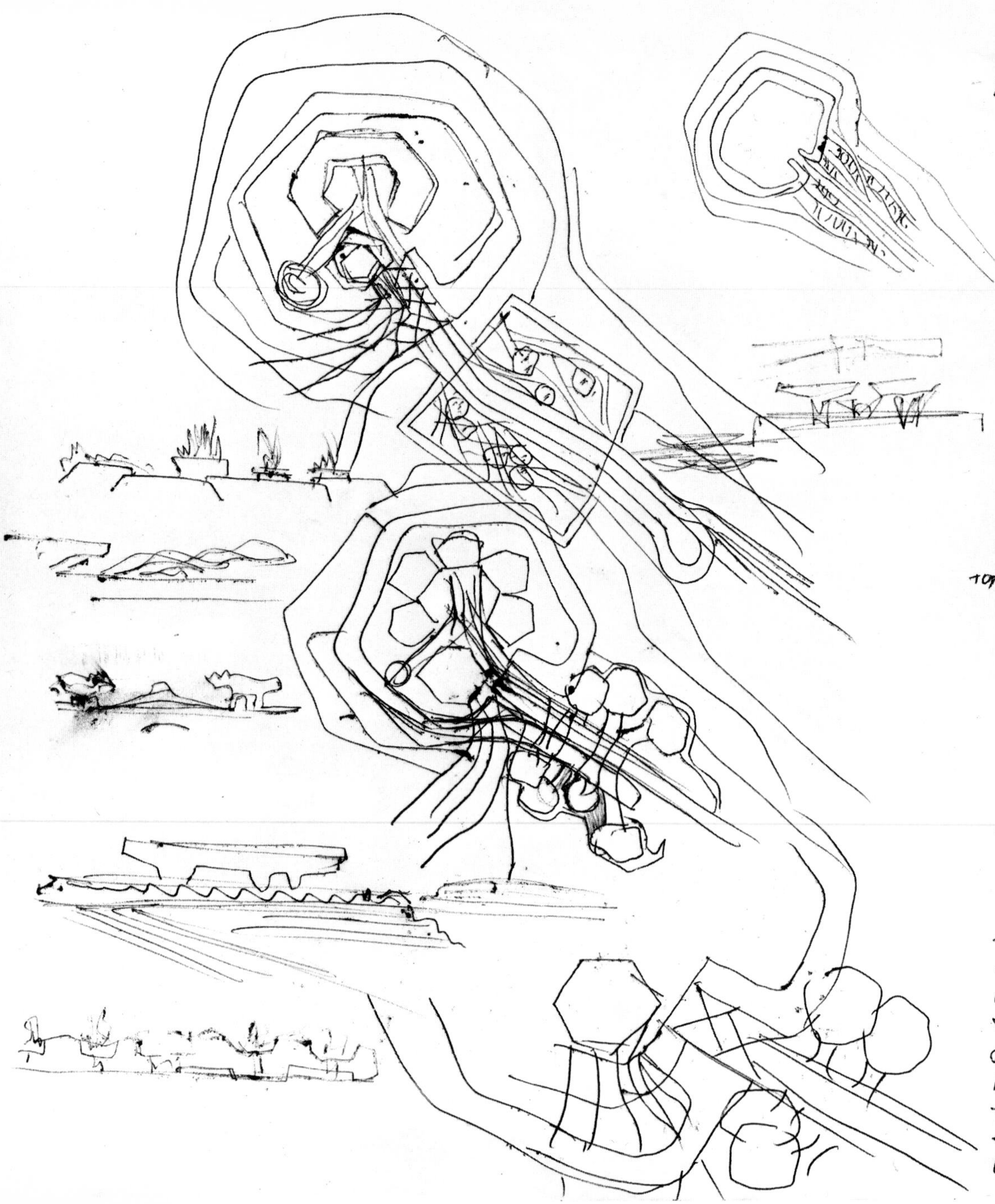

COMPELLING MAN TO ACT UNETHICALLY. TO KNOW IT. (SONATA OF DESPAIR

THE PRECEDING ARE THE REALITIES. FACING METAPHYSICAL MAN & AS SUCH ARE DISCARDED BY THE EFFICIENT MAN. THEY ARE NONETHELESS THE ONLY REASON BY WHICH THERE IS A GAP OF SUBSTANCE BETWEEN ANIMALITY & MANLINESS. WHAT DISQUALIFIES MAN AS A GOOD ANIMAL IS ITS DEMONSTRATE CAPACITY & PERSISTENCE IN BEING & PRODUCING EVIL THUS CONTRARY TO THE ORGANIC INNOCENCE OF NATURE, HENCE ITS VALIDITY. THE ANIMAL MAN IS A DARK SPEK TO BE BRUSH ASIDE BY THE GODS IF EVER THEY EXISTED

TO BE DIRECTLY PERTINENT AS TO TOM ARCHITECTURE WITHOUT FALLING IN ROLE OF RULE GIVER I WOULD SAY THAT TOTEMS CAN SUBSTITUTE A SUSTAINED LONGING FOR A COMPREHENSIVE COHERENCE EMBRACING EACH SINGLE EXPRESSION AS A LONG REMEMBERANCE OF ITS OWN PRESENCE ON THE ENVIRONMENT.

ACCORDING TO ONES OWN POWER THIS WILL DEFINE THE FIELD OF ONES OWN ACTION AS A LIMITED BUT ENLIGHTENED ENDEAVOUR.

THIS WILL ALSO CLEARLY INDICATE THE RESPONSABILITY FOR THE FEW GIFTED ONES SO OFTEN ILL SERVING THEIR OWN VIRTUE BY DISREGARDING A SUBSERVIENT WILL & A MACULATED INTEGRITY. OR IT IS THAT 'ARCHITECTURE' REALLY ESCAPE THEM? & WHAT THEY RETAIN OF IT IS AN AGGREGATE OF

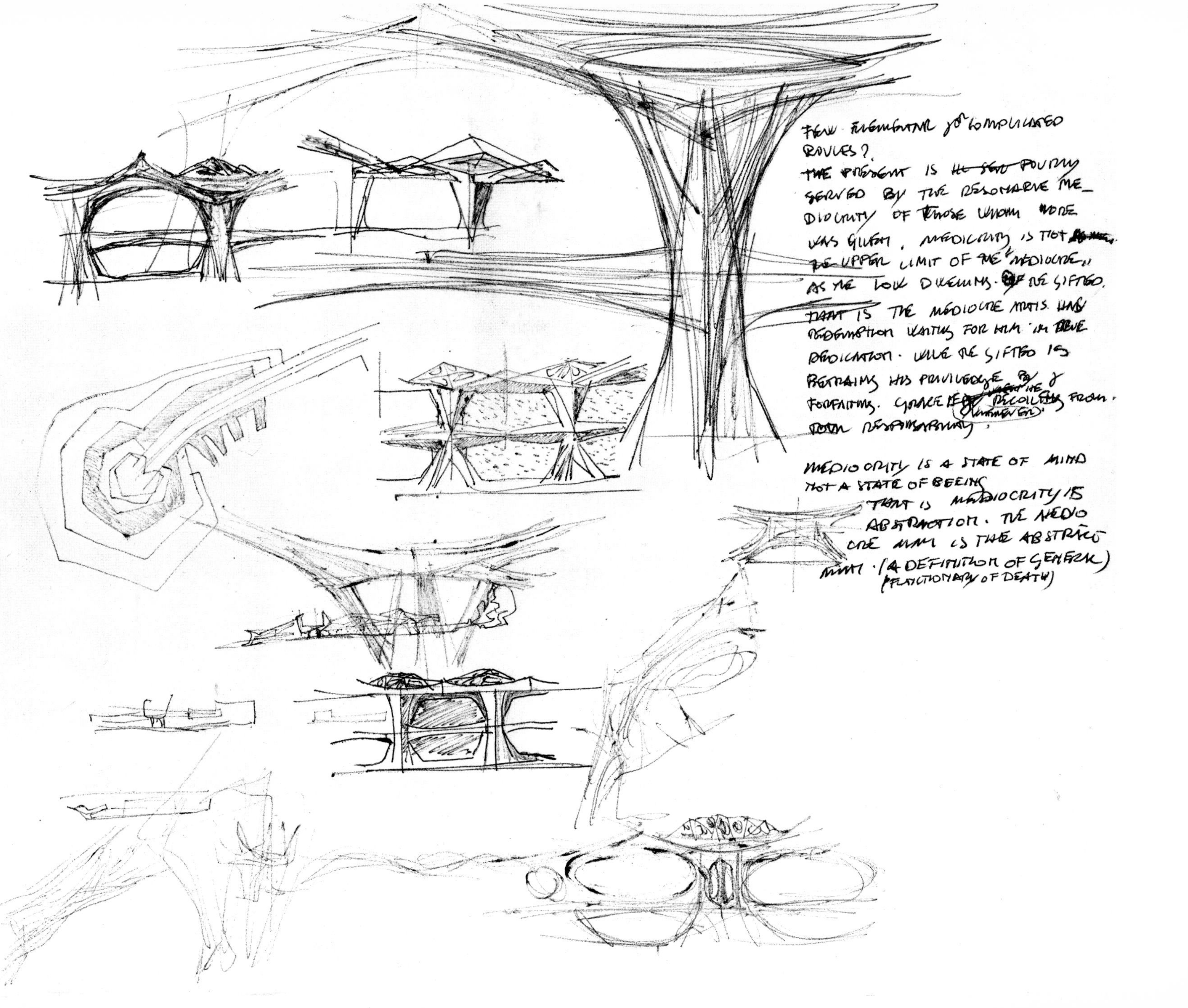
THE PRESENT IS POURLY
SERVED BY THE RESONANCE ME_
DIOCRITY OF THOSE WHOM MORE
WAS GIVEN. MEDIOCRITY IS NOT
THE UPPER LIMIT OF THE MEDIOCRE,
AS THE LOW DILEMMA OF THE GIFTED.
THAT IS THE MEDIOCRE MAN'S
REDEMPTION WAITING FOR HIM IN TRUE
DEDICATION. WHILE THE GIFTED IS
BETRAYING HIS PRIVILEGE BY
FORFAITING.
FROM
RESPONSABILITY.
MEDIOCRITY IS A STATE OF MIND
NOT A STATE OF BEEING
THAT IS MEDIOCRITY IS
ABSTRACTION. THE MEDIO
CRE MAN IS THE ABSTRACT
MAN. (A DEFINITION OF GENERAL)
(DICTIONARY OF DEATH)

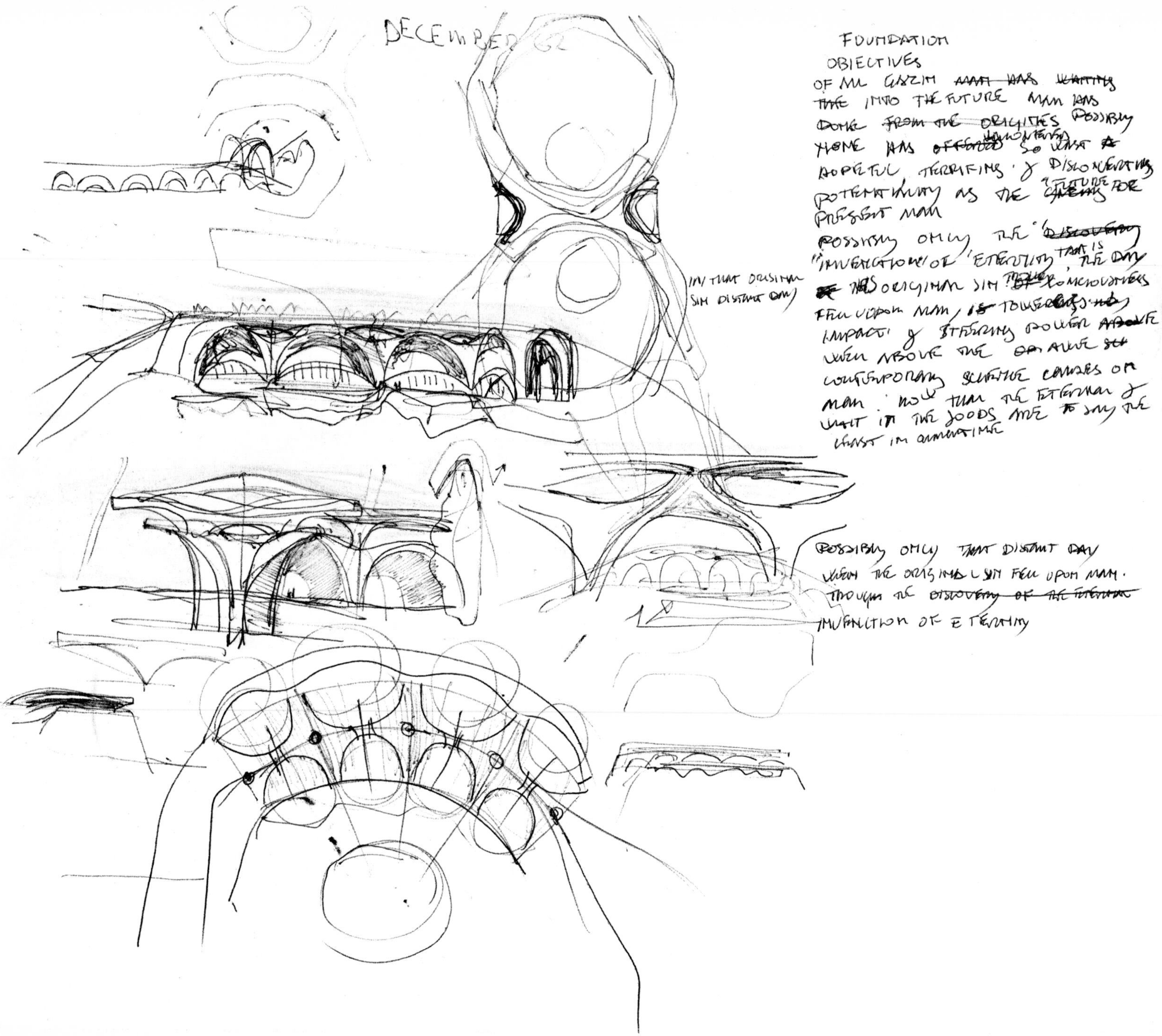
DECEMBER 62
FOUNDATION
OBJECTIVES
INTO THE FUTURE
PRESENT MAN
POSSIBLY ONLY THAT DISTANT DAY
WHEN THE ORIGINAL SIN FELL UPON MAN.
INVENTION OF ETERNITY

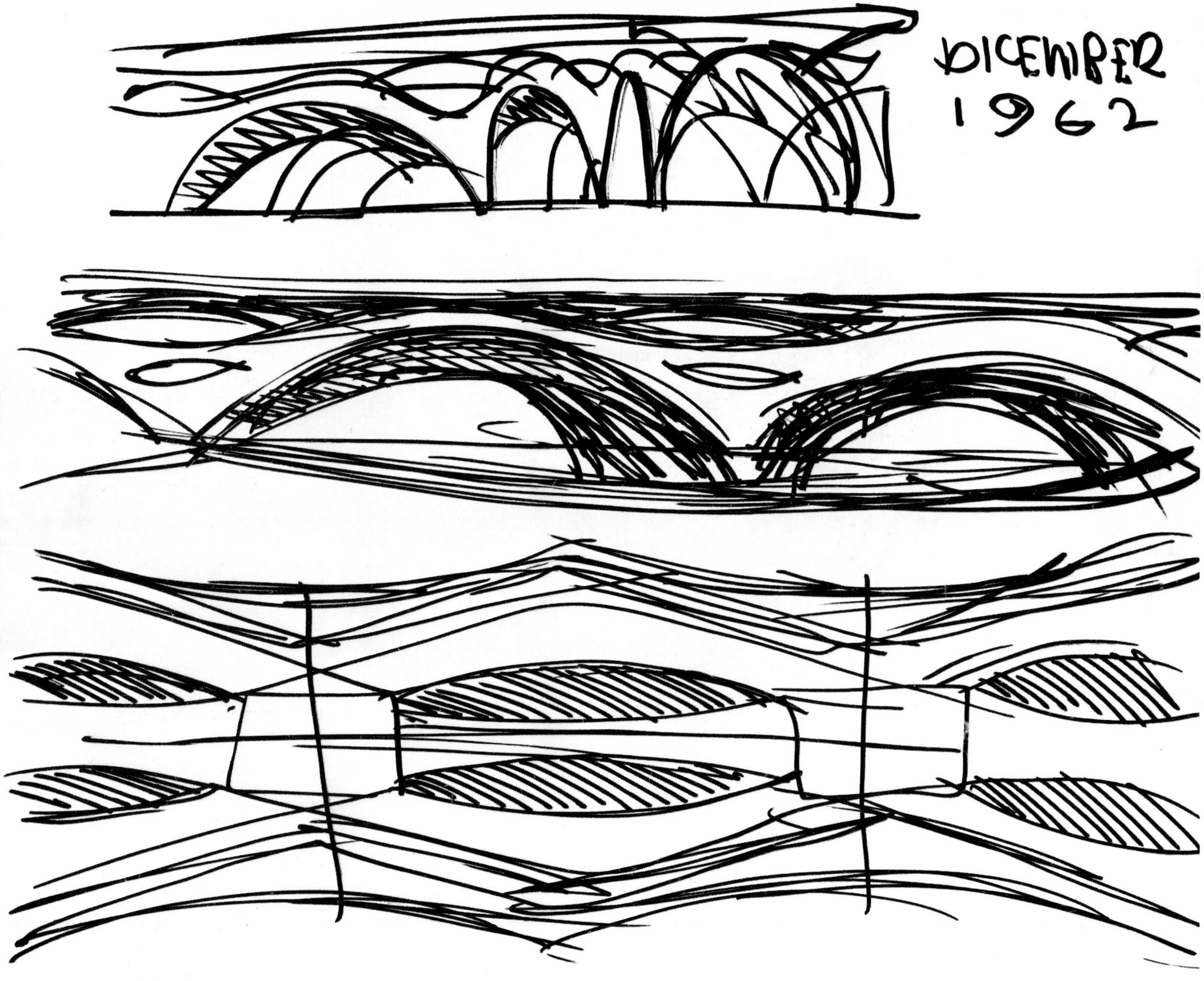
DICEMBER
1962

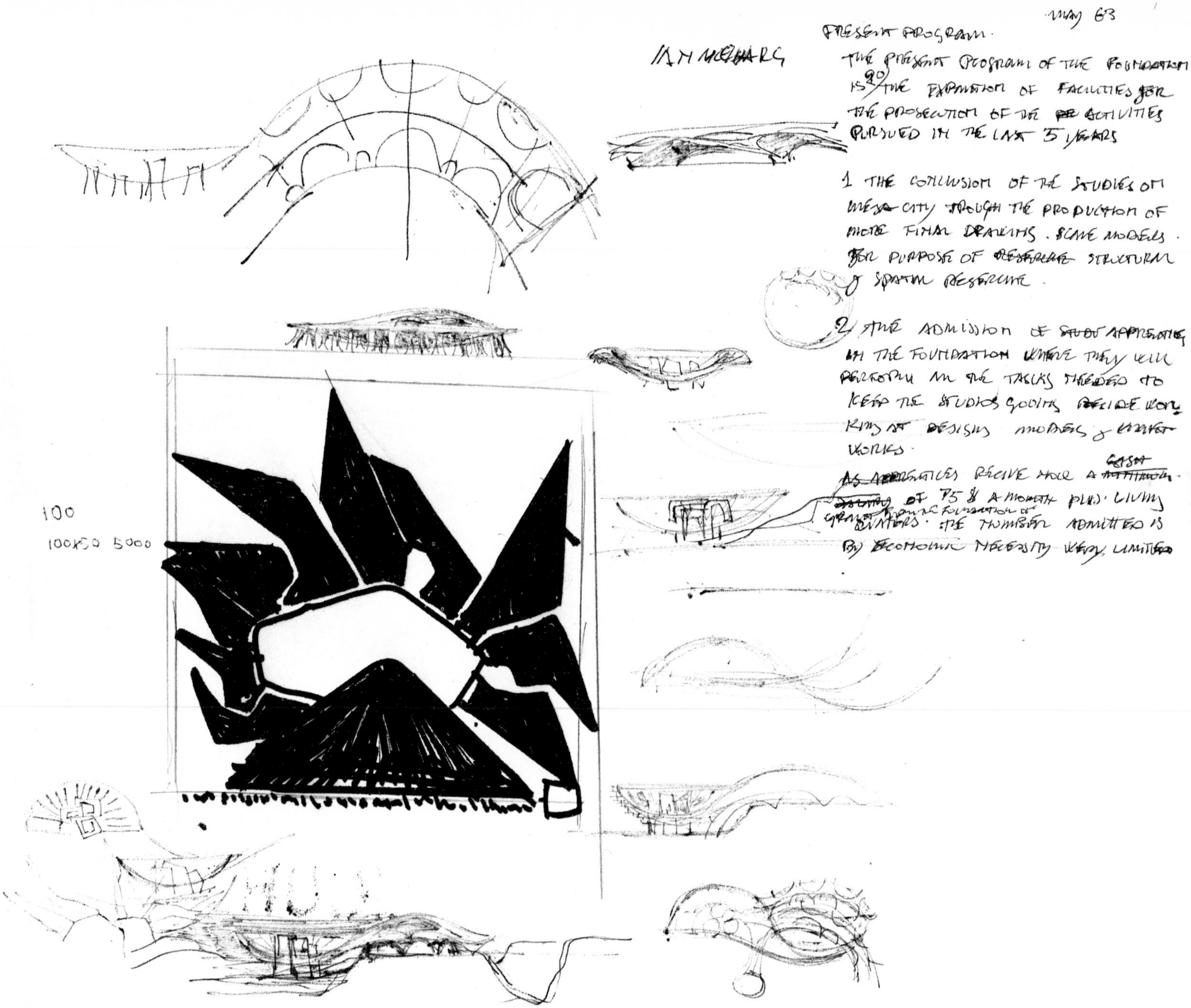
May 63
IAN MCHARG
PRESENT PROGRAM.
THE PRESENT PROGRAM OF THE FOUNDATION IS 90% THE EXPANSION OF FACILITIES FOR THE PROSECUTION OF THE ACTIVITIES PURSUED IN THE LAST 5 YEARS
1 THE CONCLUSION OF THE STUDIES ON MESA CITY THROUGH THE PRODUCTION OF MORE FINAL DRAWINGS. SCALE MODELS. FOR PURPOSE OF STRUCTURAL & SPATIAL RESEARCH.
2 THE ADMISSION OF STUDENT APPRENTICES IN THE FOUNDATION WHERE THEY WILL PERFORM ALL THE TASKS NEEDED TO KEEP THE STUDIOS GOING BESIDE WORKING AT DESIGNS MODELS & CRAFT WORKS.
APPRENTICES RECEIVE NOW A CASH OF 75 $ A MONTH PLUS LIVING QUARTERS. THE NUMBER ADMITTED IS BY ECONOMIC NECESSITY VERY LIMITED
100
100x50 5000

CARS. NOTES:
GROOPINGS & AUTORITY TWO ASPECTS OF MAN'S ~~ABILITY~~ CAPACITY TO "CONSTRUCT"

GROOPINGS ⟶ ESCAPE
AUTORITY ⟶ DOGMA
ARE THE TWO INVOLUTIVE ASPECTS. (ESCAPE & DOGMA),
INVENTIVENESS AS SUBSTITUTE FOR "WISDOM" (BIOLOGICAL & SOCIAL CONTINUITY),
SEE THE "EXPERIENCE" OF THE AMERICAN SOCIETY. FORMED BY UPROOTED POPULATION OF EUROPE, INTELLECTUALLY RESOLVING ECOLOGICAL PROBLEMS TROUGH MECHANICS (OR & SLAVERY) THE INTELLECTUALIZATION OF A SLOWLY ACQUIRED WISDOM, THE IGNORANCE OF IT AT THAT & THE VACUUM LEFT FILLED WITH THIS NEW PHENOMENON: "PRACTICAL SCIENCE"
AN INSTANCE OF EMERGENCE TROUGH STRIFE

—

THE SUBURBIA & THE CORAL COLONY: COMMON DENOMINATOR: CELLULAR IDENTITY, LOW COMPLEXITY, "AMORPHISMS" (RELATIVE)
IF ONE TAKES AWAY FROM THE CORAL COLONY THE FLUID MEDIUM CARRYING ALL THAT IS NEEDED IN & OUT OF EACH CELL & CONSTITUTING THE PLASMA OF THE CELLULE, TAKE AWAY THIS OUTER BLOOD OF THE CELL ITSELF & TRY TO SUBSTITUTE IT WITH WIRES PIPES RADIATIONS, CONVEYERS ETC & ONE HAS THE INSIDE POOR MECHANICAL TRANSLATION OF AN ECOLOGICAL FEAT

35 m
1cm = 5 m

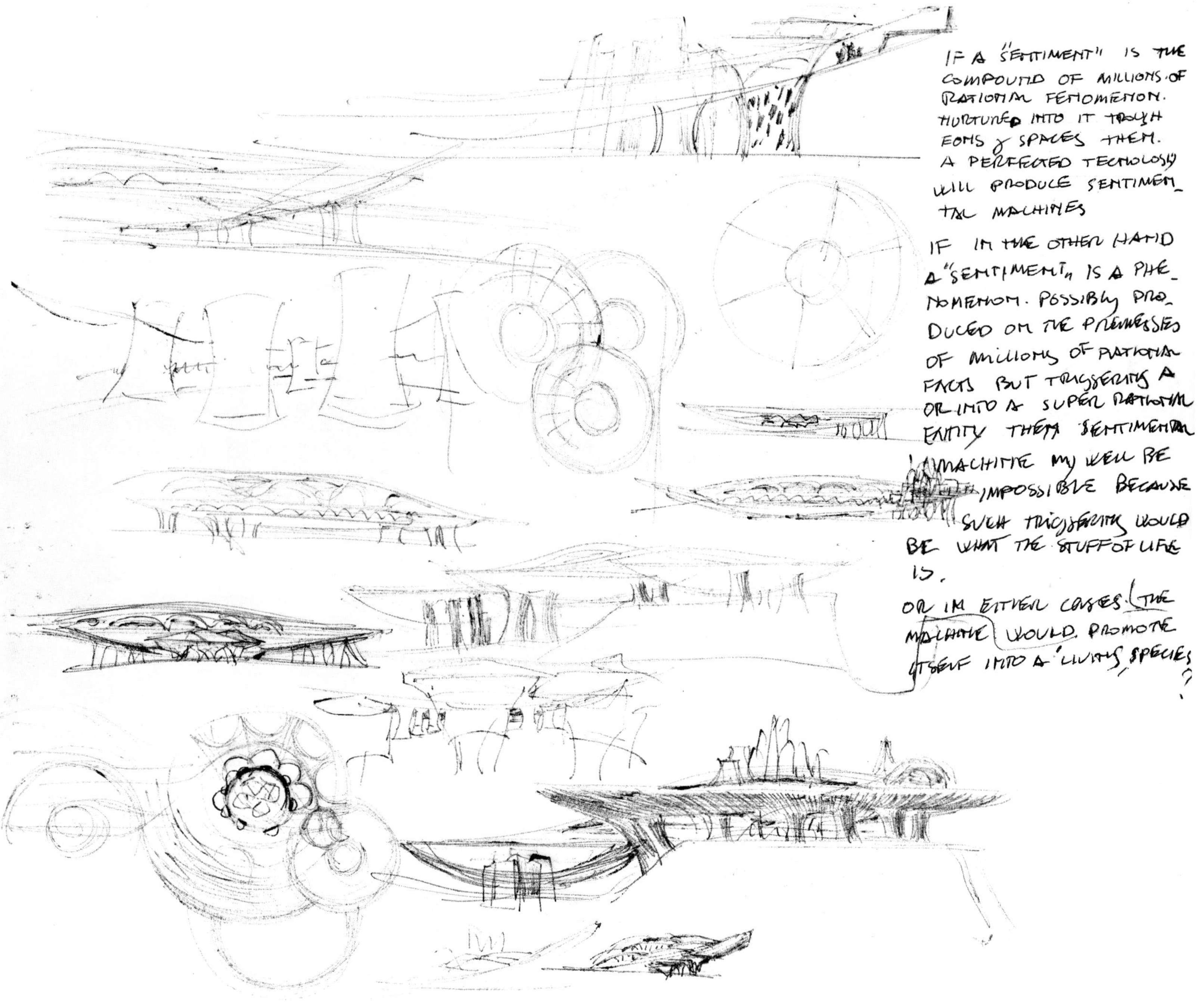
IF A "SENTIMENT" IS THE
COMPOUND OF MILLIONS OF
RATIONAL FENOMENON.
NURTURED INTO IT TROUGH
EONS & SPACES THEM.
A PERFECTED TECNOLOGY
WILL PRODUCE SENTIMEN_
TAL MACHINES
IF ON THE OTHER HAND
A "SENTIMENT" IS A PHE_
NOMENON. POSSIBLY PRO_
DUCED ON THE PREMISSES
OF MILLIONS OF RATIONAL
FACTS BUT TRIGGERING A
OR INTO A SUPER RATIONAL
ENTITY THEN SENTIMENTAL
MACHINE MAY WELL BE
IMPOSSIBLE BECAUSE
SUCH TRIGGERING WOULD
BE WHAT THE STUFF OF LIFE
IS.
OR IN EITHER CASES THE
MACHINE WOULD PROMOTE
ITSELF INTO A "LIVING" SPECIES
?

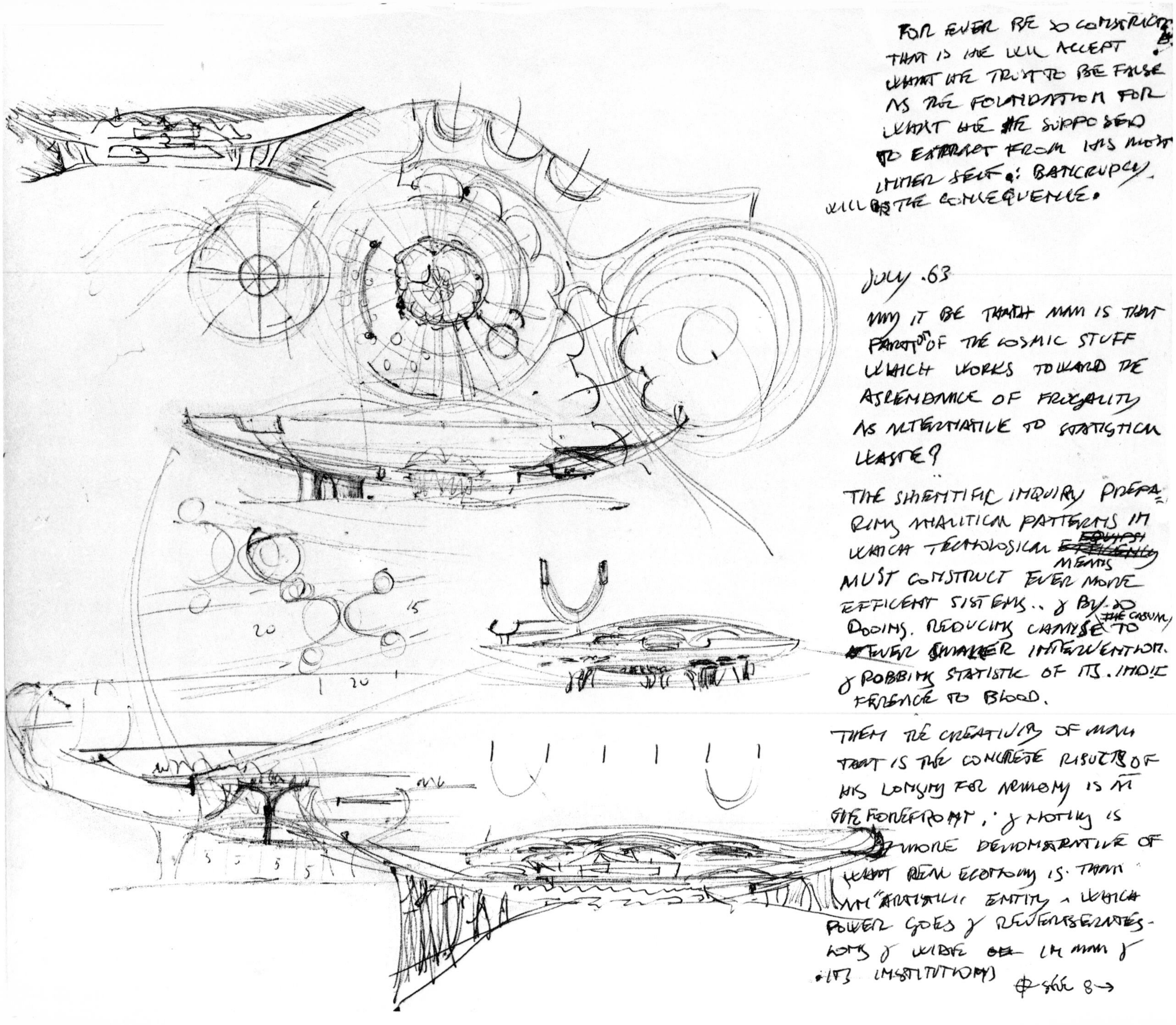
FOR EVER BE SO CONSTRICTED
THAT IS WE WILL ACCEPT
WHAT WE TRUST TO BE FALSE
AS THE FOUNDATION FOR
WHAT WE ARE SUPPOSED
TO EXTRACT FROM HIS MOST
INNER SELF. BANKRUPTCY
WILL BE THE CONSEQUENCE.
JULY .63
MAY IT BE THAT MAN IS THAT
PART OF THE COSMIC STUFF
WHICH WORKS TOWARD THE
ASCENDANCE OF FRUGALITY
AS ALTERNATIVE TO STATISTICAL
LEASTE?
THE SCIENTIFIC INQUIRY PREPA-
RING ANALITICAL PATTERNS IN
WHICH TECHNOLOGICAL MEANS
MUST CONSTRUCT EVER MORE
EFFICENT SISTEMS.. & BY SO
DOING, REDUCING CHANCE TO THE CASUAL
EVER SMALLER INTERVENTION.
& ROBBING STATISTIC OF ITS. INDIF-
FERENCE TO BLOOD.
THEN THE CREATIVITY OF MAN
THAT IS THE CONCRETE RESULTS OF
HIS LONGING FOR HARMONY IS IN
THE FOREFRONT, & NOTHING IS
MORE DEMONSTRATIVE OF
WHAT REAL ECONOMY IS THAN
AN "ARTISTIC" ENTITY, WHICH
POWER GOES & REVERBERATES-
ONS & WIDE IN MAN &
ITS INSTITUTIONS
SEE 8 →

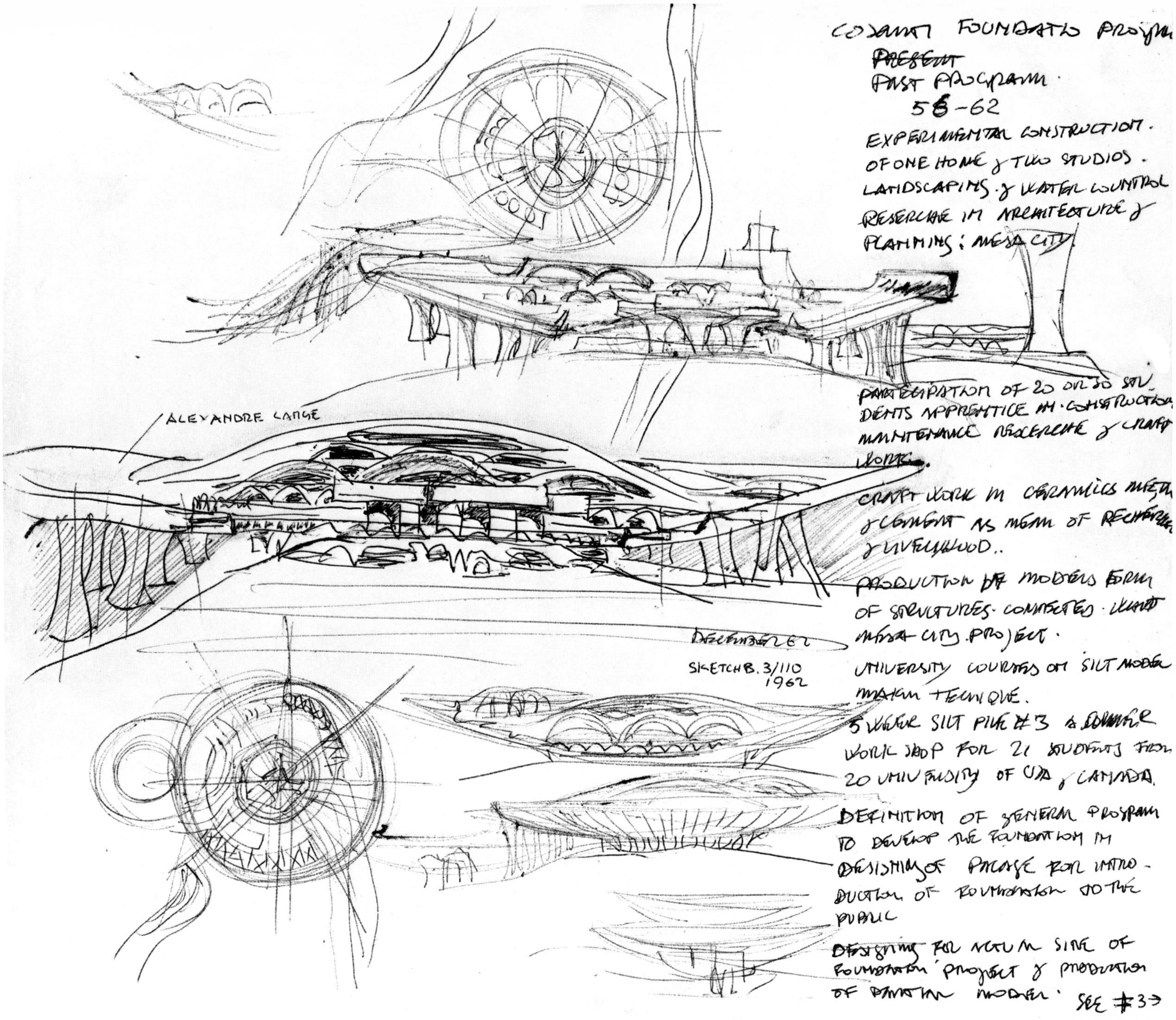
COSANTI FOUNDATION PROGRAM
PRESENT
PAST PROGRAM.
56-62
EXPERIMENTAL CONSTRUCTION.
OF ONE HOME & TWO STUDIOS.
LANDSCAPING & WATER CONTROL
RESEARCH IN ARCHITECTURE &
PLANNING: MESA CITY
PARTICIPATION OF 20 OR 30 STU-
DENTS APPRENTICE IN CONSTRUCTION
MAINTENANCE RESEARCH & CRAFT
WORK.
CRAFT WORK IN CERAMICS METAL
& CEMENT AS MEAN OF RESEARCH
& LIVELIHOOD..
PRODUCTION OF MODELS FORM
OF STRUCTURES CONNECTED WITH
MESA CITY PROJECT.
UNIVERSITY COURSES ON SILT MODEL
MAKING TECHNIQUE.
5 WEEK SILT PILE #3 A SUMMER
WORK SHOP FOR 21 STUDENTS FROM
20 UNIVERSITY OF USA & CANADA.
DEFINITION OF GENERAL PROGRAM
TO DEVELOP THE FOUNDATION IN
DESIGNING OF PACKAGE FOR INTRO-
DUCTION OF FOUNDATION TO THE
PUBLIC
DESIGNING FOR ACTUAL SITE OF
FOUNDATION PROJECT & PRODUCTION
OF PARTIAL MODEL. SEE #33
ALEXANDRE LANGE
DECEMBER 62
SKETCH B. 3/110
1962

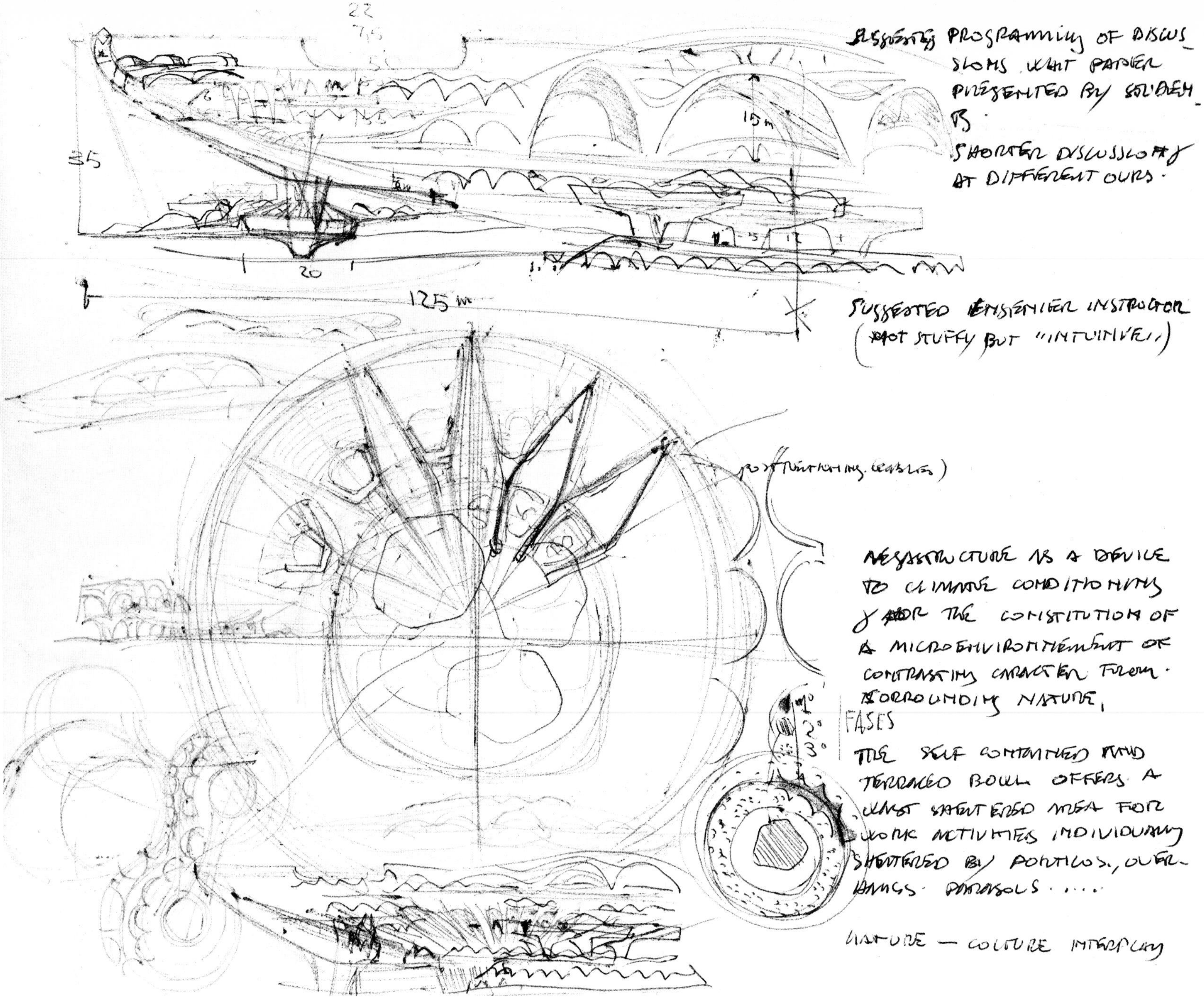
PROGRAMMING OF DISCUSSIONS
PRESENTED BY
SHORTER
AT DIFFERENT OURS.
35
15 m
20
125 m
SUGGESTED
(NOT STUFFY BUT
FASES
1°
2°
3°
THE SELF
TERRACED BOWL OFFERS A
WORK ACTIVITIES
PARASOLS
NATURE — CULTURE INTERPLAY

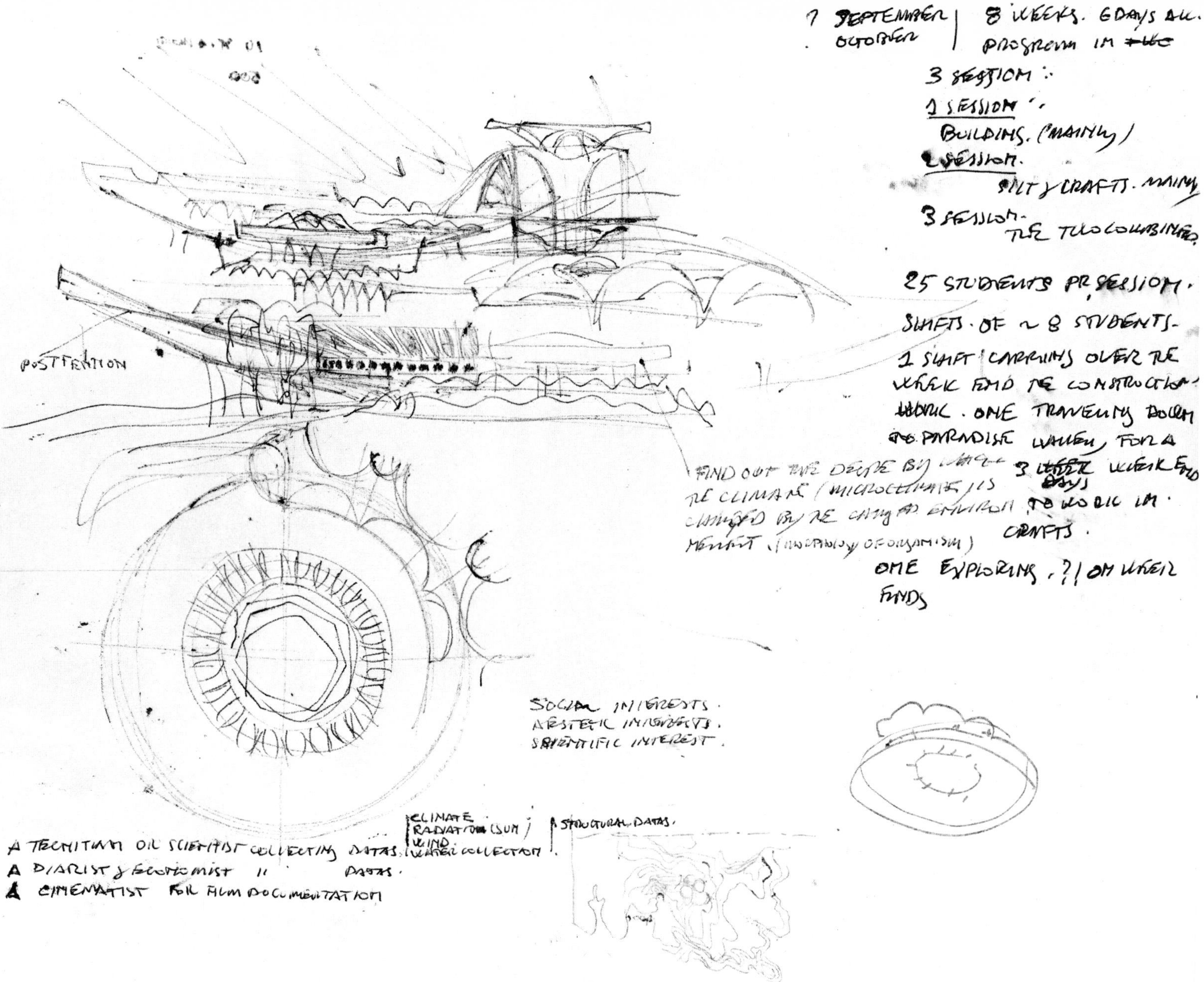
7 SEPTEMBER
OCTOBER
8 WEEKS. 6 DAYS ALL
PROGRAM IN
3 SESSION :
1 SESSION :
BUILDINGS. (MAINLY)
2 SESSION.
ART & CRAFTS. MAINLY
3 SESSION.
THE TWO COMBINED.
25 STUDENTS PR SESSION.
SHIFTS OF ~ 8 STUDENTS.
1 SHIFT CARRYING OVER THE WEEK END THE CONSTRUCTION WORK. ONE TRAVELING DOWN TO PARADISE VALLEY, FOR A 3 DAYS WEEK END TO WORK IN CRAFTS.
ONE EXPLORING ?? ON WEEK ENDS
FIND OUT THE DEGREE BY WHICH THE CLIMATE (MICROCLIMATE) IS CHANGED BY THE CHANGED ENVIRONMENT (INTERPLAY OF ORGANISM)
POSTTENSION
SOCIAL INTERESTS.
AESTETIC INTERESTS.
SCIENTIFIC INTEREST.
A TECHNICIAN OR SCIENTIST COLLECTING DATAS.
CLIMATE
RADIATION (SUN)
WIND
WATER COLLECTION
STRUCTURAL DATAS.
A DIARIST & ECONOMIST " DATAS.
A CINEMATIST FOR FILM DOCUMENTATION

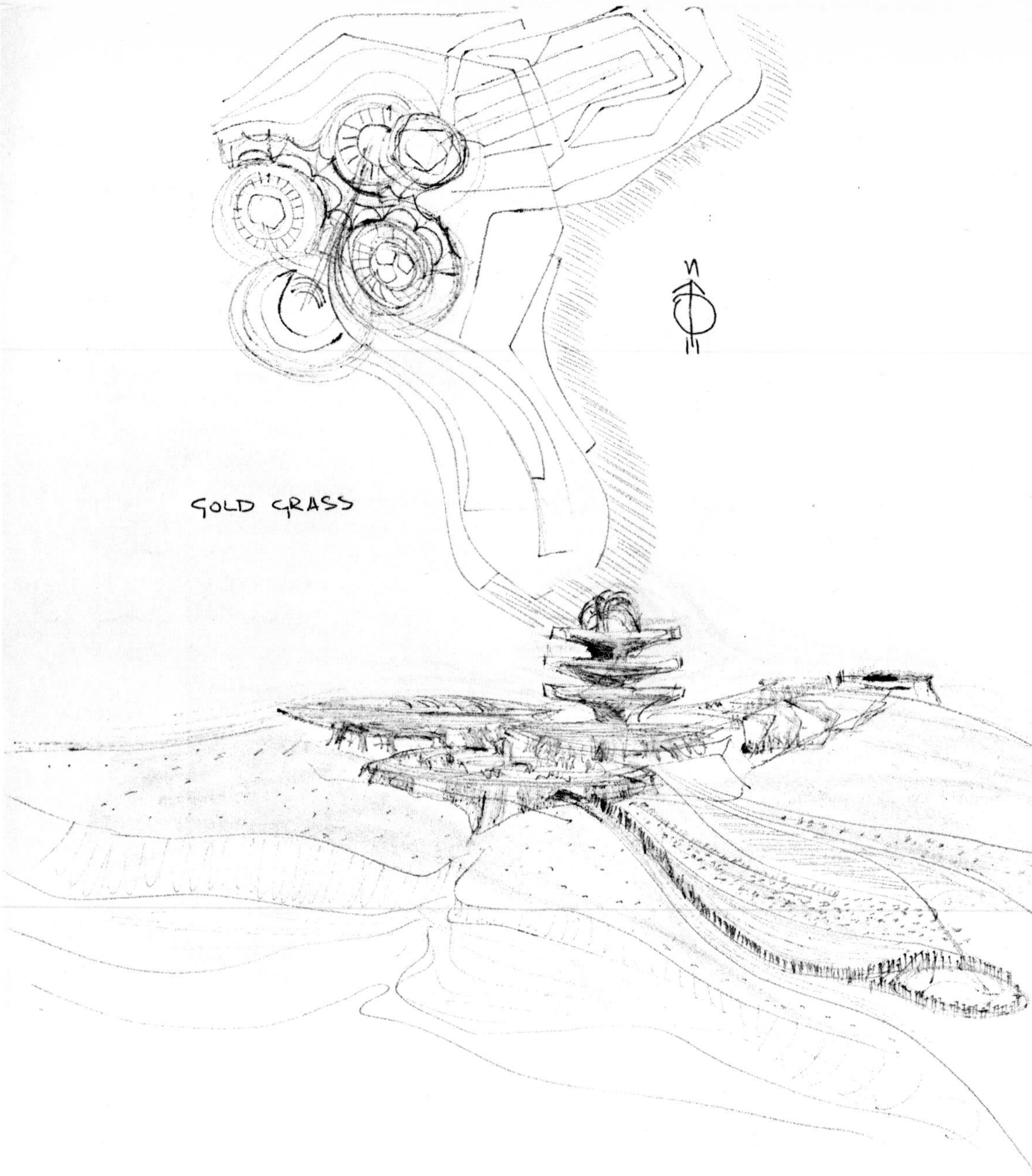

FUTURE PROGRAM. SEE F. PAPER.

THE TECHNICAL "EXPLOSION" HAS PHISICALLY PARALLELED THE BREA-KING DOWN ACCOURING IN THE "SOUL" OF MAN.

PARTICLE OF SOUL ARE THUS RIDING ON BITS OF MATTER CLEAVERLY ORGANIZED IN. CONSOUMER GOODS

THE CONSUMTION OF MAN & THINGS, IS DIRECT CONSEQUE-NCE (? OR CAUSE) OF THE POLITIQUE OF PRODUCTION.

WE DO NOT PRODUCE OUT OF NEED ANY MORE. WE MUST CONSUME BECAUSE PRODUCTION SO DICTATES.

THIS MATERIALIZATION OF EXISTENCE WELL REFLECTS THE ATOMIZATION OF VALUES.

WE LIVE AN EXPLODED CIVILISATION

UNLESS MAGNETS OF "COLTURE" AQUIRE ENOUGH FORCE TO RETRIVE & CLUSTER AROUND THEMSELVES. THE MORE DEMANDING "SOULS", AS IN OTHER TIMES AND CONDI-TIONS DID THE "NEW" ORDERS OF THE CHURCH. THIS ATOMISATION WILL APPROXIMATE MORE AND MORE THE AMOURPHOUS CONDI-TION OF CAOS THAT RECOGNIZE ONLY THE LAWS OF STATISTICS. IS MAN A STATISTICAL PHENO-MENON? AND IF SO IS THERE A NEXT STEP THAT WILL FREE HIM FROM THIS CONDITION?

FIVE YEARS CYCLES FESTIVALS MUSIC & DANCE
DRAMA & OPERA
MOVIE & PHOTOGRAPHY
FINE ARTS & CRAFTS
DESIGN - INDUSTRY

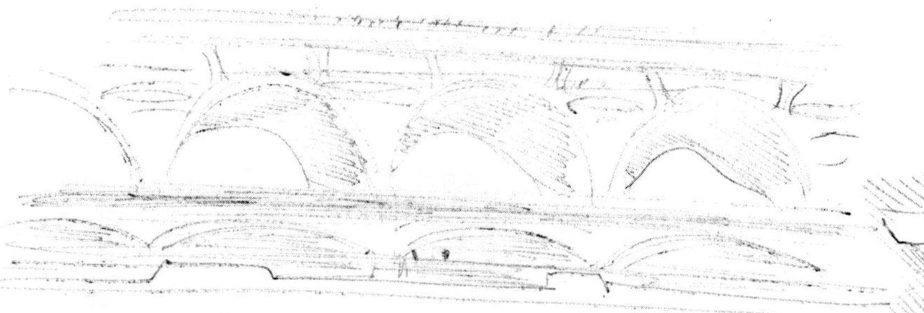

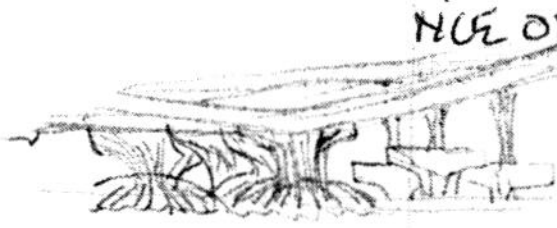

SEE 8 ← ⊕ IN SUCH CONTEST MAN'S DEFIANCE OF STATISTICAL TRUTH IS MAN QUEST FOR ITS OWN ORIGINAL & SIGNIFICANT DIVINITY

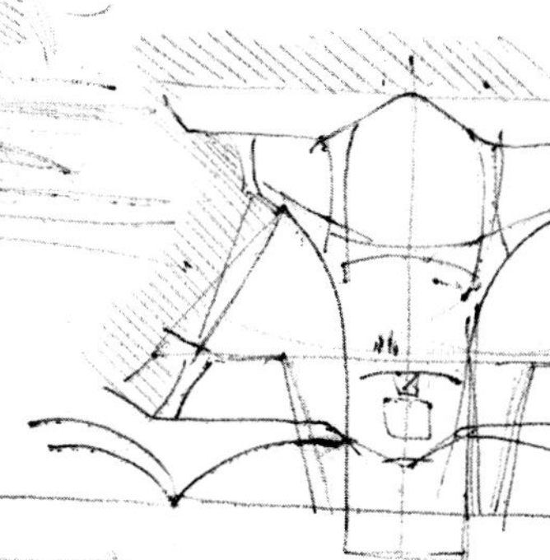

HOW MUCH UNDOING ~~[illegible]~~ OF THAT WHICH IT IS DOING THE DOING TO PRODUCE THAT WHICH IS NOT IS POSSIBLY A PIVOTAL PROBLEM? IS ACCEPTANCE OF THE "REAL" THE BEST PREMISES FOR THE CONSTRUCTION OF THE "DIVINE"? OR IS A CAREFUL DISCRIMINATION OF THE REAL THE NEEDED STARTING PLATEAU. OR IS THE TOTAL REJECTION OF THE "REAL" SUCH PLATEAU?

SCIENTIFIC REALITY IS A VERY FOREIGN WORLD TO MAN ~~[illegible]~~. NONE OF THE RELIGIOUS SERIOUS MINDS OF THE PAST WOULD HAVE FORSEEN IT, THUS THEIR OCCASIONAL, OR NOT SO, REJECTION OF THE MATERIAL WORLD CAN HARDLY BE CONSIDERED UTTERLY

REALITY IS NOT THE WORLD OUR SENSES OFFER TO US. YET UP TO YESTERDAY THOSE SENSES WERE OUR "CONNECTIVITY" WITH THE SUBSTANCE OF WHAT THEY SENSED.

NOW SCEPTICISM ABOUT MAN'S GOODNESS IS JOINED BY MISTRUST ON THE TRUTHFULNESS OUR SENSES ARE ENDOWED WITH.

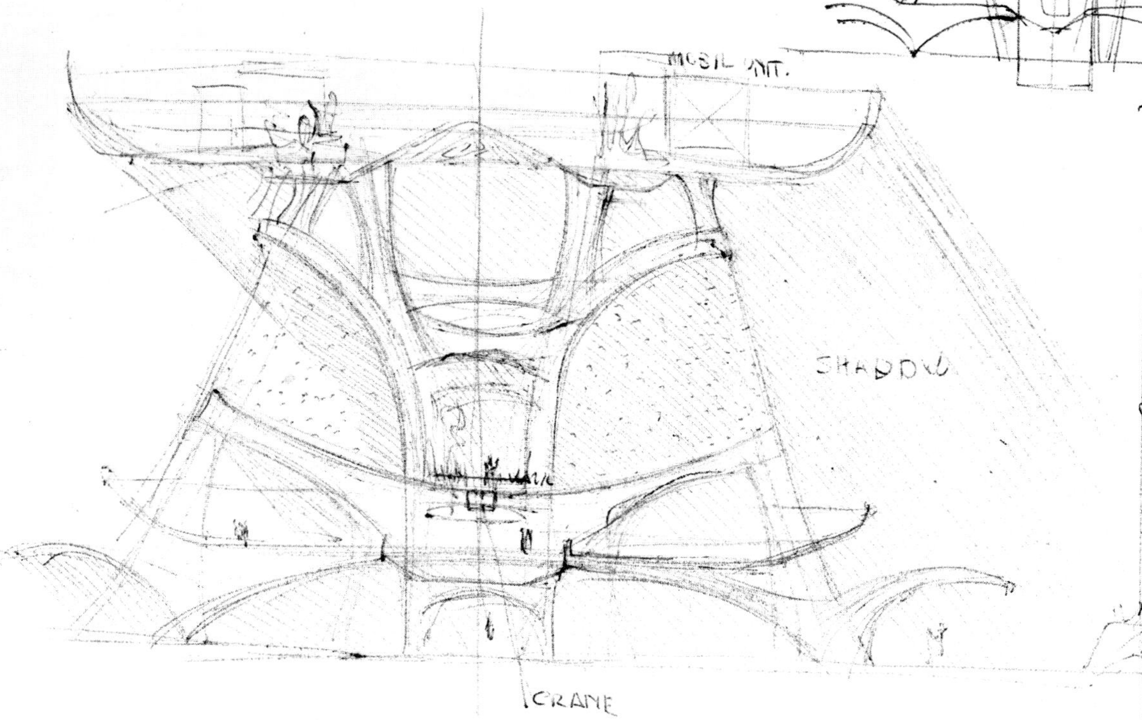

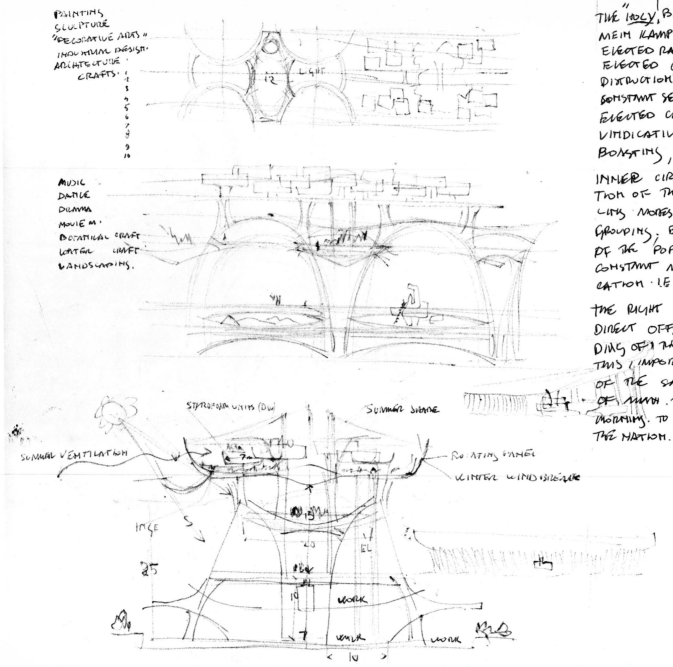

PAINTINGS
SCULPTURE
"DECORATIVE ARTS"
INDUSTRIAL DESIGN
ARCHITECTURE
CRAFTS
1
2
3
4
5
6
7
8
9
10

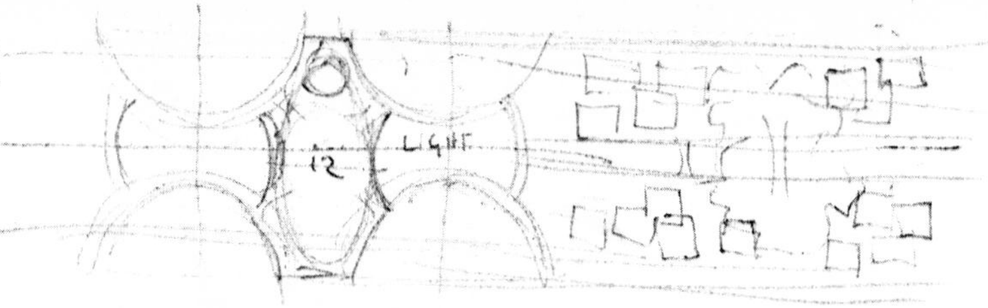

MUSIC
DANCE
DRAMA
MOVIE M.
BOTANICAL CRAFT
WATER CRAFT
LANDSCAPING

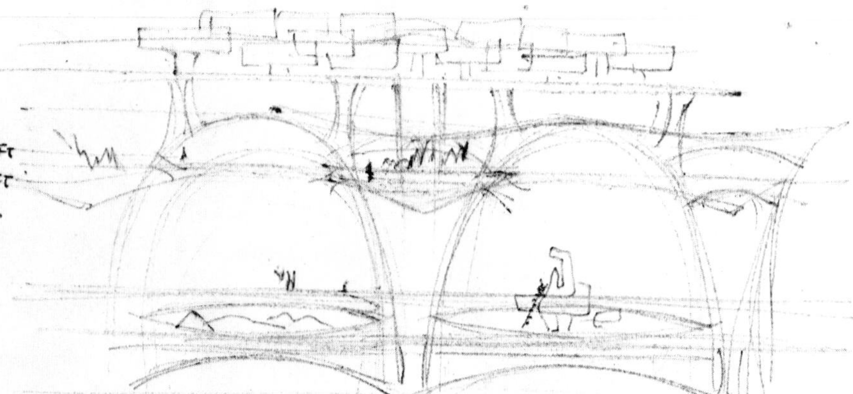

AUGUST 63

THE "HOLY ? BIBLE" OR JEOUHA MEIN KAMPF!
ELECTED RACE, GUIDED BY AN ELECTED GANG, GENOCIDE, DISTRUCTION, SAVAGERY, REVENGE, CONSTANT SELF PRISE! THE ELECTED CILDREN OF A SAVAGE VINDICATIVE, JEALOUS, RESENTFUL, BOASTING, PETTY, CRUEL .. GOD

INNER CIRCLE DIRECT EMANATION OF THE GODHEAD CONTROLLING MORES, ECONOMY, ETHICS, GROUPINGS, BREEDINGS, BELIEFS OF THE POPULATION BY THE CONSTANT MENACE OF SCOMMUNICATION I.E. DEATH.

THE RIGHT EXTREMISTS OF USA DIRECT OFFSPRING OF THE READING OF THE "HOLY" BIBLE.
THIS IMPORTANT DOCUMENT OF THE SAVAGE IPOCRISY OF MAN. TO BE READ EVERY MORNING. TO THE INFANTS OF THE NATION.

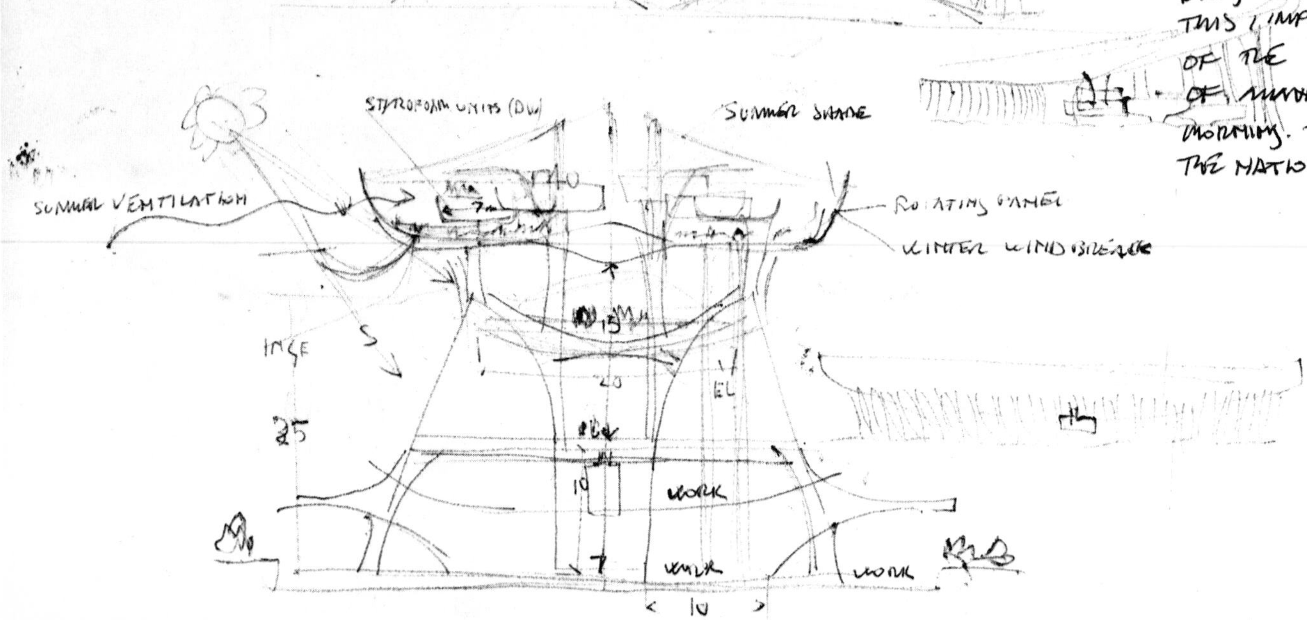

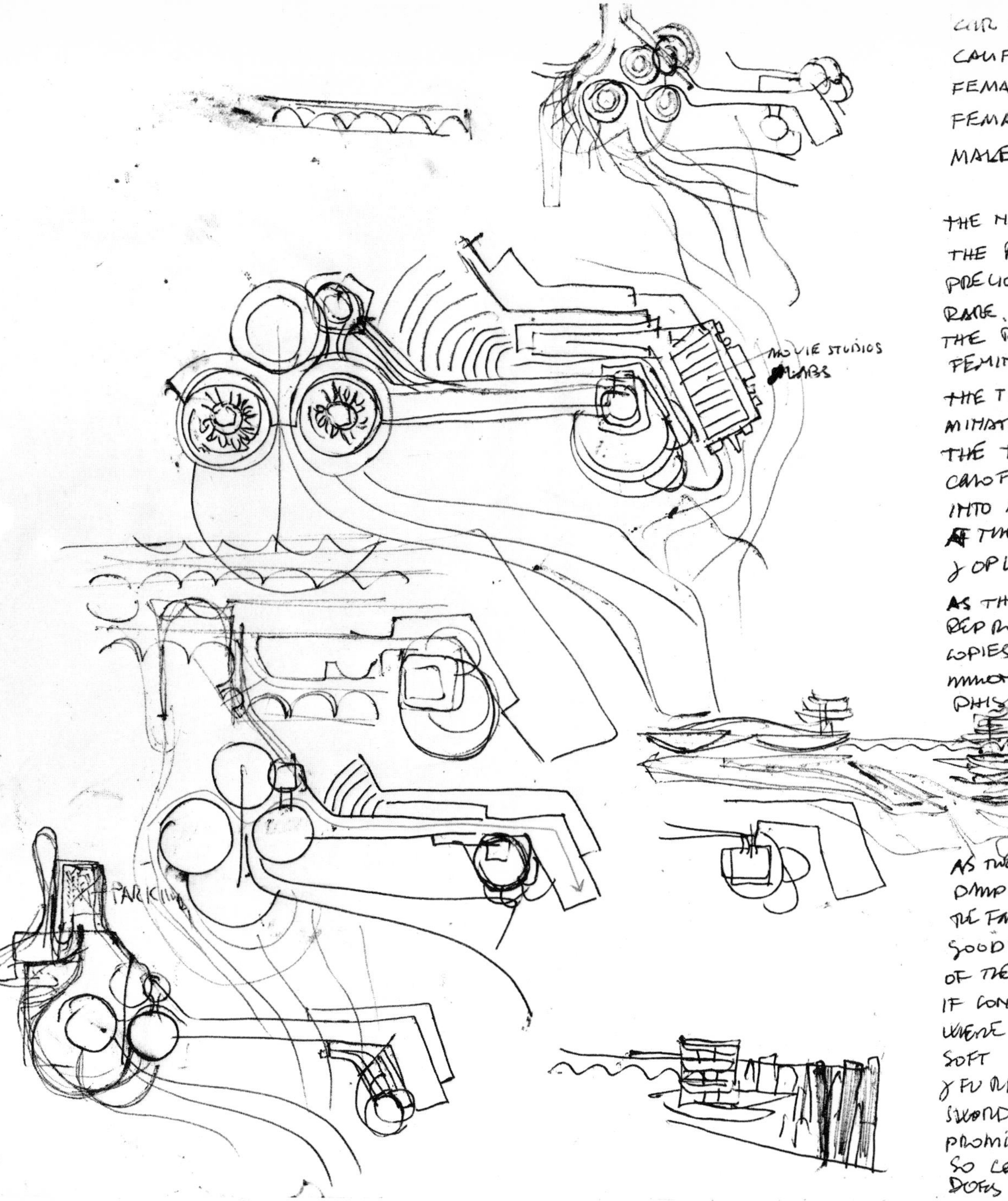

CAR NOTES. AUGUST 1963

CALIFORNIA & ARIZONA

FEMALE & MALE

FEMALE → FEMININE

MALE → MASCULINE
↘ EFFEMINATE

THE NATURE OF THE FEMININE:
THE PRECIOUSNESS OF THE GENTLE.
PRECIOUSNESS ~~AS~~ THAT WHICH IS
RARE.
THE RARE EFFEMERALS OF THE
FEMININE WORLD
THE TIDAL FUTILITY OF THE EFFE-
MINATE WORLD
THE TRANSFORMATION OF THE
CALIFORNIAN NATURE (COAST)
INTO AN EFFEMINATE WORLD
~~AT~~ THE INVITATION OF A MILD
& OPULENT ECOLOGY ~~BALANCE~~

AS THE RARE DECAYES BY SELF
REPRODUCTION IN CHEAPER & CHEAPER
COPIES AMORPHISMS. GROWTHS CO-
MMON: THE EFFEMINATE AMOR-
PHISM OF A CONDITION. WHERE-
IN THE FEMININE IS KILLED
BY THE EMASCULATED
MASCULINE

AS THE STERILE MALE DRIVE IS
DAMPENED THEN. BROUGHT TO
THE FALSE PORT. BY THE ~~EQUIVOCAL~~
GOOD BUT DISTORTED INTENTION
OF THE FALSIFIED FEMININE (AS
IF CONCEPTION OR THE ACT OF LOVE
WHERE THE ENCOUNTER OF TWO
SOFT ENERGIES, NOT THE ANGUISHED
& FURIOUS SEEKING OF A FEMININE
SWORD WAITING. ENVELOPMENTS.
PROMISES OF WARMTH).
SO CONSTRUCTION, FOR INSTANCE,
DOES NOT OFFER THE MALE MORAL

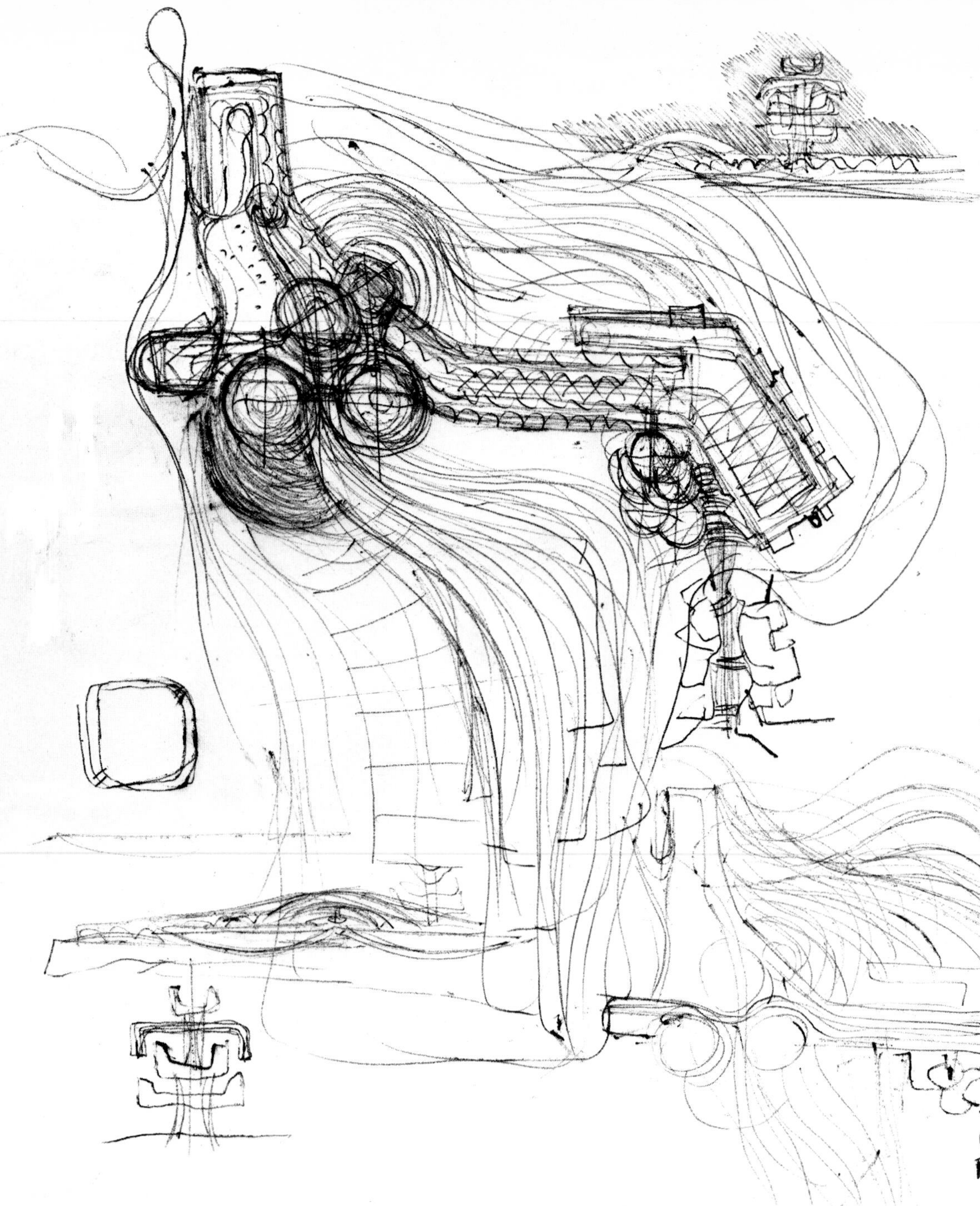

OF PROTECTIVE STRENGTH
WAITING WHICH THE FEMININE WILL SING
HER PRECIOUS. POEMS.

HIGH PITCHED HONEST ARROGANCE MIGHT
HAVE BEEN CAUSAL (EFFECT OF
PATERNAL 'CARE') IN BREEDING.
THE OPEN PLAN WHERE THE EFFEMI-
NATE (AMOURPHISM) SEEDS MALE
& FEMALE INDIFFERENTLY WITH
STERILITY.

- - - - -

AS THE DESERT OPENS UNDER YOU
FROM THE SAN DIEGO MOUNTAINS.
IN THE LAND STILL NOMINALLY
CALIFORNIAN. THE PRESENCE OF
A TREMENDOUS MALE GOD. IS
FELT. A . DIVINITY OF
FORBEARANCE & UNREMITTING BEAUTY
A WORLD DEMANDING OF THE MASCULINE
ITS. STRENUOUS SEEKING. FROM THE
FEMININE THE GRACE OF GENTLE-
NESS; MAKING. A TAME BEAST OF IT

BLEEDING & EMASCULATE,
BLEEDING WHITE BLOOD ON CRIMSON
LONGINGS.
LIKE DUSTY GRAVEL THE LAUGHING
OF INDIFFERENCE THE WOLF INDIFFE-
RENCE OF THE WOLF GASPES IN
DUMB RESONANCE! LATHSOME.
SISTER WATER, A WARMTHER TO
WEDGE THE DESOLATE ENMITY.

. . . .

AND A LEGION OF WILLS. THE NAME
RING OF THE LOST SACRIFICES, THE
FOCUSED BLADE OF THE OLDEST
BLOOD THE DESPERATE EXHAUSTION.
TO PUNCTURE THE BLADDER & THE
RUSH OF SISTER WOMEN. THE
FLOOD OF ATONEMENT
TEMPORARY

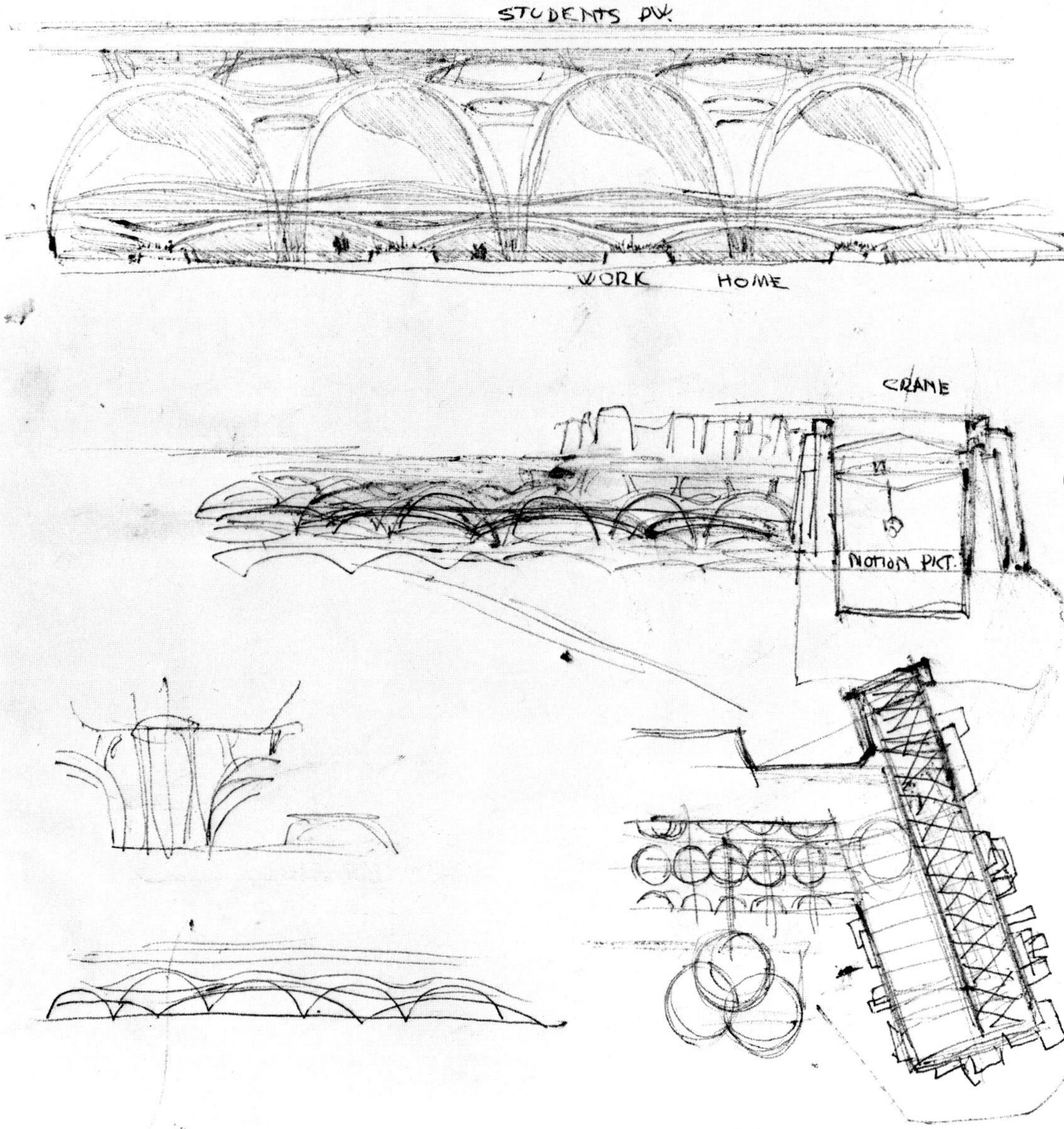

SEPTEMBER 63
ON RICCI

1 TRUST IN FUNDAMENTAL GODNESS & SEMPLICITY INHERENT TO LIFE & MAN "IF WE JUST LET GO"!

2 BASIC DISTRUST ON THE PRESENT CONDITION OF MAN & SOCIETY

3 MOMENTS OF INCREDIBLE NAIVETÉ THAT RISOLVE VERY COMPLEX PROBLEMS. BY OVEROVERSEMPLIFICATION

4 THE LONGING FOR UNITY - COMMUNITY TENDS TO CONFUSE DIFFERENT "CATEGORIES" INTO A INDECIFRABLE ONENESS.

5 THE "SINGLE TISSUE" OF THE EARTH-CITY HAS FRIGHTENING CONNOTATIONS.

6 CELLULAR (ATOMISTIC) VISION OF LIFE ANONIMOUS. & MAN TOOL TO UNKNOWN (NOT YET EXISTING) GODS.

7 ANONIMITY AS A PRIMORY QUASI IDENTITY BETWING INDIVIDUALS (TOO MANY TIME DENIED) LEAVES A STUNTED VITALITY & A REFUSAL OF THE PEAKS AS WELL AS THE . . . . .

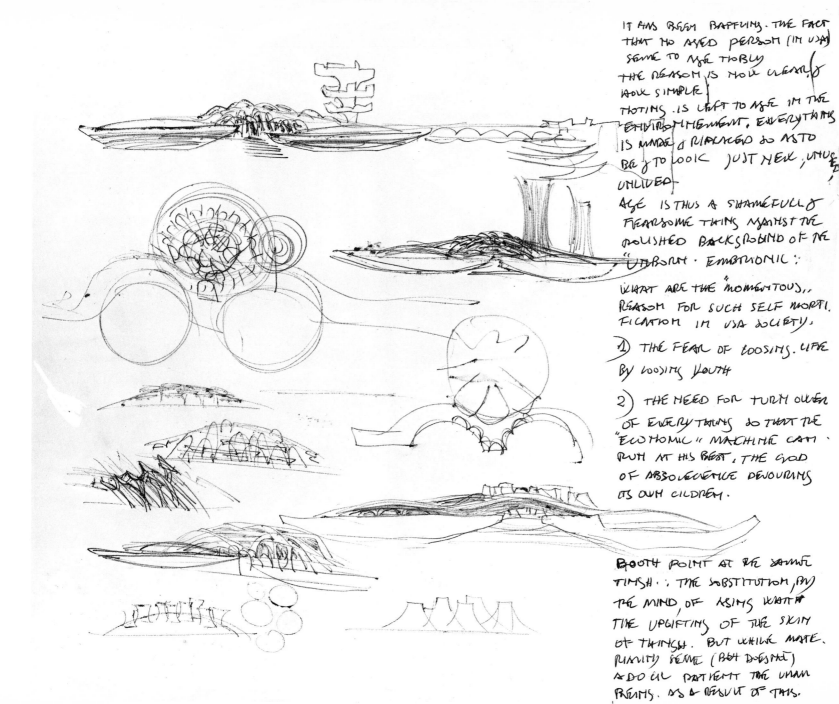

IT HAS BEEN BAFFLING. THE FACT THAT NO AGED PERSON (IN USA) SEEMS TO AGE NOBLY

THE REASON IS NOW CLEAR, & NOW SIMPLE.

NOTHING IS LEFT TO AGE IN THE ENVIRONMENT. EVERYTHING IS MADE & REPLACED SO AS TO BE & TO LOOK JUST NEW, UNUSED, UNLIVED.

AGE IS THUS A SHAMEFULL & FEARSOME THING AGAINST THE POLISHED BACKGROUND OF THE "UNBORN - EMBRIONIC".

WHAT ARE THE "MOMENTOUS" REASON FOR SUCH SELF MORTIFICATION IN USA SOCIETY.

1) THE FEAR OF LOOSING LIFE BY LOOSING YOUTH

2) THE NEED FOR TURN OVER OF EVERYTHING SO THAT THE "ECONOMIC" MACHINE CAN RUN AT HIS BEST, THE GOD OF OBSOLESCENCE DEVOURING ITS OWN CILDREN.

BOOTH POINT AT THE SAME TIMSH: THE SOBSTITUTION, BY THE MIND, OF AGING WITH THE UPGIFTING OF THE SKIN OF THINGSH. BUT WHILE MATERIALITY SEEME (BUT DOESN'T) ADOCIL PATIENT THE HUMAN BEINGS. AS A RESULT OF THIS.

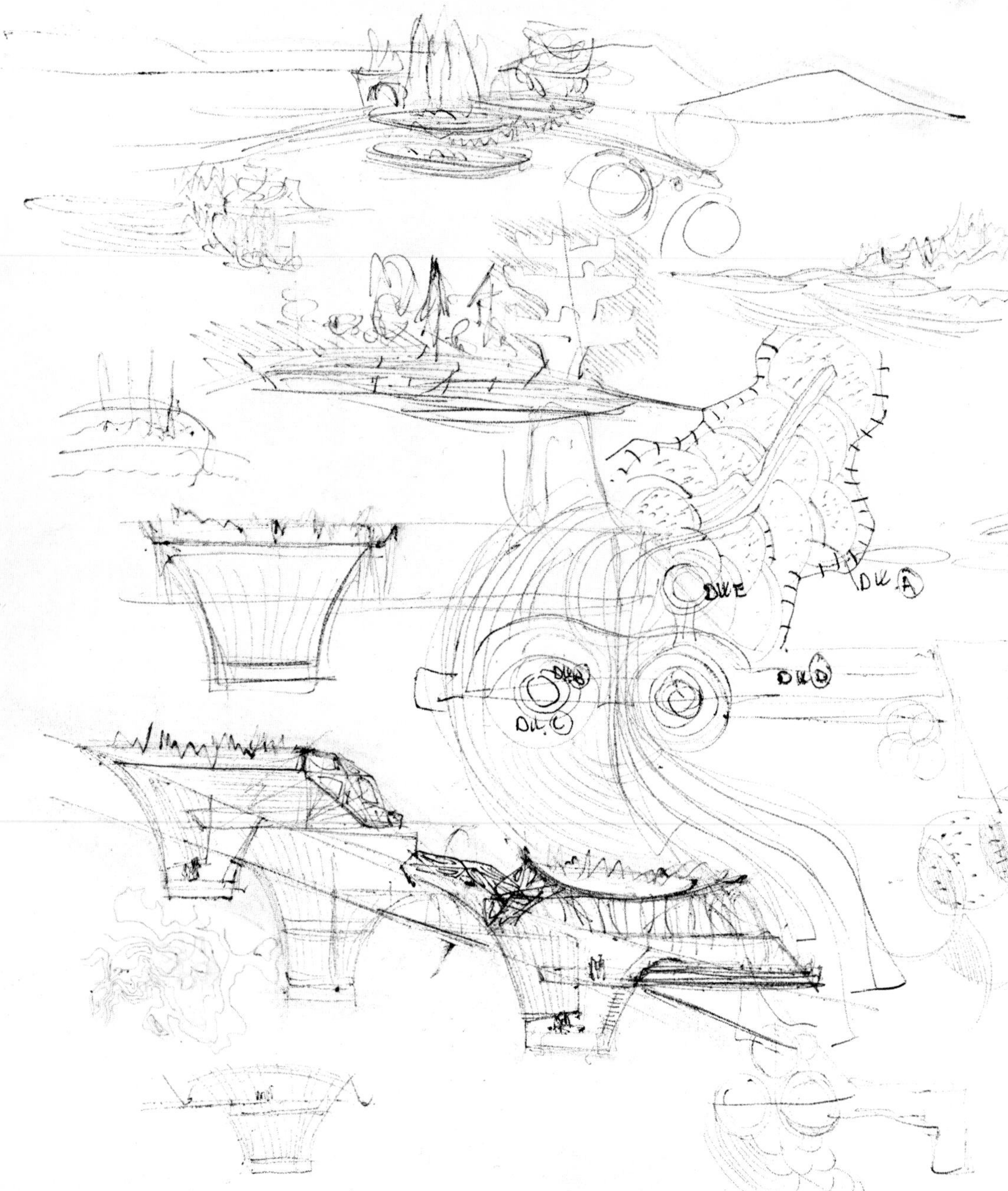

THE LESS ONE IS USED TO THE PRESENCE OF DEATH THE MORE ONE CANT ACCEPT IT COURAGEOUSLY. A THEORETICALLY FOOL PROOF LIFE WOULD ENGENDRE A GENERAL ISTERIA FOR ANY OCCASION OF DEATH & THE OCCASION OF DEATH IS AS FREQUENT AS THE OCCASION OF BIRTH.

IF BETWEEN THOSE TWO WELL KEPT ~~SECRET~~ - MISTERIES. NOTHING IS BORN OF METAPHISICAL NATURE THE BALANCE HAS NO SUBSTANCE TO SHOW & NOTHING REMAINS AS TO THE "NECESSITY" OF LIFE

THAT WHICH IS INEVITABLE MAY NOT BE NECESSARY; IT IS SO THOU UNDER THE OMNIPOTENCE OF A GOD. NOT SO IF MAN IS "FREE".

SANITY IS NOT THE DEEPROOTED QUALITY OF MAN. INSANITY IS THE FOUNDATION OF HIS EXISTENCE

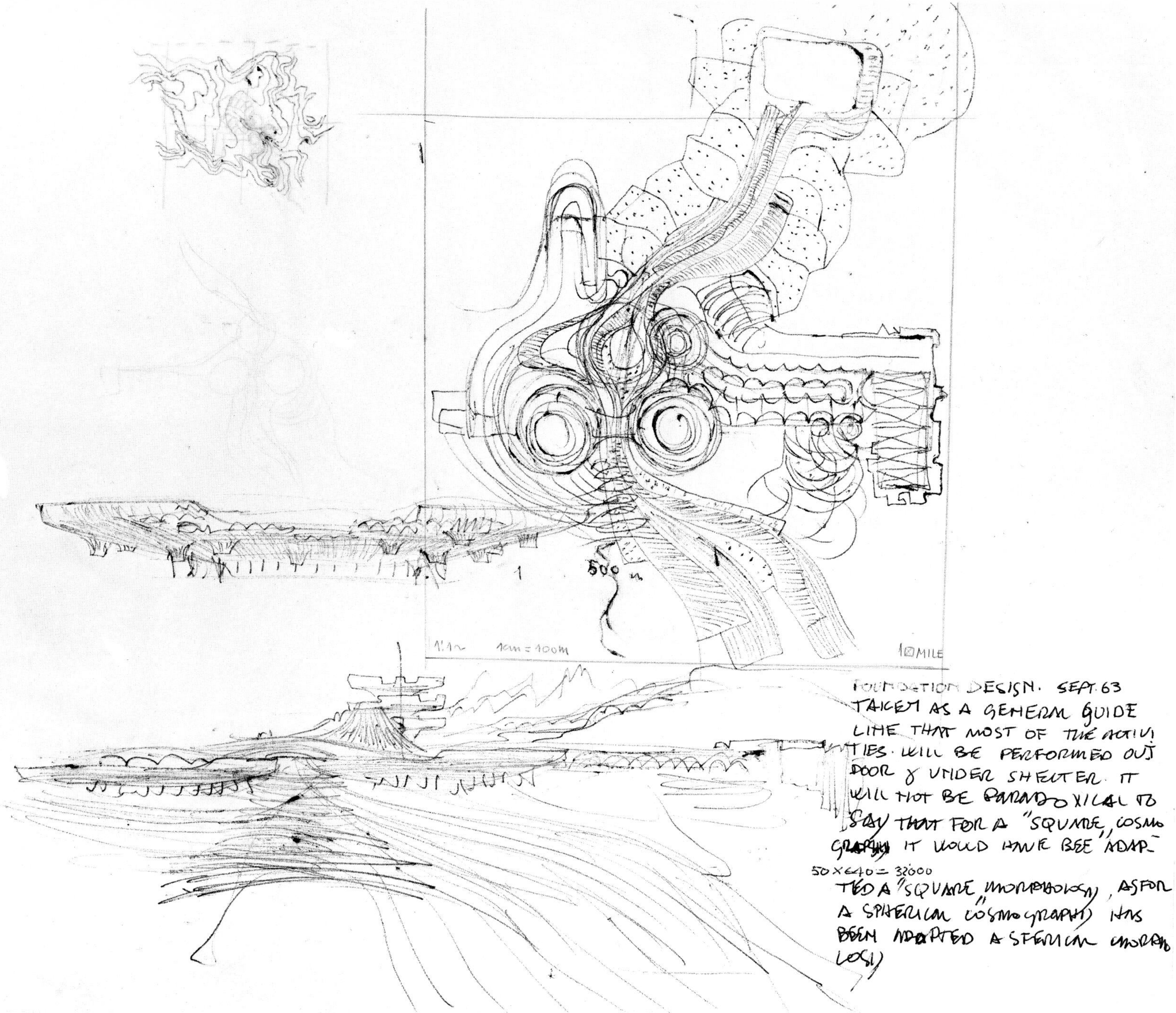
500 m
1:1 m   1cm = 100m
10 MILE
FOUNDATION DESIGN. SEPT. 63
TAKEN AS A GENERAL GUIDE
LINE THAT MOST OF THE ACTIVI
TIES. WILL BE PERFORMED OUT
DOOR & UNDER SHELTER. IT
WILL NOT BE PARADOXICAL TO
SAY THAT FOR A "SQUARE" COSMO
GRAPHY IT WOULD HAVE BEE ADAP-
50 × 640 = 32000
TED A "SQUARE" MORPHOLOGY, AS FOR
A SPHERICAL COSMOGRAPHY HAS
BEEN ADAPTED A SFERICAL MORPHO
LOGY)

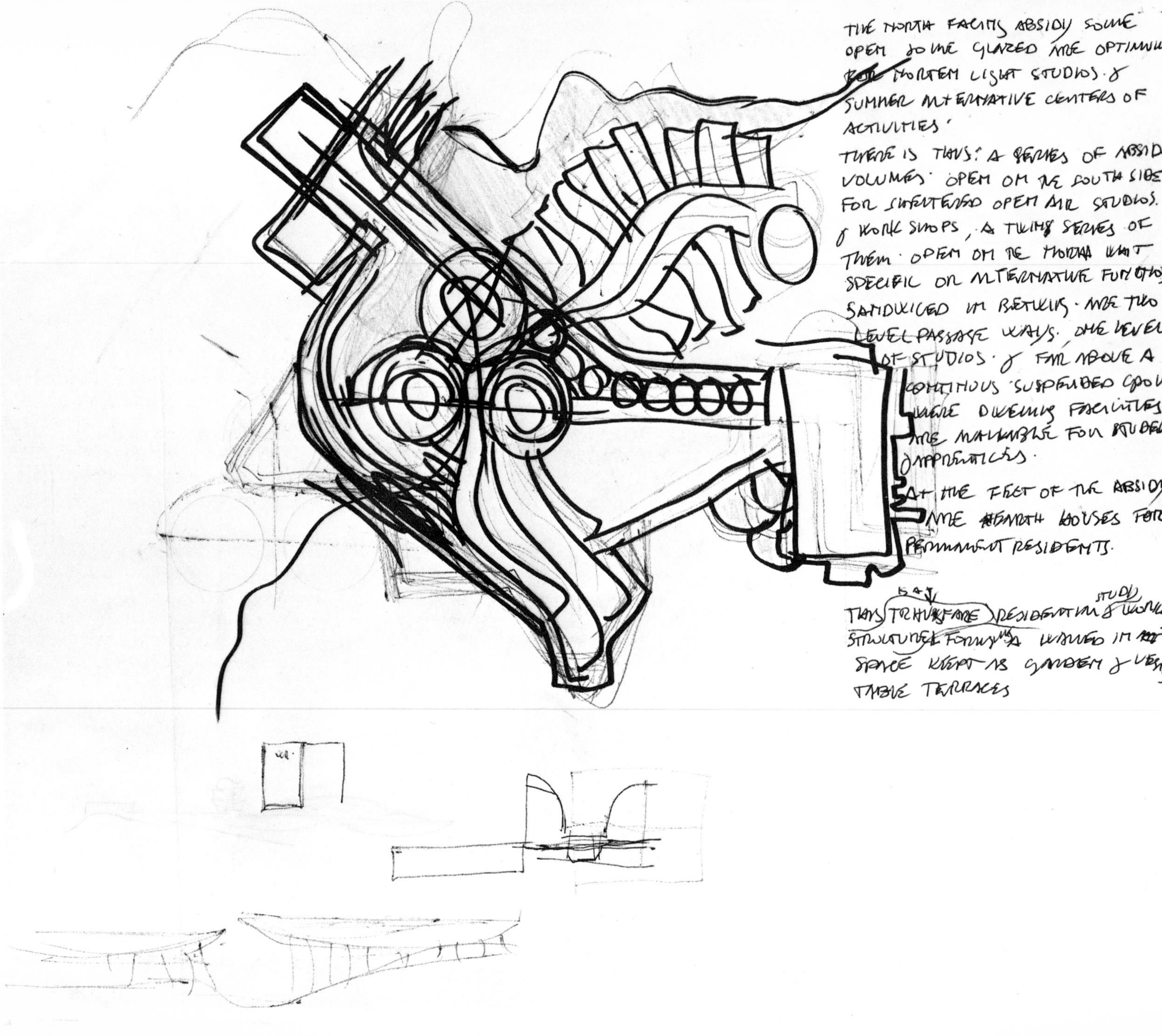
THE NORTH FACING ABSIDS SOME
OPEN SOME GLAZED ARE OPTIMUM
FOR NORTHERN LIGHT STUDIOS. &
SUMMER ALTERNATIVE CENTERS OF
ACTIVITIES.
THERE IS THUS: A SERIES OF ABSIDAL
VOLUMES. OPEN ON THE SOUTH SIDE
FOR SHELTERED OPEN AIR STUDIOS.
& WORK SHOPS, A TWIN SERIES OF
THEM. OPEN ON THE NORTH WITH
SPECIFIC OR ALTERNATIVE FUNCTIONS.
SANDWICHED IN BETWEEN. ARE TWO
LEVEL PASSAGE WAYS. ONE LEVEL
OF STUDIOS. & FAR ABOVE A
CONTINUOUS SUSPENDED GROUND
WHERE DWELLING FACILITIES
ARE AVAILABLE FOR STUDENTS
& APPRENTICES.
AT THE FEET OF THE ABSIDS
ARE HEARTH HOUSES FOR
PERMANENT RESIDENTS.
THUS THE RESIDENTIAL & STUDIO WORKING
STRUCTURE FORMS A WEAVED IN
SPACE KEPT AS GARDEN & VEGE
TABLE TERRACES

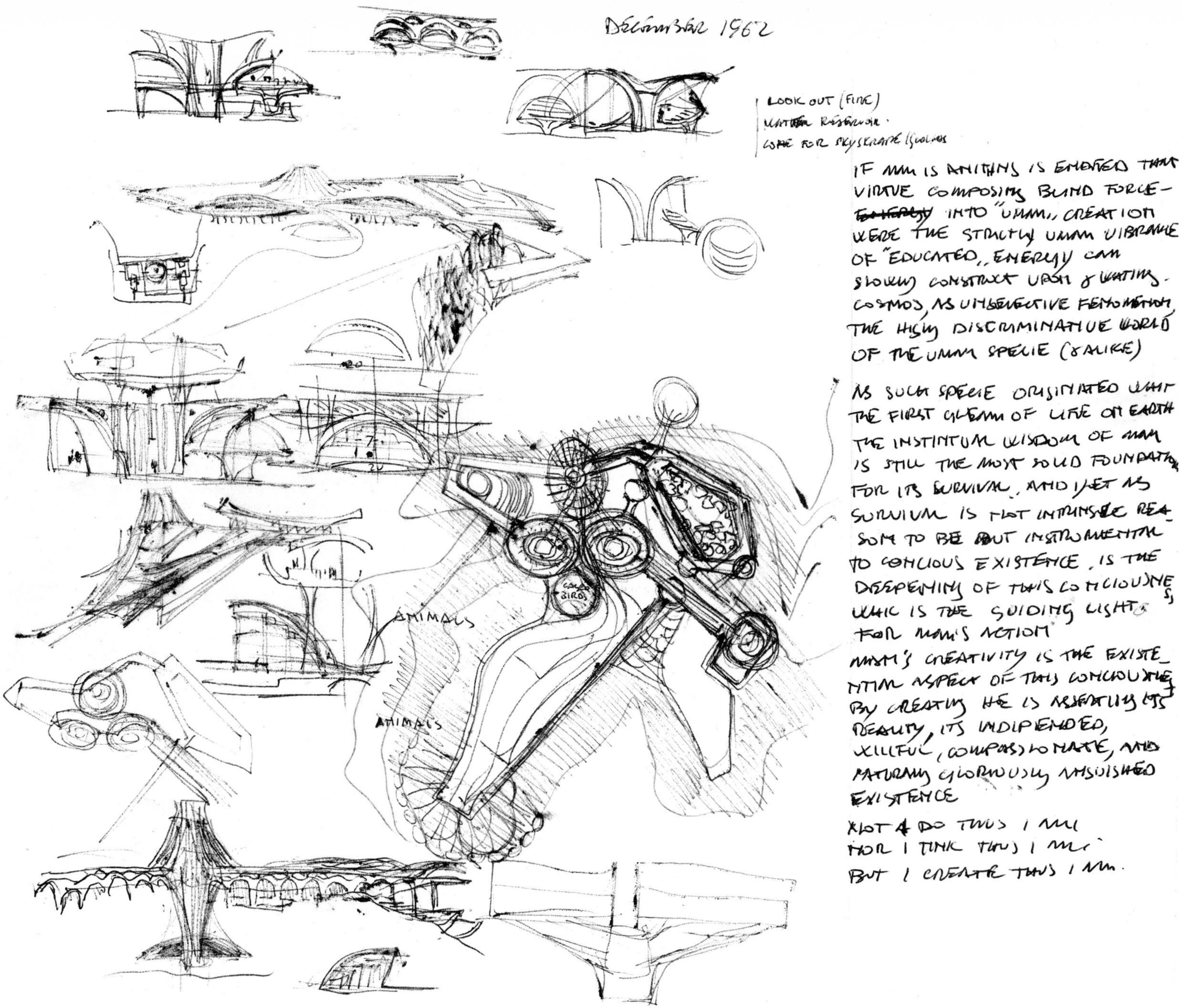
DECEMBER 1962
LOOK OUT (FIRE)
WATER RESERVOIR
IF MAN IS ANYTHING IS EMERGED THAT
VIRTUE COMPOSING BLIND FORCE-
INTO "MAN" CREATION
WERE THE STRICTLY MAN VIBRANCE
OF "EDUCATED" ENERGY CAN
SLOWLY CONSTRUCT UPON A WAITING
COSMOS, AS UNSELECTIVE FENOMENON,
THE HIGH DISCRIMINATIVE WORLD
OF THE MAN SPECIE (& ALIKE)
AS SUCH SPECIE ORIGINATED WITH
THE FIRST GLEAM OF LIFE ON EARTH
THE INSTINTUAL WISDOM OF MAN
IS STILL THE MOST SOLID FOUNDATION
FOR ITS SURVIVAL. AND YET AS
SURVIVAL IS NOT INTRINSIC REA-
SON TO BE BUT INSTRUMENTAL
TO CONCIOUS EXISTENCE, IS THE
DEEPENING OF THIS CONCIOUSNESS
WHICH IS THE GUIDING LIGHT
FOR MAN'S ACTION
MAN'S CREATIVITY IS THE EXISTE-
NTIAL ASPECT OF THIS CONCIOUSNESS
BY CREATING HE IS ASSERTING ITS
REALITY, ITS INDIPENDED,
WILLFUL, COMPASSIONATE, AND
NATURALLY GLORIOUSLY ANGUISHED
EXISTENCE
NOT I DO THUS I AM
NOR I TINK THUS I AM
BUT I CREATE THUS I AM.
ANIMALS
ANIMALS

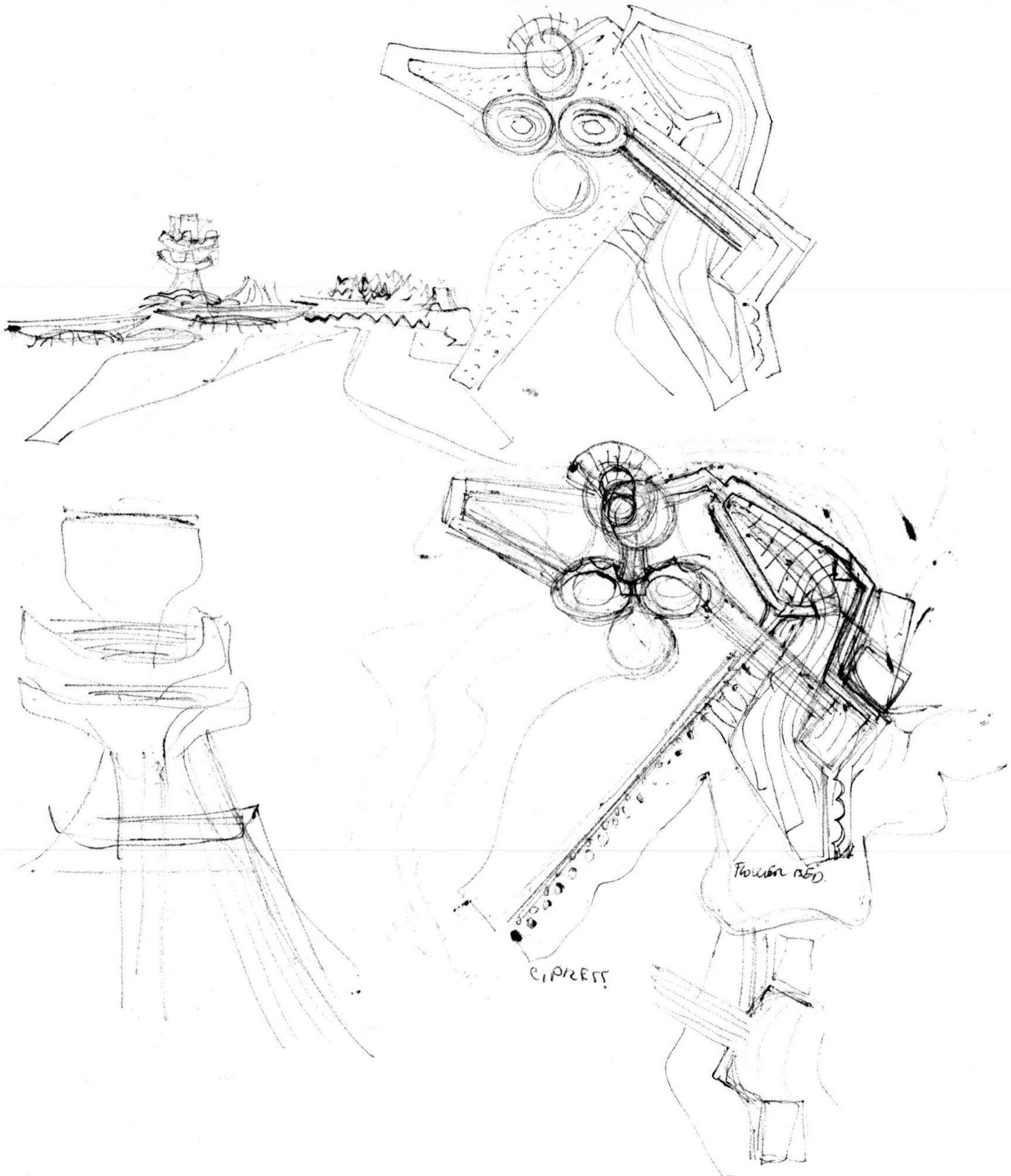

FLOWER BED.
CIPRESS

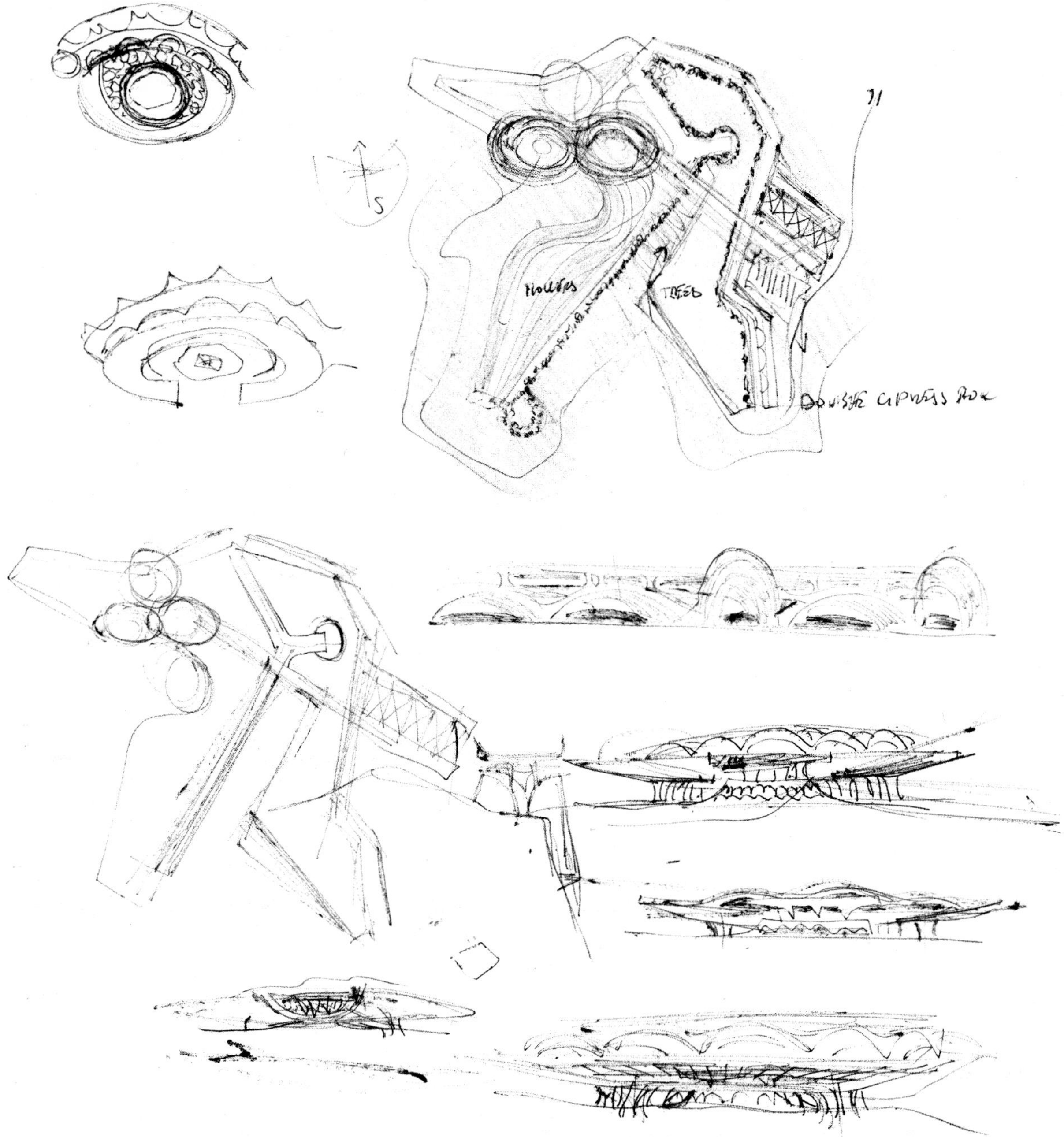
FLOWERS
TREES
DOUBLE CYPRESS ROW

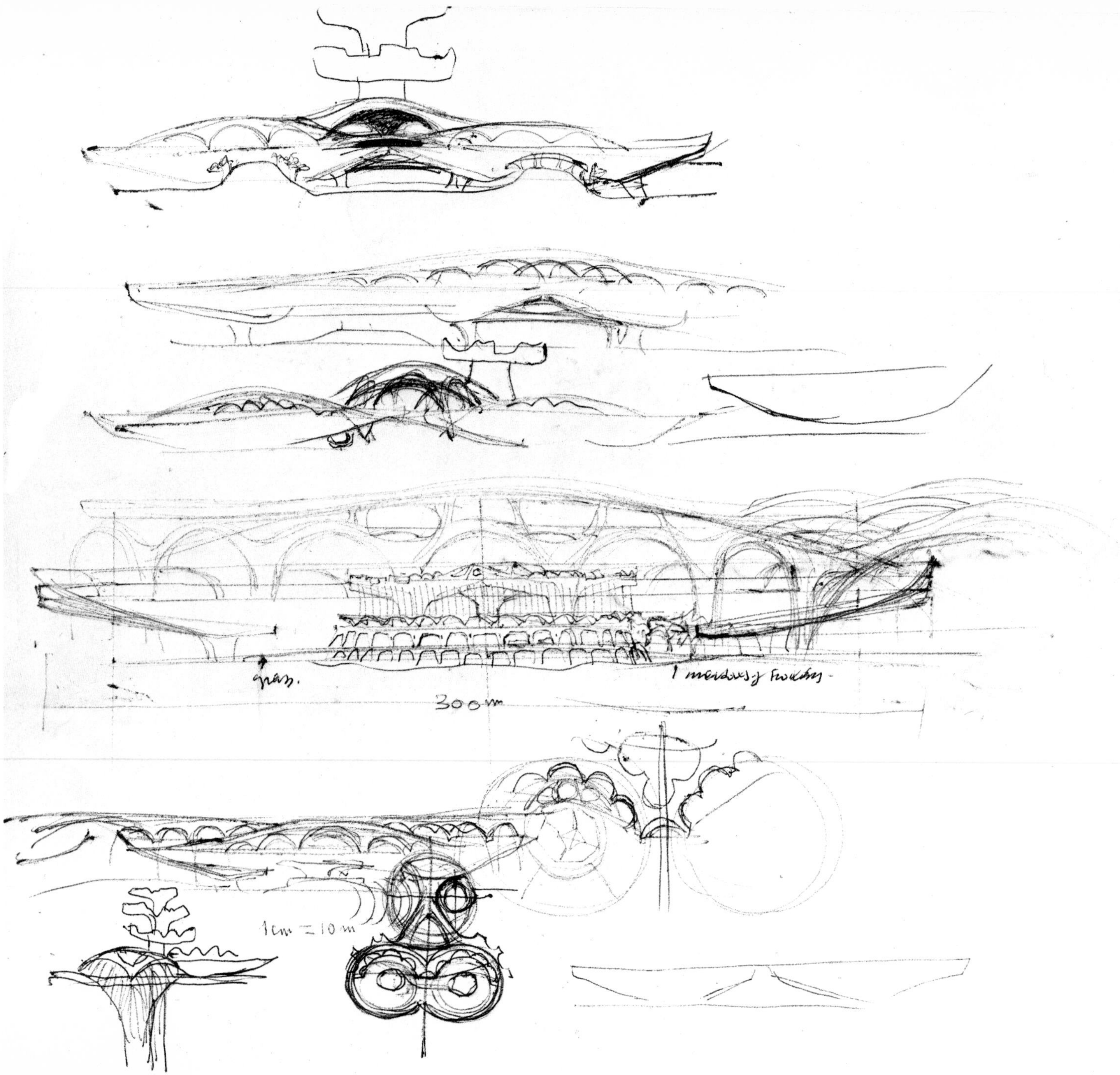
grass.
meadows
300m
1cm = 10m

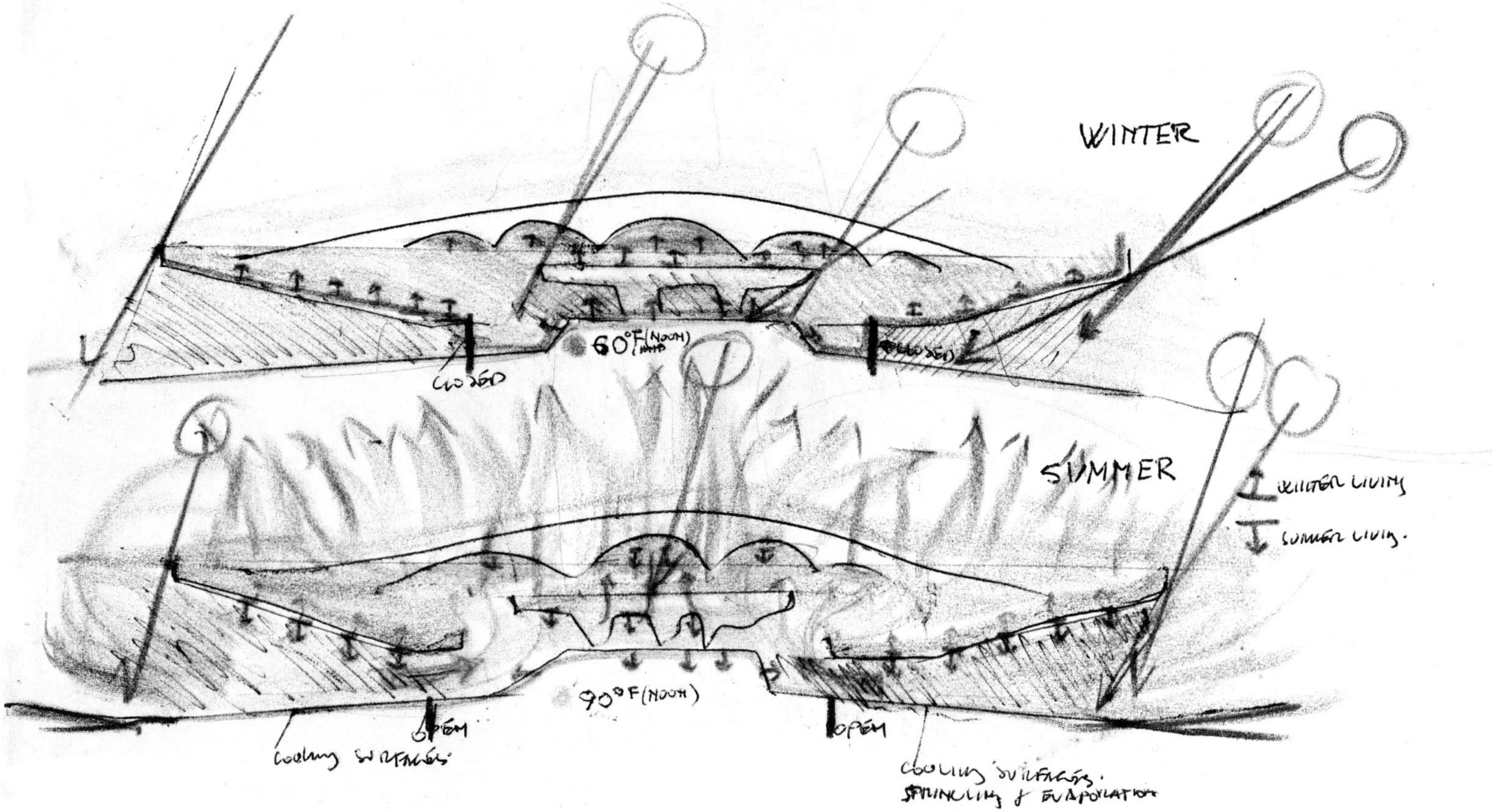
WINTER
60°F (NOON)
CLOSED
SUMMER
winter living
summer living
90°F (NOON)
OPEN
OPEN
cooling surfaces
cooling surfaces.
sprinkling & evaporation

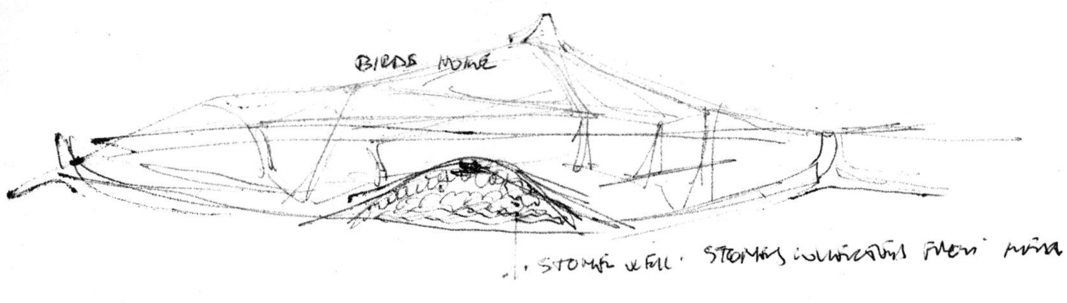
BIRDS HOME

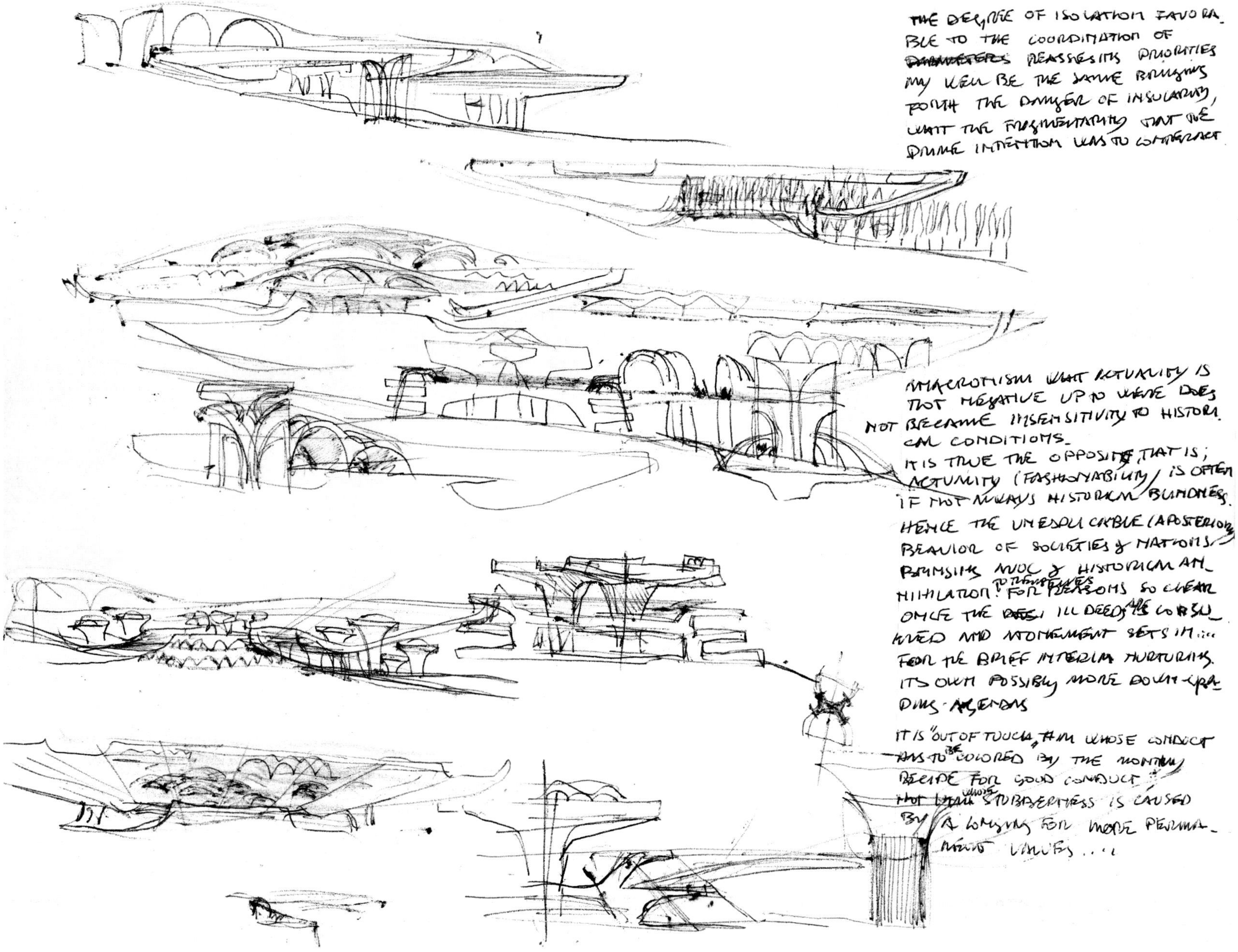
THE DEGREE OF ISOLATION FAVORA-
BLE TO THE COORDINATION OF
REASSESSING PRIORITIES
MAY WELL BE THE SAME BRINGING
FORTH THE DANGER OF INSULARITY,
WITH THE FRAGMENTATION THAT THE
PRIME INTENTION WAS TO COUNTERACT
ANACRONISM WHAT ACTUALITY IS
NOT NEGATIVE UP TO WHERE DOES
NOT BECAME INSENSITIVITY TO HISTORI-
CAL CONDITIONS.
IT IS TRUE THE OPPOSITE, THAT IS;
ACTUALITY (FASHIONABILITY) IS OFTEN
IF NOT ALWAYS HISTORICAL BLINDNESS.
HENCE THE UNEXPLICABLE (APOSTERIORI)
BEHAVIOR OF SOCIETIES & NATIONS
BRINGING HAVOC & HISTORICAL AN-
NIHILATION TO THEMSELVES FOR REASONS SO CLEAR
ONCE THE ILL DEEDS ARE CONSU-
MED AND ATONEMENT SETS IN....
FOR THE BRIEF INTERIM NURTURING
ITS OWN POSSIBLY MORE DOWN-GRA-
DING AGENDAS
IT IS "OUT OF TOUCH" HIM WHOSE CONDUCT
HAS TO BE COLORED BY THE MONTHLY
RECIPE FOR GOOD CONDUCT
WHOSE STUBBORNNESS IS CAUSED
BY A LONGING FOR MORE PERMA-
NENT VALUES....

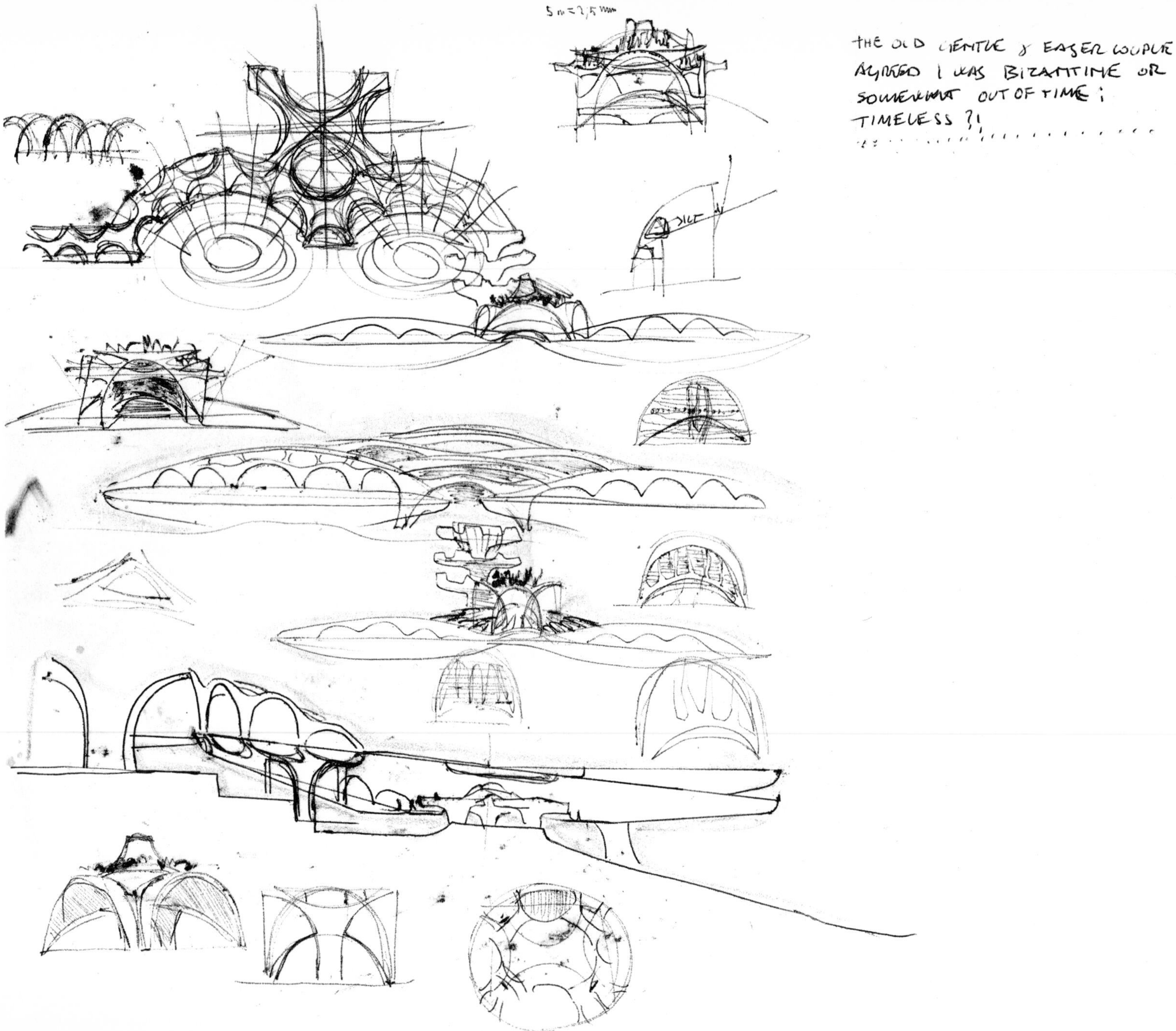
5 m = 2,5 mm
THE OLD GENTLE & EAGER COUPLE AGREED I WAS BIZANTINE OR SOMEWHAT OUT OF TIME; TIMELESS ?!

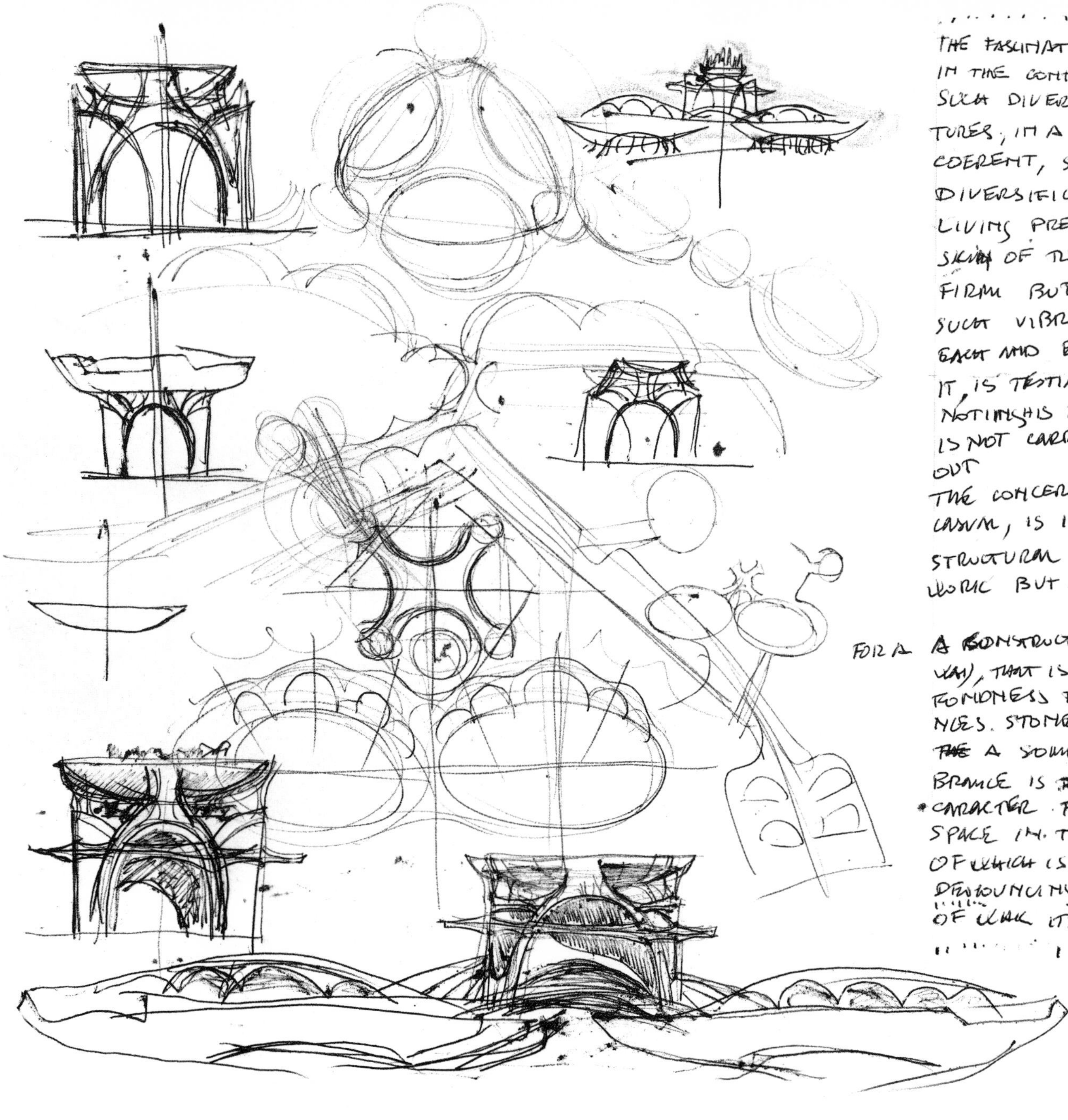

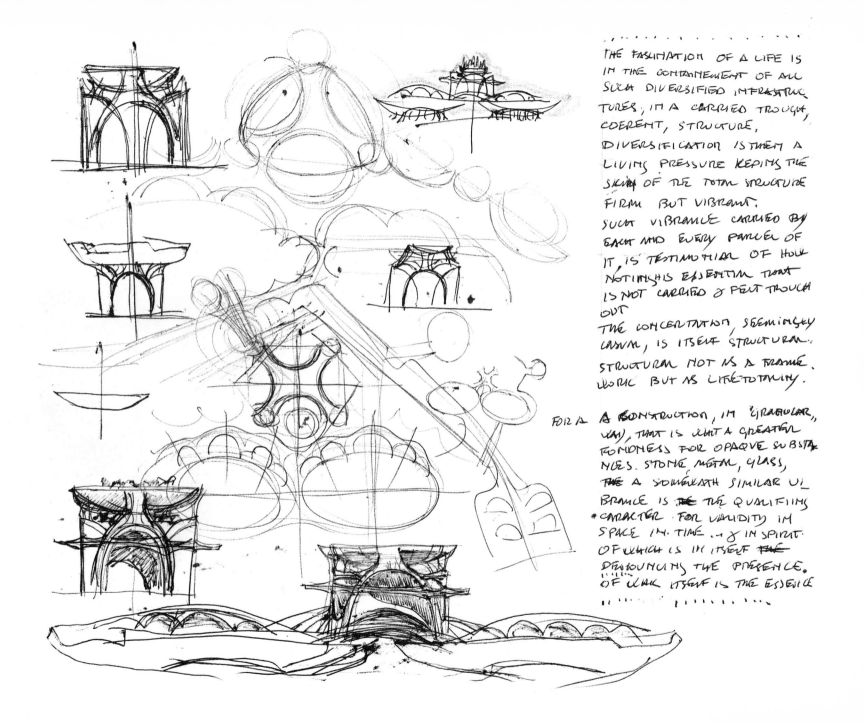

THE FASCINATION OF A LIFE IS
IN THE CONTAINEMENT OF ALL
SUCH DIVERSIFIED INFRASTRUC
TURES, IN A CARRIED TROUGH,
COERENT, STRUCTURE.
DIVERSIFICATION IS THEN A
LIVING PRESSURE KEPING THE
SKIN OF THE TOTAL STRUCTURE
FIRM BUT VIBRANT.
SUCH VIBRANCE CARRIED BY
EACH AND EVERY PARCEL OF
IT, IS TESTIMONIAL OF HOW
NOTHING IS ESSENTIAL THAT
IS NOT CARRIED & FELT TROUGH
OUT
THE CONCENTRATION, SEEMINGLY
CASUAL, IS ITSELF STRUCTURAL.
STRUCTURAL NOT AS A FRAME
WORK BUT AS LIFE-TOTALITY.

FOR A A CONSTRUCTION, IN "GRANULAR"
WAY, THAT IS WHIT A GREATER
FONDNESS FOR OPAQUE SUBSTA
NCES. STONE, METAL, GLASS,
~~THE~~ A SOMEWATH SIMILAR VI
BRANCE IS ~~THE~~ THE QUALIFIING
CARACTER FOR VALIDITY IN
SPACE IN TIME ... & IN SPIRIT.
OF WHICH IS IN ITSELF ~~THE~~
DENOUNCING THE PRESENCE.
OF WHAT ITSELF IS THE ESSENCE

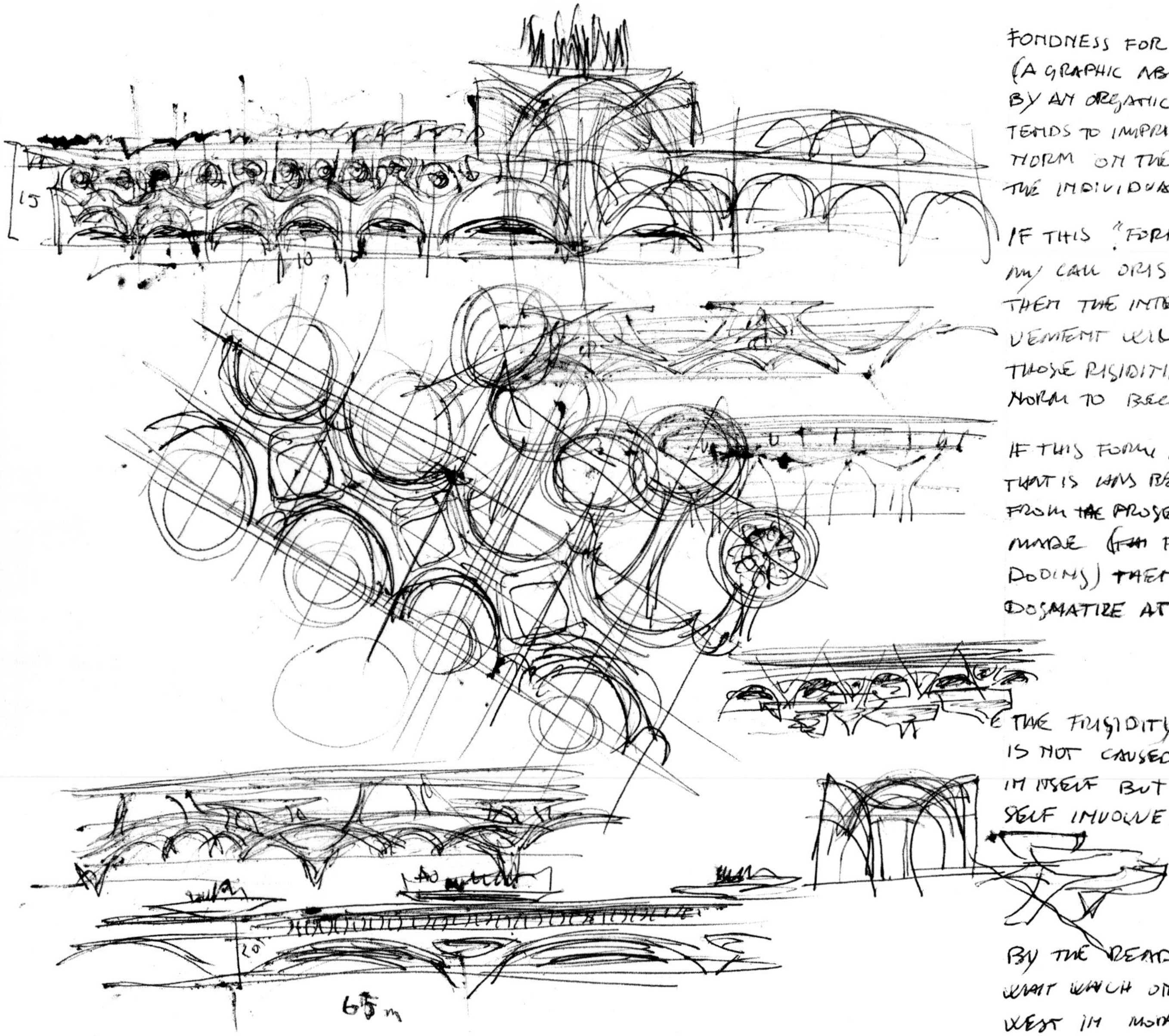

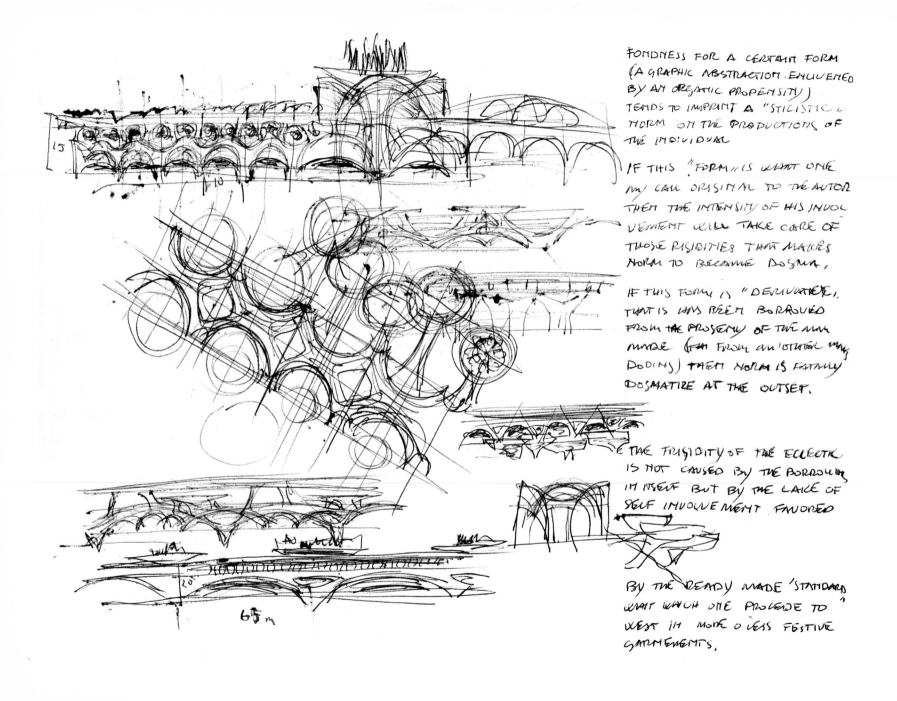

FONDNESS FOR A CERTAIN FORM (A GRAPHIC ABSTRACTION ENLIVENED BY AN ORGANIC PROPENSITY) TENDS TO IMPRINT A "STILISTIC" NORM ON THE PRODUCTIONS OF THE INDIVIDUAL

IF THIS "FORM" IS WHAT ONE MAY CALL ORIGINAL TO THE AUTOR THEN THE INTENSITY OF HIS INVOLVEMENT WILL TAKE CARE OF THOSE RIGIDITIES THAT MAKES NORM TO BECOME DOGMA.

IF THIS FORM IS "DERIVATIVE", THAT IS HAS BEEN BORROWED FROM THE PROGENY OF THE MAN MADE (OR FROM AN'OTHER MAN DOINGS) THEN NORM IS FATALLY DOGMATIZE AT THE OUTSET.

THE FRIGIDITY OF THE ECLECTIC IS NOT CAUSED BY THE BORROWING IN ITSELF BUT BY THE LACK OF SELF INVOLVEMENT FAVORED

BY THE READY MADE 'STANDARD' WHAT WHICH ONE PROCEEDE TO VEST IN MORE O LESS FESTIVE GARMEMENTS.

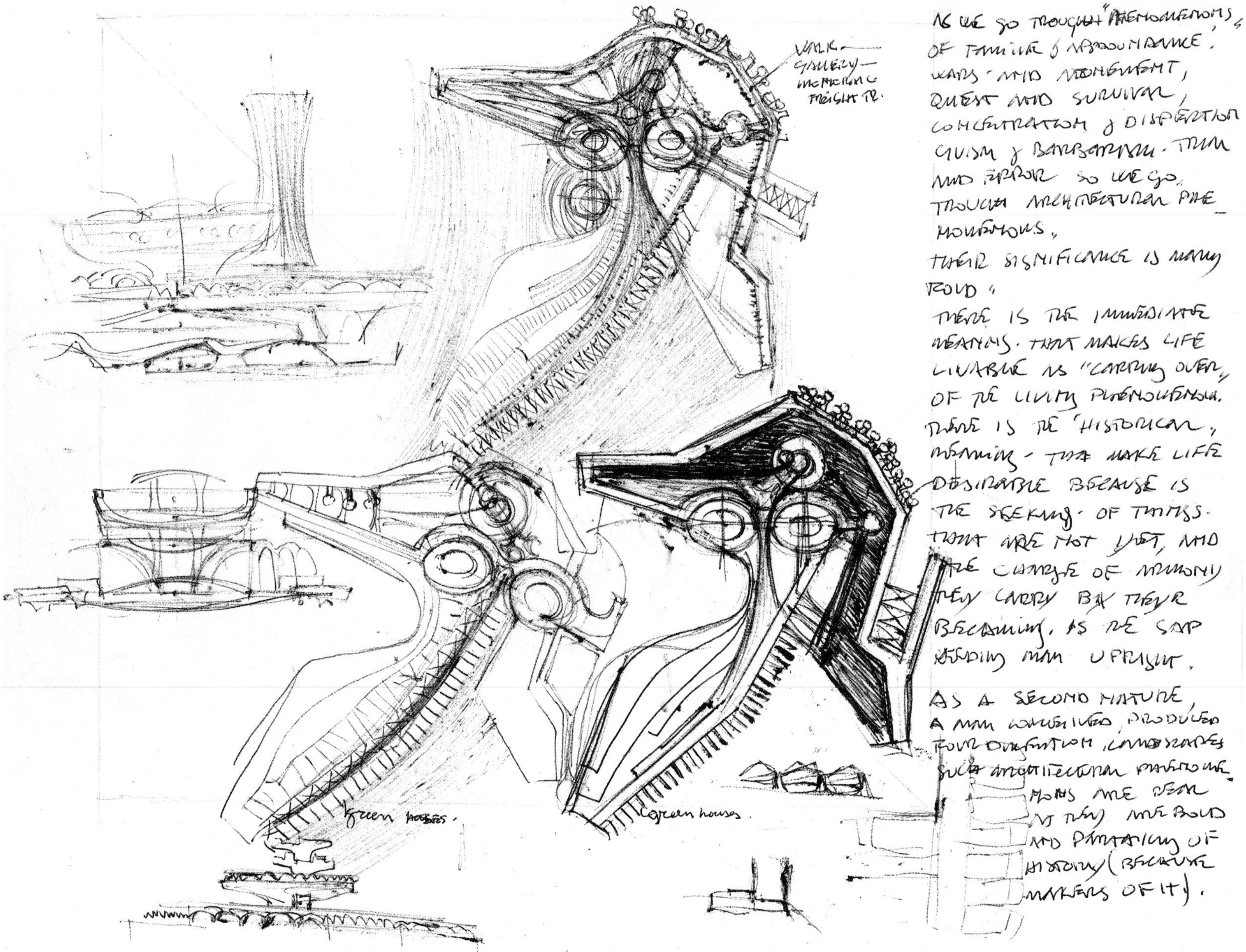
WALK-
GALLERY—
FREIGHT TR.
AS WE GO TROUGH "PHENOMENONS,,
OF FAMINE & ABBOUNDANCE.
WARS AND MOVEMENT,
QUEST AND SURVIVAL,
CONCENTRATION & DISPERTION
CIVISM & BARBARISM. TRIAL
AND ERROR SO WE GO.
TROUGH ARCHITECTURAL PHE_
NOMENONS.
THEIR SIGNIFICANCE IS MANY
FOLD.
THERE IS THE IMMEDIATE
MEANING. THAT MAKES LIFE
LIVABLE AS "CARRING OVER,,
OF THE LIVING PHENOMENON.
THERE IS THE 'HISTORICAL,
MEANING - THAT MAKE LIFE
DESIRABLE BECAUSE IS
THE SEEKING OF THINGS.
THAT ARE NOT YET, AND
THE CHARGE OF MEMORY
THEY CARRY BY THEIR
BECAMING, AS THE SAP
KEEPING MAN UPRIGHT.
AS A SECOND NATURE,
A MAN CONCEIVED, PRODUCED
FOUNDATION, LANDSCAPES
SUCH ARCHITECTURAL PHENOME-
NONS ARE REAL
AS THEY ARE BOLD
AND PARTAKING OF
HISTORY (BECAUSE
MAKERS OF IT).
green houses.
green houses

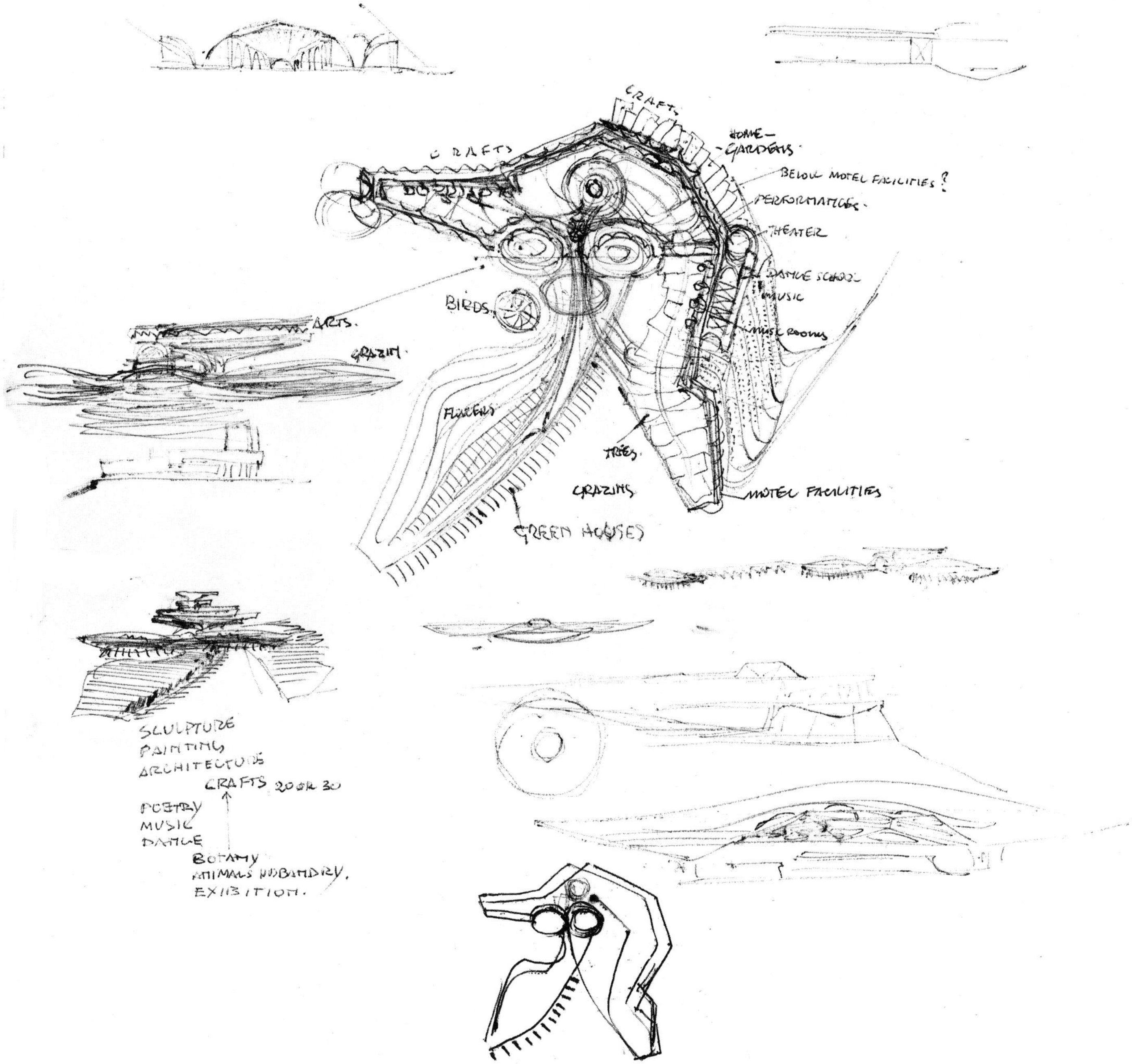
CRAFTS
CRAFTS
HOME-GARDENS
BELOW MOTEL FACILITIES ?
PERFORMANCES
THEATER
DANCE SCHOOL
MUSIC
MUSIC ROOMS
BIRDS
ARTS.
GRAZIN
FLOWERS
TREES
GRAZING
MOTEL FACILITIES
GREEN HOUSES
SCULPTURE
PAINTING
ARCHITECTURE
CRAFTS
POETRY
MUSIC
DANCE
BOTANY
ANIMALS HUSBANDRY.
EXHIBITION.

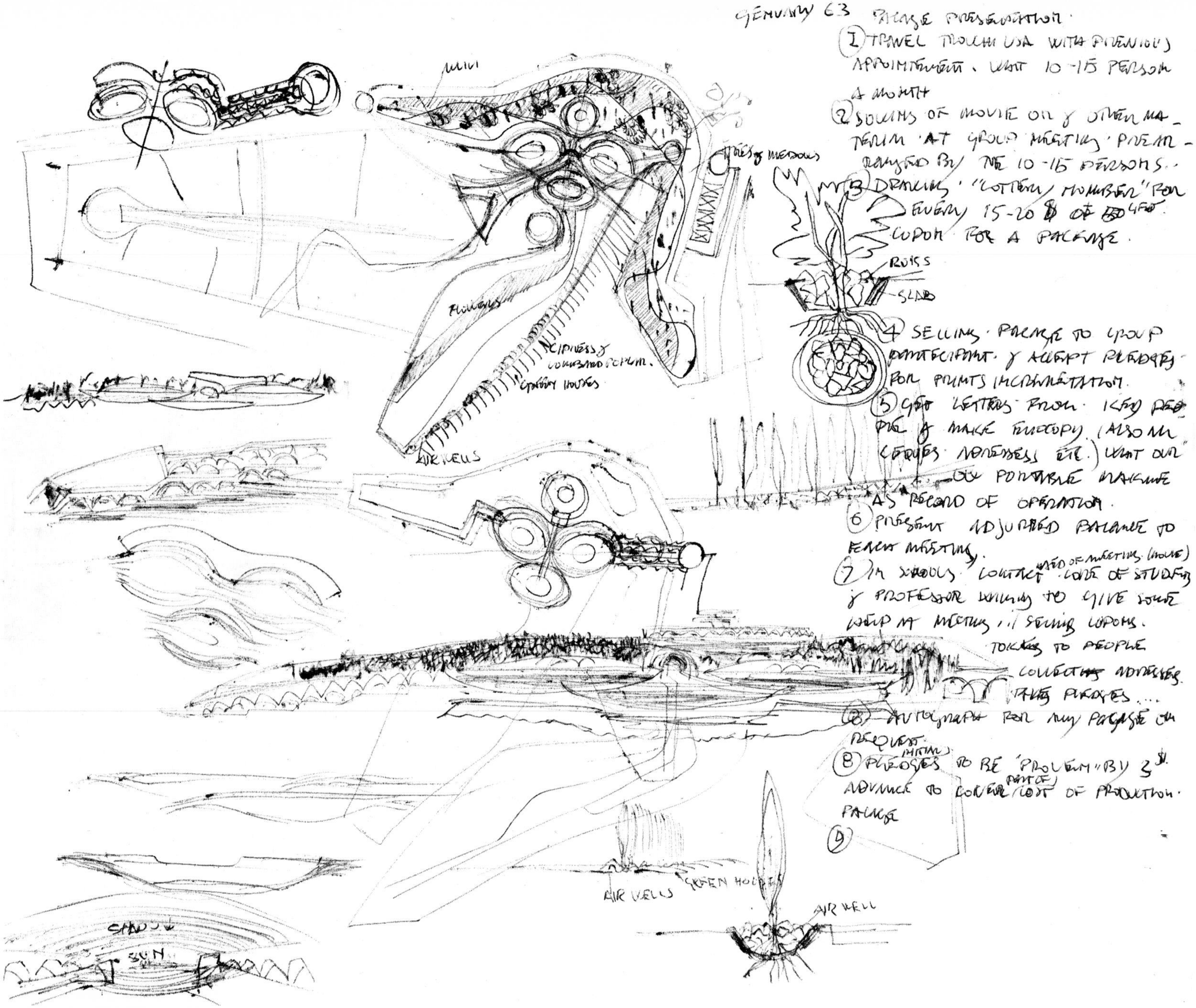
JANUARY 63
PACKAGE PRESENTATION
1 TRAVEL THROUGH USA WITH PREVIOUS APPOINTMENT. VISIT 10-15 PERSON A MONTH
2 SHOWING OF MOVIE ON & OTHER MATERIAL AT GROUP MEETING PREARRANGED BY THE 10-15 PERSONS.
3 DRAWING "LOTTERY NUMBER" FOR EVERY 15-20 $ OF COUPON FOR A PACKAGE.
4 SELLING PACKAGE TO GROUP PARTICIPANT & ACCEPT PLEDGES FOR PRINTS INCREMENTATION.
5 GET LETTERS FROM KEY PEOPLE & MAKE FILMCOPY (ALSO NAMES ADDRESSES ETC.)
AS RECORD OF OPERATION.
6 PRESENT ADJUSTED BALANCE TO EACH MEETING.
7 IN SCHOOLS CONTACT CORE OF STUDENTS & PROFESSOR WILLING TO GIVE SOME HELP AT MEETING, IN SELLING COUPONS.
TALKING TO PEOPLE
COLLECTING ADDRESSES
TAKE PLEDGES....
AUTOGRAPH FOR ANY PACKAGE ON REQUEST.
8 PLEDGES TO BE "PROVEN" BY 3 $ ADVANCE TO COVER COST OF PRODUCTION PACKAGE
9
TREES & MEADOWS
ROCKS
SLAB
FLOWERS
CYPRESS & LOMBARD POPLAR
GREEN HOUSES
AIR WELLS
SAND
SUN
AIR WELL

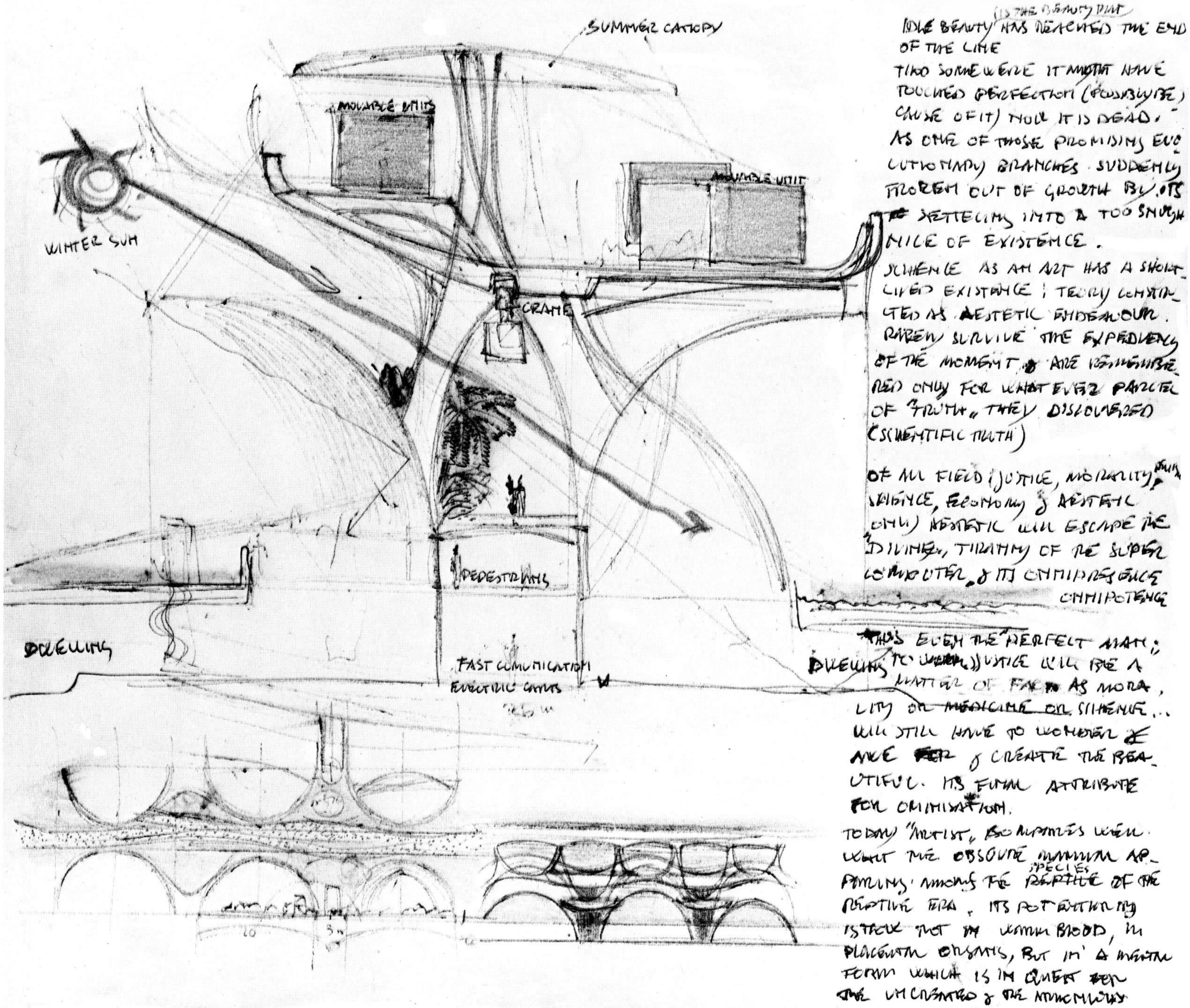
SUMMER CANOPY
MOVABLE UNITS
MOVABLE UNIT
WINTER SUN
CRANE
PEDESTRIANS
DWELLING
FAST COMMUNICATION
ELECTRIC CARTS
DWELLING
OF THE LINE
AS ONE OF THOSE PROMISING EVO
LUTIONARY BRANCHES SUDDENLY
FROZEN OUT OF GROWTH BY ITS
SETTELING INTO A TOO SNUGH
NICHE OF EXISTENCE.
SCIENCE AS AN ART HAS A SHORT-
LIVED EXISTANCE
AESTETIC ENDEAVOUR.
OF TRUTH THEY DISCOVERED
(SCIENTIFIC TRUTH)
OF ALL FIELD; JUSTICE, MORALITY,
SCIENCE, ECONOMY & AESTETIC
ONLY AESTETIC WILL ESCAPE THE
TIRANNY OF THE SUPER
COMPUTER & ITS OMNIPRESENCE
OMNIPOTENCE
THUS EVEN THE PERFECT MAN;
JUSTICE WILL BE A
MATTER OF FACT AS MORA-
LITY OR MEDICINE OR SCIENCE...
WILL STILL HAVE TO WONDER
& CREATE THE BEA-
UTIFUL. ITS FINAL ATTRIBUTE
FOR OMINISATION.
THE OBSCURE
SPECIES
REPTILE OF THE
REPTILE ERA
IN WARM BLOOD, IN
PLACENTAL ORGANS, BUT IN A MENTAL
FORM WHICH IS IN QUEST FOR
THE UNCREATED & THE UNKNOWN

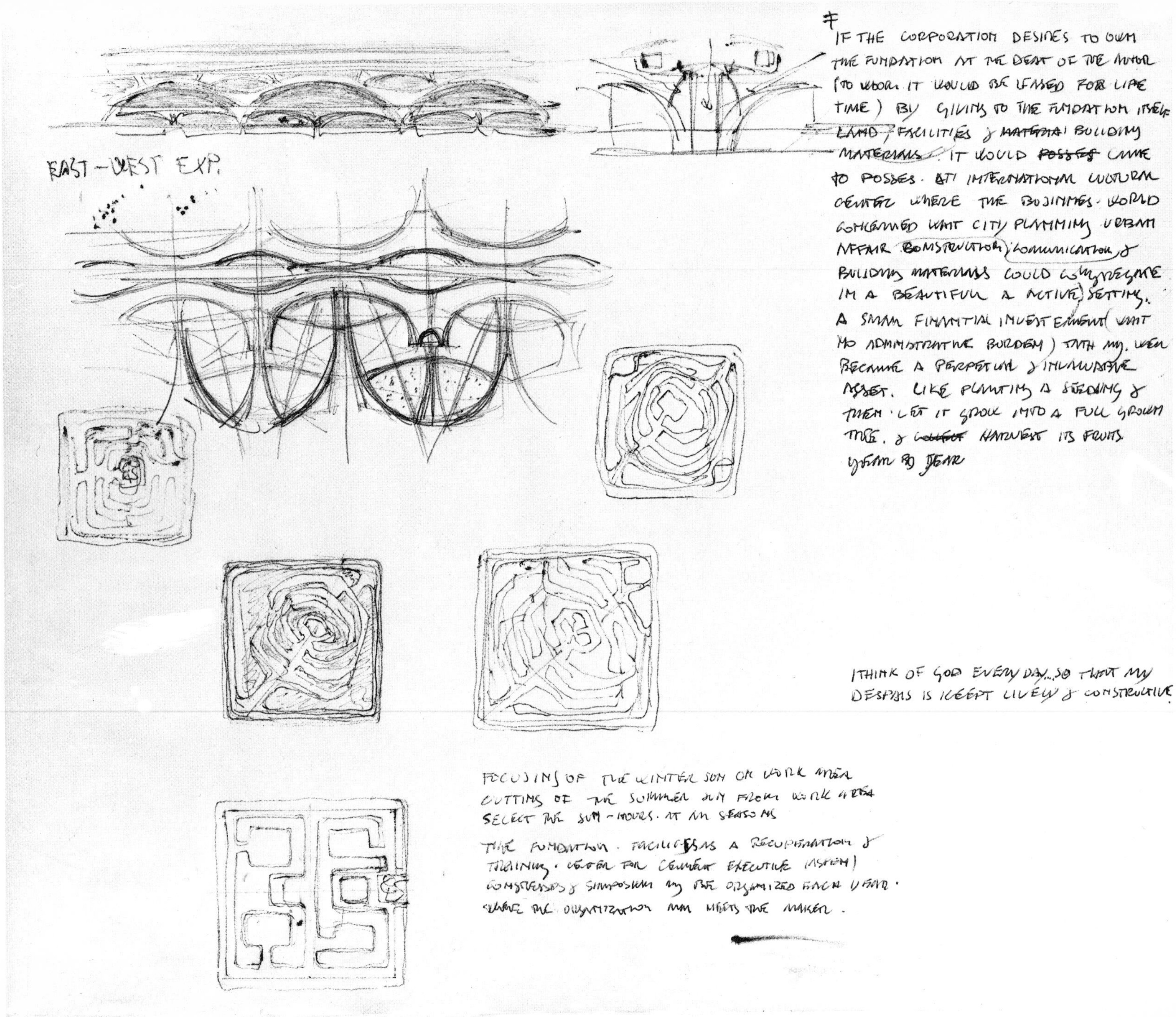
EAST-WEST EXP.
IF THE CORPORATION DESIRES TO OWN
THE FUNDATION AT THE DEAT OF THE AUTOR
(TO WHOM IT WOULD BE LEASED FOR LIFE
TIME) BY GIVING TO THE FUNDATION ITSELF
LAND, FACILITIES & BUILDING
MATERIALS. IT WOULD CAME
TO POSSES AN INTERNATIONAL CULTURAL
CENTER WHERE THE BUSINNES WORLD
CONCERNED WHIT CITY PLANNING URBAN
AFFAIR CONSTRUCTION COMMUNICATION &
BUILDING MATERIALS COULD CONGREGATE
IN A BEAUTIFUL & ACTIVE SETTING.
A SMALL FINANTIAL INVESTEMENT (WHIT
NO ADMINISTRATIVE BURDEN) WITH MY WORK
BECAME A PERPETUAL & INVALUABLE
ASSET. LIKE PLANTING A SEEDING &
THEN LET IT GROW INTO A FULL GROWN
TREE, & HARVEST ITS FRUITS
YEAR BY YEAR
I THINK OF GOD EVERY DAY... SO THAT MY
DESPAIR IS KEEPT LIVELY & CONSTRUCTIVE
FOCUSING OF THE WINTER SUN ON WORK AREA
CUTTING OF THE SUMMER SUN FROM WORK AREA
SELECT THE SUN-HOURS AT ALL SEASONS
THE FUNDATION FACILITIES AS A RECUPERATION &
TRAINING CENTER FOR CURRENT EXECUTIVE (ASPEN)
CONGRESSES & SIMPOSIUM MAY BE ORGANIZED EACH YEAR.
WHERE THE ORGANIZATION MAN MEETS THE MAKER.

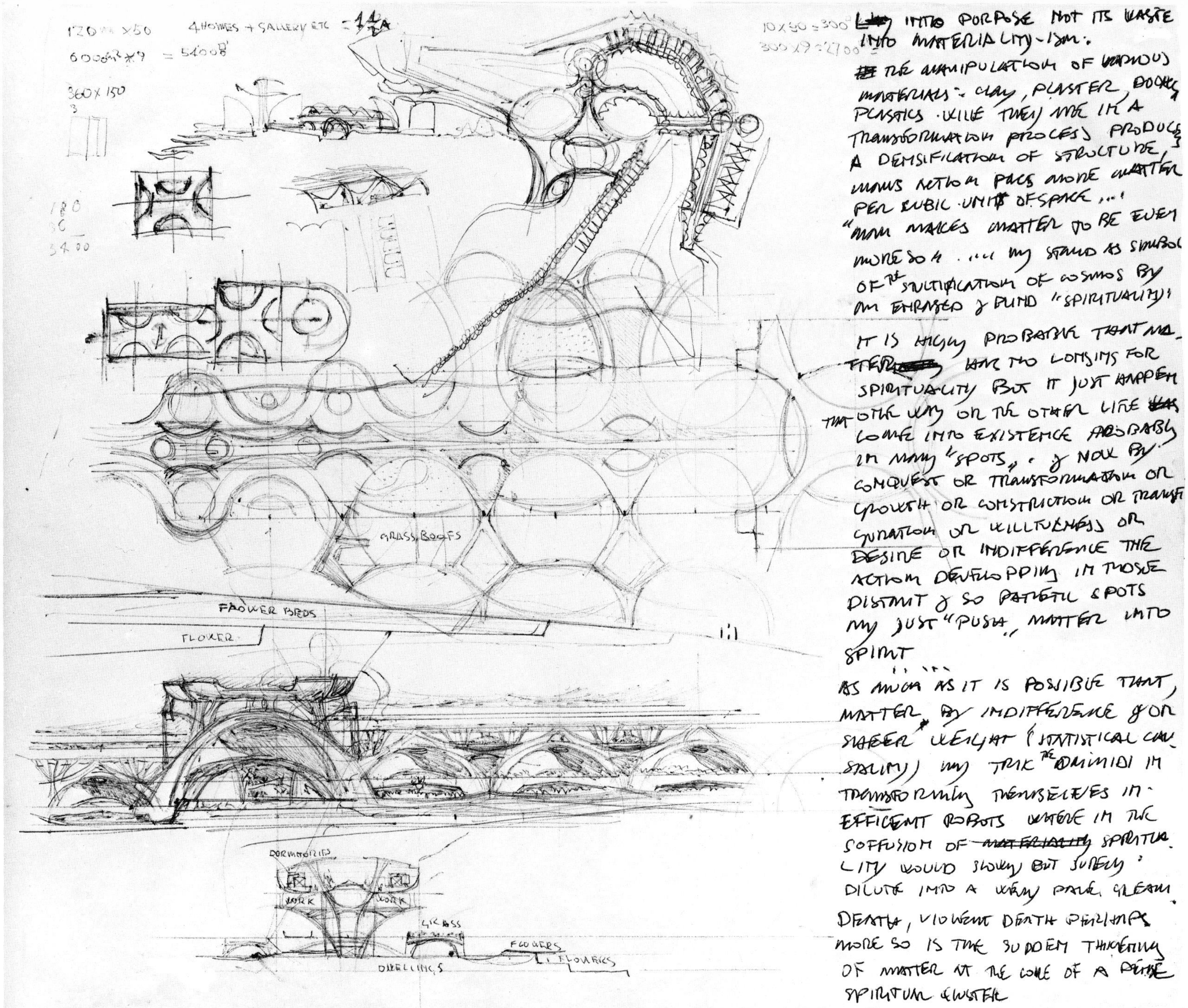
INTO PURPOSE NOT ITS WASTE
INTO MATERIALITY-ISM.
THE MANIPULATION OF VARIOUS
MATERIALS - CLAY, PLASTER, BOOKS
PLASTICS - WHILE THEY ARE IN A
TRANSFORMATION PROCESS PRODUCE
A DENSIFICATION OF STRUCTURE,
MANS ACTION PACKS MORE MATTER
PER CUBIC UNIT OF SPACE ...
"MAN MAKES MATTER TO BE EVEN
MORE SO A ..... MY STAND AS SYMBOL
OF THE STULTIFICATION OF COSMOS BY
AN EMBRASED & BLIND "SPIRITUALISM"
IT IS HIGHLY PROBABLE THAT MATTER
HAS NO CONSCIENCE FOR
SPIRITUALITY BUT IT JUST HAPPEN
THAT ONE WAY OR THE OTHER LIFE
COME INTO EXISTENCE PROBABLY
IN MANY "SPOTS" & NOW BY
CONQUEST OR TRANSFORMATION OR
GROWTH OR CONSTRICTION OR TRANSFIGURATION OR WILLFULNESS OR
DESIRE OR INDIFFERENCE THE
ACTION DEVELOPPING IN THOSE
DISTANT & SO PATHETIC SPOTS
MAY JUST "PUSH" MATTER INTO
SPIRIT
AS MUCH AS IT IS POSSIBLE THAT,
MATTER BY INDIFFERENCE &/OR
SHEER WEIGHT (STATISTICAL CONSTANCY) MAY TRICK THE ANIMIDI IN
TRANSFORMING THEMSELVES IN
EFFICIENT ROBOTS WHERE IN THE
SOFFUSION OF SPIRITUALITY WOULD SLOWLY BUT SURELY
DILUTE INTO A VERY PALE GLEAM.
DEATH, VIOLENT DEATH PERHAPS
MORE SO IS THE SUDDEN THICKENING
OF MATTER AT THE CORE OF A DENSE
SPIRITUAL CLUSTER
GRASS ROOFS
FLOWER BEDS
FLOWER
DORMITORIES
WORK
WORK
GRASS
FLOWERS
FLOWERS
DWELLINGS
120 x 50
4 HOMES + GALLERY ETC
10 x 30 = 300
300 x 9 = 2700
6000 x 9 = 54000
360 x 150

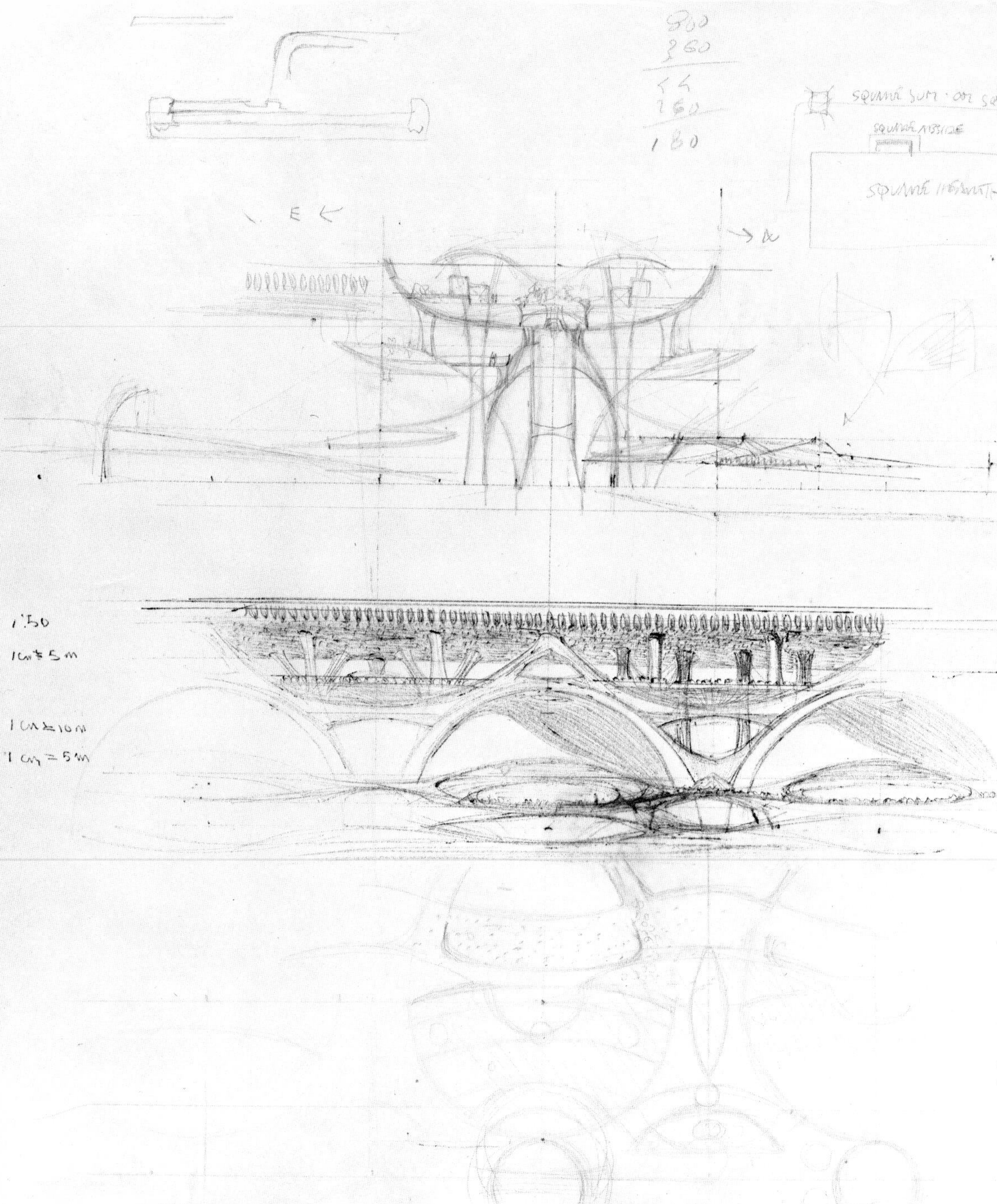

ONE FINDS STRUCTURE IN STATISTICAL
ACCUMULATION (THE WASTE OF COSMOS)
THE OTHER IN SOME KIND OF
SELF INFLICTED "RESPONSABILITY"
THIS RESPONSABILITY BECOMES
MORE & MORE DEMANDING WITH
THE INCREASE OF COMPLEXITY OF
THE DISCRIMINATING & MORE INDI
VIDUALISED PORTION OF THE STUFF
OF THE UNIVERSE (BEFORE SAID CASUAL)

THE PASSAGE FROM THE ~~CASUAL~~ STATISTICAL
TO THE DISCREMINATIVE IS THE
STEPPING UP FROM THE MATERIA
LITY OF THE UNIVERSE TO THE
PROTO-SPIRITUALITY OF THE LIVING.

REALITY SHOWS THAT ALL STATISTICAL
PROMOTED NOTIONS ARE UNHUMAN
THAT IS THE CLOSER ONE CAN GET
TO THE HUMANLESS UNIVERSE OF VALUE.

EXTREME IN THIS CONTEXT WAS
HITLER & THE NAZIS STATISTICAL
MIND: A POSSIBLY LEGITIMATE
AVERSION FOR SOME CARACTER
REFERABLE IN THE SEMITIC CARA
CTER TRIGGERED A STATISTICAL
PROCESS WHICH LOGIC AND THE TOTAL SAME
INDIFFERENCE TOWARD ETHICS THAT
COSMOS HAS, CREATURES BECAME
ABSTRACT ENTITIES TO DISPOSE
OF AS TO BRING ABOUT A STATISTICAL
"DREAM" OF PURITY.
~~IN THIS~~ NAZISM WAS HIGHLY TECHNOLO
GICAL IN SPIRIT, IT CARRIED OUT
FAITHFULLY THE RULES TO WHICH
TECHNOLOGY ABIDES

AND NOT INCIDENTALLY BUT PERHAPS
FATALLY IS THIS SAME PENCHANT OF
TECHNOLOGY TOWARD STATISTICAL
RESOLUTIONS THE INNER CONTRADDI
CTION OF OUR "PROGRESSIVE"

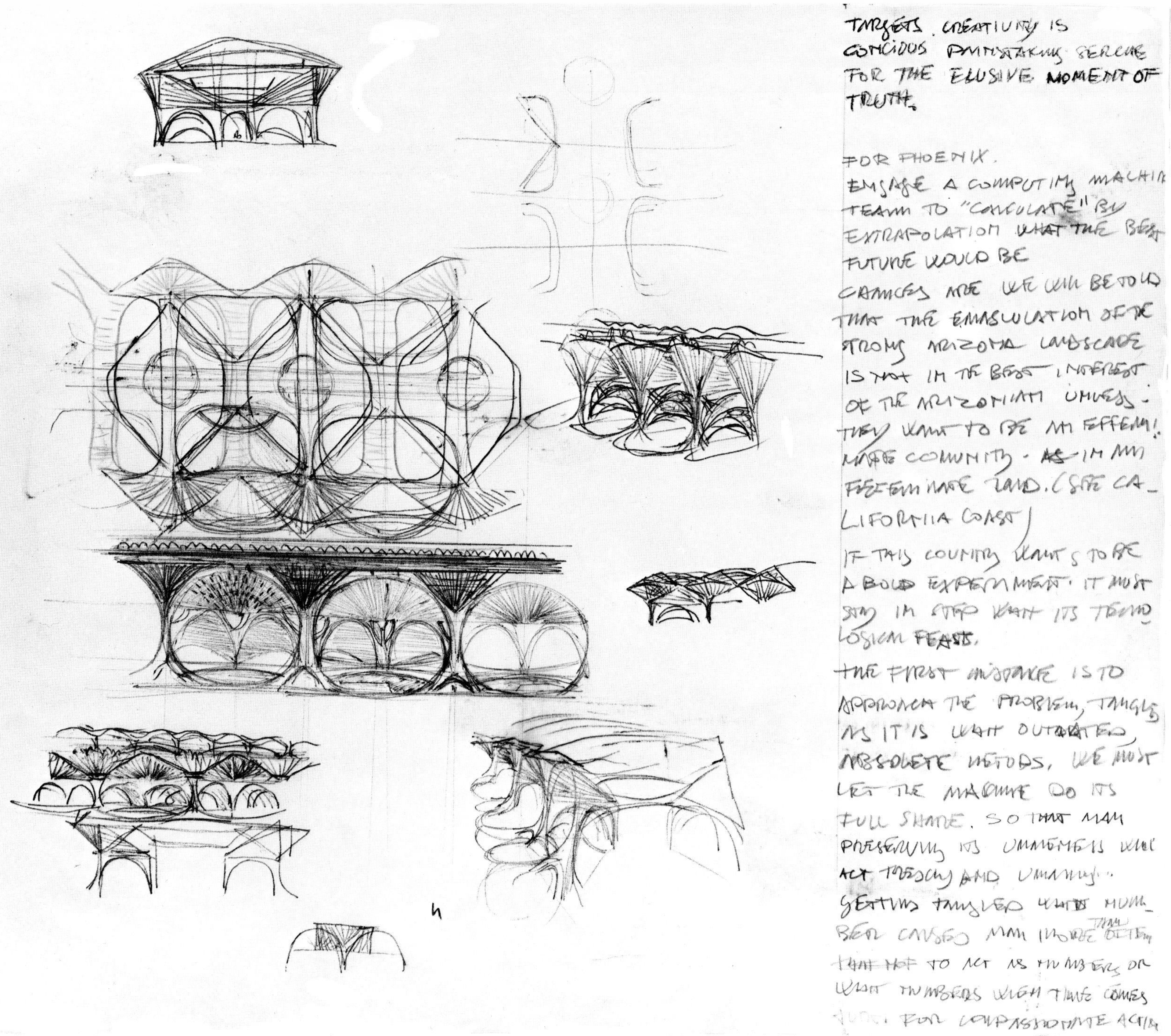
TARGETS. CREATIVITY IS
CONSCIOUS PAINSTAKING SEARCH
FOR THE ELUSIVE MOMENT OF
TRUTH.
FOR PHOENIX.
ENGAGE A COMPUTING MACHIN
TEAM TO "CALCULATE" BY
EXTRAPOLATION WHAT THE BEST
FUTURE WOULD BE
CHANCES ARE WE WILL BE TOLD
THAT THE EMASCULATION OF THE
STRONG ARIZONA LANDSCAPE
IS NOT IN THE BEST INTEREST
OF THE ARIZONIAN UNLESS -
THEY WANT TO BE AN EFFEMI-
NATE COMMUNITY - IN AN
EFFEMINATE LAND. (SEE CA-
LIFORNIA COAST)
IF THIS COUNTRY WANTS TO BE
A BOLD EXPERIMENT IT MUST
STAY IN STEP WITH ITS TECHNO-
LOGICAL FEATS.
THE FIRST INSTANCE IS TO
APPROACH THE PROBLEM, TANGLED
AS IT IS WITH OUTDATED,
OBSOLETE METHODS, WE MUST
LET THE MACHINE DO ITS
FULL SHARE. SO THAT MAN
GETTING TANGLED WITH NUM-
BER CAUSED MAN MORE THAN OFTEN
TO ACT AS NUMBERS OR
WITH NUMBERS WHEN TIME COMES
FOR COMPASSIONATE ACTION

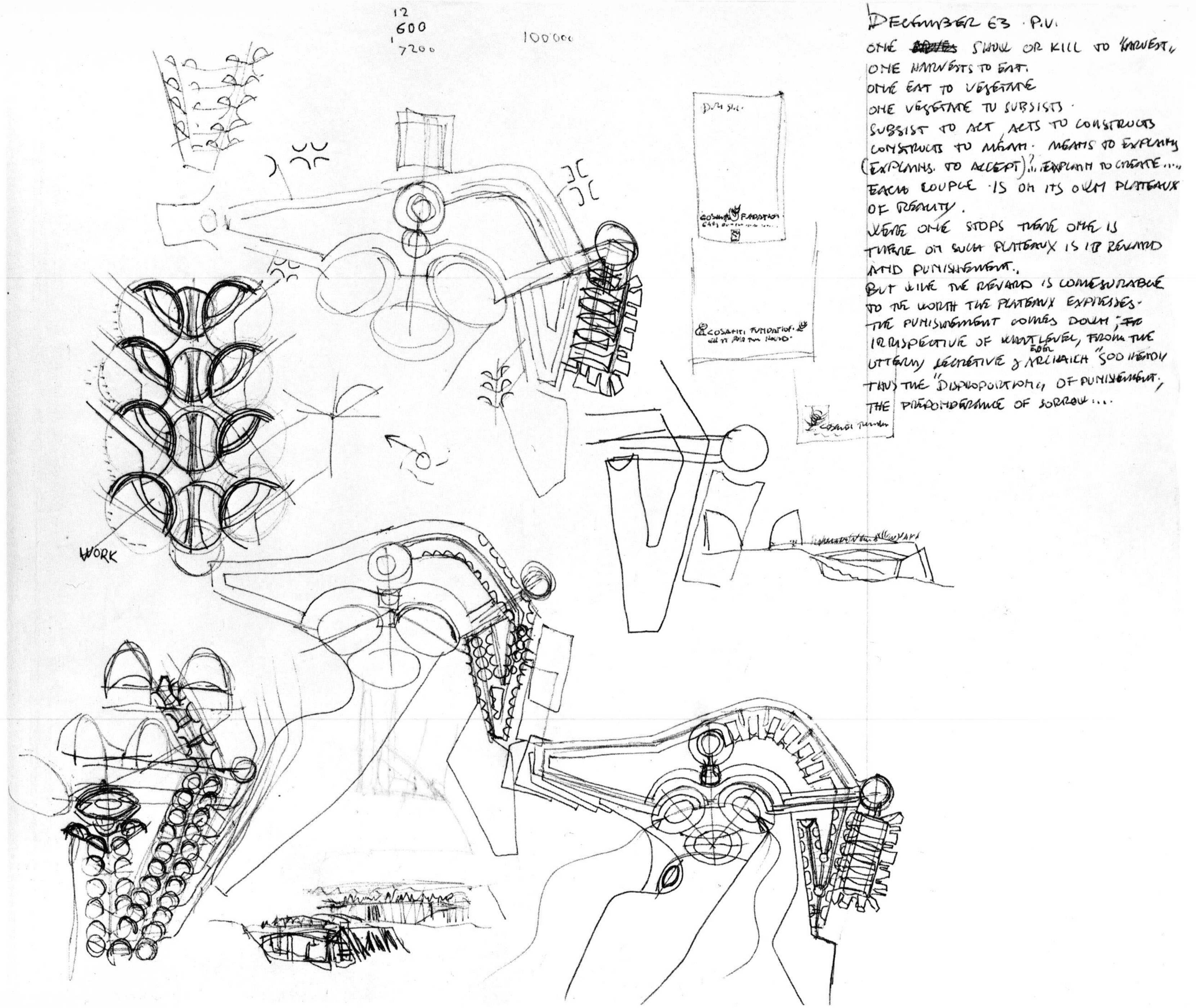
12
600
7200
100'000
DECEMBER 63 · P.V.
ONE SHOW OR KILL TO KARVEST,
ONE HARVESTS TO EAT.
ONE EAT TO VEGETATE
ONE VEGETATE TO SUBSISTS ·
SUBSIST TO ACT, ACTS TO CONSTRUCTS
CONSTRUCTS TO MEAN · MEANS TO EXPLAINS
(EXPLAINS TO ACCEPT)? EXPLAIN TO CREATE ....
EACH COUPLE IS ON ITS OWN PLATEAUX
OF REALITY.
WERE ONE STOPS THERE ONE IS
THERE ON SUCH PLATEAUX IS ITS REWARD
AND PUNISHMENT.
BUT WHILE THE REWARD IS COMMENSURABLE
TO THE WORTH THE PLATEAUX EXPRESSES·
THE PUNISHMENT COMES DOWN;
IRRISPECTIVE OF WHAT LEVEL, FROM THE
UTTERLY SECRETIVE & ARCHAICH "SOD HEMOV"
THUS THE "DISPROPORTIONALITY" OF PUNISHMENT,
THE PREPONDERANCE OF SORROW...
WORK

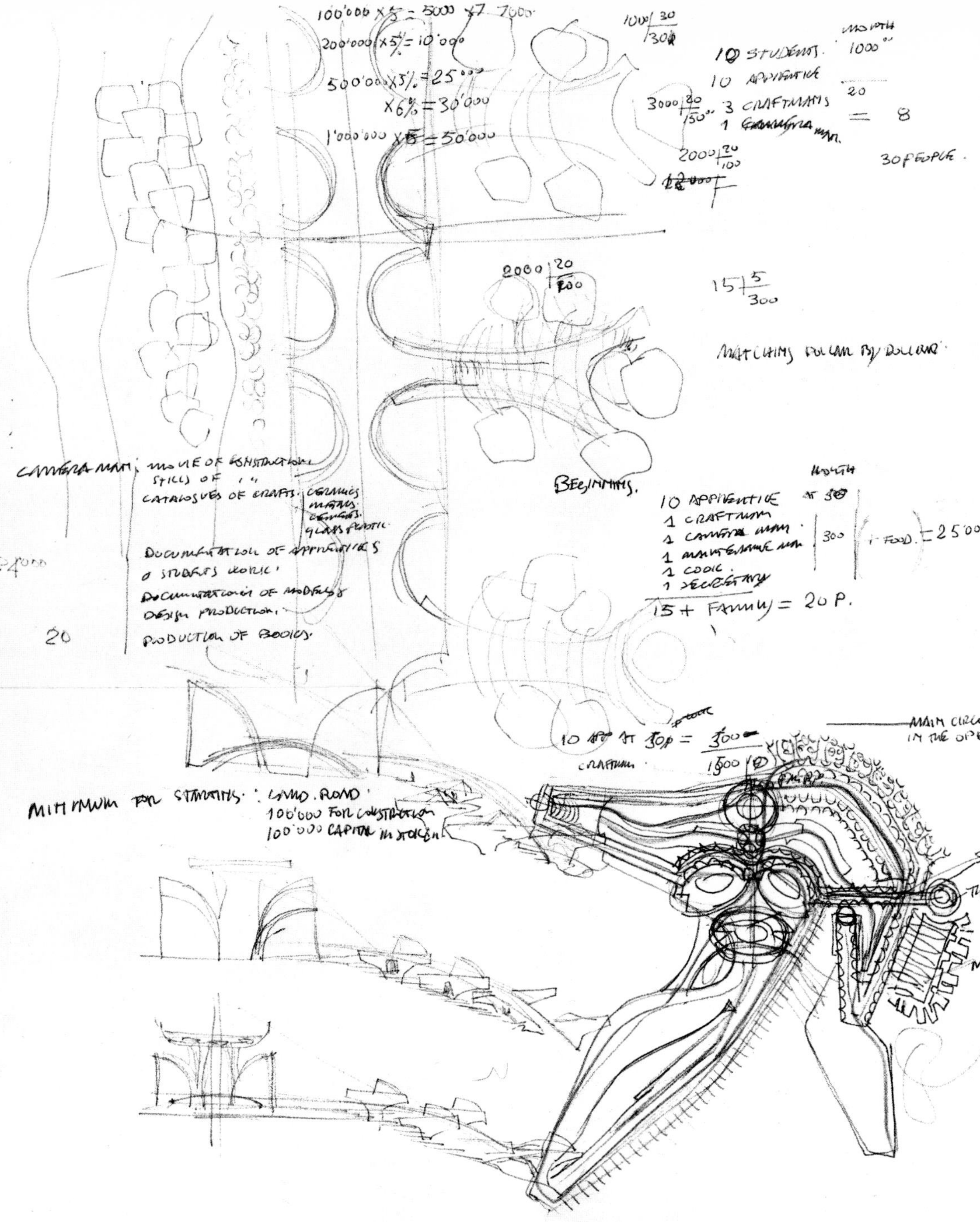

DECEMBER 63 P.V.
SPOON
TYPEWRIGHTER
RINS.

DECEMBER 63

FATE IS THE STATISTICAL STRUCTURE OF MATTER.

AS A MATERIAL BODY ANY LIVING THING IS TIGHTLY MOVED BY FATE

ANY LIVING THING IS A BATTLEGROUND BETWINS. FATE, THE STATISTICAL STRUCTURE OF MATERIALITY, AND THE WILL TOWARD CONCIOUSNESS

CONCIOUSNESS IS THE COUNTERWISE MOVEMENT AGAINST FATE SET UP IN MATERIALITY BY THE BIOLOGICAL FENOMENON

THE DEGREE OF LIVELINESS IS THE DEGREE BY WHICH CONCIOUSNESS DEFEATS THE PURPOSLESNESS OF FATE.

LIFE IS PURPOSEFULNESS
FATE IS MEANINGLESSNESS, THE RANDOM RATIONALITY OF STATISTIC

GOD IS A PROJECTION THAT CONCIOUSNESS MAKES OF ITS PURPOSEFULNESS ON THE COSMIC VASTNESS OF FATE MATERIALIZED INTO MATTER.

FATE IS REALITY DEPRIVED OF THE LIFE FENOMENON

BUT CONCIOUSNESS CAN SUSTAIN ITS QWEST ONLY IF STANDING ON THE PLATFORM THAT ONLY FATE - MATERIALITY CAN FOURNISH

THIS MY BE WHY "STRUCTURE" IS THE INDISPENSABLE NECESSITY FOR CONCIOUSNESS

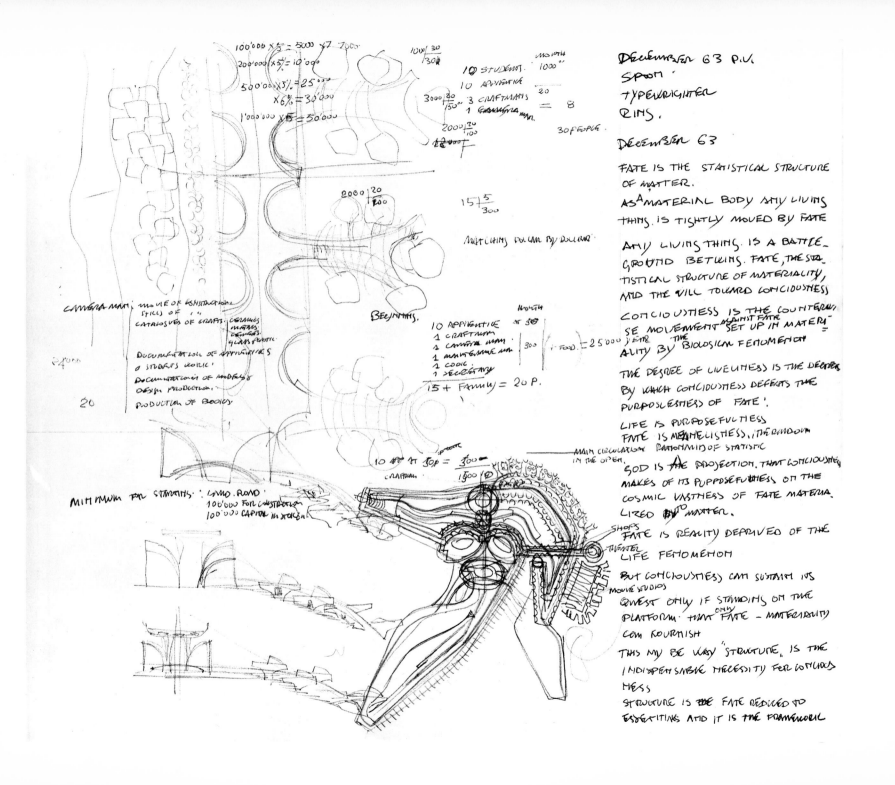

STRUCTURE IS FATE REDUCED TO ESSENTIALS AND IT IS THE FRAMEWORK

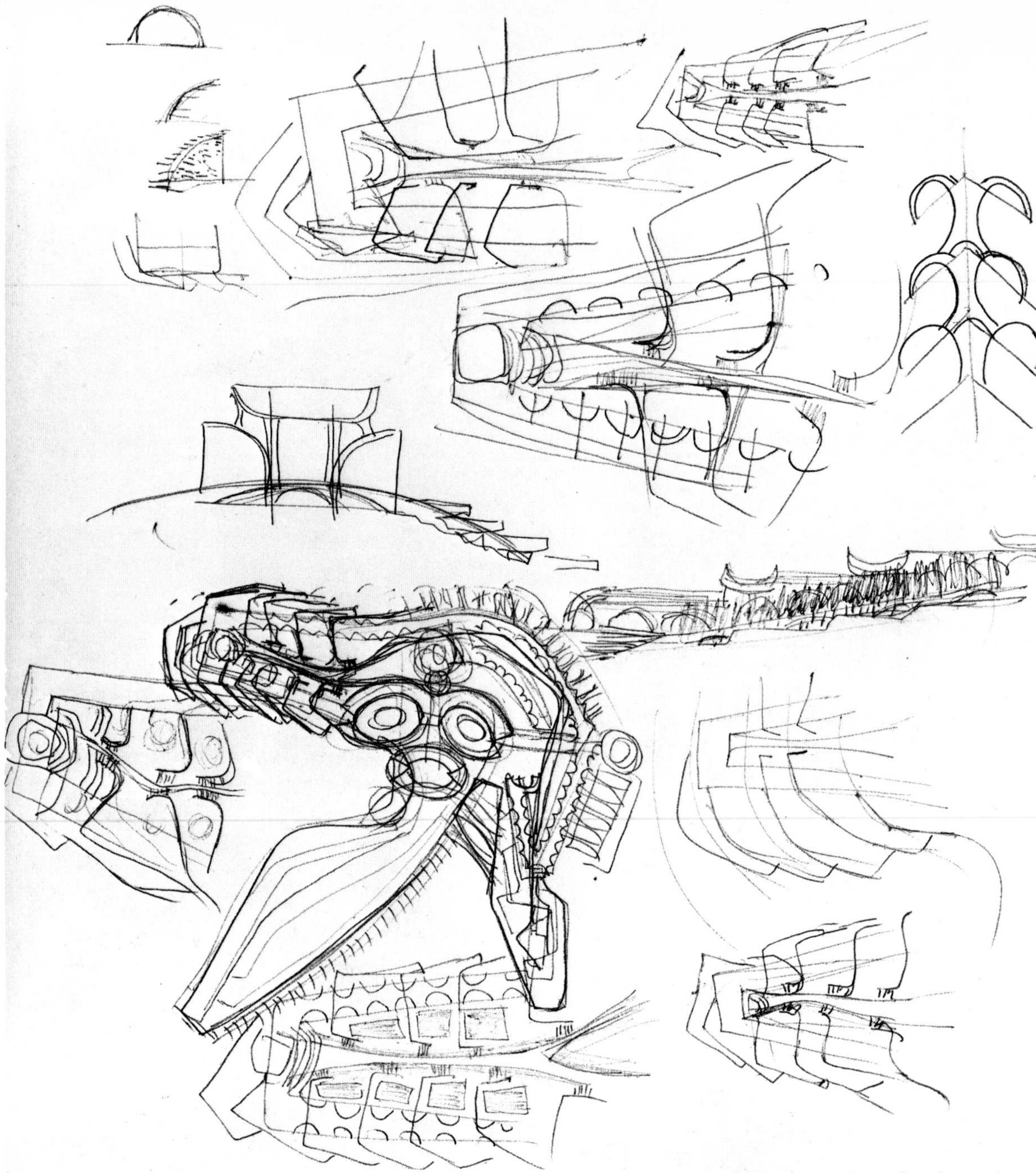

NEEDED BY CONCIOUSNESS TO168
PURSUE ITS QUEST
IN THE DOWN FALL (ENTROPY) OF FATE THE VOICE, WITH, OF STRUCTURE IS THE MUSIC AMONG SOUNDS SOUGHT BY CONCIOUSNESS STEP BY STEP SO AS TO BULID THE LADDER OF THE CREATIVE & THE COMPASSIONATE

TO PUT SENSE TO ONE'S ACTIONS ONE MUST RECEDE & REACH FOR THE SECOND "CAUSE) LA "CAUSA SECONDA"
LA CAUSA SECONDA WHATEVER MAY BE THE CAUSA PRIMA, MAY READS:
FATE IS THE STATISTICAL CONDITION OF MATTER

FATE WILL STOP ANY MAN AT ANY MOMENT.
BUT "THAT" MAN WILL BE FOUND THERE BY FATE NOT PUT THERE BY IT
THE TRUTH OF THIS IS CARRIED INSTANT BY INSTANT BY THE WILL INTERVENING ON THE GIVEN TO MODIFIE IT (IN ITS OWN IMMAGE)

GENUARY 64

WHEN MEN ARE INTERCHANGEABLE THEY ARE NO MORE INDISPENSABLE THUS THEIR LONELINESS
THE CITY POPULATED BY LONELY CREATURE IS ONLY A PHISICAL PHENOMENON. THERE IS CONTIGUITY WITHOUT RECIPROCITY THAT IS NO ONE, NOR THING, ENGROSSES IN THE WARMTH OF THE OTHER, PHISICAL DISTANCES MAY BE MEASURED IN FOOTS OR INCES BUT EVERY CREATURE IS A DESPERATE SELF GROOPING IN A UNFRIENDLY DESERT.
THE CITY MUST BE BORN IN THE "COLLECTIVE" SOUL TO GROWTH ON

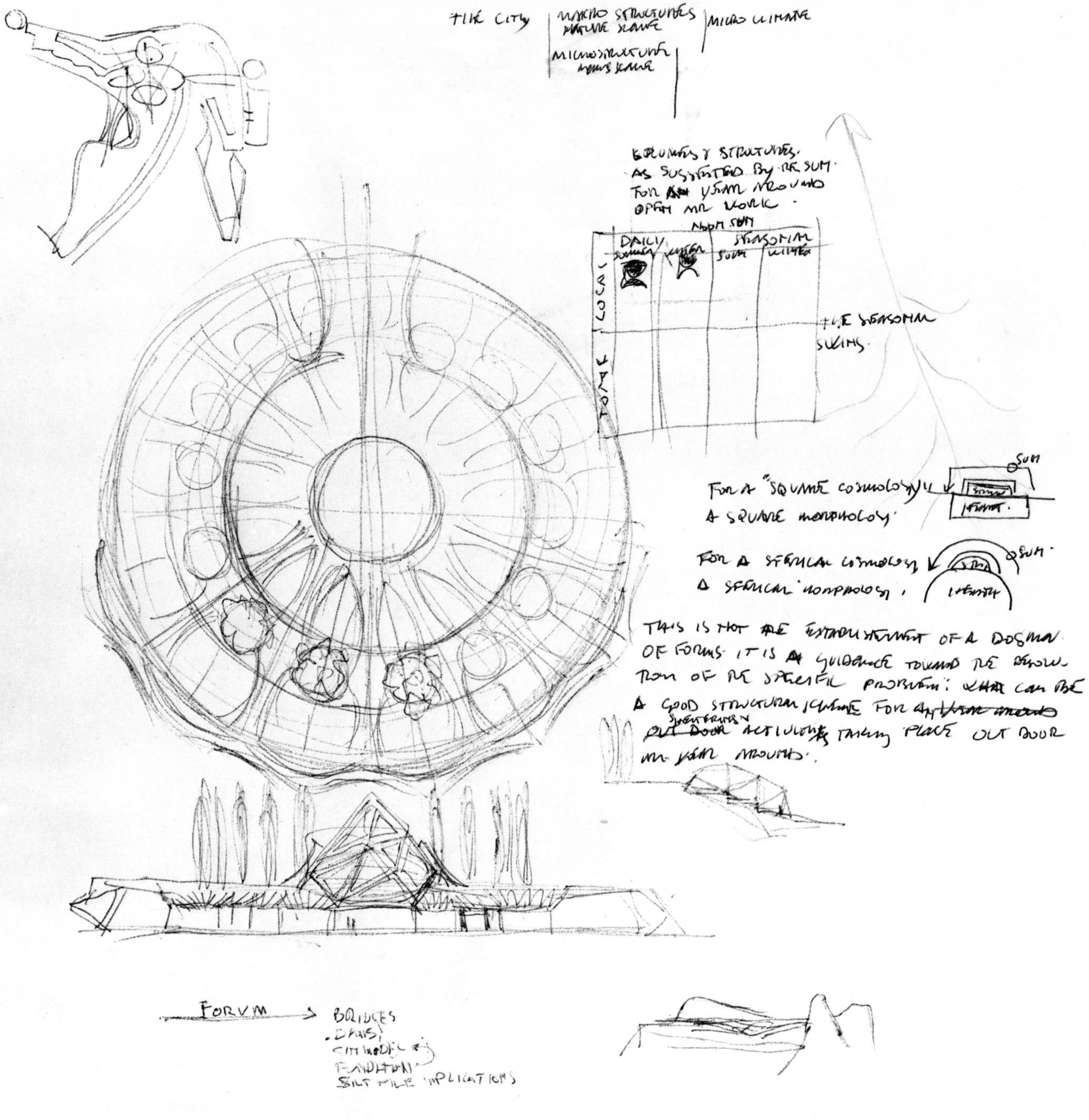
THE CITY
MACRO STRUCTURES
NATURE SCALE
MICRO CLIMATE
MICROSTRUCTURE
MANS SCALE
VOLUMES & STRUCTURES
AS SUGGESTED BY THE SUN
FOR ALL YEAR AROUND
OPEN AIR WORK.
NOON SUN
DAILY
SEASONAL
SUMMER
WINTER
SUMMER
WINTER
LOCAL
THE SEASONAL
SWINGS.
SUN
FOR A "SQUARE COSMOLOGY"
A SQUARE MORPHOLOGY.
FOR A SPHERICAL COSMOLOGY
A SPHERICAL MORPHOLOGY.
SUN.
THIS IS NOT THE ESTABLISHMENT OF A DOGMA
OF FORMS. IT IS A GUIDANCE TOWARD THE RESOLU-
TION OF THE SPECIFIC PROBLEM: WHAT CAN BE
A GOOD STRUCTURAL SCHEME FOR
ACTIVITIES TAKING PLACE OUT DOOR
ALL YEAR AROUND.
FORUM
BRIDGES
DAMS
SILT FILL IMPLICATIONS

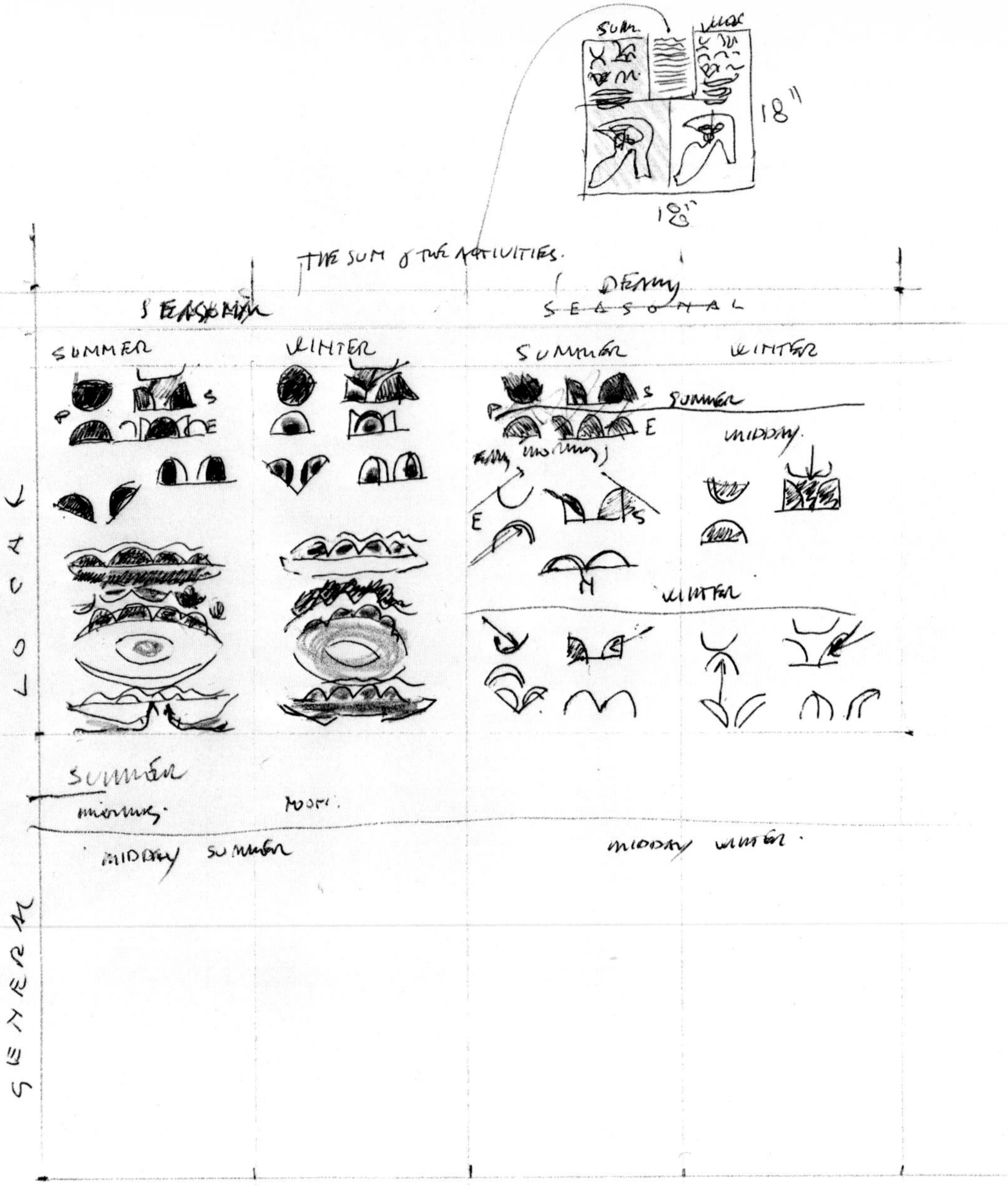
THE SUM OF THE ACTIVITIES.
SEASONAL
SUMMER
WINTER
SUMMER
WINTER
LOCAL
GENERAL
MIDDAY SUMMER
MIDDAY WINTER
18"
18"

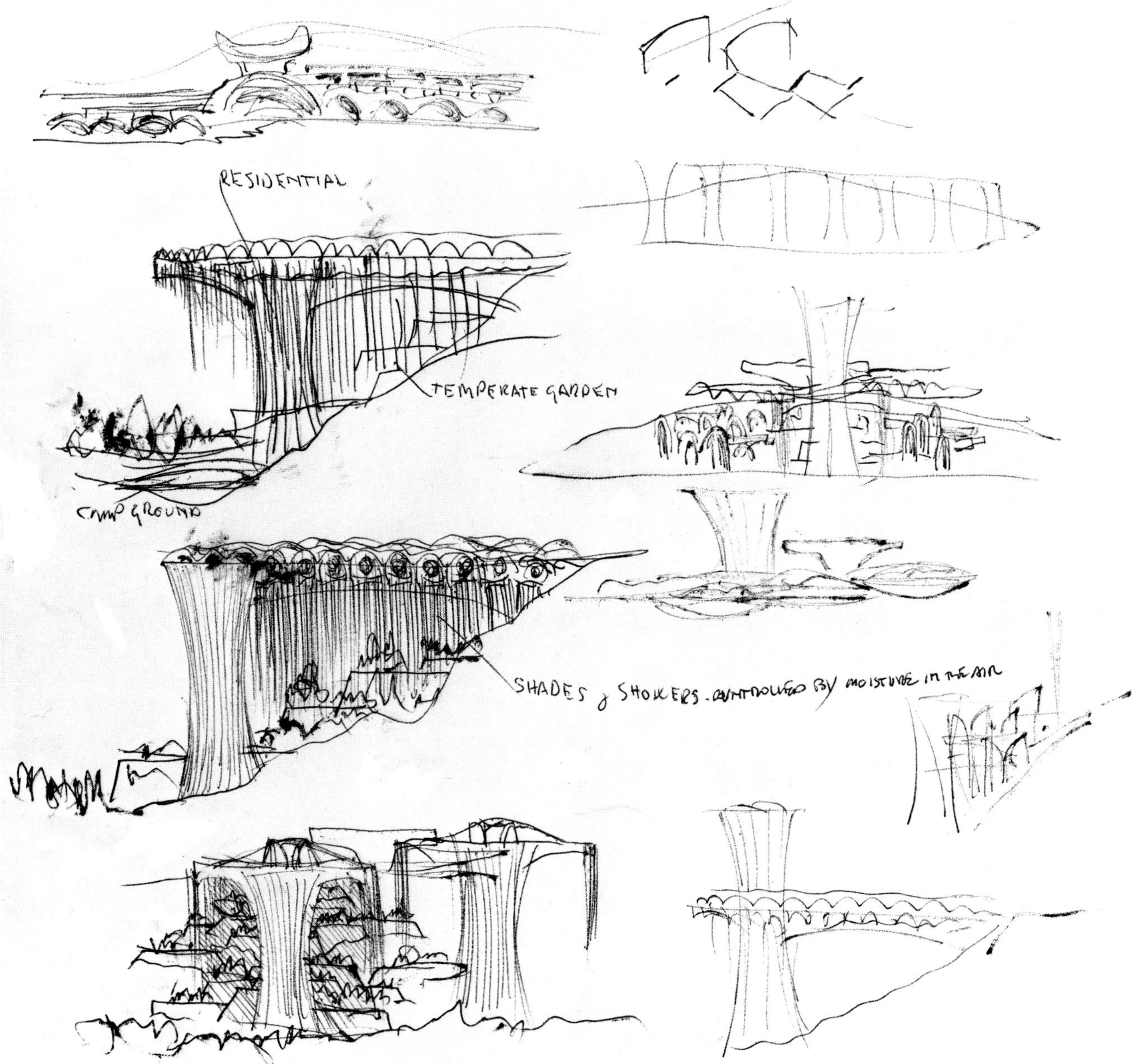
RESIDENTIAL
TEMPERATE GARDEN
CAMP GROUND
SHADES & SHOWERS - CONTROLLED BY MOISTURE IN THE AIR

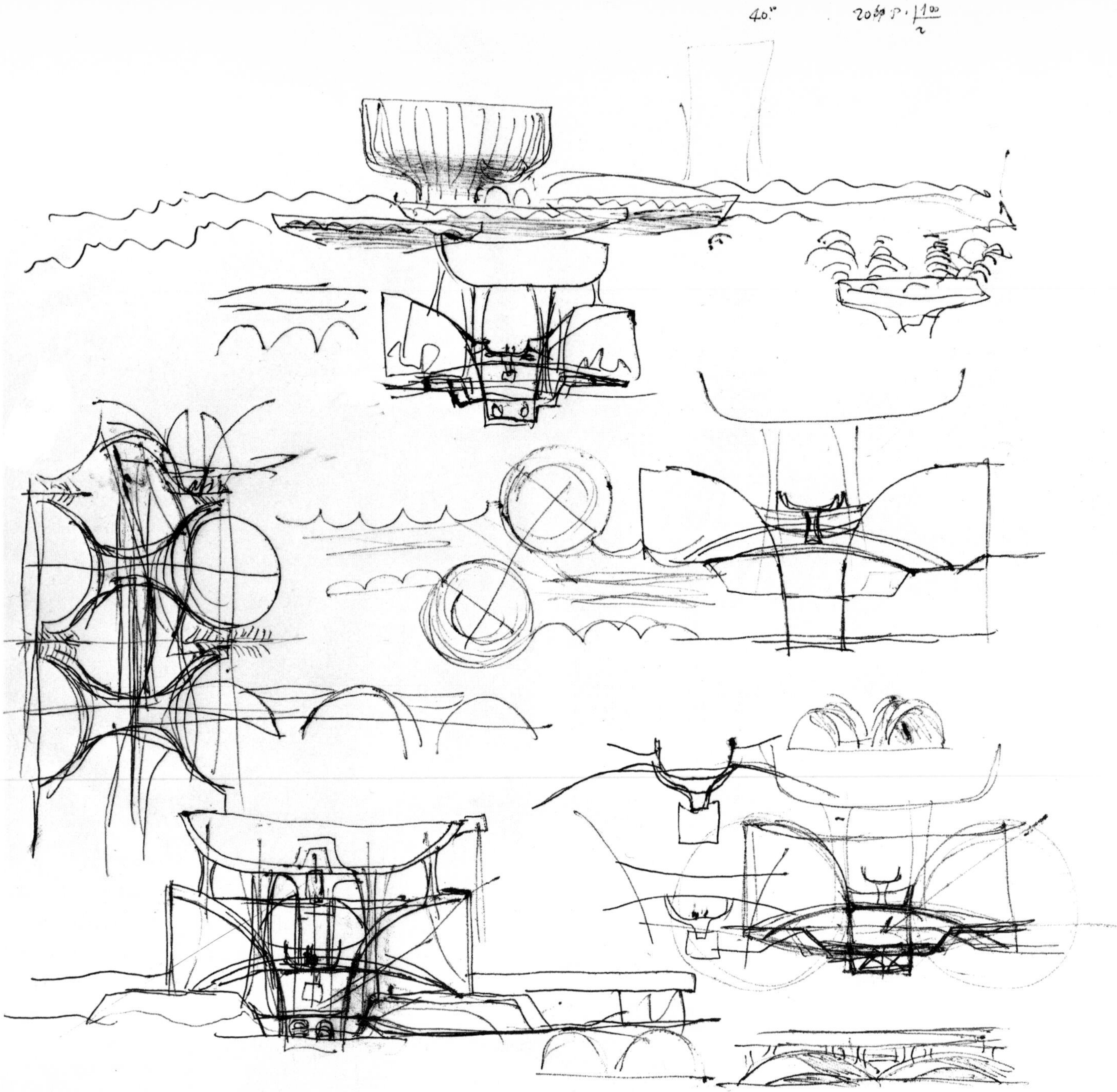

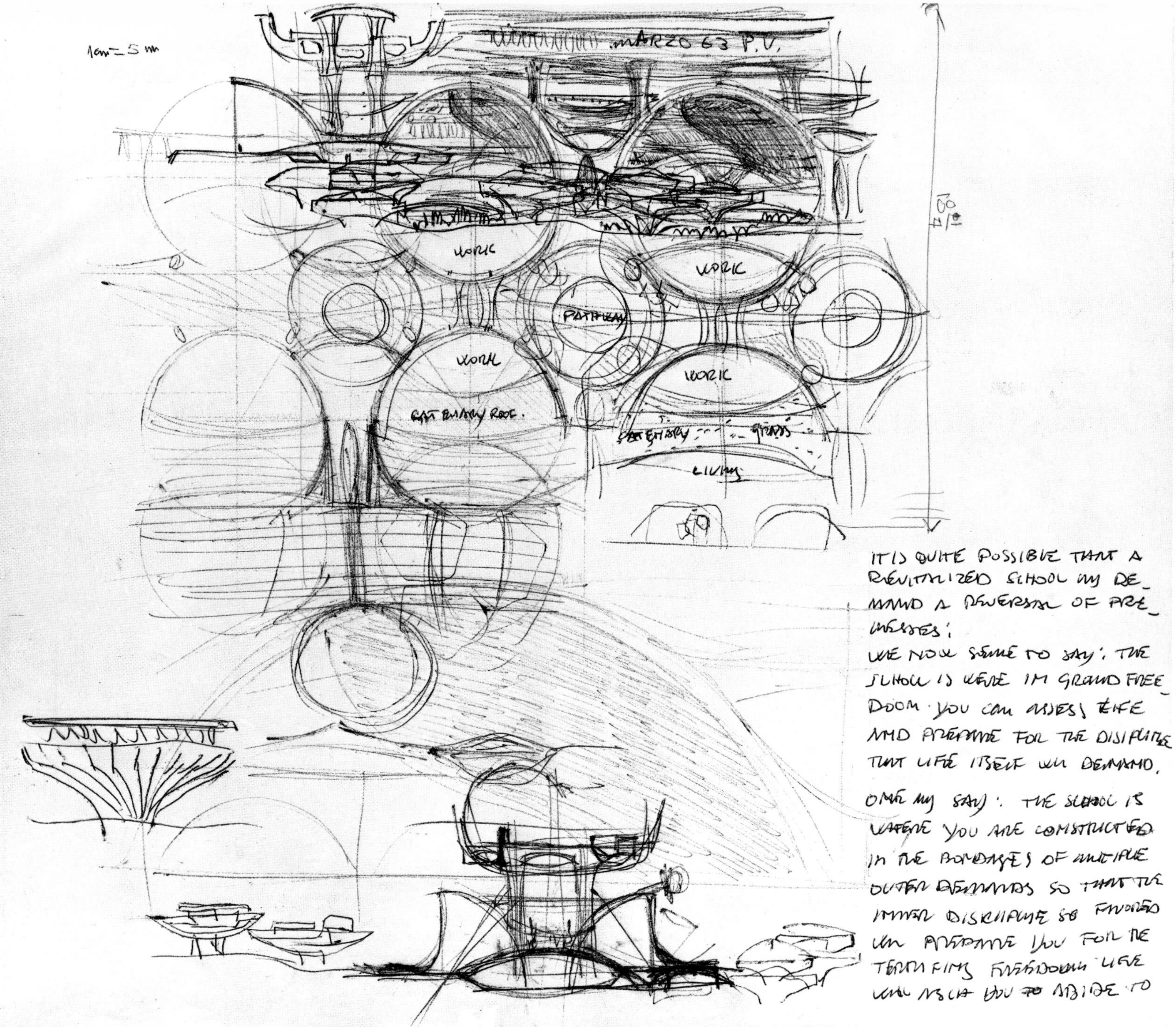
1cm = 5 m
MARZO 63 P.V.
WORK
WORK
PATHWAY
WORK
WORK
CATENARY ROOF.
CATENARY
LIVING
IT IS QUITE POSSIBLE THAT A
REVITALIZED SCHOOL MAY DE_
MAND A REVERSAL OF PRE_
MISES;
WE NOW SEEM TO SAY: THE
SCHOOL IS WHERE IN GRAND FREE_
DOOM YOU CAN ASSESS LIFE
AND PREPARE FOR THE DISCIPLINE
THAT LIFE ITSELF WILL DEMAND.
ONE MAY SAY: THE SCHOOL IS
WHERE YOU ARE CONSTRICTED
IN THE BONDAGES OF MULTIPLE
OUTER DEMANDS SO THAT THE
INNER DISCIPLINE SO FAVORED
WILL PREPARE YOU FOR THE
TERRIFYING FREEDOM LIFE
WILL ASK YOU TO ABIDE TO

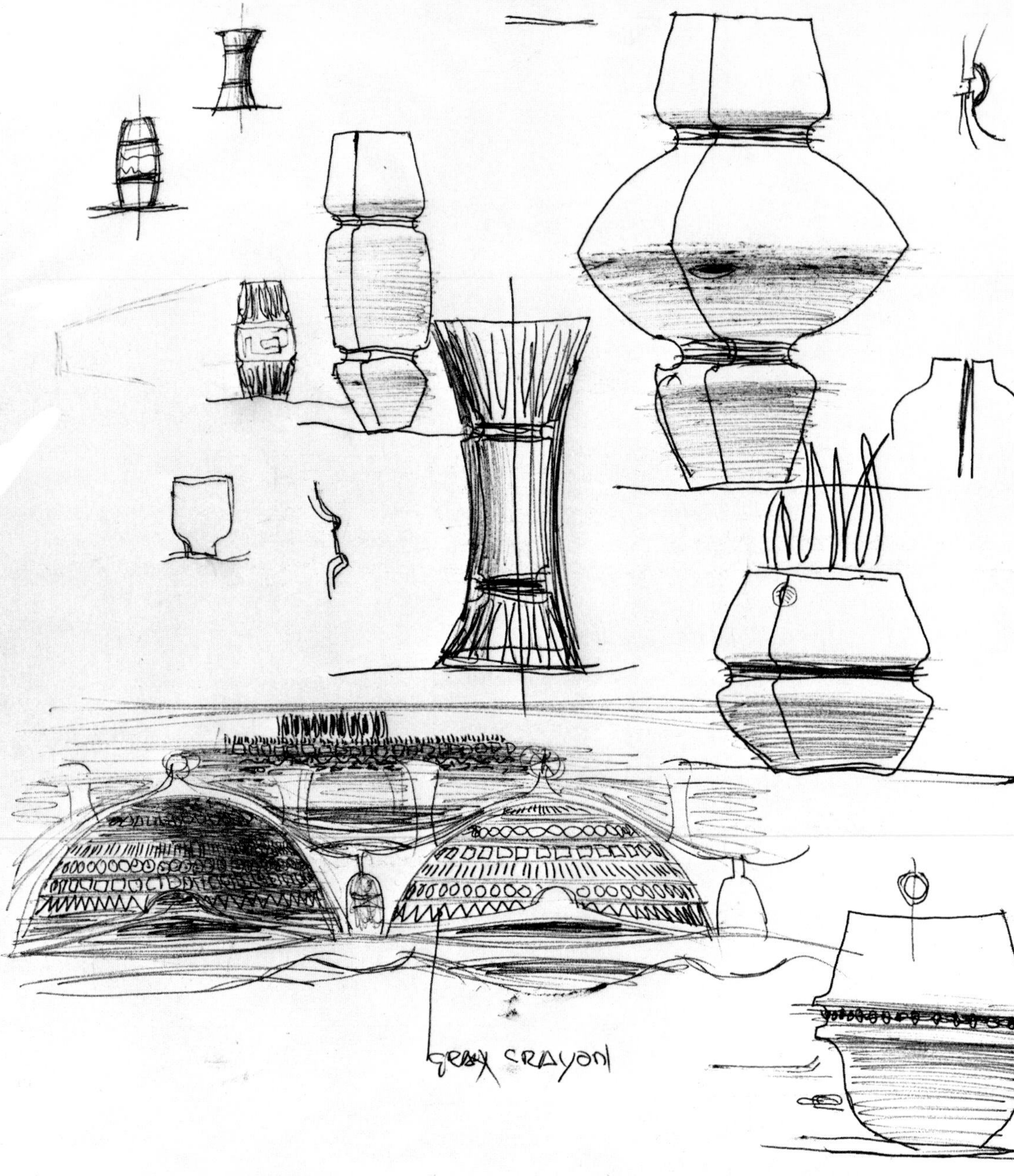

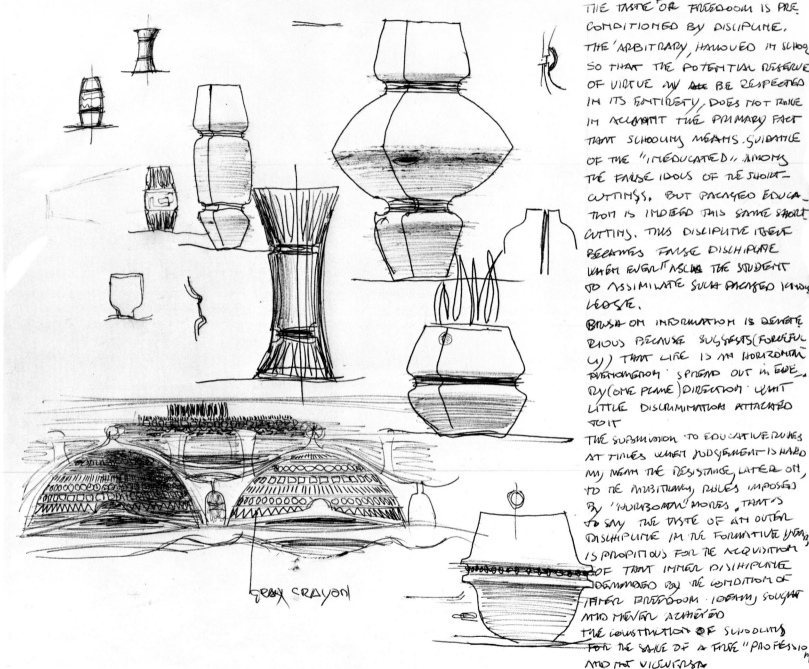

THE TASTE FOR FREEDOOM IS PRE-
CONDITIONED BY DISCIPLINE.
THE 'ARBITRARY', HALLOWED IN SCHOOL
SO THAT THE POTENTIAL RESERVE
OF VIRTUE MAY BE RESPECTED
IN ITS ENTIRETY, DOES NOT TAKE
IN ACCOUNT THE PRIMARY FACT
THAT SCHOOLING MEANS GUIDANCE
OF THE "INEDUCATED" AMONG
THE FALSE IDOLS OF THE SHORT-
CUTTINGS. BUT PACKAGED EDUCA-
TION IS INDEED THIS SAME SHORT-
CUTTING. THUS DISCIPLINE ITSELF
BECOMES FALSE DISCIPLINE
WHENEVER "INSIST" THE STUDENT
TO ASSIMILATE SUCH PACKAGED KNOW-
LEDGE.
BRUSH ON INFORMATION IS DELETE-
RIOUS BECAUSE SUGGESTS (FORCEFUL-
LY) THAT LIFE IS AN HORIZONTAL
PHENOMENON SPREAD OUT IN EVE-
RY (ONE PLANE) DIRECTION WITH
LITTLE DISCRIMINATION ATTACHED
TO IT
THE SUBMISSION TO EDUCATIVE RULES
AT TIMES WHEN JUDGEMENT IS HARD-
LY MEAN THE RESISTANCE, LATER ON,
TO THE ARBITRARY RULES IMPOSED
BY "HORIZONTAL" MORES, THAT IS
TO SAY THE TASTE OF AN OUTER
DISCIPLINE IN THE FORMATIVE YEARS,
IS PROPITIOUS FOR THE ACQUISITION
OF THAT INNER DISCIPLINE
DEMANDED BY THE CONDITION OF
INNER FREEDOOM IDEALLY SOUGHT
AND NEVER ACHIEVED
THE CONSTRUCTION OF SCHOOLING
FOR THE SAKE OF A TRUE "PROFESSION"
AND NOT VICEVERSA

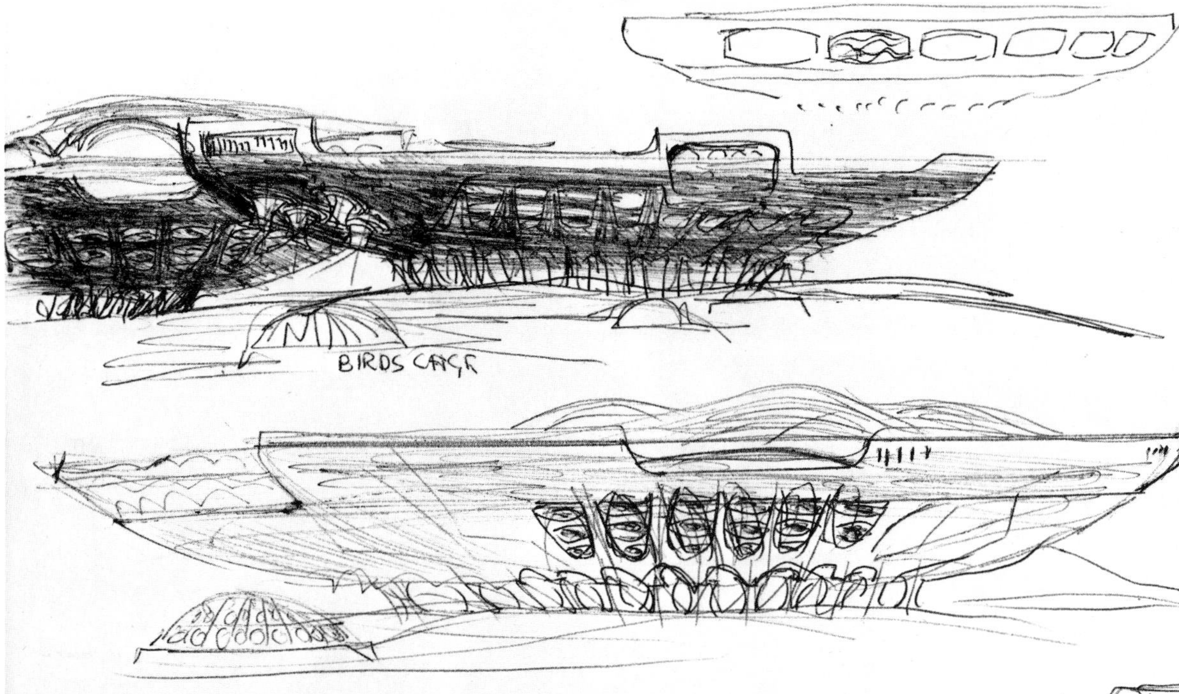

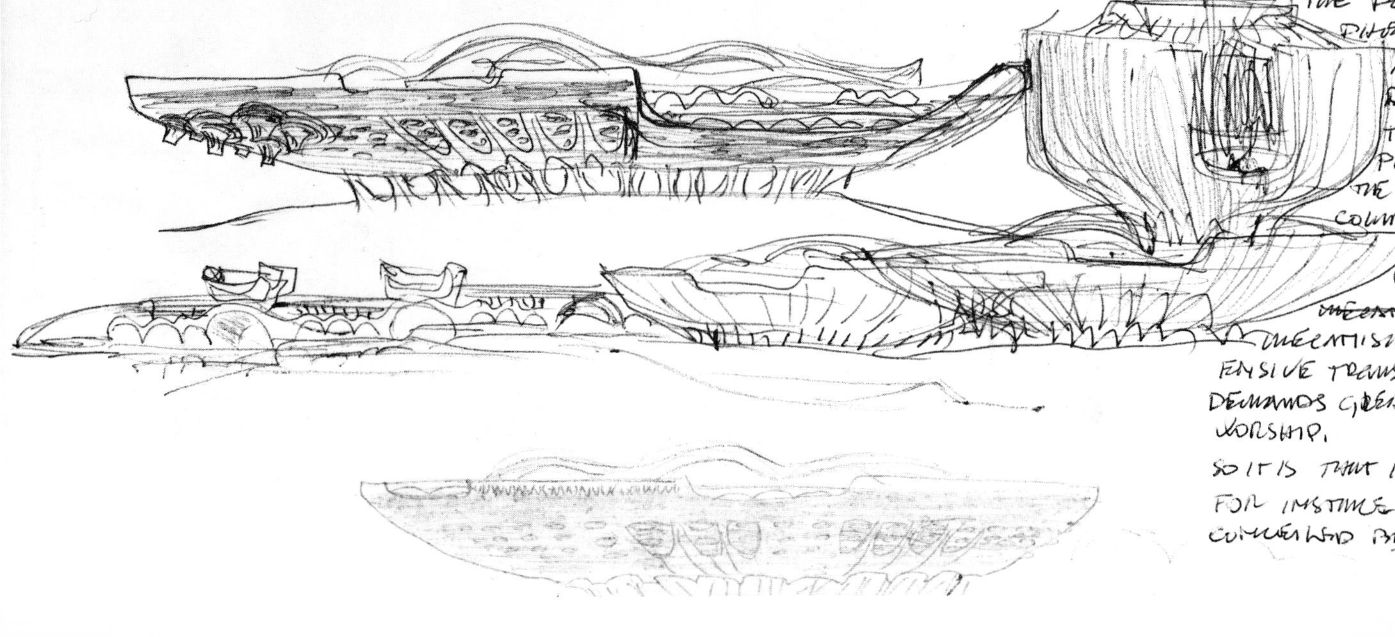

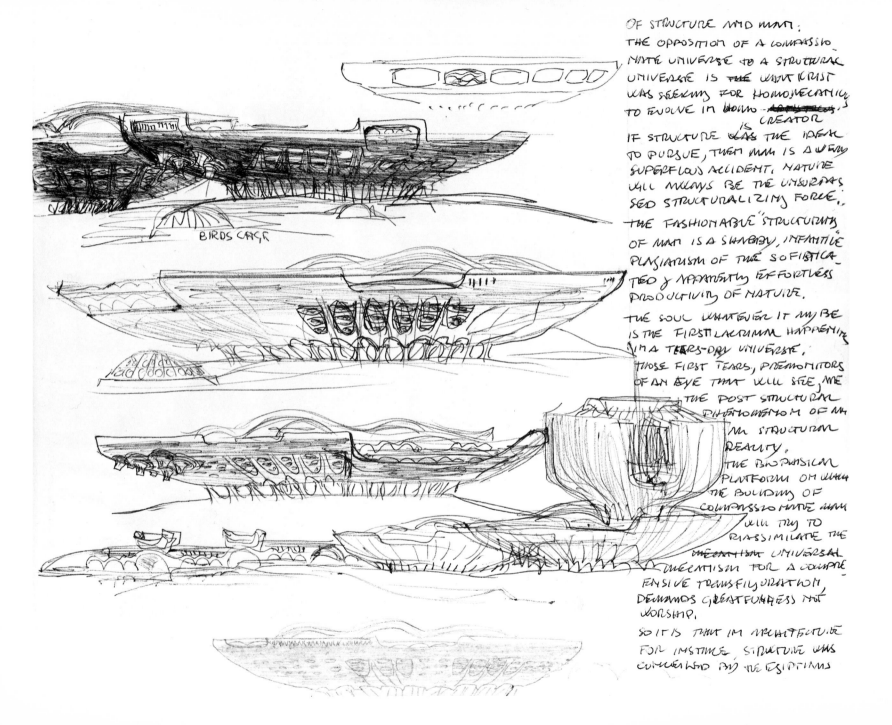

OF STRUCTURE AND MAN:
THE OPPOSITION OF A COMPASSIO-
NATE UNIVERSE TO A STRUCTURAL
UNIVERSE IS ~~THE~~ WHAT KRIST
WAS SEEKING FOR HOMO MECANICUS
TO EVOLVE IN HOMO-[illegible]: CREATOR
IF STRUCTURE ~~WAS~~ IS THE IDEAL
TO PURSUE, THEN MAN IS A VERY
SUPERFLOUS ACCIDENT, NATURE
WILL ALWAYS BE THE UNSURPAS-
SED STRUCTURALIZING FORCE.
THE FASHIONABLE "STRUCTURING"
OF MAN IS A SHABBY, INFANTILE
PLAGIARISM OF THE SOFISTICA-
TED & APPARENTLY EFFORTLESS
PRODUCTIVITY OF NATURE.
THE SOUL WHATEVER IT MAY BE
IS THE FIRST LACRIMAL HAPPENING
IN A TEARS-DRY UNIVERSE.
THOSE FIRST TEARS, PREMONITORS
OF AN EYE THAT WILL SEE, ARE
THE POST STRUCTURAL
PHENOMENON OF AN
AN STRUCTURAL
REALITY.
THE BIOPHYSICAL
PLATFORM ON WHICH
THE BUILDING OF
COMPASSIONATE MAN
WILL TRY TO
RIASSIMILATE THE
~~MECANISM~~ UNIVERSAL
MECANISM FOR A COMPRE-
ENSIVE TRANSFIGURATION,
DEMANDS GREATFULNESS NOT
WORSHIP.
SO IT IS THAT IN ARCHITECTURE
FOR INSTANCE, STRUCTURE WAS
CONCEIVED BY THE EGIPTIANS

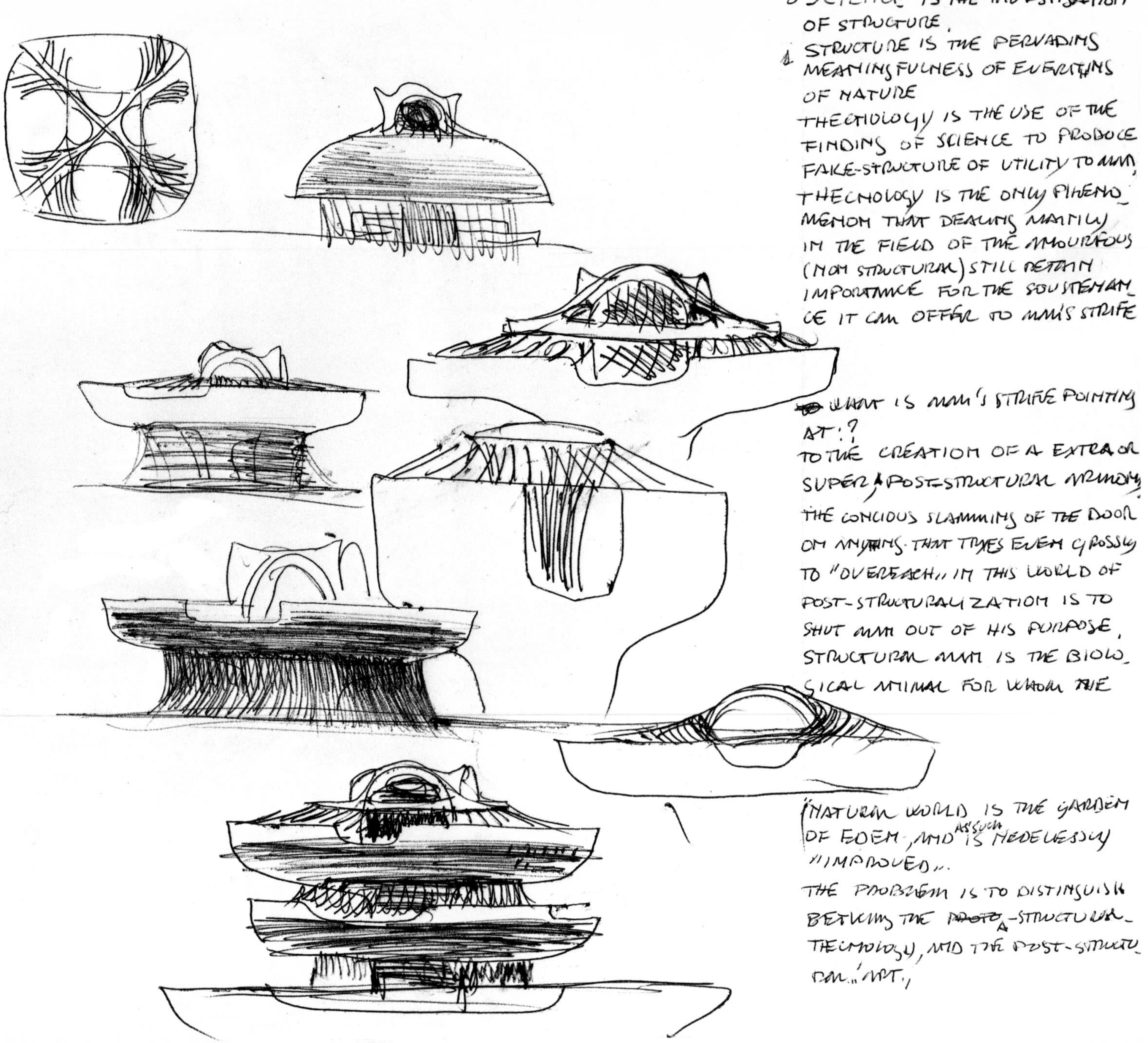
2 SCIENCE IS THE INVESTIGATION OF STRUCTURE.
1 STRUCTURE IS THE PERVADING MEANINGFULNESS OF EVERYTHING OF NATURE
THECHNOLOGY IS THE USE OF THE FINDING OF SCIENCE TO PRODUCE FAKE-STRUCTURE OF UTILITY TO MAN,
THECNOLOGY IS THE ONLY PHENO_MENON THAT DEALING MAINLY IN THE FIELD OF THE AMOURFOUS (NON STRUCTURAL) STILL RETAIN IMPORTANCE FOR THE SOUSTENAN_CE IT CAN OFFER TO MAN'S STRIFE
WHAT IS MAN'S STRIFE POINTING AT:?
TO THE CREATION OF A EXTRA OR SUPER, POST-STRUCTURAL ARMONY,
THE CONCIOUS SLAMMING OF THE DOOR ON ANYTHING THAT TRYES EVEN GROSSLY TO "OVEREACH" IN THIS WORLD OF POST-STRUCTURALIZATION IS TO SHUT MAN OUT OF HIS PURPOSE,
STRUCTURAL MAN IS THE BIOLO_GICAL ANIMAL FOR WHOM THE
"NATURAL WORLD IS THE GARDEN OF EDEN, AND AS SUCH IS NEEDLESSLY "IMPROVED".
THE PROBLEM IS TO DISTINGUISH BETWEEN THE PROTO A-STRUCTURAL THECNOLOGY, AND THE POST-STRUCTU_RAL "ART"

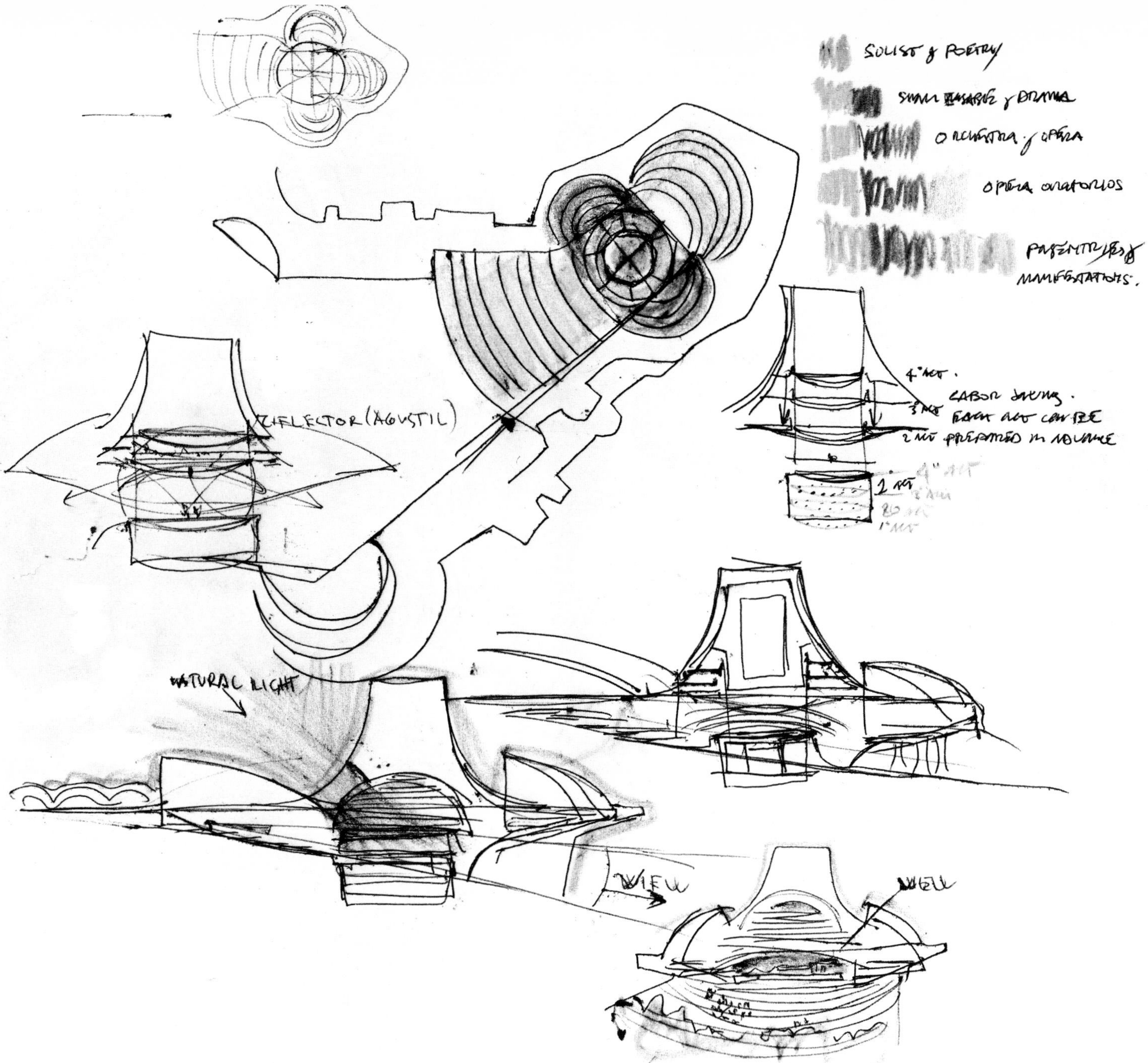
SOLIST y POETRY
SMALL ENSABLE y DRAMA
ORCHESTRA y OPERA
OPERA ORATORIOS
PAGEANTRIES y MANIFESTATIONS.
4° ACT.
LABOR SAVING.
3 ACT EACH ACT CAN BE
2 ACT PREPARED IN ADVANCE
1 ACT
REFLECTOR (ACOUSTIC)
NATURAL LIGHT
VIEW
VIEW

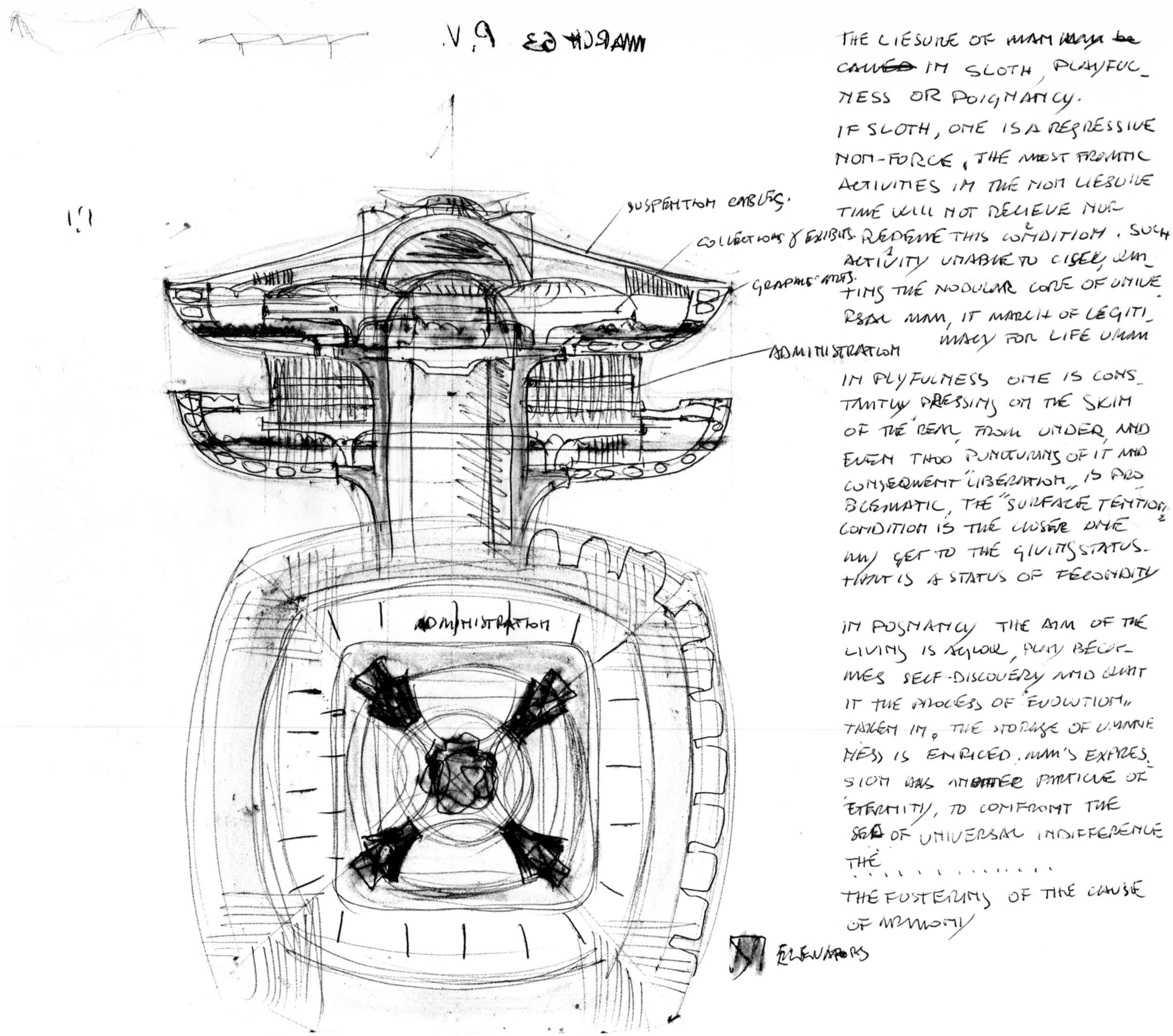
MARCH 63 P.V.
SUSPENTION CABLES.
COLLECTIONS & EXIBITS.
GRAPHIC ARTS.
ADMINISTRATION
ADMINISTRATION
ELEVATORS
THE LIESURE OF MAN may be caused IN SLOTH, PLAYFUL-
NESS OR POIGNANCY.
IF SLOTH, ONE IS A REGRESSIVE
NON-FORCE, THE MOST FRANTIC
ACTIVITIES IN THE NON LIESURE
TIME WILL NOT RELIEVE NOR
REDEEME THIS CONDITION. SUCH
ACTIVITY UNABLE TO CISEL, WAN-
TING THE NODULAR CORE OF UNIVE-
RSAL MAN, IT MARCH OF LEGITI-
MACY FOR LIFE UMAN
IN PLYFULNESS ONE IS CONS-
TANTLY PRESSING ON THE SKIN
OF THE REAL FROM UNDER, AND
EVEN THOO PUNCTURING OF IT AND
CONSEQUENT "LIBERATION" IS PRO-
BLEMATIC, THE "SURFACE TENTION"
CONDITION IS THE CLOSER ONE
MAY GET TO THE GIVING STATUS.
THAT IS A STATUS OF FECONDITY
IN POIGNANCY THE AIM OF THE
LIVING IS AGLOW, PLAY BECO-
MES SELF-DISCOVERY AND WHAT
IT THE PROCESS OF "EVOLUTION"
TAKEN IN, THE STORAGE OF UMANNE
NESS IS ENRICED. MAN'S EXPRES-
SION WAS ANOTHER PARTICLE OF
ETERNITY, TO CONFRONT THE
SEA OF UNIVERSAL INDIFFERENCE
THE . . . .
THE FOSTERING OF THE CAUSE
OF HARMONY

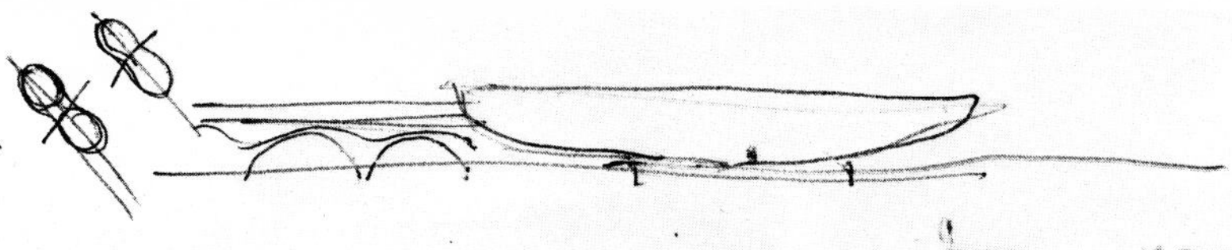

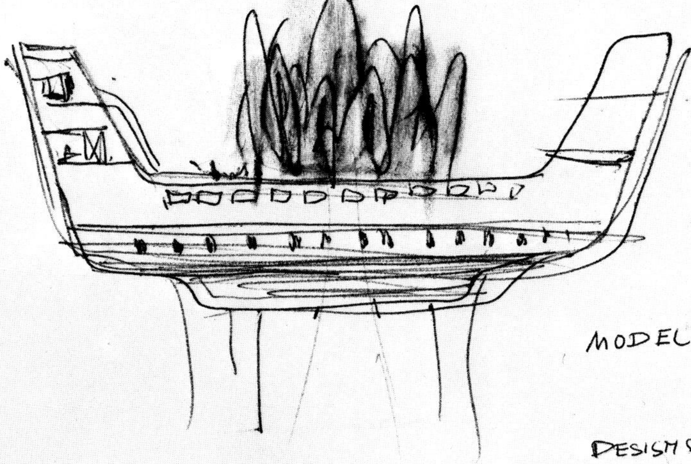

(FILL IN) SEPTEMBER 65

MAN EVOLVES BY ARCHETYPE, THE PECULIARLY VENTURESOME NATURE OF REFLECTION (CONSCIOUSNESS) PUTS IMPATIENCE AND URGENCY IN THE BLOOD-STREAM OF THE SPECIES. THUS, WHILE NATURE PATIENTLY IF BLINDLY PURSUE PERFECTION THROUGH UNENDING TIME, MAN ACHIEVES BY SKETCHES OF WHAT IS THE POSSIBLE. THE SKETCHES STAND AS ARCHETYPE OF POSSIBLE PERFECTION.

PLATO'S "IDEAS" ARE THE IDEALIZATION OF THE HASTY DEFINITION OF FAUSTIAN MAN. JOURNEYING FROM CONCEPTION TO CONCEPTION. TOO HURRIED FOR PREGNANCY AND NURSING.

HENCE THE PARTHENON THE FRUIT OF LENGTHY REFINEMENT IS STILL NOTHING BUT A SOFISTICATE ARCHETYPE OF SOMETHING NEVER TO BE CREATED. IN THIS CONTEXT IT IS (PARTHENON) THE HORSE AS IT MAY HAVE BEEN IN THE QUATERNARY ERA.

THE TREE OF EVOLUTIVE NEO-NATURE IS THUS LOOKING AS ONE OF THOSE OVER TRIMMED (?) PLANTS PLAGUED BY COUNTLESS STUBBS, STRANGELY UNBALANCED AND DISTORTED.

UNSEEN AT FIRST SIGHT ARE LOCAL SPLENDORS, THE AESTETIC QUALITY CONSIGNAL TO IT, THAT COMPASSIONATE WILL IS ABLE TO CREATE. IN SOME OF THE –

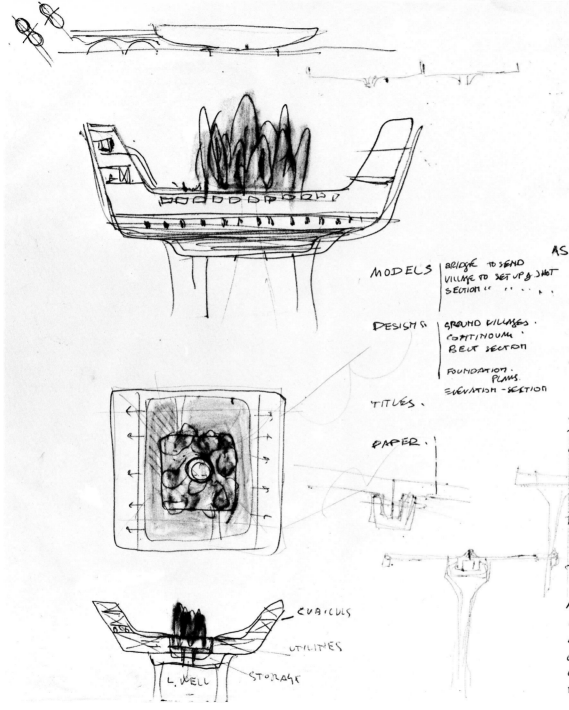

MODELS | BRIDGE TO SEND
VILLAGE TO SET UP & SHOT
SECTION " " "

DESIGNS: | GROUND VILLAGES.
CONTINUOUM.
BELT SECTION

FOUNDATION. PLANS.
ELEVATION-SECTION

TITLES.

PAPER.

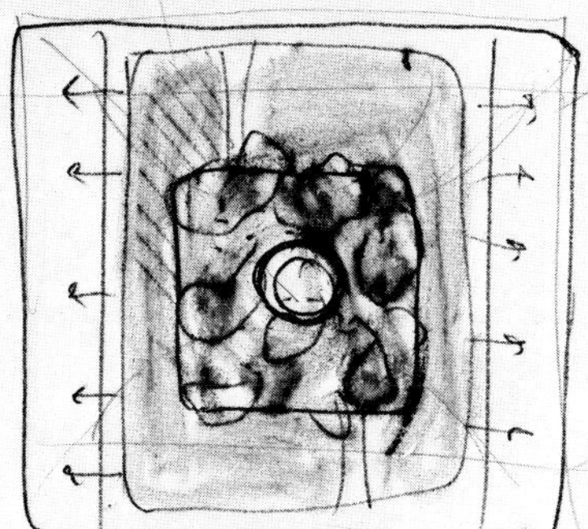

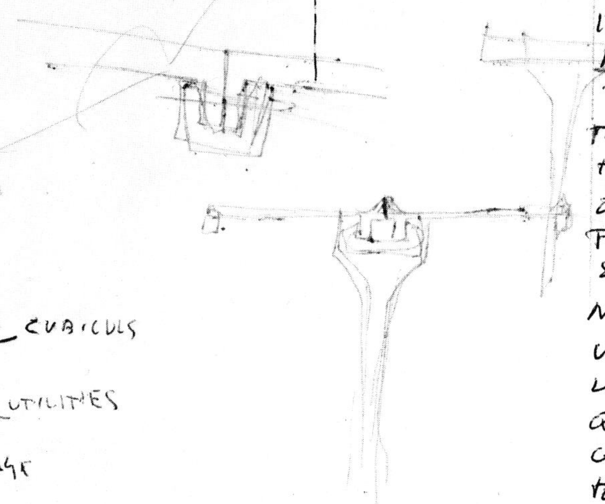

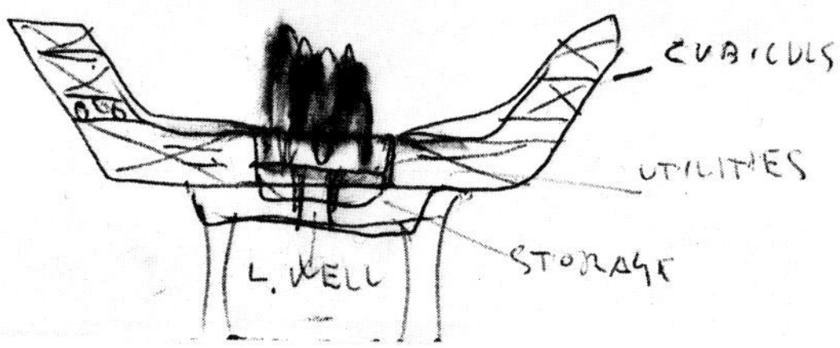

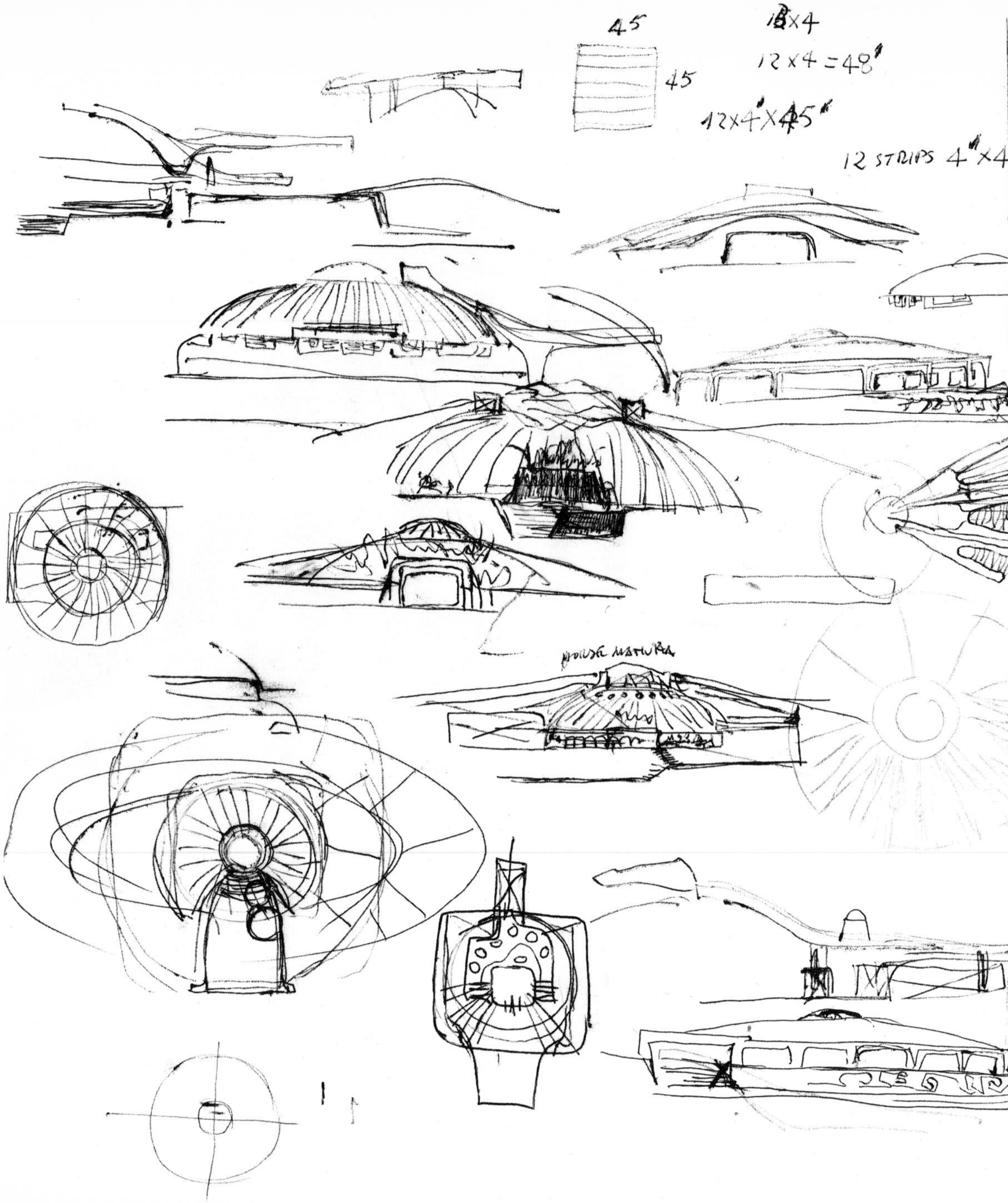

SEPTEMBER 65

IF mental communication (EXTRA sensory perception) demonstrate itself as real and as instantaneous. That is not limited to THE maximum of the light speed. The structure of the universe would "collapse," SPACE WOULD BE A FICTION IN THE WORLD OF THE MIND. THAT IS IT WOULD EXIST IN THE PROTO THINKING UNIVERSE.

LIVING SOMEWHERE WOULD MEAN BEING THERE WITHOUT. THUS THE INTERGALACTIC SPACES WOULD NO INTERFERE ON THE CONQUEST OF THE UNIVERSE. THAT IS THEIR REAL MEANING WOULD HAVE RESIDED IN A TEMPORARY DEFICIENCY OF LIFE: ITS INABILITY TO ACT DIRECTLY THROUGH THE MIND BUT ONLY THROUGH THE PHYSICAL THAT IS LIGHT SPEED, ABIDING UNIVERSE:

WHAT SPACE COLLAPSED WHAT WOULD BE OF TIME? TIME IS A RATIO OF CHANGE. A RATIO OF CHANGE IS AGAIN. DIRECT DEPENDENCE ON THE SPEED OF COMMUNICATION; WITH THIS SPEED NULLIFIED BY INSTANTANEITY. TIME WOULD ALSO COLLAPSE.

THE UNIVERSE PAST, PRESENT FUTURE, WHAT THE HERE AND THERE ARE IN A POINT.: SOD ?

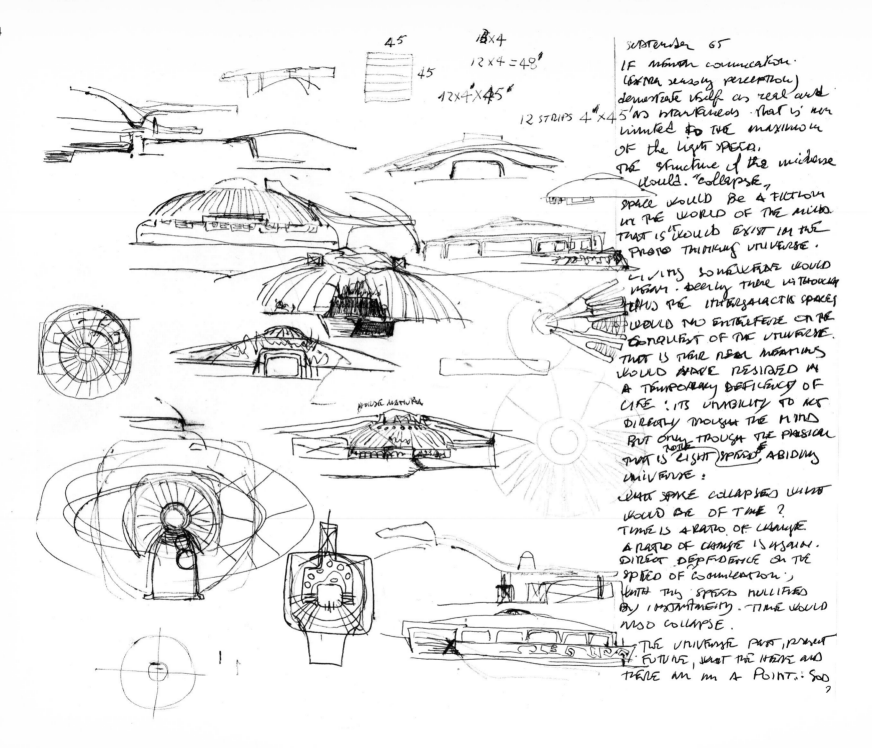

1970
In reviewing the material for publication, I realized that my optimism was not confirmed wherever it was related to outside help, but it has been doubly confirmed by the actual performance of Cosanti. This is a boost for self-reliance, and I mean not only myself but the large group of people who have carried on with dedication and discipline the task of doing, developing, and producing.

The following pages are about posters, pots, bells, and diagrams of reliance on others and other institutions.

3-12-1959

COMPRENSIVELY AS A CONSCIENCE AWARE OF THE UNBROKEN NETWORK OF PAIN, SORROW ANGUISH & TRAGEDY PERVASIVELY EXTENDED ON EVERY THING. ONE IS PRONE TO MALEDICTION MORE THAN DISPOSED TO VENERATION

ONLY OUR BUILT IN ORGANIC MACHINE OF FORGETFULNESS CAN EXPLAIN OUR CAPACITY FOR SURVIVAL & OUR ABILITY TO SMILE

THE REAL GRASP OF THE "VOLUME" OF DESPERATION EXUDED BY THE LIVING, MOMENT AFTER MOMENT IS PROBABLY ONE OF THE CAUSES OF MADNESS (IF NOT THE MAIN ONE)

& ABOVE THE EXTRA ILL FATES MANY A MAN UNDERGO IS THE "GREAT EQUALIZER" THE INESCAPABLE MOMENT-ETERNITY OF NO RESIDUAL AFTERMATH THE HALTING OF EXISTENCE (BODILY?) THE ENTERING SUDDEN & TOTAL INTO THE INCOGNITO THUS THE NON VERIFIABLE, DEATH

ON A LEVEL WHERE STATISTICS, PERCENTAGES, LAW OF AVERAGE & SO ON CANNOT CANCEL EVEN FOR A MOMENT, EVEN THE SMALLEST SORROW, ONE HAS WELL TO LOOK FOR A REASON KINDLY EXPLAINING NOT TO SAY JUSTIFYING THE PRESENCE OF THE CRUELTY OF THINGS COMING.
NOT (CAUSE) AT LEAST AFTER COMPASSION & CHARITY MADE THEIR WAY INTO LIFE, EVEN WHEN ONE COMPREHEND THEIR APPARENCE CONDITIONED TO THE (DOES) EXISTENCE OF ANGUISH & DESPERATION.

POSSIBLY MAN'S INTENSITY IS THE ACTIVATING AGENT OF MAN'S ANGUISH, POSSIBLY THE FOOLISHNESS OF SEARCHING, QUESTIONING, PLEADING FOR KNOWLEDGE, THE "ORIGINAL SIN" OF ASSERTING A WILL

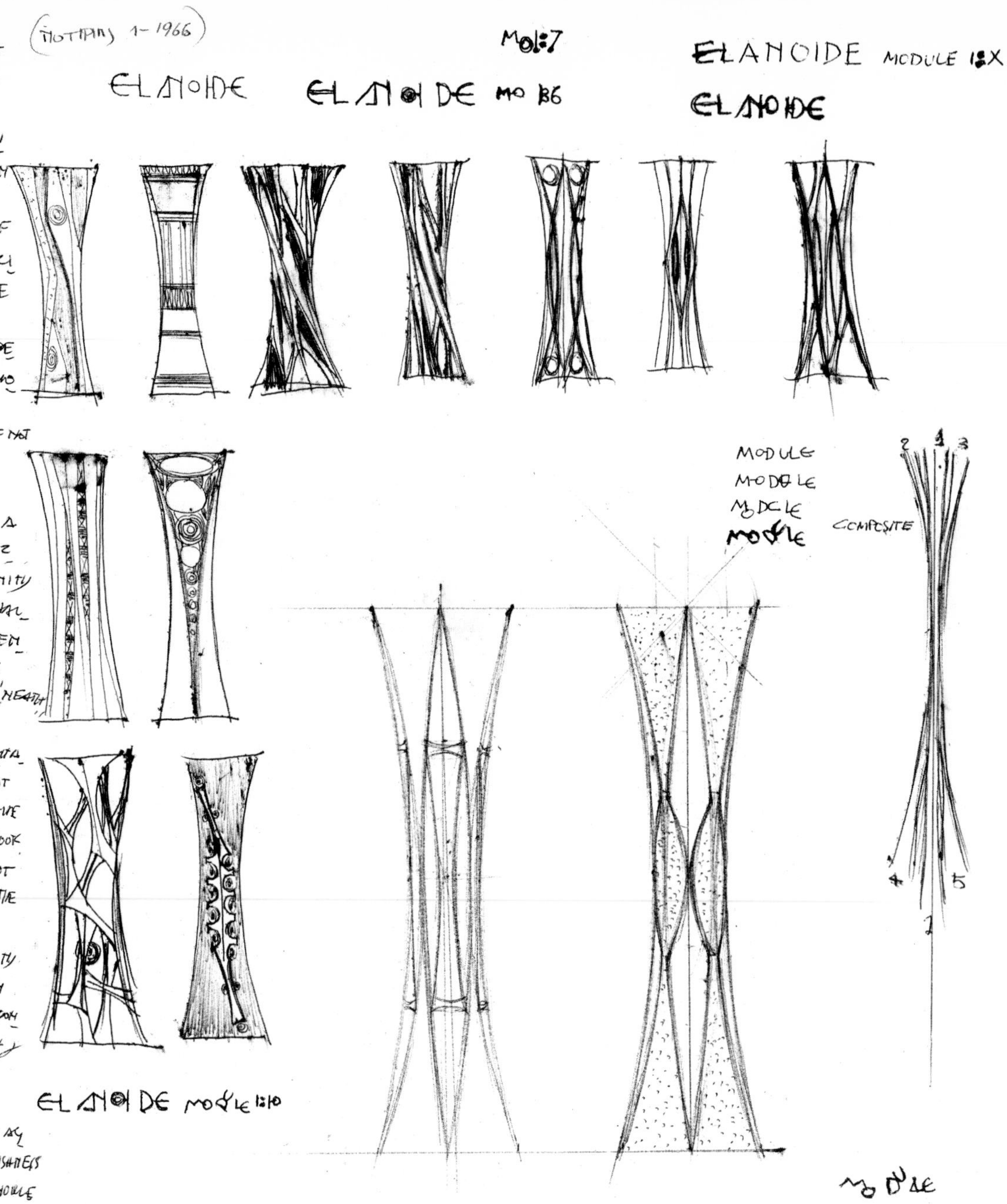

AS ONE FIND MORE & MORE NECESSARY TO RULE ON THE "FREEDOM" OF THE FREE ENTREPRISER SO AS TO DEVERATE ~~SOLVE~~ THE SHARDNESS OF THE EGO FROM THE BODY SOCIAL, CANNALING IT EVENTUALLY IN THE ~~FEEDS~~ LIMBOS OF MASS VIOLENCE BY THE TRAIN OF PSICOLOGICAL PARTECIPATION: MASS SPORT & MASS SPECTACLES OF VIOLENCE...

SO IS THE OTHER FINDING HARDER TO RESIST OR IGNORE THE PROTEST OF THIS SAME EGO, THUS HAVING TO CONCEDE NOW HERE NOW THERE A MORE INDIVIDUAL EXPRESSION OF THE BODY SOCIAL ~~SOCIAL~~

THE 20 YEARS OF A FASE IN THE AFORE LEAP ~~METAFORE~~ MAY THEN BE SOMEHOW IGNORED IN THE METAFORE OF THE TWO CONTENDENT LEAPING IN OPPOSITE DIRECTION TO REACH THE OPPONENT IDEALOGICAL POSITION USA. TOWARD SOCIALISM. USSR TOWARD DEMOCRACY

WHAT EITHER ONE WILL REACH WILL NOT BE EITHER SOCIALISM NOR DEMOCRACY. IN PART BECAUSE OF THE MOVING OF LIFE IN PART BECAUSE OF THE MALICIOUSNESS OR IGNORANCE OF MAN.

AS THE GOOD AMERICAN FEELS INSULTED OR WORSE TO BE FOUND "SOCIALISTIC" & THE GOOD COMUNIST IS ASHAMED OF ITS PROPENSITY TO GLOBAL PRIVACY.

ONE MAY WISH HERE TO THE SOVIET THAT THEIR LANDING WILL BE ON A BETTER LAND THAN THE ONE USA HAS PLANTED & REACHED.
WHILE USA BLAMES ON SOVIET THE MATERIALISM OF THE ECONOMIC MEANING

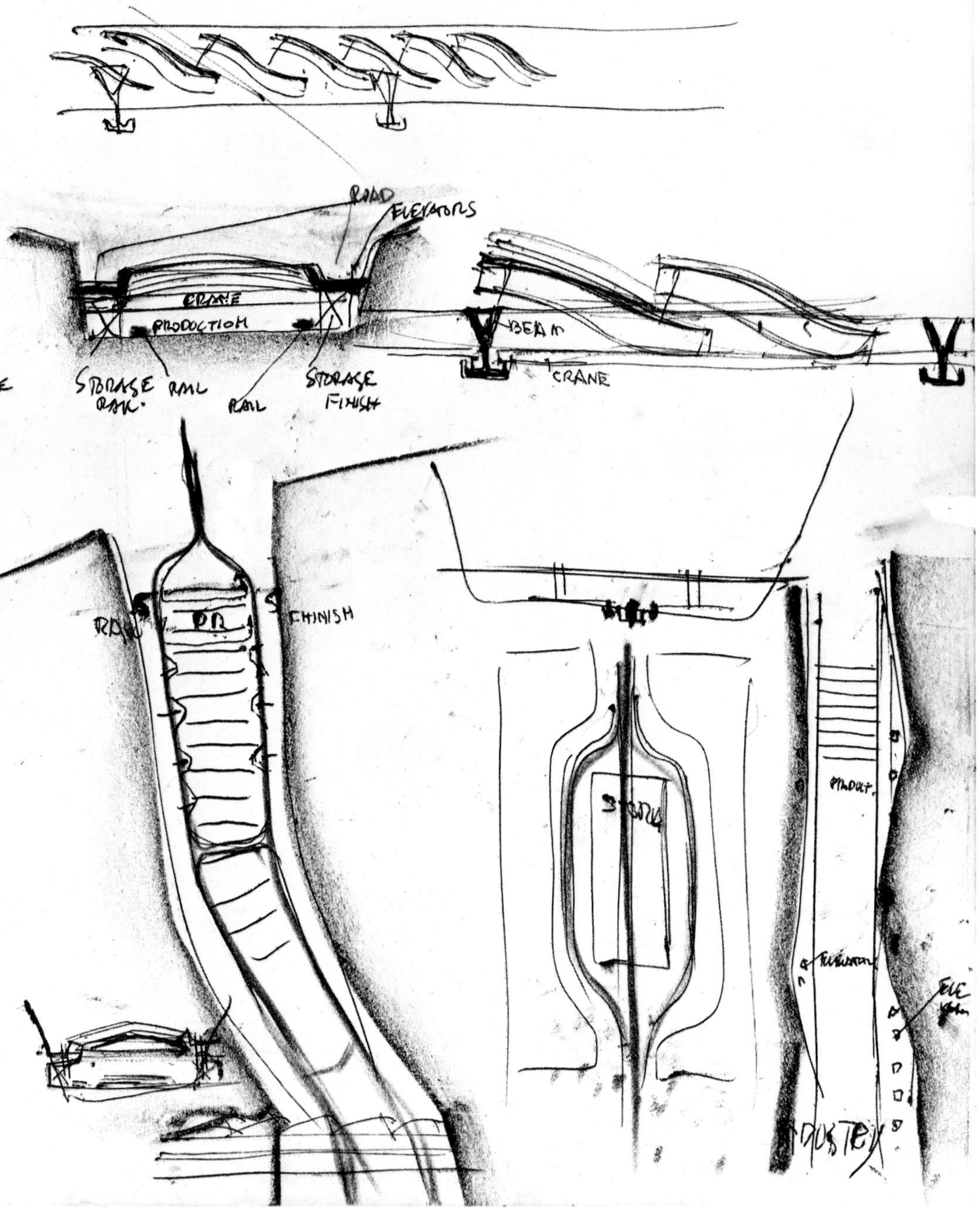

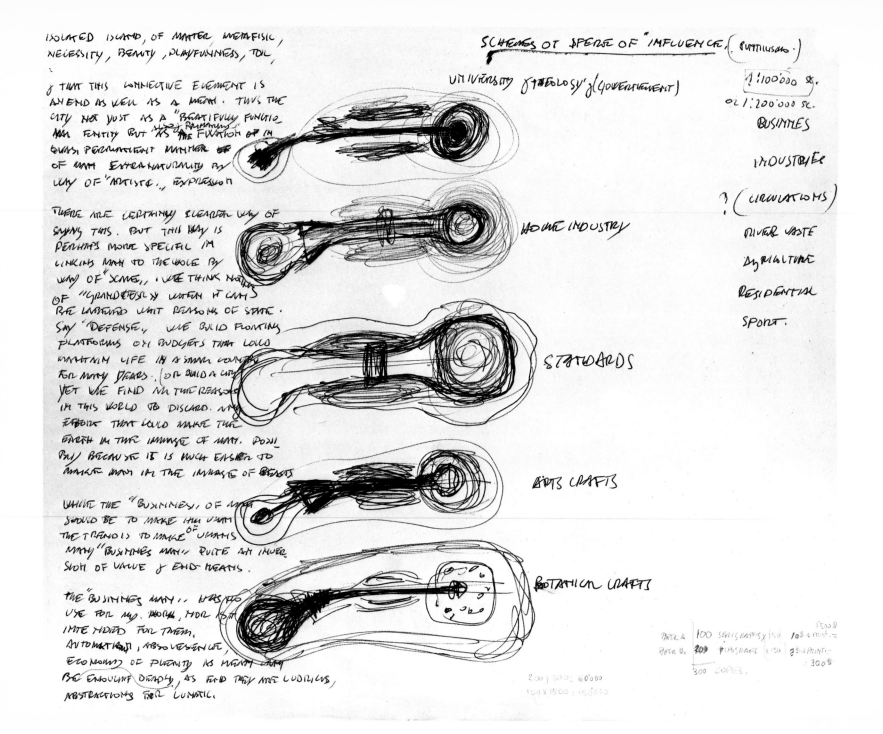

ISOLATED ISLAND, OF MATTER, METAFISIC, NECESSITY, BEAUTY, PLAYFULNESS, TOIL,

& THAT THIS CONNECTIVE ELEMENT IS AN END AS WELL AS A MEAN. THUS THE CITY NOT JUST AS A "BEAUTIFULLY FUNCTIONAL ENTITY BUT ALSO & PRIMARILY" AS THE FIXATION OF IN QUASI PERMANENT MANNER OF OF MAN EXTRANATURALITY BY WAY OF "ARTISTIC" EXPRESSION

THERE ARE CERTAINLY CLEARER WAY OF SAYING THIS. BUT THIS WAY IS PERHAPS MORE SPECIFIC IN LINKING MAN TO THE WHOLE BY WAY OF "SCALE", I WE THINK NOTHING OF "GRANDEUR" WHEN IT CAN BE LABELED WITH REASONS OF STATE. SAY "DEFENSE" WE BUILD FLOATING PLATFORMS ON BUDGETS THAT COULD MAINTAIN LIFE IN A SMALL COUNTRY FOR MANY YEARS. (OR BUILD A CITY) YET WE FIND ALL THE REASONS IN THIS WORLD TO DISCARD ANY EFFORT THAT COULD MAKE THE EARTH IN THE IMAGE OF MAN. POSSIBLY BECAUSE IT IS MUCH EASIER TO MAKE MAN IN THE IMAGE OF BEASTS

WHILE THE "BUSINNES" OF MAN SHOULD BE TO MAKE HIM HUMAN THE TREND IS TO MAKE OF HUMANS MANY "BUSINNES MAN" QUITE AN INVERSION OF VALUE & END-MEANS.

THE "BUSINNES MAN" HAS NO USE FOR MY WORK, NOR IS IT INTENDED FOR THEM. AUTOMATION, OBSOLESCENCE, ECONOMY OF PLENTY AS MEANS CAN BE ENOUGH DEADLY, AS END THEY ARE LUDRICUS, ABSTRACTIONS FOR LUNATIC.

SCHEMES OT SPERE OF "INFLUENCE". (PUNTILLISMO.)

UNIVERSITY & THEOLOGY & (GOVERNEMENT)

1:100'000 SC.

OR 1:200'000 SC.

BUSINNES

INDUSTRIES

? (CIRCULATIONS)

RIVER WASTE

AGRICULTURE

RESIDENTIAL

SPORT.

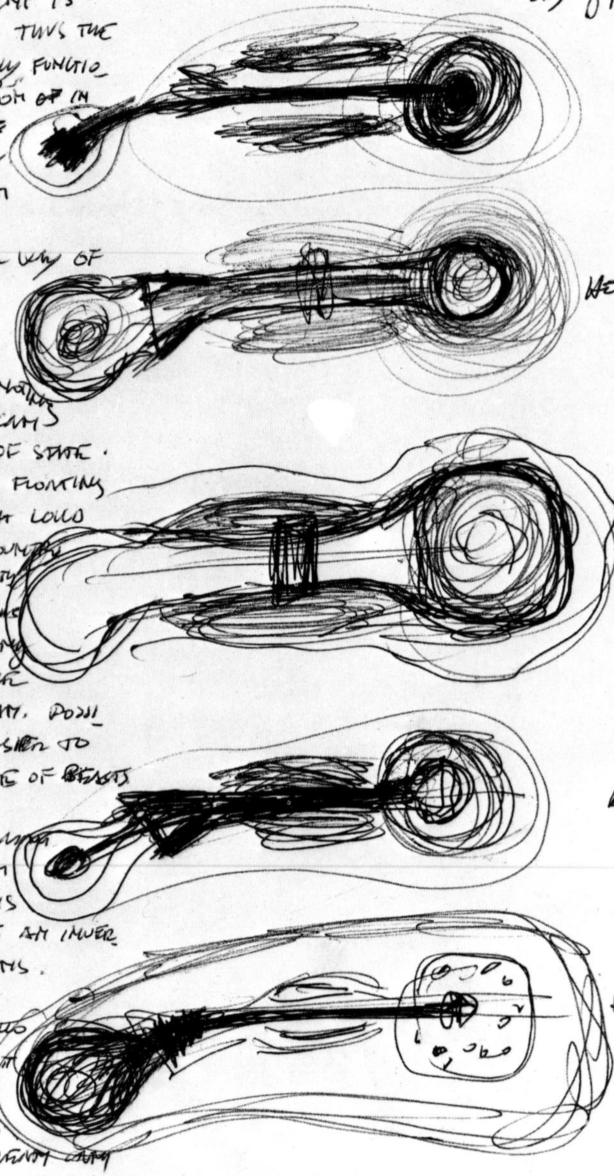

PAPER A | 100 SERIGRAPHS x 150 | 10$ A PRINT = 1500$
PAPER B. | 200 LITOGRAFS (x 150) | 2$ A PRINT = 300$
300 COPIES.

200 x 300 = 60'000
100 x 1500 = 150'000

1962

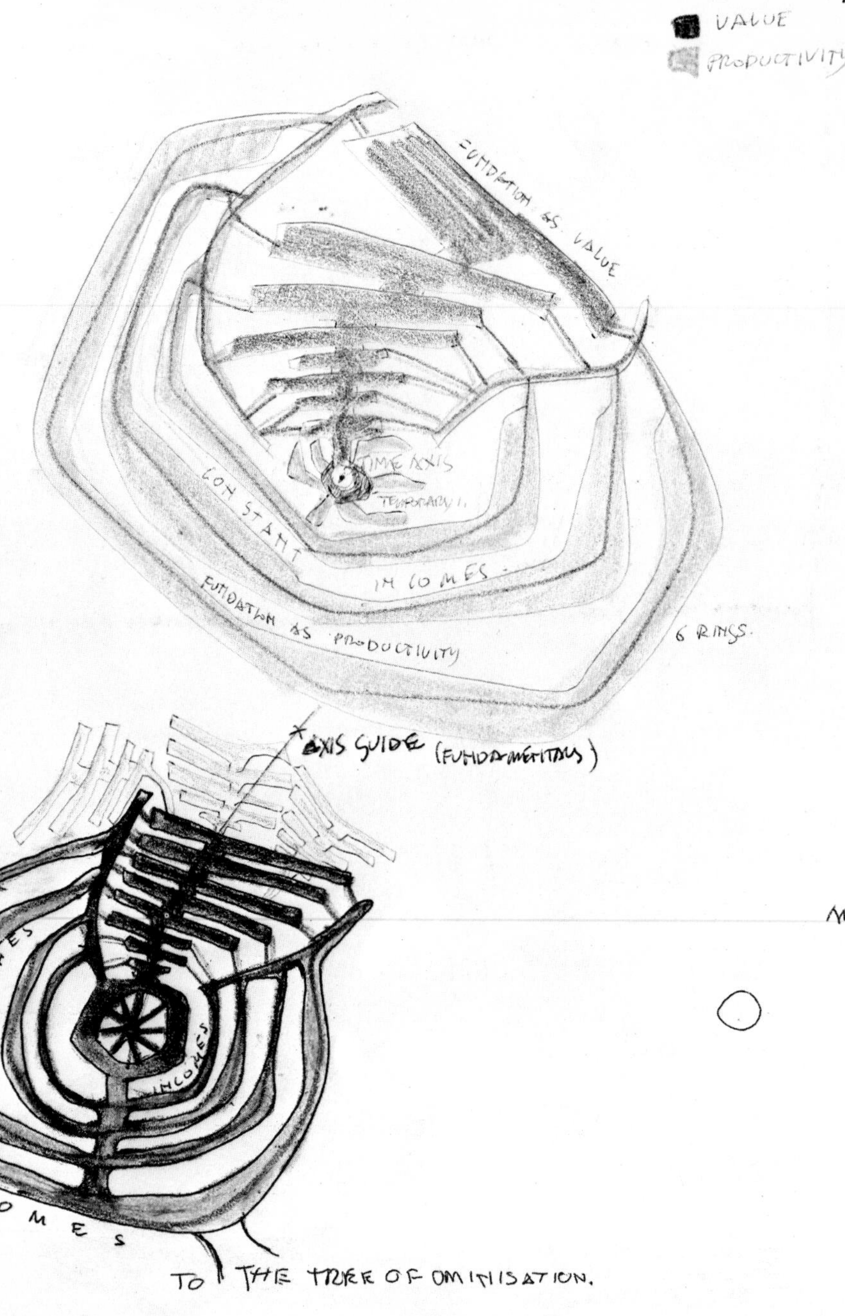

LA CONCEZIONE
LA VASTA CONOSCENZA DI UNA STRUTTURA
PERVASIVA DI TUTTO L'UNIVERSO CHE
SPARUTEZZA E IL SENTIMENTO CHE
DI QUESTA SPAZIALITÀ L'UOMO NE SARÀ
UN GIORNO SE NON IL FATTORE
DETERMINANTE, QUALE COSTRUTTORE
DELLA PROPRIA INCREMENTANTE DIVINITÀ,
PONE IL PROBLEMA DELL'ARCHITETTURA
IN QUELLA CATE-
GORIA CHE DELLE COSE "NATURALI"
UTILIZZA LA POTENZIALITÀ UMANIZ-
ZANTE SÌ DA CREARE ENTRO
UN UNIVERSO FISICO, NON
MENO SOSTANZIALE E PERVASIVO
UN UNIVERSO METAFISICO
ARCHITETTURA, LA MANIFESTAZIONE
MACROSMICA DELL'ARTIFICIALITÀ
PER CUI L'UOMO ASSECONDANDO
INSURGENZE INTERIORI, INFONDENDO
LA GRAZIA DELLA PIETÀ NELLA
SORDITÀ DELLA MATERIA, RICERCAN-
DO UNA RISOLUZIONE ALL'INCOMBENZA
DELLA ACCIDENTALITÀ STATISTICA,
FORZANDO EMOZIONALITÀ NELLA
CRUDELE SEQUENZA DELL'INDIFFE-
RENZA COSMICA,
O . . . . . . —
ARCH. QUALE L'INFINITESIMO
MORMORIO DI UNA SPIRITUALITÀ
PERMANENTE MATERIA ED ENERGIA
PROSSIMA A STRARIPARE DAI
CONFINI TERRESTRI E SOLARI

SE DALLA GENERICITÀ TEORETICA IN NON
DALLA STERILITÀ DELL'ASTRATTO, NON
È PUR REALE LA "CONCRETEZZA"
DI UNA FRAMMENTARIA RISOLVENZA,
DOVE RISOLVENZA NON È DA SPE-
RARE SE NON IN UNA VASTA,
LUNGAMENTE INCOLATA FERVIDA CALDAMENTE CONCRETA
EFFUSIONE, COMPRENSIVA DELLA [illegible]

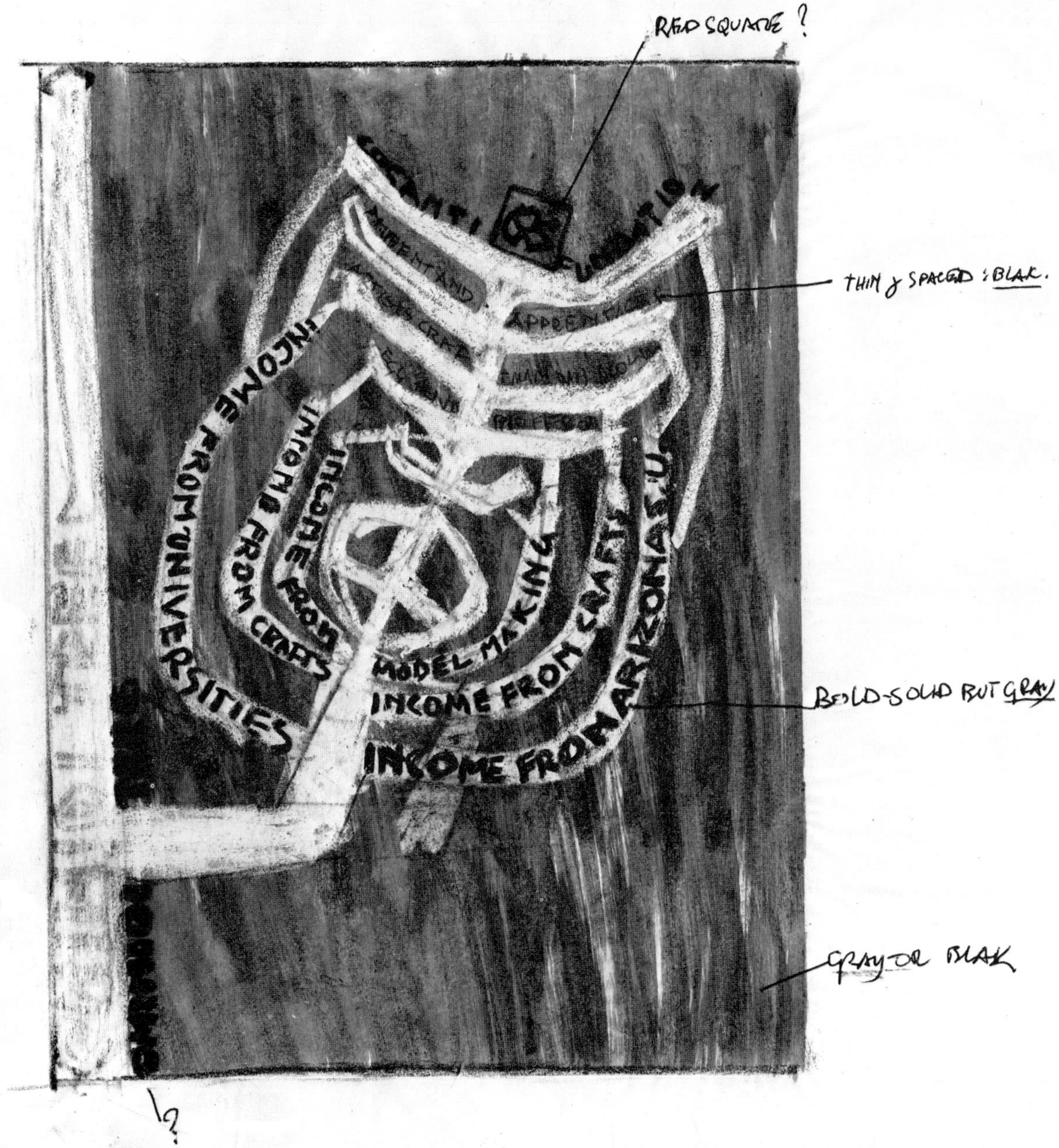
RED SQUARE ?
THIN & SPACED : BLAK.
BOLD-SOLID BUT GRAY
GRAY OR BLAK
INCOME FROM UNIVERSITIES
INCOME FROM CRAFTS
INCOME FROM
MODEL MAKING
INCOME FROM CRAFTS
INCOME FROM ARIZONA U.

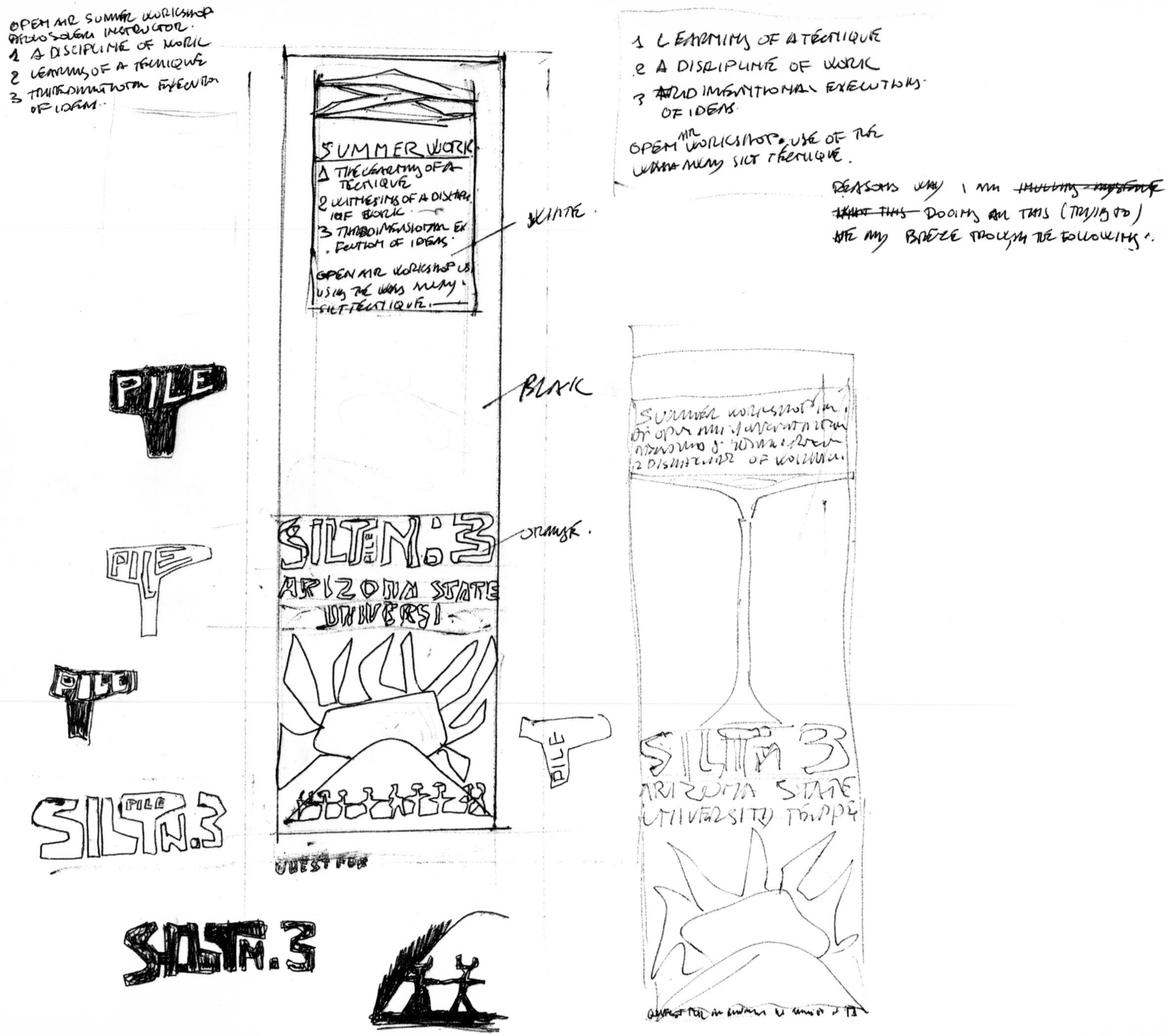
OPEN AIR SUMMER WORKSHOP
1 A DISCIPLINE OF WORK
2 LEARNING OF A TECNIQUE
OF IDEAS
SUMMER WORK
OPEN AIR WORKSHOP
WHITE
BLACK
ORANGE
PILE
SILT N.3
ARIZONA STATE
QUEST FOR
1 LEARNING OF A TECNIQUE
2 A DISIPLINE OF WORK
OF IDEAS
SILT TECNIQUE

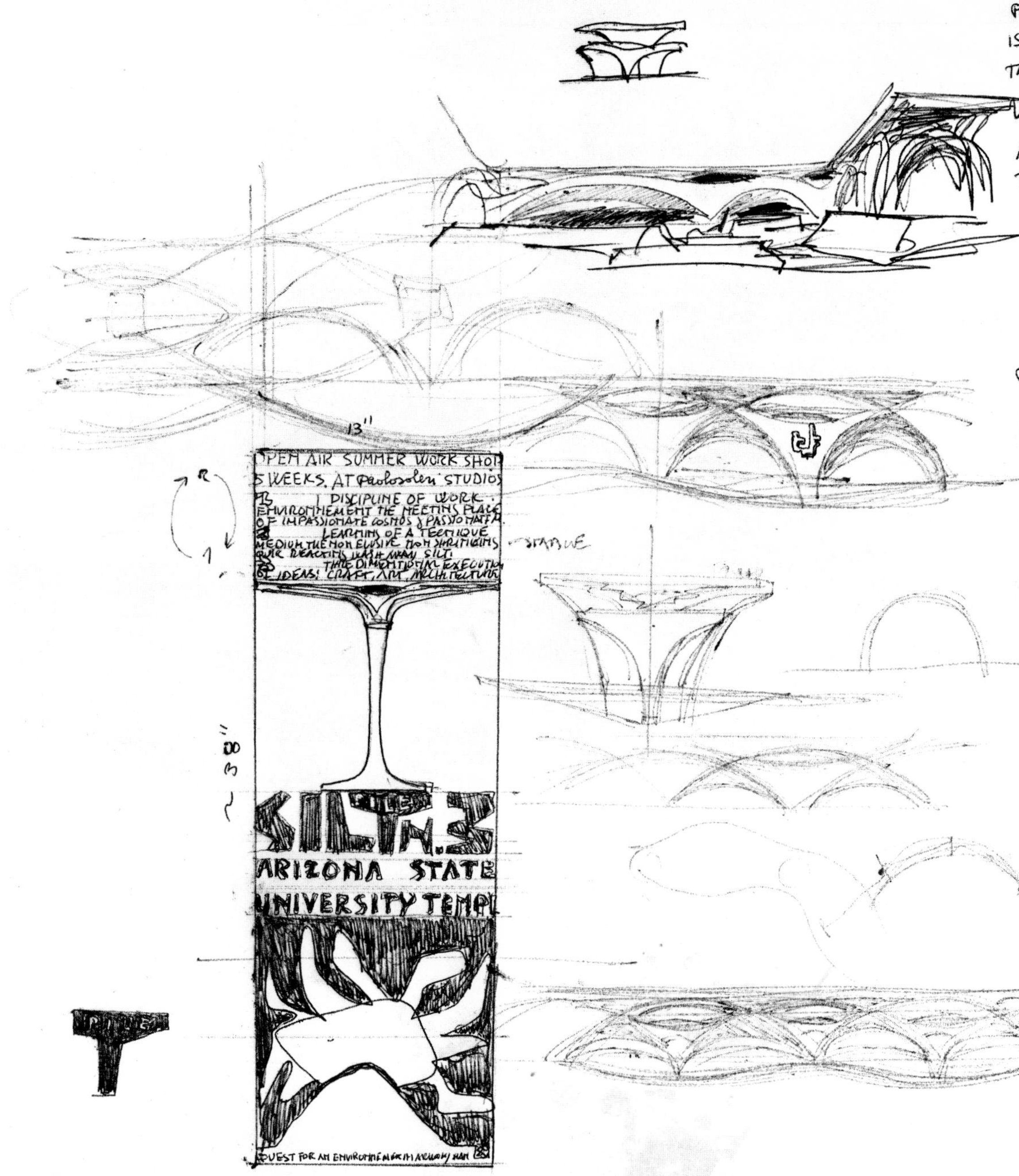

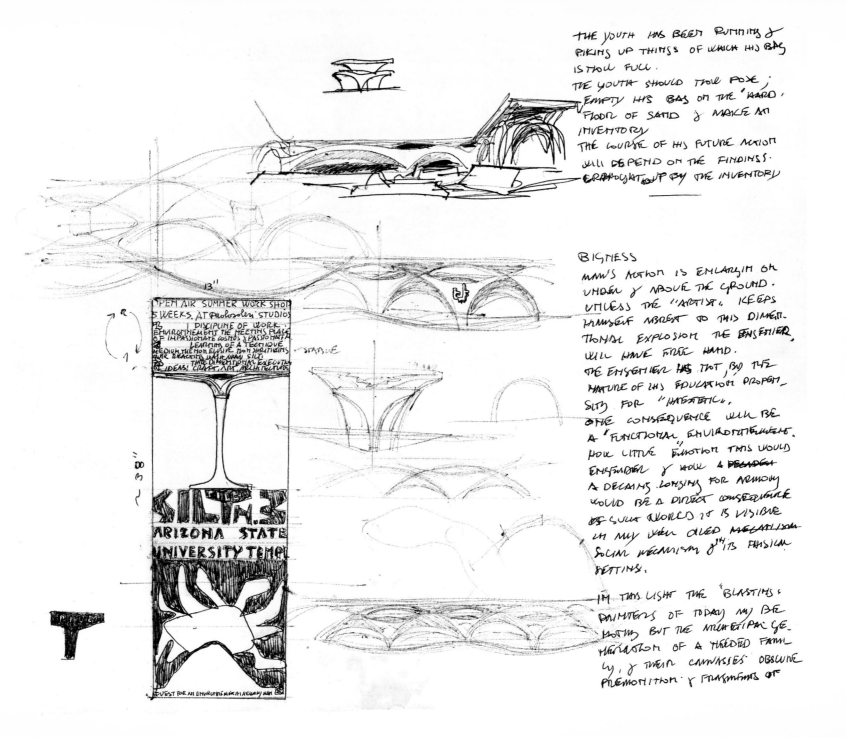

THE YOUTH HAS BEEN RUNNING & PIKING UP THINGS OF WHICH HIS BAG IS NOW FULL.
THE YOUTH SHOULD NOW POSE; EMPTY HIS BAG ON THE "HARD" FLOOR OF SAND & MAKE AN INVENTORY
THE COURSE OF HIS FUTURE ACTION WILL DEPEND ON THE FINDINGS BROUGHT ABOUT BY THE INVENTORY

BIGNESS

MAN'S ACTION IS ENLARGIN ON UNDER & ABOVE THE GROUND. UNLESS THE "ARTIST" KEEPS HIMSELF ABREAST TO THIS DIMENTIONAL EXPLOSION THE ENGENIER WILL HAVE FREE HAND.
THE ENGENIER HAS NOT, BY THE NATURE OF HIS EDUCATION PROPENSITY FOR "AESTETIC".
ONE CONSEQUENCE WILL BE A "FUNCTIONAL" ENVIRONMEMENT. HOW LITTLE EMOTION THIS WOULD ENGENDER & HOW A ~~DECADEN~~ A DECAING LONGING FOR ARMONY WOULD BE A DIRECT CONSEQUENCE OF SUCH WORLD IT IS VISIBLE IN MY WELL OILED ~~MECANISM~~ SOCIAL MECANISM & IN ITS PHISICAL SETTING.

IN THIS LIGHT THE "BLASTING" PAINTERS OF TODAY MY BE NOTHING BUT THE ARCHETIPAL GENERATION OF A NEEDED FAMILY, & THEIR CANVASSES OBSCURE PREMONITION & FRAGMENTS OF

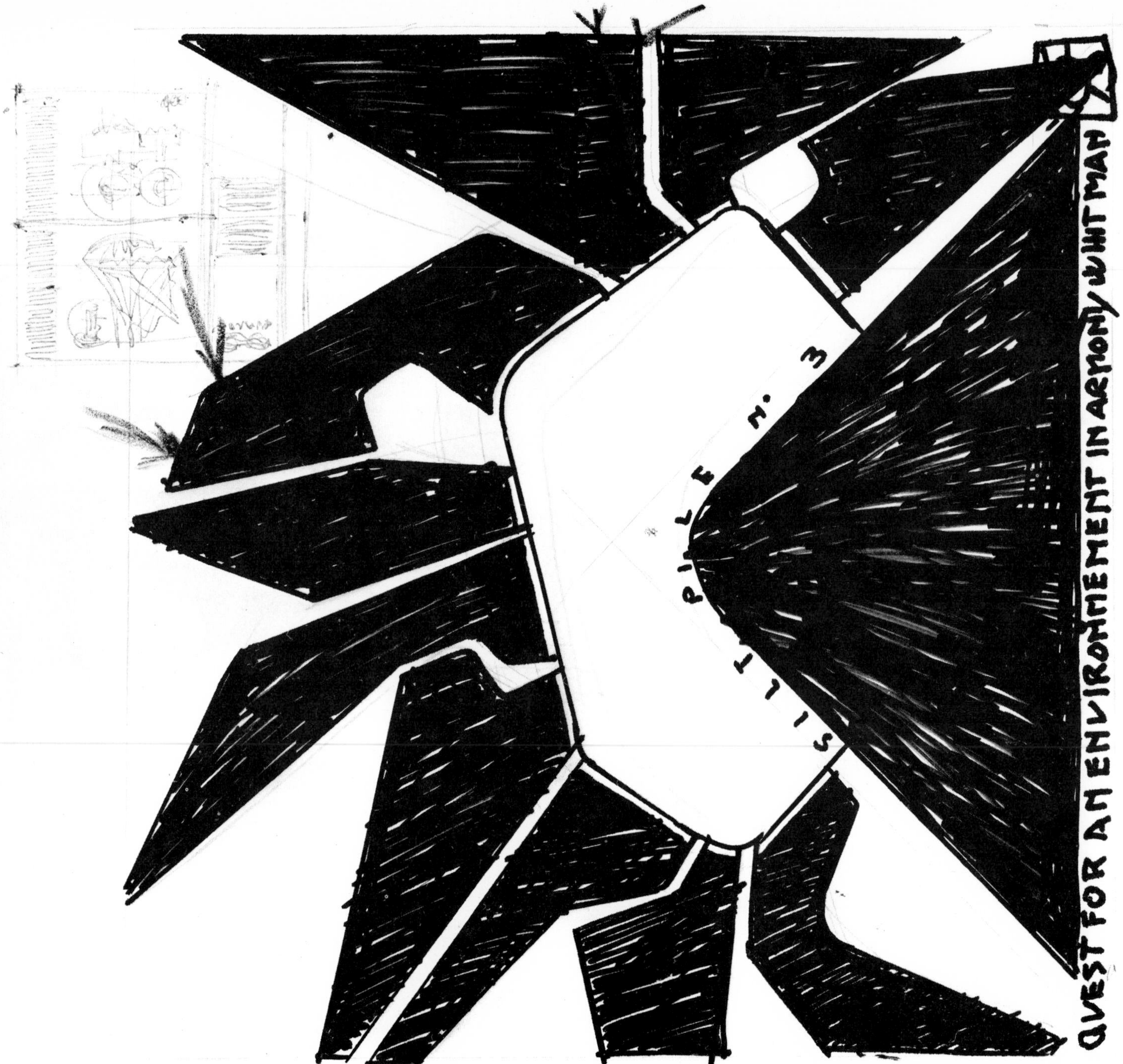
SILT PILE N. 3
QUEST FOR AN ENVIRONMEMENT IN ARMONY/WHITMAN

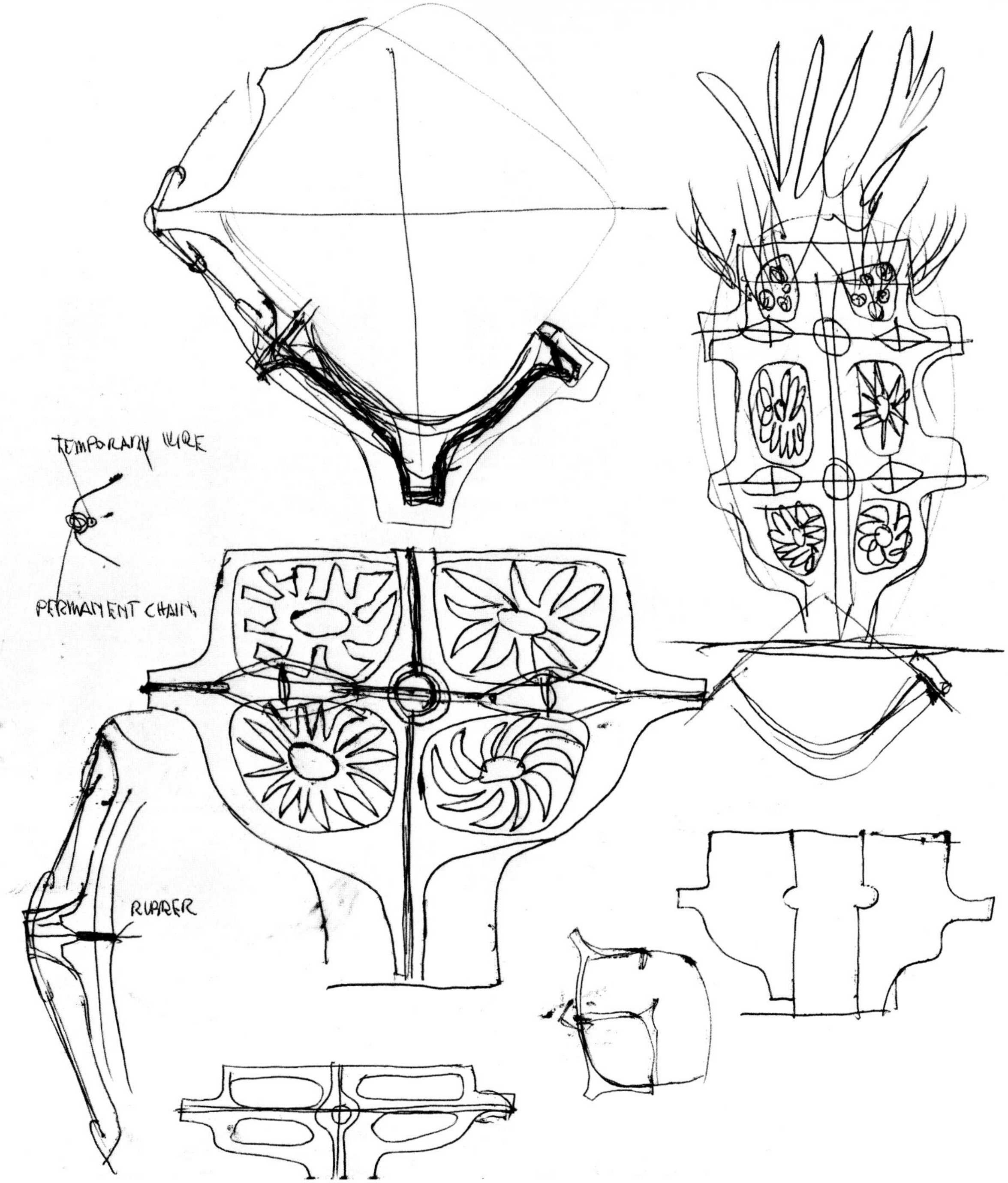
TEMPORARY WIRE
PERMANENT CHAIN
RUBBER

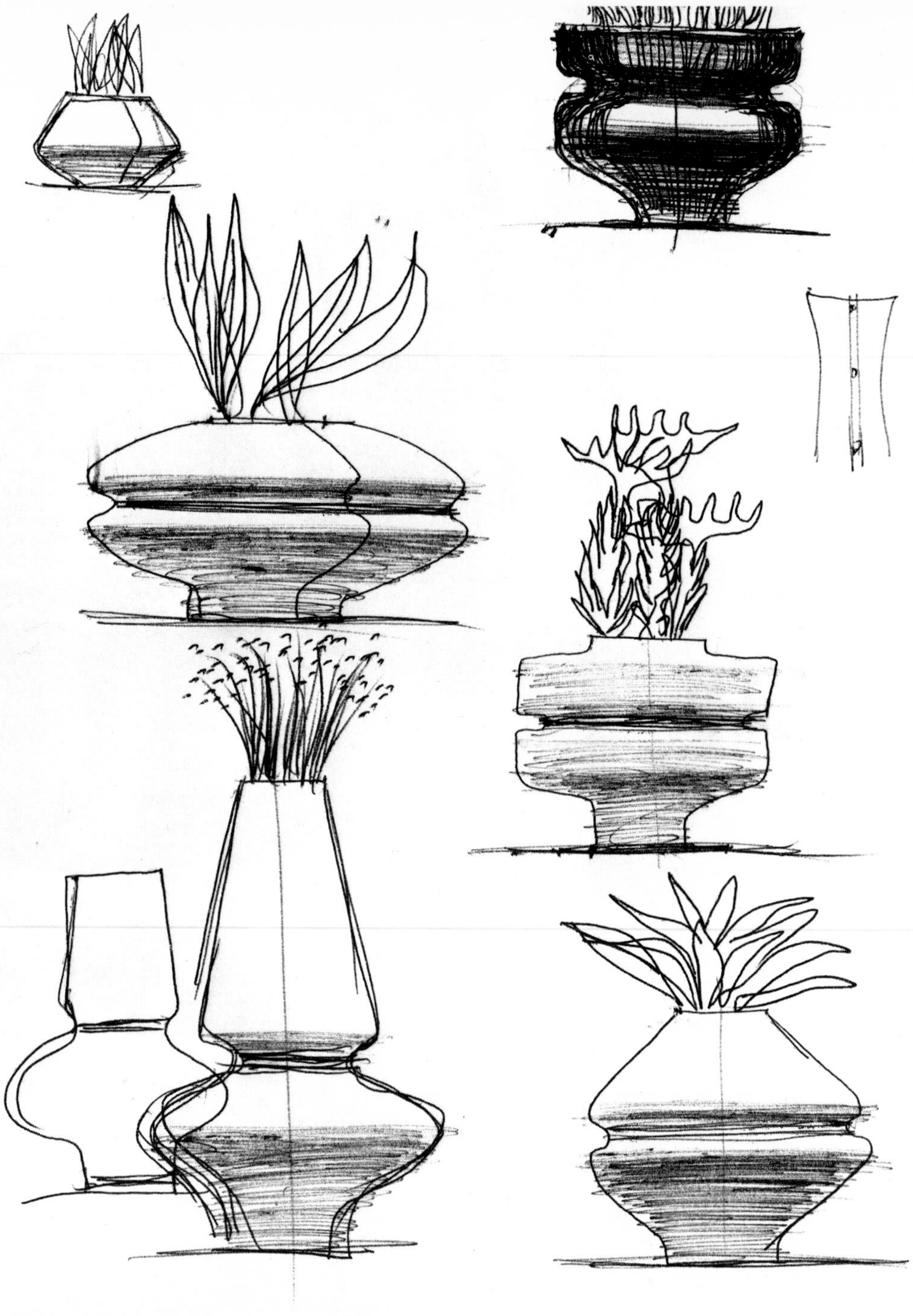

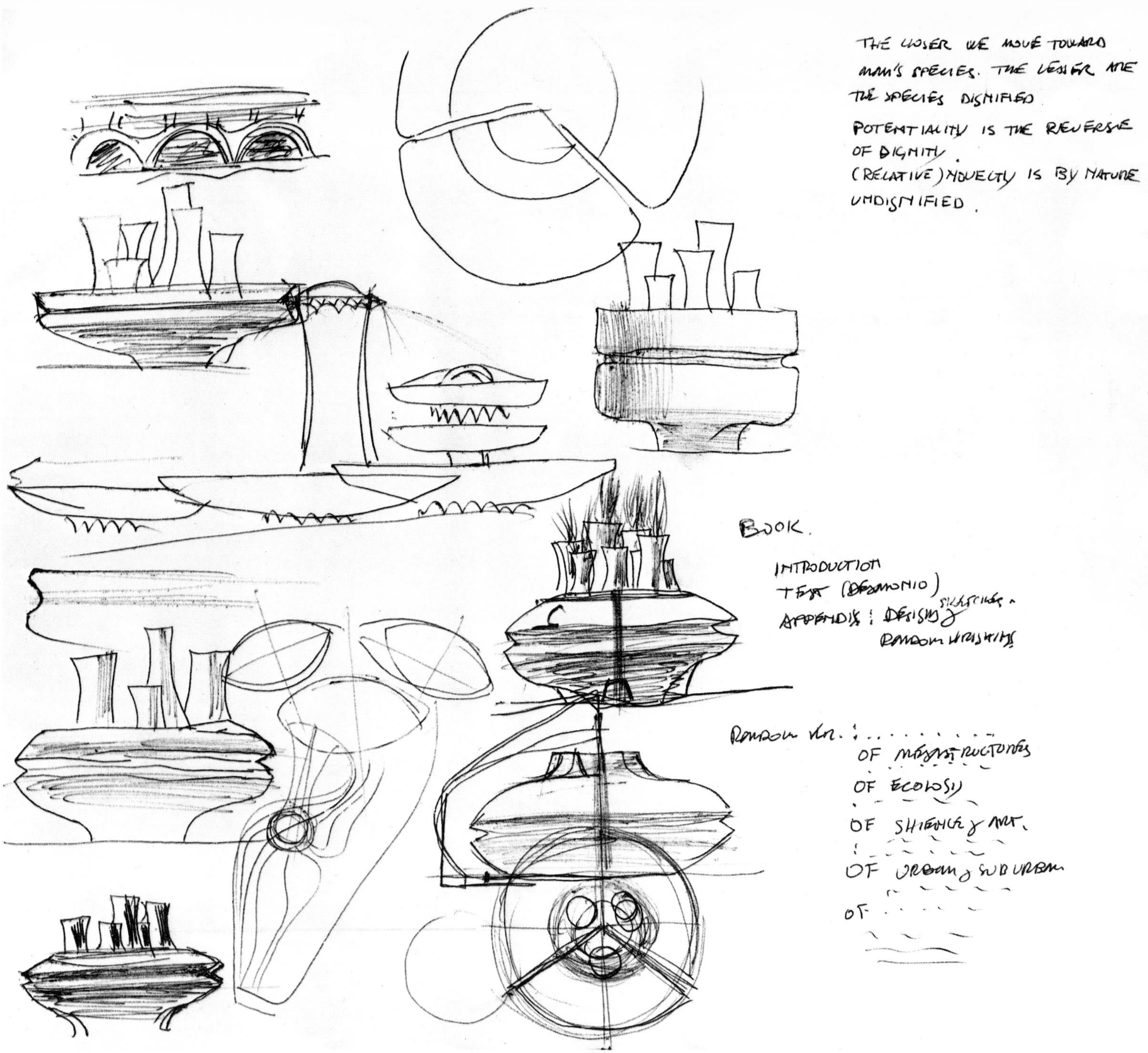
THE CLOSER WE MOVE TOWARD
MAN'S SPECIES. THE LESSER ARE
THE SPECIES DIGNIFIED
POTENTIALITY IS THE REVERSE
OF DIGNITY.
(RELATIVE) NOVELTY IS BY NATURE
UNDIGNIFIED.
BOOK.
INTRODUCTION
APPENDIX: DESIGNS & SKETCHES
RANDOM WRITINGS
RANDOM WR.
OF MEGASTRUCTURES
OF ECOLOGY
OF SCIENCE & ART.
OF URBAN & SUBURBAN
OF

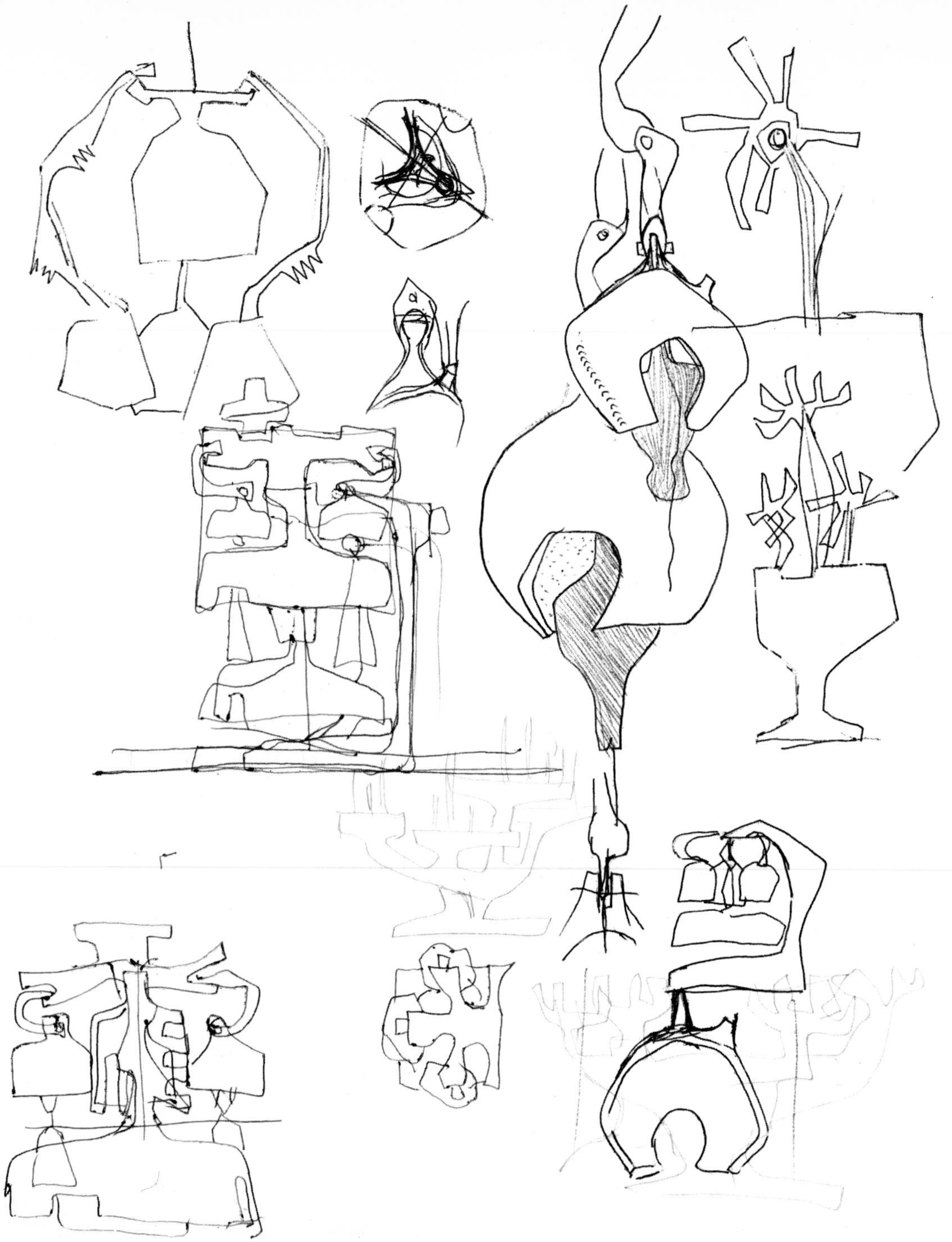

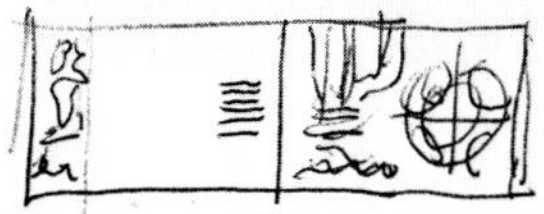

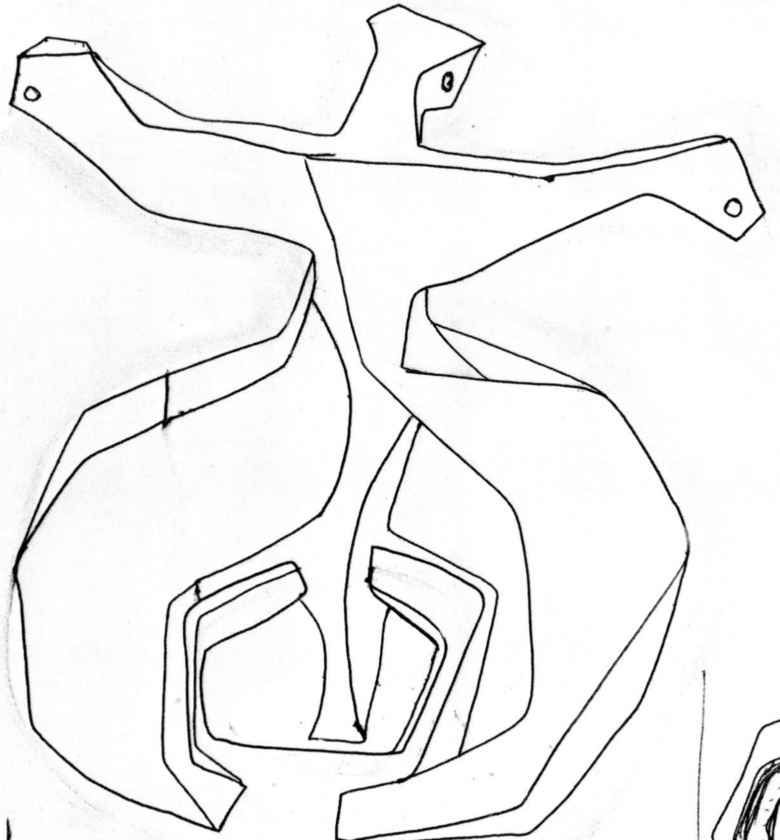

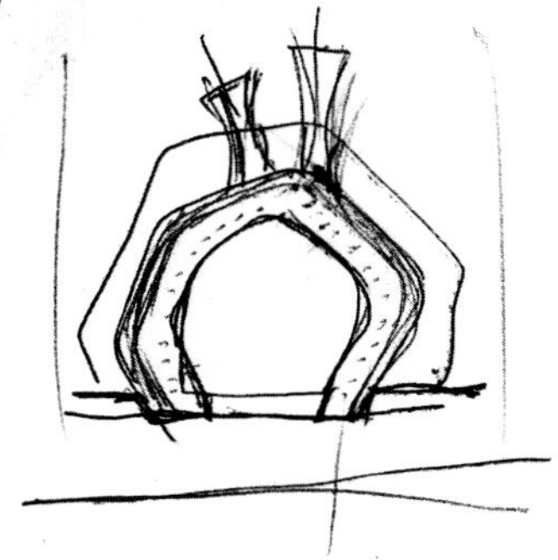

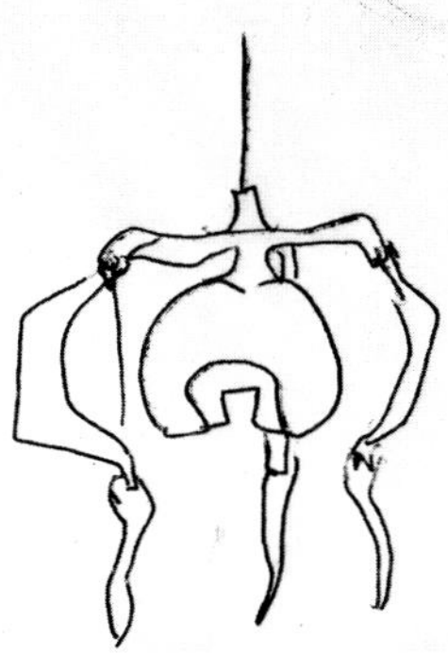

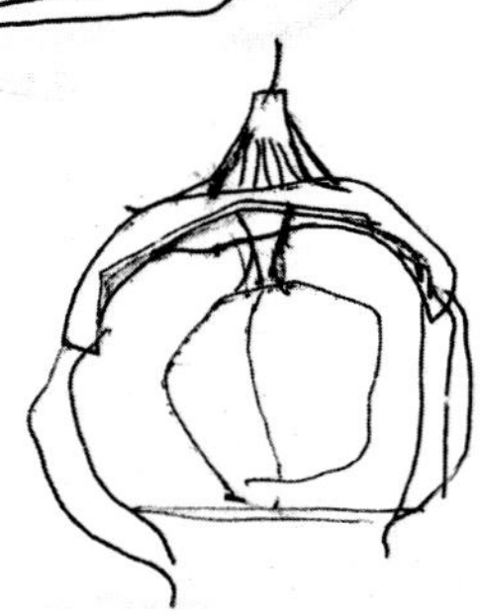